PHYSICAL REHABILITATION:

ASSESSMENT AND TREATMENT

Second Edition

DEDICATION

To Catherine Perry Wilkinson
*. . . physical therapist, educator,
mentor, and friend.*

PHYSICAL REHABILITATION:
ASSESSMENT AND TREATMENT

Second Edition

SUSAN B. O'SULLIVAN, M.S., P.T.
Assistant Professor
Department of Physical Therapy
University of Lowell
College of Health Professions
Lowell, Massachusetts

THOMAS J. SCHMITZ, M.S., P.T.
Assistant Professor
Program in Physical Therapy
Columbia University
College of Physicians and Surgeons
New York, New York

F. A. Davis Company ● Philadelphia

Printed in the United States of America

Last digit indicates print number: 10 9 8 7

Library of Congress Cataloging-in-Publication Data

O'Sullivan, Susan B.
    Physical rehabilitation.

    Includes bibliographies and index.
    1. Physical therapy.   I. Schmitz, Thomas J.
II. Title.
RM700.088   1988   615.8′2   88–7070
ISBN 0–8036–6698–5

PREFACE

Our goal in undertaking the second edition of *Physical Rehabilitation: Assessment and Treatment* was to develop a comprehensive textbook offering state-of-the-art perspectives on the rehabilitation management of adult patients. Although principally intended and carefully formulated to meet the educational needs of physical therapy students, we believe *Physical Rehabilitation: Assessment and Treatment* will also serve as a valuable resource for physical therapists inexperienced in rehabilitation procedures as well as for the other students and health care professionals involved in rehabilitation settings. This second edition is extensively updated and emphasizes effective intervention strategies by integrating scientific and medical information with physical therapy assessment, planning, and treatment procedures. From the shared clinical experience of the editors, the content selected represents the theories and treatment approaches most commonly utilized by physical therapists whose practice involves rehabilitation management of the adult patient.

Organized into 30 chapters, the conceptual basis of *Physical Rehabilitation: Assessment and Treatment* is established at the outset with three chapters examining clinical decision making, psychologic aspects of adjustment to physical disability, and the influence of values on patient care. Thus, the reader is directed early on to developing an understanding of the whole patient and to building effective problem-solving skills.

Next, chapters 4 through 13 consider specific assessment procedures common to the rehabilitation setting. These include new chapters on the assessment of vital signs, musculoskeletal deficits, and gait and motor control, as well as coverage of rapidly developing topics such as electromyography. This material is supported by new content in chapters 14 and 15, outlining strategies for improving motor control and gait training with assistive devices.

Subsequent chapters (16 through 30) examine the assessment and treatment of specific clinical problems. Each chapter addresses the clinical features and characteristics of a major medical condition commonly encountered in rehabilitation settings. Conditions covered include coronary artery disease, stroke, peripheral vascular disease, rheumatoid arthritis, multiple sclerosis, Parkinson's disease, burns, and traumatic spinal cord injury. A new chapter has been added on traumatic head injury. Coverage of special topics for physical therapists includes prosthetics, orthotics, and wheelchair prescription as well as techniques in biofeedback and transcutaneous electrical nerve stimulation.

To facilitate and to reinforce the learning of key concepts, every chapter of *Physical Rehabilitation: Assessment and Treatment* now includes an initial set of learning objectives, an introduction, a succinct summary, study questions for self-assessment, and a glossary. In addition, many chapters provide supplemental reading lists as resources for further investigating the theories and treatment strategies presented. An equally important feature of this second edition is the numerous photographs and line drawings which have been carefully selected and placed to illustrate and to reinforce the concepts and techniques presented in the text.

Finally, a primary strength of this book lies in the input it received from numerous talented professionals dedicated to improving patient care. Seventeen authorities from different clinical specialties contributed their unique perspectives and knowledge, widening the scope and strengthening the effectiveness of this edition. In addition, we were encouraged in our efforts by many constructive comments and suggestions from our students and valued colleagues.

Because physical therapy is a profession of frequent and often rapid advances, we will always consider this book a "work in progress." With this in mind, we look forward to—and welcome—suggestions from our readers for future editions.

SUSAN B. O' SULLIVAN
THOMAS J. SCHMITZ

ACKNOWLEDGMENTS

The authors gratefully acknowledge the following individuals who reviewed portions of the manuscript during critical stages of development. The content of this second edition reflects their constructive comments.

Michael P. Alexander, M.D.
Boston University
Boston, Massachusetts

Debbie Alton, P.T.
University Hospital
Boston, Massachusetts

Lucien Côté, M.D.
Columbia University
New York, New York

Chad L. Deal, M.D.
Case Western Reserve University
Cleveland, Ohio

Ruth Dickinson, M.A., P.T.
Columbia University
New York, New York

Jeffrey E. Falkel, Ph.D., P.T.
Ohio University
Athens, Ohio

Adele C. Germain, M.S., O.T.R.
Columbia University
New York, New York

Margaret A. Henly, M.A., P.T.
Columbia Presbyterian Medical
Center
New York, New York

Hollis Herman, M.S., P.T.
Northeastern University
Boston, Massachusetts

Rosalind Hickenbottom, Ph.D., P.T.
Ohio University
Athens, Ohio

John M. Hovde, M.A., P.T.
St. Mary's Hospital of Brooklyn
Brooklyn, New York

Timothy L. Kauffman, M.S., P.T.
Hahnemann University
Philadelphia, Pennsylvania

Alice Lewis, P.T.
Northeast Rehabilitation Center
Salem, New Hampshire

Phyllis A. Lisanti, R.N., Ph.D.
Lehman College of The City
University of New York
Bronx, New York

Prudence D. Markos, M.S., P.T.
Massachusetts General Hospital
Boston, Massachusetts

Robert F. Meenan, M.D., M.P.H.
Boston University
Boston, Massachusetts

Carolee Moncur, Ph.D., P.T.
University of Utah
Salt Lake City, Utah

Arthur J. Nelson, Ph.D., P.T.
New York University
New York, New York

Charles R. Noback, Ph.D.
Columbia University
New York, New York

Cynthia C. Norkin, Ed.D., P.T.
Ohio University
Athens, Ohio

Gay Rosenberg, M.A., P.T.
Saint Mary's Hospital for Children
Bayside, New York

Thomas Shaw, P.T.
Marino and Shaw Physical Therapy
Associates
Toms River, New Jersey

Bonnie Teschendorf, M.H.A., P.T.
Columbia University
New York, New York

Catherine A. Trombly, M.A., O.T.R.
Boston University
Boston, Massachusetts

Ann E. Veazey, M.S., P.T.
The Rehabilitation Institute at Santa
Barbara
Santa Barbara, California

Douglas J. Westphal, M.S., P.T.
Columbia Presbyterian Medical
Center
New York, New York

Catherine Perry Wilkinson, Ed.D., P.T.
Physical Therapy Educational
Consultant
White River Junction, Vermont

We are also indebted to several individuals who provided editorial assistance during the course of this project. First, we would like to thank Cynthia C. Norkin and Catherine Perry Wilkinson for their comprehensive review of the completed manuscript. Their valuable comments and suggestions helped shape the final format of this edition. We also would like to thank Jean-François Vilain, Senior Editor, Allied Health; Janet C. H. Mullen, Production Editor; Philip Ashley, Art Director; and Herbert J. Powell, Production Manager; F. A. Davis Company, for their continuous support and outstanding assistance in this project. Our thanks go also to Eileen M. McAulay, Columbia University, for her valuable typing assistance.

The authors wish to thank the following individuals who contributed their time, energy, and talent to the completion of the photographs: Christopher M. Powers, M.S., P.T., Suburban Physical Therapy Center, Cedar Grove, New Jersey; Gay Rosenberg, M.A., P.T., Saint Mary's Hospital for Children, Bayside, New York; Curtis W. Sullenger, B.A., Brooklyn, New York; Terry Futrell, M.Ed., University of Lowell Media Services, Lowell, Massachusetts; Raynard Manson, B.F.A., Center for Biomedical Communications, Columbia University, New York, New York; Kathleen Nordahl, M.Ed., P.T., Alice Lewis, P.T., and Kathy Ryan, P.T., Northeast Rehabilitation Center, Salem, New Hampshire. Our grateful thanks go also to the individuals whose photographs appear throughout the text.

CONTRIBUTORS

Adrienne Falk Bergen, P.T.
Positioning and Adaptive Equipment
Consultant
Dynamic Medical Equipment, Ltd.
Carle Place, New York

Karen E. Cullen, M.Ed., P.T.
Director of Research Programs
The Ledgeway Group, Inc.
Lexington, Massachusetts

Carol M. Davis, Ed.D., P.T.
Assistant Professor
Program in Physical Therapy
University of Miami
School of Medicine
Coral Gables, Florida

Daniel A. Dyrek, M.S., P.T.
Assistant Professor
Graduate Program in Physical
Therapy
Massachusetts General Hospital
Institute of Health Professions
Boston, Massachusetts

Joan E. Edelstein, M.A., P.T.
Senior Research Scientist and
Clinical Assistant Professor
Prosthetics and Orthotics
Department of Orthopedic
Surgery
New York University
New York, New York

Jeffrey E. Falkel, Ph.D., P.T.
Assistant Professor
School of Physical Therapy
Ohio University
College of Health and Human
Services
Athens, Ohio

Andrew A. Guccione, M.S., P.T.
Assistant Professor
Department of Physical Therapy
Boston University
Sargent College of Allied Health
Professions
Health Services Researcher
Multipurpose Arthritis Center
Boston University School of Medicine
Boston, Massachusetts

David E. Krebs, Ph.D., P.T.
Associate Professor
Graduate Program in Physical
Therapy
Massachusetts General Hospital
Institute of Health Professions
Boston, Massachusetts

Chaye Lamm-Warburg, M.A., O.T.R.
Occupational Therapy Consultant
Institute for Child Development
Hackensack Hospital
Hackensack, New Jersey
Doctoral Candidate
Teachers College
Columbia University
New York, New York

Gerald N. Lampe, P.T.
The Back Center
Overland Park, Kansas

Morris B. Lieberman, Ph.D.
Professor
Department of Psychology
Department of Guidance and
Counseling
Long Island University
Brooklyn, New York
Director of Clinical Services
Psychological and Consulting
Associates
Brooklyn, New York

Aaron Lieberman, D.S.W.
Assistant Professor
Department of Guidance and
Counseling
Long Island University
Brooklyn, New York
Administrative Director
Psychological and Consulting
Associates
Brooklyn, New York

Bella J. May, Ed.D., P.T.
Professor
Department of Physical Therapy
Medical College of Georgia
School of Allied Health Sciences
Augusta, Georgia
Co-Director
PhysioTherapy International, PC
Augusta, Georgia

Joseph McCulloch, Ph.D., P.T.
Associate Professor and Head
Department of Physical Therapy
Louisiana State University Medical
Center
School of Allied Health Professions
Shreveport, Louisiana

Virginia M. Mills, M.S., P.T.
Director of Traumatic Head Injury
Program
Braintree Hospital
Braintree, Massachusetts

Cynthia C. Norkin, Ed.D., P.T.
Associate Professor and Director
School of Physical Therapy
Ohio University
College of Health and Human
Services
Athens, Ohio

Susan B. O'Sullivan, M.S., P.T.
Assistant Professor
Department of Physical Therapy
University of Lowell
College of Health Professions
Lowell, Massachusetts
Doctoral Candidate
Boston University
Boston Massachusetts

Leslie G. Portney, M.S., P.T.
Assistant Professor
Department of Physical Therapy
Boston University
Sargent College of Allied Health
Professions
Boston, Massachusetts

Thomas J. Schmitz, M.S., P.T.
Assistant Professor
Program in Physical Therapy
Columbia University
College of Physicians and Surgeons
New York, New York

CONTENTS

Chapter 1

CLINICAL DECISION MAKING: PLANNING EFFECTIVE TREATMENTS

SUSAN B. O'SULLIVAN

OBJECTIVES

1. Describe the key elements in the clinical decision-making process.

2. Define the major responsibilities of the physical therapist in planning effective treatments.

3. Identify potential problems that could adversely affect the physical therapist's planning and delineate remediation strategies.

4. Describe two different models currently applied to clinical decision making.

INTRODUCTION

Clinical **decision making** involves a series of interrelated steps that enable the physical therapist to plan an effective treatment compatible with the needs and goals of the patient and members of the health care team. These steps include (1) assessment of the patient's present levels of function and dysfunction; (2) organization, analysis, and interpretation of the assessment data; (3) establishment of long-term and short-term goals; (4) development of an appropriate treatment plan to achieve those goals; (5) effective treatment of the patient; and (6) reassessment of the patient and treatment outcome. Important components of each step of the process include appropriate knowledge and clinical skills, effective decision-making skills, accurate documentation and effective communication with the patient and other members of the health care team (Fig. 1–1).

STEP 1. ASSESS THE PATIENT

This step includes the gathering of both subjective and objective data. Assessment begins with patient referral or initial entry and continues as an ongoing process throughout the course of rehabilitation. The medical record provides an important early source of information about the history of the patient's illness and present status. An understanding of disease processes, medical terminology, differential diagnosis using laboratory and other diagnostic tests, and medical management including pharmacology is essential. This may require the use of resource material or professional consultation in order to ensure a complete understanding of the data. Effective use of the medical record also should include a review of the professional reports of other members of the health care team.

An interview is another preliminary measure that is used to obtain information about the patient. An interview reveals information about the patient's primary complaint, the history of the present illness or injury, premorbid lifestyle, personal goals and expectations, motivation, and knowledge of the medical condition. Health habits, including exercise likes and dislikes, frequency and intensity of regular activity, also will prove helpful in planning an effective treatment program. Pertinent information about the patient's home and work environments also should be obtained. During the interview, listen carefully to what the patient says. Observe the patient closely, noting present mental and physical

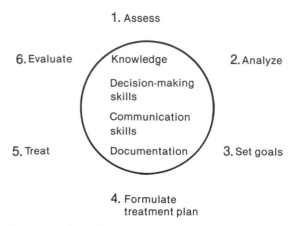

Figure 1–1. Steps in the clinical decision-making process.

function. Finally, use the interview to establish rapport, effective communication, and mutual trust. Patient cooperation serves to make a therapist's observations more valid and becomes crucial to the success of the rehabilitation program.

Once this preliminary information is gathered, a determination of the pertinent assessment procedures needed can be made through the use of screening examinations. Screening examinations allow the therapist to scan data from the body systems quickly, noting areas of deficit. Screening examinations also indicate areas requiring more detailed assessments. More definitive assessments are then used to provide objective data to determine accurately the degree of specific function and dysfunction (for example, manual muscle test, range of motion test, oxygen consumption, and so forth). Adequate training and skill in performing these procedures are crucial to ensure both validity and reliability of the tests. Failure to perform a procedure correctly can result in inaccurate data and an inappropriate treatment plan. Later chapters will focus on specific assessment procedures and will discuss issues of validity and reliability. Therapists should resist the tendency to gather excessive and extraneous data under the mistaken belief that more information is better. Unnecessary data will only confuse the picture, rendering the clinical decision making more difficult, while unnecessarily increasing the cost of care. If data are inconsistent, additional tests or assessment by another therapist may be warranted.

STEP 2. ANALYZE DATA

The assessment data must be organized and analyzed to identify a problem list. Primary problems are the direct result of the underlying disease processes, and secondary problems are the complications that may result from the effects of prolonged disability, poor management, or lack of rehabilitation intervention. Equally important is the development of an asset list which helps define the patient's present level of functional ability. The problem and asset lists then must be organized according to the functional tasks the patient will need to achieve functional independence. Decisions must be made concerning which functional tasks are realistic and

will thus become the focus of treatment. Priorities should be determined in terms of which problems are most critical to the functional task at hand and which assets need to be maximized. The therapist also will need a clear understanding of which problems can be addressed effectively in a rehabilitation program and which can not.

STEP 3. SET GOALS

Determining appropriate treatment goals is often the most difficult step in the treatment planning process, requiring skill in the interpretation of assessment data and professional judgment. **Long-term goals** define the patient's expected level of performance at the end of the rehabilitation process. They describe the functional outcomes of therapy and indicate (1) the amount of independence, supervision, or assistance required and (2) the equipment or environmental adaptation necessary to ensure adequate performance. Long-term goals usually define abilities in terms of activities of daily living, mobility within the environment, and communication or interaction within the environment.

Examples of long-term goals are

1. The patient will be independent in ambulation using an ankle-foot orthosis and a quad cane for all daily activities.

2. The patient will require close supervision in wheelchair propulsion and maximum assistance of one person in transfer activities.

3. The patient will require minimal supervision in all dressing activities.

Long-term goals are established by the rehabilitation team and reflect mutual agreement that all members of the team will work toward assisting the patient to reach these goals. The patient and family should be considered active members of the team and should be closely involved in the goal-setting process. Without direct involvement, it will be difficult to motivate the patient and to focus attention on the attainment of these goals. Many rehabilitation plans have failed miserably simply because the patient did not see the relevance of the professionals' goals or because the patient had established a very different set of goals.

Once long-term goals have been established, the next step is to determine the component skills that will be needed to attain these goals. Each component skill then becomes the objective of a **short-term goal**. The therapist should determine the appropriate sequence of sub-skills (short-term goals) and prioritize them based on an analysis of the problem and asset lists. The written goal should include an estimate of the overall level of competence and the time needed to attain the goal. Estimating how rapidly or slowly a patient will progress is a highly intuitive skill which may be difficult at first for the inexperienced therapist. Consultation with experienced professionals can often assist in this process. Goals should be directly observable or measurable and precisely defined in behavioral terms. An example of this process follows.

Long-term Goal: The patient will be independent in ambulation with bilateral knee-ankle orthoses and Loftstrand crutches for short distances of approximately 100 ft (31 M).

Short-term Goals:

1. Increase strength in shoulder depressor muscles and elbow extensor muscles in both upper extremities from good to normal within 3 weeks.

2. Increase range of motion 10 degrees in knee extension bilaterally to within normal limits within 3 weeks.

3. Achieve independence in application of lower extremity orthoses within 1 week.

4. Achieve independence in sit-to-stand activities from wheelchair to crutches within 2 weeks.

5. Improve endurance in ambulation with bilateral knee-ankle orthoses and parallel bars using a swing-through gait and increments of 50, 75, and 100 feet within 4 weeks.

6. Achieve independence in ambulation with bilateral knee-ankle orthoses and Loftstrand crutches using a swing-through gait for 50 feet within 4 weeks.

The patient is advanced through this sequence until the final end point or long-term goal is achieved. Each treatment plan usually has several long-term goals, and short-term goals or component skills may be part of more than one sequence. Thus short-term goals are often interrelated, and the final outcome of several long-term goals may be dependent upon one component skill. In formulating a treatment plan, the therapist needs to identify component skills and their relationship to treatment outcomes.

STEP 4. FORMULATE TREATMENT PLAN

Once appropriate goals have been formulated, the next step is to determine which therapeutic procedures can be used to achieve each goal. The therapist may choose from a wide variety of procedures, many of which will be discussed in this text. It is important to identify all possible treatment alternatives, to weigh carefully those alternatives, and to decide on those procedures that have the best probability of success. Therapists need to remain open to new options and to keep abreast of recent professional literature. An integrated treatment approach that provides multiple treatment options is often the one that has the greatest chance for success. Narrowly adhering to one treatment approach reduces the available treatment options and may limit or preclude success. Available clinical information should be carefully assessed and additional information sought if needed. Watts[1] suggests that clinical judgment "is clearly an elegant mixture of art and science." Professional consultation with expert clinicians may be an effective means to help a therapist sort through the complex issues involved in decision making, especially when the patient is chronically ill or has multiple disease processes or complications.

Decisions need to be formulated based upon a number of considerations, such as the patient's general health, interactions with other health professionals or family, financial costs, and length of hospitalization. Once treatment decisions are reached, a general outline of the treatment should be constructed. It should include consideration of specific modalities, therapeutic exercise procedures, assistive devices, and other specialized equipment needs. The plan should also include the strategies selected to meet the educational needs of the patient and family. An estimate should be made of the total length of treatment, the frequency (times per day or week), the duration of the treatment session, and the intensity (i.e., number of repetitions). The therapist is responsible for effective time management, and the treatment plan should include delegation of appropriate responsibilities of treatment to assistants or aides. The general outline also may consider potential discharge plans, including plans for a home visit, home program, home modifications, or potential equipment needs.

Specific treatment procedures may then be outlined. A classification schema that identifies specific components of the treatment is often helpful, especially to the inexperienced therapist. For example, components of a therapeutic exercise procedure may include a description of the activity (posture and movements), the technique (type of muscle contraction: isotonic, isometric, or eccentric), and the facilitation elements (sensory inputs) or modalities.[2] Procedures should be selected to reach individual short-term goals. Ideally, the therapist should choose procedures that accomplish more than one goal and should sequence the procedures effectively to mediate key problems first. Procedures also should be sequenced to achieve optimum motivational effects, interspacing the more difficult or uncomfortable procedures with easier ones. The therapist should include tasks that ensure success during the treatment session and, whenever possible, end each session on a positive note, helping the patient retain that positive feeling of success and look forward to the next treatment.

STEP 5. TREAT THE PATIENT

The therapist must take into account a number of factors in structuring an effective treatment session. The treatment area should be properly arranged to respect the patient's privacy, with adequate draping and positioning. The environment should be structured to reduce distractors and to focus attention on the task at hand. In applying exercise procedures, the therapist should consider good body mechanics, effective use of gravity and position, and correct application of techniques and methods of facilitation. Equipment should be gathered prior to treatment and should be in good working order. All safety precautions must be observed. The patient's pretreatment level of function or initial ready state should be assessed carefully. General state organization and homeostatic balance of the somatic and autonomic systems are important determinants of how a patient may respond to treatment. Stockmeyer[3] points out that a wide range of influences from emotional to cognitive to organic factors may affect how a patient reacts to a particular treatment. Patients with altered homeostatic mechanisms cannot be expected to react to treatment in predictable ways. Responses to treatment should be monitored carefully. Treatment modifications should be implemented as soon as needed to ensure successful performance. Therapists develop the "art of clinical practice" by learning to adjust their inputs (voice commands, manual contacts, and so forth) in response to the patient's movements.[1] Treatment thus becomes a dynamic and interactive process between patient and therapist. Shaping of behavior can be enhanced further by careful orientation to the purpose of the tasks and how they meet the patient's needs, thereby ensuring optimal cooperation and motivation.

STEP 6. ASSESS TREATMENT OUTCOME

This last step is ongoing and involves continuous reassessment of the patient and efficacy of treatment. The patient's abilities are reassessed in terms of the specific goals set forth in the treatment plan. A determination as to whether a patient has achieved the desired level of competence for each skill must be made. Two outcomes are possible: The patient reached the stated goal, or the patient did not reach the stated goal. If the goal was reached, was it the result of the treatment intervention or the result of natural improvement? In either case, new short-term goals can be written and appropriate treatment procedures selected. When long-term goals are reached or are close to being reached, discharge planning and plans for follow-up care can be initiated. If the goal has not been reached, the therapist must determine why this is so. Was the goal realistic, given the database? Was the treatment selected at an appropriate level to challenge the patient or was it too easy or too difficult? Was the patient sufficiently motivated? Were all the treatment uncertainties and constraining variables identified? With either outcome, the therapist must consider modification of the treatment plan. If the treatment was not appropriate, additional information may be sought, different treatment alternatives can be selected, or treatment goals can be modified. Long-term goals are revised if the patient progresses more rapidly or more slowly than expected. Each modification in the program is assessed in terms of its effect on the overall treatment plan. Thus, the treatment plan becomes a fluid statement of how the patient is progressing and where the patient is going. Its overall success is dependent upon the therapist's clinical decision-making skills and on engaging the patient's cooperation and motivation. Wolf[4] cautions against empiricism, that is, continuing to use a treatment simply because it works. Rather, therapists should strive to develop a concrete database upon which the validity of treatment can be substantiated. Expansion of the body of knowledge with the continued development of sound

theories of action and continued professional development are the responsibility of every therapist.

CLINICAL DECISION-MAKING MODELS

Models for clinical decision making assist the practitioner in identifying problems, recognizing relevant data, synthesizing material, and formulating conclusions. This chapter synthesizes several models, including a systems approach for treatment planning, the problem-oriented medical record (POMR), and decision analysis.

Schematically, the **systems model** is represented by the flow chart shown in Figure 1–2. This model uses a step-by-step approach, with the solution in each step dependent upon the information in the preceding one.[5,6]

In the **problem-oriented approach** originally developed by Weed[7,8] and adopted by many institutions, the patient-treatment process is divided into four phases:

Phase 1: The formation of a database, including history, physical examination, laboratory and other assessment results.

Phase 2: The identification of a specific problem list from the interpretation of the database, including specific impairment of function (physical, psychologic, social, and vocational) resulting from the disease process or from secondary associated disabilities.

Phase 3: The identification of a specific treatment plan for each of the problems described.

Phase 4: The assessment of the effectiveness of each of the plans and subsequent changes in these plans depending upon the patient's progress.

The reader will recognize many similarities between these two conceptual models. Both represent an organized approach for gathering data and determining an appropriate treatment plan.

A third model for consideration involves clinical decision analysis. **Decision analysis** is a formal discipline which had its origins in a set of economic axioms described in the late 1940s and early 1950s. Its application to operations research, management science, systems analysis, and medicine is widespread.[9–11] It is designed to consider choice under uncertainty, allowing the decision maker to integrate variables and to calculate relevant probabilities and outcomes. Keeney[11] describes the key areas on which decision analysis focuses as (1) the structure of the decision problem, (2) the alternatives, (3) the consequences associated with those alternatives, (4) the uncertainties, and (5) the preferences

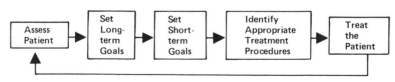

Figure 1–2. Flow chart illustrating the Systems Approach.

(values) of the decision makers. Decision analysis recognizes a series of choices, the timing of these choices, the key uncertainties or risks, and the potential benefits of each strategy. The final outcome is arrived at only after a series of "if . . . , then . . . " decisions, which allow the choices to be considered individually. Thus, the final decision best represents a realistic balance between the necessary resources and expected outcomes.[12]

The generation of a decision tree or flow diagram allows the components of the decision process to be displayed in a sequence that embodies both temporal and logical structure. Each tree may have several branching pathways (strategies) that include decision points (interventions) and chance points (events not under the decision maker's control). A tree is, therefore, progressively built from a database that includes patient symptoms, diagnostic findings, therapeutic interventions, and other relevant findings. Probabilities of various possible outcomes, when known, are entered at appropriate points. Decision trees serve to highlight various different strategies without, as Weinstein[9] points out, losing sight of the whole problem. It also highlights the critical trade-offs between the benefits and risks of treatment and potential biases, distortions, or omissions in planning[13] (Fig. 1–3). Wolf's *Clinical Decision Making in Physical Therapy*[4] is an excellent reference in aiding the reader's further understanding of this model. Several computer programs are also available to assist health professionals in constructing and analyzing decision trees and in probability calculations.[14–16]

DOCUMENTATION AND COMMUNICATION

Data included in the medical record should be meaningful (important, not just nice to have), accurate (valid and reliable), timely (recorded promptly), and systematic (regularly recorded).[17] Written documentation is formally done at the time of admission and at discharge from the program and at periodic intervals during the course of rehabilitation. The format and timing of notes may vary according to institutional policy or the needs of third party payers. In the POMR system developed by Weed, the medical record is divided into four sections, representing each of the four phases. Each member of the health care team records his/her findings and plans according to the specific problem list. Progress notes are written in **SOAP** format (subjective, objective, assessment, plan). The subjective findings are what the patient and the patient's family tell you. The objective findings are what you observe, test, or measure. The assessment includes professional judgments about the subjective/objective findings formulated into both long- and short-

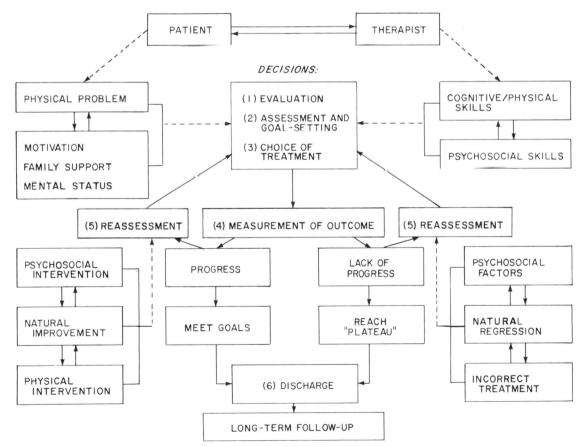

Figure 1–3. Flow chart illustrating the Decision-Making Model. From Wolf, S: *Clinical Decision Making in Physical Therapy*. Philadelphia, FA Davis, 1985, p 172.

term goals. The plan includes both general and specific aspects of treatment. Thus, the POMR highlights the relationship of the database to the treatment plan and allows the specific patient problems to become the central focus of planning.[7,8]

Computer-assisted data management systems are becoming readily available to many therapists. Software programs permit data storage and retrieval as well as statistical manipulation. The format is variable and may be consistent with the POMR system or others. An understanding of the software capabilities and of the data management system is essential in learning to use these programs.[17,18]

The therapist's plans should include goals written in objective, measurable terms. Plans and notes should be current, dated, neat, and legible. Appropriate medical terminology should be used, and confusing abbreviations or poor organization avoided. Physical therapy notes should be understandable to all who read and utilize the medical record.

Throughout the treatment planning process, the therapist should regularly communicate with other health professionals and with the patient and family. Effective communication provides an open chain of dialog and allows for full cooperation and understanding. Communication should be appropriately modified for patients of different ages, cultural backgrounds, and educational levels, and for patients with language differences and/or communication or cognitive impairments.[19]

SUMMARY

An organized process of clinical decision making allows the therapist to plan effective treatments systematically. The steps identified in this process include (1) assessing the patient, (2) analyzing the data, (3) setting goals, (4) formulating treatment plans, (5) treating the patient, and (6) assessing treatment outcomes. Inherent in this process are an appropriate knowledge base and skills in decision making, clinical practice, communication, and documentation.

QUESTIONS FOR REVIEW

1. What are the key elements in the clinical decision-making process?

2. What are the sources of information in assessing patient function and dysfunction?

3. What is the difference between a long-term goal and a short-term goal? How may they be interrelated? Practice writing examples of both.

4. How are treatment plans formulated? Describe the key steps. What factors are important to consider?

5. In assessing treatment outcome, why might a patient have failed to reach a stated goal? What actions could you as the therapist take?

6. Describe two different models for decision making. What are the stated advantages of clinical decision analysis?

7. What are the four components of the SOAP format of written documentation?

REFERENCES

1. Watts, N: Decision analysis: A tool for improving physical therapy education. In Wolf, S (ed): Clinical Decision Making in Physical Therapy. FA Davis, Philadelphia, 1985, p 8.
2. Sullivan, P, Markos, P, and Minor, M: An Integrated Approach to Therapeutic Exercise. Reston Publishing, Reston, VA, 1982.
3. Stockmeyer, S: Clinical decision making based on homeostatic concepts. In Wolf, S (ed): Clinical Decision Making in Physical Therapy. FA Davis, Philadelphia, 1985, p 79.
4. Wolf, S (ed): Clinical Decision Making in Physical Therapy. FA Davis, Philadelphia, 1985.
5. Day, D: A systems diagram for teaching treatment planning. Am J Occup Ther 27:239, 1973.
6. Olsen, S: Teaching treatment planning: A problem solving approach. Phys Ther 63:526, 1983.
7. Weed, LL: Medical Records, Medical Education and Patient Care. The Press of Case Western Reserve University, Cleveland, 1969.
8. Hill, J: Problem Oriented Approach to Physical Therapy Care—Programmed Instruction. APTA, 1111 N Fairfax St, Alexandria, VA, 1977.
9. Weinstein, M, et al: Clinical Decision Analysis. WB Saunders, Philadelphia, 1980.
10. Raiffa, H: Decision Analysis: Introductory Lectures on Choices under Uncertainty. Addison-Wesley, Reading, MA, 1968.
11. Keeney, R: Decision analysis: An overview. Operations Research 30:803, 1982.
12. Watts, N: Eighteenth Mary McMillan Lecture: The privilege of choice. Phys Ther 63:1802, 1983.
13. Eraker, S and Polister, P: How decisions are reached: Physician and patient. Ann Intern Med 97:262, 1982.
14. Pauker, S and Kassirer, J: Clinical decision analysis by personal computer. Arch Intern Med 141:1831, 1981.
15. Silverstein, M: A clinical decision analysis program for the Apple computer. Med Decis Making 3:29, 1983.
16. Lau, J, Kassirer, J, and Pauker, S: Decision maker 3.0 improved decision analysis by personal computer. Med Decis Making 3:39, 1983.
17. Johnson, G: Bases for clinical decision making: Assimilating data and marketing skills. In Wolf, S (ed): Clinical Decision Making in Physical Therapy. FA Davis, Philadelphia, 1985, p 61.
18. Hislop, H: Clinical decision making: Educational, data and risk factors. In Wolf, S (ed): Clinical Decision Making in Physical Therapy. FA Davis Company, 1985, p 25.
19. DiMatteo, M and DiNicola: Achieving Patient Compliance. Pergamon Press, New York, 1982.

GLOSSARY

Decision analysis: A systematic approach to decision making under conditions of uncertainty. Decision analysis focuses on structuring and diagramming over time the problem, the management alternatives and consequences, the uncertainties, and the preferences of the decision makers.

Long-term goals: Statements that define the patient's expected level of performance at the end of the rehabilitation process; the functional outcomes of therapy, indicating the amount of independence, supervision, or assistance required and the equipment or environmental adaptation necessary to ensure adequate performance.

Problem-oriented approach: An organized approach to the patient-treatment process characterized by four phases: (1) formation of a database, (2) identification of a specific problem list, (3) identification of a specific treatment plan, and (4) assessment of the effectiveness of treatment plans.

Short-term goals: Statements that define the component skills required to attain long-term goals, including an estimate of the overall level of patient competence and the estimated time needed to attain the goal.

SOAP notes: Progress note format utilized in the problem-oriented medical record (POMR); delineation is made among subjective findings, objective findings, assessment results, and plan of care.

Systems model: A step-by-step model of treatment planning; the solution to each problem is dependent upon information obtained in the preceding step.

Chapter 2

PSYCHOSOCIAL ADJUSTMENT TO PHYSICAL DISABILITY

MORRIS B. LIEBERMAN AND AARON LIEBERMAN

OBJECTIVES

1. Recognize the inseparability of the physical aspects from the psychologic aspects of human functioning.

2. Describe the impact of values and learning on adaptive and maladaptive coping.

3. List the stages of psychologic adjustment to loss and disability, and explain their significance.

4. Recognize the danger signs that might indicate psychopathologic adjustment of a patient.

5. Describe the behaviors that typically might be expected during the posttraumatic period.

6. Identify the contributions that physical therapists and mental health professionals can make to each other's clinical practice.

INTRODUCTION

Our understanding of what it means to be disabled can only approximate what a disabled individual might actually feel about a disability in general terms. We can not even hope to understand all the individual and unique thoughts and feelings culled from a lifetime of personal experience as they impinge on that individual. Experiences, memories, significant messages, and commands received during a lifetime, whether conscious or unconscious, organize life. They create a set of values and expectations by which one measures oneself and one's worth. They become the compass through which one steers life and relationships, and they structure the goals and foundations of that individual's world. All this occurs with the help of a functioning mind and body structure that have learned by trial and error to develop a way of coping and functioning deemed appropriate for

that individual life. Then suddenly—or gradually, depending on the nature of the disabling agent—the foundations of this structure collapse. The disabling condition, and the perception of it, disrupts the structure that had been so carefully erected. The rules and roles change, the relative independence and ability to do all the essential tasks of life may be gone. The abilities to give and to take love, care, affection, and support are altered. The relative financial stability once enjoyed may have vaporized into thin air. And the list goes on.

Intellectually we can understand the trauma, and with our ability to empathize we may even feel some of it. We may associate it with recollections of some of our own pain and loss experiences. We have overcome these; they are in the past. If it happens that we, too, have a disabling condition, we obviously have made some adjustments that the patient may yet have to make. We know the outcome of our adjustment, but to the patient who is yet to make an adjustment, "the end of the tunnel is not in sight" and therefore nonexistent. The hope for career, marriage, love, travel, independence, and financial security may all be dashed and broken into fragments. The fear of never again being able to walk, or to see, or to hear, or to move about may be consuming; when an undeserved life sentence of imprisonment within a body that can not feel or move is looming ahead, these fears can devastate the strongest among us.

Even when prognosis is excellent and promises a full return of function, will the interrupted dreams, plans, and tasks be recaptured? Will the lover wait? Will the children suspend the growth and excitement of their tender years which the deprived father or mother longs to share and to live through? During all this, who will take care of the dependent and dear ones and pay for the expensive treatment? Further, is this patient privy to all the confidence the treating professionals may have about the recovery, or does the individual have his or her own perceptions regarding the condition?

Take each one of these possibilities and try to fathom the disruption of one's emotions, and then multiply the result by all the other factors involved. We can not feel what the patient does; but we owe it to that person to learn as much as we can to understand better the pain, fears, turmoil, and emotional upheavals and implications of the disability and its role in adjustment.

ADAPTATION AS AN INTEGRATED SURVIVAL ACTIVITY

Living is a constantly ongoing adjustment and adaptation process encompassing different levels of an organism and its life. Among these, we consider **adaptation** at the physiologic, physical, psychologic, and social levels of one's functioning. Although there are indeed significant differences when we speak about one or another of these aspects of human functioning, we do have to keep in mind that even though we can delineate and define these, they are only a part of a unitary entity which functions as a whole. Any separation between levels and parts of such a system is an artificial convenience, inasmuch as no part within it is actually independent from the rest of the system.

Psychologic **adjustment** should, therefore, be viewed as a part of adjustment in general and should not be viewed as a separate entity. Overall psychologic functioning and each of its components have to be considered as aspects of a dynamic, interactive, and ongoing process of an individual's adaptation to the internal physiologic processes and the external reality. The resultant perception of life includes

1. the body total with its various genetic, electrochemical, hormonal, and neurologic configurations
2. its innate and learned mental mechanisms
3. its sociocultural, spiritual, and ethnic belief and value systems within the socioeconomic realities of the time and place with which one interacts.

NATURE AND NURTURE

As we grow and age, various sets of expectations change and evolve. The nature and direction of these changes depend upon the species specific and individual genetically inherited developmental capacities, the assigned roles proscribed by gender, and the ethnic and/or social status into which we are born. Other aspects, such as the prevailing political climate and religious beliefs, the historic period with its economic and technologic systems one lives in, and family idiosyncrasies and structure are among the contributing factors to the individual's adaptive and adjusting style. They are part and parcel of the mold from which the unique individual emerges and creates an idiosyncratic style of adaptive (or maladaptive) perceptual and conceptual functioning, a response repertoire, and a personality structure through which the individual then negotiates with his or her world.

Yet we should realize that the evolving self is in no way a passive target of all these factors. As that self evolves, it combines and channels innate drives and needs with learned or reinforced behaviors and values. These, in turn, are shaped by one's ongoing development and experience; temperament and perception; real and imagined personal competence and vulnerability; an internalized ideology, value system, and social channeling. As a result of this, and the fact that coping is an ongoing learning process that is constantly affected by the variety of social and environmental influences, the uniqueness of individual coping style is to be expected, as is the variability in one's coping effectiveness.

The individual's interaction with the internal and external reality becomes, therefore, selective, subjective, and idiosyncratic. It can be seen as the sum total of an interactional history of the individual's "nature" and "nurture." The chronology of this interactional history includes the genetic evolution that is species as well as ancestral specific, and the cultural and environmental forces that left their mark on the world into which the person was born. This shapes the individual's subjective perception of the world and of the self. It also shapes an intricate mental defense and adaptation system, resulting in a distinctive response repertoire that will be used in future coping and adjustments, the experience of which will in turn keep the response style ever changing while still resting on the developed base.

Accordingly, an individual's adjustments will depend on the thus developed ego (or self) and its defense structure, its relative strength and/or vulnerability, the adjustment style one has adopted, and the impinging stimulus. Catering to these conflicting biologic, psychologic, and social needs requires the balancing of internal and external resources. We will call this activity **coping,** even though many other names are used to describe the same balancing act. Coping is a combination of innate and learned adaptive behavior through which an individual attempts to deal with the demands of the internal and external environment and personal needs. It is an active process that is used by the individual to deal with conflicting demands and to create a state of biologic and psychologic equilibrium. The attempt to bring about such a balance and to satisfy the internal and external pressures is what **adjustment** is all about.

Such a derived idiosyncratic way of functioning is relatively stable but not static. Adaptation and coping are significantly affected by learned values and coping style. However, the resulting equilibrium may not necessarily serve the individual's survival needs nor be compatible with what society considers acceptable. Maladaption may have developed as the result of faulty perception, learned self-rejection, misguided values, or misinterpretations of reality. Deviant behavior might also be due to justified or unjustified disagreement with the surrounding set of values.

Nevertheless, whether adaptive or maladaptive, the coping response of an individual is part of an adaptation process aimed toward survival, even though the specific coping responses may be contrary to what seems best for an individual. Therefore the reader should be cognizant that it is the individual's perception of the best "survival" response to a given situation that determines reactive functioning.

In summary, it can be stated that psychologic adjustment is an intricate interactive process; that it dictates to, while being dictated by, the body mechanism and the external world one lives in; that it represents the consciously perceived self as well as unconscious motivations, emotions, drives, values, and perceptual functioning. Psychologic adjustment is therefore considered of paramount importance in any consideration of what an individual is all about. It includes the need to maintain and to develop a self-identity within a biologic and social structure of which one is a part. The psychologic adjustment of an individual might be considered crucial to what life is all about for that individual; it will determine its quality, and sometimes may even bring about its destruction. Psychologic adjustment can significantly enhance the use of one's resources for rehabilitation from a physical disability or, when it is maladaptive, be a major contributing factor to the disability.

REACTION TO INJURY AS AN ADJUSTMENT CONCEPT

Like all other adjustments, the reaction one makes to injury, illness, or loss of function is also an adjustment process that contributes to or may result in the ensuing physical disability. The resulting disability can, therefore, be considered an adjustment process to the disruptive event that interrupted the normal functioning of that individual. This implies that when an individual is confronted with a disablement, various adjustments are necessary to cope with the situation. The elicited response to the disablement may encompass most, if not all, levels of the individual's functioning. This includes the vegetative process, the autonomous nervous system and cortical responses, the hormonal response, and intrapersonal and interpersonal reactions. Above all, the response to disablement and rehabilitation depends on what the disabling condition means to the individual.

One's functioning and coping styles might help the individual adjust favorably to the newly created condition and the rehabilitation process, or they may hinder it. Acceptance of the resulting real limitations, development of compensatory functioning, adaptation to a different mode of life, and different societal roles, if required, will usually be adaptive. Unwarranted retreats to lower-level functioning, isolation or rejection of oneself, loss of self-appreciation, or even an escape into nihilism or death obviously would be considered maladaptive. For those with preexisting coping difficulties, a disability may be used as an escape from responsibility and a tool for manipulativeness; in others it may bring about further deterioration. Engel[1] reports that in some instances of emotionally dysfunctional individuals, disability may contribute positively to their overall adjustment. Moos[2] considers such findings a provocative challenge, inasmuch as most researchers tend to accentuate the negative reactions to disability, obscuring some implications of an individual's positive reaction to a disabling condition. Ehrenteil,[3] too, stresses the possible positive reaction to disability, claiming that disability may have an ego-integrative role.

Subjectivity of Disability

A person's disability or handicap is related to how the individual measures himself or herself and the handicapping condition. If a person's focus is on deficiencies rather than on assets, the extent of the disability will be increased. Much of this depends on the premorbid makeup of an individual and the unique coping repertoire, as well as to the external input about the condition.

Adjustment does not imply favorable adaptation. Adjustments are attempts to develop a fit between two or more variables. In living organisms, adjustment usually implies adapting for the sake of survival. In humans, adaptation goes beyond survival, inasmuch as our different value systems do not accept just any type of survival, or even survival itself as **adaptive.** A moral person will not consider personal survival adaptive if it is against the basic principles for which the individual stands. Society will consider **maladaptive** that which a deranged mind considers appropriate adjustment.

Many of the ways we adjust to our needs are **maladaptive.** When, for instance, we stuff ourself with food to overcome lonely feelings, or smoke to overcome tension, or get into debt for things we do not need in order to overcome inferiority feelings, we are adjusting to certain perceived needs and feelings. These are adjustments that could be considered maladaptive. Accordingly, an individual who is hurt at work and prefers to prolong the disabled status and to shirk off all responsibility for family and self might be considered maladaptive.

When a maladaptive response is the result of faulty reality testing, value judgments, misinformation, or defective neuronal brain activity, it becomes the responsibility of "responsible others" to help that individual shift the maladaptive responses to adaptive ones. Parents, spouses, clinicians, teachers, and at times society will take on the role of the "responsible others." Yet, who really knows best? We have to respect the individual's rights to make decisions unless there is indeed objective evidence that judgment faculties are faulty. We also should do our best to understand the individual's covert reasons for functioning responses. This takes special skills, objectivity, and an ability to put our own values and interests aside. If we don't, then our judgment may indeed be the one that needs correction.

Our aim as clinicians is to prevent maladaptive adjustment in our patients. For a patient who had the capacity to learn to ambulate, choosing to spend life in a wheelchair would be considered a maladaptive adjustment, but it is still an adjustment. As already stated, the terms *adjustment, coping,* and *adaptation* are given to value interpretation and do not imply a positive outcome. For the purpose of convenience, we will use the term *maladaptive* for faulty adaptation and the term *adaptive* for its opposite. We also differentiate between the terms *disability* and *disablement.* We prefer to use the term *disablement* as the actual physical condition of the individual. The term *disability,* however, is used here as the subjective functioning response of the patient.

The term *adjustment to disability* is an encompassing one, denoting an ongoing, fluid process of adjustments and readjustments at all levels of one's functioning. It can be seen as a chain reaction, inasmuch as each adjustment causes changes and is followed by other reactions. In addition, it is interactive between all levels of the person and the environment. The need to adjust to an immediate disruption of homeostatic balance during a traumatic injury is different in its intensity and urgency than the adjustment needs that arise afterward.

ADJUSTMENT TO DISABLEMENT

Among the factors contributing to disability adjustment are the extent of the injury or illness; its mode of onset; the prognosis of the physical aspect of the disability; the central processing of the brain, if affected; the social, medical, psychologic, and economic support system; and the subjective perception of the situation as well as the premorbid coping capacity of the individual.

Adjustment is obviously more dramatic during a major disabling condition, yet we must realize that even minor physical conditions are major to their owners. What is discussed here is therefore applicable to most patients seeking physical therapy intervention. Pain and reactions to injuries are subjective, and therefore adjustment might be similar regardless of the extent of injury. The difference in the adjustment need is more due to the personal perception of the meaning of the condition, but it is also dependent on the duration of the adjustment needed. Obviously an injury that ceases to have impact on the injured within a relatively short period, or that does not require any special attention or changes in one's functioning, will leave little if any scars. When the subjective reaction to a disablement is disproportionate to the level of actual damage, we can assume that such a

response is most likely triggered by some previous life trauma and/or personality structure than by the precipitating injury or illness.

Successful adjustment implies the restoration of function or the best possible approximation or compensation for the loss. We have implied that disability of physical functioning is usually accompanied by disruptions of psychologic and social functioning. Compensation for the physical loss does not necessarily bring with it a correction of the other losses which, if ignored, may actually hinder rehabilitation efforts and even increase the level of the physical limitation or contribute to additional ailments.

Our discussion of psychologic adjustment is divided into three phases of the disability. The first phase, called traumatic reaction, is the immediate period of the injury or disablement. The second phase is referred to as the posttraumatic adjustment period. The final phase, the stabilization period, is that phase when a relatively stable adjustment has been made.

The physical therapist will have little, if any, impact during the first of these stages. Therefore most of our emphasis will be on the second stage, because that is the one during which the physical therapist's intervention is at a peak. During the stabilization period which follows, the patient may still need and benefit from the guidance of the clinical team as he or she settles down to a relatively adjusted state.

The Traumatic Reaction

Although the main clinical impact of physical therapy is aimed at the posttraumatic adjustment period, it is important that the therapist be knowledgeable about the initial catastrophic reactions to the physical insult, and the interplay between the physiologic and psychologic levels of the individual's functioning at the time of the accident.

THE GENERAL ADAPTATION SYNDROME: A PHYSICAL-EMOTIONAL INTERACTION

During a catastrophic accident or an acute, severe attack of illness, the individual's response will be primarily at the physiologic level, at which physical survival takes precedence. The patient has to be catered to by the body's emergency responses from within and by the medical emergency team from without. Psychologic adjustment will most likely be extreme but not as discernible or noticeable until later. When consciousness is less affected and the insult is less catastrophic, or when the physical disablement is due to a more gradual onset (as during an illness process), the psychologic reaction may be the one most affected or noticeable. In either case an interactive feedback loop establishes itself between the physiologic and emotional functionings of the individual as a result of the ensuing **stress reaction.**

During an extreme catastrophic reaction, an organism most likely responds with what Selye[4] terms the **general adaptation response (GAS).** Selye describes GAS as the organism's defensive adaptation attempt, which is expressed through a physiologic and emotional interaction of responses aimed at dealing with real or perceived emergency situations. During this reaction there is a hormonal release of ACTH, which sets into motion an increase of physiologic responses, needed at times of emergency. However, such corticosteroid increase has an undesirable inhibitory effect on insulin and calcium, which when prolonged will create other undesirable effects, such as hypertension and digestive disturbances, as well as interfere with the immune system of the body. Selye has been able to document the devastating effect of the prolongation of this response on human mental and physical functionings. Therefore, situations that activate the sympathetic system through repeated alarms, traumas, or chronic stress may alter synaptic transmission, thus leading to anxiety and depression of function.[5]

It should, however, be noted that the physiologic and psychologic interactions to stress are not limited to catastrophic conditions only. An extensive body of research shows stress reactions present during less severe situations than those of traumatic or posttraumatic states. Everyday life frustrations, internal and external conflict situations, and changes in life conditions are major causes of stress reaction, which may have a devastating effect on one's functioning and health. This is important to the physical therapist because most of the rehabilitation effort is usually concentrated after the traumatic reaction takes place and at periods during which frustrations abound.

Posttraumatic Adjustment

It is during the posttraumatic period and the time of physical therapy that the psychologic impact of the trauma assumes major importance on the patient's functioning. Mann and Gold[6] claim that the psychologic problems after injury are as disabling as the physical ones, and they found this to be even more pronounced when the physical injury was less evident. Most of the psychologic aspects of functioning—the defenses and emotional reactions from the pretraumatic, traumatic, and posttraumatic periods—interact to create the perceptions, fears, anxieties, and behaviors with which the physical therapist has to deal.

Stabilization Period

The **stabilization period** is the third and final phase of the disability. During this time the role of the clinical team is phased out and the individual typically enters into a relatively adjusted and balanced state of living. It should be noted, however, that adjustment does not imply beneficial adaption, neither does stabilization. **Stabilization,** therefore, indicates a so-called balanced fit of one's functioning within the "world," regardless of whether it is adaptive or maladaptive. For example, an article that appeared in the *New York Times* (October 7, 1987) described an individual weighing over 1000 pounds. He has been "imprisoned" in bed for over a dec-

ade because of his body's inability to carry such weight. It can be said that he is living a stabilized and adjusted life—adjusted to a life without any movement except the frequent intake of food, which provides pleasure. It is maladaptive but nevertheless adjusted and stabilized.

All this indicates the importance of the quality the stabilization period takes on. It is this latter period during which the patient experiences the quality, and even the value, of life toward which our clinical efforts were aimed. Likewise it is the stabilization period when life again becomes meaningful or meaningless for the individual. Being alert to all the needs of the patient as well as to the signs and symptoms of maladaption during the posttraumatic adjustment period is therefore vital. This emphasizes the need for an integrated wholistic approach, which must essentially include the psychosocial aspects of disability as well as the physical. This points to a primary goal of this chapter: to alert clinicians to the wounds that illness and injury open. Interacting with the other clinical team members is paramount, therefore, in meeting the needs of the patient as an integrated human being.

THE ROLE OF COGNITION

One of the psychologic factors that affect the patient's rehabilitative functioning is cognitive make-up and the resulting perception. The most prevalent views of psychology regard cognition as one of the most significant factors in determining an individual's way of dealing with the world. Dollard and Miller[7] indicated that cognition and motives were determinants of individual functioning. Subsequent psychologic research confirmed this view and considered emotions (and stress) as arising from the individual's cognitive functioning (i.e., the person's own definition and thinking about his or her relationship with the world). This view has since been supported by numerous studies and reinforces the important role played by one's perception in dealing with the situations confronting an individual.[8-11] Selye stated, "It is not what happens to you that matters, but how you take it."[12]

Accordingly, the traumatic severity of a noxious stimulus hinges, greatly, on the individual's perception of an event and the subjective value assigned to the factors affected by it. Likewise, the ability to cope with the situation as perceived is significantly dependent on the individual's perception of personal coping ability, not less than on the actual resources available.

This indicates that the perception of an individual regarding a given situation, and the ability to cope with it effectively, is significantly determined by one's psychologic structure. Thus the choice of any adjustment toward loss of function and illness is dictated from within the personal world of an individual's belief and value system and the ensuing perception. Faulty reality appraisal and/or misguided coping strategies will create maladaptation, and, conversely, a belief in one's resources and a positve set of values may help an individual overcome a disability through actualizing previously dormant assets. (See chapter 3, Influence of Values on Patient Care: Foundation for Decision Making.) Experience shows that identical physical or physiologic damage will result in different levels of disability in different individuals.[13]

SUBJECTIVITY OF PHYSICAL DISABILITY

Understanding the psychologic adjustment of a given patient to physical disability becomes another very important tool in the armamentarium of the physical therapist. The seasoned therapist knows that an amputated limb is not a discarded anatomic part but, rather, an inseparable part of the individual even after its loss. The patient will not only feel the (phantom) sensation or pain in the lost limb but may also perceive life as worthless without it, regardless of how little the loss might objectively interfere in one's life. The prosthesis that replaces the limb may serve to balance its owner physically but fail to do so emotionally. Without the anatomic limb the patient may feel impotent, worthless, estranged, punished, guilty, unloved, and frightened.

It is doubtful that a sane person can lose an anatomic part or a function that had been a permanent part of the physical being without losing part of the psychologic self. The lack of a visible catastrophic response to such a loss would most likely indicate a defensive stance more than a negation of its presence. Thus the physical therapist can not deal with the anatomic part that is lost or dysfunctional without considering all that is or was attached, physically or mentally, to that anatomy or function.

In view of all this it seems justified to consider a patient's psychologic make-up and the intertwining of the psychologic and physical rehabilitation as major determinants in the prognosis of disability.

We can not isolate the physical body from the rest of the person and expect treatment to be successful. Of no less importance is the effect one's psychologic functioning can have on the disabling condition itself. For a better understanding of the interaction between psychologic functioning and physical disability we will differentiate between the contributing causative factors of the disability and the disability itself.

INTERACTION OF CAUSAL AND AFFECTED FACTORS IN DISABILITY OUTCOME

Traditionally we consider the causative factor of physical disability to be any external or internal agent that disrupts an individual's physical or physiologic functioning. Examples of these are a traumatic incident, an ingested poison or microorganism that causes brain damage, a degenerative disease or genetic flaw that destroys or interferes with body functions, and other such physiochemical assaults. These, then, are considered the primary causal factors of the disability. The ensuing psychologic response is considered secondary, and its effect on

the disability can be considered as a secondary contributing causal factor to the disability itself.

The disability is the end result of both the primary and secondary factors, which together shape the response of the individual. This means that the disability is not in direct proportion to the physical damage but, rather, represents the end result of the synergistic effect of the physical loss and the individual's perception and mental attitude toward this loss. Just like pain, disability is very much the result of the subjectivity of the individual. This does not imply that the physical loss itself is dependent on the mental state of the individual but, rather, that the extent of the disability hinges on that state. A limb will not regrow, regardless of what mental state the patient is in; but the chance of the prosthesis to replace the function of the lost limb will depend significantly on that state.

PSYCHOLOGIC FACTORS AFFECTING PHYSICAL CONDITIONS

Not always are physical factors the primary cause in a physical disability. The psychologic and medical literature is replete with evidence indicating emotional factors and emotional disruption as primary contributors to accidents and debilitating disease.[14-16] Charcot and Freud demonstrated the undeniable importance of psychologic factors in the development of disease.[17]

One of the earlier theories to consider emotion as the cause of illness was the psychosomatic model presented by Alexander.[14] The psychosomatic attitude was not accepted by classical medicine until the contributions of Hughlings, Jackson, Sherington, and Cannon.[18] These discoveries brought an awareness of the unity of the organism and the mind-body relationship.

Under such circumstances, the resulting physical onslaught may be secondary to the emotional state and should be treated as such. Neglect in dealing with the psychologic causal agent will enable the continuation of its malevolent effect on the individual and interfere with rehabilitation efforts. What is suggested here is that the disablement, whether owing to accident or illness, may at times have psychopathologic functioning as its primary cause.

In the previous discussion of Selye's generalized adaptation syndrome we mentioned the effect of perception and cognitive functioning on physiologic reactions. It follows that faulty perception and cognition resulting in stress will expose one to increased risks of injury and illness.[19,20] We do not wish to elaborate on this but feel that the clinician has to be knowledgeable regarding the role mental functioning plays not only in the coping with illness and injury but often as the main contributory factor in the causation of the disablement.

Such beliefs are shared by most psychologic theorists. For instance, psychodynamic theorists and practitioners consider much of physical disease and accidental injury to be the outcome of repressed or displaced mental energy.[21] Freud[22] posited the idea of "thanatos," described as a destructive, inborn drive needed for survival. Freud believed that under certain psychopathologic conditions this drive turns in toward the self and may express itself in conscious suicidal attempts and/or in unconscious self-destructive behaviors.

The third edition of the *Diagnostic and Statistical Manual of Mental Disorders* of the American Psychiatric Association[23] has assigned a special diagnostic category to the psychologic factors that affect physical conditions. The predominant symptomatology of "psychological factors affecting physical conditions" is described in the *DSM III* as any physical condition or disorder that has been triggered by a psychosocial **stressor**. The manual then states an assumption that the physical disturbance will eventually remit after the stressor ceases, or it may be replaced by a different type of adaptation (pp. 303-304).

The way psychopathologic functioning contributes to physical ailments and accidents is obviously dependent on the type of emotional disturbance that exists. Although it is beyond the aim of this chapter to provide a complete review, we will mention a few general characteristics that might affect disability.

It is obvious that during psychotic functioning when lack of reality testing and/or states of confusion are prevalent, risks of accidents and disease states are increased. Similarly, emotionally troubled individuals may be preoccupied with their problems and/or exhaust their capacity for coping with life to a degree that will interfere with their alertness and obviously their ability to take care of their own safety and health.

Some emotional disorders and personality types find their expression in dangerous behaviors, such as aggression against others and the self, or in impulsive behaviors which may result in serious injury. These would include the sociopathic, the antisocial, the impulsive, and the inadequate personality types as well as pyromaniac, psychotic, and depressed patients. Their compliance to rehabilitative efforts would also be hindered by their emotional states.

Neurotics are more prone to somatic, stress-induced physical disablement. Constant stress is not limited to those suffering from emotional dysfunction. All of us are at times given to stressful situations. It has been shown how the prolongation of such stress will eventually create physical as well as emotional dysfunction, resulting in disablement.

STRESS AND DISEASE

Research links stress to a variety of medical, social, and psychologic dysfunctions.[24,25] Stress can be defined as a state induced by a stimulus that manifests itself by virtue of one's cognitive interpretation.[25,26] The stimulus itself is considered a stressor. A **stressor** is any stimulus that evokes stress and **stress reactions** as the observable consequences of the stressor. Such a definition may appear circular to the reader, and therefore we will try to approach its explanation by analyzing stress from an adaptation point of view.

The stress response, like all other adaptation responses, aims at survival, even though its end result may be counterproductive. The stress response is an attempt to cope with a "stressor," which is a stimulus, real or imagined, and perceived as a threat to the self or to one's homeostatic balance.

An appropriate analogy to an organism's mobilization of its resources in order to fight off the "stressor enemy" is a national leadership mobilizing the country's resources against a perceived "enemy threat," which may or may not exist. Throwing all its resources toward the "war effort" and eliminating the manpower and industry needed for its peaceful maintenance may impoverish the nation to the point of collapse, rebellion, and/or a weakened condition, which may tempt a neighboring power to invade. Mobilization for defense, although taxing, is an appropriate response in face of realistic danger. When stress is the result of faulty perception, or is perpetual, the resulting exhaustion of limited resources may endanger survival. An imaginary stressor may indeed create just as genuine a stress situation as a real one might and may even give birth to a real survival threat out of the imagined one. Woolfolk and Lehrer[27] illustrate this as follows:

the individual is not a passive recipient in stressful transactions between the person and the environment, but . . . (is an active interacting participant who may even) . . . generate stress through maladaptive beliefs, attitudes and patterns of action."[p. 348]

Others similarly postulate that the appraisal of the event by the person, rather than the reality of circumstances, creates the stress, and they conclude that one's cognitive appraisal of a problem will determine the coping pattern.[28,29] Parenthetically, this development paralleled a gradual movement in psychology from that of normative research to an emphasis on individual differences.

Lazarus and Serban[30-32] considered stress as a cause of pathologic modes of adaptation that serve to produce impairment of human functioning along with cognitive and behavioral disturbances. For the sake of rehabilitative intervention it is important to realize that the interaction of personal characteristics with the external situation with which a patient is faced then creates or is created by the stress reaction. The stress level can be considered the outcome of a transaction between the individual and the environment in which there is a reciprocal interaction between these two components, namely, the person and the universe.

This interaction plays significantly in one's strategy to manage one's world and oneself. Faulty coping will result in an abundance of stressors, and an abundance of stressors will diminish one's coping ability. Considering that much of what constitutes a stressor depends on one's perceptual functioning, psychologic and emotional guidance and support may diminish the amount of stressors perceived and created. Such support from the therapeutic environment would most likely result in an increased capacity to adapt better to "life events," the major changes by which the newly disabled patient is confronted.

Much of the literature on stress and coping in general has identified major "life events" as stressors. Life events refer to major changes in lifestyle, status, role, or situation, and any such change is therefore seen as a possible stressor. This view is consistent with the notion that stress, though individually mediated, is to some degree environmentally based and/or exacerbated by environmental and social conditions. Various "life event" measures have been developed and used in assessing potential stress from the environment. One of the better-known and used is the Holmes-Rahe Social Readjustment Rating Scale[33] (Appendix A), which quantifies the effects of life changes on stress and health. Such measures of life events assume a relatively global impact and take into account only such major changes. Although there is clear validity in such an approach, a potentially more sensitive and valid measure suggested by Kanner[34] and his associates is receiving more and more recognition in recent literature. The Hassles Scale (Appendix B) requires subjects to identify the irritating and frustrating demands of everyday transactions with the environment. This approach takes into account the individual's perception or cognitive mediation of these events and is consistent with the theoretic assumption that struggle with chronic difficulties may tax coping abilities and may lead to greater difficulties in attempting to manage with the events of daily life. Empirical evidence indicates a more direct association and a greater predictability of health and emotional outcomes through the use of daily hassles measures than through the use of life events measures. It has long been established that "major alterations in social circumstances can produce deleterious effects on mental and physical well-being."[35]

With all the changes that are engendered in almost every aspect of one's functioning when disability strikes, disabled patients are more likely to expect an increase in daily hassles and a relative increase in the amount of stressors confronting them. Dealing with life becomes more taxing when disabling circumstances block one's coping style, resulting in a greater gap of the person's fit within the world and contributing more stress to an already overstressed situation.

This becomes even more profound when one of the aspects in need of adjusting is the core of the self, the self-image. In the introduction, the evolving self was shown to be part of a unitary integrated life. Part of that self is the body and the self-image, which include the **roles** one plays within the world and which can be profoundly affected by disablement. To gain better understanding, we will briefly discuss the implications of these changes.

Role and status changes are expected and accepted as part of our developmental growth. In our early life we mature, become more independent, and change. We take on new roles during the process of developing and/or moving through life situations. In later years the changes are more traumatic, inasmuch as they represent a decline of functions. This is a period during which many previously independent, mature, productive, and active adults with important roles are gradually becoming less produc-

tive, losing cherished roles and their relative independence. It is a gradual and almost expected process, yet its impact is sometimes quite devastating.[36] Something very similar happens to the disabled adult who suffers losses. The onset of disability in an adult differs, however, because it is not part of the relatively accepted life process. It is a relatively sudden and catastrophic change, with an intensity that is often of no comparison. Unlike the older person, the younger person has not had a chance to enjoy and to discharge the obligation of roles, as did the older adult. In either case, the impact and ramification of a role change is often deeply felt.

ROLE THEORY

Role theory appears to have great predictive value in explaining any area of human interaction. As Berger notes, "Role theory, when pursued to its logical conclusions, does far more than provide us with a convenient shorthand for the description of various social activities. It gives us . . . a view of man based on his existence in society."[37] Berger defines **role** as "a typified response to a typified expectation." A role, then, analogous to that of an actor in a play, is the "part" played by an individual in interaction with another individual(s) playing another "part." These related parts have in them a "script," which defines the general behaviors, feelings, and acts that belong to each part. Lebovitz[38] correctly expands the notion that roles are both the collection of rights and duties and the behavior attached to a position. It is the "pattern according to which the individual is to act in the particular situation."[37] Simply put, a role is a specified cluster of behaviors and expectations attached to each distinct, identified relationship to another person or persons. Some example of roles are male, female, athlete, patient, brother, wife, professor, and policeman. Each role carries certain expectations of behavior, dress, attitude, and so forth, and each forms a part of the individual's make-up and identity. Each individual takes on, or is assigned, many roles in the course of a lifetime which are acted out individually or simultaneously. Roles provide an identity, with predictability in social intercourse and parameters of behavioral expectations, both of the individual and of others. Roles help society and the individual create order and predictability of behavioral expectations by delimiting and defining how each individual must behave.

A role, then, is a script for behavioral limits in social interaction and a social artifact with analogous roles differing from culture to culture. It is, however, a powerful and important artifact in that it defines and prescribes a status; social, behavioral, and interactional patterns; social identity vis-a-vis the self and others; and, so doing, organizes and adds predictability to daily life. Roles are shaped and defined by the culture or society and have internal and interrelated meanings and relationships to each other within the culture that defines them. Role theory holds that these roles are not innate but, rather, learned. They are social manifestations and are defined socially. As MacCandless[39] notes, "through implicit and explicit codes, most of which have a moral, or right-wrong overtone, societies set up standards of behavior for their members."

From the individual's point of view, learning or fulfilling a role, whether ascribed or attained, is largely an unconscious, unreflective process. The powerful impact of this process on the individual lies in its unconscious nature. "The role forms, shapes, patterns both action and actor."[37] Accepting the role of female, which is difficult not to accept inasmuch as it is an ascribed role, implies accepting what society decrees as being female, including feelings, proclivities, interests, dress, and so forth. Roles, as Berger notes, "carry with them both certain actions and the emotions and attitudes which belong to these actions."[37] G.H. Mead,[40] a progenitor of role theory, asserted that the genesis of the self is the same event as the individual's discovery of society. That is to say, that in discovering and defining oneself, the individual is representing one's society in oneself and is the reflection of how society shaped and defined him or her. This notion seems analogous to Cooley's looking-glass self, whereby the child begins to define the self and develop an identity from the way others treat and interact with the child.[41]

Many proponents of role theory, such as Goffman[42] and Blumer,[43] view self-identity as developing in a negotiation process which takes place with two or more people as they establish their social roles. The self and self-identity are derived from the social roles assumed and through the evaluative and comparative process vis-a-vis the others in the social and interactive universe. One's self is defined in regard to one's roles.

All this illustrates the significance of roles and what a role change might mean to an individual. We also referred to what an individual might be going through after having sustained a severe loss of function and relative independence, change of lifestyle and self-image, alteration in social interaction, financial and vocational upheaval, and physical discomfort. How, then, does one adjust to these upsetting changes?

Obviously such adjustment will be quite individualistic and is affected by any or all of the following: preexisting coping style and conditions, the responsibility or blame one feels about the illness or injury, the value a person sets on himself or herself and the meaning of the loss, the reality of the conditions that have changed as a result of the situation, the messages received from within and without, the support/rejection balance of the current circumstances, and the functioning capacity of the body and mind.

STAGES OF ADJUSTMENT

Depending on the interactive intensity of the above factors, adjustment will be relatively rapid or prolonged, adaptive or maladaptive. The literature reviewed indicates the prevalence of a "stage" type adjustment to physical traumatization. The described stages seem to indicate that after an **initial shock** and **anxiety reaction,** most individuals go into a **denial** state, which may last from several days to several weeks. During that stage the individual may believe that the loss will be restored or may not even exist. Repression, daydreaming, or fantasy are other expressions of this stage. Denial may at times mask the depression or anxiety which is believed to be an expected outcome of the patient's current condition. When denial eventually lifts, the reaction of depression may show itself in the forms of **grief** and/or **mourning** and might be complicated by exaggerated self-blame, which may or may not be realistic. This may be followed by a projection or externalization of blame, which is considered the fourth reaction stage and is characterized by **anger** and **hostility.** Negativism, rebelliousness, opposition, and noncompliance are other forms of expression of this stage, which should culminate in an eventual **adaptive reconciliation** with or **acceptance** of the newly created reality, but may instead end up in a maladaptive retreat and **regression.**[44]

These stages are considered normal reactions that help individuals with a disabling condition deal with the severity of the abnormal state in which they find themselves.[45,46] Siller[47] considers such reactions essential for the process of living through the traumatic period and the working through of a reconstitution of a personality structure. Accordingly, unbearable effects are "displaced, delayed or disguised, suggesting a clinical picture of their absence."

These are obvious generalizations which might be used as guidelines but which have to be compromised by the reality of each individual case.[48] Although the stages might be quite similar, the content of individual reactions may differ significantly from individual to individual. As is true for the rest of the population, individuals with physical limitations are different from each other in their personal preferences. Many patients may feel vulnerable and ashamed about their helplessness and dependency, but others will feel secure and may even savor the constant need for care. Many will show resiliency, but others will not.

POSTTRAUMATIC STRESS AND OTHER DISORDERS

Apart from the less common lapses into a severe psychotic state, the more common psychopathologic reaction is the **posttraumatic stress disorder.** The third edition of the American Psychiatric Association's *Diagnostic and Statistical Manual of Mental Disorders (DSM III)* lists two subtypes of the posttraumatic stress disorder. The first is the *acute* type and the second is the *chronic* or *delayed* type. The disorder is considered acute if its appearance is within the first half year of the traumatic event and its duration is limited to a maximum of six months. The chronic type might be delayed in its appearance and lasts well over six months. For the diagnosis of posttraumatic stress disorder to be applicable, the reaction has to be the result of a "stressor [which] would evoke significant symptoms of distress in most people and is generally outside the range of common experiences."[49]

The essential feature of either diagnosis is the presence

of characteristic symptoms following a traumatic event which is generally outside the range of general human experience. Among the symptoms exhibited are one or more of the following: **dysphoria;** reexperiencing the traumatic event; numbing of responsiveness to, or reduced involvement with, the external world; and/or a variety of autonomic and cognitive symptoms.

The reexperiencing of the event is described as recurrent, painful, intrusive recollection, dreams, or nightmares, and on rare occasions, dissociative-like states during which the individual may act as if reliving the actual traumatic event. This may occur within several minutes or may last several hours or even days.

The numbing of responsiveness, also called **psychic numbing** or **emotional anesthesia,** is expressed by complaints of feeling detached or estranged from others, a loss of ability or interest in previously enjoyable activities, or the lack of any emotions or feelings. The other possible symptoms are "excessive autonomic arousal, hyperalertness, exaggerated startle response, and difficulty falling asleep."[49] Also listed in the *DSM III* are other types of sleep interruption, recurrent nightmares, impairment of memory and concentration or task completion ability, and survival guilt in those cases in which others were affected.[49]

Horowitz[50] describes the latter two types of symptoms as "intrusive" and "denial" states, respectively. The first is a hyperalert type of reaction, expressed in anticipatory anxiety, excessive alertness, and constant scanning to a point of perceiving things that are not there (hallucinations). The denial reaction is in direct contrast to the first in that it exhibits itself in a diminution of responsiveness to the condition.

Additional associated features that should alert the physical therapist to the presence of posttraumatic stress disorder are increased irritability, hostile behavior, constant tension, and somatic stress symptoms. Another emotional disability specific to the sudden onset of a disabling condition is *brief reactive psychosis* immediately following the event. The emotional turmoil and the delusions exhibited may diminish after several hours or may last several weeks.[50] In his study of post-accident individuals, Modlin[51] found that about one third of trauma patients he assessed exhibited a chronic type of free-floating anxiety, concentration and memory difficulties, nightmares, muscle tension, and sexual and social difficulties.

These are the typical posttraumatic psychopathologies commonly found among patients whose disability was associated with a catastrophic or sudden onset. Many disabilities are more gradual or an anticipated and expected outcome of illness. Patients with such conditions are also in a most vulnerable position and may succumb to similar emotional disruptions and dysfunctions. Other pathologies may be observed in these individuals. Whether sudden or gradual, the loss (or lack of developing certain normally expected abilities or functions—as is the case with congenital or early life disability) can, and will, leave psychologic wounds and scars on the individual. Even those with a gradual onset of disability will show many of these pathologies. Inasmuch as the condition progresses at a slower pace, the adjustment

requirements are not as intense. But, just like the proverbial straw that breaks the camel's back, a point may be reached that tips the balance. The balance may be tipped somewhere else—the wife who can not bear the situation any longer, or the boss who will not accept the productivity loss—and it may trigger an avalanche. These circumstances may produce an effect no less devasting then a sudden accident.

We all have breaking points and a limitation of personal resources. At periods when stress becomes more than the individual's coping repertoire is capable of handling, the fluidity of adaptive capacity may be overtaxed, resulting in a variety of maladaptive responses even in individuals who would otherwise be able to cope more appropriately. This is certainly true in disablement; the aforementioned reaction stages that the patient goes through do not always ward off the severe onslaught of the trauma, pain, dramatic life changes, and the losses experienced. Instead of the possible positive attempts at an eventual reconstruction of personality; faulty coping, severe depression, regression, and even psychosis or suicide may ensue.

Other severe psychopathologies may appear right from the onset of the trauma or even years later, including the severe depressive and anxiety disorders. Less debilitating reactions but still affecting every aspect of life include phobic avoidance, **lability,** guilt, **addictions,** and other self-defeating behaviors and the possibility of suicide. Any signs of severe reaction or lack of any reaction should be indicators of a need to consult the mental health professional. Similarly, any protraction over periods beyond those which are considered typical for mourning, anger, depression, anxiety, withdrawal, and other such behaviors should not be ignored. Lack of rehabilitative progress in patients expected to do better is a marker to be noticed. Other signs to look for are increase in alcohol intake or smoking; accident proneness; suicidal ideations and use of tranquilizers, sedatives, and other drugs; and changes in sleep and eating habits. A breakdown of cognitive functioning, or confusion, disorientation, illogical thinking, lack of reality testing, childlike dependencies, or exaggerated fears are all danger signals that require immediate attention.[52]

PHYSICAL THERAPY INTERVENTION AND THE PATIENT'S EMOTIONAL FUNCTIONING

It is imperative that the clinical staff be alert to the implication of these disorders and the adjustment process. It is important that the clinician be able to differentiate between what can be expected, considering a given specific illness or injury, and the pathologic reactions that are beyond the expected response to the situation. Such an awareness can have significant implications for the rehabilitation process and the future of the patient.

In dealing with disabling trauma and disease, the physical therapist stands out as a front-line clinician who is actively involved with the rehabilitative effort. The patient will usually spend more time and be more intimately involved with a particular physical therapist than with most other health professionals. As a result, the physical therapist may be more apt to notice and to effect changes in the emotional problems of the patient. The therapist who is alert to the psychologic dynamics of adjustment and maladjustment, and how these interact with each other and the rehabilitative effort, can be expected to have a synergistic effect on the treatment process which in turn will make clinical practice that much more rewarding. In many instances it may mean the difference between effective ameliorative therapy and propelling the patient into a satisfactory life adjustment through the maximization of his dormant potentials.

Thus, one must consider rehabilitation as much more than the physical restoration, replacement, or acceptance of physical loss. Trieshman considers rehabilitation as "the process of learning to live with one's disability in one's own environment."[52] We add here that the learning should include the use and shifting of one's premorbid, underutilized, or unrealized potentials. As aptly stated by Trieshman, the learning process dynamic is one "that starts at the moment of injury and continues for the remainder of the person's life. There is no definable end point that can be labelled 'rehabilitated' or 'adjusted' because, as with all people in all areas of life, disabled persons are continually learning to adapt to their environment." Like everyone else, individuals with physical limitations have to be able to gain some rewards and some fulfillment in life in order to "continue to endure the fatigue and frustration that life with a physical disability may include."[53]

It becomes imperative, therefore, that the physical and medical treatment objectives contain the restoration of the "secondary damage" created by the psychologic reaction to the physical disability. Restoration of physical function, training in activities of daily living, and vocational retraining will go that far and no more. Even successful psychotherapy within the walls of the hospital will not assure successful reintegration of the patient with the premorbid environment. Until the hospitalized individual is prepared for reintegration to the outside life, discharge may become counterproductive. The patient and the family have to be prepared for the social, emotional, and sexual adjustments they will have to face within the home and community. Until then, rehabilitation should not be considered complete. The changes from the patient role to the nonpatient role can be as devastating as the initial change to the patient role and may result in significant levels of depression, anxiety, and lack of social integration as exhibited in the studies by Berk and Feibel[54] and Udin and Keith.[55]

INTERACTIVE CLINICAL TEAM APPROACH

Having considered the enormity of the problem and the uniqueness of each patient, it becomes clear that the task of rehabilitation demands as deep an understanding of psychosocial dynamics as a clinician can possibly gain. Consideration must be given to the individual patient's background, status, roles, values, perception of the disabling condition, and personal philosophy of life. The success of physical therapy intervention will be enhanced by attention to these factors in relation to the specific rehabilitation task at hand. Above all, listen to what the patient says—in words, in expressions, in kidding around, or in crying. Listen to and observe the interactions with others and the self; with other patients, with the staff, with friends and family. Each of these opportunities will provide clues to the patient's emotional status, and the therapist must be alert to them.

By collecting all these data and becoming familiar with the scientific findings about human psychology, we can develop the tools needed to treat the physical body without interference from the emotional disruptions that accompany our endeavors to help our patients. We can turn many of these disruptions around and use them to our advantage in the rehabilitation process.

To this end a cooperative effort between the many disciplines involved in the rehabilitative effort is essential. Such integration of the methodology of physical therapy with those of the other health professionals, with an awareness of each profession's boundaries and limitations, will engender team work and provide the patient a better chance for maximizing compensatory functioning and reestablishing a place in the world. Albeit, this will be a place adjusted to the reality of the new circumstances imposed by the disability.

This underscores the importance of the team approach of clinicians from the various disciplines. Rehabilitation is an encompassing term that includes many disciplines, and each one of which specializes in different aspects of the rehabilitative effort. It may, therefore, be tempting for each therapist to let the others "do their things": Let the occupational therapist deal with the upper extremity or functional needs of the patient; let the speech therapist deal with communication; and let the psychologist or psychiatrist deal with the emotional problems the patient is facing—thus leaving the physical therapist to do what he or she is trained to do best. The "fly in the ointment" is that the return of physical functioning can seldom succeed unless the emotional aspects of the patient's functioning are considered and psychologic techniques incorporated into the treatment. This is not to say that the therapist should go beyond the boundaries of his or her profession when treating patients. The psychologist should not do physical therapy per se and neither should the physical therapist treat or diagnose emotional illness. However, the use of some psychologic techniques and an alertness to emotional problems must be taken into consideration in order to optimize physical therapy intervention.

The interactive team approach can enhance rehabilitation work by the sharing of each other's expertise in a cooperative effort. The mental health professional can hardly be effective without the communication of the physical therapist about the latter's observations of the patient. In return, the mental health worker can help the physical therapist through assessment of the patient's intellectual capacity and measures of motivation and emotional functioning. The mental health professional also can provide advice about patient management and the use of psychologic techniques for direct or indirect intervention with problem patients and problems with patients. The mental health care professional also can provide suggestions on utilization of specific psychological techniques for stress and pain management; assist with discharge planning; and intervene through family therapy and the use of social and natural support networks (environmental support systems).

EVALUATION AND PSYCHOLOGIC TESTING

A thorough assessment of the patient's psychologic and social functioning can significantly contribute toward a better understanding of the patient's needs, fears, anxieties, and capacities. It may guide the therapeutic effort toward a more rapid and appropriate recovery effort and may prevent unnecessary frustrated attempts toward unrealistic goals. The importance of assessment is underlined by our experience of witnessing the catastrophe that ensued when ambulation was achieved in a cognitively limited and dysfunctional patient who then ambulated on a flight of stairs as though the stairs were part of the landing. Cognitive assessment prevented further endangerment. Proper consideration of psychologic rehabilitative capacity will also prevent the frustration and eventual loss of motivation shared by the patient, the family, and staff when rehabilitative efforts are exerted beyond the capacity of the patient.

Such assessment has been proven to provide information about the patient's emotional adjustment to the disablement, personal assets and liabilities, perceptual-motor abilities, cognitive functioning, and personality structure. These can then be used to understand coping barriers, and behavioral difficulties better and to develop strategies for dealing with the overt and covert interpersonal and intrapersonal difficulties. Beals and Hickman[56] showed that the prediction of psychologic assessment regarding the return to work of back-injured workers was more predictive than that of physicians. The Halstead–Reitan Neuropsychologic Battery has been shown capable of detecting brain damage better than electroencephalography, x-ray examinations, the brain scan, or neurologic assessments (Filskov and Goldstein[57]). Tsushima and Wedding[58] found the Halstead–Reitan Neuropsychological Battery to be similar in accuracy to that of a computerized axial tomography (CAT) scan. These authors also found neuropsychologic assessments to be more sensitive in detecting subtle brain damage than clinical medical assessments. Such subtle damage may have no gross medical implications but should prove of great importance for rehabilitation inasmuch as it may seriously interfere with learning capacity. Psychologic assessment is especially helpful in identifying subjective symptomatology and hypochondriacal or malingering behaviors and can be especially useful when dealing with such complaints as pain, headaches, or vertigo.

Such assessments require the specialized expertise of the psychologist, psychiatrist, and clinical social worker.

These assessments are geared toward individual patient need. Although not all-inclusive, the following list highlights the major areas of consideration in a mental health assessment.

1. Present and premorbid intellectual, emotional, and coping functioning
2. Present and premorbid psychopathologies and personality structure and diagnosis of levels of depression, anxiety, and other mental disabilities
3. Assessment of suicidal, decompensation, and other risks
4. Degree of organicity and cognitive disability and its relationship to the patient's rehabilitative capacity
5. Symbolic meaning of the disability and loss and the compensatory reserves that can be elicited
6. Frustration tolerance, motivation, and secondary gain interference
7. Pain, stress, and tolerance assessment
8. Assessment of vocational interests and background and present functioning capacity
9. Sexual attitudes and dysfunction
10. Assessment of the present and premorbid family, social and economic status, and the natural support network (environmental support systems)

This is by no means a complete list and is rather limited to what we consider most significant for the process of rehabilitation. The derived findings of these assessments can direct the rehabilitative efforts toward the areas that can benefit most from therapeutic intervention.

PATIENT MANAGEMENT

Within the constraints of this discussion we will mention some intervention methods and techniques aimed at overcoming the psychologic disruptions and motivating a patient toward recovery.

Apart from the direct treatment of the patient, the mental health clinician can guide the physical therapist in the use of psychologic and behavior-modification principles to assist in patient management and the rehabilitation effort. The results of the mental health assessment can highlight strengths and weaknesses that should be used or corrected, respectively. By merit of professional training, the mental health clinician is usually experienced with the intervention methods that can be used in overcoming the deficiencies exhibited.

It is, however, important that the physical therapist realize there are different specializations within the field of mental health. Brief descriptions are provided below.

1. The *psychiatrist* is a medically trained physician specializing in mental disorders and their treatment.
2. The *clinical psychologist* has doctoral training in the field of clinical psychology and is trained in diagnosis, assessment, and treatment of personality and emotional dysfunctions.
3. The *clinical social worker* is trained in the assessment and intervention of environmental, social, and family dysfunctions and their interaction with the individual's adjustment and functioning.

4. The *occupational therapist* is trained in assessment of psychosocial and cognitive function. Emphasis is on the relationship between deficits in these areas and associated functional impairments.

5. Other counselors, such as art therapists, dance and movement therapists, vocational counselors, rehabilitation counselors, psychiatric nurses, and pastoral counselors, specialize in their distinct areas.

Within these professions there are multiple subspecialties. They include neuropsychology and neuropsychiatry, psychoanalysis, behavioral medicine and behavior modification, forensic psychiatry and psychology, geriatrics, group therapy, family and marital therapy, sex therapy, stress and pain reduction, biofeedback, and hypnotherapy.

Mental health clinicians also can render significant help in dealing with special problems. For example, discharge planning and the use of environmental support groups have proven to be of invaluable help in mainstreaming patients back to a comparative integrated life. The significance of self-help groups as an effective resource for reintegration into society has been documented by Lieberman and Borman.[59] Another area of great concern is the sexual functioning or the lack of it during disability. This and other areas of emotional impact should be dealt with in conjunction with the mental health clinicians specializing in these areas. All these services should be used to facilitate bringing about a new intrapsychic, interpersonal, and environmental harmony if we are to succeed with the rehabilitative effort. Neglect of these will create stumbling blocks, many of which may negate any effort toward rehabilitation or adjustment.

SUMMARY

Psychologic adjustment to physical disability is a uniquely personal experience, dependent upon lifelong experiences, temperament, and perceptions which shape an individual's adaptive (or maladaptive) processes.

Coping skills combine both innate and learned adaptive behaviors and allow the individual to balance internal and external resources in the presence of conflicting biologic, psychologic, and social needs. Ultimately, coping responses allow for the survival of the individual, even though the outcome may be contrary to what seems best for the individual. Thus psychologic adjustment is an intricate interactive process incorporating both body mechanisms and the external world, conscious perceptions of self as well as unconscious perceptions, motivations, emotions, drives, and values.

Reactions to disability are influenced by the extent of the injury or illness, its mode of onset, the prognosis, affected brain mechanisms, support systems, and subjective perceptions. The initial reaction to a catastrophic event or illness is primarily physiologic and has been described by Selye as the general adaption response. During the posttraumatic period, the psychologic aspects of functioning assume major importance.

Stress is defined as an attempt to cope with a real or imagined stimulus—a stressor—which is perceived as a threat to one's self or one's homeostatic balance. The disabled person is more likely to experience increases in the amount of daily stressors. Role and status changes are also important parts of the disablement experience.

Adjustment may be rapid or prolonged, adaptive or maladaptive. Stages in the process of adjustment to loss and disability have been identified. Initial shock or anxiety is followed by progression through stages of denial, depression, and anger. The end result of this process may be final acceptance of the newly created reality or, instead, a maladaptive retreat and regression. Adjustment may also be characterized by posttraumatic stress syndrome or other disorders. Therapists need to recognize their characteristic danger signs.

The psychologic dynamics of adjustment can be facilitated by an interactive team approach in which the contributions of all members are maximized. Rehabilitation should be considered complete only when the patient and family are prepared for the social, emotional, and sexual adjustments they will have to face when the patient returns to home and community.

QUESTIONS FOR REVIEW

1. Describe the role of perception in the formation of disability.

2. What factors might bring about maladaptive coping in spite of an individual's attempt to best serve personal survival needs?

3. In what (conscious or unconscious) ways might a disablement serve the needs of an individual to the degree that remaining disabled might be a preference?

4. Describe the different intervention needs between the "traumatic reaction" and the "posttraumatic adjustment period."

5. Give two examples of emotional factors that may cause physical disability.

6. What importance is there to the role one plays in life and the ability to overcome disability?

7. Identify the stages of adjustment to loss or disability.

8. What behaviors should alert the physical therapist to the presence of posttraumatic stress disorder?

9. Identify contributions that a mental health clinician can make toward facilitating physical therapy intervention.

REFERENCES

1. Engel, GL: Guilt, pain and success. Psychosom Med 24:37, 1962.
2. Moos, RH: Coping with Physical Illness. Plenum, New York, 1977.
3. Ehrenteil, OF: Common medical disorders rarely found in psychotic patients. Arch Neurol Psychiatry 77:1957, 1957.
4. Selye, H: The general adaptation syndrome and the disease of adaptation. J Clin Endocrinol Metab 6:117, 1946.
5. Wittkower, ED, et al: A global survey of psychosomatic medicine. Int Psychiatry 7:576, 1969.
6. Mann, AM and Gold, EM: Psychological sequelae of accident injury: A medico-legal quagmire. Can Med Assoc 95:1359, 1966.
7. Dollard, J and Miller, NE: Personality and Psychotherapy: An Analysis in Terms of Learning, Thinking and Culture. McGraw-Hill, New York, 1950.
8. Ellis, A: Humanistic Psychology: The Rational-Emotive Approach. Julian, New York, 1973.
9. Lazarus, R: Psychological Stress and the Coping Process. McGraw-Hill, New York, 1966.
10. Greenfield, N and Sternbach, R (eds): Handbook of Psychophysiology. Holt, Rinehart & Winston, New York, 1972.
11. Kirtz, S and Moos, RH: Physiological effects of social environments. Psychosom Med 36:96, 1974.
12. Selye, H: Stress in Health and Disease. Butterworth's, Reading, MA, 1976.
13. Bourestom, N and Howard, M: Personality characteristics of three personality groups. Arch Phys Med Rehabil 46:626, 1965.
14. Alexander, F: Studies in Psychosomatic Medicine. Ronald Press, New York, 1948.
15. Alexander, F: Psychosomatic Medicine: Its Principles and Applications. Norton, New York, 1950.
16. Engel, GL and Schmale, S: Psychoanalytic theory of somatic disorder: Conversion, specificity, and the disease onset situation. J Psychoanal Assoc 15:344, 1967.
17. Wittkower, ED, et al: A global survey of psychosomatic medicine. Int Psychiatry 576, 1969.
18. Dunbar, F: Emotions and bodily changes, ed 3. Columbia University Press, New York, 1947.
19. Henry JP and Stephens, P: Stress, health and the social environment. Springer-Verlag, New York, 1977.
20. Eisler, R and Polak, P: Social stress and psychiatric disorder. Journal of Mental and Nervous Disease 153:227, 1971.
21. Wolff, HG and Itace, CC (eds): Life Stress and Bodily Disease. Williams & Wilkens, Baltimore, 1950.
22. Freud, S: Civilization and Its Discontents, ed and tr by J. Strachey. WW Norton, New York, 1962.
23. American Psychiatric Association: Diagnostic Statistical Manual of Mental Disorders, ed 3. APA, Washington, DC, 1980.
24. Woolfolk, RL and Lehrer, PM: Principles and Practice of Stress Management. Guilford Press, New York, 1984.
25. Kirtz, S and Moos, RH: Physiological effects of social environments. Psychosom Med 36:96, 1974.
26. Ellis, A: Humanistic Psychology: The Rational-Emotive Approach. Julian, New York, 1973.
27. Woolfolk, RL and Lehrer, PM: Principles and Practice of Stress Management. Guilford Press, New York, 1984.
28. Lazarus, RS: Patterns for Adjustment. McGraw-Hill, New York, 1976.
29. Malmo, RB: Overview and indexes. In Greenfield, N and Sternbach, R (eds): Handbook of Psychophysiology. Holt, Rinehart & Winston, New York, 1972, p 967.
30. Lazarus, RS: Psychological Stress and the Coping Process. McGraw-Hill, New York, 1966.
31. Lazarus, RS: The concept of stress and disease. In Levi, L (ed): Society, Stress and Disease, vol 1. Oxford University Press, London, 1971, p 53.
32. Serban, G: Stress in schizophrenics and normals. B J Psychiatry 126:397, 1975.
33. Holmes, T and Rahe, R: The Social Readjustment Scale. J Psychosom Res 11:213, 1967.
34. Kanner, AD, et al: Comparison of two modes of stress management: Daily hassles and uplifts versus major life events. J Behav Med 4:1, 1981.
35. Woolfolk, RL and Lehrer, PM: Principle and Practice of Stress Management. Guilford Press, New York, 1984, p 346.
36. Sheehy, G: Passages: Predictable Crises of Adult Life. Bantam Books, New York, 1974.
37. Berger, PL: Invitation to Sociology: A Humanistic Perspective. Anchor Books, New York, 1963.
38. Labovitz, S: An Introduction to Sociological Concepts. John Wiley & Sons, New York, 1977.
39. MacCandless, BR: The Socialization Process. In Seidman, JM (ed): The Child: A Book of Readings. Holt, Rinehart & Winston, New York, 1969, p 42.
40. Mead, GH: Mind, Self, and Society. University of Chicago Press, Chicago, 1934.
41. Cooley, CH: Human Nature and the Social Order, rev ed. Charles Scribner's Sons, New York, 1922.
42. Goffman, E: The Presentation of Self in Everyday Life. Anchor, New York, 1959.
43. Blumer, H: Symbolic Interactionism: Perspective and Method. Prentice-Hall, Englewood Cliffs, NJ, 1969.
44. Siller, J: Psychological situation of the disabled with spinal cord injuries. Rehabil Lit 30:290, 1969.
45. Hohmann, G: Psychological aspects of treatment and rehabilitation of the spinal injured person. Clin Orthop 112:81, 1975.
46. Kerr, W and Thompson, M: Acceptance of disability of sudden onset in paraplegia. International Journal of Paraplegia 10:94, 1972.
47. Siller, J: Psychological situation of the disabled with spinal cord injuries. Rehabil Lit 30:290, 1969.
48. Berger, S and Garrett, J: Psychological problems of the paraplegic patient. J Rehabil 18:15, 1952.
49. American Psychiatric Association: Diagnostic and Statistical Manual of Mental Disorders, ed 3. APA, Washington, DC, 1980.
50. Horowitz, MJ: Stress-response syndromes: Post-traumatic and adjustment disorders. In Cooper, AM, Frances, AJ, and Sacks, MH (eds): The Personality Disorders and Neuroses. JB Lippincott, Philadelphia, 1986, p 409.
51. Modlin, HC: The post-accident and anxiety syndrome: The psychosocial aspects. Am J Psychiatry 123:1008, 1967.
52. Horowitz, MJ: Stress-response syndromes: Post-traumatic and adjustment disorders. In Cooper, AM, Frances, AJ, and Sacks, MH (eds): The Personality Disorders and Neuroses. JB Lippincott, Philadelphia, 1986, p 409.
53. Trieshman, RB: Spinal Injuries: Psychological, Social and Vocational Adjustment. Pergamon Press, Elmsford, NY, 1980.
54. Berk, S and Feibel, J: The unmet psychological and family needs of stroke survivors. Paper presented at the American Congress of Rehabilitation Medicine, New Orleans, November 1978. In Trieshman, RB: Spinal Injuries: Psychological, Social and Vocational Adjustment. Pergamon Press, Elmsford, NY, 1980.
55. Udin, H and Keith, R: Patients' daily activities after discharge from a rehabilitation hospital, Paper presented at American Congress of Rehabilitation Medicine, New Orleans, November 1978. In Trieshman, RB: Spinal Injuries: Psychological, Social and Vocational Adjustment. Pergamon Press, Elmsford, NY, 1980.
56. Beals, RK and Hickman, NW: Industrial injuries of the back and extremities. J Bone Joint Surg 54A:1593, 1972.
57. Filskov, SB and Goldstein, SG: Diagnostic validity of the Halstead-Reitan Neuropsychological Battery. J Consult Clin Psychol 42:382, 1974.
58. Tsushima, WT and Wedding, D: A comparison of the Halstead-Reitan Neuropsychological Battery and computerized tomography in the identification of brain disorder. American Journal of Nervous and Mental Disease 167:704, 1979.
59. Lieberman, M and Borman, L: Self-Help Groups for Coping with Crises. Jossey-Bass, San Francisco, 1979.

SUPPLEMENTAL READINGS

Adamson, JD and Schmale, AH, Jr: Object loss, giving up, and the object of psychiatric disease. Psychonomic Medicine 27:557, 1965.

Ader, R (ed): Psychoneuroimmunology. Academic Press, New York, 1981.

Anderson, TR and Cale, TM: Sexual counseling of the physically disabled. Postgrad Med 58:117, 1975.

Cannon, WB: Bodily Changes in Pain, Hunger, Fear and Rage. Charles T Branford, 1950.

Chigier, E: Sexual Adjustment of the Handicapped. Proceeding Preview of the 12th World Congress of Rehabilitation International. Sydney, Australia, 1972.

Chigier, E (ed): Sex and the Disabled. The Israel Rehabilitation Annual, 1977.

Cook, R: Sex education program service model for the multihandicapped adult. Rehabil Lit 35:264, 1974.

Eisenberg, MG and Falconer, J: Current trends in sex education programming for the physically disabled: Some guidelines for implementation and evaluation. Sexual Disabilities 1:6, 1978.

Ford, AB and Orfirer, AP: Sexual behavior and the chronically ill patient. Medical Aspects of Human Sexuality 1:51, 1967.

Krantz, DS and Glass, DC: Personality, behavior patterns, and physical illness: Conceptual and methodological issues. In Gentry, DW (ed): Behavioral Medicine. Guiford Press, New York, 1984.

Lazarus, RS and Folkman, S: Coping and Adaptation. In Gentry, DW (ed): Behavioral Medicine. Guiford Press, New York, 1984.

Lieberman, MA: Adaptive process in late life. In Datan, N and Ginsberg, LH (eds): Life-span Developmental Psychology. Academic Press, New York, 1975.

Menninger, K: The Vital Balance: The Life Process in Mental Health and Illness. Viking, New York, 1963.

Plutchik, R and Kellerman, H (eds): Theories of Emotion. Academic Press, New York, 1980.

Syme, LS: Sociocultural factors in disease etiology. In Gentry, DW (ed): Behavioral Medicine. Guiford Press, New York, 1984.

GLOSSARY

Adaptation (adaptive): Process by which an organism adjusts to contend with a new situation or environment.

Adaptive reconciliation (acceptance): The fifth and final reaction stage of adjustment to physical disability or loss; during this stage the disability or loss is no longer considered as an obstacle to be overcome but as one of many personal characteristics; approaches to meeting personal needs with respect to realities of the life situation have been reconciled.

Addiction: Physical and/or psychologic dependence on a substance (usually alcohol or drugs) with use of increasing amounts.

Adjustment: Alignment of one's inner needs with the realities of personal capabilities and/or environment; may be adaptive or maladaptive.

Anger (and hostility): The fourth reaction stage of adjustment to physical disability or loss; manifested by animosity, negativism, rebelliousness, opposition, antagonism, and noncompliance.

Brief reactive psychosis: Temporary response to a disabling condition which may last several hours to several weeks; characterized by emotional turmoil, delusions, hallucinations, personality disintegration, and loss of contact with reality.

Coping: The process of dealing with difficulties or changes within one's life or environment.

Denial: The second reaction stage of adjustment to physical disability or loss; an unconscious defense mechanism in which the existence of unpleasant realities is blocked from conscious awareness.

Dysphoria: Unrest; exaggerated feeling of depression; may be accompanied by anxiety.

General adaptation response (GAS): An organism's immediate response to an extreme catastrophe; a defensive adaptation response aimed at dealing with real or perceived emergency situations; characterized by release of adrenocorticotropic hormone and an increase of physiologic responses needed at times of emergency.

Grief: The third reaction stage of adjustment to physical disability or loss; distinguished by mental suffering, sorrow, and regret. SYN: Mourning.

Initial shock (and anxiety reaction): The first reaction stage of adjustment to physical disability or loss; characterized by disbelief, tension, feelings of impending danger, and an inability to acknowledge that the traumatic event has occurred.

Lability: Emotional instability; manifested by alterations or fluctuations in emotional state.

Maladaption (maladaptive): Difficulty or inability of an organism to contend with a new environment; faulty adaptation.

Posttraumatic stress disorder: Psychopathologic reaction to a traumatic event; symptoms exhibited may include reexperiencing the traumatic event; numbing of responsiveness to, or reduced involvement with, the external world, and/or a variety of autonomic, dysphoric, or cognitive symptoms. The *acute type* appears within the first half year of the event, with a maximum duration of six months. The *chronic type* may be delayed in its appearance and lasts well over 6 months.

Psychic numbing (or emotional anesthesia): Feelings of detachment or estrangement from others; loss of ability or interest in previously enjoyable activities; lack of emotions or feelings.

Regression: A return or retreat to a former state; a defense mechanism to illness or life frustration; characterized by appearance of less mature behaviors which were successful in earlier periods of the individual's life.

Role: Characteristic pattern of behavior developed in response to the expectations of a reference group or other individual.

Stress reaction: A response to a stressor (e.g., accident, illness, or life frustration); influenced by the interaction between the individual's physiologic and psychologic states.

Stressor: Any factor or condition capable of producing stress.

APPENDIX A HOLMES-RAHE SOCIAL READJUSTMENT SCALE

Rank	Life Event	Mean Value
1	Death of spouse	100
2	Divorce	73
3	Marital separation	65
4	Jail term	63
5	Death of close family member	63
6	Personal injury or illness	53
7	Marriage	50
8	Fired at work	47
9	Marital reconciliation	45
10	Retirement	45
11	Change in health of family member	44
12	Pregnancy	40
13	Sex difficulties	39
14	Gain of new family member	39
15	Business readjustment	39
16	Change in financial state	38
17	Death of close friend	37
18	Change to different line of work	36
19	Change in number of arguments with spouse	35
20	Mortgage over $10,000	31
21	Foreclosure of mortgage or loan	30
22	Change in responsibilities at work	29
23	Son or daughter leaving home	29
24	Trouble with in-laws	29
25	Outstanding personal achievement	28
26	Wife begin or stop work	26
27	Begin or end school	26
28	Change in living conditions	25
29	Revision of personal habits	24
30	Trouble with boss	23
31	Change in work hours or conditions	20
32	Change in residence	20
33	Change in schools	20
34	Change in recreation	19
35	Change in church activities	19
36	Change in social activities	18
37	Mortgage or loan less than $10,000	17
38	Change in sleeping habits	16
39	Change in number of family get-togethers	15
40	Change in eating habits	15
41	Vacation	13
42	Christmas	12
43	Minor violations of the law	11

From Holmes and Rahe,[33] with permission.

APPENDIX B THE HASSLES SCALE

Directions: Hassles are irritants that can range from minor annoyances to fairly major pressures, problems, or difficulties. They can occur few or many times.

Listed in the center of the following pages are a number of ways in which a person can feel hassled. First, circle the hassles that have happened to you *in the past month.* Then look at the numbers on the right of the items you circled. Indicate by circling a 1, 2, or 3 how SEVERE each of the *circled* hassles has been for you in the past month. If a hassle did not occur in the last month, do NOT circle it.

Hassles	Severity 1. Somewhat severe 2. Moderately severe 3. Extremely severe		
(1) Misplacing or losing things	1	2	3
(2) Troublesome neighbors	1	2	3
(3) Social obligations	1	2	3
(4) Inconsiderate smokers	1	2	3
(5) Troubling thoughts about your future	1	2	3
(6) Thoughts about death	1	2	3
(7) Health of a family member	1	2	3
(8) Not enough money for clothing	1	2	3
(9) Not enough money for housing	1	2	3
(10) Concerns about owing money	1	2	3
(11) Concerns about getting credit	1	2	3
(12) Concerns about money for emergencies	1	2	3
(13) Someone owes you money	1	2	3

		Severity 1. Somewhat severe 2. Moderately severe 3. Extremely severe	
Hassles			
(14) Financial responsibility for someone who doesn't live with you	1	2	3
(15) Cutting down on electricity, water, etc.	1	2	3
(16) Smoking too much	1	2	3
(17) Use of alcohol	1	2	3
(18) Personal use of drugs	1	2	3
(19) Too many responsibilities	1	2	3
(20) Decisions about having children	1	2	3
(21) Non-family members living in your house	1	2	3
(22) Care for pet	1	2	3
(23) Planning meals	1	2	3
(24) Concerned about the meaning of life	1	2	3
(25) Trouble relaxing	1	2	3
(26) Trouble making decisions	1	2	3
(27) Problems getting along with fellow workers	1	2	3
(28) Customers or clients give you a hard time	1	2	3
(29) Home maintenance (inside)	1	2	3
(30) Concerns about job security	1	2	3
(31) Concerns about retirement	1	2	3
(32) Laid-off or out of work	1	2	3
(33) Don't like current work duties	1	2	3
(34) Don't like fellow workers	1	2	3
(35) Not enough money for basic necessities	1	2	3
(36) Not enough money for food	1	2	3
(37) Too many interruptions	1	2	3
(38) Unexpected company	1	2	3
(39) Too much time on hands	1	2	3
(40) Having to wait	1	2	3
(41) Concerns about accidents	1	2	3
(42) Being lonely	1	2	3
(43) Not enough money for health care	1	2	3
(44) Fear of confrontation	1	2	3
(45) Financial security	1	2	3
(46) Silly practical mistakes	1	2	3
(47) Inability to express yourself	1	2	3
(48) Physical illness	1	2	3
(49) Side effects of medication	1	2	3
(50) Concerns about medical treatment	1	2	3
(51) Physical appearance	1	2	3
(52) Fear of rejection	1	2	3
(53) Difficulties with getting pregnant	1	2	3
(54) Sexual problems that result from physical problems	1	2	3
(55) Sexual problems other than those resulting from physical problems	1	2	3
(56) Concerns about health in general	1	2	3
(57) Not seeing enough people	1	2	3
(58) Friends or relatives too far away	1	2	3
(59) Preparing meals	1	2	3
(60) Wasting time	1	2	3
(61) Auto maintenance	1	2	3
(62) Filling out forms	1	2	3
(63) Neighborhood deterioration	1	2	3
(64) Financing children's education	1	2	3
(65) Problems with employees	1	2	3
(66) Problems on job due to being a woman or man	1	2	3
(67) Declining physical abilities	1	2	3
(68) Being exploited	1	2	3
(69) Concerns about bodily functions	1	2	3

Hassles	Severity 1. Somewhat severe 2. Moderately severe 3. Extremely severe		
(70) Rising prices of common goods	1	2	3
(71) Not getting enough rest	1	2	3
(72) Not getting enough sleep	1	2	3
(73) Problems with aging parents	1	2	3
(74) Problems with your children	1	2	3
(75) Problems with persons younger than yourself	1	2	3
(76) Problems with your lover	1	2	3
(77) Difficulties seeing or hearing	1	2	3
(78) Overloaded with family responsibilities	1	2	3
(79) Too many things to do	1	2	3
(80) Unchallenging work	1	2	3
(81) Concerns about meeting high standards	1	2	3
(82) Financial dealings with friends or acquaintances	1	2	3
(83) Job dissatisfactions	1	2	3
(84) Worries about decisions to change jobs	1	2	3
(85) Trouble with reading, writing, or spelling abilities	1	2	3
(86) Too many meetings	1	2	3
(87) Problems with divorce or separation	1	2	3
(88) Trouble with arithmetic skills	1	2	3
(89) Gossip	1	2	3
(90) Legal problems	1	2	3
(91) Concerns about weight	1	2	3
(92) Not enough time to do the things you need to do	1	2	3
(93) Television	1	2	3
(94) Not enough personal energy	1	2	3
(95) Concerns about inner conflicts	1	2	3
(96) Feel conflicted over what to do	1	2	3
(97) Regrets over past decisions	1	2	3
(98) Menstrual (period) problems	1	2	3
(99) The weather	1	2	3
(100) Nightmares	1	2	3
(101) Concerns about getting ahead	1	2	3
(102) Hassles from boss or supervisor	1	2	3
(103) Difficulties with friends	1	2	3
(104) Not enough time for family	1	2	3
(105) Transportation problems	1	2	3
(106) Not enough money for transportation	1	2	3
(107) Not enough money for entertainment and recreation	1	2	3
(108) Shopping	1	2	3
(109) Prejudice and discrimination from others	1	2	3
(110) Property, investments or taxes	1	2	3
(111) Not enough time for entertainment and recreation	1	2	3
(112) Yardwork or outside home maintenance	1	2	3
(113) Concerns about news events	1	2	3
(114) Noise	1	2	3
(115) Crime	1	2	3
(116) Traffic	1	2	3
(117) Pollution	1	2	3

HAVE WE MISSED ANY OF YOUR HASSLES? IF SO,
WRITE THEM IN BELOW.

(118) _____

ONE MORE THING: HAS THERE BEEN A CHANGE IN
YOUR LIFE THAT AFFECTED HOW YOU ANSWERED
THIS SCALE? IF SO, TELL US WHAT IT WAS.

From Kanner, et al.[34] with permission.

Chapter 3

INFLUENCE OF VALUES ON PATIENT CARE: FOUNDATION FOR DECISION MAKING

CAROL M. DAVIS

OBJECTIVES

1. Identify what a value is and how it directs human behavior.

2. Recognize how humans acquire values.

3. Identify how values influence the choices of patients and health professionals.

4. Distinguish between value-directed behavior that enhances healing and value-directed behavior that is likely to interfere with healing.

INTRODUCTION

Initially, one might question the logic of including a chapter on values in a text related to management of adult rehabilitation patients. The fact is, the entire book is devoted to educating the reader about the proper decisions to make in the rehabilitation process. Values play a critical role in most decision making, and to omit this aspect of decision making would be unwise.

Providing an operating definition of a *value* poses something of a challenge. Many interpretations have been made and several authors have provided a variety of definitions.[1-7] For the purposes of this chapter, a value is defined as an inner force that provides the standards by which patterns of choice are made. For example, if people value the safety of their lives, among other acts they will probably choose to wear a seatbelt while driving or riding in an automobile. That choice is guided by the importance they place on their safety, or by their value of safety.

Because values are internal and difficult to measure, they have not been studied as vigorously as other aspects of human behavior. One can not see a value; one can only feel it working. Values play a particularly important role in influencing our choices. The importance of this influence is emphasized when one considers that *knowing* the right thing to do and *doing* it are two separate phenomena. The first has to do with knowledge or cognition, the second with values or attitudes. This text is aimed at teaching the "knowing" aspect; this chapter, however, is devoted to elucidating the value aspect in choosing.

Most choices are value based; some decisions seem more difficult to make than others. Difficulty may arise when the therapist must resolve a values dilemma, when two seemingly equal goals or choices compete with one another. Difficulty also may arise when the therapist's values conflict with the values of the patient, the patient's family, colleagues, the larger health care system, and/or society. This chapter further defines values, describes how we acquire our values, and illustrates the influence values have on decisions. In addition, the influence that patient's values have on therapist's decisions is explored; examples of common difficult decisions in rehabilitation are provided. Finally, the role communication plays in the process of making difficult choices is discussed.

PROCESS OF DECISION MAKING

How choices are made is different from *what* choices are made. The latter can be viewed as the answer or the solution, the former describes a process. Decision making or choosing in rehabilitation is sometimes composed of nothing more than a reactive, instinctive stimulus-response effort, or haphazard trial-and-error guessing. But more often, making the right decision, choosing the best alternative, results from professionally educated problem solving. One type of problem solving in health care is termed **clinical reasoning.** When a therapist first sees a patient, the process of clinical reasoning begins. Various questions are asked in sequence to assess the patient's problem fully and, inevitably, to decide on the most appropriate treatment for this particular person at this point in time.

The greater part of professional education in health care is devoted to developing good clinical reasoners. The best instructors bravely refuse to give the "right" answer and encourage students to learn the process of discovery. In this way, students rise above the technical level of training. They are encouraged to become professionals capable of responding to complex patient situations by carefully reading the literature, questioning, touching, testing, and listening with the "third ear" to what is said as well as to what is left unsaid.

Problem solving is fundamental to our daily lives as human beings. We often don't realize we're problem solving because the process is so habitual, so subconscious. Just deciding what to have for breakfast can involve an intricate multistep process:

What shall I have for breakfast?
What's in the kitchen?
    Cereal, eggs, bacon, pancakes, juice, toast.
How hungry am I?
    Starved!
How much time do I have?
    Thirty minutes.
What did the scale say?
    5 lbs over.
That does it; juice and dry toast!

The answer to this problem-solving process was based on identifying the importance of one value over others. The fact that the scale revealed 5 excess pounds became the determining factor for making the final choice. Another person might have made the same choice but for a different reason:

How much time do I have?
    5 minutes
No time to eat! I'll have toast and juice and eat it on the way!

Most choices result from prioritizing values. The more we know about our values, the more we learn and understand our science, and the more we know about the facts of the situation, the easier it is to make a decision that seems best.[1]

Deciding what to eat for breakfast is a decision-making process of a different sort than deciding whether a patient is a good candidate to receive an above-knee prosthesis. The differences are important. The first, what to eat, is a personal choice; the second, whether to recommend a prosthesis, is a professional decision. The first is a choice that bears little consequence for the chooser if the less-than-best decision is made. However, the decision about the prosthesis has profound consequence for another person if the less-than-best decision is made. The first example, what to eat for breakfast, is more accurately viewed as a value preference or a **nonmoral value** choice; the prosthesis decision is made up largely of several moral-value-laden decisions. **Moral values,** such as justice, honesty, compassion, integrity, all reflect a way of relating to human beings, and thus moral values carry more importance than value preferences, because humans are more important than food, or music, or what we wear.[2]

When we study to become professionals, part of the professional socialization process involves the adoption of values that usually overlap with our personal values. At times, however, they might conflict with them. Professional responsibility, we learn, requires that we put the patient's needs before our own and act in ways that show we deserve the patient's trust.[3] Let's take a closer look at what a value is and how we obtain our personal and professional values.

VALUES AND VALUING

A **value** can not be seen directly, and it can not be measured. Values are constructs (moral schemes) that are made up of beliefs, emotions, and attitudes about what is best and what is not good. We can view values only indirectly by asking a person what he or she values, or, even more important, by watching another person's behavior. Values are reflected in our actions, especially the pattern of our actions over a period of time. Thus one might say, "I value honesty," but we might wonder how much when he or she knowingly cheats on income tax returns over a period of 5 years. Another value obviously has priority over honesty for this person.

Values, at times, cooperate and, at times, conflict with each other. A dilemma exists when we have difficulty choosing which value should have priority. For example, respect for life is the central value for advocates of a woman's right to choose abortion as well as for those opposed to abortion. The difference in opinion and belief of these two groups is not the value of life, but the importance of the mother's life over the fetus's life. The anti-abortionists claim the primacy of the fetus's life above all considerations; the reproductive-freedom advocates claim the primacy of the mother's choice for the quality of her life and resist outside interference with her right to choose.

People are not born with values, but they are born with instincts and needs. Values are acquired from those who socialize us, primarily parents and family, and, for many, religion. The initial learning of values takes the form of "following the rules" that parents believe will minimize personal pain and conflict, maximize pleasure and meaning, and promote harmony and peace in the home.

Adolescents, as a part of natural maturation, test the values of the home by breaking rules and trying out forbidden behavior. This process marks the beginning of a transformation in which value-based rules followed to avoid punishment become internalized and, upon reflection, are adopted as one's own. Most people end up with a very similar set of values as that of their parents. However, for some, the difference in the way they prioritize their values causes a distancing between themselves and certain family members. One example of children prioritizing their values differently from their parents is the son who is the first in four generations not to study law.

The values of health professionals take on a different priority from the values of other professionals whose primary satisfaction in work comes not from helping people directly but largely from working with ideas or inanimate objects. Likewise, although all physical therapists seem to display a very similar set of values, it might be conjectured that one of the key differences that distinguishes different specialists—for example, sports physical therapists from those devoted to caring for brain-injured patients—is the way in which the specialist prioritizes values. The sports therapist focuses professional goals upon a population with needs very different from those of brain-injured patients.

We make our most meaningful choices based on what attracts us and leads us to growth and self-fulfillment, a life of pleasure and meaning.[4] Being aware of our values helps us make informed and consistent choices that lead to personal and professional satisfaction. This is part of the process physical therapists undergo as they search out a specialty area of interest following their first few years in clinical practice.

CODE OF ETHICS

The set of moral norms adopted by a professional group to direct value-laden choices in a way consistent with professional responsibility is termed a **Code of Ethics.** One might follow the code without internalizing it, just as small children follow the "rules of the house." For the code of ethics to function as a set of professional values, one must reflect on it and decide that it, indeed, forms a values complex around which one is willing to organize professional choices. Thus, as was previously stated, reflection is necessary to the internalization of values to make them truly one's own.[6,7] The choices that then follow this internalization are likely to be consistent with one's basic beliefs, show coherence, are likely to be authentic or genuine, and are adequate to the task of decision making. Those who make the smoothest transitions into professional practice are likely to be those whose personal values and priorities greatly overlap with the values inherent in their chosen professional practice. Given that one's basic human survival needs are met, the more one reflects on one's choices and upon which choices result in the good and meaningful life, the more one is apt to experience consistent reward from opportunities.

THE VALUES OF PATIENTS AS A FACTOR IN CARE

Patients come to physical therapy as whole persons in need of professional help and guidance. All people can be viewed as possessing four quadrants of need that comprise the whole: the physical, the psychologic, the intellectual, and the spiritual. It could be said that a more meaningful and peaceful life results when choices are made that respond equally to the demands of all four quadrants of need. Central to the work of Carl Jung is the belief that a healthy personality results from obtaining a *balance* between thinking and feeling and between intuition and sensation.[8]

Patients come to physical therapy at various stages in their lives and with a unique history of having made thousands of choices. Over time the therapist comes to realize that some patients display a life pattern of meaningful, consistent, well-thought-out choices; others reveal a life of capricious, noncentered, unorganized value-based behavior. Often patients' poor choices have directly or indirectly brought them to therapy; for example, the young patient with quadriplegia who drove into a tree while drunk. Many patient problems in movement and function that are encountered in rehabilitation are not the result of "fate," but result from a lifetime of choices that placed other values as higher priority than the physical, or than the prevention of illness and injury. The more physical therapists become aware of how much control people actually have over their state of wellness and health, the more difficult it becomes for some therapists to remain nonjudgmental about their patients. It is exceedingly difficult for some clinicians, for example, to remain nonjudgmental while treating a chronic smoker for emphysema or a tremendously obese patient for hip and knee joint problems.

THE INFLUENCE OF VALUES ON THE PRIMARY GOAL OF PATIENT CARE

When a feeling of criticism and negative judgment of a patient occurs within health practitioners, they must be aware of it and consciously work not to let it affect their behavior. The primary goal of health practitioners is to help *all* people recover or maintain their health so they may function at the highest, most independent, most autonomous level possible day to day. If the primary goal is to achieve optimal health and healing, certain values seem to promote that goal more than others. One way to ascertain values that promote health and healing is to describe behavior between a therapist and patient that does the very opposite, or that interferes with health and healing. Putting yourself in the place of the patient, what therapist behaviors would *interfere* with your progress toward getting well or healing? Table 3.1 presents a sample list of very obvious behaviors that would detract from a patient's ability to function optimally in a therapeutic setting. Also included are a list of possible negative values which might underlie each of these behaviors.

Behaviors and underlying values that *facilitate* healing might be described as the exact opposite of those that detract from healing (Table 3.2). These therapist behaviors, it seems, would obviously help restore a patient's hope, promote progress toward recovery, and assist with achieving the highest possible level of independent function.

Many of us who would read the list of negative behaviors (see Table 3.1) that detract from healing would respond, "I'd never behave in such a way with my patients!" But, in fact, a huge gap exists between knowing the right thing to do, wanting to do it, and actually doing it.

Essential to a "therapeutic use of self" is the capacity to feel **compassion** for those who suffer. Compassion is quite different from **pity,** wherein a person feels sorry for those who are less fortunate. The compassion of the mature health professional is fueled with imagination, or the ability to envision what is possible from the other person's perspective. Imaginative understanding involves **self-transposal** (a cognitive attempt to put oneself in the place of another) at the least and **empathy** (identification with another's experience) at the most. As healers, therapists must not block but, rather, must allow empathy to occur, a momentary "crossing over" into the patient's frame of reference. Thus compassion is a very personal, intimate experience that is built on "trust, honesty, and the time and willingness to listen."[10]

Let's examine some patient care situations that require professional choice that may result in a less-than-optimal prioritizing of our professional and personal values.

VALUE-LADEN SITUATIONS IN REHABILITATION

What would you do, and *why,* if this situation happened to you?

Joyce, a 22-year-old college student was referred to physical therapy following surgical removal of her left leg owing to osteogenic sarcoma. Other than generalized weakness from chemotherapy, surgery, and bedrest and incisional pain and soreness, she was in "good health" on her arrival to the rehabilitation center.

You have been treating her for 6 weeks, having begun therapy from her admission to the rehabilitation center. Preoperative training was given in the acute setting; you have assisted her with preprosthetic training, strengthening, prosthetic training and acceptance, and gait training. She has been progressing well.

Joyce is intelligent and inquisitive, yet somewhat stubborn. Two weeks before discharge you notice an increasing tendency on her part to be careless and to take unnecessary risks, like hopping on one foot rather than donning her prosthesis. In addition, she admits to thinking that her daily strengthening exercises are stupid and that, after discharge, she may just throw the prosthesis away and depend on a wheelchair. Even crutches are too much bother.

You feel confused and frustrated. You've invested a great

Table 3–1 THERAPIST BEHAVIORS AND POSSIBLE UNDERLYING VALUES THAT *DETRACT* FROM THE HEALING PROCESS

Therapist Behaviors That *Interfere or Detract* from the Healing Process	Negative Values That Might Underlie Each Behavior
1. Acting cool or aloof, obviously paying more attention to other patients.	1. a. Prejudice: to prejudge or to classify a person as belonging to a larger group and thus to believe things about that person that one believes about the larger group b. Indifference: lack of interest or concern; aloofness, detachment
2. Overly criticizing you (the patient) so you feel as if nothing you do is right.	2. a. Prejudice b. Perfectionism: the doctrine that the perfection of moral character is a person's highest good and that freedom from imperfection is attainable c. Lack of flexibility
3. Treating you as an object rather than as a person with feelings of pain and worry and insecurity.	3. Depersonalization: to detract from an individual's uniqueness; to fail to honor a person's individuality
4. Treating you as if you were a child, incapable of really understanding anything that is said.	4. Patronizing: to adopt an air of condescension
5. Being unable or unwilling to help you in your exercises; leaving you alone most of the time.	5. a. Indifference b. Prejudice
6. Making fun of you in your presence and behind your back.	6. Depersonalization
7. Telling others things you've shared in confidence.	7. Breaking confidentiality: not keeping another person's trust private and secret
8. Not letting you work on your own. Always needing to supervise you or to tell you what to do next.	8. Fostering dependence
9. More often than not guessing about what is best for you. Admitting he or she "isn't sure" what to do, but "let's not let that stop us."	9. Failure to recognize and to act on one's limits of knowledge
10. Always fitting you in as if everything else in the therapist's life is more important than you are.	10. Placing selfish interest over patient's needs

Table 3–2 THERAPIST BEHAVIORS AND POSSIBLE UNDERLYING VALUES THAT
FACILITATE THE HEALING PROCESS

Therapist Behaviors That *Facilitate or Promote* the Healing Process	Positive Values That Might Underlie Each Behavior
1. Offering you (the patient) the same amount of attention offered other patients, so it balances out from day to day.	1. Justice: the quality of impartiality or fairness
2. Accepting your weaknesses along with your strengths and verbally reinforcing the desired behaviors.	2. Unconditional positive regard; acceptance
3. Always treating you as a person with feelings and being sensitive to those feelings each day.	3. a. Respect: the act of giving particular attention to a person; worthy of high regard b. Compassion: sympathetic consciousness of another's situation and the desire to be of effective help in relieving a painful situation
4. Explaining things at your level, not oversimplifying or making things too complex.	4. a. Respect b. Accurate and sensitive communication
5. Always reachable yet never fostering dependence; encouraging independent activity.	5. a. Autonomy: a quality or state of self-governance; independence b. Dignity: the quality of being worthy, honored, esteemed; to have distinction as a person
6. Never using humor inappropriately, never laughing *at* you, but encouraging you to be able to laugh, sometimes even at yourself.	6. Appropriate humor, nondefensive humor
7. Always keeping your confidence.	7. Confidentiality: keeping another person's trust private and secret
8. Fostering your own independent activity without letting you feel stranded.	8. Autonomy
9. Realizing when he or she needs the advice of someone else and asking for help in a timely fashion.	9. Recognizing the limits to one's knowledge, knowing when to get help or to refer; honesty
10. Making you feel special, cherished, and unique; showing individual concern for you and your progress.	10. a. Compassion b. Sensitivity to your uniqueness

deal of energy into the successful rehabilitation of this person and her behavior at this point seems ignorant and manipulative. Her refusal to cooperate with your suggestions angers you; you feel that her basic laziness in requesting a wheelchair existence represents settling for a quality of life that is less than optimal and selfish. You feel as if you've failed to help her realize her full adult potential.

You feel overstressed with the demands of your work.

Once the patient care day has begun, therapists seldom find or take the time to reflect on the larger issues, those which hover on the fringe of the work consciousness. Instead, therapists tend to focus on the immediate situation in front of them, quickly gathering data and problem solving as they go. Joyce's growing problem of reluctance could be viewed as a peripheral issue at first, one the therapist hoped would pass without needing to be confronted. But as her discharge date becomes closer, the therapist is forced to respond to what appears to be regressive behavior.

The therapist's responses may reveal one or more of several thoughts and feelings. Especially when under stress, one may become impatient and angry and lecture Joyce to "grow up." The therapist may feel personal failure and frustration and, in a condescending way, let her know he or she expected far more reward for the efforts placed in her successful rehabilitation. These are often automatic, emotion-based responses based on a value of spontaneous honesty and the right to express feelings regardless of the impact that expression may have on others. The therapist is unhappy and wants the situation to change but doesn't know how to change it, so the therapist displays poor impulse control and aggressively "lets off steam."

As "human" as this choice may seem, more mature

behavior is required of health professionals. No longer may they claim the luxury of spontaneous outburst, for the impact of the therapists' outbursts rarely solves value-based problems and often creates larger ones. Obviously, this is not conducive to healing.

Upon reflection, one realizes that Joyce's regressive behavior may likely reveal inner conflict, fear, and/or depression. If one puts oneself in her place, it's not difficult to come to some understanding that a person under these circumstances might be afraid and might seek a safer existence in a wheelchair. The value of compassion, funded by empathy and self-transposal, elevates the problem-solving process to a *professional choice* to sit down and to discuss this issue comprehensively with Joyce, referring her to the social worker for psychologic support and counseling, if necessary. Nonjudgmental concern and understanding are foundational to healing. In addition, health professionals caring for adults must accept that occasionally they will encounter a patient who is unwilling to cooperate with their suggestions and who resists their attempts to offer therapeutic care and advice. With the value of patient autonomy in mind, the professional's role is not to assume a paternalistic stance indicating "I know what's better for you than you do," but instead to outline as clearly, creatively, and accurately as possible the predictable results of the choices the patient is making. Patients must have control over their own lives to the greatest extent possible.

These guidelines exist in their purest sense when therapists are treating adult patients who are not suffering from confusion, mental or intellectual disorders, or significant depression. With children or adults who do suffer the conditions mentioned, therapists must aim for the greatest extent of autonomous choice possible and focus appropriate attention on parents and family care givers.

Reactive care, characterized by on-the-spot problem solving and decision making, is an unavoidable part of rehabilitation. However, the greater the number of our decisions that are based on reaction rather than on proaction or well-thought-out alternatives, the more idiosyncratic, inconsistent, and erratic our behavior will seem. Part of professional responsibility is to anticipate possible problems and to think through alternatives in advance. Likewise, the more that therapists base their decisions on scientific evidence and the more that they reflect on the values behind alternative choices, the more apt they are to experience consistent, scientific-based decisions reflective of the highest professional care. These decisions are inevitably more conducive to healing.

Triage situations always pull forth value priorities. A decision as simple as who to see first of three new inpatient referrals requires a value-based choice. What factors seem important in making the decision among these three new patients?

1. 80-year-old, frail elderly woman with osteoporosis admitted following surgery to repair a fractured hip. Room 300.

2. 30-year-old man with severe low back pain secondary to possible herniated disk. Room 201.

3. 53-year-old woman who had a mild heart attack three weeks ago, admitted for cardiac rehabilitation. Room 302.

How would you decide, at 8 AM, which of these three patients to see first? What facts seem to make a difference? The patient's age? His or her location in the hospital (closest versus farthest away from where you are now)? Your existing patient load and schedule? Your subconscious or conscious aversion to certain patients, such as those with low back pain or the elderly? If our primary goal in rehabilitation is to help patients recover their health so that they might function at the highest, most independent level possible, how can we use this goal to help direct our choices?

Putting the patient's needs first seems to be critical to this decision. The therapist's choice should not be based solely on personal convenience. What additional facts are needed? Putting oneself in the place of the patient, one comes to realize that the existence of certain factors calls forth our immediate attention. One factor that readily comes to mind that demands our immediate consideration is responding to patients in pain. Pain can totally consume one's attention and will take immediate priority in our choices. Responding first to patients in severe discomfort seems very important in sequencing the order of treatments. The therapist needs to find out which of these three individuals may have had a difficult night and is most in need of attention for relief of pain.

SUMMARY

Professional rehabilitative care requires problem solving that is proactive, based on scientific data, which demonstrates a consistent, conscious value of choosing behavior that is conducive to healing. Clinicians must become "informed reasoners"[2] who have systematically gathered the facts, have recognized potential choices and values dilemmas, and have taken the time to weigh which choice is most conducive to the healing process.

Central to this process is the courage to confront seemingly peripheral factors that therapists are tempted to hope will go away. Likewise central to this process is the willingness to put oneself in the place of the patient. Pellegrino[9] cautions us not to be so egocentric as to treat others simply as we would like to be treated. Instead, he suggests that the Golden Rule of health care should be to give each patient the opportunity to tell you what his or her needs or wants are, as you would want them to give you.

Finally, sensitive and accurate communication is required. In health, people feel alive by their connectedness to the world, and in illness they feel cut off, fragmented, and uninterested in the world. As healers, the therapists' role then becomes one of entering the patient's context of meaning. By using human-to-human skills of listening accurately to words and feelings; by communicating trust, truth, respect, interest, and caring; by explaining in ways that are relevant and intelligible to the patient; and by being sensitive to the patient's values, the therapist facilitates the patient's hope and strong belief that he or she is the patient's advocate in the world. In other words, the therapist helps the patient do what is necessary to feel once more alive in the world, connected, and hopeful of recovery to a meaningful life. Even in the face of chronic debilitating disease, terminal illness, or irreversible paralysis there is a sense that the therapist can help patients feel reconnected to the possibility of a life with meaning.

The behaviors that enhance the therapeutic moment flow out of placing the person and his or her meaning of what is wrong central to any and all attempts to offer help. Behaviors that emerge from valuing a patient's humanity—sensitive and accurate listening, respect, trust, compassion, and problem solving, to name a few—work to reinforce autonomy and dignity and to restore a patient's hope and personal control of his or her life as therapists simultaneously apply their scientific knowledge and skill.[11]

This is what is required of health care professionals in day-to-day patient care. To do less is to render less than compassionate, professional help. Reflecting, coming to better know the right thing to do, and consistently doing it result in a professional life of growth and meaning.

QUESTIONS FOR REVIEW

1. A person's values are difficult to identify. How can one know what a person values?

2. How are values related to behavior?

3. A belief is not a value, but beliefs direct our values. If a person believes fairness is good, what values can you predict the individual will hold?

4. What is the difference between a moral and a nonmoral value?

5. Give an example of a nonmoral value choice; of a moral value choice.

6. What is the difference between behavior that agrees with a code of ethics and behavior that is value based?

7. What is our obligation as health professionals when a patient refuses to take our suggestions and recommendations for healing?

8. What role does communication play in making value-based decisions in rehabilitation?

REFERENCES

1. Purtilo, RB and Cassel, CK: Ethical Dimensions in the Health Professions. WB Saunders, Philadelphia, 1981.
2. Wehlage, G and Lockword, AL: Moral relativism and values education. In Purpel, D and Ryan K (eds): Moral Education—It Comes with the Territory. McCutchen, Berkeley, CA, 1976.
3. Pelligrino, ED: What is a profession? J Allied Health 12:161, 1983.
4. Morrill, RL: Teaching Values in College. Jossey-Bass, San Francisco, 1980.
5. Henerson, ME, Morris, LL, and Fitz-gibbon, M: How to Measure Attitudes. Sage Publications, Beverly Hills, 1978.
6. Beck, C: A philosophical view of values and value education. In Hennessy, T (ed): Values and Moral Development. Paulist Press, New York, 1976.
7. Raths, LE, Harmin, M, and Simon, SB: Values and Teaching. Charles E Merrill, Columbus, OH, 1966.
8. Jung, CG: The Structure and Dynamics of the Psyche. Pantheon, New York, 1960.
9. Pellegrino, ED and Thomasma, DC: A Philosophical Basis of Medical Practice. Oxford University Press, New York, 1981.
10. Pence, GE: Can compassion be taught? J Med Ethics 9:189, 1983.
11. Davis, CM: The influence of values on patient care. In Payton OD (ed): Psychosocial Aspects of Clinical Practice. Churchill Livingstone, New York, 1986, p 119.

SUPPLEMENTAL READINGS

Brammer, LM: The Helping Relationship, ed 3. Prentice-Hall, Englewood Cliffs, NJ, 1985.
Cassell, E: The Healer's Art. JB Lippincott, Philadelphia, 1976.
Collins, M: Communication in Health Care, ed 2. CV Mosby, St Louis, 1983.
Davis, CM: Affective education for the health professions. Phys Ther 61:1587, 1981.
Frankena, W: Ethics, ed 2. Prentice-Hall, Englewood Cliffs, NJ, 1973.
Howard, J and Strauss, A: Humanizing Health Care. John Wiley & Sons, New York, 1975.
Kestenbaum, V (ed): The Humanity of the Ill. University of Tennessee Press, Knoxville, 1982.
Payton, OD (ed): Psychosocial Aspects of Clinical Practice. Churchill Livingstone, New York, 1986.
Pence, GE: Ethical Options in Medicine. Medical Economics, Oradell, NJ, 1980.
Purtilo, RB and Cassel, CK: Ethical Dimensions in the Health Professions. WB Saunders, Philadelphia, 1981.
Purtilo, RB: Health Professional/Patient Interaction. WB Saunders, Philadelphia, 1984.
Ramsey, P: The Patient as Person. Yale University Press, New Haven, 1970.

GLOSSARY

Association: Strong feelings of identification with another person.

Autonomy: A quality or state of self-governance; independence.

Clinical reasoning: A problem-solving process based on identifying the importance of one value over others; process of prioritizing values in formulating a response to a situation.

Code of Ethics: A set of moral norms adopted by a professional group to direct value-laden choices in a way consistent with professional responsibility.

Compassion: Sympathetic consciousness of another's situation and the desire to alleviate pain or suffering.

Confidentiality: Keeping another person's trust private and secret.

Depersonalization: To detract from an individual's dignity or worth; failure to honor a person's uniqueness.

Dignity: The quality of being worthy, honored, esteemed; to have distinction as a person.

Empathy: A three-stage process that includes (1) identification with another's experience or situation, (2) a shared experience with another person, and (3) a reclaiming of one's individuality separate from the shared moment.

Identification: Close personal association with another person leading to a feeling of sameness.

Indifference: Lack of interest or concern; aloofness, detachment.

Justice: The quality of impartiality or fairness.

Moral values: Values that dictate how one interacts with or treats another human being, which reflect a person's basic uniqueness, dignity, and worth.

Nonmoral values: Values that do not reflect how one treats another person but reflects esthetic, political, intellectual, personal, or social choices.

Patronizing: To adopt an air of condescension.

Perfectionism: The doctrine that the perfection of moral character is a person's highest good and that freedom from imperfection is attainable.

Pity: Sympathetic heartfelt sorrow: shared feeling wherein the individual pitied is deemed "less than" the one pitying.

Prejudice: To prejudge or to classify a person as belonging to a larger group and thus to believe things about that person that one believes about the larger group.

Respect: The act of giving particular attention to a person; worthy of high regard.

Self-transposal: The attempt to put oneself cognitively in the place of the other; to "walk in another person's shoes."

Sympathy: Feeling at one with another's feelings.

Value: An inner force that provides the standards by which patterns of choice are made.

Chapter 4

VITAL SIGNS

THOMAS J. SCHMITZ

OBJECTIVES

1. Identify the reasons for monitoring vital signs.

2. Explain the importance of monitoring vital signs in establishing a database of patient information.

3. Recognize the importance of monitoring vital signs as a method of assessing patient response to selected treatment activities.

4. Describe the common techniques for monitoring: temperature, pulse, respiration, and blood pressure.

5. Identify normative values or ranges for each vital sign.

6. Describe the normal variations in vital signs and the factors that influence these changes.

7. Describe methods for recording data obtained from monitoring vital signs.

INTRODUCTION

The ability to monitor vital signs accurately is an important component of general physical therapy assessment skills. Although frequently considered a nursing responsibility, results from a vital signs assessment have important implications for physical therapy management.

The *vital signs,* also referred to as the *cardinal signs,* generally include temperature, pulse, respiration, and blood pressure. These signs are important indicators of the body's physiologic status and reflect the function of internal organs. Variations in vital signs are a clear indicator that some change in the patient's physiologic status has occurred.

The purposes of obtaining information related to vital signs include

1. Establishing a database of values for an individual patient

2. Assisting in goal setting and treatment planning
3. Assisting with assessment of patient response to treatment
4. Contributing to assessment of effectiveness of treatment activities

In assessing vital signs it is important to note that "normal" values are specific to an individual. Although average or normative values have been established, some individuals will typically or "normally" display higher or lower values than those represented by these normative figures. This addresses the importance of monitoring vital signs as a *serial* process. Vital sign measurements yield the most useful information when performed and recorded at *periodic intervals* rather than as a one-time assessment. This type of serial recording allows changes in patient status or response to treatment to be monitored over time as well as indicates an acute change in physiologic status at a specific point in time.

An additional factor to consider is that many variables

influence the vital signs. These may include time of day, time of the month, exercise, age, sex, weight, metabolic conditions, general health status, pain, and drug intake.[1,2]

BODY TEMPERATURE

Body temperature represents a balance between the heat produced or acquired by the body and the amount lost. Because humans are warm-blooded, or **homoiothermic**, body temperature remains relatively constant despite changes in the external environment. This is in contrast to cold-blooded, or **poikilothermic**, animals (such as reptiles) in which body temperature varies with that of their environment.

Thermoregulatory System

The purpose of the thermoregulatory system is to maintain a relatively constant internal body temperature. This system monitors and acts to maintain temperatures that are optimal for normal cellular and vital organ function. The thermoregulatory system consists of three primary components: the thermoreceptors, the regulating center, and the effector organs (Fig. 4–1).[3]

THERMORECEPTORS

The thermoreceptors provide input to the temperature-regulating center located in the hypothalamus. The regulating center is dependent upon information from thermoreceptors to achieve constant temperatures. Once this information reaches the regulatory center, it is compared with a "set point" standard or optimal temperature value. Depending on the contrast between the "set" value and incoming information, mechanisms may be activated either to conserve or to dissipate heat.[3]

Afferent temperature input is provided to the regulating center by both *peripheral* and *central* thermoreceptors. The peripheral receptors, composed primarily of free nerve endings, have a high distribution in the skin (cutaneous thermoreceptors). However, thermoreceptors also have been located in the spinal cord, abdomen, and may possibly be present in other deep structures not yet identified.[3,4] The cutaneous thermoreceptors demonstrate a larger distribution of cold to warmth receptors and are sensitive to rapid changes in temperature.[5] Signals from these receptors enter the spinal cord through afferent nerves and travel to the hypothalamus via the lateral spinothalamic tract.[3,6]

The central thermoreceptors are located in the hypothalamus. These thermoreceptors are sensitive to temperature changes in blood perfusing the hypothalamus. These cells also can initiate responses either to conserve or to dissipate heat. They are particularly sensitive to core temperature changes and monitoring body warmth.[5,6]

REGULATING CENTER

The temperature-regulating center of the body is located in the hypothalamus. The hypothalamus functions to coordinate the heat production and loss processes, much like a thermostat, ensuring an essentially constant and stable body temperature. By way of influence over the effector organs, the hypothalamus achieves a relatively precise balance between heat production and heat loss. In a healthy individual, the hypothalamic thermostat is set and carefully maintained at $37°C \pm 1°C$ ($98.6°F \pm 1.8°F$).[5] In situations in which input from thermoreceptors indicates a drop in temperature below the "set" value, mechanisms are activated to conserve heat. Conversely, a rise in temperature will activate mechanisms to dissipate heat. These responses are activated through hypothalamic control over the effector organs. Input to the effector organs is transmitted through nervous pathways of both the somatic and autonomic nervous system.[3,6]

EFFECTOR ORGANS

The effector organs respond to both increases and decreases in temperature. The primary effector systems

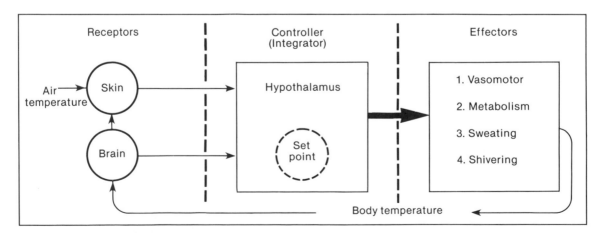

Figure 4–1. The three primary elements of the thermoregulatory system: the *receptors,* which provide thermal input regarding body temperature; the *hypothalamic control center,* which coordinates heat production and loss processes; and the *effector organs,* which regulate heat loss, conservation, and dissipation mechanisms. From Judy, WJ,[3] p 536, with permission.

include vascular, metabolic, and skeletal muscle (shivering) responses and sweating. These effector systems function either to increase or to dissipate body heat.

Conservation and Production of Body Heat

When body temperature is lowered, mechanisms are activated to conserve heat and to increase heat production. Heat conservation and production mechanisms are described below.

Vasoconstriction of Blood Vessels. The hypothalamus activates sympathetic nerves, which results in vasoconstriction of cutaneous vessels throughout the body. This significantly reduces the lumen of the vessels, decreasing blood flow near the surface of the skin where it would normally be cooled. Thus the amount of heat lost to the environment is decreased.

Decrease in or Abolition of Sweat Gland Activity. To reduce or to prevent heat loss by evaporation, sweat gland activity is diminished. Sweating is totally abolished with cooling of the hypothalamic thermostat below approximately 37°C (98.6°F).[4]

Cutis Anserina or Piloerection. Also a response to cooling of the hypothalamus, this heat conservation mechanism is commonly described as "gooseflesh." The term means "hairs standing on end." Although of less significance in man, in lower mammals with greater hair covering, this mechanism functions to trap a layer of insulating air near the skin, decreasing heat loss.

The body also responds to decreased temperature with several mechanisms designed to produce heat. These mechanisms are activated when the body thermostat falls below approximately 37°C (98.6°F).[4] Heat production mechanisms are described below.

Shivering. The *primary motor center for shivering* is located in the posterior hypothalamus. This area is activated by cold signals from the skin and spinal cord. In response to cold, impulses from the hypothalamus activate the efferent somatic nervous system, which results in increased tone of skeletal muscles. As the tone gradually increases to a certain threshold level, shivering (involuntary muscle contraction) is initiated and heat is produced. This reflex shivering can be at least partially inhibited through conscious cortical control.[6]

Hormonal Regulation. The function of hormonal influence in thermal regulation is to increase cellular metabolism, which subsequently increases body heat. Increased metabolism occurs through circulation of two hormones from the adrenal medulla: *norepinephrine* and *epinepherine.* Circulating levels of these hormones, however, are of greater significance in maintaining body temperature in infants than in adults. Heat production by these hormones can be increased in an infant by as much as 100 percent as opposed to 10 to 15 percent in an adult.[4]

A second form of hormonal regulation involves increased output of thyroxine by the thyroid gland. Thyroxine increases the rate of cellular metabolism throughout the body. This response, however, occurs only as a result of prolonged cooling, and heat production is not immediate.[5] The thyroid gland requires several weeks to hypertrophy before new demands for thyroxine can be achieved.

Loss of Body Heat

Excess heat is dissipated from the body through four primary methods: radiation, conduction, convection, and evaporation.

Radiation is the transfer of heat by electromagnetic waves from one object to another. This heat transfer occurs through the air between objects that are not in direct contact. Heat is lost to surrounding objects that are colder than the body. For example, loss of heat to a wall or surrounding room objects.

Conduction is the transfer of heat from one object to another through a liquid, solid, or gas. This type of heat transfer requires direct molecular contact between two objects, such as sitting on a cold surface or heat lost in a cool swimming pool. Heat is also lost by conduction to air.

Convection is the transfer of heat by movement of air or liquid (water). This form of heat loss is accomplished secondary to conduction. Once the heat is conducted to the air it is then moved away from the body by convection currents. Use of a fan or a cool breeze provide convection currents. Heat loss by convection is most effective when the air or liquid surrounding the body is continually moved away and replaced.

Evaporation is the conversion of a liquid to a vapor. This form of heat loss occurs on a continual basis through the respiratory tract and through perspiration from the skin. Evaporation provides the major mechanism of heat loss during heavy exercise. Profuse sweating provides a significant cooling effect on the skin as it evaporates. In addition, this cooling of the skin functions to further cool the blood as it is shunted from internal structures to cutaneous areas.

Abnormalities in Body Temperature

INCREASED BODY TEMPERATURE

An elevation in body temperature is generally believed to assist the body in fighting disease or infection. **Pyrexia** is the elevation of normal body temperature, more commonly referred to as **fever. Hyperpyrexia** and **hyperthermia** are terms that describe an extremely high fever, generally above 41.1°C (106°F).[7]

Pyrexia occurs when the "set" value of the hypothalamic thermostat rises. This elevation is caused by the influence of fever-producing substances called **pyrogens.** Pyrogens are secreted primarily from toxic bacteria or are released from degenerating body tissue.[4] The effects of these pyrogens result in fever during illness. As a result of the new, higher thermostat value, the body responds by activating its heat conservation and production mechanisms. These mechanisms raise body temperature to the new, higher value over a period of several hours. Thus a fever, or **febrile state,** is produced.

The clinical signs and symptoms of a fever vary with

the level of disturbance of the thermoregulatory center and with the specific stage of the fever (onset, course, or termination). These signs and symptoms[1,8,9] may include general malaise, headache, increased pulse and respiratory rate, chills, piloerection, shivering, loss of appetite **(anorexia)**, pale skin which later becomes flushed and hot to the touch, nausea, irritability, restlessness, constipation, sweating, thirst, coated tongue, decreased urinary output, weakness, and insomnia. With higher elevations in temperature (hyperpyrexia), disorientation, confusion, convulsions, or coma may be seen. These latter symptoms are more common in children under the age of five and believed to be related to the immaturity of the nervous system.[9]

Three specific stages have been identified describing the course of a fever.

1. *Invasion or onset* is the period of either gradual or sudden rise until the maximum temperature is reached.

2. *Fastigium or stadium* (course) is the point of highest elevation of the fever. Once maximum temperature is reached, it remains relatively stable.

3. *Difervescence* (termination) identifies the period during which the fever subsides and temperatures move toward normal. This drop in temperature can occur suddenly (crisis) or gradually (lysis).

LOWERED BODY TEMPERATURE

Exposure to extremes of cold produces a lowered body temperature called **hypothermia.** With prolonged exposure to cold there is a decrease in metabolic rate, and body temperature gradually falls. As cooling of the brain occurs, there is a depression of the thermoregulatory center. The function of the thermoregulatory center becomes seriously impaired when body temperature falls below approximately 34.4°C (94°F) and completely lost with temperatures below 29.4°C (85°F).[4] The body's heat regulatory and protection mechanism is therefore lost.

Symptoms of hypothermia include decreased pulse and respiratory rates, cold and pale skin, cyanosis, decreased cutaneous sensation, depression of mental and muscular responses, and drowsiness which may eventually lead to coma.[1,4,9] If left untreated, the progression of these symptoms may lead to death.

Factors Influencing Body Temperature

A statistical average or norm of 37°C (98.6°F) taken orally has been established for body temperature in an adult population. However, body temperature is most accurately presented as a range. A range of values is more representative of normal body temperature as certain everyday circumstances (e.g., time of day) or activities (e.g., exercise) influence the body's temperature. In addition, some individuals typically run a slightly higher or lower body temperature than depicted by a statistical average. Therefore, deviations from the average will be apparent from individual to individual as well as between measures taken from a single subject under varying circumstances.

TIME OF DAY

The term **circadian rhythm** describes a 24-hour cycle of normal variations in body temperature. Certain predictable and regular changes in temperature occur on a daily basis. Body temperature tends to be lowest in the early morning hours between 4 AM and 6 AM and highest in the late afternoon and early evening hours between 4 PM and 8 PM.[8] These regular changes in body temperature are influenced significantly by both digestive processes and level of skeletal muscle activity. For individuals who work at night, this pattern is usually inverted.[9]

AGE

Compared with adults, infants demonstrate a higher normal temperature because of the immaturity of the thermoregulatory system. They are particularly susceptible to environmental temperature changes, and their body temperature will fluctuate accordingly. Young children also average higher normal temperatures because of heat production associated with increased metabolic rate and high physical activity levels. Elderly populations tend to demonstrate lower than average body temperatures. Lower temperatures in elderly populations are associated with a variety of factors, including lower metabolic rates, decreased subcutaneous tissue (which normally insulates the body against heat loss), decreased physical activity levels, and inadequate diet.

EMOTIONS

Extremes in emotions will increase body temperature as a function of increased glandular secretions with a subsequent increase in metabolism.[1]

EXERCISE

The effects of exercise on body temperature are an important consideration for physical therapists. Strenuous exercise significantly increases body temperature because of increased metabolism. Active muscle contractions are an important and potent source of heat production. During exercise, body temperature increases are proportional to the relative intensity of the work load.[5] Vigorous exercise can increase the metabolic rate by as much as 20 to 25 times that of the basal level.[5]

MENSTRUAL CYCLE

Increased levels of progesterone during ovulation cause body temperature to rise 0.3° to 0.5°C (0.5° to 0.9°F). This slight elevation is maintained until just prior to the initiation of menstruation, at which time it returns to normal levels.[9]

PREGNANCY

Owing to increased metabolic activity, body temperature remains elevated approximately 0.5°C (0.9°F). Temperature returns to normal after parturition.

EXTERNAL ENVIRONMENT

Generally, warm weather tends to increase body temperature, and colder conditions decrease body temperature. Environmental conditions influence the body's ability to maintain constant temperatures. For example, in hot humid environments the effectiveness of evaporative cooling is severely diminished because the air is already heavily moisture laden. Other forms of heat dissipation are also dependent on environmental factors such as movement of air currents (convection). Clothing also can be an important external consideration because it can function both to conserve and to facilitate release of body heat. The amount and type of clothing is important. To dissipate heat, absorbent, loose-fitting, light-colored clothing is most effective. To conserve heat, several layers of lightweight clothing to trap air and to insulate the body are recommended.

LOCATION OF MEASUREMENT

Rectal temperatures are from 0.3° to 0.5°C (0.5° to 0.9°F) higher than oral temperatures; axillary temperatures are approximately 0.3°C (0.5°F) lower than oral.[7]

INGESTION OF WARM OR COLD FOODS

Oral temperatures will be affected by oral intake, including smoking. Patients should refrain from smoking and/or eating for at least 15 minutes (preferably 30 minutes) prior to an oral reading.

Assessing Body Temperature

TYPES OF THERMOMETERS

Clinical Glass Thermometer

Traditionally, temperatures have been taken by use of a glass thermometer. It consists of a glass tube with a bulbous tip filled with mercury. Once the bulb is in contact with body heat, the mercury expands and rises in the glass column to register body temperature. Reflux of mercury back down the tube is prevented by a narrowing of the base. The device must be shaken vigorously to return the mercury to the bulb before the next use.

Glass thermometers are calibrated in either (or both) Celsius and Fahrenheit scales. The range is from approximately 34°C (93°F) to 42.2°C (108°F), with slight variations among different manufacturers. The calibrations are in degrees and tenths of a degree. As such, each long line represents a full degree and each short line indicates 0.1 degrees on the Celsius thermometer and 0.2 degrees on the Fahrenheit thermometer. When recording temperatures it is common practice to round the fractions of degrees to the nearest whole number.

There are three different shapes of bulbous ends on glass thermometers, depending on their intended use (Fig. 4–2). A *blunt* tip can be used for both oral and rectal temperatures. The *elongated* end is for oral or axillary measures, and the *rounded* tip is for rectal measures.[1]

Electronic Thermometers

This type of thermometer provides a rapid (several-second) measure of body temperature. It consists of a portable battery-operated unit, an attached probe, and plastic disposable probe covers (Fig. 4–3). The units provide a flashed, digital display of body temperature or a stationary scale and needle marker.[1] An important advantage of these thermometers is the low chance of cross-infection, inasmuch as the probe covers are used only once.

A variety of small, hand-held electronic thermometers are also commercially available. The units are typically about 6 inches in length with a tapered design (Fig. 4–4). One end of the device is narrow and serves as the probe. The opposite end is broad and houses the battery. These thermometers also provide a flashed, digital display of body temperature. A few models allow use with disposable covers.

Chemical Thermometers

These instruments are used similarly to a clinical glass thermometer because they are placed under the patient's tongue. They consist of a series of calibrated dots impregnated with a temperature-sensitive chemical. After removal, the dots are examined for color changes and the corresponding temperature reading. They are disposed of after use.

Temperature-Sensitive Tape

Heat-sensitive tape or disks respond to body temperature by changing color. They are frequently used with pediatric patients. The forehead and abdomen are com-

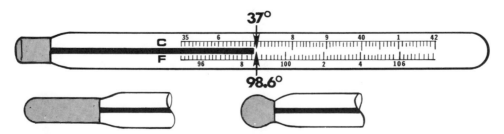

Figure 4–2. Clinical glass thermometer illustrating the three shapes of bulbous ends. The blunt end *(top)* can be used for both oral and rectal temperatures. The elongated *(bottom, left)* is for oral measures, and the rounded end *(bottom, right)* is for rectal measures. From Saperstein, AB and Frazier, MA,[1] p 456, with permission.

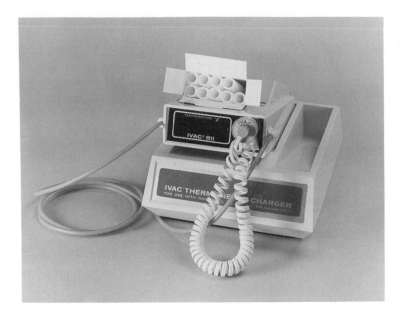

Figure 4–3. Electronic thermometer. Components include a battery-powered unit with a digital display, a probe, and disposable probe covers. Courtesy of IVAC Corporation, San Diego, CA.

mon placement sites. The temperature readings are nonspecific and are usually confirmed with a more precise measure if deviations are noted.

PROCEDURE FOR ASSESSING BODY TEMPERATURE

For purposes of establishing baseline data and assessing response to treatment, physical therapists generally use oral monitoring. However, in situations in which oral temperatures may be contraindicated, an axillary measure may substitute. Both procedures will be described.

Assessing Oral Temperature: Clinical Glass Thermometer

A. Wash hands.
B. Assemble equipment.
    1. An oral thermometer.
    2. Soft tissue to wipe thermometer.
    3. Worksheet and pen or pencil to record collected data.
C. Procedure.
    1. Explain procedure and rationale in terms appropriate to the patient's understanding.
    2. Assure patient comfort.

3. The thermometer should be held firmly between the thumb and forefinger at the end opposite the bulb.
4. If the thermometer has been soaked in a disinfectant solution, rinse under cold water.
5. Dry the thermometer using a clean tissue, wiping from the bulb *toward* the fingers in a rotating fashion.
6. Hold the thermometer at *eye level* and rotate until the column of mercury is clearly visible; note the level of the column.
7. If necessary, shake the thermometer until the mercury is below 35°C (95°F). While holding the thermometer securely, use quick, downward motions of the wrist, which will effectively lower the column.
8. Ask patient to open mouth, and place thermometer at the posterior base of the tongue to the right or left of the frenulum. Instruct patient to close the lips (not teeth) around thermometer to hold it in place.
9. Leave the clinical glass thermometer in place for 7 to 8 minutes. It should be noted that considerable discrepancy exists in the literature regarding the length of time the thermometer should be left in place. Times vary from 5 to 10 minutes.
10. Remove the thermometer.

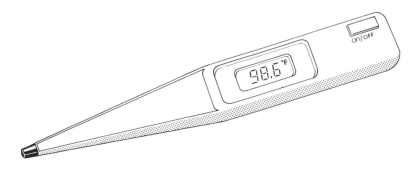

Figure 4–4. Hand-held electronic thermometer.

11. Using a clean tissue wipe the thermometer *away* from the fingers in a rotating fashion.
12. Hold the thermometer at *eye level,* rotate until mercury is clearly visible, and read the highest point on the scale to which the mercury has risen.
13. Record results.
14. Thermometer should be returned to appropriate area for disinfecting.

Assessing Oral Temperature: Electronic Thermometer

A. Wash hands.
B. Assemble equipment.
  1. An electronic thermometer unit.
  2. Disposable probe cover.
  3. Worksheet and pen or pencil to record collected data.
C. Procedure.
  1. Explain procedure and rationale in terms appropriate to the patient's understanding.
  2. Assure patient comfort.
  3. Turn on power unit (some units require a warm-up period).
  4. Place disposable cover over probe.
  5. Ask patient to open mouth, and place the covered probe at the posterior base of the tongue to the right or left of the frenulum. Instruct patient to close the lips (not teeth) around the probe and hold it in place.
  6. Electronic thermometer probes should be left in place following manufacturer's instructions for that particular unit (frequently between 10 and 45 seconds).
  7. Remove probe and dispose of cover.
  8. Temperature reading is obtained from digital readout or scale.
  9. Record results.

Assessing Axillary Temperature

Although less accurate, axillary temperatures are used when oral temperatures are contraindicated. Such situations might include **dyspnea,** surgical procedures involving the mouth or throat, very young children, and delirious or irrational patients. In these circumstances axillary measures are considered safer. Axillary temperatures are approximately 0.6°C (1.1°F) lower than oral.[10] The following procedure should be used.

A. Wash hands.
B. Assemble equipment.
  1. An oral clinical glass thermometer is usually used.
  2. Soft tissue to wipe thermometer.
  3. A towel to dry axillary region (moisture will conduct heat).
  4. Worksheet and pen or pencil to record collected data.
C. Procedure.
  1. Follow procedure steps 1 through 7 for assessing oral temperature with a clinical glass thermometer.
  2. Expose axillary region. If any moisture is present, the area should be gently towel dried with a patting motion (vigorous rubbing will increase temperature of the area).
  3. Place the thermometer in the axillary region between the trunk and upper arm (Fig. 4–5). The patient's arm should be placed tightly across the chest to keep the thermometer in place (asking the patient to move his or her hand toward the opposite shoulder is often a useful direction). If the patient is disoriented or very young, the thermometer must be held in place.
  4. Leave thermometer in place for 10 minutes.
  5. Remove thermometer.
  6. Using a clean tissue, wipe the thermometer *away* from the fingers in a rotating fashion.
  7. Hold the thermometer at *eye level,* rotate until mercury is clearly visible, and read the highest point on the scale to which the mercury has risen.
  8. Record results. Generally, a temperature reading is assumed an oral measure unless otherwise noted. An axillary temperature is designated by a circled A after the temperature (e.g., 95°F Ⓐ). Similarly, a circled R indicates a rectal measure (e.g., 99°F Ⓡ).
  9. Thermometer should be returned to appropriate area for disinfecting.

Thermometer

Figure 4–5. Positioning for monitoring axillary temperature.

PULSE

The **pulse** is the wave of blood in the artery created by the contraction of the left ventricle. With each contraction, blood is pumped into an already full aorta. The inherent elasticity of the aortic walls allows expansion and acceptance of the new supply. The blood is then forced out and is surged through the systemic arteries. It is this wave or surge of blood that is felt as the pulse. A healthy adult heart beats an average of 70 times per minute, which provides continuous circulation of approximately 5 to 6 liters of blood through the body.

The pulse can be palpated wherever a superficial artery can be stabilized over a bony surface. In monitoring the pulse, specific attention is directed toward assessing three parameters: rate, rhythm, and volume.

The *rate* is the number of beats per minute. A pulse range of 60 to 80 is considered normal for an adult. However, multiple factors will influence the pulse rate, including age, sex, emotional status, and physical activity level. Body size and build also influence pulse rate.[2,10] Tall, thin individuals generally have a slower pulse rate than those who are obese or have stout frames.

The *rhythm* describes the intervals between beats. In a healthy individual, the rhythm is *regular* or *constant* and indicates that the time intervals between beats are essentially equal.

The *volume* (force) refers to the amount of blood pushed through the artery during each ventricular contraction. The quantity (volume) of blood within the vessel produces the force of the pulse. Normally, the force of each beat is equal. With a higher blood volume, the force of the pulse is greater and with lower volumes is weaker. The volume is assessed by *how easily the pulse can be obliterated.* With an increased volume the pulse is difficult to obliterate and is termed a **bounding** or **full** pulse; a feeling of high tension is noted. With lower volumes, the pulse is easily obliterated and termed **weak** or **thready.**

In addition to rate, rhythm, and volume, the *quality or feel* of the arterial wall should be assessed. Typically, a vessel will feel smooth, elastic, soft, flexible, and relatively straight. With advancing age, vessels may demonstrate sclerotic changes. These changes frequently cause the vessels to feel twisted, hard, or cordlike with decreased elasticity and smoothness.

Factors Influencing Pulse

Essentially, any factor that alters the metabolic rate will also influence heart rate. Several factors are of particular importance when considering pulse rate.

AGE

Fetal pulse rates average 120 to 160 beats per minute.[1] The pulse rates for a newborn range between 70 to 170, with an average of 120 beats per minute. Pulse rate gradually decreases with age until it stabilizes in adulthood. The average adult pulse rate is generally considered to be between 60 and 80 beats per minute. However, much wider variations, from 50 to 100 beats per minute, are considered within a normal range for adults.

SEX

Men and boys typically have slightly lower pulse rates than women and girls.

EMOTIONS

Responses to a variety of emotions (e.g., grief, fear, anxiety, or pain) activate the sympathetic nervous system, with a resultant increase in pulse rate.

EXERCISE

Oxygen demands of skeletal muscles are significantly increased during physical activity. At rest, only 20 to 25 percent of the available muscle capillaries are open.[4] During vigorous exercise, extensive vasodilation causes all capillaries to open. The heart rate increases to provide additional blood flow to the muscle and to meet the increased oxygen requirement. For physical therapists, monitoring a patient's pulse rate is an important method of assessing response to exercise. Typically, the pulse rate will increase as a function of the intensity of the activity. A linear relationship exists between pulse rate and intensity of work load. To use the pulse rate effectively, both the patient's resting and predicted maximal heart rates must be determined.[11] Maximum heart rate values are determined by an exercise stress test or by using the formula for age-adjusted maximum heart rate: maximum heart rate = 220 minus age (see chapter 16: Coronary Artery Disease). Generally, pulse rates during a 15-to-30-minute therapeutic exercise program for a healthy individual should not exceed 60 to 70 percent of predicted maximum heart rate.[12]

In assessing pulse rate response to exercise, level of aerobic fitness also must be considered. Both resting and submaximal exercise heart rates are typically lower in trained subjects. In response to an identical exercise intensity, a sedentary person's heart rate will demonstrate greater acceleration when compared with a trained individual. Although the metabolic requirements of an activity are the same, the lower heart rate response in a trained subject occurs secondary to a more efficient (increased) stroke volume. The linear relationship between pulse rate and work load exists for both trained and untrained subjects. However, the rate of rise will differ. When compared with a sedentary person, the trained individual will achieve a higher work output and greater oxygen consumption before reaching a specified submaximal heart rate.[5]

SYSTEMIC OR LOCAL HEAT

During periods of fever, the heart rate will increase. The body will attempt to dissipate heat by vasodilation of peripheral vessels. Heart rate will increase to shunt blood flow to cutaneous areas for cooling. Local applications of thermal modalities (such as a hot pack) also will elevate heart rate to provide increased circulation to cutaneous areas secondary to arteriolar and capillary dilation.

Assessing the Pulse

A peripheral pulse can be monitored at a variety of sites on the body. Superficial arteries located over a bony surface are easiest to palpate and are referred to as "pulse points." These pulse sites, their locations, and some common indications for use are described below.

1. *Temporal:* superior and lateral to the outer canthus of the eye; used when radial pulse is inaccessible.

2. *Carotid:* on either side of the anterior neck below the ear lobe and between the sternocleidomastoid muscle and the trachea; used in cardiac arrest, in infants, and to monitor blood flow to brain.

3. *Brachial:* medial aspect of the antecubital fossa; used to monitor blood pressure.

4. *Radial:* radial aspect of the wrist at the base of the thumb; easily accessible, used for routine pulse monitoring.

5. *Femoral:* inguinal region; used in cardiac arrest and to monitor lower extremity circulation.

6. *Popliteal:* behind the knee (usually easier to palpate with slight knee flexion); used to monitor lower extremity circulation and blood pressure.

7. *Pedal (dorsalis pedal):* dorsal, medial aspect of foot; used to monitor lower extremity circulation.

In addition to the peripheral sites, the apical pulse may be monitored by auscultation (listening), using a stethoscope directly over the apex of the heart. Apical pulses are used when other sites are inaccessible (e.g., medical or surgical contraindications) or difficult to locate and to palpate, such as in newborns and some cardiac patients. See Figure 4–6 for diagram of pulse locations.

PROCEDURES FOR ASSESSING PULSE

A site should be selected that will not cause discomfort and subsequently alter the pulse rate.[2] Additionally, site location will be influenced by the specific patient diagnosis and/or the reasons for pulse monitoring. Peripheral pulses are monitored by palpation, using the tips of the first three fingers. Pulse rates obtained from the apex of the heart require use of a stethoscope.

Assessing Peripheral Pulses

A. Wash hands.
B. Assemble equipment.
   1. A watch with a second hand.
   2. Worksheet and pen or pencil to record collected data.
C. Procedure.
   1. Explain procedure and rationale to patient in terms appropriate to his or her understanding.
   2. Assure patient comfort.
   3. Select the pulse point to be monitored.
   4. Place the first three fingers squarely and firmly over

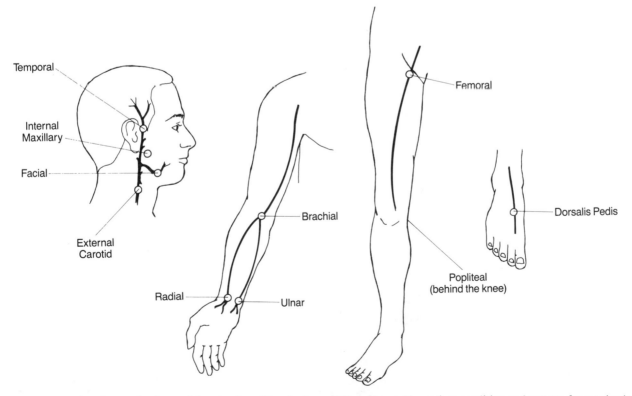

Figure 4–6. Common sites for monitoring peripheral pulses. Site selection will be influenced by patient condition and reasons for monitoring pulse.

the pulse site; use only enough pressure to feel the pulse accurately (if the pressure is too great it will occlude the artery).

5. Count the pulse for 30 seconds and multiply by 2; if any irregularities are noted, a full 60-second count should be taken; note the rhythm, volume, and quality or feel of the vessel.
6. Record results.

Assessing Apical Pulse

A. Wash hands.
B. Assemble equipment.
   1. A stethoscope.
   2. Antiseptic wipes for cleaning ear pieces and diaphragm of stethoscope before and after use.
   3. A watch with a second hand.
   4. Worksheet and pen or pencil to record collected data.
C. Procedure.
   1. Explain procedure and rationale to patient in terms appropriate to his or her understanding.
   2. Assure patient comfort.
   3. Use antiseptic wipe to clean the ear pieces and diaphragm of the stethoscope.
   4. Locate the site where pulse will be monitored; the apical pulse is located approximately 3.5 inches (8.9 cm) to the left of the midsternum, in the fifth intercostal space, within an inch of the midclavicular line drawn parallel to the sternum.[7] These

landmarks are guides to locating the apical pulse. On some individuals a stronger pulse may be noted by altering placement of the stethoscope (e.g., placement in the fourth or sixth intercostal space).

5. Warm the diaphragm of the stethoscope in the palm of hand.
6. Place stethoscope in ears such that the ear attachments are tilted forward.
7. Place diaphragm over the apex of heart. Count the pulse for 60 seconds; the pulse will be heard as a "lubb-dubb." The "lubb" represents closure of the atrioventricular (tricuspid and mitral) valves. The "dubb" represents closure of the semilunar (aortic and pulmonic) valves.[8,10]
8. Record results.
9. If the same examiner is using the stethoscope again, it is not necessary to clean the ear pieces; the diaphragm should always be cleaned.

Assessing the Apical-Radial Pulse

Typically, the apical and radial pulse values are the same. However, in some situations (e.g., cardiac disease or vascular occlusion) blood pumped from the left ventricle may not be reaching the peripheral site or may be producing a weak or imperceptible pulse. The apical pulse in such cases would be stronger than the radial.

To monitor the apical-radial pulse, two people are needed to *simultaneously* monitor each of the two pulses for 60 seconds. The results from the two assessments are

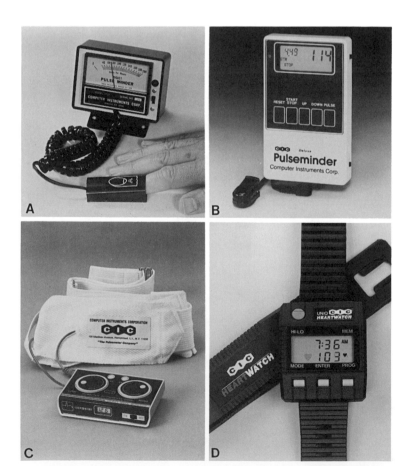

Figure 4–7. Sample models of electronic pulsemeters. (*A*) Stationary scale and needle marker readout with finger sleeve sensor, (*B*) ear-lobe clip sensor with digital display, (*C*) chest strap sensor with digital display, and (*D*) wireless chest strap sensor with wristwatch display. Courtesy of Computer Instruments Corporation, Hempstead, New York.

then compared. The difference between the two counts is called the **pulse deficit.** This type of monitoring provides additional information regarding status of the cardiovascular system.

Electronic Pulse Monitoring

Electronic pulsemeters (Fig. 4–7) use sensors to detect the pulse. Pulsemeters have gained expanded use in prescribed exercise and training programs because they provide a practical, accurate method of continual pulse monitoring. The devices consist of small, battery-operated units which can be strapped to the patient's wrist, waist, or bracketed to a piece of exercise equipment. Most units incorporate a lead wire with a distal sensor. The sensors are typically housed in a finger sleeve, earlobe clip, or chest strap attachment. Some pulsemeters are equipped with more than one type of sensor. This feature allows selection of a sensor appropriate to the activity (e.g., an ear-lobe clip or chest strap would be preferable to a finger sleeve for monitoring an activity that involved upper extremity movement). Pulse values are provided by a digital display or a stationary scale and needle marker.

Some pulsemeters provide wireless transmission from a chest sensor strap to a wristwatch display. Other units provide pulse values by placing the thumb firmly against a flat metal sensor. Various additional options are available on these units and differ with the model and manufacturer. Among the more common features are the ability to preset the upper and lower limits of the pulse

rate for a specific activity and an auditory signal when pulse values move outside the target range.

RESPIRATION

The primary function of respiration is to supply the body with oxygen for metabolic activity and to remove carbon dioxide. The respiratory system, consisting of a series of branching tubes, brings atmospheric oxygen into contact with the gas exchange membrane of the lungs, the alveolus. Oxygen is then transported throughout the body via the cardiovascular system.

The Respiratory System

Air enters the body by way of the nose and pharynx, where it is warmed, filtered, and humidified. It is then moved to the larynx, trachea, bronchi, and bronchioles (Fig. 4–8). The terminal bronchioles then branch into the respiratory bronchioles. Attached to their walls is the functional gas exchange unit of the lungs, the alveolus.

INSPIRATION

Inspiration is initiated by contraction of the diaphragm and intercostal muscles. During contraction of these muscles, the diaphragm moves downward and the intercostals lift the ribs and sternum up and outward.

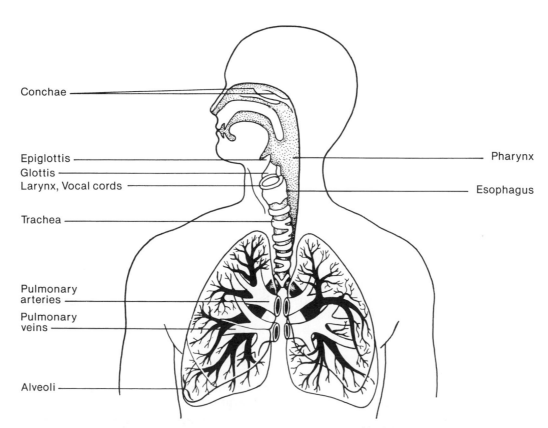

Figure 4–8. The respiratory pathways. From Guyton, AC,[4] p 299, with permission.

The thoracic cavity is thus increased in size and allows for lung expansion.

EXPIRATION

During relaxed breathing, expiration is essentially a passive process. Once the respiratory muscles relax, the thorax returns to its resting position, and the lungs recoil. This ability to recoil occurs through the inherent elastic properties of the lungs.

Regulatory Mechanisms

Regulation of respiratory function is a complex process. It involves multiple components of both neural and chemical control and is closely integrated with the cardiovascular system.

Breathing is controlled by the *respiratory center,* which lies bilaterally in the pons and medulla.[13,14] The respiratory muscles are controlled by motor nerves whose cell bodies are located in this area. This respiratory center provides control of both the rate and the depth of breathing in response to the metabolic needs of the body.

Both *central* and *peripheral* chemoreceptors influence respiration. *Central* chemoreceptors located in the respiratory center are sensitive to changes in either carbon dioxide or hydrogen concentration levels of arterial blood. An increase in either carbon dioxide levels or hydrogen ions will stimulate breathing.[4] *Peripheral* chemoreceptors are located at the bifurcation of the carotid arteries (carotid bodies) and in the arch of the aorta (aortic bodies). These receptors are sensitive to the partial pressure of oxygen (PaO_2) in the arterial blood. When PaO_2 levels in arterial blood drop, afferent impulses carry this information to the respiratory center. Motor neurons to the respiratory muscles are stimulated to increase **tidal volume** (amount of air exchanged with each breath) or with very low oxygen levels also to increase the respiratory rate.[6] An increase in respiration occurs from these peripheral chemoreceptors only when PaO_2 levels fall to approximately 60 mmHg (from a normal level of about 90 to 100 mmHg).[13] This results from the receptors being sensitive only to PaO_2 levels in plasma and not total oxygen in blood.[6]

Respiration also is influenced by a protective stretch mechanism called the *Hering-Breuer reflex.* Stretch receptors throughout the walls of the lungs monitor the amount of entering air. When overstretched, these receptors send impulses to the respiratory center to inhibit further inhalation. Impulses stop at the end of expiration so that another inspiration can be initiated.[4,13,14] Respiration also is stimulated by vigorous movements of joints and muscle (exercise) and is strongly influenced by voluntary cortical control.

Factors Influencing Respiration

Multiple factors can alter normal, relaxed, effortless respiration. As with temperature and pulse, any influence that increases the metabolic rate also will increase the respiratory rate. Increased metabolism and subsequent demand for oxygen will stimulate increased respiration. Conversely, as metabolic demands diminish, respirations also will decrease. Several influencing factors are of particular importance when assessing respiration. These include age, body size, stature, exercise, and body position.

AGE

The respiratory rate of a newborn is between 30 and 60 per minute. The rate gradually slows until adulthood, when it ranges between 12 and 18 per minute.[15] In elderly populations the respiratory rate increases owing to decreased elasticity of the lungs and decreased efficiency of gas exchange.[8]

BODY SIZE

Men generally have a larger vital capacity than women; adults larger than adolescents and children.

STATURE

Tall, thin individuals generally have a larger vital capacity than stout or obese subjects.

EXERCISE

Respiratory rate and depth will increase as a result of increased oxygen consumption and carbon dioxide production.

BODY POSITION

The supine position can significantly affect respiration and predispose the patient to stasis of fluids. The two influential factors are compression of the chest against the supporting surface and increased volume of intrathoracic blood.[8] Both these factors will limit normal lung expansion.

In addition to these factors, respiration also may be affected by drug intake, certain disease states, and the patient's emotional status.

Parameters of Respiratory Assessment

In assessing respiration, four parameters are considered: rate, depth, rhythm, and character.

The *rate* is the number of breaths per minute. Either inspirations or expirations should be counted, but not both. The normal adult respiratory rate is 12 to 18 per minute. The rate should be counted for 30 seconds and multiplied by 2. If any irregularities are noted, a full 60-second count is indicated.

The *depth* of respiration refers to the amount (volume) of air exchanged with each breath. Normally, the depth of respirations are the same, producing a relatively even, uniform movement of the chest. The normal adult tidal volume is approximately 500 ml of air. The depth of respiration is assessed by observation of chest movements. It is usually described as *deep* or *shallow,* depending on whether the amount of air exchanged is greater or less than normal.[2] With deep respirations a large volume of air is exchanged; with shallow respirations a small amount of air is exchanged with minimal lung expansion or chest wall movement.

The *rhythm* refers to the regularity of inspirations and expirations. Normally, there is an even time interval between respirations. The respiratory rhythm is described as *regular* or *irregular.*

The *character* of respirations refers to deviations from normal, quiet, effortless breathing. Two important deviations that alter the character of breathing are the *amount of effort* required and the *sound* produced during respiration.

Difficult or labored breathing is called **dyspnea.** Dyspneic patients require increased, noticeable effort to breath. This is frequently evident by increased activity noted in accessory respiratory muscles such as the intercostals and abdominals. Use of these muscles helps increase effectiveness of respiration. The intercostals assist in raising the ribs to expand the thoracic cavity; the abdominals assist function of the diaphragm. Additional muscles that may provide accessory functions in respiration are the sternocleidomastoid, pectoralis major and minor, scalene, and the subclavius.

The sound of breathing is also important in assessing the character of respirations. Several relevant terms related to respiratory sounds are described below.

1. **Wheezing:** a whistling sound produced by air passing through a narrowed bronchi or bronchiole; it may be heard on both inspiration and expiration but is more prominent on expiration; apparent with emphysema and asthmatic patients.

2. **Stridor:** a harsh, high-pitched crowing sound which occurs with upper airway obstructions caused by narrowing of the glottis or trachea (e.g., tracheal stenosis, presence of a foreign object).

3. **Rales:** rattling, bubbling, or crackling sounds which occur owing to secretions in the air passages of the respiratory tract. They may be heard with the ear but are most accurately assessed by use of a stethoscope.

4. **Sigh:** a deep inspiration followed by a prolonged, audible expiration; occasional sighs are normal and function to expand alveoli. Frequent sighs are abnormal and may be indicative of emotional stress.

5. **Stertorous:** a snoring sound owing to secretions in the trachea and large bronchi.

In addition to the rate, depth, rhythm, and character, several distinctive *patterns* of respiration have been described. The more common include the following.

1. **Cheyne-Stokes respirations:** a pattern characterized by a gradual increase in rate and depth followed by a gradual decrease. Periods of apnea occur between cycles. Considered a serious symptom, this respiratory pattern is often noted as death approaches. This pattern is also associated with severe congestive heart failure, renal failure, drug overdose, meningitis, and unaccustomed exposure to high altitudes.[7,16]

2. **Kussmaul's respirations:** a gasping, labored pattern with both increased rate and depth; associated with metabolic acidosis and renal failure.

3. **Biot's respirations:** pattern that alternates between periods of apnea and hyperpnea (increased rate and

depth).[7] Associated with meningitis and central nervous system disorders, which cause increased intracranial pressure.[7,16]

4. **Apneustic breathing:** prolonged inspiration with short, ineffective expiration; seen in lesions of the pons.[7]

5. **Paradoxical respirations:** lung inflation occurs on expiration, and deflation occurs on inspiration; may occur in open pneumothorax or in paralysis of diaphragm.[7]

Procedure for Assessing Respiration

Considering that respiration is under both voluntary (cortical) and involuntary control, it is important that the patient is unaware that respiration is being assessed. Once aware of the assessment, usual breathing characteristics may be altered. Therefore, it is often recommended that respirations be observed immediately after taking the pulse. After monitoring the pulse, the fingers can remain in place at the pulse site, and respiration can be assessed. With the use of this technique the patient's conscious attention will not be drawn to the respiratory assessment. Ideally, respiration should be assessed with the chest exposed. If this is not possible, or if respirations can not be easily observed through clothing, maintain fingers on the radial pulse site and place the patient's arm across the chest. This will allow limited palpation without drawing conscious input from the patient.

ASSESSING RESPIRATION

A. Wash hands.
B. Assemble equipment.
   1. A watch with a second hand.
   2. Worksheet and pen or pencil to record collected data.
C. Procedure.
   1. Assure patient comfort.
   2. Expose chest area if possible; if area can not be exposed and respirations are not readily observable, place patient's arm across chest and keep your fingers positioned as if continuing to monitor the radial pulse.
   3. Count the respirations (either inspirations or expirations, but not both) for 30 seconds and multiply by 2; if any irregularities are noted, count for a full 60 seconds.
   4. Observe the depth, rhythm, character, and pattern of respiration.
   5. Return clothing if chest has been exposed.
   6. Record results.

BLOOD PRESSURE

Blood pressure refers to the force the blood exerts against a vessel wall. Because liquid flows only from a higher to a lower pressure, the pressure is highest in the arteries, lower in the capillaries, and lowest in veins.[17] Inasmuch as the heart is an *intermittent* pulsatile pump, pressure is measured at both the highest and lowest points of the pulse. These points are represented by the **systolic** (ventricular contraction) and **diastolic** (ventricular relaxation) pressures. The systolic pressure is the highest pressure exerted by the blood against the arterial walls. The diastolic pressure (which is constantly present) is the lowest pressure. The difference between the two pressures is called the **pulse pressure.**

Regulatory Mechanisms

The *vasomotor center* is located bilaterally in the lower pons and upper medulla. It transmits impulses through sympathetic nerves to all vessels of the body.[6] The vasomotor center is tonically active, producing a slow, continual firing in all vasoconstrictor nerve fibers. It is this slow continual firing that maintains a partial state of contraction of the blood vessels and provides normal *vasomotor tone.*[4] The vasomotor center assists in providing a stable arterial pressure required to maintain blood flow to body tissue and organs. This occurs by way of its close connection to the cardiac controlling center in the medulla (because changes in cardiac output will influence blood pressure). Additionally, the vasomotor and cardiac controlling centers require input from afferent receptors.

AFFERENT RECEPTORS

Input regarding blood pressure is provided primarily by *baroreceptors* and *chemoreceptors.* The *baroreceptors* (pressoreceptors) are stimulated by stretch of the vessel wall from alterations in pressure. These receptors have a high concentration in the walls of the internal carotid arteries above the carotid bifurcation and in the walls of the arch of the aorta. The areas where baroreceptors are located in the carotid arteries are called *carotid sinuses* and monitor blood pressure to the brain. Their locations on the aortic arch are called *aortic sinuses* and are responsible for monitoring blood pressure throughout the body.

In response to an increase in blood pressure the baroreceptor input to the vasomotor center results in an inhibition of the vasoconstrictor center of the medulla and excitation of the vagal center.[4] This results in a decreased heart rate, decreased force of cardiac contraction, and vasodilation with a subsequent drop in blood pressure. The baroreceptor input during a lowering of blood pressure would produce the opposite effects.

The *chemoreceptors* are stimulated by reduced arterial oxygen concentrations, increases in carbon dioxide tension, and increased hydrogen ion concentrations.[18] These receptors lie close to the baroreceptors. Their locations in the carotid artery are called *carotid bodies,* and on the aortic arch they are termed *aortic bodies.*

Impulses from these receptors travel to the brain (cardioregulatory and vasomotor centers) via afferent pathways in the vagus and glossopharygneal nerves. Efferent impulses from these centers, in response to alterations in blood pressure, will alter heart rate, strength of cardiac contractions and size of blood vessels.[18]

Factors That Influence Blood Pressure

Many factors influence pressure. As with all vital signs, blood pressure is represented by a range of normal values and will yield the most useful data when monitored over a period of time. Several important factors that should be considered when assessing blood pressure include blood volume, diameter and elasticity of arteries, cardiac output, age, exercise, and arm position.

BLOOD VOLUME

The amount of circulating blood in the body directly effects pressure. Blood loss (e.g., hemorrhage) will cause pressure to drop. Conversely, an increased blood volume (e.g., blood transfusion) will cause the pressure to rise.

DIAMETER/ELASTICITY OF ARTERIES

The size (diameter) of the vessel lumen will provide either increased peripheral resistance (vasoconstriction) or decreased resistance (vasodilation) to cardiac output. The elasticity of the vessel wall also influences resistance. Normally the expansion and recoil properties of the arterial walls provide a continuous, smooth flow of blood into the capillaries and veins between heart beats. With age, these properties are diminished. Thus, there is a higher resistance to blood flow with resultant increase in systolic pressure. Because the flexibility and recoil properties are diminished, there is a lower diastolic pressure.

CARDIAC OUTPUT

When increased amounts of blood are pumped into the arteries, the walls of the vessels distend, resulting in a higher blood pressure. With lower cardiac output, less blood is pushed into the vessel, and there is a subsequent drop in pressure.

AGE

Blood pressure varies with age (Table 4–1). It normally rises after birth and reaches a peak during early puberty.

Table 4–1 VARIATIONS IN BLOOD PRESSURE WITH AGE

Age	Normal Blood Pressure (mmHg)
Newborn	40 to 70 systolic
1 month	80 systolic, 45 diastolic
6 months	90 systolic, 60 diastolic
2 years	80 to 90 systolic, 55 to 65 diastolic
4 years	100 to 115 systolic, 55 to 75 diastolic
6 years	105 to 125 systolic, 60 to 80 diastolic
8 years	105 to 125 systolic, 65 to 80 diastolic
10 years	110 to 135 systolic, 65 to 80 diastolic
12 years	115 to 135 systolic, 65 to 80 diastolic
14 years	120 to 140 systolic, 70 to 85 diastolic
Adult	110 to 140 systolic, 60 to 80 diastolic
Elderly	Same as for an adult, or slightly higher systolic and slightly lower diastolic

From Kozier and Erb,[20] p 487, with permission of the publisher.

By age 17 or 18, the adult blood pressure has been reached. The normal, average adult blood pressure is usually considered 120/80 mmHg (the top number indicates systolic pressure; the bottom, diastolic pressure).

EXERCISE

Physical activity will increase cardiac output, with a consequential linear increase in blood pressure. Greater increases are noted in systolic pressure owing to the proportional change in pressure gradient of peripheral vessels during vasodilation. Blood pressure increases are proportional to intensity of the work load.

ARM POSITION

Blood pressure may vary as much as 20 mmHg by altering arm position.[19] For consistency of measures, the patient should be sitting with the arm in a horizontal, supported position at heart level.[19] If patient condition or type of activity precludes these positions, alterations should be carefully documented.

As with other vital signs, factors such as fear, anxiety, or emotional stress also will cause an increase in blood pressure.

Assessing Blood Pressure

EQUIPMENT

The equipment required for taking blood pressure includes a *blood pressure cuff,* a *sphygmomanometer,* and a *stethoscope* (Fig. 4–9). The blood pressure cuff is an airtight, flat rubber bladder which can be inflated with air. The bladder is covered with cloth that extends beyond the length of the bladder. There are two tubes that extend from the cuff. One is attached to a rubber bulb, which has a valve used to maintain or to release air from the cuff. The second tube is attached to a manometer (portion of sphygmomanometer that registers the pressure reading).

The cuffs may be secured on the patient's extremity by Velcro, snaps, or hooks, and many are wrapped to keep in place.[20] They come in a variety of sizes. Obtaining an appropriate size cuff is important. The cuff should cover approximately one half to two thirds of the patient's upper arm or leg and should be long enough to encircle the limb.[20] Cuffs that are too narrow will show inaccurately high readings, and cuffs that are too wide, inaccurately low. Generally, the cuff width should be 20 percent wider than the diameter of the limb. A typical adult cuff width is 4.5 to 5.5 inches (12 to 14 cm) with a bladder length of 9 inches (23 cm).[2]

The sphygmomanometer registers the blood pressure reading. There are two types: *aneroid manometers* and *mercury manometers* (see Figure 4–9). The aneroid manometer registers the blood pressure by way of a circular calibrated dial and needle. The mercury manometer registers blood pressure on a mercury-filled calibrated cylinder. At the uppermost portion of the mercury column is a convex curve called the *meniscus.* A reading is

obtained by viewing the meniscus *at eye level.* If not observed directly at eye level, an inaccurate reading will be obtained.

The stethoscope is used to listen to the sounds over the artery as pressure is released from the cuff. It includes an amplifying mechanism (diaphragm) and ear pieces connected by rubber tubing. There are two types of diaphragms: a bell-shaped and a flat disk shape. Stethoscopes may have a single type of diaphragm or a combination of the two (see Figure 4–9). The bell-shaped diaphragms are generally recommended for assessing blood pressure.[21] By a combination of listening through the stethoscope and watching the manometer, the blood pressure reading is obtained.

Electronic sphygmomanometers are also commercially available. They contain a microphone and transducer built into the cuff.[10] Thus the need for a stethoscope is eliminated. A flashing light or audible "beep" indicates both the systolic and diastolic pressures.

KOROTKOFF'S SOUNDS

When assessing blood pressure, a series of sounds are heard through the stethoscope called *Korotkoff's sounds.* Initially when pressure is applied in the cuff, the blood flow is occluded and no sound is heard through the stethoscope. As the pressure is gradually released, a series of five phases or sounds have been identified.[21]

Phase 1: the first clear, faint, rhythmic tapping sound which gradually increases in intensity; period when blood initially flows through the artery; systolic pressure.

Phase 2: a murmur or swishing quality is heard.

Phase 3: sounds become crisp and louder.

Phase 4: sound is distinct, abrupt muffling; soft blowing quality; first diastolic pressure.

Phase 5: sounds disappear; second diastolic pressure.

Controversy exists as to the point of true diastolic pressure (phase 4 versus phase 5). The American Heart Association recommends use of the fifth phase as the most accurate index of diastolic pressure in adult populations.[21] Recording only one diastolic pressure (phase 5) is common practice in most clinical settings. For example, a blood pressure reading with a systolic pressure of 120 and a second diastolic reading of 76 would be recorded as 120/76. In facilities where both diastolic pressures are routinely documented, three numbers are recorded. For example, a systolic pressure of 120, a first diastolic reading of 80 and a second of 76 would be recorded as 120/80/76.

PROCEDURE FOR ASSESSING BLOOD PRESSURE

A primary consideration in assessing blood pressure is that it should be done in a minimal amount of time. The blood pressure cuff acts as a tourniquet. As such, venous pooling and considerable discomfort to the patient will occur if the cuff is left in place too long.

The brachial artery is the most common site for blood pressure monitoring and will be described in detail. A description for monitoring lower extremity blood pressure is also presented.

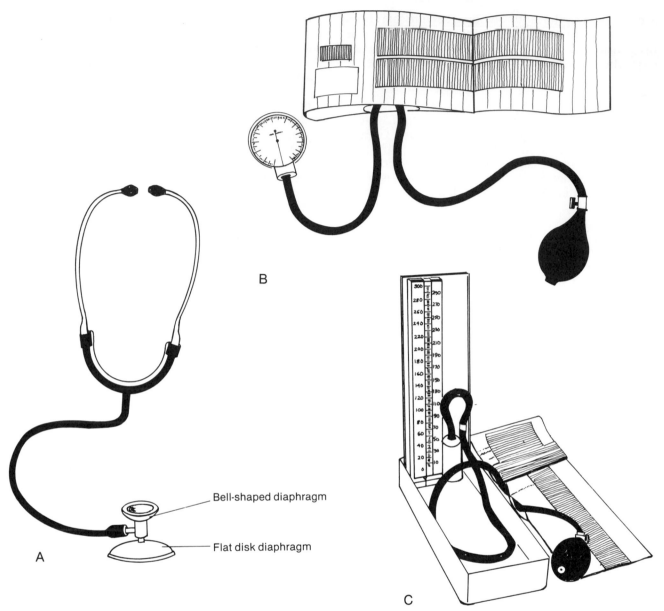

Figure 4–9. Blood pressure equipment includes (*A*) a stethoscope (note that this stethoscope has a combination of both a bell-shaped and a flat disk diaphragm) and either (*B*) an aneroid manometer and cuff or (*C*) mercury manometer and cuff.

Assessing Brachial Artery Pressure

A. Wash hands.
B. Assemble equipment.
  1. A stethoscope.
  2. A sphygmomanometer with a blood pressure cuff (size of cuff should be appropriate for size of extremity).
  3. Antiseptic wipes for cleaning ear pieces and diaphragm of stethoscope before and after use.
  4. Worksheet and pen and pencil to record collected data.
C. Procedure.
  1. Explain procedure and rationale to patient in terms appropriate to his or her understanding.
  2. Assist the patient to the desired position (the sit-

ting position is recommended);[19] assure patient comfort.
  3. Expose the arm and place at heart level with the elbow extended.
  4. Wrap the blood pressure cuff around arm approximately 2.5 to 5 cm (1 to 2 inches) above the antecubital fossa; the center of cuff should be in line with the brachial artery (Fig. 4–10).
  5. Check that the sphygmomanometer registers zero.
  6. Use an antiseptic wipe to clean the ear pieces and diaphragm of the stethoscope.
  7. Place the ear pieces of stethoscope (tilting forward) into ears; the tubes of the stethoscope should not be crossed and should hang freely.
  8. Locate and palpate the brachial artery in the ante-

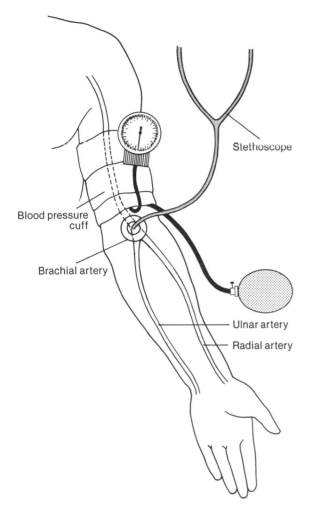

Figure 4–10. Placement of the blood pressure cuff and stethoscope for monitoring brachial artery pressure.

cubital fossa; place the diaphragm of the stethoscope over the artery (see Figure 4–10).
9. Close the valve of the blood pressure cuff (turn clockwise).
10. Pump the blood pressure cuff until the manometer registers approximately 20 mmHg above the anticipated systolic pressure.
11. Release the valve carefully, allowing air out slowly; air should be released at a rate of 2 to 3 mmHg per heart beat.
12. Watch the manometer closely and note the point at which the first sound is heard (a mercury manometer *must* be viewed at eye level); this is the point where blood first begins to flow through the artery and represents the **systolic pressure;** deflections in the dial or column of mercury will now be noted.
13. Continue to release air carefully. Note the point on the manometer when the sound first becomes muffled; this is the first **diastolic pressure.**
14. Continue to release air gradually.
15. Note the point on the manometer when the sound disappears and deflection ceases; this is recorded as the *second diastolic pressure.*

16. Allow remainder of air to release quickly.
17. If the same examiner is using the stethoscope again, it is not necessary to clean the ear pieces; however, the diaphragm of stethoscope should always be cleaned between patients.
18. Record results.

Assessing Popliteal (Thigh) Pressure

Lower extremity readings are indicated in situations in which comparison between the upper and lower extremities is warranted, such as peripheral vascular disease. They also are used when upper extremity pressures are contraindicated, such as following trauma or surgery.

Essentially, the procedure is the same as that for assessing pressure at the brachial artery, with the following variations:
1. The patient is placed in a prone position with slight knee flexion.
2. The popliteal artery is used to monitor pressure; in comparison with the brachial artery, the popliteal artery usually yields higher systolic and lower diastolic values.
3. A wide cuff is used (approximately 18 cm [17 inches]). This is placed around the lower third of the thigh. The center of the cuff should be in line with the popliteal artery.

RECORDING RESULTS

For purposes of physical therapy documentation, many therapists include vital signs data directly within the narrative format of their note. The most important element in recording this information is that it allows easy comparison from one entry to the next. The date, time of day, patient position, examiner's name, and equipment used all should be clearly indicated.

Traditionally, nursing personnel have used graph sheets to record vital sign information. If practicing in a facility where such forms are used, they will be useful in providing recent vital sign data. Familiarity with the specific recording system is important. Several methods are used and generally include some variation of open and closed circles, connecting lines and/or color codes. A sample of such a sheet is presented in Figure 4–11. Modifications of this type of form also may be useful for documenting response to physical therapy treatment.

SUMMARY

Values obtained from monitoring vital signs provide the physical therapist with important information about the patient's physiologic status. Results from these measures assist in establishing a database of values for an individual patient. They also assist in goal setting, treatment planning, assessment of patient response to treatment, and periodic reassessment to determine the effectiveness of treatment interventions.

The procedure for assessing each vital sign has been

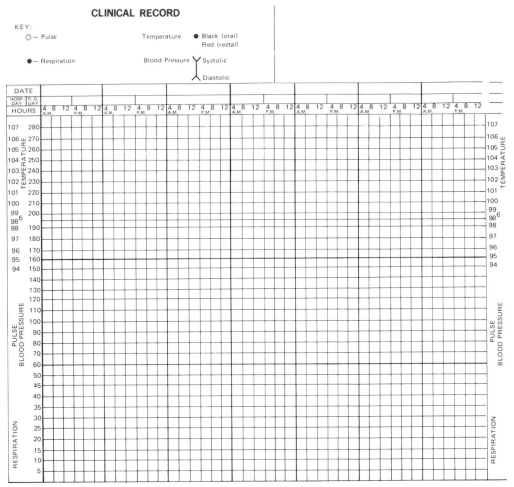

Figure 4–11. Graphic record sheet for recording vital signs. From Saperstein, AB and Frazier, MA,[1] p 483, with permission of the publisher.

presented. Because multiple factors influence vital signs, the most useful data are obtained with measures taken at periodic intervals rather than at a one-time assessment. This will allow changes in patient status or response to treatment to be monitored over time as well as indicate an acute change in status at a specific point in time.

For purposes of physical therapy assessments, documentation of vital sign data is typically included within the narrative format of the note. Use of a graph to record this information may prove a useful adjunct to the physical therapy record. *Regardless of the system of documentation selected, of critical importance is that it allows easy comparison of serial entries over time.*

QUESTIONS FOR REVIEW

1. Identify the reasons for monitoring vital signs.
2. Why are vital sign values more significant when monitored as a *serial* process versus a *one-time* assessment?
3. Describe the primary mechanisms by which the body conserves and produces heat.
4. Differentiate the four primary heat loss mechanisms: radiation, conduction, convection, and evaporation.
5. Describe daily occurrences that can either increase or decrease body temperature.
6. Describe the procedure for assessing oral temperature using a standard clinical glass thermometer.
7. Describe the procedure for assessing axillary temperatures using a standard clinical glass thermometer.
8. Define pulse rate, rhythm, and volume.
9. What factors influence the pulse?
10. Describe the procedure for assessing both radial and apical pulses.
11. What parameters are addressed during a respiratory assessment? Define each.
12. What factors will influence respiration?

13. Describe the following respiratory patterns: Cheyne-Stokes, Kussmal's, apneustic breathing, and paradoxical breathing.

14. Describe the procedure for assessing respiration.

15. What factors influence blood pressure?

16. What are the five phases of Korotkoff's sounds?

17. What changes will be noted in blood pressure readings if an inappropriate size cuff is used?

18. Describe the procedure for assessing blood pressure with use of a stethoscope and sphygmomanometer.

REFERENCES

1. Saperstein, AB and Frazier, MA: The assessment of vital signs. In Saperstein, AB and Frazier, MA (eds): Introduction to Nursing Practice. FA Davis, Philadelphia, 1980, p 452.
2. Wolf, L, Weitzel, MH, and Fuerst, EL: Fundamentals of Nursing, ed 6. JB Lippincott, New York, 1979.
3. Judy, WJ: Energy metabolism, temperature regulation and exercise. In Selkurt, EE (ed): Basic Physiology for the Health Sciences, ed 2. Little, Brown & Co, Boston, 1982, p 513.
4. Guyton, AC: Human Physiology and Mechanisms of Disease, ed 4. WB Saunders, Philadelphia, 1987.
5. McArdle, WD, Katch, FI, and Katch, VL: Exercise Physiology: Energy, Nutrition, and Human Performance, ed 2. Lea & Febiger, Philadelphia, 1986.
6. Berger, RA: Applied Exercise Physiology. Lea & Febiger, Philadelphia, 1982.
7. Thomas, CL (ed): Taber's Cyclopedic Medical Dictionary, ed 15. FA Davis, Philadelphia, 1985.
8. Kozier, B and Erb, G: Fundamentals of Nursing: Concepts and Procedures, ed 2. Addison-Wesley, Menlo Park, CA, 1983.
9. Watson, JE (ed): Medical-Surgical Nursing and Related Physiology, ed 2. WB Saunders, Philadelphia, 1979.
10. DuGas, BW: Introduction to Patient Care: A Comprehensive Approach to Nursing, ed 4. WB Saunders, Philadelphia, 1983.
11. Lunsford, BR: Clinical indicators of endurance. Phys Ther 58:704, 1978.
12. Amundsen, LR: Assessing exercise tolerance: A review. Phys Ther 59:534, 1979.
13. Wilson, LM and Price, SA: Normal respiratory function. In Price, SA and Wilson, LM (eds): Pathophysiology: Clinical Concepts of Disease Processes, ed 3. McGraw-Hill, 1986, p 481.
14. Selkurt, EE: Respiration. In Selkurt, EE (ed): Basic Physiology for the Health Sciences, ed 2. Little, Brown & Co, 1982, p 324.
15. Jarvis, CM: Monitoring the pulse, respiration and blood pressure and understanding their significance. In Sorensen, KC and Luckmann, J (eds): Basic Nursing: A Psychophysiologic Approach. WB Saunders, Philadelphia, 1979, p 660.
16. Jarvis, CM: Vital signs: How to take them more accurately and understand them more fully. Nursing 76 (6):31, April 1976.
17. Diekelmann, N, et al: Fundamentals of Nursing. McGraw-Hill, New York, 1980.
18. Ford, PJ: Anatomy of the cardiovascular system. In Price, SA and Wilson, LM (eds): Pathophysiology: Clinical Concepts of Disease Processes, ed 3. McGraw-Hill, 1986, p 329.
19. Webster, J, et al: Influence of arm position on measurement of blood pressure. Br Med J 288:1574, 1984.
20. Kozier, B and Erb, G: Techniques in Clinical Nursing: A Comprehensive Approach. Addison-Wesley, Menlo Park, CA, 1982.
21. Kirkendall, WM, et al: Recommendations for Human Blood Pressure Determination by Sphygmomanometers. American Heart Association, Dallas, 1980.

SUPPLEMENTAL READINGS

Adelman, EM: When the patient's blood pressure falls . . . What does it mean? What should you do? Nursing 80 (10):26, 1980.

Andzel, WD and Busuttil, C: Metabolic and physiological responses of college females to prior exercise, varied rest intervals and a strenuous endurance task. J Sports Med 22:113, 1982.

Amundsen, LR, et al: Exercise response during wall-pulley versus bicycle ergometer work. Phys Ther 60:173, 1980.

Astrand, P-O and Rodahl, K: Textbook of Work Physiology: Physiological Bases of Exercise, ed 3. McGraw-Hill, New York, 1986.

Baruch, IM and Mossberg, KA: Heart-rate response of elderly women to nonweight-bearing ambulation with a walker. Phys Ther 63:1782, 1983.

Britten, MX: Monitoring body temperature and understanding its significance. In Sorensen, KC and Luckmann, J (eds): Basic Nursing: A Psychophysiologic Approach. WB Saunders, Philadelphia, 1979, p 626.

Bye, PTP, Farkas, GA, and Roussos, CH: Respiratory factors limiting exercise. Ann Rev Physiol 45:439, 1983.

Driscoll, DJ, et al: Functional single ventricle: Cardiorespiratory response to exercise. JACC 4:337, 1984.

Duffin, J and Bechbache, RR: The changes in ventilation and heart rate at the start of treadmill exercise. Can J Physiol Pharmacol 61:120, 1982.

Duncan, G, Johnson, RH, and Lambie, DG: Role of sensory nerves in the cardiovascular and respiratory changes with isometric forearm exercise in man. Clin Sci 60:145, 1981.

Green, JF: Fundamental Cardiovascular and Pulmonary Physiology, ed 2. Lea & Febiger, Philadelphia, 1987.

Greer, M, Dimick, S, and Burns, S: Heart rate and blood pressure response to several methods of strength training. Phys Ther 64:179, 1984.

Guyton, AC: Textbook of Medical Physiology, ed 7. WB Saunders, Philadelphia, 1986.

Hedemark, LL and Kronenberg, RS: Chemical regulation of respiration: Normal variations and abnormal responses. Chest 82:488, 1982.

Iveson-Iveson, J: Students' forum—vital signs 4: Blood pressure. Nurs Mirror 154:41, 1982.

Iveson-Iveson, J: Students' forum—vital signs 2: Pulse taking. Nurs Mirror 154:28, 1982.

Iveson-Iveson, J: Students' forum—vital signs 3: Respiration. Nurs Mirror 154:31, 1982.

Jennett, S, Lamb, JF, and Travis, P: Sudden large and periodic changes in heart rate in healthy young men after short periods of exercise. Br Med J 285:1154, 1982.

Jette, DU: Physiological effects of exercise in the diabetic. Phys Ther 64:339, 1984.

May, GA and Nagle, FJ: Changes in rate-pressure product with physical training of individuals with coronary disease. Phys Ther 64:1361, 1984.

McKelvy, PL, Stein, CA, and Bertini, AB: Heart-rate response to a conditioning program for young, alcoholic men. Phys Ther 60:184, 1980.

Mountcastle, VB (ed): Medical Physiology, vol I, ed 14. CV Mosby, St Louis, 1980.

Mountcastle, VB (ed): Medical Physiology, vol II, ed 14. CV Mosby, St Louis, 1980.

Sodeman, WA and Sodeman, TM (eds): Sodeman's Pathologic Physiology: Mechanisms of Disease, ed 7. WB Saunders, Philadelphia, 1985.

Wenger, NK (ed): Exercise and the Heart. FA Davis, Philadelphia, 1985.

Vander, AJ, Sherman, JH, and Luciano, DS: Human Physiology: The Mechanisms of Body Function, ed 4. McGraw-Hill, New York, 1985.

GLOSSARY

Apnea: Absence of respirations, usually temporary in duration.

Anorexia: Loss of appetite.

Blood pressure: Tension exerted by the blood on the walls of a vessel.

Bradycardia: Abnormally slow (low) pulse rate; below approximately 50 beats per minute.

Bradypnea: Decreased respiratory rate; less than 10 breaths per minute.

Circadian rhythm: Variations in vital sign values that occur on a regular and predictable 24-hour cycle.

Cyanosis: Dusky, bluish, gray, or dark purple tinge of the skin and mucous membranes; caused by abnormally high amounts of reduced hemoglobin in the blood.

Diastole: Period of relaxation of the ventricles of the heart; the muscle fibers lengthen and the heart dilates.

Diastolic pressure: The pressure of the blood during relaxation (diastole) of the ventricles.

Dyspnea: Difficult or labored breathing, sometimes accompanied by pain; normal following vigorous physical activity.

Eupnea: Normal, effortless breathing.

Febrile: Pertaining to a fever; state of elevated body temperature.

Fever: Elevated body temperature.

Fever, types of
1. **Intermittent fever:** Temperatures alternate between pyrexia and normal or subnormal temperatures within a 24-hour period; an intermittent fever with fluctuations between high and low temperatures is termed a **hectic** fever.
2. **Remittent fever:** Fluctuations in temperature above normal without returning to normal between fluctuations.
3. **Sustained (constant) fever:** Consistently elevated temperature with little or no fluctuation.
4. **Relapsing (recurrent) fever:** Periods of pyrexia that alternate with normal temperatures; periods may last for a day or more.

Homoiotherm: An animal whose body temperature remains relatively constant regardless of the temperature of the external environment; a warm-blooded animal.

Hyperpnea: Increased rate and depth of respiration.

Hyperpyrexia: Extremely high fever; temperature reading of 41.1°C (106°F) or greater.

Hypertension: Higher than normal blood pressure.

Hyperthermia: Extremely high fever; temperature reading of 41.1°C (106°F) or greater.

Hyperventilation: Increase in the rate and depth of respiration.

Hypopnea: Abnormal decrease in both rate and depth of respiration.

Hypotension: Lower than normal blood pressure.

Hypothermia: Body temperature below average normal range.

Hypoventilation: Decrease in the rate and depth of respiration.

Orthopnea: Difficulty breathing in positions other than upright sitting and standing.

Poikilotherm: An animal whose body temperature varies with that of the external environment; a cold-blooded animal.

Pulse, common terms used to describe
1. **Bigeminal:** Two regular pulse beats followed by a long pause.
2. **Bounding:** A pulse that is difficult to obliterate; usually owing to high blood volume within vessel; artery has a feeling of tension on palpation (SYN: full, high-tension).
3. **Dicrotic:** A pulse that feels double on palpation; caused by prolonged ending of the pulse wave; also may be perceived as a weak wave between two beats.
4. **Intermittent:** Pulse that occasionally skips a beat.
5. **Irregular:** Pulse that varies in both force and rate.
6. **Thready:** Fine and barely perceptible pulse; easily obliterated (SYN: filiform, weak).
7. **Trigeminal:** Three regular pulse beats followed by a pause.
8. **Waterhammer:** Strong, jerky pulse of short duration which suddenly collapses (SYN: Corrigan's pulse).
9. **Weak:** Fine and barely perceptible pulse; easily obliterated (SYN: filiform, thready).

Pulse deficit: The difference between the apical and radial pulses.

Pulse pressure: The difference between the diastolic and systolic pressures.

Pyrexia: Increased body temperature; fever.

Pyrogen: Fever-producing substance.

Systole: Period during which the ventricles of the heart are contracting.

Systolic pressure: The pressure of the blood during contraction (systole) of the ventricles.

Tachycardia: Abnormally rapid (high) pulse rate; over approximately 100 beats per minute.

Tachypnea: Increased respiratory rate; greater than 24 breaths per minute.

Tidal volume: Volume or amount of air exchanged with a single breath.

Vital signs: The signs of life; that is, pulse, body temperature, respiration, and blood pressure (SYN: cardinal signs).

Chapter 5

ASSESSMENT AND TREATMENT PLANNING STRATEGIES FOR MUSCULOSKELETAL DEFICITS

DANIEL A. DYREK

OBJECTIVES

1. Describe a brief rationale for the onset of musculoskeletal dysfunction and its relationship to pain, tissue dysfunction, and functional impairment.

2. Identify the principles of the musculoskeletal assessment process.

3. Define the type of forces used to provoke tissues and structures during a musculoskeletal assessment.

4. Describe techniques for provocation of select tissues and structures.

5. Describe the components of the generic assessment process for upper and lower quarter musculoskeletal pain and dysfunction.

6. Describe the individual goals of a generic treatment strategy for musculoskeletal pain and tissue dysfunction.

INTRODUCTION

This chapter presents principles and strategies of musculoskeletal assessment and treatment planning. The material is relevant to any patient with a deficit of musculoskeletal origin. Orthopedic or musculoskeletal problems exist with any type of movement dysfunction regardless of which body system might be responsible for the patient's problem. The musculoskeletal component may be primarily responsible for the chief complaint, a contributing factor to it, or perhaps a result of it. The physical therapist must be knowledgeable and skilled in performing a thorough orthopedic screening assessment. Therefore, material in this chapter is appropriate for the therapist working with any type of patient population, including patients with neurologic, cardiopulmonary, or musculoskeletal conditions; burns; or any other condition in which movement dysfunction is present.

This chapter begins by identifying the goals of the musculoskeletal assessment and introduces the concept of the prerequisite knowledge base which the therapist must possess prior to assessing the patient. The forces applied during assessment and their effects, the differential assessment of tissue, and types of mobility deficits are discussed. A generic screening examination outline and assessment section serve to further illustrate the assessment process. The chapter concludes with a discussion of treatment goals and strategies.

PRINCIPLES OF ASSESSMENT

Purpose of the Assessment

The three primary purposes of the musculoskeletal physical therapy assessment are (1) to identify the specific lesion responsible for the patient's chief complaint of pain and functional impairment, (2) to assess the integrity and performance of the involved tissues and structures, and (3) to determine the patient's functional ability during daily occupational and recreational activities.

The first purpose of the assessment stems from the fact that pain is commonly the primary reason a patient seeks treatment. The initial goal is to identify the source of the pain by performing *provocation tests* (application of controlled external forces to impose an internal load) to isolated tissues and structures known to be capable of causing the patient's symptoms. Maitland[1] describes this process, in relation to examining joints, as identifying a **comparable sign**. The sign is the result of the provocation test, that is, pain, tenderness, restricted motion, or muscle spasm. The sign must correspond to the patient's symptoms. It is used as an indicator of treatment efficacy by re-examining it after treatment.

The second purpose of the examination is to assess the integrity and functional status of the involved tissues and structures. The tissues of the body combine to form a structure that performs a function. The clinician examines the structure to assess its ability to perform its role. For example, muscle fibers and collagen tissue compose the structure of the myotendon unit. Its function is to provide movement of body parts. The clinician assesses the strength of the myotendon unit. The muscle is examined for its torque-producing capacity, and the tendon is examined for its load-transmitting capacity. The clinician continues by examining other structures that ultimately combine with the myotendon unit to provide a means of function for the body as a whole.[2]

The third purpose is to assess the functional abilities of the patient during activities of daily living, occupational tasks, and leisure activities. The ultimate goal of physical therapy practice is to restore the maximal functional status of the patient as permitted by the integrity and performance of the tissues and structures of the body.

Periodic re-examination of the comparable sign, the functional status of the tissues, and the overall functional abilities of the patient provides a more objective measure of progress than measurement of a patient's symptoms. Symptoms can fluctuate widely in frequency, intensity, location, and correlation with activity. The patient's psychologic, cultural, and environmental influences can affect the perception of symptom behavior and intensity. The symptoms alone can be a misleading indicator of treatment success in dealing with mechanical lesions of the musculoskeletal system.

This concept is illustrated in the following example. A wheelchair-dependent patient with a spinal cord injury complains of diffuse shoulder pain. The musculoskeletal assessment of the shoulder complex reveals that the spe-

cific lesion causing the pain is a tendonitis of a rotator cuff. The assessment of the functional status of the tissues and structures reveals diminished strength and abnormal glenohumeral capsular length and flexibility. These factors result in impairment of joint mobility. All of the above deficits culminate in the functional loss of the patient being unable to propel a wheelchair. Several comparable signs may be identified in this example. The first is reproduction of the patient's pain from application of manual resistance to the involved myotendon unit, resulting in tensile stress to the lesion. The second is the elicitation of pain by passive range of motion toward internal rotation to stretch the involved tissue to again cause a tensile load. The third sign is restricted shoulder abduction, resulting in pain from impingement of the rotator cuff. A fourth sign is the restricted anteroinferior glide of the humeral head on the glenoid fossa owing to capsular fiber shortening resulting in reduced abduction. Throughout a course of treatment, these four signs, identified in the initial exam, are reassessed periodically to measure the effect of treatment.

The clinical decision-making process involved in assessing musculoskeletal tissues as the source of pain is often unclear territory. Many of the individual musculoskeletal tests are unreliable in incriminating a specific tissue as the cause of pain or dysfunction. This makes the first goal of the orthopedic examination a difficult task. A single positive test does not confirm the presence of a lesion. Confirmation may be obtained by correlating the results of multiple tests, and by performing multiple tests administered over a period of time to test the variability of a test response. Several repetitions may be made during a single examination session or during subsequent sessions with the patient.[3]

The reader is referred to chapter 1 for further reading on the process of making clinical decisions.

Because of the lack of clear and immediate confirmation of the patient's problem, the clinician may have to establish a provisional assessment on which to plan treatment. The patient's response to treatment is continually monitored by the therapist; if progress is occurring, treatment should continue based on the initial provisional assessment. If, however, no benefit is being derived, the therapist must re-examine the patient and establish an alternative plan of care. The assessment of a patient's condition may be confirmed only after treatment is successful (Fig. 5–1).

Skill is required to choose the necessary tests while avoiding the loss of valuable time with irrelevant tests. This process is promoted by performing a thorough patient interview so that a provisional assessment of the patient's condition can be made prior to the actual physical examination. Subsequently, the physical therapist selects tests that correlate with the suspected etiologies of the patient's primary complaint.

The model of musculoskeletal dysfunction presented in Figure 5–2 provides a framework which is used throughout this chapter. It provides an outline for the etiology of tissue dysfunction, impairment of musculoskeletal structures, and functional disability of the patient.

EXAMINATION PROCESS FOR THE PATIENT WITH MUSCULOSKELETAL DEFICIT

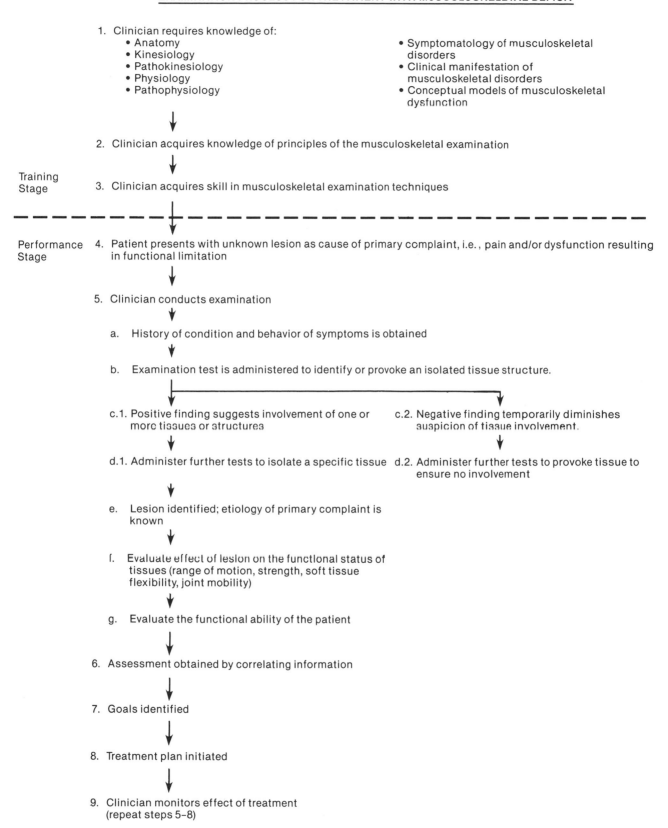

1. Clinician requires knowledge of:
   - Anatomy
   - Kinesiology
   - Pathokinesiology
   - Physiology
   - Pathophysiology
   - Symptomatology of musculoskeletal disorders
   - Clinical manifestation of musculoskeletal disorders
   - Conceptual models of musculoskeletal dysfunction

2. Clinician acquires knowledge of principles of the musculoskeletal examination

Training Stage

3. Clinician acquires skill in musculoskeletal examination techniques

Performance Stage

4. Patient presents with unknown lesion as cause of primary complaint, i.e., pain and/or dysfunction resulting in functional limitation

5. Clinician conducts examination

   a. History of condition and behavior of symptoms is obtained

   b. Examination test is administered to identify or provoke an isolated tissue structure.

   c.1. Positive finding suggests involvement of one or more tissues or structures

   c.2. Negative finding temporarily diminishes suspicion of tissue involvement.

   d.1. Administer further tests to isolate a specific tissue

   d.2. Administer further tests to provoke tissue to ensure no involvement

   e. Lesion identified; etiology of primary complaint is known

   f. Evaluate effect of lesion on the functional status of tissues (range of motion, strength, soft tissue flexibility, joint mobility)

   g. Evaluate the functional ability of the patient

6. Assessment obtained by correlating information

7. Goals identified

8. Treatment plan initiated

9. Clinician monitors effect of treatment (repeat steps 5–8)

Figure 5–1. Examination process for the orthopedic patient.

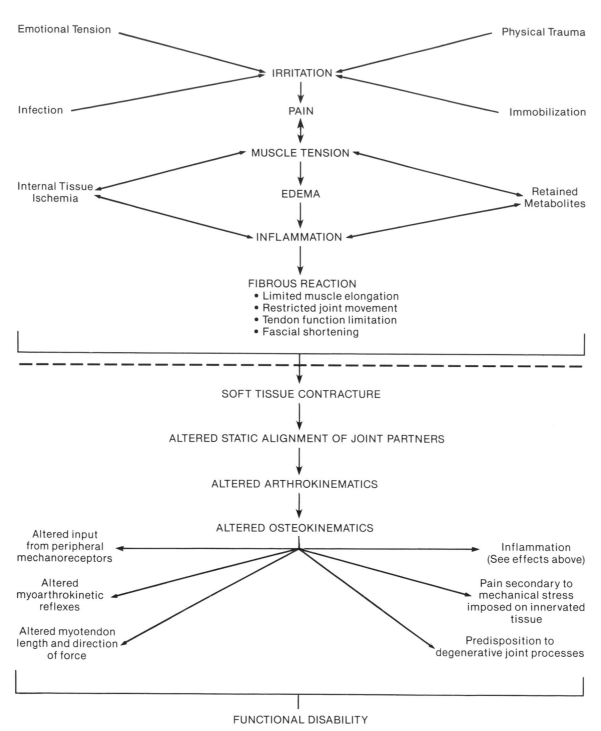

Figure 5–2. Model of musculoskeletal dysfunction.

Prerequisite Knowledge Base

Prior to conducting a musculoskeletal assessment, the clinician must possess a thorough knowledge of anatomy, kinesiology, pathokinesiology, physiology, pathophysiology, and symptomatology and physical presentation of musculoskeletal disorders. With this knowledge, the examiner has the information to effectively plan and execute the assessment process. For example, as a patient relates his or her history to the skilled therapist, the therapist can mentally prepare a list of possible disorders, pathophysiologic or pathokinesiologic in nature, that could exist as the primary cause of the patient's problem. The tests necessary to provoke the tissues of the body segment under consideration are dictated by the list of possible abnormal conditions. The clinician can focus the examination process based on each individual patient's history of problems and present symptoms. The clinician also can eliminate specific tests as inappropriate, given a thorough history and report of symptoms. Objectivity, however, must be exercised to avoid biased suspicion of a specific pathology as the cause of the patient's problem. Inexperienced therapists may look and test for what they expect to be present instead of remaining objective during the examination. The experienced examiner will continually compare physical findings with the established mental list of suspected conditions and will readily add or delete such conditions as the examination proceeds. Payton[3] and Barrows and Tamblyn[4] provide further insight into the reasoning process used in clinical practice.

The physical therapist should have prerequisite knowledge of the areas of musculoskeletal assessment described below.

CLINICAL MANIFESTATIONS OF GENERAL MUSCULOSKELETAL CONDITIONS

Many common musculoskeletal conditions may be found during the examination of different lesions. Muscle spasm, soft tissue density abnormalities, tenderness in various portions of contractile and noncontractile tissue, effusion, and edema are a few examples of common musculoskeletal conditions. The clinician must be knowledgeable of the symptoms the patient will describe in each case and learn to recognize the manner of clinical presentation for each condition.

For example, swelling as a symptom described by the patient can present two ways, as either edema or effusion. **Edema** is the presence of excessive fluid in the soft tissues of the body and is external to the joint capsule. **Effusion** is excessive fluid within the joint. The therapist must learn to differentiate between these two types of swelling to effectively manage the course of treatment.

CLINICAL MANIFESTATIONS OF SPECIFIC MUSCULOSKELETAL CONDITIONS

The physical signs and symptoms of the numerous possible lesions in the body segment under consideration must be known. Given this knowledge, the therapist can clarify the patient's report of symptoms through careful and meticulous interviewing, thereby promoting a concise list of conditions as the possible causes of the patient's problem.

For example, the therapist must know the signs and symptoms for various lesions that may be responsible for pain in the elbow region. Then the therapist can mentally compare the patient's signs and symptoms with the possible lesions capable of transmitting pain to the elbow. The tissues and structures and related body parts must be considered during this comparison process. From this process, the most probable causes of the patient's complaint can be identified, and an assessment process planned and performed which will narrow the possibilities to a single clear assessment.

NATURAL COURSE OF GENERAL AND SPECIFIC MUSCULOSKELETAL CONDITIONS

Once the patient's problem has been identified, clinical decision making proceeds. The natural course of a lesion is the path that it will follow if no clinical intervention occurs. Basically, the clinician must decide whether the condition and its sequelae can heal optimally independently of treatment or if it requires a therapeutic program.

For example, a diagnosis of an isolated muscle strain may not require any treatment other than rest. Rest diminishes the physical stress to the lesion and promotes healing of the muscle tissue. The patient is scheduled for re-examination after the estimated time period necessary to allow the lesion to heal. This re-examination allows the therapist to examine for residual deficits which may impair function and elicit pain in the future.

A second example illustrates the need to alter the natural course of a lesion through an aggressive treatment program. The patient with hemiplegia found to have chronic effusion of the talocrural joint due to a contracture may have permanent and progressive symptoms. Permanent damage to soft tissue and joint structures of the talocrural joint and surrounding area can occur by the weight-bearing force imposed on the altered joint. Secondarily, pain and reflex inhibition of neighboring musculature may occur in this patient. Therefore, intensive restorative musculoskeletal treatment should be implemented as a component of the total rehabilitation program.

Awareness of the natural course for a known condition also allows the clinician to determine the potential efficacy of treatment measures. A realistic prognosis can then be formulated for the patient, and appropriate treatment goals and plan can be established.

ELEMENTS OF THE EXAMINATION PROCESS

Types of Force Applied during the Examination Process

The musculoskeletal examination process seeks to provoke isolated tissues and structures of the musculoskeletal system, including peripheral nerves, to determine their role in the patient's pain and dysfunction. Tissue provocation is accomplished by the examiner applying a controlled external force to impose an internal load on the tissue. This internal load is called **stress.** The mechanical effect of the stress, that is, deformation of the tissue, is referred to as **strain.** The application of stress, and its resultant effect of strain, is the foundation by which the examiner can reproduce the patient's pain and identify abnormal tissue responses and integrity.

Different types of tissue demonstrate unique stress/strain curves based on their physical composition. Figure 5–3 illustrates the relative behavior of three different types of tissue. The clinician must acquire the skill to determine the normalcy of the response for numerous

A

Stress

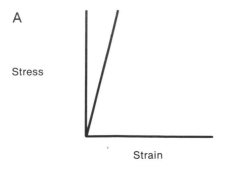

Strain

Hard tissue—minimal strain occurs as stress
increases. (Example: bone)

B

Stress

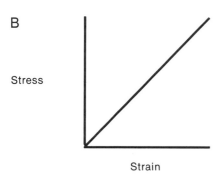

Strain

Firm tissue—strain increases proportionately
with an increase in stress.
(Example: ligament)

C

Stress

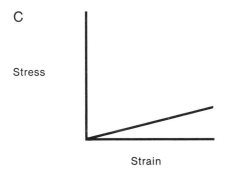

Strain

Soft tissue—strain occurs readily with minimal
stress. (Example: muscle)

Figure 5–3. Relative stress/strain curves for three different tissue types.

tissues. (The reader is referred to the Supplemental Readings for further information on the mechanical behavior of connective tissue.)

During the examination process, the clinician controls the variables of applying an external force while palpating and observing the response of the tissue. The external force can be modified by altering the

1. magnitude of the force
2. duration of force application
3. velocity of application

4. frequency of application
5. location of force application and the degree of pretest tension in the tissue
6. direction of force(s) application

Each of these variables can be manipulated by the examiner to thoroughly assess a specific tissue.

Several examples to illustrate this concept follow.

1. A low-magnitude stretching force may be insufficient to elicit pain in a tissue with a low-grade inflammatory process; however, a higher-magnitude force may elicit the patient's symptom.

2. A short duration load on internal tissue caused by stretching may not yield a pain response in a condition of chronic scar tissue, whereas a prolonged duration of load may elicit pain.

3. A slow velocity of force application may fail to elicit signs and symptoms, whereas a high rate of force application may yield positive findings.

4. A single application of a force may not elicit pain, but repetitive applications of the same magnitude of force may then elicit the patient's pain.

5. The importance of the location of force application and the degree of pretest tension in the tissue can be illustrated by considering the condition of patellar tendonitis. A positive finding of tenderness may be found only at the tendoperiosteal attachments, a weak link in the force transmission system, versus in the body of the tendon. Also the degree of knee flexion, which alters the degree of tendon stretch, will affect the level of load in the tendon prior to adding additional stress by palpation. For example, palpation of the tendon may not elicit tenderness with the knee in full extension with the tendon in a relatively slack position; but palpation may reveal tenderness with the knee in the 90 degree angle position of knee flexion in which the tendon is more tense.

6. The direction of force applied by the examiner will affect how the tissue is loaded and, therefore, the results of the test. For example, referring again to a case of patellar tendonitis, a palpation force applied perpendicular to the anterior tendon in the sagittal plane may be negative, whereas a "shear" force applied perpendicular to the medial or lateral edge of the tendon in the coronal plane may elicit a positive pain response. (Points 5 and 6 illustrate the concept of assessing tissue flexibility and its ability to resist tissue deforming loads in the sagittal, coronal, and horizontal planes and within the long axis of the tissue.)

The therapist must consider each of the variables and their combinations during the application of a force to a tissue for the purpose of examination. Only then can the clinician eliminate the tissue as a source of the patient's complaint. The types of tissue response and their clinical significance are discussed in this chapter in the section on tissue response.

COMPRESSION

Compression is a load that pushes the fibers of a material together along its long axis; it results in, or tends to cause, a shortening and widening of the material (Fig. 5–4A).[5,6] Clinically, the application of a compression load can approximate two tissues or structures, creating

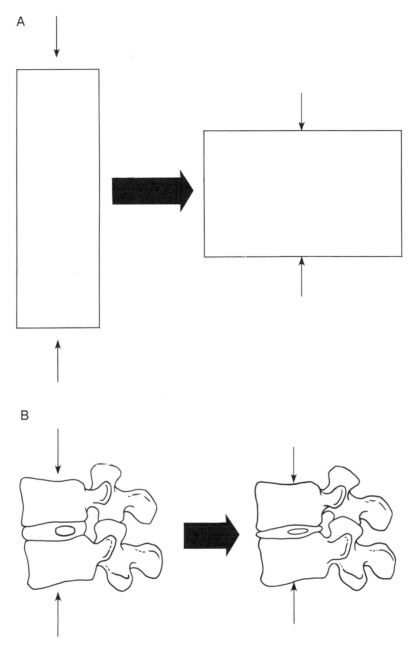

Figure 5–4. (*A*) Compression load applied to a solid deformable object. (*B*) Compression load applied to a vertebral segment resulting in deformation of the intervertebral disk.

abnormal location or intensity of force and subsequently eliciting tissue irritation and pain (Fig. 5–4B). Examples are the loading of articular cartilage in the weight-bearing joints of the lower extremity while standing, or a component of the load imposed on the intervertebral disk while sitting (see Figure 5–4B). During examination, compression loads are applied to joint surfaces to elicit pain and to determine the quality of the joint surface.[7]

TENSION

Tension occurs when an internal load imposed by forces acting in opposite directions results in the tendency to elongate or the actual elongation of the fibers in

a material. The elongation is accompanied by narrowing of the fiber (Fig. 5–5A). Tension is imposed on the quadriceps mechanism when it is passively stretched during simultaneous hip extension and knee flexion. Tension also occurs while applying resistance to the contraction of a muscle. Clinically, tension imparted to a joint will distract the joint surfaces (see Figure 5–5B). The capsuloligamentous component of the joint will be subject to a tensile load. The application of this load can be used diagnostically to determine the presence of tissue inflammation in the fibers of the capsule as indicated by the elicitation of pain. The clinical application of this type of load can be used for therapeutic purposes to restore the length of capsular fibers in the presence of a contracture.

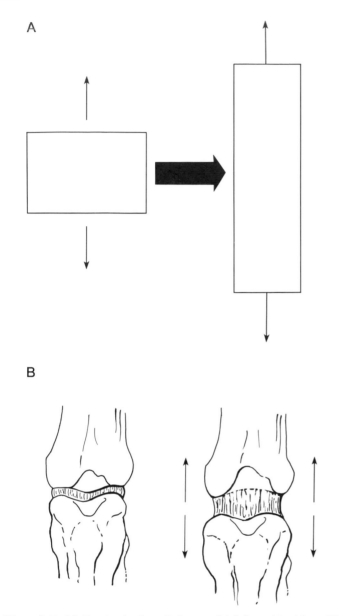

Figure 5–5. (*A*) Tension load applied to a solid deformable object. (*B*) Tension load applied to the capsuloligamentous tissue of a joint resulting in elongation of the tissue and distraction of the joint surfaces.

BENDING

Bending occurs when the application of a load imposed along the length of a tissue or structure causes deformation around an axis perpendicular to the long axis of the material. The bending effect will occur at an unsupported point in the material. A pattern of deformation occurs characterized by the creation of a tension load on the convex surface and a compression load on the concave side of the material (Fig. 5–6A). For example, a force imposed medially on the thigh creates a laterally directed load, resulting in bending of the femur (see Fig. 5–6B). A high magnitude load which exceeds the intrinsic strength of the bone would result in a fracture. A load applied for a long duration could result in remodeling of the bone until it assumed a static curved contour.

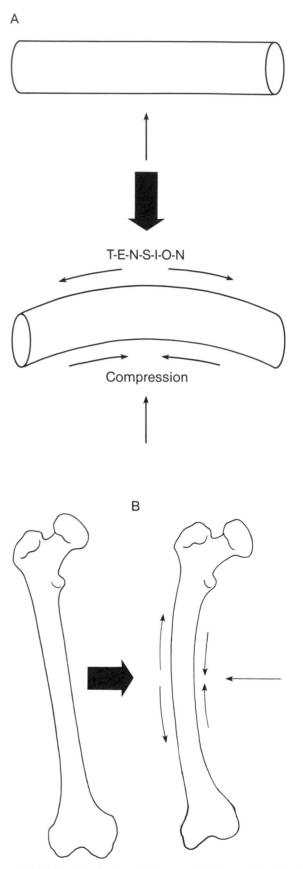

Figure 5–6 (*A*) Bending load applied to a solid deformable object. (*B*) Bending load applied to the femur. A force applied medially to the thigh creates a laterally directed load, resulting in bending of the femur.

TORSION

Torsion is a force that creates a twisting of the material around its long axis (Fig. 5–7). For example, rotation of one vertebral segment imposes a torsional load on the intervertebral disk. Repetitive high-magnitude torsional loading to the disk can result in tissue failure or tears of its outer ring, the annulus fibrosis. Subsequently the vertebral segment can develop an altered degree and pattern of motion allowing the segment to become a source of symptoms.

Clinically, the loads applied are often a combination of the forces described above. Through the skillful application of these forces, the examiner attempts to selectively load skin-fascia, muscle, tendon, myotendon and tendoperiosteal junctions, capsule, ligament, bursa, joint surfaces, and select peripheral nerves. The ability to isolate the force to a specific tissue or structure is influenced by accessibility; therefore, some body parts, such as the spine, are more difficult to examine than others.

Tissue Responses

The application of external force to tissue of the musculoskeletal system permits the therapist to detect the tissue in which pain originates and the quantity and quality of tissue resistance.

TISSUE REACTIVITY

The external force applied by the clinician imposes an internal load to the tissue. Inflamed tissue subjected to such load can evoke the perception of pain by the stimulation of peripheral mechanoreceptors. As will be explained in the next section, active, passive, and resisted motions will impose an internal tissue load. Normal healthy tissue will not evoke pain when subjected to a load, unless a force of sufficient magnitude to cause tissue damage is applied. The clinician assesses the degree of **tissue reactivity** during the examination. This information will assist in categorizing the lesion, that is, acute, subacute, or chronic, and secondarily to determine the appropriate level of force the patient could sustain during treatment without aggravating symptoms and the condition of the tissue. The degree of tissue reactivity also should be considered when advising the patient on safe levels of participation in activities of daily living and occupational tasks.

In addition to monitoring the patient's report of pain, the quality of resistance during passive motion imparted by the tissue to the palpating fingers is assessed by the clinician. Several characteristics of the resistance should be considered:

1. the presence of pain accompanying the resistance
2. the point in the range where resistance is felt
3. the type of resistance

TISSUE RESISTANCE

Tissue resistance to passive motion may be felt at several points in the range of motion: prematurely, normal, latent, or absent. A predicted range of motion exists for the tested body segment in comparison with the opposite extremity, other joints of the body, and in regard to the general population. If the end point of resistance is met

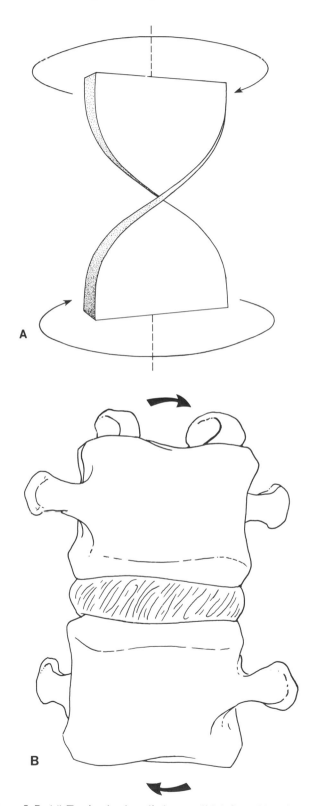

Figure 5–7. (*A*) Torsion load applied to a solid deformable object. (*B*) Torsion load applied to an intervertebral disk.

prematurely, then the tissue or joint is restricted. Similarly, when the resistance occurs at some point beyond the predicted range, the tissue or joint has excessive length or is hypermobile, respectively. The anticipated resistance to motion can be absent, as in the case of a total rupture of a ligament. The appropriate treatment plan is dictated by the individual finding. If restricted tissue is found during examination, stretching techniques should be performed to restore tissue length and flexibility. In the presence of articular tissue elongation resulting in a hypermobile joint or elongated soft tissue, suitable treatment would be to provide stability to the joint via strengthening-stabilizing exercises, an orthosis, or surgical repair.

Pain

The pattern of pain accompanying resistance during passive range of motion yields valuable diagnostic and prognostic information. Cyriax[8] describes three patterns that can occur:

1. *Pain before resistance.* Pain occurs prior to reaching the extreme of available motion. This pattern is suggestive of an acute inflammatory lesion of either extra-articular or articular origin.

2. *Pain simultaneous with resistance.* Suggestive of a subacute inflammatory process.

3. *Resistance prior to pain.* Pain is not elicited at the point of resistance, rather, overpressure must be applied to elicit pain; that is, a greater force to passively stretch the tissues beyond the physiologic range. A normal synovial joint can tolerate overpressure without eliciting pain. This pattern is indicative of a mild or chronic lesion that could tolerate aggressive treatment.

Thorough assessment of a joint requires that the pattern of pain and resistance be correlated with the point where the normal resistance to motion is expected to occur.

Type of Resistance: End-Feels

The type of resistance, that is, the **end-feel,** felt by the examiner when passively stretching a joint and its associated soft tissues provides important diagnostic and prognostic information. The end-feel is felt at the extreme of the available range of motion as the clinician imposes **overpressure** to the joint and tissues. Numerous authors have described various end-feels.[8,10] Both physiologic and pathologic end-feels exist in peripheral and spinal joints.

Normal End-feels. Kaltenborn describes three normal physiologic end-feels that possess an elastic quality of varying degrees:

1. *Soft.* Limitation is due to soft tissue approximation (e.g., knee flexion) or soft tissue stretching (e.g., ankle dorsiflexion with knee extension).

2. *Firm.* Limitation of action is due to soft tissue stretching of the less resilient capsule and ligament (e.g., external rotation of the humerus).

3. *Hard.* Limitation is due to bone-on-bone approximation (e.g., elbow extension).

Table 5–1 presents a summary of normal end-feels.

Table 5–1 NORMAL END-FEELS[1,11–14]

Type	Anatomic Limitation to Motion	Joint Motion Example
1. Hard	Bone in contact with bone	Elbow extension
2. Soft	Soft tissue approximation	Elbow and knee flexion
3. Firm	Joint capsule	Shoulder and hip rotation
	Muscle	Hip flexion with the knee extended (straight leg raise)
	Ligaments	Forearm supination

Adapted from Norkin, CC and White, JD: *Measurement of Joint Motion: A Guide to Goniometry.* FA Davis, Philadelphia, 1985.

Pathologic or Abnormal End-feels. A pathologic end-feel may be the normal type of resistance anticipated for the joint under examination but occurring prematurely or late in the range of motion, or it could be an abnormal type of resistance for the joint.

Examples of pathologic end-feels are

1. *Muscle spasm.* Characterized by a fairly abrupt stop with a mild "rebounding" sensation.

2. *Boggy.* Soft, "mushy" resistance (example: effusion).

3. *Springy.* A "rubbery" rebound with firm unyielding resistance (example: displaced meniscus at the tibiofemoral joint).

4. *Empty.* The patient voluntarily prevents the passive motion or requests the motion to cease secondary to severe pain. No tissue resistance is felt by the examiner.

5. *Capsular.* Firm limitation, yet resilient with maintained force; occurs prematurely in the range of motion.

6. *Bony block.* A sudden, abrupt limitation of motion; no "giving" sensation occurs with prolonged pressure (example: an osteophyte limiting joint motion).

7. *Laxity.* Loose; excessive mobility beyond the normal anatomic range of motion.

Differential Assessment of Soft Tissue Lesions by Motion

Three types of motion, active, passive, and resistive—provide valuable information by isolating the source of the patient's symptoms and assessing the functional status of tissues and structures. The results of each motion test are compared to reveal the

1. location, type, and intensity of pain
2. type of tissue responsible for the reproduction of pain
3. location of the lesion
4. strength
5. willingness and ability of the patient to perform a motion

Cyriax[8] developed the following scheme to assess soft tissue lesions. He classified tissues as either inert or contractile and explained how they reacted to the three types of motion. **Contractile tissues** make up the myotendinous unit and its attachments—specifically muscle, tendon, periosteum, and the bursa. These tissues can elicit pain when internal tension is produced by a muscle contraction during active and resistive motion, and by the stretch imposed on the tissue during passive motion. **Noncontractile tissues,** also known as **inert tissues,** are those which are not capable of a contraction and therefore are not inherently capable of producing their own internal load; the load must be applied by a passive force external to the tissue. The inert tissues are the joint capsule, ligaments, fascia, bursa, nerves (peripheral and root), dura mater, blood vessels, articular cartilage, and bone.

Subsequently, Cyriax elucidated the following results of selectively applying tension to the two types of tissue by each motion.
1. *Active movement.* Active movement involves the loading of inert and contractile tissue simultaneously, so a specific type of tissue can not be incriminated as the location of the lesion. However, this motion does serve a useful purpose. It can grossly identify
   a. the body segment where pain is originating
   b. the patient's ability and willingness to move
   c. where in the range of motion the pain occurs
   d. the effect of movement on the intensity of pain
   e. the pattern of motion—normal or abnormal
   f. the amount of functional movement available to the patient to execute ADL and occupational tasks
2. *Passive movement.* Passive movement tests the inert structures. The clinician controls which structure is loaded and then applies overpressure at the extreme of the available range of motion. The pattern of pain accompanying the onset of resistance should be noted. Passive motion provides a gross assessment of the length of extra-articular and periarticular soft tissue.
3. *Active and passive motion combinations.* Two specific patterns of active and passive motions exist to identify further the type of tissue responsible for the symptoms.
   a. Active and passive motions are restricted and/or painful in the same direction. This pattern is indicative of a capsular or arthrogenic lesion.
   b. Active and passive actions are restricted and/or painful in opposite directions. This pattern is indicative of a contractile tissue lesion. Resistive motion is indicated to further incriminate the tissue.
4. *Resistive movement.* The manual application of resistance to motion performed by the patient permits the clinician to assess strength and to isolate contractile tissue as a source of pain.

Strength is assessed as a gross indicator of the contractile tissue's ability to produce torque. The clinician uses the information for diagnostic purposes and as a predictor of functional ability.

Strength is assessed by resisting an isometric contraction performed midway between the available ranges of motion. This point is chosen to avoid simultaneously loading inert tissue, which chould result in pain and impair the patient's ability to produce maximal resistance. A grading system is provided in Table 5–2 for clinical recording of the strength assessment. Specific positions are utilized to isolate individual muscles for testing.[11]

Following a gross assessment of strength as described

Table 5–2 NUMERICAL GRADING SYSTEM FOR STRENGTH ASSESSMENT

0	No palpable or observable contraction.
1	Trace muscle contraction is palpable; no body part motion is observed.
2	Full range of motion with gravity eliminated; minimal range of motion is present against gravity.
3	Full range of motion is present against gravity.
4	Full range of motion is present against gravity with considerable resistance to motion provided by examiner.
5	Full range of motion is present against gravity with strong resistance to motion provided by examiner.

$(+)$ and $(-)$ symbols can be used to provide finer discrimination between the above criteria.

above, the clinician can test for strength under various conditions to more adequately assess the contractile tissue function. A determination can be made of the effect of myotendon length on strength by examining it in shortened and lengthened positions. Other variables of manual testing such as velocity of resistance, duration, and repetitions can be manipulated by the examiner. Advanced strength assessment using equipment such as an isokinetic dynamometer permits testing of the variables already discussed under concentric, isometric, and eccentric conditions.

Resistance to motion also can be used to test the contractile tissue as a source of pain. The controlled application of resistance to contractile tissue creates an internal load to the tissue. The load can reproduce the patient's typical pain when an inflammatory lesion is present. This is what Maitland describes as a "comparable sign."[1]

Resisted motion is used to aid in the assessment of tissue reactivity. The technique is identical to the strength testing consideration addressed above. When assessing for tissue reactivity, it is of critical importance to ensure that the isometric contraction is resisted at the midpoint of a joint's range of motion. This will prevent the loading of inert tissue which must be avoided. The force created by the resisted contraction will compress the articular surfaces; however, articular cartilage, an inert tissue, is not innervated, so it can not elicit pain.

Four patterns of pain and strength exist to provide additional information regarding the tissue:
   1. Painful and strong indicates a minor lesion.
   2. Painful and weak indicates a major lesion.
   3. Painless and weak indicates a lesion of neurologic origin or a total rupture of a myotendinous unit.
   4. Painless and strong indicates normal function.

Capsular and Noncapsular Patterns of Restricted Motion

When testing the patient's range of motion, the clinician must be aware of the possible capsular and noncapsular patterns of restricted motion that can occur in a joint. The assessment of the patient's lesion and its therapeutic management are dependent on the therapist's ability to differentiate between these two sources of restricted mobility.

Cyriax[8] has described a **capsular pattern** as a characteristic pattern of restricted motion owing to a diffuse arthrogenic etiology. The length and flexibility of capsular fibers are impaired in this pattern secondary to an intra-articular inflammatory process. Fibrosis of the capsular tissue occurs as a natural sequela of the healing process in inflamed tissue. The resulting capsular pattern of restriction is specific for each joint, regardless of the initial cause or underlying disease generating the inflammation. Table 5–3 lists capsular patterns of the upper and lower extremity joints as identified by Cyriax.

The capsular pattern must be contrasted to a pattern of limitation resulting from reasons other than a capsular contracture. The **noncapsular pattern** can be caused by random ligamentous adhesions, internal joint derangement, and extra-articular lesions, such as a shortened muscle. Diffuse arthritis, that is, circumferential inflammation of the joint, and its sequelae, are not present in this pattern. So, unlike the capsular pattern for a given joint, the noncapsular pattern is variable. For example, two noncapsular patterns of restricted knee motion can occur in directly opposite directions. The pattern for the knee joint owing to internal derangement caused by a

torn meniscus can be a loss of extension. However, a lack of flexion is demonstrated in the presence of a shortened quadriceps mechanism.

The two patterns are not mutually exclusive of one another. The clinician must examine for both and design treatment strategies to address all components of restricted motion.

Accessory Joint Motion

Extremity and spinal synovial joints and some cartilaginous joints possess accessory joint motion. This type of motion is the necessary "slack" in a mechanical system, whether it is in man or in a manmade system. For example, a kitchen drawer is capable of sliding on its tracks, however, on closer inspection one finds that some play in the sliding mechanism permits a degree of side-to-side and up-and-down movement. The play is essential for normal operation of the drawer. The joints of the body require the same "slack" or joint play.

The joint play exists because

1. Articular surfaces are not perfectly congruent; that is, the shape of the opposing joint surfaces are not symmetrical.

2. Strict degrees of freedom of motion do not exist. The concept of a joint complex moving around another to a maximum of three axes is a basic but inadequate explanation of joint mechanics. Innumerable axes exist in a joint during the range of motion of bone shafts.

Accessory joint motion is a prerequisite for normal, full asymptomatic and friction-free movement. It is not under voluntary control. The term **arthrokinematics** refers to this accessory joint motion, that is, the intrinsic, intracapsular motion occurring between adjacent joint surfaces. A loss of accessory joint motion (i.e., joint dysfunction) can result in a loss of range of motion and **osteokinematics,** the rotatory motion of a bone shaft. Normal accessory joint motion can not be restored by the muscle activity of active or resisted motion nor by passive rotatory motion. An exception to this situation would be when the soft tissue restriction responsible for the joint dysfunction possesses low tensile strength. In most cases, the intrinsic mechanics of a joint must be passively restored by the clinician. The techniques of joint mobilization are used for examination and treatment of accessory joint motion.

Attempts to restore osteokinematic range of motion or strength prior to restoring the accessory joint motion can result in joint inflammation, pain, effusion, hemarthrosis, capsuloligamentous laxity, and fracture. It is hypothesized that the prolonged use of an extremity demonstrating joint dysfunction can result in degenerative joint disease.

An example to illustrate this is the observable lack of digit mobility in a patient two months after tissue trauma to the finger. The restricted motion may be accompanied by pain, effusion, and impaired function. On closer examination, the second metacarpophalangeal joint exhibits an osteokinematic restriction of flexion. An accessory joint motion assessment demonstrates impaired anterior gliding and distraction of the proximal

Table 5–3 CAPSULAR PATTERNS OF EXTREMITY JOINTS

Shoulder (glenohumeral joint)	Maximum loss of external rotation
	Moderate loss of abduction
	Minimum loss of internal rotation
Elbow complex	Flexion loss is greater than extension loss
Forearm	Full and painless
	Equally restricted in pronation and supination in presence of elbow restrictions[9]
Wrist	Equal restrictions in flexion and extension
Hand	
Carpometacarpal joint I	Abduction and extension restriction
Carpometacarpal joints II–V[9]	Equally restricted in all directions
Upper extremity digits	Flexion loss is greater than extension loss
Hip	Maximum loss of internal rotation, flexion, abduction
	Minimal loss of extension
Knee (tibiofemoral joint)	Flexion loss is greater than extension loss
Ankle (talocrural joint)	Plantarflexion loss is greater than extension loss
Subtalar joint	Restricted varus motion
Midtarsal joint	Restricted dorsiflexion, plantarflexion, abduction and medial rotation
Lower extremity digits	
Metatarsalphalangeal joint I	Extension loss is greater than flexion
Metatarsalphalangeal joints II–V	Variable, tend toward flexion restriction
Interphalangeal joints	Tend toward extension restriction

phalanx on the metacarpal. The first goal of treatment is to restore the anterior glide and distraction of the phalanx. In the absence of extracapsular contributions to restricted motion, achievement of this goal may restore the joint flexion, reduce the pain, permit the effusion to resolve, and improve the functional use of the hand. The need for additional treatment measures would be assessed on an individual basis.

Screening Assessment

The following sections pertain to the process of conducting a screening assessment of the upper and lower quarters of the body. The concept of structuring an assessment process by body quadrants is clinically appropriate because

1. Pain is commonly referred from a lesion site to another location.

2. Multiple tissues and structures of a body quadrant are capable of referring pain to the same location.

3. A regional examination permits differential assessment of the tissues and structures for identification of the actual lesion site.

The upper quarter consists of all structures and soft tissues superior to the third thoracic segment; that is, the craniocervicomandibular complex, the cervicothoracic spine, tissues of the superior thorax, and the entire upper extremity. Neck motions require the participation of the superior thoracic vertebrae, hence the inclusion of the first three thoracic vertebrae in the upper quarter. The lower quarter consists of the inferior thoracic spine and the associated soft tissues and structures, the entire lumbopelvic region, and one of the lower extremities. The inferior thoracic region (to approximately T-10) is included in the lower quarter owing to its neurologic sensory contribution to the lumbopelvic region and its facet joint alignment which permits it to function like an extension of the lumbar spine (Table 5–4).

Table 5–4 COMPONENTS OF THE UPPER AND LOWER QUARTERS OF THE BODY

Upper Quarter (includes the bone, articular cartilage, capsuloligamentous complex, muscles, tendon, periosteum, nerves, dura, blood vessels, and fascia)
1. Cranium
2. Temperomandibular joints
3. Cervical spine
4. Superior thoracic spine (to approximately T3-4)
5. Ribs
6. Sternum
7. Upper extremity*—clavicle, scapula, brachium, antebrachium, wrist, hand, digits

Lower Quarter
1. Inferior thoracic spine† (from approximately T10)
2. Lumbar spine
3. Pelvis—sacrum and ilia
4. Lower extremity—thigh, leg, ankle, foot, digits

*The body quarter is referred to as left or right by the side of the extremity under examination.

†The relative importance of the midthoracic region to the patient's symptoms will determine the extent of the examination to be conducted in this region.

Exceptions exist to a strict dichotomy between the upper and lower quarters of the body; for example, a total body postural assessment is indicated in the examination of either quarter. The relative importance of the midthoracic area to the patient's symptoms will determine the depth of the assessment to be conducted in this region.

For purposes of this discussion, only the major points of a screening assessment for either body quarter will be addressed. The reader is encouraged to consult the Supplemental Readings for further examination techniques.

PATIENT INTERVIEW FOR HISTORY AND SUBJECTIVE REPORT

A thorough interview of the patient permits the therapist to establish a mental list of provisional diagnoses which promotes a coordinated and logical examination sequence. The physical examination will either support or weaken the possible diagnoses until one is identified as the primary etiology. Throughout the examination process the therapist continually adds or deletes provisional diagnoses as the source of the patient's symptoms.

The examiner must acquire skill in guiding an interview so that contradictory or vague information can be clarified without eliciting responses that the patient feels are expected to occur. The interviewer must remain objective; for only without bias to any particular diagnosis can the patient be examined adequately.

The initial step in the interview is obtaining the history of the patient's primary complaint which establishes a background to better understand present symptoms. The evolution of the problem—its behavior over time, the effect of previous treatment, and so forth—allows various lesions to be suspected as the etiology of the complaint. Next, the subjective report is conducted in which the patient describes current symptoms. The symptoms and their behavior are noted to permit a comparison with those of known problems; this aids in establishing and refining a mental list of possible lesions. Symptoms can fluctuate over time and with activity or different postures, so it is the responsibility of the examiner to obtain a thorough understanding of the patient's symptoms. If symptoms appear to fluctuate widely, then the clinician needs to question the patient about them over a longer duration of morbidity until a clear pattern is determined. Similarly, the therapist must consider the effect of a wide scope of activities and postures when symptoms initially appear to be either erratic or unaffected by the patient's present activity level.

The documentation of symptoms at the time of the initial examination establishes a baseline from which the effect of treatment can be monitored. However, it should be noted that the success of initial treatment measures is not based solely on the status of symptoms. During early stages of intervention, the effect of treatment may be based on the status of neuromusculoskeletal tissues and the integrated mechanics of soft tissues and joint structures, with an anticipated change in symptoms to follow.

History of Present Condition

The following outline can guide the examiner in obtaining a thorough history of the present condition and a subjective report of symptoms from the patient. The information is appropriate for the examination of the upper or lower body regions.

1. Patient's age and sex.
2. If the patient has been referred by a physician or dentist, obtain the physician's assessment and the reason for the referral to physical therapy.
3. Briefly delineate the patient's primary complaint.
4. Obtain the history of the present condition.
   a. Date of initial onset and any related exacerbations.
   b. Mode of onset—traumatic, acquired, or congenital. Identify the specific precipitating event whenever a traumatic onset is reported by the patient.
   c. Dates and results of previous examinations by other health care practitioners, medical tests, and medical imaging studies.
   d. Dates and results of previous treatment measures. Inquire about the effect of rest, physical modalities, medication, manual treatment, exercise, orthotics, injection, and surgery (include date, procedure, and postoperative course).
5. Past medical history—obtain information regarding any problems or events related to the primary complaint.
   a. Musculoskeletal or neurologic trauma, disease or dysfunction of a local or related body part.
   b. Any known congenital anomalies.
   c. Previous surgery on a related body segment.
6. Secondary medical problems—inquire whether any deficits exist in the following body systems:
   a. Cardiac
   b. Respiratory
   c. Neurologic
   d. Vascular
   e. Metabolic
   f. Dermatologic
   g. Visual
   h. Gastrointestinal/genitourinary
   i. Endocrine
7. Medication—type, frequency, dosage, and effect. The examiner should be aware that
   a. Present use of analgesic or anti-inflammatory agents may reduce the level of symptoms during the initial examination.
   b. Prolonged use of corticosteroid drugs is associated with osteopenia and reduced tensile strength of connective tissue, that is, ligaments. These adverse effects of medication must be considered as possible contributing factors to the patient's complaint. If these problems are suspected, the examiner should avoid applying excessive force over the lever of a long bone shaft to prevent a fracture or ligament tear.
   c. The use of anticoagulant medication may render the patient susceptible to confusions and hemarthrosis. Consequently, the clinician should monitor the application site and magnitude of force applied during both examination and treatment when the patient is using this type of medication.
8. Occupation—obtain an ergonomic description of the work environment, tasks, activities, and postures. Inquire about the level of psychologic tension perceived by the patient related to occupational responsibilities (when appropriate to the primary complaint).
9. Social situation.
   a. Marital and family status.
   b. Home architecture (see chapter 13: Environmental Assessment).

Subjective Report of Symptoms

The goal of this section is to obtain a description of the patient's pain and/or physical problem through information provided voluntarily by the patient and elicited by the therapist during the interview (enumerated below).

1. Anatomic location of primary and secondary pain sites (Fig. 5-8).
2. Description of pain sensation(s).
3. Frequency and duration of pain.
4. The effect of time, rest, activities of daily living, and occupational demands on the pain or problem. Generic questions useful in obtaining this information follow:
   - Where is your pain? Does it ever "travel"? Has your pain always been in the present location?
   - What does your pain feel like? Is it always the same? If not, what changes it?
   - Do you always have pain? If so, does it fluctuate, and what causes it to do so? If you don't continually have pain, when are you free of pain? Full of pain?
   - Has your pain/problem been getting worse, staying the same, or getting better since it started?
   - If activity affects your pain, then describe which activities worsen or improve your symptoms.
   - Do you experience joint swelling? Spasm? Joint clicking or crepitus? If so, is pain associated with it?
5. Motor or sensory symptoms—obtain information suggestive of upper or lower neuron deficits.
   Questions useful in obtaining this information include:
   - Do you experience any weakness? If so, where and when? Is it constant or intermittent?
   - Do you experience numbness, tingling, burning, shooting pain, or any patches of sensitive skin? If so, where and when?
   - Do you experience hot or cold sensations in your arms or legs?
   - Do you experience any muscle twitching?
   - Do you sometimes drop objects?
   - Do your arms or hands shake when you reach to pick up an object? When you are at rest?
6. Vascular symptoms or signs.
   - Do you experience constant or intermittent discoloration of your hands and feet? If so, when? Skin breakdown?
   - Do you experience hot or cold sensations in your arms or legs?

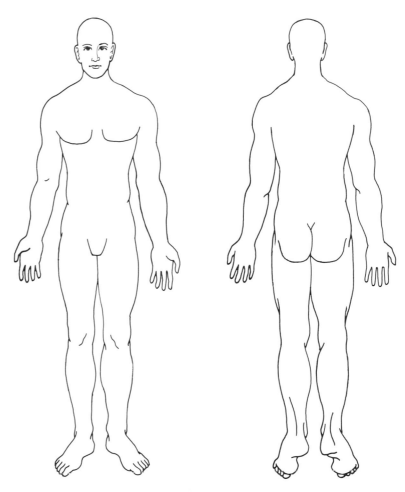

Figure 5–8. Body chart: This type of chart can supplement the patient's verbal description of the location of the pain.

- Do you experience swelling in your arms or legs?
7. Functional assessment—identify the patient's past and present levels of function and the effect of functional activity on the behavior of symptoms (see chapter 12: Functional Assessment).
   a. Activities of daily living
      - Hygiene
      - Dressing
      - Food acquisition
      - Food preparation
      - Household maintenance
      - Ability to use transportation services
      - Ambulation
   b. Occupational tasks—identify the effect of the occupational demands (as identified under the section History of the Present Condition, above) on the patient's symptoms.
   c. Recreational activity—identify the type and frequency of activity.
   The therapist should correlate the physical requirements of functional tasks with the patient's symptoms and physical status. This comparison allows recommendations for safe and asymptomatic levels of activity.
8. Obtain the patient's physiologic and functional goals to be derived from treatment.
The information above must be supplemented with additional questions based on suspected etiologies. Comprehension of the knowledge base, described earlier in this chapter as being prerequisite to the performance of an examination, is essential to interview the patient adequately.

Musculoskeletal Examination

The purpose of this section of the assessment process is to examine for normal and abnormal findings of the musculoskeletal and peripheral neurologic systems. The information already provided in this chapter should be applied during the examination process.

The components of the screening examination are outlined below.

1. *Vital signs.* When appropriate, assess heart rate, blood pressure, and respiratory rate (see chapter 4: Assessment of Vital Signs).
2. *Mental status.* Assess the patient's orientation to time, place, and person.
3. *Inspection.*
   a. Posture. Conduct a total body postural assessment. Perform this with the patient in a standing position to impose a weight-bearing load on the body.

   A triplanar assessment is conducted for all body segments, joints, and bone shafts. Triplanar assessment refers to visual inspection of body parts in

the sagittal, coronal, and horizontal planes. Inspection should be performed from anterior, posterior, and lateral views.

A plumb line should be used to establish a central reference point for inspection from each view. The proximal fixation points for the plumb line are

- Mental protuberance of the mandible for the anterior view
- Anterior margin of the mastoid process on the temporal bone for the lateral view
- External occipital protuberance (inion) on the occipital bone for the posterior view

The therapist should compare the observed findings with normal postural alignment.

b. Extremity girth. Measure to assess for muscle atrophy or hypertrophy and swelling. The circumference of the limb should be measured at regular intervals along the long axis of the body part. A prominence of bone is used as a reproducible landmark for reassessment of the patient's status.

c. Soft tissue edema. Assess for extra-articular soft tissue swelling.

d. Joint effusion. Assess for intracapsular joint swelling.

e. Skin condition. Observe for dry or moist skin, callus formation, flaking, color changes, hair distribution, and uniformity of appearance.

f. Nail condition. Observe for broken or ridged nails; the size, color, and any abnormal shape such as club-shape (convex) or spoon-shape (concave) should also be noted. Conditions of the nail are indicative of its nutritional status.

g. Muscle spasm, guarding, and protective splinting. Each is characterized by abnormal timing, degree, or duration of isolated muscle contraction. Spasm is present when a constant contraction exists with the body part in both weight-bearing and non-weight-bearing positions. Muscle guarding is characterized by constant contraction while the body part is weight-bearing, voluntarily moved, or subject to external forces, but is absent in a non-weight-bearing position. Protective splinting is a brief reflexive contraction of muscle that occurs during movement.

h. Observe general body movement during the interview portion of the examination. Inspect and observe for postures used by the patient to relieve symptoms, and for postures capable of contributing to symptoms.

4. *Palpation.*

a. Assess for soft tissue tenderness, flexibility, and density—including skin, fascia, muscle, ligament, and tendon. Apply palpatory forces parallel and perpendicular to the long axis of the structure.

b. Examine for joint line tenderness and masses.

c. Swelling should be noted and a differentiation made between edema and effusion.

d. Temperature of the skin should be assessed, using the back of the palpating hand over a lesion or the distal extremities.

5. *Range of motion.*

a. Active and passive range of motion is assessed for

the joint(s) primarily and secondarily contributing to the problem.[12] Note presence of capsular versus noncapsular patterns of restricted motion.

b. Note end-feel and pain response during passive range of motion with overpressure (see section on Tissue Response).

c. Assess accessory joint motion, its end-feel and pain response.[1,9]

6. *Muscle strength.*

a. Conduct a thorough assessment of strength by manual resistance to the body segment under examination.[11] Note the elicitation of pain from manual resistance applied to contractile tissues.

b. Conduct a gross assessment of strength for body segments related to the area possessing the primary lesion. If deficits are identified, then conduct a more thorough assessment.

c. Observe for compensatory trunk or limb movements in the presence of muscle weakness.

d. When appropriate, assess muscle torque capabilities at a higher level of function by conducting an isokinetic dynamometry assessment of strength under concentric and eccentric loading conditions at varying velocities of movement.[13,15]

7. *Neurologic assessment.*

a. Sensation. Basic forms of sensation to be routinely assessed are superficial tactile sensation (light touch), superficial pain (pin prick), temperature, and vibration (see chapter 6: Sensory Assessment).

b. Motor. Conduct an upper or lower quadrant myotomal assessment, depending on the body region under examination. A positive finding of weakness may indicate involvement of a specific nerve level (Table 5–5).

c. Deep tendon reflexes. Test the muscle stretch reflex as elicited by a rapid striking of the muscle's tendon. The deep tendon reflexes routinely assessed in each quarter are found in Table 5–6.

d. Pathologic reflexes. Assess for upper motor neuron disease or lesions of the corticospinal tracts. For

Table 5–5 MYOTOMES

Upper Quarter Myotomes

Level	Action to be tested	Muscle
C-5	Shoulder abduction	Deltoid
C-5, C-6	Elbow flexion	Biceps
C-7	Elbow extension	Triceps
C-8	Ulnar deviation	Flexor carpi ulnaris Extensor carpi ulnaris
T-1	Digit abduction/adduction	Interossei

Lower Quarter Myotomes

Level	Action to be tested	Muscle
L-2, L-3	Hip flexion	Iliopsoas
L-3, L-4	Knee extension	Quadriceps
L-5	Ankle dorsiflexion	Anterior tibialis
	Extension of great toe	Extensor hallucis longus
S-1	Plantarflexion	Gastrocnemius

Table 5–6 DEEP TENDON REFLEXES

	Root Level	Muscle	Peripheral Nerve
Upper quarter:	C5-6	Biceps	Musculocutaneous
	C5-6	Brachioradialis	Radial
	C-7	Triceps	Radial
Lower quarter:	L3-4	Quadriceps	Femoral
	S1	Gastrocnemius	Sciatic (tibial)

The degree of reflex activity is graded on a 0 to 4 scale. Grades are awarded based on a predicted response and comparison of responses between body halves.

0 = no reflex response
1 = minimal response
2 = moderate response
3 = brisk, strong response } normal range
4 = clonus

example, the Babinski reflex is elicited by stroking the lateral plantar surface of the foot. A positive response is extension of the first digit and fanning of the other digits.

e. Proprioception. Assess for passive motion sense and static position sense. *Passive motion sense* (kinesthesia) is the ability of the patient to perceive the direction of passive limb or digit movement without visual stimuli. The patient can be asked to describe verbally the commencement, direction, or cessation of motion or to mimic the direction and degree of motion with the contralateral body part. *Static position sense* is the ability of the patient to mimic the position of a body part after the therapist has passively moved the part.

f. Peripheral nerve provocation tests. The examiner imposes an external force on an isolated peripheral nerve, thereby creating internal load in the nerve. A positive finding of pain or paresthesia can be elicited in a compressed or inflamed nerve. For example, to elicit the ulnar nerve tinel sign, the nerve is palpated within the groove between the medial epicondyle of the humerus and the ulna bone of the medial elbow region. A positive finding is local tenderness and referred pain and/or paresthesia along the distal route of the nerve.

8. *Specific tests.* An important section of the examination involves the execution of select musculoskeletal tests. The type of tests and extent of testing are dependent on the nature of the chief complaint, symptoms, and previous physical examination results.

a. In the presence of spinal pain, the therapist should elect to perform passive intervertebral mobility testing (PIVM). This procedure assesses the quantity of motion at a vertebral segment. The quality of accompanying tissue responses, as discussed earlier in this chapter, is important to monitor.

b. Ligament stress tests use the application of varus and valgus stress to the elbow complex to assess the medial and lateral collateral ligaments. The degrees of varus and valgus motion, joint gapping,

and pain are compared with the contralateral extremity.

These tests are performed routinely for a few joints but for others would be dependent on earlier examination results.

c. When the therapist suspects the presence of a thoracic outlet syndrome, a full battery of tests would be performed. The tests attempt to differentiate between vascular and neurogenic causes of thoracic outlet syndrome. Representative tests include the Adson's test, pectoralis minor test, costoclavicular test, and quadrant maneuver.

9. *Gait.* Conduct a triplanar assessment of each body region (see chapter 11: Gait Analysis).

10. *Function.* Conduct an interview regarding, and when feasible assess, the patient's ability to perform activities of daily living, occupational tasks, and recreational activities. Assess for limitations secondary to pain, endurance, strength, or mobility restrictions. Assess for modifications in the method of task performance, assistive devices, or home/work environment that the patient may have made to facilitate functional abilities.

Assessment Summary

The examination process is completed with the formulation of a determination of the patient's chief complaint and its contributing factors. The completed assessment is a summary of all pertinent historical, subjective, and physical findings. It is a correlation of normal and abnormal findings to establish a specific identification of the patient's primary complaint, that is, pain and/or dysfunction. The examination findings are compared against known pathologies for the body segment under consideration. As mentioned earlier in this chapter, the therapist must develop a thorough knowledge base of musculoskeletal and peripheral neurologic pathologies. The symptoms and clinical manifestations of these pathologies must be known before they can be used for comparison in the examination process. The completed assessment will dictate the goals and course of treatment.

The primary factors to be included are

1. The mode of onset—traumatic, acquired, or congenital

2. The primary etiology of the chief complaint, that is, pain and/or functional limitation; a diagnosis

3. The stage of symptoms

4. Contributing factors to the primary etiology

5. Prognosis from physical therapy measures

6. Duration and frequency for the course of treatment

The mechanism of onset for the patient's symptoms assists the therapist in determining the prognosis, goals, and treatment plan. The prognosis for restoring a patient's comfort and functional capacity can be limited by the presence of congenital deficits of the musculoskeletal system. For example, a patient who suffers a sprain of the medial collateral ligament in the knee can experience a delay in healing secondary to the presence of a congenital valgus deformity, which imposes excessive mechanical stress to the medial tissues of the knee. In contrast to this situation, the prognosis is more favorable if the sprain is unaccompanied by congenital deficits. Generally, a patient who reports a specific recent event as the initial cause of symptoms may have a more favorable prognosis than the patient with an insidious onset. Naturally, all the variables of duration of symptoms, mechanism of onset, extent of tissue involvement, effect of previous treatment, and the clarity in delineating the effect of activity and static postures on symptoms will influence the prognosis.

The assessment should establish the stage of the patient's condition. The basic classifications of acute, subacute, and chronic conditions provide valuable information regarding the patient's ability to tolerate mechanical loads such as those imposed by daily activity or by a therapist during treatment. The classification of a patient's condition is assisted by considering the duration of symptoms since the time of initial onset. An acute stage of symptoms may exist for 48 to 72 hours post onset; whereas the subacute stage may persist from 2 weeks to several months after the onset of initial symptoms. Symptoms can be considered chronic after approximately 3 to 6 months. The significance of the duration of symptoms, however, may not allow a clear assessment of the patient's condition. For example, the patient may be experiencing an acute exacerbation of a chronic lesion at the time of the initial examination. The classification of the condition implies the degree of reactivity of involved tissues to forces applied during routine activities of daily living, occupational tasks, and recreational activity. Similarly, it permits the clinician to estimate the amount of force, frequency, and duration of a treatment plan without exceeding the tolerance of the tissue and subsequently aggravating the symptoms. The physical therapist involved in treatment of musculoskeletal pain and dysfunction must acquire the skill to determine the reactivity of tissue inasmuch as the basis of treatment often is to impose physical force. For example, a patient with a spinal cord injury who reports the onset of shoulder pain only after propelling a wheelchair over a 5-mile racecourse obviously has a shoulder that is less reactive to mechanical stresses than the patient who develops acute shoulder pain after performing a transfer from bed to a wheelchair. The former patient can be expected to tolerate a more aggressive treatment approach than that for the latter patient.

Another implication of classifying the reactivity of a lesion is to assist the clinician in establishing a prognosis. The acute lesion can be expected typically to demonstrate more spontaneous improvement than that of the chronic lesion. Conversely, chronic symptoms of low intensity and mildly reactive to mechanical loads imposed by daily activities can be expected to respond less dramatically to treatment.

In addition to formulating a prognosis for recovery, classification of the lesion allows the clinician to determine the goals of treatment for the patient. A goal of obtaining a pain-free functional status for the patient with a 2-year history of shoulder pain and dysfunction may be inappropriate, whereas it would be feasible to expect the industrial worker with a recent initial episode of shoulder pain to achieve such a goal.

Treatment also can be based appropriately on the stage of the lesion. The methods, frequency, duration, and intensity of treatment are chosen with the knowledge of the patient's ability to tolerate the effects of these variables on his or her tissues and perception of pain.

A treatment approach should be formulated to address specific problems in the diagnosis. Treatment must address a specific lesion since the treatment of symptoms can result in frustration for both the patient and the therapist. Symptoms are an unreliable sole indicator for the effect of treatment because they are subject to variability in intensity, location, and behavior. For example, glenohumeral joint dysfunction, which can occur in the patient with hemiplegia secondary to a central nervous system disorder, commonly refers pain to the lateral brachium. Ultrasound treatment administered to the site of pain may yield minimal or temporary results under the best of conditions. The ultrasound could be directed, however, at the *underlying source* of pain. Rather than for pain relief, it could be used instead to promote collagen extensibility by application to the anteroinferior capsule of the joint in the axilla. Ultrasound can assist in the restoration of tissue length and flexibility, which permits normal glenohumeral arthrokinematics and osteokinematics and subsequently the relief from pain.

A clear cause-and-effect relationship between a lesion and symptoms cannot always be made during an initial examination. Instead, the assessment may establish a provisional diagnosis, subject to confirmation only after treatment has succeeded in resolving the symptoms. In this case, the effects of treatment must be monitored continually and modified as appropriate, and flexibility must be exercised by the therapist to modify the provisional assessment. In the realm of musculoskeletal dysfunction, the therapist may be confronted with the inability to develop a "comparable sign" and instead must develop a hypothesis for treatment based on identified tissue and lesions.

TREATMENT GOALS AND STRATEGIES

The treatment goals and strategies should correlate with the deficits identified by the clinician in the assessment section of the examination. The therapist must be aware of all possible treatment goals that can be established for any patient who possesses a musculoskeletal problem. Table 5–7 lists nine generic treatment goals that should be considered during the treatment planning process.

The promotion of soft tissue healing by improving the nutritional status of the involved body part is fundamental to any treatment plan, whether acute or chronic problems are present. The nutritional status is improved by altering the circulatory status of a tissue site, and it may be altered for different purposes. One approach is to increase circulation to an area exhibiting reduced vascularity. For example, the ischemia produced by a mus-

Table 5-7 GENERIC TREATMENT GOALS

1. Promote healing by improving the nutritional status of tissue.
2. Restore or prevent the loss of soft tissue flexibility and length for contractile and noncontractile tissue.
3. Restore or prevent the loss of normal joint alignment.
4. Restore or prevent the loss of normal joint mobility.
5. Promote normal myoarthrokinetic reflexes.
6. Promote normal motor control.
7. Resolve pain and associated symptoms.
8. Prevent recurrence of the lesion.
9. Restore the functional ability of the patient.

cle spasm causes the retention of metabolites which act as a chemical irritant to the tissue and further promote the spasm (see Figure 5–2). The application of modalities or manual techniques to increase circulation can reduce the tissue ischemia. Another method of improving the tissue's nutritional status is to decrease the circulation to an inflamed area. The purpose is to prevent excessive coagulation of blood and the resulting fibrotic reaction. Excessive fibrosis results in a loss of tissue and structural length and flexibility, as in the contracture of a myotendon unit. The clinician must be aware of the need to consider this latter method, not only in the acute lesion but also in the acute exacerbation of tissues in an underlying chronic condition.

The restoration of soft tissue flexibility and prevention of deficits are key elements in the treatment of musculoskeletal dysfunction. Healing by fibrosis is the normal response to tissue trauma. Because fibrosis causes shortening of the collagenous structure inherent in musculoskeletal soft tissue, the therapist must continually be aware of preventing this shortening or restoring the flexibility of soft tissue. Soft tissue is a three-dimensional structure, and its pliability must be examined and treated in each dimension. Theoretically, for each dimension of length, width, and depth, the flexibility must be assessed in a plane parallel to that dimension. However, in the body the examination and treatment of all three dimensions can not always be performed, owing to limited access to some tissues. Manual techniques can be used to restore flexibility by applying mechanical forces to impose tensile and shear loads on contractile and noncontractile tissues. The techniques also can be used to elicit neurophysiologic responses to facilitate the lengthening of innervated contractile soft tissue. Modalities can be used prior to the application of manual techniques to prepare the tissues for stretching; for example, the application of ultrasound to increase collagen extensibility.[16] The restoration of flexibility will enable the tissue to tolerate physical stress, thereby reducing the internal load and the subsequent inflammatory reaction and stimulation of nociceptors.

Normal static joint alignment should be restored to ensure an initial proper axis from which motion can be initiated. Absence of joint alignment permits excessive loading of neighboring soft tissue and articular surfaces and impairment of arthrokinesia and osteokinesia. Examples of joint malalignment are the anterior displacement of the humeral head relative to the glenoid fossa as observed in the patient with laxity of the anterior glenohumeral joint capsule, and the posterior tibial subluxation on the femur as seen in a patient after prolonged immobilization of the knee.

The restoration of joint mobility—that is, normal arthrokinesia and osteokinesia—is necessary to prevent abnormal soft tissue loading of the joint capsule, ligaments, synovial lining, and articular surfaces. Excessive or abnormally directed loading can lead to pain, capsular laxity, effusion, hemarthrosis, and eventually degenerative joint disease. Subsequently, the patient's level of function is impaired.

The promotion of normal **myoarthrokinetic reflexes**[17] is achieved through goals 1, 2, 3, and 4 listed in Table 5–6. For example, joint effusion causes an inhibitory effect on surrounding musculature,[18] and ligamentous laxity is purported to decrease the normal protective response muscle imparts to a joint when it is subjected to physical stress,[19] the latter occurring secondary to a sensory loss from the ligament.

The restoration of normal motor control involves multiple factors of strength, mobility, controlled mobility, stability, and skill. Chapters 9 and 14 provide a detailed discussion of motor control; however, there are some points relevant to the musculoskeletal system that should be included here. Strength involves the production of torque with sufficient magnitude and duration at functional velocities during concentric and eccentric modes of muscle contraction. Strength occurs as a result of peripheral contractile tissue and structural capabilities linked with central neural control. Joint stability is obtained through passive tissue tension by an intact ligament of normal length and tensile strength, and through dynamic contraction of agonist and antagonistic muscle groups throughout the range of motion. Treatment is aimed at obtaining optimum stability of joints and mobility of the body's lever arms. The physical therapist should be concerned with the peripheral and central aspects of motor control for the total rehabilitation of the patient.

The reduction of pain and associated symptoms is accomplished primarily by achieving the goals already described. However, when these goals are unattainable, the clinician may elect to alter the perception of pain through the neuromodulation of peripheral sensory information, such as the use of transcutaneous electrical nerve stimulation (TENS). The clinician must consider other factors that affect the perception of pain. In addition to the physiologic factors described in the generic goals, emotional, social, psychologic, cultural, and environmental influences can alter the perception of pain. When the clinician recognizes that multiple factors are influencing the patient's pain, consideration should be given to referring the patient to other health care practitioners for a team approach to pain management.

The patient must assume the major role in preventing a recurrence of the problem. It is the responsibility of the therapist to educate the patient regarding the nature of the lesion. The patient should be aware of the effect of mechanical stresses imposed on the body part under consideration by daily activity and occupational tasks. This information enables the patient to prevent recurring pain through altering the method of executing tasks, modifying the environment, and using equipment to assist in performing the task.

The functional status of the patient is improved or restored by achieving the goals already described. In addition, the therapist seeks to improve the patient's functional status by conducting training sessions in which the patient practices the proper biomechanical execution of daily and occupational tasks in a simulated environment.

The nine generic goals are applied to three categories of musculoskeletal lesions in Table 5–8. The three plans function as a strategy for treatment of musculoskeletal tissue and structural deficits. They are provided to serve as

1. A treatment planning guide for the clinician.
2. A framework on which new knowledge and skills can be added during the professional development of a therapist.
3. A basis for the analysis of the rationale for various treatment techniques and modalities.

The order of the goals under each category provides a sequential treatment plan. However, based on the needs of the individual patient, the clinician should modify the plan as necessary.

SUMMARY

The goal of this chapter has been to promote an understanding of the principles, content, and strategies of the assessment and treatment planning process for the patient with musculoskeletal dysfunction. The areas with which the therapist must become familiar in order to perform a thorough examination were discussed. The therapist must know and understand the etiology, symptoms, physical manifestations, and natural course of musculoskeletal conditions. The application and effect of the tools used for the examination process and the wide realm of tissue responses to physical tests also must be understood. With this knowledge base, the clinician can begin to test components and identify deficits of the musculoskeletal system.

Table 5–8 TREATMENT STRATEGIES

1. Soft tissue lesion without a mechanical deficit.
Promote tissue nutrition.
↓
Alter mechanical tissue load.
↓
Prevent formation of soft tissue restrictions.
↓
Promote motor control.
↓
Restore previous or maximal functional status.

2. Soft tissue restriction without an articular deficit.
(The first two steps below are appropriate if soft tissue inflammation is present.)
Promote tissue preparation.
↓
Restore contractile and noncontractile tissue flexibility and length via tensile and shear loading.
↓
Promote motor control.
↓
Restore previous or maximal functional status.

3. Articular deficit with soft tissue lesion and/or restriction.
↓   ↓
Promote tissue nutrition.   Promote tissue preparation.
↓   ↓
Alter mechanical tissue load.   Restore tissue flexibility and length.
↓
Prevent formation of soft tissue restrictions.
↘   ↙
Restore proper static joint alignment.
↓
Restore normal joint mobility.
↓
Restore motor control.
↓
Restore previous or maximal functional status.

Treatment planning for the patient with musculoskeletal deficits begins with the formation of goals based on the assessment. Identification of strategies for achieving these goals is the next step. This chapter provides the reader with generic goals and strategies for consideration in treating a wide variety of musculoskeletal conditions.

QUESTIONS FOR REVIEW

1. Outline a conceptual model of musculoskeletal tissue dysfunction and its sequelae.
2. Outline the generic steps of an examination process.
3. Describe how active, passive, and resistive motion can be used as an assessment tool.
4. Describe the possible responses of soft tissue and structures to provocation tests conducted during a physical examination.
5. Define and provide three examples of a capsular pattern.
6. Define "end-feel" and list five characteristic types.

7. Provide three reasons for thoroughly interviewing a patient to obtain a history of the problem and a subjective report of the symptoms.
8. List the components of a screening examination for the musculoskeletal system.
9. Describe the purpose and components of the assessment section of a musculoskeletal examination.
10. List nine generic treatment goals appropriate for treatment of the patient with musculoskeletal pain and dysfunction.

11. Provide a sequential treatment plan using the goals identified in question #10 for the following:
   a. A soft tissue lesion without a mechanical deficit
   b. A soft tissue restriction without an articular deficit
   c. An articular deficit with soft tissue inflammation and/or restriction

REFERENCES

1. Maitland, GD: Peripheral Manipulation. Butterworths, Boston, 1977.
2. Caillet, R: Soft Tissue Pain and Disability. FA Davis, Philadelphia, 1977.
3. Payton, CD: Clinical Reasoning Process in Physical Therapy. Phys Ther 65:924, 1985.
4. Barrows, HS and Tamblyn, RM: Problem-Based Learning: An Approach to Medical Education. Springer Publishing, New York, 1980.
5. Rodgers, MM and Cavanagh, PR: Glossary of biomechanical terms, concepts, and units. Phys Ther 64:1886, 1984.
6. White, AA and Panjabi, MM: Clinical Biomechanics of the Spine. JP Lippincott, Philadelphia, 1978.
7. Maitland, GD: The hypothesis of adding compression when examining and treating synovial joints. J Orthop Sports Phys Ther 2:7, 1980.
8. Cyriax, J: Textbook of Orthopaedic Medicine, vol. 1. Diagnosis of Soft Tissue Lesions, ed 8. Bailliere Tindall, London, 1983.
9. Kaltenborn, FM: Mobilization of the Extremity Joints: Examination and Basic Treatment Techniques. Olaf norlis bokhandel, Oslo, Norway, 1980.
10. Grieve, GP: Mobilization of the Spine, ed 3. Churchill Livingstone, New York, 1979.
11. Daniels, L and Worthingham, C: Muscle Testing: Techniques of Manual Examination. WB Saunders, Philadelphia, 1980.
12. Joint Motion: Method of Measuring and Recording. American Academy of Orthopaedic Surgeons, Chicago, 1985.
13. Moffroid, M and Whipple, R: Specificity of speed of exercise. Phys Ther 50:1699, 1970.
14. Perrine, J and Edgerton, VR: Muscle force-velocity and power-velocity relationships under isokinetic loading. Med Sci Sports 10:159, 1978.
15. Winter, DA, Wells, RP and Orr, GW: Errors in the use of isokinetic dynamometers. Eur J Appl Physiol 46:397, 1981.
16. Lehman, JF, et al: Effects of therapeutic temperatures on tendon extensibility. Arch Phys Med 51:481, 1970.
17. Wyke, B: The neurology of joints. Am Roy Coll Surg Engl 41:35, 1967.
18. Spencer, JD, Hayes, KC, and Alexander, IJ: Knee joint effusion and quadriceps reflex inhibition in man. Arch Phys Med Rehabil 65:171, 1984.
19. Kennedy, JC, Alexander, IJ, Hayes, KC: Nerve supply of the human knee and its functional importance. Am J Sports Med 10:329, 1982.

SUPPLEMENTAL READINGS

Akeson, WH, et al: Collagen cross linking alterations in joint contractures: Changes in periarticular connective tissue collagen after nine weeks of immobilization. Connect Tissue Res 5:15–19, 1970.
Bowling, RW and Erhard, R: Letter to the editor. Bull Ortho Sports Med APTA 4:8, 1979.
Broding, H: Principles of examination and treatment in manual medicine. Scand J Rehab Med 11:181, 1979.
Butler, DL, et al: Biomechanics of ligaments and tendons. Exerc Sports Sci Rev 6:126–282, 1979.
Coates, H and King, A: The Patient Assessment: A Handbook for Therapists. Churchill Livingstone, New York, 1982.
Cohen, S and Viellion, G: Patient assessment: Examining joints of the upper and lower extremities. Am J Nurs 81(4) 763, 1981.
Corrigan, B and Maitland GD: Practical Orthopaedic Medicine. Butterworth, Boston, 1983.
Curwin, S and Stanish, WD: Tendonitis: Its Etiology and Treatment. DC Heath, Lexington, MA, 1984.
Cyriax, JH and Cyriax, PH: Illustrated Manual of Orthopaedic Medicine. Butterworth, London, 1983.
Darnell, MW: A proposed chronology of events for forward head posture. J Cranioman Prac 1:49, 1983.
Davies, GJ, Malone, T, and Bassett, FH: Knee examination. Phys Ther 60:1565, 1980.
DonTigny, R: Letter to the editor. Bull Ortho Sports Med APTA 4:8, 1979.
Ebner, M: Connective Tissue Massage: Theory and Therapeutic Application. Robert E Krieger, Huntington, NY, 1975.
Eddy, DM and Clanton, CH: The art of diagnosis: Solving the clinicopathological exercise. N Engl J Med 306:1263, 1982.
Erhard, R and Bowling, R: The recognition and management of the pelvic component of low back and sciatic pain. Bull Ortho Sec APTA 2:4, 1977.
Friedman, MH and Weisberg, J: Application of orthopedic principles in evaluations of the temporomandibular joint. Phys Ther 62:597, 1982.
Fulkerson, JP: Awareness of the retinaculum in evaluating patellofemoral pain. Am J Sports Med 10:147, 1982.
Goodridge, JP: Muscle energy technique: Definition, explanation, methods of procedure. J Am Osteopath Assoc 81:249, 1981.
Gould, JA and Davies, GJ: Orthopaedic and Sports Physical Therapy. CV Mosby, St Louis, 1985.
Gozna, ER and Harrington, IJ: Biomechanics of Musculoskeletal Injury. Williams & Wilkins, Baltimore, 1982.
Grieve, EFM: Mechanical dysfunction of the sacroiliac joint. Int Rehabil Med 5:46, 1983.
Grieve, GP: The sacroiliac joint. Physiotherapy 62:384, 1976.
Grieve, GP: Common Vertebral Joint Problems. Churchill Livingstone, New York, 1981.
Grieve, GP: Lumbar instability. Physiother 68:2, 1982.
Hoke, B, Howell, D, and Stack, ML: The relationship between isokinetic testing and dynamic patellofemoral compression. J Orthop Sports Phys Ther 4:150, 1983.
Hoppenfeld, S: Physical Examination of the Spine and Extremities. Appleton-Century-Crofts, New York, 1976.
Hubbard, RP: Mechanical behavior of connective tissue. In Greeman, PE (ed): Concepts and Mechanisms of Neuromuscular Functions. Springer-Verlag, New York, 1984.
Janda, V: Muscle Function Testing. Butterworth, Boston, 1983.
Kapandji, IA: The Physiology of the Joints, vol 1: Upper Limb, 1982. Vol. 2: Lower Limb, 1971. Vol 3: The Trunk and Vertebral Column, 1974. Churchill Livingstone, New York.
Kessler, RM, and Hertling, D: Management of Common Musculoskeletal Disorders: Physical Therapy Principles and Methods. Harper & Row, Philadelphia, 1983.
Kirkaldy-Willis, WH and Hill, RJ: A more precise diagnosis for low back pain. Spine 4:102, 1979.

Lamb, D: The neurology of spinal pain. Phys Ther 59:971, 1979.

Little, RW: Biomechanics Modeling and Concepts. In Greenman, PE (ed): Concepts and Mechanisms of Neuromuscular Functions. Springer-Verlag, New York, 1984.

Magee, DJ: Orthopaedic Physical Assessment. WB Saunders, Philadelphia, 1987.

Maigne, R: Low back pain of thorocolumbar origin. Arch Phys Med Rehabil 61:389, 1980.

Maitland, GD: Vertebral Manipulation. Butterworth, Boston, 1977.

Maitland, GD: Examination of the cervical spine. Aust J Physiother 25:29, 1979.

Maitland, GD: Musculo-skeletal Examination and Recording Guide, ed 3. Lauderdale Press, Glen Osmond, South Australia, 1981.

McKenzie, RA: The Lumbar Spine: Mechanical Diagnosis and Therapy. Spinal Publications, Waikanae, New Zealand, 1981.

Mennell, JM: Joint Pain. Little, Brown & Co, Boston, 1964.

Mitchell, FL, Moran, PS, and Pruzzo, NA: An Evaluation and Treatment Manual of Osteopathic Muscle Energy Procedures. Mitchell, Moran, and Pruzzo, Valley Park, MO, 1979.

Moll, JMH, Liyanange, SP, and Wright, V: An objective clinical method to measure lateral spinal flexion. Rheum Phys Med 11:225, 1972.

Nelson, MA, et al: Reliability and reproducibility of clinical findings in low back pain. Spine 4:97, 1979.

Paris, SB: Anatomy as related to function and pain. Orth Clin N Amer 14:475, 1983.

Polley, HF and Hunder GG: Pneumatologic Interviewing and Physical Examination of the Joints. WB Saunders, Philadelphia, 1978.

Radakovich, M and Malone, T: The superior tibiofibular joint: The forgotten joint. J Orthop Sports Phys Ther 3:129, 1982.

Ritter, MA and Gosling, C: The Knee: A Guide to the Examination and Diagnosis of Ligament Injuries. Charles C Thomas, Springfield, IL, 1979.

Rocabado, M: Biomechanical relationship of the cranial, cervical, and hyoid regions. J Cranioman Prac 1:61, 1983.

Smidt, GL and Rogers, MW: Factors contributing to the regulation and clinical assessment of muscular strength. Phys Ther 62:1283, 1982.

Steindler, A: Kinesiology of the Human Body under Normal and Pathological Conditions. Charles C Thomas, Springfield, IL, 1955.

Tank, R and Halbach, J: Physical therapy evaluation of the shoulder complex in athletes. J Orthop Sports Phys Ther 3:108, 1982.

Tomberlin, JP, Eggart, JS, and Callister, L: The use of standardized evaluation forms in physical therapy. J Orthop Sports Phys Ther 5:348, 1984.

Travell, JG and Simons, DG: Myofascial Pain and Dysfunction: The Trigger Point Manual. Williams & Wilkins, Baltimore, 1983.

Urban, LM: The straight-leg-raising test: A review. J Orthop Sports Phys Ther 2:117, 1981.

Vidik, A: Functional properties of collagenous tissue. Rev Connect Tis Res 6:127–215, 1973.

Wadsworth, GT: Wrist and hand examination and interpretation. J Orthop Sports Phys Ther 5:108, 1983.

Weismantel, A: Evaluation and treatment of sacroiliac joint problems. Bull Ortho Sports Med APTA 3:5, 1978.

Woerman, AL and Binder-Macleod, SA: Leg length discrepancy assessment: Accuracy and precision in five clinical methods of evaluation. J Orthop Sports Phys Ther 5:230, 1984.

Wolf, SL: Clinical Decision Making in Physical Therapy. FA Davis, Philadelphia, 1984.

Zohn, DA and Mennell, JM: Musculoskeletal Pain: Diagnosis and Physical Treatment. Little, Brown & Co, Boston, 1976.

GLOSSARY

Arthrokinematics: The intrinsic, usually intracapsular, articular motion occurring between adjacent joint surfaces; a prerequisite for normal, pain-free osteokinematics.

Bending: A deformation around an axis perpendicular to the long axis of a material caused by the imposition of a load along the length of a tissue; results in a tension load on the convex surface and a compression load on the concave surface.

Capsular pattern: A characteristic pattern of restricted osteokinematics secondary to fibrosis of the joint capsule, resulting in its loss of flexibility and length; accompanied by an impairment of arthrokinematics.

Comparable sign: A term advocated by Maitland[7] to describe a positive finding—that is, restricted movement, pain, or muscle spasm—found during assessment; the sign relates to or is "comparable to" the patient's symptoms.

Compression: A load that pushes the fibers of a material together along its long axis; it results in, or tends to cause, a shortening and widening of the material.

Contractile tissue: The myotendonous unit, that is, muscle, tendon, and tendoperiosteal attachment; transmits the internal load created during contraction of a muscle.

Edema: In an orthopedic context, refers to extra-articular soft tissue swelling.

Effusion: In an orthopedic context, refers to intracapsular swelling of a joint.

End-feel: The characteristic quality of resistance imparted to the examiner's hands while applying passive overpressure to a joint and its associated soft tissues; can be normal or abnormal.

Myoarthrokinetic reflex: Neurophysiologic reflexes elicited by loading of the joint capsule and ligaments; can either facilitate or inhibit the musculature.

Noncapsular pattern: A limitation of joint motion which results from other than a capsular pattern of restriction; for example, internal derangement of the knee.

Noncontractile tissue: Inert tissue incapable of contraction; includes the joint capsule, ligaments, fascia, bursa, nerves (peripheral and root), dura mater, blood vessels, articular cartilage, and bone; can be loaded only by internal passive force.

Osteokinematics: The movement occurring between two bones; involves rotatory motion of bone around an axis; the extracapsular motion of one bone moving in relation to another stable bone.

Overpressure: The passive force applied to a joint and its associated soft tissues to stress the joint partners beyond the physiologic range of motion; used to determine the type of end-feel, the status of soft tissue and joint structures, and the presence of pain in response to mechanical deformation of tissue.

Provocation test: The application of controlled external forces to impose an internal load on isolated tissues and structures.

Strain: The deformation that occurs to material subject to loading, that is, stress; can cause lengthening or shortening of the structure.

Stress: The internal load produced in a structure by an external force.

Tension: An internal load imposed by forces acting in opposite directions resulting in a tendency to elongate, or the actual elongation of the fibers in a material.

Tissue reactivity: The tolerance of tissue to an internal load created by the external force of the examiner; indicated by the patient's perception of pain intensity.

Torsion: A force that creates a twisting of the material around its long axis.

Chapter 6

SENSORY ASSESSMENT

THOMAS J. SCHMITZ

OBJECTIVES

1. Identify the purposes of performing a sensory assessment.

2. Describe the classification and function of the receptor mechanisms involved in the perception of sensation.

3. Identify the spinal pathways that mediate sensation.

4. Identify the general guidelines for completing a sensory assessment.

5. Describe the testing protocol for assessment of each sensory modality.

INTRODUCTION

Disturbances of the sensory system pose significant functional implications for the patient. Impairment of sensation may be associated with any disease or trauma affecting the nervous system.[1] This impairment can result from dysfunction at any point within the sensory system, from the receptor, or the peripheral nerve to the spinal cord, nuclei, sensory tracts, brainstem, thalamus, or sensory cortex.[1-3] Examples of diagnoses that generally demonstrate some level of sensory impairment include disease or injury to peripheral nerves or spinal cord, burns, hemiplegia, arthritis, multiple sclerosis, fractures, and head trauma or disease. This list, which is not all inclusive, indicates the wide variety of disorders that may present with some element of sensory deficit and the importance of a thorough knowledge of techniques for assessing sensation.

Another area of concern related to alterations in sensory function are the neurosensory changes that occur during the normal aging process. Decreased acuity of many sensations occurs or is considered likely to occur with normal aging.[4-6] Documented findings include a decreased response to tactile[7] and vibratory stimuli,[8] decreased two-point discrimination,[9,10] decreased kines-

thetic awareness,[4] and minimal alterations in the perception of pain.[11] These changes frequently appear in the presence of age-related visual or hearing losses which impair compensatory capabilities. In addition, some medications may influence further the distortion of sensory input.[6] Knowledge of anticipated age-related changes of the sensory system will improve the therapist's ability to interpret test results from older patients.

Considering the close relationship between sensory input and motor output, detailed information related to sensory status is a critical factor in treatment planning. For example, a patient who has decreased awareness of where a limb is in space may be unable to execute appropriate motor responses during a program of therapeutic exercise or to safely accomplish some functional activities. Consequently, treatment designed for this patient must be adjusted either to improve or to accommodate the sensory deficit.[1] Additionally, insensitive body parts, particularly the hands and feet, are often subjected to injury. This is evident by the frequent occurrence of burns, cuts, lacerations, and bruises on insensitive limbs.[12] Knowledge of the patient's sensory deficit will guide the therapist in appropriately educating the patient about the impairment and precautions that should be taken to avoid injury.

Sensory testing is usually a component of the overall initial examination. Because sensory deficits will influence motor performance, the sensory assessment generally is completed prior to tests that involve elements of active motor function (such as manual muscle testing, active range of motion, functional assessments, and so forth). Sensory tests are also an important component of periodic reassessment to determine the effectiveness of the rehabilitation program.[13]

The purposes of performing a sensory assessment are to

1. Determine the level of sensory feedback affecting movement (including influence of sensory deficits on performance of functional activities or use of adaptive equipment and prosthetics or orthotics).

2. Provide a basis for initiating a program of desensitization (use of tactile stimuli to decrease hypersensitivity) or sensory retraining (learning the sensation of a movement or sensory stimuli).

3. Determine the need for instruction in techniques to compensate for the sensory loss, such as use of visual cues during movement.[1,14]

4. Assure patient safety and prevent secondary complications (for example, prevention of burns during application of hearing modalities, prevention of decubitus ulcers, and so forth).

5. Formulate goals and to plan for appropriate therapeutic intervention.

6. Help determine, over a period of time, the effects of rehabilitation, surgical or medical management.[15]

Prior to a discussion of specific testing protocol, a brief review of the sensory system is warranted. The following section presents an overview of the approaches to classification of the sensory system: divisions and types of sensory receptors, and the pathways that mediate sensory signals.

CLASSIFICATION OF THE SENSORY SYSTEM

Portions of the sensory system have been classified for both descriptive and functional purposes. In 1920, Henry Head[17] grossly divided tactile sensations into two systems, the **protopathic** and **epicritic** systems. Head theorized that the protopathic system was designed for protection, to warn or to defend the organism against potential harm.[18] This system was concerned with unpleasant sensations such as pain; extreme changes in temperature;[19] and diffuse, unpleasant light touch sensations such as itching or tingling.[18]

The epicritic system, believed to be a phylogenetically newer system, was considered to exert a controlling function over the protopathic system.[20] The epicritic system was described as concerned with highly discriminative sensations such as localization of cutaneous stimuli, object recognition,[18] two-point discrimination, and subtle changes in temperature.[19] Although both systems could mediate the perception of pain, it was the protopathic system that was identified as most concerned with pain messages, often producing a motor response.[20]

Another classification system divides sensation into three categories with reference to the type or location of the receptor which responds to a particular stimulus. The three divisions include the *superficial, deep,* and *combined*[19] sensations. **Exteroceptors** are the sensory receptors responsible for the superficial sensations. They receive stimuli from the external environment via the skin and subcutaneous tissue.[21] Exteroceptors are responsible for the perception of pain, temperature, light touch, and pressure.[19,21] **Proprioceptors** are the sensory receptors responsible for deep sensations. These receptors receive stimuli from muscles, tendons, ligaments, joints,[19,21] and fascia[21] and are responsible for position and movement **(kinesthesia)** sense.

The combination of both the superficial and deep sensory mechanisms makes up the third category of combined, or cortical,[22] sensations. These sensations require information from both the exteroceptive and proprioceptive receptors as well as intact function of cortical sensory association areas. The combined (cortical) sensations include stereognosis, two-point discrimination, vibration, barognosis, graphesthesia, tactile localization, recognition of texture, and bilateral simultaneous stimulation.[1,19,22]

Sensations also have been classified according to the system by which they are mediated to higher centers. Sensations are mediated by either the *anterolateral spinothalamic* or the *dorsal column–medial lemniscal* system.[2,18,20,21,23] The anterolateral spinothalamic system responds to stimuli that are potentially harmful in nature. It contains slowly conducting fibers of small diameter, some of which are unmyelinated.[23,24] The system is concerned with transmission of thermal and nocioceptive[21] information and mediates pain, temperature, crudely localized touch,[2,23,24] tickle, itch, and sexual sensations.[25] The dorsal column-medial lemniscal system (also referred to as the dorsal column system) is considered to be involved with responses to more discriminative sensations. It contains faster conducting fibers of large diameter with greater myelination.[2] This system mediates the sensations of discriminative touch and pressure sensations, vibration, movement and position sense.[2,21,24,25] The two systems are not independent but integrated to function together.

Classification of Sensory Receptors

The sensory receptors frequently are divided according to their structural design and the type of stimulus to which they preferentially respond.[2] These divisions include (1) *mechanoreceptors,* which respond to mechanical deformation of the receptor or surrounding area; (2) *thermoreceptors,* which respond to changes in temperature; (3) *nocioceptors,* which respond to noxious stimuli and result in the perception of pain; (4) *chemoreceptors,* which respond to chemical substances and are responsible for taste, smell, oxygen levels in arterial blood, carbon dioxide concentration and osmolality of body fluids; and (5) *photic (electromagnetic) receptors,* which respond to light within the visible spectrum.[2,25]

It is important to note that pain is not limited to simuli received from nocioceptors, because other types of receptors and nerve fibers contribute to this sensation. High intensities of stimuli to any type of receptor may be perceived as pain (for example, extreme heat or cold, and high-intensity mechanical deformation).[2]

TYPES OF SENSORY RECEPTORS

A composite list of the general classification of sensory receptors is presented in Table 6–1. Note that this list also includes the receptors responsible for electromagnetic (visual) and chemical stimuli.

Cutaneous Sensory Receptors

Cutaneous receptors are located at the terminal portion of the afferent fiber.[2] These include free nerve endings, hair follicle endings, Merkel's disks, Ruffini endings, Krause's end-bulbs, Meissner's corpuscles, and Pacinian corpuscles. The density of these sensory receptors varies for different areas of the body. For example,

Table 6–1 CLASSIFICATION OF SENSORY RECEPTORS

I. Mechanoreceptors
  A. Cutaneous sensory receptors
    1. Free nerve endings
    2. Hair follicle endings
    3. Merkel's disk
    4. Ruffini endings
    5. Krause's end-bulbs
    6. Meissner's corpuscles
    7. Pacinian corpuscles
  B. Deep sensory (joint) receptors
    1. Muscle spindle
    2. Golgi tendon organs
    3. Free nerve endings
    4. Pacinian corpuscles
    5. Joint receptors
      a. Golgi-type endings
      b. Free nerve endings
      c. Ruffini endings
      d. Paciniform endings
II. Thermoreceptors
  A. Cold
    1. Cold receptors
  B. Warmth
    1. Warm receptors
III. Nocioceptors
  A. Pain
    1. Free nerve endings
    2. Extremes of stimuli to other sensory receptors
IV. Electromagnetic receptors
  A. Vision
    1. Rods
    2. Cones
V. Chemoreceptors
  A. Taste
    1. Receptors of taste buds
  B. Smell
    1. Receptors of olfactory nerves in olfactory epithelium
  C. Arterial oxygen
    1. Receptors of aortic and carotid bodies
  D. Osmolality
    1. Probably neurons of supraoptic nuclei
  E. Blood CO_2
    1. Receptors in or on surface of medulla and in aortic and carotid bodies
  F. Blood glucose, amino acids, fatty acids
    1. Receptors in hypothalamus

Adapted from Guyton, AC.[25]

there are many more tactile receptors in the fingertips than in the back. These areas of higher receptor density correspondingly display a higher cortical representation in somatic sensory area I.[26] Receptor density is a particularly important consideration in interpreting the results of a sensory assessment for a given body surface. Figure 6–1 presents a diagram of the cutaneous sensory receptors and their respective locations within the various layers of skin.

1. *Free nerve endings.* These receptors are found throughout the body. Stimulation of free nerve endings results in the perception of pain, temperature, touch,[2] pressure, tickle, and itch sensations.[25]

2. *Hair follicle endings.* At the base of each hair follicle a free nerve ending is entwined. The combination of the hair follicle and its nerve provides a sensitive receptor. These receptors are sensitive to mechanical movement and touch.[2]

3. *Merkel's disks.* These receptors are located below the epidermis in hairy and glabrous skin. They are sensitive to low-intensity touch as well as to velocity of touch. They provide for the ability to perceive continuous contact of objects against the skin and are believed to play an important role in both two-point discrimination and localization of touch.[25]

4. *Ruffini endings.* Located in the deeper layers of the dermis, these encapsulated endings are involved with the perception of touch and pressure. They are particularly important in signaling continuous states of skin deformation.[27]

5. *Krause's end-bulb.* These receptors are located in the dermis. They are believed to have a contributing role in the perception of touch and pressure.[28]

6. *Meissner's corpuscles.* Located in the dermis, these encapsulated nerve endings contain many nerve filaments within the capsule. They are in high concentration in the fingertips, lips, and toes—areas that require high levels of discrimination. These receptors play an important role in discriminative touch and the recognition of texture.[2,27]

7. *Pacinian corpuscles.* These receptors are located in the subcutaneous tissue layer of the skin and in deep tissues of the body (including tendons and soft tissues around joints). They are stimulated by rapid movement of tissue and are quickly adapting. They play a significant role in the perception of deep touch and vibration.[2,21,25]

Deep Sensory Receptors

The *deep sensory receptors* are located in muscles, tendons, and joints.[2,23,25,27] They include both muscle and joint receptors. They are concerned primarily with posture, **position sense, proprioception,** muscle tone and speed, and direction of movement. The deep sensory receptors include the muscle spindle, Golgi tendon organs, free nerve endings, Pacinian corpuscles, and joint receptors.

Muscle Receptors

1. *Muscle spindles.* The muscle spindle fibers (intrafusal fibers) lie in a relatively parallel position to the muscle fibers (extrafusal fibers). They monitor changes

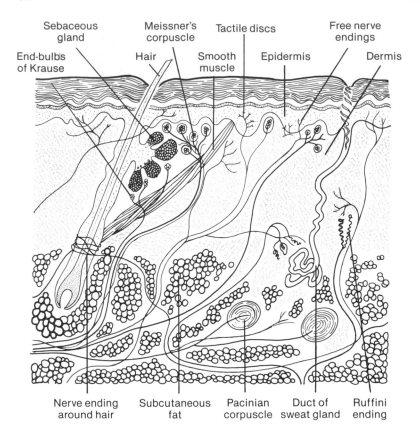

Figure 6–1. Schematic representation of the skin and its receptors. The receptors are located in the three layers of skin: the epidermis, dermis, and the subcutaneous layer. From Gardner, E,[21] p 222, with permission of the publisher. Originally modified from Woollard, Weddell, and Harpman, J Anat 74:441, 1940.

in muscle length as well as velocity of these changes. The muscle spindle plays a vital role in position and movement sense and in motor learning.

2. *Golgi tendon organs.* These receptors are located in series at both the proximal and distal tendonous insertions of the muscle. The Golgi tendon organs function to monitor tension within the muscle. They also are considered to provide a protective mechanism by preventing structural damage to the muscle in situations of extreme tension. This is accomplished by inhibition of the contracting muscle and facilitation of the antagonist.

3. *Free nerve endings.* These receptors are within the fascia of the muscle. They are believed to respond to pain and pressure.

4. *Pacinian corpuscles.* Located within the fascia of the muscle, these receptors respond to vibratory stimuli and deep pressure.

Joint Receptors

1. *Golgi-type endings.* These receptors are located in the ligaments and function to detect the rate of joint movement.

2. *Free nerve endings.* Found in the joint capsule and ligaments, these receptors are believed to respond to pain and crude awareness of joint motion.

3. *Ruffini endings.* Located in the joint capsule and ligaments, Ruffini endings are responsible for the direction and velocity of joint movement.

4. *Puciniform endings.* These receptors are found in the joint capsule and primarily monitor rapid joint movements.

Transmission of Sensory Signals

Somatic sensory information enters the spinal cord through the dorsal roots. Sensory signals are then carried to higher centers via ascending pathways from one of two systems: the *anterolateral spinothalamic system* or the *dorsal column–medial lemniscal system.*

ANTEROLATERAL SPINOTHALAMIC SYSTEM

The spinothalamic tracts are diffuse pathways concerned with nondiscriminative sensations such as pain, temperature, tickle, itch, and sexual sensations. This system is activated primarily by mechanoreceptors, thermoreceptors, and nocioceptors and is composed of afferent fibers which are small and slowly conducting. Sensory signals transmitted by this system do not require discrete localization of signal source or precise gradations in intensity.[2,19,25]

After originating in the dorsal roots, the fibers of the spinothalamic system cross to the opposite anterolateral segment of the white matter (Fig. 6–2) and ascend diffusely in the anterior and lateral white columns. They demonstrate a diffuse pattern of termination at all levels of the lower brainstem as well as at the thalamus.[2,19,27]

Compared with the dorsal column–medial lemniscal system, the anterolateral spinothalamic pathways make up a cruder, more primitive system. The spinothalamic tracts are capable of transmitting a wide variety of sensory modalities. However, their diffuse pattern of termination results in only crude abilities to localize the source

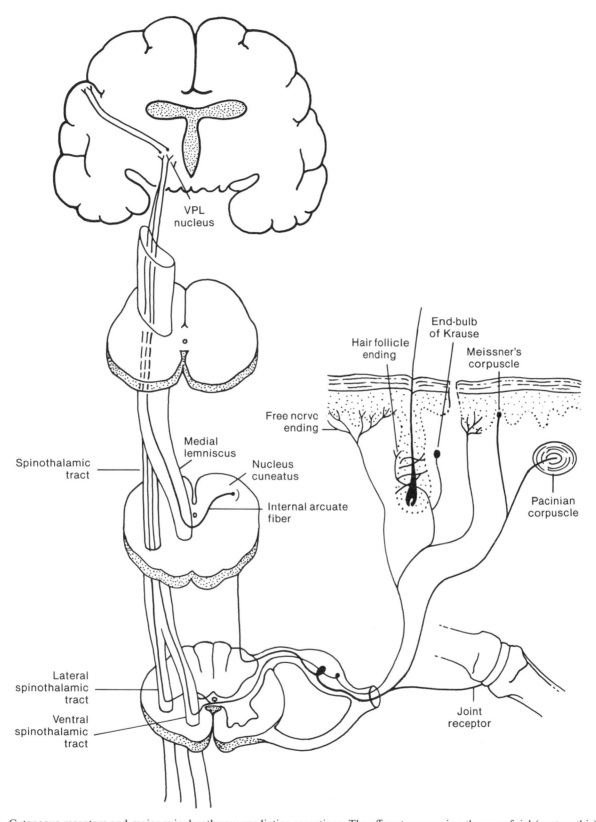

Figure 6–2. Cutaneous receptors and major spinal pathways mediating sensations. The afferents conveying the superficial (protopathic) sensations are small, slow conducting, and travel via the spinothalamic tracts. The afferents conveying the discriminative sensations are larger, faster conducting, and travel via the dorsal-lemniscus pathway. Branches for reflexes and pain and temperature have been omitted. From Brown, DR,[2] p 230, with permission of the publisher. Originally adapted from Netter, F: *The CIBA Collection of Medical Illustrations. I. The Nervous System.* CIBA Chemical Co, Summit, NJ, 1972.

of a stimulus on the body surface and poor intensity discrimination.[27]

The three major tracts of the spinothalamic system include the (1) *anterior (ventral) spinothalamic tract,* which carries the sensations of crudely localized touch and pressure; (2) the *lateral spinothalamic tract,* which carries pain and temperature; and (3) the *spinoreticular tract,* which is involved with diffuse pain sensations.[2,19,25]

DORSAL COLUMN–MEDIAL LEMNISCAL SYSTEM

This system is responsible for transmission of discriminative sensations received from specialized mechanoreceptors. Sensory modalities that require fine gradations of intensity and precise localization on the body surface are mediated by this system. Sensations transmitted by the dorsal column–medial lemniscal pathway include discriminative touch, **stereognosis,** tactile pressure, **barognosis, graphesthesia,** recognition of texture, kinesthesia, **two-point discrimination,** proprioception, and vibration.[2,19,25]

This system is composed of large, rapidly conducting fibers. After entering the dorsal column the fibers ascend to the medulla and synapse with the dorsal column nuclei (nuclei gracilis and cuneatus). From here they cross to the opposite side and pass up to the thalamus through bilateral pathways called the *medial lemnisci.* Each medial lemniscus terminates in the ventral posterolateral thalamus. From the thalamus, third-order neurons project to the somatic sensory cortex (see Figure 6–2).[2,19,25]

GENERAL GUIDELINES FOR SENSORY ASSESSMENTS

The testing procedure consists of two components: (1) application of the stimulus and (2) patient response to the stimulus. During the sensory assessment, the following information should be gathered.

1. The type of sensation affected.
2. The quantity of involvement (e.g., number of extremities or body surface areas affected).
3. The degree of involvement (e.g., absent, impaired, delayed responses, **hyperasthesia,** and so forth).
4. Localization of the exact boundaries of the sensory impairment (this will assist in determining location of the lesion).
5. The patient's subjective feelings about changes in sensation.

The patient's ability to comprehend instructions and to communicate responses is crucial to accurate sensory testing. As such, general knowledge of the patient's cognitive status and hearing and visual acuity is required. Several simple preliminary tests may be warranted to make these determinations if the therapist is unfamiliar with the patient.

Rapid tests for mental orientation typically involve asking the patient questions related to *time* (date, day of the week, or season of the year), *place* (present location, home address, name of the city or state) and *person* (the patient's own name and age, identification of family members or other individuals known to the patient). Simple tests for memory might involve requests for information related to both long-term and short-term recall; for example, requesting information pertaining to place of birth or historical facts as well as what was eaten for breakfast or repetition of a series of numbers. A gross hearing assessment can be made by observing the patient's response to conversation. The therapist also should note how alterations in volume and tone of verbal directions influence patient response. Finally, a gross assessment of visual acuity may be necessary. This can be assessed quickly by asking the patient to read a standard eye chart or to identify the time from a wall clock. Peripheral field vision can be tested by sitting directly in front of the patient with outstretched arms. The index fingers should be extended and gradually brought toward midline of the patient's face. The patient is asked to identify when the therapist's approaching finger(s) is first seen. Differences between right and left visual field acuity should be noted carefully. Depth perception may be grossly checked by holding two pencils or fingers in front of the patient. The patient is asked to identify the foreground object.

Findings from these gross assessments will guide the therapist in preparation for formal sensory testing. Because the sensory tests require a patient response to the stimulus, disoriented patients generally can not be accurately tested. However, vision, hearing, or speech deficits will not adversely affect test results if appropriate adaptations are made in providing instructions and indicating responses. Such modifications include use of increased visual cues and/or manual contacts.

Patient education prior to the sensory assessment is also an important consideration. A full explanation of the purpose and goals of the testing should be provided. The patient also should be informed that his or her cooperation is necessary in order to obtain accurate test results.

During the assessment, the patient should be in a comfortable, relaxed position in a quiet room. Both the prone and supine positions will be required in order to assess each side of the body.[29] Preferably, the tests should be performed when the patient is well rested. Considering the high level of concentration required, fatigue has been noted to affect results of some sensory tests adversely.[30] A "trial run" or demonstration of each procedure should be performed just prior to the actual test. This will orient and inform the patient regarding the procedure and exactly what to anticipate during the testing.

Some method of occluding the patient's vision during the testing should be used (vision should not be occluded during the explanation and demonstrations). Visual input is prevented because it may compensate for a sensory deficit and thus decrease the accuracy of test results. The traditional methods of occluding vision are by use of a blindfold (a small folded towel can be used effectively) or by asking the patient to keep the eyes closed. These methods are practical in most instances. However, in situations of central nervous system dysfunction, a patient may become anxious[14] or disoriented[1] if vision is occluded for a long period of time. In these situations a small screen[1,14] or folder[14] may be preferable to avoid visual input. Whatever method is used, it should be removed between the tests while directions and demonstrations are provided.

The superficial (exteroceptive) sensations are usually assessed first, inasmuch as they consist of more primitive responses, followed by the deep (proprioceptive) and combined (cortical) sensations. If a test indicates impairment of the superficial responses, it is likely that some impairment of the more discriminative (deep and combined) sensations also will be noted.

The tests should be carried out following the main sensory nerves and their segmental (dermatome) supply. The **dermatomes** are the cutaneous areas that correspond to the spinal segments that provide their innervation (Fig. 6–3). Dermatome charts do not represent discrete boundaries because some overlap of innervation exists at the borders of adjacent dermatomes. However, the charts are useful as a reference during testing, and they provide a method for recording results.[1]

Sensory tests are usually performed in a distal to proximal direction. This progression will conserve time, particularly when dealing with localized lesions involving a single extremity where deficits tend to be more severe distally. It is generally not necessary to test every segment of each dermatome; testing general body areas is sufficient. However, once a deficit area is noted, testing must become more discrete and the exact boundaries of the impairment should be identified. A skin pencil may be useful to mark the boundaries of sensory change directly. This information should be transferred later to a gross sensory assessment form (Table 6–2) and graph-

ically presented on the dermatome chart (see Figure 6–3) for inclusion in the medical record. Most often the dermatome charts are completed using a color code (i.e., each color represents a different sensation). The colors used to plot each sensation are then coded at the bottom of the page. In some instances hatch marks of varying density are used to represent gradations in sensory impairment (i.e., the closer together, the greater the sensory impairment). With this method, a completely colored-in area indicates no response to a given sensation. With varied or "spotty" sensory loss it is not uncommon that more than one dermatome chart is required to completely depict all test findings.

During testing, the application of stimuli should be applied in a random, unpredictable manner with variation in timing.[1] This will improve accuracy of the test results by avoiding a consistent pattern of application which might provide the patient "clues" to the correct response. During application of stimuli, consideration must be given also to skin condition. Scar tissue or callused areas are generally less sensitive and will demonstrate a diminished response to sensory stimuli.

Equipment

In order to perform a sensory assessment the following equipment and materials are required:

1. A large-headed pin (providing one sharp and one dull end).
2. Two test tubes with stoppers.
3. A camel hair brush, a piece of cotton, or a tissue.

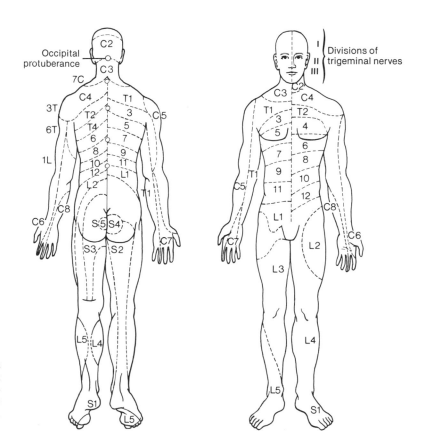

Figure 6–3. The dermatome chart represents the cutaneous areas supplied by a single dorsal root and its ganglia. Note that the trunk demonstrates a sequential, segmental pattern of innervation, and that the extremities present an irregular pattern as segmental innervation migrates distally. From Gilroy, J and Meyer, JS,[29] p 58, with permission of the publisher.

Table 6–2 GROSS SENSORY ASSESSMENT FORM

This form provides a general record of the type, severity, and location of the sensory impairment(s). It should be used in conjunction with one or more dermatome charts which graphically outline the exact boundaries of the deficit. The designations P and D may be added to the grading key to indicate either a proximal (P) or a distal (D) location of the deficit on the limb or body part.

Name: _____ Date: _____
Examiner: _____

Key to Grading*
1. Intact: normal, accurate response
2. Decreased: delayed response
3. Exaggerated: increased sensitivity or awareness of the stimulus after it has ceased
4. Inaccurate: inappropriate perception of a given stimulus
5. Absent: no response
6. Inconsistent or ambiguous: response inadequate to assess sensory function accurately

*(Separate notation should be made for assessment of the face. Abnormal responses should be briefly described in the comments section. NA indicates that the test is not appropriate for the given body area.)

Sensations	Upper Extremity		Lower Extremity		Trunk		Comments
	Right	Left	Right	Left	Right	Left	
Superficial							
Pain (sharp/dull discrimination)	_____	_____	_____	_____	_____	_____	
Temperature	_____	_____	_____	_____	_____	_____	
Light touch	_____	_____	_____	_____	_____	_____	
Pressure	_____	_____	_____	_____	_____	_____	
Deep (Proprioceptive)							
Movement sense	_____	_____	_____	_____	NA	NA	
Position sense	_____	_____	_____	_____	NA	NA	
Combined (Cortical)							
Tactile localization	_____	_____	_____	_____	_____	_____	
Two-point discrimination	_____	_____	_____	_____	_____	_____	
Bilateral simultaneous stimulation	_____	_____	_____	_____	_____	_____	
Vibration	_____	_____	_____	_____	_____	_____	
Stereognosis	_____	_____	_____	_____	_____	_____	
Barognosis	_____	_____	NA	NA	NA	NA	
Graphesthesia	_____	_____	NA	NA	NA	NA	
Recognition of texture	_____	_____	NA	NA	NA	NA	

4. A variety of small commonly used articles such as keys, coins, pencils, and so forth.

5. An anesthesimeter or an electrocardiogram (ECG) caliper[30] with the tips sanded to blunt the ends[31] and a small ruler.

6. A series of small weights of the same dimension but representing graduated increments in weight.

7. Samples of fabrics of various textures such as cotton, wool, or silk (approximately 4 × 4 inches [10 × 10 cm]).

8. Tuning fork and earphones (to reduce auditory clues).

Reliability of Sensory Testing

As with all assessment procedures, the reliability of sensory testing is an important consideration for physical therapists. Currently, there are few systematic reports of data collection related to reliability of sensory tests. In a study by Kent,[32] the upper limbs of 50 adult patients with hemiplegia were tested for sensory and motor deficits. Three sensory tests were administered and then repeated by the same examiner within 1 to 7 days. Results revealed a high reliability for both stereognosis (r = 0.97) and position sense (r = 0.90). A low reliability was reported for two-point discrimination, with correlation coefficients ranging from 0.59 to 0.82, depending on the body area tested.

Although limited published data are available related to reliability measures, several approaches can be used to improve this aspect of the tests. These include (1) use of consistent guidelines for completing the tests; (2) administration of the tests by trained, skillful examiners; and (3) subsequent retests performed by the same individual. It also should be noted that the reliability of sensory tests will be further influenced by the patient's understanding of the test procedure and the patient's ability to communicate results.[1]

The recent studies by Nolan[13,15,33] have generated some renewed interest in both the reliability and the validity of sensory testing in general. Additional research related to standardization of testing protocols, development of quantitative approaches to collecting information, and establishment of additional normative data for various age groups will improve the reliability, validity, and future clinical application of test results.

Testing Protocol

This section presents the individual tests for assessment of sensation. The tests are subdivided for superficial, deep, and combined sensations.

SUPERFICIAL SENSATIONS

Pain (Sharp/Dull Discrimination)

Test. A large-headed pin is used (providing one sharp end and one dull end). Both stimuli (sharp and dull ends of pin) are applied in random fashion. To avoid summation of impulses, the stimuli should not be applied too close to each other or in rapid succession. In order to maintain a uniform pressure with each successive application of stimuli, the pin should be held firmly and the fingers allowed to "slide" down the pin once in contact with the skin. This will avoid the chance of gradually increasing pressure during application.

Response. The patient is asked to indicate when a stimulus is felt and to reply "sharp," "dull," or "unable to tell." All areas of the body should be tested.

Temperature

Test. Two test tubes with stoppers are required for this assessment; one should be filled with hot water and the other with crushed ice. Ideal temperatures for cold are between 41°F (5°C) and 50°F (10°C) and for hot, between 104°F (40°C) and 113°F (45°C). Caution should be exercised to remain within these ranges, because exceeding these temperatures may elicit a pain response and consequently inaccurate test results. The test tubes are randomly placed in contact with the skin area to be tested. All skin surfaces should be tested.

Response. The patient is asked to indicate when a stimulus is felt and to reply "hot," "cold," or "unable to tell."

It should be noted that clinical usefulness of thermal testing may be problematic. Nolan[30] points out that the tests are extremely difficult to duplicate on a day-to-day basis owing to rapid changes in temperature once the test tubes are exposed to room air. Although a simple test to perform, assessing changes over time is not practical unless a method of monitoring temperature of the test tubes is used.[30]

Light Touch

Test. For this test a camel hair brush, piece of cotton, or a tissue is used. The area to be tested is lightly touched or stroked.

Response. The patient is asked to indicate when he or she recognizes that a stimulus has been applied by responding "yes" or "now."

Pressure

Test. The therapist's thumb or fingertip is used to apply a firm pressure on the skin surface. This pressure should be firm enough to indent the skin[1,14] and to stimulate the deep receptors.[1]

Response. The patient is asked to indicate when he or she recognizes that a stimulus has been applied by responding "yes" or "now."

DEEP (PROPRIOCEPTIVE) SENSATIONS

Proprioception includes both **position sense** and **movement sense (kinesthesia).** Position sense is the awareness of the position of joints at rest. Movement sense or kinesthesia is the awareness of movement. Although these sensations are closely related, they should be assessed individually.

Movement Sense (Kinesthesia)

Test. This test assesses the *perception of movement.* The extremity or joint(s) to be assessed is moved passively through a range of motion. As discussed earlier, a trial run or demonstration of the procedure should be performed prior to actual testing. This will ensure that the patient and the therapist agree on terms to describe the direction of movements.

Response. The patient is asked to indicate verbally the direction of movement *while the extremity is in motion.* The patient is asked to describe the direction and range of movement in terms previously discussed with the therapist (i.e., "up," "down," "in," "out," "full range of motion," "partial range of motion," and so forth). The patient may also respond by simultaneously duplicating the movement with the opposite extremity. This second approach, however, is usually impractical with proximal lower extremity joints owing to potential stress on the low back. During testing, movement of larger joints is usually discerned more quickly than smaller joints. The therapist's grip should remain constant, preferably over bony prominences to reduce tactile stimulation.

Position Sense

Test. This test assesses *joint position sense.* The extremity or joint(s) to be assessed is moved through a range of motion and held in a static position. Again, caution should be used with hand placements to avoid excessive tactile stimulation.

Response. While the extremity or joint(s) under assessment is held in a *static position* by the therapist, the patient is asked to describe the position verbally or duplicate the position of the extremity or joint(s) with the opposite extremity.

COMBINED (CORTICAL) SENSATIONS

Stereognosis

Test. Testing for object recognition will require use of items of differing size and shape. A variety of small, easily obtainable and culturally familiar objects are used for this assessment. These objects may include keys, coins, combs, safety pins, pencils, and so forth. Individual objects are placed in the patient's hand. The patient is allowed to manipulate the object and is asked to identify the item verbally. The patient should be allowed to handle several sample test items during the explanation and demonstration of the procedure.

Response. The patient is asked to name the object verbally. For patients with speech deficits the items can be selected from a group after each test.

Tactile Localization

Test. This test assesses the ability to localize touch sensation on the skin. Using a fingertip, the therapist touches different skin surfaces. After each application of a stimuli the patient is given time to respond.

Response. The patient is asked to identify the location of the stimuli by touch or verbal description. The patient's eyes may be open during the response component of this test.[1] Tactile localization may be tested separately or included with other tests[1] (e.g., localization of sharp/dull or light touch sensations). The distance between the application of the stimulus and the site indicated by the patient should be measured and recorded.

Two-Point Discrimination

Test. This test assesses the ability to perceive two points applied to the skin simultaneously. It is a measure of the smallest distance between two stimuli (applied simultaneously and with equal pressure) which can still be perceived as two distinct stimuli.[30] This assessment is among the most practical and easily duplicated test for cutaneous sensation. Recently, two-point discrimination has been the subject of a series of important studies by Nolan.[13,15,33] The purpose of his research was to establish normative data on two-point discrimination for young adults. His sample consisted of 43 college students ranging in age from 20 to 24. Values from his studies are presented in Table 6–3 for the upper extremity, Table 6–4 for the lower extremity, and Table 6–5 for the face and trunk. These findings are consistent with earlier, less extensive studies on two-point discrimination in the upper limb.[31,34] Normative values are extremely useful in interpreting test results from sensory assessments, as well as from other types of assessments. However, the results from these studies[13,15,33] must be used cautiously, inasmuch as they relate to a specific population. They should not be generalized for interpreting data from older or younger patients.

Several instruments have been described for use in measuring two-point discrimination. These include a reshaped paper clip,[35] an eye caliper,[31] a Boley gauge,[31] and an anesthesimeter.[1,30] The ECG caliper (a compass-type device) has been identified as a particularly practical, inexpensive, and easily obtained tool for measuring two-point discrimination.[30] Prior to use for two-point discrimination testing, the tips of the ECG caliper should be lightly sanded to form blunt ends.[31] This will ensure that the tactile stimulus will not be perceived as painful.

During the test procedure the two ends are applied to the skin simultaneously. With each successive application, the two ends are gradually brought closer together until the stimuli are perceived as one. The smallest distance between the stimuli that is still perceived as two distinct points is measured with a ruler and recorded. To increase validity of the test it is appropriate to alternate the application of two stimuli with the random applica-

Table 6–4 TWO-POINT DISCRIMINATION VALUES FOR THE LOWER EXTREMITY (N = 43)

Skin Region	($\overline{X}$) mm	s
Proximal—anterior thigh	40.1	14.7
Distal—anterior thigh	23.2	9.3
Mid—lateral thigh	42.5	15.9
Mid—medial thigh	38.5	12.4
Mid—posterior thigh	42.2	15.9
Proximal—lateral leg	37.7	13.0
Distal—lateral leg*	41.6	13.0
Medial leg	43.6	13.5
Tip of great toe	6.6	1.8
Over 1–2 metatarsal interspace	23.9	6.3
Over 5th metatarsal	22.2	8.6

*N = 41.

From Nolan, MF,[13] with permission of the American Physical Therapy Association.

Table 6–3 TWO-POINT DISCRIMINATION VALUES FOR THE UPPER EXTREMITY (N = 43)

Skin Region	$\overline{X}$ (mm)	s
Upper—lateral arm	42.4	14.0
Lower—lateral arm	37.8	13.1
Mid—medial arm	45.4	15.5
Mid—posterior arm	39.8	12.3
Mid—lateral forearm	35.9	11.6
Mid—medial forearm	31.5	8.9
Mid—posterior forearm	30.7	8.2
Over 1st dorsal interosseous muscle	21.0	5.6
Palmar surface—distal phalanx, thumb	2.6	0.6
Palmar surface—distal phalanx, long finger	2.6	0.7
Palmar surface—distal phalanx, little finger	2.5	0.7

From Nolan, MF,[33] with permission of the American Physical Therapy Association.

Table 6–5 TWO-POINT DISCRIMINATION VALUES FOR THE FACE AND TRUNK (N = 43)

Skin Region	$\overline{X}$ (mm)	s
Over eyebrow	14.9	4.2
Cheek	11.9	3.2
Over lateral mandible	10.4	2.2
Lateral neck	35.2	9.8
Medial to acromion process	51.1	14.0
Lateral to nipple	45.7	12.7*
Lateral to umbilicus	36.4	7.3†
Over iliac crest	44.9	10.1‡
Lateral to C7 spine	55.4	20.0†
Over inferior angle of scapula	52.2	12.6†
Lateral to L3 spine	49.9	12.7†

*n = 26.
†n = 42.
‡n = 33.

From Nolan, MF,[15] with permission of the American Physical Therapy Association.

tion of only a single stimulus. It is also important to consider that perception of two-point discrimination varies considerably for different individuals and body parts, being most refined in the distal upper extremities. Nolan[13] also noted a high level of two-point discrimination in the great toe. In testing for two-point discrimination, both intraindividual[13] and interindividual[13,15,33] variations in perception of the stimulus must be considered.

Response. The patient is asked to identify the perception of "one" or "two" stimuli.

Bilateral Simultaneous Stimulation

Test. This test assesses the ability to perceive a simultaneous touch stimulus on opposite sides of the body; proximally and distally on a single extremity; or proximally and distally on one side of the body. The therapist simultaneously (and with equal pressure) (1) touches identical locations on opposite sides of the body, (2) touches proximally and distally on opposite sides of the body, and (3) touches proximal and distal locations on the same side of the body. The term *extinction phenomena* is used to describe a situation in which only the proximal stimulus is perceived, with "extinction" of the distal.

Response. The patient verbally states when he or she perceives a touch stimulus and the number of stimuli felt.

Vibration

Test. The test for vibration assesses the ability to perceive a vibratory stimulus. The base of a vibrating tuning fork is placed on a bony prominence (such as the sternum, elbow, or ankle). If intact, the patient will perceive the vibration. If there is impairment, the patient will be unable to distinguish between a vibrating and nonvibrating tuning fork. Therefore, there should be a random application of vibrating and nonvibrating stimuli. Earphones may be used for this test procedure to reduce auditory clues from the vibrating fork.

Response. The patient is asked to respond by verbally identifying the stimulus as vibrating or nonvibrating each time the base of the fork is placed in contact with a bony prominence.

Several additional tests for the combined (cortical) sensations include barognosis, graphesthesia, and recognition of texture. However, these tests are usually not performed if stereognosis and two-point discrimination are found to be intact.[22]

Barognosis

Test. To assess for recognition of weight, a series of small objects of the same size but of graduated weight is used. The therapist may choose to place a series of different weights in the same hand one at a time, or to place a different weight in each hand simultaneously.

Response. The patient is asked to identify the comparative weight of objects in a series (i.e., to compare the relative weight of the object with the previous one), or when the objects are placed in both hands simultaneously the patient is asked to compare the weight of the two objects. The patient responds by indicating that the object is "heavier" or "lighter."

Graphesthesia

Test. The recognition of letters, numbers, or designs traced on the skin is assessed by the use of the eraser end of a pencil. A series or combination of letters, numbers, or designs is traced on the palm of the patient's hand (with the bottom of the figure at the base of the patient's hand). Between each separate drawing the palm should be gently wiped with a soft cloth to clearly indicate a change in figures to the patient. This test is also a useful substitute for stereognosis when paralysis prevents grasping an object.

Response. The patient is asked to identify verbally the figures drawn on the skin. For patients with speech deficits the figures can be selected (pointed to) from a series of line drawings.

Recognition of Texture

Test. This test assesses the ability to differentiate among various textures. Suitable textures may include cotton, wool, or silk. The items are placed individually in the patient's hand. The patient is allowed to manipulate the sample texture.

Response. The patient is asked to identify the individual textures as they are placed in the hand. They may be identified by name (e.g., silk, cotton) or by texture (e.g., rough, smooth).

SUMMARY

Sensory assessments provide important information related to the status of the sensory system. Results from these tests assist in goal setting, treatment planning, and periodic reassessment to determine the effectiveness of treatment intervention. Individual tests for assessment of each sensation have been presented. Reliability of these test procedures can be improved by careful adherence to consistent guidelines, administration of tests by trained individuals, and subsequent retests performed by the same examiner. Documentation of test results should address the type(s) of sensation affected, the quantity and degree of involvement, and localization of the exact boundaries of the sensory deficits. Finally, it should be emphasized again that additional research related to sensory testing is warranted. The development of standardized protocols, reliability measures, and additional normative data will significantly improve the clinical applications of data obtained from sensory assessments.

QUESTIONS FOR REVIEW

1. Describe the purposes of performing a sensory assessment. Identify when a sensory assessment should be completed (in terms of sequencing with respect to other initial examinations such as manual muscle testing, functional tests, and so forth). Identify four patient groups or diagnoses that would routinely warrant a sensory assessment.
2. Identify
   a. The five classifications of sensory receptors and the types of stimuli to which they respond.
   b. The cutaneous and joint receptors, their location, and types of stimuli to which they respond.
   c. The spinal pathways and the sensations they mediate.
3. Describe
   a. The type of information that should be gathered during a sensory assessment.
   b. The materials required to complete the assessment.
   c. How you would prepare the patient for the sensory testing.
   d. The sequence or progression of testing you would follow.
4. For each of the three groups of sensations—superficial, deep, and combined—describe each sensory test, providing both the test procedure and directions for patient response.
5. Describe the method(s) you would use to record the results of your assessment.

REFERENCES

1. Scott, AD: Evaluation and treatment of sensation. In Trombly, CA (ed): Occupational Therapy for Physical Dysfunction, ed 2. Williams & Wilkins, Baltimore, 1983, p 38.
2. Brown, DR: Neurosciences for Allied Health Therapies. CV Mosby, St Louis, 1980.
3. Minor, MAD and Minor, SD: Patient Evaluation Methods for the Health Professional. Reston Publishing, Reston, Virginia, 1985.
4. Colavita, FB: Sensory Changes in the Elderly. Charles C Thomas, Springfield, MA, 1978.
5. Corso, JF: Aging Sensory Systems and Perception. Praeger Publishers, New York, 1981.
6. Jackson-Klykken, O: Brain function, aging, and dementia. In Umphred, DA (ed): Neurological Rehabilitation. CV Mosby, St Louis, 1985, p 515.
7. Thornbury, JM and Mistretta, CM: Tactile sensitivity as a function of age. J Gerontology 36:34, 1981.
8. Verrillo, RT: Age related changes in the sensitivity to vibration. J Gerontology 35:185, 1980.
9. Bolton, CF, Winkelmann, RK, and Dyck, PJ: A quantitative study of Meissner's corpuscles in man. Neurology 16:1, 1966.
10. Gellis, M and Pool, R: Two-point discrimination distances in the normal hand and forearm. Plastic and Reconstructive Surgery 59:57, 1977.
11. Harkins, SW, Price, DD, and Martelli, M: Effects of age on pain perception: Thermonociception. J Gerontology 41:58, 1986.
12. Wood, H: Prevention of deformity in the insensitive hand: The role of the therapist. Am J Occup Ther 23:487, 1969.
13. Nolan, MF: Limits of two-point discrimination ability in the lower limb in young adult men and women. Phys Ther 63:1424, 1983.
14. Pedretti, LW: Evaluation of sensation, perception, and cognition. In Pedretti, LW (ed): Occupational Therapy: Practice Skills for Physical Dysfunction, ed 2. CV Mosby, St Louis, 1985, p 99.
15. Nolan, MF: Quantitative measure of cutaneous sensation: Two-point discrimination values for the face and trunk. Phys Ther 65:181, 1985.
16. Umphred, DA and McCormack, GL: Classification of common facilitory and inhibitory treatment techniques. In Umphred, DA (ed): Neurological Rehabilitation. CV Mosby, St Louis, 1985, p 72.
17. Head, H: Studies in Neurology, vol 2. Oxford University Press, London, 1920.
18. Ayers, AJ: Sensory Integration and Learning Disorders. Western Psychological Services, Los Angeles, 1972.
19. Chusid, JG: Correlative Neuroanatomy and Functional Neurology, ed 19. Lange Medical Publications, Los Altos, CA, 1985.
20. Ayers, AJ: Tactile functions: Their relation to hyperactive and perceptual motor behavior. Am J Occup Ther 18:6, 1964.
21. Gardner, E: Fundamentals of Neurology: A Psychophysiological Approach, ed 6. WB Saunders, Philadelphia, 1975.
22. Paine, RS and Oppe, TE: Neurological examination of children. Clinics in Developmental Medicine, vols 20–21. Spastics Society Medical Education and Information Unit in Association with William Heinemann Medical Books, London, 1966.
23. Werner, JK: Neuroscience: A Clinical Perspective. WB Saunders, Philadelphia, 1980.
24. Farber, SD: Neurorehabilitation: A Multisensory Approach. WB Saunders, Philadelphia, 1982.
25. Guyton, AC: Human Physiology and Mechanisms of Disease, ed 4. WB Saunders, Philadelphia, 1987.
26. Guyton, AC: Basic Human Neurophysiology, ed 3. WB Saunders, Philadelphia, 1981.
27. Guyton, AC: Textbook of Medical Physiology, ed 7. WB Saunders, Philadelphia, 1986.
28. Noback, CR: Personal communication, August 12, 1985.
29. Gilroy, J and Meyer, JS: Medical Neurology, ed 3. Macmillan, New York, 1979.
30. Nolan, MF: Clinical assessment of cutaneous sensory function. Clinical Management in Physical Therapy 4(2):26, 1984.
31. Werner, JL and Omer, GE: Evaluating cutaneous pressure sensation of the hand. Am J Occup Ther 24:347, 1970.
32. Kent, BE: Sensory-motor testing: The upper limb of adult patients with hemiplegia. Journal of the American Physical Therapy Association 45:550, 1965.
33. Nolan, MF: Two-point discrimination assessment in the upper limb in young adult men and women. Phys Ther 62:965, 1982.
34. Moberg, E: Evaluation of sensibility in the hand. Surg Clin North Am 40(2):357, 1960.
35. Moberg, E: Emergency Surgery of the Hand. E & S Livingstone, Ltd, London, 1967.

SUPPLEMENTAL READINGS

Adams, JH, Corsellis, JAN, and Duchen, LW (eds): Greenfield's Neuropathology, ed 4. John Wiley & Sons, New York, 1984.

Adams, RD and Victor, M: Principles of Neurology, ed 3. McGraw-Hill, New York, 1985.

Albe-Fessard, D and Fessard, A: Recent advances on the neurophysiological bases of pain sensation. ACTA Neurobiol Exp 35:715, 1975.

Appel, SH (ed): Current Neurology, volume 5. John Wiley & Sons, New York, 1984.

Asbury, AK, McKhann, GM, and McDonald, WI (eds): Diseases of the Nervous System, vol 1. WB Saunders, Philadelphia, 1986.

Asbury, AK, McKhann, GM, and McDonald, WI (eds): Diseases of the Nervous System, volume 2. WB Saunders, Philadelphia, 1986.

Bender, MB, Stacy, C, and Cohen, J: Agraphesthesia: A disorder of directional cutaneous kinesthesia or a disorientation in cutaneous space. Journal of the Neurological Sciences 53:531, 1982.

Burgess, PR, et al: Signaling of kinesthetic information by peripheral sensory receptors. Ann Rev Neurosci 5:171, 1982.

Dannenbaum, R and Dykes, RW: Evaluation of cutaneous sensation in myelodysplastic children, using electrical stimulation. Developmental Medicine and Child Neurology 26:184, 1984.

Dellon, AL: Evaluation of Sensibility and Re-education of Sensation in the Hand. Williams & Wilkins, Baltimore, 1981.

Dellon, AL: The moving two-point discrimination test: Clinical evaluation of the quickly-adapting fiber/receptor system. J Hand Surg 3:474, 1978.

Dellon, AL, Curtis, RM, and Edgerton, MT: Evaluating recovery of sensation in the hand following nerve injury. The Johns Hopkins Medical Journal 130:235, 1972.

Dyck, PJ, et al: Clinical versus quantitative evaluation of cutaneous sensation. Arch Neurol 33:651, 1976.

Dyck, PJ, Schultz, PW, and O'Brien, PC: Quantitation of touch-pressure sensation. Arch Neurol 26:465, 1972.

Dykes, RW: Parallel processing of somatosensory information: A theory. Brain Res Rev 6:47, 1983.

Elfant, IL: Correlation between kinesthetic discrimination and manual dexterity. Am J Occup Ther 31:23, 1977.

Huss, AJ: Sensorimotor Approaches. In Hopkins, HL and Smith, HD (eds): Willard and Spackman's Occupational Therapy, ed 6. JB Lippincott, Philadelphia, 1983, p 107.

Iggo, A and Andres, KH: Morphology of cutaneous receptors. Ann Rev Neurosci 5:1, 1982.

Kandel, ER and Schwartz, JH (eds): Principles of Neural Science, ed 2. Elsevier Science, New York, 1985.

McCloskey, DI: Kinesthetic sensibility. Physiological Reviews 58:763, 1978.

Merzenich, MM and Kaas, JH: Principles of organization of sensory-perceptual systems in mammals. Prog Psychobiol Physiol Psychol 9:1, 1980.

Moberg, E: Criticism and study of methods for examining sensibility in the hand. Neurology 12:8, 1962.

Mulder, DW, et al: Motor neuron disease (ALS): Evaluation of detection thresholds of cutaneous sensation. Neurology 33:1625, 1983.

Norrsell, U: Behavioral studies of the somatosensory system. Physiol Rev 60(2):327, 1980.

Russell, EW: Tactile sensation—an all-or-none effect of cerebral damage. J Clin Psychol 36:858, 1980.

Schmidt, RF (ed): Fundamentals of Sensory Physiology, ed 3. Springer-Verlag, New York, 1986.

GLOSSARY

Abarognosis: Inability to recognize weight.

Allesthesia: Sensation experienced at a site remote from point of stimulation.

Analgesia: Complete loss of pain sensibility.

Anesthesia: Loss of sensation.

Astereognosis: Inability to recognize the form and shape of objects by touch (syn: tactile agnosia).

Barognosis: Ability to recognize weight.

Causalgia: Painful, burning sensations, usually along the distribution of a nerve.

Dermatome: Cutaneous areas that correspond to the spinal segments providing their innervation.

Epicritic system: Division of sensory system described by Head (1920); refers to highly discriminative nerve fibers which allow perception of fine sensory stimuli.

Exteroceptors: Sensory receptors that provide information from the external environment.

Graphesthesia: Recognition of numbers, letters, or symbols traced on the skin.

Hypalgesia: Decreased sensitivity to pain.

Hyperalgesia: Increased sensitivity to pain.

Hyperesthesia: Increased sensitivity to sensory stimuli.

Hypesthesia: Decreased sensitivity to sensory stimuli.

Interoceptor: Sensory receptors that provide information about the body's internal environment (such as oxygen levels and blood pressure).

Kinesthesia (movement sense): Sensation and awareness of active or passive movement.

Pallesthesia: Ability to perceive or to recognize vibratory stimuli.

Paresthesia: Abnormal sensation such as numbness, prickling, or tingling without apparent cause.

Position sense: Sensation and awareness of static positions of a joint or body segment.

Proprioception: Sensation and awareness of body position and movements.

Proprioceptors: Sensory receptors responsible for deep sensations; found in muscles, tendons, ligaments, joints, and fascia.

Protopathic system: Division of sensory system described by Head (1920); refers to nerve fibers that allow perception of crude, nondiscriminative, poorly localized sensations such as pain and temperature.

Reliability: The level of consistency of either a measuring instrument or a testing method.

Sensation: The appreciation of stimuli through the organs of special sense (e.g., eyes, ears, nose), the peripheral cutaneous sensory system (e.g., temperature, taste, touch), or internal receptors (e.g., muscle, joint receptors).

Stereognosis: The ability to recognize the form of objects by touch.

Thalamic syndrome: Vascular lesion of the thalamus resulting in sensory disturbances and partial or complete paralysis of one side of the body; associated with severe, boring pain. Sensory stimuli may produce an exaggerated, prolonged, and/or painful response.

Thermanalgesia: Inability to perceive heat.

Thermanesthesia: Inability to perceive sensations of heat and cold.

Thermesthesia: Ability to perceive heat and cold sensations; temperature sensibility.

Thermhyperesthesia: Increased sensitivity to temperature.

Thermhypesthesia: Decreased temperature sensibility.

Two-point discrimination: Ability to recognize two blunt points applied to the skin simultaneously.

Validity: The degree to which an instrument or tool measures what it is designed to measure; the degree to which an assessment instrument or tool is able to predict future behavior.

Chapter 7

ASSESSMENT AND TREATMENT PLANNING STRATEGIES FOR PERCEPTUAL DEFICITS

CHAYE LAMM-WARBURG

OBJECTIVES

1. Explain why it is essential for physical therapists to be familiar with the signs of perceptual dysfunction.

2. Describe how visual disturbances affect the ability of the patient to participate in rehabilitation.

3. Explain how a patient can be assisted to compensate for body scheme/body image disorders.

4. Describe how spatial relations can affect the patient's ability to follow directions.

5. Explain the effect of the various agnosias on the patient's ability to recognize stimuli in the environment.

6. Differentiate between ideomotor, ideational, and constructional apraxia. Describe how a patient with apraxia might behave in response to different instructional sets commonly employed in rehabilitation.

7. Describe how the psychologic, emotional, and cognitive status of a patient with perceptual impairment may affect participation in assessment and treatment sessions.

INTRODUCTION

Adequate treatment of a patient with brain damage depends upon understanding the perceptual motor process—a chain of events through which the individual selects, integrates, and interprets stimuli from the body and the surrounding environment. A normally functioning system is a necessary key to successful interaction with the environment. The result of a malfunctioning system is ineffectual behavior.[1]

The primary objective of this chapter is to introduce the reader to concepts relating to perceptual dysfunction following brain damage. An important focus for the physical therapist should be on understanding how a particular perceptual disability might be manifested, and how assessment and treatment of movement disorders might be altered in a manner consistent with the abilities and limitations of the patient.

Disorders in the perceptual domain must be considered in order to assess fairly the patient's true residual abilities. For example, using sets of directions that would confuse the patient during a specific assessment (such as sensation, range of motion [ROM], manual muscle test [MMT], transfers, or gait analysis) may paint a picture of more or different disability than that which actually exists. Improper assessment sets the stage for useless therapy. Often the first clue to a perceptual problem appears during a routine, initial sensory-motor assessment. Awareness of the possibility and nature of perceptual deficits will signal the therapist to reorient the tone of the assessment. Throughout this chapter, the patient with hemiplegia in whom brain damage has occurred as a result of a stroke has been used to exemplify perceptual dysfunction.

RESPONSIBILITIES OF THE PHYSICAL AND OCCUPATIONAL THERAPISTS

Occupational therapists are the members of the rehabilitation team especially trained to assess and to treat perceptual dysfunction. They are responsible for the selection and administration of an appropriate constellation of assessment tools, accurate interpretation of results, and formulation of an overall program for perceptual rehabilitation.

In the hospital setting, the physical therapist is often the first member of the rehabilitation team to see a patient with brain injury. The physical therapist must understand the nature of perceptual dysfunction and recognize that individuals in certain diagnostic categories, such as stroke and traumatic head injury, are likely to behave in ways that indicate the presence of particular perceptual problems.[2] When this occurs the physical therapist should be aware that, whenever possible, it is appropriate to refer the patient to occupational therapy for assessment and remediation.

The assessment tools described in this chapter are included in order to assist the reader in understanding the nature of the different perceptual disabilities. They are not meant to be used as a substitute for an intensive assessment by a trained occupational therapist when one is available.

An understanding of perceptual dysfunction may go a long way toward alleviating much of the potential frustration that often accompanies treatment of a patient with brain damage, most of which is the result of inappropriate expectations of the therapist, the patient, and the family. Furthermore, by collaboration with the occupational therapist, with other members of the rehabilitation team, and with the family, consistent treatment strategies may be developed and carried out with obvious benefits to the patient.

SENSATION AND PERCEPTION

The terms "perception" and "sensation" are often confused with each other. **Sensation** may be defined as the appreciation of stimuli through the organs of special sense (e.g., eyes, ears, nose, and so forth), the peripheral cutaneous sensory system (e.g., temperature, taste, touch,

and so forth), or internal receptors (e.g., deep receptors in muscles and joints).[3]

Perception cannot be viewed as independent of sensation. However, the quality of perception is far more complicated than the recognition of the individual sensations.[3] Perception is the ability to select those stimuli that require attention and action, to integrate those stimuli with each other and with prior information, and finally to interpret them. The end result of this process enables the individual to make sense out of a complex and constantly changing internal and external sensory environment. Perceptual ability is clearly a prerequisite for learning,[4] and rehabilitation is largely a learning process.[5] Thus, it is not surprising that patients with perceptual disorders are limited in the ability to learn self-care and activities of daily living (ADL) skills; hence, as a group, they are more limited in their potential for achieving independence.[6,7]

In any rehabilitation program geared toward achievement of maximum independence by patients, there is a compelling need for therapists to learn to recognize behavior related to perceptual deficits. The therapist's modification of a treatment approach in light of these deficits will ensure that patients receive the full benefit of both assessment and treatment.[4]

CLINICAL INDICATORS

A perceptual deficiency ought to be suspected, assessed, or ruled out as a cause of diminished functioning in all patients suffering from brain damage, including those with stroke and traumatic head injury. It is a particularly likely culprit in cases in which the patient seems unable to participate fully in self-care tasks and has difficulty participating in physical therapy for reasons that cannot be accounted for by lack of motor ability, sensation, or comprehension. Perceptual dysfunction must be differentiated from premorbid cognitive perceptual deficits[8] and the general confusion and emotional sequelae which often accompany stroke and brain injury.

Often patients with perceptual difficulties will display the following characteristics: inability to do simple tasks independently or safely, difficulty in initiating or completing a task, difficulty in switching from one task to the next, and a diminished capacity to locate visually or to identify objects that seem obviously necessary for task completion. Additionally, they may be unable to follow simple one-stage instructions despite apparently good comprehension. They tend to make the same mistakes over and over. Activities may take an inordinately long time to complete, or they may be done impulsively. Patients may hesitate many times, appear distracted and frustrated, and exhibit poor planning. They are frequently inattentive to one side of the body and extrapersonal space, and they may deny the presence or extent of the disability. These characteristics, all or some of which may be present, often make participation in ADL and active therapy seem an insurmountable problem. They will be explained and expanded upon throughout the remainder of this chapter.

Two typical scenarios will be presented to give the reader a concrete idea of when perceptual dysfunction should be suspected. The first is a patient with a right hemisphere stroke who presents clinically with a left hemiparesis and with good speech. Upon observation in the nursing unit, the patient appears to have functional strength in the unaffected right extremities and fair return on the affected left side. Yet the patient seems to have difficulty with simple ROM activities even in the intact extremities, appearing confused and unable to move the arm up or down upon command. The patient can not seem to follow instructions on walking with a quad cane, constantly confusing the proper step sequence, and is unable to maneuver a wheelchair around the corner without crashing into the wall.

This patient should not be dismissed as uncooperative, intellectually inferior, or confused. Rather, the therapist should have the patient assessed by the occupational therapist for perceptual dysfunction. In this instance, the patient is likely to be having difficulty in **spatial relations, right-left discrimination,** and **vertical disorientation,** or perhaps left-sided neglect and **apraxia.** Further observation and assessment should reveal the precise cause of the difficulties.

Another example is a patient with left hemisphere damage and a resulting right hemiparesis and mild aphasia. The patient can respond reliably to yes or no questions and is able to follow simple one-stage commands such as "put the pencil on the table" or "give me the cup." However, if asked to point to the arm, or asked to imitate the therapist's movements during an active ROM assessment even with the unaffected limbs, the patient does not respond and appears totally uncooperative. During therapy the same patient is on a mat table. The therapist explains and then demonstrates the proper techniques for rolling to one side. The patient does not move. However, a moment later when his wife arrives, the patient quickly initiates rolling in an attempt to sit up and to greet his wife.

The astute therapist will realize that this patient may not be confused, stubborn, or uncooperative, as indeed he may appear. Rather, he may be suffering from a lack of awareness of body structure and relationship of body parts **(somatagnosia),** as evidenced by the assessment incident, and an inability to perform a task upon command or to imitate gestures **(ideomotor apraxia),** as demonstrated in the rolling episode.

ALTERATIONS IN BRAIN INPUT FOLLOWING BRAIN DAMAGE AND HOSPITALIZATION

The brain that has been damaged functions as a whole, just as it does in individuals without brain damage. When one part is damaged, the behavior observed is not merely the result of the brain operating precisely as in the intact individual minus the "function" of the area that was subject to anoxia. Rather, it is an outward manifestation of the reorganization of the entire central nervous system (CNS) at multiple levels working to compensate

for the loss.[9] It is important to realize that the patient must cope with a nervous system operating without normal sensory input at all levels, both cortical and subcortical.[9] Normal responses to environmental stimuli are difficult to obtain when the input upon which they have to act is deranged or incomplete. Recovery of function can be attributed to structural reorganization of the CNS into a new dynamic system widely dispersed within the cerebral cortex and lower formations.[10]

When a patient is hospitalized (with or without brain damage), it is important to realize that the inputs impinging on that patient's nervous system are radically different from the ones normally received. On the one hand, the environment is sensorially impoverished. There is no variation in temperature and lighting, and familiar background noises (e.g., familiar telephones, airplanes, dogs, and buses) are missing. On the other hand, an enormous array of unfamiliar noises are present: nurses talking, loudspeakers, and the whir of machines. Strange and different smells and unfamiliar, unavoidable, and unpleasant sights abound. Often, because of motor impairment, the patient can not move around to seek or to escape inputs; therefore, everything bombards the nervous system. Even if orienting responses are preserved, there is a profound sense of loss of control. This sensory derangement compounds the problems faced by the patient with brain damage, because those very abilities that enable the individual to select, to filter out, and to integrate incoming sensations in order to organize the self for appropriate action often fail in this sensorially bizarre environment.

To gain insight into the experience of the patient under such circumstances, it is enlightening to browse through the biographic and autobiographic reports of some noted neurologists and neuropsychologists, themselves victims or relatives of victims of cerebral vascular accidents. Particularly instructive are the reports of Bach-y-Rita,[11] Brodal,[12] and Gardner.[13]

THE PURPOSE OF ASSESSMENT

The presence of perceptual dysfunction must be confirmed if it is suspected to be interfering with the patient's ability to carry out functional activities[14] or to participate in any aspect of the rehabilitation program. It is often difficult to correlate perceptual deficits gleaned from testing with functional loss.[7,15] Therefore, formal testing is indicated only when there is a functional loss unexplained by motor deficit, sensory deficit, or deficient comprehension. It should be noted that not all areas of functional loss are typically detected within the hospital setting. It is not uncommon for the patient to perform adequately in self-care skills but then break down on higher-level tasks, such as driving, banking, or planning a meal. When appropriate, competence in these areas should be considered within the context of an ADL assessment.

The purpose of assessment is to determine which perceptual abilities are intact and which are limited. Understanding the manner in which a particular deficit influences task performance will foster the application of a therapeutic strategy in which intact capabilities may be used to compensate for or to overcome deficits.[7]

Failure in the performance of a task may result from any number of processes underlying perception. For example, a patient's inability to complete a jigsaw puzzle may result from an inability to see the picture (visual defect—**hemianopsia**) or difficulty in attending to one half of the picture (**unilateral neglect**). The patient may be incapable of listening to the instructions (attentional deficit), unable to know what the pieces are for (organizational deficit), or unable to manipulate them (**apraxia**). Although it is often difficult to implicate reliably one or another of these problem areas, the therapist must be aware of the different deficits that may produce a similar pattern of behavior.[14,16]

Assessment is not an end in itself.[14] Careful assessment paves the way for realistic and cost-effective treatment.[7] Continuous monitoring of the patient's perceptual status will ensure the use of appropriate treatment regimens and their modification when necessary.

PSYCHOLOGIC AND EMOTIONAL CONSIDERATIONS AFFECTING RESPONSE TO ASSESSMENT AND TREATMENT

Psychologic and emotional considerations play an important role in the patient's ability to cope with disability in general, as well as in the response to testing and assessment materials. The therapist needs to be aware of behaviors that typically reflect a patient's psychologic difficulties rather than particular perceptual abilities. Psychologic adjustment to disability depends upon many factors, including age, vocational status, education, economic situation, attitude toward the reactions of others,[5] family support, and feelings of competence prior to the onset of disease.

When assessing psychologic status the following should be noted: whether the patient is confused; what the level of comprehension is for verbal instructions (written and spoken); whether communication is enhanced through the use of visual cues and demonstration; the ability to recognize errors; cooperation and initiative—whether the patient is realistic about capabilities and goals; and emotional stability.[5] Disturbances of emotional response are evidenced by rapid and frequent mood changes and low frustration tolerance. Difficult tasks may cause a catastrophic reaction.

The patient's ability to detect relevant cues from the environment, or to discriminate between relevant and irrelevant stimuli (necessary for perceptual competence) may be adversely influenced by poor judgment, fatigue, and prior expectations. Poor judgment is a major contributor to accidents in patients with hemiplegia. This is related in part to the diminished awareness by these patients as to what they are and are not capable of doing. The ambiguity of having one set of limbs that work normally and one set that is not functional is one of the factors that may lead the patient to rely on solutions to the

problems of daily living that are familiar but now inappropriate.[17]

Anxiety over capabilities may inhibit maximum performance. The patient's capacity to learn is enhanced if anxiety can be reduced.[5] Motivation is influenced by many factors, among them premorbid personality. It is of utmost importance for the therapist to structure the therapeutic environment so that the patient will be positively motivated to learn to the maximum ability.[5] To this end, therapeutic tasks should be structured to ensure success, thereby diminishing frustration.

The frontal lobes of both hemispheres are involved in planning, abstract reasoning, and foresight.[3] Therefore, patients with frontal lobe involvement may present with additional symptoms. Family and hospital staff may complain of the patient's apparent apathy, poor or unreliable judgment, difficulty adapting to new situations, and/or lack of attention to the needs and feelings of others. In addition, a few of the symptoms experienced by patients with frontal lobe involvement may result in a diminished capacity for learning.[18] These are

1. Problems in starting. There appears to be a decrease in spontaneity, slower rate of activity, and decreased initiation. This may make the patient appear "lazy."

2. Problems in stopping. There appears to be a disinhibition of inappropriate responses. Overreacting and impulsiveness are common. An example of impulsiveness is when a patient neglects to lock the wheelchair brakes before standing, attempts to walk unaided when assistance is clearly needed, or touches a hot stove. The patient may or may not have perceptual deficiencies which complicate the ability to lock a wheelchair, or to learn to walk, but the impulsive tendencies add a further complication: the patient does not take the time to use the information available through intact senses to generate an appropriate response. Rather, the patient acts in the most habitual manner, failing to assess which is the most appropriate (safest) method for accomplishing the goal. The combination of perceptual deficits and poor judgment limits the ultimate degree of independence that a patient can achieve.[3]

3. Difficulties in making mental or behavioral shifts. The patient may have difficulty shifting attention from one thing to another, may perseverate both mentally and motorically, and appear inflexible.

4. Lack of self-awareness. The patient does not recognize errors, can not project the effect behavior may have on others, and displays a general lack of social awareness.

5. Concrete thinking. The patient lacks insight and takes everything at face value. Typically, the patient displays a lack of ability to plan, to use foresight, and to sustain goal-directed behavior. Ability to use or to form abstract concepts is impaired. Patients who have difficulty solving problems in abstract ways tend to function more adequately in familiar surroundings.[3]

The combination of impulsiveness, poor judgment, poor planning ability, and lack of foresight, particularly problematic in patients with left hemiplegia, does not bode well for independent functioning. These disabilities may diminish somewhat with the passage of time.[3]

Cognitive/Intellectual Deficits

One of the difficulties in assessing the outcome of perceptual tests is differentiating the results from cognitive or intellectual deficits. A number of the most common problem areas are delineated below.

MEMORY

Memory can be defined as "a mental process that allows the individual to store experiences and perceptions for recall at a later time."[19] All memory is not localized in one particular place in the nervous system; rather, many and perhaps all regions of the brain may contain neurons with the proper plasticity for memory storage.[20]

There are three stages of memory. **Immediate recall** involves retention of information that has been stored for a few seconds. **Short-term memory** mediates retention of events or learning that has taken place within a few hours or days. **Long-term memory** consists of early experiences and information acquired over a period of years.

The adequacy of memory functions can be assessed by having the patient recall lists or collections of objects that have just been presented (immediate recall), teaching the patient a new verbal or visual task and asking him or her to recall it a few hours or a day later (short-term memory), and requesting the patient to recall personal historical events (long-term memory). Frequently there is a loss of short-term memory following stroke, which particularly interferes with the patient's ability to benefit from rehabilitation, especially those activities involving the use of new and heretofore unfamiliar techniques.[14]

It is advisable to question the patient's family as to premorbid memory, inasmuch as many patients in the stroke-prone age group already have begun to experience declining memory as part of the aging process.

ATTENTIONAL DEFICITS AND DISTRACTABILITY

The inability of many patients with hemiplegia to pay attention during therapy is a frequent complaint of therapists. **Attention** is the ability to select and to attend to a specific stimulus while simultaneously suppressing extraneous stimuli. A patient who is inattentive or distractable will have difficulty in processing and assimilating new information or techniques.[19]

Diller and Weinberg[21] suggest that attention is not a unitary phenomenon. They have demonstrated that different aspects of attention seem to be impaired depending on the type of task and the side of the stroke. Tasks investigated required either scanning, searching the environment for clues; or spanning, retaining several bits of information at the same time. In addition, tasks could be divided into those requiring visual processing and those requiring verbal processing. As could be expected, on tasks that required auditory scanning, the performance of patients with right hemiplegia (generally language impaired) was inferior to that of those with left hemiplegia. And on tasks that required visual scanning, the performance of patients with left hemiplegia (generally impaired for visuospatial tasks) was inferior to that of those with right hemiplegia.

However, on spanning tasks, the findings were not as clear-cut. On verbal spanning tasks, in which the stimuli were not present at all times (i.e., they required verbal rehearsal) the patients with right hemiplegia did poorly. On verbal tasks in which the stimuli were present at all times, they performed adequately, because they could rely on the use of visual input to succeed in the task. Patients with left hemiplegia could not retain visual information long enough to succeed in the scan tasks but were able to use verbal rehearsal to improve their performance in the visual span tasks.

Clinically, ability to attend to a task (or to succeed in it by any measure) has significance for the therapist. Diller and Weinberg[21] suggest that to improve the performance, the patient with left hemiplegia should be trained to scan the visual environment. A patient scanning too quickly should be advised to slow down. Patients with right hemiplegia should be spoken to more slowly to afford them the chance to process verbal information.[21] This study also highlights the notion of encouraging patients with left hemiplegia to use verbalization to improve performance in visual tasks, and of encouraging the patient with right hemiplegia to use visualization techniques to attend to verbal tasks.

For many patients, inability to attend to significant stimuli is compounded by distraction from nonimportant stimuli in the environment. Often noise is the most distracting stimulus, causing irritability and diminished concentration. Ideally, distractable patients should be assessed in a noise-free, visually uninteresting environment.

Some additional tools that may be used for the remediation of attentional deficits and distractability are environmental restructuring, setting time limits or speed limits, amplification of stimuli, and making the crucial stimuli salient to the patient.[22] The environment can be structured by having the patient initially perform some aspect of therapy in a nondistracting setting and then slowly increasing potentially distracting elements, both visual and auditory, as patient tolerance improves.[4] For patients who have difficulty reading as a result of diminished concentration abilities, a card with a slit large enough for only one line to appear can be placed over the page while the patient reads. The slit is enlarged as the patient is able to tolerate more extraneous stimuli.[14]

ENVIRONMENT, CONTENT, AND LIMITATIONS OF THE FORMAL PERCEPTUAL ASSESSMENT

Environment

The patient should be sitting comfortably and wearing glasses and/or a hearing aid if needed. Ideally the room should be quiet and free of distraction. The therapist should be positioned opposite or next to the patient.[14]

Content

Age, sex, and hand dominance should be noted.[23] Perceptual dysfunction needs to be differentiated from sensory loss, language impairment, hearing loss, motor loss (weakness, spasticity, incoordination), visual disturbances (poor eyesight, hemianopsia), disorientation, and lack of comprehension. The patient should not be misjudged because of a cultural bias, such as a lack of experience in taking tests. Premorbid intellectual ability should be ascertained from an interview with family or friends, inasmuch as intellectual abilities may affect performance on some of the assessments and the patient's behavior in general. Premorbid memory should be determined as well.

Specific assessment tools will be described following each deficit in the section entitled "The Perceptual Deficits." Scoring on a particular task is either intact, impaired, or absent. The quality of the patient's response to the test media (e.g. how the task is approached, how and why the error is made) is as important to note as the success or failure in completing the task. Some aspects of response in the testing situation or during ADL can be referred to as the patient's individual "perceptual style." Included under this rubric are the patient's perceptual strategy, response to various cues, rate of performance, and consistency of performance.[24]

Limitations of Formal Perceptual Assessment

The performance of a patient who has had a stroke may vary from day to day; a single assessment session is, therefore, usually unreliable.[2] A number of short sessions scheduled on successive days are preferable. To enhance its practical value, perceptual testing must be done in conjunction with observation in self-care and ADL skills, in which the patient's judgment and discriminative abilities with regard to real life tasks can be determined. It is not uncommon for patients to test poorly for visual perceptual skills but to perform adequately in ADL with minimal effort or assistance.[22]

Technical issues surrounding formal assessment abound. There are little normative data on the sensory, motor, and perceptual abilities of the age group most prone to stroke.[25] Few test batteries or assessment tools have been examined experimentally in the adult post-stroke population and found to be both reliable and valid. Ideally, a test instrument should be able to define perceptual dysfunction as an entity, to define its components, and to predict recovery of functional independence accurately. Perhaps the greatest challenge would be the development of an assessment battery of which the results would indicate specific avenues of therapeutic intervention. One promising instrument under current investigation is the St. Mary's Evaluation.[26] It is based upon a high factor analytic loading of measures of **body scheme, figure ground, position in space, spatial relations,** and **astereognosis.**

The specific assessment tools that will be suggested below are used widely in the clinic. Most, however, are not standardized. The same holds true for treatment techniques. A few assessment devices are standardized on children but not adults. They are useful, however, for examining the quality of response to the test stimuli.

WALL'S ASSESSMENT AND TREATMENT PROCESS

It has been established that better functional results are achieved more quickly when patients are treated as soon as possible after the onset of any disability.[14,25] However, as with assessment techniques, there is a lack of conclusive evidence supporting specific treatments of isolated perceptual deficits. The treatment techniques that are suggested here for each disability area are those that appear to be of value in current clinical practice.

A six-stage program for the treatment of cognitive-perceptual-motor dysfunction has been outlined by Wall[7] and is presented as a succinct way of summarizing the assessment and treatment process.

1. Assessment

A thorough assessment of the patient in whom deficits are suspected is necessary in order to identify the specific perceptual problems. Assessment techniques will be included in the section describing specific perceptual deficits.

2. Time

It must be recognized that natural progress in overcoming or compensating for perceptual deficits may be slow but will be forthcoming in the first few weeks and months.

It is also necessary to recognize that it takes time for the patient, especially an elderly patient, to respond to therapy. Rushing either the assessment or the treatment will lead to frustration, which in turn will inhibit success. A great deal of patience is required on the parts of both the therapist and the patient.

3. Education

Education for the patient, family, and friends is essential for continuity of care. It is necessary to supply accurate information to all who interact with the patient. They should understand why it is inadvisable or impossible for the patient to do some things safely or independently, and why other things must be done in a specific way. Explaining why the patient behaves in a particular way reduces the likelihood of inappropriate expectations from those without the background to know that brain damage affects not only how the patient moves but how he or she experiences and thus responds to the world.

Feedback is essential in patient education. The

patient's own feedback may be inaccurate owing to perceptual and cognitive dysfunctions. Thus, the individual may be unaware that a task has not been accomplished or that it has not been performed in the safest or most efficient manner. The therapist must provide this feedback in the form of "knowledge of results" (KR), and "knowledge of performance" (KP). Knowledge of results is information regarding whether or not the patient accomplished the goal. Knowledge of performance is information regarding the manner in which the goal was reached.[27]

The form in which this feedback is delivered depends upon the specific limitations and strengths of the patient. For example, the physical therapy goal for a patient with left hemiplegia and visual perceptual involvement might be to walk to the end of the parallel bars. Knowledge of results would consist of a verbal confirmation by the therapist concerning whether or not the patient reached the end of the parallel bars. Knowledge of performance might include comments by the therapist concerning the correctness of the patient's visual scanning, positioning of the lower extremities, correct posture, and appropriate use of the upper limbs. For the verbally impaired patient the feedback would have to be visual. Tactile input also can be used effectively for patients with either right or left hemiplegia. A combination of inputs, using a number of sensory modalities, often facilitates patient success at a given task.

4. The Therapeutic Relationship

The patient must be addressed as an adult, and not patronized. He or she must be regarded as a principal participant in both the assessment and the treatment process. Open communication among the patient, staff, and family should be established early and maintained. In situations in which the perceptual deficit does not interfere with assimilation of information, the patient should have a major role in the decision-making process regarding the goals of therapy.

5. The Therapeutic Program

Three major approaches to perceptual rehabilitation are commonly employed. They are the **transfer of training approach,** the **sensorimotor approach,** and the **functional approach.** These have been delineated and described by Siev, Freishtat, and Zoltan.[28] The theoretic bases of these approaches will be explained in this section. Specific applications will be offered in the treatment suggestions following the description of individual perceptual deficits. These three models are not mutually exclusive—many therapists use a combination, guiding their selection by their clinical expertise and the patient's response to the various techniques. The functional approach will be emphasized because this is the most useful of the three for the physical therapist.

A fourth approach, tentatively termed **cognitive reha-**

bilitation, is a promising area of research which will be briefly mentioned.

THE TRANSFER OF TRAINING APPROACH

The underlying theory of the transfer of training approach is that practice in one task with particular perceptual requirements will enhance performance in other tasks with similar perceptual demands. Thus, doing specifically selected perceptual exercises, such as pegboard activities, parquetry blocks, puzzles, and the like, will facilitate improved performance in ADL and self-care activities. For example, Diller and coworkers[29] found that patients with left hemiplegia who received training in block design improved in their organization of eating behavior when compared with a control group. More recently Young and associates[30] demonstrated that training patients with left hemiplegia in block design, in addition to visual scanning and visual cancellation tasks, generalized to improvements in reading and writing, although no specific training in writing was offered. The available research is so sparse that it is difficult to assess the efficacy of this mode of treatment as a whole. However, if it is believed that such exercises would be beneficial, they can be incorporated into other components of the treatment program, such as those aimed at maintaining sitting or standing balance, weight-bearing exercises, or functional use of the affected extremities.

THE SENSORIMOTOR APPROACH

The Ayres model for treatment based upon neurophysiologic and development principles is the basis for the sensorimotor approach.[31,32] It was developed for the treatment of cognitive and perceptual problems in children. The underlying assumption is that by offering specific sensory stimulation and carefully controlling the subsequent motor output, one can influence the way in which the brain organizes and processes sensations. Integration of sensorimotor functions (tactile, proprioceptive, vestibular, and so forth) proceeds in a developmental sequence in the normal child. It is proposed that recapitulation of this pattern facilitates integration of these functions in the learning-disabled child, and in other pediatric populations as well.[31,32]

Some of the treatment modalities employed are rubbing or icing to provide tactile input, the use of resistance and weight bearing to impart proprioceptive input, and the use of spinning to provide vestibular input. Following the controlled sensory input, an adaptive motor response is required by the patient in order to integrate the sensations provided by the therapist. The use of compensatory or **splinter skills** (skills acquired in a manner inconsistent with, or incapable of being integrated with, those already present) is rigorously avoided in favor of remediating underlying deficits. For more detailed information the reader is referred to the work of Ayres.[31,32]

There are a number of problems with the application of this approach to adult populations. The treatment process is ordinarily quite lengthy. In addition, specific assessment and treatment regimens have been developed for and standardized on children, who presumably have sufficiently pliable nervous systems to be influenced by this form of therapy. The neurophysiologic literature is replete with examples of the ability of younger patients to compensate neurologically for abilities that would be completely lost in mature individuals with similar lesions.[10,33,34] Furthermore, a fully developed adult with diffuse cerebral damage may have other complicating medical concerns that actually contraindicate the use of some modalities employed by this therapeutic school. Many therapists are enthusiastically awaiting results of ongoing research using the Ayres approach in the post-stroke population.

THE FUNCTIONAL APPROACH

The basic premise of the functional approach is that repetitive practice of specific functional skills will enhance the patient's independence in those specific tasks. The proponents of this approach (this author included) favor emphasis on the remediation of the functional problem over the treatment of its underlying cause. For example, a patient with difficulty in depth and distance perception, who is therefore unable to navigate a flight of stairs, would be made aware of the problem and practice techniques to ensure the ability to climb stairs safely. However, problems might still be displayed in depth and distance perception in other areas of daily function.

In the functional approach, therapy is viewed as a learning process that takes into consideration the unique strengths and limitations of the individual patient. It is composed of two complementary components: compensation and adaptation. To compensate for the disability, the patient first has to be made aware of deficiencies (**cognitive awareness**) and then taught how to make allowances for them using intact sensations and perceptual skills. The patient should be taught specific techniques and assisted in developing functional habits. For example, if the patient has homonymous hemianopsia, the therapist should explain that because of the visual problem, the patient is seeing only one half of the environment. The patient should then be shown how to turn the head to compensate for the deficit. Environmental scanning would be incorporated into general therapy sessions as well. A few general suggestions when teaching compensatory techniques are (1) use simple directions, (2) establish and carry out a routine, (3) do each activity in a consistent manner, and (4) employ repetition as much as necessary.

Adaptation refers to the alteration of the environment. For example, if the patient cannot differentiate between right and left, or tends to neglect the left side of the body, a piece of red tape on the left shoe during gait training will allow the patient to attend better to the left side and thus to follow the therapist's instructions more accurately. The therapist can use the functional approach to assist patients in improving specific motor skills related to treatment goals.

There are several inherent benefits to the functional approach. First, the patient will be in the hospital for only a limited amount of time. Therefore, it seems most efficacious to concentrate on goal-directed, real-life activities inasmuch as independent performance of these activities is the ultimate goal of therapeutic intervention. Second, the activities are age appropriate and concrete and are clearly relevant to the patient's concerns. For this reason they tend to be the most "motivating." Third, tasks can be incorporated into the entire hospital experience. Dressing can be reinforced at bedside by the nursing staff, and eating skills can be reinforced at the appropriate times.

The major limitation of this approach is that the methods learned in one task can not be generalized to the performance of another task. It has been criticized as the teaching of "splinter skills," in which the causes of the dysfunction are not addressed, and an all-encompassing approach to other accompanying disorders is not considered.

COGNITIVE REHABILITATION

Cognitive rehabilitation focuses on how brain-injured individuals acquire and use knowledge. It is an approach that attempts to address memory, high language disorders, and perceptual dysfunction under one umbrella.[35] Information processing, problem solving, awareness, judgment, and decision making are among the areas addressed. The therapist using a cognitive remediation approach might be concerned with the patient's perceptual style, including perceptual strategy, response to different types of cues, and rate and consistency of task performance.[24] Diller and Gordon[36] provide a review of the literature pertaining to intervention strategies for cognitive deficits.

6. Discharge Planning and Continuity of Care

Once areas of perceptual dysfunction have been ascertained and remediation techniques have been implemented, the therapist will be able to advise the family as to the patient's need for assistance and to recommend appropriate plans for discharge.

IMPLICATIONS FOR TREATMENT

Data Collection and Task Analysis

The use of systematic data collection provides the scientific basis to guide treatment. Its importance can not be overemphasized with respect to all facets of therapeutic intervention, including perceptual remediation.

Task analysis is the breakdown of an activity or task into its component parts and a delineation of the specific motor, perceptual, and cognitive abilities necessary to perform each component. Task analysis is another tool that is critical to appropriate therapeutic intervention. For example, the strength, ROM, and balance abilities necessary to accomplish bed mobility and ambulation activities can be clearly defined by the physical therapist.

However, the specific perceptual and cognitive requirements of each step needed to perform these two tasks may not be known. Without a knowledge of the perceptual requirements for successful completion of a task, the therapist can not simplify the task for the patient and progressively upgrade it.

Visual Disturbances

Visual deficit is one of the most common forms of sensory loss affecting the patient with hemiplegia,[14] although it often receives little attention.[37] The lesion resulting in a stroke may affect the eye, the optic radiation, or the visual cortex, representing the reception, transmission, and appreciation, respectively, of any visual array. Visual disturbances commonly encountered by patients with hemiplegia are poor eyesight, diplopia, homonymous hemianopsia, damage to the visual cortex, and retinal damage. It is important to be aware of the presence of these deficits so as not to confuse them with visual perceptual deficiencies, and in order that they be taken into account during the course of therapeutic intervention.

Poor visual acuity is a frequent finding following stroke or head injury, even in the absence of other visual problems.[14] Therefore, it is recommended that the patient receive a comprehensive eye examination and have his or her eyeglass prescription checked.

Diplopia, or double vision, is often present following a stroke. The patient sees two of the entire environment. Diplopia is usually the result of decreased range of motion in one eye. Treatment usually consists of range of motion exercises for the eye muscles. In addition, the patient usually is instructed to wear a patch on alternate eyes until the condition clears. If the condition does not clear, the optometrist may recommend prisms.

Homonymous hemianopsia is probably the most common visual deficit affecting patients with hemiplegia,[14] occurring most frequently following damage to the middle cerebral artery near the internal capsule.[3] Recent studies indicate that the frequency of hemianopsia following a right-hemisphere stroke is as high as 46 percent.[38,39] In addition, there is a significant correlation between the presence of visual field deficits and visual neglect.[40] Most important, the presence of a visual field deficit is a significant prognostic sign, predicting both a higher death rate following stroke and poorer performance in ADL,[41] even following rehabilitation.[42]

Figure 7–1 demonstrates the normal functioning of the visual fields, in which the left side of the environment (the house) is perceived by the nasal retina of the left eye and the temporal retina of the right eye, and the right side of the environment (the tree) is perceived by the nasal retina of the right eye and the temporal retina of the left eye.[3]

The lesion producing homonymous hemianopsia interrupts inflow to the optic pathways on one side of the brain; this produces a loss of the outer half of the visual field from one eye and the inner half of the visual field of the other eye. The result is a loss of incoming information from half of the visual environment (left or right) contralateral to the side of the lesion. Thus the loss of the

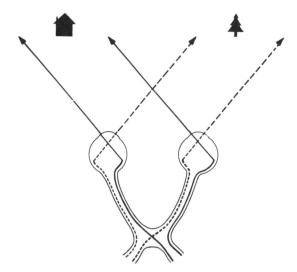

Figure 7–1. Normally functioning visual system; right and left visual fields. See text for explanation. From Sharpless, JW,[3] p 247, with permission of the publisher.

left half of the visual field accompanies left hemiplegia, and loss of the right visual field accompanies right hemiplegia. Figure 7–2 illustrates visual field deficits associated with a number of lesions to the visual system.

The presence of homonymous hemianopsia may inhibit performance in many daily activities. The patient is usually unaware of the condition and does not automatically compensate by turning the head unless specifically instructed. One of the dangers involved in this condition is illustrated in Figure 7–3.

The presence of homonymous hemianopsia is a hindrance to the performance of many activities of daily living. When presented with a tray of food, a patient with right homonymous hemianopsia may attend to the plate and fork on the left side and fail to "see" the knife, spoon, and cup on the right side of the plate (Fig. 7–4). Often a patient will read only one half of the page—to the midline or from the midline.

Because of its prevalence, it is essential for the therapist to assess for the presence or absence of hemianopsia. A number of techniques are currently employed. Jones[14] suggests that the therapist sit opposite the patient about 3 feet away and hold two pens behind the head, one in each hand (Fig. 7–5). The patient should have one eye covered. The therapist should instruct the patient to gaze directly at him or her and to indicate when and where the pens appear. The therapist should maintain the gaze and bring one pen from outside his or her own visual field slowly into view. The therapist then must note whether the patient sees the pen at the same time that the therapist does, or only when the pen has come close to or has crossed the midline. The test should be repeated from each side—right and left, from above, and from below.

An alternate method suggested by Pedretti[43] is to stand behind the seated patient and instruct the patient to look straight ahead at some object placed 6 to 10 feet away. The therapist holds a pencil or small flashlight behind the patient's head and slowly brings it into the patient's

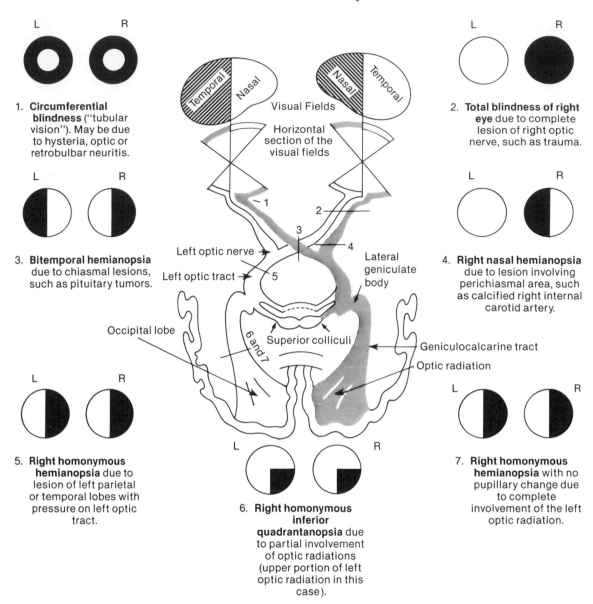

Figure 7–2. Visual field deficits and associated lesion sites. From Chusid, JG,[44] p 114, with permission of the publisher.

peripheral visual field in a semicircular arc (Fig. 7–6). The pencil or flashlight is held about 15 inches from the patient's head. The procedure should be repeated a number of times to verify the accuracy of the response. Notation is made as to whether the patient sees the pencil or flashlight when it is in the periphery or only when it is near the front of the eyes. Responses may be recorded graphically as in Figure 7–7.

Often the patient can be taught to compensate for hemianopsia by being made aware of the deficit and being instructed to turn the head to the affected side.[43] Patients usually require constant reminders at first, which may be tapered off over time. Early in therapy, items (e.g., eating utensils, writing implements) should be placed where the patient is most apt to see them (on the intact side). They can be moved progressively to the midline and then to the affected side, if appropriate. The nursing staff should be made aware of the condition and requested to place the patient's essential bedside needs

such as telephone, tissues, and so forth within the intact visual field. The therapist initially should sit on the patient's intact side when instructing or giving demonstrations and should alternate this with the affected side so that the patient receives maximum stimulation. Of course, the patient will have to be reminded to turn the head at first. For reading, a red line can be drawn on the left side of the page for patients with left hemiplegia. Red tape can be placed on the floor, mat, or parallel bars to attract the patient to the side of the environment that tends to be ignored. The patient should be taught to look for these cues. These external cues can be slowly tapered off over time. Exercises that require motor crossing of the midline can be used to reinforce visual crossing of the midline and turning of the head.[23]

Eye movement disorder is another area of visual dysfunction common to patients who have had a stroke. Eye movements, which are controlled by the extraocular muscles, are used to detect, to identify, and to derive

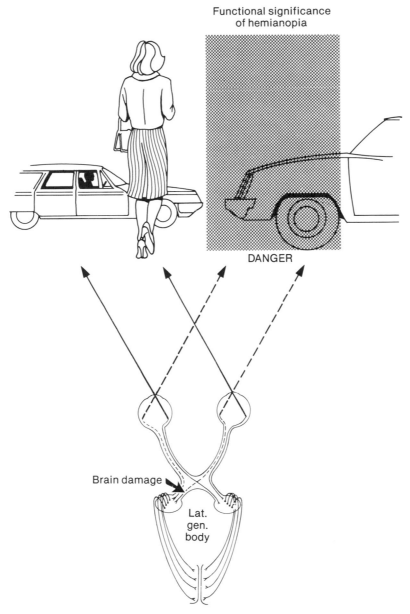

Figure 7–3. The functional significance of hemianopsia—it may lead to accidents. From Tobis, JS and Lowenthal, M,[5] p 78, with permission of the publisher.

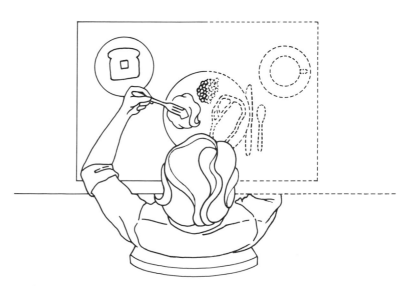

Figure 7–4. A table setting as it might appear to a patient with right homonymous hemianopsia following a stroke. The dotted lines indicate that she may be unable to locate her knife, spoon, cup, and so forth. From Sharpless, JW,[3] p 248, with permission of the publisher.

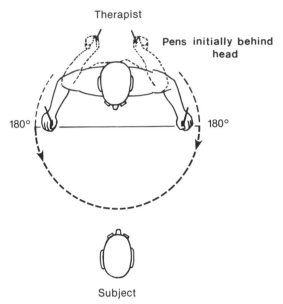

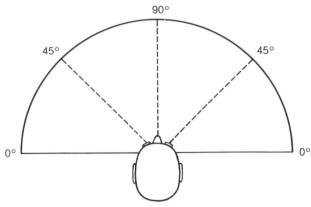

Figure 7–7. Graph for recording degrees of estimated visual field deficit. From Pedretti, LW, [43] p 110, with permission.

Figure 7–5. Method for assessing hemianopsia. See text for explanation. Modified from Pedretti, LW,[43] p 110, with permission of the publisher.

meaning from objects and visual signs in the environment. They allow a person to become oriented to and to explore the critical visual aspects of the environment.[9] Two types of eye movements are important to assess: (1) **fixation,** which allows the patient to maintain focus on an object as it is brought nearer or farther away; and (2) **ocular pursuits,** which enable the eyes to follow a moving object. Often the eyes will not follow a moving object visually, although the patient seems aware of the presence of that object and can locate it if asked. The patient is visually hypoactive. Eye movement disorder often

accompanies visual-perceptual dysfunction and is frequently related to attentional deficits.[22]

Aside from the visual sensory deficits outlined above, many patients suffer from visual-perceptual dysfunction. Damage to areas of the cortex upon which visual information converges with information from other senses may interfere with the recognition and interpretation of visual information, even though the visual stimuli may have arrived at the visual cortex uninterrupted. A total failure to appreciate incoming visual sensory information owing to a lesion in the cortex is referred to as **cortical blindness.** There is no statistical correspondence between the presence of visual field cuts and the presence of visual-perceptual disorders.[37] Similarly, there is no correspondence between **aphasia,** age, and time since infarct and measures of visual-perceptual dysfunction.[37] However, within the realm of visual perceptual disorders there is a significant difference between the performances of patients with right hemiplegia and those with left hemiplegia. Patients with left hemiplegia frequently have been found to perform more poorly on measures of visual perceptual dysfunction than patients with right hemiplegia. Thus, therapists should be aware of the possibility of visual-perceptual deficits particularly in the left hemiplegic population. Specific examples of visual-perceptual dysfunction are included within the four categories of perceptual disorders described in the following section.

Perceptual Deficits

This section is divided into four parts: disorders of body scheme and body image; spatial relations syndrome; agnosia; and apraxia, as outlined in Table 7–1. Each category encompasses a constellation of perceptual deficits which are grouped together for ease of understanding. Information pertaining to each deficit will be organized identically. Individual deficits will be defined (1), and clinical examples will be offered (2). An approximate lesion area will be identified (3), although for some disorders controversy exists as to the actual area of the cortex involved in producing a specific perceptual deficit, and to its laterality. When a cerebral hemisphere is des-

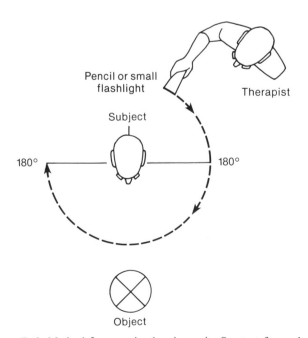

Figure 7–6. Method for assessing hemianopsia. See text for explanation. Modified, from Pedretti, LW,[43] p 110, with permission.

ignated it refers to the majority of cases cited in the literature. Exceptions do occur. Table 7–2 presents a compilation of perceptual disabilities associated with lesions of the right or left hemisphere of the brain. Finally, assessment methods in current use will be offered (4), as well as suggestions which the therapist may employ (5).

The value of dwelling upon probable areas of cortical damage is controversial. The indication of cortical loci is an attempt at relating the study of neuroanatomy to actual patient behavior related to perceptual dysfunction. It does not imply that the author is a strict localizationist. An examination of cortical loci will give the reader a sense of which perceptual deficits are likely to be seen together.

As therapists, we are required to assist the patient to bridge the gap between maladaptive behavior and independent function in activities of daily living. Whether or not the area of the brain purported to produce a particular dysfunction appears damaged on a computerized axial tomography (CAT) scan or other neurologic or radiologic test is not a key determinant of the rehabilitative approach to therapy. The patient's approach to task performance and the relative strengths or weaknesses of the patient (motorically, cognitively, and perceptually), which the therapist ascertains through thorough observation and assessment, are much more pertinent to the selection of appropriate therapeutic strategies than locus of the lesion.

Assessment tools are described for each perceptual disability in order to enhance the reader's awareness of the complexity of behavior ascribed to perceptual deficiencies. Familiarity with the tools used to assess perceptual dysfunction can serve as an aid in communication between physical and occupational therapists engaged in the treatment of the same patient.

The following section also includes specific treatment suggestions from the sensorimotor, transfer of training, and functional approaches described previously. The treatment techniques most relevant are those dealing with the functional approach and adaptation of the environment. In these sections examples are given as to how to facilitate the patient's success within a treatment session. Information is provided on how the therapist might gear language, demonstrations, feedback, and use of media and environment to the individual needs of the perceptually impaired patient.

BODY SCHEME/BODY IMAGE DISORDERS

Body image is defined as a visual and mental image of one's body that includes feelings about one's body, especially in relation to health and disease.[7,28] The term **body scheme** refers to a postural model of the body, including the relationship of the body parts to each other and the relationship of the body to the environment. Body awareness is derived from the integration of tactile, proprioceptive, and interoceptive sensations in addition to the individual's subjective feelings about the body.[1] An awareness of body scheme is considered one of the essential foundations for the performance of all purposeful motor behavior.[54] The two terms body image and body scheme are often used interchangeably.[49] Therefore, when researching this topic, close attention should be paid to the particular definition put forth by the author. Specific disturbances of body image and body scheme are **somatagnosia,** visual or **unilateral spatial neglect,** right-left discrimination, **finger agnosia,** and **anosognosia.**

Somatagnosia/Body Scheme Impairment

1. **Somatagnosia,** or impairment in body scheme, is a lack of awareness of the body structure and the relationship of body parts on one's self or on others. Patients with this deficit may display difficulty following instructions that require distinguishing body parts and may be unable to imitate movements of the therapist.[7] Often patients report that the affected arm or leg feels unduly heavy.[23] Lack of proprioception may underlie or compound this disorder.[2] Body scheme impairment is also termed **autopagnosia.**[55]

2. Clinically, the patient may have difficulty performing transfer activities because of not knowing what the therapist is referring to in instructions; for example, "Pivot on your leg and reach for the armrest with your hand." Often a patient with a body scheme disorder will have difficulty dressing. In addition, patients may have a hard time participating in exercises that require some body parts to be moved in relation to other body parts; for example, "Bring your arm across your chest and touch your shoulder."

3. The lesion site is the dominant parietal lobe,[44] or posterior temporal lobe.[45] Thus this disorder is seen primarily with right hemiplegia. However, impairment in body scheme may also occur in left hemiplegia.

Table 7–2 PERCEPTUAL DISABILITIES: SITE AND SIDE OF LESION

Lobe Vascular Supply*	Left Hemisphere Deficits (Dominant)	Right Hemisphere Deficits (Non-Dominant)

Temporal lobe
  Internal carotid artery
  Posterior cerebral artery
  Middle cerebral artery
	Somatagnosia[45]†
	Auditory agnosia[45]
	Ideomotor apraxia[44]
	Ideational apraxia[45]
	Constructional apraxia[46]
	Disorders of speech[46]
	Acalculia[46]
		Unilateral neglect[46]
		Constructional apraxia[46]
		Difficulty recognizing complex or incomplete visual stimuli[18]

Occipital lobe Posterior cerebral artery	Visual object agnosia[44] Simultagnosia[45] Prosopagnosia[47] Color agnosia[46] Constructional apraxia[18] Right homonymous hemianopsia[44] Sensory aphasia[44] Alexia[18] Agraphia[18] Acalculia[18]	Visual object agnosia[44] Color agnosia[44] Topographical disorientation[46] Depth and distance perception[48] Prosopagnosia[47] Dressing apraxia[45] Left homonymous hemianopsia[18] Symbol agnosia[18] Complex visual hallucinations[18]

Parietal lobe
  Internal carotid artery
  Anterior cerebral artery
  Posterior cerebral artery
  Middle cerebral artery
	Somatagnosia[44]
	Right-left discrimination[49]
	Finger agnosia[50]
	Gerstmann's syndrome[44]
	Visual object agnosia[46]
	Visual spatial agnosia[46]
	Astereognosis[18]
	Ideomotor apraxia[52]
	Ideational apraxia[45]
	Constructional apraxia[53]
	
	Aphasia[18]
	Alexia[18]
	Agraphia[18]
	Acalculia[18]
	Diminished logic[2]
		Unilateral neglect[46]
		Right-left discrimination[49]
		Finger agnosia[50]
		Anosognosia[44]
		Spatial relations syndrome[51]
		Figure ground discrimination[45]
		Form constancy[18]
		Position in space[18]
		Topographic disorientation[46]
		Vertical disorientation[18]
		Visual object agnosia[18]
		Visual spatial agnosia[18]
		Astereognosis[18]
		Dressing apraxia[45]
		Difficulty comprehending the emotional tone of language[20]

Frontal lobe‡
  Internal carotid artery
  Middle cerebral artery
  Anterior cerebral artery
	Motor aphasia‡
	Agraphia
	Verbal apraxia
	Motor apraxia
		Motor amusia
		Motor apraxia

*References for vascular supply are Lezak,[18] Chusid,[44] and McFie.[45]
†Superscripts refer to numbered references at end of chapter.
‡References for frontal lobe and motor aphasia information are Lezak,[18] Siev et al,[28] and Chusid.[44]

4. Assessment techniques:

a. The patient is requested to point to the appropriate body parts as named by the therapist on himself or herself,[54,55] on the therapist, and on a picture or puzzle of a human figure. For example, "Show me your feet. Show me your chin. Point to your back." The words "right" and "left" should not be used because they may lead to an inaccurate diagnosis in the case of a patient who has difficulty with right-left discrimination. Aphasia should be ruled out as a cause of poor performance.

b. The patient is asked to imitate movements of the therapist. For example, the therapist touches his or her cheek, arm, leg, and so forth. A mirror-image response is acceptable.[28,55]

c. The patient is requested to answer questions about the relationship of body parts. For example, "Are your knees below your head? Which is on top of your head, your hair or your feet?" For aphasic patients, questions should be phrased to require a yes or no or true or false response.[54] Patients with intact function in this area should respond correctly most of the time and within a reasonable period of time. Those patients with receptive aphasia are particularly likely to do poorly on tests for somatagnosia.[55]

5. Treatment suggestions:

a. The sensorimotor approach attempts to associate sensory input with an adaptive motor response.[28] Facilitation of body awareness is accomplished through sensory stimulation to the body part affected. For example, the patient is asked to rub the appropriate body part with a rough cloth as the therapist names it or points to it.[23]

b. With the transfer of training approach, the patient

verbally identifies body parts or points to pictures of them as the therapist touches them.[23]

Unilateral Visual or Spatial Neglect

1. Unilateral spatial neglect, sometimes termed visual hemi-inattention when referring to the visual component, is the inability to register and to integrate stimuli and perceptions from one side of the body and the environment. This is usually the left side of the body, and for purposes of this discussion, we will assume that it is the left. As a result, the patient ignores the left side of the body and stimuli occurring in the left personal space. This may occur despite intact visual fields or concomitantly with right or left homonymous hemianopsia, but it is not caused by it.[48] Frequently the patient has sensory loss on the affected side, compounding the problem. Although the patient with left-sided hemianopsia has actual loss of vision from the left visual field of both eyes, he or she may be aware of the problem and compensate automatically or learn to compensate by turning the head. The patient with visual neglect has intact vision but seems unaware of the problem and does not attempt to compensate spontaneously by turning the head. More time seems to be required in learning to compensate for this disability than with hemianopsia. There is great difficulty in integrating stimuli from the left half of the body and personal space for use in ADL. As with hemianopsia, the patient with visual spatial neglect often avoids crossing the midline visually or motorically.[23] It is important for the therapist to be familiar with this disorder inasmuch as it is a frequent clinical finding following a right hemisphere stroke.[38]

2. Clinically, the patient ignores the left half of the body when dressing and forgets to put on the left sleeve or left pants leg. Often a male patient will forget to shave the left half of his face. A woman may neglect to put makeup on the left side of her face.[56] The patient may neglect to eat from the left half of a plate and will start reading a newspaper from the middle of the line. Typically, the patient bumps into objects on the left side or tends to veer right when walking or propelling a wheelchair.

3. The right nondominant hemisphere[48] in the parieto-occipital association area.[18]

4. Assessment techniques:

a. Draw a man or draw a clock.[57] The patient is asked to copy simple drawings of a house, a tree, a man, and/or a clock. The drawings done by a patient with this deficit will have parts missing from the left half of the picture or be lacking in detail (Fig. 7–8). Differentiate these drawings from those likely to be produced by a patient suffering from **constructional apraxia,** in which most parts would be present but not in correct relation to each other. In addition, many patients with constructional apraxia (usually those with left hemisphere damage) will improve when copying a model, but those with unilateral neglect (usually right hemisphere damage) will not.

b. The patient is asked to read aloud. It should be noted if words are missed on the left half of the page or if there is hesitation at the beginning of a line.[58]

Examiner's drawings   Patient's drawings

Figure 7–8. Assessment for unilateral neglect. *(Left)* Therapist's drawing of a house and a flower. *(Right)* Impaired copying by a patient with unilateral neglect following a stroke. From Siev, E, Freishtat, B, and Zoltan, B,[28] p 61, with permission.

5. The purpose of therapy is to increase awareness of the left side of the body and space.

a. Cognitive awareness (based upon Weinberg and coworkers[59]): The patient is taught to be aware of the deficit through the method of visual scanning. This technique is used to assist the patient to become aware of the imbalance in perception of the two sides of space. The patient practices turning toward the left and shifting the eyes to the left (visual scanning). With experience, the patient will begin to trust visual cues to guide action. For example, a patient does not shave properly on his left (affected) side. When asked to touch both sides of his face, or to look in the mirror, he will not notice that anything is amiss. However, after being trained to systematically scan the visual environment, starting with the left side of his face, the patient may notice the unshaven side in the mirror. Subsequently, when asked to touch both sides of his face, he will confirm that one side is unshaven and take appropriate action.

A comprehensive and systematic training program for the treatment of right-brain-damaged patients, including the problem of left-sided neglect, has been developed over the past 15 years at the Department of Rehabilitation Medicine at New York University Medical Center in New York. For a detailed description of this program the reader is referred to Gordon and associates[56] and Weinberg and colleagues.[59,60]

b. Using the functional approach, repeated practice is used in particular areas of difficulty in ADL, such as transferring from a wheelchair or eating. The following steps are recommended by Stanton and associates.[61] Break down the activity into small components. Have the patient practice each one in sequence until a criterion level has been reached. Then taper the cues. Finally, arrange the activity into larger components. Keeping ongoing records of progress will assist the therapist in guiding treatment appropriately. Encourage verbal self-cuing in verbally intact patients. It is worthwhile to refer to the aforementioned article for further details concerning the systematic implementation of therapeutic procedures.

c. Adapt the environment. The patient is addressed and given demonstrations from the unaffected side. The nursing staff should place the patient's call button, telephone, and other essential paraphernalia on the unaffected side. A bold red line may be drawn on the side of the page that will be neglected.[62] A mirror may be placed in front of the patient while dressing or ambulating to draw attention to the neglected side.

d. Using the sensorimotor approach, the therapist stimulates the left side of the patient's body using a rough cloth, ice, or other material. The patient is reminded to watch what the therapist is doing. Next, the patient stimulates the affected side himself (herself) while watching.[23]

e. With the transfer of training approach, the patient participates in tasks that make it necessary to look toward the affected side,[60] such as watching television with the screen appropriately placed. For example, the television can be placed initially at the midline and progressively moved toward the affected side. A brightly colored tape track may be placed along the floor and the patient instructed to walk or to guide the wheelchair along it.[28]

Right-Left Discrimination

1. A disorder in **right-left discrimination** is the inability to identify the right and left sides on one's own body or on that of the examiner.[49] This includes the inability to execute movements in response to verbal commands that include the terms "right" and "left." Patients are often unable to imitate movements.[49]

2. Clinically, the patient can not tell the therapist which is the right arm and which is the left. The right shoe can not be discerned from the left shoe, and the patient is unable to follow instructions using the concept of right-left, such as "turn right at the corner." The patient can not discriminate the right from the left side of the therapist.

3. The lesion site is the parietal lobe of either hemisphere.[49] A close relationship between aphasia (usually owing to left hemisphere damage) and deficits in right-left discrimination has been reported. In nonaphasic patients (usually those with right hemisphere damage), a relationship has been reported between general mental impairment and right-left discrimination.[55]

4. The patient is asked to point to body parts upon command: right ear, left foot, right arm, and so forth.[43] Six responses should be elicited on the patient's own body, on that of the therapist, and on a model or picture of the human body.[55] To rule out somatagnosia, the patient should be tested first without the directional component.

5. Treatment techniques:

a. In giving instructions to the patient the words "right" and "left" should be avoided. Instead, pointing or providing cues using distinguishing features of the limb are more effective (e.g., "the arm with the watch"). These guidelines are particularly salient for therapists teaching locomotion or transfers, when confusing instructions may yield dangerous results.

b. Adapt the environment. The right side of all common objects such as shoes and clothing should be marked with red tape or seam binding.[62]

Finger Agnosia

1. **Finger agnosia** can be defined as the inability to identify the fingers on one's own hands or on the hands of the examiner.[49] This includes difficulty in naming the fingers upon command, identifying which finger was touched, and, by some definitions, mimicking finger movements. This deficit usually occurs bilaterally and is more common on the middle three fingers.[63] Finger agnosia correlates highly with poor dexterity in tasks that require movements of individual fingers in relation to each other[28] such as buttoning, tying laces, and typing. Bilateral finger agnosia with right-left discrimination, agraphia, and acalculia is termed Gerstmann's syndrome.[49] Gerstmann's syndrome usually is associated with a focal lesion of the dominant hemisphere in the region of the angular gyrus.[44]

2. Finger agnosia may be the result of a lesion located in either parietal lobe,[50] in the region of the angular gyrus, or in the supramarginal gyrus.[45] It is often found in conjunction with an aphasic disorder,[55] or with general mental impairment.[49,55]

3. A portion of Sauguet's test assessment[55] is recommended.

a. The patient is asked to name the fingers touched by the therapist, with the eyes open (five times) and if successful, with vision occluded (five times).

b. The patient is asked to point to the fingers named by the therapist on the patient's own hands (10 times), on the therapist's hands (10 times), and on a schematic model (10 times).

c. The patient is asked to point to the equivalent finger on a picture which is life size as each finger is touched by the therapist (Fig. 7–9).

d. The patient is asked to imitate finger movements; for example, curl the index finger, touch the thumb to the middle finger.

4. Treatment suggestions:

a. To apply sensory integrative principles, the patient's discriminative tactile systems (touch and pressure) are stimulated. A rough cloth can be used to rub the dorsal surface of the affected arm, hand, and fingers, and the ventral surface of the affected fingers. Pressure can be applied to the ventral surface of the hand. For details, see Siev, Freishtat, and Zoltan.[28]

b. To use the transfer of training approach, the patient is quizzed on finger identification.[28]

Anosognosia

1. **Anosognosia** is a severe condition including denial, neglect, and lack of awareness of the presence or severity of one's paralysis.[57,64,65] Presence of this disability may compromise rehabilitation potential greatly, because it limits the patient's ability to recognize the need for, and thus to use, compensation techniques.

2. Typically, the patient maintains that there is nothing wrong and may disown the paralyzed limbs and refuse to accept responsibility for them. The patient may claim

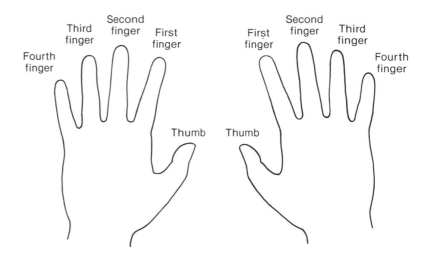

Figure 7–9. Hand chart for testing for finger agnosia (reduced from life size). Fron Siev, E, Freishtat, B, and Zoltan, B,[28] p 68, with permission.

that the limb has a mind of its own or that it was left at home, or in a closet. It has been observed that patients suffering from anosognosia have a tendency to cover the paretic arm.[66]

3. The lesion is usually located in the nondominant parietal lobe,[45] in the region of the supramarginal gyrus.[44]

4. Anosognosia is assessed by talking to the patient. The patient is asked what happened, whether paralysis is present, how it feels, and why the limbs can not be moved. A patient with anosognosia may deny the paralysis, say that it is of no concern, and fabricate reasons that the limbs won't move the way they should.

5. It is extremely difficult to compensate for this condition. Safety is of paramount importance in the treatment and discharge planning for patients suffering from anosognosia, because they typically do not acknowledge that they are disabled and will therefore refuse to be careful.[3]

SPATIAL RELATIONS SYNDROME

This syndrome encompasses a constellation of deficits that have in common difficulty in perceiving the relationship between objects in space or the relationship between the self and two or more objects.[28] Research suggests that the right parietal lobe has the primary role in space perception.[51] Thus a spatial relations deficit most frequently occurs in patients with right-sided lesions and resulting left hemiparesis.[45]

Spatial relations syndrome includes disorders of figure ground discrimination, **form constancy,** spatial relations, **position in space,** and **topographical disorientation.** Additional visuospatial deficits, such as depth and distance perception, will be discussed in this section. **Constructional apraxia** and **dressing apraxia** are sometimes viewed as spatial relations problems.[28]

Figure Ground Discrimination

1. A disorder in visual **figure ground discrimination** is the inability to distinguish visually a figure from the background in which it is embedded. Functionally, it interferes with the patient's ability to locate, visually, objects that are not well defined. The patient has diffi-

culty ignoring irrelevant visual stimuli and can not always select the appropriate cue to which to respond.[43] This often leads to distractability, resulting in a shortened attention span,[1] frustration, and decreased independent and safe functioning.[7]

2. Clinically, the patient cannot locate items in a pocketbook or drawer, locate buttons on a shirt, or distinguish the armhole from the remainder of a shirt. The patient may not be able to tell when one step ends and another begins on a flight of stairs, especially when walking down.

3. The predominant lesion is generally in the nondominant parietal lobe[45] but may be located in any part of the brain.[31]

4. Assessment techniques:

a. Ayres Figure Ground Test (subtest of the Southern California Sensory Integration Tests)[67]: The subject must distinguish the three objects in an embedded test picture, from a possible selection of six items as in Figure 7–10. It was originally standardized on children but may be useful in identifying perceptual disorders in brain-damaged adults.[18] Normative data have recently become available for normal adult males.[68]

b. Functional tests: A white towel can be placed on a white sheet, and the patient is asked to find the towel. The patient can be asked to point out the sleeve, buttons, and collar of a white shirt or to pick out a spoon from an unsorted array of eating utensils. It is necessary to rule out poor eyesight, hemianopsia, visual agnosia, and poor comprehension to improve the validity of these assessment techniques.

5. Treatment techniques:

a. Compensation through cognitive awareness: The patient is taught to become aware of the nature of the deficit. The patient should be cautioned to examine an array of objects slowly and systematically and should be instructed to use other, intact senses (for example, touch) to differentiate between objects. For example, when learning to lock a wheelchair, the patient should be advised to locate the brake levers by touch rather than by searching for them visually.

b. Adaptation and simplification of the environment: Red tape may be placed over the Velcro strap of the shoe or orthosis to aid the patient in locating it. Very few items should be placed in the patient's drawers or

Figure 7–10. An example of the figure-ground perception test. From Ayres, AJ.[67] Copyright © 1972 by Western Psychological Services. Excerpted from the Figure-Ground Perception Test Plates of the *Southern California Sensory Integration Tests (SCSIT)* and reprinted by permission of the publisher, Western Psychological Services, 12031 Wilshire Boulevard, Los Angeles, California, 90025, USA.

nightstand, and they should always be replaced in the exact location each time. Brightly colored tape can be used to mark the edges on stairs.

c. With the functional approach, repeated practice is used in each specific area of difficulty. The same procedure should be used each time, incorporating verbal cues and touch as adjuncts to vision.

d. Using the transfer of training approach, the therapist should arrange for practice in visually locating objects in a simple array (such as three very different objects), and progress to more difficult ones (four or five dissimilar objects or three similar ones).

Form Constancy

1. Impairment in **form constancy** is the inability to perceive or to attend to subtle differences in form and shape. The patient is likely to confuse objects of similar shape

or not to recognize an object placed in an unusual position.

2. Clinically, the patient may confuse a pen with a toothbrush, a vase with a water pitcher, or a cane with a crutch, and so forth.

3. The lesion site is the parieto-temporo-occipital region (posterior association areas) of the nondominant lobe.[18]

4. A number of items similar in shape and different in size are gathered. The patient is asked to identify them. One set of items might be pencil, pen, straw, toothbrush, watch, and the other might be key, paper clip, coins, and ring. Each object is presented several times in different positions (upside down, for example). Visual object agnosia must be ruled out as a cause for poor performance by first presenting objects separately and asking the patient to identify them or to demonstrate how they are used.

5. Treatment suggestions:

a. With the transfer of training approach, the patient should practice describing, identifying, and demonstrating the usage of similarly shaped and sized objects. The patient should sort like objects and should be assisted to focus on differentiating cues.

b. To achieve cognitive awareness and compensation, the patient must be made aware of the specific deficit. If the patient can read, often used and confused objects can be labeled. The patient should be encouraged to use vision, touch, and self-verbalization in combination.

Spatial Relations Deficit

1. A **spatial relations deficit**, or spatial disorientation, is the inability to perceive the relationship of one object in space to another object or to one's self. This may lead to, or compound, problems in constructional tasks and dressing.[43] Crossing the midline may be a problem for patients with spatial relations deficits.[23]

2. Clinically, the patient might find it difficult to place the cutlery, plate, and spoon in the proper position in setting the table. The patient may be unable to tell the time from a clock, owing to difficulty in perceiving the relative positions of the hands, as illustrated in Figure 7–11, or the patient may not know how to position arms, legs, and trunk in relation to the wheelchair when transferring.

3. The lesion site is predominantly the nondominant parietal lobe.[18]

4. Assessment techniques:

a. The therapist draws a picture of a clock and then asks the patient to fill in the numbers and to draw in the hands to designate a particular time.[43] Responses indicative of impaired perception of spatial relations are illus-

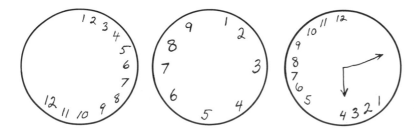

Figure 7–11. Responses to the draw-a-clock test, which may be indicative of defective perception of spatial relations. From Pedretti, LW,[43] p 109, with permission.

trated in Figure 7–11. Patients with poor eye–hand coordination can be requested to place markers in the appropriate positions instead of drawing numbers.

b. Two or three objects (such as matchsticks or pencils) are placed on a piece of paper in a particular pattern. The patient is asked to duplicate the pattern.

c. To improve the validity of these assessments, unilateral neglect and hemianopsia should be ruled out as the causes of poor performance. If these are present, position the stimulus array appropriately.

5. Treatment suggestions:

a. Using the transfer of training approach to improve the ability to orient one's self to other objects, the patient can be given instructions on positioning himself or herself in relation to the therapist or another object; for example, "Sit next to me," "Go behind the table," "Step over the line." In addition, the therapist can set up a maze of furniture. Having the patient copy block or matchstick designs of increasing difficulty will increase awareness of the relationship between one object (block or matchstick) and the next.

b. With the sensorimotor approach, if the patient avoids crossing the midline, activities that require crossing the midline both motorically and visually can be incorporated into other therapeutic activities. One specific activity is to have the patient hold a dowel with both hands. The therapist guides it from the uninvolved side to the involved side. Later, the patient can progress to manipulating the dowel with only verbal or visual cues, and finally guiding it independently.[23]

Position in Space

1. A deficit in the perception of **position in space** is the inability to perceive and to interpret spatial concepts such as up, down, under, over, in, out, front, and behind.

2. Clinically, if a patient is asked to raise the arm "above" the head during a range of motion assessment or if asked to place the feet "on" the footrests, the patient may behave as if he or she does not know what to do.

3. The lesion is located in the nondominant parietal lobe.[45]

4. To assess function, two objects are used, such as a shoe and a shoe box. The patient is asked to place the shoe in different positions in relation to the shoe box; for example, in the box, below the box, or next to the box. Alternatively, the patient is presented with two objects and asked to describe their relationship. For example, a toothbrush can be placed in a cup, under a cup, and so forth, and the patient asked to indicate the location of the toothbrush.

Another mode of assessment is to have the patient copy the therapist's manipulations with an identical set of objects. For example, the therapist hands the patient a comb and a brush. The therapist then takes an identical set and places them in a particular relationship to each other, such as the comb on top of the brush. The patient is requested to arrange his or her comb and brush the same way. Success in this task may represent sufficient ability to use position in space functionally.

Figure ground difficulty, apraxia, incoordination, and lack of comprehension should be ruled out when performing these assessments. Objects should be positioned

to avoid compounding of results with hemianopsia and unilateral spatial neglect.

5. Treatment suggestions:

a. To use the transfer of training approach, three or four identical objects are placed in the same orientation (wrist weights, combs, mugs, and so forth). An additional object is placed in a different orientation. The patient is asked to identify the odd one, and then to place it in the same orientation as the other objects.

b. The sensorimotor approach used for treatment of spatial relations is the same used for treatment of disorders of position in space.

Topographic Disorientation

1. Topographic disorientation refers to difficulty in understanding and remembering the relationship of one place to another.[28] As a result the patient is unable to get from one place to another, with or without a map.[54] This disorder is frequently seen in conjunction with other difficulties in spatial relations.[28]

2. Clinically, the patient can not find the way from the hospital floor to the physical therapy clinic despite being shown time after time. The patient can not describe the spatial characteristics of familiar surroundings, such as the layout of the bedroom at home.[48]

3. The lesion site is the occipito-parietal lobe of the nondominant hemisphere.[14,46]

4. The patient is asked to describe or to draw a familiar route, such as the block on which he or she lives, the layout of his or her house, or a major neighborhood intersection.[48] The impaired patient will be unable to succeed in this task.

5. Treatment suggestions:

a. Using the transfer of training approach, the patient practices going from one place to the another, following verbal instructions. Initially, simple routes should be used, and then more complicated ones.[28]

b. With the functional approach, important routes in the hospital or in the patient's home are repeatedly practiced.

c. Adapt the environment. Necessary or important routes can be marked with colored dots. The spaces between the dots are gradually increased and eventually eliminated as improvement takes place.[28] This is an example of taking a normally right-hemisphere task and (because there is right-sided damage) converting it into a left-hemisphere task. In this instance we take the spatial task of remembering routes (right-hemisphere task) and substitute sequential landmarks (sequencing is typically a left-hemisphere strength) to accomplish the same goal (getting from place to place).

d. To gain cognitive awareness, the patient must be instructed not to leave the clinic, room, or home unattended, because he or she may get lost.

Additional Visuospatial Deficits

Depth and Distance Perception

1. The patient with deficits in these areas experiences defective judgment of direction, distance, and depth. Spatial disorientation may be involved in faulty distance perception. Impaired depth perception, along with hemi-

anopsia, is one of the most common visual disturbances following a stroke.[69]

2. Clinically, the patient may have difficulty navigating stairs, may miss the chair when attempting to sit, or may continue pouring once a glass is filled.[1,28]

3. This may occur with a lesion in the right, nondominant hemisphere,[48] particularly in the occipital lobe.[18]

4. Assessment techniques:

   a. For a functional assessment of distance perception, the patient is asked to take or to grasp an object that has been placed on a table. The object is then held in front of the patient, in the air, and the patient is asked to grasp it. The impaired patient will overshoot or undershoot.[28]

   b. To assess depth perception functionally, the patient can be asked to fill a glass of water. A patient with a depth perception deficit may continue pouring once the glass is filled.[28]

5. Treatment suggestions:

   a. Help the patient become aware of the deficit (cognitive awareness). Stress the importance of walking cautiously, especially on the stairs.

   b. With the transfer of training approach, the patient is requested to place the feet on designated spots during gait training.[23] Also, blocks can be arranged in piles of 2 to 8 inches. The patient is asked to touch the top of the piles with the foot. This is done to reestablish a sense of depth and distance.[23]

   c. With the functional approach, practice in compensation for disturbances in depth and distance perception occurs intrinsically in many ADL activities.[69]

Vertical Disorientation

1. Vertical disorientation refers to a distorted perception of what is vertical. Displacement of the vertical position can contribute to disturbance of motor performance, both in posture and and in gait.[70] This is not influenced by presence or absence of homonymous hemianopsis.[7] Scores on one test for visual perception of the vertical position were found to correlate with differences in walking ability.[37]

2. An example of the way in which a person with distorted verticality views the world and the way this may affect posture is depicted in Figure 7–12.

3. The lesion site is in the nondominant parietal lobe.

4. The therapist holds a cane vertically and then turns it sideways to a horizontal plane. The patient is handed the cane and asked to turn it back to the original position. If the patient's perception of the vertical position is distorted, the cane will most likely be placed at an angle, representing the patient's conception of the world around.[14]

5. The patient must be made aware of the disability. The patient should be instructed to compensate by using touch for proper self-orientation, especially when going through doorways, in elevators, and on the stairs.

AGNOSIA

Agnosia is the inability to recognize familiar objects using one or more of the sensory modalities, while often retaining the ability to recognize the same object using other sensory modalities.[44] All types of agnosia represent an impairment in the transmission of the sensory signal to the conceptual level.

Visual Object Agnosia

1. **Visual object agnosia** is the most common form of agnosia.[58] It is defined as the inability to recognize familiar objects despite normal function of the eyes and optic tracts.[72] One remarkable aspect of this disorder is the readiness with which the patient can identify an object once it is handled (i.e., information is received from another sensory modality).[58] Visual object agnosia may occur with or without hemianopsia.[44] The patient may not recognize people, possessions, and common objects. Specific types of visual agnosia are described below.

Simultagnosia, also known as Balint's syndrome,[18] is the inability to perceive a visual stimulus as a whole. The patient perceives an entire array one part at a time. The lesion is in the dominant occipital lobe.[45]

Prosopagnosia was traditionally considered to be the inability to recognize faces as being familiar. This phenomenon is now thought to be related to any visually ambiguous stimulus the recognition of which depends upon evoking a memory context, such as different species of birds or different makes of cars. Prosopagnosia is usually accompanied by visual field defects. Bilateral functionally symmetrical occipital lesions are thought to be responsible for this deficit.[47]

Color agnosia is the inability to recognize colors; it is not color blindness. The patient is unable to name colors or to identify them upon command, although the ability to name objects is retained.[48] Color agnosia is frequently associated with facial or other visual object agnosias.[18,48] It is usually the result of a dominant hemisphere lesion.[46] The simultaneous occurrence of left-sided hemianopsia,

Degree of verticality

Figure 7–12. Vertical disorientation may contribute to disturbances of posture and gait. From Tobis, JS and Lowenthal, M,[5] p 37, with permission.

alexia, and color agnosia is a classic occipital lobe syndrome.[46]

2. The lesions associated with visual object agnosias are thought to occur in the occipito-temporo-parietal **association areas** of either hemisphere, which are responsible for the integration of visual stimuli with respect to memory.[44] The exact nature of the disability may be determined by the laterality of the lesion.[45] Color agnosia frequently accompanies diffuse dementia.[46]

3. To assess this disorder, several common objects are placed in front of the patient. The patient is asked to name the objects, to point to an object named by the therapist, or to demonstrate its usage. It is important to rule out aphasia and apraxia, although this is not easily done.

4. Treatment suggestions:

a. Using the transfer of training approach, drills can be used to practice discrimination between faces that are important to the patient (using photographs), in discrimination between colors, and common objects. The therapist should assist the patient in picking out salient visual cues for relating names to faces.

b. With compensation techniques, the patient is instructed to use intact sensory modalities—such as touch or audition—to distinguish people and objects.

Auditory Agnosia

1. Auditory agnosia refers to the inability to recognize nonspeech sounds or to discriminate between them. This rarely occurs in isolation from other communication disorders.[18]

2. For example, the patient can not tell the difference between the ring of a doorbell and that of a telephone, or between a dog barking and thunder.

3. The lesion is located in the dominant temporal lobe.[45]

4. Assessment is usually carried out by a speech therapist. The patient is asked to close the eyes and to identify the source of various sounds. The therapist rings a bell, honks a horn, rings a telephone, and so forth, and asks the patient to identify the sound (verbally or by pointing to a picture).

5. Treatment generally consists of drilling the patient on sounds, but this has not been found to be particularly effective.[15]

Tactile Agnosia or Astereognosis

1. **Tactile agnosia,** or **astereognosis,** is the inability to recognize forms by handling them, although tactile, proprioceptive, and thermal sensations may be intact. This condition commonly causes difficulties in ADL, inasmuch as many self-care activities that are normally done in the absence of constant visual monitoring require the manipulation of objects. If tactile agnosia is present in combination with unilateral neglect or sensory loss, performance in ADL may be severely hampered.[7]

2. If a patient is handed an object (key, comb, safety pin) with vision occluded, the patient will fail to recognize it.

3. The lesion is in the parieto-temporo-occipital lobe (posterior association areas) of either hemisphere.[18]

4. In assessment, the patient is asked to identify objects placed in the hand by examining them manually without visual cues (see chapter 6).

5. Treatment suggestions:

a. With the transfer of training approach, the patient practices feeling various common objects, shapes, and textures with vision occluded. The patient is instructed to immediately look at the object for visual feedback and note special characteristics of the object.

b. To achieve cognitive awareness, the patient is made aware of the deficit and is instructed in visual compensation.

APRAXIA

Apraxia is a disorder of voluntary learned movement. It is characterized by an inability to perform purposeful movements, which can not be accounted for by inadequate strength, loss of coordination,[73] impaired sensation,[3,44] or attentional difficulties.[74] The patient is unable to accomplish the task even though the instructions are understood.[44,75]

Ideomotor and **ideational apraxias** are generally thought to be the result of dominant hemisphere lesions and may be particularly difficult to assess in the aphasic patient. Although aphasia and apraxia often occur together, there is not a strong correlation between the severity of the aphasia and the severity of the apraxia. **Apraxia** is a disorder of skilled movement and not a language disorder.[75] **Dressing apraxia** and **constructional apraxia** occur with lesions in either hemisphere.

Ideomotor Apraxia

1. **Ideomotor apraxia** refers to a breakdown between concept and performance.[3] There is a disconnection between the idea of a movement and its motor execution.[69] It appears that information cannot be transferred from the areas of the brain that conceptualize to the centers for motor execution. Thus the patient with ideomotor apraxia is able to carry out habitual tasks automatically and describe how they are done but is unable to perform a task upon command and is unable to imitate gestures.[2] Patients with this form of apraxia often perseverate;[44] that is, they repeat an activity or a segment of a task over and over, even if it is no longer necessary or appropriate. This makes it difficult for them to finish one task and then to go on to the next.[3] Patients with ideomotor apraxia appear most handicapped when requested to perform tasks that require use of many implements and that have many steps. This form of apraxia can be demonstrated separately in the facial areas, upper extremity, lower extremity, and for total body movements.[73] Apraxic patients are often observed to be clumsy in their actual handling of objects.[74] Impairment is often suspected when observing the patient in ADL or during a routine motor assessment.

2. Several examples follow:

The patient is unable to "blow" on command. However, if presented with a lit match, the patient will spontaneously blow it out.[69]

The patient may fail to walk if requested to in the traditional manner. However, if a cup of coffee is placed on a table at the other end of the room and the patient is told, "please have some coffee," the patient is likely to traverse the room to get it.[2]

A male patient is asked to comb his hair, he may be able to identify the comb and even tell you what it is used for. However, he will not actually use the comb appropriately when it is handed to him. Despite this observation in the clinic, his wife reports that he combs his hair spontaneously every morning.

A female patient is asked to squeeze a dynamometer. She appears not to know what to do with it, although her comprehension is adequate, the task has just been demonstrated, and it is clear that she has adequate strength.

3. The lesion is generally found in the dominant supramarginal gyrus.[44,52]

4. Assessment techniques:

a. The Goodglass and Kaplan[73] test for apraxia is comprised of universally known movements, such as blowing, brushing teeth, hammering, shaving, and so forth. It is based on what the authors consider a hierarchy of difficulty for apraxic patients. First the patient is told, "Show me how you would bang a nail with a hammer." If the patient fails to do this or uses his or her fist as if it were a hammer, the patient is asked, "Pretend to hold the hammer." If the patient fails following this instruction, the therapist demonstrates the act and asks the patient to imitate. The apraxic patient typically will not improve after demonstration but will improve with use of the actual implements.[75] Ability to correct one's self upon following verbal suggestions is considered to be counterindicative of apraxia.

b. The therapist sits opposite the patient. The patient is asked to imitate different postures or limb movements.[67] The apraxic patient is unable to imitate postures. Additional apraxia tests may be found in Heilman.[75]

5. Treatment suggestions:

a. Anderson and Choy[23] suggest the modification of instructional sets as follows: Speak slowly and use the shortest possible sentences. One command should be given at a time, and the second command should not be given until the first task is completed. When teaching a new task, it should be broken down into its component parts. One component is taught at a time, physically guiding the patient through the task if necessary. It should be completed in precisely the same manner each time. When all the individual units are mastered, an attempt to combine them should be made. A great deal of repetition may be necessary.[7] Family members must be advised to use the exact approach found to be successful in the clinic. Performing activities in as normal an environment as possible is also helpful.

b. Using the sensorimotor approach, multiple sensory inputs are used on the affected body parts in order to enhance the production of appropriate motor responses.[76] The reader is referred to the work of Okoye[76] for additional details on this approach.

Ideational Apraxia

1. **Ideational apraxia** is a failure in the conceptualization of the task.[3] It is an inability to perform a purposeful motor act, either automatically or upon command, because the patient no longer understands the overall concept of the act,[7] can not retain the idea of the task,[44] and can not formulate the motor patterns required.[3] Often the patient can perform isolated components of a task but can not combine them into a complete act. Furthermore, the patient can not verbally describe the process of performing an activity, describe the function of objects, or use them appropriately.

Sharpless[3] claims that ideational apraxia is an unusual complication of stroke and is often present concomitantly with agnosias.

2. For example, when presented in the clinic with a toothbrush and toothpaste and told to brush the teeth, the patient may put the tube of toothpaste in the mouth, or try to put toothpaste on the toothbrush without removing the cap. Furthermore, the patient may be unable to describe verbally how toothbrushing is done. Similar phenomena may be evident in all aspects of ADL (washing, meal preparation, and so forth) and so may limit the safety and potential independence of the patient.[7] It has been shown that patients with ideational apraxia test poorly in the clinical situation and appear more able to perform ADL at the appropriate time and in a familiar setting.[76]

3. The lesion causing ideational apraxia is thought to be in the dominant parietal lobe.[45] This deficit also may be seen in conjunction with diffuse brain damage, such as cerebral arteriosclerosis.[44,45]

4. Assessment techniques:

a. The tests for ideational apraxia are essentially the same as those for ideomotor apraxia. The major difference to be expected in response is that the patient with ideomotor apraxia can perform a motor act spontaneously and automatically at the appropriate time, but the patient with ideational apraxia is unable to do so.

5. The treatment techniques used are the same as those for ideomotor apraxia. Nevertheless, "the efficacy of any treatment approach for this disorder is doubtful."[15]

Constructional Apraxia

1. **Constructional apraxia** is characterized by faulty spatial analysis and conceptualization of the task.[3] It is most evident in the inability to produce two or three dimensional forms by drawing, constructing, or arranging blocks or objects spontaneously or upon command.[77] It hampers the patient's ability to manipulate the environment effectively because of an inability to construct things from component parts. Although able to understand and to identify the individual components, the patient can not place them into a correct meaningful relationship.[3]

This deficit is found in patients with lesions to either hemisphere, but upon testing there is a difference in the quality of their responses.[53,78] Patients with right-sided lesions appear to be more severely affected than those with left brain involvement.[78] They clearly lack the visuospatial ability to succeed in a task. Additionally, they lack perspective, are unable to place a figure in the appropriate position in space, and seem unable to analyze parts in relationship to each other.[78,81]

Patients with left-hemisphere damage seem to lack the analytic or planning ability necessary to initiate and perform movements in sequence to complete a constructional task.[69] In a study by McFie and Zangwill,[53] the left-lesioned group (in contrast to the right-lesioned group) rarely presented with unilateral neglect or topographic disorientation but often demonstrated impairment in constructional tasks concomitant with general intellectual impairment.

The presence of constructional apraxia is thought to be related to body scheme disorders, often resulting in difficulty in dressing and diminished performance in other ADL skills[82,83]

2. For example, a patient understands all about sandwiches and what they are for but is unable to put one together.

3. Lesions are located in the posterior parietal lobe of either hemisphere.[53] Constructional apraxia is more common and more severe in patients with right-hemisphere lesions. Right-sided lesions that result in constructional apraxia tend to be less diffuse than left-sided lesions.[78]

4. Assessment techniques:

a. The patient is asked to copy a drawing of a house, a flower, or a clock face. Figure 7–13 depicts typical drawings of a house done by patients with left- and right-hemisphere lesions, respectively.

b. The patient is requested to copy geometric designs (e.g., circle, square, or T shape).

c. The patient is instructed to copy block bridges, matchstick designs, or pegboard configurations. Initially only three pieces are used and a progression is made to use of more.

Visuoconstructive difficulties found with right- and left-sided lesions demonstrate qualitative differences, as described above. In response to the assessment materials, patients with right-sided damage tend to draw on the diagonal and neglect the left side of the page.[78] They draw pieces of the picture without any coherent relationship to each other. Thus their drawings tend to be complex, yet unrecognizable.[53] They have immense difficulty with copying or constructing anything in three dimensions and are not helped by the presence of a model or by landmarks in a picture.[81] They do not generally improve with practice.[81]

In contrast, the drawings of patients with left-hemisphere damage are usually more recognizable.[78] They are characterized by great simplicity.[53] Patients with left-side lesions draw slowly and hesitatingly,[53] are often unable to draw angles, and have general difficulty in execution.[80] In contrast to that of right-hemisphere stroke victims, their performance often improves with the aid of a model,[78] the use of landmarks in drawing, and with repeated trials.[81] Short-term visual memory impairment is thought to be associated with constructional apraxia in patients with right-sided lesions.[51] The reader is encouraged to consult Warrington and coworkers,[51,77] who provide a comprehensive review of constructional apraxia, including many examples of the drawings of patients with right and left hemiplegia.

Verbal and comprehensional difficulties, poor manual dexterity and the presence of homonymous hemianopsia must be ruled out during assessment for this disorder.

5. With the transfer of training approach, the patient is asked to practice copying geometric designs, both by drawing and by building. Initially, simple patterns are used, progressing to the more complex.[28] Patients with left-hemisphere lesions may benefit from the use of landmarks, and then their gradual withdrawal as skill improves.[81]

Dressing Apraxia

1. **Dressing apraxia** is the inability to dress one's self properly owing to a disorder in body scheme or spatial relations,[18] rather than difficulty in motor performance or incoordination.

2. For example, the patient puts on clothes upside down, inside out, or backward; does not align buttons properly; puts both legs into one pant leg; neglects to dress one side of the body. Geometric patterns may add to the confusion.[3]

3. The lesion site is the nondominant occipital or parietal lobe.[45]

4. Clinical observation is the most effective method of assessment. The patient should be asked to dress and to undress. The patient is observed for the problems described above.

Since dressing apraxia and constructional apraxia exhibit a high degree of correlation, tests for constructional apraxia are sometimes performed.[82,83]

Figure 7–13. Impaired responses to the draw-a-house test for constructional apraxia. Note the differences in response between the patient with a left *(A)* versus a right *(B)* hemisphere lesion. From Siev, E, Freishtat, B, and Zoltan, B,[28] p 39, with permission.

A   Left hemisphere lesion   B   Right hemisphere lesion

5. Using the functional approach, the therapist develops a set sequence and pattern for dressing and has the patient practice the exact same routine daily. A key to successful performance is proper positioning of garments. One suggestion, for example, is to have the patient drape his or her shirt or blouse over the back of a chair and slide into it. Other guides are to start always from the bottom button, to mark the right side of all garments and shoes, and to color code the inside and the outside of garments.

SUMMARY

Perception—the process by which an individual selects, integrates, and interprets stimuli from the body and surrounding environment—is critical to the normal functioning of each human being. The patient with brain damage may be lacking in those abilities which allow one to make sense of and to respond appropriately to the outside world. It is essential for the physical therapist to be able to recognize when a patient is suffering from some type of perceptual dysfunction and to have the requisite tools to understand the causes of the behavior.

This chapter has attempted to provide an overview of the perceptual dysfunctions which may occur following brain damage, particularly that resulting from a stroke, and how they can affect the functioning of the patient, particularly within the context of the rehabilitation setting. The importance of differentiating perceptual dysfunction from problems related to lack of motor ability, inadequate sensation, poor language skills, and simple uncooperativeness has been emphasized.

Treatment in the form of adaptation of the physical environment and instructional sets and the teaching of compensatory techniques has been singled out as the most effective avenue for intervention. Although alluded to in a very abbreviated fashion, activity analysis and systematic data collection remain two of the most powerful tools at the disposal of the therapist attempting to develop a firm rationale for, and empirically to justify, the efficacy of any treatment regimen selected.

QUESTIONS FOR REVIEW

1. Describe the relationship between sensation and perception. How does perceptual impairment interfere with rehabilitation?

2. Differentiate between the roles of the occupational therapist and the physical therapist in the treatment of perceptual dysfunction following stroke.

3. What behaviors should prompt the therapist to suspect that a patient may have perceptual difficulties?

4. How does the hospital setting compound the difficulties faced by the patient who is attempting to make sense out of the environment following a stroke?

5. Describe some of the psychologic and emotional consequences of stroke that may affect the patient's performance during assessment and treatment sessions.

6. What behaviors are found following frontal lobe damage that may interfere with the ability to participate in rehabilitation?

7. Describe three stages of memory and assessment methods for each.

8. Explain how attentional deficits and distractability interfere with task performance. Under what circumstances would patients with left hemiplegia typically appear more handicapped? Under what circumstances would patients with right hemiplegia appear more handicapped? Suggest appropriate cues to facilitate improved performance.

9. Describe and differentiate between the two components of feedback: KR and KP. How should feedback for patients with right hemiplegia differ from that for patients with left hemiplegia?

10. Describe the theories underlying the transfer of training, the sensorimotor, and the functional approaches to the treatment of the perceptually disabled. Define and give clinical examples of compensation, adaptation, and cognitive awareness.

11. Define task analysis. Describe how this technique can be used to improve therapy.

12. Define and diagram homonymous hemianopsia. Give examples of how this disorder can interfere with the patient's success in ADL and therapeutic tasks. Describe ways in which the physical therapist can assist the patient to compensate.

13. Define body scheme and body image. Enumerate and describe five disorders that can be grouped in this category. Are they commonly found in patients with right or left hemiplegia?

14. Describe unilateral neglect. Give clinical examples of its manifestation. Describe how this disorder is assessed, and how it is differentiated from homonymous hemianopsia and constructional apraxia. Describe how the physical therapist can structure treatment sessions to help the patient compensate for this disability.

15. What is anosognosia? Why are safety considerations of paramount importance in dealing with the patient with anosognosia?

16. Describe spatial relations syndrome. Does it usually occur in patients with right hemiplegia or left hemiplegia? Describe disorders in figure ground discrimination, form constancy, spatial relations, position in space, and topographic disorientation. Give clinical examples of each.

17. Describe how the physical therapist might structure assessment and treatment sessions to facilitate successful participation of the patient with deficits in spatial relations and position in space.

18. Describe how faulty depth and distance perception and vertical disorientation affect ambulation, posture, and participation in other ADL. How can the physical therapist assist in the remediation of these conditions?

19. Define agnosia. Differentiate between the agnosias affecting vision, audition, and touch.

20. Differentiate between ideomotor and ideational apraxias, and offer clinical examples for each. Describe how the therapist can modify instructional sets to facili-

tate more successful participation of the patient in various tasks.

21. Define constructional apraxia and give clinical examples. Describe how patients with right versus left hemiplegia respond differently to drawing tasks.

REFERENCES

1. Halperin, E and Cohen, BS: Perceptual-motor dysfunction. Stumbling block to rehabilitation. Maryland Med J 20:139, 1971.
2. Johnstone, M: Restoration of Motor Function in the Stroke Patient, ed 2. Churchill Livingstone, New York, 1983.
3. Sharpless, JW: Mossman's A Problem Oriented Approach to Stroke Rehabilitation, ed 2. Charles C Thomas, Springfield, IL, 1982.
4. Spencer, EA: Functional restoration. In Hopkins, HL and Smith, HD (eds): Willard and Spackman's Occupational Therapy, ed 6. JB Lippincott, Philadelphia, 1983, p 353.
5. Tobis, JS and Lowenthal, M: Evaluation and Management of the Brain-Damaged Patient. Charles C Thomas, Springfield, IL, 1960.
6. Lehmann, JF, et al: Stroke rehabilitation: Outcome and prediction. Arch Phys Med Rehab 56:383–389, 1975.
7. Wall, N: Stroke rehabilitation. In Logigian, MK (ed): Adult Rehabilitation: A Team Approach for Therapists. Little, Brown & Co, Boston, 1982, p 225.
8. Adams, GF: Capacity after stroke. Br Med J 1:91, 1973.
9. Luria, AR: Higher Cortical Functions in Man. Basic Books, New York, 1966.
10. Moore, J: Neuroanatomical considerations relating to recovery of function following brain injury. In Bach-y-Rita P (ed): Recovery of Function: Theoretical Considerations for Brain Injury Rehabilitation. University Park Press, Baltimore, 1980, p 9.
11. Bach-y-Rita, P: Brain plasticity as a basis for therapeutic procedures. In Bach-y-Rita, P (ed): Recovery of Function: Theoretical Considerations for Brain Injury Rehabilitation. University Park Press, Baltimore, 1980, p 225.
12. Brodal, A: Self-observations and neuroanatomical considerations after a stroke. Brain 76:675, 1973.
13. Gardner, H: The Shattered Mind: The Person After Brain Damage. Alfred A. Knopf, New York, 1975.
14. Jones, M: Approach to Occupational Therapy, ed 3. Butterworths, London, 1977.
15. Siev, E and Freishtat, BF: Perceptual Dysfunction in the Adult Stroke Patient: A Manual for Evaluation and Treatment. Charles B Slack, Thorofare, NJ, 1976.
16. Sahs, AL, Hartman, EC, and Aronson, SM (eds): Guidelines for Stroke Care. DHEW Pub (HRA) 76-14017, US Department of Health, Education, and Welfare, Washington, DC, 1976.
17. Diller, L and Weinberg, J: Evidence for accident prone behavior in hemiplegic patients. Arch Phys Med Rehab 51:358, 1970.
18. Lezak, MD: Neuropsychological Assessment, ed 2. Oxford University Press, New York, 1983.
19. Strub, RL and Black, FW: The Mental Status Examination in Neurology, ed 2. FA Davis, Philadelphia, 1985.
20. Kupferman, I: Hemispheric asymmetries and the cortical localization of higher cognitive and affective functions. In Kandel, ER and Schwartz, JH (eds): Principles of Neuroscience, ed 2. Elsevier, New York, 1985, p 673.
21. Diller, L and Weinberg, J: Differential aspects of attention in brain-damaged persons. Perceptual and Motor Skills 35:71, 1972.
22. Abreu, BC: Interdisciplinary approach to the adult visual perceptual function-dysfunction continuum. In Abreu BC (ed): Physical Disabilities Manual. Raven Press, New York, 1981, p 151.
23. Anderson, E and Choy, E: Parietal lobe syndromes in hemiplegia: A program for treatment. Am J Occup Ther 24 (1):13, 1970.
24. Toglia, J and Abreu, BC: Cognitive Rehabilitation. Supplement to Workshop: Management of Cognitive-Perceptual Dysfunction in the Brain-Damaged Adult. Sponsored by Braintree Hospital, Braintree, MA, and Cognitive Rehabilitation Associates, New York, NY, May, 1987.
25. Carr, JH and Shepherd, RB: A Motor Relearning Programme for Stroke. Aspen, Rockville, MD, 1983.
26. Harlowe, D and Deusen, JV: Construct validation of the St Mary CVA evaluation: Perceptual measures. Am J Occup Ther 38:184, 1984.
27. Gentile, AM: A working model of skill acquisition with special reference to teaching. Quest Monograph 17:61, 1972.
28. Siev, E, Freishtat, BF, and Zoltan, B: Perceptual and Cognitive Dysfunction in the Adult Stroke Patient: A Manual for Evaluation and Treatment, rev ed. Charles B Slack, Thorofare, NJ, 1986.
29. Diller, L, Ben-Yishay, Y, and Gerstman, L: Rehabilitation, monograph 50: Studies in cognition and rehabilitation in hemiplegia. New York University Medical Center, New York, 1974.
30. Young, GC, Collins, D, and Hren, M: Efficacy of pairing scanning training with block design training in the remediation of perceptual problems in left hemiplegics, J Clin Neuropsychol 42:312, 1983.
31. Ayres, JA: Sensory Integration and Learning Disorders. Western Psychological Services, Los Angeles, 1972.
32. Ayres, JA: Sensory Integration and the Child. Western Psychological Services, Los Angeles, 1980.
33. Finger, S and Stein, DG: Brain Damage and Recovery: Research and Clinical Perspectives. Academic Press, New York, 1982.
34. Laurence, S and Stein, DG: Recovery after brain damage and the concept of localization of function. In Finger, S (ed): Recovery from Brain Damage: Research and Theory. Plenum Press, New York, 1978, p 369.
35. Giantusos, R: What is cognitive rehabilitation? J Rehab 46:36, 1980.
36. Diller, L and Gordon, WA: Intervention strategies for cognitive deficits in brain-injured adults. J Consul Clin Psychol 49:822, 1981.
37. Van Ravensberg, CD, et al: Visual perception in hemiplegic patients. Arch Phys Med Rehab 65:304, 1984.
38. Hier, DB, Mondlock, J, and Caplan, LR: Behavioral abnormalities after right hemisphere stroke. Neurology 33:337, 1983.
39. Kertesz, A and Dobrowolski, S: Right hemisphere deficits: Lesion size and location. J. Clin Neuropsychol 3:283, 1981.
40. Hier, DB, Mondlock, J, and Caplan, LR: Recovery of behavioral abnormalities after right hemisphere stroke. Neurology 33:345, 1983.
41. Haerer, AF: Visual field defects and the prognosis of stroke patients. Stroke 4:163, 1977.
42. Feigenson, JS, et al: Factors influencing outcome and length of stay in a stroke rehabilitation unit, part I. Stroke 8:651, 1977.
43. Pedretti, LW: Evaluation of sensation, perception and cognition. In Pedretti, LW (ed): Occupational Therapy: Practice Skills for Physical Dysfunction, ed 2. CV Mosby, St Louis, 1985, p 99.
44. Chusid, JG: Correlative Neuroanatomy and Functional Neurology, ed 19. Lange Medical Publications, Los Altos, CA, 1985.
45. McFie, J: The diagnostic significance of disorders of higher nervous activity. In Vinken, PJ and Bruyn, GW (eds): Handbook of Clinical Neurology, vol 4. Disorders of Speech, Perception, and Symbolic Behavior. American Elsevier, New York, 1969, p 1.
46. Hecaen, H: Aphasic, apraxic, and gnostic syndromes. In Vinken, PJ and Bruyn, GW (eds): Handbook of Clinical Neurology, vol 4. Disorders of Speech, Perception, and Symbolic Behavior. American Elsevier, New York, 1969.
47. Damasio, AR, Damasio, HD, van Hoesen, GW: Prosopagnosia: Anatomical basis and behavioral mechanism. Neurology 32:331, 1982.
48. Benton, A: Visuoperceptive, visuospatial, and visuoconstructive disorders. In Heilman, KM and Valenstein, E (eds): Clinical Neuropsychology. Oxford University Press, New York, 1979, p 186.
49. Benton, A: Body scheme disturbances: Finger agnosia and right-left discrimination. In Heilman, KM and Valenstein, E (eds): Clinical Neuropsychology. Oxford University Press, New York, 1979, p 141.

50. Gainotti, G: Emotional behaviour and hemispheric side of the lesion. Cortex 8:41, 1972.
51. Warrington, EK and James, M: Disorders in visual perception in patients with localized cerebral lesions. Neuropsychologia 5:253, 1967.
52. Hecaen, H and Sauguet, J: Cerebral dominance in left-handed subjects. Cortex 7:19, 1971.
53. McFie, J and Zangwill, OL: Visual-constructive disabilities associated with lesions of the left cerebral hemisphere. Brain 83:243, 1960.
54. Macdonald, J: An investigation of body scheme in adults with cerebral vascular accident. Am J Occup Ther 14:72, 1960.
55. Sauguet, J, Benton, AL, and Hecaen, H: Disturbances of the body scheme in relation to language impairment and hemispheric locus of lesion. J Neurol Neurosurg Psychiatry 34:496, 1971.
56. Gordon, WA, et al: Perceptual remediation in patients with right brain damage: A comprehensive program. Arch Phys Med Rehab 66:353, 1985.
57. Gregory, ME and Aitkin, JA: Assessment of parietal lobe function in hemiplegia. Occup Ther 34:9, 1971.
58. Wode, DT, et al: Stroke: A Critical Approach to Diagnosis, Treatment, and Management. Yearbook Medical Publishers, Chicago, 1986.
59. Weinberg, J, et al: Training sensory awareness and spatial organization in people with right brain damage. Arch Phys Med Rehab 60:491, 1979.
60. Weinberg, J, et al: Visual scanning training effect in reading related tasks in acquired right brain damage. Arch Phys Med Rehab 58:479, 1977.
61. Stanton, KM, et al: Wheelchair transfer training for right cerebral dysfunctions: An interdisciplinary approach. Arch Phys Med Rehab 64:276, 1983.
62. Burt, MM: Perceptual deficits in hemiplegia. Am J Nurs 70:1026, 1970.
63. Hecaen, H, et al: The syndrome of apractagnosia due to lesions of the minor cerebral hemisphere. Arch Neurol Psych 75:400, 1956.
64. Friedlander, WJ: Anosognosia and perception. Am J Phys Med 46:1394, 1967.
65. Ullman, M: Disorders of body image after stroke. Am J Nursing 64:89, 1964.
66. Zankle, HT: Stroke Rehabilitation. Charles C Thomas, Springfield, IL, 1971.
67. Ayres, JA: Southern California Sensory Integration Tests. Western Psychological Services, Los Angeles, 1972.
68. Peterson, P and Wikoff, RL: The performance of adult males on the southern California figure-ground visual perception test. Am J Occup Ther 37:554, 1983.
69. Trombly, CA: Stroke. In Trombly CA (ed): Occupational Therapy for Physical Dysfunction, ed 2. Williams & Wilkins, Baltimore, 1983, p 308.
70. Levenson, C: Rehabilitation of the stroke hemiplegia patient. In Krusen, FH, Kottke, FJ, and Ellwood, PM (eds): Handbook of Physical Medicine and Rehabilitation, ed 2. WB Saunders, Philadelphia, 1971, p 521.
71. Birch, HG, et al: Somesthetic influences on perception of visual verticality in hemiplegia. Arch Phys Med Rehab 43:556, 1962.
72. Dicmonas, E: Sensory system structure and function. In Abreu, BC (ed): Physical Disabilities Manual. Raven Press, New York, 1981, p 23.
73. Goodglass, H and Kaplan, E: The Assessment of Aphasia and Related Disorders, ed 2. Lea & Febiger, Philadelphia, 1983.
74. Geschwind, N: The apraxias: Neural mechanisms of disorders of learned movement. American Scientist, 63:188, 1975.
75. Heilman, KM: Apraxia. In Heilman, KM and Valenstein, E (eds): Clinical Neuropsychology. Oxford University Press, New York, 1979, p 159.
76. Okoye, R: The apraxias. In Abreu, BC (ed): Physical Disabilities Manual. Raven Press, New York, 1981, p 241.
77. Warrington, EK: Constructional apraxia. In Vinken, PJ and Bruyn, GW (eds): Handbook of Clinical Neurology, vol 4. Disorders of Speech, Perception, and Symbolic Behavior. American Elsevier, New York, 1969, p 67.
78. Piercy, M, Hecaen, H, and de Ajuriaguerra, J: Constructional apraxia associated with unilateral cerebral lesions—left and right sided cases compared. Brain 83:225, 1960.
79. DeRenzi, E and Faglioni, P: The relationship between visuospatial impairment and construction. Cortex 3:327, 1967.
80. Gainotti, G and Taicci, G: Patterns of drawing ability in right and left hemisphere patients. Neuropsychologia 8:379, 1970.
81. Hecaen, H and Assal, G: A comparison of constructive deficits following right and left hemisphere lesions. Neuropsychologia 8:289, 1970.
82. Lorenze, EJ and Cranco, R: Dysfunction in visual perception with hemiplegia—its relation to activities of daily living. Arch Phys Med Rehab 43:514, 1962.
83. Williams, N: Correlation between copying ability and dressing activities in hemiplegia. Am J Phys Med 46:1332, 1967.

SUPPLEMENTAL READINGS

Abreu, BC and Toglia, JP: Cognitive rehabilitation: A model for occupational therapy. Am J Occup Ther 41:439, 1987.
Adams, RD and Victor, M: Principles of Neurology, ed 3. McGraw-Hill, New York, 1985.
Appel, SH (ed): Current Neurology, vol 5. John Wiley & Sons, New York, 1984.
Carpenter, MB: Core Text of Neuroanatomy, ed 2. Williams & Wilkins, Baltimore, 1978.
Goldstein, G and Ruthven, L: Rehabilitation of the Brain-Damaged Adult. Plenum Press, New York, 1983.
Kandel, ER: Central representation of touch. In Kandel, ER and Schwartz, JH (eds): Principles of Neuroscience, ed. 2. Elsevier, New York, 1985, p 316.
Kandel, ER: Processing of form and movement in the visual system. In Kandel, ER and Schwartz, JH (eds): Principles of Neuroscience, ed 2. Elsevier, New York, 1985, p 366.
Kelly, JP: Auditory system. In Kandel, ER and Schwartz, JH (eds): Principles of Neuroscience, ed 2. Elsevier, New York, 1985, p 396.
Malkmus, D: Integrating cognitive strategies into the physical therapy setting. Phys Ther 63:1952, 1983.
Smith, GW: Care of the Patient with a Stroke: A Handbook for the Patient's Family and the Nurse, ed 2. Singer, New York, 1976.
Stein, DG, Rosen, JJ, and Butters, N (eds): Plasticity and Recovery in the Central Nervous System. Academic Press, New York, 1974.

GLOSSARY

Adaptation: Alteration of the environment in order to compensate for perceptual dysfunction.

Agnosia: The inability to recognize familiar objects with one sensory modality, while retaining the ability to recognize the same object with other sensory modalities.

Anosognosia: A perceptual disability including denial, neglect, and lack of awareness of the presence or severity of one's paralysis.

Aphasia: Absence or impairment of the ability to communicate through speech, writing, or signs owing to dysfunctions of brain centers.

Apraxia: A disorder of voluntary learned movement characterized by an inability to perform purposeful movements, which can not be accounted for by inadequate strength, loss of coordination, impaired sensation, attentional deficits, or lack of comprehension.

Association areas: Areas of the cerebral cortex that border on and are connected to the primary sensory areas; analyzes and synthesizes incoming isolated sensations into a whole or gestalt, so that complex environmental displays can be perceived and acted upon.

Astereognosis: The inability to recognize objects by handling them, although tactile proprioceptive, and thermal sensations may be intact.

Attention: The ability to select and to attend to a specific stimulus while simultaneously suppressing extraneous stimuli.

Autopagnosia: Impairment of body scheme.

Body image: A visual and mental image of one's body that includes feelings about one's body, especially in relation to health and disease.

Body scheme: A postural model of one's body, including the relationship of the body parts to each other and the relationship of the body to the environment.

Cognitive awareness: The knowledge that one has a deficit.

Cognitive rehabilitation: An approach to the remediation of cognitive-perceptual skills that focuses on how the individual acquires and uses knowledge, and seeks overall strategies for the brain-damaged patient to approach task performance.

Color agnosia: An inability to recognize colors.

Compensation: An approach to the treatment of the perceptually disabled that advocates use of intact abilities and alternate methods for solution to functional problems.

Constructional apraxia: Faulty spatial analysis and conceptualization of a task. It is most evident in the inability to produce two- or three-dimensional forms by drawing, constructing, or arranging blocks or objects, spontaneously or upon command.

Cortical blindness: A total failure to appreciate incoming visual sensory information owing to a lesion in the cortex, rather than injury to the eyes.

Dressing apraxia: An inability to dress one's self properly owing to a disorder in body scheme or spatial relations, rather than difficulty in motor performance or incoordination.

Figure ground discrimination: The ability to distinguish a figure from the background in which it is embedded.

Finger agnosia: The inability to identify the fingers on one's own hands or on the hands of the examiner, including difficulty in naming the fingers upon command, identifying which finger was touched, and mimicking finger movements.

Fixation: The ability to maintain focus on an object as it is brought closer to and farther away from the eyes.

Form constancy: The ability to perceive or to attend to subtle differences in form and shape. The perceptually impaired patient is likely to confuse objects of similar shape or to fail to recognize an object placed in an unusual position.

Functional approach: An approach to the treatment of perceptually impaired individuals which advocates practice in the specific functional tasks in which the patient is deficient, in order to enhance independence.

Hemianopsia: Inability to see half the field of vision in one or both eyes.

Homonymous hemianopsia: Blindness in the outer half of the visual field of one eye and the inner half of the visual field of the other eye, producing an inability to receive information from either the right or the left half of the visual environment.

Ideational apraxia: An inability to perform a purposeful motor act, either automatically or upon command; an inability to retain the idea of the task and to formulate the necessary motor patterns. The patient no longer understands the overall concept of the act.

Ideomotor apraxia: The inability to perform a task upon command and to imitate gestures, even though the patient understands the concept of the task and is able to carry out habitual tasks automatically.

Immediate recall: The ability to remember information that has been stored for a few seconds.

Long-term memory: A compilation of early experiences and information acquired over a period of years.

Memory: A mental process that allows the individual to store experiences and perceptions for recall at a later time.

Ocular pursuits: The ability of the eyes to follow a moving object.

Perception: The process of selection, integration, and interpretation of stimuli from one's own body and the surrounding environment.

Position in space disorder: The inability to perceive and to interpret spatial concepts such as up, down, under, over, in, out, front, and behind.

Prosopagnosia: An inability to recognize faces or other visually ambiguous stimuli as being familiar and distinct from one another.

Right-left discrimination disorder: The inability to identify the right and left sides on one's own body or on that of the examiner.

Sensorimotor approach: An approach to perceptual remediation that posits that by offering specific sensory stimulation and carefully controlling the subsequent motor output, one can influence the way in which the brain organizes and processes sensations.

Short-term memory: The retention of events or learning that has taken place within a few hours or days.

Simultagnosia: The inability to perceive a visual stimulus as a whole; also known as Balint's syndrome.

Somatagnosia: Impairment in body scheme; a lack of awareness of the body structure and the relationship of body parts on one's self or on others.

Spatial relations deficit: The inability to perceive the relationship of one object in space to another object or to one's self.

Spatial relations syndrome: A constellation of deficits that have in common difficulty in perceiving the relationship between objects in space, or the relationship between the self and two or more objects.

Included are disorders of figure ground discrimination, form constancy, spatial relations, position in space, and topographic disorientation.

Splinter skill: A trained or learned skill that is acquired in a manner inconsistent with, or incapable of being integrated with, skills the individual already possesses.

Tactile agnosia: The inability to recognize forms by handling them, although tactile, proprioceptive, and thermal sensations may be intact; also known as astereognosis.

Task analysis: The breakdown of an activity or task into its component parts and a delineation of the specific motoric, perceptual, and cognitive abilities that are necessary to perform each component.

Topographic disorientation: Difficulty in understanding and remembering the relationship of one place to another.

Transfer of training approach: An approach to perceptual remediation that posits that practice in tasks with particular perceptual requirements will enhance performance in tasks with similar perceptual demands.

Unilateral spatial neglect: The inability to register and to integrate stimuli and perceptions from one side of the body and the environment (usually the left). As a result, the patient ignores that side of the body and stimuli occurring on that side of personal space.

Unilateral visual neglect: The inability to register and to integrate visual stimuli and perceptions from one side of the environment (usually the left). As a result, the patient ignores stimuli occurring in that side of personal space.

Vertical disorientation: A distorted perception of the upright (vertical) position.

Visual object agnosia: The inability to recognize familiar objects despite normal function of the eyes and optic tracts.

Chapter 8

COORDINATION ASSESSMENT

THOMAS J. SCHMITZ

OBJECTIVES

1. Identify the purposes of performing a coordination assessment.

2. Describe the common coordination deficits associated with lesions of the cerebellum, basal ganglia, and dorsal columns.

3. Define the major areas of movement capabilities tested during a coordination assessment.

4. Describe the specific tests used to assess both nonequilibrium and equilibrium coordination deficits.

5. Describe the testing protocol for performing a coordination assessment.

INTRODUCTION

Coordination is the ability to execute smooth, accurate, controlled movements. The ability to produce these movements is a complex process which is dependent on a fully intact neuromuscular system. Coordinated movements are characterized by appropriate speed, distance, direction, rhythm, and muscle tension. In addition, they involve appropriate synergist influences, easy reversal between opposing muscle groups, and proximal fixation to allow distal motion or maintenance of a posture. *Incoordination* and *coordination deficit* are general terms used to describe abnormal motor function characterized by awkward, extraneous, uneven, or inaccurate movements.[1]

Physical therapists are frequently involved in management of coordination deficits. These deficits are often related to, and indicative of, the area of central nervous system (CNS) involvement of a particular diagnosis. Some locations of CNS involvement present very classic and stereotypical deficits, but others are much less predictable. Several examples of diagnoses that typically demonstrate coordination deficits related to CNS involvement include **Parkinsonism,** multiple sclerosis,

Huntington's disease, cerebral palsy, **Sydenham's chorea,** cerebellar tumors[2] and some learning disabilities.[3-5]

The purposes of performing a coordination assessment include the following:

1. To assess the ability of muscles or groups of muscles to work together to perform a task or functional activity.

2. To assist with goal setting and formulation of treatment plans.

3. To provide a basis for developing a program of therapeutic exercise designed to improve coordination.

4. To assist in determining methods to teach, to simplify, or to adapt an activity.[4]

5. To assist in selection of adaptive equipment that may facilitate performance or improve safety of an activity.

6. Over time, to determine the effects of therapeutic intervention or drug therapy on coordinated movement.

COORDINATION DEFICITS AND CNS INVOLVEMENT

Several areas of the CNS provide input to, and act together with, the cortex in the production of coordinated movement. These include the cerebellum, basal ganglia, and dorsal (posterior) columns. Although it is incorrect to assign *all* problems of incoordination to one of these sites, lesions in these areas are responsible for many characteristic motor deficits seen in adult populations. The following sections present a brief overview of the normal function of the cerebellum, basal ganglia, and posterior columns as well as common clinical features associated with lesions in each of these areas.

Cerebellum

The primary function of the cerebellum is concerned with coordination of motor activity, equilibrium, and muscle tone. Although all of the mechanisms of cerebellar function are not clearly understood, lesions of this area have been noted to produce typical patterns of incoordination, impaired balance, and decreased muscle tone.

Several theories of function of the cerebellum related to motor activity have been established. Among the more widely held is that the cerebellum functions as a *comparator* and *error-correcting mechanism*.[6-9] The cerebellum compares the *commands for movement* transmitted from the motor cortex with the *actual motor performance* of the body segment. This occurs by a comparison of information received from the cortex with that obtained from peripheral feedback mechanisms. The motor cortex and brainstem motor structures[10] provide the commands for the intended motor response. Peripheral feedback during the motor response is provided by muscle spindles, Golgi tendon organs, joint and cutaneous receptors, the vestibular apparatus,[11] and the eyes and ears. This feedback provides continual input regarding posture and balance as well as position, rate, rhythm, and force of slow movements of peripheral body segments.[8] If the input from the feedback systems does not compare appropriately (i.e., movements deviate from intended command), the cerebellum supplies a corrective influence. This effect is achieved by corrective signals sent to the cortex which, via motor pathways, modifies or "corrects" the ongoing movement (e.g., increasing or decreasing level of activity of specific muscles).[8] The cerebellum also functions to modify cortical commands for subsequent movements.[7]

This CNS analysis of movement information, determination of level of accuracy, and provision for error correction is referred to as a **closed-loop system.**[12] It should be noted that not all movements are controlled by this system. Stereotypical movements (e.g., gait activities) and rapid, short duration movements, which do not allow sufficient time for feedback to occur, are believed to be controlled by an **open-loop system.** In this system control originates centrally from a **motor program** which is a "memory" or preprogrammed pattern of information for coordinated movement. The motor system then follows the established pattern independent of feedback or error-detection mechanisms.[12]

CLINICAL FEATURES OF CEREBELLAR DYSFUNCTION

Specific clinical findings are associated with cerebellar disease. Many of these findings either directly or indirectly influence the ability to execute accurate, smooth, controlled movements. The clinical features identified emphasize the crucial influence of the cerebellum on equilibrium, posture, muscle tone, and initiation and force of movement. The following clinical signs are manifestations of cerebellar lesions.

1. **Hypotonia** is a decrease in muscle tone. It is believed to be related to the disruption of afferent input from stretch receptors and/or lack of the cerebellum's facilitory efferent influence on the fusimotor system.[13] A diminished resistance to passive movement will be noted, and muscles may feel abnormally soft and flaccid.[14] Diminished deep tendon reflexes also may be noted.

2. **Dysmetria** is a disturbance in the ability to judge the distance or range of a movement. It may be manifested by an overestimation (**hypermetria**) or an underestimation (**hypometria**) of the required range needed to reach an object or goal.

3. **Dysdiadochokinesia** is an impaired ability to perform rapid alternating movements. This deficit is observed in movements such as rapid alternation between pronation and supination of the forearm. Movements are irregular, with a rapid loss of range and rhythm.[11]

4. **Tremor** is an involuntary oscillatory movement resulting from alternate contractions of opposing muscle groups. Two types of tremors are associated with cerebellar lesions. An **intention,** or **kinetic, tremor** occurs during voluntary motion of a limb and tends to increase as the limb nears its extended goal.[7] Intention tremors are diminished or absent at rest.[6] **Postural,** or **static, tremors** may be evident by back-and-forth oscillatory movements of the body while the patient maintains a standing posture. They also may be observed as up-and-down oscillatory movements of a limb when it is held against gravity.[11]

5. **Movement decomposition** describes a movement performed in a sequence of component parts rather than as a single, smooth activity. For example, when asked to touch the index finger to the nose, the patient might first flex the elbow, then adjust the position of the wrist and fingers, further flex the elbow, and finally flex the shoulder.

6. **Disorders of gait** involve ambulatory patterns that typically demonstrate a broad base of support. The arms may be held away from the body to improve balance. Initiation of forward progression of a lower extremity may start slowly and then unexpectedly be flung rapidly and forcefully forward, audibly hitting the floor.[15] Gait patterns tend to be generally unsteady, irregular, and staggering, with deviations from an intended forward line of progression.

7. **Ataxia** is a general, comprehensive term used to describe the combined influence of cerebellar dysfunction (especially dysmetria and decomposition of movement)[16] on gait, posture, and patterns of movement.

8. **Dysarthria** is a disorder of the motor component of speech articulation. The characteristics of cerebellar dysarthria are referred to as *scanning speech*. This speech pattern is typically slow, may be slurred, hesitant, with prolonged syllables[7] and inappropriate pauses.[6] Word use, selection, and grammar remain intact,[7,11] but the melodic quality of speech is altered.[11]

9. **Nystagmus** is a rhythmic, oscillatory movement of the eyes. Several deficits related to eye movements are associated with cerebellar lesions. Nystagmus is the most common and causes difficulty with accurate fixation. It is typically apparent as the eyes move away from a midline resting point to fix on a peripheral object. An involuntary drift back to the midline position is observed.[15] Nystagmus is believed to be linked to the cerebellum's influence on synergy and tone of the extraocular muscles.[13]

10. The **rebound phenomenon** was originally described by Gordon Holmes. It is the loss of the check reflex,[15] or check factor,[17] which functions to halt forceful active movements. Normally, when application of resistance to an isometric contraction is suddenly removed, the limb will remain in approximately the same position by action of the opposing muscle(s). With cerebellar involvement, the patient is unable to "check" the motion, and the limb will move suddenly when resistance is released. The patient may strike himself or herself or other objects when the resistance is removed.

11. **Asthenia** is a generalized muscle weakness associated with cerebellar lesions.

In addition to these characteristic clinical features of cerebellar involvement, there also may be a greater length of time required to initiate voluntary movements. Difficulty also may be observed in stopping or changing the force, speed, or direction of movement.[14]

Basal Ganglia

The basal ganglia are a group of nuclei located at the base of the cerebral cortex. The three main nuclei of the basal ganglia include the *caudate,* the *putamen,* and the *globus pallidus.* These nuclei have close anatomic and functional connections with two other subcortical nuclei that are also frequently considered as part of the basal ganglia: the *subthalmic nucleus* and the *substantia nigra.*[9,16]

Although the influences of the basal ganglia on movement are not understood as clearly as those of the cerebellum, there is evidence that the basal ganglia play an important role in several complex aspects of movement and postural control. These include the initiation and regulation of gross intentional movements and the ability to accomplish automatic movements and postural adjustments. In addition, the basal ganglia play an important role in maintaining normal background muscle tone.[18,19] This is accomplished by the inhibitory effect of the basal ganglia on both the motor cortex and lower brainstem. The basal ganglia also are believed to influence some aspects of both perceptual[20] and cognitive functions.[20,21]

Clinical observation indicates that patients with lesions of the basal ganglia typically demonstrate several characteristic motor deficits. These are (1) poverty and slowness of movement; (2) involuntary, extraneous movement; and (3) alterations in posture and muscle tone.[18,21] Common diagnostic groups that demonstrate basal ganglia involvement are Parkinsonism, Wilson's disease, and Huntington's disease.

CLINICAL FEATURES OF LESIONS OF THE BASAL GANGLIA

Disorders of the basal ganglia present a unique pattern of deficits with characteristic involuntary movements, disturbances of muscle tone and posture, and diminished postural reactions. The following clinical signs are manifestations of basal ganglia lesions.

1. **Bradykinesia** is slowed or decreased movements. It may be demonstrated in a variety of ways such as a decreased arm swing; slow, shuffling gait; difficulty initiating or changing direction of movement; lack of facial expression; or difficulty stopping a movement once begun.

2. **Rigidity** is an increase in muscle tone causing greater resistance to passive movement. Two types of rigidity may be seen: *lead pipe* and *cogwheel*. Lead pipe rigidity is a uniform, constant resistance felt by the examiner as the extremity is moved through a range of motion. Cogwheel rigidity is considered a combination of the lead pipe type with tremor. It is characterized by a series of brief relaxations or "catches" as the extremity is passively moved.

3. **Tremor** is an involuntary, rhythmic, oscillatory movement observed at rest (**resting tremor**). Resting tremors typically disappear or decrease with purposeful movement but may increase with emotional stress. Tremors associated with basal ganglion lesions (e.g., **Parkinsonism**) are frequently noted in the distal upper extremities in the form of a "pill-rolling" movement, which appears as if a pill were being rolled between the first two fingers and the thumb. Motion of the wrist and pronation and supination of the forearm may be evident. Tremors also may be apparent at other body parts as well, such as the head.[6]

4. **Akinesia** is an inability to initiate movement and is seen in the late stages of Parkinsonism. This deficit is associated with assumption and maintenance of fixed postures.[20] A tremendous amount of mental concentration and effort is required to perform even the simplest motor activity.[8]

5. **Chorea** is a characteristic movement disorder associated with **Huntington's disease.** Features of chorea include involuntary, rapid, irregular, and jerky movements; also referred to as *choreiform movements.*

6. **Athetosis** is characterized by slow, involuntary, writhing, twisting, "wormlike" movements. Frequently, greater involvement in the distal upper extremities is noted, which may include fluctuations between hyperextension of the wrist and fingers and a return to a flexed position, combined with rotary movements of the extremities. Many other areas of the body may be

involved, including the neck, face, tongue,[8] and trunk; also referred to as *athetoid movements.* Pure athetosis is relatively uncommon and most often presents in combination with spasticity, tonic spasms, or chorea.[22] Athetosis is a clinical feature of cerebral palsy.

7. **Choreoathetosis** is a term used to describe a movement disorder with features of both chorea and athetosis.

8. **Hemiballismus** is sudden, jerky, forceful, wild, flailing motions of the arm and leg of one side of the body. Primary involvement is in the axial and proximal musculature of the limb. Hemiballismus results from a lesion of the contralateral subthalmic nucleus.[14-16]

9. **Dystonia** involves twisting, sometimes bizarre, movements caused by involuntary contractions of the axial and proximal muscles of the extremities.[15] Torsion spasms also are considered a form of dystonia, with spasmotic torticollis being the most common.[15] If the contraction is prolonged at the end of the movement, it is termed a *dystonic posture.*[20]

Dorsal (Posterior) Columns

The dorsal (posterior) columns play an important role in both coordinated movement and posture. The dorsal columns are responsible for mediating proprioceptive input from muscles and joint receptors. Proprioceptive input includes both position sense (awareness of the position of a joint at rest) and kinesthesia (awareness of movement).

Coordination deficits associated with dorsal column lesions are somewhat less characteristic than those produced by other CNS lesions. However, they typically result in equilibrium and motor control disturbances related to the patient's lack of proprioceptive feedback. Because vision assists in both guiding movements and maintaining balance, visual feedback can be an effective mechanism to compensate partially for a proprioceptive loss. Thus, coordination and/or balance problems will be exaggerated in poorly lit areas or when the patient's eyes are closed. In addition, some noticeable slowing of voluntary movements may be observed. This occurs because visually guided motions are generally more accurate when speed of movement is reduced.

Disturbances of gait are a common finding in dorsal column lesions. The gait pattern is usually wide-based and swaying, with uneven step lengths and excessive lateral displacement. The advancing leg may be lifted too high and then dropped abruptly with an audible impact. Watching the feet during ambulation is typical[15] and is indicative of a proprioceptive loss.

Another common deficit seen with dorsal column dysfunction is **dysmetria.** As mentioned earlier, this is an impaired ability to judge the required distance or range of movement and may be noted in both the upper and lower extremities. It is manifested by the inability to place an extremity accurately or to reach a target object. For example, in attempting to lock a wheelchair brake, the patient may inaccurately judge (overestimate, or underestimate) the required movement needed to reach the brake handle. As with other coordination deficits associated with dorsal column lesions, visual guidance will reduce the manifestations of dysmetria.

TESTING PROCEDURES

Preliminary Considerations

Accurate and careful observation is an important preliminary activity to performing a coordination assessment. Inasmuch as treatment activities will be geared toward improving functional activity levels, initial observations should focus here. Prior to specific testing procedures, the patient should first be observed performing a variety of functional activities. These may include bed mobility, self-care routines (dressing, combing hair, brushing teeth), transfers, eating, writing, changing position from lying or sitting to standing, maintaining a standing position, walking, and so forth.

During the initial observation general information can be obtained which will assist in localizing specific areas of deficit. This information will include

1. Level of skill in each activity (including amount of assistance or assistive devices required).

2. The occurrence of extraneous movements, oscillations, swaying, or unsteadiness.

3. Number of extremities involved.

4. Distribution of coordination impairment: proximal and/or distal musculature.

5. Situations or occurrences that alter (increase or decrease) coordination deficits.

6. Amount of time required to perform an activity.

7. Level of safety.

From this initial observation the therapist will be guided in selecting the most appropriate tests for the deficit areas noted. An initial screening of strength, sensation, and range of motion prior to the coordination assessment will improve validity because weakness, tactile deficits, and decreased range of motion all may influence coordinated movement. It is also important to note that coordination deficits may occur in the presence of normal muscle strength and intact sensation.

When assessing elderly persons, consideration must be given to the effects of aging on several aspects of movement abilities. Typical changes include slower reaction and movement times,[23] increased postural sway,[24,25] and decreased balance.[26] These changes may be accentuated further by alterations in muscle strength, sensation, perceptual skills, and so forth. Knowledge of these anticipated changes will improve the therapist's ability to interpret results of coordination assessments for older patients.

Coordination tests generally can be divided into two main categories: *gross motor activities* and *fine motor activities.* Gross motor tests involve assessment of body posture, balance, and extremity movements involving large muscle groups. Examples of gross motor activities include crawling, kneeling, standing, walking, and running. Fine motor tests involve assessment of extremity movements concerned with utilization of small muscle groups. Examples of fine motor activities include manipulating objects with the hands and finger dexterity, which involves skillful, controlled manipulation of tiny objects.

Coordination tests can be subdivided into *nonequilibrium* and *equilibrium* tests. Nonequilibrium coordina-tion tests assess both static and mobile components of movements when the body *is not* in an upright (standing) position. These tests involve both gross and fine motor activities. Equilibrium tests assess both static and

Table 8–1 NONEQUILIBRIUM COORDINATION TESTS[3,15,17]

1. Finger to nose	The shoulder is abducted to 90 degrees with the elbow extended. The patient is asked to bring the tip of the index finger to the tip of the nose. Alterations may be made in the initial starting position to assess performance from different planes of motion.
2. Finger to therapist's finger	The patient and therapist sit opposite each other. The therapist's index finger is held in front of the patient. The patient is asked to touch the tip of the index finger to the therapist's index finger. The position of the therapist's finger may be altered during testing to assess ability to change distance, direction, and force of movement.
3. Finger to finger	Both shoulders are abducted to 90 degrees with the elbows extended. The patient is asked to bring both hands toward the midline and approximate the index fingers from opposing hands.
4. Alternate nose to finger	The patient alternately touches the tip of the nose and the tip of the therapist's finger with the index finger. The position of the therapist's finger may be altered during testing to assess ability to change distance, direction, and force of movement.
5. Finger opposition	The patient touches the tip of the thumb to the tip of each finger in sequence. Speed may be gradually increased.
6. Mass grasp	An alternation is made between opening and closing fist (from finger flexion to full extension). Speed may be gradually increased.
7. Pronation/supination	With elbows flexed to 90 degrees and held close to body, the patient alternately turns the palms up and down. This test also may be performed with shoulders flexed to 90 degrees and elbows extended. Speed may be gradually increased. The ability to reverse movements between opposing muscle groups can be assessed at many joints. Examples include active alternation between flexion and extension of the knee, ankle, elbow, fingers, and so forth.
8. Rebound test	The patient is positioned with the elbow flexed. The therapist applies sufficient manual resistance to produce an isometric contraction of biceps. Resistance is suddenly released. Normally, the opposing muscle group (triceps) will contract and "check" movement of the limb. Many other muscle groups can be tested for this phenomenon, such as the shoulder abductors or flexors, elbow extensors, and so forth.
9. Tapping (hand)	With the elbow flexed and the forearm pronated, the patient is asked to "tap" the hand on the knee.
10. Tapping (foot)	The patient is asked to "tap" the ball of one foot on the floor without raising the knee; heel maintains contact with floor.
11. Pointing and past pointing	The patient and therapist are opposite each other, either sitting or standing. Both patient and therapist bring shoulders to a horizontal position of 90 degrees of flexion with elbows extended. Index fingers are touching or the patient's finger may rest lightly on the therapist's. The patient is asked to fully flex the shoulder (fingers will be pointing toward ceiling) and then return to the horizontal position such that index fingers will again approximate. Both arms should be tested, either separately or simultaneously. A normal response consists of an accurate return to the starting position. In an abnormal response, there is typically a "past pointing," or movement beyond the target. Several variations to this test include movements in other directions such as toward 90 degrees of shoulder abduction or toward 0 degrees of shoulder flexion (finger will point toward floor). Following each movement, the patient is asked to return to the initial horizontal starting position.
12. Alternate heel to knee; heel to toe	From a supine position, the patient is asked to touch the knee and big toe alternately with the heel of the opposite extremity.
13. Toe to examiner's finger	From a supine position, the patient is instructed to touch the great toe to the examiner's finger. The position of finger may be altered during testing to assess ability to change distance, direction, and force of movement.
14. Heel on shin	From a supine position, the heel of one foot is slid up and down the shin of the opposite lower extremity.
15. Drawing a circle	The patient draws an imaginary circle in the air with either upper or lower extremity (a table or the floor also may be used). This also may be done using a figure-eight pattern. This test may be performed in the supine position for lower extremity assessment.
16. Fixation or position holding	Upper extremity: The patient holds arms horizontally in front. Lower extremity: The patient is asked to hold the knee in an extended position.

Tests should be performed first with eyes open and then with eyes closed.
Abnormal responses include a gradual deviation from the "holding" position and/or a diminished quality of response with vision occluded.
Unless otherwise indicated, tests are performed with the patient in a sitting position.

dynamic components of posture and balance when the body *is* in an upright (standing) position. They involve primarily gross motor activities and require observation of the body in both static (stationary) and mobile (body in motion) postures.

Coordination tests focus on assessment of movement capabilities in five main areas: (1) *alternate or reciprocal motion,* which tests ability to reverse movement between opposing muscle groups; (2) *movement composition, or synergy,* which involves movement control achieved by muscle groups acting together; (3) *movement accuracy,* which assesses the ability to gauge or to judge distance and speed of voluntary movement; (4) *fixation or limb holding,* which tests the ability to hold the position of an individual limb or limb segment; and (5) *equilibrium and posture holding,* which assesses the ability to maintain balance and upright body posture.

Table 8–1 presents a sample of tests appropriate for nonequilibrium coordination testing, and Table 8–2 presents suggested tests for assessing equilibrium coordination. It should be noted that a single test is often appropriate to assess several different deficit areas, and areas may be tested simultaneously to conserve time. The tests contained here are intended as samples and are not all-inclusive. Other activities may be developed that are equally effective in assessing a particular deficit and may be more appropriate for an individual patient. It also should be emphasized that careful observation during performance of functional activities (e.g., self-care routines, wheelchair propulsion, transfers, and so forth) often provide an effective means for assessing many coordination deficits.

The two subdivisions of coordination tests presented here (nonequilibrium and equilibrium) have traditionally been used for providing structure and organization to administration of the tests. However, it should be noted that the "nonequilibrium" division presents something of a misnomer, inasmuch as elements of posture and balance are required during these tests. Although each subdivision places particular emphasis on certain components of movement, *there will clearly be overlap between assessment findings from the two subdivisions.*

Table 8–3 includes selected coordination deficits and suggested tests that would be appropriate to assess the given problem.

Testing Protocol

The following progression should be used in performing a coordination assessment.

1. *Gather equipment.*
   a. Coordination assessment form.
   b. Pen or pencil to record data.
   c. Stopwatch (for timed performance).
   d. Two chairs.
   e. Mat or treatment table.
   f. Method of occluding vision (if needed).

2. *Select location.* The most appropriate setting is a quiet, well-lit room, free of distractions.

3. *Test selection.* Tests should be selected (see Tables 8–1 and 8–2) to assess the specific components of movement appropriate for the individual patient. This activity will be guided by an initial observation of functional activities completed *prior to* formal coordination testing.

4. *Patient preparation.* Preferably, testing should be conducted when the patient is well rested. The testing procedures should be fully explained to the patient. Each coordination test should be described and demonstrated by the therapist prior to actual testing. Because testing procedures require mental concentration and some physical activity, fatigue, apprehension or fear may adversely influence test results.

5. *Testing.* Generally, nonequilibrium tests are completed first, followed by the equilibrium tests. Attention should be directed toward carefully guarding the patient during testing; use of a safety belt may be warranted. During the testing activities the following questions can be used to help direct the therapist's observations. The findings should be included in the *comment* section of the assessment form.
   a. Are movements direct, precise, and easily reversed?

Table 8–2 EQUILIBRIUM COORDINATION TESTS

1. Standing in a normal, comfortable posture.
2. Standing, feet together (narrow base of support).
3. Standing, with one foot directly in front of the other (toe of one foot touching heel of opposite foot).
4. Standing on one foot.
5. Arm position may be altered in each of the above postures (i.e., arms at side, over head, hands on waist, and so forth).
6. Displace balance unexpectedly (while carefully guarding patient).
7. Standing, alternate between forward trunk flexion and return to neutral.
8. Standing, laterally flex trunk to each side.
9. Walking, placing the heel of one foot directly in front of the toe of the opposite foot.
10. Walk along a straight line drawn or taped to the floor; or place feet on floor markers while walking.
11. Walk sideways and backward.
12. March in place.
13. Alter speed of ambulatory activities (increased speed will exaggerate coordination deficits).
14. Stop and start abruptly while walking.
15. Walk in a circle, alternate directions.
16. Walk on heels or toes.
17. Normal standing posture. Observe patient both with patient's eyes open and with patient's eyes closed (or vision occluded). If patient is able to maintain balance with eyes open but not with vision occluded, it is indicative of a proprioceptive loss. This inability to maintain an upright posture without visual input is referred to as a positive **Romberg sign.**

Table 8–3 SAMPLE TESTS FOR SELECTED MOTOR DEFICITS CONTRIBUTING TO COORDINATION PROBLEMS

Deficit	Sample Test
1. Dysdiadochokinesia	Finger to nose Alternate nose to finger Pronation/supination Knee flexion/extension Walking with alternations in speed
2. Dysmetria	Pointing and past pointing Drawing a circle or figure eight Heel on shin Placing feet on floor markers while walking
3. Movement decomposition	Finger to nose Finger to therapist's finger Alternate heel to knee Toe to examiner's finger
4. Hypotonia	Passive movement Deep tendon reflexes
5. Tremor (intention)	Observation during functional activities (tremor will typically increase as target is approached) Alternate nose to finger Finger to finger Finger to therapist's finger Toe to examiner's finger
6. Tremor (resting)	Observation of patient at rest Observation during functional activities (tremor will diminish significantly or disappear)
7. Tremor (postural)	Observation of normal standing posture
8. Asthenia	Fixation or position holding (upper and lower extremity) Application of manual resistance to assess muscle strength
9. Rigidity	Passive movement Observation during functional activities Observation of resting posture(s)
10. Bradykinesia	Walking, observation of arm swing Walking, alter speed and direction Request that a movement or gait activity be stopped abruptly Observation of functional activities
11. Disturbances of posture	Fixation or position holding (upper and lower extremity) Displace balance unexpectedly in sitting or standing Standing, alter base of support Standing, one foot directly in front of the other Standing on one foot
12. Disturbances of gait	Walk along a straight line Walk sideways, backward March in place Alter speed of ambulatory activities Walk in a circle

b. Do movements occur within a reasonable or normal amount of time?

c. Does increased speed of performance affect level (quality) of motor activity?

d. Can continuous and appropriate motor adjustments be made if speed and direction are changed?

e. Can a position or posture of the body or specific extremity be maintained without swaying, oscillations, or extraneous movements?

f. Are placing movements of both upper and lower extremities exact?

g. Does occluding vision alter quality of motor activity?

h. Is there greater involvement proximally or distally? On one side of body versus the other?

i. Does the patient fatigue rapidly? Is there a consistency of motor response over time?

6. *Documentation.* The results of each test activity should be recorded.

RECORDING TEST RESULTS

Protocol for assessing and recording results from coordination tests vary considerably among institutions and individual therapists. Owing to the nature of the assessment and the wide variation in types and severity of deficits, observational coordination assessments are not highly standardized. However, a number of standardized tests are available for upper extremity assessment. These tests assess specific components of manual dexterity through the use of functional or work-related tasks. Many of these tests were developed originally to assess personnel for recruitment to various employment activities. Several examples of these tests are discussed later in this chapter.

Several options are available for recording results from a coordination assessment. A *coordination assessment form* is frequently useful to provide a composite picture of the deficit areas noted. These forms are often developed within clinical settings. They may be general (a sample is included in the appendix to this chapter) or specific to a given group of patients, such as those with head injuries.[27] Generally, these forms tend to lack reliability testing. However, they do provide a systematic method of data collection and documentation. These forms frequently include some type of rating scale in which level of performance is weighted using an arbitrary scale. An example of such a scale follows:

4—Normal performance.

3—Movement accomplished with only slight difficulty.

2—Moderate difficulty is demonstrated in accomplishing activity, movements are arrhythmical, and performance deteriorates with increased speed.

1—Severe difficulty noted; movements are very arrhythmical; significant unsteadiness, oscillations, and/or extraneous movements are noted.

0—Unable to accomplish activity.

A score from the rating scale would then be assigned to each component of the coordination assessment. An advantage of using rating scales is that they provide a mechanism for qualitatively describing patient performance. However, several inherent limitations exist in using such scales. Often the descriptions are not reflective of exact patient performance. Or the rating scale may not be defined adequately or detailed appropriately, thus decreasing reliability of repeated or interexaminer testing. Frequently, coordination forms include a *comments* section. This component of the form allows for additional narrative descriptions of patient performance. Using a combination of a rating scale and narrative comments or summary will ensure that all deficit areas are adequately documented.

The use of a series of *timed tests* is another approach to assessing coordination. Because accomplishing an activity in a reasonable amount of time is a component of performance, the length of time required to accomplish certain activities is recorded by use of a stopwatch. A few standardized measurement tools have been developed based on timed activities. However, specific timed performance measures may be incorporated into a more general assessment form as well.

Computer assisted force-plates also have been used to measure one component of equilibrium coordination. This approach provides a qualitative assessment of sway (a measure of postural stability).[28,29] The force-plates are capable of monitoring fluctuations in vertical pressure exerted by the feet. They offer the important advantage of providing an objective measure of postural stability.

Finally, although a more costly method, *videotape recordings* have been used effectively for periodic assessment of coordination deficits. Videotapes provide a permanent, visual record of patient performance. They are particularly useful for assessing treatment and/or drug management via preintervention and postintervention recordings.

Although several options for documenting results are available, a written record using some type of assessment form is most common. An important consideration in establishing a protocol for recording test results is that each therapist is interpreting the form and/or rating scale in the same manner. This will require developing an instrument that is well defined, with distinct rating scale categories. Training sessions for new staff members and periodic reviews for the entire staff will improve interrater reliability.

STANDARDIZED INSTRUMENTS FOR ASSESSING MANUAL DEXTERITY AND COORDINATION

Several standardized tests have been developed to assess upper extremity coordination and hand dexterity through the use of functional activities. Many of these tests include normative data to assist with interpretation of test results. Strict adherence to the prescribed method of administration is imperative when using standardized tests. Any deviations from the established protocol will affect the validity and reliability of the measures and consequently make comparisons with published norms invalid. Skill of the examiner is another important consideration. The tests should be administered by an individual specifically trained in administration and interpretation of results. Subsequent retests should be performed by the same individual. These standardized tests are particularly useful in providing objective measures of patient progress over time. Several examples of these tests are described below.

The *Jebsen-Taylor Hand Function Test*[30] measures hand function using seven subtests of functional activities: writing, card turning, picking up small objects, simulated feeding, stacking, picking up large lightweight objects, and picking up large heavy objects. The test is easy to construct, to administer, and to score. Normative data are included related to age, sex, maximum time, and hand dominance. It allows assessment of hand function in seven common activities of daily living.

The *Minnesota Rate of Manipulation Test*[31,32] was originally designed to select personnel for jobs requiring manual arm and hand dexterity. This test assesses ability in five operations: placing, turning, displacing, one-hand turning and placing, and two-hand turning and placing. The test requires use of a form board with wells and round disks. Available from American Guidance Service, Inc., Publishers Building, Circle Pines, MN, 55014.

The *Purdue Pegboard*[32,33] test assesses dexterity by placement of pins in a pegboard and assembly of pins, washers, and collars. There are several subtests, including right-hand prehension, left-hand prehension, prehension test with both hands, and assembly. The test has been used to select personnel for industrial jobs that require manipulative skills. Normative values are available, and both unilateral and bilateral dexterity can be assessed. This test requires use of a testing board, pins, collars, and washers. Available from Science Research Associates, Inc., 359 East Erie Street, Chicago, IL, 60611.

The *Crawford Small Parts Dexterity Test*[1,32] uses the manipulation of small tools as a component of the test. The test uses pins, collars, and screws as well as a board into which these small objects fit. Use of tweezers is required both to place the pins in holes and to place a collar over the pin. The screws must be placed with the fingers and screwed in using a screwdriver. This test has been useful in prevocational testing. Normative data are available. This test is scored by time. Available from Psychological Corporation, 304 East 45th Street, New York, NY 10017.

There are a variety of other standardized and commercially distributed tests available. Selection should be based on the individual needs of a given facility and the diagnostic groups most frequently seen. Additionally, careful assessment should be made of criteria used for standardization of the testing instrument.

SUMMARY

Coordination assessments provide the physical therapist with important information related to motor performance. They assist in identifying the source of motor deficits (although some clinical findings may not be attributable to a single area of CNS involvement). They also assist in goal setting and treatment planning and with periodic reassessment to determine the effectiveness of treatment interventions. Because observational coordination tests are not highly standardized, the potential for error and misinterpretation of results exists. Sources of potential error can be reduced by use of well-defined rating scales, administration of tests by skilled examiners, and subsequent retesting performed by the same therapist.

A variety of observational coordination assessments have been presented. The majority of these tests can be used to assess more than one type of motor deficit. Documentation should include the type, severity, and location of the deficit as well as factors that alter the quality of performance. It is evident that multiple influences affect movement capabilities. As such, the results of coordination tests must be carefully considered with respect to data obtained from other assessments such as sensation, muscle strength, tone, and range of motion.

QUESTIONS FOR REVIEW

1. Describe the clinical features of coordination deficits associated with lesions of the cerebellum, basal ganglia, and dorsal columns.

2. Explain the purpose of an initial observation of the patient prior to a formal coordination assessment. What type of activities should be observed? What information should be gathered?

3. Identify and describe the five general areas of movement capabilities assessed during a coordination assessment.

4. Differentiate between the types of activities included in equilibrium versus nonequilibrium coordination tests.

5. What questions related to patient performance should be considered during a coordination assessment to help direct the examiner's observations?

6. Define each of the following terms. Identify at least two coordination tests that would be appropriate for each deficit. Explain the testing protocol you would use for each.
   a. Dysdiadochokinesia
   b. Dysmetria
   c. Movement decomposition
   d. Tremor
      Intention
      Resting
      Postural
   e. Rigidity
   f. Bradykinesia

REFERENCES

1. Scott, AD: Evaluation of motor control. In Trombly, CA (ed): Occupational Therapy for Physical Dysfunction, ed 2. Williams & Wilkins, Baltimore, 1983, p. 46.
2. Lombardo, MC: Central nervous system tumors. In Price, SA and Wilson, LM (eds): Pathophysiology: Clinical Concepts of Disease Processes, ed. 3. McGraw-Hill, New York, 1986, p 819.
3. DeHaven, GE, Mordock, JB, and Loykovich, JM: Evaluation of coordination deficits in children with minimal cerebral dysfunction. Phys Ther 49:153, 1969.
4. Johnson, JH: Children with physical and orthopedic disabilities. In Clark, PN and Allen, AS (eds): Occupational Therapy for Children. CV Mosby, St Louis, 1985, p 406.
5. Kendrick, KA and Hanten, WP: Differentiation of learning disabled children from normal children using four coordination tasks. Phys Ther 60:784, 1980.
6. Brown, DR: Neurosciences for Allied Health Therapies. CV Mosby, St Louis, 1980.
7. Ghez, C and Fahn, S: The cerebellum. In Kandel, ER and Schwartz, JH (eds): Principles of Neural Science, ed 2. Elsevier Science, New York, 1985, p 502.
8. Guyton, AC: Human Physiology and Mechanisms of Disease, ed 3. WB Saunders, Philadelphia, 1982.
9. Lavine, RA: Neurophysiology: The Fundamentals. DC Heath, Lexington, MA, 1983.
10. Ghez, C: Introduction to the motor systems. In Kandel, ER and Schwartz, JH (eds): Principles of Neural Science, ed 2. Elsevier Science, New York, 1985, p 429.
11. Urbscheit, NL: Cerebellar dysfunction. In Umphred, DA (ed): Neurological Rehabilitation. CV Mosby, St Louis, 1985, p 452.
12. Schmidt, RA: Motor Control and Learning: A Behavioral Emphasis. Human Kinetics, Champaign, IL, 1982.
13. Werner, JK: Neuroscience: A Clinical Perspective. WB Saunders, Philadelphia, 1980.
14. Nolte, J: The Human Brain: An Introduction to Its Functional Anatomy. CV Mosby, St Louis, 1981.
15. Chusid, JG: Correlative Neuroanatomy and Functional Neurology, ed 19. Lange Medical Publications, Los Altos, CA, 1985.
16. Gilman, S and Winans, SS: Manter and Gatz's Essentials of Clinical Neuroanatomy and Neurophysiology, ed 6. FA Davis, Philadelphia, 1982.
17. DeJong, RN: The Neurologic Examination, ed 3. Harper & Row, New York, 1970.
18. Henneman, E: Motor functions of the brainstem and basal ganglia. In Mountcastle, VB (ed): Medical Physiology, vol 1, ed 14. CV Mosby, St Louis, 1980, p 787.
19. Guyton, AC: Basic Human Neurophysiology, ed 3. WB Saunders, Philadelphia, 1981.
20. Melnick, ME: Basal ganglia disorders: Metabolic, hereditary, and genetic disorders in adults. In Umphred, DA (ed): Neurological Rehabilitation. CV Mosby, St Louis, 1985, p 416.
21. Cote, L and Crutcher, MD: Motor functions of the basal ganglia and diseases of transmitter metabolism. In Kandel, ER and Schwartz, JH (eds): Principles of Neural Science, ed 2. Elsevier Science, New York, 1985, p 523.
22. Schanzenbacher, KE: Diagnostic problems in pediatrics. In Clark, PN and Allen, AS (eds): Occupational Therapy for Children. CV Mosby, St Louis, 1985, p 78.
23. Hodgkins, J: Influence of age on the speed of reaction and movement in females. Gerontol 17:385, 1962.
24. Brocklehurst, JC, Robertson, D, and James-Groom, P: Clinical correlates of sway in old age—sensory modalities. Age Ageing 11:1, 1982.
25. Sheldon, JH: The effect of age on the control of sway. Gerontology Clinics 5:129, 1963.
26. Bohannon, RW, et al: Decrease in timed balance test scores with aging. Phys Ther 64:1067, 1984.

27. Cruz, VW: Evaluation of coordination: A clinical model. Clinical Management in Physical Therapy 6(3):6, 1986.
28. Thyssen, HH, et al: Normal ranges and reproducibility for the quantitative Romberg's test. Acta Neurol Scandinav 66:100, 1982.
29. Jansen, EC, Larsen, RE, and Olesen, MB: Quantitative Romberg's test: Measurement and computer calculation of postural stability. Acta Neurol Scand 66:93, 1982.
30. Jebsen, RH, et al: An objective and standardized test of hand function. Arch Phys Med Rehab 50:311, 1969.
31. Fess, EE: Documentation: Essential elements of an upper extremity assessment battery. In Hunter, JM, et al, (eds): Rehabilitation of the Hand, ed 2. CV Mosby, St Louis, 1984, p 49.
32. Smith, HD: Assessment and evaluation—specific evaluation procedures. In Hopkins, HL and Smith, HD (eds): Willard and Spackman's Occupational Therapy, ed 6. JB Lippincott, New York, 1983, p 149.
33. Baxter, PL and Ballard, MS: Evaluation of the hand by functional tests. In Hunter, JM, et al (eds): Rehabilitation of the Hand, ed 2. CV Mosby, St Louis, 1984, p 91.

SUPPLEMENTAL READINGS

Adams, JH, Corsellis, JAN, and Duchen, LW (eds): Greenfield's Neuropathology, ed 4. John Wiley & Sons, New York, 1984.
Adams, RD and Victor, M: Principles of Neurology, ed 3. McGraw-Hill, New York, 1985.
Appel, SH (ed): Current Neurology, vol 5. John Wiley & Sons, New York, 1984.
Asbury, AK, McKhann, GM, and McDonald, WI (eds): Diseases of the Nervous System, vol 1. WB Saunders, Philadelphia, 1986.
Asbury, AK, McKhann, GM, and McDonald, WI (eds): Diseases of the Nervous System, vol 2. WB Saunders, Philadelphia, 1986.
Connolly, BH and Michael, BT: Performance of retarded children, with and without Down syndrome, on the Bruininks Oseretsky Test of Motor Proficiency. Phys Ther 66:344, 1986.
Cools, AR, et al: Cognitive and motor shifting aptitude disorder in Parkinson's disease. Neurol Neurosurg Psychiatry 47:443, 1984.
Keshner, EA: Reevaluating the theoretical model underlying the neurodevelopmental theory. Phys Ther 61:1035, 1981.
Lombardo, MC: The nervous system. In Price, SA and Wilson, LM (eds): Pathophysiology: Clinical Concepts of Disease Processes, ed 3. McGraw-Hill, New York, 1986, p 711.
Kornse, DD, et al: Developmental apraxia of speech and manual dexterity. J Commun Disord 14:321, 1981.
Kottke, FJ: From reflex to skill: The training of coordination. Arch Phys Med Rehabil 61:551, 1980.
Kottke, FJ: Therapeutic exercise to develop neuromuscular coordination. In Kotkke, FJ, Stillwell, GK, and Lehmann, JF (eds): Krusen's Handbook of Physical Medicine and Rehabilitation, ed 3. WB Saunders, Philadelphia, 1982, p 403.
Kottke, FJ, et al: The training of coordination. Arch Phys Med Rehabil 59:567, 1978.
Kraft, GH: Movement disorders. In Basmajian, JV and Kirby, RL (eds): Medical Rehabilitation. Williams & Wilkins, Baltimore, 1984, p 162.
Potter, CN and Silverman, LN: Characteristics of vestibular function and static balance skills in deaf children. Phys Ther 64:1071, 1984.
Salmoni, AW, Schmidt, RA, and Walter, CB: Knowledge of results and motor learning: A review and critical reappraisal. Psychol Bull 95:355, 1984.
Schmidt, RA: Past and future issues in motor programming. Research Quarterly for Exercise and Sport 51:122, 1980.
Mayo Clinic and Mayo Foundation: Clinical Examinations in Neurology, ed 5. WB Saunders, Philadelphia, 1981.
Thomas, JR: Acquisition of motor skills: Information processing differences between children and adults. Research Quarterly for Exercise and Sport 51:158, 1980.

GLOSSARY

Akinesia: An inability to initiate movement; seen in the late stages of Parkinsonism.

Asthenia: A generalized muscle weakness associated with cerebellar lesions.

Asynergia: Loss of ability to associate muscles together for complex movements.

Ataxia: A general term used to describe uncoordinated movement; may influence gait, posture, and patterns of movements.

Athetosis: Slow, involuntary, writhing, twisting, "worm-like" movements; clinical feature of cerebral palsy. (Syn: athetoid movements)

Bradykinesia: Abnormally slow movements.

Chorea: Involuntary, rapid, irregular, jerky movements; clinical feature of Huntington's disease. (Syn: choreiform movements)

Choreoathetosis: Movement disorder with features of both chorea and athetosis; frequently seen in cerebral palsy.

Closed-loop system (Servomechanism, Servo): A movement control process that employs feedback against a reference for correctness for computation of error, and subsequent movement correction.

Dysarthria: Disorder of the motor component of speech articulation.

Dysdiadochokinesia: Impaired ability to perform rapid alternating movements.

Dysmetria: Impaired ability to judge the distance or range of a movement.

Dyssynergia: Impaired ability to associate muscles together for complex movement; decomposition of movement.

Dystonia: Impaired or disordered tonicity; tone fluctuates in an unpredictable manner from low to high.

Hemiballismus: Sudden, jerky, forceful, wild, flailing motions of one side of the body.

Huntington's disease: A degenerative disease of the basal ganglia and cerebral cortex with hereditary transmission as an autosomal dominant trait. Onset is usually after the age of 30 and is frequently fatal within 5 to 15 years after onset. The disease is characterized by choreiform movements; disturbances of tone, posture, and gait; and dementia.

Hyperkinesia: A general term used to describe abnormally increased muscle activity or movement; restlessness.

Hypermetria: Excessive distance or range of a movement; an overestimation of the required motion needed to reach a target object.

Hypokinesia: A general term used to describe decreased motor responses (especially to a specific stimulus); sluggishness, listlessness.

Hypometria: Shortened distance or range of a movement; an underestimation of the required motion needed to reach a target object.

Hypotonia (hypotonus): Reduced muscle tension below normal resting levels.

Motor program: A set of prestructured commands that when initiated results in the production of a coordinated movement sequence.

Movement decomposition: Performance of a movement in a sequence of component parts rather than as a single smooth activity.

Nystagmus: Rhythmic, oscillatory movement of the eyes.

Open-loop system: A control mechanism that uses preprogrammed instructions to regulate movement independent of a feedback and error-detection process.

Parkinsonism: A degenerative disease with primary involvement of the basal ganglia; characterized by tremors, rigidity, bradykinesia, and impairments of posture, balance, and gait. Onset is typically in the fifth or sixth decade of life. (Syn: Paralysis agitans)

Rebound phenomenon: Absence of a check reflex; when resistance to an isometric contraction is suddenly removed, the body segment moves forcibly in the direction in which effort was focused.

Rigidity: Increase in muscle tone; results in greater resistance to passive movement. Resistance is felt as constant and uniform (lead-pipe rigidity), or as jerky "catches" (cogwheel rigidity).

Romberg sign: Inability to maintain standing balance when vision is occluded.

Sydenham's chorea: Childhood disease associated with rheumatic fever. The disease is self-limiting, and recovery is usually complete; characterized by involuntary, abrupt, jerky, extraneous movements and disturbances of balance and gait; impairments of speech and memory also may be apparent.

Tremor: An involuntary oscillatory movement resulting from alternate contractions of opposing muscle groups.

Intention (or kinetic) tremor: Occurs during voluntary motion.

Postural (static) tremor: Back-and-forth oscillatory movements of the body while patient maintains a standing posture.

Resting tremor: Present when involved body segment is at rest; typically disappears or decreases with purposeful movement.

Wilson's disease: A hereditary disease associated with faulty copper metabolism; characterized by degenerative changes in the brain, cirrhosis of the liver, a greenish-brown pigmentation of the cornea (Kayser-Fleischer ring), personality changes, festinating gait, flexed postures, dystonia, tremors, involuntary movements, and dysphagia. (SYN: hepatolenticular degeneration)

APPENDIX A   SAMPLE COORDINATION ASSESSMENT FORM

Name: _____

Examiner: _____ Date _____

PART I NONEQUILIBRIUM TESTS

Key to Grading

5. Normal performance.
4. Minimal impairment: able to accomplish activity with slightly less than normal speed and skill.
3. Moderate impairment: able to accomplish activity, but coordination deficits very noticeable; movements are slow, awkward and unsteady.
2. Severe impairment: able only to initiate activity without completion.
1. Activity impossible.

Grade:Left	Coordination Test	Grade:Right	Comments
	Finger to nose		
	Finger to therapist's finger		
	Finger to finger		
	Alternate nose to finger		
	Finger opposition		
	Mass grasp		
	Pronation/supination		
	Rebound test of Holmes		
	Tapping (hand)		
	Tapping (foot)		
	Pointing and past pointing		
	Alternate heel to knee; heel to toe		
	Toe to examiner's finger		
	Heel on shin		
	Drawing a circle (hand)		
	Drawing a circle (foot)		
	Fixation/position holding (upper extremity)		
	Fixation/position holding (lower extremity)		

Additional comments:

PART II EQUILIBRIUM TESTS
Key to Grading
4. Able to accomplish activity.
3. Can complete activity; minor physical contact guarding required to maintain balance.
2. Can complete activity; significant (moderate to maximal) contact guarding required to maintain balance.
1. Activity impossible.

Grade	Coordination Test	Comments
	Standing: normal comfortable posture	
	Standing: normal comfortable posture with vision occluded	
	Standing: feet together	
	Standing on one foot	seconds L( ); R( )
	Standing: forward trunk flexion and return to neutral	
	Standing: lateral trunk flexion	
	Walk: place heel of one foot in front of toe of the opposite foot	
	Walk: along a straight line	
	Walk: place feet on floor markers	
	Walk: sideways	
	Walk: backward	
	Walk: in a circle	
	Walk: on heels	
	Walk: on toes	

Additional comments:

NOTE: Notations should be made under comments
section if
1. Lack of visual input renders activity impossible or
   alters quality of performance.
2. Verbal cuing is required to accomplish activity.
3. Alterations in speed affect quality of performance.
4. An excessive amount of time is required to complete
   activity.
5. Changes in arm position influence equilibrium tests.
6. Any extraneous movements, unsteadiness, or
   oscillations are noted in head, neck, or trunk.
7. Fatigue alters consistency of response.

Chapter 9

MOTOR CONTROL ASSESSMENT

SUSAN B. O'SULLIVAN

OBJECTIVES

1. Identify the purposes and components of a motor control assessment.

2. Identify the central nervous system control mechanisms associated with motor control.

3. Describe common motor control deficits.

4. Describe specific assessment procedures and tests used to evaluate motor control deficits.

5. Identify complicating factors that may influence the results of a motor control assessment.

INTRODUCTION

Motor behavior evolves from a complex set of neurologic and mechanical processes which determine the nature of our movements. Some movements are genetically predetermined and become apparent through processes of normal growth and development. Examples of these include the reflex patterns that predominate during much of our early life. Other movements, termed **motor skills,** are learned through interaction and exploration of the environment. Thus practice and experience are important variables in defining motor learning and motor skill development. Both reflex patterns and motor skills are subject to control by the central nervous system (CNS), which organizes vast amounts of sensory information and produces the commands necessary for coordinated movement.[1] Several levels of CNS command hierarchies can be identified (Fig. 9–1). In general, the higher centers (association cortex) develop the plan or strategy for movement. The middle centers (basal ganglia, cerebellum, and sensorimotor cortex) elaborate the plan by packaging the needed movements and postures. The lowest centers (spinal cord) provide information about the environment and performance and translate the plan into specific muscle actions. Movements are fur-

ther modified by stretch reflex activity.[2] These levels of control must be viewed as a flexible rather than a rigid hierarchy, with ongoing interactions supporting movement. Subsystems are continuously adjusted, with control of movement distributed throughout the system.[3] Damage to the CNS interferes with motor control processes. Lesions affecting the higher centers essentially remove their coordinating influence on the lower centers. The term **release phenomenon** has been used to refer to this process. The movements that result are more reflex in nature and stereotyped, but learned skills become disorganized or impossible. Alterations in tone and postural and movement control can be expected.[4–6]

The assessment of motor control dysfunction is a multifaceted process which seeks to identify areas of deficit in peripheral or central function. Thus a number of assessments must be considered here.

Assessment of motor control functions is based largely upon a subjective appraisal of function which is frequently a difficult process for the beginning student. The key to successful assessment and reassessment is careful, systematic observation and accurate recording of results. Several examples of rating systems and assessment forms are provided.

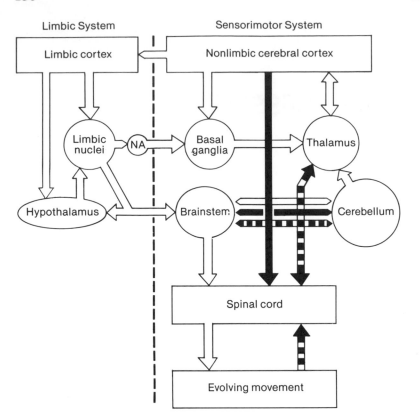

Figure 9–1. Diagram of major components of the limbic and sensorimotor systems. Each system can adjust its output based on comparison of what is needed and what is actually happening. The cerebellar circuit and, presumably, the hypothalamic circuit serve as comparators and adjusters. Not shown are detailed parts, crossing of pathways, and interneuronal relays at all levels. Filled arrows indicate output (efferent) connections of sensorimotor system; checkered arrows represent input (afferent) connections. From Brooks, V: *Motor control—how posture and movements are governed.* Phys Ther 63:667, 1983, with permission.

MENTAL STATUS

In patients with CNS lesions, mental status may be affected. Cognitive deficits can range from loss of consciousness to memory deficits, poor judgment, short attention span, distractability, or difficulties in information processing and learning. A detailed assessment by a clinical neuropsychologist may be necessary to obtain a complete and accurate picture of these deficits.[7,8]. Lack of attention to cognitive problems by the physical therapist can render an assessment of motor control in a brain-damaged patient invalid and unreliable. Prior to an examination of sensorimotor function, consideration must be given to a simple means of assessing cognitive function.

The patient's ability to follow directions and to understand the task should be ascertained. If memory and short-term learning are impaired, instructions should be kept to brief concise phrases. New tasks may pose greater problems for the patient than tasks that are familiar. Complex tasks can be broken down into component parts to simplify them and to ensure successful performance. Arranging the environment by reducing distractors also may be necessary to ensure maximum performance during assessment. Demonstration and positive feedback can assist the patient to understand what is expected and can be used to improve performance. Whenever modifications and cognitive strategies are necessary, they should be recorded in the patient's chart.[9]

One example of a widely adopted instrument to assess cognitive function in patients with head injury is the **Levels of Cognitive Functioning** developed by Hagen, Malkmus and Durham.[10] This tool, also known as the **Rancho Los Amigos Scale,** is presented in Table 9–1. It catego-

rizes neurobehavioral responses along a continuum that designates neurologic recovery and increasing cognitive integrity. Patient responses range from decreased response levels (II,III) to agitated (IV), confused (V,VI), or automatic response levels (VII,VIII). The level of function is determined by observing patient responses to stimulation and environmental manipulation. The presenting stimuli can include visual, auditory, olfactory, cutaneous, gustatory, and kinesthetic stimuli. Environmental manipulation includes the structuring of the treatment environment to reduce or to eliminate extraneous noises and visual stimuli. Patients in different stages of recovery vary in their responses and tolerance to stimulation. At the early levels, arousing stimuli are given, but in the later stages, calming stimuli and environmental structure are important. The therapist records the type of stimulation presented, the environmental context in which it was presented, and the behavioral responses of the patient including type, frequency, consistency, and duration. The behaviors then are categorized according to the descriptors presented in the scale. The therapist, as well as other members of the rehabilitation team, is then able to determine the approximate level of cognitive recovery and the appropriate modifications needed for successful treatment.[10,11]

COMMUNICATION ABILITY

Communication disorders may occur in patients with CNS lesions. The speech and language pathologist has the primary role in assessment, diagnosis, and treatment of these deficits. Problems can range from articulation deficits and dysarthria to receptive and expressive lan-

Table 9–1 LEVELS OF COGNITIVE FUNCTIONING

Level	Behaviors Typically Demonstrated
I.	No response: Patient appears to be in a deep sleep and is completely unresponsive to any stimuli.
II.	Generalized response: Patient reacts inconsistently and nonpurposefully to stimuli in a nonspecific manner. Responses are limited and often the same regardless of stimulus presented. Responses may be physiological changes, gross body movements, and/or vocalization.
III.	Localized response: Patient reacts specifically but inconsistently to stimuli. Responses are directly related to the type of stimulus presented. May follow simple commands in an inconsistent, delayed manner, such as closing eyes or squeezing hand.
IV.	Confused-agitated: Patient is in heightened state of activity. Behavior is bizarre and nonpurposeful relative to immediate environment. Does not discriminate among persons or objects; is unable to cooperate directly with treatment efforts. Verbalizations frequently are incoherent and/or inappropriate to the environment; confabulation may be present. Gross attention to environment is very brief; selective attention is often nonexistent. Patient lacks short-term and long-term recall.
V.	Confused-inappropriate: Patient is able to respond to simple commands fairly consistently. However, with increased complexity of commands or lack of any external structure, responses are non-purposeful, random, or fragmented. Demonstrates gross attention to the environment, but is highly distractible and lacks ability to focus attention to a specific task. With structure, may be able to converse on a social-automatic level for short periods of time. Verbalization is often inappropriate and confabulatory. Memory is severely impaired, often shows inappropriate use of objects; may perform learned tasks with structure but is unable to learn new information.
VI.	Confused-appropriate: Patient shows goal-directed behavior, but is dependent on external input for direction. Follows simple directions consistently and shows carry-over for relearned tasks with little or no carry-over for new tasks. Responses may be incorrect due to memory problems but appropriate to the situation; past memories show more depth and detail than recent memory.
VII.	Automatic-appropriate: Patient appears appropriate and oriented within hospital and home settings; goes through daily routine automatically, but frequently robot-like with minimal-to-absent confusion, but has shallow recall of activities. Shows carry-over for new learning, but at a decreased rate. With structure is able to initiate social or recreational activities; judgment remains impaired.
VIII.	Purposeful and appropriate: Patient is able to recall and integrate past and recent events and is aware of and responsive to environment. Shows carry-over for new learning and needs no supervision once activities are learned. May continue to show a decreased ability relative to premorbid abilities, abstract reasoning, tolerance for stress, and judgment in emergencies or unusual circumstances.

From Malkmus, D,[11] with permission.

guage dysfunction (aphasia). A speech and language assessment generally includes an examination of cognitive skills (tests of attention, memory, and thought processing) and language skills (speaking, reading, and writing). In many cases the communication problems seen with brain damage are the result of combined dysfunction of both the cognitive and language systems. Auditory or visual receptive problems also can significantly impair performance on a physical therapy assessment. Therefore, it becomes crucial to identify an appropriate means of communicating with the patient. This may include simplifying verbal or written instructions or using alternate forms of communication such as gestures, pantomine, or communication boards. A common error is to assume that the patient understands the task at hand when the patient really has no idea what is expected. To ensure accuracy of testing, frequent checks for comprehension should be performed throughout the assessment. For example, the use of message discrepancies (saying one thing and gesturing another) can be used to test the patient's level of understanding.[9,12]

AROUSAL

An assessment of **arousal** or central state of alertness is important in determining the degree to which an individual is able to respond. Low arousal is associated with sleep or drowsiness, and high arousal is associated with extreme excitement. Measurements of autonomic nervous system (ANS) function are frequently used to determine levels of arousal and to establish baseline values for a number of body functions. The ANS functions to maintain equilibrium (homeostasis) among visceral functions and to initiate actions designed to adapt and to protect the individual under varying circumstances (Table 9–2). These "fight-or-flight" responses are initiated whenever the individual perceives a threat or danger. The major control centers for the ANS are in the spinal cord, brainstem, and hypothalmus. Additional influences may originate from the cortex and limbic system.[5,13]

Autonomic and somatic systems interact and influence each other through the action of the brainstem and more specifically the reticular formation (RF).[14] This structure is primarily responsible for controlling the overall level of CNS activity, including wakefulness and sleep, arousal and attentive states. Sensory stimuli influence the RF and initiate arousal responses, and motor systems become engaged in carrying out the commands of the RF in producing fight-or-flight responses. Balanced interaction of the autonomic and somatic systems allows for reactive yet stable responses of an individual.

An imbalance in the ANS, with the sympathetic system dominant, results in an individual with high arousal. Specific responses include hyperalertness, increased heart rate (HR), increased blood pressure (BP), increased respiratory rate (RR), dilated pupils, and sweating. Although a certain level of arousal is necessary for optimal motor performance, high levels cause a deterioration in performance. This is referred to as the inverted-U theory or the Yerkes-Dodson law.[1]

Excess levels of arousal also can yield unexpected responses. This theory was originally proposed by Wilder as the **Law of Initial Value (LIV)**.[15] It states, "The higher the initial value (IV) of a function, the less change will occur in response to a function-increasing stimulus, and the lower the IV of a function the less change will occur in response to a function-decreasing stimulus . . . When the IV of a function is well beyond the midrange, there is an increasing tendency for no response or a reversal of response."[16] For example, patients at either end of an arousal continuum (either very high or very low) may not respond to stimulation or may respond with a para-

Table 9–2 AUTONOMIC EFFECTS ON VARIOUS ORGANS OF THE BODY

Organ	Effect of Sympathetic Stimulation	Effect of Parasympathetic Stimulation
Eye: Pupil	Dilated	Constricted
Ciliary muscle	Slight relaxation	Contracted
Glands: Nasal	Vasoconstriction and slight secretion	Stimulation of thin, copious secretion (containing many enzymes for enzyme-secreting glands)
Lacrimal		
Parotid		
Submaxillary		
Gastric		
Pancreatic		
Sweat glands	Copious sweating (cholinergic)	None
Apocrine glands	Thick, odoriferous secretion	None
Heart: Muscle	Increased rate	Slowed rate
	Increased force of contraction	Decreased force of atrial contraction
Coronaries	Dilated (β_2); constricted (α)	Dilated
Lungs: Bronchi	Dilated	Constricted
Blood vessels	Mildly constricted	? Dilated
Gut: Lumen	Decreased peristalsis and tone	Increased peristalsis and tone
Sphincter	Increased tone	Relaxed
Liver	Glucose released	Slight glycogen synthesis
Gallbladder and bile ducts	Relaxed	Contracted
Kidney	Decreased output	None
Bladder: Detrusor	Relaxed	Excited
Trigone	Excited	Relaxed
Penis	Ejaculation	Erection
Systemic blood vessels:		
Abdominal	Constricted	None
Muscle	Constricted (adrenergic α)	None
	Dilated (adrenergic β)	
	Dilated (cholinergic)	
Skin	Constricted	None
Blood: Coagulation	Increased	None
Glucose	Increased	None
Basal metabolism	Increased up to 100%	None
Adrenal cortical secretion	Increased	None
Mental activity	Increased	None
Piloerector muscles	Excited	None
Skeletal muscle	Increased glycogenolysis	None
	Increased strength	

From Guyton, A,[5] with permission.

doxical or reversed response (opposite to the expected reaction). Stockmeyer[16] suggests that this may explain the reactions of labile patients who seem to lack the homeostatic controls for normal function. Another example is when stressed or fatigued individuals are stimulated, they are much more likely to respond with exaggerated fight-or-flight responses. Figure 9–2 depicts the compensatory shifts in initial values designed to maintain a stable system.

Assessment of baseline levels of central state should, therefore, precede other aspects of a motor control assessment. Critical factors in obtaining a baseline assessment of homeostatic control mechanisms include (1) a representative sampling of ANS responses, includ-

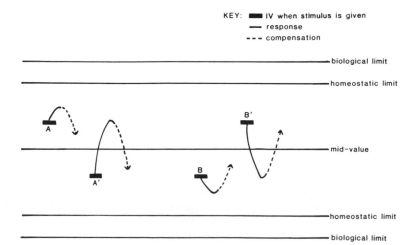

Figure 9–2. Compensation for deviations from the initial value occur back toward mid-values in a stable system. (A) IV high, function-raising stimulus yields small response. (A′)IV low, function-raising stimulus yields a large response. (B) IV low, function-decreasing stimulus yields a small response. (B′)IV high, function-decreasing stimulus yields a large response. From Stockmeyer, S,[16] p 84, with permission.

ing HR, BP, RR, pupil dilation, and sweating; (2) a determination of patient reactivity, including the degree of response, rate of response to sensory stimulation; and (3) a determination of compensatory mechanisms in response to physiologic stressors.[16] Careful monitoring during motor performance also can assist in determining homeostatic stability. More specific guidelines for assessment of vital functions can be found in chapter 4. Sensory-motor responses then can be examined in light of this information. Strong, weak, or paradoxical responses may be influenced by central regulatory mechanisms attempting to maintain or to restore homeostatic balance. Wide fluctuations in responses may be the result of an initial state that is so extreme it alters normal homeostatic control mechanisms.[17,18]

SENSORY FUNCTION

Sensory information is a critical component of motor control because it provides the necessary feedback used to monitor performance. This is referred to as the *closed-loop* system of motor control. Schmidt[1] defines this as "a control system employing feedback, a reference of correctness, computation of error, and subsequent correction in order to maintain a desired state of the environment." *Servomechanism* or *servoloop* are other terms used to refer to this type of control. A variety of feedback sources are used to monitor movement, including eyes, ears, vestibular apparatus, muscle, tendon and joint proprioceptors, and touch receptors. The CNS analyzes all available movement information, determines error, and institutes appropriate corrective action when necessary. Thus a thorough sensory examination of each of these systems is an important part of a motor control assessment.

The primary role of closed-loop systems of motor control appears to be the monitoring of constant states such as posture and balance, and the control of slow movements or those requiring a high degree of accuracy. Feedback information is also essential for the learning of new motor tasks. Patients who have deficits in any of the movement monitoring sensory systems may be able to compensate with other sensory systems. For example, the patient with major proprioceptive losses can use vision as an error-correcting system to maintain a stable posture. When vision is occluded, however, postural instability becomes readily apparent (e.g., positive Romberg test). Significant sensory losses and inadequate compensatory shifts to other sensory processes may result in severely disordered movement responses. The patient with proprioceptive losses and severe visual disturbances such as diplopia (commonly seen in the multiple sclerosis patient) may be unable to maintain a stable posture. An accurate motor control assessment, therefore, requires that the therapist not only assess each individual sensory system but also look at the total integration of these systems in the control of posture and movement. Control of posture, balance, slow (ramp) movements, tracking tasks, or new motor tasks provide the ideal challenge in which to monitor feedback control and closed-loop processes.

Control of rapid (ballistic) movement sequences and stereotypic actions such as those seen in gait, on the other hand, appear to be monitored by a different set of control processes, termed *open-loop systems.* In this situation, the control originates centrally from a *motor program* or a set of preprogrammed instructions for coordinated movement which act independent of feedback information and error-detection processes.[1] Motor control assessment also should include a number of well-learned, rapid movement sequences.[1,19,20]

Many motor tasks are achieved through a combination of both open-loop and closed-loop processes. A central program defines the movement while feedback functions to monitor and to modify the movement as needed. In assessing the integrated action of both control models, the therapist needs to ascertain the balance between feedback guidance and motor programming. For example, in performing learned tasks, how much feedback control is needed to complete the movement? If an unexpected load or challenge to the movement is introduced, how quickly does the patient respond with the apropriate adjustment?

PERCEPTUAL FUNCTION

Perceptual motor function is defined as the selection, integration, and interpretation of sensory stimuli from the body and the surrounding environment. It is critical to motor performance, motor learning, and successful interaction with the environment. The occupational therapist has the primary role in assessment, diagnosis, and treatment of these deficits. Deficits frequently can go undetected, produce ineffectual behaviors, and influence the results of a motor control assessment. Perceptual problems always should be suspected when the patient has great difficulty in accomplishing a task even though specific causes (e.g., spasticity, weakness) can not be identified. Perceptually impaired patients also display difficulty in doing simple tasks independently and safely, in completing tasks, and in switching from one task to another. These patients tend to make the same mistakes over and over again and often show a diminished capacity to locate visually or to identify objects that seem necessary for task completion. They also experience difficulty in following simple instructions even though comprehension is good. Perceptually impaired individuals are often impulsive, distractable, and frustrated, and exhibit poor planning ability. Patients who are inattentive to one side of the body or who deny the presence or extent of disability also must be suspected of perceptual dysfunction. The therapist should be aware of the specific disorders that are likely to include perceptual dysfunction.[21] See chapter 7 for a thorough discussion of this topic.

MOTOR FUNCTION

Tone

An assessment of muscle **tone** seeks to identify the resting tension and responsiveness of muscles to passive elongation or stretch. Because muscles rarely work in isolation, the term *postural tone* is preferred by some clinicians to describe the pattern of muscular tension that exists throughout the body and affects groups of muscles.[22] Tone is categorized as **hypertonus,** increased above normal resting levels, or **hypotonus,** decreased below normal resting levels.

TONAL ABNORMALITIES

Hypertonus

Clinically, forms of hypertonus include spasticity, rigidity, or spasms. In **spasticity,** there is increased resistance to sudden passive movement. The response produced is velocity dependent. The quicker the stretch, the stronger the response of a spastic muscle. Spasticity results from upper motor lesions in the motor cortex or its extrapyramidal projections. One type of alteration in supraspinal control is dependent upon afferent input and results in excessive drive to gamma motoneurons. In these cases, the hyperactive muscle spindle activity results in hyperactive phasic and tonic stretch reflexes. Spasticity that does not depend upon afferent input is alpha driven, with the alpha motoneurons receiving the excessive drive from the CNS.[13]

Continued passive stretch of a spastic muscle may produce a sudden relaxation or letting go, termed the **claspknife phenomenon.** Stretch may also produce **clonus,** characterized by spasmodic alterations of muscle contraction and relaxation occurring at a regular frequency. Clonus is frequently seen in the calf muscles but also may occur in other areas of the body such as the jaw or wrist.[23,24]

In *rigidity,* resistance is increased to all motions, rendering body parts stiff and immovable. Rigidity is relatively constant and independent of the velocity of a stretch stimulus. Brainstem lesions can produce either **decerebrate rigidity** or **decorticate rigidity,** whereas basal ganglia lesions produce Parkinsonian rigidity. **Decerebrate rigidity** refers to sustained contraction and posturing of the trunk and limbs in a position of full extension.[5] **Decorticate rigidity** refers to sustained contraction and posturing of the trunk and lower limbs in extension and the upper limbs in flexion.[5] Both decerebrate rigidity and decorticate rigidity result from alterations in control of the stretch reflex arc (gamma rigidity) and resemble an exaggerated form of spasticity. In Parkinson's disease, disordered function of the basal ganglia produces a different type of rigidity. Both agonist and antagonist muscles remain tightly contracted throughout movement and do not respond to sudden movements with intense and increased resistance from the stretch reflexes. This type of rigidity may be more the result of excess activation of alpha motoneurons than gamma motoneurons. Patients with Parkinsonism may demonstrate the **cogwheel phenomenon,** which is a rachet-like response to passive movement characterized by an alternate giving and increased resistance to movement. Constant rigidity in patients with Parkinsonism is termed leadpipe rigidity.[13,23,25]

Spasm refers to spontaneous, involuntary, and convulsive contraction of selected muscle groups. Spasms can occur anywhere in the body and result in abnormal sustained postures. When spasms are strong and painful, they are termed *cramps.* Spasms can be caused by a number of factors, including extrapyramidal involvement and hypoparathyroid tetany.[26]

Hypotonus

Hypotonia or **flaccidity** are the terms used to define decreased or absent muscular (postural) tone. Resistance to passive movement is diminished, stretch reflexes are dampened, and limbs are easily displaced (floppy) with frequent hyperextensibility of joints. Movements are generally impaired with weakness (paresis) or paralysis. Hypotonia can be produced by upper motor neuron lesions affecting the cerebellum or pyramidal tracts, causing a loss of descending facilitatory influences on the spinal gamma and alpha motoneurons.[13] Hypotonia also can occur as a temporary state, termed **spinal shock** or **cerebral shock,** depending upon the location of the injury to the CNS. The duration of the CNS depression that occurs with shock is highly variable and typically is followed by an emerging hyperreflexic, hypertonic state. Lower motor neuron lesions affecting the peripheral nervous system can produce symptoms of muscle weakness or paralysis, fasciculations, hypotonia, hyporeflexia, and atrophy.[25,27]

Dystonia is defined as impaired or disordered tone and is commonly associated with involuntary movement disorders of the basal ganglia such as hepatolenticular degeneration (Wilson's disease) or athetosis. Dystonic movements are typically slow, sinuous (writhing), sustained, and involuntary. Tone fluctuates in an unpredictable manner from low to high. **Dystonic posturing** refers to an abnormal, involuntary sustained posture maintained by powerful tonic contractions of muscles. Dystonia represents an abnormal hypertonic state and is commonly seen in dystonia musculorum deformans or spasmodic torticollis (wry neck).[13,28]

TONAL ASSESSMENT

Tone can be influenced by a number of factors, including (1) position and interaction of tonic reflexes, (2) stress and anxiety, (3) volitional effort and movement, (4) drugs, and (5) state of the CNS. The therapist should consider the impact of each of these factors in arriving at a determination of tone. Tonal assessment requires repeated examinations, because fluctuations in tone are common owing to the constantly changing state of CNS excitability.[16,22] Qualitative assessment can be considered in three phases: initial observation, assessment of passive movement and myotatic (stretch) reflexes, and voluntary movement control.

Initial Observation

Initial observation of the patient can reveal the presence of abnormal movements or posturing of the limbs or body. Stereotyped movement patterns (abnormal synergies) are suggestive of the presence of tone abnormalities. Involuntary fluctuating movements may be indicative of dystonia, and complete absence of spontaneous movements may be indicative of flaccidity. Careful assessment should be made relative to the effect of the patient's body and head positions on tone. For example, the patient who is supine with the lower limb stiffly held in extension and plantarflexion can be suspected of having increased extensor tone owing to the tonic labyrinthine reflex. Symmetrical and asymmetrical tonic neck reflexes and supporting reactions also commonly influence tone. Posturing in fixed, antigravity positions (e.g., arm held fixed against the body in flexion, adduction, and supination) is also suggestive of spasticity. Limbs that appear floppy and lifeless (e.g., leg rolled out to the side in external rotation) may be indicative of a low tone condition. Palpation may yield information about the resting state of muscles. Consistency, firmness, and turgor can be examined and the responsiveness to touch noted.[29]

Passive Motion Testing

Assessment of passive movements and myotatic reflexes reveals information about the responsiveness of muscles to a stretch stimulus. Because these responses should be examined in the absence of voluntary control, the patient is instructed to relax, letting the therapist support and move the limb. All movements are assessed, with particular attention given to those identified as problematic in the initial observation period.

During a passive movement test, the therapist should maintain firm and constant manual contacts, moving the limb randomly and at a slow and steady rate. When tone is normal, the limb moves easily and the therapist is able to alter direction and speed without feeling abnormal resistance. The limb is responsive and feels light. Hypertonic limbs generally feel stiff and resistant to movement, and flaccid limbs feel heavy and unresponsive. Older adults may find it difficult to relax; their stiffness should not be mistaken for spasticity.[28] Altering the speed of movement can be used to distinguish spasticity from other hypertonic states. Faster movements intensify the response and increase the amount of resistance offered by a spastic muscle. Rigidity offers a more constant resistance to all rates of movements. A sudden letting go is indicative of the clasp-knife phenomenon. Clonus is always assessed using a quick stretch stimulus. For example, ankle clonus is tested by sudden dorsiflexion of the foot.

A **drop test (placing test)** can be used to test the integrity of automatic proprioceptive reactions of the limbs. The arm or leg is raised (placed) by the therapist into an antigravity position and suddenly dropped. A normal limb momentarily falls, then catches and maintains the position as intact proprioceptors react to prevent it from falling. Hypertonic limbs are resistant to the stretch stimulus and demonstrate a delay in the downward movement, and hypotonic limbs fall abruptly.[22]

A determination of tone should be made based upon a comparison with the responses of a normal limb. Therapists need to be familiar with the wide range of normal responses of tonicity in order to develop an appropriate frame of reference to assess abnormality. In cases of localized or unilateral dysfunction (e.g., hemiplegia), comparison with the unaffected, "normal" limb is common. These comparisons may not be reliable, however, inasmuch as abnormal findings have been reported on these supposedly normal extremities.[31] Responses should be averaged (over a number of trial movements) and recorded using a standardized scoring key. A sample scoring key to assess tonal responses follows:

0 Absent response (flaccidity)
1 Decreased response (hypotonia)
2 Normal response
3 Exaggerated response (mild to moderate hypertonia)
4 Sustained response (severe hypertonia)

Reliability of repeated testing can be improved by being consistent in the application of the stretch stimulus, postures, and environments.

Voluntary Movement Control

Assessment of voluntary movement control can reveal additional information about the influence of tonal abnormalities on motor control. During the performance of mobility activities (e.g., sitting up, transfers), movements should be carefully observed and analyzed for tonal interference. This qualitative assessment yields important indirect evidence of tonal dysfunction. Strong efforts are likely to produce increased arousal and hypertonic responses. Quantitative scoring systems designed to assess independence in activities of daily living (ADL) can assist in arriving at meaningful conclusions. Specifically, the time it takes to complete an activity may reveal important information about hypertonicity. Scoring systems have been developed that attempt to assess the influence of spasticity on voluntary control, ranging from the absence of voluntary movement or total **synergy** movements to normal voluntary control.[22,32–34] These assessments allow some objective measurement of function but provide only an indirect estimation of tone. Because other problems may be the cause of poor functional scores (e.g., decreased range of motion, motor control), the therapist must use this information as an adjunct to other tonal assessments.

Other Measures

Several other assessments have been used clinically to assess tone. The application of prolonged local cold has been shown to decrease muscle spindle firing and gamma spasticity. Therefore there is a decrease in the strength of the stretch reflexes and resistance to passive movement following prolonged icing.[35] Vibration also has been used to assess tonicity and to help in the diagnosis of certain neurologic conditions. The application of an electrically driven vibratory stimulus normally elicits the **tonic vibration reflex (TVR),** a sustained contraction of the muscle being vibrated. Deep tendon reflexes also are inhibited. Normal individuals are able to voluntarily inhibit the vibration reflex, but those with spasticity are not. In moderate and severe spasticity, vibratory suppression of the deep tendon reflexes is considerably less than normal. Finally, vibration may produce abrupt timing abnormalities (jerky onset) and an irradiation or spreading of the tonic contraction to include other muscles, such as antagonists.[23,36] Electromyography (EMG) also has been used to augment the clinical assessment of tone. Collection of EMG data during passive motion tests and voluntary movements can reveal information about abnormal or heightened muscle responses. Specifically, critical velocity thresholds and phasic versus tonic stretch reflex dysfunctions in spasticity have been investigated.[24]

Reflexes and Reactions

TENDON (MUSCLE STRETCH) REFLEXES

Tendon taps are used to assess the deep tendon reflexes (DTR) by percussing the muscle tendon directly either with the tips of the therapist's fingers or with a reflex hammer. Typical reflexes examined include the jaw, biceps, brachioradialis, triceps, patellar, hamstring, and ankle. Use of standardized postures allows the therapist to isolate and examine radicular integrity accurately. Testing of the DTR also reveals information regarding hypertonic or hypotonic muscle states. In testing, there is a wide range of responses of the DTR that is considered normal. Repeated practice with a large number of different subjects will enhance the examiner's ability to assess function. Stretch reflex responses are highly variable and may be dampened or exaggerated by a number of factors, including central state and patient anticipation of the strike of the hammer. If stretch reflexes are difficult to elicit, responses usually can be enhanced by specific maneuvers. In the *Jendrassik maneuver,* the patient hooks together the fingers of the hands and attempts to pull them apart. While this pressure is maintained, the reflex is tested. Additional maneuvers include clenching the teeth or a contralateral fist when upper extremity reflexes are being tested.[28,30] For a summary of stretch reflex tests, see Table 9–3.

Table 9–3 REFLEX ASSESSMENT—MYOTATIC AND SUPERFICIAL REFLEXES

Myotatic Reflexes (Stretch)	Stimulus (S)	Response (R)
Jaw (trigeminal n)	Patient is sitting, with jaw relaxed and slightly open. Place finger on top of chin; tap downward on top of finger in a direction which causes the jaw to open.	Jaw rebounds.
Biceps (C5-C6)	Patient is sitting with arm flexed and supported. Place thumb over the biceps tendon in the cubital fossa, stretching it slightly. Tap thumb or directly on tendon.	Slight contraction of muscle (elbow flexes) normally occurs.
Triceps (C7-C8)	Patient is sitting with arm supported in abduction, elbow flexed. Palpate triceps tendon just above olecranon. Tap directly on tendon.	Slight contraction of muscle (elbow extends) normally occurs.
Hamstrings (L5S1S2)	Patient is prone with knee semiflexed and supported. Palpate tendon at the knee. Tap on finger or directly on tendon.	Slight contraction of muscle (knee flexes) normally occurs.
Patellar (L2-L4)	Patient is sitting with knee flexed, foot unsupported. Tap tendon of quadriceps muscle between the patella and tibial tuberosity.	Contraction of muscle (knee extends) normally occurs.
Ankle (S1-S2)	Patient is prone with foot over the end of the plinth or sitting with knee flexed and foot held in slight dorsiflexion. Tap tendon just above its insertion on the calcaneus. Maintaining slight tension on the gastroc-soleus group improves the response.	Slight contraction of muscle (foot plantarflexes) normally occurs.

Scoring Key for Myotatic Reflexes: 0   No response
1+ Decreased response
2+ Normal response
3+ Exaggerated response
4+ Clonus

Superficial Reflexes (Cutaneous)	Stimulus (S)	Response (R)
Plantar (S1, S2)	With a large pin or fingertip, stroke up the lateral side of the foot, moving from the heel to the base of the little toe and then across the ball of the foot.	Normal response is plantarflexion of the great toe, sometimes the other toes with slight inversion and flexion of the distal foot. Abnormal response, termed a + Babinski, is extension of the great toe with fanning of the four other toes (typically seen in upper motor neuron lesions).
Chaddock	Stroke around lateral ankle and up lateral aspect of foot to the base of the little toe.	Same as for plantar.
Abdominal (T7-12)	Position patient in supine position, relaxed. Make quick, light stroke with a large pin or fingertip over the skin of the abdominals from the periphery to the umbilicus (test each abdominal quadrant separately).	Localized contraction underlying the stimulus, causing the umbilicus to move toward the quadrant stimulated.

SUPERFICIAL CUTANEOUS REFLEXES

Superficial reflexes are elicited with a noxious stimulus, usually a light scratch. Reflexes tested include the plantar reflex, confirming toe signs (Chaddock), and superficial abdominal reflexes. The plantar reflex is tested for the presence of a Babinski response. A noxious stroking stimulus is applied on the sole of the foot along the lateral surface of the foot and up across the ball of the foot. A normal response consists of flexion of the big toes, sometimes of the other toes, or no response at all. An abnormal response (positive Babinski) consists of extension (dorsiflexion) of the big toe, sometimes with fanning of the other toes. In adults, it is always indicative of corticospinal dysfunction. The Chaddock sign is elicited by stroking around the lateral ankle and up the lateral aspect of the foot. It also produces extension of the big toe and is considered a confirmatory toe sign. The superficial abdominal reflex is elicited with quick, light strokes over the skin of the abdominal muscles. A localized contraction underlying the stimulus is produced with a resultant deviation of the umbilicus toward the area stimulated. An abnormal response consists of no response or a strong, delayed response.[30] Examples of superficial reflex tests are summarized in Table 9–3.

DEVELOPMENTAL REFLEXES AND REACTIONS (POSTURAL REFLEXES)

A developmental reflex assessment reveals information about the function and integration of the developmental reflexes. Assessment begins with an examination of the primitive and tonic reflexes. These reflexes are normally present during gestation or infancy and become integrated by the CNS at an early age. Once integrated, these reflexes are not generally recognizable in their pure form. They do continue, however, as "adaptive fragments of behavior," underlying normal motor control and aiding volitional movement.[37] In adults, they are more readily apparent under conditions of fatigue or effort[38,39] or following damage to the CNS.[32,40] The reflexes in this category include (1) **spinal level or elemental reflexes:** flexor withdrawal, extensor thrust, crossed extension; and (2) **brainstem level or tuning reflexes:** tonic neck, tonic labyrinthine, and associated reactions. Spinal level reflex responses are generally the simplest to observe and are typically judged by their appearance as part of an overt movement response. Brainstem reflexes, on the other hand, serve to bias the musculature and may not be visable through movement responses. In fact, movement rarely is produced but, rather, is more typically influenced through tonal adjustments. Thus the term "tuning reflexes" is an appropriate description of their function.[37]

To obtain an accurate assessment, the therapist must be concerned with several factors. The patient must be positioned appropriately to allow for the predicted movement response. An adequate test stimulus is essential, including both adequate magnitude and duration of stimulation. Keen observation skills are needed to detect what may be subtle movement changes and to distinguish normal responses from abnormal responses. Obligatory and sustained responses that dominate motor behavior are always considered abnormal in the adult patient. Palpation skills can assist in identifying tonal changes not readily apparent to the eye. Objective scoring of responses is essential. A sample reflex scoring key suggested by Caputo[41,42] follows:

0   Absent
1 + Tone change: slight, transient with no movement of the extremities
2 + Visible movement of extremity
3 + Exaggerated, full movement of extremities
4 + Obligatory and sustained movement, lasting for more than 30 seconds

Higher level reactions (righting, equilibrium, protective) are controlled by centers in the midbrain and cortex and are important components of normal postural control and movement. The term **reaction** is commonly used to refer to those reflexes which appear during infancy or early childhood and remain throughout life.[43] **Righting reactions** serve to maintain the head in its normal upright posture (face vertical, mouth horizontal) or to maintain the normal alignment of the head and trunk. Assessment procedures focus on positioning or manipulating the body and observing the automatic adjustments necessary to restore normal alignment and head position. **Equilibrium reactions** serve to maintain balance in response to alterations in the body's center of gravity and/or base of support. They can be tested by using a movable surface which alters the patient's base of support with respect to the center of gravity (termed tilting reactions). Equilibrium boards or gymnastic balls are commonly used to assess tilting reactions. Equilibrium reactions also can be tested by altering the patient's position through voluntary movements or by manual displacement. In either situation the center of gravity is altered with respect to the base of support and the patient is forced to make the automatic adjustments necessary to maintain balance (termed *postural fixation reactions*). Protective reactions (protective extension reactions) serve to stabilize and to support the body in response to a displacing stimulus in which the center of gravity exceeds the base of support. Thus the arms or legs extend in an effort to support the body weight as the body lowers (falls) to the support surface.

Reflex testing procedures have been effectively described by a number of authors.[40,43–45] A summary of these assessment procedures is provided in Table 9–4, and a sample recording form is presented in Table 9–5.

Stages of Motor Control

A developmental perspective of normal motor skill development provides an appropriate focus for the assessment of posture and movement control. These processes have been well investigated and described by many authors.[46–53] The stages of motor control initially described by Rood[54] and further elaborated on by Stockmeyer[55] incorporate normal developmental processes and provide a useful clinical framework for the assess-

Table 9–4 REFLEX ASSESSMENT—DEVELOPMENTAL REFLEXES

Primitive/Spinal Reflexes	Stimulus	Response
Flexor withdrawal	Noxious stimulus (pinprick) to sole of foot. Tested in supine or sitting position.	Toes extend, foot dorsiflexes, entire leg flexes uncontrollably. Onset: 28 weeks gestation. Integrated: 1–2 months.
Crossed extension	Noxious stimulus to ball of foot of extremity fixed in extension; tested in supine position.	Opposite lower extremity flexes, then adducts and extends. Onset: 28 weeks gestation. Integrated: 1–2 months.
Traction	Grasp forearm and pull up from supine into sitting position.	Grasp and total flexion of the upper extremity. Onset: 28 weeks gestation. Integrated: 2–5 months.
Moro	Sudden change in position of head in relation to trunk: drop patient backward from sitting position.	Extension, abduction of upper extremities, hand opening, and crying followed by flexion, adduction of arms across chest. Onset: 28 weeks gestation. Integrated: 5–6 months.
Startle	Sudden loud or harsh noise.	Sudden extension or abduction of arms, crying. Onset: birth. Integrated: persists.
Grasp	Maintained pressure to palm of hand (palmer grasp) or to ball of foot under toes (plantar grasp).	Maintained flexion of fingers or toes. Onset: palmer: birth; plantar: 28 weeks gestation. Integrated: palmer: 4–6 months; plantar: 9 months.

Tonic/Brainstem Reflexes	Stimulus	Response
Asymmetrical tonic neck (ATNR)	Rotation of the head to one side	Flexion of skull limbs, extension of the jaw limbs, "bow and arrow" or "fencing" posture. Onset: birth. Integrated: 4–6 months.
Symmetrical tonic neck (STNR)	Flexion or extension of the head.	With head flexion: flexion of arms, extension of legs; with head extension: extension of arms, flexion of legs. Onset: 4–6 months. Integrated: 8–12 months.
Symmetrical tonic labyrinthine (TLR or STLR)	Prone or supine position.	With prone position: increased flexor tone/flexion of all limbs; with supine: increased extensor tone/extension of all limbs. Onset: birth. Integrated: 6 months.
Positive supporting	Contact to the ball of the foot in upright standing position.	Rigid extension (cocontraction) of the lower extremities. Onset: birth. Integrated: 6 months.
Associated reactions	Resisted voluntary movement in any part of the body.	Involuntary movement in a resting extremity. Onset: birth–3 months. Integrated: 8–9 years.

Midbrain/Cortical Reflexes	Stimulus	Response
Neck righting action on the body (NOB)	Passively turn head to one side; tested in supine.	Body rotates as a whole (log rolls) to align the body with the head. Onset: 4–6 months. Integrated: 5 years.
Body righting acting on the body (BOB)	Passively rotate upper or lower trunk segment; tested in supine.	Body segment not rotated follows to align the body segments. Onset: 4–6 months. Integrated: 5 years.
Labyrinthine head righting (LR)	Occlude vision; alter body position by tipping body in all directions.	Head orients to vertical position with mouth horizontal. Onset: birth–2 months. Integrated: persists.
Optical righting (OR)	Alter body position by tipping body in all directions.	Head orients to vertical position with mouth horizontal. Onset: birth–2 months. Integrated: persists.
Body righting acting on head (BOH)	Place in prone or supine position.	Head orients to vertical position with mouth horizontal. Onset: birth–2 months. Integrated: 5 years.
Protective extension (PE)	Displace center of gravity outside the base of support.	Arms or legs extend and abduct to support and to protect the body against falling. Onset: arms: 4–6 months; legs: 6–9 months. Integrated: persists.

Table 9–4 *continued.*

Midbrain/Cortical Reflexes	Stimulus	Response
Equilibrium reactions—tilting (ER)	Displace the center of gravity by tilting or moving the support surface (e.g., with a movable object such as an equilibrium board or ball).	Curvature of the trunk toward the upward side along with extension and abduction of the extremities on that side; protective extension on the opposite (downward) side. Onset: prone 6 months; supine 7–8 months; sitting 7–8 months; quadruped 9–12 months; standing 12–21 months. Integrated: persists.
Equilibrium reactions—postural fixation	Apply a displacing force to the body, altering the center of gravity in its relation to the base of support; can also be observed during voluntary activity.	Curvature of the trunk toward the external force with extension and abduction of the extremities on the side to which the force was applied. Onset: prone 6 months; supine 7–8 months; sitting 7–8 months; quadruped 9–12 months; standing 12–21 months. Integrated: persists.

Table 9–5 MOTOR BEHAVIOR INVENTORY

CHART A.

Pt. Name: _____ Location: _____

I.D. No. or S.S. No.: _____ Age: _____ Sex: _____ Diagnosis: _____

_____ Complications: _____

INSTRUCTIONS: ALL RESPONSES ARE RECORDED AS THE AVERAGE OF FIVE (5) TRIALS; STANDARDIZED POSTURES AND ENVIRONMENT ARE USED; THE STIMULI ARE APPLIED CONSISTENTLY.

REFLEX KEY: 0—Normal; 1—Decreased; 2—Absent; 3—Exaggerated; 4—Sustained

	No. 1 Date:		No. 2 Date:		No. 3 Date:		No. 4 Date:		No. 5 Date:		No. 6 Date:	
	R	L	R	L	R	L	R	L	R	L	R	L
I. REFLEXES A. Deep Tendon Jerk												
Ankle (PF)												
Knee (Bx)												
Elbow (FL)												
Elbow (Ex)												
Wrist (FL)												
DTR Summary Score:												
B. Passive Resistance Stretch												
Ankle (PF)												
Knee (Ext)												
Elbow (FL)												
Elbow (Ext)												
Wrist (FL)												
Passive Resistance Summary Score:												
C. Clonus Ankle (PF)												
Wrist (FL)												
Clonus Summary Score:												
D. Plantar Stimulation												
(Babinski) Plantar (FL)												
Extensor												
Babinski Summary Score:												
E. Hoffman Response												
(Hand and Fingers)												
F. Grasp Response												
Traction												
Primitive												
True												
Grasp Response Summary Score:												
Reflex Summary Score:												

Table 9–5 *continued.*

CHART B.

Pt. Name: _____ Location: _____

I.D. No. or S.S. No.: _____ Age: _____ Sex: _____ Diagnosis: _____

_____ Complications: _____

INSTRUCTIONS: ALL RESPONSES ARE RECORDED AS THE AVERAGE OF FIVE (5) TRIALS: STANDARDIZED POSTURES AND ENVIRONMENT ARE USED; THE STIMULI ARE APPLIED CONSISTENTLY.

KEY: 0—Absent; 1—Tone change in extremity; 2—Visible movement of extremity; 3—Full movement of extremities; 4—Obligatory and sustained movement

	No. 1 Date:		No. 2 Date:		No. 3 Date:		No. 4 Date:		No. 5 Date:		No. 6 Date:	
II. PRIMITIVE RESPONSES	R	L	R	L	R	L	R	L	R	L	R	L
A. Spinal												
Flexor withdrawal _____												
Extensor thrust _____												
Crossed extension _____												
Spinal Summary Score:												
B. Tuning Responses (Brainstem)												
Asymmetric tonic neck$_L^R$ _____												
Symmetric tonic neck$_{DF}^{VF}$ _____												
Asymmetric tonic labyrinthine$_L^R$ _____												
Symmetric tonic labyrinthine _____												
Associated arm _____												
Leg _____												
Tuning Response Summary Score:												

III. RIGHTING RESPONSES
   KEY: 0—Present with complete motion; 1—Moves with incomplete motion; 2—Moves with inconsistent mass pattern; 3—Moves always with mass pattern

A. Derotational												
Neck on trunk _____												
Legs on trunk												
B. Labyrinthine												
Sitting (side to side) _____												
Sitting (forward and back)												
C. Optical												
Sitting (side to side) _____												
Sitting (forward and back)												
D. Moro												
Sudden extension of head												
Righting Responses Summary Score:												

ment and treatment of patients with motor control deficits. They will, therefore, become a major conceptual frame of reference for many of the procedures discussed in this chapter. These stages include (1) **mobility,** (2) **stability,** (3) **controlled mobility,** and (4) **skill.**

MOBILITY

The initial stage of motor control is characterized by the development of functional **mobility.** During early development, generally the first three months of life, many of the infant's movements are spontaneous, random, and rhythmic, occurring at regular and brief intervals. They tend to be relatively brisk, full-range, and not well controlled. The term *random* may not be accurate, however, because evidence suggests that spontaneous movements may in fact be related to the spatial and temporal organization of more advanced motor patterns. For example, spontaneous kicking may be a forerunner to walking.[56] Mobility movements are also **reflex** based and serve a large protective function for the newborn. As development progresses, control shifts from reflexive to voluntary. One of the essential requirements for this stage of motor control is the ability to initiate the movement, requiring adequate activation of muscles. The second requirement is the ability to move through the range, requiring adequate strength, ROM, and flexibility.

Assessment of mobility function in the adult patient seeks to determine the availability of adequate range through active and passive ROM testing and muscle

Table 9–5 *continued.*

CHART C.

Pt. Name: _____ Location: _____

I.D. No. or S.S. No.: _____ Age: _____ Sex: _____ Diagnosis: _____

_____ Complications: _____

IV. BALANCE REACTIONS
  KEY: 0—Present with all components; 1—Pattern lacking some component; 2—Pattern lacking all components; 3—Patterns opposite to normal

	No. 1 Date:	No. 2 Date:	No. 3 Date:	No. 4 Date:	No. 5 Date:	No. 6 Date:
A. Prone on Forearms						
Weight transfer (side to side)						
Weight bearing						
Protective response						
Prone Summary:						
B. Sitting (feet unsupported)						
Weight transfer (side to side)						
Weight bearing						
Protective response						
Sitting Summary:						
C. Standing (feet parallel)						
Weight transfer						
Weight bearing						
Protective response						
D. Standing on Left Leg						
Protective response						
E. Standing on Right Leg						
Protective response						
Standing Summary:						
Balance Reaction Summary Score:						

From Nelson, A,[29] with permission.

function through reflex, tonal, and movement observations. Several developmental activities can be used to assess mobility function. Commonly used activities include (1) withdrawal patterns of either the arm or leg (flexor withdrawal, supine withdrawal), (2) rolling over, and (3) the assumption of pivot prone (prone extension). Inasmuch as full extension from the prone position is not a comfortable position for many older individuals, assumption of a modified extension pattern in sidelying or sitting may be more appropriate. In observing the movements, the therapist must determine if the patient can initiate the appropriate movement responses independently and complete the available range.

STABILITY

The second stage of motor control is concerned with the development of **stability.** Stability is defined as the ability to maintain a steady position in relation to gravity. This also has been referred to as static equilibrium[53] or static postural reactions.[22] The emergence of both righting and equilibrium reactions contributes to the ability to maintain body position. Throughout the first year of life, the infant learns to control posture in progressively more upright and weight-bearing positions. As postures become more upright, the child's base of support becomes smaller while the center of gravity becomes higher. The number of weight-bearing joints also is increased. Three important progressions of change can be identified: (1) the development of head control, (2) the development of sitting, and (3) the development of standing (Fig. 9–3). Collectively, they represent the emergence of static postural control, an essential prerequisite for further development of dynamic movement control.

The development of stability control can be broken down into two phases: **tonic holding** and **cocontraction.**[55] **Tonic holding** is defined as the activation of postural muscles in the fully shortened range. The term *shortened held resisted contraction (SHRC)* frequently is used to refer to the action of postural muscles during this activity. Muscle spindle stretch sensitivity is believed to be enhanced as a result of the effects of gravity or resistance and the recruitment of static gamma motoneurons. **Cocontraction** refers to the simultaneous contraction of

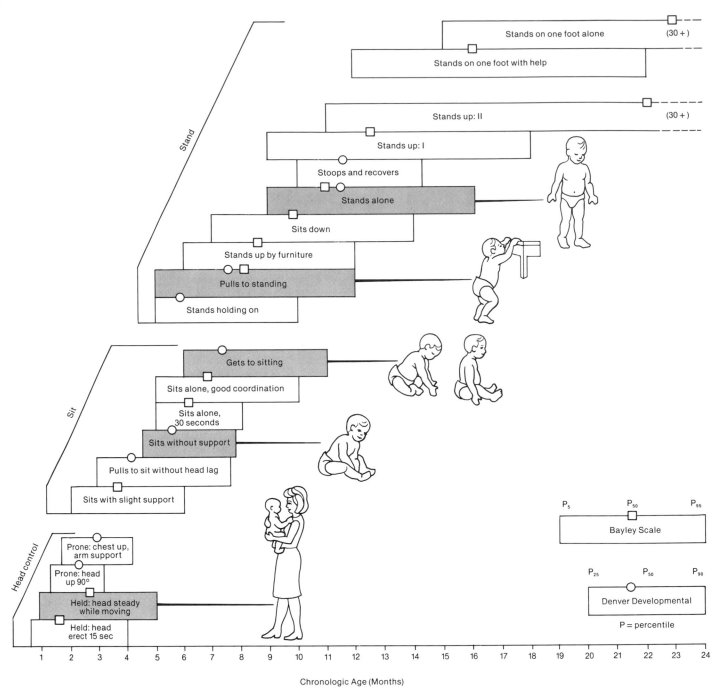

Figure 9–3. Developmental progressions of change: postural control. From Keogh, J and Sugden, D,[53] p 32, with permission.

both agonist and antagonist muscles and optimally functions to support the body in weight-bearing postures. The action of the postural extensors is of special importance in the development of cocontraction. The stretch applied to the extensors as they move from the shortened range to the mid range activates both primary and secondary spindle endings. This may help set up the pattern of cocontraction through the activation of both flexors via the spindle secondary endings and extensors via the spindle primary endings.[55] The assumption of weight-bearing postures also activates joint receptors, which add to the facilitation of stabilizing muscles around the joint.

Assessment of stability control in the adult patient begins with an examination of tonic holding ability. The patient is asked to sustain an isometric contraction of the postural muscles in the shortened range against resistance. Pivot prone (extension of head, trunk, and extremities) position or modified pivot prone (extension in sidelying or sitting) position is frequently used as a test activity to assess the function of the postural extensors. Full flexor withdrawal (withdrawal supine) also can be used to assess flexor holding, but this is of less clinical significance than the action of the extensors in examining stability control. The therapist assesses how long the patient is able to maintain the response and observes the quality of control. Smooth and sustained holding is indicative of adequate control, and jerky and unsustained holding is indicative of poor control. Muscles that cannot hold in the shortened range against gravity or slight manual resistance can not be expected to support the body weight in more stressful upright weight-bearing postures. If tonic holding is adequate, the therapist can progress to an assessment of cocontraction stability control in weight-bearing postures. Frequently used postures include neck cocontraction (midline head control in prone position), prone on elbows, quadruped, sitting, and kneeling or standing.

During normal development, postural control generally progresses in a cephalo-caudal direction.[53] Head control precedes upper trunk/upper extremity control, which precedes lower trunk/lower extremity control. The adult patient, however, may not conform to this sequence, inasmuch as deficits arise depending on the specific areas of the CNS affected. For example, the patient with a cerebral vascular accident (CVA) may demonstrate good control of the lower trunk and lower extremity, but deficits may be more evident in the upper body and upper extremity. The therapist must select the postures to be examined based upon the specific needs of each patient. Criteria for adequate stability control include (1) the ability to hold the posture without support, (2) the ability to sustain the posture for an adequate time, and (3) the ability to control the posture as evidenced by a minimal amount of postural sway.

CONTROLLED MOBILITY

The third stage of motor control development is concerned with the ability to change position and to achieve a new position while maintaining postural control. Several different terms have been used clinically to describe this stage. Rood used the phrase "mobility superimposed on stability" to refer to movement of the proximal segments while the distal segments (hands, knees and/or feet) were fixed.[55] This has been shortened to **controlled mobility** by some authors.[57,58] Bobath[22] refers to it as **dynamic postural control** achieved through well-coordinated patterns of movement and tonal changes. **Dynamic equilibrium** and/or **motion stability** also have been used to refer to this ability to maintain body control while the body is in motion.[53] Thus, the development of postural control progresses along a continuum from static to dynamic control. Skilled motor function requires a balanced interaction between both static control and dynamic control.

Assessment of controlled mobility in the adult patient focuses on an observation of the postural responses obtained during movement. Initially, weight shifting or rocking movements in any of the developmental weight-bearing postures can be used to test this function. The patient is positioned in the posture (e.g., prone on elbows or sitting) and instructed to move slowly. The movements tested can include rocking from side to side, forward/backward, diagonally, or rotatively. The movements are assessed for smoothness and control of timing and range. Full range of motion and balanced control in

all directions are expected. Because control of weight shifting precedes control of unilateral weight-bearing postures, rocking is thought to be an important activity in promoting the development of mature equilibrium reactions.[55] Patients who are unable to perform simple rocking movements may be suspected of having faulty or incomplete equilibrium reactions.

Once control in weight shifting is demonstrated, the therapist can assess the patient's ability to assume the posture independently. The terms *assumption of upright postures* or *movement transitions* have been used to describe these movements. This is a more difficult movement test because it requires the patient to move through a greater range of movement and against maximum effects of gravity. The patient must assume the posture (e.g., getting into the quadruped position from the supine position) without assistance or support. The therapist observes whether the test item can be completed. If assistance is required, the type and amount is recorded. The quality of the movement response also is noted, including an observation of the overall coordination of spatial and temporal components. Inasmuch as there is considerable variation among normal individuals, the therapist needs to be familiar with the wide range of normal responses in order to ascertain deviations from the normal. A major distinguishing factor between normal and abnormal responses is typically the degree to which rotation around the longitudinal axis is incorporated into the movement pattern.[22] Normal movements flow easily, with maximum rotation, but abnormal movements do not. Abnormal patterns are also more stereotyped and frequently influenced by the presence of primitive or tonic reflexes and abnormal tone.

Testing of controlled mobility can then focus on *static-dynamic control*. This is defined as the ability to shift weight onto one side and free the opposite limb for non-weight-bearing, dynamic activities. Unilateral weight bearing places even greater demands for dynamic stability than seen with rocking, because the support limb assumes full weight bearing while the dynamic limb constantly challenges control. Equilibrium reactions are essential for success in static-dynamic activities.

SKILL

The fourth and highest level of motor control is termed **skill**. **Skill** is a coordinate movement evidenced by the discrete distal motor function superimposed upon proximal stability.[55] Dynamic stability of the trunk and proximal joints is maintained during activities, which allows for interaction and exploration of the environment. Examples of skill level activities include (1) oromotor functions of chewing, swallowing, speech; (2) hand functions of grasp and manipulation; and (3) locomotion (ambulation). Figures 9–4 and 9–5 document the developmental progressions of change for manual control and locomotion. Movements of the extremities during this stage differ from movements seen in earlier stages in that they are regulated with precise spatial and temporal timing. Fitts,[59] a noted investigator of motor skills, defined a skilled response as an organized, goal-directed sequence of activities that effectively utilizes feedback to produce

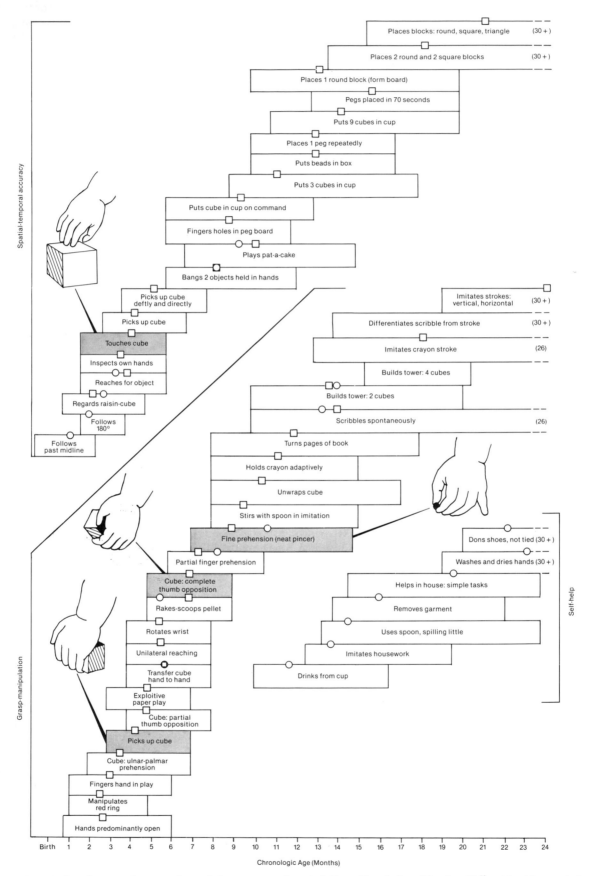

Figure 9–4. Developmental progressions of change: manual control. From Keogh, J and Sugden, D,[53] p 46, with permission.

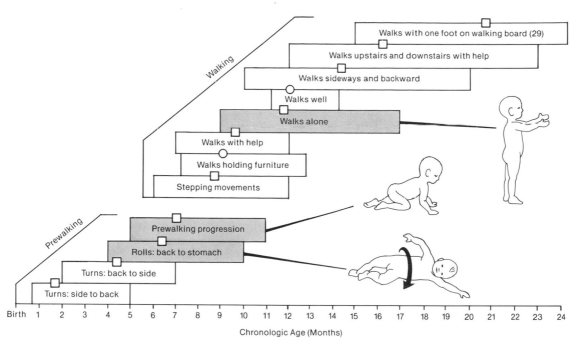

Figure 9-5. Developmental progressions of change: locomotion. From Keogh, J and Sugden, D,[53] p 38, with permission.

finely coordinated movement. Bobath[22] uses the term **normal postural reflex mechanism** to refer to the same level of control. She distinguishes the component parts as (1) normal postural tone; (2) normal reciprocal interaction of muscles, including proximal fixation/distal mobility, automatic postural adaptation of muscles, and precise timing and direction; and (3) automatic movement patterns (righting, equilibrium, protective reactions). Though the descriptions vary slightly, the reader may recognize common elements in defining the skill level of motor control. Several other factors of skilled performance are important. A skilled individual is able to perform both discrete or continuous movement sequences. A skilled individual is able to move in an environment that is stable, performing **closed skills,** or in a changing environment, performing **open skills.** A skilled individual is able to perform single or simultaneous movement sequences. Thus the skilled individual is able to move with precise control (e.g., feeding or dressing), to maintain movement sequences for extended periods (e.g., walking or running), to perform equally well in different types of environments (e.g., in the clinic or at home), and to combine different movement sequences (e.g., walking while reaching for an object).[53,60]

Skill level control in the adult patient can be assessed using many of the developmental activities previously described. In rolling, the patient is instructed to roll over and is observed for overall smoothness and controlled interaction of body movements (flexion, rotation, and extension). Inasmuch as skilled rolling emerges once body-on-body righting reactions mature, a segmental trunk pattern is expected. For example, the shoulder precedes hip, or vice versa. A log-rolling pattern in which the shoulder and hip move together as one unit is indicative of lower-level control and may be suggestive of hypertonicity. Trunk counterrotatory movements

(adversive movements) consist of moving the hip forward while simultaneously moving the shoulder backward, or its reverse, and also can be used to demonstrate a skill level of trunk control.[57] Counterrotatory trunk control should first be tested in sidelying. If present, control then can be challenged with increasingly more difficult postures, including creeping, kneeling, standing, and walking.

Skill level function of the upper extremities can be assessed by having the patient demonstrate manual control in combination with proximal postural control. Tasks that require fine motor control or finger dexterity are selected. These can include many ADL tasks, such as buttoning a shirt or writing with a pencil, or the coordination test items listed in chapter 8. Assessment by the therapist focuses on the degree of control of both distal and proximal segments. The arms and trunk should be held steady and controlled while the distal segments successfully perform the task. Bimanual control can be tested by having the patient perform activities with both hands doing the same task (symmetrical control) or by having both hands perform different tasks (asymmetrical control). Manual control also should be assessed using several different postures (e.g., progressing in order of difficulty from sitting to standing and walking).

Assessing control of locomotion includes an examination of both prewalking and walking skills. An infant uses crawling (in the prone position) or **creeping** (in the quadruped position) as early forms of locomotion. Crawling is typically not tested in the adult patient, but creeping may be included. Care must be taken, however, in selecting this as a test item because many older patients with arthritic changes in their knees find the quadruped position uncomfortable. When assessing creeping, the therapist should focus particular attention on the sequences of arm and leg movements and on the counterrotatory action of the trunk. Patterns are described as either **homo-lateral (ipsilateral),** with the leg and arm of one side alternating with the leg and arm of the other side, or **contralateral (reciprocal),** with the right leg and left arm alternating with the left leg and right arm. The reciprocal pattern is the more difficult and representative of higher-level control.

An investigation of walking skills includes an assessment of the determinants of gait during level walking. Stepping movements and all walking variations, including stopping/starting, different speeds, sideward, backward, crossed-leg, stairclimbing, and uneven terrains, are assessed. Because walking represents a continuous movement sequence, the ability to sustain a consistent walking pattern over time should be noted. Examination of postural control during ambulation focuses on an observation of the base of support (step width and step length) and the position and movement of the upper extremities. Widely spaced steps and arms held out to the side or elevated in a high guard position are indicative of decreased balance control. A skilled gait pattern includes a normal heel-toe sequence with trunk counterrotation and reciprocal arm swing. A more complete description of normal gait parameters and gait analysis can be found in chapter 11. A sample motor control recording form is provided in Table 9–6.

Voluntary Movement Control

Ontogenetic development of movement patterns progresses from mass or total patterns of movement to selective movement control. This process may be reversed, however, in cases of injury to the CNS. Mass patterns reemerge while selective movement control becomes disordered or disappears completely. The term **synergy** is frequently used in these instances to refer to the stereotyped movement patterns that emerge following brain damage. This is not to be confused with the normal cooperative action of certain muscles defined as synergetic action. Abnormal synergies are highly predictable and restricted. They can be elicited either by reflex action as

Table 9–6 MOTOR CONTROL RECORDING FORM

Patient's name: _____ Patient's number: _____

Physician: _____ Diagnosis: _____

Therapist: _____ Date: _____

Score: N = level of control normal; P = level of control present but of poor quality; O = level of control absent

| Posture | Mobility | | Stability | | Controlled Mobility | | |
	ROM	Initiate Motion	Tonic Holding	Co-contraction	Weight Shifting	Static/Dynamic	Skill
Sidelying/rolling							
Sitting							
Pivot prone							
Prone on elbows							
Quadruped							
Hooklying/lower trunk rotation							
Kneeling							
Half kneeling							
Modified plantigrade							
Standing/walking							

Comments:

From Minor, M and Minor, S,[58] with permission.

an associated reaction or voluntarily. For example, in hemiplegia, four distinct synergies have been identified—flexion and extension synergies in both upper and lower extremities.[32] The reader is referred to Table 17–3 for a complete description of these patterns.

Assessment of abnormal patterns is typically descriptive. The therapist must be able to identify and to describe the pattern, identifying the strong linkages occurring between muscle groups. For example, elbow, wrist, and finger flexion always occur when shoulder flexion is initiated. Therapists also need to identify when these patterns occur, under what circumstances, and what movement variations are possible. As CNS recovery progresses, synergies become more variable and may

Table 9–7 MOTOR BEHAVIOR INVENTORY

Pt. Name: _____ Location: _____

I.D. No. or S.S. No.: _____ Age: _____ Sex: _____ Diagnosis: _____

_____ Complications: _____

V. VOLUNTARY MOVEMENTS
  KEY: 0—Present with all components; 1—Present with insufficient motion or speed; 2—Present with partial mass patterns (synergy); 3—Present only in mass pattern (synergy); 4—No movement possible

	R	L	R	L	R	L	R	L	R	L	R	L
A. Supine Position												
1. Hip extension with knee flexion												
2. Ankle dorsiflexion with knee extended												
3. Knee flexion with hip extended												
4. Hold extended arm in elevated position when placed there												
5. Flexion of elbow												
6. Extension of elbow												
7. Flexion of wrist												
8. Flex and extended wrist												
9. Supination of forearm (elbow flexed at 90°)												
10. Pronation of forearm (elbow flexed at 90°)												
11. Rolling to left side												
12. Rolling to right side												
B. Sitting Position												
1. Abduct arm to side (with elbow extended)												
2. Supinate forearm (elbow flexed trunk fixed)												
3. Pronate forearm (without adduction)												
4. Externally rotate (extended arm)												
5. Flex elbow and touch shoulder same side												
6. Extend elbow (return from same shoulder)												
7. Flex elbow to opposite shoulder												
8. Extend (or return) to original position												
9. Extend wrist with fingers flexed												
10. Extend wrist with fingers extended												
11. Perform palmar prehension												
C. Standing Position												
1. Stand on both legs (30 sec)												
2. Stand on left leg (30 sec)												
3. Stand on right leg (30 sec)												
4. Alternating stepping in place (record seconds for 8 steps or 4 cycles)												
5. Stand on left leg and lift toes												
6. Stand on right leg and lift toes												
Voluntary Summary Score:												
Total Motor Inventory Summary Score:												

From Nelson, A,[29] with permission.

reemerge only under certain conditions such as stress or fatigue. Lessening of synergy dominance and more variation of available movements become hallmarks of sequential recovery. Patients firmly locked into synergy patterns can not isolate individual movements. Standard manual muscle testing procedures therefore are *not* appropriate because the movements do not correspond to the expected individual muscle actions. Objective measures that attempt to quantify synergy patterns use the criteria of available range obtained within the predicted course of the synergy pattern. The Brunnstrom Hemiplegia Classification and Progress Record is based upon this system.[32] Other methods of assessment focus on the degree to which movements can deviate from the predicted synergy patterns. The Bobath hemiplegia assessment is based upon this approach.[22] Inasmuch as spasticity frequently interacts with synergy patterns, tone should be carefully assessed both before and during synergy movements. A motor behavior inventory of voluntary movements is provided in Table 9–7.

Learning Factors

Learned skills comprise a large part of our movement repertoire. Individual differences in sensorimotor experiences account for a significant part of the variation in underlying motor abilities and skill acquisition which exists between individuals. An assessment of motor control must, therefore, consider sources of individual differences in order to arrive at an accurate starting point for treatment planning. Important elements include preferential learning style, interests, personality characteristics, problem-solving abilities, and other preexisting psychosocial behavioral patterns.[61] These elements can be determined best by talking with the patient and family and using careful listening and observation skills. The medical chart also provides an important source of information concerning relevant premorbid history.

Individual differences also may focus upon a particular mode of sensory processing. For example, an individual may rely heavily on visual processing and demonstration in order to perform a task. Others may depend more upon auditory processing, talking themselves through a movement task. Still others rely more on kinesthetic processing, feeling their way through the movement. Familiarity with the task may structure the type of sensory processing perferred. Fitts[59] identified three distinct phases of motor learning: (1) early or cognitive phase, (2) associated or intermediate phase, and (3) the final or autonomous phase of learning. Predominence of sensory processing mechanisms varies according to the stage of learning. In the early stage, visual demonstration, auditory instructions, and manual guidance can contribute to learning the general idea or cognitive map of the task. For most individuals, visual-spatial processing appears to predominate. During the middle stage, organization of the movement pattern is accomplished more through concentration on proprioceptive feedback with less emphasis on visual or verbal guidance. During the last stage, refinement of the movement task occurs through more automatic and less cognitive processing of kines-

thetic cues.[19] Thus preferential modes of sensory processing vary according to task familiarity and stage of motor learning. The term *preferential* is used to indicate a preferred mode of processing and not the total exclusion of other forms of processing.

A thorough understanding of each of these factors allows the therapist to structure the therapeutic environment and therapist-patient interaction appropriately. Successful motor performance may depend less on underlying patient ability than on overall interest, cooperation, and motivation.

OBJECTIVE MEASURES

Dynamometry

An **isokinetic dynamometer** is an instrument which controls the velocity of a moving limb, keeping it at a constant rate, while accommodating maximum resistance as the part moves through the range. For example, the speed control on a Cybex II Isokinetic Dynamometer can be set between 0 to 300 degrees per second velocity while the range of torque output monitored is between 0 and 448 Newton meters.[62] The use of an isokinetic dynamometer during a motor control assessment allows the therapist to monitor several important characteristics of performance including torque output, range of motion or arc of excursion attained, rate of tension development, and the time intervals between reciprocal action of muscles. Thus it provides a quantitative assessment of torque control, timing, and reciprocal muscle action. Patients with neurologic deficit typically demonstrate decreased torque development, decreased limb excursion, extended times to peak torque development and the time peak torque is held, increased time intervals between reciprocal contractions, and/or problems in torque development at higher speeds.[31] For example, many patients with hemiplegia are unable to develop tension above 70 to 80 degrees per second. When this value is compared with the speed needed for normal walking (100 degrees per second), reasons for gait difficulties become readily apparent.[29] When available, normative data can provide an appropriate reference to assess and to interpret patient data.[63–71] For example, Watkins and associates[31] studied a group of patients with hemiplegia and found, in addition to many of the above changes, diminished torque values on the supposedly normal extremities.[31] These findings cast doubt as to the validity of using the uninvolved side in patients with hemiplegia as a reference for normal control.[31] Although additional research is needed, isokinetic dynamometry has already provided useful and objective information about the movement problems of selected patients. Continued application of dynamometry in the area of motor control assessment is needed.

Videotape Analysis

The qualitative analysis of movement patterns can be assisted by the use of video equipment. Patient responses recorded on videotape provide a permanent record of motor performance and allow the therapist the opportunity to compare responses over time. Recordings made at 3, 6, and 9 months of recovery can be compared easily without complete reliance on the therapist's memory or written notes. Videotapes also can be viewed repeatedly at different speeds to thoroughly investigate motor control during different activities. For example, a patient's performance in a task such as sitting up from the supine position can be observed first at regular speeds, then at slow-motion speeds. Stop-action or freezing a frame also can be used to isolate a problematic point in the movement sequence. This may be particularly helpful for the inexperienced therapist in improving both the quality and reliability of observations. Direct assessment of patient performance without videotape capabilities does not permit this detailed analysis. Moreover, repeated trials may needlessly tire the patient while yielding a significant decrease in performance. Videotapes can be used to provide a feedback for the patient, increasing awareness of a particular motor problem and assisting an appropriate corrective action. Sequential videotape recordings over the course of rehabilitation provide visual documentation of patient progress and can be important motivational tools in therapy.[72-74]

SUMMARY

A detailed motor control assessment analyzes a number of different factors, ranging from peripheral factors of range of motion, muscle power, and sensation to more central ones of tone, reflexes, and overall patterns of recruitment, timing, and organization within the CNS. Classical clinical testing of individual sensorimotor systems can yield valuable information about the integrity of these components. However, normal motor control models focus upon the integrated action of the CNS controlling these systems, yielding a complexity of behavioral responses. Our theoretic understanding of the CNS and its control processes is both incomplete and imperfect. Therapists must, therefore, be constantly aware of the changing knowledge of neuroscience in order to incorporate new ideas into their therapeutic approach to both assessment and treatment. Some aspects of control have withstood the test of time and are widely accepted. Both genetically defined reflex movements and learned skills comprise the basis of our posture and movement repertoire. Further, different levels of processing within the CNS provide the basis for automatic and volitional control of posture and movement. Assessment of motor control is a difficult process critically related to the therapist's ability to observe, analyze, and categorize behavior accurately. An understanding of normal development and movement control mechanisms is essential to this process. Determining the causative factors responsible for abnormal movement patterns must be based upon a comparison of expected or normal responses with the patient's abnormal ones. This can be achieved best by a systematic and thorough approach to behavioral assessment.

QUESTIONS FOR REVIEW

1. What are the two types of movement patterns which comprise our movement repertoire? How does the assessment of each differ? In normal patients? In patients with motor control deficits?

2. How can mental status, sensation, perception, communication ability, and central state or arousal influence a motor control assessment?

3. Define closed-loop processes of motor control. How do they differ from open-loop processes? How do they influence a motor control assessment?

4. What are the major types of tonal abnormalities? Define each. Describe the procedures used to assess each.

5. What influences may have impact on an assessment of tone? How can the assessment be structured to identify these factors appropriately?

6. Describe the four major levels of motor control. How should an assessment of each level be structured? Name two activities that could be used to assess each level and describe key factors that you would use to guide your assessment.

7. What are abnormalities in voluntary movement control? How can they be assessed?

8. What role do learning factors have in motor performance? How can they be assessed?

9. Describe the role of dynamometry in the assessment of motor control. Do the same for the role of videotapes.

10. What are the major difficulties in arriving at an accurate assessment of motor control? How can the assessment be structured to alleviate or to reduce their impact?

REFERENCES

1. Schmidt, R: Motor Control and Learning. Human Kinetics, Champaign, IL, 1982.
2. Brooks, V: The Neural Basis of Motor Control. Oxford University Press, New York, 1986.
3. Bernstein, N: The Coordination and Regulation of Movement. Pergamon Press, London, 1967.
4. Jackson, H: On some implications of dissolution of nervous system. Med Press Circular 2:411, 1882.
5. Sherrington, C: The Integrative Action of the Nervous System. Charles Scribner's Sons, New York, 1906.
6. Guyton, A: Basic Neuroscience. WB Saunders, Philadelphia, 1987.

7. Griffith, E: Types of disability. In Rosenthal, M, et al (eds): Rehabilitation of the Head-Injured Adult. FA Davis, Philadelphia, 1983.
8. Beh-Yishay, Y and Diller, L: Cognitive deficits. In Rosenthal, M, et al (eds): Rehabilitation of the Head-Injured Adult. FA Davis, Philadelphia, 1983.
9. Fowler, R and Fordyce, W: Stroke: Why Do They Behave That Way? American Heart Association, Dallas, 1974.
10. Hagen, C, Malkmus, D, and Durham, P: Levels of cognitive functioning. In Rehabilitation of the Head Injured Adult: Comprehensive Physical Management. Professional Staff Association of Rancho Los Amigos Hospital, Downey, CA, 1979.
11. Malkmus, D: Integrating cognitive strategies into the physical therapy setting. Phys Ther 63:1952, 1983.
12. Smith, R: Speech and language assessment. In Rosenthal, M, et al (eds): Rehabilitation of the Head-Injured Adult. FA Davis, Philadelphia, 1983.
13. Somjen, G: Neurophysiology—the essentials. Williams & Wilkins, Baltimore, 1983.
14. Dell, P: Reticular homeostasis and critical reactivity. In Moruzzi, B, Fessard, A, and Jasper, HH (eds): Progress in Brain Research, vol 1. Brain Mechanisms. Elsevier, New York, 1963.
15. Wilder, J: Basimetric approach (law of initial value) to biological rhythms. Ann NY Acad Sci 98:1211, 1961.
16. Stockmeyer, S: Clinical decision making based on homeostatic concepts. In Wolf, S (ed): Clinical Decision Making in Physical Therapy. FA Davis, Philadelphia, 1985.
17. Farber, S: Neurorehabilitation—A Multisensory Approach. WB Saunders, Philadelphia, 1982.
18. Heiniger, M and Randolph, C: Neurophysiological Concepts in Human Behavior. CV Mosby, St Louis, 1981.
19. Sage, G: Introduction to Motor Behavior: A Neuropsychological Approach, ed 2. Addison-Wesley, Reading, MA, 1977.
20. Stelmach, G (ed): Motor Control Issues and Trends. Academic Press, New York, 1976.
21. Siev, E, Freishtat, B, and Zoltan, B: Perceptual and Cognitive Dysfunction in the Adult Stroke Patient, ed 2. George B. Slack Thorofare, NJ, 1986.
22. Bobath, B: Adult Hemiplegia: Evaluation and Treatment, ed 2. Wm Heinemann Medical Books, London, 1978.
23. Bishop, B: Spasticity: Its physiology and management. Part III. Identifying and assessing the mechanisms underlying spasticity. Phys Ther 57:385, 1977.
24. Burke, D: Stretch reflex activity in the spastic patient. In Buser, P, Cobb, W, and Okuma, I (eds): Kyoto Symposia (EEG Suppl No 36), Elsevier Biomedical Press, Amsterdam, 1982.
25. Gilroy, J and Holliday, P: Basic Neurology. Macmillan, New York, 1982.
26. Chusid, J: Correlative Neuroanatomy and Functional Neurology, ed 18. Lange Medical Publishers, Los Altos, CA, 1982.
27. Mountcastle, V (ed): Medical Physiology, ed 14. CV Mosby, St Louis, 1980.
28. Weiner, W and Goetz, C (eds): Neurology for the Non-Neurologist. Harper & Row, Philadelphia, 1981.
29. Nelson, A: Motor assessment. In Rosenthal, M, et al (eds): Rehabilitation of the Head-Injured Adult. FA Davis, Philadelphia, 1985.
30. Barrows, H: Guide to Neurological Assessment. JB Lippincott, Philadelphia, 1980.
31. Watkins, M, Harris, B, and Kozlowski, B: Isokinetic testing in patients with hemiparesis. Phys Ther 64:184, 1984.
32. Brunnstrom, S: Movement Therapy in Hemiplegia. Harper & Row, New York, 1970.
33. Ashburn, A: A physical assessment for stroke patients. Physiotherapy 68:109, 1982.
34. Evans, C: The practical evaluation of handicap after severe stroke. Physiotherapy 67:199, 1981.
35. Griffith, E: Spasticity. In Rosenthal, M, et al (eds): Rehabilitation of the Head-Injured Adult. FA Davis, Philadelphia, 1985.
36. Bishop, B: Vibratory stimulation. Part II. Vibratory stimulation as an evaluation tool. Phys Ther 55:28, 1975.
37. Easton, T: On the normal use of reflexes. Am Sci 60:591, 1972.
38. Hellebrandt, F, Schade, M, and Carns, M: Methods of evoking the tonic neck reflexes in normal human subjects. Am J Phys Med 35:144, 1956.
39. Hellebrandt, F and Waterland, J: Expansion of motor patterning under exercise stress. Am J Phys Med 41:56, 1962.
40. Bobath, B: Abnormal Postural Reflex Activity Caused by Brain Lesions. Wm. Heinemann Medical Books, London, 1965.
41. Capute, A, et al: Primitive Reflex Profile. University Park Press, Baltimore, 1978.
42. Capute, A, et al: Primitive reflex profile: A pilot study. Phys Ther 58:1061, 1978.
43. Barnes, M, Crutchfield, C, and Heriza, C: The Neurophysiological Basis of Patient Treatment, vol 2. Reflexes in Motor Development. Stokesville Publishing, Atlanta, 1978.
44. Fiorentino, M: Normal and Abnormal Development. The Influence of Primitive Reflexes on Motor Development. Charles C Thomas, Springfield, IL, 1972.
45. Fiorentino, M: Reflex Testing Methods for Evaluating CNS Development, ed 2. Charles C Thomas, Springfield, IL, 1973.
46. Bayley, N: The development of motor abilities during the first three years. Monographs of the Society for Research in Child Development 1 (1, serial #1), 1935.
47. Gesell, A and Amatruda, C: Developmental Diagnosis. Harper, New York, 1941.
48. McGraw, M: The Neuromuscular Maturation of the Human Infant. Hafner Press, New York, 1945.
49. Peiper, A: Cerebral Function in Infancy and Childhood. Consultants Bureau Enterprises, New York, 1963.
50. Connolly, K (ed): Mechanisms of Motor Skill Development. Academic Press, New York, 1970.
51. Milani-Comparetti, A and Gidone, E: Pattern analysis of motor development and its disorders. Dev Med Child Neurol 9:631, 1967.
52. Illingworth, R: The Development of the Infant and Young Child. Normal and Abnormal. E & S Livingstone Ltd., London, 1975.
53. Keogh, J and Sugden, D: Movement Skill Development. Macmillan, New York, 1985.
54. Rood, M: The use of sensory receptors to activate, facilitate, and inhibit motor response, autonomic and somatic in developmental sequence. In Sattely, C (ed): Approaches to Treatment of Patients with Neuromuscular Dysfunction. William Brown, Dubuque, IO, 1962.
55. Stockmeyer, S: An interpretation of the approach of Rood to the treatment of neuromuscular dysfunction. Am J Phys Med 46:900, 1967.
56. Thelan, E, Bradshaw, G, and Ward, J: Spontaneous kicking in month-old infants: manifestation of a human central locomotor program. Behav Neural Biol 32:45, 1981.
57. Sullivan, P, Markos, P, and Minor, M: An Integrated Approach to Therapeutic Exercise. Reston, Reston, VA, 1982.
58. Minor, M and Minor, S: Patient Evaluation Methods for the Health Professional. Reston, Reston, VA, 1985.
59. Fitts, P and Posner, M: Human Performance. Brooks/Cole, Belmont, CA, 1969.
60. Gentile, A, et al: The structure of motor tasks. Movement 7:11, 1975.
61. Umphred, D: Conceptual model of an approach to the sensorimotor treatment of the head-injured client. Phys Ther 63:1983, 1983.
62. Isolated Joint Testing and Exercise: A Handbook for Using the Cybex II and U.B.X.T. Cybex, Div of Lumex, Inc., 2100 Smithtown Ave, Ronkonkoma, NY 11779, 1981.
63. Watkins, M and Harris, B: Evaluation of isokinetic muscle performance. Clin Sports Med 2:37, 1983.
64. Holmes, J and Gordon, J: Isokinetic strength characteristics of the quadriceps femoris and hamstring muscles in high school students. Phys Ther 64:914, 1984.
65. Armstrong, L, et al: Using isokinetic dynamometry to test ambulatory patients with multiple sclerosis. Phys Ther 63:1274, 1983.
66. Griffin, J, McClure, M, and Bertorini, T: Sequential isokinetic and manual muscle testing in patients with neuromuscular disease: a pilot study. Phys Ther 66:32, 1986.
67. Simmons, J, Roth, D, and Merta, R: Calculation of disability using the Cybex II system. Orthopedics 5:181, 1982.
68. Goslin, B and Charteris, J: Isokinetic dynamometry: normative data for clinical use in lower extremity (knee) cases. Scand J Rehabil Med 11:105, 1979.
69. Murray, M, et al: Strength of isometric and isokinetic contractions: knee muscles of men aged 20 to 86. Phys Ther 60:412, 1980.
70. Mira, A, Carlisle, K, and Greer, R: A critical analysis of quadriceps function after femoral shaft fracture in adults. J Bone Joint Surg (Am) 62:61, 1980.

71. Watkins, M, et al: Effect of patellectomy on the function of the quadriceps and hamstrings. J Bone Joint Surg (Am) 65:390, 1983.
72. Stichbury, J: Assessment of disability following severe head injury. Physiotherapy 61:268, 1975.
73. Turnbull, G and Wall, J: The development of a system for the clin-
ical assessment of gait following stroke. Physiotherapy 71:294, 1985.
74. Pink, M: High speed video applications in physical therapy. Clinical Management 5:14, 1985.

GLOSSARY

Aphasia: Absence or impairment of the ability to communicate through speech, writing or signs due to dysfunction of brain centers.

Arousal (central state): An internal state of alertness or excitement.

Brainstem reflexes (tuning reflexes, attitudinal reflexes): Reflexes organized by lower brainstem centers of control; e.g., tonic neck, tonic labyrinthine, associated reactions.

Cerebral shock: Transient hypotonia following injury to the brain.

Clasp-knife phenomena: A sudden relaxation or letting go of a spastic muscle in response to a stretch stimulus.

Clonus: Spasmodic alteration of muscular contraction and relaxation.

Closed skills: Motor skills performed in a stable, predictable environment.

Cogwheel phenomenon: A rachet-like response to passive movement seen in patients with rigidity; characterized by an alternate presence and release of resistance to movement.

Controlled mobility (dynamic postural control; dynamic equilibrium, motion stability): The third stage of motor control characterized by the maintenance of postural control during weight shifting and movement.

Creeping: Movement progression in the quadruped (all fours) position.

Homolateral creeping: An ipsilateral creeping pattern in which the arm and leg of one side of the body move together and alternate with the opposite arm and leg.

Contralateral (reciprocal) creeping: A creeping pattern in which the contralateral arm and leg alternates with the opposite movement pair.

Decerebrate rigidity (decerebration): Sustained contraction of extensor muscles of all four limbs resulting from a lesion in the brainstem between the red nucleus and vestibular nuclei.

Decorticate rigidity (decortication): Sustained contraction of extensor muscles in the lower limbs and flexor muscles in the upper limbs resulting from a brainstem lesion between the cortex and red nucleus.

Drop test (placing test): A test used to assess the integrity of automatic proprioceptive reactions; the limb is raised to a new position and suddenly dropped.

Dystonic posturing: Abnormal involuntary sustained posturing of the body maintained by powerful contractions of muscles.

Equilibrium reactions: Automatic responses which serve to maintain or regain balance during posture and movement; provides for restoration of center of gravity (c-o-gr) within the base of support (b-o-s) when balance is displaced.

Flaccidity: State of absent or decreased muscle tone.

Hypertonus: Excess muscular tone or tension.

Hypotonus: Reduced muscular tone or tension.

Isokinetic dynamometer: An exercise device which controls the velocity of a limb, keeping it at a constant rate while offering accommodating resistance through the range of motion.

Law of Initial Value (LIV) of Wilder: A law describing the relationship between a stimulus and a change in a function from its pre-stimulus level; expressed as: the higher the initial value of a function, the less change will occur in response to a function-increasing stimulus, and the lower the initial value of a function, the less change will occur in response to a function-decreasing stimulus.

Levels of cognitive functioning (Rancho Los Amigos Scale): A rating scale which categorizes neurobehavioral responses along a continuum of neurologic recovery and increasing cognitive integrity.

Mobility: The first stage of motor control characterized by random full range movements; reflex based.

Motor skill: A movement dependent upon practice and experience for its execution.

Normal postural reflex mechanism: A term used by Bobath to refer to the skill level of postural control, comprised of 5 essential components: 1) normal postural tone; 2) normal reciprocal interaction of muscles; and 3) righting reactions; 4) equilibrium reactions; and 5) protective reactions.

Open skills: Motor skills performed in a constantly changing, unpredictable environment.

Postural tone: A pattern of muscular tone or tension that exists throughout the body and affects groups of muscles.

Primitive reflexes: An involuntary movement response to a stimulus which is present before or at birth and normally integrated by the first six months of life.

Reaction: An involuntary movement response to a stimulus which appears in infancy and remains present throughout life.

Reflex: A genetically defined involuntary movement response to a stimulus.

Release phenomenon: Release of the lower brainstem and spinal control centers from the modulating influence of higher centers; seen in brain damage affecting the higher centers.

Righting reaction: An involuntary movement response

to a stimulus that serves to maintain the normal alignment of the head and body in space.

Rigidity: Stiffness, tenseness, inability to bend or to be bent.

Skill: The fourth and highest level of motor control characterized by coordinate movement; discrete distal motor control superimposed upon proximal stability.

Spasms: Involuntary and convulsive muscular contraction; when strong and painful, called cramps.

Spasticity: Increased tone or contraction of muscle causing stiff awkward movements; the result of an upper motor neuron lesion.

Spinal reflex (elemental reflex): An involuntary movement response to a stimulus organized on a spinal cord level of control; e.g. flexor withdrawal, and extensor thrust, crossed extension.

Spinal shock: Transient hypotonia following injury to the spinal cord.

Stability: The second stage of motor control characterized by the ability to maintain a steady position in relation to gravity. It is comprised of two substages:

Tonic holding: Activation of postural extensor muscles in the fully shortened range.

Cocontraction: Simultaneous contraction of both agonist and antagonist muscles necessary to stabilize and support the body.

Synergy: Normal association of functionally linked muscles which produce coordinated movement. In some neurological conditions, a stereotyped mass pattern of movement in which muscles are abnormally linked together in predictable movement patterns; typically seen in hemiplegia.

Tone (muscle): The resistance of muscles to passive elongation or stretch.

Tonic vibration reflex (TVR): A sustained contraction of muscle in response to a vibratory stimulus.

Chapter 10

ELECTROMYOGRAPHY AND NERVE CONDUCTION VELOCITY TESTS

LESLIE PORTNEY

OBJECTIVES

1. Describe the instrumentation system used to record electromyographic (EMG) data for clinical and kinesiologic uses.

2. Describe the general methodology used to perform an EMG and nerve conduction velocity (NCV) examination.

3. Describe the characteristics of normal and abnormal EMG potentials.

4. Describe the EMG and NCV findings typically seen with neuromuscular disorders.

5. Discuss the implications of clinical EMG findings for goal setting and treatment planning in rehabilitation.

6. Discuss the relationship between EMG and force with different types of contractions.

7. Discuss procedural, technical, and physiologic considerations for interpreting clinical and kinesiologic electromyographic data.

8. Describe the uses of kinesiologic EMG for clinical assessment and treatment of patients with neuromuscular or musculoskeletal dysfunction.

INTRODUCTION

Luigi Galvani presented the first report on electrical properties of muscles and nerves in 1791.[1] He demonstrated muscle activity following stimulation of neurons and recorded potentials from muscle fibers in states of voluntary contraction in frogs. This information was disregarded for close to a century, as conflicting theories were accepted, and did not become part of medical technology until the early portion of this century when instrumentation was developed to make recording such activity reliable and valid. Today **electromyography** (EMG) is used to assess the scope of neuromuscular disease or trauma and as a kinesiologic tool to study muscle function.

As an assessment procedure, clinical electromyography involves the detection and recording of electrical potentials from skeletal muscle fibers. **Nerve conduction velocity (NCV)** tests determine the speed with which a peripheral motor or sensory nerve conducts an impulse. Together with other clinical assessments, these two electrodiagnostic procedures can provide information about the extent of nerve injury, muscle disease, and the prognosis for surgical intervention and rehabilitation. These data can be valuable for diagnosis and determination of rehabilitation goals for patients with musculoskeletal and neuromuscular disorders.

Kinesiologic EMG is used extensively to study muscle activity and to establish the role of various muscles in specific activities. Although the concepts are the same, the focus of kinesiologic EMG is quite different from that of clinical EMG in terms of instrumentation requirements and data analysis techniques. Basmajian and De Luca[2] have provided a thorough review of literature in this area.

CONCEPTS OF ELECTROMYOGRAPHY

Electromyography is, in essence, the study of motor unit activity. Motor units are composed of one anterior horn cell, one axon, its neuromuscular junctions, and all the muscle fibers innervated by that axon (Fig. 10–1). The single axon conducts an impulse to all its muscle fibers, causing them to depolarize at relatively the same time. The depolarization produces electrical activity, which is manifested as a **motor unit action potential** (MUAP) and recorded graphically as the *electromyogram*. It is often reassuring to a patient to realize that electromyography only records electrical activity already present in contracting muscle, as opposed to introducing electrical energy into the body. The reader is encouraged to review the anatomy and physiology of the neuromuscular system as a basis for further discussion of electromyographic data.

Instrumentation

Recording the electromyogram requires a system including **electrodes** that pick up electrical potentials (activity) from contracting muscle (INPUT PHASE), an amplifier which processes the small electrical signal (PROCESSOR PHASE), and a display (OUTPUT PHASE), which allows visualization and listening to

sounds emitted, allowing complete analysis of data (Fig. 10–2).

INPUT PHASE

Electrodes

Several types of **electrodes** can be used to monitor the myoelectric signal. **Surface electrodes** are used to test nerve conduction velocity and in kinesiologic investigations. They are generally considered adequate for monitoring large superficial muscles or muscle groups. They are not considered selective enough to record activity accurately from individual **motor units** nor from specific small or deep muscles.[3] **Fine-wire indwelling electrodes** can be used for kinesiologic study of small and deep muscles. *Needle electrodes* are necessary to record single motor unit potentials for clinical EMG.

Surface electrodes are small metal disks, most commonly made of silver-silver chloride,[4] that are applied to the skin overlying the appropriate muscle (Fig. 10–3). They are usually attached with adhesive collars or tape. In a *bipolar arrangement,* two electrodes are placed over one muscle, usually over the belly, in a longitudinal direction with respect to the muscle fibers.[5]

Electrode gel is applied beneath surface electrodes to facilitate conduction of electrical potentials. Often, some skin preparation is necessary to reduce **skin resistance,** which can interfere with the quality of recording. This may include washing, rubbing with alcohol, and abrading the superficial skin layer to remove dead dry skin cells. However, with advances in instrumentation technology, amplifiers may have sufficient input **impedance** and electrodes may be of sufficient conductivity that skin preparation may not be necessary.

Fine-wire indwelling electrodes were introduced in the early 1960s for kinesiologic study of small and deep muscles.[6] They are handmade using two strands of small diameter wire (approximately 100 μm) coated with a polyurethane or nylon insulation, which are threaded through a hypodermic needle. The tips of the wires are bared 1 to 2 mm and bent back against the needle shaft (Fig. 10–4). The needle is inserted into the muscle belly and immediately withdrawn, leaving the wires imbedded in the muscle. Because of the small diameter of these wires—as thin as a hair—subjects cannot feel the presence of the wires in the muscle. These wires form a bipolar electrode configuration that can record from a localized area and that is capable of picking up single motor unit potentials. Fine-wire electrodes are necessary when monitoring activity from deep muscles, such as the soleus, or small or narrow muscles, such as the finger flexors.[3] They may not be as useful for larger muscles because they sample motor unit activity from such a small area of the muscle.

A needle electrode is required for clinical EMG, so that single motor unit potentials can be recorded from different parts of a muscle. The first studies of motor unit activity were done by Adrian and Bronk[7] in 1929 using a **concentric (coaxial) needle electrode.** This electrode consists of a stainless steel cannula, similar to a hypodermic needle, through which a single platinum wire is threaded

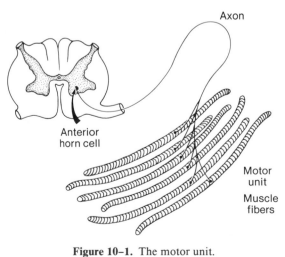

Figure 10–1. The motor unit.

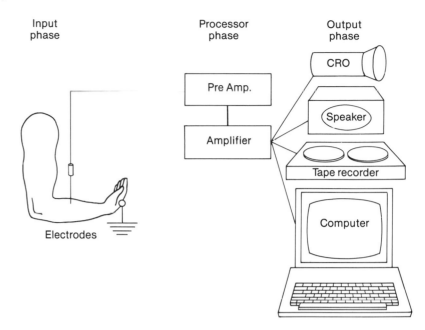

Input phase · Processor phase · Output phase

CRO · Pre Amp. · Speaker · Amplifier · Tape recorder · Computer

Electrodes

Figure 10-2. The EMG recording system, with needle electrode in forearm and ground electrode on dorsum of hand.

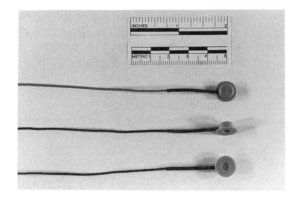

Figure 10-3. Surface electrodes: Silver-silver chloride surface electrodes (Beckman type).

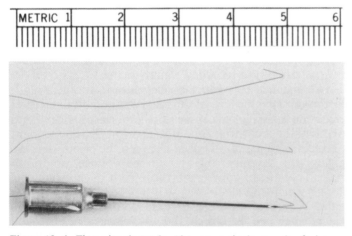

Figure 10-4. Fine-wire electrode. Above two single strands of wire are shown with different lengths of hooks, which appear as they might in muscle. Insulation is removed from the tips of the wires, and hooks created to keep wires imbedded while the needle is withdrawn from the muscle. The hypodermic needle at the bottom shows usual configuration before wires are inserted. Note: Wires have been slightly extracted from needle at tip. Reproduced from Soderberg, Glandcook, TM,[10] p 1814, with permission.

(Fig. 10-5). The cannula shaft and wire are insulated from each other, and only their tips are exposed. The wire and the needle cannula act as electrodes with the difference of potential between them recorded. A bipolar arrangement also may be used, with two wires threaded through the cannula (see Figure 10-5). The bared tips of both wires act as the two electrodes, the needle serving as a ground and as a mechanism to introduce the wires into the muscle. These electrodes are not useful for kinesiologic study because of the discomfort caused by the needle remaining in the muscle during contraction.

Another commonly used approach for clinical EMG is monopolar recording, in which a single fine needle (**monopolar needle electrode**), insulated except at the tip, is inserted into the muscle. A second surface electrode, placed on the skin near the site of insertion, serves as the **reference electrode.** These electrodes are less painful than concentric electrodes because they are much smaller in

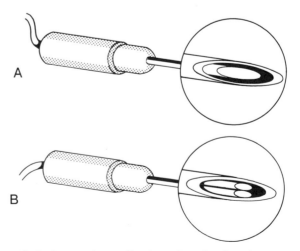

Figure 10-5. Concentric needle electrodes, showing single *(A)* and bipolar *(B)* wire configurations.

diameter. Because monopolar configurations record much larger potentials than bipolar, the type of electrode must be specified to avoid misinterpretation of data relative to the size of potentials and the area of pickup.

Any one of these types of needle electrodes can be used for a clinical EMG examination. Fine-wire electrodes are not appropriate for use in clinical EMG because the examiner does not have good control over placement of the electrode and the electrode cannot be moved within the muscle once it is placed. Guidelines for insertion of electrodes have been published,[8] and anatomic references should always be consulted to assure accurate and safe placement when using needles. Because they pierce the skin, all needle and fine-wire electrodes must be sterilized.

In addition to the **recording electrodes** (either surface or needle), a **ground electrode** must be applied to provide a mechanism for canceling out the interference effect of external electrical noise such as that caused by fluorescent lights, broadcasting facilities, diathermy equipment, and other electrical apparatus. The ground electrode is a surface plate electrode attached to the skin near the recording electrodes, but usually not over muscle.

The Myoelectric Signal

An electrode is a transducer, a device for converting one form of energy into another. Electrodes convert the bioelectric signal resulting from muscle or nerve depolarization into an electrical potential capable of being processed by an amplifier. It is the *difference of electrical potential* between the two recording electrodes that is processed.

The unit of measurement for difference of potential is the **volt.** The **amplitude,** or height, of potentials is usually measured in microvolts (10^{-6} volts). The greater the difference of potential seen by the electrodes, the greater the amplitude, or voltage, of the electrical potential. The amplitude of a MUAP is usually measured peak-to-peak; that is, from the highest point to the lowest point.

It is of interest to analyze the process by which a motor unit potential is transmitted to an amplifier in order to understand how such potentials can be interpreted. Because of the dispersion of the fibers in a single motor unit, the muscle fibers from several motor units may be interspersed with one another (Fig. 10–6). Therefore, when one motor unit contracts, the depolarizing fibers are not necessarily close together. Consequently, a needle or surface electrode cannot be situated precisely within or over any one motor unit.

As all the fibers of a single motor unit contract almost synchronously, the electrical potentials arising from them travel through body fluids, as a result of the excellent conducting properties of the electrolytes surrounding the fibers. This process is called **volume conduction.** The electrical activity will flow through the conducting medium, the volume conductor, in all directions—not just in the direction of the inserted needle electrode or of the surface electrodes on the skin. Fibrous tissue, fat, and blood vessels act as insulation against the flow. Therefore, the actual pattern of the flow of electrical activity within the volume conductor is not predictable.[9] The sig-

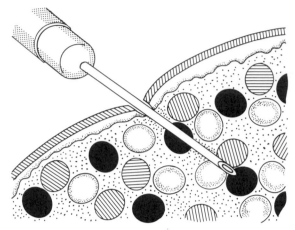

Figure 10–6. Cross-sectional view of muscle belly with needle electrode inserted. Differently shaded fibers represent different motor units.

nals that do reach the electrode are transmitted to the amplifier. All others are simply not recorded, although they are present. The activity produced by all individual fibers contracting at any one time is summated because it reaches the electrode at relatively the same time. Electrodes only record potentials they pick up, without differentiating their origin. Therefore, if two motor units contract at the same time from the same or adjacent muscles, the activity from fibers of both units will be summated and recorded as one large potential.

What variables, then, influence how much electrical activity is recorded by the electrodes and, therefore, the size and shape of the recorded potential? First, the proximity of the electrodes to the fibers that are firing will affect the amplitude and **duration.** Fibers that are further away will contribute less to the recorded potential. Second, the number and size of the fibers in the motor unit will influence the size of the potential. A larger motor unit will produce more activity. Third, the distance between the fibers will affect the output, because if the fibers are very spread out, less of their total activity is likely to reach the electrodes. The size of the electrodes may also be a consideration. If the recording surface is larger, the electrodes will pick up from a larger area, making the size of the recorded signal greater.

The distance between the electrodes is another major factor affecting the size of the recorded potential. Greater electrode spacing will increase the surface, width, and depth of the recording area. Because voltage is dependent on the difference of potential between the electrodes, the greater the distance, the greater the voltage, or amplitude. There is, of course, a critical limit to this distance, above which the electrodes will not be able to record a valid signal. Some surface electrode assemblies have been developed in which the two electrodes are fixed within a casing, standardizing interelectrode distance (see Figure 10–3).[2,10] Needle electrodes have a fixed distance between the wires and the needle shaft, which never changes even when the electrode is moved. Fine-wire indwelling electrodes are the least reliable in this aspect, inasmuch as there is little control over the interwire distance within the muscle. The wires are often prone to changing position within the muscle after repeated contractions, compromising the validity of the signals.

The effect of interelectrode distance explains the higher amplitude potentials seen with monopolar recording. The reference electrode is usually a significant distance away from the active recording electrode on a neutral area, thereby recording 0 potential. The difference of potential, then, between the reference and active recording electrodes is much larger than that seen between two electrodes placed over the muscle. It should be clear, however, that this greater EMG signal does not represent a greater amount of motor unit activity. It is of greater voltage, and may potentially be distorted because of the greater interelectrode distance.

The shape, size, and duration of the recorded motor unit potential is actually a graphic representation of the electrical activity being picked up by the electrodes, relative to the structure of the motor unit and the electrode placement (Fig. 10–7). Therefore, with a given electrode placement, each motor unit potential will look distinctly different. The implications of this process for repeated EMG testing should be evident. It is impossible to recognize a motor unit potential as the same one if electrodes have been reinserted or moved because the spatial and temporal relationships between the electrodes and the muscle fibers cannot be validly duplicated. This holds true for surface electrodes as well, although reapplication of surface electrodes has been shown to be more reliable than reinsertion of wire electrodes.[11]

Another important consideration is the ability of elec-

trodes to record activity selectively from a single muscle. Because of volume conduction, electrical activity from nearby contracting muscles other than the muscle of interest may reach the electrodes and be processed simultaneously. There is no way to distinguish this activity by looking at the output signal. Careful electrode placement and spacing, and choice of size and type of electrode will help control such "cross talk" or electrical "overflow."[2]

Artifacts

The EMG signal should be a true representation of motor unit activity occurring in the muscle of interest. Unfortunately, many excess signals, or **artifacts,** can be recorded simultaneously, distorting the electromyogram.

Movement Artifact. All electrodes are composed of a metallic detecting surface, which is in contact with an electrolyte. This electrolyte may be the conductive electrode gel placed between a surface electrode and the skin, or it may be the tissue fluids surrounding an inserted needle or fine-wire electrode. An ion exchange occurs at the interface between the electrode and the electrolyte, which is recorded as a bioelectric event when a difference of potential exists between the two electrodes.[12] If no muscle activity is present, therefore, and the ionization that exists at each electrode/electrolyte interface is stable, then no difference of potential exists, resulting in **electrical silence.**

If, however, some disturbance occurs at one or both electrode/electrolyte interfaces, producing a difference of potential, a low frequency AC signal will be recorded that does not represent EMG activity. This signal is called a **movement artifact.** It may result from movement of the skin beneath a surface electrode, pressure on or movement of the electrodes, or it may be caused by movement of a needle or fine-wire electrode within a contracting muscle. Most movement artifact occurs at frequencies below 10 to 20 **Hz** and can be eliminated with firm fixation of the electrodes and proper filtering of the signal (see discussion of **Bandwidth** in the next section).

Movement of electrode cables also can cause a high-voltage, high-frequency artifact, resulting from disturbance of the electromagnetic field that surrounds the conducting lead wires. These artifacts are not easily filtered. Some recording systems have small preamplifiers that attach directly to the electrode sites, eliminating lengthy cables. Care must be taken to reduce these artifacts and not to interpret such signals as motor unit activity. Artifacts will be discussed again in the section on kinesiologic EMG.

Power Line Interference. The human body acts as an antenna, attracting electromagnetic energy from the surrounding environment. This energy is most commonly drawn from power lines and electrical equipment operating under an alternating current at 60 cycles per second (60 Hz). An artifact caused by this **interference current** resembles a sine wave and can cause a constant hum in the recorded signal if it is not eliminated through appropriate amplification techniques.

Electrocardiogram (ECG). A third type of artifact, from pulse or ECG, occurs when electrodes are placed on the trunk, upper arm, or upper thigh. These are generally

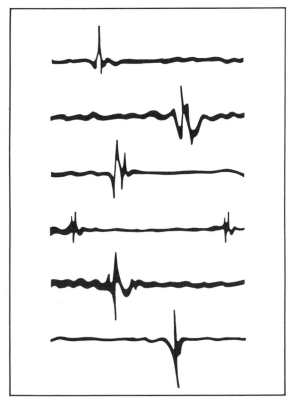

Figure 10–7. Single motor unit potentials, as seen on an oscilloscope.

regular signals, and the amplifier system may not be able to eliminate them. Their amplitude will vary, depending on placement of electrodes.

PROCESSOR PHASE

Before the graphic motor unit potential can be visualized, it is necessary to amplify the small myoelectric signal. An **amplifier** converts the electrical potential seen by electrodes to a voltage signal large enough to be displayed. In order to choose an appropriate amplifier and to interpret this output correctly, several characteristics of amplifiers should be considered.

Common Mode Rejection Ratio (CMRR)

The recording electrodes transmit electrical potentials arising from contracting motor units to two sides of a **differential amplifier,** each electrode supplying input to one side. The *difference of potential* between each input and ground is processed in opposite directions. The *difference* between these signals is amplified and recorded, hence the name of the amplifier. If the two electrodes receive equal signals, no activity is recorded. Electrical **noise** is transmitted to both ends of the differential amplifier, that is, a *common* signal. **Noise** is defined as any unwanted signal that is detected along with the wanted signal.[2] Noise is generated by static electricity present in the air, and by 60 Hz signals from power lines, fluorescent lights, electrical appliances or modalities, radio signals, and so forth. The noise, being equal at both ends of the amplifier, is canceled out when the difference of potential between the two sides is recorded.

In reality, however, the noise is not eliminated completely. Some of the recorded voltage will reflect noise. The **common mode rejection ratio (CMRR)** is a measure of how much the desired signal voltage is amplified relative to the unwanted signal.[4] A CMRR of 1000:1 indicates that the wanted signal is amplified 1000 times more than the noise. CMRR also may be expressed in decibels (1000:1 = 60 dB). The higher this value the better. A CMRR of greater than 100 dB is generally desired.

Signal-to-Noise Ratio

Noise also can be inherently generated by the electronic components of an amplifier, including resistors, transistors, and integrated circuits. This noise is often manifested as a hissing sound on an **oscilloscope.** The factor that reflects the ability of the amplifier to limit this noise relative to the amplified signal is the **signal-to-noise ratio:** the ratio of the wanted signal to the unwanted signal.

Gain

This characteristic refers to the amplifier's sensitivity; that is, its ability to amplify signals. The *gain* refers to the ratio of the output signal level to the input level.[10] A higher gain will make a smaller signal appear larger on the display. A greater sensitivity is required for clinical EMG in which individual motor units must be distinctly visible and their amplitude measured.

Input Impedance

Impedance refers to a property of resistance, or opposition to current flow, that occurs in alternating current circuits (such as an amplifier). Electrodes provide one source of impedance, affected by such variables as electrode material, size of the electrode, length of the leads, and the electrolyte. If the electrode impedance is too great, the signal will be attenuated. Electrode impedance can be reduced by using larger electrodes of good conductivity with shorter leads. Fine-wire and needle electrodes generally have much greater impedance than surface electrodes, owing to their much smaller surface area.

Body tissues, including adipose tissue, blood, and skin also provide a source of resistance to the electrical field. Resistance and impedance are measured in units called ohms. Skin impedance can be measured with an ohmmeter and its value reduced by proper preparation. Most researchers have reported acceptable skin impedance under 20,000 ohms, although with proper preparation and good electrodes, resistance can usually be reduced to between 1000 and 5000 ohms. Some skin areas, such as those with darker pigments or those that are more exposed, generally have higher impedance. Skin impedance obviously is a concern only with surface electrodes.

Impedance is also present at the input of an amplifier. Due to the direct relationship between voltage and impedance (based on Ohm's law), the muscle action potential is effectively divided into voltage changes at the electrode and amplifier input terminals. If the impedance at the amplifier is greater than the impedance at the electrode, the voltage drop will be greater at the amplifier (the recorded potential) and more accurately represent the true signal voltage. If the electrode impedance is too great, the voltage will drop at the source of the signal and less of the electrical energy will be transmitted to the amplifier. Therefore, the amplifier input impedance should be substantially greater (at least 1000 times) than the impedance recorded at the electrodes. An input impedance of 1 megohm is acceptable for surface electrodes but should be greater with fine-wire and needle electrodes.[10] Because skin resistance contributes to the impedance measured at the electrodes, greater input impedance decreases the need for skin preparation with surface electrodes.

Bandwidth

The EMG waveforms processed by an amplifier are actually the summation of signals of varying frequencies, measured in **Hertz** (1 Hz = 1 cycle per second). A MUAP can be likened to a piano chord, which is composed of many notes, each at a different frequency (sound). If we vary the notes, the chord will sound different. Similarly, the shape and amplitude of an action potential are, in part, a function of the frequencies that compose the waveform.

Amplifiers usually have variable filters that can be adjusted to limit the range of frequencies they will process. The frequency **bandwidth** delineates the highest and lowest frequency components that will be processed, or the upper and lower cut-off frequencies. If the full range of frequencies that make up the major portion of a waveform are not processed, the potential will be distorted. Amplifiers should be able to respond to signals between 10 and 10,000 Hz in order to record nerve and muscle potentials accurately for clinical EMG.[13-15] For kinesiologic purposes, however, in which specific waveform characteristics are not of major interest, a bandwidth of 10 to 1,000 Hz is adequate for surface electrodes, and 20 to 20,000 Hz for fine-wire electrodes.[10] Limiting signals within these frequency ranges is also helpful for reducing the effects of low- and high-frequency artifacts.

OUTPUT PHASE

The amplified signals must be displayed in a useful fashion. The type of output used is dependent on the type of information desired and instrumentation available.

Clinical EMG Displays

A *cathode ray oscilloscope (CRO)* is usually used for visual display in clinical EMG. A loudspeaker transforms the myoelectric signals into sound. Tape recorders have been used to record both the CRO image and the sound, to be played back at a later time for review. Many newer units incorporate computers that provide for digitizing the signal for storage and conversion back to analog signals for later display. Ink pen-writers are not appropriate for electrodiagnostic purposes because the pens have inherent frequency limitations that do not allow faithful reproduction of the motor unit potentials.

The cathode ray oscilloscope contains a **cathode ray tube** (Fig. 10–8). An electron gun in the rear of the tube projects an electron beam toward the interior of the screen, which is coated with a phosphorescent material. The electron beam causes this material to glow on contact, producing the lighted image we see on the screen. Two sets of plates, vertical and horizontal, are located in the body of the tube. The vertical plates are controlled by the amplifier from which the signal is being transmitted. They will deflect the electron beam in a vertical direction, proportional to the amplitude, or voltage, of the input signal. The horizontal plates control the speed of the **sweep** of the beam, or its movement across the screen. Therefore, the vertical plates control the display of the signal voltage and the horizontal plates control the display of the signal duration. These are usually expressed in microvolts (μV) and milliseconds (msec), respectively. By convention, a negative deflection goes above the baseline, and a positive vertical deflection moves below the baseline.

The exterior front of the oscilloscope screen is usually covered with a grid, forming vertical and horizontal divisions. The value of these divisions, relative to the displayed signal, can be manipulated by controls on the front panel of the CRO. The *gain* of the amplifier can be varied, making the vertical divisions equal to different voltages. For example, if a 10 μV signal is processed by the amplifier, the display may be set for this potential to be two divisions high. Therefore, each division represents 5 μV. However, if one wants the potential to look larger, the **sensitivity** must be increased. Therefore, one can turn up the gain, so that 10 μV would now have an excursion of five divisions. Each division would then represent 2 μV. The size of the input signal itself has not changed, only the size of the display. The higher the sensitivity, the larger the given signal will look. Therefore, when trying to display very small potentials, the sensitivity must be high. This will cause artifacts and noise to increase in size as well.

In similar fashion, the horizontal divisions may have varied values. A **sweep** speed control may increase or decrease the rate at which the beam travels across the oscilloscope screen, changing the time per division, usually read in milliseconds. A given potential may look more or less spread out. Again, the actual **duration** of the potential does not change, only the value of each horizontal division.

An oscilloscope may have a storage capability, allow-

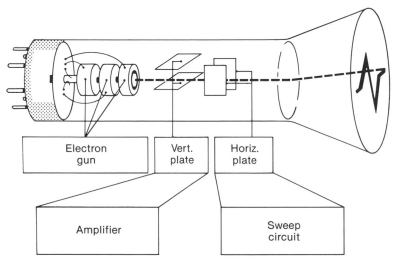

Figure 10–8. The cathode ray tube.

ing potentials to remain on the screen for indefinite periods. Alternatively, a camera can be connected to the oscilloscope with its shutter triggered by the sweep of the oscilloscope. Photographs can then be made of the test results for a permanent record. Some electromyographs have a built-in camera that can transpose the image on the screen onto photosensitive paper. Electromyographs also can be interfaced with computers that perform complex analyses of motor unit potentials and send results to a printer.

A loudspeaker provides the sound of the motor unit potential. The signal relayed from the amplifier can be transformed into sound in the same way that any radio signal is processed. For the same reason that every motor unit potential will look different, it also will sound different. Normal and abnormal potentials have distinctive sounds that are helpful in their differential identification. These will be described in the next section.

Electromyographs traditionally have been equipped with an FM magnetic tape recorder, which enables the electromyographer to maintain a permanent recording of the test results, both sound and image, to be played back on the oscilloscope for detailed analysis and reference. With the onset of computerization, this addition is not seen as often today.

Kinesiologic EMG Displays

Several types of recorders are used in kinesiologic study. The pen or chart recorder has been used historically, providing a permanent written record of the output. These recorders have limitations in terms of frequency response and are useful only when integrated or averaged waveforms are generated. An oscilloscope often is used in conjunction with a pen recorder to allow visual inspection of raw signals for artifacts.

Recorders also are available with a mechanism for focusing light beams, instead of pens, across photosensitive paper, creating the image of the EMG signal. These light beams are not subject to the same frequency limitations as pens and can record raw EMG signals at frequencies adequate for kinesiologic and clinical study.

Present technology allows the recording of raw and integrated EMG signals on magnetic tape, or sampling using a computer and printer. Several inexpensive analog-to-digital convertors are available for use with microcomputers, as well as the software needed to perform motion analysis using EMG data.

CLINICAL ELECTROMYOGRAPHY

The Electromyographic Examination

An electromyographic examination usually involves observation of muscle action potentials from several muscles in different stages of muscle contraction. The specific muscles to be tested are determined by the examiner according to the identified clinical problem. If a peripheral nerve lesion is suspected, the muscles innervated by that nerve will be studied. Examiners can test muscles whose innervations arise from a single nerve root to determine site of injury. When the extent of injury is questioned, muscles that appear unaffected may be examined as well. Each patient's case must be studied and the test planned accordingly.

Initially, the patient is asked to relax the muscle to be examined during insertion of the needle electrode. Insertion into a contracting muscle is uncomfortable, but bearable. At this time, the electromyographer will observe a spontaneous burst of potentials, which possibly is caused by the needle breaking through muscle fiber membranes. This is called **insertion activity** and normally lasts less than 300 msec.[13,14] This activity also is seen during examination as the needle is repositioned in the muscle. It usually stops when the needle stops moving. Insertion activity can be described as normal, reduced, or increased. It is considered a measure of muscle excitability and may be markedly reduced in fibrotic muscles or exaggerated when denervation or inflammation is present (Fig. 10–9).[14]

Following cessation of insertion activity, a normal relaxed muscle will exhibit **electrical silence,** which is the absence of electrical potentials. The baseline recorded usually will be slightly wavy as a result of the high amplifier sensitivity, which causes the baseline to reflect electrical noise from external and internal sources. These wavy deflections are readily distinguished from muscle potentials. Observation of silence in the relaxed state is an important part of the EMG examination. Potentials arising spontaneously during this period are significant abnormal findings. It is often difficult for a patient to relax sufficiently to observe complete electrical silence. However, the potentials seen will be distinct motor unit potentials, whereas **spontaneous potentials** can be differentiated by their low amplitude, shape, and sound. Sedation of a patient in order to achieve this relaxation is not

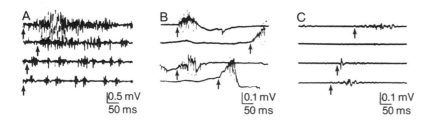

Figure 10–9. Increased *(A)*, normal *(B)*, and decreased *(C)*, insertion activity induced by movements of the needle electrode (indicated by arrows). The tracings were obtained from the first dorsal interosseus in a patient with tardy ulnar palsy *(A)*, tibialis anterior in a control subject *(B)*, and fibrotic deltoid of a patient with severe dermatomyositis *(C)*. Reproduced from Kimura, J,[14] p 248, with permission.

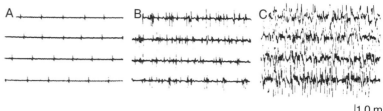

Figure 10–10. Normal recruitment of the triceps brachii in a 44-year-old healthy man. Activity was recorded during minimal contraction *(A)* where single motor unit activity is evident; during moderate contraction *(B)* when motor units are recruited; and during maximal contraction *(C)* when an interference pattern is visible. Reproduced from Kimura, J,[14] p 248, with permission.

|1.0 mV
10 ms

practical because voluntary movement will be hampered.

One exception to finding no activity in normal resting muscle occurs when the needle is in the end-plate region. Such activity may be reflected as constant low-amplitude

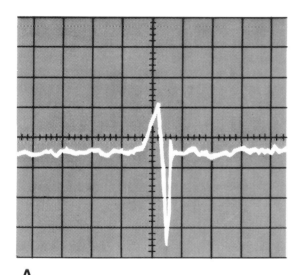

A

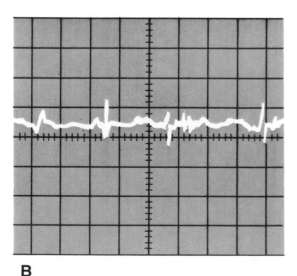

B

Figure 10–11. Single motor unit action potentials. The characteristics of amplitude, duration, and shape are examined by the electromyographer. *(A)* Normal biphasic potential, *(B)* Normal triphasic potentials. Reproduced from Yanof, HM,[77] p 438, with permission.

noise or high-amplitude intermittent spikes. It usually disappears by repositioning the needle slightly. *End-plate potentials* may be excessive in denervated muscle.[14]

After observing the muscle at rest, the patient is asked to contract the muscle minimally (Fig. 10–10). This weak effort should cause individual motor units to fire. These motor unit potentials are assessed with respect to *amplitude, duration, shape, sound,* and *frequency* (Fig. 10–11). These five parameters are the essential characteristics that will distinguish between normal and abnormal potentials.

It should be reiterated at this time that a motor unit potential is actually the summation of electrical potentials from all the fibers of that unit close enough to the electrodes to be recorded. The voltage amplitude is affected by the number of fibers involved. The duration and shape are functions of the distance of the fibers from the electrodes, the more distant fibers contributing to terminal phases of the potential.

NORMAL MOTOR UNIT ACTION POTENTIALS (MUAP)

In normal muscle, the amplitude of a single motor unit action potential may range from 300 μV to 5 mV, peak-to-peak, recorded with a concentric needle. The amplitude is primarily determined by a limited number of fibers located close to the electrode tip.[14] Therefore, motor units must be sampled from different sites in order to determine their amplitude accurately.

The total **duration,** measured from initial baseline deflection to return to baseline, will normally range from 3 to 16 msec. Duration is a function of the synchrony with which individual muscle fibers fire within a motor unit. This is affected by the length and conduction velocity of the axon terminals and muscle fibers.[14] Duration can be affected significantly by electrical activity originating in fibers distant to the electrode.

The typical shape of a MUAP is diphasic or triphasic, with a **phase** representing a section of a potential above or below the baseline. It is not abnormal to observe small numbers of **polyphasic action potentials,** having four or more phases, in normal muscle. However, when polyphasic potentials represent more than 10 percent of a muscle's output, it may be an abnormal finding.

The normal motor unit will fire up to 15 times per second with strong contraction. The identifying sound is a clear, distinct thump.[13]

Increasing gradation of contraction will allow the electromyographer to observe the pattern of *recruitment* in the muscle. With greater effort, increasing numbers of motor units fire at higher frequencies, until the individual potentials are summated and can no longer be recognized, and an **interference pattern** is seen (see Figure 10–10). This is the normal finding with a strong contraction. Highest amplitudes for interference patterns typically vary between 2 mV and 5 mV.

An electromyographer, therefore, assesses insertion activity and activity with the muscle at rest and in states of minimal, moderate, and maximal contraction. The needle electrode is moved to different areas and depths of each muscle to sample different muscle fibers and motor units. This is necessary because of the small area from which a needle electrode will pick up electrical activity, and because the effects of pathology may vary within a single muscle. Up to 25 different points within a muscle may be examined by moving and reinserting the needle electrode.

ABNORMAL POTENTIALS

Spontaneous Activity

Because a normal muscle at rest exhibits electrical silence, any activity seen during the relaxed state can be considered abnormal. Such activity is termed *spontaneous* because it is not produced by voluntary muscle contraction. Four types of spontaneous potentials have been identified and will be described here: **fibrillation potentials, positive sharp waves, fasciculations,** and **repetitive discharges.**

Fibrillation Potentials. **Fibrillation potentials** are believed to arise from spontaneous depolarization of a single muscle fiber.[9,13,14] This theory is supported by the small amplitude and duration of the potentials. They are not visible through the skin. Fibrillation potentials may result from spontaneous discharges of denervated muscle fibers owing to hypersensitivity to small quantities of circulating acetylcholine.[16] Alternative explanations also have been proposed, suggesting that slowly changing membrane potentials of metabolic origin will periodically reach critical thresholds, creating a spike potential.[17]

Fibrillation potentials may have up to three phases, and their spikes may vary in amplitude from 20 to 300 μV, with an average duration of 2 msec (Fig. 10–12).[18] Their sound is a high-pitched click, which has been likened to rain falling on a roof or wrinkling tissue paper.[14,19] Fibrillation potentials have been recorded at frequencies up to 30 per second.[9,13,14]

Fibrillation potentials are classically indicative of lower motor neuron disorders, such as peripheral nerve lesions, anterior horn cell disease, radiculopathies, and polyneuropathies with axonal degeneration. They also are found to a lesser extent in myopathic diseases such as muscular dystrophy, dermatomyositis, polymyositis, and myasthenia gravis.

Positive Sharp Waves. **Positive sharp waves** have been observed in denervated muscle at rest, usually accompanied by fibrillation potentials. However, they also are reported in primary muscle disease, especially muscular dystrophy and polymyositis.[13,20] The waves are typically diphasic, with a sharp initial positive deflection

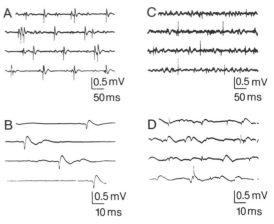

Figure 10–12. Spontaneous activity of the anterior tibialis in a 68-year-old woman with amyotrophic lateral sclerosis. Positive sharp waves *(A,B)* have a consistent configuration with a sharp positive deflection followed by a long-duration low-amplitude negative deflection *(B)*. Fibrillation potentials *(C,D)* are low-amplitude biphasic spikes. Reproduced from Kimura, J,[14] p 268, with permission.

(below baseline) followed by a slow negative phase (Fig. 10–12). The negative phase is of much lower amplitude than the positive phase, and of much longer duration—sometimes up to 100 msec.[13,19] The peak-to-peak amplitude may be variable, with voltages approaching 1 mV. The discharge frequency may range from 2 to 100 per second. The sound has been described as a dull thud. Positive sharp waves may be the result of single fiber discharges near the electrode tip or a synchronized discharge of several denervated fibers.[13,21] They are probably recorded from damaged areas of muscle fiber,[13] or they may be initiated by mechanical stimulation by the electrode within the muscle itself.[21]

Recent evidence indicates that fibrillation potentials and positive sharp waves also may be present with upper motor neuron lesions, creating a need for alternative explanations for their occurrence.[22–26] Spielholtz and colleagues[27] observed both types of potentials in patients with spinal cord lesions and attributed their occurrence to the lack of some trophic factor from higher centers to the anterior horn cell. This connection is lost with peripheral denervation. In upper motor neuron lesions the anterior horn cell itself is denervated, resulting in similar EMG findings. Spielholtz suggests that these findings may explain observation of fibrillations and positive sharp waves with myopathies, suggesting that muscle disease also affects the neuron. Johnson and associates[24] proposed a similar hypothesis to explain finding spontaneous potentials in patients following cerebral vascular accident.

Bilateral slowing of nerve conduction velocities in the ulnar and peroneal nerves also has been documented in patients with hemiplegia, supporting the hypothesis of lower motor neuron involvement.[28] Similar findings were not obtained, however, in a study of patients with cerebral palsy.[29] These findings also have been disputed by others, who have not confirmed the presence of spontaneous EMG activity in hemiplegic patients.[30,31] Further study is obviously needed to clarify the effect of upper

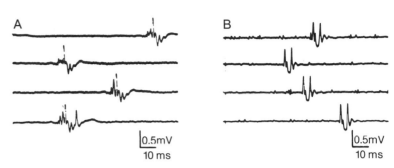

Figure 10–13. Fasciculation potentials in two patients with polyneuropathy. Recordings were obtained from the tibialis anterior in both, showing a very polyphasic potential of long duration *(A)* and a double-peaked complex discharge *(B).* Fasciculation potentials are not always abnormal in waveform as shown here and are usually indistinguishable in shape from voluntarily activated motor unit potentials. Reproduced from Kimura, J,[14] p 271, with permission.

motor neuron involvement on lower motor neuron function.

Investigators also have demonstrated spontaneous potentials in normal muscles of healthy subjects, primarily in muscles of the feet.[32] They suggest that pathologic changes involving axonal loss, segmental demyelination, and collateral sprouting may be associated with aging or mechanical trauma to the feet. Their findings have important clinical implications in that interpretation of the pattern of EMG and other assessments is necessary in order to determine pathology accurately.

Fasciculations. **Fasciculations** are spontaneous potentials seen with irritation or degeneration of the anterior horn cell, nerve root compression, and muscle spasms or cramps. They are believed to represent the involuntary asynchronous contraction of a bundle of muscle fibers or a whole motor unit. Although their origin is not clearly known, there is evidence that the spontaneous discharge originates in the spinal cord or anywhere along the path of a peripheral nerve, causing contraction of the muscle fibers.[33]

Fasciculations are often visible through the skin, seen as a small twitch. They are not by themselves a definitive abnormal finding, however, inasmuch as they also are seen in normal individuals, particularly in calf muscle, eyes, hands, and feet. When seen with other abnormal factors, fasciculations do contribute information relative to pathology. The amplitude and duration of these potentials may be similar to a motor unit potential (Fig. 10–13). They may be diphasic, triphasic, or polyphasic. Their firing rate is usually irregular, up to 50 per second. Their sound has been described as a low-pitched thump.[9,13]

Repetitive Discharges. **Repetitive discharges,** also called *bizarre high-frequency discharges,* are seen with lesions of the anterior horn cell and peripheral nerves and with myopathies. The discharge is characterized by an extended train of potentials of various form (Fig. 10–14). The distinguishing feature that differentiates these discharges from other spontaneous potentials is their frequency, which usually ranges from 5 to 100 impulses per second. The amplitude can vary from 50 μV to 1 mV, and duration may be up to 100 msec.[14] Repetitive discharges that increase and decrease in amplitude in a waxing and waning fashion are typical of myotonias and sound like a "dive bomber." High-frequency discharges are probably triggered by movement of the needle electrode within unstable muscle fibers, or by volitional activity.[13]

Abnormal Voluntary Potentials

Polyphasic potentials may be considered abnormal, but they are elicited upon voluntary contraction, not at rest. They are typical of myopathies and peripheral nerve involvement. In primary muscle disease these potentials are generally of smaller amplitude than normal motor units, and of shorter duration. These multiphasic changes occur because of the decrease in the number of active muscle fibers within the individual motor units owing to pathology. Although the entire unit will fire during voluntary contraction, fewer fibers are available in each unit to contribute to the total voltage and duration of the potential. The polyphasic configuration is a result of the slight asynchrony of muscle fibers within a motor unit. This phenomenon is probably caused by the difference in the length of the terminal branches of the axon extending to each individual fiber. The effects of this are normally not seen because the time differences are so slight. However, when some fibers are no longer contracting, these differences become more apparent, resulting in a fragmentation of the motor unit potential (Fig. 10–15).[13]

Polyphasic potentials also may be seen following regeneration of a peripheral nerve. As some muscle fibers become reinnervated, they will generate action potentials with voluntary contraction. However, there are significantly fewer fibers acting than were present in the original unit, and these fibers will clearly reflect asynchronous depolarization. These polyphasic potentials are also much smaller in amplitude and duration than normal

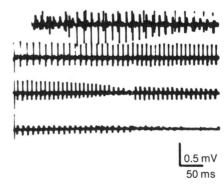

Figure 10–14. Repetitive discharge from the right anterior tibialis in a 39-year-old man with myotonic dystrophy. The waxing and waning quality of these discharges is evident. Reproduced from Kimura, J,[14] p 265, with permission.

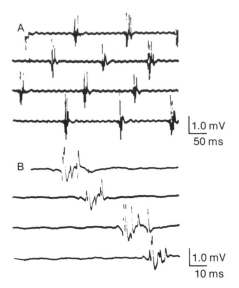

Figure 10–15. Polyphasic motor unit potentials from the anterior tibialis in a 52-year-old man with amyotrophic lateral sclerosis (recorded at fast *(A)* and slow *(B)* sweep speeds. Reproduced from Kimura, J.[14] p 278, with permission.

units. They have been termed *nascent motor units.* Although they are considered abnormal potentials, they are a positive finding with peripheral nerve lesions.

Some forms of neuropathic involvement, such as anterior horn cell disease, will result in hypertrophy of an intact motor unit by collateral sprouting of axons to fibers of denervated motor units, forming **giant motor units.** Because these sprouts are of small diameter and have slow conduction velocities, there is a dispersion in the recorded potential, increasing amplitude and duration and resulting in a polyphasic shape. These have been called giant potentials. If this situation is sufficiently prevalent, the interference pattern may be increased in amplitude.

Sources of Error in Clinical Electromyography

The subjective techniques used for electromyographic examination leave several avenues for error in performing and reporting the tests.[34,35] An understanding of potential errors will facilitate valid and reliable interpretation of test results.

Interpretation of when insertion activity is reduced or increased is dependent upon electrode position as well as subjective estimation. When the muscle is supposedly at rest, a trained observer must be able to distinguish spontaneous potentials from **single motor unit potentials** generated out of anxiety. The examiner must be able to judge the level of the patient's effort in order to determine validly if recruitment is normal and an interference pattern is achieved.[35] The electromyographer also must be able to distinguish different motor unit potentials and assess their amplitude, duration, and shape.

In terms of technique, it is obvious that inaccurate

electrode placement will distort the recorded potentials. In EMG examinations, great care must be taken to ensure appropriate placement of the needle electrode within the muscle. Anatomic anomalies must be considered. This becomes especially important because of volume conduction, when small or thin muscles are tested, such as those in the hand. Electrodes can be inserted too far, penetrating deeper muscles and thereby providing false information.

The interpretation of electromyographic potentials also provides opportunity for error. In electromyography, an experienced eye is needed to identify abnormal potentials accurately. It is also important to report them in appropriate terminology so that they are properly communicated. Fibrillation potentials and positive sharp waves were once called "denervation potentials." This did not distinguish the two types of potentials, nor is it an accurate expression in many cases. Similarly, an experienced examiner also must be able to judge when the number of polyphasic potentials is above normal percentages.

Nerve Conduction Velocity Tests

Hodes, Larabee, and German[36] first developed the technique for calculating the conduction velocity of the ulnar nerve in 1948. Dawson and Scott[37] further refined the procedure a year later, recording nerve potentials from the ulnar and median nerves through the skin at the wrist. This electromyographic technique has since become a valuable tool for assessing abnormalities and lesions of peripheral nerve, as well as localizing the site of involvement.

Nerve conduction velocity tests involve direct stimulation to initiate an impulse in motor or sensory nerves. The **conduction time** is measured by recording evoked potentials either from the muscle innervated by the motor nerve or from the sensory nerve itself. Nerve conduction velocity can be tested on any peripheral nerve that is superficial enough to be stimulated through the skin at two different points. Most commonly it is performed on the ulnar, median, peroneal, and posterior tibial nerves; less commonly on the radial, femoral, and sciatic nerves. Complete guidelines for performing nerve conduction velocity tests are available in several references.[38–40]

INSTRUMENTATION

Although electromyography records the spontaneous or volitional potentials of motor units, nerve conduction measurements involve **evoked potentials,** produced by direct electrical stimulation of peripheral nerves. The instrumentation, therefore, includes a stimulator in addition to all the components of the electromyograph already described (Fig. 10–16).

The stimulating electrode is typically a two-pronged bipolar electrode with the **cathode** (−) and the **anode** (+) extending from a plastic casing (Fig. 10–17). A single cathodal stimulating electrode also can be used in con-

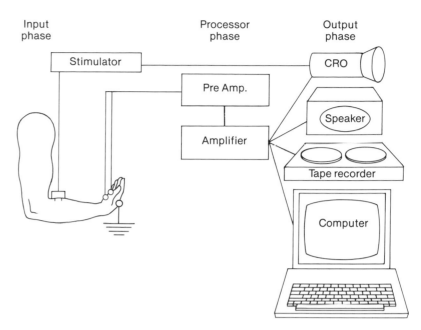

Figure 10–16. Recording system for nerve conduction velocity test, showing addition of the stimulator. The stimulating electrode is positioned over nerve trunk. Surface electrodes record potentials over thenar muscles. Ground electrode is placed on dorsum of hand. Note the connection between the stimulator and the CRO, which is the triggering mechanism for the oscilloscope sweep.

junction with an inactive electrode. A needle electrode can be used to stimulate the nerve. The stimulus is provided by a square wave generator, with pulses typically delivered at a duration of 0.1 msec and a frequency of 1 pulse per second (up to 20 pps). The intensity needed will vary with the nerve and the individual patient, usually between 150 and 300 V and 20 to 40 mA.[14]

A trigger mechanism is incorporated into the recording system, so that the oscilloscope sweep is triggered by the stimulator. This means that the sweep begins when the stimulus is delivered, producing a **stimulus artifact** on the screen with each successive stimulus. This allows the measurement of time from stimulus onset to response. The sweep makes one complete excursion across the screen for each pulse put out by the stimulator.

MOTOR NERVE CONDUCTION VELOCITY (MNCV)

Stimulation and Recording

Recording potentials directly from a peripheral nerve makes monitoring of purely sensory or motor fibers impossible. Therefore, to isolate the potentials conducted by motor axons of a mixed nerve, the evoked potential is recorded from a distal muscle innervated by the nerve. Although the stimulation of the nerve will evoke sensory and motor impulses, only the motor fibers will contribute to the contraction of the muscle. For the ulnar nerve the test muscle is the abductor digiti minimi; for the median nerve, the abductor pollicis brevis; for the peroneal nerve, the extensor digitorum brevis; and for

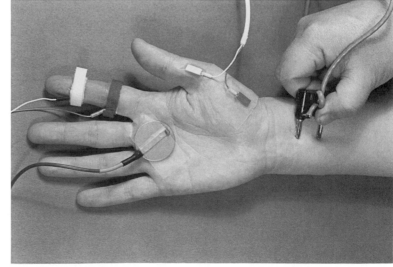

Figure 10–17. Setup for motor and sensory conduction velocity tests of the median nerve. Recording electrodes are placed over the muscle belly of the abductor pollicis brevis for motor conduction, and ring electrodes are placed over the proximal and distal interphalangeal joints of the second digit for sensory conduction. The ground electrode is located between the stimulating and recording electrodes on the hand. The nerve is stimulated at the wrist (shown) and at the elbow to obtain motor latencies. Only stimulation at the wrist is necessary for sensory latency. Reproduced from Kimura, J,[14] p 108, with permission.

the posterior tibial nerve, the abductor hallicus or abductor digiti minimi.

Surface electrodes usually are used to record the evoked potential from the test muscle, although needle electrodes may be used when responses are very weak. The surface electrodes should be small—less than 1 cm in diameter. One recording electrode, the **active electrode,** (sometimes called the **pick-up electrode**) is placed over the belly of the test muscle. Correct location of this electrode is important to the accuracy of the test, and the belly of the muscle should be palpated carefully, preferably against slight resistance. The second recording electrode, the **reference electrode,** is taped over the tendon of the muscle, distal to the active electrode. The skin should be cleaned with alcohol to reduce skin resistance before applying electrodes. A **ground electrode** is placed over a neutral area between the **recording electrodes** and the stimulation sites, usually over the dorsum of the hand or foot, or over the wrist or ankle. The skin over the stimulation sites also should be cleaned with alcohol to decrease resistance to the stimulus pulse, making the procedure more comfortable for the patient.

For purposes of illustration, the test procedure for the MNCV of the median nerve will be described. The technique is basically the same for all nerves, except for the sites of stimulation and placement of the recording electrodes. The active electrode is taped over the belly of the test muscle, the abductor pollicis brevis, and the reference electrode is taped over the tendon just distal to the metacarpophalangeal joint. The stimulating electrode is placed over the median nerve at the wrist, just proximal to the distal crease on the volar surface, with the cathode directed toward the recording electrodes (Fig. 10–17). The **cathode** is the stimulating electrode (usually black) and the **anode** is the inactive electrode (usually red). It is important that the cathode be directed toward the recording electrodes to stimulate depolarization toward the muscle (**orthodromic conduction**).

At the moment the stimulus is produced, the **stimulus artifact** is seen at the left of the screen. The trigger mechanism controls this and it will, therefore, always appear in the same spot on the screen, facilitating consistent measurements. This spike is purely mechanical and does not represent any muscle activity (Fig. 10–18).

The stimulus intensity starts out low and is slowly increased until the **evoked potential** is clearly observed. When the stimulating electrode is properly placed over the nerve, all muscles innervated distal to that point will contract, and the patient will see and feel his hand "jump." The intensity is then increased until the evoked response no longer increases in size. At that time the intensity is increased further by about 25 percent to be sure that the stimulus is *supramaximal.* Because the intensity must be sufficient to reach the threshold of all motor fibers in the nerve, a supramaximal stimulus is required. It is also essential that the cathode be properly placed over the nerve trunk so that the stimulus reaches all the motor axons.

As in the electromyogram, the potentials seen on the **oscilloscope** represent the electrical activity picked up by the recording electrodes. The signal will represent the difference of electrical potential between the active and ref-

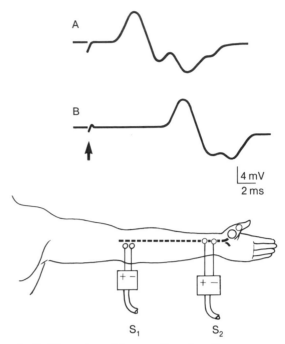

Figure 10–18. Illustration of the recording of median nerve motor conduction velocity, with the M wave recorded following stimulation at the wrist and elbow. Nerve conduction time from the elbow to the wrist can be determined as the latency difference between the distal and proximal stimulations. The MNCV is then calculated by dividing the surface distance between the two points by the latency difference.

erence electrodes. When the supramaximal stimulus is applied to the median nerve at the wrist, all the axons in the nerve will depolarize and begin conducting an impulse, transmitting the signal across the motor endplate, initiating depolarization of the muscle fibers. During these events the two recording electrodes do not record a difference of potential because no activity is taking place beneath the electrodes. When the muscle fibers begin to depolarize, the electrical potentials are transmitted to the electrodes through the volume conductor, and a deflection is seen on the oscilloscope. This is the **evoked potential,** which is called the **M wave** (Fig. 10–18). The M wave represents the summated activity of all motor units in the muscle responding to stimulation of the nerve trunk. The amplitude of this potential is, therefore, a function of the total voltage produced by the contracting motor units. The initial deflection of the M wave is the negative portion of the wave, above the baseline.

Although not done as often, nerve conduction velocity tests can be performed on more proximal segments of the nerve trunk by stimulating at more proximal points, such as Erb's point and the axilla.

Calculation of Motor Conduction Velocity

The point at which the M wave leaves the baseline indicates the time elapsed from the initial propagation of the nerve impulse to the depolarization of the muscle fibers beneath the electrodes. This is called the response **latency.** The latency is measured in milliseconds from the stimulus artifact to the onset of the M wave. This time alone is not a valid measurement of nerve conduction because it incorporates other events besides pure nerve conduction; namely, transmission across the myoneural junction and generation of the muscle action potential. Therefore, these extraneous factors must be eliminated from the calculation of the nerve conduction velocity. There is also evidence that the distal segments and terminal branches of nerves conduct at much slower rates than the main axon,[36,41] and **conduction velocity** should reflect only the speed of conduction within the nerve trunk.

To account for these distal variables, the nerve is stimulated at a second, more proximal point. This will produce a response similar to that seen with distal stimulation (Fig. 10–18). The stimulus artifact will appear in the same spot on the screen, but the M wave will originate in a different place because the time for the impulses to reach the muscle would, obviously, be longer. Subtraction of the **distal latency** from the **proximal latency** will determine the **conduction time** for the nerve trunk segment between the two points of stimulation. Conduction velocity is determined by dividing the distance between the two points of cathodal stimulation (measured along the surface) by the difference between the two latencies (velocity = distance/time).

$$\text{Conduction velocity} = \frac{\text{Conduction distance}}{\text{Proximal latency} - \text{distal latency}}$$

Conduction velocity is always expressed in meters per second, although conduction distance is usually measured in centimeters and latencies in milliseconds. These units must be converted during calculation.

To compute the motor nerve conduction velocity for the test illustrated in Figure 10–18, the proximal and distal latencies are determined by measuring the time from the stimulus artifact to the initial M wave deflection, according to the calibration scale, or sweep speed. The **conduction time** is calculated by taking the difference between these latencies. **Conduction distance** is then determined by measuring the length of the nerve between the two points of stimulation. For example,

Proximal latency   7 msec
Distal latency   2 msec
Conduction distance 30 cm

$$\text{Conduction velocity} = \frac{30 \text{ cm}}{7 \text{ msec} - 2 \text{ msec}} = \frac{30 \text{ cm}}{5 \text{ msec}}$$

Conduction velocity = 60 meters per second

Interpretation of the motor nerve conduction velocity is made in relation to normal values, which are usually expressed as mean values, standard deviations, and ranges. Norms have been determined by many investigators in different laboratories. Even so, average values seem to be fairly consistent. The motor nerve conduction velocity for the upper extremity has a fairly wide range, with values reported from 45 to 70 M/sec. The average normal value is about 60 M/sec. For the lower extremity, the average value is about 50 M/sec. Distal latencies and

average normal amplitudes of M waves also are found in such tables but must be viewed with caution, inasmuch as technique, electrode setup, instrumentation, and patient size can affect these values. The reader is referred to more comprehensive discussions for complete tables of normal values.[13,39,42,43]

It is important to note that the value calculated as the conduction velocity is actually a reflection of the speed of the fastest axons in the nerve. Although all axons are stimulated at the same point in time, and supposedly fire at the same time, their conduction rates vary with their size. Not all motor units will contract at the same time, inasmuch as some receive their nerve impulse later than others. Therefore, the initial M wave deflection represents the contraction of the motor unit, or units, with the fastest conduction velocity. The curved shape of the M wave is reflective of the progressively slower axons reaching their motor units at a later time.

In addition to latencies, the M wave itself can provide useful information about the integrity of the nerve or muscle. Three parameters should be assessed: amplitude, shape, and duration. Any change occurring in these characteristics is called **temporal dispersion.** These parameters reflect the summated voltage produced by all the contracting motor units over time within the test muscle. Therefore, if the muscle is partially denervated, fewer motor units will contract following nerve stimulation. This will cause the M wave amplitude to decrease. Duration may change depending on the conduction velocity of the intact units. Similar changes also may be evident in myopathic conditions, in which all motor units are intact but fewer fibers are available in each motor unit.

The shape of the M wave also can be variable. Deviation from a smooth curve need not be abnormal, and it is often useful to compare the proximal and distal M waves with each other as well as with the contralateral side. They should be similar. In abnormal conditions, changes in shape may be the result of a significant slowing of conduction in some axons, repetitive firing, or asynchronous firing of axons following a single stimulus.

SENSORY NERVE CONDUCTION VELOCITY (SNCV)

Sensory neurons demonstrate the same physiologic properties as motor neurons, and conduction velocity can be measured in a similar way. However, some differences in technique are necessary to differentiate between sensory and motor axons. Although sensory fibers can be tested regarding **orthodromic conduction** (normal physiologic direction) or **antidromic conduction** (opposite to normal conduction), orthodromic measurements appear to be more common. For the same reason that motor axons are examined by recording over muscle, sensory axons are either stimulated or recorded from digital sensory nerves. This eliminates the activity of motor axons from the recorded potentials.

Stimulation and Recording

The **stimulation electrode** used for motor conduction velocity tests can be used for sensory tests, or the stimulus may be provided by ring electrodes placed around the base of the middle of the digit innervated by the nerve (see Figure 10–17). The recording electrodes can be surface or needle electrodes. Surface electrodes are placed over the nerve trunk where it is superficial to the skin. The active electrode is placed distally, and a ground electrode is usually set between the stimulating and recording electrodes.

The electrode positions can be reversed, measuring **antidromic conduction.** If electrode sites are consistent, the latencies should be essentially equivalent in both directions. Orthodromic stimulation of fingertips appears to be more uncomfortable than stimulation of the nerve trunk.[13]

Sensory potentials for the median and ulnar nerves can be recorded at the wrist and elbow. The ulnar nerve also can be monitored at the axilla, although it is rather unreliable and difficult to differentiate between median and ulnar nerves. In lower extremities, the toes can be stimulated and sensory potentials recorded at various sites along the tibial and sciatic nerves. Sensory examination has been reported to be more difficult in the lower extremities because of anatomic variations.[13] The path of the main nerve trunk often can be determined by electrical stimulation and observation of motor responses.

Calculation of Sensory Conduction Velocity

Latencies are usually measured from the stimulus artifact to the peak of the evoked potential, rather than to the initial deflection, because of the uneven baseline seen with sensory tests (Fig. 10–19). The baseline is more uneven because sensory tests require much greater amplifier sensitivity than do motor tests, which allow more noise to interfere with recording. Although sensory conduction velocity can be determined in the same way as motor conduction velocity (dividing distance by difference between latencies), often latencies are sufficient measurements, because terminal branching does not seem to be a significant limitation. Therefore, the latency essentially represents sensory nerve conduction activity only.

Normal SNCV ranges between 45 and 75 m/sec. Amplitude, measured with surface electrodes, may be 10 to 60 μV, and duration should be short—less than 2 msec. Sensory-evoked potentials are usually sharp, not rounded like the M wave. Sensory nerve conduction velocities have been found to be slightly faster than motor nerve conduction velocities because of the larger diameter of sensory nerves.[44]

Because the amplitude of sensory potentials can be so low, even under normal conditions, the potential can be hidden in the erratic baseline, making it difficult to distinguish from the noise. In their early studies, Dawson and Scott[37] used photographic superimposition to overlay 100 sweeps. Because the stimulus artifact and the evoked potential will appear in the same place with each sweep, the random background noise looks dispersed and the evoked response is brighter on film. More sophisticated instrumentation has been developed that can process repetitive sweeps, averaging only the signals that appear at the same time frame and enabling the noise to be canceled out and the response to be reinforced. Electronic averagers then display the evoked potential clearly. These systems are often computerized today, allowing the potential to be clearly delineated from the random noise.

SOURCES OF ERROR IN CONDUCTION VELOCITY TESTS

For nerve conduction measurements, proper placement of both recording and stimulating electrodes is essential for reliable measurement. The active electrode should be directly over the muscle belly so that the M wave will be an accurate representation of full motor unit activity. Some leeway exists, however, before conduction velocity values are significantly affected.[45]

When patients are not able to contract the test muscle voluntarily, the electromyographer must be able to locate the muscle belly accurately. The electrodes also may record volume-conducted potentials from neighboring muscles, resulting in misinterpretation of the output.[46] If the stimulating electrode is not directly over the nerve trunk, all axons may not be stimulated, or axons from adjacent nerves may be stimulated instead. Consideration must be given to the possibility of anomalous innervation for the same reason.

In addition to placement concerns, the intensity of the

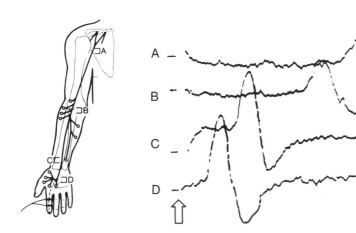

Figure 10–19. Sensory nerve conduction study of the median nerve. The sites of stimulation shown include elbow *(A)*, wrist *(B)*, and palm *(C)*. Digital potentials are recorded antidromically, using ring electrodes placed around the second digit. The arrow indicates the stimulus artifact. From Kimura, J: *Electrodiagnosis in Diseases of Nerve and Muscles: Principles and Practice.* FA Davis, Philadelphia, 1983, p 107, with permission.

stimulus is important. A submaximal stimulus may not be sufficient to reach the threshold of all axons in the nerve. This will significantly increase the latency obtained. The supramaximal stimulus that is required also may be of great enough intensity to cause spread of the stimulus pulse to other nerves.

Errors can occur in the calculation of the conduction velocity. The measurement of the distance between stim-

ulation sites (conduction distance) must be accurate. This is of special concern when the nerve trunk does not follow a perfectly straight path, as with the ulnar and radial nerves. The position of the limb will greatly affect these measurements as well. When measuring latencies, the location of the initial deflection of the M wave may be somewhat subjective.[47] In addition, the actual determination of the latency time must be exact. A permanent

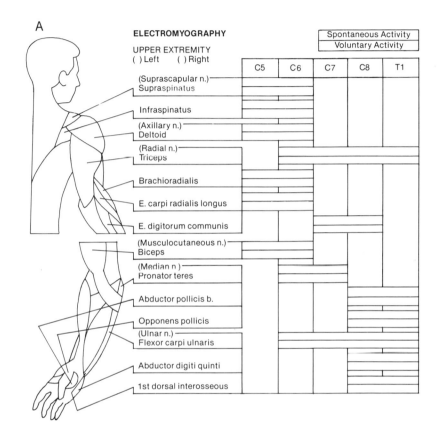

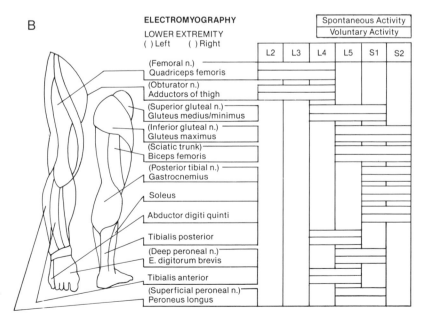

Figure 10–20. Sample report form for EMG. The pictorial form demonstrates the relative position and peripheral nerve and root innervation of the commonly tested upper extremity and lower extremity muscles. Information about spontaneous and voluntary activity can be recorded for each muscle. Reproduced from Brumback, et al: *Pictorial report form for needle electromyography.* Phys Ther 63:224, 1983, with permission.

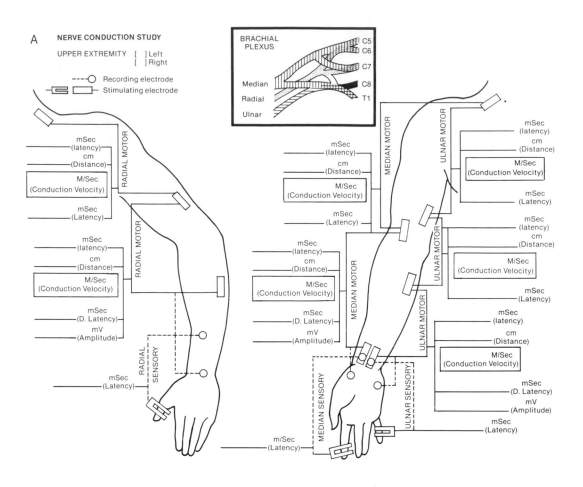

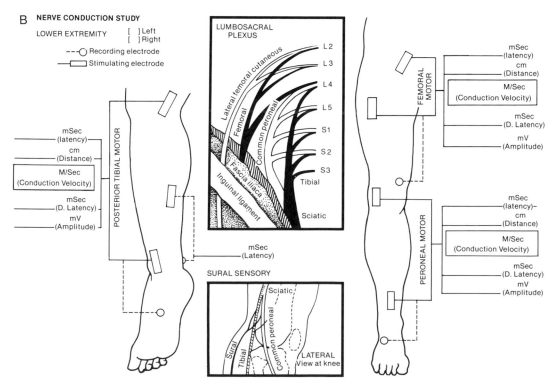

Figure 10–21. Sample report form for nerve conduction studies, containing listings of latencies, electrode distances, potential amplitudes and calculated conduction velocities, followed by interpretation. Forms for upper and lower extremity show relationship of anatomy to NCV data. Reproduced from Brumback, RA, et al: *Pictorial report form for nerve conduction studies.* Phys Ther 61:1457, 1981, with permission.

recording of some kind, such as film or computer print-out, is preferable to reading off the oscilloscope, where parallax errors are readily made. It is also easy to make errors in calculation of the nerve conduction velocity. Omission of distal latencies and distance between electrodes also can be considered an error in reporting, inasmuch as these values are necessary to the assessment of normal versus abnormal results.

In sensory nerve conduction velocity tests, care must be taken when placing electrodes, so that antidromic motor responses or volume-conducted activity is not recorded with the sensory potentials. If this occurs, the latency, shape, and duration of the evoked sensory potential will be affected significantly.

Other factors also must be considered when interpreting test results. *Age* and *temperature* are the two most influential factors that can cause variations in conduction velocity. Nerve conduction is slowed considerably in infants, young children, and elderly individuals. At birth the motor nerve conduction velocity is approximately half normal adult values and gradually increases until it reaches adult rates at 5 years of age.[48,49] Motor and sensory conduction velocities have been shown to decrease slightly following age 35, with larger significant differences noted after age 70.[50,51]

Lower temperature also can decrease motor and sensory conduction velocities significantly.[52] Drops of 1° C (34° F) in intramuscular temperature have been correlated with changes of 2 to 2.4 M/sec in conduction velocity. It is advisable to warm a cool limb prior to examination to stabilize the limb's temperature.

Echternach[35] has written a thorough discussion of measurement issues related to EMG and NCV that will be helpful to anyone interested in these test procedures.

Reporting the Results of the Clinical EMG Examination

The performance of reliable and valid electromyographic examinations requires extensive experience and expertise related to biomedical instrumentation, as well as to neuromuscular anatomy and pathology. The material presented here, however brief, is intended to provide sufficient background for the reader to use information from an electromyographic report intelligently and to apply these data to other aspects of patient care specifically related to prognosis, goal setting, and treatment planning. With this in mind, it seems appropriate to review how such reports are presented.

The EMG report typically is found in patients' charts or medical records. The essential data include (1) the specific muscle or muscles tested, including side of body and the innervation of these muscles; (2) the response seen during electrode insertion; (3) the response at rest (spontaneous activity, specifying type of potentials or electrical silence); and (4) responses with voluntary contraction (motor unit potentials and recruitment) (Fig. 10–20). The data provided should relate to the five parameters of electrical potentials previously described: amplitude, duration, shape, sound, and frequency.

Reports of nerve conduction measurements should include (1) location of recording and stimulating electrodes; (2) the calculated velocity, in meters per second; (3) the distal latency and distance between recording and stimulating electrodes; and (4) the amplitude and duration of the M wave or evoked sensory potential (Fig. 10–21). Comments should follow the data, stating the impression or implications of findings.

It is extremely important to stress here that diagnoses should not be made solely on the basis of electromyographic data. All other appropriate assessment procedures performed on the patient are used to provide a complete picture of the patient's disorder. These include a history and laboratory tests, as well as physical therapy assessments, such as the manual muscle test, sensory tests, a range of motion test, and so forth. Electrodiagnostic findings will often provide objective evidence to support clinical observations.

CLINICAL IMPLICATIONS OF ELECTROMYOGRAPHIC TESTS

Typical findings with neurogenic or myogenic disorders can be described (Fig. 10–22). The following discussion will focus on selected disorders that typify EMG and NCV results, and their implications for assessment and treatment planning.

Disorders of the Peripheral Nerve

PERIPHERAL NERVE LESIONS

Lesions of the peripheral nerve fall into three categories: neuropraxia, axonotmesis, and neurotmesis. They may be due to traumatic injury or entrapment. Clinically, such disorders typically cause weakness and atrophy of all muscles innervated distal to the lesion. Sensory findings often occur first, but they may not be as definitive as motor deficits in localizing the site of the lesion.[14] Electromyographic data can assist in the identification and prognosis of such cases.

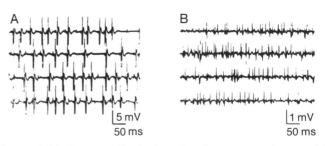

Figure 10–22. Large-amplitude, long-duration motor unit potentials from the first dorsal interosseus *(A)* compared with relatively normal motor unit potentials from orbicularis oculi *(B)* in a patient with polyneuropathy. Note discrete single unit interference pattern during maximal voluntary contraction. Reproduced From Kimura, J,[14] p 281, with permission.

Neuropraxia

This lesion involves some form of local blockage, stopping or slowing conduction across a specific point in the nerve. Conduction above and below the lesion is usually normal. Compression disorders are the most common types of neuropraxic lesions, such as Bell's palsy (facial nerve), Saturday night palsy (radial nerve compression in spiral groove), pressure over the peroneal nerve at the fibula head, and carpal tunnel syndrome (median nerve entrapment). Nerve conduction velocity tests can detect evidence of demyelinization prior to axonal degeneration, which may occur with long-standing compression. Nerve conduction measurements usually will reveal increased latencies across the compressed area but normal conduction velocity above and below. In acute conditions with no denervation, the EMG will be normal at rest. This should be considered a positive prognostic sign. The interference pattern may be decreased or absent if there is severe blockage.

Axonotmesis

With *axonotmesis* the neural tube is intact, but axonal damage has occurred. This may be a progressive condition as a result of long-standing neuropraxia, or it may occur from traumatic lesions. The deficit in nerve conduction velocity will depend partly on the number of axons affected. If the larger diameter fibers remain intact, the conduction velocity may be normal. However, M wave amplitude will be decreased because fewer motor units are contracting. Fibrillation potentials and positive sharp waves are typically seen on EMG 2 to 3 weeks following denervation, depending on the distance of the axon from the cell body.

Neurotmesis

Neurotmesis involves total loss of axonal function, with disruption of the neural tube. Conduction ceases below the lesion. A conduction velocity test cannot be performed because no evoked response can be elicited. Recovery is dependent on proper orientation of axons as they regenerate. Spontaneous potentials will appear with the muscle at rest, and no activity is produced with attempted voluntary contraction.

Regeneration of peripheral nerves will be signaled by the presence of small polyphasic potentials (nascent units) with voluntary contraction. These may be seen before clinical recovery is evident through results of clinical assessment such as the manual muscle test. After clinical recovery is established, polyphasic potentials may persist, often as giant potentials, owing to collateral sprouting. Rehabilitation goals for patients with peripheral nerve injuries can be influenced by results of serial EMG findings. Evidence of regeneration will suggest that motor function is improving, and treatment plans should address minimal exercise for the weak and easily fatigued muscles. Positive signs of regeneration also will help in setting realistic long-term goals for functional recovery.

POLYNEUROPATHIES

Polyneuropathies typically result in sensory changes, distal weakness, and hyporeflexia. Neuropathies can be related to general medical conditions, such as diabetes, alcoholism, renal disease, or malignancies; they may result from infections, such as leprosy or Guillain-Barré syndrome; they may be associated with metabolic abnormalities, such as malnutrition or the toxic effects of drugs or chemicals.[14]

Neuropathic conditions may be manifested as axonal damage or demyelination of axons. With *axonal lesions,* recruitment will be severely affected. A partial interference pattern may be observed with maximal effort, or single motor unit potentials may still be identifiable (see Figure 10–22). The motor unit duration and amplitude may be decreased. Fibrillation potentials, positive sharp waves, and fasciculations are typical (see Figure 10–12).

With *demyelinization,* nerve conduction measurements will often provide the most useful data. Sensory fibers are often affected before motor fibers, and significant slowing of sensory conduction velocity may be seen. The evoked potential will typically be reduced in amplitude.

Electrophysiologic findings usually correlate with clinical signs in patients with neuropathic involvement.[53] Some differences exist between types of neuropathies in terms of relative onset of sensory and motor symptoms and nerve conduction changes. Electromyographic findings are usually nonsignificant if axonal damage is not a factor. Often electrophysiologic changes are seen before clinical manifestations, with sensory nerves affected before motor nerves,[14] making the electromyogram unremarkable. The SNCV test may then provide the most helpful information. Clinicians will find such information useful in following progression or remission of the existing condition.

Motor Neuron Disorders

Motor neuron disorders most commonly involve degenerative diseases of the anterior horn cells. These include poliomyelitis, syringomyelia, and a few diseases that are characterized by degeneration of both upper and lower motor neurons, such as amyotrophic lateral sclerosis, progressive muscular atrophy, and progressive bulbar palsy.[54] Spinal muscular atrophies are another classification of motor neuron disease.[55] The reader is referred to comprehensive texts to review clinical features of these diseases.[14,56]

Diseases of the anterior horn cell are classically indicated by fibrillation potentials and positive sharp waves at rest (see Fig. 10–12), and by reduced recruitment with voluntary contraction, owing to loss of motor neurons. Single motor unit action potentials can still be seen with maximal effort, called a **single motor unit pattern.** Polyphasic motor unit potentials of increased amplitude and duration are typically seen later in the course of the disease (see Figure 10–15), owing to reinnervation and collateral sprouting.[57] Motor nerve conduction velocity may be slowed, depending on the distribution of degeneration among motor fibers, but sensory-evoked potentials are unaffected.

Myopathies

In primary muscle diseases, such as the dystrophies or polymyositis, the motor unit remains intact, but degeneration of muscle fibers is evident. Therefore, the number of fibers innervated by one axon is diminished. Motor nerve conduction is typically normal, although the amplitude of the M wave will be decreased because fewer fibers are responding to stimulation. Sensory nerve potentials and neuromuscular transmission are normal.[14] In early stages the EMG examination shows prolonged insertion activity, perhaps owing to the instability of muscle fibers or of the muscle membrane itself. Fibrillations and positive sharp waves are also seen, sometimes with repetitive discharges. Voluntary contraction typically elicits short duration and low amplitude polyphasic potentials, reflecting random loss of muscle fibers.[14] Less than maximal effort will require early recruitment, and an interference pattern is evoked because more motor units are needed to create the necessary tension within the muscle (Fig. 10–23). The total amplitude of the interference pattern, however, will be diminished.

In advanced stages of polymyositis and muscular dystrophy, when contractile tissue is replaced by fibrous and other tissues, no electrical potentials may be seen at all. On insertion the needle will meet some resistance as it enters the fibrotic tissue. Motor nerve conduction measurements also will be impossible under such conditions because no evoked potential can be elicited.

Inasmuch as most myopathies are progressive, clinicians will find EMG and MNCV findings helpful in documenting the extent of deterioration over time. Electromyography will help delineate the distribution of the involvement, assisting the therapist in focusing treatment and planning adaptations for functional activities.

Myotonia

Myotonia is a disorder characterized by delayed relaxation of previously contracted muscle.[13] It results in a pathologic muscle stiffness. Myotonia dystrophica exhibits EMG changes typical of myopathy as well. Myotonic disorders do not have a known etiology, although recent studies suggest a defect in the sarcolemmal membrane causing after-depolarization following activation of the muscle membrane.[58]

As a part of the generalized membrane abnormality, myotonia may result in mildly slowed MNCV[59] and a marked reduction in motor unit activity.[60] However, the typical EMG response in myotonia is the persistence of high-frequency repetitive discharges with alternately increasing and decreasing amplitude (see Fig. 10–14). This "waxing and waning" is a distinctive feature, producing the classic "dive bomber" sound. These trains of potential can discharge at frequencies up to 150 pulses per second. The myotonic discharge follows voluntary contraction, or it may be provoked by needle insertion or movement. Myotonic symptoms can be abolished or lessened pharmacologically.[13]

Myasthenia Gravis

Myasthenia gravis and myasthenic syndrome are disorders of neuromuscular transmission, characterized by weakness following repetitive contractions, and recovery following rest or administration of an anticholinesterase. *Myasthenia gravis* is thought to be an autoimmune disorder,[61] often associated with other immunologic diseases.[14] It is characterized by weakness and excessive fatigability, often confined to ocular muscles, or palatal and pharyngeal muscles.[62]

Myasthenic syndrome often is associated with small cell carcinoma of the bronchus and is more prevalent in males. Weakness and fatigability primarily affect the lower extremities, particularly the pelvic girdle and thigh muscles.[11]

Myasthenic disorders demonstrate a normal EMG at rest, although fibrillation potentials and positive sharp waves may be present in severely affected muscles, indicating loss of innervation. Motor unit potentials will appear normal at first and then progressively decrease in amplitude with continued effort. Repetitive stimulation during a motor nerve conduction test will cause progressive decreases in the amplitude of the M wave (Fig. 10–24). Pharmacologic intervention often will normalize the response.

Radiculopathy

Nerve root involvement, or radiculopathy, is not an uncommon condition at all spinal levels. Electromyography can often assist in identifying this condition by determining the etiology for radiating pain, persistent weakness, hyporeflexia, and fasciculations. Sensory symptoms accompany motor signs and may range from mild paresthesias to complete loss of sensation.

The fundamental feature in the determination of motor nerve root involvement is the delineation of the distribution of abnormal findings within muscles receiv-

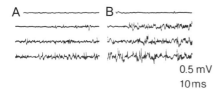

A ——————— B ——————

0.5 mV
10 ms

Figure 10–23. Low-amplitude, short-duration motor unit potentials recorded during minimal voluntary contraction from the biceps brachii *(A)* and tibialis anterior *(B)* in a 7-year-old boy with Duchenne dystrophy. A high number of discharging motor units during minimal contraction reflect early recruitment. Reproduced from Kimura, J,[14] p 282, with permission.

1-11-79

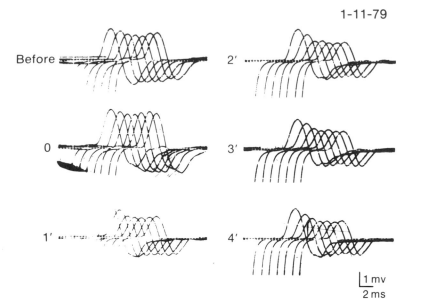

$$\overline{\lceil} 1\,mv$$
2 ms

Figure 10–24. Decremental evoked motor responses before and after voluntary exercise in a patient with generalized myasthenia gravis. The median nerve was stimulated at the rate of 3 per second for seven shocks in each train. The M wave was recorded from the thenar muscles. Comparing the amplitude of the last response with the amplitude of the first, the decrement was 25 percent at rest. Reproduced from Kimura, J,[14] p 196, with permission.

ing their peripheral innervation from the same myotome. For example, abnormal potentials seen in the extensor muscles of the hand may suggest involvement of the radial nerve. However, if the biceps brachii is examined (musculocutaneous nerve), as well as the opponens pollicis (median nerve), and these muscles also exhibit some abnormal electromyographic potentials, the common feature could be considered the C6 nerve root. These findings would have significant implications for treatment planning in terms of addressing the cause of muscle weakness or fatigue.

Electromyographic abnormalities are those typical of neuropathic involvement. Compression of a nerve root can result in irritation or degeneration of nerve fibers. If the lesion is of sufficient severity and duration, the electromyogram will show increased insertion activity, fibrillation potentials, and positive sharp waves at rest, and low-amplitude polyphasic potentials. In later stages, high-amplitude polyphasic potentials may appear, reflecting reinnervation. Electromyography is especially valuable in differentiating between disorders of the peripheral nerve trunk and more proximal involvement. Electromyography may be more useful than nerve conduction velocity studies, which might not show any remarkable changes at distal segments of these peripheral nerves unless diffuse degeneration has occurred.

KINESIOLOGIC ELECTROMYOGRAPHY: USE IN THE CLINIC

In addition to being a standard tool for neuromuscular assessment, electromyography can be an extremely useful adjunct to clinical practice. Physical therapists have become increasingly involved in the use of kinesiologic EMG to examine muscle function during specific purposeful tasks or therapeutic regimens.[63] For this purpose, therapists are no longer concerned with examining single motor unit potentials, but instead we need to look at patterns of muscle response, onset and cessation of activity, and the level of muscle response in relation to effort, type of muscle contraction, and position. Therapists can use EMG to assess the ability of exercises to facilitate or to inhibit specific muscle activity, and thereby to determine if treatment goals are being realized.[64,65] With the growing need for validation of treatment effectiveness, EMG presents an objective means for scientific documentation.

A wealth of kinesiologic literature exists, much of it involving the use of EMG. Professional journals include many articles concerned with clinical questions and techniques. The therapist should have a basic understanding of kinesiologic EMG in order to assess methods and data analysis procedures used in kinesiologic EMG studies.

Although the principles of recording and instrumentation are the same for clinical and kinesiologic EMG, several additional factors must be considered in order to interpret kinesiologic EMG data.

Instrumentation

ELECTRODES

As described earlier, surface and fine-wire indwelling electrodes are used in kinesiologic study, although surface electrodes are used more often in clinical situations. Once a muscle is chosen for study, its size and location must be considered in choosing and applying or inserting electrodes. Based on previous discussions of volume conduction and the factors affecting the motor unit potential, the following determinations must be made: (1) electrode size, (2) interelectrode distance, (3) location of electrode sites (including the ground), and (4) skin preparation (for surface electrodes).

Smaller muscles obviously require the use of smaller electrodes, with a small interelectrode distance. If electrodes are too far apart, even on larger muscles, activity from nearby muscles may be recorded. This crosstalk would confound interpretation of the output by making activity look greater than it actually was. The electrodes should be located over or within the muscle belly as much as possible to record from the main mass of the muscle. If they are located poorly, levels of activity recorded with strong contractions may not be accurately indicative of the muscle's activity. The ground electrode should be located reasonably close to the recording electrodes, preferably on the same side of the body. Skin should be prepared to reduce impedance, although newer amplifiers may have sufficient input impedance to negate this need.

Many investigators and clinicians have found it efficient to use palpation for locating electrode sites, if the subject can voluntarily contract the muscle to facilitate this process.[65-68] However, if repeated measurements are attempted, requiring reapplication of electrodes, this method may be unreliable. When electrodes are not oriented to the muscle in the same way with repeated testing, the output will look different even with identical levels of contraction. Many investigators have used electrical stimulation of motor points to locate optimal electrode sites.[69-71] Some have marked the skin with indelible solutions to be able to relocate electrodes.[11] Others have used body landmarks and measured specific distances to standardize application sites (Fig. 10-25).[72-74] These measurements are often most time-efficient, but they do not always accommodate to individual anatomic differences. Basmajian and Blumenstein[75] have provided guidelines for placement of surface electrodes for use with biofeedback that can be useful for kinesiologic study as well, as long as individual variation in body parameters and muscle bulk are taken into consideration.

The distance between electrodes also must be standardized so that repeated analysis of EMG is valid. If electrodes are further apart at a second session, the same level of contraction may produce higher amplitude readings. When placement criteria are specified, researchers have shown fairly good test-retest reliability for surface electrodes,[11,76] although submaximal contractions have demonstrated better reproducibility than maximal contractions.[68] Reapplication of indwelling electrodes is less reliable because of the difficulty of consistently locating a needle within muscle tissue with reinsertion.[11]

When using surface electrodes, the therapist also must consider problems related to the displacement of skin overlying muscle during movement. The spatial relationship between the electrodes and the muscle can change greatly as a muscle contracts through its range. This will, of course, affect the EMG signal. The electrode sites should be determined with this in mind. Such problems are often seen when monitoring the biceps brachii or scapula muscles, for instance. Electrodes should be applied to the skin with the limb or body part positioned as it will be positioned during the procedure.

SIGNAL CONDITIONING

For clinical EMG the *raw signal* is displayed, allowing visual examination of the size and shape of individual

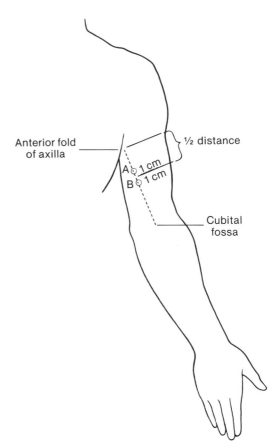

Figure 10-25. Example of standardized electrode placement for the biceps brachii. A line is drawn from the anterior axillary fold to the center of the cubital fossa, and a point marked at the center of this line. Electrodes are then placed 1 cm above and below this point along the line.

muscle and nerve potentials. For kinesiologic EMG, however, the therapist is generally interested in looking at overall muscle activity during specific activities, and quantification of the signal is often desired in order to describe and to compare changes in the magnitude and pattern of muscle response.

Several forms of output can be useful for this purpose. Computer-processed raw data can be displayed on a monitor or printout. Raw EMG data can be displayed on an oscilloscope (Fig. 10-26) or ink chart recorder at a gain and sweep speed that allows visualization of the total muscle activity. Remember, however, that the raw EMG signal can not be faithfully reproduced on an ink chart recorder because of the inertia of the pens, which prevents them from being able to process high-frequency components. Pens generally cut signals off above 70 and 100 Hz. Even with these limitations, however, the raw data can be examined for general patterns and changes. Fiber optic recorders operate without such limitations and can faithfully reproduce the myoelectric signal.

The EMG signal also can be manipulated electronically in several ways to facilitate quantification and to eliminate problems of processing raw data (Fig. 10-27). One way is **rectification**. The signal is *full-wave rectified* by electronically causing both the negative and positive portions of the raw signal to appear above the baseline.

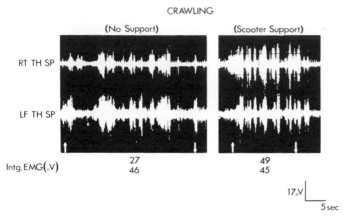

CRAWLING

(No Support)   (Scooter Support)

RT TH SP

LF TH SP

Intg. EMG(ₚV)   27   49
                     46   45

17ₚV
5 sec

Figure 10–26. The EMG activity recorded from the right and left thoracic paraspinal regions (RT TH SP, LF TH SP) during floor and scooter crawling. Arrows indicate duration of EMG sampling, and numbers refer to integrated EMG values of upper and lower traces, respectively. (From Wolf, SL, Edwards, DI, and Shutter, LA,[65] p 223, 1986, with permission.)

The rectified signal is then put through a series of circuits and filters to be presented in a "smoothed" format. One format is a *linear envelope,* which describes a curve outlining the peaks of the full wave rectified signal.[15] Many authors and electronic equipment companies call this an "integrated" signal, but that is a misnomer, because the linear envelope is a moving average of the EMG output over time.

Another type of circuit provides a mathematically *integrated* signal through accumulation of electrical energy on a capacitor, or condensor. This process is called **integration.** Integrated EMG (IEMG) is defined as the area under the curve.[15] These curves can be processed in several ways (see Figure 10–27). The simplest method is integration throughout the period of muscular activity. The total accumulated activity can be determined for a series of contractions or a single contraction. The slope of the curve, or ramp, is a direct function of the amount of electrical energy being processed.

Alternatively, the condensor can be set to discharge at predetermined intervals based on time or voltage amplitude. Time intervals can be set so that the capacitor resets to zero on a regular basis, within periods as small as 200 msec or as long as 10 sec. The height of each peak, or ramp, then represents the accumulated activity over

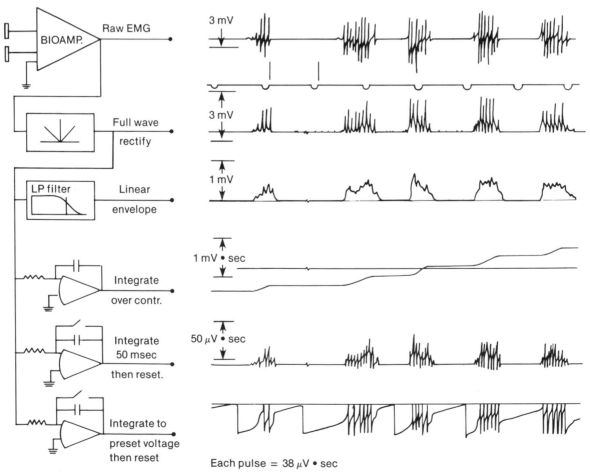

Figure 10–27. Illustration of the raw electromyogram and several methods of signal processing. The raw EMG was full-wave rectified and expressed as a linear envelope and integrated data. Reproduced from Winter, DA: *Biomechanics of Human Movement.* John Wiley & Sons, New York, 1979, p 140, with permission.

that time interval. Integration also can be based on a preset voltage level. When the condensor reaches this voltage, it resets to zero, without regard to time. If the EMG signal is very weak, the condensor may continue to collect electrical energy for indefinite periods until its discharge threshold is finally reached. The frequency with which the condensor resets is an indication of the level of EMG activity. Each ramp also can be depicted as a pulse and the frequency of pulses counted to determine the level of activity (Fig. 10–28).

A third method is determination of the *root-mean-square (RMS)*, an electronic average representing the square root of the average of the squares of the current or voltage over the whole cycle.[77] Root-mean-square provides a nearly instantaneous output of the power of the EMG signal[10,15] and is considered the preferable output form by some researchers.[2] These averaged or integrated signals also can be displayed by a meter, light bar, or speaker, as they are in most biofeedback devices. An analysis of the *frequency spectra* (called Fourier analysis) that comprise the motor unit waveform is a fourth method used to interpret changes in motor unit activity. Variations in **frequency** characteristics can be identified with fatigue[78] and abnormalities of the neuromuscular system.[79]

Technology has advanced sufficiently today that microcomputers are now readily applied to the processing of conditioned signals, including integration and display. Personal computers can be adapted easily to interface with electromyographs of all types. The EMG signal can be stored, averaged, and sampled in a variety of ways to permit detailed and complete analysis.

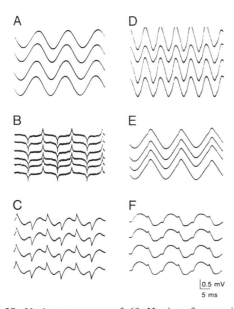

Figure 10–28. Various patterns of 60 Hz interference induced by nearby electrical applicances. They include common 60 Hz interference *(A),* 60 Hz interference with spikes probably induced by high impedance of the recording electrode *(B),* typical 60 Hz interference from fluorescent lights *(C),* 120 Hz interference from a diathermy unit *(D),* and 60 Hz interference from a heat lamp *(E,F).* Reproduced from Kimura, J,[14] p 51, with permission.

ARTIFACTS

When observing processed output, one must be aware that this processed signal is a summation or average of all activity being recorded, including potential artifacts and cross-talk from other muscles. Artifacts will be processed along with the EMG signal, and no differentiation can be discerned on the output. These artifacts can be of sufficient voltage to distort the output signal markedly. It is not unusual for a researcher to observe the raw signal on an oscilloscope and to monitor artifacts at the same time that integrated data are being recorded.

Therapists must, therefore, remain aware of conditions that may cause artifacts during recording and take precautions where possible. For example, if hamstring muscle activity is being monitored during an activity in the sitting position, pressure on the electrodes on the posterior aspect of the thigh may cause movement artifact. Some form of padding under the thigh, placed proximal and distal to the electrodes, can help alleviate this pressure. For activities requiring broad movements, electrode cables should be taped down as much as possible, either to a table or chair or along the limb itself, to avoid artifacts caused by their movement.

Care should be taken when applying electrodes that no gel oozes out beneath the adhesive collar or tape. If gel from both electrodes should contact, the circuit may be shorted and no difference of potential will be recorded. If attachments become loose, a 60 Hz signal will be recorded, interfering with the EMG signal. Electrodes with broken or frayed connections cause the same outcome. Electrodes often break beneath the protective tubing that connects the electrode itself to the lead wire. If raw data are not monitored, this condition may not be noticed. Other equipment in the area also may be the source of electrical interference. Diathermy, electrical stimulators, and vibrators are examples of devices that can contribute to noise. Sometimes, using isolated power lines will help with this situation. When the noise is too great, laboratories need to be shielded in copper.

Artifacts also can occur owing to a pulse or ECG signal, especially if one is recording from the trunk, upper arm, or upper thigh. Correct application of the ground electrode and use of an amplifier with appropriate bandwidth, input impedance, and CMRR should help reduce these potentials but may not be able to eliminate them. Electrocardiogram artifacts are generally fairly regular, however, and their effect may be successfully canceled out with normalization procedures. If a frequency analysis is being performed, however, this signal, typically generating frequency characteristics up to 100 Hz, will provide significant interference.

If the raw signal can be observed, the following general guidelines will be helpful in identifying artifacts. Electrical noise, such as 60 Hz interference, is a regular signal, usually appearing in the form of a sine wave (see Figure 10–28). It may make a loud buzzing noise and will be seen or heard even when the muscle is not contracting. Cable artifact results in wide, large amplitude spikes. Movement of electrodes often causes the baseline to appear wavy but does not generally interfere with the amplitude of the signal to any marked degree.

AMPLIFIERS

Many clinicians have access to instrumentation that will monitor EMG signals. Most biofeedback devices can be used for kinesiologic monitoring of EMG, as can a clinical EMG with an oscilloscope. Sometimes chart recorders will be available; polygraphs designed for use with EEG will often be able to monitor EMG data. The therapist should be aware of the input impedance, frequency bandwidth, and gain of an amplifier, so that a reasonable portion of the EMG signal can be recorded validly.

Although amplifiers that provide an integrated output display are easier to use (such as those on most biofeedback devices), raw data viewed on an oscilloscope can still be useful.[65] The major disadvantage of using raw data is that they are not quantitative, and it may be difficult to discern small changes in amplitude. However, many clinicians find the raw signal helpful because it allows them to visualize the bursts of activity and periods of silence better.

QUANTIFYING EMG

Quantification of raw EMG signals can be difficult because the signals are often erratic. Subjective rating scales have been used to grade the relative amplitude of the raw signal, using numeric gradings from 0 to 4 (Fig. 10–29). Readings of 0 and 1 indicate no or insignificant activity; grade 2, moderate activity; and grades 3 and 4, major or marked contraction of the test muscle.[80,81] These scales are useful for making gross comparisons of one muscle's EMG level during different activities within a single test session. The level of grade 4 should be determined by obtaining a reading during a maximal contraction. All further comparisons are then made relative to that level. This method is reasonably useful with isometric contractions, when the level of EMG stays fairly consistent within a contraction. However, with movement, the variation in level of EMG throughout the contraction can make this form of analysis very difficult.

Integrated EMG, recorded on a chart recorder, can be quantified by using a planimeter to measure the area under the curve, which is often expressed in arbitrary units for comparison. Cumulative IEMG can be analyzed by measuring the total voltage accumulated over a set time interval, relative to a known signal. Computer analysis allows sampling of either raw or integrated data at specific intervals (such as 100 samples/second).

Electromyography also can be analyzed in relation to the onset and cessation of activity, without regard to amplitude. Some permanent recording is helpful if computerized data are not obtained, to determine the latency of responses between different muscles or relative to some other parameter, such as the command to move.

More subjective quantification can be accomplished with biofeedback devices that have a meter or light bar, allowing monitoring of the voltage level of output. Although permanent recordings of these values may not be available, the therapist can use the readings to approximate the level of activity. Because these values tend to change rapidly, it is often helpful to observe the highest or lowest value or the range of values achieved during a particular activity and to use these scores for comparison purposes. Trying to get more specific than that may be misleading, unless the levels of contraction are very uniform and values can be easily determined from the display.

NORMALIZATION

The purpose of quantifying the EMG signal is usually to compare activity between sessions, muscles, or subjects. Because of the variability inherent in EMG procedures, and the interindividual differences in anatomy and movement characteristics, some form of *normalization* is necessary in order to validate these comparisons. This is usually done by first recording the EMG of a muscle during a maximal voluntary contraction (MVC), or some known submaximal level of contraction (against a known weight), and then expressing all other EMG values as a percentage of this contraction. This "control" value serves as a standard against which all

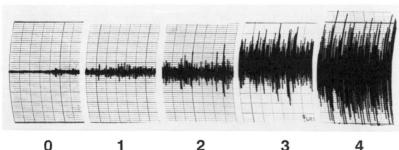

0   1   2   3   4

Figure 10–29. One scheme for subjective grading of raw EMG, showing a five-grade basis for data analysis. Grade 0 indicates zero activity; grade 1, minimal activity; grade 2, moderate activity; grade 3, marked activity; grade 4, maximal activity. Reproduced from Long, GL and Brown, ME,[80] p 1689, with permission.

comparisons can be made, even if test values exceed the control. In this way subjects and muscles can be compared, and activity on different days can be correlated by repeating the control contraction at each test session. This helps eliminate some of the problems related to reapplication of electrodes as well. Although no standard method has been developed for this control contraction, many investigators use manual muscle test positions, resisting isometric contractions either manually or against some fixed resistance. Others have used isotonic contractions against a known weight, or maximal isokinetic efforts.

The Relationship between EMG and Force

The relationship between the EMG and muscle tension has been studied since 1952,[82,83] and it continues to be the subject of many investigations. It is generally accepted that a direct relationship exists between the EMG activity and muscular effort, but this relationship must be discussed in terms of muscle length and type of contraction.

ISOMETRIC CONTRACTIONS

Several early studies have demonstrated that when muscle maintains a constant length, the EMG output varies directly with muscle tension. Many investigators have documented a linear relationship between muscle tension and integrated EMG.[82–84] Others have reported curvilinear relationships.[67,76,85–87] The linear slope, or the degree of nonlinearity, seems to vary with the muscle tested, with the joint position or muscle length, with electrode placements, and with the method of measurement of force.[67,85,86,88] Even though the use of different methods makes comparisons of these studies difficult, they all support the general conclusion that an increase in EMG output is observed with increasing muscle tension as long as the muscle length does not change (i.e., during an isometric contraction).[86,89] This relationship exists with spasticity as well, although the slope of the relationship appears greater than normal, indicating that more motor units are recruited at higher tension levels than in the normal muscle.[90]

When muscle length is varied, however, this relationship does not hold. Generally, less EMG activity is seen with greater tension as a muscle is lengthened and, conversely, greater EMG activity is seen with decreased tension as a muscle is shortened (Fig. 10–30).[83] Theoretically, therefore, we can assume that fewer motor units are needed to produce the same level of tension in the lengthened position.

ISOTONIC CONTRACTIONS

The relationship between EMG and force is further confounded during isotonic contractions, defined as contractions producing average constant force or torque.[15] When muscle length continually changes during movement, several factors must be considered. The force-length relationship of the muscle varies throughout the contraction, thereby constantly altering the motor unit activity in proportion to tension. The axis of rotation of the joint changes as the limb moves through range, changing the movement of the arm and resulting force components. The movement of the skin over the muscle and the variation in shape of the muscle as it contracts also will affect the spatial relationship between the electrodes and muscle fibers, changing the amount of electrical activity actually recorded at different muscle lengths. It is difficult, therefore, to quantify muscle activity validly when movement is occurring.

The EMG–force relationship also has been examined in terms of eccentric and concentric contractions. Eccentric, or lengthening, contractions use elastic elements and metabolic processes more efficiently than concentric contractions.[91,92] Therefore, for the same amount of muscle tension, an eccentric contraction will require fewer motor units—that is, less overall EMG activity—than a concentric contraction.

The rate of muscle shortening is another consideration. Studies have shown that during eccentric contractions the level of EMG activity remains constant for a given load, independent of velocity of the contraction.[89,93] Concentric EMG activity, however, is greater for a given force as velocity is increased, probably reflecting a need for greater recruitment to accommodate for a faster contraction time. However, only when velocity is kept constant is the EMG activity proportional to tension.[93] Therefore, with isotonic movement at uncontrolled velocity, EMG output will not be a direct reflection of muscle tension. This is an important point when we consider clinical applications of EMG.

FATIGUE

When a muscle exhibits localized fatigue following repeated contractions, one might expect to see a decrease in overall EMG output. The opposite is generally observed, however. We typically see an increase in EMG amplitude as a muscle fatigues.[84] In an attempt to maintain the level of active tension in the muscle, additional motor units are recruited and active motor units fire at increasing rates to compensate for the decreased force of contraction of the fatigued fibers. This has been substantiated in many studies using submaximal contractions.[84,94–96] Following maximal contraction, when the entire motor unit pool is supposedly recruited, force declines and the EMG stays constant.[97] This suggests that fatigue is occurring within the muscle but that the maximal number of motor units is still contracting. Eventually, however, as the contraction continues, the contractile elements within the muscle will fail and simultaneously the EMG will start to decrease.[94] Electromyographic indications of fatigue can occur very quickly, within the first 60 seconds of both submaximal and maximal contractions.[94,95,97,98]

Researchers have observed both linear[84,86,94,97] and nonlinear[67,99] EMG–force relationships during fatiguing contractions. The slope of this relationship varies with the degree of fatigue.[100] Studies also have demonstrated a relationship between predominance of fiber type within

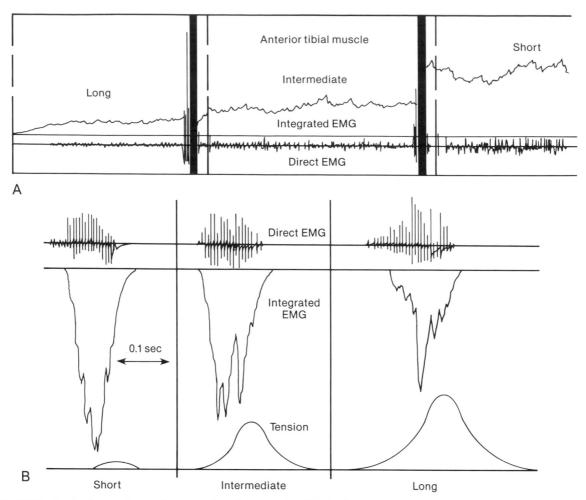

Figure 10–30. *(A)* Maximal voluntary isometric contraction of the anterior tibialis of a normal subject with the muscle at different lengths. Note the rise in EMG activity as the muscle is progressively shortened. The integrated EMG is really a linear envelope. *(B)* EMG activity of the triceps brachii of a cineplastic amputee, illustrating the same effect. (From Inman, VT, et al,[83] p 193, with permission.)

a muscle and its EMG fatigue characteristics.[67,95] Muscles composed of primarily type I (slow twitch) fibers fatigue at a slower rate and demonstrate only small increases in EMG activity.[67]

Electromyographic evidence of fatigue and endurance also may be manifested as changes in the frequency characteristics of the motor unit potential. By measuring frequency shifts in the electrical potentials of an impaired muscle during treatment, the therapist can determine if the muscle is being sufficiently exercised.[2] If the characteristic frequency decreases, the muscle is exhibiting evidence of fatigue, and therefore is truly being exercised. If the frequency does not change, then synergists may be responsible for the force being generated and the involved muscle is not receiving the benefits of the treatment. If a decrease in the frequency is seen at first, and then abruptly levels off without a decrease in output force, the involved muscle may have stopped participating, and other muscles may have taken over to generate the force. Such a technique could be helpful in discriminating which muscles are truly contributing to the force output that is measured over a joint. Of course, appropriate instrumentation for recording and analysis must be available. This type of data will not be analyzed on conventional EMG units or biofeedback devices.

EMG AND "STRENGTH"

The above factors are of great significance for interpreting EMG amplitude during activities that require muscles to operate at different lengths or speeds, or that use different types of contractions. Those who use EMG to study muscle function during activities are often tempted to make statements regarding the muscle's "strength." Although this term is used clinically, it must be used with caution. Strength is a construct that must be defined as torque or force produced under a specific set of conditions. Clinicians must be very careful, therefore, about concluding that a muscle is "working harder" or that a muscle is "stronger" just because the EMG activity is greater. Within a single session, when electrode positions remain constant, the position of the limb, the type of contraction, and the speed of movement will affect the level of EMG activity recorded.

The significance of these factors becomes apparent when comparisons are made between isometric exercises performed at different joint angles. Electromyographic activity recorded from a single muscle positioned at different points in the range may have varied amplitudes but may indeed represent contractions of similar tension levels. Therefore, the EMG, which records motor unit activity, must be distinguished from muscle tension, which is a function of contractile processes. Therapists often use the term "optimal" to describe a biomechanically advantageous position for a muscle. However, EMG could be lower at this optimal position because fewer motor units are required to create a given level of force. Greater EMG activity may actually indicate that a muscle's efficiency is decreased.

Therapists should also be cognizant of the fact that EMG can record activity of individual muscles, whereas the force or torque measured across a joint may represent the resultant interaction of agonists, antagonists, and synergists. Adjacent muscles make differential contributions to the strength, stability, and coordination of a contraction. The EMG of the agonist may not necessarily be a valid representation of activity around a joint. Therefore, EMG data can not be expected to provide direct information about an individual muscle's "strength."

Therapists also must resist the temptation to make inferences about *muscle tone* based on EMG activity. Normal muscle "tonus" refers to resting tension within a muscle resulting from elastic and viscoelastic properties of muscle fibers.[101] Tone also reflects the reflex responsiveness or readiness of a muscle to contract. Essential to a definition of tone is the fact that even though a relaxed muscle shows no electrical activity on EMG, it still maintains a passive state of tone.[102] Therefore, tone is not a function of motor unit activity and can not be measured with EMG. This means that when the term *spasticity* is used to indicate a state of hypertonus, it actually refers to the potential for an overactive muscle response to a stimulus[102] and not to motor unit activity, per se. Like a normal muscle at rest, a "relaxed" spastic muscle will exhibit electrical silence. This is true of spastic and rigid muscles of patients with Parkinsonism as well.[104]

Although there is evidence that lower motor neuron changes are evident on EMG, with upper motor neuron dysfunction[24,26,27] such activity is not consistently seen[30,31] and would not be of sufficient amplitude to be picked up with surface electrodes. We can, for kinesiologic purposes, consider a spastic muscle "normal" in terms of peripheral innervation. When a muscle contracts, be it normal or hypertonic, a normal motor unit pattern will be recorded on EMG. The level of motor unit activation will affect the amplitude of the signal directly.

Clinical Applications

Therapists can use EMG as an adjunctive approach in a wide variety of applications for assessment and treatment. With an appreciation for concepts of recording and limitations of interpretation previously discussed, the therapist will find EMG a valuable clinical tool to help validate intervention. This approach should be differentiated from EMG biofeedback, in which EMG is used to provide information to the patient to allow the patient to learn to control his or her own neuromuscular responses. Kinesiologic applications involve the use of EMG to provide information to the therapist, to identify activity that would otherwise go undetected, to allow for adjustment of technique or position, and to provide

information about the effectiveness of a specific procedure.

The following discussion illustrates a few examples of the clinical applications of kinesiologic EMG.

SELECTING A MUSCLE

Because activities or functional movements are generally performed by muscle groups, decisions about which muscle or muscles to monitor can be difficult. Therapists are often limited to one or two recording channels and must, therefore, choose muscles that are representative of the group or that are considered prime movers. One must be careful not to assume an active muscle is "responsible" for a movement, however, when all participants are not monitored. It may be necessary to repeat the activity several times, each time monitoring a different set of muscles, in order to get a better sense of what is happening around a joint.

If muscles are closely situated, such as finger flexors or intrinsic hand muscles, electrodes can be placed to record from the entire muscle group. The therapist must determine which muscles combine to perform the movement and interpret output in terms of a general pattern of muscle activity. Of course, the EMG signal can not then be attributed to any one muscle, and it is not possible to determine which muscle contributed more or less to the total output. When the activity of a single muscle is of interest, surface electrodes should be placed as close together as possible over the muscle belly, to avoid recording overflow activity from adjacent musculature.

MOTOR CONTROL

It has been established that it is not possible to "measure" tone with surface electrodes. It is possible, however, to monitor the level of motor unit activity facilitated by a stimulus such as passive stretch,[66] by a treatment modality, or with changes in position (assuming that the muscle length has not changed significantly). Clinicians must be aware, however, that the EMG cannot distinguish voluntary contraction from reflex activity and that the output could be a function of both.[105]

Associated reactions, or *exercise overflow,* also can be monitored with EMG. Exercise overflow refers to EMG activity recorded in unexercised muscles during contraction in another body part. Overflow activity to ipsilateral or contralateral muscles or body parts can be observed on EMG even when overt movement does not occur.[106–108] Such muscle activity can be monitored while adjusting an applied load, during position changes, or during resistive exercise.

Although a few authors have concluded that exercise overflow does not occur to any appreciable degree in normals,[2,109] others have clearly demonstrated such activity in this population.[106,107,110,111] Discrepancies exist because some investigators have based their conclusions on a limited amount of data, monitoring only selected muscles. One must be careful not to make broad generalizations about directions of overflow or primary sites of overflow unless many muscles are tested. Even if the muscle chosen to be monitored is not active, others may be.

Studies of patients with spasticity have consistently shown, however, that overflow does indeed occur to a marked degree,[112] often with reactions occurring in predictable patterns on the involved side.[113] Investigators who have stabilized the overflow extremity so that the overflow muscles were resisted have demonstrated much higher levels of activity[107] than those who have left the overflow limb free.[109] Electromyography can help the therapist judge the level of response, although caution must be exercised in interpreting why the overflow activity is present. In addition to neurophysiologic responses, some overflow may be occurring as a function of stabilization requirements. These issues are hard to separate, and EMG will not discriminate between them.

Many techniques are used to influence muscle activity. Equipment such as electrical stimulators and vibrators can be problematic when used in conjunction with EMG because they can cause 60 Hz interference. These instruments generally need to be turned off in order to monitor the EMG response following application. Tapping may be effectively performed over a tendon without much interference, but tapping over the muscle belly can cause movement artifact. Other techniques, such as cryotherapy, resistance, positioning, and so forth will generally not interfere with valid EMG recording, although the therapist must always be concerned with movement artifacts in setting up procedures.

ASSESSMENTS

Manual Muscle Test

Electromyography can be used to assess the degree of effort during isometric break tests. It also can assist in identifying substitutions. However, caution must be exercised in intepreting a muscle as "substituting" for a prime mover when it is a synergist or stabilizer. Silence should not be expected in muscles surrounding the "tested muscle." Overflow electrical activity from adjacent muscles also may be recorded at the electrodes of the test muscle, and the output will then be interpreted incorrectly. Putting electrodes on several surrounding muscles allows for some differentiation. If muscles are close together, however, surface electrodes may not be able to provide sufficient differentiation, even if they are spaced close together.

Equilibrium Reactions

Electromyography can be used to assess amplitude and timing of onset of supporting muscle groups in order to describe patterns of response. This can be done in sitting or standing. Weight-bearing patterns can be examined objectively by monitoring lower extremity musculature, particularly hip and ankle muscles.[114] Treatment strategies may address facilitation or inhibition of specific muscle groups to enhance balance reactions and weight shifting. Therapists are encouraged to read the literature describing normal EMG patterns[2] and to use EMG in the clinic to clarify the effect of intervention. For example, do muscles respond in consistent patterns? Is activity sporadic or constant? This may be most useful in tests in which balance is purposely perturbed, because in normal standing or sitting positions, supporting musculature is minimally active.[115]

Gait

Electromyography can be useful to assess muscle activity during gait if instrumentation allows simultaneous and coordinated tracking of the activity, for example, film, videotape, electrogoniometers, or contact foot switches to delineate swing and stance phases. Speed of walking must be considered in terms of the effect on EMG. Therapists can refer to many studies that report normal patterns of EMG during gait,[116–118] recognizing that these "norms" are ideal models and that an individual patient will probably not match them. Gait is a prime example of a situation in which functional performance must be the major consideration, and EMG used only for information purposes. A patient may ambulate without functional difficulty, even though the EMG pattern at the knee is not "normal." The complex interactions between muscles in an activity like gait must also be considered, and recognition must be given to the varied patterns that may result in normal functional movement.

Procedurally, length of electrode leads can limit the distance walked, and in many cases this will result in cable artifacts. Telemetry has been used with some success to allow free walking. Many biofeedback units have straps that allow patients to carry them while walking, which also helps limit this problem. Electrode assemblies with preamplifiers that are attached over the muscle will protect against cable artifacts are well.

Passive Movement

Electromyography can help identify whether movements are truly passive. In this situation EMG can act as a feedback device to both the therapist and the patient. Electrode placement need not be specific to monitor general activity around the joint. Passive stretch to a normal relaxed muscle does not elicit appreciable EMG activity, regardless of speed of movement,[119,120] indicating that patients can voluntarily relax to allow full passive motion to occur.

MOVEMENT PATTERNS

Therapists can use EMG to observe the effect of treatment on patterns of muscle response.[108] When movement can not be observed, EMG can be particularly useful as a measurement tool. For example, agonist–antagonist relationships can be examined, and cocontraction or reciprocal inhibition can be documented. Specific therapeutic procedures, such as traction[121] or approximation, and activities such as mat exercises or PNF patterns[122] can be studied and the pattern of muscle activity more objectively determined than by visual observation alone. Muscle interactions can be examined during isokinetic exercise as well,[123] in which velocity of movement can be controlled and range of motion easily tracked.

Therapeutic concepts must be operationally defined,

however. For example, how much activity must be present in a group of muscles around a joint for "cocontraction" to be present? Must all the muscles be equally active? Must an antagonistic muscle be totally silent for reciprocal inhibition to have occurred? Is a muscle an antagonist by virtue of being attached on the opposite side of a joint, or is it defined by its action? Can a muscle normally considered an antagonist be a synergist? The answers to these questions are not clear, and how a therapist defines them for clinical use will be important in the setup and interpretation of the EMG. Using a maximal voluntary contraction as a reference, or control contraction, for interpreting muscle activity can help with these issues.

Looking at patterns of timing also can be useful in many situations. Levels of skill,[123] coordination,[124] and balance[125] often are determined by assessing timing of onset of muscle activity as well as of amplitude. Researchers have seen decreased cocontraction (or decreased antagonist/synergist activity) with improvements in these parameters. Some form of permanent output is helpful for measurement, because timing differences can often be less than 1 second. A few authors have used EMG changes as evidence of motor learning, showing distinct patterns emerging in agonist/antagonist activity with practice.

When two-joint muscles are a part of a movement pattern, their activity will reflect action at one or both joints, depending on biochemical and functional parameters.[126] The interpretation of the EMG can become tentative when one is not clear what contribution a muscle is making at each joint. Muscles such as the hamstrings and rectus femoris are major examples. When the length–tension relationships are affected by changes at both ends of a muscle, it can be difficult to judge whether the EMG is adequately representing the muscle's function. Therapists should make every effort to limit movement to one joint and to stabilize the other when movement is necessary. This consideration also should be given to muscles whose function is primarily at one joint, but whose tendons cross two joints, such as finger and wrist flexors, long head of biceps femoris and gastrocnemius.

RECRUITING SPECIFIC MUSCLES

Because strength is generally measured across a joint and represents the resultant torque generated by many muscles, EMG can help determine whether a specific muscle is participating in the action. For example, EMG has been used to assess the differential contribution of portions of the quadriceps femoris to knee extension,[81] to assess the role of the vastus medialis in patellar syndromes,[127,128] and to demonstrate the effect of varying hip and knee positions on this activity.[128–131] Electromyography has been used to determine if specific muscles are active during performance of PNF patterns[106,122] and to document the effect of spasticity on such patterns in hemiplegic patients.[113]

Therapists often want to determine which exercises or positions will best recruit specific muscles. Electromyography can assist in making the determination. Clinicians have used EMG to observe the effect of body position during specific exercises in order to minimize stress on low back musculature;[132] they have examined the ability of specific knee extension exercises to recruit selectively portions of the quadriceps femoris;[74,128,133] and they have demonstrated that specific musculature can be isolated during activities using voluntary control.[73]

SUMMARY

These are but a few examples of the variety of clinical situations in which EMG can help the therapist judge the effect of treatment and the validity of assessments in terms of muscle response. Therapists must use EMG wisely, however, recognizing its limitations as a measurement tool. Electromyography shows that a muscle is working, not *why* it is working, and can be interpreted only as a measure of motor unit activity. Electromyography can not determine that a treatment is "effective" in the sense of achieving predicted functional outcomes. By itself EMG can not provide information as to whether a muscle has gotten stronger or weaker, or if it is hypertonic or hypotonic. Under most circumstances, with repeated testing over short periods, small changes will be difficult to assess. These must be determined through clinical assessment. But the EMG can provide information during treatment or assessment that may increase efficacy. It is a form of feedback for the therapist that can be invaluable in situations in which overt movement or muscle contraction is not observable.

Kinesiologic literature abounds with studies concerning the use of EMG to determine muscle function under different conditions.[2,65] Therapists should be familiar with this body of literature in order to interpret and to use EMG data. These studies can be used also as guides for setting up EMG as part of treatment plans. One must be critical of EMG studies, however, many of which demonstrate methodologic faults that can invalidate findings. In addition, the results of EMG studies may not always be generalized to a specific patient and should not be considered the "correct" responses in all cases. Obviously, the therapist's clinical judgment must prevail when observing responses of individual patients.

The clinician is encouraged to explore the uses of EMG whenever response of superficial muscles is of interest. As long as the limitations of interpretation of EMG are kept in mind, this tool can be a major adjunct to therapeutic intervention and assessment.

QUESTIONS FOR REVIEW

1. What are the basic components of a recording system for EMG and NCV tests?

2. What characteristics should be considered when choosing an amplifier for monitoring EMG?

3. What are the stages in a clinical EMG examination?

4. Describe how motor and sensory NVC are calculated.

5. What are the typical EMG and NCV findings with peripheral nerve lesions, myopathy, and motor neuron disease?

6. What are the possible causes of movement artifact? How can these effects be reduced or eliminated?

7. Describe four types of signal conditioning for EMG.

8. Describe a method for quantifying raw EMG.

9. What is the effect of changing muscle length on the relationship between EMG and force?

10. What type of changes are seen in the EMG signal when a muscle becomes fatigued?

11. Assume that you are including EMG to monitor muscle response as a component of a treatment program. What considerations are important for setting up your procedure in terms of

a. Choice and placement of electrodes?

b. Type of contractions?

c. Patient position?

d. Timing of activities?

e. How the EMG will be interpreted?

REFERENCES

1. Green, RM: Commentary on the Effect of Electricity on Muscular Motion. Elizabeth Licht, Cambridge, 1953.
2. Basmajian, JV and De Luca, CJ: Muscles Alive, ed 2. Williams & Wilkins, Baltimore, 1985.
3. Perry, J, Easterday, CS, and Antonelli, DJ: Surface versus intramuscular electrodes for electromyography of superficial and deep muscles. Phys Ther 61:7, 1981.
4. Strong, P: Biophysical Measurements. Tektronix, Beaverton, OR, 1973, p 295.
5. Zuniga, EM, Truong, XT, and Simons, DG: Effects of skin electrode position on averaged electromyographic potentials. Arch Phys Med Rehabil 50:264, 1969.
6. Basmajian, JV and Stecko, G: A new bipolar electrode for electomyography. J Appl Physiol 17:849, 1962.
7. Adrian, ED and Bronk, DW: The discharge of impulses in motor nerve fibers. J Physiol (Lond) 67:119, 1929.
8. Goodgold, J: Anatomical Correlates of Clinical Electromyography. Williams & Wilkins, Baltimore, 1974.
9. McDermott, JF, Modoff, WL, and Boyle, RW: Electromyography. General Practitioner 27:103, 1963.
10. Soderberg, GL and Cook, TM: Electromyography in biomechanics. Phys Ther 64:1813, 1984.
11. Komi, PV and Buskirk, ER: Reproducibility of electromyographic measurements with inserted wire electrodes and surface electrodes. Electromyography 4:357, 1970.
12. Geddes, LA: Electrodes and the Measurement of Bioelectric Events. John Wiley & Sons, New York, 1972.
13. Goodgold, J and Eberstein, A: Electrodiagnosis of Neuromuscular Diseases, ed 2. Williams & Wilkins, Baltimore, 1978.
14. Kimura, J: Electrodiagnosis in Diseases of Nerve and Muscle: Principles and Practice. FA Davis, Philadelphia, 1983.
15. Units, Terms and Standards in the Reporting of EMG Research. Montreal, Canada, Ad Hoc Committee of the International Society of Electrophysiological Kinesiology. Department of Medical Research, Rehabilitation Institute of Montreal, August 1980.
16. Denny-Brown, D and Pennybacker, JB: Fibrillation and fasciculation in voluntary muscle. Brain 61:311, 1938.
17. Li, CL, Shy, GM, and Wells, J: Some properties of mammalian skeletal muscle fibres with particular reference to fibrillation potentials. J Physiol (Lond) 135:522, 1957.
18. Buchthal, F and Rosenfalck, A: Spontaneous electrical activity of human muscle. EEG Clin Neurophysiol 20:321, 1966.
19. Eisen, AA: Electromyography and nerve conduction as a diagnostic aid. Orthop Clin North Am 4:885, 1973.
20. Pearson, CM: Polymyositis. Ann Rev Med 17:63, 1966.
21. DeLisa, JA, Kraft, GH, and Gans, BM: Clinical electromyography and nerve conduction studies. Orth Rev 7:75, 1978.
22. Brandstater, ME and Dinsdale, SM: Electrophysiological studies in the assessment of spinal cord lesions. Arch Phys Med Rehabil 57:70, 1976.
23. Goldkamp, O: Electromyography and nerve conduction studies in 116 patients with hemiplegia. Arch Phys Med Rehabil 48:59, 1967.
24. Johnson, EW, Denny, ST, and Kelly, JP: Sequence of electromyographic abnormalities in stroke syndrome. Arch Phys Med Rehabil 56:468, 1975.
25. Kruger, KC and Waylonis, GW: Hemiplegia: Lower motor neuron electromyographic findings. Arch Phys Med Rehabil 54:360, 1973.
26. Taylor, RG, Kewalramani, LS, and Fowler, WM: Electromyographic findings in lower extremities of patients with high spinal cord injury. Arch Phys Med Rehabil 55:16, 1974.
27. Spielholtz, NI, et al: Electrophysiological studies in patients with spinal cord lesions. Arch Phys Med Rehabil 53:558, 1972.
28. Takebe, K, et al: Slowing of nerve conduction velocity in hemiplegia: Possible factors. Arch Phys Med Rehabil 56:285, 1975.
29. Takebe, K and Basmajian, JV: Motor and sensory nerve conduction velocities in cerebral palsy. Arch Phys Med Rehabil 57:158, 1976.
30. Chokroverty, S and Median, J: Electrophysiological study of hemiplegia. Arch Neurol 35:360, 1978.
31. Alpert, S, et al: Absence of electromyographic evidence of lower motor neuron involvement in hemiplegic subjects. Arch Phys Med Rehabil 52:179, 1971.
32. Falck, B and Alaranta, H: Fibrillation potentials, positive sharp waves and fasciculation in the intrinsic muscles of the foot in healthy subjects. J Neurol Neurosurg Psychol 46:681, 1983.
33. Wettstein, A: The origin of fasciculations in motorneuron disease. Ann Neurol 5:295, 1979.
34. Johnson, EW, Fallon, TJ, and Wolfe, CV: Errors in EMG reporting. Arch Phys Med Rehabil 57:30, 1976.
35. Echternach, JL: Measurement issues in nerve conduction, velocity and electromyographic testing. In Rothstein, JM (ed): Measurement in Physical Therapy. Churchill Livingstone, New York, 1985, p 281.
36. Hodes, R, Larabee, MG, and German, W: The human electromyogram in response to nerve stimulation and the conduction velocity of motor axons. Arch Neurol Psychiat 60:340, 1948.
37. Dawson, GD and Scott, JW: The recording of nerve action potentials through the skin in man. J Neurosurg Psychiatr 12:259, 1949.
38. Smorto, MP and Basmajian, JV: Clinical Electroneurography: An Introduction to Nerve Conduction Tests. Williams & Wilkins, Baltimore, 1972.
39. DeLisa, JA and MacKenzie, K: Manual of Nerve Conduction Velocity Techniques. Raven Press, New York, 1982.
40. Ma, DM and Liveson, JA: Nerve Conduction Handbook. FA Davis, Philadelphia, 1983.
41. Trojaborg, W: Motor nerve conduction velocities in normal subjects with particular reference to the conduction in proximal and distal segments of median and ulnar nerves. EEG Clin Neurophysiol 17:314, 1964.
42. Sutherland, S: Nerve and Nerve Injuries. Williams & Wilkins, Baltimore, 1968.
43. Mayer, RF: Nerve conduction studies in man. Neurology 13:1021, 1963.
44. Dawson, GD: The relative excitability and conduction velocity of sensory and motor nerve fibers in man. J Physiol (Lond) 131:436, 1956.

45. Currier, DP: Placement of recording electrode in median and peroneal nerve conduction studies. Phys Ther 55:365, 1975.
46. Gassell, MM: Sources of error in motor nerve conduction studies. Neurology, 14:825, 1964.
47. Maynard, FM and Stolov, WC: Experimental error in determination of nerve conduction velocity. Arch Phys Med Rehabil 43:362, 1972.
48. Thomas, JE and Lambert, EH: Ulnar nerve conduction velocity and H-reflex in infants and children. J Appl Physiol 15:1, 1960.
49. Gamstorp, I: Normal conduction velocity of ulnar, median and peroneal nerves in infancy, childhood and adolescence. Acta Paediatrica (Suppl 146)68, 1963.
50. Buchthal, F and Rosenfalck, A: Evoked action potentials and conduction velocity in human sensory nerves. Brain Res 3:1, 1966.
51. Norris, AH, Shock, NW, and Wagman, IH: Age changes in the maximum conduction velocity of motor fibers of human ulnar nerves. J Appl Physiol 5:589, 1953.
52. Halar, EM, DeLisa, JA, and Soine, TL: Nerve conduction studies in upper extremities: Skin temperature corrections. Arch Phys Med Rehabil 64:412, 1983.
53. Braddom, RL, Hollis, JB, and Castell, DO: Diabetic peripheral neuropathy: A correlation of nerve conduction studies and clinical findings. Arch Phys Med Rehabil 58:308, 1977.
54. Rose, FC: Clinical aspects of motor neuron disease. In Rose, FC (ed): Motor Neuron Disease. Grune & Stratton, New York, 1977, p 1.
55. Gardner-Medwin, D and Walton, JN: A classification of the neuromuscular disorders and a note on the clinical examination of the voluntary muscles. In Walton, JN (ed): Disorders of Voluntary Muscle, ed 2. Little, Brown & Co, Boston, 1969, p 411.
56. Brooke, MH: A Clinician's View of Neuromuscular Diseases. Williams & Wilkins, Baltimore, 1977.
57. Wohlfart, G: Collateral regeneration from residual motor nerve fibers in amyotrophic lateral sclerosis. Neurology 7:124, 1957.
58. Rowland, LP: Pathogenesis of muscular dystrophies. Arch Neurol 33:315, 1976.
59. Caccia, MR, Negri, S, and Parvis, VP: Myotonic dystrophy with neural involvement. J Neurol Sci 16:253, 1972.
60. McComas, AJ, Campbell, MJ, and Sica, REP: Electrophysiological study of dystrophia myotonica. J Neurol Neurosurg Psychiatry 34:132, 1971.
61. Simpson, JA: Myasthenia gravis: A new hypothesis. Scott Med J 5:419, 1960.
62. Perlo, VP, et al: Myasthenia gravis: Evaluation of treatment in 1355 patients. Neurology 16:431, 1966.
63. Physical Therapy Advanced Clinical Competencies: Clinical Electrophysiology. Chapel Hill, NC, Clinical Electrophysiology Council, Board for Certification of Advanced Clinical Competence, 1984.
64. Soderberg, GL and Cook, TM: An electromyographic analysis of quadriceps femoris muscle setting and straight leg raising. Phys Ther 63:1434, 1983.
65. Wolf, SL, Edwards, DI, and Shutter, LA: Concurrent assessment of muscle activity (CAMA): A procedural approach to assess treatment goals. Phys Ther 66:218, 1986.
66. Sahrmann, SA and Norton, BJ: Stretch reflex of the biceps and brachioradialis muscles in patients with upper motor neuron syndrome. Phys Ther 58:1191, 1978.
67. Woods, JJ and Bigland-Ritchie, B: Linear and non-linear surface EMG/force relationships in human muscles. Am J Phys Med 62:287, 1983.
68. Yang, JF and Winter, DA: Electromyography reliability in maximal and submaximal isometric contractions. Arch Phys Med Rehabil 64:417, 1983.
69. Walmsley, RP: Electromyographic study of the phasic activity of peroneus longus and brevis. Arch Phys Med Rehabil 58:65, 1977.
70. Currier, DP: Maximal isometric tension of the elbow extensors at varied positions. Part 2. Assessment of extensor components by quantitative electromyography. Phys Ther 52:1265, 1972.
71. Komi, PV and Vittasalo, JHT: Signal characteristics of EMG at different levels of muscle tension. Acta Physiol Scand 96:267, 1976.
72. Davis, JF: Manual of Surface Electromyography. Wright-Patterson Air Force Base, OB, WADC Technical Report 59-184, 1959, p 15.
73. Mayhew, TP, Norton, BJ, and Sahrmann, SA: Electromyographic study of the relationship between hamstring and abdominal muscles during a unilateral straight leg raise. Phys Ther 63:1769, 1983.
74. Soderberg, GL and Cook, TM: An electromyographic analysis of quadriceps femoris muscle setting and straight leg raising. Phys Ther 63:1434, 1983.
75. Basmajian, JV and Blumenstein, R: Electrode Placement for EMG Biofeedback. Williams & Wilkins, Baltimore, 1980.
76. Graham, GP: Reliability of electromyographic measurements after surface electrode removal and replacement. Percept Motor Skills 49:215, 1979.
77. Yanof, HM: Biomedical Electronics, ed 2. FA Davis, Philadelphia, 1972.
78. Lindstrom, LR, Magnusson, R, and Petersen, I: Muscular fatigue and action potential conduction velocity changes studied with frequency analysis of EMG signals. Electromyography 4:341, 1970.
79. Muro, MM, et al: Surface EMG power spectral analysis of neuromuscular disorders during isometric and isotonic contractions. Am J Phys Med 61:244, 1982.
80. Long, GL and Brown, ME: Electromyographic kinesiology of the hand: Muscles moving the long finger. J Bone Joint Surg 46-A:1683, 1964.
81. Basmajian, JV, Harden, TP, and Regenos, EM: Integrated actions of the four heads of quadriceps femoris: An electromyographic study. Anat Rec 172:15, 1972.
82. Lippold, OCJ: The relation between integrated action potentials in a human muscle and its isometric tension. J Physiol 117:492, 1952.
83. Inman, VT, et al: Relation of human electromyogram to muscular tension. EEG Clin Neurophysiol 4:187, 1952.
84. Edwards, RG and Lippold, OCJ: The relation between force and integrated electrical activity in fatigued muscle. J Physiol (Lond) 132:677, 1956.
85. Clamann, HP and Broecker, KT: Relation between force and fatigability of red and pale skeletal muscles in man. Am J Phys Med 58:70, 1979.
86. Vredenbregt, J and Rau, G: Surface electromyography in relation to force, muscle length and endurance. In Desmedt, JE (ed): New Developments in Electromyography and Clinical Neurophysiology, vol 1. Karger, Basel, Switzerland, 1973, p 606.
87. Zuniga, EN and Simons, DG: Nonlinear relationship between averaged electromyogram potential and muscle tension in normal subjects. Arch Phys Med Rehabil 50:613, 1969.
88. Lawrence, JH and De Luca, CJ: Myoelectric signal vs force relationship in different human muscles. J Appl Physiol 54.1653, 1983.
89. Heckathorne, CW and Childress, DS: Relationships of the surface electromyogram to the force, length, velocity, and contraction rate of the cineplastic human biceps. Am J Phys Med 60:1, 1981.
90. Tang, A and Rymer, WZ: Abnormal force–EMG relations in paretic limbs of hemiparetic human subjects. J Neurol Neurosurg Psychiatry 44:690, 1981.
91. Doss, WS and Karpovich, PV: A comparison of concentric, eccentric and isometric strength of elbow flexors. J Appl Physiol 20:351, 1965.
92. Knuttgen, HG, Petersen, FB, and Klausen, K: Exercise with concentric and eccentric muscle contractions. Acta Paediat Scand (Suppl) 217, 1971.
93. Bigland, B and Lippold, OCJ: The relation between force, velocity and integrated electrical activity in human muscles. J Physiol (Lond) 123:214, 1954.
94. Currier, DP: Measurement of muscle fatigue. Phys Ther 49:724, 1969.
95. Hakkinen, K and Komi, PV: Electromyographic and mechanical characteristics of human skeletal muscle during fatigue under voluntary and reflex conditions. EEG Clin Neurophysiol 55:436, 1983.
96. deVries, HA: Method for evaluation of muscle fatigue and endurance from electromyographic fatigue curves. Am J Phys Med 47:125, 1968.
97. Bigland-Ritchie, B, et al: Central and peripheral fatigue in sustained maximum voluntary contractions of human quadriceps muscle. Clin Sci Molec Med 54:609, 1978.
98. Hagberg, M: Electromyographic signs of shoulder muscular fatigue in two elevated arm positions. Am J Phys Med 60:111, 1981.
99. Petrofsky, JS, et al: Evaluation of the amplitude and frequency

components of the surface EMG as an index of muscle fatigue. Ergonomics 25:213, 1982.

100. Lenman, JAR: Quantitative electromyographic changes associated with muscular weakness. J Neurol Neurosurg Psychiatry 22:306, 1959.
101. Griffith, ER: Spasticity. In Rosenthal, M, et al (eds): Rehabilitation of the Head-Injured Patient. FA Davis, Philadelphia, 1983, p 125.
102. Basmajian, JV: New views on muscular tone and relaxation. Can Med Assoc J 77:203, 1957.
103. Brooks V: The Neural Basis of Motor Control. Oxford University Press, New York, 1986.
104. Shimazu, H, et al: Rigidity and spasticity in man: Electromyographic analysis with reference to the role of the globus pallidus. Arch Neurol 6:10, 1962.
105. Nelson, AJ: Motor assessment. In Rosenthal, M, et al (eds): Rehabilitation of the Head-Injured Adult. FA Davis, Philadelphia, 1983, p 241.
106. Barry, G: An EMG Study of Contralateral Overflow during Varied Intensities of Isometric Knee Extension. Master's thesis. Boston University, Boston, MA, 1983.
107. Portney, LG, Sullivan, PE, and Bachelder, ME: Analysis of exercise overflow to preferred and non-preferred limbs. (Abstract) Phys Ther 64:749, 1984.
108. Sullivan, PE, Markos, PD, and Minor, MAD: An Integrated Approach to Therapeutic Exercise: Theory and Clinical Application. Reston Publishing, Reston, VA, 1982.
109. Gregg, RA, Mastellone, AF, and Gersten, JW: Cross exercise—A review of the literature and study utilizing electromyographic techniques. Am J Phys Med 36:269, 1957.
110. Devine, KL, LeVeau, BF, Yack, HJ: Electromyographic activity recorded from an unexercised muscle during maximal isometric exercise of the contralateral agonists and antagonists. Phys Ther 61:898, 1981.
111. Markos, PD: Ipsilateral and contralateral effects of proprioceptive neuromuscular facilitation techniques on hip motion and electromyographic activity. Phys Ther 59:1366, 1979.
112. Hopf, HC, Schlegel, HJ, and Lowitzsch, K: Irradiation of voluntary activity to the contralateral side in movements of normal subjects and patients with central motor disturbances. Eur Neurol 12:142, 1974.
113. Russell, AS: Electromyographic activity during proprioceptive neuromuscular facilitation in normal and hemiplegic patients. Master's thesis. Stanford University, 1971.
114. Nelson, AJ: Strategies for improving motor control. In Rosenthal, M, et al (eds): Rehabilitation of the Head-Injured Adult. FA Davis, Philadelphia, 1983.
115. Basmajian, JV and Bentzon, JW: An electromyographic study of certain muscles of the leg and foot in the standing posture. Surg Gynecol Obstet 98:662, 1954.

116. Waters, RL and Morris, JM: Electrical activity of muscles of the trunk during walking. J Anat 111:191, 1972.
117. Radcliffe, CW: The biomechanics of below-knee prostheses in normal, level, bipedal walking. Artif Limbs 6:16, 1962.
118. Shiavi, R, et al: Variability of electromyographic patterns for level-surface walking through a range of self-selected speeds. Bulletin of Prosthetic Research 10:5, 1981.
119. Leavitt, LA and Beasley, WC: Clinical application of quantitative methods in the study of spasticity. Clin Pharmacol Ther 5:918, 1964.
120. Bierman, W and Ralston, HJ: Electromyographic study during passive and active flexion and extension of the knee of the normal human subject. Arch Phys Med Rehabil 46:71, 1965.
121. Svendsen, DA and Matyas, TA: Facilitation of the isometric maximum voluntary contraction with traction: A test of PNF prediction. Am J Phys Med 62:27, 1983.
122. Sullivan, PE and Portney, LG: Electromyographic activity of shoulder muscles during unilateral upper extremity proprioceptive neuromuscular facilitation patterns. Phys Ther 60:283, 1980.
123. Osternig, LR, et al: Electromyographic patterns accompanying isokinetic exercise under varying speed and sequencing conditions. Am J Phys Med 63:289, 1984.
124. Hobart, DJ, Kelley, DL, and Bradley, LS: Modification occurring during acquisition of a novel throwing task. Am J Phys Med 54:1, 1975.
125. Person, RS: An electromyographic investigation on coordination of the activity of antagonist muscles in man during the development of a motor habit. Pavlov J Higher Nervous Activity 8:13, 1958.
126. Nashner, LM: Balance adjustments of humans perturbed while walking. J Neurophysiol 44:650, 1980.
127. Fujiwara, M and Basmajian, JV: Electromyographic study of two-joint muscles. Am J Phys Med 54:234, 1975.
128. Portney, LG, Sullivan, PE, and Daniell, JL: EMG activity of vastus medialis oblique and vastus lateralis in normals and patients with patellofemoral arthralgia. Phys Ther (Abstract) 66:808, 1986.
129. Mariani, PP and Caruso, I: An electromyographic investigation of subluxation of the patella. J Bone Joint Surg 61-B:169, 1979.
130. Reynolds, L, et al: EMG activity of the vastus medialis oblique and the vastus lateralis in their role in patellar alignment. Am J Phys Med 62:61, 1983.
131. Wheatley, MD and Jahnke, WS: Electromyographic study of the superficial thigh and hip muscles in normal individuals. Arch Phys Med Rehabil 32:508, 1951.
132. Blackburn, SE and Portney, LG: EMG activity of back musculature during Williams' flexion exercises. Phys Ther 61:878, 1981.
133. Blanpied, P and LeVeau, BF: The effects of a short-arc quadricep strengthening program on the EMG activity of the VMO and the VL muscles. Phys Ther (Abstract) 66:808, 1986.

SUPPLEMENTAL READINGS

Basmajian, JV and Blumenstein, R: Electrode Placement for EMG Biofeedback. Williams & Wilkins, Baltimore, 1980.
Basmajian, JV and De Luca, CJ: Muscles Alive, ed 5. Williams & Wilkins, Baltimore, 1985.
Echternach, JL: Measurement issues in nerve conduction velocity and electromyographic testing. In Rothstein, JM (ed): Measurement in Physical Therapy. Churchill Livingstone, New York, 1985, p 281.
Goodgold, J and Eberstein, A: Electrodiagnosis of Neuromuscular Diseases, ed 2. Williams & Wilkins, Baltimore, 1978.
Kimura, J: Electrodiagnosis in Diseases of Nerve and Muscle: Principles and Practice. FA Davis, Philadelphia, 1983.

Soderberg, GL: Kinesiology: Application to Pathological Motion. Williams & Wilkins, Baltimore, 1986.
Soderberg, GL and Cook, TM: Electromyography in biomechanics. Phys Ther 64:1434, 1984.
Units, Terms and Standards in the Reporting of EMG Research. Montreal, Canada, Ad Hoc Committee of the International Society of Electrophysiological Kinesiology. Department of Medical Research, Rehabilitation Institute of Montreal, August 1980.
Woods, JJ and Bigland-Ritchie, B: Linear and non-linear surface EMG/force relationships in human muscles. Am J Phys Med 62:287, 1983.

GLOSSARY

Amplifier: A device used to process an electrical signal, converting it to a voltage output which can be displayed. A **differential amplifier** is characterized by two input terminals, each of which is reference to ground. The differential input virtually eliminates the effect of electrical noise in the recording system.

Amplitude: Of an action potential, the maximum voltage difference between two points, usually measured baseline to peak or peak to peak; expresses the level of the signal activity.

Anode: The positive terminal of a source of electrical currrent.

Antidromic conduction: Propagation of an action potential in a direction opposite to the normal (orthodromic) direction for that fiber, i.e., conduction along motor fibers toward the spinal cord, and conduction along sensory fibers away from the spinal cord.

Artifact: A voltage signal generated by a source other than the one of interest. See **stimulus artifact, movement artifact.**

Bandwidth: Frequency response of an amplifier, referring to the limits on the range of signal frequencies processed; for example, 10 to 1000 Hz.

Cathode: The negative terminal of a source of electrical current.

Common mode rejection ratio (CMRR): A proportion expressing an amplifier's ability to reject unwanted noise while amplifying the wanted signal; for example, a ratio of 1000:1 indicates that the wanted signal will be amplified 1000 times more than noise. It can also be expressed in decibels (1000:1 equals 60 dB).

Conduction distance: Distance measured (in cm) between two points of stimulation along a nerve in a nerve conduction velocity test.

Conduction time: Time difference between the distal and proximal latencies in a nerve conduction velocity test; that is, the time it takes for an impulse to travel between the two points of stimulation along a nerve trunk. Measured in milliseconds.

Conduction velocity: Speed of propagation of an action potential along a nerve or muscle fiber. Calculated in meters/second by dividing the **conduction distance** by the **conduction time.** The calculated velocity represents conduction velocity of the fastest axons in the nerve.

Duration: The period of time in which an action potential occurs; measured as the interval from the first deflection from the baseline to its final return to the baseline.

Electrical silence: The absence of measurable electromyographic activity, typically recorded at rest in normal muscles.

Electrode: A device capable of recording electrical potentials or conducting electricity to provide a stimulus.

Concentric (coaxial) needle electrode: Recording electrode consisting of a steel cannula through which is threaded a single platinum wire which is insulated from the needle shaft. The wire and shaft are bared at the tip, and the potential difference between them is recorded in the presence of electrical activity. The electrode also can be configured with two wires (bipolar) threaded through the cannula, recording the difference of potential between these wires.

Fine-wire indwelling electrode: Small-diameter insulated wire strands inserted into the muscle belly by means of a hypothermic needle.

Ground electrode: An electrode connected to a common source, used to reduce the effect of electrical noise in a recording system; an arbitrary zero potential reference point.

Monopolar needle electrode: A solid wire, usually of stainless steel, coated, except at its tip, with insulating material. Voltage is measured between the tip of the needle and some other electrode usually placed on the skin (**reference electrode**).

Recording electrode (active electrode): Needle or surface electrode used to record electrical activity from nerve and muscle.

Reference electrode: In motor nerve conduction velocity testing the electrode placed over the tendon of the test muscle. In monopolar recording of EMG, the inactive electrode placed over a neutral area.

Stimulating electrode: Device used to apply electrical current to stimulate propagation of a nerve impulse or muscle contraction; requires positive (anode) and negative (cathode) terminals.

Surface electrode: Small metal disks, most commonly made of silver-silver chloride, applied to the skin overlying appropriate muscle.

Electromyography (EMG): The recording and study of the electrical activity of muscle. It is commonly used to refer to nerve conduction studies as well. The electromyograph is the instrument used to record and to display the electromyogram.

Evoked potential: Waveform elicited by a stimulus.

Fasciculation potential: A random, spontaneous twitching of a group of muscle fibers which may be visible through the skin. The amplitude, configuration, duration, and frequency are variable.

Fasciculations: Spontaneous potentials seen with irritation or degeneration of the anterior horn cell, nerve root compression, and muscle spasms or cramps.

Fibrillation potential: Electrical activity associated with fibrillating muscle, reflecting the activity of a single muscle fiber; associated with denervation and myopathy. Classically, these potentials are biphasic spikes of short duration (less than 5 msec), with a peak-to-peak amplitude less than 1 mV, a firing rate ranging from 1–50 Hz, and a high-pitched regular sound likened to "rain on the roof."

Frequency: Number of complete cycles of a repetitive waveform in 1 second; measured in Hertz (Hz).

Giant motor units: Motor unit potentials with a peak-to-peak amplitude and duration much greater than normal ranges; often seen following collateral sprouting with regeneration of peripheral nerves.

Hertz (Hz): Unit of frequency representing cycles per second.

Impedance: The property of a substance that offers resistance to current flow in an alternating current circuit. Skin, electrodes, and amplifier input terminals provide sources of impedance to EMG potentials.

Insertion activity: Electrical activity caused by insertion or movement of a needle electrode in a muscle. Can be described as normal, reduced, increased, or prolonged.

Integration: Mathematical processing of a rectified electromyographic signal that allows quantification. Integration can be performed over set intervals or within preset voltage threshold levels.

Interference pattern: Electrical activity recorded from a muscle during maximal voluntary effort, in which identification of each of the contributing motor unit potentials is not possible.

Latency: In nerve conduction velocity tests, the interval between onset of a stimulus and the onset of a response, measured from the stimulus artifact to the onset of the M wave.

Distal latency: The time (in msec) for an action potential to travel from the distal point of stimulation along a nerve to the recording electrode.

Proximal latency: The time (in msec) for an action potential to travel from the proximal point of stimulation along a nerve to the recording electrode.

Motor unit: The anatomic unit of an anterior horn cell, its axon, the neuromuscular junctions, and all the muscle fibers innervated by that axon.

Motor unit action potential (MUAP): Action potential reflecting the electrical activity of a single motor unit; characterized by its amplitude, configuration, duration, frequency, and sound.

Movement artifact: An electrical signal resulting from the movement of the recording electrodes or their cables.

M wave: A compound action potential evoked from muscle by a single electrical stimulus to its motor nerve.

Myotonic discharge: A high-frequency discharge, characterized by repetitive firing (20–80 Hz) of biphasic or monophasic potentials recorded after needle insertion or after voluntary muscle contraction; typical features include a waxing and waning amplitude and frequency and a sound likened to a "dive bomber."

Nerve conduction velocity (NCV): The speed with which a peripheral motor or sensory nerve conducts an impulse.

Noise: An unwanted electrical signal that is detected along with the desired signal.

Orthodromic conduction: Propagation of an action potential in the same direction as physiologic conduction; that is, motor nerve conduction away from the spinal cord and sensory nerve conduction toward the spinal cord.

Oscilloscope: A device for displaying electronic signals on a screen, composed of a cathode ray tube (CRT) within which horizontal and vertical beams strike a phosphorescent surface, allowing visualization of the signal. Control of values of vertical and horizontal divisions permit quantification of amplitude and duration of signals.

Phase: That portion of a wave between the departure from and the return to the baseline.

Polyphasic action potential: An action potential having five or more phases.

Positive sharp wave: A form of electrical potential associated with fibrillating muscle fibers, recorded as a biphasic, positive-negative action potential initiated by needle movement and recurring in uniform patterns. The initial positive phase is of short duration (less than 5 msec) and large amplitude (up to 1 mV); the second negative phase is of long duration (10–100 msec) and low amplitude.

Rectification: A process whereby the negative portion of an electromyographic wave is inverted and superimposed on the positive portion, so that the signal is seen only above the baseline. This allows further processing and integration.

Repetitive discharges (bizarre high-frequency discharges): An extended train of potentials, generally 5 to 100 impulses per second, commonly seen in lesions of the anterior horn cell and peripheral nerves, and with myopathies.

Sensitivity: Characteristic of a system, expressing its ability to record and to display signals of different sizes, usually expressed as a range; for example, 20 uV to 30 mV.

Signal-to-noise ratio: The relationship (proportion) between the signal power and the power of the noise.

Single motor unit pattern: An interference pattern recorded at maximal effort when single motor unit potentials can still be identified.

Skin resistance: The opposition to electrical conduction offered by skin cells and other substances on the skin, usually necessitating some form of skin preparation prior to application of surface electrodes.

Spontaneous potentials: Action potentials recorded from muscle or nerve at rest after insertional activity has subsided, when no voluntary contraction or external stimuli are present.

Stimulus artifact: A potential recorded at the time the stimulus is applied.

Sweep: Horizontal movement of a phosphorescent beam across the face of an oscilloscope.

Temporal dispersion: Distortion of duration, amplitude, or shape of the M wave potential in a motor nerve conduction velocity test.

Volt: The difference of potential between two points; the unit of measurement for EMG amplitude.

Volume conduction: Spread of current from a potential source through a conducting medium, such as body tissues.

Chapter 11

GAIT ANALYSIS

CYNTHIA NORKIN

OBJECTIVES

1. Define the terms used to describe normal gait.

2. Define reliability and validity in relation to gait analysis.

3. Describe the variables that are assessed in each of the following types of gait analyses: kinematic qualitative anaylsis, kinematic quantitative analysis, and kinetic analysis.

4. Describe and give examples of the common deviations found in gait.

5. Describe and give examples of methods used for assessing kinematic and kinetic variables.

6. Compare and contrast the advantages and disadvantages of kinematic qualitative and kinematic quantitative gait analyses.

7. Describe the model for observational gait analysis presented in this chapter.

INTRODUCTION

One of the major purposes of the rehabilitative process is to help patients achieve as high a level of functional independence as possible within the limits of their particular disabilities. Human locomotion or gait is one of the basic components of independent functioning that is commonly affected by either disease processes or injury. Therefore, the goal of many physical therapy treatment programs is to restore or to improve a patient's ambulatory status.

Content of Gait Analysis

In order to set realistic treatment goals and to develop and implement a treatment plan directed toward improving or restoring a patient's gait, the physical therapist must be able to assess ambulatory status. The assessment should include

1. An accurate description of the gait pattern and gait variables.
2. An identification and description of all gait deviations.
3. An analysis of the deviations and identification of the mechanisms responsible for producing abnormalities in gait.
4. A determination of the need for assistive devices.

Furthermore, the assessment should provide objective data that can be used as a basis for formulating realistic treatment goals and assessing progress toward those goals.

Selection of a Gait Analysis

Gait is a complex activity, and a large amount of the physical therapy literature is devoted to methods of analyzing gait.[1-14] The type of gait analysis that the clinician selects depends upon the purpose of the analysis, the type of equipment that is available, and the knowledge, skills, and experience of the clinician.

The purpose of a gait analysis may include, but is not limited to, the following: assessment of the fit of a lower extremity prosthesis,[1] comparison of the effects of different types of assistive devices,[2] determination of the need for an orthotic device,[3] and assessment of the need for increasing endurance or gait velocity. To determine the need for an orthotic adjustment, the therapist may need to assess the forces acting during gait. To determine if a patient should increase ambulating endurance, the therapist needs to assess time and distance variables as well as physiologic parameters.

The type of equipment necessary for performing a gait analysis depends upon the purpose of the analysis, equipment availability, and the amount of time that the therapist can expend. Equipment used in a gait analysis may be as simple as a pencil and paper[4] or as complex as an electronic imaging system with force plates embedded in the floor.[5,6]

The knowledge, skills, and experience of the therapist are essential ingredients in any gait analysis. The therapist must be aware of the types of analyses that are available and which assessment methods are reliable and valid so that the appropriate method may be selected. The therapist must have a knowledge and understanding of the **kinematics, kinetics,** and neural control of normal and pathologic human locomotion in order to analyze and to interpret the data obtained from an assessment.

Types of Analyses

The types of gait analyses in use today can be classified under two broad categories: kinematic and kinetic. Kinematic gait analyses are used to describe movement patterns without regard for the forces involved in producing the movement.[4] Kinetic gait analyses are used to determine the forces that are involved in gait.[15] In some instances, kinematic and kinetic gait variables may be assessed in one analysis. A kinematic gait analysis consists of a description of movement of the body as a whole and/or body segments in relation to each other during gait. Kinematic gait analyses can be either qualitative or quantitative.

KINEMATIC QUALITATIVE GAIT ANALYSIS

The most common method used in the clinic is a **qualitative gait analysis.** This method usually requires only a small amount of equipment and a minimal amount of time.

Definition of Variables

The primary variable that is assessed in a qualitative kinematic analysis is **displacement,** which includes a description of patterns of movement, deviations from normal, body postures, and joint angles at specific points in the gait cycle. **Linear displacement** is measured in meters, whereas rotational displacement is measured in degrees. An example of **rotational displacement** would be the amount of knee flexion and extension that occurs during the gait cycle. Four different reference systems are used in describing displacement:

1. Absolute spatial system: the environment is used as a reference.

2. Relative system: the position of one body segment is described in relation to another body segment.

3. Absolute reference system: the body segment is described in reference to the vertical or horizontal position.

4. Relative reference system: the excursion of a body segment from one position to another is described (e.g., the ankle passes through a 35 degree excursion from relative dorsiflexion to relative plantarflexion).[15]

Gait Terminology

To assess gait a therapist must be familiar with the terminology used to describe gait. Usually gait is described in reference to the activities of one extremity. The largest unit used to describe gait is called a *gait cycle.* In normal walking a gait cycle commences when the heel of the reference extremity contacts the supporting surface. The gait cycle ends when the heel of the same extremity contacts the ground again. The gait cycle is divided into two phases, **stance** and **swing,** and two periods of **double support.** In normal gait the stance phase, which constitutes 60 percent of the gait cycle, is defined as the interval in which the foot of the reference extremity is in contact with the ground. The swing phase, which constitutes 40 percent of the gait cycle, is that portion in which the reference extremity does not contact the ground. The term double support refers to the two intervals in a gait cycle in which body weight is being transferred from one foot to the other and both right and left feet are in contact with the ground at the same time (Fig. 11–1).

Step and **Stride** are considered to be quantitative variables and will be discussed in the kinematic quantitative gait section. However, a definition of these variables is necessary for a comprehensive overview of gait terminology. Two steps, a *right step* and a *left step,* comprise a stride, and a stride is equal to a gait cycle. A step may be defined in two dimensions: distance and time. **Step length** is the distance from the point of heel strike of one extremity to the point of heel strike of the opposite extremity, whereas **stride length** is the distance from the point of heel strike of one extremity to the point of heel strike of the same extremity. **Stride time** and **step time** refer to the length of time required to complete a step and a stride, respectively (Fig. 11–2).

Traditionally, each phase of gait (stance and swing) has been divided into the following units: stance (*heel strike, footflat, midstance, heel off,* and *toe off*) and swing (*acceleration, midswing,* and *deceleration*). Recently, the subdivisions within phases have been redefined and a new terminology developed at Rancho Los Amigos Medical Center (RLA). In the new terminology the subdivisions are named as follows: stance (*initial contact, loading response, midstance, terminal stance,* and *preswing*) and

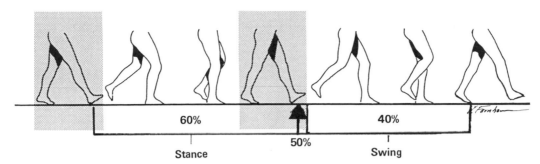

Figure 11–1. The two periods of double support overlap the stance phases of the two lower extremities for about 22 percent of the gait cycle at a normal walking speed. The stance phase constitutes 60 percent of the gait cycle, and the swing phase constitutes 40 percent of the cycle at normal walking speed. Increases or decreases in walking speeds will alter the percentages of time spent in each phase. (From Norkin, C, and Levangie, P,[24] with permission.)

swing (*initial swing, midswing,* and *terminal swing*).[16] The similarities and differences between the two terminologies are presented in Table 11–1.

The normal angular rotations at the joints in each portion of both swing and stance phases as well as normal muscle activity and function are presented in Tables 11–2 to 11–6. The clinician should be familiar with normal ranges and patterns of motion in order to identify deviations from normal. The clinician also should be familiar with normal muscle activity and function in order to perform an analysis of the causes of the deviations.

Methods of Assessment

The most common method of performing a kinematic qualitative analysis is through observation. Some of the most well-known observational gait analysis schemes have been developed by Brunnstrom,[17] and at New York University Post-Graduate Medical School Prosthetics and Orthotics,[18] Temple University,[19] and at Rancho Los Amigos Medical Center.[5,16] Daniels and Worthingham[20] included a procedure for observational gait analysis at the end of their manual muscle testing text, and the first edition of this text[21] included a worksheet for observational gait analysis. In general, these protocols provide

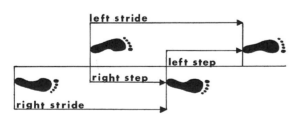

Figure 11–2. Two strides—a right stride and a left stride—are shown in the diagram. Right stride length (illustrated by the arrow) is the distance between the point of contact of the right heel (at the lower left corner of the diagram) and the next contact of the right heel. Left stride length is the distance between the point of contact of the left heel (at the top left of the diagram) to the point of contact of the next left heel. Each stride contains two steps, but only both steps in the left stride are labeled. The left stride contains a right step and a left step. The right step length (shown in the middle of the diagram) is the distance between left heel contact to the point of right heel contact. Left step length is the distance between right heel contact and the next left heel contact. Step and stride times refer to the amount of time required to complete a step and to complete stride, respectively.

Table 11–1 GAIT TERMINOLOGY

Traditional	Rancho Los Amigos
Stance Phase	
Heel strike: The beginning of the stance phase when the heel contacts the ground. The same as initial contact.	Initial contact: The beginning of the stance phase when the heel or another part of the foot contacts the ground.
Foot flat: Occurs immediately following heel strike, when the sole of the foot contacts the floor. This event occurs during loading response.	Loading response: The portion of the stance phase from immediately following initial contact until the contralateral extremity leaves the ground.
Midstance: The point at which the body passes directly over the reference extremity.	Midstance: The portion of the stance phase that begins when the contralateral extremity leaves the ground and ends when the body is directly over the supporting limb.
Heel off: The point following midstance at which time the heel of the reference extremity leaves the ground. Heel off occurs prior to terminal stance.	Terminal stance: The portion of the stance phase from midstance to a point just prior to initial contact of the contralateral extremity.
Toe off: The point following heel off when only the toe of the reference extremity is in contact with the ground. Toe off occurs during preswing.	Preswing: The portion of stance from the initial contact of the contralateral extremity to just prior to the lift off of the reference extremity. This portion includes toe off.
Swing Phase	
Acceleration: The portion of beginning swing from the moment the toe of the reference extremity leaves the ground to the point when the reference extremity is directly under the body.	Initial swing: The portion of swing from the point when the reference extremity leaves the ground to maximum knee flexion of the same extremity.
Midswing: Portion of the swing phase when the reference extremity passes directly below the body. Midswing extends from the end of acceleration to the beginning of deceleration.	Midswing: Portion of the swing phase from maximum knee flexion of the reference extremity to a vertical tibial position.
Deceleration: The swing portion of the swing phase when the reference extremity is decelerating in preparation for heel strike.	Terminal swing: The portion of the swing phase from a vertical position of the tibia of the reference extremity to just prior to initial contact.

Table 11–2 ANKLE AND FOOT: STANCE PHASE, SAGITTAL PLANE ANALYSIS

Portion of Phase	Normal Motion	Normal Moment	Normal Muscle Activity	Result of Weakness	Possible Compensation
Heel strike to foot flat	0°–15° plantarflexion	Plantarflexion	Pretibial group acts eccentrically to oppose plantarflexion moment and thereby to prevent foot slap by controlling plantarflexion.	Lack of ability to oppose the plantarflexion moment causes the foot to slap the floor.	To avoid foot slap and to eliminate the plantarflexion moment, heel strike may be avoided and either the foot placed flat on the floor or placed with the toes first at initial contact.
Foot flat through midstance	15° plantarflexion to 10° dorsiflexion	Plantarflexion to dorsiflexion	Gastrocnemius and soleus act eccentrically to oppose the dorsiflexion moment and to control tibial advance.	Excessive dorsiflexion and uncontrolled tibial advance.	To avoid excessive dorsiflexion, the ankle may be maintained in plantarflexion.
Midstance to heel off	10°–15° dorsiflexion	Dorsiflexion	Gastrocnemius and soleus contract eccentrically to oppose the dorsiflexion moment and control tibial advance.	Excessive dorsiflexion and uncontrolled forward motion of tibia.	The ankle may be maintained in plantarflexion. If the foot is flat on the floor, the dorsiflexion moment is eliminated and a step-to gait is produced.
Heel off to toe off	15° dorsiflexion to 20° plantarflexion	Dorsiflexion	Gastrocnemius, soleus, peroneus brevis, peroneus longus, flexor hallicus longus contract to plantarflex the foot.	No roll off.	Whole foot is lifted off the ground.

the therapist with a systematic approach to observational gait analysis by directing attention to a specific joint or body segment during a given point in the gait cycle. Most of these schemes are in the form of checklists or profiles in which the examiner notes the presence or absence of a particular deviation or critical event at a particular point in the patient's gait cycle.

The Temple University method uses a scoring system that consists of the following: present, inconsistent, bor- derline, occurs throughout, absent, limited, and exagger- ated. This system is used to rate 48 gait deviations. The Temple system also includes a section for assessing time and distance measures, that is, velocity, step length, step time, and width of base of support.[19] The observational gait analysis method formulated by New York Univer- sity Post-Graduate Medical School Prosthetics and Orthotics includes 13 gait deviations, which are rated on a three-point scale: 0—not noticeable, +—just notice-

Table 11–3 ANKLE AND FOOT: SWING PHASE, SAGITTAL PLANE ANALYSIS

Portion of Phase	Normal Motion	Normal Moment	Normal Muscle Action	Result of Weakness	Possible Compensation
Acceleration to midswing	Dorsiflexion to neutral	None	Dorsiflexors contract to bring the ankle into neutral and to prevent the toes from dragging on the floor.	Foot drop and/or toe dragging.	Hip and knee flexion may be increased to prevent toe drag, or the hip may be hiked or circumducted. Sometimes vaulting on the contralateral limb may occur.
Midswing to deceleration	Neutral	None	Dorsiflexion.	Foot drop and/or toe dragging.	Hip and knee flexion may be increased to prevent toe drag. The swing leg may be circumducted, or vaulting may occur on the contralateral side.

Table 11–4 KNEE: STANCE PHASE, SAGITTAL PLANE ANALYSIS

Portion of Phase	Normal Motion	Normal Moment	Normal Muscle Action	Result of Weakness	Possible Compensation
Heel strike to foot flat	Flexion 0°–15°	Flexion	Quadriceps contracts initially to hold the knee in extension and then eccentrically to oppose the flexion moment and control amount of flexion.	Excessive knee flexion because the quadriceps cannot oppose the flexion moment.	Plantarflexion at ankle so that foot flat instead of heel strike occurs. Plantarflexion eliminates the flexion moment. Trunk lean forward eliminates the flexion moment at knee and therefore may be used to compensate for quadriceps weakness.
Foot flat through midstance	Extension 15°–5°	Flexion to extension	Quadriceps contracts in early part, and then no activity is required.	Excessive knee flexion initially.	Same as above in early part of midstance. No compensation required in later part of phase.
Midstance to heel off	5° of flexion to 0° (neutral)	Flexion to extension	No activity required.		None required.
Heel off to toe off	0°–40° flexion	Extension to flexion	Quadriceps required to control amount of knee flexion.		

Table 11–5 KNEE: SWING PHASE, SAGITTAL PLANE ANALYSIS

Portion of Phase	Normal Motion	Normal Moment	Normal Muscle Action	Result of Weakness	Possible Compensation
Acceleration to midswing	40°–60° flexion	None	Little or no activity in quadriceps. Biceps femoris (short head), gracilis, and sartorius contract concentrically.	Inadequate knee flexion.	Increased hip flexion, circumduction, or hiking.
Midswing	60°–30° extension	None			
Deceleration	30°–0° extension	None	Quadriceps contracts concentrically to stabilize knee in extension in preparation for heel strike	Inadequate knee extension.	

Table 11–6 HIP: STANCE PHASE, SAGITTAL PLANE ANALYSIS

Portion of Phase	Normal Motion	Normal Moment	Normal Muscle Action	Result of Weakness	Possible Compensation
Heel strike to foot flat	30° flexion	Flexion	Erector spinae, gluteus maximus, hamstrings.	Excessive hip flexion and anterior pelvic tilt owing to inability to counteract flexion moment.	Trunk lean backward to prevent excessive hip flexion and to eliminate the hip flexion moment. (See Fig. 11–5).
Foot flat through midstance	30° flexion to 5° (neutral)	Flexion to extension	Gluteus maximus at beginning of period to oppose flexion moment, then activity ceases as moment changes from flexion to extension.	At the beginning of the period, excessive hip flexion and anterior pelvic tilt owing to inability to counteract flexion moment.	At beginning of the period, subject may lean trunk backward to prevent excessive hip flexion; however, once the flexion moment changes to an extension moment, the subject no longer needs to incline the trunk backward.
Midstance to heel off		Extension	No activity.	None.	None required.
Heel off to toe off	10° of hyperextension to neutral	Extension	Illiopsoas, adductor, magnus, and adductor longus.	Undetermined.	Undetermined.

able, and + +—very noticeable. The Rancho Los Amigos technique involves a systematic assessment of the movement patterns of the following body segments at each point in the gait cycle: ankle, foot, knee, hip, pelvis, and trunk. The Rancho Los Amigos form is similar to the Temple form in that the Rancho form consists of 48 descriptors of common gait deviations such as toe drag, excessive plantarflexion and dorsiflexion, excessive varus or valgus at the knee or foot, hip hiking, and trunk flexion. The observing therapist must decide whether or not a deviation is present and note the occurrence and timing of the deviation on the form.[16]

Considerable training and constant practice are necessary to develop the observational skills that are necessary for performing any observational gait analysis. Therapists who wish to learn the Rancho method may elect to attend a workshop or the therapist can learn through study. Forms for recording an assessment, and practice gait film strips useful for learning how to use the recording form, may be obtained by writing to Rancho Los Amigos.[16] However, prior to selecting a particular assessment method the therapist should attempt to obtain information regarding the method's reliability and validity.

Reliability

Reliability as applied to gait analysis refers to the level of consistency of either a measuring instrument (footswitches, forceplates, and electrogoniometers) or a method of analysis (observational gait checklists and formulas for measuring stride length). To determine if a measuring instrument is reliable, the measurements obtained from successive and repeated use of the instrument must be consistent. For example, if an electrogoniometric measurement of a normal subject's knee flexion range of motion during the swing phase is 60 degrees on every Monday morning for 2 months, the instrument is said to be reliable. If, however, the measurement obtained on the first Monday is 60 degrees, 30 degrees on the second Monday morning, and 40 degrees on the third Monday morning, the instrument would be considered to have very low reliability.

To make a definitive determination of the reliability of an instrument, one would have to make certain that factors that could influence the measurement are ruled out (e.g., that the subject has not injured his or her knee during the week or that the placement of the instrument has not changed).

To determine whether an assessment method is reliable, two different forms of reliability need to be determined: *intratester and intertester reliability*. The *intratester reliability* of an assessment method can be determined by examining the consistency of the results obtained when one individual uses a particular method repeatedly. For example, Sue Jones, P.T., uses a particular method to assess a student physical therapist's gait. Sue repeats her assessment at 1-week intervals for 2 months and obtains the same results during each analysis. In this instance the method would be considered as having high intratester reliability because the results obtained by the same person are consistent over time.

Intertester reliability is determined by looking at the consistency of the data obtained from repeated analyses performed by a number of different persons. If the results obtained by the numerous examiners are in agreement, the method has high intertester reliability.

Generally the reliability of existing observational gait analyses is low or moderate because of difficulties involved in trying to observe and to make accurate judgments about the motions occurring at numerous body segments. Also, therapists differ in their observational skills. Only moderate reliability between therapists (intertester reliability) was found when a modification of the New York University (NYU) orthotic gait analysis method was used to assess the gait of 10 hemiplegic patients. The authors suggest that training of therapists in gait analysis is necessary to improve reliability.[22] In another study only moderate interrater and intrarater reliability was found when three physical therapists with at least 5 years' experience used an observational gait form created from the NYU, Temple, and Rancho schemes to evaluate the gaits of 15 disabled children with knee-ankle-foot orthoses (KAFOs).[23] The reliability of the Rancho Los Amigos observational gait analysis technique has not been published. Gronley and Perry[5] report that differences among raters are resolved through discussion and consensus.

Validity

The other aspect of gait analysis that must be considered is *validity*. *Validity* refers to the degree that a measurement reflects what it is supposed to measure. If a test instrument purports to measure a patient's functional ambulation ability, one would expect that the test would predict the patient's performance on functional ambulation skills. If the test does not predict a patient's functional ambulation skills, the test may not be considered valid. Unfortunately, many of the methods used for observational gait analysis have not been tested for reliability and validity.

The reader should attempt to determine if the reliability and validity of an instrument or method of analysis has been determined by either looking in the literature or by contacting other investigators who are using the particular method or instrument. If the instrument or method has not been tested, the therapists may wish to perform their own tests for reliability and validity.

Advantages and Disadvantages

The advantages of observational gait analyses are that they require little or no instrumentation, are inexpensive to use, and can yield general descriptions of gait variables. The disadvantages are that the technique, being dependent upon the therapist's observational skills, is subjective and has only moderate reliability.

When using any type of observational gait analysis, therapists should seriously consider either filming or videotaping the patient's gait. A visual record is especially important when using the Rancho format because of the time involved in assessing a large number of deviations at six different body parts. Most patients can not walk continuously for the length of time required to complete a detailed full body observational analysis. Videotape records of a patient's initial assessment and reassessment can be used to provide evidence of progress and as a means of determining reliability of the assessment instrument. Observational gait analysis may be a useful tool to determine the quality of a patient's gait and to identify common deviations but should be used in conjunction with quantitative measures to document progress toward goals adequately. Examples of the process involved in an observational gait analysis will be presented in the following section.

Models for Kinematic Gait Analysis and Assessment of Variables

The purpose of this section is to present a model and some examples of the process involved in an observational gait analysis. The first step in the process involves the identification and accurate description of the patient's gait pattern and any deviations. The second step involves a determination of the causes. To identify and to describe a patient's gait, the therapist must have a good knowledge of gait terminology, an accurate mental picture of normal gait postures and normal displacements of the body segments in each portion of the two phases of gait and in each plane of analysis (saggital and frontal). To determine the causes of a patient's gait pattern and specific deviations, the therapist must know the normal roles and functions of muscles during gait and the normal forces involved.[24] A patient's deviations from normal occur because of an inability to perform the tasks of walking in a normal fashion. For example, a patient with a foot drop can not use the dorsiflexors to attain the normal neutral position of the ankle necessary to clear the floor during swing nor the normal amount of hip and knee flexion to shorten the leg. Therefore the patient must compensate for the inability to dorsiflex the ankle by some method such as increasing the amount of hip and knee flexion above the normal amount; that is, by **circumduction** of the entire limb (Fig. 11–3) or by *hiking* the hip (Fig. 11–4). The type of compensation that a particular individual uses depends upon the specific disability. Circumduction or hip hiking may be used if the patient has either a stiff knee or extensor thrust which prevents use of increased knee flexion to raise the plantarflexed foot above the floor. Increased hip and knee flexion may be used if the patient has an isolated problem in the ankle. Consequently, in addition to knowledge of the effects of single joint or muscle dysfunction, the therapist needs to be aware of the effects of neurologic deficits on gait.

Tables 11–2 to 11–7 provide a review of the normal sagittal plane joint displacements, moments of force, and muscle activity and function as well as the results of isolated muscle weaknesses and possible compensations. Tables 11–8 to 11–14 present a few of the common deviations observed in a sagittal plane analysis and probable causes for the deviations. Tables 11–15 and 11–16

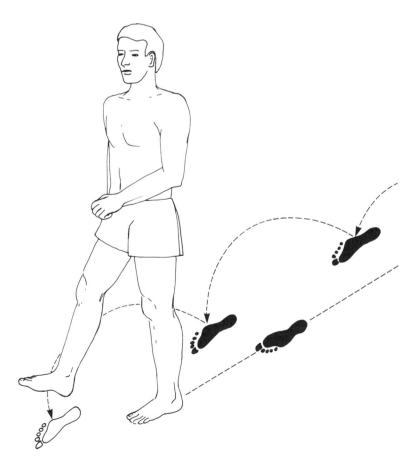

Figure 11–3. Circumduction of the patient's right lower extremity is used as a mechanism for advancing the swing leg. The patient uses a combination of external rotation and abduction to move the limb away from the body. This combination of motions is followed by adduction and internal rotation to bring the leg back toward the body. Circumduction may be used as a method of advancing the limb in the absence of hip flexors or in the case of a stiff knee.

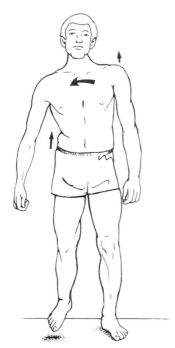

Figure 11–4. The subject in the diagram is using a contraction of the quadratus lumborum to hike his right hip. Hip hiking elevates the extremity so that the foot can clear the floor during the swing phase.

provide sample gait analysis recording forms. If the reader decides to use the gait analysis recording forms presented in this text, reliability tests should be conducted because these forms are presented only as guides and have not been tested.

In Tables 11–2 to 11–7, the phase of gait, the normal joint displacements, moments of force, and muscle activity are presented in the first four columns, and the effects of muscle weakness and possible compensations are presented in the last two columns. (The reader should be aware that only the effects of isolated muscle weaknesses and associated compensations are presented.) The intent of the tables is to provide some of the facts about normal gait that the therapist needs to keep in mind when observing gait and an example of how to proceed with an

analysis of the causes of an atypical gait pattern or particular deviation.

Tables 11–8 to 11–14 present some of the common gait deviations, as well as possible causes and analyses. Notice that the sample recording form presented in Table 11–16 is formatted in the same manner as Tables 11–8 to 11–14. Therefore, the clinician can use the sample analyses presented in the tables as guides.

OBSERVATIONAL GAIT ANALYSIS

Directions for performing an observational gait analysis are enumerated below.

1. Select the area in which the patient will walk, and measure the distance that you want the patient to cover.

2. Position yourself so that you have an unobstructed view of the subject. If filming, the camera should be positioned to view the patient's lower extremities and feet as well as the head and trunk from both the sagittal and frontal perspectives.

3. Select the joint or segment that you wish to assess first (e.g., ankle and foot), and mentally review the normal displacement patterns and muscle functions.

4. Select either a sagittal plane observation (view from the side) or a frontal plane observation (view from the front and/or back).

5. Observe the selected segment during the initial part of the stance phase and make a decision about the position of the segment. Note any deviations from the normal pattern.

6. Observe either the same segment during the next part of the stance phase or another segment at the initial part of the stance phase. Progress through the same process as in number five.

7. Repeat the process described in number 6, above, until you have completed an assessment of all segments in the sagittal and frontal planes. Remember to concentrate on one segment at a time in one part of the gait cycle. Do not jump from one segment to another or from one phase to another.

8. Always perform observations on both sides (right and left). Although only one side may be involved, the other side of the body may be affected.

Table 11–7 HIP: SWING PHASE, SAGITTAL PLANE ANALYSIS

Portion of Phase	Normal Motion	Normal Moment	Normal Muscle Activity	Result of Weakness	Possible Compensation
Acceleration to midswing	20°–30° flexion	None	Hip flexor activity to initiate swing illiopsoas, rectus femoris, gracilis, sartorius, tensor fascia lata.	Diminished hip flexion causing an inability to initiate the normal forward movement of the extremity and to raise the foot off the floor.	Circumduction and/or hip hiking may be used to bring the leg forward and to raise the foot high enough to clear the floor.
Midswing to deceleration	30° flexion to neutral	None	Hamstrings.	A lack of control of the swinging leg. Inability to place limb in position for heel strike.	

Table 11-8 COMMON DEVIATIONS, ANKLE AND FOOT: STANCE PHASE, SAGITTAL PLANE ANALYSIS

Portion of Phase	Deviation	Description	Possible Causes	Analysis
Initial contact	Foot slap	At heel strike, forefoot slaps the ground.	Flaccid or weak dorsiflexors or reciprocal inhibition of dorsiflexors; atrophy of dorsiflexors.	Look for low muscle tone at ankle. Look for steppage gait (excessive hip and knee flexion) in swing phase.
	Toes first	Toes contact ground instead of heel. The tiptoe posture may be maintained throughout the phase, or the heel may contact the ground.	Leg length discrepancy; contracted heel cord; plantarflexion contraction; spasticity of plantarflexors; flaccidity of dorsiflexors; painful heel.	Compare leg lengths and look for hip and/or knee flexion contractures. Analyze muscle tone and timing of activity in plantarflexors. Check for pain in heel.
	Foot flat	Entire foot contacts the ground at heel strike.	Excessive fixed dorsiflexion; flaccid or weak dorsiflexors; neonatal/proprioceptive walking.	Check range of motion at ankle. Check for hyperextension at the knee and persistence of immature gait pattern.
Midstance	Excessive positional plantarflexion	Tibia does not advance to neutral from 10° plantarflexion.	No eccentric contraction of plantarflexors; could be due to flaccidity/weakness in plantarflexors; surgical overrelease, rupture, or contracture of Achilles tendon.	Check for spastic or weak quadriceps; hyperextension at the knee; hip hyperextension; backward- or forward-leaning trunk. Check for weakness in plantarflexors or rupture of Achilles tendon.
	Heel lift in midstance	Heel does not contact ground in midstance.	Spasticity of plantarflexors.	Check for spasticity in plantarflexors, quadriceps, hip flexors, and adductors.
	Excessive positional dorsiflexion	Tibia advances too rapidly over the foot, creating a greater than normal amount of dorsiflexion.	Inability of plantarflexors to control tibial advance. Knee flexion or hip flexion contractures.	Look at ankle muscles, knee and hip flexors, range of motion, and position of trunk.
	Toe clawing	Toes flex and "grab" floor.	Could be due to a plantar grasp reflex that is only partially integrated; could be due to positive supporting reflex; spastic toe flexors.	Check plantar grasp reflex, positive supporting reflexes, and range of motion of toes.
Push-off (heel off to toe off)	No roll off	Insufficient transfer of weight from lateral heel to medial forefoot.	Mechanical fixation of ankle and foot. Flaccidity or inhibition of plantarflexors, inverters, and toe flexors. Rigidity/cocontraction of plantarflexors and dorsiflexors. Pain in forefoot.	Check range of motion at ankle and foot. Check muscle function and tone at ankle. Look at dissociation between posterior foot and forefoot.

Table 11-9 COMMON DEVIATIONS, ANKLE AND FOOT: SWING PHASE, SAGITTAL PLANE ANALYSIS

Portion of Phase	Deviation	Description	Possible Causes	Analysis
Swing	Toe drag	Insufficient dorsiflexion (and toe extension) so that forefoot and toes do not clear floor.	Flaccidity or weakness of dorsiflexors and toe extensors. Spasticity of plantarflexors. Inadequate knee or hip flexion.	Check for ankle, hip, and knee range of motion. Check for strength and muscle tone at hip, knee, and ankle.
	Varus	The foot is excessively inverted.	Spasticity of the invertors. Flaccidity or weakness of dorsiflexors and evertors. Extensor pattern.	Check for muscle tone of invertors and plantarflexors. Check strength of dorsiflexors and evertors. Check for extensor pattern of the lower extremity.

Table 11–10 COMMON DEVIATIONS, KNEE: STANCE PHASE, SAGITTAL PLANE ANALYSIS

Portion of Phase	Deviation	Description	Possible Causes	Analysis
Initial contact (heel strike)	Excessive knee flexion	Knee flexes or "buckles" rather than extends as foot contacts ground.	Painful knee; spasticity of knee flexors or weak or flaccid quadriceps. Short leg on contralateral side.	Check for pain at knee; tone of knee flexors; strength of knee extensors; and leg lengths; anterior pelvic tilt.
Foot flat	Knee hyperextension (genu recurvatum); see Figure 11–6	A greater than normal extension at the knee.	Flaccid/weak quadriceps and soleus compensated for by pull of gluteus maximus. Spasticity of quadriceps. Accommodation to a fixed ankle plantarflexion deformity.	Check for strength and muscle tone of knee and ankle flexors, and range of motion at ankle.
Midstance	Knee hyperextension (genu recurvatum)	During single limb support, tibia remains in back of ankle mortice as body weight moves over foot. Ankle is plantarflexed.	Same as above.	Same as above.
Push-off (heel off to toe off)	Excessive knee flexion	Knee flexes to more than 40° during push off.	Center of gravity is unusually forward of pelvis. Could be due to rigid trunk, knee/hip flexion contractures; flexion-withdrawal reflex; dominance of flexion synergy in middle recovery from CVA.	Look at trunk posture, knee and hip range of motion, and flexor synergy.
	Limited knee flexion	The normal amount of knee flexion (40°) does not occur.	Spastic/overactive quadriceps and/or plantarflexors.	Look at tone in hip, knee, and ankle muscles.

GAIT ANALYSIS IN NEUROMUSCULAR DISORDERS

The gait patterns of individuals with neuromuscular deficits are influenced primarily by abnormalities in muscle tone, influences of nonintegrated early reflexes, diminished influence of righting and equilibrium reactions, diminished dissociation among body parts, and diminished coordination. If proximal stability (cocontraction of the postural muscles of the trunk) is threatened by atypically low or high muscle tone, or muscle tone that fluctuates, the control of controlled mobility is lost. In gait, a loss of control over the sequential timing of muscular activity may result in asymmetrical step and stride lengths. In addition, deviations from normal posture and motion may occur such as forward or backward trunk leaning (Fig. 11–5), excessive flexion or extension at the hip and knee in the stance phase, and diminished dorsiflexion or excessive plantarflexion.

In the presence of multiple muscle involvement or neurologic deficits that affect balance, coordination, and muscle tone, the deviations observed and the analysis of these deviations will be more complex than indicated in the tables. Examples of gait patterns observed in association with spasticity and with hypotonus follow.

An individual with hypertonic diplegic cerebral palsy may have a posteriorly tilted pelvis, forward flexion of the upper trunk, protracted scapulae, and somewhat excessive neck extension. Excessive hip flexion, adduction, and internal rotation may be observed during stance and may be accompanied by either excessive knee flexion or hyperextension. If excessive knee flexion occurs during stance, dorsiflexion at the ankle may be exaggerated during late stance/preswing in order to advance the tibia over the ankle and to clear the toes and forefoot from the ground after push-off (heel off to toe off).

In other individuals, hyperextension at the knee occurs in stance and may be accompanied by plantarflexion and

Table 11–11 COMMON DEVIATIONS, KNEE: SWING PHASE, SAGITTAL PLANE ANALYSIS

Portion of Phase	Deviation	Description	Possible Causes	Analysis
Acceleration to midswing	Excessive knee flexion	Knee flexes more than 65°	Diminished preswing knee flexion, flexor-withdrawal reflex, dysmetria.	Look at muscle tone in hip, knee, and ankle. Test for reflexes and dysmetria.
	Limited knee flexion	Knee does not flex to 65°	Pain in knee, diminished range of knee motion, extensor spasticity. Circumduction at the hip.	Assess for pain in knee and knee range of motion. Test muscle tone at knee and hip.

Table 11–12 COMMON DEVIATIONS, HIP: STANCE PHASE, SAGITTAL PLANE ANALYSIS

Portion of Phase	Deviation	Description	Possible Causes	Analysis
Heel strike to foot flat	Excessive flexion	Flexion exceeding 30°.	Hip and/or knee flexion contractures. Knee flexion caused by weak soleus and quadriceps. Hypertonicity of hip flexors.	Check hip and knee range of motion and strength of soleus and quadriceps. Check tone of hip flexors.
Heel strike to foot flat	Limited hip flexion	Hip flexion does not attain 30°.	Weakness of hip flexors. Limited range of hip flexion. Gluteus maximus weakness.	Check strength of hip flexors and extensors. Analyze range of hip motion.
Foot flat to midstance	Limited hip extension	The hip does not attain a neutral position.	Hip flexion contracture, spasticity in hip flexors.	Check hip range of motion and tone of hip muscles.
	Internal rotation	An internally rotated position of the extremity.	Spasticity of internal rotators. Weakness of external rotators. Excessive forward rotation of opposite pelvis.	Check tone of internal rotators and strength of external rotators. Measure range of motion of both hip joints.
	External rotation	An externally rotated position of the extremity.	Excessive backward rotation of opposite pelvis.	Assess range of motion at both hip joints.
	Abduction	An abducted position of the extremity.	Contracture of the gluteus medius. Trunk lateral lean over the ipsilateral hip.	Check for abduction pattern.
	Adduction	An adducted position of the lower extremity.	Spasticity of hip flexors and adductors such as seen in spastic diplegia. Pelvic drop to contralateral side.	Assess tone of hip flexors and adductors. Test muscle strength of hip abductors.

inversion at the ankle and foot (Fig. 11–6). Electromyographic recordings may show prolonged activity in the quadriceps and in the gastroc-soleus muscle groups. The hamstrings and gluteal and dorsiflexor muscle groups may be reciprocally inhibited.

In each of the above cases, there is insufficient dissociation between the pelvic and shoulder girdles as evidenced by markedly decreased longitudinal trunk rotation. Weight shift is accomplished by lateral flexion with slight extension of the weight-bearing side of the body being accomplished by lateral extension. The ground force application lines are excessively displaced from the centers of rotation at the hips and knees (Fig. 11–7).

In individuals with low muscle tone in the trunk, proximal stability (tonic extension and cocontraction of axial muscles) is diminished. The pelvis may be anteriorly tilted so that the upper trunk is slightly extended. The scapulae may be retracted and the head may be forward. The hip may be flexed during stance and the knee may be hyperextended accompanied by plantarflexion at the

Table 11–13 COMMON DEVIATIONS, HIP: SWING PHASE, SAGITTAL PLANE ANALYSIS

Portion of Phase	Deviation	Description	Possible Causes	Analysis
Swing	Circumduction	A lateral circular movement of the entire lower extremity consisting of abduction, external rotation, adduction, and internal rotation.	A compensation for weak hip flexors or a compensation for the inability to shorten the leg so that it can clear the floor.	Check strength of hip flexors, knee flexors, and ankle dorsiflexors. Check range of motion in hip flexion, knee flexion, and ankle dorsiflexion. Check for extensor pattern.
	Hip hiking	Shortening of the swing leg by action of the quadratus lumborum.	A compensation for lack of knee flexion and/or ankle dorsiflexion. Also may be a compensation for extensor spasticity of swing leg.	Check strength and range of motion at knee, hip, and ankle. Also check muscle tone at knee and ankle.
	Excessive hip flexion	Flexion greater than 20°–30°.	Attempt to shorten extremity in presence of footdrop. Flexor pattern.	Check strength and range of motion at ankle and foot. Check for flexor pattern.

Table 11–14 COMMON DEVIATIONS, TRUNK: STANCE, SAGITTAL PLANE ANALYSIS

Portion of Phase	Deviation	Description	Possible Causes	Analysis
Stance	Lateral trunk lean	A lean of the trunk over the stance extremity (gluteus medius gait/trendelenberg gait). See Figure 11–7.	A weak or paralyzed gluteus medius on the stance side can not prevent a drop of pelvis on the swing side, so a trunk lean over the stance leg helps compensate for the weak muscle. A lateral trunk lean also may be used to reduce force on hip if a patient has a painful hip.	Check strength of gluteus medius and assess for pain in the hip.
	Backward trunk lean	A backward leaning of the trunk, resulting in hyperextension at the hip (gluteus maximus gait).	Weakness or paralysis of the gluteus maximus on the stance leg. Anteriorly rotated pelvis.	Check for strength of hip extensors. Check pelvic position.
	Forward trunk lean	A forward leaning of the trunk, resulting in hip flexion.	Compensation for quadriceps weakness. The forward lean eliminates the flexion moment at the knee. Hip and knee flexion contractures.	Check for strength of quadriceps.
		A forward flexion of the upper trunk.	Posteriorly rotated pelvis.	Check pelvic position.

Table 11–15 GAIT ANALYSIS RECORDING FORM

Fixed Postures Observed During Gait

Patient's name _____ Age _____ Sex _____

Head	Tilt	To the right _____	To the left _____
		Forward _____	Backward _____
Trunk	Lean	To the right _____	To the left _____
		Forward _____	Backward _____
Pelvis	Tilt	To the right _____	To the left _____
		Anterior _____	Posterior _____
Hip	Flexion	On the right _____	On the left _____
		Bilateral _____	
	Extension	On the right _____	On the left _____
		Bilateral _____	
	Abduction	On the right _____	On the left _____
		Bilateral _____	
	Adduction	On the right _____	On the left _____
		Bilateral _____	
	External rotation	On the right _____	On the left _____
		Bilateral _____	
	Internal rotation	On the right _____	On the left _____
		Bilateral _____	
Knee	Flexion	On the right _____	On the left _____
		Bilateral _____	
	Extension	On the right _____	On the left _____
		Bilateral _____	
	Hyperextension	On the right _____	On the left _____
		Bilateral _____	
	Valgum	On the right _____	On the left _____
		Bilateral _____	
	Varum	On the right _____	On the left _____
		Bilateral _____	
Ankle/foot	Dorsiflexion	On the right _____	On the left _____
		Bilateral _____	
	Plantarflexion	On the right _____	On the left _____
		Bilateral _____	
	Varus	On the right _____	On the left _____
		Bilateral _____	
	Valgus	On the right _____	On the left _____
		Bilateral _____	
	Pes planus	On the right _____	On the left _____
		Bilateral _____	
	Pes cavus	On the right_____	On the left _____
		Bilateral _____	

Table 11–16 RECORDING FORM FOR OBSERVATIONAL GAIT ANALYSIS

Patient's name _____ Age _____ Sex _____ Height _____ Weight _____
Diagnosis _____
Footwear _____ Assistive devices _____
Date _____ Therapist _____

DIRECTIONS: Place a check in the space opposite the deviation if the deviation is observed.

Body Segment	Deviation	Stance HS R	L	FF R	L	MST R	L	HO R	L	TO R	L	Swing ACC R	L	MSW R	L	DEC R	L	Possible Cause	Analysis
Ankle and foot Observations In the sagittal plane	None																		
	Foot flat																		
	Foot slap																		
	Heel off																		
	No heel off																		
	Excessive plantarflexion																		
	Excessive dorsiflexion																		
	Toe drag																		
	Toe clawing																		
	Contralateral vaulting																		
Observations in the frontal plane	Varus																		
	Valgus																		
Knee Observations in the sagittal plane	None																		
	Excessive flexion																		
	Limited flexion																		
	No flexion																		
	Hyperextension																		
	Genu recurvatum																		
	Diminished extension																		

207

Table 11–16 *continued.*

Body Segment	Deviation	Stance HS		FF		MST		HO		TO		Swing ACC		MSW		DEC		Possible Cause	Analysis
		R	L	R	L	R	L	R	L	R	L	R	L	R	L	R	L		
Observations in the frontal plane	Varum																		
	Valgum																		
Hip	None																		
Observations in the sagittal plane	Excessive flexion																		
	Limited flexion																		
	No flexion																		
	Diminished extension																		
Observations in the frontal plane	Abduction																		
	Adduction																		
	External rotation																		
	Internal rotation																		

	Circumduction										
	Hiking										
Pelvis	None										
Observations in sagittal plane	Anterior tilt										
	Posterior tilt										
	Increased backward rotation										
	Increased forward rotation										
	Limited backward rotation										
	Limited forward rotation										
	Drops on contralateral side										
Trunk	None										
Observations in frontal plane	Backward rotation										
	Lateral lean										
	Forward rotation										
	Backward lean										
	Forward lean										

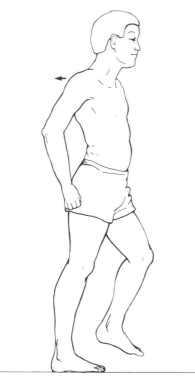

Figure 11–5. The subject leans or lurches his trunk posteriorly to eliminate the flexion moment at the hip. This type of deviation during gait is often referred to as a gluteus maximus gait because the trunk lean backward is used as a compensation in patients with a weak gluteus maximus.

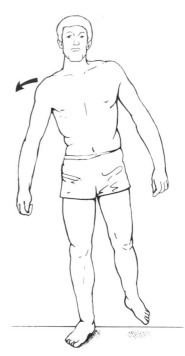

Figure 11–7. The patient is leaning his trunk over the right hip in an attempt to compensate for a weak gluteus medius on the right. This type of gait is often called a gluteus medius gait. (See Table 11–14.)

ankle. The foot may be pronated with the majority of the body weight being borne on the medial border. Frequently these individuals show diminished longitudinal trunk rotation and sluggish equilibrium reactions in the trunk. They tend to rely on protective extension reactions of the limbs to maintain balance. The staggering reactions of the lower extremities may be pronounced. Stride length and step length may be uneven. Gait may be wide based and unsteady. Although the gait patterns in neurologic gait may be complex and an analysis of the causes may be difficult, a detailed observational gait analysis can provide valuable data.

Generally, in order to analyze gait patterns in persons who have sustained neurologic damage, the following preliminary questions need to be asked:

1. How does the position of the head influence muscle tone in the trunk and the limbs?

2. How does weight bearing influence muscle tone in the upper and lower extremities?

3. What is the position of the pelvis and shoulder?

KINEMATIC QUANTITATIVE GAIT ANALYSIS

Kinematic **quantitative gait analyses** are used to obtain information on time and distance gait variables. The data obtained through these analyses are quantifiable and therefore provide the therapist with baseline data that can be used to plan treatment programs and to assess progress toward goals or goal attainment. The fact that the data are quantifiable is important because third-party payers are demanding that therapists use measurable data when they are assessing patients, setting goals and

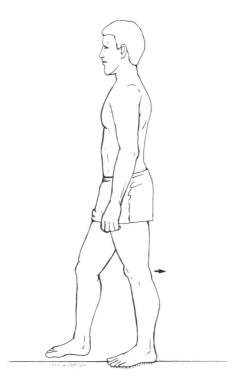

Figure 11–6. The patient's knee is thrust into a hyperextended position during single limb support. The tibia remains in back of the ankle mortise as the body weight moves over the foot.

documenting the effects of a treatment program. However, data derived from qualitative observations may be necessary to classify degrees of motor impairment and to check on the validity of the quantitative variables measured. Therefore both qualitative and quantitative gait analyses should be performed to provide a comprehensive picture of an individual's gait.

Variables

The variables measured in a quantitative gait analysis are listed and described fully in Table 11–17.

Because distance and time variables are affected by a number of factors such as age, sex, height,[25–27] weight, level of maturation,[28] and type of foot gear, attempts have been made to take these factors into account. Ratios such as stride–length divided by functional lower extremity length are used to normalize for differences in patients' leg lengths. Step length divided by the subject's height is used in an attempt to normalize differences among patients' heights. Other ratios are used to assess symmetry; for example, right swing time divided by left swing time or swing time divided by stance time. Sutherland and coworkers[28] list the ratio of pelvic span to ankle spread as one of the determinants of mature gait in children.

In a situation in which a patient can not ambulate independently (either with or without assistive devices), subordinate locomotor variables may be assessed using the Functional Ambulation Profile (FAB).[29] The following variables are evaluated by using a stopwatch to determine the amount of time required either to accomplish a task or to maintain a position:

bilateral stance time
uninvolved stance time
involved stance time
dynamic weight transfer rate
parallel bar ambulation

Recently the National Institute of Handicapped Research funded a project to develop a uniform data system for medical rehabilitation. An instrument called the Functional Independence Measure (FIM) Locomotion Scale is one of the first parts of the system to be published. The FIM scale of functional levels for locomotion includes the following four levels of primary categories:

4.0—Complete independence
3.0—Modified independence
2.0—Modified dependence
1.0—Complete dependence

Three subcategories are included under 3.0—modified independence (supervision, minimal assistance, and moderate assistance).[30]

METHODS USED FOR MEASURING VARIABLES

The recent physical therapy literature contains a number of studies describing techniques for measuring time and distance gait variables[9–14] as well as studies investigating the uses and reliability of different methods of measurement.[31] Two types of variables (time and dis-

tance) are frequently included in a kinematic quantitative gait analysis and are necessary for the interpretation of kinetic and electromyographic (EMG) data. The techniques and equipment required for measurement of these variables range from simple to complex. The time requirements also vary, and the therapist must be familiar with different methods of assessing these variables in order to select the method most appropriate to each situation. Prior to selecting a method of measurement, the therapist should understand the variable in question and how that variable is related to the patient's gait.

Distance Variables

Variables such as degree of foot angle, width of base of support, step length, and stride length can be assessed simply and inexpensively in the clinic by recording the patient's footprints during gait. Many different methods for recording footprints have been described in the literature, for example, the absorbent paper method;[8] commercially available carbon paper system;[4] painting,[7] inking,[31] or chalking of the feet; and felt-tipped markers attached to the shoes.[13] Other more expensive methods for assessing these variables include imaging systems, foot switches, cinematography, video and time-lapse photography.

Walkways for recording footprints may be created either by the application of various materials to the floor or by using an uncarpeted floor or hallway. A few of the materials used to create walkways include absorbent paper,[8] commercially produced carbon paper, and aluminum.[14] In the absorbent paper method, three layers of material are placed over a carpeted floor to form a walkway. The first layer is brown paper, the second layer is moistened paper or terry cloth, and the third layer is absorbent paper such as a paper tablecloth. When the subject walks along the walkway, the pressure of the body weight causes the water from the second layer to be absorbed by the dry top layer. The therapist outlines the footprints with a felt-tipped pen immediately following the walking trial. The resulting record permits measurement of step and stride lengths, stride width, and foot angle. The commercially made carbon paper and aluminum paper provide a similar type of footprint record.

Other simple methods of recording footprints require the application of paints, ink, or chalk to the bottom of the patient's foot or shoe or the attachment of inked pads or other markers. For example, the bottoms of a patient's feet may be covered with Tempera paint[7] prior to walking along a paper-covered walkway, or a felt-tipped marker may be taped to the back of a patient's shoe.[13] In both methods, measurements of step length, stride length, step width, and foot angle may be obtained.

Another way of obtaining step length and stride length data is by placing a grid pattern on the floor.[10] A strip of masking tape about 30 cm wide and 10 meters long is laid down in a straight line. The tape is marked off in 3 cm increments for its entire length, and the segments are numbered consecutively so that the patient's heel strikes can be identified. The therapist calls out the heel strike locations from the numbers on the grid pattern and the numbers are recorded by a tape recorder. Cadence and

Table 11–17 GAIT VARIABLES: QUANTITATIVE GAIT
ANALYSIS

Variable	Description
Speed	A scalar quantity that has magnitude but not direction.
Free speed	A person's normal walking speed.
Slow speed	A speed slower than a person's normal speed.
Fast speed	A rate faster than normal.
Cadence	The number of steps taken by a patient per unit of time. Cadence may be measured in centimeters as the number of steps per second $$\text{Cadence} = \frac{\text{number of steps}}{\text{time}}$$ A simple method of measuring cadence is by counting the number of steps taken by the patient in a given amount of time. The only equipment necessary is a stopwatch, paper, and pencil.
Velocity	A measure of a body's motion in a given direction.
Linear velocity	The rate at which a body moves in a straight line.
Angular velocity	The rate of motion in rotation of a body segment around an axis.
Walking velocity	The rate of linear forward motion of the body. This is measured in either centimeters per second or meters per minute. To obtain a person's walking velocity, divide the distance traversed by the time required to complete the distance. $$\text{Walking velocity} = \frac{\text{distance}}{\text{time}}$$ Walking velocity may be affected by age, level of maturation, height, sex, type of footwear, and weight. Also, velocity may affect cadence, step, stride length, and foot angle as well as other gait variables.
Acceleration	The rate of change of velocity with respect to time. Body acceleration has been defined by Smidt and Mommens[2] as the rate of change of velocity of a point posterior to the sacrum. Acceleration is usually measured in meters per second per second (m/s^2).
Angular acceleration	The rate of change of the angular velocity of a body with respect to time. Angular acceleration is usually measured in radians per second per second (radians/s^2).
Stride time	The amount of time that elapses during one stride; that is, from one foot contact (heel strike if possible) until the next contact of the same foot (heel strike). Both stride times should be measured. Measurement is usually in seconds.
Step time	The amount of time that elapses between consecutive right and left foot contacts (heel strikes). Both right and left step times should be measured. Measurement is in seconds.
Swing time	The amount of time during the gait cycle that one foot is off the ground. Swing time should be measured separately for right and left extremities. Measurement is in seconds.
Double support time	The amount of time spent in the gait cycle when both lower extremities are in contact with the supporting surface. Measured in seconds.
Cycle time (stride time)	The amount of time required to complete a gait cycle. Measured in seconds.
Step length	The linear distance between two successive points of contact of the right and left lower extremities. Usually a measurement is taken from the point of heel contact at heel strike of one extremity to the point of heel contact of the opposite extremity. If a patient does not have a heel strike on one or both sides, the measurement can be taken from the heads of the first metatarsals. Measured in centimeters or meters.

Table 11–17 *continued.*

Variable	Description
Width of walking base (step width)	The width of the walking base (base of support) is the linear distance between one foot and the opposite foot. Measured in centimeters or meters.[7]
Foot angle (degree of toe out or toe in)	The angle of foot placement with respect to the line of progression. Measured in degrees.[7]
Bilateral stance time	The length of time up to 30 seconds that a person can stand upright in the parallel bars bearing weight on both lower extremities.
Uninvolved stance time	The length of time up to 30 seconds that an individual can stand in the parallel bars while bearing weight on the uninvolved lower extremity (involved extremity is raised off the supporting surface).
Involved stance time	The length of time up to 30 seconds that an individual can stand in the parallel bars on the involved lower extremity (uninvolved lower extremity is raised off the supporting surface).
Dynamic weight transfer rate	The rate at which an individual standing in the parallel bars can transfer weight from one extremity to another. Measured in seconds from the first lift-off to the eighth lift-off.
Parallel bar ambulation	Length of time required for an individual to walk the length of the parallel bars as rapidly as possible. Two trials are averaged to obtain this measurement. Measurement is in seconds.

velocity as well as step and stride lengths may be obtained from this method.

Temporal Variables

In all of the above listed methods of assessing stride and step lengths, temporal variables such as cadence, velocity, and stride times may be calculated. The distance that the subject walks and the time taken to complete the distance from the first heel strike on the measured distance to the last heel strike can be measured. Cadence can be determined by dividing the number of steps taken during the walking trial by the elapsed time between the first and last heel strikes. Velocity can be calculated by taking the total distance between the first and last heel strikes and dividing it by the elapsed time for the distance. In order to obtain a normal walking speed, the patient should be allowed to take a few steps prior to the beginning of any measurements.

Instrumented Systems

Acceleration can be measured by using a device called an **accelerometer.** Accelerometers are transducers that measure the effects of a force. Usually three accelerometers are required to measure acceleration in the three planes of motion (sagittal, frontal, and horizontal). Accelerometers are expensive, and the data generated are difficult to analyze. Joint displacement can be measured with goniometry. Two types of goniometers are available: a polarized light goniometer called a polgon[32] and an electrogoniometer, which is called an elgon.[12] The polgon is composed of sensors containing photoelectric cells with polarized gratings in front of the cells. These sensors are placed on the body segments being assessed. An optical projector illuminates the subject as he or she walks, and the sensors emit electrical signals as the sensors move relative to each other. The electrogoniometer is a potentiometer that converts movement into an electrical signal that is proportional to the degree of movement.

Data obtained from both the polgon and the elgon can be displayed either as angle/angle diagrams[32] or on a strip chart recorder. Angle/angle diagrams are produced by plotting the angular sagittal plane displacements of adjacent joints against each other. Strip chart recorders provide a record of the displacement patterns of gait.

Other instrumented methods of assessing temporal and distance measures include a gait mat developed at Moss Rehabilitation Center's Rehabilitation Engineering Department in Philadelphia. The mat has a series of switches embedded in it which can be scanned by a microprocessor to yield temporal data. **Foot switches** of various types can be purchased and placed either inside or outside of a patient's shoes. The foot switches consist of transducers and a semiconductor and are used to signal such events as heel strike. One type of foot switch device that has been used to assess both temporal and loading variables is the Krusen Limb Load Monitor.[9] Originally this device was designed to monitor the amount of weight that a patient placed on an affected extremity. When the weight exceeded a predetermined magnitude, the instrument emitted a warning signal. Recently, the device has been modified and used to obtain data on temporal and loading gait variables. This device consists of a pressure-sensitive force plate that can be worn within a patient's shoe. It can be connected to a strip chart recorder to yield a permanent record of temporal and distance gait variables.[9]

Imaging systems such as the **light-emitting diode (LED)** system for assessing sagittal-plane motion and temporal and distance variables have been used at the University of Iowa. The system consists of LEDs, foot switches, and a 35 mm single-frame color-slide photographic technique.[11]

Electromyography is used to analyze the timing and peak activity of muscle activity during gait.[33–35] Usually electromyography is used in combination with other instrumentation to identify the particular portion of the gait cycle in which the muscle activity occurs.[36]

Reliability

Reliability of the absorbent paper and felt-tipped pen methods has not been reported. In a study of 61 neurologically impaired patients, Holden and associates[31] used ink footprints on a paper-covered walkway. High interrater and test-retest reliability was reported using the inked footprint method to determine the following variables: velocity, cadence, step length, and stride length. These workers also found a strong linear relationship between the variables and a Functional Ambulation Classification test protocol that was developed at Massachusetts General Hospital. The grid pattern method of gait analysis is reported to be a feasible clinical research tool as well as a good method for quantitative analysis of temporal and distance measures.[10] Soderberg and Gabel[11] report that the LED system has high interrater and intrarater reliability for temporal and distance measures. Test-retest reliability coefficients for Nelson's functional ambulation profile also are reported to be high.[29]

ADVANTAGES AND DISADVANTAGES

The primary advantages of assessing temporal and distance measures are that these measures can be assessed simply and inexpensively in the clinic and that they yield an objective and reliable baseline upon which to formulate goals and to assess progress or lack of progress toward goals. For example, gait patterns displayed by patients with arthritis often are characterized by a reduced rate and range of knee motion compared with those of normal subjects, and they have a slower than normal gait velocity. Brinkmann and Perry[37] found that following joint replacement the rate and range of knee motion and gait velocity increased above preoperative levels but did not reach normal levels. Usually increases in measures such as cadence and velocity indicate improvement in a patient's gait. However, comparisons with normal standards are appropriate only if the goal of treatment is to restore a normal gait pattern (e.g., for a patient recovering from a meniscectomy). Comparisons with normal standards may not be appropriate for a patient who has had a cerebral vascular accident. The appropriate norms for a hemiplegic patient's gait may be either a hemiplegic population of similar age, sex, and involvement or the patient's pretreatment gait. Therapists need to be extremely cautious when selecting a norm or standard by which to measure patient progress. Significant differences have been found in temporal and distance measures among healthy young women (age 20 to 35 years) and healthy elderly women (age 60 to 84 years). Step length and velocity of gait in the younger age group were significantly greater than step and stride length and velocity in the older women.[38] Therefore, one way to determine if the standard is appropriate is to compare the characteristics of the population used to establish the norm with the patient's characteristics. For example, is the age of the patient in the same range as the sample population? Is the patient's sex the same as that of the sample population? Holden and colleagues[39] recommend that gait performance goals for patients with neurologic problems not only should be based upon norms derived from patients with the same diagnosis but also should consider etiologic factors, type of ambulation aid, and functional category.

Temporal and distance measures may be critical factors in determinations of a patient's independence in ambulation. For example, a certain velocity of gait may need to be achieved in order to cross a local street within the limit of the time allotted by a crossing light or to walk a certain distance in order to shop in the local supermarket. Changes in velocity may affect step length, cadence, and other gait variables. Therapists need to survey the patient's community to determine the distances and time requirements for accessing stores and public buildings prior to making a judgment about a patient's functional ambulation status.[40]

Few disadvantages exist regarding quantitative gait analysis except for the expense involved in instrumentation and the fact that a certain amount of uncertainty exists about how to normalize for leg length, height, age, sex, weight, level of maturation, and disability.[41] Temporal and distance assessments should be used as an integral part of or in conjunction with both observational and kinetic assessments to provide a complete picture of gait. A sample recording form for time and distance variables is presented in Table 11–18.

KINETIC GAIT ANALYSIS

Kinetic gait analyses are directed toward assessment and analysis of the forces involved in gait. Although kinetic gait analyses have been used primarily for research purposes, they may be used clinically in the future. A complete review of kinetic gait analysis methods is beyond the scope of this chapter, but a few of the major variables are presented and described in Table 11–19.

The instrumentation required to assess kinetic variables is complex and expensive. Force plate systems are necessary for performing kinetic gait assessments, and such systems cost in the range of $10,000 to $50,000.[43] If a therapist wishes to use an instrumented system, he or she should contact one of the facilities that are using such systems, such as the Mayo Clinic in Minnesota or Rancho Los Amigos Medical Center in California.

Energy Cost during Ambulation

An additional consideration in the analysis of gait is the relative energy cost of the patient's gait pattern. Energy cost is assessed most accurately by measurement of the amount of oxygen consumption, carbon dioxide production, and pulmonary ventilation used during ambulation. Although these procedures are the most

Table 11–18 GAIT ANALYSIS RECORDING FORM: TEMPORAL AND DISTANCE MEASURES

Patient's name _____ Age _____ Sex _____

Height _____ Weight _____

Diagnosis: _____

Ambulatory aids: Yes _____ No _____

Type: Crutch(es) _____ Cane(s): R _____ Walker: _____

L _____

Other: _____

Date													
Therapist's initials													
Distance walked													
Distance from first to last heel strike													
Elapsed time (time from first to last heel strike)													
Walking velocity (distance walked divided by elapsed time)													
Left stride length (distance between two consecutive left heel strikes)													
Right stride length (distance between two consecutive right heel strikes)													
Left step length (distance between a right heel strike and the next consecutive left heel strike)													
Right step length (distance between a left heel strike and the next consecutive right heel strike)													
Step length difference (difference between right and left step lengths)													
Cadence (total number of steps taken divided by the elapsed time)													
Width of walking base (perpendicular distance between right and left heel strike)													
Left foot angle (angle formed between a line bisecting the left foot and the line of progression)													
Right foot angle (angle formed between a line bisecting the right foot and the line of progression)													
Right stride length to right lower extremity length (right stride length divided by right lower extremity length)													
Left stride length to left lower extremity length (left stride length divided by left lower extremity length)													

The therapist may wish to obtain averages for stride and step lengths, width of walking base and foot angles.

accurate, they also require expensive instrumentation. Therefore the physical therapist needs a simple method to estimate the energy cost of a patient's gait. The relative energy cost of gait can be estimated by monitoring heart rate during ambulation. Heart rate is directly and linearly related to oxygen consumption during exercise[43] and can provide information as to how the patient's cardiovascular system is adapting to the stress of ambulation.

Table 11–19 GAIT VARIABLES: KINETIC GAIT ANALYSIS

Variable	Description
Ground (floor) reaction forces	Vertical, anterior-posterior, and medial-lateral forces created as a result of foot contact with the supporting surface. These forces are equal in magnitude and opposite in direction to the force applied by the foot to the ground. Ground reaction forces are measured with force platforms in newtons (N) or pound force.
Torque (moment of force)	The turning or rotational effect produced by the application of a force. The greater the perpendicular distance of the point of application of a force from an axis of rotation, the greater the turning effect, or torque, produced. Torque is calculated by multiplying the force by the perpendicular distance from the point of application of the force and the axis of rotation. Torque = force × perpendicular distance or moment arm. Measurement is in newton meters.
Joint forces	The forces between articular surfaces that are created by muscle, gravity, and inertial forces. These forces are measured in newtons.
Work	Work is the product of the force applied and the distance the object moves in the direction of the force. Work = force × distance

The most accurate way to assess heart rate is to use a telemetry system that produces beat-by-beat information as well as electrocardiographic activity. The intensive care or cardiac care units in many hospitals have telemetry systems that could be utilized for monitoring a patient during gait. If the therapist does not have access to telemetry monitoring, heart rate responses to ambulation can be assessed by palpation of the radial or carotid arteries. A pulse measurement should be taken at rest, just prior to ambulation, immediately postambulation, and at various intervals after ambulation (1 minute, 3 minutes, and 5 minutes). The palpation method allows the therapist to determine how hard the heart had to work to accomplish a given gait activity and how long the heart takes to return to resting level.

SUMMARY

The ability to perform a meaningful gait analysis that accurately describes a patient's gait will provide important quantifiable information necessary for adequate treatment planning. This chapter introduced the kinematic gait variables that the physical therapist can assess inexpensively and easily in a clinical setting and provided a model for performing an observational gait analysis.

For most purposes, kinematic analysis and heart rate monitoring will yield the information necessary for routine clinical use. The reader is encouraged to consult the references at the end of the chapter for additional information.

QUESTIONS FOR REVIEW

1. Describe each of the three different types of gait analysis (kinematic qualitative, kinematic quantitative, and kinetic).
   a. List the variables assessed in each of the three types of gait analyses.
   b. Select one variable from each type of analysis and describe a method of assessment.
2. Explain the difference between intratester and intertester reliability and give examples of how a test might be set up for each form of reliability.

3. Compare the advantages of a kinematic qualitative gait analysis with the advantages of a kinematic quantitative analysis.
4. Using the model presented in Tables 11–1 to 11–11, perform an observational gait analysis that includes both identification of observed deviations and an analysis to determine the causes of the deviations.
5. What factors must be considered when assessing time and distance variables?

REFERENCES

1. Ogg, LH: Gait analysis for lower-extremity child amputees. Phys Ther 45:940, 1965.
2. Smidt, GL and Mommens, MA: System of reporting and comparing influence of ambulatory aids on gait. Phys Ther 60:551, 1980.
3. Zachazewski, JE, Eberle, ED, and Jefferies, ME: Effects of tone-inhibiting casts and orthoses on gait. Phys Ther 62:453, 1982.
4. Craik, RL and Otis, CA: Gait assessment in the clinic. In Rothstein, JM: Measurement in Physical Therapy. Churchill Livingstone, London, 1985.
5. Gronley, JK and Perry, J: Gait analysis techniques. Rancho Los Amigos Hospital Gait Laboratory. Phys Ther 64:1831, 1984.
6. Laughman, RK, et al: Objective clinical evaluation of function. Phys Ther 64:35, 1984.
7. Shores, M: Footprint analysis in gait documentation: An instructional sheet format. Phys Ther 60:1163, 1980.
8. Clarkson, BH: Absorbent paper method for recording foot placement during gait. Phys Ther 63:345, 1983.
9. Wolf, SL and Binder-Macleod, SA: Use of the krusen limb load

monitor to quantify temporal and loading measurements of gait. Phys Ther 62:976, 1982.
10. Robinson, JL and Smidt, GL: Quantitative gait evaluation in the clinic. Phys Ther 61:351, 1981.
11. Soderberg, GL and Gabel, RH: A light emitting diode system for the analysis of gait: A method and selected clinical examples. Phys Ther 58:426, 1978.
12. Little, H: Gait analyses for physiotherapy departments: A review of current methods. Physiotherapy 67:334, 1981.
13. Czerny, K: A clinical method of quantitative gait analysis. Phys Ther 63:1125, 1983.
14. Chodcra, JD: Analysis of gait from footprints. Physiotherapy 60:179, 1974.
15. Rodgers, MM and Cavanagh, PR: Glossary of biomechanical terms, concepts, and units. Phys Ther 64:82, 1984.
16. Pathokinesiology Service and Physical Therapy Department: Normal and Pathological Gait Syllabus. Professional Staff Association of Rancho Los Amigos Hospital, Downey, California, 1981.
17. Brunnstrom, S: Movement Therapy in Adult Hemiplegia. Harper & Row, New York, 1970.
18. Lower Limb Prosthetics. New York University Medical Center Post-Graduate Medical School Prosthetics and Orthotics, New York, 1981.
19. Bampton, S: A guide to the visual examination of pathological gait. Temple University Rehabilitation Research and Training Center #8, Moss Rehabilitation Hospital, Philadelphia, 1979.
20. Daniels, L and Worthingham, C: Muscle Testing: Techniques of Manual Examination, ed 5. WB Saunders, Philadelphia, 1986.
21. O'Sullivan, S, Cullen, K, and Schmitz, T: Physical Rehabilitation: Evaluation and Treatment Procedures. FA Davis, Philadelphia, 1981.
22. Goodkin, R and Diller, L: Reliability among physical therapists in diagnosis and treatment of gait deviations in hemiplegics. Percept Mot Skills 37:727, 1973.
23. Krebs, D, Edelstein, J, and Fishman, S: Observational gait analysis reliability in disabled children. Phys Ther (Abstract) 64:741, 1984.
24. Norkin, C and Levangie, P: Joint Structure and Function: A Comprehensive Analysis. FA Davis, Philadelphia, 1983.
25. Finley, FR, Cocy, K, and Finizie, R: Locomotive patterns in elderly women. Arch Phys Med Rehabil 50:140, 1969.
26. Murray, M, et al: Walking patterns in normal men. J Bone Joint Surg (AM) 46A:335–360, 1964.
27. Murray, M, Kory, R, and Sepic, S: Walking patterns of normal women. Arch Phys Med Rehabil 51:637, 1970.
28. Sutherland, DH, et al: The development of mature gait. J Bone Joint Surg 62A:336, 1980.
29. Nelson, AJ: Functional ambulation profile. Phys Ther 54:1059, 1974.
30. Morton, T: Uniform data system for rehab begins: First tool measures dependence level. Progress Report, American Physical Therapy Association 15:14, October 1986.
31. Holden, MK, et al: Clinical gait assessment in the neurologically impaired, reliability and meaningfulness. Phys Ther 64:35, 1984.
32. Grieve, DW, Leggett, D, and Wetherstone, B: The analysis of normal stepping movements as a possible basis for locomotor assessment of the lower limbs. J Anat 127:515, 1978.
33. Lyons, K, et al: Timing and relative intensity of hip extensor and abductor muscle action during level and stair ambulation. Phys Ther 63:1597, 1983.
34. Waters, RL, et al: Electromyographic gait analysis before and after operative treatment for hemiplegic equinus and equinovarus deformity. J Bone Joint Surg 64A:284, 1982.
35. Peat, M, et al: Electromyographic temporal analysis of gait: Hemiplegic locomotion. Arch Phys Med Rehabil 57:421, 1976.
36. Sutherland, DH, Cooper, L, and Daniel, D: The role of ankle plantar flexors in normal walking. J Bone Joint Surg 62A:355, 1980.
37. Brinkmann, JR and Perry, J: Rate and range of knee motion during ambulation in healthy and arthritic subjects. Phys Ther 65:7, 1985.
38. Hageman, PA and Blanke, DJ: Comparison of gait of young women and elderly women. Phys Ther 66:1382, 1986.
39. Holden, MK, Gill, KM, and Magliozzi, MR: Impaired patients. Phys Ther 66:1530, 1986.
40. Lerner-Frankiel, MB, et al: Functional community ambulation: What are your criteria? Clinical Management 6:12, 1986.
41. Inman, VT, Ralston, HJ, and Todd, F: Human Walking. William & Wilkins, Baltimore, 1981.
42. Yack, HJ: Techniques for clinical assessment of human movement. Phys Ther 64:17, 1984.
43. Astrand, PO and Rodahl, K: Textbook of Work Physiology. McGraw-Hill, New York, 1977, p 617.

GLOSSARY

Acceleration: The rate of change of velocity with respect to time. Body acceleration has been defined by Smidt and Mommens[2] as the rate of change of velocity of a point posterior to the sacrum. Acceleration is usually measured in meters per second per second (m/s^2).

Angle/angle diagrams: Diagrams in which angular displacements of adjacent joints in the sagittal plane are plotted against each other.

Angular acceleration: The rate of change of the angular velocity of a body segment with respect to time. Angular acceleration is usually measured in radians per second per second ($radians/s^2$).

Accelerometer: A device used to measure the vertical, anterior-posterior, and medial-lateral accelerations of body segments.

Angular velocity: The rate of motion in rotation of a body segment around an axis.

Bilateral stance time: The length of time (up to 30 seconds) that a subject can stand upright in the parallel bars bearing weight on both lower extremities.

Cadence: Number of steps per unit of time; may be measured in centimeters as the number of steps per second (cadence = number of steps/time). A simple method of measuring cadence is by counting the number of steps taken by the patient in a given amount of time. The only equipment necessary is a stopwatch, paper, and pencil.

Circumduction: A circular motion of the swinging leg that includes the hip motions of abduction, external rotation, adduction, and internal rotation. This gait deviation may be used to compensate for inadequate hip or knee flexion and/or insufficient dorsiflexion.

Cycle time (stride time): The amount of time required to complete a gait cycle; measured in seconds.

Displacement: The change in position of the body as a whole (**linear,** or **translational, displacement**) or its segments (**rotational displacement**). **Linear,** or **translational, displacement** is measured in meters, whereas **rotational displacement** is measured in degrees.

Double support time: The period of the gait cycle when both lower extremities are in contact with the supporting surface (double support); measured in seconds.

Dynamic weight transfer rate: The speed at which an individual standing in the parallel bars can transfer weight from one extremity to another; measured in seconds from the first liftoff to the eighth liftoff.

Foot angle: Degree of toe out or toe in; the angle of foot placement with respect to the line of progression; measured in degrees.

Free speed: Defined as an individual's normal walking speed.

Ground (floor) reaction forces: Vertical, anterior-posterior, and medial-lateral forces created as a result of foot contact with the supporting surface. These forces are equal in magnitude and opposite in direction to the force applied by the foot to the ground. Ground reaction forces are measured with force platforms in newtons (N) or pound force.

Involved stance time: The length of time (up to 30 seconds) that an individual can stand in the parallel bars on the involved lower extremity (uninvolved lower extremity is raised off the supporting surface).

Joint forces: The forces between articular surfaces that are created by muscle, gravity, and inertial forces; measured in Newtons.

Kinematics: A description of the type, amount, and direction of motion; does not include the forces producing the motion.

Kinetics: The study of the forces that cause motion.

Light-emitting diode (LED): System for assessing sagittal-plane motion and temporal and distance variables. The system consists of LEDs, foot switches, and a 35 mm single-frame color-slide photographic technique.

Linear velocity: The rate at which a body moves in a straight line.

Parallel bar ambulation: Length of time required for an individual to walk the length of the parallel bars as rapidly as possible. Two trials are averaged to obtain this measurement; measured in seconds.

Qualitative gait analysis: The identification and description of gait patterns.

Quantitative gait analysis: The measurement in distance and time of gait variables.

Speed: A scalar quantity; has magnitude but not direction. **Slow speed** is a speed slower than an individual's normal speed; **fast speed** is a rate faster than normal.

Stance phase: The portion of gait in which one extremity is in contact with the ground. The phase is divided into the following segments: heel strike, foot flat, midstance, heel off, and toe off. The Rancho Los Amigos divisions are initial contact, loading response, midstance, terminal stance, and preswing.

Step: Consists of two dimensions; a distance (**step length**) and time (**step time**); two steps comprise a stride.

Step length: The linear distance between two successive points of contact of the right and left lower extremities. Usually a measurement is taken from the point of heel contact at heel strike of one extremity to the point of heel contact of the opposite extremity. If a patient does not have a heel strike on one or both sides, the measurement can be taken from the heads of the first metatarsals; measured in centimeters or meters. Both right and left step lengths should be obtained. When the right foot is leading, it is a right step. When the left foot is leading, it is a left step.

Step time: The number of seconds between consecutive right and left foot contacts; both right and left step times should be measured.

Stride: Consists of two dimensions; a distance (**stride length**) and a time (**stride time**).

Stride length: The linear distance between two consecutive foot contacts of the same lower extremity. Usually a measurement is taken from the point of one heel contact at heel strike and the next heel contact of the same extremity. However, stride length may be measured by using other events such as two consecutive toe offs; measured in centimeters or meters. Both right and left stride lengths should be measured.

Stride time: The number of seconds that elapses during one stride (from one foot contact until the next contact of the same foot). Stride time is synonymous with **cycle time.** Both right and left stride times should be measured.

Swing phase: The phase of gait during which the reference limb is not in contact with the supporting surface.

Swing time: The number of seconds during the gait cycle that one foot is off the ground. Swing time should be measured separately for right and left extremities.

Torque (moment of force): The turning or rotational effect produced by the application of a force. The greater the perpendicular distance of the point of application of a force from an axis of rotation, the greater the turning effect or torque produced. Torque is calculated by multiplying the force by the perpendicular distance from the point of application of the force and the axis of rotation:

$$\text{Torque} = f \times \text{perpendicular distance or moment arm}$$

Measurement is in newton meters.

Uninvolved stance time: The length of time (up to 30 seconds) that an individual can stand in the parallel bars while bearing weight on the uninvolved lower extremity (involved extremity is raised off the supporting surface).

Velocity: A measure of a body's motion in a given direction.

Walking velocity: The rate of linear forward motion of the body; measured in either centimeters per second or meters per minute:

$$\text{Walking velocity} = \text{distance/time}$$

Walking velocity may be affected by age, level of maturation, height, sex, type of footwear, and weight. Also, velocity may affect cadence, step, stride length, and foot angle as well as other gait variables.

Width of walking base (step width; base of support): The linear distance between one foot and the opposite foot; measured in centimeters or meters.

Work: The application of a force through a distance; accomplished whenever a force moves an object through a distance.

$$\text{Work} = \text{force} \times \text{distance}$$

Chapter 12

FUNCTIONAL ASSESSMENT

ANDREW A. GUCCIONE, KAREN E. CULLEN, AND SUSAN B. O'SULLIVAN

OBJECTIVES

1. Discuss the concepts of health status, impairment, functional disability, and handicap.

2. Define functional activity, and discuss the purposes and components of a functional assessment.

3. Select activities and role performances appropriate to a particular individual's characteristics and condition to assess functional status.

4. Compare and contrast some of the characteristics of various tests, including physical function tests and multidimensional functional assessment instruments.

5. Identify factors to be considered in the selection of testing instruments.

6. Compare and contrast various scoring methods used.

7. Discuss the issues of reliability and validity as they relate to functional assessment.

INTRODUCTION

The ultimate objective of any rehabilitation program is to return the individual to as normal and full a lifestyle as possible or, alternatively, to maintain or to maximize remaining function.[1] For a patient with a fractured arm, this may be a reasonably simple process: improve range of motion and strength and reestablish skills in dressing and feeding. For the patient with a stroke, the task is much more complex because the problems are much more extensive and complicated. In both instances, the therapist begins with a systematic assessment of each body system, planning treatments to reduce or to eliminate the problems identified and measuring the progress of those treatments. However, in the end, the final common denominator for assessing the success of each program is the attainment or reattainment of optimal function. It is the heart of all rehabilitation efforts.

Functional activities are those activities identified by an individual as essential to support physical and psychologic well-being as well as to create a personal sense of meaningful living. They require the integration of both cognitive and affective resources with motoric skills. Functional activity, therefore, is a patient-referenced concept and dependent on what the individual identifies as important. It is not totally individualistic, however, for there are certain categories of activities that are common to everyone. Eating, sleeping, elimination, and hygiene seem to be major activities of survival and protection common to all animals. Particular to humans are the evolutionary advancements of bipedal locomotion and complex hand activities. Work and recreation provide a social framework for the performance of these functional activities.

This chapter presents a conceptual framework for assessing functional status and introduces the reader to terminology used in the field. It presents an overview of the purposes of functional assessment and the range and rigor of formal test instruments currently available. Considerations in test selection and principles of administration are also presented.

A CONCEPTUAL FRAMEWORK

Chronically ill and disabled persons represent a large segment of the population in this country. Approximately 35 million individuals suffer from physical or mental impairments that limit their capacity to perform some daily functional activity.[2] Historically, these individuals have been categorized or classified according to their medical diagnoses. Thus the disease and its clinical manifestations can serve to define and to stereotype the individual who has a functional deficit. The term **disease** is used here to refer to a pathologic condition of the body that presents a particular group of signs and symptoms that sets that condition apart as abnormal. Medical assessment procedures such as physical examination and laboratory tests are the primary tools to delineate the problems created by disease. Focus on a biomedical model, with emphasis on the characteristics of disease (etiology, pathology, manifestations), may result in the medical labeling of individuals; for example, as amputees, paraplegics, arthritics, or CVAs. This model virtually ignores the equally important social, psychologic, and behavioral dimensions of **illness**. Illness is used here to refer to the forms of personal behavior that emerge when the reality of having a disease is internalized and experienced by an individual.[3] These factors often play a key role in determining the success or failure of rehabilitation efforts well beyond the nature of the medical disease that prompted a patient's referral to physical therapy.

A broader conceptual framework is necessary to fully understand the concepts of health and functional disability. Terms such as well-being, quality of life, and **functional status** are often used interchangeably to describe health status. There is, however, no clear understanding of what these terms mean. The most global def-

inition of **health** has been provided by the World Health Organization (WHO). This organization defined health as "a state of complete physical, mental, and social well-being, and not merely the absence of diseases and infirmity."[4] Although such global definitions are useful as philosophic statements, they lack the precision necessary for a clinician or researcher. Factors that are often used to define health in more measurable terms include (1) **physical signs,** (2) **symptoms,** and (3) **functional disability.**[5] Full consensus on the meaning of these terms, however, has not been reached. More recently, WHO has adopted an International Classification of Impairments, Disability, and Handicaps (ICIDH).[6] The goal was to promote the use of consistent terminology and to provide a framework for discourse among health professionals. The definitions presented in this chapter are reflective of that classification system.

Nagi[7,8] and Wood[9,10] and Badley[10] have been influential in developing models that explicate health status and disability (Fig. 12–1 represents a modification of their work). The conceptual framework used in this chapter for understanding health status begins with the pathology or disease process that mobilizes the body's defenses and response mechanisms. Physical signs and symptoms indicate the body's attempts to cope with this attack on its normal functioning. **Physical signs** are the directly observable or measurable changes in an individual's organs or systems. **Symptoms** are the more subjective reactions to the changes experienced by the individual. Thus the individual demonstrates an elevated blood pressure (a physical sign) and reports feeling dizzy (a symptom). **Impairments** evolve as the natural consequence of pathology or disease and are defined as "any loss or abnormality of anatomical, physiological, or psychological structure of function."[10] The partial or complete loss of a limb or an organ, or any disturbance in body part, organ, or system function are examples of impairments. Impairments may be temporary or permanent and represent an overt manifestation (exteriorization) of the pathologic state. Physical therapists are primarily concerned with impairments of the musculoskeletal, neuromuscular, and cardiopulmonary systems.[11] A **functional disability** is the inability of an individual to

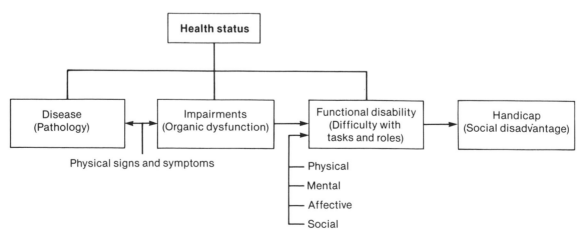

Figure 12–1. A conceptual framework for understanding functional status assessment.

function normally as the result of impairment. The presumed "cause-and-effect" relationship between having an impairment and experiencing a disability is strictly logical. For example, physical therapists may assume that the fact that a patient can not bathe independently is causally linked to the fact that the individual has lost upper extremity range of motion. The return of function following remediation of the impairment of joint mobility is then considered clinical evidence of a causal relationship between an impairment and disability. Although deficits in behavioral or motor skills or alterations in social function may typically exist in certain disease categories, the exact empirical relationship between a particular set of impairments and a specific functional disability is not yet known. Patients with the same disease and the same impairments may not have the same disability. The illness will be particular to the individual. Thus examination of functional status, defined as the normal or characteristic performance of a task or role by an individual, is a broad-based, multidimensional process that must be linked to the other tests and measurements used by a physical therapist in assessing a patient.[11]

Four main categories of function have been delineated: **physical function, mental function, affective function** and **social function. Physical function** refers to those sensory-motor skills necessary for the performance of usual daily activities. Getting out of bed, walking, climbing stairs, and bathing are examples of physical functions. Physical therapists are traditionally most involved with this category of functional assessment and treatment. Tasks concerned with daily self-care such as feeding, dressing, hygiene, and physical mobility are called **basic activities of daily living** (BADL). Advanced skills that are considered vital to an individual's independent living in the community are termed **instrumental activities of daily living** (IADL). These include a wide range of high-level skills such as managing personal affairs, cooking and shopping, home chores, and driving. **Mental function** refers to the intellectual or cognitive abilities of an individual. Factors such as initiative, attention, concentration, memory, problem solving, or judgment are important components of normal mental function. **Affective function** refers to the affective skills and coping strategies needed to deal with the everyday "hassles" as well as the more traumatic and stressful events each person encounters over the course of a lifetime. Factors such as self-esteem, attitude toward body image, anxiety, depression, and the ability to cope with change are examples of affective functions. Finally, **social function** refers to an individual's ability to interact successfully with others in the performance of social roles and obligations. Categories of roles and activities that are relevant to assessing an individual's social function include the degree of social interaction, including participation in recreational activities and clubs; social behaviors, such as telephoning or visiting relatives or friends; and social roles created and sustained through interpersonal relationships specific to one's personal life and occupation.[11]

The term **handicap** describes the "disadvantage for a given individual resulting from an impairment or a disability that limits or prevents the fulfillment of a role that is normal (depending on age, sex, social and cultural factors) for that individual."[10] A handicap is characterized by a discordance between the actual performance of an individual on a particular task or role and the performance expected by the community. This "standard" reflects the cultural, social, economic, and environmental consequences of a disability. Although an individual may have a particular impairment that results in a functional deficit, the negative value placed by others on that disability makes a person handicapped. In some instances, a person who is functioning independently may still be handicapped owing to the social stigma of using an assistive device such as a wheelchair. Physical therapists can help change social attitudes and environmental restrictions like architectural barriers that stigmatize individuals as "handicapped."

ASSESSMENT OF FUNCTION

Purpose of Functional Assessment

Analysis of function focuses on the measurement and classification of functional abilities and **functional activities** and the identification of functional limitations.[12] In essence, it is a measure of change in how a person does certain tasks or fulfills certain roles in the various dimensions of living previously described. Functional assessment is accomplished via a test or battery of tests, the results of which can be used as (1) an information base for setting realistic function-oriented treatment goals, (2) an indicator to the patient of current abilities that documents progression toward more complex functional levels, (3) an index for decisions on admission and discharge from a rehabilitation or extended care facility or to determine needs for community services, (4) a guide for determining the safety of an individual in performing a particular task and the risk of injury with continued performance, (5) a formalized instrument to assess the effectiveness of a specific treatment intervention (rehabilitative, surgical, or medical) on function.

General Considerations

Physical therapists possess a unique body of knowledge related to the identification, remediation, and prevention of movement dysfunction. Thus they are actively involved in the assessment of physical function through the use of performance-based tests. Other members of the rehabilitation team, including the occupational therapist, nurse, rehabilitation counselor, and recreational therapist, are also typically involved in administering functional assessments. A few tests are designed to be completed collectively by the team. Other tests are compiled in separate sections by specific health professionals and housed together in the patient's chart. Where teams exist, physical therapists are typically responsible for the assessment of bed mobility, transfers, balance, and locomotion (wheelchair, ambulation, and elevation activities). Occupational therapists are typically involved in the assessment of feeding, bathing, dressing, homemaking, and use of adaptive devices for upper extremity activities. Overlap among team members exists, however. For example, the assessment of toilet transfers may be done by the physical therapist, occupational therapist, or the nurse as a component of a general bowel and bladder program. In these instances, the testing should be coordinated to reduce duplication and unnecessary patient stress. In noninstitutional settings or where there is no team, the physical therapist may be responsible for all items on a physical function test.

Types of Instruments

A functional assessment may be administered by the therapist who observes the patient during the performance of an activity or by a trained interviewer. Relevant data also may be collected by patient self-assessment. Irrespective of the particular instrument used, there are several basic considerations to be kept in mind. The patient should be assessed when he or she is not fatigued. The setting chosen must be conducive to testing, free of distractions, and, if possible, similar to the actual environment in which the patient must eventually perform. The patient should be told if the test is to take several sessions.

PERFORMANCE-BASED ASSESSMENTS

A **performance-based assessment** may be used both as an initial tool and as an ultimate indicator of the success of the rehabilitation program. Therefore, this assessment is administered during the early phase of rehabilitation, usually following testing of sensation, range of motion, strength, motor control, and coordination. Retesting should occur at regular intervals to document the presence or absence of progress.

During the administration of the test, each task is presented, and the patient is asked to perform; for example, "Push your wheelchair over to that red chair and stop." The patient is given no other instructions or assistance unless he or she is unable or unsure of how to perform, then only as much direction or assistance as is needed is given. Appropriate safety procedures should be taken during the session so that the patient does not attempt tasks that are potentially dangerous.

INTERVIEWER ASSESSMENTS

To maximize accuracy in assessing function, interviewers should be taught to administer a specific questionnaire by someone trained to use that instrument. Interviewers should practice until they have reached a high degree of agreement with expert assessors of the same cases. Periodic retraining may be necessary if interviewers do not have frequent practice administering the instrument.

Interviewer assessments should be designed so that questions are asked in a standard format and answers are recorded as specified. Ad lib prompting for answers is discouraged because it tends to bias results. The interview should be scheduled with the patient in advance and conducted in an environment conducive to complete concentration. Interviews may be conducted by phone or in person, but when they are used as a pretest and a posttest, the mode of administration should be kept constant.[14,15]

SELF-ADMINISTERED ASSESSMENTS

The critical issue in the ability of a **self-administered assessment** to capture function correctly and completely lies in providing clearly worded questions without language bias, concise directions on completing the questions, and a format that encourages accurate reporting of answers to all questions. Long paper-and-pencil tests may be difficult for those with upper extremity disability. It is also important to know when the patient has had the help of others to complete the test.[14-16]

Instrument Formats and Parameters

Grading criteria are specific to the format of the particular functional test being administered. Few, if any, are perfect. None seems to be universally applicable to all patients with equal success.

NUMERIC OR LETTER-GRADE FORMAT

A few tests use numeric or letter grades that are assigned to describe qualitatively the degree to which a person can perform the task. Most commonly, the scales are **ordinal,** or **rank-order,** scales and may run from 0 to 5, 1 to 5, or the like, in ascending or descending order. Letter grades are awarded in the same way. The system is identical to the one used with manual muscle testing. The primary drawback in using such a system to score function is that the category definitions are often not exactly descriptive of the patient's function or ability to perform the task. In addition, they are not quantitative and can not be added or subtracted,[17] an important mistake that is often made.

CHECKLIST FORMAT

A **checklist format** with a description of various functional tasks is simply scored as able to complete (present; checked) or not able to complete (absent; not checked). The results are not quantitative and require interpretation for a notion of improvement.

SUMMARY OR ADDITIVE SCALE FORMAT

The **summary,** or **additive, scale** grades a specific series of skills, awards points for part or full performance, and totals the performance score as a percentage of 100 points or as a fraction, such as $^{60}/_{100}$ or $^{9}/_{24}$ and so forth.

Table 12-1 BARTHEL INDEX

Date _____
Initial _____

FEEDING
10 = Independent. Able to apply any necessary
        device. Feeds in reasonable time.
 5 = Needs help (e.g., for cutting).   _____
BATHING
 5 = Independent   _____
PERSONAL TOILET
 5 = Independently washes face, combs hair,
        brushes teeth, shaves (manages plug if electric).   _____
DRESSING
10 = Independent. Ties shoes, fastens fasteners,
        applies braces.
 5 = Needs help, but docs at least half of work in
        reasonable time.   _____
BOWELS
10 = No accidents. Able to use enema or
        suppository, if needed.
 5 = Occasional accidents or needs help with enema
        or suppository.   _____
BLADDER
10 = No accidents. Able to care for collecting device
        if used.
 5 = Occasional accidents or needs help with device.   _____
TOILET TRANSFERS
10 = Independent with toilet or bedpan. Handles
        clothes, wipes, flushes or cleans pan.
 5 = Needs help for balance, handling clothes or
        toilet paper.   _____
TRANSFERS—CHAIR AND BED
15 = Independent, including locks wheelchair, lifts
        footrests.
10 = Minimum assistance or supervision.
 5 = Able to sit, but needs maximum assistance to
        transfer.   _____
AMBULATION
15 = Independent for 50 yards. May use assistive
        devices, except for rolling walker.
10 = With help 50 yards.
 5 = Independent with wheelchair for 50 yards if
        unable to walk.   _____
STAIR CLIMBING
10 = Independent. May use assistive devices.
 5 = Needs help or supervision.   _____
                                                              Totals _____

A score of zero (0) is given in any category in which the patient does not achieve the stated criterion.
(From Mahoney, FI and Barthel, DW: *Functional evaluation: The Bartel index.* Md State Med J
14:61–65, 1965, with permission.)

Examples are the Granger and Barthel (Table 12-1) scales.[18,19] The danger in these summary scores is that one might incorrectly assume (1) normal function is absolute and equivalent to a set number, and (2) such scores can be compared via mathematic operations. It may well be that a patient who scores $^{60}/_{100}$ at admission and a $^{90}/_{100}$ at discharge is indeed better. However, it would be incorrect to assume that he is 33 percent improved or within 10 percent of normal. Neither conclusion is sound.

VISUAL ANALOG SCALE FORMAT

Visual, or **linear, analog scales** attempt to represent measurement quantities in terms of a straight line placed horizontally or vertically on paper (Fig. 12–2). The end points of the line are labeled with descriptive terms to anchor the extremes of the scale and to give reference to any point in the continuum between. The ends of the scale should not be so extreme that they are never cho-

Figure 12–2. This is a visual analog scale for measuring pain and disease symptoms. The patient is instructed to mark the line at the point that corresponds to the degree of pain or severity of symptom that is being experienced.

sen. Commonly the lines are 10 cm in length, but distances of 15 and 20 cm are also used. The subject is asked to bisect the line at a point representing his or her position on the scale. The score is then obtained by measuring from the zero mark to the mark bisecting the scale. The score is treated as ordinal data.[17,20,21]

VISUAL RECORDING FORMAT

With ever-increasing technology, new tools are available to record changes in function. Although more costly than other methods, videotaping or filming has the capacity to represent functional abilities precisely as the patients perform them. Thus it allows the therapist to assess changes in quality of performance as well as the number of activities completed. Visual recordings are appropriate methods for assessing and validating the effectiveness of new drugs or treatment approaches and are useful to patients in depicting the true extent of their disability. They are also useful in training staff to score tasks reliably by reaching agreement on observed performance.

TIME PARAMETER

The timing of a series of activities is often used when a given speed of performance is required or an improvement in performance speed is expected. Probably the most common example is in premedication and post-medication assessments of patients with Parkinsonism who are placed on levodopa therapy. Examples of activities that may be timed include (1) walking a set distance, (2) writing one's signature, (3) donning an article of clothing, and (4) crossing a street during the time of a "Walk" light. Scores of timed tests should not be taken as absolute but rather as one measure of performance. Furthermore, it may not always be clear what is being measured. For example, the patient may get dressed quickly, within seconds, but do so with poorly coordinated movements and a low-quality result. When the task is slowed down, the movements become more coordinated, with a more satisfactory end result, but time increases. Or as a patient with a head injury recovers, extraneous movements decrease, as does the time required to complete a task. Time also can be used as a measure of endurance. It provides objective evidence of the ability of the cardiopulmonary system to support sustained activity. Certain medical conditions that affect energy expenditure may require proper pacing for successful completion of a functional activity. Thus time scores alone do not yield the complete picture. When taken with other performance measures, they do provide an added dimension to the assessment.

DESCRIPTIVE PARAMETERS

Therapists should use descriptive terms that are well defined and nonambiguous. Meanings of descriptive terms should be clear to all others using the medical record. Table 12–2 provides a sample set of acceptable

Table 12–2 FUNCTIONAL ASSESSMENT AND IMPAIRMENT TERMINOLOGY

DEFINITIONS
1. **Independent:** patient is able consistently to perform skill safely with no one present.
2. **Supervision:** patient requires someone within arm's reach as a precaution; low probability of patient having a problem requiring assistance.
3. **Close guarding:** person assisting is positioned as if to assist with hands raised but not touching patient; full attention on patient; fair probability of patient requiring assistance.
4. **Contact guarding:** therapist is positioned as with close guarding with hands on patient but not giving any assistance; high probability of patient requiring assistance.
5. **Minimum assistance:** patient is able to complete majority of the activity without assistance.
6. **Moderate assistance:** patient is able to complete part of the activity without assistance.
7. **Maximum assistance:** patient is unable to assist in any part of the activity.

DESCRIPTIVE TERMINOLOGY
A. Bed mobility
  1. Independent—no cuing* is given
  2. Supervision ⎫
  3. Minimum assistance ⎪
  4. Moderate assistance ⎬ may require cues
  5. Maximum assistance ⎭
B. Transfers; ambulation
  1. Independent—no cuing is given
  2. Supervision ⎫
  3. Close guarding ⎪
  4. Contact guarding ⎪
  5. Minimum assistance ⎬ may require cues
  6. Moderate assistance ⎪
  7. Maximum assistance ⎭
C. Balance
  1. Normal: patient is able to maintain position with therapist maximally disturbing balance
  2. Good: patient is able to maintain position with moderate disturbance from therapist
  3. Fair: patient is able to maintain position for short periods of time unsupported
  4. Poor: patient attempts to assist but requires assistance from other person to maintain position
  5. No balance: patient is unable to assist in maintaining position

*Types of Cues
1. Verbal
2. Visual
3. Tactile
NOTE: In some instances (e.g., a person with a memory deficit, short attention, learning disability, visual loss), a decrease in the amount of cues may represent treatment progress, even though the level of dependence remains the same. Interim progress notes can denote these changes by citing frequencies (e.g., 2 out of 3 tries) or an arbitrarily defined rank order scale (e.g., always/occasionally/rarely).

terms and definitions. Additional terms used to qualify function include **dependence, endurance,** and **difficulty.**

Unless otherwise noted, the term **dependence** means human assistance. However, the use of any and all equipment should be noted if used during the performance of a functional task; for example, independent in ambulation with axillary crutches or independent in dressing with adapted clothing and long-handled shoe-horn.

Endurance refers to the energy consumption required to complete the functional task. Measurements of endurance generally include heart rate, respiratory rate, and blood pressure both at rest (baseline measurements) and during the most stressful elements of the functional task; for example, "heart rate increased to 120 per minute with ambulation; no significant increase in respiratory rate." In addition, the patient's perception of exertion and overt signs of fatigue, such as shortness of breath, also should be noted.

Difficulty is a hybrid term that suggests that an activity poses an extra burden for the patient, regardless of dependence level. It is unclear whether it is a measure of overall perceptual motor skill, coordination, efficiency, or a combination of measures.

Additional factors that are frequently used to qualify functional performance include (1) pain, (2) time of day, (3) medication level, and (4) environment.

Interpreting Test Results

Clearly, the single most important consideration in functional assessment is using the test results correctly to establish and to revise treatment goals and the treatment plan. The therapist should carefully delineate the contributing factors that result in the functional deficit. When diminished ability is evident, the therapist must attempt to ascertain the cause of the problem. Some important questions to ask include

1. What are the normal movements necessary to perform the task?

2. Which impairments inhibit performance or completion of the task? For example, do factors such as poor motor planning and execution, decreased strength, decreased range of motion, or altered tone impair function?

3. Are the patient's problems the result of communication or perceptual, visual, auditory, or cognitive involvement? Does poor memory or fatigue impair ability?

A few tasks may need to be analyzed more precisely. Activities can be broken down into subordinate parts, or subroutines. A **subordinate part** is defined as an element of movement without which the task cannot proceed safely or efficiently. For example, bed mobility includes the following subordinate parts: (1) scooting in bed (changing position for comfort or skin care and getting to the edge), (2) rolling onto the side, (3) lowering legs, (4) sitting up, (5) balancing over the edge of the bed, and (6) getting out of bed. A functional loss of independent bed mobility may result from an inability to perform any or all of these subroutines. These are not only checkpoints for assessing patients, but they also later form the basis of a training program. The more involved the patient or the slower the learner, the more the functional task may need to be broken down into subordinate parts.

Abbreviated assessment findings of two cases follow.

Case A	Case B
36 y.o. male construction worker	72 y.o. female housewife
dx. traumatic right below-knee amputation; post fracture left femur	dx. CVA with right hemiplegia with global aphasia

Partial Assessment Findings

strength: decreased all extremities following prolonged immobilization	flaccid paralysis right extremities
functional disability: unable to transfer from bed to wheelchair	unable to transfer from bed to wheelchair

Although the functional disability in each case is in fact identical, the contributing factors, short-term and long-term goals, and the treatment approach would be markedly different. In Case A, the inability to transfer can reasonably be attributed to decreased strength. When ameliorated, it is likely that the patient will go on to achieve a long-term goal of independent ambulation with a prosthesis. Case B has factors that can not be addressed solely through physical therapy. In addition, it may be difficult to determine whether it is the paralysis or the aphasia that compromises efforts to assess and to improve function. Although a similar goal of independence in wheelchair mobility and transfers may be proposed, frequent reassessment may demonstrate that functional deficits persist, despite improvement in motor function. In that case, the impairments in comprehension and language function may be the more important contributing factors. Thus the design of rehabilitation programs is based upon the impairments that presumably underlie the functional deficits. If remediation of the impairment does not solve the functional problem, the therapist needs to reexamine the initial clinical impression by looking for other potentially causative factors.

Assessing the Quality of Instruments

Within the rehabilitation setting, many tools have been developed primarily for in-house use and may have spread from facility to facility as staff have moved. In most instances, the instruments underwent many modifications and the original sources have been lost. Other tests have been designed more rigidly and tested in clinical trials, assessing the instrument's metric properties and providing documentation of **reliability, validity,** and scoring scheme in the literature. If the reliability and validity of instruments are not established, little faith can be put in the results obtained or in the conclusions drawn from the results.[14] A poorly constructed instrument can produce data that are questionable, if not worthless.[22] Considering the purposes of functional assessment, the importance of these concepts becomes clear.

RELIABILITY

A reliable instrument measures a phenomenon dependably, time after time, accurately, predictably, and without variation.[14] If a functional assessment or any test is not reliable, the patient's initial baseline status or the true effect of treatment can be concealed. The instrument should be reliable from session to session and should have strong *interrater reliability*—agreement among multiple observers of the same event. If a particular patient is assessed by several therapists in the course of treatment, or reassessed over time to determine long-term change, the reliability of the functional assessment tool must be known.

The single greatest flaw in the clinical use of most types of functional tests is the tendency toward poor interrater reliability. To use functional assessments with maximum accuracy, (1) all therapists in a facility must be retrained periodically to ensure similarity in grading, (2) individual grades must be defined clearly and must be mutually exclusive, and (3) grading criteria must be strictly adhered to and easy to administer.

VALIDITY

Validity is a more complex concept. A valid instrument measures what it purports to measure.[15] There are different types of validity. The critical concept is whether the functional assessment measures all the important or specified dimensions of function. For example, does an index designed to admit or to discharge patients on the basis of function truly represent just that? In essence, can the interpretations of the results be trusted as measures of the intended parameter?[21,22] If there is a **"gold standard"**—an unimpeachable measure of a phenomenon, such as a laboratory test with normative values—then a new instrument designed to provide the same assessment can be tested against the results of this standard. The degree to which the two agree will establish some measure of validity. In the measurement of function, although there is no one "gold standard," some of the more recently developed instruments have undergone extensive testing of their measurement properties. Cross comparisons between these instruments have established validity scores. The issue of validity is particularly relevant for self-assessed instruments. The validity of some self-assessed instruments has been determined by comparison with clinician ratings.

OTHER FACTORS

In addition to reliability and validity, a measure of functional status should be (1) sufficiently sensitive to reflect changes in patient status, (2) concise enough to be clinically useful, and (3) complete enough to give an adequate overview of the patient's function.

Considerations in Selection of Instruments

There are a large number of instruments that have been developed to assess and to classify functional ability. Given the plethora of instruments that currently exist, it is quite reasonable to ask how these instruments compare with one another. It is important to remember that no instrument is perfect for all patients or all situations. No instrument can assess all the items potentially relevant to a particular individual and provide the perfect composite picture. For example, one instrument may provide an extensive assessment of BADL but not

deal with affective or social dimensions. Another may investigate social functioning while omitting some activities of daily living (ADL) tasks. Many items overlap from instrument to instrument. For example, a question on the ability to ambulate is a common item found in most physical function instruments. Although instruments may cover the same kind of activity, the questions posed about the performance of the same activity may be quite different. For example, one instrument may investigate the degree of difficulty and of human assistance required to "dress yourself, including handling of closures, buttons, zippers, snaps." Another may ask, "How much help do you need in getting dressed?" Differences also may exist in the time frames sampled in the various instruments. For example, the period of time sampled may range from nonspecific to short term (as little as a week) to long term (as long as a month). Instruments that assess only short-term objectives may not relate well to the long-term objectives of a rehabilitation program.[13]

Some formal, standardized instruments for assessing function summarize detailed information about a complex area of function into an overall index score. Use of these instruments facilitates the interpretation of complex data and enables the clinician to perform cross-disease, cross-program, and cross-population comparisons of function. Instruments that lack this feature lose some of their clinical utility and appeal. Caution must be exercised in considering only summated scores, however, because potentially important individual differences in functional ability can be masked. Two patients with the same numeric score might be quite different in their functional deficits.

Critical questions to ask, therefore, in selecting an instrument include

1. What are the domains or categories that the assessment instrument focuses on?

2. How adequately does the instrument measure the domain or domains being sampled?

3. What areas of physical function are included? Does the instrument measure BADL? IADL?

4. What aspect of function is being measured? Is the level of dependence-independence considered? Length of time required to complete the functional task? Degree of difficulty? Influence of pain?

5. What is the time frame sampled in the assessment?

6. What is the mode of administration?

7. What type of scoring system is used?

8. Are multiple instruments necessary to provide a more complete assessment? Extrapolating items from a variety of instruments may provide the kind of data desired but should be considered only with caution inasmuch as this process may result in a loss of reliability or validity.

Factors such as the theoretic orientation of the user, the purpose for using the instrument, and the relevance of particular functional items to certain patient populations all enter into the decision-making process. In the final analysis, the choice of instrument may be dictated by practical considerations. For example, self-report instruments, which rely on information from the patient, is limited in use to mentally competent individuals.

Time and resources for administration also may influence test selection. In any case, there are many suitable instruments available for assessing functional status.

Selected Instruments Assessing Physical Function

BARTHEL INDEX

The Barthel Index specifically measures the degree of assistance required by an individual on 10 items of mobility and self-care ADL[19] (see Table 12–1). Levels of measurement are limited to either complete independence or needing assistance. Each performance item is assessed on an ordinal scale with a specific number of points assigned to each level or ranking. Variable weightings were established by the developers of the Barthel Index for each item based upon clinical judgment or other implicit criteria. An individual who uses human assistance in eating, for example, would receive 5 points; independence in eating would receive a score of 10 points. A single global score, ranging from 0 to 100, is calculated from the sum of all weighted individual item scores, so that a 0 equals complete dependence in all 10 activities, and 100 equals complete independence in all 10 activities. The Barthel Index has been used widely to monitor functional changes in individuals receiving inpatient rehabilitation. Although its psychometric properties have not been fully assessed, the Barthel Index has achieved high correlations with other measures of physical disability.[24]

KENNY SELF-CARE EVALUATION

The Kenny Self-Care Evaluation uses professional observation to investigate the dependence of individuals in performing 17 activities divided over six major categories: bed mobility, transfers, locomotion, dressing, personal hygiene, and feeding[25,26] (Table 12–3). Each categoric scale contains five levels that rank the degree of assistance required to accomplish a given task. A score of 0 to 4 is calculated for each category. A global score is created by summing all the scale scores. The global score ranges from 0 for the completely dependent individual to 24 points for the totally independent individual. All items are weighted equally. The use of the Kenny Self-Care Evaluation is hampered by the amount of professional time required to observe patient performance of such a large spectrum of selected activities throughout the day. The construction of the locomotion category also confuses the overall independence of the wheelchair-bound patient with that of an ambulatory individual. Either individual may be fully independent in all the other self-care activities, yet the wheelchair user will always receive the lower overall score, despite an equiv-

Table 12–3 The Kenny Self-Care Evaluation

From Schoening, H, et al: Numerical scoring of self-care status of patients. Arch Phys Med Rehabil 60:689, 1965, p. 691, with permission.

alent capacity for self-care and independent living. The measurement properties of the Kenny Self-Care Evaluation have not been reported.

KATZ INDEX OF ACTIVITIES OF DAILY LIVING

Katz's Index of ADL focuses on patient performance and the degree of assistance required in six categories of basic ADL: bathing, dressing, toileting, transfering, continence, and feeding[27,28] (Table 12–4). Using both direct observation and patient self-report over a two-week period, the examiner scores 1 point for each activity that is performed without human help. A 0 score is given if the activity is performed with human assistance or is not performed. Activity scores are combined to form a cumulative scale in letter grades (A through G) in order of increasing dependency. An individual's global letter score indicates an exact pattern of responses to the list of items. A score of B in the Katz Index, for example, means that the individual is independent in performing all but one of the six basic ADL categories. On the other hand, a score of D means that the individual is independent in all but bathing, dressing, and one additional function. The combination of categoric deficits in the Katz Index represents its developers' theoretic orientation. The developers of the Katz Index assumed a developmental and hierarchical organization of function in constructing their instrument. This organizational model is based on the empirically noted integration of neurologic and locomotor responses that is seen in children. One version of the scale demonstrated agreement ratios of 0.68 and 0.98 between different professional raters. Test-retest reliability of respondent self-reports produced intraclass correlation coefficients ranging from 0.61 to 0.78.[29] The Katz Index, originally developed for use with institutionalized patients, has been adapted for use in community-based populations.[30] A major disadvantage of using the Katz Index in rehabilitation settings is its failure to include an item on ambulation. The predictive validity of the instrument for long-term survival also has been reported.[28]

Table 12–4 THE KATZ INDEX OF INDEPENDENCE IN ADL

Name _____ Day of evaluation _____
For each area of functioning listed below, check description that applies. (The word "assistance" means supervision, direction, or personal assistance.)

Bathing—either sponge bath, tub bath, or shower.

☐	☐	☐
Receives no assistance (gets in and out of tub by self if tub is usual means of bathing)	Receives assistance in bathing only one part of the body (such as back or a leg)	Receives assistance in bathing more than one part of the body (or not bathed)

Dressing—gets clothes from closets and drawers—including underclothes, outer garments and using fasteners (including braces if worn)

☐	☐	☐
Gets clothes and gets completely dressed without assistance	Gets clothes and gets dressed without assistance except for assistance in tying shoes	Receives assistance in getting clothes or in getting dressed, or stays partly or completely undressed

Toileting—going to the "toilet room" for bowel and urine elimination, cleaning self after elimination, and arranging clothes

☐	☐	☐
Goes to "toilet room," cleans self, and arranges clothes without assistance (may use object for support such as cane, walker, or wheelchair and may manage night bedpan or commode, emptying same in morning)	Receives assistance in going to "toilet room" or in cleansing self or in arranging clothes after elimination or in use of night bedpan or commode	Doesn't go to room termed "toilet" for the elimination process

Transfer

☐	☐	☐
Moves in and out of bed as well as in and out of chair without assistance (may be using object for support such as cane or walker)	Moves in and out of bed or chair with assistance	Doesn't get out of bed

Continence

☐	☐	☐
Controls urination and bowel movement completely by self	Has occasional "accidents"	Supervision helps keep urine or bowel control; catheter is used, or is incontinent

Feeding

☐	☐	☐
Feeds self without assistance	Feeds self except for getting assistance in cutting meat or buttering bread	Receives assistance in feeding or is fed partly or completely by using tubes or intravenous fluids

Table 12–4 *continued.*

The Index of Independence in Activities of Daily Living is based on an evaluation of the functional independence or dependence of patients in bathing, dressing, going to toilet, transferring, continence, and feeding. Specific definitions of functional independence and dependence appear below the index.

A—Independent in feeding, continence, transferring, going to toilet, dressing, and bathing.
B—Independent in all but one of these functions.
C—Independent in all but bathing and one additional function.
D—Independent in all but bathing, dressing, and one additional function.
E—Independent in all but bathing, dressing, going to toilet, and one additional function.
F—Independent in all but bathing, dressing, going to toilet, transferring, and one additional function.
G—Dependent in all six functions.
Other—Dependent in at least two functions, but not classifiable as C, D, E, or F.
Independence means without supervision, direction, or active personal assistance, except as specifically noted below. This is based on actual status and not on ability. A patient who refuses to perform a function is considered as not performing the function, even though he is deemed able.

Bathing (sponge, shower, or tub)
Independent: assistance only in bathing a single part (as back or disabled extremity) or bathes self completely
Dependent: assistance in bathing more than one part of body; assistance in getting in or out of tub or does not bathe self
Dressing
Independent: gets clothes from closets and drawers; puts on clothes, outer garments, braces; manages fasteners; act of tying shoes is excluded
Dependent: does not dress self or remains partly undressed
Going to toilet
Independent: gets to toilet; gets on and off toilet; arranges clothes; cleans organs of excretion (may manage own bedpan used at night only and may or may not be using mechanical supports)
Dependent: uses bedpan or commode or receives assistance in getting to and using toilet

Transfer
Independent: moves in and out of bed independently and moves in and out of chair independently (may or may not be using mechanical supports)
Dependent: assistance in moving in or out of bed and/or chair; does not perform one or more transfers
Continence
Independent: urination and defecation entirely self-controlled
Dependent: partial or total incontinence in urination or defecation; partial or total control by enemas, catheters, or regulated use of urinals and/or bedpans
Feeding
Independent: gets food from plate or its equivalent, into mouth (precutting of meat and preparation of food, as buttering bread, are excluded from evaluation)
Dependent: assistance in act of feeding (see above); does not eat at all or parenteral feeding

Reprinted by permission of *The Gerontologist/The Journal of Gerontology* 10:20, 1970.

FUNCTIONAL STATUS INDEX

The Functional Status Index (FSI) is derived partially from the original Katz Index. It is a self-report instrument that conceptualizes functional disability along the dimensions of dependence, difficulty, and pain encountered in the performance of 18 physical and social activities during the preceding seven days[5,31,32] (see chapter 21, appendix A for FSI). These activities were culled from an original inventory of 45 items covering five categories: gross mobility, hand activities, personal care, home chores, and interpersonal activities. The FSI, designed to assess functional outcomes in noninstitutionalized, chronically disabled populations, includes a wide range of basic and instrumental ADL. Functional dependence is assessed on a 5-point scale where a score of 1 equals complete independence, 2 designates the use of equipment, 3 designates the use of human assistance, 4 designates the use of equipment and human assistance, and 5 indicates complete dependence. Pain and difficulty are measured on separate 4-point scales that grade these dimensions in terms of increasing severity. Scores for each subindex of function can be tabulated to provide three summated ratings of dependence, difficulty, and pain. The FSI is available in interviewer and self-administered formats in long and short versions. It can be completed in less than 30 minutes in its long form.

The FSI subindexes of function demonstrated acceptable reliability ratings: test-retest reliability ratings ranged from 0.69 to 0.77, and interobserver reliability ratings ranged from 0.72 to 0.78 across the three dimensions. Construct validity coefficients for the global indexes on each dimension ranged from 0.87 to 0.98.[29] The FSI has been used for patients with rheumatoid arthritis to investigate the effectiveness of inpatient care[33] and as a measure of functional change in a study of aerobic exercise training.[34] The investigators in the latter study concluded that the tasks specified in the FSI may not be sensitive to detecting change when patients have previously modified their ADL to meet their particular needs.

SUMMARY OF PHYSICAL FUNCTION TESTS

No single physical function instrument covers all areas of physical function, and no single item is found in all instruments (Table 12–5). Even items that appear to assess the same function may, depending on how the instrument is constructed, be concerned with a different aspect of physical performance.[29] For example, in considering ambulation, the FSI can distinguish between human and mechanical assistance, whereas the Barthel Index indicates disability only when human assistance is needed for walking. Item comparability across instruments must always be carefully assessed. The Barthel and Kenny instruments provide the most detailed measures of personal care. In the area of mobility, the Kenny Instrument provides more coverage than any other instrument, whereas the Katz Index considers only one area of physical mobility. The FSI is the only instrument

Table 12–5 ITEMS COVERED IN SELECTED PHYSICAL FUNCTION INSTRUMENTS

	Barthel	Kenny	Katz	FSI
BADL				
Personal Care				
Bathing	+	+	+	+
Toileting	+	+	+	–
Grooming	+	+	–	–
Dressing	+	+	+	+
Feeding	+	+	+	–
Hand functions	–	–	–	+
Mobility				
Bed				
Activities	–	+	–	–
Sitting	–	+	–	–
Standing	–	+	–	–
Transfers	+	+	+	+
Ambulation	+	+	–	+
Wheelchair	–	+	–	–
Inclines/stairs	+	+	–	+
IADL				
Indoor				
Home chores	–	–	–	+
Outdoor				
Home chores	–	–	–	+
Travel/drive car	–	–	–	+
Social activities				
Vocational	–	–	–	+
Avocational	–	–	–	+
Impairments				
Upper extremity motion	–	–	–	–
Lower extremity motion	–	–	–	–
Continence	+	+	+	–

discussed that investigates a broad array of activities and tasks, including BADL, IADL, and social activity.

Multidimensional Functional Assessment Instruments

Further research has resulted in the emergence of newer instruments to measure broad components of health status. Although wider in scope than physical function instruments, these instruments do not provide a comprehensive assessment of health as the concept has been previously discussed (see Figure 12–1). Most concentrate on two or three dimensions of a patient's function, with very limited—if any—attention to the signs and symptoms of disease or resultant impairments. Therefore, to some degree the term *health status* frequently used to describe these instruments is a misnomer, inasmuch as these instruments actually measure function and not overall health. Used in conjunction with traditional clinical methods of assessing signs and symptoms, multidimensional functional status instruments can add an important comprehensive view of a patient's function to the overall health assessment process. In this respect they add a crucial, and previously missing, component in assessing the health of individuals with a disability. A few of these instruments representative of the current "state of the art" are discussed below.

THE SICKNESS IMPACT PROFILE

The Sickness Impact Profile (SIP) was developed to address the need for an instrument that was precise enough to detect changes in perceived function.[35-40] Intended for use across types and severities of illness, it is designed to detect small impacts of illness. The SIP contains 136 items in 12 categories of activities. These include sleep and rest, eating, work, home management, recreation, ambulatory mobility, body care and movement, social interaction, alertness, emotional behavior, and communication. A sample SIP measure of affective functioning specific to emotional behavior is found in Table 12–6. The entire test can be either self-administered or administered by an interviewer in 20 to 30 minutes. Sickness impact profile scores are percentage ratings based on the ratio of the summed scale scores to the summed values of all SIP items. Higher scores indicate greater dysfunction.

The SIP test-retest reliability coefficients range from 0.75 to 0.92 for the overall score and from 0.45 to 0.60 for items checked.[37] Validity has been assessed using subjective self-assessment, clinician assessment, and subject's scores on other instruments. Correlations that are relevant to establishing multiple forms of validity range from a low of 0.35 to a high of 0.84.[36] The SIP has been used to describe the physical and psychosocial functions of individuals in an outpatient setting in relation to the duration of disease.[41] There are, however, some concerns regarding its use and suitability in certain kinds of studies. In assessing disability, SIP focuses only on ability versus inability to perform an activity; for example, "I am not going into town." It neglects the range of performance in between, with some potential loss of precision. The SIP also combines many functional activities into a single item, which may also reduce its discriminatory ability, such as "I have difficulty doing handwork; for example, turning faucets, using kitchen gadgets, sewing, carpentry." A few investigators have noted that the SIP may be more sensitive to detecting deterioration of status than to improvement, which may diminish its suitability as an instrument for monitoring individuals over time.[42]

Table 12–6 SICKNESS IMPACT PROFILE (SIP): AFFECTIVE FUNCTION

PLEASE RESPOND TO (CHECK) *ONLY* THOSE STATEMENTS THAT YOU ARE *SURE* DESCRIBE YOU TODAY AND ARE RELATED TO YOUR STATE OF HEALTH.

1. I say how bad or useless I am; for example, that I am a burden on others. _____
2. I laugh or cry suddenly. _____
3. I often moan and groan in pain or discomfort. _____
4. I have attempted suicide. _____
5. I act nervous or restless. _____
6. I keep rubbing or holding areas of my body that hurt or are uncomfortable. _____
7. I act irritable and impatient with myself; for example, talk badly about myself, swear at myself, blame myself for things that happen. _____
8. I talk about the future in a hopeless way. _____
9. I get sudden frights. _____

CHECK HERE WHEN YOU HAVE READ ALL STATEMENTS ON THIS PAGE ☐

Reprinted by permission of Marilyn Bergner, Ph.D.

THE FUNCTIONAL STATUS QUESTIONNAIRE

The Functional Status Questionnaire (FSQ), adapted from existing functional disability instruments, is a brief self-administered assessment instrument designed to screen and to monitor changes in function among primary care patients.[43] It contains measures of basic and intermediate ADL, psychologic function, work performance, social activity, and quality of social interaction. There are also six single items covering age, bed disability days, restricted activity days, satisfaction with health, work role limitations, number of close friends, and frequency of social contact. A sample section of the FSQ which deals specifically with social functioning items is included in Table 12–7. The FSQ can be completed in 15 minutes and computer-scored to produce a one-page report, which includes six summated-rating scores and six single-item scores. Scores are transformed into values between 0 and 100 and displayed on a visual analog scale.

In several administrations, correlations between the six scale scores and the six single-item scores as well as the respondent's age were all significant and in the expected directions, suggesting that the FSQ validly measures what it was designed to assess.[43] The FSQ has been used in a multicenter study of the impact of providing functional status data to clinicians on subsequent patient care and outcomes.[44]

THE MULTILEVEL ASSESSMENT INSTRUMENT (MAI)

As part of their research at the Philadelphia Geriatric Center, Lawton and coworkers[45,46] developed a model for assessment for older individuals based on competence or ability to perform in the areas traditionally recognized as components of health status. These include physical health, cognition, activities of daily living (ADL), time use or formal social activity, and social interaction and support. Psychologic well-being is understood as personal adjustment in terms of morale and psychiatric symptoms and, unlike many other instruments, is distinct from cognitive functioning. This is a relevant distinction in a geriatric population in which deficits in mental processes such as memory or calculation may exist separate from factors related to morale or psychologic outlook. This instrument also investigates the perceived quality of the individual's residential environment and the adequacy of economic resources. Taken in their entirety, these domains represent the interests of the entire health care team. The IADL battery from the MAI is found in Table 12–8.

The subscale properties of the MAI are fully investigated and do not depend on an interviewer's summary judgments, as do a few other multidimensional instruments. Because it was developed expressly to address the salient characteristics of the elderly and was tested a significant number of times in comparison with other

Table 12–7 FUNCTIONAL STATUS QUESTIONNAIRE (FSQ): SOCIAL FUNCTIONING

Social/role function	During the past month have you:
Work performance (for those employed, during the preceding month)	Done as much work as others in similar jobs?* Worked for short periods of time or taken frequent rests because of your health? Worked your regular number of hours?* Done your job as carefully and accurately as others with similar jobs?* Worked at your usual job, but with some changes because of your health? Feared losing your job because of your health?
Responses: all of the time (1), most of the time (2), some of the time (3), none of the time (4).	
Social activity	Had difficulty visiting with relatives or friends? Had difficulty participating in community activities, such as religious services, social activities, or volunteer work? Had difficulty taking care of other people such as family members?
Responses: usually did with no difficulty (4), some difficulty (3), much difficulty (2), usually did not do because of health (1), usually did not do for other reasons (0).	
Quality of interaction	Isolated yourself from people around you? Acted affectionate toward others?* Acted irritable toward those around you? Made unreasonable demands on your family and friends? Gotten along well with other people?*
Responses: all of the time (1), most of the time (2), a good bit of the time (3), some of the time (4), a little of the time (5), none of the time (6).	

Single item questions

Which of the following statements best describes your work situation during the past month? *Responses:* working full-time; working part-time; unemployed, looking for work; unemployed because of my health; retired because of my health; retired for some other reason.

During the past month, how many days did illness or injury keep you in bed all or most of the day? *Response:* 0–31 days.

During the past month, how many days did you cut down on the things you usually do for one-half day or more because of your own illness or injury? *Response:* 0–31 days.

During the past month, how satisfied were you with your sexual relationships? *Responses:* very satisfied, satisfied, not sure, dissatisfied, very dissatisfied, did not have any sexual relationships.

How do you feel about your own health? *Responses:* very satisfied, satisfied, not sure, dissatisfied, very dissatisfied.

During the past month, about how often did you get together with friends or relatives, such as going out together, visiting in each other's homes, or talking on the telephone? *Responses:* every day, several times a week, about once a week, two or three times a month, about once a month, not at all.

*Scores are reversed. (From Jette et al,[43] with permission.)

Table 12–8 THE MULTILEVEL ASSESSMENT INSTRUMENT (MAI): INSTRUMENTAL ACTIVITIES OF DAILY LIVING (IADL)

Can you use the telephone
  without help ☐
  with some help ☐
  Are you completely unable to use the telephone? ☐
Can you get to places out of walking distance
  without help ☐
  with some help ☐
  Are you completely unable to travel unless special
    arrangements are made? ☐
Can you go shopping for groceries
  without help ☐
  with some help ☐
  Are you completely unable to do any shopping? ☐
Can you prepare your own meals
  without help ☐
  with some help ☐
  Are you completely unable to prepare any meals? ☐
Can you do your own housework
  without help ☐
  with some help ☐
  Are you completely unable to do any housework? ☐
Can you do your own handyman work
  without help ☐
  with some help ☐
  Are you completely unable to do any handyman work? ☐
Can you do your own laundry
  without help ☐
  with some help ☐
  Are you completely unable to do any laundry at all? ☐
If you had to take medicine, can you do it
  without help (in the right doses at the right time) ☐
  with some help (take medicine if someone prepares it for you
    and/or reminds you to take it) ☐
  Are you/would you be completely unable to take your own
    medicines? ☐
Can you manage your own money
  without help ☐
  with some help ☐
  Are you completely unable to handle money? ☐

Reprinted by permission of Powell Lawton, Ph.D.

instruments, it is extensively used, particularly for studies assessing psychologic well-being among the elderly.[47–53] All of its scales have been tested and may be used as modular assessment batteries either separately or together.

The MAI scales are currently available in long, middle, and short versions. The long forms of the scales have all been validated by comparison with clinicians' ratings. These versions of the MAI scales also have the highest reported test-retest correlations, ranging from 0.73 to 0.95. Intraclass correlations between interviewer and clinician administrations ranged from 0.58 to 0.88 on the various subscales. The full MAI administered by an interviewer takes approximately 50 minutes.

SUMMARY OF MULTIDIMENSIONAL FUNCTIONAL ASSESSMENT INSTRUMENTS

For the purposes of illustration, three multidimensional instruments have been presented. Choice of a multidimensional instrument carries the same caveats men-

tioned for instruments assessing physical function. No instrument assesses all potentially relevant items. Table 12–9 presents a comparison of items covered. In the physical function area, questions on the ability to ambulate and on mobility restrictions/confinement are the only items these instruments have in common. Aspects of physical function not covered in any of these instruments include bed activities and dexterity. The FSQ and the MAI include more BADL items than the SIP and also are more complete in the areas of social functions. The SIP and FSQ investigate occupational items, whereas the MAI does not. Finally, the SIP and MAI present a more complete assessment of affective functions than does the FSQ.

SUMMARY

This chapter has presented a conceptual framework for understanding health status and disability. The traditional medical model with its narrow focus on disease and its symptoms fails to consider the broader social, psychologic, and behavioral dimensions of illness. All these factors have impact on an individual's functional

Table 12–9 ITEMS COVERED IN SELECTED MULTIDIMENSIONAL FUNCTIONAL DISABILITY INSTRUMENTS

	SIP	FSQ	MAI
Signs	−	−	−
Symptoms	+	+	+
Physical function			
Bed activities	−	−	−
Transfers	−	−	+
Ambulation	+	+	+
Dexterity	−	−	−
Mobility restriction/ confinement	+	+	+
BADL			
Bathing	+	+	+
Grooming	−	−	+
Dressing	−	+	+
Feeding	−	+	+
Toileting	−	−	+
IADL			
Indoor home chores	+	+	+
Outdoor home chores/shopping	+	+	+
Community travel/drive car	+	+	+
Work/school	+	+	−
Affective function			
Anxiety	−	+	+
Depression	−	+	+
Emotional control	+	−	−
Self-esteem	−	−	+
Intellectual functioning	+	−	+
Communication	+	−	−
Sleep/rest	+	−	−
Vitality	−	−	+
Positive well-being	−	−	+
General health perceptions	−	+	+
Social function			
Interaction	+	+	+
Support/network	−	+	+
Activity/leisure	+	+	+

status. Functional assessment, therefore, must be viewed as a broad, multidimensional process. Four main categories of function have been delineated: physical, mental, affective, and social. Instrumentation has been presented that addresses the physical dimension, the area of assessment physical therapists are traditionally most involved with, as well as multiple dimensions. Finally, specific aspects of functional assessment have been discussed, including purpose, selection of instruments, aspects of test administration, interpretation of test results, and assessment of instrument quality.

QUESTIONS FOR REVIEW

1. How do functional status and functional assessment relate to health status?

2. Your rehabilitation facility has decided to use the Kenny Evaluation of Self-Care. How can reliability be ensured so that the results can be used with confidence in both treatment planning and research?

3. What criteria can be used in the selection of a functional instrument?

4. Discuss the uses, advantages, and disadvantages of performance-based assessments, interviewer assessments, and self-administered assessments.

5. Explain how environment and fatigue and other related issues affect a functional assessment. Suggest ways to control these factors in the clinic.

6. Identify the major types of scoring systems used in functional assessments. What are some common errors in interpretation of testing results?

7. Review Tables 12–2 through 12–9. Hypothesize a caseload in a rehabilitation facility and indicate how and when you could use each of these instruments with your proposed population. Describe the advantages and disadvantages of each.

8. Using one of the instruments, develop a set of results and use them to set treatment goals and to formulate a treatment plan.

9. For each of the following, identify particular physical tasks relevant to that individual's functional status.

    a. a 22-year-old female file clerk
    b. a 31-year-old male physical therapist
    c. a 39-year-old female homemaker with children
    d. a 45-year-old male construction worker
    e. a 56-year-old female school teacher
    f. a 65-year-old male journalist

10. Discuss the relationships among disease, impairment, disability, and handicap.

REFERENCES

1. Williams, T (ed): Rehabilitation in the Aging. Raven Press, New York, 1984.
2. Granger, C and Gresham, G (ed): Functional Assessment in Rehabilitation Medicine. Williams & Wilkins, Baltimore, 1984, p vii.
3. Duckworth, D: The need for a standard terminology and classification of disablement. In Granger, C and Gresham, G (ed): Functional Assessment in Rehabilitation Medicine. Williams & Wilkins, Baltimore, 1984.
4. World Health Organization (WHO): The First Ten Years of the World Health Organization. World Health Organization, Geneva, 1958.
5. Jette, A: Concepts of health and methodological issues in functional assessment. In Granger, C and Gresham G (ed): Functional Assessment in Rehabilitation Medicine. Williams & Wilkins, Baltimore, 1984.
6. World Health Organization (WHO): International Classification of Impairments, Disabilities, and Handicaps. World Health Organization, Geneva, 1980.
7. Nagi, S: Disability and Rehabilitation. Ohio State University Press, Columbus, OH, 1969.
8. Nagi, S: Some conceptual issues in disability and rehabilitation. In Sussman, M: Sociology and Rehabilitation. Ohio State University Press, Columbus, OH, 1965.
9. Wood, P: The language of disablement: A glossary relating to disease and its consequences. Int Rehab Med 2:86, 1980.
10. Wood, P and Badley, E: Setting disablement in perspective. Int Rehab Med 1:32, 1978.
11. Jette, A: State of the art in functional status assessment. In Rothstein, J (ed): Measurement in Physical Therapy. Churchill Livingstone, New York, 1985.
12. Granger, C: A conceptual model for functional assessment. In Granger, C and Gresham, G: Functional Assessment in Rehabilitation Medicine. Williams & Wilkins, Baltimore, 1984.
13. Liang, M, Cullen, K, and Larson, M: In search of a more perfect mousetrap (health status or quality of life instrument). J Rheum 9:775, 1982.
14. Kerlinger, F: Foundations of Behavioral Research, ed 3. Holt, Rinehart & Winston, New York, 1986.
15. Currier, D: Elements of Research in Physical Therapy. Williams & Wilkins, Baltimore, 1979.
16. Thorndike, R: Educational Measurement, ed 2. American Council on Education. Washington, DC, 1976.
17. Michels, E: Measurement in physical therapy: On the rules for assigning numerals to observations. Phys Ther 63:209, 1983.
18. Granger, C and Greer, D: Functional status measurement and medical rehabilitation outcomes. Arch Phys Med Rehabil 57:103, 1976.
19. Mahoney, F and Barthel, D: Functional evaluation: The Barthel index. Md State Med J 14:61, 1965.
20. Scott, J and Huskisson, E: Graphic representation of pain. Pain 2:175, 1976.
21. Revel, S, et al: The reliability of a linear analogue for evaluating pain. Anaesthesia 31:1191, 1976.
22. Hasselkus, B and Safrit, M: Measurement in occupational therapy. Am J Occup Ther 30:429, 1976.
23. Kaufert, J: Functional ability indices: Measurement problems in assessing their validity. Arch Phys Med Rehabil 64:260, 1983.
24. Granger, C, Albrecht, G, and Hamilton, B: Outcome of comprehensive medical rehabilitation: Measurement by Pulses profile and the Barthel index. Arch Phys Med Rehabil 60:145, 1979.
25. Schoening, H, et al: Numerical scoring of self-care status of patients. Arch Phys Med Rehabil 46:689, 1965.
26. Schoening, H and Iversen, I: Numerical scoring of self-care status: A study of the Kenny self-care evaluation. Arch Phys Med Rehabil 49:221, 1968.
27. Katz, S, et al: Studies of illness in the aged. The Index of ADL: A

standardized measure of biological and psychosocial function. JAMA 185:914, 1963.

28. Katz, S, et al: Progress in the development of the Index of ADL. Gerontologist 10:20, 1970.

29. Liang, M and Jette, A: Measuring functional ability in chronic arthritis. Arthritis Rheum 24:80, 1981.

30. Branch, L, et al: A prospective study of functional status among community elders. Am J Public Health 74:266, 1984.

31. Jette, A: Functional capacity evaluation: An empirical approach. Arch Phys Med Rehabil 61:85, 1980.

32. Jette, A: Functional Status Index: Reliability of a chronic disease evaluation instrument. Arch Phys Med Rehabil 61:395, 1980.

33. Shope, J, et al: Functional status outcome after treatment of rheumatoid arthritis. Clin Rheumatol Practice 1:242, 1983.

34. Harkon, T, et al: Therapeutic value of graded aerobic exercise training in rheumatoid arthritis. Arthritis Rheum 28:32, 1985.

35. Gilson, B, et al: The Sickness Impact Profile: Development of an outcome measure of health care. Am J Public Health 65:1304, 1975.

36. Bergner, M, et al: The Sickness Impact Profile: Validation of a health status measure. Med Care 14:57, 1976.

37. Pollard, W, et al: The Sickness Impact Profile: Reliability of a health status measure. Med Care 14:146, 1976.

38. Carter, W, et al: Validation of an interval scaling: The Sickness Impact Profile. Health Serv Res 11:516, 1976.

39. Bergner, M, et al: The Sickness Impact Profile: Development and final revision of a health status measure. Med Care 19:787, 1981.

40. Deyo, R, et al: Measuring functional outcomes in chronic disease: A comparison of traditional scales and a self-administered health status questionnaire in patients with rheumatoid arthritis. Med Care 21:180, 1983.

41. Deyo, R, et al: Physical and psychosocial function in rheumatoid arthritis. Clinical use of a self-administered health status instrument. Arch Intern Med 142:879, 1982.

42. MacKenzie, C, et al: Can the Sickness Impact Profile measure change: An example of scale assessment. J Chronic Dis 39:429, 1986.

43. Jette, A, et al: The functional status questionnaire: Reliability and validity when used in primary care. J Gen Int Med 1:143, 1986.

44. Calkins, D, et al: Functional status study: Initial results of a clinical trial. Clin Res 33:244A, 1985.

45. Lawton, M, et al: A research and service oriented multilevel assessment instrument. J Gerontol 37:91, 1982.

46. Lawton, M: Environment and other determinants of well-being in older people. Gerontologist 23:349, 1983.

47. Hinrichsen, G: The impact of age-concentrated, publicly assisted housing on older people's social and emotional well-being. J Gerontol 40:758, 1985.

48. Scheidt, R: A taxonomy of well-being for small-town elderly: A case for rural diversity. Gerontologist 24:84, 1984.

49. Ward, R, Sherman S, and LaGory, M: Informal networks and knowledge of services for older persons. J Gerontol 39:216, 1984.

50. Weinberger, M, et al: The effects of positive and negative life changes on the self-reported health status of elderly adults. J Gerontol 41:114, 1986.

51. Windley, P and Scheidt, R: Service utilization and activity participation among psychologically vulnerable and well elderly in rural small towns. Gerontologist 23:283, 1983.

52. Wolinsky, F, et al: Measurement of the global and functional dimensions of health status in the elderly. J Gerontol 39:88, 1984.

GLOSSARY

Activities of daily living (ADL): Activities necessary for daily self-care, personal maintenance, and independent community living.

Affective function: Affective skills and coping strategies needed to deal with everyday stresses as well as the more traumatic and difficult events each person encounters over the course of a lifetime; includes such factors as self-esteem, attitude toward body image, anxiety, depression, and the ability to cope with change.

Basic activities of daily living (BADL): Tasks concerned with daily self-care, such as feeding, dressing, hygiene, and physical mobility.

Checklist format: Assessment tool in which a description of various tasks is simply scored as completed or not completed.

Dependence: Requiring some level of human assistance.

Difficulty: Hybrid term that suggests that an activity poses an extra burden for an individual, regardless of dependence level.

Disease: Pathologic condition of the body that presents a group of characteristic signs and symptoms that sets the condition apart as abnormal.

Endurance: Energy consumption required to complete a functional task.

Functional activities: Activities identified by an individual as essential to support physical and psychologic well-being as well as to create a personal sense of meaningful living.

Functional disability: Inability of an individual to function normally as the result of impairment.

Functional status: Normal or characteristic performance of a task or role by an individual.

Gold standard: Accepted, accurate measure of a particular phenomenon that can serve as a verifying norm for other measures.

Handicap: Social disadvantage for a given individual resulting from an impairment or a disability that limits or prevents the fulfillment of a role or task that is considered normal (relative to age, sex, social, and cultural factors).

Health: State of complete physical, mental, and social well-being, and not merely the absence of disease and infirmity.

Illness: Forms of personal behavior that emerge as the reality of having a disease is internalized and experienced by an individual.

Impairments: Any loss or abnormality of anatomic, physiologic, or psychologic structure or function; the natural consequence of pathology or disease.

Instrumental activities of daily living (IADL): Advanced skills considered vital to an individual's independent living in the community, including managing personal affairs, cooking and shopping, home chores, and driving.

Interviewer assessment: Process in which the assessor interviews or questions a subject and records answers.

Mental function: Intellectual or cognitive abilities of an individual, including initiative, attention, concentration, memory, problem solving, and judgment.

Ordinal scale (or rank order): Classification scheme that rates observations in terms of the relationship between items (i.e., less than, equal to, or greater than).

Performance-based assessment: Assessment of a particular skill based on observation of an actual attempt, as opposed to acceptance of a self-report of skill level.

Physical function: Sensory-motor skills necessary for the performance of usual daily activities.

Physical signs: Directly observable or measurable changes in an individual's organs or systems as a result of pathology or disease.

Reliability: Degree to which an instrument can consistently measure the same parameter in multiple trials.

Self-administered assessment: Survey or series of questions so constructed that it can be answered directly by the respondent without additional input or direction.

Social function: Ability to interact successfully with others in the performance of social roles and obligations; includes social interactions, behaviors, and roles.

Subordinate part: Element of movement without which the task cannot proceed safely or efficiently.

Summary (or additive) scale: Approach to grading a specific series of skills by awarding points for part or full performance; totals the performance score as a percentage of 100 or as a fraction.

Symptoms: Subjective reactions to the changes experienced by an individual as a result of pathology or disease.

Validity: The degree to which data or results of a study are correct or true.

Visual (or linear) analog scale: Linear rating designed to capture a subject's judgment of his or her position on a continuum. A line is presented horizontally or vertically on paper, with the end points anchored with descriptive words representing the extremes of the parameter of interest.

Chapter 13

ENVIRONMENTAL ASSESSMENT

THOMAS J. SCHMITZ

OBJECTIVES

1. Describe the purposes of an environmental assessment.

2. Describe the activities involved in preparation for an on-site visit.

3. Identify the components of an environmental assessment.

4. Describe the significance of environmental accessibility for the differently abled individual.

5. Value the importance of an environmental assessment as an integral part of overall rehabilitation planning.

INTRODUCTION

A primary goal of rehabilitation is for the patient to return to a former environment and lifestyle. In order to achieve this goal, continuity of accessibility must exist among forms of transportation, building entrances, and building interiors. The value of any one of these components is diminished without access to the others. An accessible building is useless if suitable transportation to and from the facility is not available. With total accessibility as a goal, environmental assessments must address the multiple but individual requirements of each patient. These include the housing, social, recreational, educational, and employment needs of the patient.

The purposes of an environmental assessment are multiple and serve to

1. Assess the degree of safety, level of function, and comfort of the patient in the home, community, and work environment.

2. Make realistic recommendations to the patient, family, employer, and/or government agencies and third-party payers regarding environmental accessibility.

3. Assess the patient's need for additional adaptive equipment.

4. Assist in preparing the patient and family for discharge from the hospital and to help determine whether further services may be required (i.e., outpatient treatment, home health services, and so forth).

The environmental assessment may be done through either an on-site visit or an interview. The on-site visit is preferable because it allows assessment of performance in the actual environment in which the activities must be accomplished. On-site visits are often useful in reducing patient, family, and employer fear concerning the patient's ability to function independently. The on-site visit also provides an excellent opportunity for the therapist to make recommendations regarding altering, coping with, or adapting specific **environmental barriers.** Considering the time and costs involved with on-site visits, an on-site visit preceded by an interview is often the best way to assess the patient's environment.

Although the therapist may want to visit the patient's home and workplace, if applicable, an interview with the patient and family may be all that is needed to provide suggestions and guidelines for some aspects of the environmental assessment (e.g., general community access). Because it is usually not feasible for the therapist to

The author acknowledges the assistance of Douglas J. Westphal, M.S., P.T., in locating resource material for this chapter.

assess all aspects of the patient's total environment, family involvement is particularly important in assuring that the goal of maximum accessibility is met. Prior to the patient's discharge, the therapist should guide and encourage the family in an investigation of access to community recreational and educational facilities, the availability of public transportation, and the accessibility of local shopping facilities.

ON-SITE ASSESSMENT

Preparations for the On-Site Visit

During the patient's hospitalization, the family should be encouraged to make several visits to the physical and occupational therapy departments. These visits serve several functions. They provide the family an opportunity to become familiar with the patient's capabilities and limitations. They give the family time to learn safe methods of assisting with ambulation, transfers, exercise, and functional activities. During these visits the therapist also will have an opportunity to instruct the family in the use of adaptive equipment. The time spent in family education will facilitate the patient's transition from the hospital to the home and community. When realistic, weekend passes for the patient should be encouraged prior to the on-site assessment. During these visits problems not previously anticipated by the therapist or family may be uncovered. Emphasis can then be placed on solving these problems prior to actual discharge.

Preceding the on-site assessment, information should be gathered about several important areas that will influence both the preparation for and the types of suggestions made during the visit. This information should include

1. Knowledge of the family's interrelations (especially the family's attitude toward the patient and the extent of their desire to have the patient return home).

2. The family's attitude toward the hospital and staff (which may influence receptivity to suggested modifications to the home).

3. Knowledge of the projected prognosis for the patient's disability (e.g., whether the disability is static or progressive, and what long-term functional capabilities are expected).

4. General knowledge of the physical structure of the living space (house, apartment, number of levels, stairs, railings, and so forth).

5. Detailed information about the patient's present level of function as judged by all disciplines working with the patient (occupational therapy, physical therapy, speech, and so forth).

6. Information about the patient's insurance coverage and financial situation (in terms of capacity to modify environment).

7. Knowledge of the patient's future plans (gainful employment, school, vocational training, and so forth).

This information can be gathered from interviews with the patient, family conferences, medical records, social service interviews, and specific assessment procedures. Once this information is gathered, decisions can be made

concerning the amount of **adaptive equipment** required for the on-site visit, whether an assessment of the patient's work environment will be required, and the appropriate team members to accompany the patient on the visit.

Home Assessment

Ideally, the physical and occupational therapists should accompany the patient on the home visit. They assume shared responsibility for assessing the patient's functional level at home. Depending on the specific needs of the patient and/or family, a speech therapist, social worker, or nurse also may be included on the home visit. The visit should be broken into two components. The first portion should deal with accessibility of the dwelling's exterior, and the second half should be concerned with an assessment of the home's interior. A tape measure and home assessment form are valuable tools during the visit. Many rehabilitation departments develop their own home assessment forms to meet the particular needs of their patient population. The forms help organize the visit and are useful in directing attention to all necessary details. A variety of home assessment forms are available. A sample is provided in Appendix A. This form can be expanded or modified, depending on the specific needs of the individual or patient population.

One method of accomplishing the interior assessment is to begin with the patient in bed as though it were morning. Simulation of all daily activities, including dressing, grooming, bathroom activities, and preparation of meals can ensue. The patient should attempt to perform all transfer, exercise, ambulation, self-care, and homemaking activities as independently as possible to facilitate the assessment. This will provide an additional opportunity to teach the family how and when to assist the patient.

Upon arrival at the home for the on-site visit, the patient may need to rest for a short while before beginning the assessment. This is an important consideration, because many patients become very excited and/or emotional when returning home after a lengthy absence. This may be true even if previous passes were issued for weekend home visits.

The following considerations are offered as suggestions for home assessments. This list is neither exhaustive nor inclusive for every diagnosis. It is intended to direct attention to some of the most common concerns encountered during home visits.

EXTERIOR ACCESSIBILITY: GENERAL CONSIDERATIONS

1. It is important to note whether the house or apartment is owned or rented. The type and ownership of the home may preclude any modifications the patient or family may require.

2. The relative permanence of the dwelling should be considered. If the patient plans to move in the near

future, it will influence the type of modifications recommended (e.g., installing permanent ramps versus removable ones, or paving a gravel driveway).

EXTERIOR ACCESSIBILITY: SPECIFIC CONSIDERATIONS

Route of Entry

1. If there is more than one entry to the dwelling, the most accessible should be selected (closest to driveway, most level walking surface, least stairs, available handrails, and so forth).

2. Ideally, the driveway should be a smooth, level surface with easy access to the home. Walking surfaces to the entrance should be carefully assessed. Cracked and uneven surfaces should be repaired or an alternate route selected.

3. The entrance should be well lighted and provide adequate cover from adverse weather conditions.

4. The height, number, and condition of stairs should be noted. Ideally, steps should not be greater than 7 inches (17.5 cm) high with a depth of 11 inches (27.9 cm).[1] **Nosings,** or "lips," on the stairs are often problematic and should be removed or reduced, if possible. The steps also should have a nonslip surface.

5. Handrails should be installed, if needed. In general, the handrails should measure 32 inches (81.3 cm) in height, and at least one handrail should extend 18 inches (45.7 cm) beyond the foot and top of the stairs.[1] Modifications in height measurements will be required for particularly tall or short individuals.

6. If a ramp is to be installed, there should be adequate space. The recommended **grade** for wheelchair ramps is 12 inches in ramp length for every inch of threshold height.[2] Ramps should be a minimum of 48 inches (121.9 cm) wide with a nonslip surface.[3] Handrails also should be included on the ramp (32 inches [81.3 cm] in height) and extend 12 inches (30.5 cm) beyond the top and bottom of the ramp.[2]

Entrance

1. For wheelchair users, the entrance should have a platform large enough to allow the patient to rest and to prepare for entry. This platform area is particularly important when a ramp is in use. It provides for safe transit from the inclined surface to the level surface. If a wheelchair user is required to open a door that swings out, this area should be at least 5 feet × 5 feet (153 cm × 153 cm). If the door swings away from the patient, a space at least 3 feet (91.5 cm) deep and 5 feet (153 cm) wide is required.[1]

2. The door locks should be accessible to the patient. The height of the locks should be assessed as well as the amount of force required to turn the key. Alternative lock systems (e.g., voice- or card-activated or push buttons) may be an important consideration for some patients.

3. The door handle should be turned easily by the patient. Rubber doorknob covers or lever-type handles

(slip-on models are available) are often easier to use for patients with limited grip strength.

4. The door should open and close in a direction that is functional for the patient. A cane may be hung outside the door to help the wheelchair user close the door when leaving.

5. If there is a raised **threshold** in the doorway, it should be removed. If removal is not possible, the threshold should be lowered to no greater than ½ inch (1.27 cm) in height, with **beveled** edges.[1] If needed, weatherstripping the door will help prevent drafts.

6. The doorway width should be measured. Generally, 32 inches (81.3 cm)[2] to 34 inches (86.3 cm)[1] is an acceptable doorway width to accommodate most wheelchairs.

7. If the door is weighted to aid in closing, the pressure should not exceed 8 pounds in order to be functional for the patient.[1]

8. **Kick plates** may be added to doors subject to frequent use by wheelchair users or individuals using ambulatory assistive devices. The kick plate should measure 12 inches (30.5 cm) in height from the bottom of the door.[1]

INTERIOR ACCESSIBILITY: GENERAL CONSIDERATIONS

Furniture Arrangement

1. Sufficient room should be made available for maneuvering a wheelchair or ambulating with an assistive device.

2. Clear passage must be allowed from one room to the next.

3. Unrestricted access should be provided to electrical outlets, telephones and wall switches.

Floors

1. All floor coverings should be glued or tacked to the floor. This will prevent bunching or rippling under wheelchair use.

2. Scatter rugs should be removed.

3. Use of nonskid waxes should be encouraged.

Doors

1. Raised thresholds should be removed to provide a flush, level surface.

2. Doorways may need to be widened to allow clearance for a wheelchair or assistive device. In instances in which this is not possible, wheelchair users may benefit from a narrowing device attached directly to the chair. This allows the width of the chair to be temporarily reduced by turning a crank handle.

3. Doors may have to be removed, reversed, or replaced with curtains or folding doors.

4. As mentioned earlier in regard to exterior doors, handles should be assessed also inside the home. Rubber doorknob covers or lever-type handles may be important considerations. **Knurled** surface door handles are used on interiors of buildings and dwellings when frequented by

visually impaired persons. These abrasive, knurled surfaces indicate that the door leads to a hazardous area and alerts the individual to danger.

Stairs

1. All indoor stairwells should have handrails and should be well lighted (battery-operated wall lamps are a practical supplement to electrical light sources).

2. For patients with decreased visual acuity or age-related visual changes, contrasting textures on the surface of the top and bottom stair(s) will alert them that the end of the stairwell is near. Circular bands of tape also can be placed at the top and bottom of the handrail for the same purpose.

3. Many patients with visual impairment will benefit also from bright, contrasting color markers on the border of each stair.

Heating Units

1. All radiators, heating vents, and hot-water pipes should be appropriately screened off to prevent burns, especially for patients who have sensory impairments.

2. Adaptations may be required to allow patient access to heat controls (e.g., use of reachers or enlarged, extended, or adapted handles on heat-control valves).

INTERIOR ACCESSIBILITY: SPECIFIC CONSIDERATIONS

Bedroom Area

1. The bed should be stationary and positioned to provide ample space for transfers. Stability may be improved by placing the bed against a wall or in the corner of the room (except when the patient plans to make the bed). Additional stability may be achieved by placing rubber suction cups under each leg.

2. The height of the sleeping surface must be considered to facilitate transfer activities. The height of the bed may be raised by use of wooden blocks with routed depressions to hold each leg. The use of another mattress or box spring also will provide additional height to the bed. Blocks may be used to raise the height of chairs.

3. The mattress should be carefully assessed; it should provide a firm, comfortable surface. If the mattress is in relatively good condition, a bed board inserted between the mattress and box spring may suffice to improve the sleeping surface adequately. If the mattress is badly worn, a new one should be suggested.

4. A bedside table or cabinet might be suggested; it will be useful to hold a lamp, a telephone, necessary medications, and a call bell if assistance is needed.

5. The closet clothes bar may require lowering to provide accessibility. The bar should be lowered to 52 inches (132 cm) from the floor.[1] Wall hooks also may be a useful addition to the closet area and should be placed between 40 inches (101.6 cm) and 56 inches (142.2 cm) from the floor.[1] Shelves also can be installed at various levels in the closet (Fig. 13–1). The highest shelf should not exceed 45 inches (114.3 cm) in height.[1] Clothing and

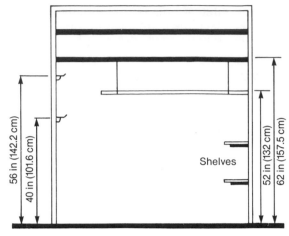

Figure 13–1. Closet modifications to provide accessibility for a wheelchair user. (From Cotler, SR, and De Graff, AH,[1] p 57. Used with permission.)

grooming articles frequently used by the patient should be placed in the most easily accessible bureau drawer.

6. A portable commode, urinal, or bedpan also may be an appropriate consideration.

Figure 13–2 illustrates the basic components and dimensions of a wheelchair-accessible bedroom.

Bathroom Area

1. If the door frame prohibits passage of a wheelchair, the patient may transfer at the door to a chair with **casters** attached. As mentioned earlier, another solution to this problem may be to order a wheelchair adaptor that allows the width of the chair to be adjusted.

2. An elevated toilet seat will facilitate transfer activities.

3. **Grab bars** (securely fastened to a reinforced wall) will assist in both toilet and tub transfers. Grab bars should be 1.5 inches (3.8 cm)[1,2] in diameter and be knurled. For use in toilet transfers, the bars should be mounted horizontally 33 inches (83.8 cm) to 36 inches (91.4 cm)[2] from the floor (Fig. 13–3). The length of the grab bars should be between 24 inches (61 cm) and 36 inches (91.4 cm) on the back wall and 42 inches (106.7 cm) on the side wall.[2] For use in tub transfers they should be mounted horizontally 24 inches (61 cm) high measured from the floor of the tub.[3]

4. A tub seat may be recommended for bathing. Many types of commercially produced tub seats are available. In selecting a tub seat, function and safety are primary considerations. The tub seat should provide a wide base of support with suction feet, a back rest, and a relatively long seating surface to facilitate transfers in and out of the tub (Fig. 13–4).

5. A bathmat or nonskid adhesive strips may be placed on the floor of the tub (these are easily attainable at most hardware stores).

6. Additional bathroom considerations may include handspray attachment to the bathtub faucet, a governor to regulate the hot-water temperature, enlarged faucet

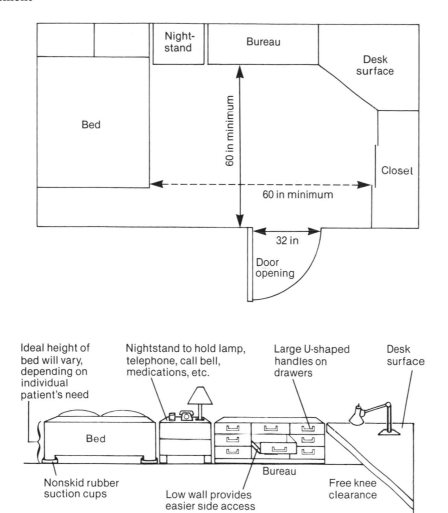

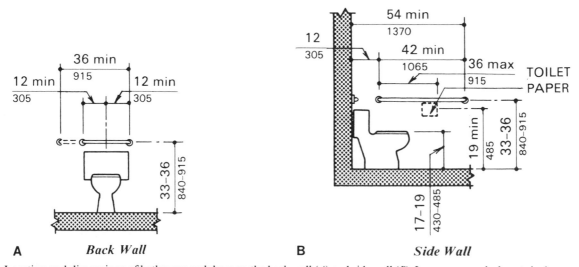

Figure 13–2. Sample dimensions and features of a bedroom area providing access for an individual using a wheelchair.

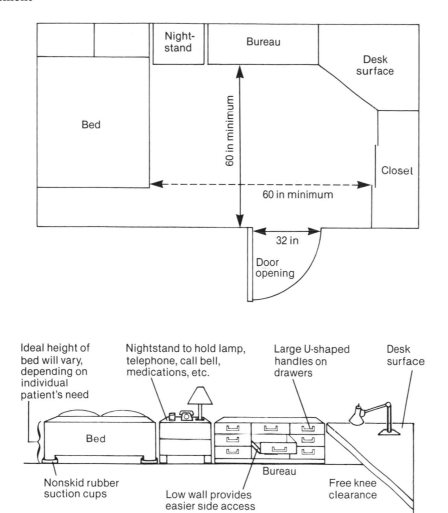

A   *Back Wall*   **B**   *Side Wall*

Figure 13–3. Location and dimensions of bathroom grab bars on the back wall (*A*) and side wall (*B*). Larger numerals denote inches, smaller numerals, millimeters. (From American National Standards Institute,[2] p 46, with permission.)

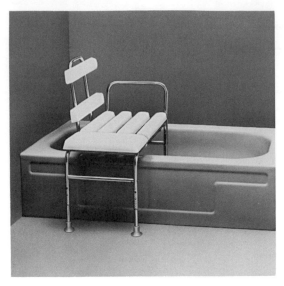

Figure 13–4. Shown here is a tub seat that provides a wide base of support with suction feet, a back rest, and a long seating surface to facilitate transfers. (Courtesy of Lumex, Inc., Bay Shore, NY.)

handles on the tub or sink, and a towel rack and toilet articles that are within easy reach of the patient.

7. An enlarged mirror over the sink also may be useful. A wall mirror with an adjustment hinge to tilt the top away from the wall facilitates use from a sitting position. Hinged-wall, gooseneck, or accordian fold-up mirrors (with one side magnified) are also helpful for close work.

8. Hot-water pipes under the sink should be insulated to avoid burns.

Figure 13–5 illustrates the basic components and minimum space requirements of an accessible bathroom.

Kitchen

1. The height of counter tops (work space) should be appropriate for the wheelchair user; the armrests should be able to fit under the working surface. The ideal height of counter surfaces should be no greater than 31 inches (79 cm) from the floor with a knee clearance of 27.5 inches (69.8 cm) to 30 inches (76.2 cm).[1] Counter space should provide a depth of at least 24 inches (61 cm).[1] All surfaces should be smooth to facilitate sliding of heavy items from one area to another. Slide-out counter spaces are useful in providing an over-the-lap working surface. For ambulatory patients, stools (preferably with back and foot rests) may be placed strategically at the main work area(s).

2. A small cart with casters may be suggested to improve ease of movement of articles from refrigerator to counter and other such activities.

3. The height of tables also should be checked and may have to be raised or lowered.

4. Equipment and food storage areas should be selected with optimum energy conservation in mind. All frequently used articles should be within easy reach, and unnecessary items should be eliminated. Additional storage space may be achieved by installation of open shelv-

ing or use of peg boards for pots and pans. If shelving is added, adjustable shelves are preferable and should be placed 16 inches (41 cm)[3] above the counter top.

5. Electric stoves are generally preferable to open-flame gas burners. Controls may require adaptation and should be located on the front border of the stove (to eliminate the need for reaching across the burners). Burners that are placed beside each other provide a safer arrangement than those placed one behind the other. A burn-proof counter surface adjacent to the burners will facilitate movement of hot items once cooking is completed. Smooth, ceramic cooktop surfaces also reduce the amount of lifting required while cooking. If cooktops provide knee clearance beneath, exposed or potential contact surfaces must be insulated.[2]

6. A split-level cooking unit is generally more easily accessible than a single, low-level combined oven-and-burner unit.

7. A counter-top microwave oven also may be an important consideration for some patients.

8. The sink may be equipped with large blade-type handles, and a spray-hose fixture often provides improved function. Shallow sinks 5 to 6 inches (12.7 cm to 15.2 cm)[1,3] in depth will improve knee clearance below. As in the bathroom, hot-water pipes under the kitchen sink should be insulated to prevent burns.

9. Dishwashers should be front loading, with pull-out shelves.

10. Access to the refrigerator will be enhanced by use of a side-by-side (refrigerator/freezer) model.

11. A smoke detector and one or more easily accessible, portable fire extinguishers should be available.

Figure 13–6 presents sample features of a kitchen designed for a wheelchair user.

Workplace Assessment

An investigation of the workplace is an important component of the environmental assessment. The most effective means of assessing the patient's work environment is an on-site visit. The specificity of the patient's job will dictate many of the types of functional activities that will be needed to perform the required tasks. When assessing level of function in the work environment, the principles of energy conservation are of prime importance in maximizing the worker's efficiency and comfort. Capabilities should be weighed against the physical demands of the work environment, and the therapist, using knowledge of adaptive equipment and ergonomics, may suggest changes appropriate to the situation.

Many of the assessments and adaptive strategies employed in the home will be used in the work environment as well. Several considerations specific to the work setting are described below.

1. A parking space should be available within a short distance of the building if the patient plans to drive to and from work. Parking spaces should be a minimum of 96 inches (243.8 cm) wide, with an adjacent access aisle 60 inches (152.4 cm) wide.[2] The location should be clearly marked as a handicapped parking area.

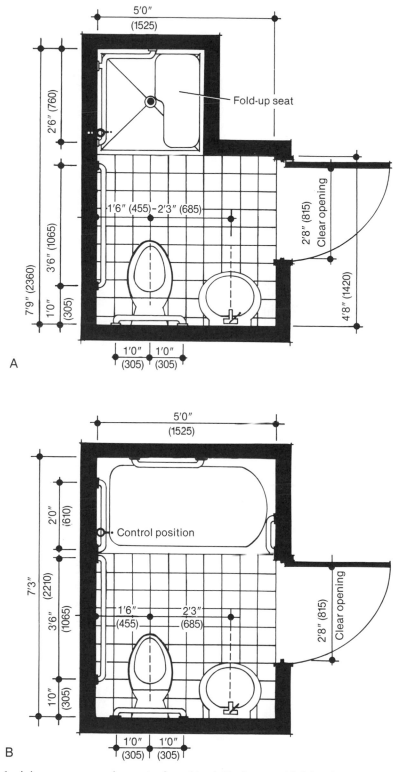

Figure 13–5. Sample features and minimum space requirements of a residential bathroom with (A) a shower stall and (B) a bathtub. The dotted line indicates lengths of wall that require reinforcement to receive grab bars or supports. (From Nixon, V: *Spinal Cord Injury: A Guide to Functional Outcomes in Physical Therapy Management.* Aspen Systems Corporation, Rockville, MD, 1985, p 186, with permission.)

2. External accessibility of the building should be addressed using guidelines similar to those presented for home exteriors.

3. The immediate work area should be carefully exam-

ined. This will include lighting, seating surface (if other than a wheelchair), and the height and size of the work counter (some patients may benefit from a variable-height or tilting work surface). Access to supplies or

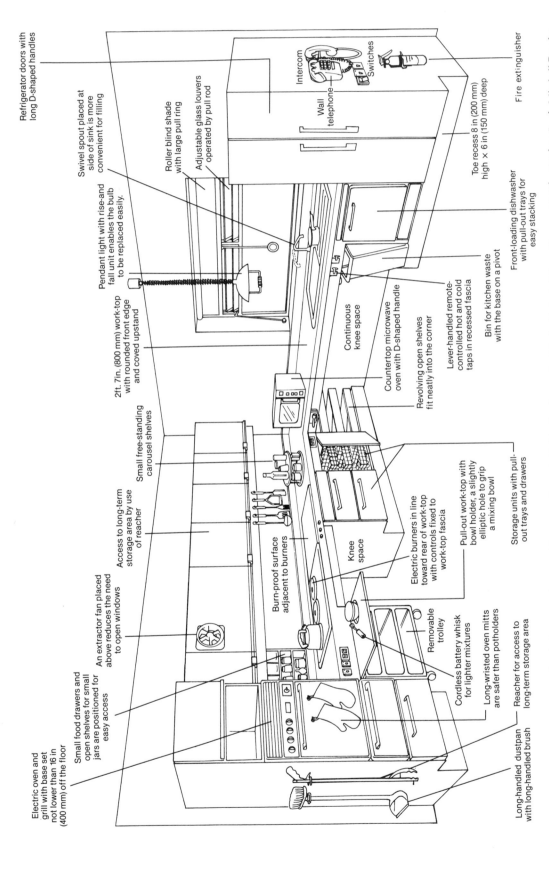

Figure 13–6. Sample features of a kitchen area that provides access for an individual using a wheelchair. (Adapted from Conran, T: *The Kitchen Book.* Mitchell Beazley, 1977, pp 118–119.)

Refrigerator doors with long D-shaped handles

Swivel spout placed at side of sink is more convenient for filling

Roller blind shade with large pull ring

Adjustable glass louvers operated by pull rod

Intercom

Wall telephone

Switches

Fire extinguisher

Pendant light with rise-and fall unit enables the bulb to be replaced easily.

Toe recess 8 in (200 mm) high × 6 in (150 mm) deep

Front-loading dishwasher with pull-out trays for easy stacking

2 ft. 7 in. (800 mm) work-top with rounded front edge and coved upstand

Continuous knee space

Countertop microwave oven with D-shaped handle

Revolving open shelves fit neatly into the corner

Lever-handled remote-controlled hot and cold taps in recessed fascia

Bin for kitchen waste with the base on a pivot

Small free-standing carousel shelves

Access to long-term storage area by use of reacher

An extractor fan placed above reduces the need to open windows

Small food drawers and open shelves for small jars are positioned for easy access

Electric oven and grill with base set not lower than 16 in (400 mm) off the floor

Burn-proof surface adjacent to burners

Knee space

Electric burners in line toward rear of work-top with controls fixed to work-top fascia

Pull-out work-top with bowl holder, a slightly elliptic hole to grip a mixing bowl

Storage units with pull-out trays and drawers

Removable trolley

Cordless battery whisk for lighter mixtures

Long-wristed oven mitts are safer than potholders

Reacher for access to long-term storage area

Long-handled dustpan with long-handled brush

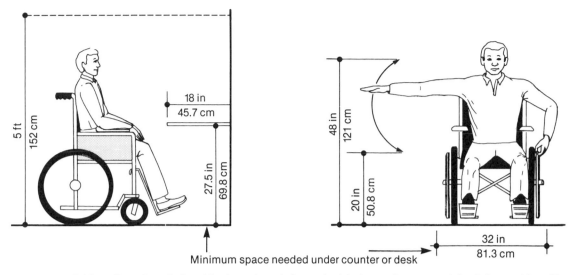

Figure 13–7. Maximum available unilateral vertical and horizontal reach for a wheelchair user from an upright sitting position. (From Cotler, SR, and De Graff, AH,[1] p 9, with permission.)

materials should be considered with respect to the patient's vertical and horizontal reaching capabilities. From an upright wheelchair sitting position, the vertical range (Fig. 13–7) of reach is from 20 inches (50.8 cm) to 48 inches (121.9 cm).[1] The maximum functional horizontal reach is considered 18 inches (45.7 cm) from the edge of a desk or work surface.[1] For patients with good trunk control, reaching capacity will be increased.

4. Access to public telephones, drinking fountains, and bathrooms should be addressed.

A variety of building survey forms have been developed to facilitate the on-site assessment of the workplace. These forms assist with attending to all necessary details during the visit. A sample of such a form is provided in Appendix B.

Community Assessment

To attain the goal of full accessibility for the patient, the availability of community resources, services, and facilities must be investigated. As mentioned earlier, when direct involvement by the therapist is not possible, this may best be accomplished by providing the family with guidelines for exploring access to local facilities. Another important consideration is to refer the patient and/or the family to community organizations such as the Arthritis Foundation, National Easter Seal Society, or the Veterans Administration. These groups can provide information on services available to disabled residents of the community. Individuals who are returning to school should be encouraged to contact the campus disabled student services office. Information will be offered on housing, disabled student services, and general campus resources.

Two important areas that warrant attention when investigating community resources are the availability of appropriate transportation and accessibility of area social, religious, educational, cultural, and shopping facilities.

TRANSPORTATION

Currently the availability of accessible public transportation varies considerably among geographic vicinities. As such, careful exploration by the patient and family will be needed to determine what resources are obtainable in specific locales. Some communities provide part-time service of partially or completely accessible buses. These include the so-called kneeling buses equipped with a hydraulic unit that lowers the entrance to curb level for easier boarding. Some buses, although fewer in number, are designed with hydraulic lifts to allow direct entry by a wheelchair user. In communities where these buses are available, they typically operate on specific time schedules and are frequently limited to highly trafficked routes. Careful planning is usually necessary to benefit from such service.

Unfortunately, the majority of public transportation systems in the United States do not allow use by non-ambulatory individuals or by those with limited ambulatory capacity. Most urban transit systems are virtually inaccessible to differently abled individuals. As an alternative, many areas provide door-to-door van transportation to disabled residents of the community. Again, availability of such services may be scarce in some locations.

Some patients will want to master driving an adapted automobile or van. This, of course, will improve opportunities for community travel significantly. Motor vehicle adaptations are selected based on the physical capabilities of the individual. Common adaptive equipment includes *hand controls* to operate the brakes and the accelerator; *steering wheel attachments,* such as knobs or universal cuffs, for individuals with limited grip strength; *lifting units* to assist with placement of the wheelchair into the vehicle; and, for patients with quadriplegia or high-level paraplegia, *self-contained lifting platforms* for entry to a van while remaining seated in a wheelchair.

For patients whose capacity for long-distance ambulation is limited and/or whose endurance is low, com-

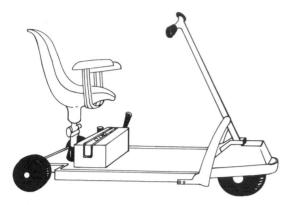

Figure 13–8. Motorized cart suitable for outdoor travel.

mercially available city-going electric carts (Fig. 13–8) may be a practical alternative for travel within reasonable proximity of the home.

ACCESS TO COMMUNITY FACILITIES

A few elements considered for workplace assessment warrant attention for general community access, as well. Briefly, these area facilities should be assessed for the availability of appropriate parking areas, beveled curbs, external and internal structural accessibility of buildings, availability of accessible public telephones, drinking fountains, bathrooms, and restaurants. Theaters, auditoriums, and lecture halls must be considered with respect to accessible seating areas. Locations of emergency exits also should be noted for all facilities. In addition to these general considerations, stores and shopping areas also should be inspected for access to merchandise (especially for wheelchair users), appropriate isle widths, and adequate space at checkout counters.

Another useful source of information on community access are the guidebooks offered by many larger cities. These books provide information on accessibility of hotels, restaurants, transportation, and cultural and recreational facilities.[4] These publications usually can be obtained from the city's chamber of commerce, the mayor's office for the handicapped, or the office of tourism. Combined use of such guides and phoning ahead for details of accessibility will facilitate travel both within and outside the local community.

Follow-up Report

Upon completion of the environmental assessment, a final combined report should be compiled. This report consists of information obtained from the home and, if applicable, the workplace assessment. Information should be included about the measures taken to explore general community accessibility.

Documentation of the on-site visit should incorporate a completed home assessment or building survey form. Additional information that should be provided includes:

1. A description of the methods used to assist the patient in ambulation or functional activities.

2. A description of the type and quantity of adaptive equipment required (including source and cost).

3. Suggested structural modifications with precise specifications.

4. Recommended changes in furniture arrangements, floor coverings, and so forth.

Documentation related to community access entails a verification that the patient is aware of available community resources. The sources of this information, as well as whether the therapist was directly or indirectly involved in assessment, should be documented.

The completed report should then be included as part of the patient's medical record. Copies of the report should be submitted to the patient's family, the physician, third-party payer(s), and any community-based health care or social service agencies that will be providing care upon discharge.

FUNDING FOR ENVIRONMENTAL MODIFICATIONS

The patient and family may require assistance in locating appropriate financial resources to achieve **environmental accessibility.** Typically, the social service department within the rehabilitation facility will provide direction in this area. Potential sources of funding include private insurance companies, Veterans Administration Housing Grants, the Division of Vocational Rehabilitation (DVR), and the Worker's Compensation Commission.

An important consideration is that not all patients will have current housing that is amenable to modification (e.g., an individual who previously lived in a third-floor walk-up apartment and is now a wheelchair user). In such instances, the local Housing and Urban Department (HUD) office will be an important resource. This office can provide a listing of already accessible housing within the community. Because there are often waiting lists for such dwellings, early application is warranted.

Finally, some "creative funding" for specific items (such as specialized adaptive equipment not covered by other resources) may be available through private organizations or foundations. Considerable time, research, and perseverance may be required in locating a receptive organization. General suggestions the patient and family might consider in seeking assistance include contacting local businesses or corporate-giving offices, civic or service clubs, churches or synagogues, labor unions, Jaycees, and the Knights of Columbus.[5]

LEGISLATIVE ACTION RELATED TO ENVIRONMENTAL ACCESS

In recent years much attention has been focused on the importance of environmental accessibility. Through legislation and a variety of private organizations, significant strides have been made in this area. The Architectural Barrier Act of 1968 (P.L. 90-480) provided that certain buildings that were financed by federal funds be designed and constructed "to insure that physically handicapped persons will have ready access to, and use of, such buildings [p 719]."[6] The Rehabilitation Act of 1973 provided that access must be established in all federally funded buildings and transportation facilities constructed since 1968.[7] Because many federally funded institutions provided low compliance with the 1973 Rehabilitation Act, an amendment was passed in 1978.[8] The Comprehensive Rehabilitation Services Amendments (P.L. 95-602) of 1978 strengthened the enforcement of the original 1973 Rehabilitation Act.[8] The Architectural and Transportation Barriers Compliance Board is the governing body responsible for enforcing this legislation.[4]

Another important item of legislation related to environmental accessibility is the Public Buildings Act of 1983, which functioned to establish public building policies for the federal government. This act (section 307) provided several amendments to the Architectural Barrier Act of 1968, which further strengthened and delineated the importance of accessibility. The term *fully accessible* in this act was defined as

> the absence or elimination of physical and communications barriers to the ingress, egress, movement within, and use of a building by handicapped persons and the incorporation of such equipment as is necessary to provide such ingress, egress, movement, and use and, in a building of historic, architectural, or cultural significance, the elimination of such barriers and the incorporation of such equipment in such a manner as to be compatible with the significant architectural features of the building to the maximum extent possible [p 373]."[9]

In response to recent legislation related to accessibility, several important publications have been developed to assist in the planning and/or modification of existing facilities.[1-3] These publications offer specifications for making facilities accessible to and usable by differently abled people.

Despite the recent gains made in architectural accessibility, many barriers continue to exist. Inasmuch as most public transportation systems were built before 1968, accessibility is not required by law.[4] Other areas that continue to be problematic include revolving doors, designs of many supermarkets and shopping areas (barrier imposed by checkout areas and items displayed on high shelves);[8] lack of available parking spaces; multiple levels of stairs at the entrance to some buildings; and the design of many theaters and auditoriums that do not have specifically designated areas for wheelchair users.[4]

Although increasing numbers of buildings are being designed to provide accessibility, this area warrants further involvement from therapists. Both physical and occupational therapists have important knowledge and skills to enable them to provide valuable input into the modification and/or initial planning of barrier-free designs.

SUMMARY

Information obtained from an environmental assessment is an important factor in facilitating the patient's transition from the rehabilitation setting to the home and community. Such assessments assist in determining the level of patient access, safety, and function within specific components of the environment. They also assist in determining the need for additional treatment interventions, environmental modifications, out-patient services, and adaptive equipment. Additionally, they assist in preparing the patient, family, and/or colleagues for the individual's return to a given setting.

This chapter has presented a sample approach to environmental assessment. Common environmental features that typically warrant consideration have been highlighted. Inasmuch as a return to a former environment is often a primary goal of rehabilitation, early consideration of these issues is warranted. Collaboration among team members, the patient, and family will ensure an optimum and highly individualized approach to community reintegration.

QUESTIONS FOR REVIEW

1. Identify the purposes of an environmental assessment.
2. What information should be obtained prior to an on-site visit? Identify possible sources of this information.
3. Who should be involved in the on-site visit?
4. Identify the components of a home assessment (i.e., what specific aspects of the dwelling's interior and exterior should be assessed?)
5. Explain the importance of an environmental assessment in overall rehabilitation planning.
6. Describe the information that should be included in the follow-up report once the environmental assessment is complete.

REFERENCES

1. Cotler, SR and DeGraff, AH: Architectural Accessibility for the Disabled of College Campuses. New York State University Construction Fund, 194 Washington Ave, Albany, NY 12210, 1976.
2. American National Standards Institute: American National Standard for Buildings and Facilities—Providing Accessibility and Usability for Physically Handicapped People. American National Standards Institute, 1430 Broadway, New York, NY 10018, 1986.
3. Building Design Requirements for the Physically Handicapped, rev ed. Eastern Paralyzed Veterans Association, 432 Park Avenue South, New York, NY 10016, undated.
4. Trombly, CA: Environmental Evaluation and Commuity Integration. In Trombly, CA (ed): Occupational Therapy for Physical Dysfunction, ed 2. Williams & Wilkins, Baltimore, 1983, p 493.
5. Corbet, B (ed): National Resource Directory: An Information Guide

for Persons with Spinal Cord Injury and Other Physical Disabilities. National Spinal Cord Injury Association, 149 California Street, Newton, MA, 02158, 1985.

6. Architectural Barriers Act, Public Law 90-480, 1968.

7. Silver, M: Federal compliance board under fire. Accent on Living 22(1):24, 1977.

8. Ross, EC: New rehabilitation law. Accent on Living 23(3):23, 1978.

9. Public Buildings Act, 98th Congress, 1st session, 1983.

SUPPLEMENTAL READINGS

Baum, CM: Nationally speaking: Independent living—a critical role for occupational therapy. Am J Occup Ther 34(12):773, 1980.

Bednar, MJ (ed): Barrier-Free Environments. Dowden, Hutchinson & Ross, Stroudsburg, PA, 1977.

Berube, B: Barrier-free design—making the environment accessible to the disabled. Can Med Assoc J 124(1):68, 1981.

Collings, GD: Barrier free access: Right or privilege. Phys Ther 56(9):1029, 1976.

Costa, FJ and Sweet, M: Barrier-free environments for older Americans. Gerontologist 16:404, 1976.

Francis, RA: The development of federal accessibility law. J Rehab 49(1):29, 1983.

Frieden, L: Independent living models. Rehabil Lit 41(7–8):169, 1980.

Green, I, et al: Housing for the Elderly: The Development and Design Process. Van Nostrand Reinhold, New York, 1975.

Laurie, G: Housing and Home Services for the Disabled: Guidelines and Experiences in Independent Living. Harper Row, New York, 1977.

Penton, J: Living with disability: Housing. Nurs Times (Suppl), 74(33):11, 1979.

Randall, M: Locating rehabilitation product information through ABLEDATA. Occupational Therapy in Health Care 1(4):47, 1984.

Raschko, BB: Housing Interiors for the Disabled and Elderly. Van Nostrand Reinhold, New York, 1982.

Rostron, J and Rostron, PM: Assessment techniques for rehousing or adaptations for severely physically disabled adults. Int J Nurs Stud 15(4):203, 1978.

Speidel, LK: Air transportation and the disabled: Current and future trends. Occupational Therapy in Health Care 1(4):55, 1984.

Taira, ED: An occupational therapist's perspective on environmental adaptations for the disabled elderly. Occupational Therapy in Health Care 1(4):25, 1984.

Wamboldt, JJ: Computer environmental control units for the severely physically disabled: A guide for the occupational therapist. Occupational Therapy in Health Care 1(4):155, 1984.

GLOSSARY

Adaptive equipment: Devices or equipment designed and fabricated to improve performance in activities of daily living.

Beveled: Smooth, slanted angle between two surfaces; for example, a slant or inclination between two uneven surfaces to allow easier passage of a wheelchair.

Casters: Small revolving wheels on the legs of a chair; such a chair may allow mobility in an area that is unable to accommodate a wheelchair; term also refers to the small front wheels of a wheelchair.

Environmental accessibility: Absence or removal of physical barriers from the entrance and within a building or dwelling to allow use by differently abled individuals.

Environmental barrier: Any component of a dwelling, structure, or vehicle that prevents use of the facility or service by a differently abled individual (e.g., revolving doors, stairways, narrow doorways).

Grab bars: Wall supports used to assist patient in both toilet and tub transfers; can be mounted vertically, horizontally, or diagonally.

Grade, gradient: Degree of inclination or slope of a ramp.

International symbol of access: Symbol widely used to indicate that a building and its facilities are accessible.

Kick plate: Metal guard plate attached to the bottom of a door.

Knurled surface: Roughened area, often in a criss-crossed pattern; used on either doorknobs or **grab bars.** On doorknobs it is used to provide tactile clues to visually impaired patients to indicate that passage leads to an area of danger. On grab bars it is used to improve grasp and to prevent slipping.

Nosing: Edge or brim of a step that projects out over the lower stair surface.

Threshold: Elevated surface on floor of doorway; a doorsill.

APPENDIX A HOME ASSESSMENT FORM

TYPE OF HOME

_____ Apartment.
         Is elevator available? _____
         What floor does patient live on?
         _____

_____ One floor home.
_____ Two or more floors.
_____ Does patient live on first floor, second floor, or use all floors of home?
_____ Basement. Does patient have or use basement area?

ENTRANCES TO BUILDING OR HOME

Location   Front Back Side (Circle one)
   Which entrance is used most frequently or easily?
   _____
   Can patient get to entrance? _____
Stairs
   Does patient manage outside stairs? _____
   Width of stairway _____
   Number of steps _____ Height of steps _____
   Railing present as you go up. R _____ L _____
   Both _____
   Is ramp available for wheelchair patient? _____
Door
   Can patient unlock, open, close, lock door? (Circle for yes)
   If doorsill is present, give height _____ and material
   _____
   Width of doorway _____
   Can patient enter _____ leave _____ via door?
Hallway
   Width of hallway _____
   Are any objects obstructing the way? _____

APPROACH TO APARTMENT OR LIVING AREA
(Omit if not applicable)
Hallway
   Width _____
   Obstructions? _____
Steps
   Does patient manage? _____
   Width of stairway _____
   Number of steps _____ Height of steps _____
   Railing present as you go up? R _____ L _____
     Both _____
   Is ramp available? _____
Door
   Can patient unlock, open, close, lock door? (Circle one)
   Doorsill? Give height _____ material _____
   Width of doorway _____
   Can patient enter _____ leave _____ via door?
Elevator
   Is elevator present? _____ Does it land flush with door? _____
   Width of door opening _____
   Height of control buttons _____
   Can patient manage elevator alone? _____

INSIDE HOME

Note width of hallways and of door entrances.
Note presence of doorsills and height.
Note if patient must climb stairs to reach room.

Can patient move from one part of the house to another?
   Hallways _____
   Bedroom _____
   Bathroom _____
   Kitchen _____
   Living room _____
   Others _____
Can patient move safely?
   Loose rugs _____
   Electrical cords _____
   Faulty floors _____
   Highly waxed floors _____
   Sharp-edged furniture _____
Note areas of particular danger for patient.
   Hot-water pipes _____
   Radiators _____

BEDROOM

   Is light switch accessible? _____
   Can patient open and close windows? _____
Bed
   Height _____ Width _____
   Both sides of bed accessible? _____ Headboard present? _____ footboard? _____
   Is bed on wheels? _____ Is it stable? _____
   Can patient transfer from wheelchair to bed? _____ and bed to wheelchair? _____
   Is night table within patient's reach from bed? _____ Is telephone on it? _____
Clothing
   Is patient's clothing located in bedroom? _____
   Can patient get clothes from dresser? _____ closet? _____ elsewhere? _____

BATHROOM

Does patient use wheelchair _____ walker _____ in bathroom?
Does wheelchair _____ walker _____ fit into bathroom?
Light switch accessible _____ Can patient open and close window? _____
What material are bathroom walls made of? _____
   If tile, how many inches does it extend from the floor beside the toilet? _____
How many inches from the top of the rim of the bathtub? _____
Does patient use toilet? _____
   Can patient transfer independently to and from toilet?
   _____
   Does wheelchair wheel directly to toilet for transfers?
   _____
   What is height of toilet seat from floor? _____
   Are there bars or sturdy supports near toilet? _____
   Is there room for grab bars? _____
Can patient use sink? _____ What is height of sink?
   _____
   Is patient able to reach and turn off faucets? _____

Is there knee space beneath sink? _____
Is patient able to reach necessary articles? _____
    mirror? _____ electrical outlet? _____
Bathing
Does patient take tub bath? _____ shower? _____
    sponge bath? _____
If uses tub, can patient safely transfer without
    assistance? _____
Bars or sturdy supports present beside tub? _____
Is equipment necessary? (tub seat, handspray attach-
    ment, tub rail, no-skid strips, grab rails, other
    _____)
Can patient manage faucets and drain plug? _____
Height of tub from floor to rim _____
Is tub built in _____ or on legs _____?
Width of tub from the inside _____
If uses separate shower stall, can patient transfer inde-
    pendently and manage faucets? _____
If patient takes sponge bath, describe method.

LIVING ROOM AREA

Light switch accessible? _____ Can patient open and
    close window? _____
Can furniture be rearranged to allow manipulation of
    wheelchair? _____
Can patient transfer from wheelchair to and from
    sturdy chair? _____ Height of chair _____
Can patient transfer from wheelchair to and from
    sofa? _____ Height of sofa _____
Can ambulatory patient transfer to and from chair?
    _____ sofa? _____
Can patient manage television and radio? _____

DINING ROOM

Light switch accessible? _____
Is patient able to use table? _____ Height of table
    _____

KITCHEN

What is the table height? _____ Can wheelchair fit
    under? _____
Can patient open refrigerator door and take food?
    _____
Can patient open freezer door and take food? _____
Sink
Can patient be seated at sink? _____
Can patient reach faucets? _____ Turn them on and
    off? _____
Can patient reach bottom of basin? _____
Shelves and cabinets
Can patient open and close? _____
Can patient reach dishes, pots, silver, and food?
    _____

Comments:

Transport
Can patient carry utensils from one part of kitchen to
    another? _____

Stove
Can patient reach and manipulate controls? _____
Light pilot on oven? _____
Manage oven door? _____
Place food in oven and remove? _____
Manage broiler door? _____
Put food in and remove? _____
Other Appliances
Can patient reach and turn on appliances? _____
Can patient use outlets? _____
Counter space: Is there enough for storage and work
    area?
    _____
    Diagram (include stove, refrigerator, sink, table,
        counters, others if applicable)

LAUNDRY

If patient has no facilities, how will laundry be managed?
Location of facilities in home or apartment and descrip-
    tion of facilities present:

Can patient reach laundry area? _____
Can patient use washing machine and dryer? _____
    Load and empty? _____
    Manage doors and controls? _____
Can patient use sink? _____
    What is height of sink? _____
    Able to reach and turn on faucets? _____
    Knee space beneath sink? _____
    Able to reach necessary articles? _____
Is laundry cart available? _____
Can patient hang clothing on line? _____
Ironing board
    Location:
        Is it kept open? _____
        If not kept open, can patient set up and take down
            ironing board? _____
    Can patient reach outlet? _____

CLEANING

Can patient remove mop, broom, vacuum, pail from
    storage? _____
Use equipment? (mop, broom, vacuum and so forth)
    _____

EMERGENCY

Location of telephone in house:

Could patient use fire escape or back door in a hurry if alone? _____
Does patient have neighbors', police, fire and physician's numbers? _____

OTHER

Will patient be responsible for child care? _____

If so, give number of children _____ and ages: _____

Will patient do own shopping? _____
    Is family member or friend available? _____
    Is delivery service available? _____
Does family have automobile? _____
Is family member or friend available to help with lawn care, change high light bulb, and so forth? _____

APPENDIX B BUILDING SURVEY FORM

Name of building: _____ Date of survey: _____
Location: _____ Surveyor: _____

	Yes	No
PARKING AREA		
1. Are handicapped parking spaces with adequate wheelchair transfer space designated?	___	___
2. Are curb cutouts available and appropriately labeled?	___	___
3. Are parking spaces easily accessible to walkway without requiring negotiating behind parked cars?	___	___
4. Indicate number of available handicapped parking spaces. _____		

ENTRANCES TO BUILDING

1. Is at least one major entrance available for use by the handicapped?   ___ ___
2. Does the entrance provide access to a level where elevators are available?   ___ ___

ELEVATORS

1. Is a passenger elevator available?   ___ ___
2. Does the elevator reach all levels of the building?   ___ ___
3. Are control buttons (both inside and outside of the elevator) no more than 48 inches (122 cm) from the floor?   ___ ___
4. Are control buttons raised and easy to push?   ___ ___
5. Is an emergency telephone accessible?   ___ ___

PUBLIC TELEPHONES

1. Are an appropriate number of phones available and accessible to handicapped individuals?   ___ ___
2. Are they dial or pushbutton? _____
3. Is the height of the dial mechanism no more than 44 inches (112 cm) from the floor?   ___ ___
4. Is a receiver volume control available?   ___ ___

FLOOR SURFACES

1. Are surfaces nonslip?   ___ ___
2. If carpeting is present, is it tightly woven and securely glued to floor (to prevent rippling under wheelchair)?   ___ ___

REST ROOMS

1. Is there an adequate number of rest rooms available and accessible to the handicapped?   ___ ___
2. Is there at least 48 inches (122 cm) between inside wall and partitions enclosing toilet?   ___ ___
3. Is entrance to cubicle at least 48 inches (122 cm) wide?   ___ ___
4. Are grab bars present and securely mounted?   ___ ___
5. Is height of seat not more than 17.5 inches (44.5 cm)?   ___ ___
6. Is toilet paper holder within easy reach?   ___ ___
7. Is adequate turning space (6 ft × 6 ft [183 cm × 183 cm]) available in main area of rest room?   ___ ___
8. Is there adequate space for clearance of knees under sink?   ___ ___
9. Are drain and hot-water pipes covered or shielded to avoid burns?   ___ ___
10. Are faucet handles large (blade type) and accessible?   ___ ___

WATER FOUNTAINS

1. Is the fountain height appropriate for use by someone in a wheelchair?   ___ ___
2. Are controls push button or blade type? _____
3. Is a foot control available?   ___ ___
4. Is adequate space (at least 3 ft [92 cm]) provided near fountain to permit wheelchair mobility?   ___ ___

(From Cotler, SR, and DeGraff, AH: *Architectural Accessibility for the Disabled of College Campuses.* New York State University Construction Fund, Albany, New York, 1976.)

Chapter 14

STRATEGIES TO IMPROVE MOTOR CONTROL

SUSAN B. O'SULLIVAN

OBJECTIVES

1. Briefly describe a conceptual model of motor behavior, defining the contributions of each of the following mechanisms to movement: sensation, attention, arousal, perception, decision making, and movement control.

2. Identify the major theories of recovery of function following lesions to the central nervous system.

3. Briefly describe a conceptual model of motor learning.

4. Compare and contrast the three phases of motor learning: cognitive, associative, and autonomous.

5. Briefly describe a conceptual model of motor development, including
   a. major sequences of motor development
   b. characteristics of development in four major stages: mobility, stability, controlled mobility, and skill.

6. Formulate a clinical decision-making model that incorporates planning based on motor behavior, motor learning, and motor development processes.

7. Identify appropriate treatment strategies for patients with deficits in motor control.

INTRODUCTION

Developing strategies designed to improve motor control requires a thorough understanding of motor behavior, motor learning, and motor development processes. A conceptual model that ties these three areas together provides a useful framework for planning and allows the therapist to approach clinical problem solving in a more systematic manner. Patients frequently demonstrate motor control deficits in more than one area of function. Careful, ongoing assessment of motor behaviors and the environmental situations in which they occur provides an appropriate base for initiating therapeutic intervention. Many of these assessment procedures are discussed in preceding chapters. In physical therapy, a number of different treatment approaches and techniques have been developed to address a multiplicity of motor control problems. Use of a clinical decision-making model based upon normal function allows the blending of therapeutic approaches and the development of an optimal treatment plan designed to meet the individual needs of the patient.[1-3]

A CONCEPTUAL MODEL OF MOTOR BEHAVIOR

Motor behavior is the complex interaction of many body parts, which involves the processing of sensory information, integration, and decision making by neural control centers, and execution of appropriate motor responses. Sensory input is received by sensory receptors and transmitted to appropriate centers in the central nervous system (CNS) where it is interpreted and translated into an appropriate motor program. The motor program is then executed, selected muscles are engaged, and movement is initiated. The execution is guided by feedback processes. An example of a model of neural behavior is presented in Figure 14–1. Successful motor performance depends upon intact functioning of each of the component parts.[4–7]

Sensory Processes

Several general concepts are important to an understanding of sensory processing. First, the various types of sensory receptors demonstrate differential sensitivity. Each receptor is highly sensitive to one type of stimulus but is relatively insensitive to other stimuli at normal intensities. Use of appropriate intensities of sensory stimulation ensures that only the desired receptors are stimulated. Excess stimulation can activate unwanted sensory receptors and produce undesired responses, including generalized arousal or sympathetic fight-or-flight reactions. Another special characteristic of sensory receptors is their adaptation to stimuli over time. Generally, they can be divided into two categories, slow receptors and rapidly adapting receptors. In treatment, fast-adapting, or phasic, receptors such as touch receptors are generally more effective in initiating movement sequences; slow-adapting, tonic, receptors—such as joint receptors, golgi tendon organs, and muscle spindles—are more effective in monitoring movement responses. Sensory information is transmitted to the CNS over different types of nerve fibers. Type A fibers are large-diameter, myelinated fibers that conduct at an extremely rapid rate. Type C fibers have smaller diameters, are unmyelinated, and conduct at slower velocities. Rapidly conducted information such as the proprioceptive signals carried in some type A fibers provides an appropriate base for motor control training. Certain body segments such as the face, palms of the hands, and soles of the feet demonstrate both high concentrations of tactile receptors and increased representation in the sensory cortex. These areas are highly responsive to stimulation and are closely linked to both protective and exploratory functions.[6,8]

Sensory Stimulation Techniques

Sensory stimulation techniques can be used to facilitate, to activate, or to inhibit movement responses. The

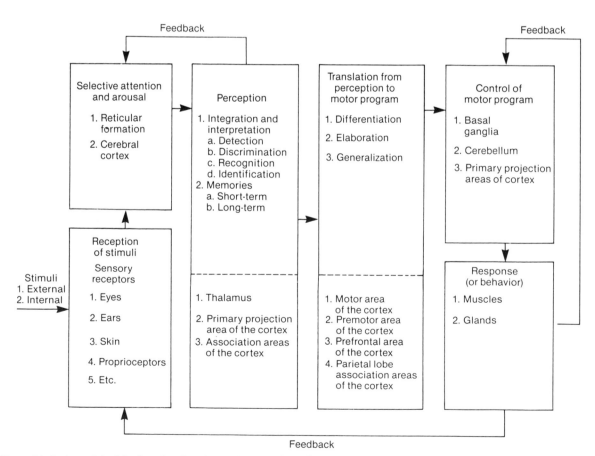

Figure 14–1. A model of the functional and neural mechanisms for motor behaviors. (From Sage, G.[4] p 189, with permission.)

distinction here is important. **Facilitation** refers to the enhanced capacity to initiate a movement response through increased neuronal activity and altered synaptic potential. An applied stimulus may lower the synaptic threshold but may not be of sufficient amount to produce an observable movement response. **Activation** refers to the actual production of a movement response and implies reaching a critical threshold level for neuronal firing. **Inhibition** refers to the decreased capacity to initiate a movement response through altered synaptic potential. The synaptic threshold is raised, making it more difficult for the neuron to fire and to produce movement.

Movements produced as a result of sensory stimulation are reflex in nature and cannot be considered representative of normal motor control. Rather, they serve as a bridge between absent or disordered control and normal control. Several general guidelines are important. First, sensory stimulation techniques can be additive. That is, several inputs applied simultaneously—such as **quick stretch, resistance,** and verbal commands, which are commonly combined in proprioceptive neuromuscular facilitation (PNF)—may produce the desired motor response, whereas use of a single stimulus may not. This demonstrates properties of **spatial summation** within the CNS. Repeated application of the same stimulus (e.g., repeated quick stretches) also may produce the desired motor response, whereas a single stimulus does not, representing properties of **temporal summation** within the CNS. Once a desired motor response is obtained, repeated active movement will serve to reinforce and to strengthen the response. Sensory stimulation should be withdrawn gradually until the patient can perform the activity completely without it. Repeated use of sensory stimulation long after it is necessary can result in movements that become stimulus dependent. This further limits the patient's ability to move independently and to regain normal control.

The application of a given sensory stimulation technique does not always produce the predicted response. The response to stimulation is unique to each patient and dependent upon a number of different factors, including level of intactness and general state of the CNS, and the specific level of activity of the motoneurons in question.[9,10] For example, a depressed, hypoactive patient may require large amounts of stimulation to achieve the desired response, but a hyperactive patient may require very little, if any, stimulation to generate a movement response. The intensity, duration, and frequency of stimulation need to be adjusted to meet the individual needs of the patient. Unpredicted responses also can be the result of poorly applied or incorrect techniques. For example, an inadequate vibrator that produces a low-frequency vibratory discharge (5 to 50 Hz) stimulates low-frequency receptors in the skin and can cause a withdrawal response. The normal high-frequency stimulus produces selective activation of spindle primary endings and reflex contraction of the muscle vibrated.

Very little controlled research is available to guide the therapist in the application of sensory stimulation techniques. Therefore it is critical that keen observational skills and good judgment be applied to each clinical situation. Initial selection of stimuli should be based upon a careful assessment of the patient and the environment. The selection and application of a specific stimulus requires an accurate knowledge of neurophysiologic mechanisms and predicted responses. Careful observation during application can be compared with the therapist's knowledge of expected responses. If the responses are not as expected, adjustment in either stimulus intensity, duration, or frequency may be necessary to improve the response. If no response is obtained or if the opposite of what is expected emerges, continued stimulation is generally not indicated. Stockmeyer[11] points out that absent or paradoxic effects may represent unstable baseline function and homeostatic instability of somatic and autonomic functions. In the presence of these alterations of function, continued sensory stimulation serves only to increase the disorganization of the CNS.

Sensory stimulation techniques can be grouped according to the sensory system and the receptors that are activated preferentially during application of the stimuli. Thus techniques are commonly classified as primarily proprioceptive, exteroceptive, vestibular, or special (affecting the special senses of vision, hearing, or smell). A few techniques provide combined inputs and therefore fall into more than one area. Techniques also have been classified according to the nature of the response. Margaret Rood,[12] a pioneer in the use of sensory stimulation techniques, grouped stimuli as either phasic or tonic and closely linked them to the type of motor pattern, mobility or stability, that was sought in treatment.

PROPRIOCEPTIVE STIMULATION TECHNIQUES

Proprioceptive stimulation techniques act through muscle or joint proprioceptors to alter movement responses. Table 14–1 provides a summary of the proprioceptive stimulation techniques discussed in this section.

Quick Stretch

Quick stretch facilitates muscle contraction and acts primarily through the muscle spindle primary endings (IA). These endings are sensitive to both length and velocity changes in muscle and produce reflex facilitation of the muscle being stretched (agonist muscle) and its synergists while providing inhibition to antagonists. Specific therapeutic techniques include tapping directly over the muscle belly or tendon and applying a light, quick stretch to a muscle, optimally applied in the lengthened range. These techniques produce a relatively short-lived contraction and can be enhanced by the application of resistance.

Resistance

Resistance, or maintained stretch, serves to recruit both alpha and gamma mononeurons and thus enhances both intrafusal and extrafusal muscle contraction. Contraction without resistance can result in unloading of the muscle spindle and decreased facilitation of movement from the stretch reflexes. This is particularly true as the

Table 14-1 PROPRIOCEPTIVE STIMULATION TECHNIQUES

Stimulus	Response	Consideration
Quick Stretch		
Activates Muscle spindles: 　IA endings (rate or change in length) Input to higher centers (cerebellum, parietal cortex) *Techniques* Quick stretch, tapping: muscle belly or tendon	Monosynaptic facilitation of agonist Polysynaptic facilitation of synergists, inhibition of antagonist	Low threshold response Relatively short-lived contraction: the addition of resistance perpetuates contraction Applied in lengthened range: initiates contraction IA effects are similar in flexors and extensors Adverse effects in hypertonia; augments spasticity
Prolonged Stretch		
Activates Muscle spindles: IA + II endings (length), golgi tendon organs (Ib), joint receptors Input to higher centers *Techniques* Slowly applied, maintained stretch, particularly in lengthened ranges Splinting, casting, weight-bearing positions Reflex-inhibiting patterns (NDT) gravity/position	Inhibition or dampening of muscle response; dampens contraction, dampens muscle tone IA response: monsynaptic facilitation of agonist II response: polysynaptic facilitation of specific muscles, depending on muscle of origin Ib response: inhibition of agonist, facilitation of antagonist	Higher threshold response Response may be dependent upon type of muscle: flexor or extensor Extensor: tonic muscles may be more responsive to inhibitory effects owing to possible II inhibition; increased GTOs Flexor: phasic muscles may be initially facilitated, with sustained stretch more inhibitory
Resistance/Maintained Stretch		
Activates Muscle spindles (IA + II), GTOs (Ib) Recruits both alpha and gamma motoneurons *Techniques* Manual Gravity, body weight Mechanical	Facilitates intrafusal and extrafusal contraction; response proportional to magnitude of resistance Enhances stretch sensitivity (increased fusimotor drive) of muscle to any type of stretch Hypertrophies extrafusal muscle fibers Enhances kinesthetic awareness	Facilitation effects more pronounced with isometric and eccentric contractions May be inhibitory to hypotonic postural muscles (lacking in stretch sensitivity) With maximal resistance 　Irradiation to ipsilateral or contralateral muscle groups may occur (overflow effects) 　Overflow may be detrimental in hypertonia Slow, maintained contraction optimal for physiologic extensors
High-Frequency Vibration		
50 or 100-300 Hz Low amplitude (1-2 mm) *Activates* Muscle spindles: IA fibers; (II's + Ib's are poor vibration receptors) TVR is supported by higher centers—reverberating polysynaptic pathways Also activates Pacinian corpuscles in skin, subcutaneous tissues, bone, teeth, fluid chambers, soft tissue membranes *Technique* Electric vibrators (battery-driven vibrators may provide ineffective stimulus)	Tonic vibration reflex (TVR) Autogenic facilitation of agonist with reciprocal inhibition of antagonist. Ia endings fire at frequency of vibration (nonadapting); response is similar to repeated quick stretches Inhibition or dampening of monosynaptic stretch reflexes owing to presynaptic inhibition at AHC Light vibration to skin can suppress other cutaneous sensations (tactile hypersensitivity, pain)	The higher the frequency of vibrator, the stronger the response Firm, gentle pressure optimal Duration: short, repeated periods 10–15 sec on/off optimal; (peaks 30–60 sec) ***Response is enhanced with*** 1. Active contraction: isometric or isotonic 2. Placing muscle in lengthened range 3. Position: reflex support 4. Certain drugs (stimulants) 5. Resistance (prolongs response) 6. Vibrating at myotendinous junction 7. Slight cooling enhances TVR, cold dampens TVR ***Precautions*** 1. Heat or friction effects (burning, itching) with continual vibration in one spot 2. Vibration to bone may cause irradiation to other muscles 3. Individual variability among normal subjects (mood) 4. May be contraindicated in very young children (immature CNS); hypertonicity, tremor, UMN lesions

Table 14–1 *continued.*

Stimulus	Response	Consideration
Low-Frequency Vibration (5 to 50 Hz) *Activates* Receptors in skin, low threshold IIs, Ibs *Technique* Electric vibrators	**Response** Flutter response May cause alarming effects: vertigo, nausea, and protective withdrawal Inhibition of muscle vibrated	1. Weak battery-powered vibrators; excessive pressure decreases Hz vibration effectiveness
Approximation (telescoping) *Activates* Joint receptors (static, type I) *Techniques* Joint compression applied in weight-bearing postures Manually applied compression Weight belts or cuffs	Facilitates postural extensors Enhanced joint awareness	Apply in range of function: mid to shortened ranges Contraindicated in inflamed joints
Traction *Activates* Joint receptors (phasic, Type II) *Techniques* Manual traction to joint surfaces Frequently combined with stretch of adjacent muscles	Facilitates agonists; enhances movement Enhanced joint awareness	Useful to initiate flexor patterns Slow, sustained traction to painful joints often relieves muscle spasm and pain; i.e., joint mobilization
Inhibitory Pressure *Activates* Tactile receptors (group II cutaneous afferents); may also activate spindle afferents (IA & II) and GTOs (Ib) *Techniques* Firm, constant pressure, especially to long tendons Positioning at extreme of range may enhance response Use of mechanical devices: Firm object in hand—cones; splints	Inhibition (dampens muscle tone)	Weight-bearing postures may provide inhibition; i.e., quadruped position inhibitory to quadriceps, long finger flexors Hypotonic muscles may be further inhibited in weight-bearing postures

movement progresses into the shortened ranges during concentric contractions. Isometric contractions, however, demonstrate less muscle spindle stretch lag and unloading effects and are more responsive to resistance. Recruitment is directly proportional to the amount of resistance applied. Thus slight resistance results in a small number of motor units firing, and maximum resistance results in a large number of motor units firing. Resistance also improves motor control by enhancing kinesthetic awareness and increasing strength. If applied in excess to hypertonic muscles, resistance can produce detrimental effects, including increased tone and synergistic activity. Therefore it should be applied with caution and can be contraindicated in some patients. Therapeutically, resistance can be applied manually, mechanically, or through the effective use of gravity and body weight.

Prolonged Stretch

Firm, **prolonged stretch** generally produces inhibition or dampening of muscle responses. This type of stimulus is thought to activate golgi tendon organs and joint receptors, resulting in autogenic inhibition of the muscle being stretched. Spindle secondary endings also may be activated inasmuch as they are more sensitive to absolute length changes and operate at a higher threshold than the primary endings. The reflex action of these endings is less clearly understood. Although previously thought to facilitate flexors and to inhibit extensors, their action is now thought to be more diverse. These endings also can provide autogenic facilitation of either extensor or flexor muscles, depending upon the activity of spinal interneurons. Thus their reflex action is variable and can be switched by the CNS.[13,14] Activation of secondary endings in their inhibitory extensor mode may explain why in some cases prolonged stretch is more effective in inhibiting extensor muscles than flexor muscles. Therapeutically, prolonged stretch can be applied manually, mechanically, or through the use of gravity and position. Inhibitory splinting or casting techniques and the **reflex-inhibiting patterns** used in Bobath's neurodevelopmental treatment (NDT) approach use these natural inhibitory mechanisms to gain new range and movement.[15,16] To optimize treatment effectiveness, application in the lengthened range is desired.

Inhibitory Pressure

Firm, moderate **inhibitory pressure** applied to the tendon of muscle results in inhibition of muscle tone. The response is relatively short lived, with adaption to a sustained stimulus occurring fairly quickly.[17] Several types of tactile receptors normally detect touch and pressure and provide activation of A-beta (group II) cutaneous afferents. Deep pressure also may activate muscle spindle afferents (Ia and II) and golgi tendon organs (Ib). Inhibitory pressure can be applied manually or through positioning and adaptive devices such as cones or splints. Postures such as a kneeling or a quadruped position can be used to provide inhibition to the quadriceps muscle and thus can be used to dampen tone in spasticity. Sitting with extended arm support or quadruped with the hand open and flat provides inhibitory input to the long finger flexors of the hand. Pressure inhibition techniques are incorporated into many therapeutic procedures including NDT reflex-inhibiting patterns.

Vibration

Muscle spindle primary endings (Ia) are highly sensitive to **vibration.** The high-frequency stimulus arises from an electrically driven vibrator that optimally operates at a frequency of 100–200 Hz and an amplitude of 1 to 2 mm. The response to vibration, known as the *tonic vibration reflex* (TVR), is sustained contraction of the vibrated muscle. Phasic stretch reflexes are also inhibited. The TVR is mediated through both spinal and suprasegmental pathways and is supported by higher centers. It represents a more complex response than the phasic stretch reflex discussed previously. Vibration effects peak within 30 seconds and last as long as the stimulus is applied. Vibration also can facilitate muscle responses for a brief time after the stimulus is removed through mechanisms of synaptic posttetanic potentiation.[18]

Clinically, vibration can be applied to hypotonic muscles to enhance contraction. Because the response is maintained, vibration is an ideal stimulus to apply to weak postural muscles whose primary function is one of **tonic holding.** Vibration also can be used to inhibit muscles when applied to the antagonist muscles through mechanisms of normal reciprocal innervation. Certain factors enhance vibration, including applying the stimulus on the tendon or myotendinous junction, on a lengthened muscle, or on a muscle that is voluntarily contracting, resisted, or in a reflex supported position. Slight cooling or chemical stimulants also enhance vibration, and cold and depressants dampen the TVR. Several precautions also should be noted. Use of a weak, battery-operated vibrator or too much pressure can result in a low-frequency stimulus (5 to 50 Hz). This type of stimulus may activate spindle secondary endings and golgi tendon organs and may thus have an inhibitory effect on muscles. Low-frequency vibration also can produce an alarming reaction, resulting in a protective or withdrawal response. Vibrators held in one area too long can cause friction and heating effects. The recommended duration is 1 to 2 minutes. Vibration to bone may be uncomfortable and can irradiate to other muscles, often producing an undesired facilitation of those muscles. Vibration can enhance abnormal movement patterns and hypertonicity and is generally contraindicated in neurologic conditions with spasticity, tremor, ataxia, and seizures. It is also contraindicated in the very young child with an immature CNS.[18–21]

Pacinian corpuscles are also velocity sensitive and highly responsive to a high-frequency vibratory stimulus. Vibration applied lightly to the skin therefore activates these tactile receptors. Repetitive stimulation over a large skin area can be used clinically to suppress other cutaneous sensations. Some forms of tactile hypersensitivity and pain can be suppressed in patients using superficial vibration. Activation of large primary afferents and the gate theory are possible explanations for the resulting inhibition.

Approximation and Traction

Joint receptors respond to both **approximation** and **traction** forces. **Approximation,** or compression, of the joint surfaces activates tonic joint receptors and facilitates holding responses of postural muscles. The compressive forces that are inherent in an activity such as standing cause reflex facilitation of the muscles needed to stabilize the body. Inasmuch as muscles are normally called upon to stabilize the body in mid to shortened ranges, the compression stimulus is typically applied in the position of function. Therapeutically, use of weight-bearing postures and/or manually applied compression can be used to facilitate these responses. For example, approximation directed downward through the head and spine can be applied in the sitting or standing position. Approximation directed downward through the pelvis and hip joint can be applied in postures of kneeling or standing. Weight cuffs or belts can be added to increase normal approximation forces and to promote stability.

Traction forces that distract the joint surfaces activate the more phasic joint receptors and along with stretch enhance movement responses. In PNF patterns, traction and stretch are used to initiate flexor patterns or pulling motions, and approximation and stretch are used to initiate extensor patterns or pushing motions.[22] Both traction and approximation improve joint awareness and thus can be effective stimuli for enhancing motor control. They are contraindicated in patients with acute inflammatory joint conditions. Traction applied through gentle mobilization can provide some relief of pain and improved range of motion in less acute situations.

EXTEROCEPTIVE STIMULATION TECHNIQUES

Exteroceptive stimulation techniques enhance movement responses through activation of sensory receptors in the superficial and subcutaneous layers of the skin. Table 14–2 provides a summary of the principal exteroceptive techniques. Several different types of receptors detect the tactile sensations of touch, pressure, and tissue deformation, including free nerve endings, Meissner's corpuscle, Merkel's disks, hair end-organs, Ruffini's end-

Table 14–2 EXTEROCEPTIVE STIMULATION TECHNIQUES

Stimulus	Response	Considerations
Light Touch		
Activates Fast adapting skin receptors, sensory C, some A fibers, alpha motor neurons CNS-higher centers (cortex ANS, limbic system, brainstem) *Techniques* Manually applied: brief, light stroke; brief swipe with ice cube; painful stimulus, light pinching	Phasic, protective withdrawal reflexes (spinal level) After discharge reactions: maintained withdrawal, increased arousal, emotional responses: arousal and protection	Low threshold response Effects are immediate Accommodates rapidly (quick-adapting); give stimulus intermittently with pauses between stimulus Stimulus *brief* in duration Effective in initially mobilizing muscles Response should be immediately resisted to maintain contraction May not be a potent stimulus in mature, intact CNS. Contraindicated in patients demonstrating generalized arousal, autonomic instability.
Repetitive Brushing		

Activates
 Free nerve endings, sensory C, some A fibers; diffuse, tonic volley in spinal cord, and higher centers
 Techniques
 Battery-operated brush
	Response highly variable
	 Enhanced stretch sensitivity of muscle spindles (gamma biasing)
	 Reduction of pain
	 Can also cause arousal responses
		Prolonged brushing (3–5 min) over painful site: may reduce pain via presynaptic inhibition in dorsal horn
		 Brushing skin overlying muscle may facilitate muscle
		 Enhances static holding of postural extensors may have immediate and long latency responses
		 Difficult to assess appropriateness, effectiveness
		 Contraindicated
		   In very young children with immature CNS
		   Patients with generalized arousal, autonomic instability. hyperexcitable state

Prolonged Icing		
Activates Thermo receptors; decreased neuromuscular transmission, spindle firing, metabolic rate *Techniques* Ice chips, ice wraps Icepak Immersion in cold water	Inhibition of muscles, postural tone Decreased pain	Careful monitoring is necessary Cold may be adversive to some patients Contraindicated in patients with sensory deficits, generalized arousal, autonomic instability, vascular problems
Neutral Warmth (35°–37°C)		
Activates Thermoreceptors: ANS (parasympathetic) Brainstem (RF) *Techniques* Wrapping body or body part with towels, ace wraps Application of clothes—gloves, socks, tightly fitting clothing Tepid baths Air splints	Retention of body heat Generalized inhibition of postural tone Decreased pain, increased relaxation	Applied for moderate duration: 10–20 min Patients with increased sympathetic activity respond effectively. Avoid overheating—may see rebound effects
Maintained Touch		
Activates Tactile receptors Sensory fibers ANS; brainstem RF *Techniques* Firm manual contacts/pressure to midline abdomen, back Firm pressure to lips, palms, soles	Calming effect—promotes parasympathetic responses generalized inhibition	Useful with patients who overreact to sensory stimulation in general Apply to hypersensitive areas to normalize responses (desensitize) Avoid brief stimuli (light touch) Often effective when used with other maintained stimuli such as vibration
Slow Stroking		
Activates ANS brainstem RF *Technique* To posterior, primary rami (PPR) over sympathetic ganglion	Decreases muscle tone generally Calming effect—promotes parasympathetic responses	Clinically, very useful in aroused sympathetic patients

Table 14-2 *continued.*

Stimulus	Response	Considerations
Slow Stroking		
Use flat hand, firm moving pressure, alternating strokes for 3–5 minutes; just lateral to vertebral column from cervical to sacral regions		
Manual Contacts		
Activates Skin receptors, sensory fibers (A and C) spinal and higher centers *Technique* Direct firm contact	Segmental facilitation of muscles Activation of motor cortex	Light, intermittent touch facilitates movement Firm, maintained touch facilitates holding Location, timing, and pressure important

organs, and Pacinian corpuscles. Pain is detected by free nerve endings, and thermal sensations are detected by specific thermal receptors and free nerve endings. Most transmit their information in large myelinated A-beta (group II) fibers, providing the CNS rapid access to incoming sensory information. Free nerve endings, however, transmit over the slower conducting A-delta (group III) fibers and the unmyelinated C fibers (group IV).[6]

Manual Contacts

Manual contacts are integral to the success of most techniques designed to improve motor control. Direct, firm contact over the desired muscles facilitates the agonist to contract and alters synergistic, antagonist muscle function through activation of spinal level reciprocal innervation mechanisms and cortical level stimulation.[23,24] Manual contacts can be used to facilitate and to give direction to movement responses, to provide security and support to unstable body segments, or to alter tone. In general, **light,** intermittent **touch** facilitates movement responses, and firmer, **maintained touch** facilitates sustained, holding responses. Accurate placement of the therapist's hands directly over contracting muscles is critical to treatment success. Similarly, the therapist needs to anticipate the movement's end position and alter the hand position when necessary to allow for unrestricted movement through the range of motion.

Light Touch

Light touch can be used to elicit phasic withdrawal responses. The reaction is a spinal level reflex called the flexor reflex or withdrawal reflex. It is most frequently elicited by a noxious stimulus, such as a pinprick, although almost any type of cutaneous stimulus, including touch, can initiate the reaction. The information is transmitted over both A and C fibers and through polysynaptic spinal pathways, causing facilitation of the muscles needed for withdrawal and inhibition of the antagonists. The exact pattern of withdrawal is dependent upon the location of the stimulus and the most effective combination of muscle actions needed to escape it. A strong or painful stimulus also produces pronounced after-discharge effects within the spinal cord, which allow the limb to be maintained in its withdrawal position for sev-

eral seconds while the rest of the CNS is mobilized. Supraspinal effects result from transmission of the information to the cortex via lemniscal pathways and to the brainstem via the nonspecific spinothalamic connections. Here the principal effects are perception of threatening stimuli and initiation of arousal/protective responses.[6]

Therapeutically, light touch can be applied manually using a brief light stroke, light pinching, or a brief swipe of an ice cube. Sensory areas of high receptor density (hands, face) are more responsive to this type of stimulation than areas of low density. Inasmuch as the response is brief, resistance should be added to enhance and to maintain the contraction. The addition of proprioceptive stimuli also serves to moderate the exteroceptive signals and alters the nature of the response. Light touch stimuli can be effective in initially mobilizing muscles in patients with mobility problems. Because of the potential for widespread brainstem interaction, they are contraindicated in patients demonstrating generalized arousal or autonomic instability.[8,12]

Repetitive Brushing

Repetitive brushing is a technique originally devised by Rood to stimulate tactile receptors in order to facilitate movement responses. A battery-powered brush is used to stimulate the dermatomal area of a given muscle repetitively. Free nerve endings detect the stimulus and transmit the information over largely C and some A-delta fibers. The CNS effects are diverse and believed to occur both on spinal and brainstem levels. Immediate facilitation of muscles results from reflex activation on the spinal cord level. Enhanced spindle sensitivity is theorized to result from activation of the reticular formation and its outflow to gamma motoneurons. Responses, therefore, may be both immediate, within 30 seconds, and long lasting, owing to the reverberating circuits within the brainstem. Rood suggested that an optimal response may be obtained up to 30 minutes following brushing.[25] Research evidence supporting this technique has been scant and nonconclusive.[26-28] Clinically, it is difficult to assess either the appropriateness or the effectiveness of brushing as a stimulation technique. It is possible that brushing may produce therapeutic responses in some patients with impaired neural function, as reported by Rood.[8,12] Because the responses to stimulation are less predictable and dependable than other types of stimulation, such as vibration, this technique is seldom used.

Prolonged Icing

Prolonged icing can be used to provide localized inhibition of postural tone and pain. Cold can be applied in a variety of ways, including ice chips, iced turkish towels, ice packs, or immersion in cold baths. The inhibitory effects are due to decreased rates of neuronal and spindle firing and decreased metabolic rates of the cooled tissues. Because many patients may have adversive effects including sympathetic arousal and withdrawal, prior testing for adversive reactions and careful monitoring is necessary.

Attention

Selective attention mechanisms allow an individual to attend to relevant cues of both the task and the environment while screening out irrelevant ones. Information selected for processing is augmented while other irrelevant information is inhibited. Control of attention mechanisms is influenced by stimulus intensity, novelty, past experience or memory, motivation, and expectancy. Ongoing processing of sensory information also influences attention mechanisms and enhances continued neural transmission. Thus the sensations that immediately precede a sensory cue can make it easier for subsequent sensations to be received. In treatment, consistency in emphasizing normal sensations of tone and movement as stressed by Bobath may make succeeding movements easier and enhance the development of motor control.[15,16] Complexity of task demands or fatigue also can influence attentiveness, substantially decreasing performance in repetitive situations.

Neural control sites for selective attention include both the cortex and reticular formation. Thus both conscious and subconscious modes of control exist. The reticular formation may have an important role in gating or filtering sensory information from the periphery. The cortex in turn is capable of monitoring and modifying the actions of the reticular formation.

STRATEGIES TO IMPROVE ATTENTION

Processing of information by the CNS requires selective attention. These mechanisms allow an individual to concentrate on relevant task and environmental stimuli while screening out all or most other stimuli. Because there is a limit to central processing capacity, it is important to structure and to limit carefully information presented to the patient. Good verbal commands using adequate volume and inflection can provide an effective means of directing attention.[29] The therapist can ensure that the important parts of the skill are attended to by identifying key task elements. During early learning, environmental distractors should be reduced, and, if possible, complex skills broken down into their component parts. As learning progresses, the whole task and its component parts should be practiced. The environment also

can be modified during late learning to increase the number of distractors and to promote development of advanced skills.[4,5]

Patients with severe attentional deficits are unable to attend to important stimuli and often appear erratic in thought and action. Consistency must become the hallmark of treatment. The treatment schedule, setting, procedures, verbal instructions, and therapist should be consistent from day to day. Activities that work within the limitations of the patient's attention span should be planned. Thus short periods of treatment and simple repetitive activities are more beneficial than longer and more complex ones. Activities of interest to the patient are generally more successful than novel ones. Instructions also should be kept short and simple. Combining instructions with demonstration is frequently a more effective strategy to engage the patient's attention than verbal instructions alone. Key factors in achieving success in treatment are the establishment of a daily routine and the prompt reinforcement of desired behaviors.[30-33]

Patients who perseverate appear to get stuck on a thought or action and persist in repeating themselves over and over again. These patients should be guided gently into a new activity. Use of interesting activities can help refocus attention, and use of well-defined sequences of activities can help limit perseveration episodes. Successful completion of each part of the sequence should be positively reinforced.[33]

Arousal

Arousal refers to the overall level of alertness of the CNS. Low arousal is associated with sleep or drowsiness, and high arousal is associated with extreme excitement. Arousal mechanisms maintain the body in a general state of readiness and prepare the individual to respond. A number of factors influence general state, including emotions, time of day, or fatigue. Stimulus-specific arousal responses, however, are activated by cortical activity (thinking) and by novel, unexpected, or threatening stimuli.

Major neural control centers for arousal exist within the reticular formation (RF) of the brainstem. Sensory information is transmitted to the RF over sensory pathways. The RF in turn monitors this information and activates the necessary neural centers as needed. It has direct interaction with most neural control centers, including the cortex and the autonomic nervous system. A certain level of arousal is necessary for optimal motor performance. High states of arousal cause a deterioration in performance, and low states fail to yield the necessary responsiveness needed for effective performance. This is referred to as the **inverted U theory,** or the **Yerkes-Dodson law.**[5]

Excess levels of arousal also can yield unexpected or paradoxic responses. Wilder (1967) proposed a theory to explain the influence of prestimulus levels on responses, termed *Law of Initial Value (IV)*. It states,

the higher the IV of a function, the less change will occur in response to a function-increasing stimulus, and the lower the IV of a function, the less change will occur in response to a function decreasing stimulus. When the IV of a function is well beyond the midrange, there is an increasing tendency for no response or a reversal of response.[11]

For example, a patient with a head injury who is extremely agitated may not appear to respond to the addition of a new environmental stimuli. Inasmuch as the patient is already hyperkinetic, an increase in motor activity is not observed. With further stimulation, the patient may respond by lapsing into unconsciousness (a reversal of response). Thus the state of the CNS affects the reaction of somatic systems to external stimuli.

Optimal arousal improves motor performance and motor learning. Poor selectivity of sensory cues can be found with low levels of arousal, and increased distractibility and poor decision making are characteristic of excessive arousal levels. Performance and learning are impaired in both situations. Different motor tasks may require different levels of arousal. For example, high arousal levels improve performance on rapid, power activities. However, the same level of arousal decreases performance on fine motor or precision tasks. Tasks that require a high degree of steadiness or decision processing also are impaired by high arousal levels. Examples of these include postural holding responses and complex motor skills. The term *open skill* describes a motor activity performed in a situation in which the number of environmental distractions is high. Open skills are more impaired by high arousal levels than are *closed skills*, which are motor skills performed in a relatively consistent environment. Optimal arousal levels also vary according to the stage of learning, with the higher arousal levels more disruptive during early learning.[4,5]

STRATEGIES TO IMPROVE AROUSAL LEVELS

Decreased Arousal Levels

Patients with brain damage may show decreased alertness and arousal levels. These patients benefit from an organized sensory stimulation program designed to improve generalized response levels. Stimulation periods should be kept brief, often 5 to 10 minutes, and interspersed throughout the day to balance rest with activity. Different types of stimulation can be provided, including auditory, visual, cutaneous, kinesthetic, olfactory, and gustatory stimuli. Table 14–3 presents a sample listing of the types of stimuli available. Sensitivity to the patient's responses will help determine the optimal times for treatment, general length of the session, and the type of stimulation that proves most beneficial. Premorbid interests often provide an important source of information in determining which stimuli are most meaningful to the patient. Overstimulation should be avoided. Stimuli should be presented carefully one at a time, and extraneous environmental stimuli should be minimized. Verbal explanations should be kept brief and to the point, focusing the patient on the specific stimuli. Malkmus[31] recommends keeping a 24-hour record of the types of sensory stimuli used, the individuals who applied them,

Table 14–3 SENSORY STIMULI USED IN MODIFYING AROUSAL LEVELS

Low Arousal State Sensory Stimuli High Intensity, High Frequency Intermittent, Phasic	Response Brief, Phasic Generalized Arousal
Auditory verbal commands brisk music different sounds	Orientation to sound
Visual stationary targets tracking targets (horizontal and vertical) bright colors	Orientation to objects
Cutaneous light, moving touch perioral region, midline abdomen different textured, shaped materials	Activation of total withdrawal patterns
Kinesthetic upright positioning (wheelchair, tilt table) ROM, ADL tasks	Orientation to environment and body
Vestibular fast movements: angular or transient linear acceleration mobile surfaces (large ball, bolster, equilibrium board)	Increased tone Increased postural reactions
Olfactory/gustatory different scents, tastes noxious odors	Orientation to stimuli

High Arousal State Sensory Stimuli Low Intensity, Low Frequency Maintained, Tonic	Response Maintained, Tonic Generalized Calming
Auditory soft, soothing voice soft music quiet environment Visual soft, low lights Cutaneous maintained touch neutral warmth slow stroking down PPR	Decreased tone, decreased activity
Kinesthetic highly structured activity	Organized responses

and the patient's responses. Once responsiveness increases, the therapist should have the patient begin to discriminate particular types of stimuli and to respond with specific motor responses. Thus, touching two different textured objects, discriminating between them, and then holding the one selected requires the patient to make choices and to initiate actions. Response times are frequently delayed, so extra time should be allowed for the patient to respond.[30,33]

Increased Arousal Levels

Agitated patients who demonstrate excess levels of arousal also benefit from a controlled application of sensory techniques. Frequently, sources of stimulation from the environment precipitate bouts of agitation and disorganization. The patient is generally unable to process stimuli effectively and is similarly unable to control responses, which are often bizarre and combative. Careful assessment can reveal the offending stimuli and those which have a calming influence. The environment should be modified to eliminate or to reduce irritative stimuli. Thus treatment can be given in the quiet of the patient's room rather than in a noisy gym. Because unexpected surprises often precipitate outbursts, consistency in total management is very important. Establish a daily routine and provide an overall structure. Each new activity should be explained carefully before the activity is attempted. During the execution of the task, verbal reassurances and manual guidance are often helpful to the patient. When agitated outbursts occur, the therapist should calmly redirect the patient's attention away from the cause of irritation. Often selection of a task over which the patient has some control will help the patient regain composure. The therapist should provide a model for calm, controlled behavior and reward each successful effort with positive reinforcement.[32,33]

STIMULATION TECHNIQUES

The application of therapeutic stimuli for the aroused patient attempts to restore homeostatic balance by reducing hyperkinetic, fight-or-flight responses and promoting generalized relaxation. Several different types of stimuli can be effective, including **maintained touch, slow stroking, neutral warmth, slow vestibular stimulation,** or **inverted positioning.** In general, they are applied in a slow, maintained or rhythmical, repetitive manner and are thought to produce a calming effect by influencing brainstem activity and parasympathetic outflow.

Maintained Touch

Maintained touch can be used to desensitize hypersensitive areas and to reduce phasic withdrawal responses. It is therefore effective in patients who overreact to tactile stimulation in general. Firm maintained manual contacts are used to apply pressure to the abdomen or back and to sensitive areas, typically the palms, soles of the feet, or perioral region (lips). As previously mentioned, brief, light types of stimulation, which could elicit avoidance responses, are avoided. Maintained pressure to the midline abdomen or back also may have a calming effect.[25]

Slow Stroking

Slow stroking over the posterior primary rami (PPR) of the back is thought to produce a generalized calming effect. This procedure consists of firm, alternate strokes using a flat hand over the paravertebral muscles distally from the cervical to sacral regions. As one hand begins at the top of the spine, the other hand is reaching the bottom of the opposite side. It is continued for 3 to 5 minutes, or until relaxation occurs.

Neutral Warmth

Neutral warmth is an inhibitory technique first suggested by Rood.[12] It involves the retention of body heat, with temperatures generally in the moderate range between 35° to 37° C.[34] Neutral warmth can be achieved by wrapping the patient in turkish towels or thermal blankets; applying snug-fitting clothing such as gloves, tights, sweaters; or using a tepid bath or shower. The principal effects are a generalized inhibition of postural tone and a reduction of pain owing to the activation of parasympathetic responses. In general, a moderate duration of application, 10 to 20 minutes, is sufficient to produce relaxation effects though the duration is dependent upon the individual responses of each patient. Wrapping the spastic upper extremity of patients with hemiplegia has been found to be an effective technique in improving joint range of motion.[35] Wrapping also may enhance relaxation and decrease pain in some patients with rheumatoid arthritis who demonstrate increased sympathetic responses.[25]

Vestibular Stimulation

Vestibular stimulation techniques can be used to alter arousal levels, tone, and motor performance. Table 14–4 presents a summary of these techniques. The vestibular apparatus has two specialized sets of receptors, which are concerned with equilibrium. One set of receptors is located in the cristae ampullaris of the semicircular canals and is primarily concerned with detection of angular acceleration and velocity. The other sets of receptors are found in the macula of the utricule and in the macule of the saccule and are primarily concerned with the detection of head position and linear acceleration. The vestibular portion of cranial nerve VIII transmits most of the information to the vestibular nuclei, where widespread neuronal connections originate to the cerebellum, cortex, brainstem, reticular formation and autonomic nervous system, medial longitudinal fasciculus and cranial nerve nuclei, and spinal cord. Other fibers of cranial nerve VIII pass directly to the cerebellum. Because of the diffuse connections with many other structures within the CNS, vestibular stimulation has the potential to influence widespread functions. Stimulation can result in a decrease or increase in tone and movement of the head, trunk, and extremities. Stimulation also can influence coordinated eye movements and produce nystagmus, nausea or vomiting.[6,7]

Slow vestibular stimulation can be achieved through gentle, repetitive rocking movements, slow linear movements, or rolling. Mobile equipment such as a large ball, bolster, hammock, or rocking chair can be used to provide effective stimulation. The developmental postures of sidelying and sitting are ideal for achieving movement without the harmful effects of tonic reflex activity. Rocking is also commonly done in on-elbows and quadruped postures. Slow rolling movements should stress rotation within the body axis, particularly when truncal hypertonicity exists. The upper trunk rotates on the lower trunk, producing a segmental trunk pattern. Passive movements are used to initiate the treatment, and active

Table 14–4 VESTIBULAR STIMULATION TECHNIQUES

Stimulus	Response	Consideration
Slow, Maintained Vestibular		
Activates Otolith organs (response to maintained linear acceleration and head position) Semicircular canals Tactile, proprioceptors assist higher centers: brainstem outflow *Techniques* Slow, repetitive rocking: rocking chair, gymnastic ball, bolster Slow, continuous movements: rolling patterns, handling techniques	Generalized inhibition of postural tone Soothing, calming effect; decreased arousal	Slow, low intensity, repetitive stimuli Useful with hypertonic, hyperactive, anxious patients
Fast, Irregular Vestibular		
Activates Semicircular canals (respond to changes in angular acceleration) Otolith organs Tactile, proprioceptors assist higher centers: brainstem outflow *Techniques* Fast spinning: mesh net, hammock, scooter board, spinning chair,	Generalized facilitation of postural tone Promotes head righting, postural extension from prone position Increased arousal, attention Postrotary nystagmus	Rapid, high intensity, irregular accelerating and decelerating stimuli Useful with hypotonic patients; children with Down's syndrome, sensory integrative dysfunction; patients with deficient motor skills (hemiplegia, cerebral palsy) Helps overcome akinesia in Parkinsonism Adverse reactions may include behavioral changes, seizures, or sleep disorders
Inverted Position		
Activates Carotid sinus (pressure sensitive), medullary centers, ANS Vestibular apparatus; extereoceptors, proprioceptors assist *Techniques* Lower patient's head in relation to trunk: Prone over large ball, stool, bolster Inverted positioning apparatus Squat position, head down Sitting, head tipped down	Depressor effect on medullary centers (decreased BP, HR, respiratory rate) Generalized decrease in postural tone; soothing, calming effect Activation of postural extensors of neck, trunk and proximal joints	Requires careful monitoring because of ANS responses Contraindicated in certain patients with cardiovascular disease, unstable intracranial pressures (head injury) Useful with hyperactive, hypertonic, or aroused patients and with some hypertensive patients Facilitation of postural extensors (vibration, tapping) can assist positioning extensor responses

movements should be encouraged as soon as possible. All these movements produce a soothing, calming effect and a generalized inhibition of postural tone through interaction with the reticular formation and autonomic nervous system.[36] A slow, even, rhythmical pattern is important to provide low-intensity stimulation.

Inverted Head Position

The **inverted head position,** or **tonic labyrinthine inverted response,** involves tipping the head down in relation to the trunk. This can be achieved using the prone posture and equipment such as a large ball, stool, or specially constructed inverted frame. Adult patients can be stimulated by tipping them forward from a sitting posture. The effect of the head-down position is twofold. First baroreceptors in the carotid sinus are stimulated, producing generalized depression of sympathetic responses and facilitation of parasympathetic responses. Hypertonicity is therefore reduced.[37] The second major effect of the inverted head position is stimulation of the vestibular apparatus, which produces a generalized facilitation of postural extensors.[38] The facilitatory effects of the inverted position can be enhanced by the addition of other therapeutic stimuli used to improve **tonic holding,** such as **vibration.** Because prolonged positioning can decrease blood pressure dramatically and increase intracranial pressure, careful monitoring of vital signs is necessary. Patients who experience difficulty breathing, ringing in the ears, elevated heart rate, sweating, or nausea should be returned to the normal upright position immediately.[25,39]

Fast vestibular stimulation promotes a generalized facilitation of postural tone, normalized postural reactions and motor control, and increased arousal and attention. Therapeutically, stimulation can be achieved using a variety of equipment, including a mesh net or hammock, tilt board, scooter board, nystagmus board, or spinning chair. Both linear motions (forward-backward, side-to-side, or up-and-down) and angular motions (rolling, spinning) can be used. In general, the stimuli given are rapid, high intensity, and irregular (accelerating and decelerating). Patient responses should be monitored carefully, inasmuch as adverse reactions such as behavioral changes, seizures, or sleep disorders have been noted.[39] Benefits have been noted in diverse groups of patients, including those with hypotonicity, sensory integrative dysfunction, cerebral palsy, hemiplegia, Parkinson's disease, and Down's syndrome.[40-43]

Perception

Perceptual processes allow the sorting out and organization of incoming sensory stimuli into meaningful data. Sage[4] defines the essential steps of perception as the "detection, discrimination, recognition, and identification of incoming information for an interpretation." Perceptual processes thus require interaction of sensory systems with memory processes. Long-term memory stores are searched, and meaning is attached based on past sensory experiences. Individual differences exist in preferred modes of perceptual processing, in processing abilities, and in consistency of response over time. For example, many individuals rely heavily on visual processing, but others rely more on auditory or kinesthetic signals. Some individuals can process sensory cues faster than other individuals, resulting in faster reaction times on timed movement tasks. Intraindividual differences may result from the inability of an individual to adapt to different environmental situations, failing to screen out background signals from relevant ones. Perceptual deficits and therapeutic strategies for remediation are discussed more fully in chapter 7.

Decision Making

Perceptual responses are translated into commands for movement responses. Memory patterns in the sensory and sensory association areas are searched and an appropriate pattern found. The term **sensory engram** is frequently used to describe the memory store of different sensorimotor experiences. The CNS then translates the engram into action by calling up the various motor components needed to reproduce the movement. Thus the sensory engram activates the motor components of the brain and controls the pattern of activity established.[6] The motor areas of the cortex are also organized. A *motor program* (or *motor engram*) describes a set of prestructured commands that, when initiated, results in the production of a coordinated movement sequence.[5]

Motor programs are developed through experience and learning. Movement sequences are differentiated into component parts (patterns of movement), stored, and then called up as movement demands arise. Learning a new movement sequence is made easier by the presence of existing motor programs. These programs can be called up in different sequential orders and modified, resulting in the new motor pattern.

Neural control centers for motor programs are quite varied. The premotor association areas in the frontal and parietal cortex, the basal ganglia, and the lateral hemisphere of the cerebellum all contribute to the formation of motor programs.[44-47]

Movement Control

Command sequences for movement are executed by the primary motor cortex acting on segmental motor centers in the brainstem and spinal cord. Different modes of control are possible.

OPEN-LOOP CONTROL PROCESSES

Motor programs can be run off virtually without the influence of peripheral feedback. This is referred to as an *open-loop control* process[5] (Fig. 14–2). Examples of movements controlled in this manner include the execution of well-learned, rapid movement sequences such as playing the piano. Here the finger movements occur too rapidly to allow for feedback modification to occur. Deafferented limbs also demonstrate open-loop control processes, inasmuch as movement is generally possible without feedback though overall performance deteriorates. Thus preprogrammed movements exist and can be executed without the benefit of feedback analysis and correction.

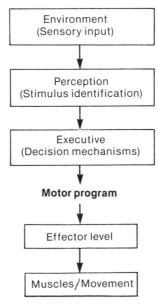

Figure 14–2. Open-loop motor control system.

CLOSED-LOOP CONTROL PROCESSES

Closed-loop control is defined as movement control that employs feedback against a reference for correctness.[5] Movement error is determined, and subsequent corrections are made[48] (Fig. 14–3). Visual, vestibular, muscle, and joint proprioceptors along with selected touch receptors provide the primary information for movement analysis and correction. Prior to movement, feedback is used to provide valuable information about the starting position and movement readiness. During the movement, feedback (termed **knowledge of performance,** or **KP**) allows for error detection and movement modification. After the movement, feedback (termed **knowledge of results,** or **KR**) assists in apprising the overall success of the movement and ensuring motor learning. Examples of movements controlled largely by feedback processes include the movements necessary to maintain posture and balance. Closed-loop control maintains the body at a constant state and controls body position. New motor skills that must be learned, such as tennis, skiing, or tracking, and fine motor tasks also require a high degree of feedback and closed-loop control.[49–51]

AN INTEGRATED CONTROL MODEL

The complexity of human motor behavior negates any simplistic model of movement control. Schmidt[5] suggests that both open-loop and closed-loop processes operate as part of a larger general motor system. Motor programs provide the generalized code for motor events, and feedback mechanisms refine and perfect movement.

Either may assume a predominate role, depending upon the task at hand. For example, motor programs are critical for the execution of fast movements, whereas feedback processes play a key role in the execution of slow movements. Both may operate within a given movement but at different times and with different functions. This has been expressed as an **intermittent control hypothesis.** Thus these two modes of operation can act either alone or together, yielding patterns of motor behavior that are uniquely complex while remaining flexible.[5]

Neural control centers responsible for organizing and controlling movement are varied. The three main higher centers that operate together include the cortex, the cerebellum, and the basal ganglia. The sensorimotor cortex mediates sensory input and organizes voluntary initiation of movement through its direct connections with the spinal neurons. The basal ganglia closely modulates cortical output and along with the cortex initiates and regulates gross intentional movements of the body, including involuntary and postural movements. It also appears preferentially active in the control of slow movements. The cerebellum serves a comparator function, checking the plan for the intended movement sent down from the cortex (termed **efferent copy**) with the feedback arising during movement execution.[47] Any discrepancy between the two immediately results in commands for movement modification to be returned to other centers. The cerebellum is preferentially active in controlling the coordination and timing of movement sequences and rapid movements. Feedback loops exist within all levels of the CNS and allow the system to be fully operational. Long loops allow interaction between peripheral feedback/spinal mechanisms and higher-level control centers,

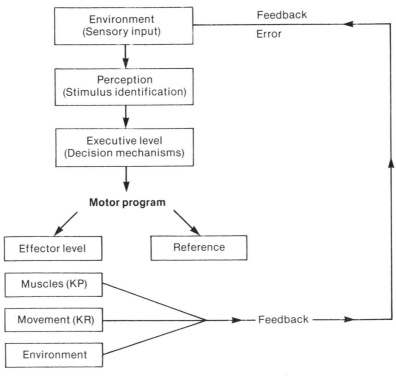

Figure 14–3. Closed-loop motor control system.

whereas short loops allow for smooth interaction between neural control centers.[5,6,45–47]

MECHANISMS OF RECOVERY FROM CNS LESIONS

Recovery of function occurs following injury to the central nervous system (CNS). Even patients with extensive brain damage can demonstrate quite remarkable recovery. Thus the brain is capable of major adaptation and reorganization. This is frequently termed lesion-induced **neural plasticity.** Although the exact mechanisms of recovery are unknown, several theories have been proposed. These include (1) **diaschisis,** (2) **redundancy,** (3) **vicarious function,** (4) **functional reorganization,** and (5) **behavioral substitution.** Recovery of function is most likely due to the collective action of several different mechanisms rather than to any single mechanism.[52–58]

Diaschisis theory refers to the early, spontaneous recovery that occurs secondary to the resolution of cerebral shock. Immediately following an injury, temporary loss of function may result from edema or extracellular bleeding. Function is affected in areas of the CNS that may be quite distant from the site of the original lesion. As these factors resolve, function is restored. This explains spontaneous recovery that occurs during the initial weeks and months following injury.

Redundancy theory refers to ability of the CNS to control function with only part of the neural system intact. Thus when damage occurs to an area, other parts of the system normally active in controlling the function take over and assume greater responsibility in controlling the activity. Lashley[59] used the term *equipotentiality* to refer to the idea that control of function occurs by a given area. Central nervous system deficits can be overcome if part of the region remains intact. Thus the smaller the lesion, the greater the capacity for the remaining tissues in the area to assume functional control.

Vicarious function refers to the capacity of the brain to take on functions normally controlled by other areas. For example, a function like speech is typically controlled by the left hemisphere in most individuals. If damage occurs to this area before speech patterns are firmly established, children are able to develop speech using right hemisphere function.[60]

Functional reorganization refers to the ability of the CNS to alter its structural organization following injury. *Collateral sprouting* is a term used to describe growth of viable neurons within the CNS to occupy synaptic sites of degenerating neurons. This improves functional organization by reestablishing interneuronal synaptic connections. Some, though not all, areas of the brain have the capacity for collateral sprouting and synaptic reclamation. Evidence for terminal sprouting (regeneration) and denervation supersensitivity (increased sensitivity to neurotransmitters at the receptor sites of denervated synapses) also exists.[52]

Behavioral substitution refers to the ability to achieve the same goal by substituting an entirely different motor strategy. For example, an intact motor pattern is selected and reorganized to perform a task previously accomplished by the damaged one. Substitution also can occur if the sensory cues are altered to control the same movement pattern. For example, a patient with impaired proprioception may learn to position the body appropriately to achieve a stable sitting posture using vision and a long mirror.

Several important points are worth emphasizing. Central nervous system recovery is a dynamic and evolving process. Plasticity appears greatest during the early phases of recovery and decreases over time. The presence of learned motor skills before an injury may make relearning easier following the injury. Recovery can be enhanced through effective treatment strategies. Repeated practice of desired motor behaviors stimulates adaptation and reorganization. Finally, recovery does not necessarily mean restoration of normal function. The behavioral manifestations of patients with residual disability represent both loss of function and reorganization of function within the CNS.[52]

A CONCEPTUAL MODEL OF MOTOR LEARNING

Motor learning has been defined as "a set of processes associated with practice or experience leading to relatively permanent changes in skilled behavior."[5] Although structural changes within the CNS occur with learning, they are not directly observable. Rather, we infer learning through observed changes in behavior. These changes can include alterations in the amount of attention or effort, improvements in timing and coordination, or increases in speed. Retention of task ability over time is another frequently used parameter to assess learning. Performance is not always an accurate reflection of the amount of learning that has taken place. Factors such as fatigue or poor motivation may cause performance to deteriorate. Learning, however, should be viewed as a relatively permanent event, the result of changes in the hierarchical, spatial, and temporal organization of the nervous system. Motor learning is the direct result of practice and experience and is highly dependent upon sensory information and feedback processes. The relative importance of the different types of sensory information varies according to the phase of learning. For most individuals the need for visual information predominates during early learning, and proprioceptive information becomes more important during later phases. Individual differences do exist, however, and may influence both the rate and the degree of learning possible. The pioneering work of Fitts and Posner[61] has led to the identification of three distinct phases of learning. These phases are discussed in the following sections and are summarized in Table 14–5.

Phases of Motor Learning

COGNITIVE OR EARLY PHASE

During the initial, **cognitive phase** of learning the major task at hand is to develop an overall understand-

Table 14–5 PHASES OF MOTOR LEARNING AND TRAINING STRATEGIES

Cognitive Phase	Associated Phase	Autonomous

Patient develops an understanding of task:
  Knows task demands
  Assesses abilities
  Develops strategies
  Performs successive approximations of
    task
  Involves stimulus selection,
    discrimination, perceptual organization,
    development of a motor program
	Patient practices movement pattern
	Spatial and temporal components of
	  movement are organized
	Extraneous movements, errors decrease
	Dependence on visual feedback
	  decreases
	Dependence on proprioceptive feedback
	  increases
	Cognitive monitoring decreases
	Motor program becomes refined
		Patient practices and refines finer
		  aspects of movement
		Spatial and temporal components
		  become highly organized
		Movement becomes increasingly
		  autonomous, requiring little
		  cognitive monitoring
		Control is shifted from higher to
		  lower centers

Training Strategies	*Training Strategies*	*Training Strategies*

Develop task understanding of "cognitive
  map"
Demonstrate task at ideal performance
  speed
Break complex tasks down into
  component parts; teach parts and whole
Have patient verbalize task components
  and requirements (mental practice)
Manually guide patient through
  movement
Direct attention to critical task elements–
  movement cues, overall sequence; point
  out similarities to other learned tasks
Organize practice:
  have patient look at movement (vision
    important)
Stress slow, controlled movement
Structure environment for development
  of closed skills
Use reinforcements (praise) for *correct*
  performance, do not cue on errors
  which are largely inconsistent at this
  time, avoid verbal bombardment
	Organize practice
	Identify movement errors, intervene
	  when errors become consistent
	Give feedback:
	  Knowledge of performance
	  Knowledge of results
	  Correct early in movement or
	    immediately after
	Emphasize proprioceptive feedback,
	  "feel of movement"
	Modify environment: practice in
	  environment where task will be
	  performed; gradually progress toward
	  practice in an open (changing)
	  environment
		Organize practice
		Identify movement errors, prescribe
		  corrections
		Stress refinement of skill,
		  consistency of performance
		Promote development of open
		  skills, performance in an open
		  (changing) environment, provide
		  distractions

ing of the skill. This is frequently termed the *cognitive map* or *cognitive plan*. This phase requires a large amount of cortical input in order to determine the specific task demands and to decide upon an appropriate course of action. The learner assesses his or her own abilities and develops strategies that might allow successful completion of the task. A trial-and-error process quickly reveals which strategies are going to be successful and which ones will not. Performance, therefore, is generally uneven during this phase. Processing of sensory cues and perceptual-motor organization eventually leads to the selection of a motor program that proves reasonably successful. Inasmuch as the learner progresses from an initially disorganized and often clumsy pattern to more organized movements, learning can be readily observed during this phase. The learner also progresses from primarily visually guided movement to more proprioceptively guided movements as he or she develops the "feel" or "sensations" of the correct pattern.

ASSOCIATIVE OR INTERMEDIATE PHASE

During the middle, **associative phase** of learning, refinement of the motor program is achieved through practice. Spatial and temporal aspects become organized

as the movement develops into a coordinated pattern. Performance improves with greater consistency and fewer errors and extraneous movements. The learner is now concentrating on how to do the movement rather than on what movement to do. Proprioceptive cues become increasingly important while dependence on visual cues decreases. Learning in this phase can persist for varying lengths of time, depending upon a number of factors. The nature of the task, the prior experience and motivation of the learner, and the organization of practice and teaching strategies used can influence learning.

AUTONOMOUS OR FINAL PHASE

During the final, **autonomous phase** of learning, movements become refined and highly coordinated. Little or no conscious attention is needed to execute the movements, hence the name autonomous. Neural control is shifted from higher to lower centers. This frees the individual to concentrate on other tasks while continuing to perform the movement pattern. Movements are virtually error-free, with little interference from environmental distractions. The learner can perform the movements equally well in a closed or stable environment or in an open, constantly changing one. Thus the learner is able to succeed in performing closed and open skills equally.

Strategies to Improve Motor Learning

Motor learning can be facilitated through the use of effective training strategies.[4,5,63-65] Several general factors are inherent in the learning process.

MOTIVATION

Motivation is crucial to the success of any training program. The patient must fully understand the purpose of the task at hand and want to master it. Planning that involves the patient and family in mutual goal setting can greatly enhance the desire to achieve those goals. Continued motivation also can be enhanced by the effective use of feedback during treatment. Treatment successes are important and can be highlighted through the use of carefully planned positive reinforcements. Balancing the more difficult tasks with easier ones allows the patient to experience feelings of success interspersed with frustrations. The therapist also should plan each therapy session to end on a positive, successful note. The patient can then feel encouraged about overall efforts and eager to continue therapy.

PRACTICE

Practice is essential for motor learning and the development of motor programs. Without practice, learning is impossible; with effective structuring of practice, learning is enhanced. Two basic types of practice schedules exist, massed or distributed. **Massed practice** refers to a prolonged period of practice time with infrequent rest times. **Distributed practice** refers to an alternating sequence of rest and practice sessions in which the rest time equals or exceeds the practice time. Both result in motor learning, though one may be more advantageous in certain circumstances than the other. Distributed practice is preferable when the learner's capacity for sustained performance is poor; when the task is complex, long, or energy costly; or when motivation is low. It is also preferable when the learner has a short attention span, poor concentration, or fatigues easily. Because this applies to many patients undergoing rehabilitation, particularly during the early phases of learning, this is a frequently used practice schedule. Massed practice can be useful when the patient's motivation or skill levels are high and when the patient has adequate attention and concentration. Fatigue should be avoided, however, inasmuch as it can interfere with performance and possibly learning. During the later phases of learning, varied practice schedules can be used to improve learning.

Practice of related or similar movement skills may improve performance in other desired skills. This has been termed **transfer of learning** and can be a useful strategy in promoting learning. The most frequently used application of this principle is practicing component parts of a motor activity before practicing the integrated whole. This is not always a successful strategy, however, and is dependent upon the nature of the learner and the task. If the task is complex with highly independent parts

or if the learner has a limited memory or attention, then learning can be enhanced through this method of practice. If the task has highly integrated, dependent parts or is relatively simple, then practice of the integrated whole will be more successful. Skilled learners with adequate attention spans and memories generally do better in practicing the integrated whole. The integration of motor programs is made easier by practice, which includes appropriate timing of all subroutines. In tasks that require speed and accuracy, both should be emphasized. Stressing accuracy first and then speed may not result in adequate transfer of learning and appropriate timing. For example, when gait movements are practiced stressing only accuracy at very slow speeds, the normal timing needed for ambulation may then be difficult to achieve. As a result, the patient walks with a slow deliberate gait pattern. If the parts-to-whole method is used, it is important to practice both the parts alternately and then the whole in order to ensure adequate transfer. Thus, within the same session the patient should practice each of the component parts, then the integrated whole. Delaying practice of the whole for days or weeks can interfere with transfer effects and learning.

Transfer effects also can be incorporated into treatment by having the patient practice the desired movements using the contralateral extremities. For example, in hemiplegia the more normal extremities (uninvolved side) can be engaged in practice of the desired movement patterns first. This enhances formation of the necessary motor programs, which can then be used to control the same movements on the opposite, involved extremities. This method can not, however, substitute for lack of movement potential of the affected extremities. Contralateral practice is also frequently used to see if the patient understands the desired movement. Thus, the patient is asked to demonstrate the movement. Transfer can be improved if the number of repetitions of the contralateral extremities is increased and actual training of those limbs is promoted.

FEEDBACK

Feedback is critical to motor learning and can be either **intrinsic,** occurring as a natural result of the movement; or **augmented,** providing additional or extra sensory cues. Proprioceptive signals are an example of a type of intrinsic feedback, and verbal commands are an effective form of augmented feedback. During therapy both intrinsic and augmented feedback can be manipulated to enhance motor learning. It is important to use precise, accurate feedback and to assist the learner in perceiving and classifying the sensory cues necessary for movement. Delayed feedback can cause movement disturbances, and too much feedback can be confusing and can cause feedback dependence.

Ongoing feedback provides the learner with important information about the quality of the movement produced **(knowledge of performance).** Feedback also provides information about the end result or overall success of the movement response **(knowledge of results).** Both KP and KR are important for motor learning and performance. The therapist should, therefore, carefully pair KP and KR with the movement task. The goal of therapy is to have the patient perform the correct movements while achieving the desired objectives. For example, a transfer incorrectly performed is as undesirable a treatment result as the production of movement patterns that do not result in a successful transfer.

Strategies also vary according to the specific phase of learning. Thus the plan to facilitate motor learning in the early cognitive phase should differ from a plan for training in the later stages. Table 14–5 presents a summary of some of these differences. It is important to recognize that overlap exists and that patients in transitional phases may benefit from a combination of training strategies.

TRAINING STRATEGIES FOR THE COGNITIVE PHASE

The overall goal during this phase of learning is to facilitate task understanding and to organize early practice. Learning can be facilitated through three basic methods of instruction: demonstration, verbal instructions, and manual guidance. Demonstration should stress correct performance, preferably at ideal performance speeds. This helps the patient arrive at an accurate reference of correctness. If the task is complex, it can be broken down into its component parts and one step attempted at a time. The relationship of the individual parts to the whole should be emphasized, however, by repeated demonstration of the integrated whole. The therapist is the most frequent—though not the only—source of demonstration. Highly skilled patient demonstrators or audiovisual materials such as videotapes or films also can be used.

Verbal instructions provide another important source for early learning. Here the therapist describes the task. Similarities to other previously learned tasks should be identified, inasmuch as this will aid in structuring the motor program. Have the patient also describe the task and its key task elements. Mental practice, a form of mental or quiet rehearsal, can further assist in movement readiness and learning. Make sure that the patient is mentally rehearsing the correct movements by having the patient first verbalize the task. Directions should focus the patient's attention on the overall movement sequence, the critical task elements, and important movement cues.

Initial practice can be enhanced by having the patient look at the movements, because vision is the primary means of error detection during this phase. Stress slow, controlled practice to ensure the patient replicates only correct movement patterns. Low effort enhances voluntary control, whereas intense effort can result in overflow to muscles not directly involved in the activity and incorrect movements. During task performance stress elimination of all unnecessary muscle activity. Verbal instructions should be kept to a minimum. Excess communication can distract the learner and frequently interferes with learning. At the conclusion of the movement task, have the patient verbalize the task and determine how well he or she did. This can further help in arriving at task understanding.

Manual guidance also can assist the patient during early learning. The therapist's hands can be used effectively to substitute for the missing elements and to ensure correct performance. Guidance is particularly helpful in slow, postural types of movements. Thus, it is an effective treatment element used in many therapeutic approaches. For example, handling techniques in Bobath's neurodevelopmental treatment effectively use guidance to assist the patient in more normal movements.[15,16] Manual guidance also can be effective in situations in which patient confidence is lacking or when vision or hearing are impaired. The supportive use of hands can allay patient fears, instill confidence, and compensate for communication impairments. The key to success in manually guided movements is knowing when to remove support and to let the patient move independently. Active participation promotes motor learning. Passive movement or dragging the patient through the movements does little to ensure learning and may actually increase dependence on the therapist.

Structuring practice sessions during the cognitive phase involves reducing irrelevant cues and keeping environmental distractions to a minimum. Early learning focuses on key task elements in a carefully structured, closed environment. The natural limits in CNS information-processing capacity will dictate the amount and speed in which elements or cues can be presented. As learning progresses, the number of elements or distractions can be gradually increased until performance approaches normal. Perceptual difficulties in processing sensory cues require additional adjustments. These are fully discussed in chapter 7.

TRAINING STRATEGIES FOR THE ASSOCIATIVE PHASE

The overall goal during this phase of learning is to improve the organization or exactness of the motor program. Frequent practice allows the spatial and temporal components of movement to become organized into a coordinated pattern. The therapist should intervene when movement errors become consistent and should prescribe the appropriate corrections. Corrections given early in the movement or immediately after are more effective than a continuous barrage of verbal instructions. Proprioceptive signals become increasingly important and should be stressed as the primary means of movement feedback. Thus the patient's attention is directed to the sensations of normal movement. The patient learns to experience the feel of the movement and to replicate those movements consistently. Knowledge of results is similarly important, inasmuch as the patient learns to appraise movement successes consistently. Videotaping the patient during performance of the movement task can enhance the accuracy of self-assessment efforts. Guided movement is less effective during this phase and may actually hinder the normal feel of movement and learning. As learning progresses, the environment should be modified gradually to provide a more realistic movement setting. Thus distractions are increased and the patient is expected to perform in a more open, changing environment.

TRAINING STRATEGIES FOR THE AUTONOMOUS PHASE

The overall goal during this phase of learning is refinement of movement. The patient is directed to practice the movements until the spatial and temporal components become highly organized. Movement errors are infrequent, and corrections should be initiated as they are identified. The therapist should stress refinement of skills and consistency of movement in a variety of environmental situations. The continued use of distractions, such as ongoing conversation, can yield important evidence of the autonomous nature of the patient's movements. The patient should be able to carry out the movements without any lessening in the quality of the performance. Moreover, the patient should be able to anticipate environmental changes accurately and to solve problems effectively to produce the appropriate solutions. It is important to remember that not all patients with motor control deficits can reach this skill level of learning. Performance may reach consistent levels within structured environments, but performance in more open environmental settings may not be possible.

A CONCEPTUAL MODEL OF MOTOR DEVELOPMENT

The development of posture and movement during the first few years of life allows the infant to learn basic control of body movements and to interact effectively with the environment. Control progresses from largely random, reflexive movements to more coordinated and purposeful ones. All children develop in a similar manner, with differences noted in the rate of development and in the quality of movements but not in the fundamental progressions of change. The development of postural control progresses through a variety of positions as the child gradually gains control of the body in more upright, antigravity postures. These progressions are summarized in Figure 9–3. The child first learns to maintain each posture, then to move easily in and out of each posture, and finally to achieve purposeful function in the posture. Development proceeds across many fronts at the same time. Thus the child begins to hold in a higher-level posture while developing important functional skills in an earlier posture. The control of posture provides the fundamental foundation for the development of locomotor and manual control. These progressions are summarized in Figures 9–4 and 9–5. Locomotor skills include the prewalking skills such as rolling, crawling, and creeping as well as upright walking. Manual skills include proximal support and stabilization of the arm and control of distal grasp and manipulation. The reader is referred to the work of noted developmental specialists such as Bayley,[66] Gesell and Amatruda,[67] McGraw,[68] Peiper,[69] Illingworth,[70] Milani-Comparetti and Gidone,[71] Connolly,[72] and Keogh and Sugden[73] for further study.

Several sequences of development are apparent and can provide a useful framework for treatment. Motor development generally proceeds in cephalocaudal and proximal-distal directions. Head control is achieved before trunk and lower extremity control. Shoulder and hip control emerge with trunk control before control of the distal extremities. Sympathetic responses predominate early in development, whereas homeostasis and controlled parasympathetic responses emerge later on. Reflex dominance and mass patterns of movement precede reflex integration and selective voluntary control of movement. Gross motor control precedes the development of fine motor control. Additional sequences include

1. Flexion and extension movements before rotation
2. Isometric movements (holding in a posture) before isotonic control (moving in a posture)
3. Eccentric control (moving out of a posture) before concentric control (moving into a posture)
4. Symmetrical movement patterns before asymmetrical movement patterns
5. Discrete movements before continuous movement sequences
6. Static control before dynamic control of posture

Stages of Development

Motor development proceeds according to stages, which identify four levels of function. These are (1) mobility, (2) stability, (3) controlled mobility, and (4) skill. These stages are both progressive and overlapping and have been extensively described by Stockmeyer.[8] They provide a useful conceptual framework for treatment planning. Table 14–6 presents a summary of the progression of these stages.

MOBILITY

The *mobility stage* is characterized by spontaneous, random movement of the limbs occurring at irregular and brief intervals. Mobility movements tend to be brisk, full range, and not well controlled. Rood[8] used the term **light work** to refer to movement of the distal segments of the limbs over the more fixed, proximal segments. Mobility movements are initially reflex based and thus serve a largely protective function for the newborn. The essential motor requirements include the ability to initiate the movement (requiring adequate activation of agonist muscles with inhibition of the antagonists) and the ability to move through the range (requiring adequate strength, range of motion, and flexibility). Classic mobility patterns include withdrawal from a stimulus, or flexor withdrawal, rolling over, and the assumption of pivot prone position. The pivot prone position is defined as a full-range prone extensor pattern of the head, trunk, lower extremities, and proximal upper extremities. Type IIB muscle fibers (fast-twitch, fast-fatigable motor units) and to a less extent type IIA muscle fibers (fast-twitch,

Table 14–6 NEUROPHYSIOLOGICAL SENSORIMOTOR APPROACH TO TREATMENT*

Progression of Motor Development				
Reciprocal Innervation Mobility	Co-innervation Stability	Heavy Work Movement Combined Mobility and Stability in Weight Bearing	Skill Combined Mobility and Stability in Nonweight Bearing

Withdrawal from
stimulus
  ↓
Flexion pattern ———→ Extension ———→ Neck co-contraction ———→ Head oriented to vertical ———→ Speech articulation
toward stimulus   pattern   ↓   plane (rotation available)   eye control
  ↓   Prone on elbows ↙
Roll

Prone on extended ———→ Weight shifting backward, ————→ Unilateral upper extremity
arms   forward, side to side   weight bearing and
All fours ↙   reaching
                      → Weight shifting forward
                        and backward
                                ↓
                             side to side ————→ Unilateral reaching during
                                              creeping
Bilateral lower ↙
extremity weight
bearing ————————→ Weight shifting in standing

Hold semisquat and ←————————————————— Cruising
squat   ↓
                → Squat to stand ————————→ Walking
                                              ↓
                                           Hands free for prehension

*Compiled by Becky Porter, MS, RPT, Indiana University Physical Therapy Program, 1978. (From Farber, S,[34] p 122, with permission.)

fatigue-resistant motor units) are well-designed to carry out these movements, generating fast contractions in a relatively short time.[74] The muscles most active in mobility patterns tend to be the flexors, adductors, and internal rotators. Because normal reciprocal innervation mechanisms must be fully operational to allow movement, this stage also has been described as the stage of reciprocal innervation.

STABILITY

Stability refers to the ability to fix or to maintain a position in relation to gravity. Two phases of stability control can be identified, **tonic holding** and **cocontraction. Tonic holding** refers to the activation of postural muscles in the fully shortened range against gravity (sometimes referred to as a **shortened held resisted contraction,** or **SHRC**). Tonic holding of the postural extensors is optimally achieved in the pivot prone (prone extension) pattern. This activity facilitates the development of muscle spindle stretch sensitivity (spindle bias) through the recruitment of static gamma motoneurons which respond to the load imposed by gravity. Optical and labyrinthine righting reactions also contribute to the development of tonic holding. **Cocontraction** is optimally achieved as the body moves from holding in full extension in the shortened range to holding in midrange postures such as neck cocontraction or prone on elbows.

Quadruped, squatting, and standing positions are also patterns in which cocontraction is developed. Stretch to stretch-sensitive extensor muscles is theorized to cause reflex facilitation of extensor muscles via the action of spindle primary endings and facilitation of flexor muscles via the action of spindle secondary endings and GTOs. Since the response of the spindle secondary endings can be quite variable,[13] the GTOs may provide the major source of assistance in the development of cocontraction. GTOs are far more prevalent in extensor muscles than in flexor muscles and are sensitive to active contraction, particularly in the lengthened range. As the extensors move into a more lengthened range, a pattern of cocontraction or coinnervation of both extensors and flexors emerges, enabling stable control of posture. Type I muscle fibers (slow-twitch, fatigue-resistant motor units) are optimally designed to participate in these sustained responses.[74] The muscles most active in stability patterns tend to be the deep postural and one-joint muscles, largely the extensors, abductors, and external rotators.

CONTROLLED MOBILITY

Controlled mobility (CM) refers to the ability to maintain postural stability while moving. Rood[8] originally described this as mobility superimposed upon stability, or **heavy work,** in which the distal segments are fixed and the proximal segments are moving. This description has been simplified to *controlled mobility* by some authors.[75] Controlled mobility activities include weight shifting forward or backward, side to side, or any combination thereof. Thus CM can be achieved in any of the previously mentioned weight-bearing postures in which initial stability control is achieved. Developmentally, control proceeds from midrange control to control throughout the range (through increments of range). The development of proximal rotatory function or rotation about the longitudinal axis of the body represents an advanced level of controlled mobility and can be achieved in side-lying, rolling, or upright postures. Control in weight shifting also proceeds from bilateral to unilateral weight bearing. Thus the child is able to shift onto an extremity and free up the opposite extremity for exploration or skill level function. The term **static-dynamic control** has been used to describe this variation. Static dynamic control represents a transitional level between controlled mobility and skill levels of control.[75]

SKILL

Skill is defined as coordinate movement and is demonstrated by discrete or continuous movement sequences superimposed upon a stable posture. Examples of skill level activities include oromotor function (chewing, swallowing, and speech) for the head, hand function (grasp and manipulation) for the upper extremities, and locomotion (ambulation) for the lower extremities. Movements differ during this stage of development from those seen in earlier stages in that they are finely tuned, with precise spatial and temporal organization and effective use of feedback. Skilled movements also allow for organized, goal-directed behaviors.[61]

ADULT DEVELOPMENT

Control of movements is a continuously evolving process that progresses throughout life. Although the fundamentals of movement are learned in childhood, acquisition of new motor skills continues throughout the lifespan. Similar progressions through the stages can be observed in adult motor skill development. Differences exist, however, in the rate of progression, the stages required, and the length of time needed in each stage. Because many of the adaptive components of movement, postural sets, or motor programs already exist, they can be called up easily to form the new motor skill. Patients who experience motor control deficits frequently demonstrate a regression in motor control with absent or incomplete control at any of the stages of development. For example, following a stroke, a patient is unable to maintain unsupported sitting for more than a few seconds and sits with a slumped, poorly controlled posture. The patient loses balance and falls over with the slightest movement adjustment in any direction. This represents poor stability control with absent controlled mobility function. One would reasonably expect that this patient's ability to perform a skill level function such as dressing in unsupported sitting also would be severely impaired. A major difference exists, however, between

the child, who has not yet developed, and the disabled adult, who has already completed development. The adult's behavior is likely to be fragmented, with residuals of intact function coexisting with areas of deficient function.

Developmental Strategies to Improve Motor Control

Developmental processes provide an important framework in determining strategies designed to improve motor control. Treatment that is based upon an accurate assessment of the patient's developmental level and models the normal sequences of development can assist the patient in regaining control more quickly and more successfully than treatment that disregards these factors. For example, a patient severely disabled by a head injury will need to regain head and trunk control before functional use of the extremities can be attempted. Sequences of activity progressing from rostral to caudal, gross to fine, or mobility to stability should be considered. Therapy should model the spiral nature of development; that is, complete mastery in one set of activities is not necessary before proceeding on to the next higher level of activity. In the adult patient it is common to be working on several different levels of activities at one time. The therapist's role is to provide an appropriate challenge for the patient, to assist as necessary in achieving the desired control, and to remove support as soon as possible in order to allow for independent function.

STRATEGIES TO NORMALIZE TONE AND TO IMPROVE REFLEX INTEGRATION

Normal voluntary control of movement is based upon the prerequisites of normal tone and reflex integration. This has been expressed as a *normal postural reflex mechanism* (NPRM). Bobath[15] identifies five essential elements of the NPRM: (1) normal tone, (2) integrated primitive reflexes and movement patterns, (3) righting reactions, (4) protective extension reactions, and (5) equilibrium reactions.[15]

Functionally, normal postural tone allows for smooth integration of agonists, antagonists, and synergists via normal mechanisms of reciprocal innervation. It also allows for optimal movement readiness and antigravity function. Abnormal tone can prevent or restrict movement, producing uncoordinated movement that is accomplished only with a great deal of effort. A number of factors can influence tone and should be controlled during treatment. These include high anxiety or stress, intense effort or resistance, pain, and overflow from other parts of the body. Positioning and interaction with primitive or tonic reflexes also may alter tone. For example, the supine position may increase extensor tone throughout, whereas the prone position may increase flexor tone. A sidelying or sitting position may therefore be better initial treatment positions than either a prone or supine position for the patient with hyperreflexia. As previously discussed, sensory stimulation techniques can be effective in reducing tone. **Prolonged icing, slow vestibular inputs** (rocking, mobile surfaces), **inverted positioning, inhibitory pressure, neutral warmth,** and **slow stroking** all have been used with some degree of success.

The pioneering work of Bobath[15,16] has resulted in a number of manual inhibition or handling techniques which can be used to influence tone. **Reflex-inhibiting patterns** attempt to control and to reverse abnormal patterns of movement through **key points of control.** The primary key points are the neck, spine, and proximal joints (shoulders and hips) although some distal key points (toes, fingers, and wrists) can be used. Altering a spastic pattern begins first with effective positioning and slow steady movement aimed at reversing or lengthening the spastic components. The inhibitory results are probably due in part to activation of GTO (Ib) endings and possibly spindle II endings. Rhythmic rotation, crossing of the midline, and active controlled movements in the new range are also an important part of handling to reduce tone and should be stressed. For the patient with hypotonia, tapping, positioning in antigravity postures, and other proprioceptive or tactile inputs can be used to increase tone.

Reflex integration refers to the normal contributions that reflexes play in the regulatory control of posture and coordination. Easton refers to these influences as adaptive fragments of behavior that comprise the basic language of the CNS's motor program.[76] As such, reflexes permit dynamic postural control. An imbalance in reflex activity can emerge following some types of brain injury. For example, in hemiplegia, the more primitive and tonic reflexes dominate, whereas higher-level righting, protective, and equilibrium reactions disappear or become disordered. Associated reactions and tonic neck and tonic labyrinthine reflexes are just a few of the reflexes that can dominate motor behavior. Concurrently primitive synergistic movement patterns consisting of primarily total flexion or total extension movements emerge. They further restrict the individual's ability to move outside these mass patterns and make isolated motor control extremely difficult or impossible.

Treatment goals designed to improve reflex integration are twofold: (1) to prevent or to reduce primitive and tonic reflex activity and (2) to promote the development of higher-level righting, protective, and equilibrium reactions. Positions, movements, or stimuli that set off primitive or tonic reflexes should be avoided carefully. During therapy, activities should stress movements out of reflex-dependent postures (i.e., reflex-inhibiting patterns) and stimulate the higher-level reactions. Patterns that promote the development of head control and segmental rotation around the longitudinal axis of the body are similarly important. Patients should practice dissociation or breaking up of mass patterns of movement in postures most conducive to these movements. For example, head control and independent head movements can be practiced in a sitting position within a controlled range of function that does not produce the corresponding change in the arm movements associated with the asymmetrical tonic neck reflex.

Adaptive equipment such as a Swiss gymnastic ball or equilibrium board can be used to stimulate righting, pro-tective, and equilibrium reactions. On the mat, weight shifting also can be effective in stimulating these reactions. A variety of weight-bearing postures can be used for this purpose, including prone on elbows, sitting, quadruped, kneeling, half-kneeling, and standing. Postures should be selected carefully on the basis of the patient's presenting level of control. The degree to which the patient's center of gravity (COG) is displaced within or outside of the base of support (BOS) determines the reaction obtained. That is, movements within the BOS will stimulate righting and equilibrium reactions, whereas movements that displace the COG outside the BOS will stimulate protective extension reactions. Range and speed of the displacements can be increased gradually as the patient's reactions improve. The successful stimulation of these reactions is also dependent upon the degree to which the patient experiences the displacement or loss of balance. If the therapist's manual contacts are too secure or predictable, these higher-level postural reactions will be difficult to elicit because the patient will be likely to feel too safe.

STRATEGIES TO IMPROVE MOBILITY

Initial mobility can be elicited through the use of low-threshold, phasic stimuli. As previously mentioned, these can include quick stretch, or light touch, quick icing, and light pinching to elicit withdrawal responses. Associated reactions and tonic reflexes also have been used in some approaches to bridge the gap between complete lack of movement and early movement attempts.[77] Inasmuch as any of these movements are reflex in nature, they should be used carefully and considered only as a temporary strategy to facilitate movement. The movements should be immediately resisted in order to add proprioceptive inputs and to perpetuate the response. The movements also can be reinforced with verbal commands, which focus the patient's attention on gaining control through voluntary effort.

Specific exercise techniques that can be used in treatment to initiate movements include **active assisted movement (AAM), rhythmic initiation (RI), repeated contractions (RC),** and **hold-relax active motion (HRAM). Active assisted movement** (guided movements, handling) involves both assisted and active movements. The therapist first passively guides the patient through the correct movement pattern several times to ensure that the patient has the correct idea of the desired movement. The patient is then asked to participate in the movement pattern actively. The therapist provides assistance only during those parts of the pattern which require assistance, while stressing active control by the patient. **Rhythmic initiation** is a similar procedure, which involves voluntary relaxation followed by passive, active assistive, and finally mildly resisted movements of the agonist pattern. Transition into the next stage is dependent upon the patient's ability to relax and to participate in the movement pattern. Rhythmic initiation is most effective in patients with hypertonia, although it can be used during the initial stages of motor learning to guide and to stimulate correct motor patterns. **Repeated contractions** involve repeated isotonic contractions of the agonist pattern. The movements are resisted slightly, and repeated stretch can be added to reinforce voluntary contraction during the weak parts of the range. **Hold-relax active motion** involves first obtaining an isometric contraction in the shortened range, followed by active relaxation and passive movement into the lengthened range. The patient is instructed to move isotonically back through the range against resistance and repeated stretch, if needed. Hold-relax active motion is applied in one direction only and can be used to enhance stretch sensitivity and contraction of a weak or hypotonic agonist.

In cases in which limitations in mobility are due to specific muscle contracture or hypertonicity, techniques can be incorporated to improve range and to decrease tone. The most widely used techniques are **contract-relax (CR), hold-relax (HR),** and **rhythmic rotation (RRo).** Both **contract-relax** and **hold-relax** involve active, resisted contractions of the range-limiting muscles within a diagonal pattern of motion (PNF pattern) followed by relaxation and active movement into the new range (agonist pattern). Hold-relax uses isometric contractions with no movement, whereas contract-relax uses an isotonic contraction of the rotators with isometric contractions of all other pattern components. **Rhythmic rotation** involves repeated, passive rotational movements of the limb or trunk following commands for active relaxation. The movements are slow and gentle, gradually working the limb or segment into the lengthened range. The reader is referred to the work of Bobath,[15,16] Voss, Ionta, and Meyers,[22] and Sullivan, Markos and Minor[75] for a more complete description of these techniques.

STRATEGIES TO IMPROVE STABILITY

Stability can be enhanced through the use of maintained tonic types of stimuli. These can include vibration, resistance, approximation, tapping, and manual contacts. The stimuli are maintained as long as they are needed to enhance the contraction. Weight bearing and antigravity postures alone and in combination with the above stimuli also can be used to stimulate proprioceptive mechanisms and holding responses in stretch-sensitive muscles. Prone on elbows, sitting, or modified plantigrade postures can be used to develop upper trunk and shoulder stability, whereas quadruped, bridging, kneeling, half-kneeling, or standing postures can be used to develop lower trunk and pelvic stability. Specific therapeutic techniques that can be applied to enhance stability include **alternating isometrics (AI), rhythmic stabilization (RS),** or **slow reversal-hold (SRH).** Alternating isometrics consists of alternate isometric contractions of first the agonists, then antagonist muscles. The patient is instructed to hold and the therapist resists the hold first in one direction, then in the other. The holding can be challenged in all directions; that is, flexion-extension, abduction-adduction, diagonally, or rotationally.[75] **Rhythmic stabilization** similarly employs isometric contractions of antagonist patterns but differs from AI in that it attempts to apply the resistance simultaneously to both muscle groups and does not allow relaxation to occur between the contractions. For example, in stand-

ing, resistance can be applied to the trunk flexors at the shoulders and to the trunk extensors at the pelvis at the same time. The therapist's hands are then switched to the opposite surfaces and the resistance is applied to shoulder extensors and pelvic flexors. This occurs without any distinct relaxation phase between opposing contractions. **Slow reversal-hold** is a technique that involves alternate isometric and isotonic contractions of both agonists and antagonists. The patient is instructed to hold, followed by stretch and resisted movement in the opposite direction ending with a corresponding hold of the antagonists. When SRH is used as a stability technique, the isometric components are stressed and the range of movement is limited. Slow-reversal hold applied through decreasing range (decrements of range) can be effective in some patients with hyperkinesia, such as athetoid patients.[22,75]

STRATEGIES TO IMPROVE CONTROLLED MOBILITY

Activities to improve controlled mobility include rocking or weight shifting in any of the previously mentioned weight-bearing postures. The movements can be stimulated in any direction; that is, flexion-extension, abduction-adduction, diagonally, or rotatory. Diagonal movements are generally more efficient inasmuch as they represent a combination of both flexion-extension and abduction-adduction movement components. Thus in a quadruped posture the patient can rock forward and diagonally over one shoulder and backward and diagonally over the opposite leg. The range of function is gradually increased and works within the patient's limits of control. More advanced controlled-mobility activities include moving into and out of postures and static-dynamic work. In static-dynamic work, the patient shifts weight over to an extremity and frees the opposite extremity for non-weight-bearing activities. For example, the patient shifts weight onto the right arm and both lower extremities in the quadruped posture and lifts the left arm up off the mat. Additional movements, such as PNF extremity patterns, can be added to the non-weight-bearing limb to increase the level of difficulty. Controlled-mobility activities challenge the patient by superimposing control of dynamic movements on stability control. Manual contacts, stretch, resistance, and verbal commands are effective stimuli in enhancing these responses.

Therapeutic techniques that can enhance controlled mobility function include **slow reversals (SR), slow reversal-hold (SRH), repeated contractions (RC),** and **agonist reversal (AR). Slow reversals** consist of alternating isotonic contractions of first agonist then antagonist patterns. The movements are reversed without any relaxation phase and resisted throughout. During the movements the patient is directed toward increasing or gaining full range of motion. **Slow reversal-hold** can be used to promote either stability (as previously mentioned) or controlled mobility. When used as a controlled mobility technique, it progresses through increments of range. **Repeated contractions** are appropriate to use as a controlled-mobility technique when muscle imbalances exist and the movements are stronger in one direction than in the other. Repeated contractions also can be applied if weakness in any part of the range exists. **Agonist reversal** is a technique that incorporates resistance to both concentric and eccentric contractions of the agonists. For example, in bridging, the assumption of the posture involves concentric contraction of the hip extensor muscles, but getting back down involves a controlled eccentric contraction. Thus agonist reversal works on control of agonist muscles using two types of contraction patterns. Common activities that require eccentric control include sit-to-stand transitions, descending stairs, and moving from kneeling to heelsitting.[22,75]

STRATEGIES TO IMPROVE SKILL

Skill-level activities should be attempted only after control in static and controlled-mobility activities has been achieved. Activities that demonstrate skilled function include locomotion (reciprocal creeping or walking), skilled hand function (grasp and manipulation), and oral-motor function. Highly coordinated patterns of movement such as the PNF extremity patterns also represent skill-level function when performed with precise timing and direction. Specific therapeutic techniques that can enhance skilled function include **slow reversals, slow reversal-hold, timing for emphasis (TE),** and **resisted progression (RP).** **Timing for emphasis** promotes normal timing of pattern components by reinforcing or resisting the stronger components to augment the weaker ones. Completion of a diagonal pattern of motion (PNF pattern) emphasizes all components with normal distal to proximal timing. When an imbalance exists, the stronger components are maximally resisted to enhance overflow and contraction of the weaker segments. The stronger components also can be isometrically "locked in" at a point in the range at which they are the strongest while repeated contractions are then applied to improve contraction of the weaker components. **Resisted progression** involves the use of stretch and resistance to enhance locomotion. The therapist's manual contacts are positioned to resist both the forward progression and the pelvic rotation. Locomotion patterns can be resisted in any direction; that is, forward-backward, sideward, or diagonally. In walking, a crossed walking pattern known as **braiding** also can be used to develop high-level skill function. Manual contacts, stretch, resistance, and verbal commands are effective in facilitating coordinated responses.[22,75] Isokinetic devices are effective to improve the temporal organization of movement. The speed of the movements can be predetermined and gradually progressed to more rapid speeds as motor control improves. A metronome can be added to maintain consistency in pacing the activity. When the velocity of movement is being stressed, the resistance is set low. Isokinetic training has been used successfully to improve the timing of reciprocal leg movements and to simulate walking.[60]

SUMMARY

This chapter has outlined a conceptual framework based on normal processes of motor behavior, motor learning, and motor development (Fig. 14-4). Clinical

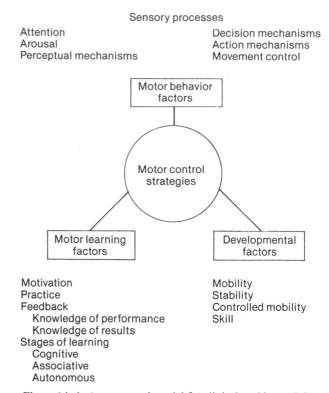

Figure 14-4. A conceptual model for clinical problem solving.

decision making for patients with motor control deficits must be based upon a comparison of normal and abnormal function in each of these areas. The therapist must be able to recognize, to categorize, and to sequence motor behaviors appropriately to develop effective treatment goals and strategies. The unique problems of each patient also require that the therapist recognize a number of interrelated factors, including individual needs, motivations, concerns, and potential for response. Movements must be assessed and undertaken within the context in which they normally occur. Peripheral inputs can be used to manipulate and to improve motor patterns. Given the tremendous variability in CNS function, however, it is unrealistic to expect that individual techniques can produce identical responses in different patients or even in the same patient under different environmental circumstances. Techniques must, therefore, be chosen carefully and monitored closely during treatment. The basic components of control must be addressed, including normal tone and reflex integration, dynamic stability, appropriate timing and sequencing of components, and the ability to generate and to release muscle tension as needed. Functional changes can result only from repetition of the desired activity. Early, frequent, and consistent practice provides the best chance for optimal treatment results. Meaningful progress may be painstakingly slow, especially in the presence of multiple and complex motor control problems. Frustrations frequently run high for both patient and therapist. Physical therapists have many skills and techniques available to assist patients. The adoption of a standardized or generalized approach to patient care can blind the clinician to the full range of treatment options available and so should be avoided.

QUESTIONS FOR REVIEW

1. Differentiate between the terms facilitation, activation, and inhibition. What criteria can be used to determine whether each has been successfully achieved?

2. What sensory stimulation techniques can be used to enhance movement (mobility)? Stability? Clinically how do you determine whether the technique is indicated?

3. What types of techniques can be used to modify arousal levels? What factors need to be considered when working with patients with low arousal levels? High arousal levels?

4. Define open-loop control processes and closed-loop processes. Describe how each may be used during normal activities.

5. Differentiate between the three different phases of motor learning. How should training strategies differ during each stage?

6. Developmental strategies form the bases of many therapeutic approaches in physical therapy. How should these strategies vary when treating the adult patient as opposed to the pediatric patient?

7. Identify three therapeutic procedures that can be used for patients with deficits in the mobility stage of motor control. Do the same for stability, controlled-mobility, and skill stages.

8. Your patient is 22 years old and is recovering from a severe head injury. List two procedures that could be used to decrease the moderate to severe spasticity that is present in trunk and proximal extremities.

REFERENCES

1. Umphred, D: Conceptual model of an approach to the sensorimotor treatment of the head-injured client. Phys Ther 63:1983, 1983.
2. Rinehart, M: Considerations for functional training in adults after head injury. Phys Ther 63: 1975, 1983.
3. Wolf, S: Clinical Decision Making in Physical Therapy. FA Davis, Philadelphia, 1985.
4. Sage, G: Introduction to Motor Behavior: A Neuropsychological Approach, ed 2. Addison-Wesley, 1977.
5. Schmidt, R: Motor Control and Learning. Human Kinetics, Champaign, IL, 1982.
6. Guyton, A: Basic Human Neurophysiology, ed 3. WB Saunders, Philadelphia, 1981.
7. Mountcastle, V (ed): Medical Physiology, vol 1, ed 14. CV Mosby, St Louis, 1980.
8. Stockmeyer, S: An interpretation of the approach of Rood to the treatment of neuromuscular dysfunction. Am J Phys Med 46:950, 1967.
9. Wilder, J: Stimulus and Response: The Law of Initial Value. John Wright and Sons, Bristol, England, 1967.
10. Dell, P: Reticular homeostasis and critical reactivity. In Moruzzi, G, Fessard, A, and Jasper, H (eds): Progress in Brain Research, vol 1: Brain Mechanisms, Elsevier, New York, 1963.
11. Stockmeyer, S: Clinical decision making based on homeostatic concepts. In Wolf, S: Clinical Decision Making in Physical Therapy. FA Davis, Philadelphia, 1985.
12. Rood, M: The use of sensory receptors to activate, facilitate, and inhibit motor response, autonomic and somatic, in developmental sequence. In Satterly, C (ed): Approaches to the Treatment of Patients with Neuromuscular Dysfunction. Wm C Brown, Dubuque, IA, 1962.
13. Urbscheit, N: Reflexes evoked by group II afferent fibers from muscle spindles. Phys Ther 59:1083, 1979.
14. Scholz, J and Campbell, S: Muscle spindles and the regulation of movement. Phys Ther 60:1416, 1980.
15. Bobath, B: Adult Hemiplegia: Evaluation and Treatment, ed 2. Wm Heinemann Medical Books, London, 1978.
16. Bobath, B: The treatment of neuromuscular disorders by improving patterns of coordination. Physiotherapy 55:1, 1969.
17. Kukula, C, et al: Effect of tendon pressure on alpha motoneuron excitability. Phys Ther 65:595, 1985.
18. Bishop, B: Vibration stimulation. I. Neurophysiology of motor responses evoked by vibratory stimulation. Phys Ther 54:1273, 1974.
19. Bishop, B: Vibratory stimulation. II. Vibratory stimulation as an evaluation tool. Phys Ther 55:29, 1975.
20. Eklund, G and Hagbarth, K: Normal variability of tonic vibration reflexes in man. Exp Neurol 16:80, 1966.
21. Goldfinger, G and Schoon, C: Reliability of the tonic vibration reflex. Phys Ther 58:46, 1978.
22. Voss, D, Ionta, M, and Myers, B: Proprioceptive Neuromuscular Facilitation, ed 3. Harper & Row, Philadelphia, 1985.
23. Hagbarth, K: Excitatory and inhibitory skin areas for flexor and extensor motoneurons. Acta Physiol Scand 26 (Suppl) 94:1, 1952.
24. Eldred, E and Hagbarth, K: Facilitation and inhibition of gamma efferents by stimulation of certain skin areas. J Neurophysiol 17:59, 1954.
25. Rood, M: Unpublished class notes from Rood workshop. Youville Hospital, Boston, 1976.
26. Spicer, S and Matyas, T: Facilitation of TVR by cutaneous stimulation. Am J Phys Med 59:223, 1980.
27. Spicer, S and Matyas, T: Facilitation of the TVR by cutaneous stimulation in hemiplegics. Am J Phys Med 60: 280, 1981.
28. Mason, C: One method for assessing the effectiveness of fast brushing. Phys Ther 65:1197, 1985.
29. Johansson, C, Kent, B, and Shepard, K: Relationship between verbal command volume and magnitude of muscle contraction. Phys Ther 63:1260, 1983.
30. Malkmus, D, Booth, B, and Kodimer, C: Rehabilitation of the Head-Injured Adult: Comprehensive Cognitive Management. Professional Staff Association of Rancho Los Amigos Hospital, Downey, CA, 1980.
31. Malkmus, D: Integrating cognitive strategies into the physical therapy setting. Phys Ther 63:1952, 1983.
32. Reinhart, M: Considerations for functional training in adults after head injury. Phys Ther 63:1975, 1983.
33. Howard, M and Bleiberg, J: A Manual of Behavior Management Strategies for Traumatically Brain-Injured Adults. Rehabilitation Institute of Chicago, Chicago, 1983.
34. Farber, S: Neurorehabilitation: A Multisensory Approach. WB Saunders, Philadelphia, 1982.
35. Twist, D: Effects of wrapping technique on passive range of motion in a spastic upper extremity. Phys Ther 65:299, 1985.
36. Pederson, D: The soothing effect of rocking as determined by the direction and frequency of movement. Can J Behav Sci 7:237, 1975.
37. Rheault, W, et al: Effects of inverted position on blood pressure, pulse rate, and deep tendon reflexes of healthy young adults. Phys Ther 65:1358, 1985.
38. Tokizane, T, et al: Electromyographic studies on tonic neck, lumbar, and labyrinthine reflexes in normal persons. Jpn J Physiol 2:130, 1951.
39. Heinger, M and Randolph, S: Neurophysiological Concepts in Human Behavior: The Tree of Learning. CV Mosby, St Louis, 1981.
40. Ottenbacher, K: Developmental implications of clinically applied vestibular stimulation: A review. Phys Ther 63:338, 1983.

41. Kanter, R, Clark, D, and Atkinson, J: Effects of vestibular stimulation in seizure-prone children. Phys Ther 62:16, 1982.
42. Fiebert, I and Brown, E: Vestibular stimulation to improve ambulation after a cerebral vascular accident. Phys Ther 59:423, 1979.
43. Chee, F, Kreutzberg, J, and Clark, D: Semicircular canal stimulation in cerebral palsied children. Phys Ther 58:1071, 1978.
44. Cheney, P: Role of cerebral cortex in voluntary movements. Phys Ther 65:624, 1985.
45. Brooks, V: Roles of cerebellum and basal ganglia in initiation and control of movements. Can J Neurol Sci 265, 1975.
46. Brooks, V: Motor control: How posture and movements are governed. Phys Ther 63:664, 1983.
47. Evarts, E: Control of voluntary movement by the brain: Contrasting roles of sensorimotor cortex, basal ganglia and cerebellum. In Buser, P, Cobb, W, and Okuma, T (eds): Kyoto Symposia. Elsevier Biomedical Press, Amsterdam, 1982.
48. Adams, J: A closed loop theory of motor learning. J Motor Behavior, 3:111, 1971.
49. Adams, J, Gopher, L, and Lintern, G: Effects of visual and proprioceptive feedback on motor learning. J Experimental Psychology 9:11, 1977.
50. Stelmach, G: Motor Control Issues and Trends. Academic Press, New York, 1976.
51. Singer, R: Motor Learning and Human Performance. Macmillan, New York, 1980.
52. Bishop, B: Neural plasticity, part 4. Lesion-induced reorganization of the CNS. Phys Ther 62:1442, 1982.
53. Luria, A: Restoration of Function after Brain Injury. Pergamon, London, 1963.
54. Bach-y-Rita, P (ed): Recovery of Function: Theoretical Considerations for Brain Injury Rehabilitation. University Park Press, Baltimore, 1980.
55. Finger, S and Stein, D: Brain Damage and Recovery. Academic Press, New York, 1982.
56. St. James-Roberts, I: Neurological plasticity and recovery from brain insult. In Reese, H and Lipsitt, L (ed): Advances in Child Development and Behavior. Academic Press, New York, 1979.
57. Goldberger, M: Motor recovery after lesions. Trends in Neural Sciences 3:288, 1980.
58. Craik, R: Clinical correlates of neural plasticity. Phys Ther 62:1452, 1982.
59. Lashley, K: Functional determinant of cerebral localization. Archives of Neurology and Psychiatry 38:371, 1937.
60. Nelson, A: Strategies for improving motor control. In Rosenthal, M, et al: Rehabilitation of the Head-Injured Adult. FA Davis, Philadelphia, 1983.
61. Fitts, P and Posner, M: Human Performance. Brooks/Cole, Belmont, CA, 1967.
62. Marteniuk, R: Motor skill performance and learnings: Considerations for rehabilitation. Physiotherapy (Can) 31:4, 1979.
63. Kottke, F: From reflex to skill: The training of coordination. Arch Phys Med Rehabil 61:551, 1980.
64. Kottke, F, et al: The training of coordination. Arch Phys Med Rehabil 59:567, 1978.
65. Carr, J and Shephard, R: A Motor Relearning Programme for Stroke. Aspen, Rockville, MD, 1983.
66. Bayley, N: The development of motor abilities during the first three years. Monographs of the Society for Research in Child Development 1 (1, serial no 1), 1935.
67. Gesell, A and Amatruda, C: Developmental Diagnosis. Harper, New York, 1941.
68. McGraw, M: The Neuromuscular Maturation of the Human Infant. Hafner Press, New York, 1945.
69. Peiper, A: Cerebral Function in Infancy and Childhood. Consultants Bureau Enterprises, New York, 1963.
70. Illingworth, R: The Development of the Infant and Young Child: Normal and Abnormal. E and S Livingstone, London, 1975.
71. Milani-Comparetti, A and Gidone, E: Pattern analysis of motor development and its disorders. Dev Med Child Neurol 9:631, 1967.
72. Connolly, K (ed): Mechanisms of Motor Skill Development. Academic Press, New York, 1970.
73. Keogh, J and Sugden, D: Movement Skill Development. Macmillan, New York, 1985.
74. Rose, S and Rothstein, J: Muscle mutability, part 1. General concepts and adaptions to altered patterns of use. Phys Ther 62:1773, 1982.
75. Sullivan, P, Markos, P, and Minor, M: An Integrated Approach to Therapeutic Exercise. Reston, Reston, VA, 1982.
76. Easton, T: On the normal use of reflexes, Am Sci 60:591, 1972.
77. Brunnstrom, S: Movement Therapy in Hemiplegia. Harper & Row, New York, 1970.

SUPPLEMENTAL READINGS

Barnes, M, Crutchfield, C, and Heriza, C: The Neurophysiological Basis of Patient Treatment. Vol II. Reflexes in Motor Development. Stokesville, Atlanta, 1978.
Bishop, B: Spasticity: Its physiology and management. Phys Ther 385, 1977.
Brooks, V: The Neural Basis of Motor Control. Oxford University Press, New York, 1986.
Carr, J and Shephard, R: Physiotherapy in Disorders of the Brain. Wm Heinemann Medical Books, London, 1980.
Charness, A: Stroke/Head Injury. Aspen, Rockville, MD, 1986.
Crutchfield, C and Barnes, J: The Neurophysiological Basis of Patient Treatment. Vol III. Peripheral Components of Motor Control. Stokesville, Atlanta, 1984.
Johnstone, M: Restoration of Motor Function in the Stroke Patient. Churchill Livingstone, New York, 1983.
Mathews, P: Mammalian Muscle Receptors and Their Central Connections. Edward Arnold, London, 1972.
Nixon, V: Spinal Cord Injury, Aspen, Rockville, MD, 1985.

GLOSSARY

Activation: A movement response produced by sensory stimulation techniques; results from the attainment of a critical threshold level of neuronal firing.

Active assisted movement (AAM): Movement performed actively by a patient with assistance provided as need.

Agonist reversal (AR): A proprioceptive neuromuscular facilitation (PNF) technique involving both resisted concentric and eccentric contractions of the agonist pattern.

Alternating isometrics (AI): A proprioceptive neuromuscular facilitation (PNF) technique involving alternate isometric contractions of first agonists, then antagonists.

Approximation: A compression force applied to a joint that facilitates cocontraction and stabilizing responses of postural muscles.

Associative phase of motor learning: The middle phase of learning in which refinement of the motor program is achieved through practice.

Autonomous phase of motor learning: The final stage of learning in which the spatial and temporal aspects of movement become highly organized through practice.

Behavioral substitution: A theory of central nervous system recovery that refers to the ability to achieve the same goal by substituting an entirely different behavioral strategy.

Braiding: A proprioceptive neuromuscular facilitation (PNF) gait activity consisting of resisted sideward crossed stepping: one leg moves across and in front of the other leg, followed by a side step of the other leg; the cycle is repeated with a step across and behind followed by a side step of the other leg.

Cocontraction: Simultaneous contraction (coactivation) of muscles on both sides of a joint (agonists and antagonists), enabling stability or dynamic stability patterns.

Cognitive phase of motor learning: The initial phase of learning in which the cognitive plan for the task is developed.

Contract-relax (CR): A proprioceptive neuromuscular facilitation (PNF) technique involving a maximally resisted contraction of the range-limiting antagonist pattern followed by active relaxation and movement into the agonist pattern. Rotators are allowed to contract isotonically while all other muscles contract isometrically.

Diaschisis theory: A theory of CNS recovery that refers to the early, spontaneous recovery secondary to the resolution of cerebral shock.

Distributed practice: An alternating sequence of rest and practice sessions in which the rest time equals or exceeds the practice time.

Efferent copy: A copy of the motor plan sent by the cortex to the cerebellum to be used as a reference for correctness.

Facilitation: The enhanced capacity to initiate a movement response through increased neuronal activity and altered synaptic potential.

Fast vestibular stimulation: Rapid, irregular stimulation of the vestibular apparatus, resulting in a generalized increase in postural tone and improved motor coordination.

Feedback: Sensory information provided to the central nervous system from the production of movement. Two general types exist:

    Augmented feedback (extrinsic feedback): Feedback that is added to that normally received during a movement task.

    Intrinsic feedback: Feedback normally received during the execution of movement.

Functional reorganization: A theory of central nervous system (CNS) recovery that refers to the ability of the CNS to alter its structural organization following injury.

Heavy work: Term used to describe motor patterns in which the distal segments are fixed and the proximal segments are moving.

Hold-relax (HR): A proprioceptive neuromuscular facilitation (PNF) technique involving a maximally resisted isometric contraction of the range-limiting

antagonist pattern followed by active relaxation and movement into the agonist pattern.

Hold-relax active motion (HRA): A proprioceptive neuromuscular facilitation (PNF) technique involving maximal isometric contraction in the shortened range followed by active relaxation, passive movement into the lengthened range and resisted movement back to the shortened range.

Inhibition: Decreased capacity to initiate a movement response through decreased neuronal activity and altered synaptic potential.

Inhibitory pressure: A maintained pressure stimulus applied to long tendons of muscle that results in autogenic inhibition.

Intermittent control hypothesis: A theory of motor control that specifies the interaction between closed loop and open loop processes in controlling movement.

Inverted head position (tonic labyrinthine inverted response): Tipping of the head down in relation to the trunk; stimulation of baroreceptors and vestibular apparatus results in a generalized depression of sympathetic activity (carotid sinus response) and generalized facilitation of postural extensors (vestibular response).

Inverted U theory (Yerkes-Dodson law): With increasing arousal, performance improves up to a point. Further increases in arousal beyond this point result in a decrease in performance.

Key points of control: Parts of the body, generally proximal components such as the head, shoulders, hips—used in neurodevelopmental treatment (NDT) to control tone and movement.

Knowledge of performance (KP): Feedback that occurs during movement and allows for error detection and movement modification.

Knowledge of results (KR): Feedback that occurs at the conclusion of movement and allows the apprisal of the overall success of the movement response.

Light touch: A brief touch stimulus that can be used to elicit a phasic withdrawal response.

Light work: A term used to describe motor patterns in which the distal segments of the limbs are moving over the fixed, proximal segments.

Maintained touch: Firm manual contacts used to apply pressure and maintained contact to sensitive areas, including the palms, soles, or lips.

Manual contacts (MC): A contact stimulus of the hands resulting in facilitation of a movement response.

Massed practice: A prolonged period of practice with infrequent rest periods.

Motor learning: A set of processes associated with practice or experience leading to a relatively permanent change in skilled behavior.

Neural plasticity: Refers to the capacity of the central nervous system for adaption and reorganization.

Neutral warmth: The retention of body warmth through wrapping or neutral baths, producing generalized inhibition and a calming effect.

Prolonged icing: A maintained cold stimulus that produces a localized inhibition of postural tone and pain.

Prolonged stretch: A maintained stretch stimulus that produces inhibition or dampening of muscle responses.

Quick stretch: A brief stretch stimulus used to facilitate muscle contraction.

Redundancy theory: A theory of central nervous system (CNS) recovery that refers to the ability of the CNS to control the same function with several different neural areas.

Reflex-inhibiting patterns: Dynamic movement patterns used in neurodevelopment treatment (NDT) to inhibit or to reverse abnormal reflex or tonal patterns while facilitating more normal movements.

Reflex integration: The normal contributions that reflexes play in the regulatory control of posture and movement.

Repeated contractions (RC): A PNF technique involving repeated, isotonic contractions of the agonist.

Repetitive brushing (fast brushing): A repetitive light touch stimulus used to facilitate movement responses.

Resistance (maintained stretch): An external load applied to muscle that results in recruitment of alpha and gamma motoneurons.

Resisted progression (RP): A PNF technique involving the use of stretch and resistance to enhance patterns of locomotion.

Rhythmic initiation (RI): A proprioceptive neuromuscular facilitation (PNF) technique involving voluntary relaxation followed by passive, active-assistive and finally mildly resisted movements of the agonist pattern.

Rhythmic rotation (RRo): A therapeutic technique used in proprioceptive neuromuscular facilitation (PNF) and neurodevelopment treatment (NDT) that involves repeated, passive rotational movements of a limb or the trunk following commands for active relaxation.

Rhythmic stabilization (RS): A proprioceptive neuromuscular facilitation (PNF) technique involving isometric contractions of antagonist patterns with resistance applied simultaneously to both agonists and antagonists.

Sensory engram: A memory store of sensorimotor experiences in the sensory cortex.

Shortened held resisted contraction (SHRC): Sustained isometric contraction of muscles in the shortened range; usually applied to postural extensors.

Slow reversals: A proprioceptive neuromuscular facilitation (PNF) technique involving alternating isotonic contractions of first agonist then antagonist patterns.

Slow reversal-hold: A proprioceptive neuromuscular facilitation (PNF) technique involving alternate isometric and isotonic contractions of both agonist and antagonist patterns: a holding response of the agonist is followed by a resisted isotonic contraction of the antagonist pattern, progressing to an isometric hold of the antagonist in the shortened range.

Slow stroking: Firm, alternate strokes applied to the back over the posterior primary rami (PPR) to promote calming and generalized inhibition.

Slow vestibular stimulation: Gentle, repetitive rocking or rolling movements which produce a generalized calming effect and inhibition of postural tone.

Spatial summation (multiple fiber summation): The capacity of the central nervous system to increase signal strength by using progressively greater numbers of neuronal fibers.

Static-dynamic control: A variation of controlled mobility in which body weight is shifted over the support limbs while one or more limbs are lifted and engaged in a dynamic motor pattern.

Temporal summation: The capacity of the central nervous system to increase signal strength by increasing the frequency of impulses in a nerve fiber.

Timing for emphasis (TE): A proprioceptive neuromuscular facilitation (PNF) technique involving an isometric hold and resistance of the stronger components of a pattern while repeated contractions are applied to the weaker components.

Tonic holding: Holding of the postural muscles (extensors) in the fully shortened range against gravity or manual resistance.

Traction: A distraction force applied to joint surfaces that facilitates phasic movement responses.

Transfer of learning: Practice of related or similar movement skills that results in improved performance of other desired skills.

Vibration: A high-frequency, low-amplitude intermittent stretch stimulus that produces the tonic vibration reflex (TVR) and results in maintained contraction of muscle.

Vicarious function: A theory of central nervous system recovery that refers to the capacity of the brain to take on functions normally controlled by other areas.

Chapter 15

GAIT TRAINING WITH ASSISTIVE DEVICES

THOMAS J. SCHMITZ

OBJECTIVES

1. Identify the components of a general gait-training program.

2. Identify the purposes of a preambulation exercise program.

3. Describe the guidelines for measuring assistive devices.

4. Describe the common gait patterns used with assistive devices.

5. Describe the techniques for guarding the patient during gait training in the parallel bars, on level surfaces, and on stairs.

INTRODUCTION

Ambulation is a primary functional goal for many patients that requires that physical therapists be able to identify problems that limit or prevent ambulation, to determine their causes, and to plan appropriate therapeutic intervention. A component of this intervention typically includes a program of gait training. The purpose of gait-training activities is to provide the patient a method of ambulation that allows maximum functional independence and safety at a reasonable energy cost.

This chapter presents a general framework of gait training with assistive devices that can be modified to meet the needs of individual patients. Several factors will be of major influence in determining the extent and type of gait-training activities required. These factors include the patient's primary diagnosis, medical history, weight-bearing status, data obtained from the physical therapist's assessment, and input from the patient regarding ambulatory goals. For example, the progression of gait-training activities indicated for an otherwise healthy individual with a non-weight-bearing tibial fracture would be very different from those developed for a patient with paraplegia.

The major elements of a gait-training program are out-lined in Table 15-1. It should be noted that the entire sequence will not be indicated for each patient. Depending on individual patient need, multiple segments may be accomplished concurrently (i.e., a more rapid progression may be indicated), or portions may be completely omitted.

PREPARATION FOR STANDING AND PARALLEL BAR PROGRESSION

Preambulation Mat Program

Preambulation exercise programs prepare the patient for assuming the upright position and typically involve a large component of mat work. Many of these mat activities are based on a developmental framework and progress from initial activities with a large base of support (BOS) and a low center of gravity (COG) through later activities which have a smaller BOS and high COG. The techniques utilized within each posture of the mat program are sequenced according to the four stages of motor control and progress from (1) *mobility,* which incorporates initiation of movement techniques, including *assist*

Table 15–1 GENERAL OUTLINE OF GAIT-TRAINING PROGRAM

A. PREAMBULATION MAT PROGRAM: Activities and techniques to
  1. Improve strength, coordination, and range of motion.
  2. Facilitate proprioceptive feedback.
  3. Develop postural stability.
  4. Develop controlled mobility in movement transitions.
  · 5. Develop dynamic balance control and skill.
B. PARALLEL BAR PROGRESSION: Instruction and training in
  1. Moving from sitting to standing and reverse.
  2. Standing balance and weight-shifting activities.
  3. Use of appropriate gait pattern, forward progression, and turning.
  *4. Moving from sitting to standing and reverse with assistive device.
  *5. Standing balance and weight-shifting activities with assistive device.
  *6. Use of assistive device (with selected gait pattern) for forward progression and turning.
C. ADVANCED PARALLEL BAR ACTIVITIES
  1. Walking sideward (sidewalking).
  2. Walking backward.
  3. Braiding.
  4. Resisted ambulatory activities.
D. INDOOR PROGRESSION: Instruction and training in
  1. Use of assistive device for ambulation on level surfaces.
  2. Elevation activities, including climbing stairs and, if available indoors, negotiating ramps and curbs.
  3. Opening doors and passing through doorways (including elevators) and over thresholds.
  4. Falling techniques (generally included for active ambulators requiring long-term use of assistive devices).
E. OUTDOOR PROGRESSION: Instruction and training in
  1. Opening doors and passing through thresholds that lead outdoors.
  2. Use of assistive device for ambulation on outdoor surfaces and uneven terrain.
  3. Elevation activities including stair climbing and negotiating ramps and curbs.
  4. Crossing a street within the time allocated by a traffic light.
  5. Entering an automobile and/or public transportation.

*Because of limited space, use of the parallel bars may not be possible. However, when adjustable-width bars are available, they provide added security for preliminary use of the assistive device. An alternative approach would be to begin use of the device *outside and next to* the parallel bars.

to position in which the therapist manually assists the patient to achieve a given posture; (2) to *stability,* characterized by the ability to maintain a posture against gravity; (3) to *controlled mobility,* which is the ability to maintain postural control during weight shifting and movement; (4) and finally to *skill,* which is the highest level of motor development, characterized by discrete motor control superimposed on proximal stability. The techniques used within each posture typically progress from assisted or guided movement to resisted.

These mat or lead-up activities (the term *lead-up* implies that the activities are preparatory for or "lead up" to ambulation) have important functional carry-over to other daily activities as well, such as relieving pressure, dressing, and bed mobility. The development of successful mat programs will require the therapist to draw on several different exercise approaches. The work of Voss,[1] Sullivan,[2] and coworkers is particularly helpful in this regard. Additionally, many other more traditional

forms of exercise provide important components of an overall program of preambulation exercises (e.g., progressive resistive exercises, sling/spring suspension techniques, and coordination exercises).

Depending on the level of patient involvement, the goals of a preambulation exercise program will be to
  1. Improve strength.
  2. Improve or maintain range of motion.
  3. Improve coordination.
  4. Facilitate proprioceptive feedback.
  5. Instruct in handling and moving the affected extremity or extremities.
  6. Develop postural stability in sitting and standing.
  7. Develop controlled mobility function as evidenced by the ability to move within postures.
  8. Develop control in movement transitions such as rolling and moving from a supine position to a sitting position.
  9. Improve trunk and pelvic control.
  10. Develop dynamic balance control, including equilibrium and protective reactions.

A general outline of suggested preambulation mat exercises follows. The activities should be sequenced from easiest to most difficult and should reflect the spiral nature of motor development; that is, total mastery of one activity is not necessary before progressing to the next higher level. With adult patients it is common to work on several levels of activities concurrently. The specific activities and techniques selected as well as the sequence of progression will be determined by goals established for the individual patient. Chapter 14 (Strategies to Improve Motor Control) should be consulted for descriptions of the individual techniques and additional treatment suggestions. The mat sequence which follows uses a progression of postures, including rolling, prone-on-elbows (and hands), hooklying and bridging, quadruped, sitting, kneeling and half kneeling, modified plantigrade, and, finally, standing.

ROLLING

A frequent initial starting point for a preambulation mat program is rolling. This activity provides a large BOS and low COG without bearing weight through the joints. Mat work may begin in a *sidelying* position at first, particularly if initiation of rolling is difficult. Resisted isometric contractions in shortened ranges (termed *shortened held resisted contraction*) are a useful early technique in sidelying. This technique uses sustained isometric contractions of the postural extensors in preparation for **cocontraction.** Manual contacts are posteriorly on the shoulder and pelvis. The patient is asked to "hold" maximally against the resistance of the therapist through increments of range. Additionally, the proprioceptive neuromuscular facilitation (PNF) techniques of **hold-relax-active movement** and **rhythmic stabilization**[1] also may be used in sidelying to facilitate cocontraction and proximal **stability.**

Rolling activities generally progress from **log rolling** to **segmental rolling. Log rolling** produces movement of the entire trunk as a unit around the longitudinal axis of the body. **Segmental rolling** is a progression from log rolling.

In segmental rolling either the upper or the lower segment of the trunk can move independently while the other segment is stabilized. As the progression continues, **counterrotation** will develop. **Counterrotation** involves simultaneous movement of the upper and lower segments of the trunk in opposite directions. Several suggested activities follow which can be used and/or combined to facilitate rolling.

1. Flexion of the head and neck with rotation may be used to assist movement from supine to prone positions.

2. Extension of the head and neck with rotation may be used to assist movement from prone to supine positions.

3. Bilateral upper extremity activities that cross the midline will produce a pendular motion and can be used to rock the body from a supine position toward a prone position. To create this momentum, both elbows are extended, the shoulders flexed to approximately 110 degrees with the hands clasped together. The upper extremities are then swung from side-to-side.

4. Crossing the ankles will also facilitate rolling. The ankles are crossed such that the upper leg is toward the direction of the roll (e.g., the right ankle would be crossed over the left when rolling toward the left).

5. Several PNF patterns are useful during early rolling activities.[1-3] The upper extremity patterns of D_1 flexion, D_2 extension, chop, and reverse chop will facilitate *rolling toward* a *prone* position. The upper extremity lifting pattern will facilitate *rolling toward* a *supine* position. To facilitate rolling in either direction, the lower extremity pattern of D_1 flexion is used consistently.[3]

PRONE-ON-ELBOWS POSITION

In the prone-on-elbows position there continues to be a large BOS and low COG. This position provides weight bearing on the elbows and forearms. The posture is useful to facilitate proximal stability via cocontraction of the glenohumeral and scapular musculature. Although head and neck control is required to assume a prone-on-elbows position, it can be further improved in this posture. The prone-on-elbows position must be used cautiously because some patients will find it difficult to tolerate the increased lordotic curve. Additionally, this position may be problematic for patients with shoulder or elbow pathology, cardiac or respiratory impairment, or hip flexor tightness.

To assist in initial assumption of the prone-on-elbows position, the patient should be in the following starting position:[4] prone, both lower extremities extended, the shoulders abducted, elbows flexed, forearms pronated, palms flat on supporting surface, and the head in a neutral position (or turned to one side for comfort). The therapist is positioned to the side of the patient or, if supporting surface permits, straddling the patient's trunk with one foot on either side of the patient's body. The therapist's hips and knees should be flexed and manual contacts placed over the pectoral muscles with fingers pointing toward the sternum. The therapist then assists to position by lifting and supporting the upper trunk as the patient adducts the shoulders to allow weight bearing on the elbows (Fig. 15–1). Several suggested activities

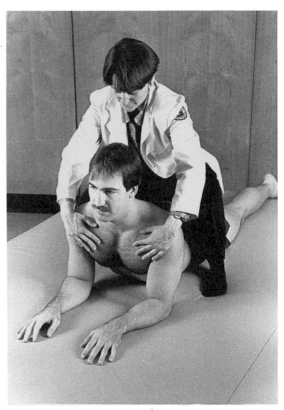

Figure 15–1. Method for assisting patient into the prone-on-elbows position.

that can be used as a progression within this posture follow.

1. Initial activities should include assisted assumption and maintenance of the posture.

2. Manually applied approximation force can be used to facilitate **tonic holding** of proximal musculature. Rhythmic stabilization or alternating isometrics may be used to increase stability of head, neck, and scapula.[2]

3. A progression can be made to independent maintenance of the posture while altering head position and depressing the scapula.

4. Weight shifting in this position will improve dynamic stability through increased joint **approximation.**[5] Weight shifting is usually easiest in a lateral direction but also may be accomplished in an anterior or posterior direction (Fig. 15–2).

5. Activities that require resisted grasp in this position such as squeezing a ball or a cone[5] will reinforce cocontraction at the shoulder.[5,6]

6. Controlled mobility activities of the scapula can be used to promote proximal dynamic stability (e.g., prone-on-elbows pushups).

7. Static-dynamic activities should be included in the prone-on-elbows position. This involves unilateral weight bearing on the static limb while the dynamic limb is freed. This will further facilitate cocontraction in the weight-bearing limb.

8. Movement within this posture can be achieved by an on-elbows forward-and-backward progression.

9. Movement into and out of the posture should be a final component of the prone-on-elbows sequence.

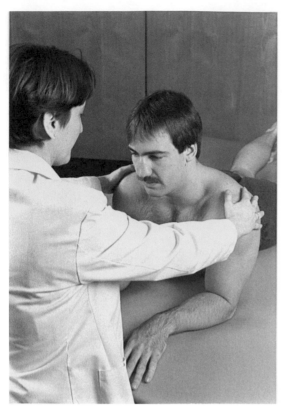

Figure 15–2. Prone on elbows. Lateral weight shifting will improve dynamic stability secondary to increased joint approximation.

PRONE-ON-HANDS POSITION

This position is considered an intermediate step between the prone-on-elbows and quadruped positions.[5] In the prone-on-hands position a smaller BOS and higher COG is achieved. Weight is now borne through the elbows to the hands and wrists. As with the prone-on-elbows position, this position also will be inappropriate for many patients owing to the excessive lordosis required to assume and to maintain the position. However, this position has several important functional implications. The functional carry-over of the prone-on-hands position include development of the initial hyperextension of the hips and low back for patients requiring this type of postural alignment during ambulation (e.g., patients with paraplegia), and standing from a wheelchair or rising from the floor with crutches and bilateral knee ankle orthoses.

To assist to the prone-on-hands position, the patient should first assume the prone-on-elbows position. The therapist's position and manual contacts are the same as for assisting to prone-on-elbows. Initially, work in this position often requires starting with the patient's supporting hand placement further away from the body (i.e., with greater than 90 degrees of shoulder flexion) until the patient becomes accustomed to the position. This type of early positioning may require contact guarding from the therapist to allow maintenance of the position. Several suggestions follow for activities that may be completed while the patient is in the prone-on-hands position.

1. Initial activities should include assisted assumption and assisted maintenance of the posture.
2. Additional approximation force can be applied through manual contacts to further facilitate tonic holding of proximal musculature.
3. Independent maintenance of the posture should be practiced; a progression can be made to maintaining the posture with alterations in head position and during scapular depression.
4. Lateral weight shifting with weight transfer between hands will increase joint approximation.
5. Resisted scapular depression and prone-on-hands push-ups may be used as strengthening exercises in this position.
6. A progression can be made to movement within this posture in both forward and lateral directions. This activity has useful functional implications for patients with paraplegia. An important example is floor-to-stand transitions. The prone-on-hands position provides the functional skills to allow the patient to reposition the body and the crutches to prepare for standing.

HOOKLYING

In this posture the patient is supine with hips and knees flexed and feet flat on the mat. This position provides a large BOS and low COG. Lower trunk rotation can be facilitated by movement of the lower extremities across the midline. It is useful in activating both the lower abdominals and low back extensors as well as increasing range of motion in the low back and hips.[2] Activities within this posture are initiated with assisted or guided movement. A progression is then made to application of resistance applied in each direction away from the midline. Manual contacts at the knees must be altered from the medial to lateral surfaces as the direction of movement is changed. Several suggestions that may be used and/or combined in the hooklying position follow.

1. Tonic holding activities within a shortened range will improve stability (shortened held resisted contraction).
2. Rhythmic stabilization may be used with manual contacts at the knees to facilitate cocontraction and stability.[1]
3. Active assisted, guided, or resisted movement in each direction away from the midline may be used to increase range of motion (Fig. 15–3).
4. Hip abduction and adduction can be facilitated by use of alternating isometrics with manual contacts at the knees.
5. The level of difficulty of this activity may be increased by decreasing the amount of hip and knee flexion and moving manual contacts for application of resistance to the ankles.[2]

BRIDGING

This activity is a progression from hooklying. It places the lower extremities in a weight-bearing position and is an important precursor to assuming the kneeling posi-

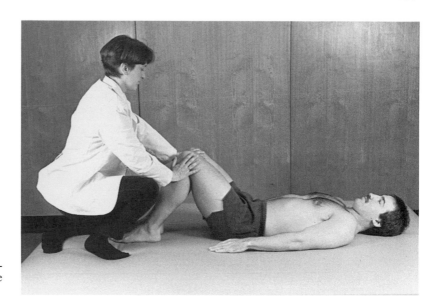

Figure 15–3. Hooklying. In this position lower trunk rotation and range of motion is facilitated by movement of the lower extremities in each direction from the midline.

tion and in developing sit-to-stand control. For this activity the patient is in a hooklying position and elevates the pelvis off the mat (Fig. 15–4). The BOS is thus reduced and the COG is raised. This activity is particularly useful for facilitating pelvic motions and strengthening the low back and hip extensors in preparation for the stance phase of gait. In addition, bridging has several important functional implications, including bed mobility, use of a bedpan, pressure relief, lower extremity dressing, and movement from a sitting to a standing position. Specific pelvic motions (e.g., pelvic forward motion, rotation, and lateral shift) required during gait also can be initiated and facilitated in this position. Several suggestions that can be used as a progression within this posture follow.

1. Initial activities will involve assisted assumption and assisted maintenance of the position. Manual contacts to assist to position are at the pelvis. Assistance dur-

ing early bridging activities also can be provided by having the patient abduct the arms on the mat to provide a larger BOS.

2. The ability to maintain, or to hold, the posture can be facilitated by use of shortened held resisted contractions. The isometric techniques of alternating isometrics and rhythmic stabilization also can be used to promote stability.

3. Independent maintenance of the posture should be practiced with a progressive decrease in the BOS provided by the upper extremities (i.e., moving arms closer to body).

4. The techniques of slow reversal and slow reversal-hold can be used to facilitate pelvic rotation and lateral shifting.[2]

5. Strengthening can be accomplished during bridging by application of resistance with manual contacts at the anterior superior iliac spines. Resistance also can be

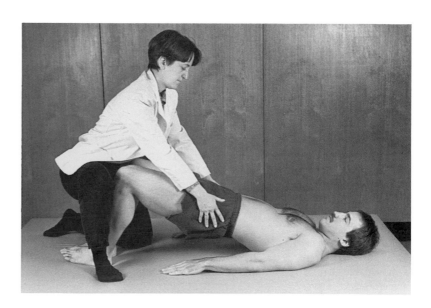

Figure 15–4. Bridging. Manual contacts at the pelvis can be used to assist or to resist pelvic elevation.

applied diagonally (greater emphasis of resistance to one side) to facilitate pelvic rotation and/or to increase range of motion selectively on one side.[1,7]

6. Bridging also can be used to facilitate hip abduction and adduction. This can be accomplished either symmetrically (resistance applied against the same motion in each extremity) or asymmetrically (resistance applied against opposing motions) by use of alternating isometrics with manual contacts at the knees.[7]

7. Several modifications to bridging can be made to make the activity more demanding by altering the BOS. These modifications include (a) performing the activity with support from only one lower extremity in preparation for weight acceptance during the stance phase of gait, and (b) decreasing the angle of hip and knee flexion (i.e., moving the feet distally).

8. A final component of the sequence is unassisted or resisted (e.g., using agonist reversal) movement into and out of the posture.

QUADRUPED POSITION

This on-all-fours position further decreases the BOS and raises the COG with weight bearing through multiple joints. The **quadruped** position is the first position in the mat progression that allows weight bearing through the hips. This posture is particularly useful for facilitating initial control of the musculature of the lower trunk and hips.

As mentioned earlier, complete mastery of each component of the mat progression is not always necessary before progressing to the next higher level. Progressions may be planned such that two postures may be overlapped and used in a mat sequence concurrently. Clinically, this is particularly true of quadruped and sitting positions (description of the sitting position follows). Although quadruped is described here first, it is not uncommon for the two postures to be reversed or worked on simultaneously.

Assumption of the quadruped position can be achieved from two positions. If the patient is able to sit, the patient may be guided into sidesitting by rotating the trunk to allow weight bearing on the hands with the elbows extended. The therapist then guides the lower trunk into the quadruped position with manual contacts on the pelvis, assisting movement of the pelvis over the knees.

The quadruped position also may be assumed from a prone-on-elbows position. Using this technique the therapist straddles the patient's lower extremities with one foot placed parallel to each thigh. With the therapist's hips and knees bent, he or she then lifts and guides the pelvis over the knees as the patient "walks" backward on elbows. Once the pelvis is positioned over the knees, the patient assumes or is assisted into weight bearing on hands with full elbow extension. Several suggested techniques and activities that can be incorporated into the quadruped position follow.

1. Initial activities involve assisted assumption and assisted maintenance of the position. If these activities are difficult, a gymnastic ball can first be used to support the patient's trunk during the movement transition from side sitting to the quadruped position and then during maintenance of the position. The ball can be placed centrally under the trunk or moved toward the upper or lower extremities, depending on the area of greatest weakness.

2. Rhythmic stabilization or alternating isometrics will facilitate cocontraction of shoulder, hip, and trunk musculature.[1]

3. Weight shifting can be used in a forward, backward, and side-to-side direction to increase weight bearing over two extremities simultaneously to improve dynamic stability.

4. Manual application of approximation force can be used to facilitate cocontraction through both upper and lower extremities.

5. For patients with spasticity, this position can be used to provide inhibitory pressure to the quadriceps and long finger flexors (using an open-hand position) to diminish tone.

6. Rocking through increments of range (forward, backward, side-to-side, and diagonally) will facilitate equilibrium and proprioceptive responses as well as increase range of motion at the proximal weight-bearing joints.[1,2]

7. Static-dynamic activities, such as freeing one or more extremities from a weight-bearing position, may be used in the quadruped position. A progression is frequently made from unweighting one upper extremity to one lower extremity to opposite upper and lower extremities simultaneously. This activity will provide greater joint approximation forces on the supporting extremities and increase dynamic holding of postural muscles (Fig. 15–5).

8. Movement within the quadruped position (**creeping**) has several important implications for ambulation. Creeping can be used to improve strength (resisted progression), facilitate dynamic balance reactions, and improve coordination and timing.

9. A final progression within the quadruped position is unassisted movement into and out of the posture.

SITTING

A program of mat activities typically includes work in the sitting position. Sitting can be used effectively to develop balance, trunk control, and weight bearing on the upper extremities. In addition, improved stability of the head and neck can be achieved in this position. Three types of sitting are often incorporated into a preambulation mat program:

1. **Short sitting.** In this position the patient's hips and knees are flexed with the feet flat on the floor.

2. **Tailor sitting** ("Indian style" sitting). This position places the hips in flexion, abduction, and external rotation, with the knees flexed and the ankles crossed.

3. **Long sitting.** In this position the hips are flexed and the knees are extended on the supporting surface.

As with the quadruped position, the sitting position provides a small BOS and high COG. However, it should be noted that the BOS for the various types of sitting is different and may influence selection for an individual patient. For example, the long sitting position provides a

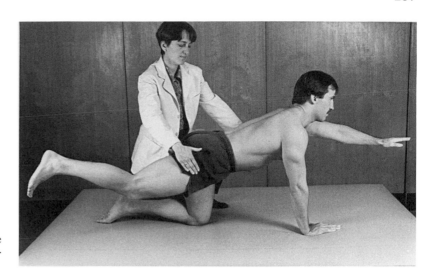

Figure 15–5. Quadruped. Static-dynamic activities facilitate dynamic holding of postural muscles by increasing weight-bearing demands on the static limbs.

relatively large BOS as compared with the short sitting position. This larger BOS in long sitting is provided by placement of the lower extremities in contact with the supporting surface.

Another factor that warrants consideration in selection of sitting postures is the range of motion required to assume the position. The long sitting position will be difficult for some patients owing to limited range of motion in the low back and/or hamstrings. Hamstring tightness in the long sitting position may also result in alterations in pelvic position, causing the patient to "sit back" on the ischia. Similarly, the tailor position will be inappropriate in situations of limited hip or knee range of motion.

The BOS in sitting may be altered by changing the position of upper extremity support. Upper extremity support may be placed posterior to the pelvis (large BOS), lateral to the pelvis (small BOS), or anterior to the pelvis (intermediate BOS). Several suggestions that can be incorporated into a progression of activities used in the sitting positions follow.

1. Initial activities will focus on assisted assumption and assisted maintenance of the position. For patients with proprioceptive loss, use of a mirror during sitting activities may provide important visual feedback.

2. Manual application of approximation force may be used at the shoulders to promote cocontraction.

3. A variety of PNF techniques may be used. Specifically, alternating isometrics and rhythmic stabilization are important in promoting early stability in this posture.[1]

4. For patients with spasticity, sitting with extended arm support with the hand open and flat will provide inhibitory input to the long finger flexors to dampen tone.

5. The position of upper extremity support may be altered with subsequent transfer of weight in each position (e.g., posteriorly, anteriorly, and laterally). This activity also will promote cocontraction as well as alter the BOS.

6. Unassisted maintenance of the posture should be included with a gradual reduction and then elimination of upper extremity support.

7. Balancing activities may be practiced in sitting without upper extremity support. The position of the upper extremities may be altered by having the patient move into shoulder flexion, abduction, and so forth while maintaining trunk balance. A progression may be made to movement of the trunk (forward, backward, and side to side) without upper extremity support. As a component of these activities the patient's balance may be manually challenged at the trunk or by passive movement of the lower extremities. Balance also may be challenged by asking the patient to practice throwing and catching a ball to and from various directions or by completing functional activities such as putting on a pair of socks, tying shoes, and so forth.

8. Unassisted movement into and out of the sitting position should be practiced.

9. When indicated, the sitting position is often used for partial instruction in self-range-of-motion exercises. Both long sitting and tailor sitting can be used for this purpose. Forward flexion of the trunk with the knees extended in long sitting will maintain length of the low back and hamstring muscles. The tailor sitting position facilitates range of motion in hip external rotation, abduction, and knee flexion, and allows easier access to the ankle and foot.

10. Sitting pushups are an important preliminary activity for transfers and ambulation as well as for improving ability in positional changes. This activity is accomplished by placing arms at sides, extending the elbows, and depressing the shoulders to lift the buttock from the mat. The activity can be initiated with bearing weight on the base of the hands placed directly on the mat and progressed to the use of pushup blocks with graded increments in height. A modification of the sitting pushup is placement of both hands on one side of the body in a long sitting position (side sitting). The patient then pushes down on both upper extremities to lift the buttocks off the mat. The functional implications of this activity are related to movement transitions from sitting to quadruped positions. It is also an important preliminary activity prior to sit-to-stand activities for patients with paraplegia (initial trunk rotation is often required before standing).

11. Movement within this posture has direct functional carry-over to transfers, ambulation, and positional changes. However, these activities require good bilateral upper extremity strength (e.g., patients with paraplegia). Movement within sitting can be accomplished by using a seated pushup in combination with movement from the head and upper body. Momentum is created by throwing the head and shoulders forcefully in the direction opposite to the desired direction of motion. For example, while performing a pushup on the mat from long sitting, simultaneous rapid and forceful extension of the head and shoulders will move the lower extremities forward; movement in a posterior direction can be achieved by use of a sitting pushup with simultaneous rapid and forceful flexion of the head and trunk. This same progression of movement is used with the **swing-to** and **swing-through gait patterns.** Movement in the sitting position also may be accomplished by hiking one hip and shifting weight forward or backward and then repeating with the opposite hip. For patients with paraplegia, these early movements within the sitting posture frequently incorporate the use of mat crutches.

12. A number of additional exercises may be included in the sitting position. With manual contacts at the shoulder, resistance may be applied to trunk extension, flexion, and rotation. Combining PNF patterns of the head, trunk, and extremities in sitting (e.g., chopping or lifting activities) can be used to improve strength as well as to assist the patient in achieving functional goals related to this posture.[2]

KNEELING

The kneeling position further decreases the BOS, raises the COG, and provides weight bearing at the hips and knees. This position is particularly useful for establishing lower trunk and pelvic control and further promoting upright balance control. The position also facilitates the lower extremity pattern (initiated during bridging) of combined hip extension with knee flexion necessary for gait activities.

It is usually easiest to assist the patient into a kneeling position from a quadruped position. From the quadruped position, the patient moves or "walks" the hands backward until the knees further flex and the pelvis drops toward the heels. The patient will be "sitting" on the heels. From this position the patient may be assisted to kneeling by using the upper extremities to climb stall bars while the therapist guides the pelvis. Another method is for the therapist to assume a heel-sitting position directly in front of the patient. The patient's upper extremities are supported on the therapist's shoulders while the therapist manually guides the pelvis. Several suggested techniques and activities that can be utilized during kneeling follow.

1. Initial activities concentrate on assisted assumption and assisted maintenance of the position.

2. Approximation force may be used at the hips to facilitate cocontraction.

3. The PNF technique of slow reversal or slow reversal-hold is effective in facilitating pelvic forward motion, lateral shifting, and rotation.[2]

4. Eccentric hip control can be facilitated by agonist reversals. This technique uses a smooth reversal between concentric and eccentric contractions. With manual contacts at the pelvis, the hips are moved into increments of flexion with a return to extension. The excursion of movement is gradually increased. This technique also improves ability to move from heel-sitting to the kneeling position.

5. Transfer of weight from one knee to the other will facilitate cocontraction on the supporting limb.

6. Balancing activities may be practiced, progressing from support with one upper extremity to balancing without upper extremity support. The patient's balance may be challenged in this position. Throwing and catching a ball from various directions also can be used as a component of these balance activities.

7. Unassisted assumption of the posture can be facilitated by use of reverse chop or lift-trunk patterns.[1]

8. Hip hiking and forward progression, or "kneel walking," while upper extremities are supported on the therapist's shoulder can be included in this position. A resisted progression can be used to facilitate forward movement. A progression is then made to a resisted progression with the upper extremities freed.

9. A variety of mat crutch activities can be used in the kneeling position (most commonly used with individuals who have sustained spinal cord injuries). Examples include weight shifting anteriorly, posteriorly, and laterally with emphasis on lower trunk and pelvic control; placing the crutches forward, backward, and to the side with weight shifts in each direction; alternately raising one crutch at a time and returning it to the mat; hip hiking; instruction in selected gait patterns and forward progression using crutches.

10. Kneeling can be used to provide inhibition to the quadriceps muscle and thus to dampen tone in patients with spasticity. Reduction of extensor tone may be an important preparatory activity to standing for some patients.

HALF-KNEELING

In half-kneeling (Fig. 15–6) the COG is the same as in kneeling; however, the BOS is widened. Greater demands are now placed on the posterior weight-bearing limb in preparation for weight acceptance during the stance phase of gait. Weight on the forward limb is now borne through the ankle. This position allows facilitation of hip extension, lateral pelvic control, and ankle movements, and it increases proprioceptive input through the foot.[8] The following techniques and activities are appropriate for use in the half-kneeling position.

1. Initial activities will include assisted assumption and assisted maintenance of the posture.

2. Rhythmic stabilization or alternating isometrics may be used in this position to improve stability. Several combinations of manual contacts[2] may be used: shoulder and pelvis; shoulder and anterior knee; and pelvis and anterior knee.

3. Anterior/posterior weight shifting in this position will facilitate range of motion of the hip, knee, and especially the ankle (see Figure 15–6).

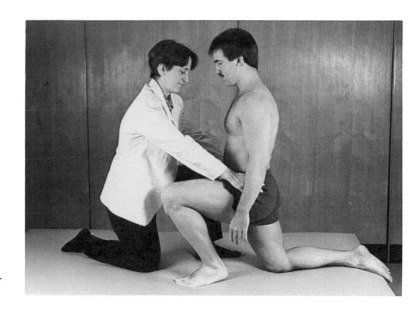

Figure 15-6. Half-kneeling. Anterior weight shifting onto forward limb.

4. Resistance may be introduced with manual contacts at the pelvis during weight shifting (e.g., slow reversal or slow reversal-hold).

MODIFIED PLANTIGRADE

Modified plantigrade (Fig. 15-7) is the next posture in the progression toward erect standing and walking. In this position there is a relatively small BOS and high COG. This posture inherently promotes stability because weight-bearing demands are placed on all joints of all four extremities. Modified plantigrade is an important precursor to walking inasmuch as it superimposes close to full weight bearing on an advanced lower extremity pattern. This pattern, required during gait, combines hip flexion with knee extension and ankle dorsiflexion.

Initial assist-to-position activities are usually easiest from a sitting position, using a chair with arms. The chair is positioned directly in front of a treatment table or other stable surface of appropriate height. A guarding belt is warranted during early transitions from sitting to plantigrade positions. A similar procedure as for any sit-to-stand transfer is used. The patient is asked or assisted to move forward in the chair. The feet should be flat on the floor and the hands placed on the armrests of the chair. The patient then pushes down on the handrests and moves toward modified plantigrade (placing one hand at a time onto the supporting surface). The therapist provides the needed level of assistance by use of the guarding belt and/or manual contacts. Several suggested activities and techniques that can be used in this posture follow.

1. Initial activities involve assisted assumption and assisted maintenance of the posture.

2. Stability can be enhanced by use of manual approximation force at both the shoulders and the pelvis. Rhythmic stabilization and alternating isometrics also can be used to promote stability in this position. Manual contacts are at the pelvis, shoulders, or shoulders and pelvis.

3. Range of motion can be increased and dynamic sta-

bility further enhanced by controlled mobility techniques such as rocking through increments of range. Rocking can be used in multiple directions (e.g., forward, backward, diagonally) and is effective in increasing weight bearing over one or more extremities. Guided weight shifting is effectively accomplished by the therapist standing behind the patient with manual contacts at the pelvis.[2]

4. A progression can be made to static-dynamic activities. Freeing one extremity will place increased demands

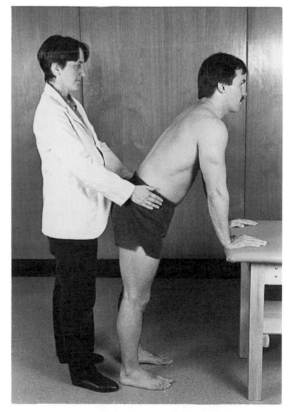

Figure 15-7. Modified plantigrade.

on the three remaining weight-bearing limbs. Lower extremity positions can be altered by stepping with the dynamic limb in both forward and backward directions. Body weight is then shifted over the dynamic limb while the static limb remains stationary. This will facilitate pelvic motion and lateral shifting. Rotation of the lower trunk also can be emphasized during static-dynamic lower extremity activities.

STANDING

The final posture in the sequence is erect standing. The BOS is small with a high COG, requiring greater balance control. Standing activities are most often initiated in the parallel bars (described in the next section). However, for many patients these activities can be initiated next to a treatment table or other supporting surface. It should be noted that patients may demonstrate sufficient stability to maintain a standing posture prior to being able to assume the position independently. The following activities and techniques can be utilized in the standing position.

1. Initial activities involve assisted assumption (described under parallel bar progression) and assisted maintenance of the position.

2. The ability to maintain the posture can be promoted by stability techniques such as rhythmic stabilization and alternating isometrics with manual contacts at the pelvis, scapula, or both scapula and pelvis.[1]

3. Guided weight shifting onto alternate lower extremities with manual contacts on the pelvis also will improve stability. Additional support may be provided by placement of the patient's hands on the therapist's shoulders. As stability improves, upper extremity support should be reduced or eliminated.

4. Controlled-mobility activities of the trunk can be practiced in standing with the feet symmetrical or in stride. Anterior-posterior, lateral, and rotational movements of the trunk can be emphasized.[2]

5. Static-dynamic activities will promote weight acceptance by advancing the dynamic limb forward and moving body weight over the advanced limb. This activity also will promote forward rotation and lateral shift of the pelvis (Fig. 15-8).

6. A progression is then made to walking, which represents the final and highest level of motor control (skill). Manual contacts can be placed at the pelvis to guide and to assist with control of pelvic movement. Upper extremity support should be gradually decreased and then eliminated. The sequence of activities in standing typically includes resisted progression; walking backward, sideways; and braiding. These activities are described in the following section.

This section presented a sample progression of mat activities to improve control within each posture. The progressive emphasis of control from proximal to distal body segments is summarized in Table 15-2. It should be noted that this basic progression will require adaptation and modification, depending on the unique needs of each individual patient. In addition to the mat progression outlined, a program of strengthening and coordination exercises are important concurrent activities during

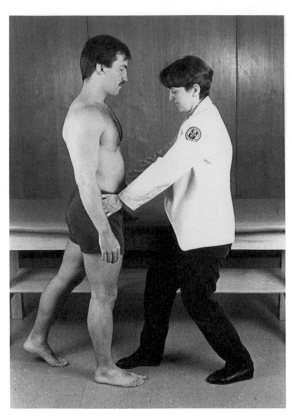

Figure 15-8. Standing. Static-dynamic activities will promote weight acceptance on the dynamic limb, forward pelvis rotation, and lateral shift.

preparation for ambulation. Transfer training and wheelchair management also can be initiated in conjunction with mat activities once the patient has begun work on movement within the sitting position. Table 15-3 presents a summary of the preambulation exercise program.

Parallel Bar Progression

Upright activities in the parallel bars can be initiated once the patient has progressed through a program of preambulation exercises. As mentioned earlier, every activity within the mat sequence will not be appropriate for each patient. Consequently, all mat activities may not be warranted or feasible before initiating upright activities.

Prior to standing, two important preliminary activities include fitting the patient with a guarding belt and adjusting the parallel bars. The initial adjustment of the parallel bars is an estimate based on the patient's height. Ideally the bars should be adjusted to allow 20 to 30 degrees of elbow flexion and come to about the level of the greater trochanter. Considering individual variations in body proportions and arm length, the elbow measurement is usually most accurate. Once the patient is standing, the height of the bars can be checked. If adjustments are required, the patient should be returned to a sitting position. The sequence of activities included in the parallel bar progression follows.

Table 15–2 FOCUS OF CONTROL WITHIN EACH POSTURE OF THE PREAMBULATION MAT PROGRESSION

Posture	Focus of Control

Rolling	Trunk
	    Segmental rotation
	    Counter rotation

Prone-on-elbows	Head Neck Upper trunk Scapula Shoulders
Prone-on-hands	Elbows (intermediate control of upper extremities)
Hooklying	Lower trunk Proximal lower extremities
Bridging	Lower trunk Hips/pelvis Lower extremities
Quadruped	Trunk Proximal and intermediate upper extremities Proximal lower extremities
Sitting	Trunk Proximal and intermediate upper extremities
Kneeling	Trunk Pelvis Proximal lower extremities
Half-kneeling	Trunk Pelvis Proximal and distal lower extremities (knee and ankle) Reciprocal control of lower extremities
Plantigrade	Trunk Proximal and intermediate control of lower extremities
Standing	Trunk Lower extremities

1. *Wheelchair placement.* The patient's wheelchair should be positioned at the end of the parallel bars. The brakes should be locked, the footrests placed in an upright position, and the patient's feet should be flat on the floor.

2. *Guarding belt.* The guarding belt should be fastened securely around the patient's waist. Guarding belts provide several critical functions. They increase the thera-

pist's effectiveness in controlling or preventing potential loss of balance; they improve patient safety; they facilitate the therapist's use of proper body mechanics in untoward circumstances; and finally, they are an important consideration regarding issues of liability. The safety implications of the guarding belt should be explained to the patient carefully.

3. *Initial instruction/demonstration.* In initiating instruction in parallel bar activities, the entire progression should be presented before breaking it into component parts. This will include instruction and demonstration in how to assume a standing position in the parallel bars, guarding techniques to be used by the therapist, the components of initial standing balance activities, the gait pattern to be used, how to turn in the parallel bars, and how to return to a sitting position. Demonstrating these activities by assuming the role of the patient during verbal explanations will facilitate learning. Each component of the parallel bar progression should then be reviewed prior to the patient's actual performance of the activity.

4. *Assuming the standing position.* To prepare for standing, the patient should be instructed to move forward in the chair. The therapist is positioned directly in front of the patient. A method of guarding should be selected that *does not* interfere with the patient's use of the upper extremities while moving to standing. One useful approach is to grasp the guarding belt anteriorly (an "underhand" grasp will provide the most security). With unilateral involvement, the therapist's opposite wrist should be placed under the axillary region on the patient's stronger or unaffected side with the hand at the lateral border of the scapula. Care should be taken not to exert any upward pressure into the axilla. Although the correct position for guarding is typically on the patient's weaker side, the therapist may stand closer to the unaffected side in order to brace or to guard the patient's sound lower extremity and to ensure one strong supporting limb. For example, this approach would be indicated in situations in which one lower extremity requires a non-weight-bearing status. If bilateral involvement exists, the therapist should be positioned more centrally in order to brace both of the patient's knees. If necessary, the patient's feet may be braced (by the therapist's feet) to prevent sliding. An alternate hand placement particularly useful with bilateral involvement is one hand under the buttock, the opposite hand on the lateral aspect

Table 15–3 PREAMBULATION EXERCISE PROGRAM: SAMPLE PROGRESSION OF PREPARATORY ACTIVITIES

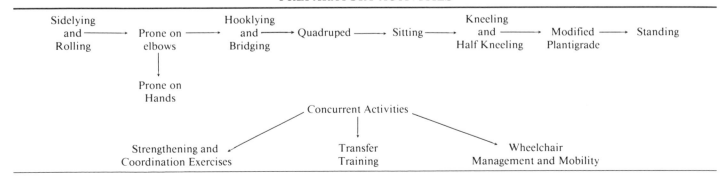

of the guarding belt or below the axilla onto the scapula and lateral-posterior chest wall.

Having moved forward in the chair with the supporting foot or feet flat on the floor, the patient should be instructed to come to a standing position by leaning forward and pushing down on the armrests of the wheelchair. The patient should *not* be allowed to stand by pulling up on the parallel bars. As the patient nears an erect posture, the hands should be released from the armrests one at a time and placed on the parallel bars. The patient's COG should be guided over the BOS to promote a stable standing posture.

5. *Initial parallel bar activities.* During parallel bar activities, the therapist usually stands inside the bars facing the patient or outside the bars on the patient's weaker side. In guarding the patient from inside the bars, one hand should grasp the guarding belt anteriorly, and the opposite hand should be in front of, *but not touching,* the patient's shoulder. From outside the bars one hand should grasp the belt posteriorly with the opposite hand in front of, *but not touching,* the patient's shoulder. This method of guarding provides effective hand placement for an immediate response should the patient's balance be lost. It also eliminates the patient's feeling of being "held back" or "pushed forward," which may occur with manual contacts at the shoulders.

The following initial balancing activities in the parallel bars can be modified relative to the patient's weight-bearing status and specific requirements of a diagnosis (e.g., use of a prosthesis or orthosis). Guarding techniques are maintained by the therapist during these activities.

a. *Standing balance.* Initially, the patient should be allowed time to become acclimated to the upright posture. During initial standing activities, the therapist should be alert to complaints of nausea or lightheadedness, which may indicate an onset of **orthostatic (postural) hypotension** caused by a drop in blood pressure. These symptoms typically disappear as tolerance to the upright posture improves. However, if the patient has been confined to bed and/or a wheelchair for a prolonged period, these symptoms may be severe. In these situations a gradual progression of tilt-table activities and careful monitoring of vital signs is warranted prior to standing.

b. *Lateral weight shift.* The patient shifts weight from side to side without altering the BOS; hand placement on the parallel bars is not altered.

c. *Anterior-posterior weight shift.* The patient shifts weight forward and backward without altering the BOS; hand placement on the parallel bars is not altered.

d. *Anterior-posterior hand placement and weight shift.* The patient moves the hands forward on the bars and shifts weight anteriorly. This is alternated with a posterior hand placement, and weight is shifted backward.

e. *Single-hand support.* The patient balances with support from only one hand on the parallel bars; hands are alternated. A progression of this activity involves gradual changes in position of the freed hand and upper extremity. For example, begin the activity by moving the freed hand several inches above the bar and gradually progress to alternate positions such as shoulder flexion, abduc-

tion, crossing the midline, and so forth. A progression can be made to balancing with both hands freed from the bars.

f. *Hip hiking.* The patient maintains the BOS and alternately hikes one hip at a time; hand placement on parallel bars is maintained. Resistance can be applied by manual contacts at the pelvis.

g. *Standing pushups.* The patient's hands are placed just anterior to the thighs on the parallel bars. Body weight is lifted by simultaneous elbow extension and shoulder depression. Additional height may be gained by forward flexion of the head. Return to the starting position is made by a controlled lowering of the body. This activity requires significant upper extremity strength, using the controlled mobility developed in preambulation activities. It is usually reserved for younger patient groups, such as those with paraplegia, and selected patients with lower extremity amputation.

h. *Stepping forward and backward.* The patient steps forward with one leg, shifts weight anteriorly, and returns to the starting position (normal BOS). This is alternated with stepping backward with one leg, shifting the weight posteriorly, and returning to the starting position. Resistance can be applied with manual contacts at the pelvis.

i. *Forward progression.* The patient begins ambulation in the parallel bars using the selected gait pattern and appropriate weight bearing on the affected lower extremity. The patient should be instructed to *push down* rather than to pull on the parallel bars while ambulating, inasmuch as this is the motion that eventually will be required with an assistive device. This will be easier if the patient is instructed to use a loose or open grip on the bars rather than a tight grip, facilitating correct use of the parallel bars and, ultimately, the assistive device.

j. *Turning.* Once the desired distance in the parallel bars has been reached, the patient should be instructed to turn toward the stronger side. For example, with a non-weight-bearing left lower extremity, the turn should be toward the right. The patient should be instructed to turn by stepping in a small circle and *not to pivot* on a single extremity. This technique will carry over to ambulation outside the bars, when pivoting will always be discouraged because of the potential loss of balance by movement on a small BOS. Guarding while turning in the parallel bars can be accomplished two ways. The therapist can remain in front of the patient, maintain the same hand positions, and turn with the patient. This will keep the therapist positioned in front of the patient. A second method is not to turn with the patient but, rather, to guard from behind on the return trip. In this method hand placements will change during the turn. Hand placement is changed gradually by first placing both hands on the guarding belt as the patient initiates the turn. One hand then remains on the posterior aspect of the belt and the freed hand is placed anterior to, *but not touching,* the shoulder on the patient's weaker side for the return trip toward the chair. Although both techniques are acceptable, the latter is probably more practical, considering the limited space available in the parallel bars.

As mentioned earlier, guarding also may be accomplished from outside the parallel bars. This positioning of the therapist is particularly useful during later stages of gait training. However, it presents several inherent problems for early training. If unilateral involvement exists, it is frequently difficult to remain close to the patient's weaker side (especially if the patient is not able to ambulate the full length of the parallel bars). In addition, the distance between the therapist and patient imposed by the intervening bar renders the therapist less effective in guarding and in using appropriate, safe body mechanics to help support the patient during periods of unsteadiness or loss of balance.

k. *Returning to the seated position.* When reaching the chair the patient should again turn as described earlier. Once completely turned, patients are typically instructed to continue backing up until they feel the seat of the chair on the back of their legs (this will require substitution with visual or auditory clues for patients with impaired sensation). At this point the patient releases the stronger hand from the parallel bar and reaches back for the wheelchair armrest. Once this hand has securely grasped the armrest, the patient should be instructed to bend forward slightly, release the opposite hand from the parallel bar and place it on the other armrest. Keeping the head and trunk forward the patient gently returns to a seated position.

6. *Advanced parallel bar activities.* Although not appropriate for every patient, several more advanced activities also can be incorporated into gait training in the parallel bars. These include the following.

a. *Resisted forward progression.* Resistance can be applied through manual contacts at the pelvis and/or shoulder as the patient walks forward.

b. *Walking backward.* Walking backward can be initiated actively and progress to application of resistance through manual contacts at the pelvis. This activity also combines hip extension with knee flexion and is particularly useful for patients with hemiplegia with synergy influence in the lower extremities.

c. *Walking sideward.* Initially, this activity is performed actively. A progression can then be made to application of resistance with manual contacts at the pelvis and thigh. Walking sideward facilitates active abduction of the moving limb combined with controlled mobility and weight bearing of the opposite supporting extremity.

d. *Braiding.* This activity requires a side-step progression with the advancing limb alternately placed anteriorly and posteriorly to the supporting limb. It incorporates lower trunk rotation as well as crossing the midline.

ASSISTIVE DEVICES AND GAIT PATTERNS

Before continuing with the progression of gait training activities outside the parallel bars, consideration will be given to (1) selection and measurement of assistive devices, and (2) selection and description of gait patterns used with each ambulatory device.

Selection, Measurement, and Gait Patterns for Use of Ambulatory Assistive Devices

There are three major categories of ambulatory assistive devices: canes, crutches, and walkers. Each have several modifications to the basic design, many of which were developed to meet the needs of a specific patient problem or diagnostic group. Assistive devices are prescribed for a variety of reasons, including problems of balance, pain, fatigue, weakness, joint instability, excessive skeletal loading, and cosmesis.[9] Another primary function of assistive devices is to eliminate weight-bearing fully or partially from an extremity. This unloading occurs by transmission of force from the upper extremities to the floor by downward pressure on the assistive device.

CANES

The function of a cane is *to widen the BOS* and *to improve balance.* Canes are *not* intended for use with restricted weight-bearing gaits (such as non- or partial-weight-bearing). Patients are typically instructed to hold a cane in the hand *opposite the affected extremity.* This positioning of the cane most closely approximates a normal reciprocal gait pattern with the opposite arm and leg moving together. It also widens the BOS with less lateral shifting of the COG than when the cane is held on the **ipsilateral** side.[10]

Contralateral positioning of the cane is particularly important in reducing forces created by the abductor muscles acting at the hip. During normal gait, the hip abductors of the stance extremity contract to counteract the gravitational moment at the pelvis on the contralateral side during swing. This prevents tilting of the pelvis on the contralateral side but results in a compressive force acting at the stance hip. Use of a cane in the upper extremity opposite the affected hip will reduce these forces. The floor (ground) reaction force created by the downward pressure of body weight on the cane counterbalances the gravitational movement at the affected hip.[11,12] Thus, the need for tension in the abductor muscles is reduced, with a subsequent decrease in joint compressive forces.

Several components of floor reaction forces creating joint compression at the hip can be reduced by use of a cane. In a study by Ely and Smidt,[13] contralateral use of a cane was found to decrease the vertical and posterior components of the floor reaction force produced by the affected foot. They noted that the reduction in vertical floor reaction peaks were probably due to a shifting of body weight toward the cane, which was a contributing factor in reducing contact force at the affected hip.

Other authors also have advocated the use of canes to reduce forces acting at the hip.[10,12,14] This concept is particularly important for activities such as stair climbing when the forces generated at the hip are significantly increased.[11] Clearly, use of a cane has important implications for hip disorders such as joint replacements or degenerative joint disease.

In addition to altering the forces on the affected extremity, canes are selected on the basis of their ability to improve gait by providing increased dynamic stability and improving balance. This is achieved by the increased BOS provided by the additional point of floor contact. The level of stability provided by canes is on a continuum. The greatest stability is provided by the broad-based canes and the least by a standard cane. The following section presents several of the more common types of canes in clinical use and identifies their advantages and disadvantages.

Standard Cane

This assistive device also is referred to as a regular or conventional cane (Fig. 15–9A). It is made of wood or plastic and has a half circle ("crook") handle. The distal rubber tip is at least 1 inch in diameter or larger.

Advantages. This cane is inexpensive and fits easily on stairs or other surfaces where space is limited.

Disadvantages. The standard cane is not adjustable and must be cut to fit the patient. Its point of support is anterior to the hand and not directly beneath it.

Standard Adjustable Aluminum Cane

This assistive device is the same basic design as the regular or standard cane (see Figure 15–9B). It is made of aluminum tubing and has a half circle handle with a molded plastic covering. The telescoping design of this

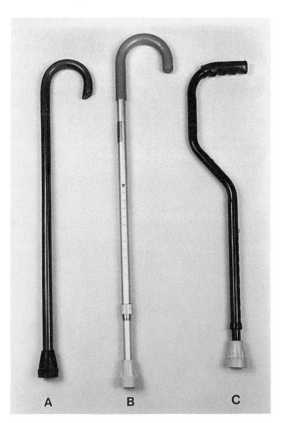

Figure 15–9. Shown here are (A) standard wooden cane, (B) standard adjustable aluminum cane, (C) adjustable aluminum offset cane.

cane enables the height to be adjusted by placing the locking-pin mechanism into the proper notch. Variations in available height range differ slightly with manufacturers. However, they are generally adjustable within the range of approximately 27 to 38.5 inches (68 to 98 cm). The distal rubber tip is at least 1 inch in diameter or larger. (*Note:* Most adjustable aluminum assistive devices use a push-button pin or notch mechanism to alter height; many include a reinforcing cuff which is tightened by a thumbscrew or a rotation sleeve).

Advantages. This cane is quickly adjustable, facilitating ease of determining appropriate height. It is particularly useful for measurement prior to altering the length of a standard cane. It is lightweight and fits easily on stairs.

Disadvantages. The point of support is anterior to the hand and not directly beneath it. This cane is also more costly than a standard cane.

Adjustable Aluminum Offset Cane

The proximal component of the body of this cane is offset anteriorly. It is made of aluminum tubing with a plastic or rubber molded grip-shaped handle (see Figure 15–9C). The telescoping design allows the height to be adjusted by a pin or notch mechanism from approximately 27 to 38.5 inches (68 to 98 cm). The distal rubber tip is at least 1 inch in diameter or larger.

Advantages. The design of this cane allows pressure to be borne over the center of the cane for greater stability. This cane also is quickly adjusted, lightweight, and fits easily on stairs.

Disadvantages. This cane is more costly than standard or adjustable aluminum canes.

Quad (Quadriped) Cane

This assistive device is constructed of aluminum and aluminum tubing. It is available in a variety of designs and base sizes, depending on the manufacturer (Figs. 15–10 and 15–11). The characteristic feature of these canes is that they provide a broad base with four points of floor contact. Each point (leg) is covered with a rubber tip. The legs closest to the patient's body are generally shorter and may be angled to allow foot clearance. On some designs the proximal portion of the cane is offset anteriorly. The handpiece is usually one of a variety of contoured plastic grips. A telescoping design allows for height adjustments. Quad canes are generally adjustable from approximately 28 to 38 inches (71 to 91 cm).

Advantages. This cane provides a broad-based support. Bases are available in several different sizes. This cane is also easily adjustable.

Disadvantages. Depending on the specific design of the cane, the pressure exerted by the patient's hand may not be centered over the cane and may result in patient complaints of instability. As a result of the broad BOS, quad canes often are not practical for use on stairs. Another disadvantage of broad-based canes is that they warrant use of a slower gait pattern. If a faster forward progression is used, the cane often "rocks" from rear legs to front legs, which decreases effectiveness of the cane.

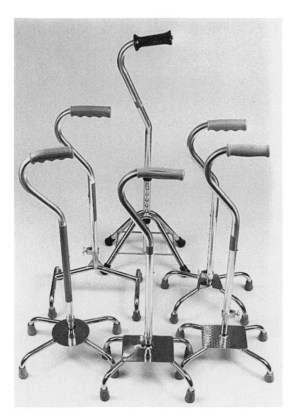

Figure 15–10. Shown here are a variety of large-based quad (quad-riped) canes.

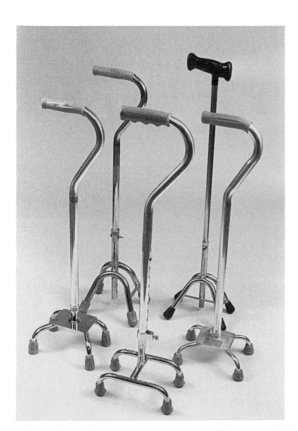

Figure 15–11. Shown here are a variety of small-based quad (quad-riped) canes.

Patients should be instructed to place all four legs of the cane on the floor simultaneously to obtain maximum stability.

Walk Cane

This cane also is constructed of aluminum and aluminum tubing (Fig. 15–12). It provides a very broad base with four points of floor contact. Each point (leg) is covered with a rubber tip. The legs farther from the patient's body are angled to maintain floor contact and to improve stability. The handgrip is molded plastic around the uppermost segment of aluminum tubing. Walk canes fold flat and are adjustable in height from approximately 29 to 37 inches (73 to 94 cm).

Advantages. Walk canes provide a very broad-based support and are more stable than a quad cane. These canes also fold flat for travel or storage.

Disadvantages. As with the quad canes, the specific design of a walk cane or handgrip placement may not allow pressure to be centered over the cane. Walk canes can not be used on most stairs. They require use of a slow forward progression and are generally more costly than quad canes.

Hand Grips

A general consideration relevant to all canes is related to handgrips. There are a variety of styles and sizes available. The type of handgrip should be judged and selected primarily on patient comfort and its ability to provide

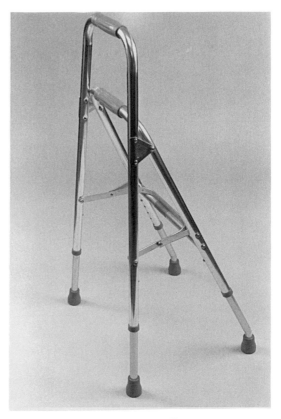

Figure 15–12. Walk cane.

adequate surface area to allow effective transfer of weight from the upper extremity to the floor. It is useful to have several styles available for assessment with individual patients.

Measuring Canes

In measuring cane height, the cane (or center of a broad-based cane) is placed approximately 6 inches from the lateral border of the toes. Two landmarks typically are used during measurement, the greater trochanter and the angle at the elbow. The top of the cane should come to approximately the level of the greater trochanter, and the elbow should be flexed to about 20 to 30 degrees. Because of individual variations in body proportion and arm lengths, the degree of flexion at the elbow is a more important indicator of correct cane height. This elbow flexion serves two important functions:[10] It allows the arm to shorten or to lengthen during different phases of gait, and it provides a shock-absorption mechanism. Finally, as with all assistive devices, the height of the cane should be assessed with consideration to patient comfort and its effectiveness in accomplishing its intended purpose.

Gait Pattern for Use of Canes

As discussed earlier, the cane should be held in the upper extremity opposite the affected limb. For ambulation on level surfaces, the cane and the involved extremity are advanced simultaneously (Fig. 15–13). The cane should remain relatively close to the body and should not be placed ahead of the toe of the involved extremity. These are important considerations, because placing the cane too far forward or to the side will cause lateral and/or forward bending, with a resultant decrease in dynamic stability.

When bilateral involvement exists, a decision must be made as to which side of the body the cane will be held. This question is most effectively resolved by a problem-solving approach with input from both the patient and therapist. Questions to be considered include
1. On which side is the cane most comfortable?
2. Is one placement superior in terms of improving balance and/or ambulatory endurance?
3. If gait deviations exist, is one position more effective in improving the overall gait pattern?
4. Is safety influenced by cane placement (e.g., during transfers, stair climbing, or ambulation on outdoor surfaces?)
5. Is there a difference in grip strength between hands? Consideration of these questions will generally provide sufficient information to determine the most effective cane placement when bilateral involvement exists.

CRUTCHES

Crutches are used most frequently to improve balance and to either relieve weight bearing fully or partially on a lower extremity. They are typically used bilaterally and function to *increase the base of support, to improve lateral stability,* and to allow the upper extremities *to trans-*

(4) Cycle is repeated.

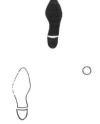

(3) The uninvolved extremity is advanced.

(2) The cane and involved extremity are moved forward simultaneously.

(1)   Starting position. In this example, the left lower extremity is the involved limb.

Figure 15–13. Gait pattern for use of cane.

fer body weight to the floor. This transfer of weight through the upper extremities permits functional ambulation while maintaining a restricted weight-bearing status. There are two basic designs of crutches in frequent clinical use: *axillary* and *forearm* crutches.

Axillary Crutches

These assistive devices also are referred to as regular or standard crutches (Fig. 15–14A). They are made of lightweight wood or aluminum. Their design includes an axillary bar, a handpiece, double uprights joined distally by a single leg covered with a rubber suction tip (which should be 1.5 to 3 inches in diameter). The single leg allows for height variations. Height adjustments for wooden and some aluminum crutches are accomplished by altering the placement of screws and wing bolts into predrilled holes. The height of the handgrips is adjusted in the same manner. Some types of aluminum crutches use a push-button pin or notch mechanism for height adjustments similar to those found on aluminum canes. Others also have patient height markers adjacent to the notches to assist in adjustment. Axillary crutches are generally adjustable in adult sizes from approximately 48 to 60 inches (122 to 153 cm), with children's and extra-long sizes available.

A modification to this basic design is the ortho crutch (see Figure 15–14B). This type of axillary crutch is made

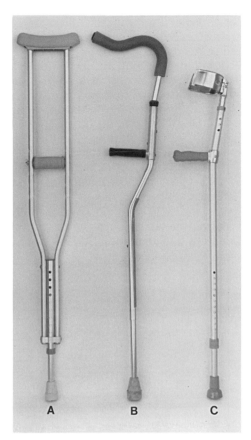

Figure 15-14. Shown here are (*A*) axillary crutch, (*B*) ortho crutch, and (*C*) forearm crutch.

of aluminum. Its design includes a single upright, an axillary bar covered with sponge-rubber padding, and a handgrip covered with molded plastic. The crutch adjusts both proximally (to alter elbow angle) and distally (to alter height of crutch). Adjustments are made using a push-button pin or notch mechanism. The distal end of the crutch is covered with a rubber suction tip.

The body of research available comparing the two designs of axillary crutches is limited. One study compared the level of energy expended during non-weight-bearing ambulation using each type of crutch.[15] The results indicated that less energy was expended with the ortho crutches than with standard axillary crutches for short periods over short distances. Although the findings of a single study have limited clinical application, the authors suggest that the results have implications for crutch selection for patients with cardiovascular involvement for short-distance ambulation.

Advantages. Axillary crutches improve balance and lateral stability and provide for functional ambulation with restricted weight bearing. They are easily adjusted, inexpensive in wood, and can be used for stair climbing.

Disadvantages. Because of the tripod stance required to use crutches and the resultant large BOS, crutches are awkward in small areas. For the same reason, the safety of the user may be compromised when ambulating in crowded areas. Another disadvantage is the tendency of some patients to lean on the axillary bar. This pressure creates the potential for damage to nervous and vascular structures in the axilla.

Platform Attachments. These attachments (Fig. 15-15) are also referred to as forearm rests or troughs. Although they are described here, they also are used with walkers. Their function is to allow transfer of body weight through the forearm to the assistive device. A platform attachment is used when weight bearing is contraindicated through the wrist and hand (e.g., some arthritic patients). The forearm piece is usually padded, has a dowl or handgrip, and has Velcro straps to maintain the position of the forearm. Trough crutches are also commercially available.

Forearm Crutches

These assistive devices are also known as Lofstrand and Canadian crutches (see Figure 15-14C). They are constructed of aluminum. Their design includes a single upright, a forearm cuff, and a handgrip. This crutch adjusts both proximally to alter position of the forearm

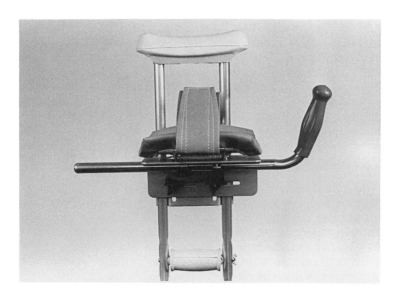

Figure 15-15. Platform attachment to axillary crutch.

cuff and distally to alter height of the crutch. Adjustments are made using a pin or notch mechanism. The available heights of forearm crutches are indicated from handgrip to floor and are generally adjustable in adult sizes from 29 to 35 inches (74 to 89 cm), with children's and extra-long sizes available. The distal end of the crutch is covered with a rubber suction tip. The forearm cuffs are available with either a medial or anterior opening. The cuffs are made of metal and can be obtained with a plastic coating.

Advantages. The forearm cuff allows use of hands without the crutches becoming disengaged. They are easily adjusted and allow functional stair-climbing activities. Many patients feel they are more cosmetic and they fit more easily into an automobile owing to the overall decreased height. They are also the most functional type of crutch for stair-climbing activities for individuals wearing bilateral knee-ankle-foot orthoses.

Disadvantages. Forearm crutches provide less lateral support owing to the absence of an axillary bar. The cuffs may be difficult to remove. These crutches are more costly than wooden axillary crutches.

Measuring Crutches

Axillary Crutches. Several methods are available for measuring axillary crutches. The most common are from a standing or a supine position. Measurement from standing is most accurate and is the preferred approach.

Standing. From the standing position in the parallel bars, crutches should be measured from a point approximately 2 inches below the axilla. The width of two fingers is often used to approximate this distance. The distal end of the crutch should come to a point 2 inches lateral and 6 inches anterior to the foot. A general estimate of crutch height can be obtained prior to standing by subtracting 16 inches from the patient's height. With the shoulders relaxed, the handpiece should be adjusted to provide 20 to 30 degrees of elbow flexion.

Supine. From this position the measurement is taken from the anterior axillary fold to a point 6 to 8 inches (5 to 7.5 cm) from the lateral border of the heel.

Forearm Crutches. Standing is the position of choice for measuring forearm crutches. From a standing position in the parallel bars, the distal end of the crutch should be positioned at a point 2 inches lateral and 6 inches anterior to the foot. With the shoulders relaxed, the height should then be adjusted to provide 20 to 30 degrees of elbow flexion. The forearm cuff is adjusted separately. Cuff placement should be on the proximal one third of the forearm, approximately 1 to 1.5 inches below the elbow.

Gait Patterns for Use of Crutches

Gait patterns are selected on the basis of the patient's balance, coordination, muscle function, and weight-bearing status. The gait patterns differ significantly in their energy requirements, BOS, and the speed with which they can be executed.

Prior to initiating instruction in gait patterns, several important points should be emphasized to the patient:

1. During crutch use, body weight should always be *borne on the hands* and not on the axillary bar. This will prevent pressure on both the vascular and nervous structures located in the axillary region.

2. Balance will be optimal by always maintaining a wide (tripod) BOS. Even when in a resting stance, the patient should be instructed to keep the crutches at least 4 inches (10 cm) to the front and to the side of each foot. Caution should be used *not* to allow the foot to achieve parallel alignment with the crutches. This will jeopardize anterior-posterior stability by decreasing the BOS.

3. When using standard crutches, the axillary bars should be held close to the chest wall to provide improved lateral stability.

4. The patient should also be cautioned about the importance of holding the head up and maintaining good postural alignment during ambulation.

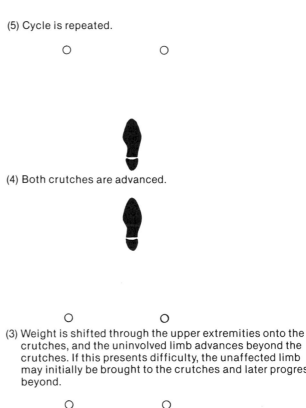

(5) Cycle is repeated.

(4) Both crutches are advanced.

(3) Weight is shifted through the upper extremities onto the crutches, and the uninvolved limb advances beyond the crutches. If this presents difficulty, the unaffected limb may initially be brought to the crutches and later progress beyond.

(2) Weight is shifted onto the uninvolved right lower extremity, and the crutches are advanced.

(1) Starting position. In this example, the left lower extremity is non-weight-bearing.

Figure 15–16. Three-point gait pattern.

5. Turning should be accomplished by stepping in a small circle rather than pivoting.

Three-Point Gait. In this type of gait three points of support contact the floor. It is used when a non-weight-bearing status is required on one lower extremity. Body weight is borne on the crutches instead of on the affected lower extremity. The sequence of this gait pattern is illustrated in Figure 15–16.

Partial-Weight-Bearing Gait. This gait is a modification of the three-point pattern. During forward progression of the involved extremity, weight is borne partially on both crutches *and* on the affected extremity (Fig. 15–17). During instruction in the partial-weight-bearing gait, emphasis should be placed on use of a normal heel-toe progression on the affected extremity. Often the term *partial-weight-bearing* is interpreted by the patient as meaning that only the toes or ball of the foot should contact the floor. Use of this positioning over a period of days or weeks will lead to heel cord tightness. Limb load monitors are often a useful adjunct to partial-weight-bearing gait training. These devices provide auditory feedback to the patient regarding the amount of weight borne on an extremity (see chapter 29).

Four-Point Gait. This pattern provides a slow, stable gait as three points of floor contact are maintained.

(4) Cycle is repeated.

(3) Weight is shifted onto the crutches and partially to the affected extremity, and the unaffected limb advances.

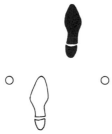

(2) Weight is shifted onto the uninvolved limb. The crutches and the affected extremity are advanced simultaneously as shown or can be broken into two components:
   (a) advance crutches, (b) advance affected extremity.

(1) Starting position. In this example, the left lower extremity is partial-weight-bearing.

Figure 15–17. Partial-weight-bearing gait: modification of the three-point gait pattern.

Weight is borne on both lower extremities and typically is used with bilateral involvement related to poor balance, incoordination, or muscle weakness. In this gait pattern one crutch is advanced and then the opposite lower extremity is advanced. For example, the left crutch is moved forward, then the right lower extremity, followed by the right crutch and then the left lower extremity (Fig. 15–18).

Two-Point Gait. This gait pattern is similar to the four-point gait. However, it is less stable because only two points of floor contact are maintained. Thus, use of this gait requires better balance. The two-point pattern more closely simulates normal gait, inasmuch as the opposite lower and upper extremity move together (Fig. 15–19).

Two additional less commonly used crutch gaits are the **swing-to** and **swing-through** patterns. These gaits are often used when there is bilateral lower extremity involvement, such as in spinal cord injuries. The swing-to gait involves forward movement of both crutches simultaneously, and the lower extremities "swing to" the crutches. In the swing-through gait the crutches are moved forward together, but the lower extremities are swung beyond the crutches. Both these crutch patterns are discussed in greater detail in chapter 26 (Traumatic Spinal Cord Injury).

WALKERS

Walkers are used to improve balance and to relieve weight bearing either fully or partially on a lower extremity. Of the three categories of ambulatory assistive devices, walkers afford the greatest stability. They *provide a wide BOS, improve anterior and lateral stability,* and *allow the upper extremities to transfer body weight to the floor.*

Walkers are typically made of tubular aluminum with molded vinyl handgrips and rubber tips. They are adjustable in adult sizes from approximately 32 to 37 inches (81 to 92 cm), with children's, youth, and tall sizes available. Several modifications to the standard design are available and are described below.

1. A folding mechanism. Folding walkers are particularly useful for patients who travel. These walkers can be easily collapsed to fit in an automobile or other storage space.

2. Handgrips. Enlarged and molded handgrips are available, which may be useful for some arthritic patients.

3. Platform attachments. This adaptation is used when weight bearing is contraindicated through the wrist and hand (described in crutch section).

4. Reciprocal walkers. These walkers are designed to allow unilateral forward progression of one side of the walker. A disadvantage of this design is that some inherent stability of the walker is lost. However, they are useful for patients incapable of lifting the walker with both hands and moving it forward.

5. Casters. This adaptation should be used very judiciously because the stability of the walker will be reduced. Walkers with front wheels (sometimes called "rolling" walkers), however, may allow functional ambulation for patients who are unable to lift and to move a

(6) Cycle is repeated.

(5) The left lower extremity is advanced.

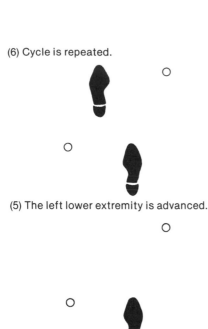

(4) The right crutch is advanced.

(3) The right lower extremity is advanced.

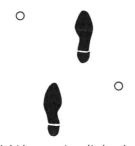

(2) The left crutch is advanced.

(1) Starting position. Weight is borne on both lower extremities and both crutches.

Figure 15–18. Four-point gait pattern.

(4) Cycle is repeated.

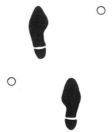

(3) The right crutch and left lower extremity are advanced together.

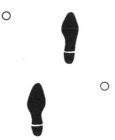

(2) The left crutch and right lower extremity are advanced together.

(1) Starting position. Weight is borne on both lower extremities and both crutches.

Figure 15–19. Two-point gait pattern.

conventional walker. Pressure brakes should always be used with casters.

6. Stair-climbing walkers. Walkers designed for use on stairs are commercially available. Regardless of design, walkers tend to be extremely unsafe on stairs and should be avoided.

Advantages. Walkers provide four points of floor contact with a side BOS. They provide a high level of stability. They also provide a sense of security for patients fearful of ambulation. They are relatively lightweight and easily adjusted.

Disadvantages. Walkers tend to be cumbersome, are awkward in confined areas, and are difficult to maneuver through doorways. They eliminate normal arm swing and can not be used safely on stairs.

Measuring Walkers

The height of a walker is measured similarly to a cane. The walker should come to approximately the greater trochanter and allow for 20 to 30 degrees of elbow flexion.

Gait Patterns for Use of Walkers

Prior to initiating instruction in gait patterns, several points related to use of the walker should be emphasized with the patient:

1. The walker should be picked up and placed down on *all four legs simultaneously* to achieve maximum stability. Rocking from the back to front legs or sliding the walker forward should be avoided because it decreases the effectiveness and safety of the assistive device.

2. The patient should be encouraged to hold the head up and to maintain good postural alignment.

3. The patient should be cautioned not to step too close to the front crossbar. This will decrease the overall BOS and may cause the patient to fall backward.

There are three types of gait patterns used with walkers. These are the full, partial, and non-weight-bearing gaits. The sequence for each pattern follows.

Full Weight Bearing

1. The walker is picked up and moved forward about an arm's length.

2. The first lower extremity is moved forward.

3. The second lower extremity is moved forward past the first.

4. The cycle is repeated.

Partial Weight Bearing

1. The walker is picked up and moved forward about an arm's length.

2. The involved lower extremity is moved forward, and body weight is transferred partially onto this limb and partially through the upper extremities to the walker.

3. The uninvolved lower extremity is moved forward past the involved limb.

4. The cycle is repeated.

Non-Weight-Bearing

1. The walker is picked up and moved forward about an arm's length.

2. Weight is then transferred through the upper extremities to the walker. The involved limb is held anterior to the patient's body but does not make contact with the floor.

3. The uninvolved limb is moved forward.

4. The cycle is repeated.

USE OF ASSISTIVE DEVICES ON LEVEL SURFACES AND STAIRS

Level Surfaces

Gait-training activities on indoor surfaces are begun once the patient has achieved appropriate skill and balance in parallel bar activities (including moving to and from standing and sitting positions, turning, and use of the selected gait pattern). Use of the parallel bars often continues concurrently with initial gait training on indoor surfaces. At this point in the progression, continued use of the parallel bars typically emphasizes advanced activities and/or work on specific deviations.

Several important preparatory activities should precede ambulation on level surfaces with the assistive device. These activities may be completed in the parallel bars for added security. However, if the width of the bars is not adjustable, the BOS of the assistive device may make movement within the bars difficult and unsafe. An alternative is to move the patient outside but *next to* the parallel bars or near a treatment table or wall. These preparatory activities include

1. Instruction in assuming the standing and seated positions with use of the assistive device. These techniques are outlined in Table 15–4 for each category of assistive device.

2. Standing balance activities with the assistive device (similar to those using the parallel bars, described earlier).

3. Instruction in use of assistive device (with selected gait pattern) for forward progression and turning.

As mentioned earlier, demonstrating these activities by assuming the role of the patient during verbal explanations is an effective teaching approach. Following the demonstration, verbal cueing and explanations can be used again to guide performance of the activity.

Following these preliminary instructions, gait training using the assistive device can be begun on level surfaces. The following guarding technique (Fig. 15–20) should be used.

1. The therapist stands posterior and lateral to the patient's weaker side.

2. A wide BOS should be maintained with the therapist's leading lower extremity following the assistive device. The therapist's opposite lower extremity should be externally rotated and follow the patient's weaker lower extremity.

3. One of the therapist's hands is placed posteriorly on the guarding belt and the other anterior to, but *not touching*, the patient's shoulder on the weaker side.

Should the patient's balance be lost during gait training, the hand guarding at the shoulder should make contact. Frequently the support provided by the therapist's hands at the shoulder and on the guarding belt will be enough to allow the patient to regain balance. If the balance loss is severe, the therapist should move in toward the patient so that the body and guarding hands can be used to provide stabilization. The patient should be allowed to regain balance while "leaning" against the therapist. If balance is not recovered and it is apparent the patient is going to fall, further attempts should not be made to hold the patient up because this is likely to result in injury to the patient and/or the therapist. In this situation the therapist should continue to brace the patient against the body and move with the patient to a sitting position to break the fall and to protect the head. It is also important to talk to the patient ("Help me lower you to the floor") so that the patient does not continue to struggle to regain balance.

Gait-training activities on level surfaces should include instruction and practice in passage through doorways, elevators, and over thresholds. When using crutches, doorways are most easily approached from a diagonal. A hand must be freed to open the door and one crutch placed in a position to hold it open. The patient then gradually proceeds through the doorway, using the crutch to open the door wider if necessary.

Because many patients using a walker or cane may have balance problems, careful assessment will determine the safest methods for passage through doorways. A patient using a walker with sufficient balance may be able to use a technique similar to that described above.

Table 15–4 BASIC TECHNIQUES FOR ASSUMING STANDING AND SEATED POSITIONS WITH ASSISTIVE DEVICES

I. CANE
   A. *Coming to standing*
      1. Patient moves forward in chair.
      2. Cane is positioned on uninvolved side (broad-based cane) or leaned against armrest (standard cane).
      3. Patient leans forward and pushes down with both hands on armrests, comes to a standing position, and then grasps cane. With use of a standard cane, the cane may be grasped loosely with fingers prior to standing and the base of the hand used for pushing down on armrests.
   B. *Return to sitting*
      1. As the patient approaches the chair, the patient turns in a small circle toward the uninvolved side.
      2. The patient backs up until the chair can be felt against the patient's legs.
      3. The patient then reaches for the armrest with the free hand, then releases the cane (broad-based) and reaches for the opposite armrest. A standard cane is leaned against the chair as the patient grasps the armrest.
II. CRUTCHES
   A. *Coming to standing*
      1. The patient moves forward in the chair.
      2. Crutches are placed together in a vertical position on the *affected* side.
      3. One hand is placed on the handpieces of the crutches; one on the armrest of the chair.
      4. The patient leans forward and pushes to a standing position.
      5. Once balance is gained, one crutch is cautiously placed under the axilla on the unaffected side.
      6. The second crutch is then carefully placed under the axilla on the affected side.
      7. A tripod stance is assumed.
   B. *Return to sitting*
      1. As the patient approaches the chair, the patient turns in a small circle toward the uninvolved side.
      2. The patient backs up until the chair can be felt against the patient's legs.
      3. Both crutches are placed in a vertical position (out from under axilla) on the *affected* side.
      4. One hand is placed on the handpieces of the crutches; one on the armrest of the chair.
      5. The patient lowers to the chair in a controlled manner.
         [*Note:* See chapter 26, Traumatic Spinal Cord Injury for alternative methods using bilateral knee ankle orthoses.]
III. WALKER
   A. *Coming to standing*
      1. The patient moves forward in the chair.
      2. The walker is positioned directly in front of the chair.
      3. The patient leans forward and pushes down on armrests to come to standing.
      4. Once in a standing position, the patient reaches for the walker, one hand at a time.
   B. *Return to sitting*
      1. As the patient approaches the chair, the patient turns in a small circle toward the stronger side.
      2. The patient backs up until the chair can be felt against the patient's legs.
      3. The patient then reaches for one armrest at a time.
      4. The patient lowers to the chair in a controlled manner.

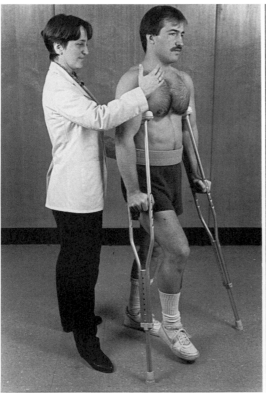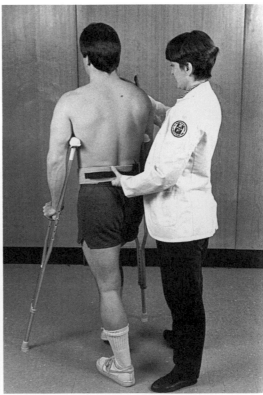

Figure 15–20. Anterior *(left)* and posterior *(right)* views of guarding technique for level surfaces, demonstrated with use of crutches. The same positioning is used with canes and walkers.

Stair Climbing

The next activity in the gait-training progression is stair climbing. Ideally, firsthand information from a home visit will provide information about the type and number of stairs the patient will be required to use. However, careful questioning of the patient and/or family members generally will provide sufficient information on which to plan. The information obtained should include the height and number of stairs, presence and stability of railings, and condition and type of floor covering or pavement leading to and on the stairs.

Several general guidelines should be relayed to the patient during instruction in stair climbing. First, if a railing is available it should *always* be used. This is true even if it requires placing an assistive device in the hand in which it is not normally used. For stair climbing with axillary crutches using a railing, both crutches are placed together under one arm. Second, the patient should be cautioned that the stronger lower extremity *always* leads going up the stairs, and the weaker or involved limb *always* leads coming down ("up with the good and down with the bad").

The progressions of stair-climbing techniques are pre-sented in Table 15–5. The following guarding technique should be used by the therapist during stair climbing.

Ascending Stairs (Fig. 15–21)

1. The therapist is positioned posterior and lateral on the affected side *behind* the patient.

2. A wide BOS should be maintained with each foot on a different stair.

3. A step should be taken only when the patient is *not* moving.

4. One hand is placed posteriorly on the guarding belt and one is anterior to, *but not touching,* the shoulder on the weaker side.

Descending Stairs (Fig. 15–22)

1. The therapist is positioned anterior and lateral on the affected side *in front* of the patient.

2. A wide BOS should be maintained with each foot on a different stair.

3. A step should be taken only when the patient is *not* moving.

4. One hand is placed anteriorly on the guarding belt and one is anterior to, *but not touching,* the shoulder on the weaker side.

Should the patient's balance be lost during stair climbing, the following procedure should be followed: First,

---

Table 15–5 STAIR-CLIMBING TECHNIQUES*

I. CANE
  A. *Ascending*
    1. The unaffected lower extremity leads up.
    2. The cane and affected lower extremity follow.
  B. *Descending*
    1. The affected lower extremity and cane lead down.
    2. The unaffected lower extremity follows.
II. CRUTCHES: THREE-POINT GAIT (non-weight-bearing gait)
  A. *Ascending*
    1. The patient is positioned close to the foot of the stairs. The involved lower extremity is held back to prevent "catching" on the lip of the stairs.
    2. The patient pushes down firmly on both handpieces of the crutches and leads up with the unaffected lower extremity.
    3. The crutches are brought up to the stair that the unaffected lower extremity is now on.
  B. *Descending*
    1. The patient stands close to the edge of the stair such that the toes protrude slightly over the top. The involved lower extremity is held forward over the lower stair.
    2. Both crutches are moved down *together* to the *front* half of the next step.
    3. The patient pushes down firmly on both handpieces and lowers the unaffected lower extremity to the step that the crutches are now on.
III. CRUTCHES: PARTIAL-WEIGHT-BEARING GAIT
  A. *Ascending*
    1. The patient is positioned close to the foot of the stairs.
    2. The patient pushes down on both handpieces of the crutches and distributes weight partially on the crutches and partially on the affected lower extremity while the unaffected lower extremity leads up.
    3. The involved lower extremity and crutches are then brought up together.
  B. *Descending*
    1. The patient stands close to the edge of the stair such that the toes protrude slightly over top of the stair.
    2. Both crutches are moved down *together* to the *front* half of the next step. The affected lower extremity is then lowered (depending on patient skill, these may be combined). *Note:* When crutches are not in floor contact, greater weight must be shifted to the uninvolved lower extremity to maintain a partial-weight-bearing status.
    3. The uninvolved lower extremity is lowered to the step the crutches are now on.
IV. CRUTCHES: TWO- AND FOUR-POINT GAIT
  A. *Ascending*
    1. The patient is positioned close to the foot of the stairs.
    2. The right lower extremity is moved up and then the left lower extremity.
    3. The right crutch is moved up and then the left crutch is moved up (patients with adequate balance may find it easier to move the crutches up together).
  B. *Descending*
    1. The patient stands close to the edge of the stair.
    2. The right crutch is moved down and then the left (may be combined).
    3. The right lower extremity is moved down and then the left.

---

*The sequences presented here describe stair-climbing techniques without the use of a railing. When a secure railing is available, the patient should be instructed to use it always.

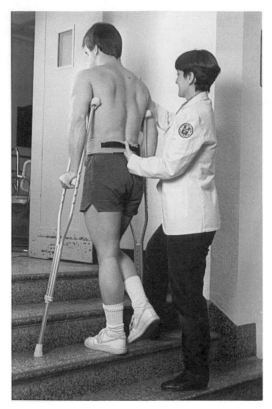

Figure 15–21. Guarding technique for ascending stairs.

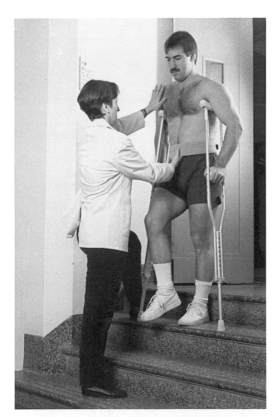

Figure 15–22. Guarding technique for descending stairs.

contact should be made with the hand guarding at the shoulder. Next, the therapist should move toward the patient to help brace the patient (the patient should *never* be pulled toward the therapist on stairs) or leaned toward the wall of the stairwell (if available). Finally, if needed, the therapist can move with the patient to sit the patient down on the stairs. Remember to inform the patient of your intentions ("I'm going to sit you down").

Curbs and Ramps

The technique for climbing curbs is essentially the same as that of climbing a single stair (see Table 15–5). A useful lead-up activity to curb climbing is provided by a series of small, free-standing, wooden platforms with nonslip coverings. These can be fabricated easily in increments of height. For additional security they can be placed next to or within the parallel bars, and a progression can be made from a 3- or 4-inch increment to a 7-inch curb height.

Ramps can be negotiated several ways. If the incline is very gradual, it may be sufficient simply to instruct the patient to use smaller steps. However, for steeper inclines the patient should be instructed to use smaller steps and to traverse the ramp (use a diagonal, zigzag pattern) for both ascending and descending.

Outdoor Surfaces

Activities on outdoor surfaces are among the final components of a gait-training progression. They must be specifically assessed to determine their appropriateness for an individual patient. Basic outdoor activities include

1. Exit and entrance through outside doors and thresholds.

2. Gait training on outdoor, uneven surfaces.

3. Curbs, ramps, and stair climbing.

4. Crossing the street in the time allotted by a traffic light.

5. Entering and exiting public or private transportation.

SUMMARY

This chapter presented a general framework of gait-training activities with a progression from suggested preambulation exercises to approaches for instruction on level surfaces and stairs. Each component of this sequence should be considered during treatment planning. Through a process of careful assessment, the appropriate elements of the mat progression, specific treatment techniques, and segments of the upright progression can be selected for an individual patient. Additional factors that will influence treatment planning include the patient's diagnosis, medical history, weight-bearing status, and input from the patient regarding ambulatory goals.

QUESTIONS FOR REVIEW

1. Identify the goals of a preambulation exercise program.

2. Outline a general parallel bar progression that would be appropriate for a patient preparing to use a partial-weight-bearing crutch gait.

3. Contrast and compare the advantages and disadvantages of each category of ambulatory assistive device: canes, crutches, and walkers.

4. Explain the method used for measuring a cane, crutches, and a walker.

5. Describe the sequence for instructing a patient to rise from and return to a sitting position with a cane, crutches, and a walker.

6. Describe therapist positioning and hand placement for guarding the patient on level surfaces and stairs.

7. Describe the sequence for the following crutch gaits: four-point, two-point, three-point, and partial-weight-bearing.

REFERENCES

1. Voss, DE, Ionta, MK, and Myers, BJ: Proprioceptive Neuromuscular Facilitation: Patterns and Techniques, ed 3. Harper & Row, Philadelphia, 1985.
2. Sullivan, PE, Markos, PD, and Minor, MAD: An Integrated Approach to Therapeutic Exercise: Theory and Clinical Application. Reston, Reston, VA, 1982.
3. Voss, DE: Proprioceptive neuromuscular facilitation (NUSTEP Proceedings). Am J Phys Med 46:838, 1967.
4. Myers, BJ: The proprioceptive neuromuscular facilitation (PNF) approach. In Trombly, CA (ed): Occupational Therapy for Physical Dysfunction, ed 2. Williams & Wilkins, Baltimore, 1983, p 105.
5. Stockmeyer, SA: An interpretation of the approach of Rood to the treatment of neuromuscular dysfunction (NUSTEP Proceedings). Am J Phys Med 46:900, 1967.
6. Trombly, CA: The Rood approach. In Trombly, CA (ed): Occupational Therapy for Physical Dysfunction, ed 2. Williams & Wilkins, Baltimore, 1983, p 74.
7. Hollis, M: Practical Exercise Therapy. Blackwell Scientific Publications, Boston, 1981.
8. Ryerson, SD: Hemiplegia resulting from vascular insult or disease. In Umphred, DA (ed): Neurological Rehabilitation. CV Mosby, St Louis, 1985, p 474.
9. Smidt, GL and Mommens, MA: System of reporting and comparing influences of ambulatory aids on gait. Phys Ther 60:551, 1980.
10. Jebsen, RH: Use and abuse of ambulatory aids. JAMA 199:63, 1967.
11. Norkin, CC and Levangie, PK: Joint Structure and Function: A Comprehensive Analysis. FA Davis, Philadelphia, 1983.
12. Elson, RA and Charnley, J: The direction of the resultant force in total prosthetic replacement of the hip joint. Med Biol Eng 6:19, 1968.
13. Ely, DD and Smidt, GL: Effect of cane on variables of gait for patients with hip disorders. Phys Ther 57:507, 1977.
14. Blount, WP: Don't throw away the cane. J Bone Joint Surg (Am) 38-A:695, 1956.
15. Hinton, CA and Cullen, KE: Energy expenditure during ambulation with ortho crutches and axillary crutches. Phys Ther 62:813, 1982.

SUPPLEMENTAL READINGS

Barnes, B: Ambulation outcomes after hip fracture. Phys Ther 64:317, 1984.

Baruch, IM and Mossberg, KA: Heart-rate response of elderly women to nonweight-bearing ambulation with a walker. Phys Ther 63:1782, 1983.

Blessey, RL, et al: Metabolic energy cost of unrestrained walking. Phys Ther 56:1019, 1976.

Bohannon, RW and Gibson, DF: Effectiveness of a rolling board treatment for improving gait. Phys Ther 66:349, 1986.

Brown, M, et al: Walking efficiency before and after total hip replacement. Phys Ther 60:1259, 1980.

Corcoran, PJ and Peszczynski, M: Gait and gait retraining. In Basmajian, JV (ed): Therapeutic Exercise, ed 4. Williams & Wilkins, Baltimore, 1984, p 285.

DePasquale, LJ: Peripheral vision used in gait training (suggestion from the field). Phys Ther 57:42, 1977.

Fillyaw, M: Modified walker for patients with polyarticular rheumatoid arthritis (suggestion from the field). Phys Ther 64:205, 1984.

Fisher, SV and Gullickson, G: Energy cost of ambulation in health and disability: A literature review. Arch Phys Med Rehabil 59:124, 1978.

Fowler, SA, et al: Color-matching technique to train children in the correct use of stairs. Phys Ther 56:903, 1976.

Ganguli, S, et al: Biomechanical approach to the functional assessment of the use of crutches for ambulation. Ergonomics 17:365, 1974.

Hoberman, M and Basmajian, JV: Crutch and cane exercises and use. In Basmajian, JV (ed): Therapeutic Exercise, ed 4. Williams & Wilkins, Baltimore, 1984, p 267.

Jankowski, LW, et al: Accuracy of methods for estimating O_2 cost of walking in coronary patients. J Appl Physiol 33:672, 1972.

Jorgensen, CS: Walker modification for patients with multiple handicaps (suggestion from the field). Phys Ther 59:1250, 1979.

Kathrins, BP and O'Sullivan, S: Cardiovascular responses during nonweight-bearing and touchdown ambulation. Phys Ther 64:14, 1984.

Klenerman, L and Hutton, WC: A quantitative investigation of the forces applied to walking-sticks and crutches. Rheumatol Rehab 12:152, 1973.

Lerner-Frankiel, M, et al: Functional community ambulation: What are the criteria: Clinical Management in Physical Therapy 6(2):12, 1986.

McBeath, AA, Bahrke, M, and Balke, B: Efficiency of assisted ambulation determined by oxygen consumption measurement. J Bone Joint Surg 56-A:994, 1974.

Najdeski, P: Crutch measurement from the sitting position (suggestion from the field). Phys Ther 57:826, 1977.

Najdeski, P: Walking path or track (suggestion from the field). Phys Ther 56:426, 1976.

Nielsen, DH, et al: Clinical determination of energy cost and walking velocity via stopwatch or speedometer cane and conversion graphs. Phys Ther 62:591, 1982.

Opara, CU, Levangie, PK, and Nelson, DL: Effects of selected assistive devices on normal distance gait characteristics. Phys Ther 65:1188, 1985.

Palmer, ML and Toms, JE: Manual for Functional Training, ed 2. FA Davis, Philadelphia, 1986.

Patterson, R and Fisher, SV: Cardiovascular stress of crutch walking. Arch Phys Med Rehabil 62:257, 1981.

Reisman, M, et al: Elbow movement and forces at the hands during swing-through axillary crutch gait. Phys Ther 65:601, 1985.

Shoup, TE, Fletcher, LS, and Merrill, BR: Biomechanics of crutch locomotion. J Biomechanics 7:11, 1974.

Smidt, GL and Wadsworth, JB: Floor reaction forces during gait: Comparison of patients with hip disease and normal subjects. Phys Ther 53:1056, 1973.

Sullivan, PE and Markos, PD: Clinical Procedures in Therapeutic Exercise. Appleton & Lange, Norwalk, CT, 1987.

Virga, K: Adapted crutches for patients with little or no hand grasp (suggestion from the field). Phys Ther 59:37, 1979.

Wadsworth, JB, Smidt, GL, and Johnston, RC: Gait characteristics of subjects with hip disease. Phys Ther 52:829, 1972.

Wells, RP: The kinematics and energy variations of swing-through gait. J Biomechanics 12:579, 1979.

GLOSSARY

Counterrotation (in rolling): Simultaneous movement of the upper and lower segments of the trunk in opposite directions.

Developmental sequence: An established pattern of developmental activities by which a child acquires the control needed for functional movement.

Elevation activities: A general term used in gait training to describe an ambulatory activity requiring movement from one level surface to another (e.g., negotiating curbs, climbing stairs or ramps).

Four-point gait: One crutch is moved forward, the opposite lower extremity is advanced, the other crutch is moved forward and opposite lower extremity advanced; slow, stable gait pattern.

Log rolling: Rolling in which movement of the entire trunk rotates as a unit around the longitudinal axis of the body.

Long sitting: Sitting with knees extended on a supporting surface.

Lordosis: Abnormally increased anterior curvature of the lumbar spine.

Orthostatic (postural) hypotension: A lower than normal drop in blood pressure related to movement to a standing position; may be severe after prolonged bedrest or confinement to a sitting position.

Partial-weight-bearing (PWB) gait: A modification of the three-point gait pattern; during stance phase on the affected extremity, weight is borne partially on the affected extremity and partially on the crutches; the crutches and affected lower extremity are advanced together, the uninvolved lower extremity steps past the crutches.

Quadruped: All-fours position; weight bearing on hands and knees.

Segmental rolling: Rolling in which the upper or lower segment of the trunk moves independently while the opposite segment is stable.

Short sitting: Sitting with knees flexed over a supporting surface such as a mat or bed.

Swing-through gait: Both crutches are moved forward together, both lower extremities then swing beyond the crutches; typically used with severe involvement or paralysis of both lower extremities.

Swing-to gait: Both crutches are moved forward together, both lower extremities then swing to the crutches; typically used with severe involvement or paralysis of both lower extremities.

Tailor sitting: Crossed-leg or "Indian style" sitting; the hips are placed in flexion, abduction, and external rotation with the knees flexed.

Three-point gait: A non-weight-bearing (NWB) gait; weight is borne on the crutches instead of on the affected lower extremity; both crutches are advanced and the unaffected lower extremity steps past the crutches.

Two-point gait: One lower extremity and the opposite crutch are advanced together; this is repeated with the other crutch and lower extremity.

Chapter 16

CORONARY ARTERY DISEASE

SUSAN B. O'SULLIVAN

OBJECTIVES

1. Define terms associated with the pathology and management of coronary artery disease.

2. Describe the etiology, pathophysiology, symptomatology, and sequela of coronary artery disease.

3. Describe diagnostic and assessment procedures commonly associated with coronary artery disease.

4. Describe the rehabilitative management of the patient with coronary artery disease.

5. Value the therapist's role in the management of patients with coronary artery disease.

INTRODUCTION

Cardiovascular diseases are the leading cause of death in the United States today, accounting for nearly one million deaths each year (51 percent of all deaths). In the United States alone, an estimated 40 million individuals are afflicted with cardiovascular diseases. Thirty-five years ago, only 5 percent of deaths were attributed to cardiovascular diseases. This marked increase is seen primarily in western industrialized societies and can be regarded as a manifestation of civilization and progress.[1,2] However, this picture appears to be changing. The American Heart Association reports an absolute decline in deaths from cardiovascular disease in recent years.[3,4] Despite this downward trend, these diseases remain the leading cause of death and morbidity in the United States. Their effect can be measured both in terms of the disabilities produced and in the economic burden placed on the patient, family, and community resulting from health care costs and loss of income.

EPIDEMIOLOGY OF CARDIOVASCULAR DISEASES

Epidemiologic studies reveal that certain risk factors are associated with the development of atherosclerosis and cardiovascular disease. Studies such as the Framingham Study in Framingham, Massachusetts, have identified a variety of personal and socioeconomic factors that increase a person's risk of developing cardiovascular disease.[4] Factors that are implicated include those associated with certain living habits: cigarette smoking; a sedentary lifestyle; a diet excessive in calories, saturated fat, **cholesterol,** and salt; and obesity. In addition, studies of psychosocial factors have identified a behavior pattern associated with the development of these diseases characterized by competitiveness, drive, and an overdeveloped sense of time urgency (type A behavior).[5,6] Other risk factors include genetic predisposition, high blood pressure, diabetes, sex (males more than females), age (middle to older ages), and the use of oral contraceptives. These risk factors permit the prediction of the likelihood of developing cardiovascular disease before the actual symptoms appear. The more risk factors an individual presents or the greater the problem with any single risk factor, the greater is the overall risk of cardiovascular disease. It is important to note that the effect of two or more risk factors is not summative in nature but, rather, multiplies the risk with each additional factor. Many of these risk factors can be modified or eliminated; for example, smoking, sedentary lifestyle, elevated blood pressure, elevated serum cholesterol, and obesity. Factors such as family history, age, and sex can not be controlled. In an effort to reduce the risk of developing cardiovascular disease, the American Heart Association recommends screening for risk factors and the routine application of preventive measures.[4] As individuals continue to modify lifestyle and maintain an interest in personal health, the incidence of coronary heart disease may continue to decrease.

CLINICAL MANIFESTATIONS OF CARDIOVASCULAR DISEASES

Arteriosclerosis, commonly called hardening of the arteries, includes a variety of conditions that cause the artery walls to thicken and to lose elasticity. The symptoms that result vary according to the type of vessel involved and the site and extent of disease within the vessel. Arteriosclerosis that affects the innermost layer of the vessels is called type I or intimal arteriosclerosis. Thickening of the intimal layer is accompanied by plaque formation, which consists of collagen, smooth muscle cells, and **lipids.** Progressive thickening of the intima occurs normally in most individuals by the age of 20. When the intimal lesion exceeds the thickness of the media or middle layer, the vessel is considered atherosclerotic. **Atherosclerosis** is defined as a form of arteriosclerosis in which the inner layers are made thick and irregular by deposits of a fatty substance. The internal channel of arteries becomes narrowed, and blood supply is reduced. Type II, or medial, sclerosis affects the middle layer of the vessel, resulting in calcification and hypertrophy. Individuals with this type of arteriosclerosis develop pipestem or rigid arteries typically in medium-size vessels such as the brachial artery. Blood flow is not usually reduced. Type III, or arteriolar, sclerosis affects small blood vessels, with characteristic changes in both the media and intima. Blood flow is reduced. This is often seen in hypertensive patients.[7]

The pathogenic process is thought to begin with an initial injury to the endothelial cells that line the blood vessels. Following this injury, platelets adhere to the vessel wall, causing proliferation of smooth muscle cells and the binding of lipids, especially low-density **lipoproteins** (LDL), at these sites. In the latter stages these fatty streaks develop into mature atherosclerotic plaques stimulated by a platelet-derived growth factor which causes continued proliferation of fibroblasts and smooth muscle cells. As this process continues, progressive narrowing of the vessel results.[7-9]

Clinical manifestations of coronary artery disease (CAD) include **ischemia, infarction, congestive heart failure,** and sudden death. **Ischemia** refers to deprivation of oxygen to the tissues. **Angina pectoris** is an example of an ischemic condition in which the heart muscle receives an insufficient supply of oxygen and blood, causing pain in the chest. Ischemic symptoms are reversible events but may herald more serious cardiovascular pathology. **Infarction,** or myocardial cell death, following a cessation of blood supply may result from occlusion or stenosis of greater than 75 percent of the supplying artery. Both **thrombosis** (the formation of a blood clot within a vessel) and **embolus** (a blood clot that forms in the blood vessels in one part of the body and travels to another) may cause myocardial infarction. Infarction is an irreversible injury. **Aneurysm** is a dilation or saclike bulging of a vessel or wall. These weakened areas may rupture, often in hypertensive patients, and cause sudden death. The leading cause of sudden death in individuals with cardiovascular diseases are electrical complications caused by **arrhythmias.** An **arrhythmia** is an irregularity or loss of normal heart rhythm. **Congestive heart failure** is the backing up of blood in the veins leading to the heart, often accompanied by accumulation of fluid in various parts of the body. Pump failure after infarction results from the heart's inability to pump out all the blood it receives.[8-11]

Typically, the patient with myocardial infarction presents with atherosclerotic involvement of two or three coronary arteries with restriction of 75 percent or more of the lumen of the vessel. The overt signs of disease normally do not occur until the obstruction is relatively severe and the disease is in its chronic stage. It also has been estimated that 25 percent of patients with CAD present with sudden death as their first and only symptom.[10] The long-term prognosis following CAD depends upon the extent and location of the existing disease.[9,11,12]

DETERMINANTS OF CORONARY ARTERY DISEASE

The clinical manifestations of CAD all represent an imbalance between the oxygen demands of the heart and the available oxygen supply. Several factors determine the myocardial oxygen demands (MVO_2). The major determinants include heart rate, contractility of the myocardium, and intramyocardial tension, which is the product of ventricular pressure and volume (Fig. 16–1).[10,11]

Oxygen supply to the heart is determined by coronary blood flow and the oxygen content of arterial blood. Blood is delivered to the myocardium by the right and left coronary arteries, which come directly from the aorta and branch into a vascular network that supplies the heart (Fig. 16–2). Familiarity with coronary circulation will improve the reader's understanding of the clinical relevance of an occlusion, inasmuch as the location will determine to a large degree any residual functional abnormalities. The right coronary artery (RCA) originates from the aorta and runs inferior in the atrioventricular sulcus. It supplies the right atrium and most of the right ventricle. It commonly branches off to the left ventricle, supplying portions of the posterior and inferior

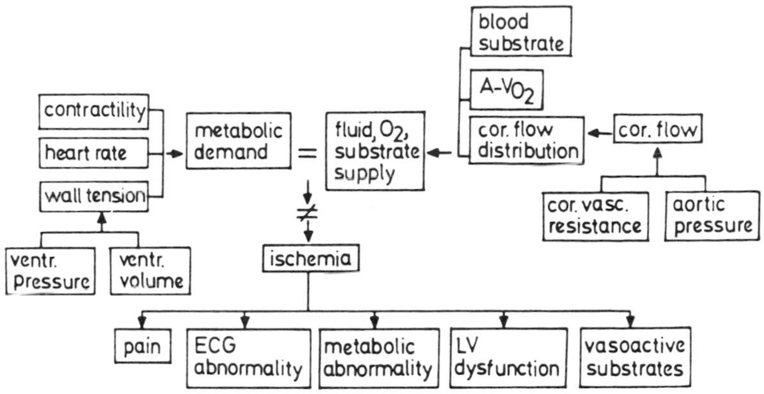

Figure 16-1. The oxygen supply–demand relationships for patients with ischemic heart disease. Supply and delivery are influenced by multiple factors. When contractility, wall tension, heart rate, or other parameters in the left side of the diagram are increased, there must be a corresponding increase in delivery. If not, ischemia may result. (Reproduced from Ellestad, M,[12] p 24, with permission.)

walls. It supplies the conduction system of the heart (sinoatrial node, atrioventricular node, and bundle of His) and the interventricular septum. The left coronary artery (LCA) also originates from the aorta and bifurcates into two branches. The left anterior descending artery supplies the anterior, superior, and lateral walls of the left ventricle and portions of the interventricular septum. It may also branch off to the right ventricle. The left circumflex artery supplies the lateral and inferior walls of the left ventricle and portions of the left atrium. It may also supply portions of the posterior wall.[9,15] Although these represent the common patterns of coronary circulation, it is important to note that the distribution of blood supply is variable from individual to individual. Because the left ventricle is the major pumping station to the body, the left coronary system, which supplies up to 70 percent of the left ventricular mass, becomes the most significant branch in terms of myocardial injury and residual functional work capacity. The most common

site of severe narrowing and infarction in the LCA is within the first 2 cm of the origin of the left anterior descending and left circumflex arteries; in the RCA, narrowing and infarction occur more frequently in the distal third of the artery.[8]

Myocardial metabolism is essentially aerobic and requires a very high rate of oxygen extraction from the blood, as well as a continuous flow of blood through the myocardium. With exercise of any level very little additional oxygen extraction can occur. Therefore, increased demands of the myocardium must be met by increasing the total volume of coronary blood flow. At rest most of the left ventricular coronary flow occurs during diastole. Thus, diastolic pressure and duration are important determinants of coronary blood flow. Tachycardia (heart rate greater than 100 beats per minute) reduces diastolic time and may significantly reduce blood flow, causing ischemia in patients with CAD.[16] Therefore, regulation of heart rate is essential if the symptoms of ischemia (angina, left ventricular dysfunction, or electrical instability) are to be prevented. Myocardial performance with increasing intensities of exercise may be altered in CAD. **Stroke volume** may decrease instead of increase, as anticipated, causing exercise-induced hypotension. This is termed *inotropic incompetence.* Heart rate may not increase linearly with increasing workload intensity as expected, or it may decrease. This response has been termed *chronotropic incompetence.* Both inotropic and chronotropic incompetence are poor prognostic indicators.[17,18]

The autonomic nervous system also influences the heart and blood vessels through both direct neural and indirect neurohumoral effects. Sympathetic fibers increase the overall activity of the heart, increasing both the rate and the force of contraction and myocardial metabolism. Parasympathetic stimulation produces the opposite effect, decreasing the overall activity and metabolism of the heart. Sympathetic stimulation also constricts coronary as well as most other arteries, causing increased flow resistance and elevating pressures. Parasympathetic stimulation has almost no effects on blood vessels, though pressures generally fall owing to decreased pumping action of the heart. Indirectly the sympathetic nervous system regulates coronary vascular resistance by stimulating the adrenal cortex to secrete catecholamines, norepinephrine, and epinephrine into

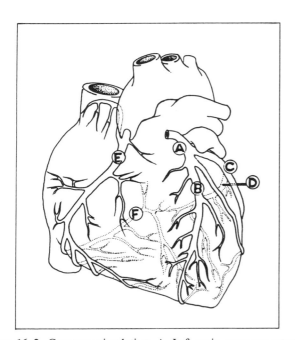

Figure 16-2. Coronary circulation. A, Left main coronary artery. B, Left anterior descending coronary artery. C, Left circumflex coronary artery. D, Posterior circumflex coronary artery. E, Right coronary artery. F, Posterior descending artery.

the circulating bloodstream. This hormonal release causes similar but more long-lasting and potent effects than direct sympathetic stimulation. Blood vessels vasoconstrict and heart activity is increased. Control of these responses is exerted by the central nervous system in the vasomotor center located in the brainstem. Arterial pressure is regulated by the vasomotor center through the baroreceptor reflex. This reflex is activated by pressure or stretch receptors located in the walls of large systemic arteries, especially prevalent in the internal carotid arteries and the aortic arch. Chemoreceptors located in the carotid and aortic bodies react to changes in arterial oxygen concentration and through brainstem activation exert a controlling influence on blood pressure as well as respiration. Stimulation of the motor cortex, hypothalamus, or other higher nervous centers can excite or inhibit the vasomotor center in response to motor activities and emotional or alarm patterns. Catecholamine levels elevated by stress or cigarette smoking can contribute to the pathogenesis of hypertension, endothelial damage, and atherosclerosis.[10]

The Patient with Angina

Angina pectoris is pain secondary to temporary, localized **ischemia.** It is usually substernal and lasts from 1 to 3 minutes, during which time the patient may complain of "burning," "indigestion," or "tightness." Other symptoms, such as dyspnea, variable pulse rate, and elevated blood pressure, also may be noted during the attack. Angina is commonly precipitated by physical exertion and/or emotional stress, although other factors such as exposure to cold or eating also may initiate it. The ischemia that results from inadequate coronary blood flow also causes depressed left ventricular function, which is evident by changes in the **electrocardiogram (ECG),** chiefly by depression of the ST segment. Angina is a reversible symptom and can be relieved by rest or the use of medications that serve to decrease the work of the heart. Commonly used drugs include nitroglycerin and **beta-adrenergic blocking agents** such as propranolol or calcium antagonists.[10,11]

Clinically, angina is assessed by determining the angina threshold, defined as the level of physical activity that usually precipitates the signs of cardiac dysfunction (pain) and electrical instability. Patients with angina typically develop symptoms at a consistent level of their rate-pressure product (heart rate × systolic blood pressure) or typically at a workload roughly corresponding to 50 to 60 percent of their age-predicted maximal oxygen uptake.[18] This information may be obtained from a personal history or by observing the patient's performance on a graded exercise test, which is a measured exercise challenge designed to determine an individual's functional capacity during physical stress. In cases of severe angina, either myocardial scintigraphy (myocardial perfusion of radionuclides and scintillation photography) or coronary arteriography (injection of radiopaque dye and x-ray examination) may be used to determine the exact location and extent of CAD and the appropriate therapeutic intervention.

The Patient with Revascularization Surgery

In cases of severe, chronically disabling CAD, balloon angioplasty (transluminal coronary angioplasty) or, more commonly, coronary artery bypass graft (CABG) may be recommended to achieve revascularization of the myocardium. Balloon angioplasty involves the threading of a balloon-tipped tube through a catheter into the coronary arteries to the point of the atherosclerotic lesion and then inflating the balloon to compress the lesion.[7] A CABG procedure usually involves bypassing one or more obstructed arteries either by the anastomosing of a vein graft from the aorta to the coronary artery at a point distal to the obstruction, or by patch grafting to widen the obstructed artery. The surgery improves the clinical status, often with a dramatic and significant reduction of pain. Significant improvement in the duration of exercise, maximal heart rate response, and the incidence of ECG ischemic changes also have been reported. Some patients do not achieve any apparent benefit greater than that with conventional drug management. The value of bypass surgery in prolonging life is controversial and is currently the object of intense study and investigation.[19,20]

The Patient with Myocardial Infarction

Myocardial infarction (MI) is the death of myocardial tissue secondary to occlusion or severe stenosis (greater than 75 percent) of a coronary artery. It is often associated with one or more of the following symptoms: severe, prolonged substernal chest pain; radiating pain to the left arm, neck, or jaw; and diaphoresis, vomiting, weakness, dyspnea, and/or anxiety. The functional damage that results is permanent, and the prognosis depends upon the artery involved, the amount of cardiac muscle tissue involved, and the patency and adequacy of the remaining circulation. Infarction places an increased load on healthy myocardial tissue, which may then become abnormal with time. Metabolic and electrical abnormalities caused by the necrosis and natural healing process result.[10,11]

Clinically, myocardial infarction is assessed by physical examination, laboratory tests, and the ECG. In the physical examination, the physician observes the patient and gathers data on physical signs. Pain is usually intense or "crushing" substernal pain which is prolonged and unrelieved by rest. It may radiate to arms, jaw, or neck. Other typical signs include nausea, sweating, and dyspnea. The heart rate may be abnormally slow (bradycardia) or fast (tachycardia). A gallop rhythm (extra S_3 and S_4 heart sounds) may or may not be heard. Laboratory tests usually reveal an elevation in the white blood cell count, erythrocyte sedimentation rate, and serum enzyme levels. Serum enzymes are the most powerful diagnostic tool of the three and many times are termed cardiac enzymes, though they are released in instances of cell death other than myocardial infarction. These enzymes include serum glutamic-oxaloacetic transaminase (SGOT), also known as aspartate aminotransferase

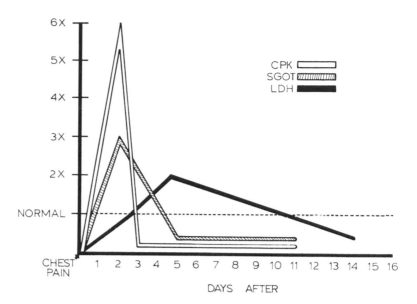

Figure 16–3. Cardiac enzyme elevation following myocardial infarction. SCPK and SGOT characteristically begin to rise early and to reach peak activity 24 hours after onset; activity returns to normal by the third to fifth days. SLDH begins to rise 12 to 24 hours following infarction and reaches peak activity by day three. Activity may remain elevated as long as 10 days after onset.

(AST), lactate dehydrogenase (LDH), and creatine phosphokinase (CPK). Figure 16–3 indicates the characteristic levels of elevation and the time frame in which they remain elevated following myocardial infarction.[21] Separation of CPK by electrophoresis or radioimmunoassay into isoenzymes has revealed a specific isoenzyme released in cardiac muscle necrosis, known as MB-CPK. It appears within 4 hours after infarction and peaks by 36 hours.[7] For the therapist working in the acute care setting, it is important to check enzyme levels daily, because any reelevation in these levels that exceeds the normal time frame could mean the presence of a new infarction or extension of the old one. Exercise is contraindicated until further diagnostic studies are completed.

The ECG changes resulting from acute myocardial infarction remain one of the most reliable cues in diagnosing infarction. These changes may appear as early as 30 minutes or, rarely, as late as 2 weeks following the insult. Characteristically, the infarcted tissue can not depolarize or repolarize and becomes a "functional hole" in the normal conduction of the myocardium. A Q wave becomes apparent in the ECG, and if its height is greater than one quarter of the size of the R wave, it is considered indicative of myocardial infarction. The muscle tissue that surrounds the infarcted area is called the *zone of injury* and causes elevation of the ST segment on the ECG. Adjacent to this area is an area of ischemic tissue that causes the T wave to invert (Figs. 16–4 and 16–5). During the recovery process, the ST segment often returns to normal within a few days, the T wave returns to normal within a few months; however, the abnormal Q wave usually remains.[22–24] The ECG can be used to localize the site of the infarction by studying the appearance of the Q waves in the 12 different leads. Because each lead picks up an electrical signal from a slightly different angle, it is possible to locate the infarcted area within certain limits. These changes are summarized in Table 16–1.

Following myocardial infarction the patient is typically admitted to the coronary care unit (CCU) and is put on complete bedrest for a brief period (averaging 3 1/2 days) and modified bedrest for the rest of the hospital

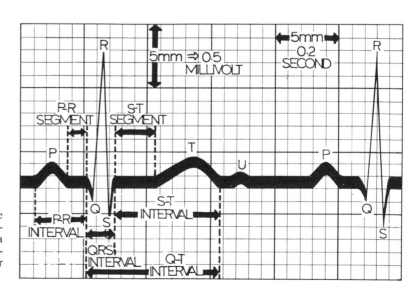

Figure 16–4. Normal electrocardiogram. An electrical impulse originates from the SA node and spreads across the atria, depolarizing them and yielding a P wave. At the AV node there is a brief 1/10 second pause followed by depolarization of the ventricles, yielding a QRS complex. The T wave represents ventricular repolarization.

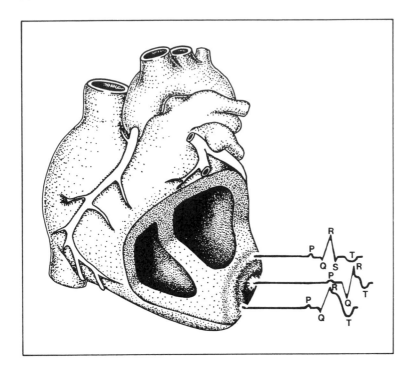

Figure 16–5. Electrocardiogram following myocardial infarction. The inner zone represents the zone of infarction, which causes a large Q wave to appear on the ECG. The middle zone represents the zone of injury, which causes elevation of the ST segment on the ECG. The outer zone represents the zone of ischemia, which causes the T wave to invert on the ECG.

stay. The patient is usually transferred from the CCU to a hospital, progressive care, or cardiac rehabilitation unit for the remainder of the hospitalization, which averages a total of 14 days.[25]

The patient may be given any of a number of medications, typically (1) antiarrhythmic agents, (2) anti-coagulant drugs, (3) antihypertensive drugs for hypertensive patients, (4) tranquilizers, (5) nitrate drugs, (6) beta-adrenergic blocking drugs, (7) antidepressant drugs, and (8) digitalis. The effects of some of the more widely used cardiac drugs are summarized in Table 16–2. Patients are also typically put on diets restricted in cholesterol, fats, and sodium and are restricted from smoking. Inasmuch as electrical complications may be numerous and represent the leading cause of sudden death, continuous ECG monitoring is instituted immediately and continues for the first few days of hospitalization; modified monitoring or radiotelemetry may be used during the remainder of the hospitalization.[25]

Following an MI, patients may develop complications. The location of the infarct and the amount of muscle tissue destroyed will determine the emergence and effect of these complications. Cardiogenic shock results from severe depression of cardiac output caused by extensive loss of cardiac muscle and is associated with a mortality rate of 80 percent. Rupture of the ventricular wall or of the papillary muscles may also occur secondary to the liquefaction stage of necrosis of the myocardium. Extension of the infarct or additional necrosis of cells of borderline viability may result in cases in which myocardial oxygen supply is greatly diminished. Papillary muscle dysfunction may result in mitral valve regurgitation and heart murmurs. Thromboemboli from peripheral or pulmonary veins may result from prolonged bedrest and inactivity.[11,26] Patients with an unstable cardiac status (significant disturbances of cardiac rhythm, heart failure, persistent or recurrent chest pain, uncontrolled hypertension or hypotension, and clinical shock) are excluded from early physical activity. Rehabilitation can be started for these patients as soon as their complications have been resolved and their condition stabilized. Without complications, patients can be referred for rehabilitation almost immediately.[18,26]

Table 16–1 ELECTROCARDIOGRAPHIC CHANGES FOLLOWING MYOCARDIAL INFARCTION

A. Sequential phases in infarction	
1. Acute	ST elevation (earliest change)
	Tall, hyperacute T waves
	New Q or QS wave
2. Evolving	Deep T wave inversions may persist; usually returns to normal (months)
	ST elevation returns to baseline (days)
	Q or QS waves may decrease in size, rarely disappear
B. Infarction type	
1. Subendocardial intramural	ST-T changes: ST depression or T wave inversion
	Without QRS changes
2. Transmural	Abnormal Q or QS waves in leads overlying the infarct
	ST-T changes
C. Infarction site	
1. Anterior infarction:	Q or QS in V1 to V4
2. Lateral infarction:	Q or QS in lead I, aVl
3. Inferior infarction:	Q or QS in leads II, III, aVf
4. Posterior infarction:	Large R waves in V1–V3
	ST depression V1, V2, or V3

Standard 12-lead electrocardiogram: leads I to III, aVr, aVl, and aVf are limb leads; V1 to V6 are chest leads.
Adapted from Goldberger and Goldberger,[22] and Conover.[23]

Table 16–2 CARDIAC AND NONCARDIAC DRUG INTERVENTIONS AND THEIR POSSIBLE EFFECT ON EXERCISE REGIMENS (THE LIST OF NAMED DRUGS IS NEITHER INCLUSIVE NOR EXHAUSTIVE)

Certified staff should be aware of the following information about each participant prior to beginning a graded test or exercise session.
1. All drugs taken by each participant.
2. The medical indications for each drug.
3. The pharmacodynamics and pharmokinetics of each drug.

	Exercise Performance	Effect Heart Rate	Blood Pressure	Effect on ECG	Effect on GXT
Antianginal nitrate agents	↑Nitrobid ↑Isordil ↑Isordic Tembids ↑Cardilate ↑Peritrate	↑Nitrobid ↑Sorbitrate ↑Ointment	↓Nitrobid ↓Sorbitrate ↓Ointment	Reduces evidence of myocardial ischemia	May delay onset of ischemic response (lower double product)
Beta blockers	↓↑Inderal ↓↑Lopressor	↓Inderal ↓Lopressor	↓Inderal ↓Lopressor	U waves may become prominent due to bradycardia	May delay onset of ischemic response (lower double product)
Antihypertensive diuretics		→Diuril, Esidrix →Enduron, Lasix →Edecrin, Aldactone →Dyrenium	↓Diuril, Esidrix ↓Enduron, Lasix ↓Edecrin, ↓Aldactone ↓Dyrenium	Prolongs QT interval, accentuates U waves if hypokalemic	May cause false-positive if hypokalemic
Vasodilator		↑Apresoline	↓Apresoline		
Central nervous system		↓Serpasil ↓Ismelin ↓Inderal	↓Serpasil ↓Ismelin ↓Inderal, Minipress ↓Aldomet, Catapres		May delay onset of ischemic response
Digitalis glycosides	↑Strophanthin-G ↑Crystodigin ↑Lanoxin	↑With toxicity or may ↓ if blocks AV node		May produce ST depression or sagging change accentuated with exercise	False-positive
Antiarrhythmics	↑Lanoxin ↑Dilantin ↓↑Xylocaine ↓↑Pronestyl ↓↑Inderal ↓↑Lopressor ↓↑Quinaglute	↑Pronestyl ↑Quinaglute ↑Norpace		ST-T wave changes, U-wave changes, widening of QRS, QT changes	Lanoxin—false-positive Quinaglute, Inderal—may delay onset of ischemic response
Tranquilizers (phenothiazines)		↑	↓	T and U wave changes	May cause false-positive
Antidepressants	Minor antiarrythmics effect	↑	↓	ST-T wave changes	May cause false-positive
Antianxiety (lithium)	No change	No change	No change	ST-T wave changes	May cause false-positive
Others Nicotine Bronchodilators Antihistamines with decongestants Thyroid Drugs Cold Remedies Alcohol		↑ ↑ ↑ ↑ ↑ ↓	↑ ↑ ↑ ↑ ↑	 No change No change No change ? ?	May cause false-positive ? No change No change ? ?

From American College of Sport Medicine,[43] with permission.

REHABILITATION FOR THE PATIENT WITH CORONARY ARTERY DISEASE

Phase 1: Inpatient Cardiac Rehabilitation

TREATMENT GOALS

1. Initiate early physical activity to
   a. Maintain present level of function and to prevent deconditioning
   b. Help allay anxiety and depression
   c. Safely progress toward independence in self-care
2. Assist in assessing the physiologic response to activity and exercise
3. Provide patient and family education

INITIAL ASSESSMENT

An initial assessment is conducted by each member of the cardiac rehabilitation team. This team typically includes a physician, nurse, physical and occupational therapists, nutritionist, psychologist, and pharmacist, although staffing patterns may vary from institution to institution.[18,26]

The first part of the initial assessment is a thorough review of the patient's chart. Items important to note include

1. Medical problems, past medical history; physician's examination
2. Medications
3. Laboratory studies
   a. Blood tests
   b. Cardiac enzymes
   c. Cholesterol, triglycerides
4. Diagnostic studies
   a. Chest x-ray examination
   b. Cardiograms (resting, exercise, vector, echo ECGs)
   c. Catheterization data
   d. Radionuclide studies
   e. Surgical report
5. Nursing notes, reports from other members of the cardiac rehabilitation team and consultants

Reviewing the chart daily will reveal any changes in the patient's cardiac status from day to day. Changes in enzyme levels, ECG patterns, or other diagnostic data may herald the emergence of complications or an extension of the infarction. These patients also may have numerous other medical problems, such as diabetes or chronic lung disease. The medical management and response to treatment of these other conditions will greatly influence clinical decision making and cardiac recovery.[27]

The therapist next should interview the patient. The patient can provide valuable information about psychosocial problems, risk factor profile, diet, knowledge of heart disease, personal goals, family relationships, and home environment. The therapist will want to pay special attention to prior lifestyle, exercise, and recreational interests and habits. Vocational information should

include type of work, average number of hours per week, attitude toward job, and work-related pressures. The patient should be questioned about anginal pain (precipitating factors, duration, frequency, methods used to relieve pain, and limitations in daily activity). The intense pain in infarction is usually time limited, generally lasting hours or the first few days. Chest wall pain following by-pass surgery is generally sharp and is influenced by respiratory movements. It is important to note that not all the information from the interview process can be secured in a single session but, rather, is obtained from a series of sessions with the patient. As the patient begins to feel better and less anxious, he or she will be able to communicate more readily, and a total picture of the present functional level, previous lifestyle, and the information necessary for effective rehabilitation planning will begin to emerge. The interview also serves to establish the very important rapport and trust between patient and therapist. This creates an environment for mutual goal setting and can ensure improved compliance in the overall rehabilitation program. The interview session also can be used to initiate early patient education. It is helpful to the patient at this point if the total cardiac rehabilitation program is outlined, so that the patient has a clear understanding of the convalescent period and the plan for resumption of normal activities. Interviews with family members also should be scheduled as needed.

The initial assessment of the patient should include a gross neuromuscular examination. Items such as range of motion, muscle strength, sensation, balance, coordination, and gait should be examined as the patient's medical condition and tolerance permits; excessive effort and straining should be avoided. Vital signs should be taken. Chest wall inspection and palpation can reveal localized areas of pain as well as respiratory patterns. Auscultation of the chest using a stethoscope reveals information about heart sounds (normal first and second heart sounds as opposed to extra heart sounds, gallop rhythm, or murmurs) and breath sounds (normal breath sounds as opposed to rales). Examination of the extremities can reveal information about peripheral pulses and edema.[26-28]

PHYSICAL ACTIVITY

The primary benefits of early physical activity or ambulation include (1) the prevention of deconditioning effects, (2) the prevention of complications such as thromboemboli, and (3) a decrease in anxiety and depression.[29,30] The harmful effects of prolonged bedrest and deconditioning have been clearly delineated by the studies of Saltin and coworkers[31] and are summarized in Table 16–3. The psychologic complications following myocardial infarction have been reported by a number of investigators, notably Cassem and Hackett.[32-34] They have identified anxiety (threat of death) and depression (threat of invalidism) as the two most common psychologic symptoms following an acute coronary event. These symptoms are best counteracted by early, supervised physical activity which allows the patient to regain control of life and to become independent in self-care

Table 16–3 DECONDITIONING EFFECTS OF PROLONGED BEDREST

A decrease in physical work capacity
An increase in the heart rate response to effort
A decrease in adaptability to change in posture which is manifest primarily as orthostatic hypotension
A decrease in the circulation blood volume (with plasma volume decreasing to a greater extent than red cell mass)
A decrease in lung volume and vital capacity
A decrease in serum protein concentration
A negative nitrogen and calcium balance
A decrease in the contractile strength of the body musculature

From Wenger, N: *Coronary Care: Rehabilitation after Myocardial Infarction.* American Heart Association, New York, 1973. By permission of the American Heart Association.

and some activities of daily living (ADL) prior to discharge. The patient is thus reassured that these activities can be performed safely at home without supervision and without fear of "overdoing it" and risking reinfarction and death. A supportive, calm, and reassuring attitude will go a long way in assisting in the patient's psychologic recovery.

It is important to note that physical training is not a goal of this phase of cardiac rehabilitation. The intensity of exercise is not sufficiently high nor is the duration of exercise long enough to produce a training effect on the cardiovascular system. The primary benefits remain the prevention of deconditioning and psychologic reassurance.

Low level in-hospital exercise programs need to be individualized, based upon the results of the initial assessment and adjusted according to each patient's limitations. Specific program components are selected on the basis of their low-intensity quality, with gradually increasing metabolic cost, safety, and dynamic nature. Activities are described in **metabolic equivalents,** or **METs,** defined as the energy requirement for basal homeostasis while the subject is awake and in a sitting position. A MET is approximately 3.5 to 4.0 ml of oxygen per kilogram of bodyweight per minute. Most programs begin with activities of around 1 MET, progress to 2 METs while the patient is in the CCU, and reach 4 METs at the time of discharge.[28] Activities include self-care and selected arm and leg exercises designed to improve flexibility, muscle tone, ambulation, and ability to climb stairs. Specific exercise progressions generally include

1. Passive to active to resistive exercise
2. Distal to intermediate to proximal joint exercises
3. Extremity to trunk exercises
4. Semisupine to sitting to standing exercises
5. Progressive increases in ambulation to stair climbing (down) and stair climbing (up)

The metabolic cost of these activities can be increased by

1. Altering the specific type of activity,
2. Increasing the time (duration) spent on the activity, or
3. Altering the position of the body.

Generally patients are seen twice a day for short durations ranging from 10 to 20 minutes each session. Exercise sessions should be coordinated with other hospital activities (such as meals, rest periods, occupational therapy, medical rounds). The sessions should always include a warm-up period with activities of gradually increasing intensity and a cool-down period with activities of gradually decreasing intensity.

One of the earliest and most widely modeled protocols is from Grady Memorial Hospital in Atlanta. This program was developed by Nanette Wenger, M.D., Charles Gilbert, M.D., and Mary Skorapa, M.D., under the auspices of the Emory University School of Medicine. The early ambulation protocol currently used at this facility is included in Table 16–4. The program has three parallel levels of activity: supervised exercise, CCU/ward activity, and educational/recreational activity. The physician approves the progression from one activity level to the next, and individual members of the cardiac team supervise specific activities and document the patient's daily progress. The program itself is not varied from patient to patient, although the time spent at each step may vary, depending upon the patient's response.[18,28]

Another program that also serves as a frequent model for cardiac rehabilitation protocols is the program of Graded Calisthenics used at Montefiore Hospital in New York. These exercises are based upon the original work of Weiss and Karpovich[35] and are primarily designed for reconditioning the skeletal muscles after periods of forced bedrest through the use of calisthenic exercises of gradually increasing intensity. The patient is progressed according to individual tolerance.[36]

Although cardiac rehabilitation protocols may vary from one institution to another, the responsibilities of the physical therapist in overseeing the exercise portion of the rehabilitation program remain fairly consistant. These include

1. Assessing the physiologic responses to exercise and activity
2. Supervising the exercise program and ambulation activities
3. Accurately charting and recording the patient's program and responses to treatment
4. Assisting in patient and family education
5. Preparing the patient for discharge and a home exercise program

ASSESSMENT OF THE PHYSIOLOGIC RESPONSES TO EXERCISE AND ACTIVITY

Heart rate (HR) is recorded before, during, and after each exercise or exercise session. Recording of the HR provides a simple, easily measurable index of myocardial oxygen consumption and myocardial work. Heart rates can be determined by measuring the ECG tracing or by palpating a peripheral pulse with a light but firm pressure. The radial pulse is the most common site used for pulse counting. Caution must be used in taking a carotid pulse, because carotid sinus pressure may be dangerous or falsely lower the pulse rate through stimulation of the baroreceptors located there. Protocols may vary as to whether the first pulse is counted as 0 (generally considered the most accurate method) or 1. The count is maintained for a short duration (10 to 15 seconds) and the

Table 16–4 IN-PATIENT REHABILITATION: 7-STEP MYOCARDIAL INFARCTION PROGRAM

Step	Date	M.D. Initials	Nurse/PT Notes	Supervised Exercise	CCU/Ward Activity	Educational-Recreational Activity
				CCU		
1	—			Active and passive ROM all extremities, in bed Teach patient ankle plantar and dorsiflexion—repeat hourly when awake	Partial self-care Feed self Dangle legs on side of bed Use bedside commode Sit in chair 15 min 1–2 times/day	Orientation to CCU Personal emergencies, social service aid as needed
2	—			Active ROM all extremities, sitting on side of bed	Sit in chair 15–30 min 2–3 times/day Complete self-care in bed	Orientation to rehabilitation team, program Smoking cessation Educational literature if requested Planning transfer from CCU
				Ward		
3	—			Warm-up exercises, 2 METs: Stretching Calisthenics Walk 50 ft and back at slow pace	Sit in chair ad lib To ward class in wheelchair Walk in room	Normal cardiac anatomy and function Development of atherosclerosis What happens with myocardial infarction 1–2 METs craft activity
4	—			ROM and calisthenics, 2.5 METs Walk length of hall (75 ft) and back, average pace Teach pulse counting	Out of bed as tolerated Walk to bathroom Walk to ward class, with supervision	Coronary risk factors and their control
5	—			ROM and calisthenics, 3 METs Check pulse counting Practice walking few stairsteps Walk 300 ft bid	Walk to waiting room or telephone Walk in ward corridor prn	Diet Energy conservation Work simplification techniques (as needed) 2–3 METs craft activity
6	—			Continue above activities Walk down flight of steps (return by elevator) Walk 500 ft bid Instruct in home exercise	Tepid shower or tub bath, with supervision To occupational therapy, cardiac clinic teaching room, with supervision	Heart attack management: Medications Exercise Surgery Response to symptoms Family, community adjustments on return home Craft activity prn
7	—			Continue above activities Walk up flight of steps Walk 500 ft bid Continue home exercise instruction; present information regarding outpatient exercise program	Continue all previous ward activities	Discharge planning: Medications, diet, activity Return appointments Scheduled tests Return to work Community resources Educational literature Medication cards Craft activity prn

From Wenger, N: *Rehabilitation of the patient with symptomatic atherosclerotic coronary disease.* In Hurst, JW (ed): *The Heart*, ed 5. McGraw-Hill, New York, 1982, p 1151, with permission.

number multiplied to calculate a minute rate. The HR should be taken immediately after exercise inasmuch as HR will fall rapidly as recovery progresses.[37]

Heart rates at rest and during exercise are limited by certain drugs, notably beta-adrenergic blocking agents and some antihypertension drugs. Thus HR is low at rest and rises very little with exercise. Certain patients with severe myocardial dysfunction also may be limited in their HR response, demonstrating chronotropic incompetence.[18] The use of HR in monitoring performance is therefore limited, and other physiologic parameters assume greater importance.

Most of the activities in phase 1 programs are of such low intensity that the HR rises very little. Heart rates are generally restricted to increases of 20 or 30 beats above resting or to target HR of 120 to 130 beats per minute. Excessive tachycardia (HR above 120 beats per minute) or bradycardia (HR below 43 beats per minute) are abnormal responses to increased intensity of work.[22] Activity should be terminated if the HR exceeds these or other predetermined end points or if it fails to increase or decreases as the work load increases. Anxious patients may experience a small anticipatory rise in HR before exercise is started, but this should level off once exercise begins.[18,26,29]

Blood pressures are routinely taken before, during, and after exercise. It is important to take blood pressures immediately after the activity—within the first 15 seconds, because pressures usually fall rapidly once an activity is stopped. Pressure taken and recorded during an activity provide the most clinically useful information because the rate-pressure product (heart rate × systolic blood pressure) is a commonly accepted index of myocardial oxygen consumption.[38,39] When blood pressures are being recorded during activity, the therapist should instruct the patient to walk in place. The patient's arm should be held in extension and elevation to about heart level, with the stethoscope placed directly over the brachial artery in the antecubital fossa. Low levels of physical activity generally cause only slight increases in blood pressures. Abnormal blood pressure responses to increased intensity of work which present contraindications to continuing exercise include (1) a failure of the systolic pressure to rise as exercise progresses, (2) a hypertensive blood pressure response (greater than 200 mmHg systolic pressure or greater than 110 mmHg diastolic pressure), or (3) a progressive fall in systolic pressure of 10 to 15 mmHg. The latter is a serious sign and may herald the development of shock.[18,26]

The therapist working with a patient with cardiac disease requires knowledge of the ECG and its interpreta-tion. Basic competencies include the ability to recognize rate disturbances, arrhythmias, and ST changes. Ventricular arrhythmias and **ST segment depressions** are closely correlated to coronary artery disease and sudden death.[13,17,40] These include certain types of **premature ventricular contractions (PVCs)**, ventricular tachycardia, ventricular fibrillation, and horizontal or downsloping ST segment depressions. A PVC originates from an ectopic pacemaker located in the myocardium outside the normal nervous conduction system. The ectopic beat occurs very early in the cycle and is followed by a long (compensatory) pause. It is also characterized by the absence of a P wave, and a slow conduction time, which produces a very wide QRS complex. Although PVCs may occasionally occur at rest and during exercise in the normal individual, they are an important concern in the patient with CAD. Potentially dangerous PVCs seen in the cardiac patient include those of high frequency (greater than five per minute), sequential (two or more consecutive discharges), multifocal (originating from more than one ectopic focus) or R on T phenomenon (occurring so early it falls on the T wave of the previous beat) (Fig. 16–6). Ventricular tachycardia is a run of more than four PVCs in rapid succession, all originating from the same focus. It characteristically produces a rapid ventricular rate (150 to 200 beats per minute), which seriously impairs cardiac output and heart function (Fig. 16–7). In ventricular fibrillation, the HR is so rapid (greater than 300 beats per minute) that the ventricles can not fill, and **cardiac output** is at a standstill. The chaotic twitching of the ventricles produces a totally irregular appearance on the ECG (Fig. 16–8) and complete **cardiac arrest.**[22–24,41]

Examination of the changes in the ST segment also may reveal persistent ischemia in the myocardium and an increased likelihood of potentially dangerous arrhythmias with resultant funtional impairment.Normally the ST segment is isoelectric or falls on the baseline. The baseline or reference line is determined by drawing a line from one PQ junction to the next PQ junction. The J point is defined as the point at which the ST segment

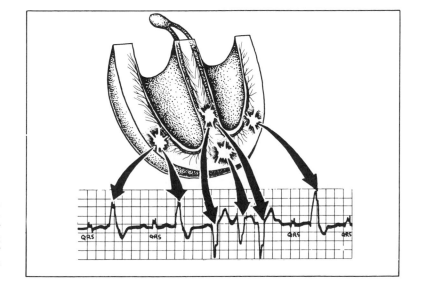

Figure 16–6. Multifocal PVCs. Multifocal PVCs originate from multiple ventricular ectopic foci or pacemakers. Each focus produces its own distinct PVC every time it fires. Like all other PVCs, it occurs early in the cardiac cycle and is followed by a compensatory pause. It is characterized by the absence of a P wave and a wide, bizarre-looking QRS complex that results from its slow ventricular conduction.

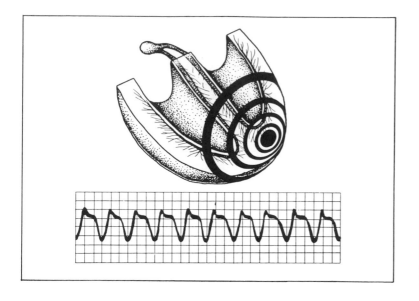

Figure 16–7. Ventricular tachycardia. Ventricular tachycardia is a run of more than four PVCs. It results from a single ventricular ectopic focus and produces a rate of 150 to 200 beats per minute. Heart function is seriously impaired.

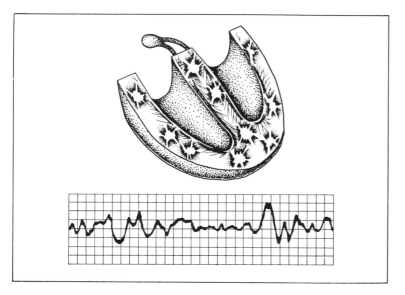

Figure 16–8. Ventricular fibrillation. Ventricular fibrillation results from many ventricular ectopic foci and produces an irregular or chaotic twitching of the ventricles. There is no effective cardiac output (cardiac arrest).

changes its slope. The magnitude of ischemic deviation (depression or elevation) is determined by measuring the distance between the J point and the baseline. Three types of abnormal ST segment depressions have been identified: (1) upsloping ST segments (1.5 mm below the baseline) and 0.06 seconds after the J point, (2) horizontal ST segments (1.0 mm below the baseline), and (3) downsloping ST segments (1.0 mm below the baseline). Both the amount and type of ischemic deviation will vary depending upon the severity of the underlying coronary artery disease (Figs. 16–9 to 16–12). [13,40]

Inasmuch as almost every known type of cardiac arrhythmia may be induced by exercise, the therapist requires competence in ECG interpretation. Less life-threatening though still serious arrhythmias include atrial arrhythmias, such as atrial tachycardia and atrial fibrillation, and conduction defects, such as first-degree, second-degree, or third-degree heart blocks. It is beyond the scope of this text to instruct the reader in interpretation of normal and abnormal ECGs. The reader is referred to Dubin's work on ECGs, [21] which is an excel-

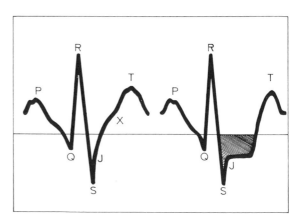

Figure 16–9. ST segment depression. Changes in the ST segment are determined by measuring the amount of deflection of the J point from the isoelectric line. This line is considered to be the baseline and is determined by a line that connects successive points at the PQ junction. This diagram illustrates ST segment depression of about 2.0 mm.

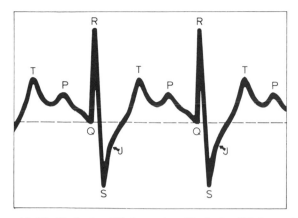

Figure 16–10. Upsloping ST depression. Upsloping ST depression is indicative of ischemia if at 0.06 second after the J point the segment is 1.5 mm or more below the baseline.

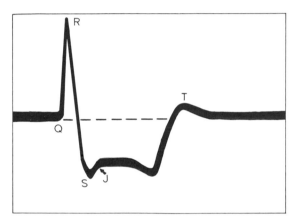

Figure 16–11. Horizontal ST depression. Horizontal or flat ST segment depression is indicative of ischemia if the segment is depressed 1 mm or more below the baseline.

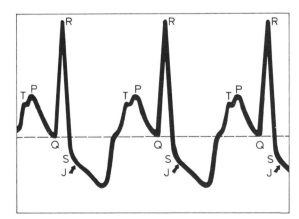

Figure 16–12. Downsloping ST depression. Downsloping ST segment depression is indicative of ischemia if the segment is depressed 1 mm or more below the baseline.

lent reference for beginning study. A thorough understanding of the types of antiarrhythmic medications and their effect on exercise performance is also necessary.[7,43]

Rhythm disturbances occurring during physical activity are monitored continuously at first via bedside

hookup to an ECG. As the patient progresses through the program, radiotelemetry of the ECG may be employed, especially during new or stressful activities or with high-risk patients. It is important to remember that telemetry assists in the identification of arrhythmias and conduction defects but can not be used reliably to detect ST segment changes.[28] The therapist must be constantly on the lookout for ischemic manifestations that may herald an intolerance to the level of physical activity prescribed. The signs and symptoms of excessive effort include (1) persistent dyspnea; (2) dizziness or confusion; (3) anginal pain; (4) severe leg claudication; (5) excessive fatigue; (6) pallor, cold sweat; (7) ataxia; or (8) pulmonary rales. Responses that may be delayed for as long as several hours include (1) prolonged fatigue, (2) insomnia, and (3) sudden weight gain owing to fluid retention. If the patient exhibits any of these symptoms, the exercise should be terminated immediately and the intensity reduced in subsequent sessions. The information should be reported and charted.[26,42–44]

The **Borg ratings of perceived exertion scale (RPE)** also has been used extensively with individuals to assess subjective rating of work intensity. It consists of a 15-point graded scale (with numbers ranging from 6 to 20) that patients use to rate their perceptions of how hard they are working. Descriptive words accompany the numbers, such as *hard,* or *very hard* (Table 16–5).[45] Both local symptoms (muscle aches, cramps, pain, or fatigue) and central symptoms (feelings of being tired or breathless) contribute to the overall feelings of work performance. In healthy, middle-aged men the numeric RPE score when multiplied by 10 corresponds to HR. High correlations with other physiologic variables such as respiratory rate and aerobic power (VO_2) also have been found. Correlations between HR and RPE are considerably lower in individuals working at low intensities, but correlations are much greater with individuals working at moderate or high workloads. This may limit the usefulness of RPE in predicting target HR to those cardiac patients who are capable of at least moderate workloads. These patients appear to be able to use RPE to estimate work intensity accurately, including those patients on beta blockers with limitations in HR responses.[46–49]

Multiple factors, including signs and symptoms, HR,

Table 16–5 BORG'S RPE-SCALE

6
7 No exertion at all
Extremely light
8
9 Very light
10
11 Light
12
13 Somewhat hard
14
15 Hard (heavy)
16
17 Very heavy
18
19 Extremely hard
20 Maximal exertion

From Borg, G,[45] with permission.

ECG changes, blood pressure, RPE and energy costs, appear to provide the safest way to determine exercise tolerance levels in patients with CAD. Reliance on any one measure while ignoring others is neither safe nor appropriate. Additional problems that might increase the predicted overall metabolic cost of an activity, thereby producing an abnormal cardiovascular response to exercise, include (1) restricted range of movement (ROM) in one or more joints, (2) specific muscle weakness, (3) chronic respiratory problems, (4) neurologic impairments, and (5) postural deviations. The physical therapist should assess these systems routinely to determine their impact on function and cardiovascular performance.

SUPERVISION OF EXERCISE PROGRAMS

Phase 1 programs are designed to provide a safe progression of activities during the patient's early convalescence. Although the exercises included are generally simple and routine, it is important to make sure that the patient performs each exercise correctly. Any alteration in how the exercise is done may change the predicted metabolic cost of the activity and produce unexpected and/or undesired cardiovascular responses. The dynamic nature of the activities and rhythmic breathing should be stressed in order to avoid the dangers of isometric exercise, breath holding, and straining. The latter is termed Valsalva's maneuver and results in increased intrathoracic-intra-abdominal pressures which impair venous return and decrease cardiac output. Isometric exercise greater than 20 percent of maximum voluntary contraction results in an increased pressure load on the heart (increased peripheral vascular resistance and sudden increases in both systolic and diastolic blood pressures). The patient with an ischemic left ventricle does not tolerate these changes well and is vulnerable to dangerous arrhythmias and angina.[16,18,19]

The exercise periods should be brief (generally 10 to 20 minutes) and should be performed twice daily. The therapist should balance the activity periods with periods of adequate rest and should schedule activity periods so that they occur at least 1 hour after meals. Also, exercise periods must be appropriately spaced to allow a rest period prior to activities supervised by other members of the cardiac rehabilitation team. The patient should be made aware of the importance of gradual warm-ups and cool-downs and in balancing activity with rest so that he or she will be able to continue this pattern after discharge. Exercise also should be avoided during periods of acute emotional stress.

Activity progression following bypass surgery is typically rapid. Specific program alterations generally include preoperative and postoperative respiratory management and arm exercises to decrease shoulder and chest wall pain. Lateral stretching of the chest that pulls on the incision site should be avoided. Incisional pain and edema, pain and numbness in the leg where the saphenous vein graft was removed can be expected during early recovery.[50] Early ambulation programs are conservative in nature and have been found to be safe.[51-53] The benefits include the reduction of both physical and psychologic complications.

Although a written rehabilitation protocol assists in structuring and documenting care and improves communication between team members, it does restrict individualized prescription of specific exercises. Although it is possible to speed up or to slow down the rate of progression through these programs according to the individual patient's needs, each patient still reaches the same predetermined end point. As physicians and therapists become more knowledgeable and skilled in monitoring and prescription procedures, more individually prescribed exercise programs will be developed with clinical end points that may vary considerably from patient to patient. Programs are also taking on patients who demonstrate more complicated clinical pictures. Thus the variability of programs within an institution may well reflect the "state of the art" and the level of training of its team members.

ACCURATE RECORDING AND CHARTING

Daily charting typically includes date, time, level of activity, position, and duration. The patient's responses to the session are recorded, including preexercise and postexercise HR and blood pressures (BP) and if monitoring is used, an exercise-obtained rhythm strip (see Table 16–6). Any significant observations concerning the patient's emotional and psychologic state, cooperation, and adherence to program regulations should also be noted. Programs that use a protocol sheet generally allow the physician to initial approval for the level of activities that are to be performed.[26]

PATIENT AND FAMILY EDUCATION

Each member of the cardiac rehabilitation team contributes to the total patient and family education program. The goals of the educational program are to (1) improve understanding of coronary disease and its management; (2) modify risk factors; (3) alleviate fears and anxieties, enabling the patient to assume some responsibility for health care; (4) teach general activity guidelines, energy conservation and self-monitoring techniques; and (5) teach cardiopulmonary resuscitation (CPR) to a family member. The program may use informal teaching or formalized group classes. Educational plans should reflect the individual learning styles, interests, and educational level of patients and family members. A variety of educational methodologies and materials (audiovisual and written) and a clear method of assessment are sound patient education practices. Lifestyle changes and long-term compliance in exercise are difficult for patients to achieve and require a consistent educational approach from all team members and family support as well.[18,26,54-57]

DISCHARGE PLANNING

The therapist should review with the patient the home exercise program, general activity guidelines and restric-

Table 16–6 IN-PATIENT EXERCISE RECORD

Date _____ Time _____ Level of activity _____ Position _____ Duration _____

PLACE RHYTHM STRIP HERE

HR Pre Ex _____ HR Post Ex _____ BP Pre Ex _____ BP Post Ex _____

Comments: _____

Date _____ Time _____ Level of activity _____ Position _____ Duration _____

PLACE RHYTHM STRIP HERE

HR Pre Ex _____ HR Post Ex _____ BP Pre Ex _____ BP Post Ex _____

Comments: _____

Date _____ Time _____ Level of activity _____ Position _____ Duration _____

PLACE RHYTHM STRIP HERE

HR Pre Ex _____ HR Post Ex _____ BP Pre Ex _____ BP Post Ex _____

Comments: _____

From *Guidelines for Cardiac Rehabilitation Centers*, American Heart Association, Greater Los Angeles Affiliate, 1982. By permission of the American Heart Association.

tions for exercising at home, monitoring procedures, and signs of exertional intolerance. Sample discharge instructions and suggestions for exercising at home are provided in Tables 16–7 and 16–8.[26]

Low-level multistage exercise testing prior to discharge may be performed. This procedure has been demonstrated to be safe and effective and provides objective information useful in prescribing exercise and activity in the early at-home period of rehabilitation (phase 2). It also helps to reassure the patient about going home and may help assess the patient's readiness to return to work. Generally the patient exercises to a predetermined end point, 60 to 70 percent of the patient's **age-predicted maximal heart rate** or to other well-defined criteria such as a target HR of 120, 4 METs or ST segment depression or angina. A more detailed description of graded exercise testing follows.[58]

Phase 2: Rehabilitation: The Subacute Phase

Phase 2 rehabilitation (subacute phase) includes the early at-home period following hospitalization, typically up to 3 months after discharge.
Treatment Goals
1. Maintain or improve discharge level of function
2. Progress toward full independence in self-care and return to work
3. Begin low-level physical training within safe limits
4. Promote psychologic recovery and risk factor modification
During the first two weeks at home the patient is advised to continue exercising at the same level at which he or she was performing in the hospital. This includes a daily period of exercise and walking. For the patient who

remains asymptomatic, the exercise duration and frequency can be increased so that by the third or fourth week the patient is exercising two to three times a day and walking for longer distances. If the response to increased duration and frequency does not produce any abnormal signs of cardiac inadequacy (as determined by the patient's own self-monitoring), progression to the next higher level of intensity may be undertaken. In general, patients with uncomplicated myocardial infarctions have a functional work capacity that ranges from 4 to 7 METs during this time. High-risk patients (i.e., patients with significant arrhythmias) benefit from continued supervision and monitoring in an out-patient cardiac rehabilitation program, generally three times per week. Maintaining continuity of supervision may assist the patient in readjustment and in lifestyle modification.[26]

Eight to twelve weeks posthospitalization the patient is typically reassessed for admission to a phase 3 rehabilitation program and returns to work. Work situations demanding energy expenditures greater than 8 to 10 METs generally preclude the patient from returning to that job situation. However, most occupations require significantly lower metabolic expenditures, and with proper **exercise prescription** and lifestyle modification, return to work can be a realistic rehabilitation goal.[59]

GRADED EXERCISE TESTING

Graded exercise testing, or **exercise tolerance testing,** is the observation and recording of the patient's cardiovascular responses during a measured exercise stress.[13,40,43] The goals of testing are (1) to observe the ECG changes representative of myocardial ischemia and coronary artery disease during known workloads and (2) to determine the functional aerobic capacity of the patient, which serves as the basis for **exercise prescrip-**

Table 16–7 SUGGESTIONS FOR EXERCISING AT HOME

Walk daily. Always include an adequate warm-up and cool-down period in each exercise session. Choose a comfortable pace.

Rest 1/2 to 1 hour twice a day for the first few weeks at home. Sleep 6 to 8 hours every night.

Space exercise and activity periods evenly with adequate periods.

Wait at least 1 hour after meals before exercising.

Avoid extremes in weather: In the winter, exercise during the warmer parts of the day; in the summer, exercise in the early morning or evening.

Avoid bursts of speed, strenuous steps or hills, and strong winds while walking.

Avoid vigorous arm and shoulder activities, especially overhead arm activity (arm activity requires more energy than leg activity).

Avoid lifting heavy weights or objects (isometric exercise).

Avoid situations and people who make you anxious or angry. Don't exercise when you feel tense. Instead, practice relaxation techniques.

If you feel tired or have chest pain, dizziness, or shortness of breath—no matter what you are doing—stop and rest.

Do not exceed your target heart rate.

Take your medications as ordered. If you need to take nitroglycerin before or during exercise, remember to do so. Any change (either increase or decrease) in certain medications may affect your exercise performance.

Don't exercise if you have an acute illness.

Adopt a pace of daily activity that is not rushed. Plan your day so that you can get everything done without being tense or hurried.

Conserve your energy whenever possible: Adapt your living situation for maximum convenience. Eliminate unnecessary tasks; plan your day in advance.

Pay attention to warning signs: Call your physician or therapist if you have any of the following:
  Pain or chest discomfort that does not go away with medication or with 15 minutes of rest
  Marked shortness of breath
  Dizziness
  Excess fatigue
  Unusual palpitations
  Overly slow or very fast heart rate that does not return to normal after a short rest period

Report to your physician immediately any signs that may be indicative of developing congestive heart failure, including:
  Swelling of your feet and ankles
  Sudden weight gain of 2 to 3 pounds when you know you have not been overeating
  Sleeping on two to three pillows at night so that you can breathe better

Adapted from Cardiac Rehabilitation Committee;[26] Cardiac Clinic–Grady Memorial Hospital;[54] and North Carolinia Myocardial Infarction Rehabilitation Program.[56]

Table 16–8 CARDIAC REHABILITATION CENTER DISCHARGE INSTRUCTIONS

Name _____ Date_____

Congratulations on your improvement and going home! Continued moderate exercise and attention to healthful living habits will facilitate your return to normal health. The following will assist you in this program. *Keep a record of your responses to exercise (attached)* and *take it with you* each time you visit your personal doctor and the cardiac rehabilitation center.

HOME EXERCISE PROGRAM
Top heart rate _____ beats/min.
Lying
  1. Move legs outward
  2. Straight arm raise
  3. Knee to chest
Sitting
  4. Toe Touch
  5. Move legs outward
  6. Move arms outward
  7. Move arms forward & backward with arms elevated
Standing
  8. Arm circles
  9. Side trunk bends
 10. Rocking on toes
 11. Slight knee bends
 12. Trunk circles
Each exercise should be repeated _____ times in a row,
_____ times a day

INSTRUCTIONS FOR WALKING

An exercise program for you began in the hospital and should be continued at home. Walking is excellent exercise. The following is a guide to be used *with the precautions* outlined for you by your physician.
A. Warm up by doing the stretching exercises (as noted above) and walk at a slow pace for _____ minutes.
B. After checking your warm-up pulse rate, resume walking at a faster pace for _____ minutes at your prescribed heart rate of _____. Check your pulse intermittently to see that it is not too fast or too slow.
C. Cool off by walking at a slow pace for _____ minutes.
Your intervals are _____
Your prescribed target heart rate is _____
If you have any questions ask the exercise therapist in charge of your cardiac rehabilitation program or call at _____.

From *Guidelines for Cardiac Rehabilitation Centers*, American Heart Association, Greater Los Angeles Affiliate, 1982. By permission of the American Heart Association.

tion. It has also been widely used to assess the effects of treatment programs. Exercise testing devices, **ergometers,** allow the precise calibration and increase of workload. These include treadmill, bicycle, or arm ergometer (Fig. 16–13). In deciding on which testing instrument to use, consideration should be given to the anticipated training program. Patients using a bicycle ergometer for training should be tested using a similar device.

The test begins with a low-level workload, which allows for a gradual warm-up period, and gradually increases to the point of cardiovascular limitation (multistage testing). Stages are usually two to three minutes in duration, allowing the patient to reach **steady state** (a work situation in which oxygen uptake equals the oxygen requirement of the tissues). Steady state work can be detected by observing the heart rate response which levels off to a constant rate (usually within three to four beats of the previous heart rate).[60] Various testing protocols have been developed; some are continuous (using a progressive increase in workload), and others are intermittent (alternating work with rest periods). Tests can also be maximal (allowing the patient to reach maximum heart rate) or submaximal (stopped at a predetermined end point or when exertional symptoms develop). Ellestad's book *Stress Testing* provides an excellent reference for further study.[12]

The exercise test is performed under direct supervision. An informed consent is obtained prior to testing. The patient first undergoes a complete medical examination, including a resting 12-lead ECG. At this time any patient who presents absolute contraindications to exercise testing is excluded (Table 16–9). During each minute

Oxygen Requirements for Step, Treadmill, and Bicycle Ergometer

Functional Class	METS	O₂ Requirements ml O₂/kg/min	Step Test — Nagle Balke Naughton 2 min stages 30 steps min	Treadmill Tests — Bruce 3 min stages		Kattus 3 min stages		Balke %grade at ¾ mph	Balke %grade at 3 mph	Bicycle Ergometer — For 70 kg body weight kgm/min
Normal and I	16	56.0	Step height increased 4 cm q 2 min					26		
	15	52.5				mph	%gr	24		
	14	49.0		mph	%gr	4	22	22		1500
	13	45.5	Height (cm)	4.2	16			20		
	12	42.0	40			4	18	18	22.5	1350
	11	38.5	36					16	20.0	1200
	10	35.0	32			4	14	14	17.5	1050
	9	31.5	28	3.4	14			12	15.0	900
	8	28.0	24			4	10	10	12.5	750
	7	24.5	20	2.5	12	3	10	8	10.0	
II	6	21.0	16			2	10	6	7.5	600
	5	17.5	12	1.7	10			4	5.0	450
III	4	14.0	8					2	2.5	300
	3	10.5	4						0.0	
	2	7.0								150
IV	1	3.5								

Figure 16–13. Oxygen requirements for step, treadmill, and bicycle ergometer. Oxygen requirements increase with work loads from bottom of chart to top in various exercise tests of the step, treadmill, and bicycle ergometer types. (Reproduced from American Heart Association,[42] with permission.)

of the exercise test and recovery, the following parameters are measured: oxygen consumption (VO₂), BP, HR, heart rhythm (ECG), RPE, and clinical observation of the patient. Figure 16–14 demonstrates the CM5 lead system, the most popular single-lead system for exercise monitoring. This lead system has proven to be the most sensitive in monitoring ischemic responses in the left ventricle as evidenced by ST changes.[13,40]

Clinical end points of exercise testing are determined

Table 16–9 CONTRAINDICATIONS TO EXERCISE TESTING

Acute myocardial infarction
Acute myocarditis or pericarditis
Rapid atrial or ventricular dysrhythmias
Second- or third-degree heart block
Congestive heart failure
High-grade left main coronary disease (or its equivalent)
Severe aortic stenosis
Uncontrolled severe hypertension
Unstable progressive angina

From the American Heart Association,[42] with permission.

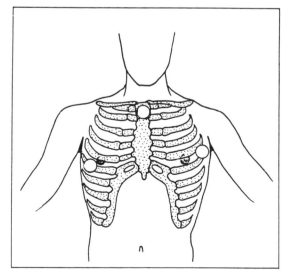

Figure 16–14. Exercise electrocardiography using a CM5 lead. One of the most widely used lead systems is a modified bipolar lead, the CM5. The positive electrode is placed in the fifth intercostal space at the left anterior axillary line, and the negative electrode is placed on the manubrium. This lead provides very sensitive monitoring and is able to detect the highest incidence of positive changes in patients with known ischemia.

by the attending cardiologist and usually include the following.

1. End points based upon emergence of disease-related symptoms; for example, significant exertional intolerance, which may be evidenced by dizziness, syncope, mental confusion, dyspnea, angina, claudication, cyanosis, or pallor. Hypotension or a fall in systolic blood pressure with increasing workloads, significant high blood pressure (greater than 240 mmHg systolic, 130 mmHg diastolic for a high or intermediate test) or intolerable leg fatigue and exhaustion would also be reasons for stopping the test.

Electrocardiographic changes include PVCs (frequent multifocal PVCs or three in a row) in sequential runs (ventricular tachycardia), paroxysmal atrial tachycardia, second or third degree atrioventricular block, or ischemic deviation of the ST segment (greater than 2 mm depression or 3 mm elevation) would be reasons for stopping the test. Cardiac patients or individuals at risk for coronary disease are usually given submaximal tests that are stopped upon attainment of a level at which exertional symptoms develop.[13,43,44]

2. End points based upon attainment of maximal performance (**age-predicted maximal heart rate** = 220 minus age). This end point is used typically for healthy individuals; many cardiac patients become symptomatic before this end point is reached and are thus unable to attain this level of exercise.

3. End points based upon attainment of a predetermined submaximal level of performance, such as 75 percent age-adjusted maximal heart rate, or an arbitrary workload, such as 4 METs or one that raises the heart rate to 130 beats per minute. These criteria are frequently used in low-level, predischarge testing.[58]

After the exercise test the patient may continue to exercise at a low level for a short time or may rest comfortably. The recovery period (the first 5 to 15 minutes after exercise) is monitored as closely as the exercise period, for in many patients ECG abnormalities develop during recovery and not during exercise. A resting ECG is taken again and compared with the pretest resting ECG.[42]

Patients who will be exercising on medications are most often tested while on those medications. Certain medications may cause difficulty in interpreting the exercise test results. For example, **digitalis** may produce a false-positive test. This is defined as an ischemic depression of the ST segment which is accentuated in patients with established coronary heart disease or is produced in a patient with no evidence of coronary heart disease. Propranolol may produce a false-negative test (the ischemic response of the ST segment is dampened or absent in patients with significant coronary artery disease) and causes a reduction in resting and exercise heart rates. This latter effect would negate the use of a submaximal heart rate as a clinical end point to the test and necessitate the determination of oxygen consumption during testing. Hypokalemia (low serum potassium) seen in patients taking diuretics also may cause an abnormal ST response and increases the likelihood of ventricular arrhythmias.[13,40,42]

Symptomatic cardiac patients usually have a work capacity of about 6 METs or less. Asymptomatic patients may range from 7 to 9 METs, and active, healthy men range from 12 to 15 METs.[43,59]

Phase 3: Rehabilitation Exercise Training

Patients entering a phase 3 rehabilitation program for high-level exercise training include those patients who have completed phase 1 and 2 programs (generally 3 to 12 months after discharge), and individuals with known coronary disease or who are at high risk for its development. These programs may be hospital- or community-based. Before beginning exercise at higher levels of intensity, a history, medical assessment, and multistage graded exercise test are required. Table 16–10 presents special precautions for exercise program candidates.

TREATMENT GOALS

1. Provide an individualized exercise program designed to produce an exercise training response within safe limits.

2. Promote psychologic recovery and risk factor modification.

3. Promote life-long commitment to physical fitness and personal health management.

Exercise training programs typically last 12 weeks and include intensive rehabilitation under the direction of a physician and close supervision by the cardiac team members. The benefits of physical training in CAD include improved exercise capacity (increased oxygen consumption and decreased heart rate/blood pressure product, allowing patients to exercise longer before reaching their angina threshold). These and other changes in improved exercise capacity are similar to those reported for healthy individuals and are summarized in Table 16–11.[18,61–63] Training programs also promote improved self-image and a reduction in anxiety and depression.[64,65] The effects of exercise on the progression of atherosclerosis and mortality remain more con-

Table 16–10 SPECIAL PRECAUTIONS FOR EXERCISE PROGRAM CANDIDATES

Uncontrolled congestive heart failure (class III or IV)
Myocarditis or cardiomyopathy within the past year
Uncontrolled hypertension
Dysrhythmias
    Second- and third-degree AV-block
    Uncontrolled atrial fibrillation
    Excessive or complex PVCs
Significant cardiac enlargement
Valvular disease, moderate to severe
Outflow tract obstructive disease (IHSS)
Recent pulmonary embolism
Anemia with hemoglobin below 10 gm/100ml
Uncontrolled metabolic disease (diabetes mellitus, thyrotoxicosis, myxedema)
Transient illness that includes acute febrile illness
Certain orthopedic disabilities
Inappropriate blood pressure response to exercise testing

From the American Heart Association,[42] with permission.

Table 16-11 POSSIBLE EFFECTS OF PHYSICAL TRAINING

Decreased heart rate at rest and during exercise
Increased rate of heart rate recovery after exercise
Increased stroke volume (blood volume pumped per heart beat)
Myocardial hypertrophy (increased size of heart muscle)
Increased myocardial oxygen supply
Increased myocardial contractility (strength of muscle contraction)
Decreased blood pressure at rest and during exercise
Increased angina threshold secondary to decreased myocardial oxygen consumption (decreased rate-pressure product)
Decreased serum lipoproteins (cholesterol, triglycerides)
Improved respiratory capacity during exercise (increased diffusion of respiratory gases, reduced residual volume, increased blood supply)
Improved functional capacity of the exercising muscles (increased skeletal muscle blood flow, improved muscle strength, increased metabolic and enzymatic function of muscle cells)
Reduced body fat, increased lean body weight (muscle mass)
Increased glucose tolerance
Improved blood fibrinolytic activity and coagulability
Improved self-confidence and sense of well-being; reduced strain and nervous tension

Adapted from Amsterdam, Wilmore, and DeMaria,[13] and Astrand and Rodah.[60]

troversial. Numerous intervention studies have failed to reveal any definitive data on improved longevity. Methodologic problems have plagued these studies, and although the evidence, such as the data obtained from the National Exercise and Heart Disease Project, are suggestive, they are by no means conclusive.[63,66] Thus the major impact of the rehabilitation programs is improvement in the quality of life for these patients. The amount of improvement in individual patients will vary considerably depending upon age, location, and degree of cardiac damage and related symptomatology, overall health, risk factors, functional work capacity, magnitude of the training stimulus, and psychosocial status. Many patients will be extremely limited in their ability to participate fully in these programs and may in fact be unable to increase their physical work capacity at all. The psychologic benefits of such programs must be weighed carefully when considering discharge or referral. Supervised exercise programs provide a significant motivational force for those patients who, if left alone, would probably stop exercising.

ASSESSMENT

The physical therapist should assess
1. The patient's premorbid history, including habitual intensity, duration and type of exercise performed, exercise likes and dislikes, recreational and vocational activities, and family support.
2. The patient's understanding of the illness, risk factors, and the effects of exercise on cardiovascular function.
3. The patient's skill and reliability in self-monitoring procedures and in recognizing the symptoms of exertional intolerance.
4. The patient's motivation and cooperation.
5. The physical status of other body systems in which disability or dysfunction might increase the predicted overall cost of metabolic activity.

THE EXERCISE PRESCRIPTION

Type

Conditioning exercises generally involve large muscle groups performing sustained, dynamic, aerobic work. These commonly include walking, jogging, running, swimming, rowing, and stationary bicycling, or any combination of these. These **aerobic exercises** are fairly easy to prescribe because the velocity is maintained and the metabolic cost of the activity is fairly constant. Conditioning activities in which the metabolic cost varies considerably from patient to patient (depending on the individual's level of skill or because of the intermittent nature of the activity) may not be as suitable, particularly in the early phases of the program. Examples of this type of aerobic activity include cross-country skiing and a variety of games and sports. They may be incorporated gradually into a training program as the patient's functional work capacity improves and exercise tolerance becomes better known.[16,43,44,67,68]

The principle of specificity of training is important to consider when trying to improve the patient's functional work capacity for a particular task or type of work. The training effect is specific to the trained skeletal muscles that are used. Thus, if the therapist is training a patient with combined paraplegia and cardiac disability and the objective is to improve cardiovascular endurance in propelling a wheelchair, sustained arm work must be used to produce the training effect. Similarly, patients returning to occupations requiring substantial amounts of arm work should also undergo an arm training program. Arm ergometers, rowing machines, or wall pulleys may be used for the dynamic activity. If arm exercises are used, it is important to consider that oxygen uptake, heart rate, and systolic blood pressure are significantly greater during arm exercise than during leg exercise at the same submaximal workload. The anginal threshold is also reached at lower workloads. The exercise prescription should be based upon the results of an arm test, and the resistance needs to be kept low to avoid a pressure response produced by the isometric component, which typically characterizes arm work.[18,69]

The principle of specificity of training also applies to the type of exercise that is used, that is, **isometric** or isotonic. Low-level resistive exercises using dumbbells or barbells may be included in the training program if the patient's strength is not adequate to meet the demand of normal activities of daily living. The therapist should utilize a low-resistance, high-repetition, dynamic routine. The exercises should be monitored closely, and the patient should be reminded to breathe rhythmically throughout the exercises. Because the blood pressure response is related to the percentage of maximal voluntary contraction, any increase in strength will result in a lower blood pressure response to any given submaximal workload. Thus the individual will be able to perform strength tasks with less strain on the heart following such training.[16,42]

Warm-up and cool-down exercises consist of flexibility exercises and generally last 5 to 10 minutes. They increase and decrease slowly in intensity to allow for gradual circulatory adjustment and to help reduce the incidence of arrhythmias. They also help minimize oxygen deficit and lactic acid accumulation and modify muscle temperature gradually. Cool-down exercises are particularly important in helping prevent venous pooling, orthostatic hypotension, and/or nausea.[42,43] The program of graded calisthenics is a good source of these exercises.[35]

Relaxation training is often included in addition to exercise training. These exercises are designed to relieve either generalized or specific muscle tension and are often given at the end of the cool-down session. Jacobson's system of progressive relaxation[70] consists of learning to tense and then to relax various muscle groups in the body. The patient is instructed to be aware of the different feelings associated with tension and relaxation.[70] Benson's relaxation response,[71] yoga, transcendental meditation, and/or biofeedback also have been used successfully in cardiac programs to help patients relax both following exercise and during stressful periods of the patient's day at home or at work. The importance of relaxation training should not be underestimated, because successful stress management coupled with permanent lifestyle modification can significantly reduce major risk factors in coronary disease.[64]

Circuit training, in which the patient spends a prescribed amount of time at an exercise station before moving on to the next, is one way in which some programs include the various types of training exercises. The exercises at each station are varied and may include either isotonic and isometric components. Rotation through the various stations generally alternates body areas (e.g., arm crank to cycle to wall pulleys to treadmill). Close monitoring should be available at each station.[42]

Intensity

The intensity of exercise prescribed is based on the results of the graded exercise test. An adequate training intensity falls within 60 to 80 percent of the patient's maximal oxygen uptake or physical work capacity.[18,42,43] Because a linear relationship exists between oxygen consumption and heart rate, the intensity also may be prescribed by using a target heart rate. (A heart rate of 85 percent maximal heart rate corresponds closely to 75 percent of maximal oxygen uptake.) The patient is instructed to achieve a heart rate between 70 and 85 percent of the highest heart rate safely achieved during the exercise test. Target heart rate also can be determined by using the heart rate range formula (Karvonen method).[43] This is an attempt to approximate heart rate and maximal oxygen uptake more closely. The formula is as follows:

$$60 \text{ to } 80\% \text{ (HR max } - \text{HR resting)} + \text{HR resting} = \text{target HR}$$

Because there is greater risk of cardiac complications such as arrhythmias and cardiac arrest with higher heart rates, the intensity should not exceed 85 percent maximum heart rate in supervised programs and 75 percent for unsupervised training. Low-level training effects have been achieved at intensities lower than 70 percent and may be suitable for unfit patients or those with a complicated medical picture. Because the duration must be increased, patient compliance may become a problem.[16]

Training regimens may be continuous or discontinuous. If discontinuous work is used, the heart rate may rise above or fall below the target heart rate, as long as the duration of each averages out to the prescribed target level. The intensity of the workload should be decreased if the heart rate rises consistently more than 4 beats per minute above the target heart rate. The workload should be increased if the heart rate falls below the target in three consecutive workloads.[15,43]

Heart rate can not be safely used to prescribe safe workloads in the presence of the following situations:

1. Isometric exercise
2. Valsalva maneuver
3. Heavy arm work
4. Environmental extremes (e.g., excessive heat, cold, or humidity)
5. Beta blockade medications
6. Pacemaker[26]

Exercise intensity is also prescribed in METs, determined as a percentage of the physical work capacity obtained from the graded exercise test. Sixty to 80 percent of the maximal metabolic work capacity is adequate to achieve an aerobic training effect. Problems can arise from using only METs to prescribe intensity of work. Very often discontinuous work must be used to achieve an average exercise intensity. For example, to jog at 7 METs a patient would have to walk part of the time at 5 METs and run part of the time at 10 METs. The high-intensity period may present hazards for some patients. Differences in overall skill or changes in speed or intensity can alter the known metabolic cost of an activity. Environmental conditions such as heat, cold, high humidity or altitude, wind, changes in terrain or running surface—such as hills—or clothing can also alter the known metabolic cost of an activity. Finally, the stress of competition (type A behavior patterns or high emotions) can increase the known metabolic cost of an activity. Thus most physicians and therapists prescribe the intensity of exercise in both METs and target heart rate. As training progresses, the workload in METs will increase in order to maintain the same target heart rate.[42,43]

Cardiovascular adaptation to work during the training session is monitored by a number of factors, including heart rate, blood pressure, rhythm disturbances, perceived exertion, and signs of exertional intolerance (all previously discussed). Continuous radiotelemetry may be indicated, particularly during the initial training sessions or with patients with complicated medical histories. Periodic ECG, pulse, pressure, and RPE monitoring are routinely taken at prescribed intervals during the training session. As training progresses, the level of monitoring decreases and the patient's responsibility in self-monitoring increases. Monitoring procedures thus provide a means of regulating the exercise prescription and adjusting intensity as needed.

DURATION

The duration of the training session varies according to patient tolerance, usually lasting 15 to 60 minutes. Ideally the patient exercises at moderate intensities and at a moderate duration, with warm-up and cool-down periods of 10 minutes each and a minimum of 15 minutes at target training intensity or target heart rate. Inasmuch as duration varies inversely with intensity, the duration must be longer with lower training intensities. Excessive workouts do not yield significant additional training benefits and only increase the likelihood of orthopedic complications and poor compliance as well as other ramifications of overtraining. As training progresses, the duration is increased first, then the intensity. Following a layoff period, both intensity and duration should be decreased. The length of the warm-up and cool-down periods should never be decreased in a high-risk group such as patients with CAD (Fig. 16–15).[42–44]

FREQUENCY

The frequency is also dependent in part upon the intensity and duration. Three to five evenly spaced workouts per week are recommended. One to two daily sessions are advisable for patients with very low functional work capacities (3 to 5 METs) who are participating in a low-level conditioning program.[42–44]

Modification of the exercise prescription by either the physician or the therapist requires careful consideration of a number of factors, including age, health status, exercise performance, recreational interests, and motivation of the patient. Table 16–12 presents reasons for temporarily reducing or deferring physical activity. The following general prescriptive considerations should be kept in mind. Patients taking medications should have their exercise prescription based upon exercise test results obtained while the patient is on those medications. Prophylactic use of nitrates prior to participation in exercise programs may be helpful in preventing symptoms and should be implemented for patients who develop angina during exercise. They do not diminish the training effect and the need for nitrates may actually be reduced or discontinued as training progresses. Patients on beta blockers will have a lower heart rate response to exercise and may have bradycardia at rest. Anginal symptoms and ECG abnormalities should be used in setting limits for the intensity of the exercise. Any change in the angina threshold or in the effect of medication on the relief of pain should be reported to the physician. Angina of increasing intensity or radiation may be indicative of a developing infarction. Exercise should be ceased immediately and the patient referred to the physician in charge or taken directly to a hospital.[13,17,18]

A supervised program provides the high-risk patient with the security of medical supervision, the support and

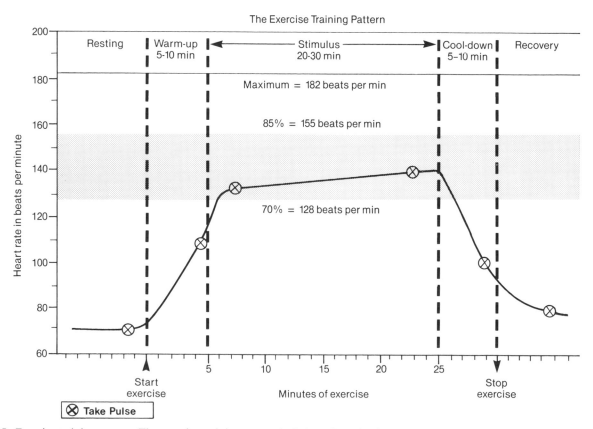

Figure 16–15. Exercise training pattern. The exercise training pattern includes a 5-to-10-minute warm-up, 20 to 30 minutes at target intensity, and 5-to-10-minute cool-down. (Reproduced from Zohman, L: *Beyond Diet . . . Exercise Your Way to Fitness and Heart Health.* CPC International, 1974, with permission.)

Table 16–12 REASONS FOR TEMPORARILY REDUCING OR DEFERRING PHYSICAL ACTIVITY

Intercurrent illness—febrile, injury, G.I.
Progression of cardiac disease
Orthopedic problem
Emotional turmoil
Severe sunburn
Alcoholic hangover
Cerebral dysfunction—dizziness, vertigo
Sodium retention—edema, weight gain
Dehydration
Environmental factors
    Weather—excessive heat or cold, humidity or wind
    Air pollution—smog, CO
Overindulgence
    Large, heavy meal within two hours
    Coffee, tea, coke (xanthines and other stimulating beverages)
Drugs—decongestants, bronchodilators, atropine, weight reducers (anorectics)

From American Heart Association, Committee on Exercise,[44] with permission.

Table 16–13 FUNCTIONAL AND THERAPEUTIC CLASSIFICATIONS OF PATIENTS WITH DISEASES OF THE HEART

Functional	Continuous-Intermittent Permissible Work Loads	Maximal
Class I	4.0–6.0 cal/min.	6.5 METs
	Patients with cardiac disease but without resulting limitations of physical activity. Ordinary physical activity does not cause undue fatigue, palpitation, dyspnea or anginal pain.	
Class II	3.0–4.0 cal/min.	4.5 METs
	Patients with cardiac disease resulting in slight limitation of physical activity. They are comfortable at rest. Ordinary physical activity results in fatigue, palpitation, dyspnea or anginal pain.	
Class III	2.0–3.0 cal/min.	3.0 METs
	Patients with cardiac disease resulting in marked limitation of physical activity. They are comfortable at rest. Less than ordinary physical activity causes fatigue, palpitation, dyspnea or anginal pain.	
Class IV	1.0–2.0 cal/min.	1.5 METs
	Patients with cardiac disease resulting in inability to carry on any physical activity without discomfort. Symptoms of cardiac insufficiency or of the anginal syndrome may be present even at rest. If any physical activity is undertaken, discomfort is increased.	
Therapeutic		
Class A	Patients with cardiac disease whose physical activity need not be restricted in any way.	
Class B	Patients with cardiac disease whose ordinary physical activity need not be restricted but who should be advised against severe or competitive efforts.	
Class C	Patients with cardiac disease whose ordinary physical activity should be moderately restricted, and whose more strenuous efforts should be discontinued.	
Class D	Patients with cardiac disease whose ordinary physical activity should be markedly restricted.	
Class E	Patients with cardiac disease who should be at complete rest or confined to bed or chair.	

Reprinted by permission of the American Heart Association, New York.

camaraderie of a group of participants with similar problems, and a safe, effective method of improving functional work capacity. Coronary risk factors also can be modified through organized educational experiences. The long-range goal of these programs is the facilitation of exercise as a lifelong habit. Motivational considerations are therefore extremely important in ensuring program compliance and in developing a commitment to continuing exercise. Because individuals become motivated when they perceive themselves in control of their own behavior, mutual goal setting is an important consideration. The patient must (1) perceive the beneficial effects of exercise and risk factor modification on his or her lifestyle and disease processes, (2) be held accountable for meeting goals, and (3) be provided with frequent feedback about successes or failures. Therapists need to be effective role models for optimal health and fitness and flexible in selecting and scheduling activities that the patient wants to do.[72–74]

Physical Training for the Patient with Chronic Disability

Patients with poor left ventricular function, congestive heart failure, or cardiomegaly are often incapacitated. These conditions are characterized by a large, dilated heart with a weakened left ventricular wall, poor contractility, decreased coronary blood flow, and decreased cardiac output. These patients often exhibit low functional work capacities and usually fall into one of the functional classifications of the American Heart Association, depending upon the severity of the disease (Table 16–13). They also may exhibit symptoms of systemic congestion (right heart failure) or pulmonary congestion (left heart failure).

Although these patients are often restricted from even moderate amounts of exercise, many can benefit from physical training. Myocardial performance remains basically unchanged, whereas overall functional capacity improves, largely owing to the enhancement of peripheral mechanisms. Assessment by exercise testing or radiotelemetry during physical activity are reliable methods of determining work capacity and monitoring physical performance. Contraindications to exercise training revealed by exercise testing include (1) early, abnormal ECG ST changes at less than 5 METs; (2) abnormal blood pressure response (exertional hypotension or hypertension greater than 200); (3) significant exertional arrhythmias; or (4) inability to achieve a peak workload of at least 2 METs.[75] Testing protocols should allow for very low initial workloads and more gradual increments. Training programs are similar (warm-ups, dynamic graded exercises, and cool-downs) with close supervision

Table 16-14 SUGGESTED INTERDISCIPLINARY STAGES FOR PATIENTS WITH CARDIOPULMONARY HISTORY AND/OR PRECAUTIONS

Stage/MET Level	ADL and Mobility	Exercise	Recreation
Stage I (1.0–1.4 METs)	*Sitting:* Self-feeding, wash hands and face, bed mobility,* Transfers Progressively increase sitting tolerance	*Supine:* (A) or (AA) exercise to all extremities (10–15 times per extremity) *Sitting:* (A) or (AA) exercise to *only* neck and LEs Include deep breathing exercise	Reading, radio, table games, (noncompetitive), light handwork
Stage II (1.4–2.0 METs)	*Sitting:* Self-bathing, shaving, grooming, and dressing in hospital Unlimited sitting *Ambulation:* At slow pace, in room as tolerated	*Sitting:* (A) exercise to all extremities, progressively increasing the number of repetitions* NO ISOMETRICS	*Sitting:* Crafts; e.g., painting, knitting, sewing, mosaics, embroidery NO ISOMETRICS
Stage III (2.0–3.0 METs)	*Sitting:* Showering in warm water, homemaking tasks with brief standing periods to transfer light items, ironing *Standing:* May progress to grooming self. *Ambulation:* May begin slow paced ambulation outside room on levels, for short distances	*Sitting:* W/C mobility limited distances *Standing:* (A) exercise to all extremities and trunk progressively increasing the number of repetitions* *May include:* 1. Balance exercises 2. Light mat activities without resistance *Ambulation:* Begin progressive ambulation program at 0% grade and comfortable pace	*Sitting:* Card playing, crafts, piano, machine sewing, typing*
Stage IV (3.0–3.5 METs)	*Standing:* Total washing, dressing, shaving, grooming, showering in warm water; kitchen/homemaking activities while practicing energy conservation (e.g., light vacuuming, dusting and sweeping, washing light clothes *Ambulation;* unlimited distance walking at 0% grade, in and/or outside*	*Standing:* Continue all previous exercise, progressively increasing 1. Number of repetitions 2. Speed of repetitions *May include* additional exercises to increase workload up to 3.5 METs, balance and mat activities with mild resistance *Ambulation:* Unlimited on level surfaces in and/or outside* progressively increasing speed and/or duration for periods up to 15–20 minutes or until target heart rate is reached* *Stairs:* May begin slow stair climbing to patient's tolerance up to two flights *Treadmill:* 1 mph at 1% grade, progressing to 1.5 mph at 2% grade* *Cycling:* Up to 5.0 mph without resistance	Candlepin bowling Canoeing—slow rhythm, pace Golf putting *Light* gardening: weeding and planting Driving*
Stage V (3.5–4.0 METs)	*Standing:* Washing dishes, washing clothes, ironing, hanging light clothes, and making beds	*Standing:* Continue exercises as in Stage IV, progressively increasing 1. Number of repetitions 2. Speed of repetitions *May Add* additional exercises to increase workload up to 4.0 METs *Ambulation:* As in stage IV, increasing speed up to 2.5 mph on level surfaces* *Stairs:* As in Stage IV and progressively increasing, if increasing to patient's tolerance *Treadmill:* 1.5 mph at 2% grade, progressing to 1.5 mph at 4% grade up to 2.5 mph at 0% grade* *Cycling:* Up to 8 mph without resistance* May use up to 7–10 lbs* of weight for UE and LE exercise in sitting	Swimming (slowly) Light carpentry Golfing (using power cart) Light home repairs
Stage VI (4.0–5.0 METs)	*Standing:* Showering in hot water, hanging and/or wringing clothes, mopping, stripping and making beds, raking	*Standing:* As in stage V *Ambulation:* As in stage V—increasing speed to 3.5 mph on level surfaces* *Stairs:* As in stage V *Treadmill:* 1.5 mph at 4–6% grade, progressing to 3.5 mph at 0% grade* *Cycling:* Up to 10 mph without resistance May use up to 10–15 lbs of weight in UE and LE exercises in sitting	Swimming (no advanced strokes) Slow dancing Ice or roller skating (slowly) Volleyball Badminton Table Tennis (non competitive) Light calisthenics

*Please refer to physician's guidelines.

Activity stages may need to be modified if the patient has other physical disabilities. A trendscriber evaluation is suggested when a patient is ready to progress to a higher level of activity.

From Spaulding Rehabilitation Hospital, Boston, MA, 1987, with permission.

maintained throughout the session. Most patients benefit from a program of graduated walking or cycle ergometry. Patients with mild chronic heart failure (class II) are generally limited to activities of daily living and walking activities of 3 to 4 METs. Patients with severe chronic heart failure (classes III and IV) are usually on bedrest or very limited physical activity—1 to 3 METs. Even modest gains in functional capacity (1 to 2 METs) can improve a patient's abilities in daily activities significantly and therefore affect overall quality of life.[76] An example of such a program is included in Table 16–14.

The physical therapist should be supportive and instructive. The patient must be taught to keep activity within the limits of exercise tolerance. Exercise that exceeds the patient's tolerance can overload the heart and result in acute failure. Patient education is often complicated by signs of memory loss and irritability that accompany decreased cerebral blood flow. These patients are often anxious or depressed and can be difficult to motivate. The therapist can have a major role in assisting the patient in overcoming these feelings through physical activity and in facilitating the patient's adjustment to chronic and even terminal disability. Additional rehabilitation goals for patients with chronic heart disease include (1) maintenance of pulmonary hygiene, adequate respiratory ventilation, and good breathing and coughing patterns; (2) prevention of venous stasis and **thrombosis** associated with prolonged bedrest; (3) prevention of decubitus ulcers associated with prolonged bedrest; and (4) control of anxiety and tension.

SUMMARY

Cardiac rehabilitation as a therapeutic measure for restoring functional capacity to patients with heart disease has progressed rapidly during the last 25 years. Programs have become more sophisticated and more individualized. Multilevel care from the acute facility to rehabilitation and community centers is available. Rehabilitation personnel have become more skilled and experienced in dealing with problems associated with cardiac disease. Research has revealed that the exercise capacity of these patients can be improved and that the programs are safe.[53,61,63,77,78] Research has also shown that these programs can significantly reduce the length of hospitalization and improve the overall functional status of the patient at discharge.[29,79,80] Evidence of the role of exercise in preventing myocardial infarction or the recurrence of other coronary events is still forthcoming. Physical therapists have an important role in monitoring and prescribing safe exercise programs for patients with a variety of cardiovascular diseases. The expert skills and experience of the therapist can be used in the acute care setting, outpatient programs, community-based programs, or in the rehabilitation setting.

QUESTIONS FOR REVIEW

1. What are the clinical manifestations of coronary artery disease? How do they differ in their pathophysiology, diagnosis, and medical management?

2. What are the critical ECG changes that herald exertional intolerance? What are the other signs and symptoms of exertional intolerance?

3. Identify and describe three life-threatening arrhythmias.

4. How do the exercise programs in phase 1, phase 2, and phase 3 differ? Do the goals differ?

5. How can exercises be modified to increase the exercise challenge for the patient with cardiac disease? In supervising exercises, what considerations are important to keep in mind?

6. Define graded exercise test. What are the clinical end points of such testing? What is the difference between predischarge testing and the testing typically done for entrance into phase 3 programs?

7. Name three motivational strategies to ensure life-long commitment to exercise. Name three effective patient education strategies.

8. What are the common psychologic reactions to mudocardial infarction? How can they best be handled?

9. What are the major elements of the exercise prescription? What factors make up each of these elements?

10. How can an exercise program be safely progressed? What factors are important in determining if a change is needed in the exercise prescriptions?

11. What evidence is present in the research literature about the effectiveness of cardiac rehabilitation programs?

12. How are programs modified for the complicated cardiac patient with pronounced left ventricular dysfunction? What are some of the additional problems this patient faces?

REFERENCES

1. American Heart Association: Heart Facts 1981. American Heart Association, Dallas, 1981.
2. Borhani, N: Epidemiology of coronary disease. In Amsterdam, EA, Wilmore, JH, and DeMaria, A (eds): Exercise in Cardiovascular Health and Disease. Yorke Medical Books, New York, 1977.
3. Kannel, W: Downward trend in cardiovascular mortality. JAMA 247:887, 1982.
4. American Heart Association: Risk Factors and Coronary Disease. American Heart Association, Dallas, 1980.
5. Jenkins, CD, Rosenman, RH, and Zyzanski, SJ: Prediction of clin-

ical coronary heart disease by a test for the coronary-prone behavior pattern. N Engl J Med 290:1271, 1974.

6. Haynes, SG, Feinleib, M, and Kannel, WB: The relationship of psychosocial factors to coronary heart disease in the Framingham Study. III. Eight-year incidence of coronary heart disease. Am J Epidemiol III:37, 1980.

7. Roberts, WC: The coronary arteries in ischemic heart disease: Fact and fancies. Triangle 16:77, 1977.

8. Sheldon, H: Boyd's Introduction to the Study of Disease, ed 9. Lea & Febiger, Philadelphia, 1984.

9. Amsterdam, EA and Mason, DT: Coronary artery disease: Pathophysiology and clinical correlations. In Amsterdam, E, Wilmore, J, and DeMaria, A (eds): Exercise in Cardiovascular Health and Disease. Yorke Medical Books, New York, 1977.

10. Davies, M and Nelson, W: Understanding Cardiology. Butterworths, Boston, 1978.

11. Bleifeld, W: Myocardial Infarction: Present knowledge and future prospects. Triangle 16:69, 1977.

12. Ellestad, M: Stress Testing: Principles and Practice, ed 2. FA Davis, Philadelphia, 1980.

13. Amsterdam, EA, Wilmore, JH, and DeMaria, AN (eds): Exercise in Cardiovascular Health and Disease. Yorke Medical Books, New York, 1977.

14. Gorlin, R: Coronary Artery Disease, vol. 11. Major Problems in Internal Medicine Series. WB Saunders, Philadelphia, 1976.

15. Dehn, MM and Mullins, CB: Physiological effects and importance of exercise in patients with coronary artery disease. Cardiovasc Med 2:365, 1977.

16. Wenger, N (ed): Exercise and the Heart, ed 2. FA Davis, Philadelphia, 1985.

17. Wenger, ND: Coronary Care: Rehabilitation of the Patient with Symptomatic Coronary Atherosclerotic Heart Disease. American Heart Association, Dallas, 1981.

18. Braunwald, E: Editorial. N Engl J Med September 1978.

19. Long, C (ed): Prevention and Rehabilitation in Ischemic Heart Disease. Williams & Wilkins, Baltimore, 1980.

20. Galen, RS: The enzyme diagnosis of myocardial infarction. Prog. Hum Pathol 6(2):141, 1975.

21. Dubin, D: Rapid Interpretation of EKGs. Cover Publishing, Tampa, FL, 1974.

22. Goldberger, A and Goldberger, E: Clinical Electrocardiography—A Simplified Approach, ed 2. CV Mosby, St Louis, 1981.

23. Conover, MB: Understanding Electrocardiography—Physiological and Interpretive Concepts, ed 3. CV Mosby, St Louis, 1980.

24. Wenger, N, et al: Physician practice in the management of patients with uncomplicated myocardial infarction: Changes in the past decade. Circulation 65:421, 1982.

25. Andreoli, KG, et al: Comprehensive Cardiac Care—A Text for Nurses, Physicians, and Other Health Practitioners, ed 5. CV Mosby, St Louis, 1983.

26. Cardiac Rehabilitation Committee, American Heart Association, Greater Los Angeles Affiliate: Guidelines for Cardiac Rehabilitation Centers, ed 2. American Heart Association, Los Angeles, 1982.

27. Schoneberger, M, Schoneberger, B, and Lunsford, B: Chart review and physical assessment prior to exercise. In Amundsen, L (ed): Cardiac Rehabilitation. Churchill Livingstone, New York, 1981.

28. Irwin, S and Blessey R: Patient Evaluation. In Irwin, S and Tecklin, J (eds): Cardiopulmonary Physical Therapy. CV Mosby, St Louis, 1985.

29. Wenger, N: Early ambulation physical activity: Myocardial infarction and coronary artery bypass surgery. Heart Lung, 13:14, 1984.

30. Wenger, N: Early ambulation: The physiologic basis revisited. Adv Cardiol 31:138, 1982.

31. Saltin, B, et al: Response to submaximal and maximal exercise after bedrest and training. Circulation 38:7, 1968.

32. Cassem, NH, and Hackett, TO: Psychological Rehabilitation of Myocardial Infarction Patients in the Acute Phase. Heart Lung 2:382, 1973.

33. Hackett, T and Cassem, N: Coronary Care: Patient Psychology. American Heart Association, New York, 1975.

34. Hackett, T and Cassem, N: Psychologic Aspects of Rehabilitation after Myocardial Infarction and Coronary Artery Bypass Surgery. In Wenger, N and Hellerstein, H (eds): Rehabilitation of the Coronary Patient, ed 2. John Wiley & Sons, New York, 1984.

35. Weiss, RA and Karpovich, PV: Energy cost of exercises for convalescents. Arch Phys Med 38:447, 1947.

36. Zohman, L and Tobis, J: Cardiac Rehabilitation. Grune & Stratton, New York, 1970.

37. Zohman, L: Practical aspects of vigorous exercise programming for coronary patients. Adv Cardiol 31:205, 1982.

38. Kitamura, K, et al: Hemodynamic correlates of myocardial oxygen consumption during upright exercise. J Appl Physiol 32:516, 1972.

39. Baller, D, et al: Comparison of myocardial oxygen consumption indices in man. Clin Cardiol 3:116, 1980.

40. Chung, EK (ed): Exercise Electrocardiography: Practical Approach. Williams & Wilkins, Baltimore, 1979.

41. Schreiner, D: Introduction to Cardiac Arrhythmia Interpretation. American Heart Association, Dallas, 1980.

42. American Heart Association: The Exercise Standards Book. American Heart Association, Dallas, 1979.

43. American College of Sports Medicine: Guidelines for Graded Exercise Testing and Exercise Prescription, ed 2. Lea & Febiger, Philadelphia, 1980.

44. American Heart Association, Committee on Exercise: Exercise Testing and Training of Individuals with Heart Disease or at High Risk for Its Development: A Handbook for Physicians. American Heart Association, New York, 1975.

45. Borg, G: An Introduction to Borg's RPE-Scale. Mouvement Publications, Ithaca, NY, 1985.

46. O'Sullivan, S: Perceived exertion—a review. Phys Ther 64:343, 1984.

47. Noble, B: Clinical applications of perceived exertion. Med Sci Sports Exerc 14:406, 1982.

48. Squires, R, et al: Effect of propranolol on perceived exertion soon after myocardial revascularization surgery. Med Sci Sports Exerc 14:276, 1982.

49. Smutok, M, Skrinar, G, and Pandolf, K: Exercise intensity: Subjective regulation by perceived exertion. Arch Phys Med Rehabil 61,569, 1980.

50. Johnson, D: The rehabilitative approach to patients undergoing coronary bypass surgery. In Wenger, N and Hellerstein, H (eds): Rehabilitation of the Coronary Patient, ed 2. John Wiley & Sons, New York, 1984.

51. Wenger, N: Early ambulation after myocardial infarction: Rationale, program components, and results. In Wenger, N and Hellerstein, H (eds): Rehabilitation of the Coronary Patient, ed 2. John Wiley & Sons, New York, 1984.

52. Harrington, K, et al: Cardiac rehabilitation: Evaluation and intervention less than 6 weeks after myocardial infarction. Arch Phys Med Rehabil, 62:151, 1981.

53. Baughman, K, et al: Early discharge following myocardial infarction—long-term follow-up of randomized patients. Arch Intern Med 142:875, 1982.

54. Cardiac Clinic—Grady Memorial Hospital: Now that Your Heart Is Healing, Let's Get Ready to Go Home. Grady Memorial Hospital, Atlanta, 1973.

55. Hollander, LL: Take Heart. Massachusetts Rehabilitation Hospital, Boston, 1977.

56. North Carolina Myocardial Infarction Rehabilitation Program: Back in Circulation. North Carolina Heart Association, Chapel Hill, NC.

57. Fardy, P, et al: Cardiac Rehabilitation—Implications for the Nurse and Other Health Professionals. CV Mosby, St Louis, 1980.

58. Johnston, B: Exercise testing for patients after myocardial infarction and coronary bypass surgery: Emphasis on predischarge phase. Heart Lung 13:18, 1984.

59. Haskell, WL: Physical activity following myocardial infarction. In Amsterdam, EA, Wilmore, JH, and DeMaria, AN (eds): Exercise in Cardiovascular Health and Disease. Yorke Medical Books, New York, 1977.

60. Astrand, P and Rodahl, K: Textbook of Work Physiology. McGraw-Hill, New York, 1978.

61. Rigotti, N, Thomas, G, and Leaf, A: Exercise and coronary heart disease. Ann Rev Med 34:391, 1983.

62. Fletcher, G: Long-term exercise in coronary artery disease and other chronic disease states. Heart Lung 13:28, 1984.

63. Eichner, E: Exercise and heart disease—epidemiology of the "exercise hypothesis." Am J Med 75:1008, 1983.

64. Bohachick, P: Progressive relaxation training in cardiac rehabilitation: Effect on psychologic variables. Nurs Res 33:283, 1984.
65. Roviaro, S, Holmes, D, and Holmsten, R: Influence of a cardiac rehabilitation program on the cardiovascular, psychological, and social functioning of cardiac patients. J Behav Med 7:61, 1984.
66. Shaw, L: Effects of a prescribed supervised exercise program on mortality and cardiovascular morbidity in patients after a myocardial infarction. National Exercise and Heart Disease Project. Am J Cardiol 48d:39, 1981.
67. Amundsen, L: Establishing activity and training levels for patients with ischemic heart disease. Phys Ther 59:754, 1979.
68. Fox, SM, Naughton, JP, and Gorman, PA: Physical activity and cardiovascular health. III. The exercise prescription: Frequency and type of activity. Mod Concepts Cardiovasc Dis 41:25, 1972.
69. Fardy, PS, Web, D, and Hellerstein, HK: Benefits of Arm Exercise in Cardiac Rehabilitation. The Physician and Sports Medicine 5:31, 1977.
70. Jacobson, E: Progressive Relaxation. University of Chicago Press, Chicago, IL, 1938.
71. Benson, H: The Relaxation Response. Avon, New York, 1975.
72. Williams, M: Motivating the patient for long-term commitment. In Fardy, P, et al: Cardiac Rehabilitation—Implications for the Nurse and Other Health Professionals. CV Mosby, St Louis, 1980.

73. Serfass, R and Gerberich, S: Exercise for optimal health: Strategies and motivational considerations. In Forum: Exercise and Health. Academic Press, New York, 1984.
74. Carmody, T, et al: Physical exercise rehabilitation: Long-term dropout rate in cardiac patients. J Behav Med 3:163, 1980.
75. Conn, E, Williams, R, and Wallace, A: Physical conditioning in coronary patients with left ventricular dysfunction. In Wenger, N and Hellerstein, H (eds): Rehabilitation of the Coronary Patient, ed 2. John Wiley & Sons, New York, 1984.
76. Kottke, T, Caspersen, C, and Hill, C: Exercise in the management and rehabilitation of selected chronic diseases. In Forum: Exercise and Health. Academic Press, New York, 1984.
77. Blumenthal, J, et al: Effects of exercise on the type A (coronary prone) behavior pattern. Psychosom Med 42: 289, 1980.
78. Hartung, GH and Rangel, R: Exercise training in post-myocardial infarction patients: Comparison of results with high risk coronary and post-bypass patients. Arch Phys Med Rehab 62:147, 1981.
79. Grant, A and Cohen, BS: Acute myocardial infarction: Effect of a rehabilitation program on length of hospitalization and functional status at discharge. Arch Phys Med Rehabil 54:201, 1973.
80. Lowenthal, SL, and McAllister, RG: Program for cardiac patients: Stress testing and training. Phys Ther 56:1117, 1976.

SUPPLEMENTAL READINGS

Amundsen, L (ed): Cardiac Rehabilitation. Churchill Livingstone, New York, 1981.
Amundsen, L.: Assessing exercise tolerance: A review. Phys Ther 59:534, 1979.
Colorado Heart Association: Exercise Equivalents. Colorado Heart Association, Denver.
DeBusk, R: Physical conditioning following myocardial infarction. Adv Cardiol 31:156, 1982.
Fletcher, GF and Cantwell, JD: Exercise and Coronary Heart Disease: Role in Prevention, Diagnosis and Treatment, ed 2. Charles C Thomas, Springfield, IL, 1979.
Fry, GJ and Jerra, K: YMCArdiac therapy: A community-based program for persons with coronary artery disease. J Cardiac Rehab 1:354, 1981.
Geer, M, et al: Physiological responses to low intensity cardiac rehabilitation exercises. Phys Ther 60:1146, 1980.
Hellerstein, HK: Rehabilitation of patients with heart disease. Postgrad Med 15:265, 1954.
Hellerstein, HK: Exercise Therapy in Coronary Disease. Bull NY Acad Med 44:1028, 1968.
Irwin, S and Tecklin, J: Cardiopulmonary Physical Therapy. CV Mosby, 1985.

Naughton, J and Hellerstein, H (eds): Exercise Testing and Exercise Training in Coronary Heart Disease. Academic Press, New York, 1973.
North Carolina Heart Association: Organizational Guidelines for Myocardial Infarction Rehabilitation Program. North Carolina Heart Association, Chapel Hill, NC.
Ogden, L: Activity guidelines for early subacute and high-risk cardiac patients. Am J Occup Ther 33:291, 1979.
Pollack, M and Schmidt, D: Heart Disease and Rehabilitation. Houghton-Mifflin, Boston, 1979.
Sivarajan, E, et al: In-hospital exercise after myocardial infarction does not improve treadmill performance. N Engl J Med 305:357, 1981.
Wenger, N and Hellerstein, H: Rehabilitation of the Coronary Patient, ed 2. John Wiley & Sons, New York, 1984.
Wilson, P, Fardy, P, and Froelicher, V: Cardiac Rehabilitation, Adult Fitness, and Exercise Testing. Lea & Febiger, Philadelphia, 1981.
Wilson, P, et al: Policies and Procedures of a Cardiac Rehabilitation Program Immediate to Long-term Care. Lea & Febiger, Philadelphia, 1978.
Yu, P, et al: Optimal resources for the care of patients with acute myocardial infarction and chronic coronary heart disease. Circulation 65:654B, 1982.

GLOSSARY

Aerobic exercise: Exercise during which the required energy is supplied by the oxygen inspired.

Age-predicted maximal heart rate: The highest heart rate attained during maximal exercise; generally considered 220 minus an individual's age in years.

Anaerobic exercise: Exercise during which the required energy is provided without use of inspired oxygen. This type of exercise is limited to short bursts of vigorous activity.

Anaerobic threshold: The point during exercise at which the metabolic demands can not be supplied solely by aerobic metabolism; the addition of anaerobic sources results in increased energy and an increase in blood lactate.

Aneurysm: A localized abnormal dilatation of a blood vessel or ventricle.

Angina pectoris: A condition in which the heart muscle receives an insufficient blood supply, causing pain in the chest and often in the left arm and shoulder. Commonly results from activity or emotion in patients with atherosclerosis.

Angiocardiography: Radiographic examination of the heart and blood vessels following injection of an opaque fluid into the bloodstream.

Antiarrhythmic agents: Agents that are used to treat cardiac arrhythmias. Commonly used drugs include lidocaine, quinidine, procainamide, disopyramide (Norpace), and phenytoin (Dilantin).

Anticoagulants: Agents that inhibit the action or formation of one or more of the clotting factors and are used to treat a variety of thromboembolic disorders. Commonly used drugs include heparin and Coumadin.

Arrhythmia or **dysrhythmia:** A loss of or an irregularity of normal heart rhythm.

Arteriosclerosis: A general term used to identify a variety of conditions that cause the artery walls to thicken and to lose elasticity; commonly called hardening of the arteries.

Asynergy: An abnormal contraction pattern (hypokinesis, akinesis, or dyskinesis) or localized wall disturbance of cardiac muscle, generally occurring in the left ventricle and resulting from coronary artery disease.

Atherosclerosis: A form of arteriosclerosis. The inner layers of artery walls are made thick and irregular by deposits of a fatty substance. The internal channel of arteries becomes narrowed and blood supply is reduced.

Beta-adrenergic blocking agent: A substance that interferes with the transmission of stimuli through pathways that normally allow sympathetic nervous stimuli to be effective. These drugs decrease heart rate, blood pressure, contractility, and stroke volume, resulting in decreased myocardial oxygen demands and decreased angina pectoris. Commonly used drugs include propranolol, metoprolol, nadolol, atenolol, and timolol.

Bundle branch block: A delay in the conduction of one or more of the bundle branches resulting in prolonged ventricular activation (evidenced by a wide QRS complex on the electrocardiogram).

Calcium channel blocking agent: A substance that inhibits the flow of calcium ions across membranes in smooth muscle. These drugs cause vasodilation and relieve angina pain and coronary artery spasm. Commonly used drugs include verapamil, nifedipine, and diltiazem.

Cardiac arrest: The heart stops beating; cessation of cardiac output and effective circulation.

Cardiac output: The amount of blood discharged from the left or right ventricle per minute.

Cardiogenic shock: Failure to maintain blood supply to the circulatory system and tissues because of inadequate cardiac output.

Catecholamines: Circulating compounds (epinephrine and norepinephrine) that are secreted by the sympathetic nervous system and the adrenal medulla; they act to increase cardiac rate, contractility, automaticity, and excitability.

Catheterization: The process of examining the heart by introducing a thin tube (catheter) into a vein or artery and passing it into the heart.

Cholesterol: A fatlike substance found in various tissues. Elevated blood levels are associated with increased risk of coronary atherosclerosis when transported by low-density lipoproteins. Cholesterol transported by high-density lipoproteins is inversely associated with coronary risk.

Congestive heart failure: A backing up of blood in the veins leading to the heart, often accompanied by accumulation of fluid in various parts of the body. Results from the heart's inability to pump out all returned blood.

Coronary bypass surgery: Surgical intervention that establishes a shunt for blood flow to "bypass" an area of obstruction.

Coronary occlusion: An obstruction or narrowing of one of the coronary arteries that hinders blood flow to some part of the heart muscle. SYN: Heart attack.

Coronary thrombosis: Formation of a clot in one of the arteries that conduct blood to the heart muscle.

Digitalis: A drug that strengthens the contraction of the heart muscle, slows the rate of contraction of the heart, and promotes the elimination of fluid from body tissues.

Ectopic pacemaker: An electrical impulse that originates from a pacemaker other than the normal conducting system. Can occur in the atria, the atrioventricular node, or in either ventricle when normal pacing fails.

Ejection fraction (EF): The difference between left ventricular end-diastolic volume and left ventricular end-systolic volume.

Electrocardiogram (ECG): A record of the electrical activity of the heart; shows waves called P,Q,R,S, and T; sometimes a U wave.

Embolus: A foreign mass present in blood vessels and conveyed by blood flow from one part of the body to another; may be liquid, solid, or gas.

Ergometer: A calibrated instrument used to determine workload during an exercise challenge; commonly a treadmill or stationary bicycle.

Exercise prescription: An individualized exercise program involving frequency, intensity, time (duration), and type (FITT).

Fibrillation: Uncoordinated contractions of the heart muscle occurring when individual muscle fibers take up independent irregular contractions; may be atrial or ventricular in origin.

Gallop rhythm: An abnormal third or fourth heart sound during tachycardia of 100 or more beats per minute.

Graded exercise testing (exercise tolerance testing, stress test): The observation and recording of an individual's cardiovascular responses during a measured exercise challenge to determine capacity to adapt to physical stress. Tests may be maximal (maximal oxygen uptake) or submaximal (a predetermined end point or when symptoms of exertional intolerance develop).

Heart block: Interference with conduction of electrical impulses from the atria to the ventricles which can be partial or complete. This can result in dissociation of the rhythms and contractions of the atria and the ventricles.

Imaging (cardiac or myocardial): The production of a picture, image, or shadow that represents the object being investigated. Noninvasive cardiac techniques including radionuclide cineangiography, myocardial perfusion scintigraphy, nuclear magnetic resonance imaging, echocardiogram.

Infarction: An area of tissue that undergoes necrosis following cessation of blood supply.

Interval training: A method of organizing an exercise training into periods of activity (peak intensity) and rest.

Ischemia: Local and temporary deficiency of blood supply to a body part owing to obstruction of the circulation.

Isometric exercise: Contraction of a muscle which is not accompanied by movement of joints that would normally be moved by that muscle's action.

Lipids: Any of various substances including fats, waxes, phosphatides, cerebrosides, and related and derived compounds; combined with proteins and carbohydrates, they constitute principal structural components of living cells.

Lipoprotein: A complex of lipid and protein molecules that transports lipids (primarily cholesterol and triglycerides) from one organ to another. Lipoproteins are classified by density as high (HDL), low (LDH), or very low (VDHL). Lipoproteins solubilize lipids that are otherwise insoluble in water and direct each type of lipid to particular body sites.

Metabolic equivalent (MET): The rate of energy expenditure requiring an oxygen consumption of 3.5 ml O_2 per kilogram body weight per minute. This unit corresponds to the basal metabolic rate while sitting.

Physical work capacity (PWC, VO_2 max, or maximal aerobic power): Physiologic maximal work performance defined as that level of performance beyond which the oxygen uptake fails to increase further with increasing work.

Premature ventricular contraction (PVC) and premature atrial contraction (PAC): Disorder of rhythm and contraction caused by an abnormal ectopic foci in the ventricle (PVC) or in the atria (PAC), which causes impulses to be discharged earlier or more frequently than those from the sinoatrial node.

Rate pressure product (RPP or double product): An index of myocardial oxygen consumption determined by the product of heart rate and mean systolic blood pressure.

Ratings of perceived exertion (Borg's RPE-Scale): A subjective assessment of the intensity of work.

Serum enzymes: Enzymes such as creatine phosphokinase (CPK), lactate dehydrogenase (LDH), and serum glutamic oxalacetic transmine (SGOT) that are released into the circulation from myocardial muscle when cell death takes place. Also called cardiac enzymes.

ST segment depression: Depression of the ST segment on the electrocardiogram which occurs in the presence of myocardial ischemia. Greater than 1 mm horizontal or downsloping and 1.5 upsloping depression is considered significant.

Steady state: A balanced physiologic state in which the oxygen uptake equals the oxygen consumption during work. It can be recognized during exercise by leveling off of the heart rate to a constant level.

Stroke volume: The amount of blood ejected by the left ventricle at each beat.

Thrombosis: The formation or presence of a blood clot (thrombus) inside a blood vessel or cavity of the heart; may occlude blood flow. If detached, the thrombosis may become an embolus.

Valsalva maneuver: An attempt to exhale forcibly with the glottis, nose, and mouth closed; causes increased intrathoracic pressure, slowing of the pulse, decreased return of blood to the heart, and increased venous pressure. Increases the likelihood of dangerous arrhythmias in patients with CAD.

Vasodilators: Drugs that cause dilation of blood vessels, often used in the treatment of angina pectoris. Commonly used drugs include nitroglycerin and isosorbide dinitrate.

Chapter 17

STROKE

SUSAN B. O'SULLIVAN

OBJECTIVES

1. Define terms associated with the pathology and management of cerebrovascular disease and stroke.

2. Describe the etiology, pathophysiology, symptomatology, and sequela of stroke.

3. Describe the diagnostic and assessment procedures commonly associated with stroke.

4. Describe the rehabilitative management of the stroke patient.

5. Value the therapist's role in the management of stroke patients.

INTRODUCTION

A cerebrovascular accident (CVA) commonly referred to as a stroke, results from restricted blood supply to the brain, causing cell damage and impaired neurologic function. Clinically, a variety of deficits are possible, including impairments of motor, sensory, mental, perceptual, and language function. Motor deficits are characterized by paralysis (**hemiplegia**) or weakness (**hemiparesis**) on the side of the body opposite the site of the lesion. Frequently the term **hemiplegia** is used generically to refer to a wide variety of problems that result from stroke. The exact location and extent of the lesion determines the neurologic picture presented by an individual patient. Strokes range from slight to severe and may be temporary or permanent.

EPIDEMIOLOGY

Stroke represents a major cause of disability and death in the United States, affecting an estimated 1,750,000 individuals and causing an estimated 180,000 deaths each year.[1] Prevalence rates in the general population (all ages combined) are between 4 and 6 per 1000, with annual incidence rates between 1 and 2 per 1000.[2] The incidence of stroke increases dramatically with age, reaching major proportions after the age of 55. For example, the annual incidence rate is 3.5 per 1000 for individuals between 55 and 64, and 9 per 1000 for individuals between 65 and 74. Although the majority of strokes affect the elderly, an estimated 20 percent of strokes occur in individuals under the age of 65. Stroke affects men and women almost equally and is more predominate in blacks than in whites, especially at younger ages.[3] Epidemiologic studies have revealed a steady decline in the incidence of stroke since the 1940s.[2] Similar downward trends also have been noted in the incidence of cardiovascular disease. Control of stroke risk factors and hypertensive therapy have been implicated in contributing to the accelerating rates of decline.

PATHOPHYSIOLOGY

A number of mechanisms may result in vascular insufficiency and stroke. The most common causes include (1) thrombus, (2) embolism, and (3) hemorrhage secondary to aneurysm or developmental abnormalities. Other less common causes include tumor, abcess, inflammatory processes such as arteritis, and trauma.

Atherosclerosis is a major contributory factor in occlusive vascular disease, producing plaque formation and progressive narrowing of the vessel. The principal sequelae of this process are stenosis, ulceration of the atherosclerotic lesions, and thrombosis. **Cerebral thrombosis** refers to the formation or development of a blood clot or thrombus within the cerebral arteries or their branches. Thrombi result from platelet adhesion and aggregation, coagulation of fibrin, and decreased fibrinolysis. It should be noted that lesions of extracranial vessels (carotid or vertebral arteries) also can produce symptoms of stroke.[4] Thrombi lead to ischemia or occlusion of an artery, with resulting infarction or tissue death (atherothrombotic brain infarction, or ABI). Thrombi also can become dislodged and travel to another site in the form of an artery-to-artery embolus.

Cerebral emboli (CE) are traveling bits of matter such as thrombi, tissue, fat, air, bacteria, or other foreign bodies which are released into the bloodstream and travel to the cerebral arteries, producing occlusion and infarction. They are commonly associated with cardiovascular disease (valvular disease, myocardial infarction, arrhythmias, congenital heart disease) or systemic disorders that produce septic, fat, or air emboli.

Hemorrhage occurs from abnormal bleeding owing to rupture of a blood vessel. **Intracerebral hemorrhage (IH)** is caused by rupture of one of the cerebral vessels with subsequent bleeding into the brain. Tissue death results from the presence of cellular constituents and chemicals in the blood, from increased pressure resulting from the enlarging clot, or from restriction of distal blood flow.[5] **Subarachnoid hemorrhage (SH)** occurs from bleeding into the subarachnoid space and may be spontaneous (rupture of a **berry aneurysm**, bleeding from an **arteriovenous malformation (AVM)**, or secondary to IH or trauma. Hypertension (HTN) is often a precipitating factor, and the affected vessel is often weakened by atherosclerosis. With massive cerebral bleeding, death often occurs within hours as a result of a rapid increase in intracranial pressure and displacement and compression of adjacent cortical tissue.

A **transient ischemic attack (TIA)** refers to the temporary interruption of blood supply to the brain. Symptoms of focal neurologic deficit may last for only a few minutes or for several hours. After the attack is over there is no evidence of residual brain damage or permanent neurologic dysfunction. Transient ischemic attacks may result from a number of different factors, including occlusive attacks, emboli, reduced cerebral perfusion (arrhythmias, decreased cardiac output, hypotension, overmedication with antihypertensive medications, **subclavian steal syndromes**) or cerebrovascular spasm. Approximately 30 percent of patients with major stroke symptoms experience a history of TIAs.[6] Thus, its major clinical significance is as a precursor to both cerebral infarction and myocardial infarction.

Atherothrombotic brain infarction is the most common cause of stroke, accounting for 57 percent of all strokes. Cerebral embolus accounts for 16 percent of strokes, and subarachnoid hemorrhage and intracerebral hemorrhage account for 10 percent and 4 percent, respectively. Transient ischemic attacks are seen in approximately 10 percent of the cases, and all other causes account for only 3 percent of strokes.[7]

Risk Factors

Cardiovascular diseases affecting the brain and heart share a number of common risk factors important to the development of atherosclerosis. These include smoking, inactivity, obesity, stress, elevated serum cholesterols (especially LDL-cholesterol), glucose intolerance (diabetes), oral contraceptives, and genetic predisposition. However, the major risk factors for the development of stroke are hypertension and impaired cardiac function. In ABI patients, 70 percent have hypertension, 30 percent coronary heart disease, 15 percent congestive heart disease, 30 percent peripheral arterial disease, and 15 percent diabetes. This coexistence of vascular problems throughout the body increases with the age of the patient. Patients with marked elevations of hematocrits are also at an increased risk of occlusive stroke owing to a generalized reduction of cerebral blood flow. Cardiac disorders, such as rheumatic heart valvular disease, endocarditis, arrhythmias (particularly atrial fibrillation), or cardiac surgery, significantly increase the risk of embolic stroke.[3] Finally, the presence of TIAs is an extremely important risk factor, inasmuch as about one third of those individuals will go on to develop a stroke within 5 years.[5] As with the cardiac risk profile, the more risk factors present or the greater the degree of abnormality of any one factor, the greater the risk of stroke.[8]

Determinants of Cerebral Blood Flow

METABOLIC CONSIDERATIONS

Cerebral blood flow (CBF) is controlled by a number of autoregulatory mechanisms that modulate a constant rate of blood flow through the brain. These mechanisms provide homeostatic balance, counteracting fluctuations in systolic blood pressure while maintaining a normal flow of 50 to 60 milliliters (ml) per 100 grams of brain tissue per minute. The brain has high oxygen demands and requires a continuous, rich perfusion of blood. Cerebral flow represents approximately 17 percent of available cardiac output.[9]

Chemical regulation of CBF occurs in response to changes in blood concentrations of carbon dioxide or oxygen. Vasodilation and increased CBF are produced in response to an increase in $PaCO_2$ or a decrease in PaO_2, whereas vasoconstriction and decreased CBF are produced by the opposite stimuli. Blood flow is also altered by changes in the blood pH. A fall in pH (increased acidity) produces vasodilation, and a rise in pH (increased alkalinity) produces a decrease in blood flow. Neurogenic regulation alters blood flow by vasodilating vessels in direct proportion to local function of brain tissue. Released metabolites probably act directly on the smooth muscle in local vessel walls. Changes in blood viscosity or intracranial pressures also may influence CBF.[9] Changes in blood pressure produce minor alterations of CBF. As pressure rises, the artery is stretched, resulting in contraction of smooth muscle in the vessel wall. The patency of the vessel is decreased, resulting in a decrease in CBF. As pressure falls, contraction lessens and CBF increases.[10] Following stroke, autoregulatory mechanisms may be impaired.[11]

ANATOMIC CONSIDERATIONS

Cerebral blood flow varies with the patency of the vessels. Progressive narrowing secondary to atherosclerosis decreases blood flow. As in coronary heart disease, symptomatic changes generally result from a restriction of flow greater than 80 percent. When an artery is obstructed, the region affected has both a central infarcted area and an edematous, hyperemic zone that surrounds the infarcted zone. Infarcts may be *pale* (anemic) or *hemorrhagic* (with leakage of blood into the infarcted area). Swelling begins soon after the insult and reaches maximum by about 4 days. The swelling then gradually subsides, generally disappearing by 3 weeks. Significant infarction and swelling can elevate intracranial pressures and produce contralateral and caudal shifts of brain structures, resulting in coma or death. This is especially likely to occur with large infarcts involving the middle cerebral artery.[6]

The symptomatology of stroke is dependent upon a number of factors, including (1) the location of the ischemic process, (2) the size of the ischemic area, (3) the nature and functions of the structures involved, and (4) the availability of collateral blood flow. Symptomatology also may depend upon the rapidity of the occlusion of a blood vessel, inasmuch as slow occlusions may allow for collateral vessels to take over, but sudden events do not.[12]

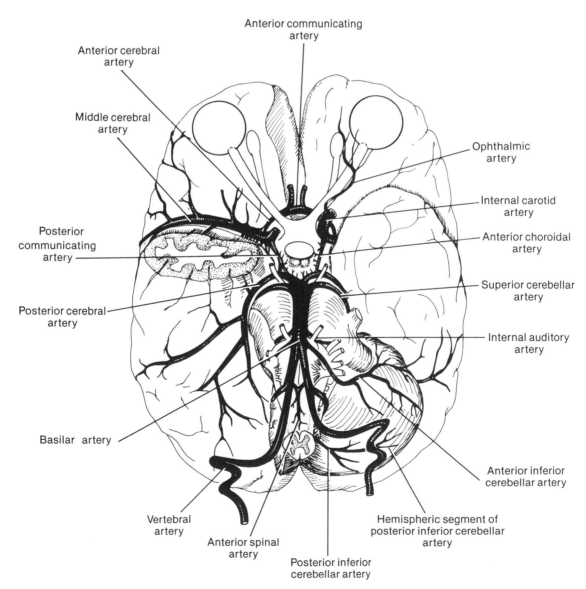

Figure 17–1. Cerebral circulation: Circle of Willis. (From DeArmond, S, et al: *A Photographic Atlas—Structure of the Human Brain,* ed 2. Oxford University Press, New York, 1976, p 171, with permission.)

Knowledge of cerebral vascular anatomy is essential to understand the symptomatology, diagnosis, and management of stroke. A brief review is therefore necessary. Extracranial blood supply to the brain is provided by right and left internal carotid arteries and by the right and left vertebral arteries. The internal carotid artery begins at the bifurcation of the common carotid artery and ascends in the deep portions of the neck to the carotid canal. It turns rostromedially and ascends into the cranial cavity. There it pierces the dura mater, branches off to the ophthalmic and anterior choroidal arteries, and then bifurcates into the middle and anterior cerebral arteries. The anterior communicating artery communicates with the anterior cerebral arteries of both sides giving rise to the rostral portion of the **circle of Willis** (Fig. 17–1). The vertebral artery is a branch off the subclavian artery and enters the vertebral foramen of the sixth cervical vertebra and travels through the foramina of the transverse processes of the upper six cervical vertebrae to the foramen magnum and into the brain. There it travels in the posterior cranial fossa ventrally and medially and unites with the vertebral artery from the other side to form the basilar artery at the upper border of the medulla. The cerebellum is supplied by three pairs of cerebellar arteries which arise off the vertebral-basilar system. At the upper border of the pons the basilar artery bifurcates to form the posterior cerebral arteries and the posterior portion of the circle of Willis. Posterior communicating arteries connect the posterior cerebral arteries with the internal carotid arteries and complete the circle of Willis.

Occlusion produces focal signs specific to the artery involved. The main arteries that supply the cerebral hemispheres and subcortical structures include the anterior, middle, and posterior cerebral arteries. Occlusions of the internal carotid and vertebral-basilar arteries also will be discussed.[9,10,13] These findings are summarized in Table 17–1.

Table 17–1 SYNDROMES RESULTING FROM OCCLUSION OF CEREBRAL ARTERIES

Artery	Structures Supplied	Clinical Signs												
		Coma	Diplopia	Homolateral Loss of Vision	Hemianopsia	Mental Confusion	Aphasia (If Dormant Side Involved)	Contralateral Hemiplegia	Contralateral Hypesthesia	Contralateral Hemianesthesia	Pseudobulbar Palsy	Flaccid Quadraplegia	Complete Anesthesia	Thalamic Syndrome
Carotid Internal	Generally, the internal carotid and its branches serve the caudal half of the brain; hindbrain, midbrain, thalamus, occipital lobes and inferior portion of the temporal lobes.			X	X		X	X		X				
Anterior Cerebral	Anterior limb of the internal capsule, caudate nucleus, putamen, corpus callosum, white matter adjacent to Broca's area and the motor and sensory cortex serving the lower extremity.					X	X	X Mostly lower extremity involvement	X Mostly lower extremity involvement	X				
Middle Cerebral	Cortex, lateral parts of frontal, temporal parietal and occipital lobes, head of caudate nucleus, putamen, external capsule, claustrum and anterior portion of internal capsule.	X			X		X	X Mostly upper extremity involvement	X Mostly upper extremity involvement	X				
Posterior Cerebral	Medial surface, occipital lobe; medial and inferior surface of temporal lobes; corpus callosum.				X		X	May be transient		X				
Posterior Occipital	Cuneus and corpus callosum.													X
Vertebral-Basilar	Medulla, pons, midbrain, and cerebellum, usually fatal.	X	X					X			X	X	X	

X indicates the presence of clinical sign.

Anterior Cerebral Artery Occlusion

The anterior cerebral artery (ACA) is the first and smaller of two terminal branches off the internal carotid artery. It supplies the medial aspect of the cerebral hemisphere (frontal and parietal lobes) and subcortical structures, including the anterior internal capsule, inferior caudate nucleus, anterior fornix, and anterior four fifths of the corpus callosum. Because the anterior communicating artery allows profusion of the proximal anterior cerebral artery from both sides, occlusion proximal to this point results in minimal deficit. More distal lesions produce deficits of contralateral hemiparesis and *cortical sensory loss* with greater involvement of the lower extremity than upper extremity or face. Initially, a contralateral grasp reflex in the upper extremity, incontinence, or stupor may occur. Extensive frontal lobe infarction produces significant behavioral changes. Right-sided damage to the frontal lobe may cause *contralateral neglect.* Damage to the supplementary motor area of the dominant hemisphere may produce *aphasia.* Impaired function of the corpus callosum may lead to hemispheric disconnection, characterized by *apraxia* and **agraphia.** Lesions of the ACA are uncommon.

Middle Cerebral Artery Occlusion

The middle cerebral artery (MCA) is the most common site of stroke. The middle cerebral artery is the second of the two main branches off the internal carotid artery and supplies the lateral aspect of the cerebral hemisphere (frontal, temporal, and parietal lobes) and subcortical structures, including the internal capsule (posterior portion), corona radiata, globus pallidus (outer part), most of the caudate nucleus, and the putamen. Occlusion results in drowsiness, contralateral hemiplegia, and cortical sensory loss of the face, arm, and leg, with the face and arm more involved than the leg. *Homonymous hemianopsia* (visual field defect) and deviation of the eyes away from the hemiplegic side also result. Infarction secondary to proximal middle cerebral artery occlusion often produces significant cerebral edema with increased intracranial pressures and may lead to brain herniation, coma, or death. Additional symptoms are dependent upon the specific hemisphere involved.

Infarction of the dominant left hemisphere following middle cerebral artery lesions typically produces aphasia. **Broca's aphasia** (expressive dysfunction) results from occlusion of the anterior main division of the middle cerebral artery affecting the lower frontal cortex (posterior inferior frontal gyrus or Broca's area) and anteroinferior parietal cortex. In addition to the general sensory-motor signs of stroke, apraxia of the buccofacial and unparalyzed left arm are also common. **Wernicke's aphasia** (receptive dysfunction) results from lesions disrupting the posterior part of the left superior temporal gyrus (Wernicke's area). Patients exhibiting **global aphasia** have severe expressive and receptive language dysfunction and typically have damage over a large portion of the middle cerebral artery, particularly affecting the perisylvian area.

Apraxia, a disorder of voluntary learned movement, is also common. Infarction of the nondominant right hemisphere typically produces a flat or expressionless affect. Disorders of **body scheme/body image, spatial relations syndrome, agnosias,** and **apraxias** are common. For further discussion, see chapter 7.

Posterior Cerebral Artery Occlusion

The two posterior cerebral arteries (PCA) arise as terminal branches of the basilar artery, and each supplies the corresponding occipital lobe and medial and inferior temporal lobe. Each also supplies the upper brainstem, midbrain, and posterior diencephalon, including most of the thalamus. Occlusion of thalamic branches produces *thalamic sensory syndromes,* including contralateral sensory loss (affecting pain and temperature the most) and persistent contralateral pain in response to any type of sensory input. Involvement of subthalamic and midbrain branches can produce a wide variety of deficits, including movement disorders (mild hemiparesis, athetoid posturing, tremor, hemiballismus) and homonymous field defects. Right-sided infarcts produce **hemianopsia**, and left-sided infarcts produce **alexia** (word blindness) and **anomia** (word-finding difficulty).

Internal Carotid Artery Occlusion

Complete occlusion of the internal carotid artery (ICA) produces clinical symptoms similar to those produced by occlusion of both the middle cerebral and the anterior cerebral arteries. Extensive cerebral edema can occur and often leads to coma and death. Incomplete occlusions can mimic the symptoms of either the middle cerebral artery (more commonly seen) or the anterior cerebral artery.

Vertebral-Basilar Artery Occlusions

Complete occlusion of the basilar artery generally produces loss of consciousness, brainstem and cranial nerve damage, and hemiplegia or quadriplegia with decerebrate or decorticate posturing. Patients frequently die but may remain comatose in a vegetative state, or they may regain consciousness but be in a *locked-in or de-efferented state.* Patients who exhibit the locked-in syndrome can not move or speak, owing to quadriparesis and lower bulbar palsy. Communication can be established, however, via vertical eye movements and blinking. Partial, or branch, occlusions produce both ipsilateral and contralateral symptoms, because some of the tracts in the brainstem will have crossed but others will have not. Cerebellar signs such as ataxia are common. Occlusion of both vertebral arteries produces symptoms of basilar artery dysfunction, but occlusion on only one side produces a lateral medullary infarction.

Interruption of blood flow by atherosclerotic plaques occurs at certain sites of predilection. These generally include bifurcations, constrictions, dilation, or angulations of arteries. The most common sites for lesions to

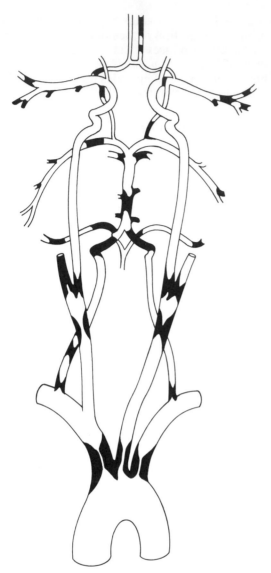

Figure 17–2. Preferred sites for atherosclerotic plaques. (From American Heart Association: *Diagnosis and Management of Stroke.* 1979, p 4, with permission.)

occur are at the origin of the common carotid artery, in the internal carotid artery at the level of the carotid sinus or at its transition into the middle cerebral artery, at the main bifurcation of the middle cerebral artery, and at the junction of the vertebral arteries with the basilar artery[6] (Fig. 17–2).

DIAGNOSIS

History and Examination

An accurate history profiling the timing of neurologic events is obtained from the patient or family members in the case of the unconscious or incommunicative patient. Of particular importance are the pattern of onset and the course of neurologic signs. A sudden onset of neurologic deficit is suggestive of subarachnoid hemorrhage or embolism, whereas a more progressive onset often indicates infarction or intracerebral hemorrhage.[5] If the symptoms are progressive over a period of hours or days, intracerebral hemorrhage typically is implicated. If the initial symptoms improve, infarction is often the cause. The physician also investigates the patient's past history, including episodes of TIAs or head trauma, presence of major or minor risk factors, medications, and pertinent family history. Any recent alterations in patient function (either transient or permanent) are thoroughly investigated.

The physical examination of the patient includes an investigation of vital signs (heart rate, respiratory rate, blood pressure) and signs of cardiac decompensation. The neurologic examination stresses function of the cerebral hemispheres, cerebellum, cranial nerves, eyes, and sensorimotor system. The presenting symptoms will help determine the location of the lesion, and comparison of both sides of the body will reveal the side of the lesion. Bilateral signs are suggestive of brainstem lesions or massive cerebral involvement.

Neurovascular tests are also performed. These include

1. Neck flexion. Meningeal irritation secondary to subarachnoid hemorrhage will produce resistance or pain to neck flexion.

2. Palpation of arteries. Both superficial and deep arteries are palpated including the temporal, facial, carotids, subclavian, brachial, radial, abdominal aorta, and lower extremity arteries.

3. Auscultation of heart and blood vessels. Abnormal heart sounds, murmurs, and bruits may be present and indicate increased flow turbulence and stenosis in a vessel.

4. Ophthalmic pressures. Abnormal pressures in the opthalmic artery may indicate problems in the internal carotid artery.

Diagnostic Tests

There are a number of routine tests that are performed. Laboratory tests assess the general state of systemic circulation and body function. Electrocardiography and x-ray examinations focus more specifically on the heart and lungs. **Computerized axial tomography** (CAT scan) of the cranium delineates alterations in brain structure. The diagnostic tests generally will include

1. Urinalysis (detects infection, diabetes, renal failure, or dehydration)

2. Blood tests—hematocrit, hemoglobin, white blood cell count and differential, platelet count

3. Erythrocyte sedimentation rate (elevated in the presence of certain vascular diseases, such as arteritis)

4. Blood sugar test

5. Serologic tests for syphilis

6. Blood chemistry profile—serum electrolytes, serum cardiac enzyme levels (elevated creatine phosphokinase—is indicative of coincidental cardiac infarction)

7. Blood cholesterol and lipid profiles

8. X-ray examination of the chest (heart size, lung tumors)

9. ECG (arrhythmias, alterations in wave forma-

tion); stroke patients may have coincidental heart disease, or stroke may cause ECG abnormalities—typically T-wave inversion, prolonged QT interval, and ST inversion.

10. **Computerized cranial axial tomography (CCT, CAT or CT scan).** Early changes following stroke reveal signs of edema and displacement of brain structures. Later changes delineate infarcted areas and changes in tissue density. The CAT scan also distinguishes between causative factors (infarction versus hemorrhage) and detects nonvascular causes of stroke. These findings have allowed more precise localization of lesions and have revolutionized the diagnosis of stroke (Fig. 17–3).

11. Cerebral angiography. Cerebral angiography involves the injection of radiopaque dye in blood vessels with subsequent roentgenography. It may be used if CAT scans are unavailable or in selected surgical cases (hemorrhages, aneurysms, and arteriovenous malformations). The risks of angiography are relatively high, with death or stroke in 1 to 2 percent of cases and minor complications in 5 to 6 percent of cases (Fig. 17–4).[6,10,14]

CLINICAL MANIFESTATIONS

Signs and Symptoms

SENSORY FUNCTION

Sensation is frequently impaired but rarely absent on the hemiplegic side. The type and extent of deficit is

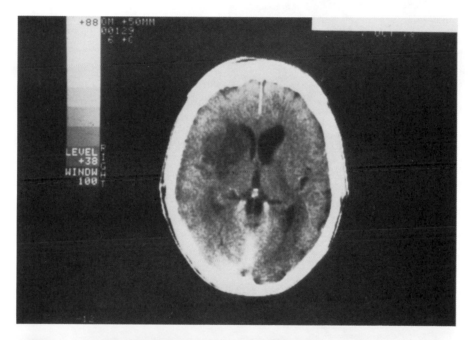

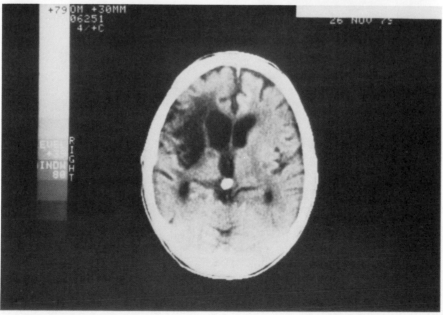

Figure 17–3. CAT scan of a patient with infarction of the middle cerebral artery territory. (From Hachinski, V, and Norris, J,[10] with permission.)

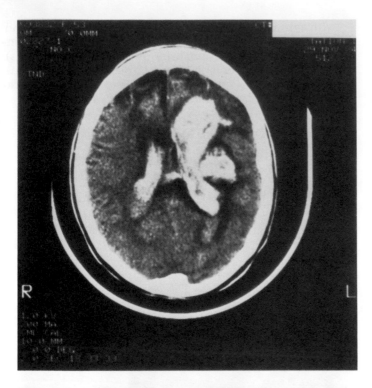

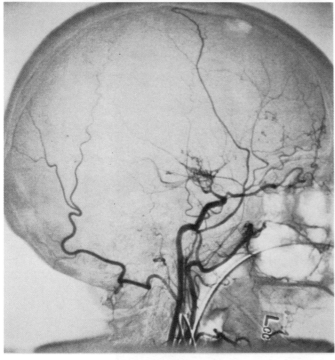

Figure 17–4. Cerebral angiography of a patient with cerebral hemorrhage secondary to bilateral moyamoya disease. (From Hachinski, V, and Norris, J,[10] p 155, with permission.)

related to the location and extent of the vascular lesion. Specific, localized areas of dysfunction are common with cortical lesions, but diffuse involvement throughout the whole side suggests deeper lesions involving the thalamus and adjacent structures. Symptoms of crossed anesthesia (ipsilateral facial impairments with contralateral trunk and limb deficits) typify brainstem lesions.[10] Proprioceptive losses are common and have a significant impact on movement abilities.[15] Loss of superficial touch, pain, and temperature are common and contrib-

ute to overall perceptual dysfunction and risk of self-injury. Patients may experience impairments in any of the combined sensations, such as two-point discrimination or stereognosis.[16]

Visual field defects such as homonymous **hemianopsia** are common in hemiplegia. The patient experiences blindness of the nasal half of one eye and the temporal half of the other eye. The term right or left is used to designate the side of the visual defect and corresponds to the hemiplegic side. Field defects contribute to the patient's overall lack of awareness of the hemiplegic side. Patients also may experience impairments in depth perception concomitant with other problems in spatial relationships (see chapter 7). **Forced gaze deviation** occurs as a result of involvement of muscles controlling eye movements. Unopposed action of eye muscles causes the eyes to deviate in the direction of the intact musculature. Patients with hemispheric lesions may look away from the hemiplegic side, whereas patients with brainstem lesions may look toward the hemiplegic side.[10]

MOTOR FUNCTION

Recovery Stages

During the early stages of stroke, flaccidity with no voluntary movement is common. Usually this is replaced by the development of spasticity and mass patterns of movement, termed *synergies.* Muscles involved in synergy patterns are often so strongly linked together that isolated movements outside the mass synergistic patterns are not possible. As recovery progresses, spasticity begins to decline and advanced movement patterns become possible. This recovery process was described by Twitchell in 1951[17] and further elaborated on by Brunnstrom (Table 17–2).[18,19] Additional studies have confirmed this recovery process.[20] Recovery stages are sequential, but not every patient will demonstrate full recovery. Patients may reach a plateau at any stage, depending on the severity of their involvement and their capacity for adaptation. Bobath describes three main recovery stages: (1) the initial flaccid stage, (2) the stage of spasticity, and (3) the stage of relative recovery.[21]

A critical concept in the management of the patient with stroke is the ability to recognize tonal changes and synergy movement patterns as separate and distinct clinical findings and to understand the interaction between the two. *Flaccidity* is usually present immediately after the stroke and is generally short-lived, lasting hours, days, or weeks. *Spasticity* emerges in about 90 percent of cases and tends to occur in predictable muscle groups, commonly the antigravity muscles. The effects of spasticity include restricted movement and static posturing of the limbs. In the upper extremity, spasticity is frequently strong in scapular retractors; shoulder adductors, depressors, and internal rotators; elbow flexors and forearm pronators; and wrist and finger flexors. In the neck and trunk, spasticity may cause slumping (increased lateral flexion) to the hemiplegic side. In the lower extremity, pelvic retractors, hip adductors and internal rotators, hip and knee extensors, plantar flexors, supinators, and toe flexors are often spastic.[19,21]

Synergy Patterns

Synergy patterns of the extremities are stereotyped, primitive movement patterns associated with the presence of spasticity. They may be elicited reflexly as associated reactions, or as voluntary movement patterns. There are two basic synergies of each extremity: a flexion synergy and an extension synergy (presented in Table 17–3). An inspection of the synergy components reveals key muscles not usually involved in either synergy, including the (1) lattisimus dorsi, (2) teres major, (3) serratus anterior, (4) finger extensors, and (5) ankle evertors. These muscles, therefore, are generally difficult to rehabilitate and represent important functional limitations for many patients in their upper extremity activities and in gait. Loss of isolated movement patterns also has important functional implications.[19,22]

Table 17–2 SEQUENTIAL RECOVERY STAGES IN HEMIPLEGIA

STAGE 1 Recovery from hemiplegia occurs in a stereotyped sequence of events that begins with a period of *flaccidity* immediately following the acute episode. *No movement of the limbs* can be elicited.

STAGE 2 As recovery begins, the basic limb synergies or some of their components may appear as associated reactions, or *minimal voluntary movement* responses may be present. At this time, *spasticity* begins to develop.

STAGE 3 Thereafter, the patient gains *voluntary control of the movement synergies,* although full range of all synergy components does not necessarily develop. *Spasticity* has further increased and may become *severe.*

STAGE 4 Some *movement combinations that do not follow the paths of either synergy* are mastered, first with difficulty, then with more ease, and *spasticity begins to decline.*

STAGE 5 If progress continues, *more difficult movement combinations* are learned as the basic limb synergies lose their dominance over motor acts.

STAGE 6 With the *disappearance of spasticity,* individual joint movements become possible and *coordination* approaches normal. From here on, as the last recovery step, normal motor function is restored, but this last stage is not achieved by all, for the recovery process can plateau at any stage.

From Brunnstrom, S: *Movement Therapy in Hemiplegia.* Harper & Row, New York, 1970, by permission.

Table 17–3 SYNERGY PATTERNS OF THE EXTREMITIES

	Flexion Synergy Components	Extension Synergy Components
Upper Extremity	Scapular retraction/ elevation or hyperextension	Scapular protraction
	Shoulder abduction, external rotation	Shoulder adduction,* internal rotation
	Elbow flexion*	Elbow extension
	Forearm supination	Forearm pronation*
	Wrist and finger flexion	Wrist and finger flexion
Lower Extremity	Hip flexion,* abduction, external rotation	Hip extension, adduction,* internal rotation
	Knee flexion	Knee extension*
	Ankle dorsiflexion inversion	Ankle plantarflexion,* inversion
	Toe dorsiflexion	Toe plantarflexion

*Generally the strongest components

Reflexes

Postural reflexes are altered, often in association with the stage of recovery in which a patient presents. During the middle stages of recovery when spasticity and synergies are strong, primitive or tonic reflex patterns may appear in a relatively pure form. Thus, movement of the head frequently elicits an obligatory change in resting tone or movement of the extremities. Flexion of the neck results in flexion of the arms and extension of the legs; extension of the neck produces the opposite responses **(symmetric tonic neck reflex—STNR)**. Head rotation to the left causes extension of the left arm and leg (skull limbs) with flexion of the right arm and leg (jaw limbs); head rotation to the right causes the reverse pattern **(asymmetric tonic neck reflex—ATNR)**. The supine posture produces an increase in extensor tone, and the prone posture increases flexor tone **(symmetric tonic labyrinthine reflex—STLR)**. Rotation of the trunk (rotation of the upper trunk with respect to the pelvis) also may influence movement of the extremities. Rotation to the hemiplegic side results in flexion of the hemiplegic upper extremity and extension of hemiplegic lower extremity. Rotation to the uninvolved side produces the opposite responses (tonic lumbar reflexes). Finally, pressure on the bottom of the hemiplegic foot may produce a strong cocontraction response of both extensors and flexors, resulting in a rigidly extended and fixed limb (positive supporting reaction).[19,21,23]

Associated reactions are commonly present. These consist of abnormal, automatic responses of the involved limb, resulting from action occurring in some other part of the body, by voluntary or reflex stimulation (e.g., yawning, sneezing, coughing, stretching). They are easier to elicit in the presence of spasticity and frequently interact with tonic reflexes. Generally, associated reactions elicit the same direction of movement in the contralateral upper extremity; that is, flexion evokes flexion. In the lower extremity, however, opposite movements are elicited; that is, flexion of one lower extremity evokes extension of the other. Specific associated reactions also have been identified. Elevation of the hemiplegic arm above the horizontal plane may elicit an extension and abduction response of the fingers (Souque's phenomenon). Resistance to abduction or adduction produces a like response in the opposite limb (adduction elicits adduction) in both upper and lower extremities (Raimeste's phenomenon). *Homolateral limb synkinesis* is the term used to describe the mutual dependency that exists between hemiplegic limbs (flexion of the arm elicits flexion of the leg on the hemiplegic side).[19,21,24]

Higher-level reactions (righting, equilibrium, protective extension) are frequently impaired or absent. A patient may be unable to maintain the head in its normal upright alignment, face vertical with the mouth in a horizontal position, in response to body position or movement. Impaired righting reactions are also evident when rotation of either the head or trunk within the body axis fails to produce a log-rolling (trunk moving as one unit) or segmental rolling (head, upper trunk, then lower trunk) pattern. Lack of equilibrium reactions may cause the patient to lose balance and to fall in response to a change of the center of gravity over the base of support. The necessary postural adjustments of the trunk and limbs are typically diminished, slow to react, or totally lacking. Protective extension of either hemiplegic limb in response to falling is commonly impaired or absent.[21,23]

Incoordination

Incoordination can result from cerebellar or basal ganglia involvement, proprioceptive losses, or motor weakness. *Ataxia* of the extremities or trunk is common in patients with cerebellar lesions. Reciprocal interaction and graded control of agonists, antagonists, and synergists may be impaired. The stretch reflex responses which allow automatic adaption of muscles to changes of posture and movement are commonly abnormal.[10,21]

Functional Movement

Functional impairments following stroke vary from patient to patient. Generally, rolling, sitting up, transfers, standing up, and walking pose significant problems for the moderate to severely involved acute stroke patient. Activities of daily living (ADL) skills such as feeding and dressing also are impaired. Success in performing functional tasks can be influenced by a number of factors, including mobility problems, mental confusion, and perceptual and language deficits.[25]

LANGUAGE FUNCTION

Language impairments frequently result from a stroke involving the middle cerebral artery and the dominant left hemisphere. (A small percentage of individuals, approximately 3 percent, demonstrate language impairment with right hemisphere lesion. These are typically left-handed individuals with mixed dominance.) Aphasia is the general term used to describe disorders of previously intact language function secondary to brain damage. Aphasia has been estimated to occur in up to 40 percent of all stroke patients.[26] Patients may experience problems in comprehension, speech, writing, gestures, or reading. Aphasia is often classified into two main types: *fluent* and *nonfluent*. Patients with nonfluent, **Broca's, aphasia** (motor aphasia) have an overall decrease in verbal communication with decreased rate, altered rhythm, and problems with articulation *(dysarthria)*. Speech is very difficult and frustrating for these patients and may lead to decreased attempts at communication. Comprehension is normal or near normal. Patients with fluent, **Wernicke's** (sensory) **aphasia,** however, often have a normal or greater than normal amount of verbal communication with an increased rate of output, normal rhythm, and articulation. These patients commonly make up words **(neologisms)** or inappropriately substitute one word for another **(verbal paraphasias),** leaving their communication ineffective and often incomprehensible. Comprehension is generally severely impaired. Patients exhibiting *global* aphasia present with both expressive and receptive difficulties and are therefore the most severely impaired. They comprise the largest group of aphasic patients (approximately 20 to 25 percent), and about 20 percent have a pure Broca's aphasia, and 15 percent have a pure Wernicke's aphasia.[26] Other types of aphasias include transcortical motor (nonfluent) or sensory (fluent), conduction (fluent), or anomic (fluent) aphasia. **Alexia** without **agraphia** refers to pure word blindness and is a rare reading disorder. Pure word deafness in which patients can hear but can not understand the spoken word also may occur. Patients with left hemisphere damage may experience **apraxia** (an inability to perform voluntary purposive movements, although there is no sensory or motor impairment). Apraxia may be *ideomotor* (movement is not possible upon command but may occur automatically), *ideational* (misuse of objects owing to an inability to perceive their correct use), or *buccofacial* (affecting oral and perioral muscles). Thus the patient may have trouble brushing teeth on command, writing, or drinking through a straw.[26–28]

PERCEPTUAL FUNCTION

Lesions of the parietal lobe of the nondominant hemisphere (typically the right hemisphere for most individuals) produce perceptual disturbances. These may include visuospatial distortions, disturbances in body image, unilateral neglect, and certain types of apraxia. Patients with visuospatial distortions may not be able to judge distance, size, position, rate of movement, form, or the relation of parts to the whole. Thus the patient may consistently bump the wheelchair into the door frame and seem unable to get through the doorway. *Topographic disorientation* refers to an inability to find the way from one area to another. The patient consistently gets lost going from one place to another. Patients also may experience difficulties in distinguishing *figure-ground relationships*. The brakes on a wheelchair may be indistinguishable from the rest of the parts of the wheel-

Table 17–4 PERCEPTUAL AND COMMUNICATION PROBLEMS IN HEMIPLEGIA: IMPLICATIONS FOR REHABILITATION

Lesion: Left Hemisphere	Hemiplegia: Right Side of Body	
Clinical Problem	*Clinical Example*	*Suggestions for Treatment*
Aphasias	Lacks functional speech	Pantomime directions
Ideomotor and ideational apraxias	Can not plan and execute serial steps in performances	Give reminders of next step in directions or manually assist limb through next motion
Number alexia	Can not recognize symbols to do simple computations	Give numeric task that might have been an automatic level, i.e., playing cards, dice, and so forth
Right-left discrimination	Unable to distinguish right from left on self or reverse on others	Train in specifics of right-left orientation of self, then reversal on external object; substitute "strong limb" or "weak limb" as necessary in directing
Slow in organization and performance	Can not remember what he or she intended to do next	Encourage quicker response by reinforcing directions

Lesion: Right Hemisphere	Hemiplegia: Left Side of Body	
Clinical Problem	*Clinical Example*	*Suggestions for Treatment*
Visuospatial	Can not orient self to changes in environment while going from one treatment area to another	Bring attention to visual landmarks (pictures, clock, and so forth) that aid in orientation
Left unilateral neglect of self	Generally unaware of objects to left and propels wheelchair into them	Remind patient to scan right to extreme left during wheelchair movements and other tasks
Body Image	Distorted awareness and impression of self	Verbally reinforce association of body parts; as deserved, give sincere compliments regarding appearance
Dressing apraxia	Applies sweater to right side, but unable to do left-side application	Give verbal directions or actually take limb through required motion
Constructional apraxia	Unable to transpose two-dimensional instructions into three-dimensional structure, as per "do-it-yourself" kits	Be sure task has purposeful meaning for patient. Use elementary concepts to guide through inability to visualize
Illusions of shortening of time	Patient arrives extremely early for appointments	Repeatedly call attention to use of watch/clock; do not give negative reward by treating patient whenever he or she comes
Number concepts— spatial type	Unable to align columns and rows of digits	Gradually progress from one column and one row in addition or subtraction; increase columns and rows; advance to multiplication and division
Rapid organization and performance	Errors from haste; may cause accidents	Provide calm environment; give patient verbal reminders to slow pace
Depth of language skills	May mention task related to prestroke occupation, but cannot go into details of it	Attempt to coordinate depth of language skills with general rehabilitation goals for individual

chair. Problems in the perception of verticality, especially in dimly lit areas, may occur. This may be evident by a patient who is constantly leaning over to one side. **Body image** (visual and mental memory of body parts) and **body scheme** (perception of precise location and relationship of body parts) may be distorted. Patients with unilateral neglect are generally unaware of what happens on the hemiplegic side. A severe form includes frank denial that the hemiplegic limbs belong to the patient. Sensory losses and hemianopia frequently contribute to this perceptual problem. Apraxia is common and may include ideomotor, ideational, dressing (unable to perform the functional tasks of dressing); or constructional (unable to construct designs in three dimensions).[29–31] The reader is referred to chapter 7 for a more complete description of these deficits. Table 17–4 summarizes common hemispheric problems in hemiplegia with implications for rehabilitation.

MENTAL FUNCTION AND BEHAVIOR

Patients with left and right hemiplegia differ widely in their behavioral styles. Those with right hemiplegia tend to be slow, more cautious, uncertain, and insecure. Thus they appear anxious and hesitant when performing tasks and often require more frequent feedback and support. They also tend to be realistic in their appraisal of their existing problems. Those with left hemiplegia tend to be quick and impulsive, frequently overestimating their abilities while minimizing or denying their problems. Safety is therefore a far greater issue with left hemiplegia, because poor judgment is common. These patients also require a great deal of feedback when learning a new task. The feedback should be focused on slowing down the activity and checking each component part of the task carefully. A patient with left hemiplegia frequently can not attend to visuospatial cues effectively, especially in a cluttered or crowded environment. Literal denial of a disability, *anosognosia,* though rare, occurs more commonly with left hemiplegia and is often accompanied by mental confusion.[31,32]

Memory problems are common. The patient with a stroke frequently has a short retention span, remembering only the first few bits of information in a series of commands. Immediate, *short-term, memory* is often impaired while long-term memory remains intact. Thus the patient can not remember the instructions for a new task given only 30 seconds ago but can remember things done 30 years ago. The patient may also have difficulties in generalizing information. Thus information learned in one setting can not be transferred to other situations. Memory problems may be specific to the hemisphere involved; right hemiplegia results in difficulty with language memory, whereas left hemiplegia results in problems with visuospatial information.[32]

Emotional lability is defined as unstable or changeable emotions and may result following acute stroke. The patient is unable to inhibit the expression of spontaneous emotions and may change quickly from laughing to crying and back to laughing again. Frequent crying is often accompanied by depression and generally diminishes over the course of time.

Sensory losses coupled with an unfamiliar environment and inactivity can lead to symptoms of sensory deprivation such as irritability, confusion, restlessness, and sometimes psychosis, delusions, or hallucinations. Nighttime may be particularly problematic. Many patients with diminished capacity are equally unable to deal with a sensory overload, produced by too much stimulation.[32]

Dementia can result from multiple infarcts of the brain. It is characterized by a generalized decline in higher cortical functions, including faulty judgments, impaired consciousness, poor memory, diminished communication, and behavioral or mood alterations. These changes are often associated with episodes of cerebral ischemia, focal neurologic signs, and hypertension. The patient may fluctuate between periods of impaired function and periods of improved or normal function.[33]

Epileptic seizures occur in a small percentage of stroke patients and are slightly more common in occlusive carotid disease (17 percent) than in middle cerebral artery disease (11 percent). Seizures also occur at the onset of cerebral hemorrhage in about 15 percent of the cases. They tend to be of the partial motor type and in some patients occur as the initial presenting symptom.[6,34]

SECONDARY PROBLEMS AND COMPLICATIONS

Psychologic Problems

The patient who has had a stroke is often frustrated by changes in the ability to sense, to move, to communicate, to think, or to act as he or she did before.[35] Common psychologic reactions include anxiety, depression, and denial. Additionally, the patient's behavior may be influenced by cognitive deficits that leave the patient irritable, inflexible, hypercritical, impatient, impulsive, apathetic, or overdependent on others. These behaviors, along with a poor social perception of one's self and environment, may lead to increasing isolation and stress.[36]

Depression is extremely common, occurring in about one third of the cases. Most patients remain significantly depressed for many months, with an average time of 7 to 8 months. The period from 6 months to 2 years after a cerebral vascular accident is the most likely time for depression to occur. Depression occurs in both mildly and severely involved patients and thus is not significantly related to the degree of impairment. However, patients with lesions in the left hemisphere experience more frequent and more severe depression than those with right hemisphere or brainstem strokes. These findings suggest that poststroke depression may not be simply a result of psychologic reaction to disability but, rather, may be related to the location of the lesion.[37,38]

Contractures and Deformities

Contracture and deformity result from loss of movement, spasticity, and improper positioning. As contractures progress, edema and pain may develop and further restrict attempts to gain motion. In the upper extremity limitations in shoulder motions are common. Patients also frequently develop contractures of the elbow, wrist, and finger flexors, and forearm pronators. In the lower extremity plantarflexion contractures are common.

Deep Venous Thrombosis

Deep venous thrombosis (DVT) and pulmonary embolism are potential complications for all immobilized patients. Common symptoms of DVT include calf pain or tenderness, swelling, and discoloration of the leg. About 50 percent of the cases do not present with clinically detectable symptoms and can be identified by phlebography or other noninvasive techniques. Anticoagulants and antiplatelet agents are the primary medical treatments, along with bedrest and elevation of the part.[10,39]

Pain

Patients with lesions affecting the thalamus (posterolateral ventral nuclei) may initially experience a contralateral sensory loss. After several weeks or months this may be replaced by a severe burning pain generalized on the hemiplegic side (thalamic pain, thalamic syndrome). Pain is increased by stimuli or contact with that side. Thalamic syndrome is extremely debilitating, and the patient generally has a poor functional outcome.[4]

Urinary and Bowel Problems

Urinary incontinence may require the temporary use of an indwelling catheter. Generally this problem improves quickly. Early removal of a catheter is desirable to prevent the development of infection. Patients are frequently impacted and may require stool softeners and low-residue diets to resolve this problem.[14]

Oral-Facial Dysfunction

Swallowing dysfunction, **dysphagia,** is a common complication after stroke, occurring in lesions affecting the medullary brainstem (cranial nerves IX and X) as well as in acute hemispheric lesions. In patients referred for detailed assessment of dysphagia, the most frequent problem seen is delayed triggering of the swallowing reflex (86 percent of patients) followed by reduced pharyngeal peristalsis (58 percent of patients) and reduced lingual control (50 percent of patients).[40] Poor jaw and lip closure, altered sensation, impaired head control, and poor sitting balance also contribute to the patient's swallowing difficulties. Most demonstrate multiple problems resulting in drooling, difficulty ingesting food, aspiration, dysarthria, and asymmetry of the muscles of facial expression. Decreased nutritional intake may result in the temporary use of a nasogastric tube for feeding. These problems have tremendous social implications, for the patient frequently feels humiliated and frustrated by their presence.[10,40,41]

Shoulder Dysfunction

Shoulder pain is extremely common following stroke, occurring in from 70 to 84 percent of patients.[42] Pain is typically present with movement and in more severe cases at rest. Several causes of shoulder pain have been proposed. In the flaccid stage, proprioceptive impairment, lack of tone, and muscle paralysis reduce the support and normal seating action of the rotator cuff muscles, particularly the supraspinatus. The ligaments and capsule thus become the shoulder's sole support. The normal orientation of the glenoid fossa is upward, outward, and forward, maintaining the superior capsule taut and stabilizing the humerus mechanically. Any abduction or forward flexion of the humerus or scapular depression and downward rotation reduces this stabilization by changing the orientation of the humerus to the glenoid fossa. Mechanical stresses resulting from traction and gravitational forces are produced. Glenohumeral friction-compression stresses also occur between the humeral head and superior soft tissues during flexion or abduction movements in the absence of normal simultaneous rotation of the arm and scapulohumeral rhythm. In the spastic stage, abnormal muscle tone contributes to poor scapular position (depression, retraction, and downward rotation) and to subluxation and restricted movement. Secondary tightness in ligaments, tendons, and the joint capsule quickly develops. Brachial plexus injury is also a potential complicating factor, as is adhesive capsulitis. Finally, poor handling and positioning of the hemiplegic arm have been implicated in producing joint microtrauma and pain owing to secondary problems in the capsule, bursa, or tendons.[42,44]

Reflex sympathetic dystrophy (RSD or shoulder-hand syndrome) occurs in approximately 12 to 25 percent of the cases.[45] The patient experiences swelling and tenderness of the hand and fingers along with shoulder pain. Sympathetic vasomotor symptoms are present and include warm, red, or glossy skin and trophic changes. The patient experiences increasing pain with movement, and further immobilization leads to increased stiffness, contracture, and atrophy of skin, bone, and muscle. In the late stages the skin is typically cool, cyanotic, and damp; fibrous and articular changes develop. The hand typically becomes contracted in metacarpophalangeal (MP) extension and interphalangeal (IP) flexion, similar to the "intrinsic minus hand." Early diagnosis and treatment is critical in preventing or minimizing the late changes of RSD. Because of close daily contact with the patient, the therapist is frequently one of the first to recognize and to report early signs and symptoms. Radionuclide bone scans (scintigraphy) can be used to confirm early symptoms of RSD reliably.[43,45]

Decreased Endurance/ Concomitant Cardiac Problems

Patients who suffer a stroke secondary to cardiac causes may demonstrate impaired cardiac output, cardiac decompensation, and serious ryhthm disorders. If these problems persist, they can directly alter cerebral perfusion and produce additional focal signs. Cardiac limitations in exercise tolerance may also result from prolonged bedrest and immobility. The patient's rehabilitation potential may be restricted, requiring diligent monitoring and careful exercise prescription by the physical therapist. These are discussed fully in chapter 16.

PROGNOSIS

The fatality rate of initial strokes varies considerably by type of stroke (atherothrombotic brain infarction, 15 percent; cerebral embolus, 16 percent; subarachnoid hemorrhage, 46 percent; and intercerebral hemorrhage, 82 percent) with an overall rate of 22 percent.[7] Thus intracranial hemorrhage accounts for the largest number of deaths following an acute episode. Approximately 60 percent of women and 52 percent of men survive 5 years, but at 10 years only 35 percent of patients who sustained stroke are still alive.[7] Survival rates are dramatically lessened by the presence of coexisting cardiovascular disease and hypertension. Survival is influenced by the age of the patient—decreasing in older age groups—and diabetes. Most patients suffer recurrent attacks, usually of the same type, and these rates are influenced by the same risk factors influencing survival.[46]

Functional recovery is largely determined by the site and extent of the lesion. The larger the lesion, the more widespread the impairment of brain function. In the early stage following stroke, improvement of symptoms may result from a decrease in cerebral edema. Thus, rehabilitation potential is more reliably assessed after the first two weeks. Neuronal recovery is also influenced by the plasticity of the central nervous system (CNS). Redundancy and reorganization allow the CNS to adjust and to redistribute function. Synaptic remodeling and collateral sprouting are just two of the recovery phenomona that occur in response to brain lesions.[47–49] Generally, the faster the recovery, the more favorable the prognosis. Most spontaneous neurologic recovery occurs within the first 6 months after the initial insult. Paralysis that remains severe after this time is not likely to improve dramatically.[50]

Stroke outcome may be adversely affected by a number of factors, including significant perceptual or cognitive dysfunction, prior stroke, nystagmus, poor motivation, and delay in initiating rehabilitation. Other less consistently related factors to outcome include an extended period of unconsciousness, significant medical problems, and hemianopsia.[51–59]

MEDICAL MANAGEMENT

Patients with TIAs are assessed to diagnose the cause of the vascular insufficiency and to institute early preventative treatment. Medical management may consist of

1. Control of blood-clotting characteristics with the short-term administration of anticoagulants (warfarin) or longer-term use of platelet-inhibiting therapy (aspirin). Vasodilators (papaverine) may be administered if vasospasm of the arterial wall is suspected.

2. Cranial arteriography if the diagnosis is uncertain or if vascular surgery is being considered.
3. Reconstructive surgery (carotid **endarterectomy** or angioplasty).[6,10,14,60,61]

Medical management of patients with strokes will vary according to whether the stroke is progressing (stroke in evolution) or completed (no new events within the preceding 24 hours). It will also vary by type of stroke, degree of neurologic deficit, and condition of the patient. The acute stroke patient requires bedrest. The primary medical concerns during this time include

1. Ensuring adequate oxygenation and circulation
2. Restoring water and electrolyte balance
3. Preventing hypoglycemia
4. Controlling seizures or infections as necessary

Unconscious or acute stroke patients may require suctioning but rarely require intubation or assisted ventilation. Oxygen therapy (nasal mask or catheter oxygen therapy) may improve clinical signs of hypoxia but is not normally indicated. Hemodilution, or blood thinning, using plasma-expanding agents (dextran) may be initiated. Anticoagulants (sodium warfarin, bishydroxycoumarin) are commonly given in cases of progressing ischemic strokes and also can prevent complications of deep venous thrombosis and pulmonary embolism. Hemorrhage is a possible complication of anticoagulation therapy, and daily prothrombin times are required to regulate the dosage of these medications. Cerebral edema is generally controlled with adrenocorticosteroids and dehydrating agents (intravenous glucose-saline solutions). If the causes of stroke are cardiac in origin, medical management focuses on control of arrhythmias, cardiac decompensation, and respiration. Management of established hypertension is especially important in patients with hemorrhagic stroke. These patients require strict control of blood pressure.[62] Active rehabilitation, including early mobilization, is initiated as soon as the patient is stabilized and before any secondary complications can develop.[5,10]

Neurosurgery is indicated in cases of intracranial bleeding causing elevated intracranial pressures, because death may result from brain herniation and brainstem compression. Generally, superficial or lobar lesions (subdural hematoma, aneurysm) are more amenable to neurosurgery, but central hemorrhages are not. Surgery of the extracranial vessels (**endarterectomy**) in patients with progressing or unstable strokes is associated with high mortality and morbidity and is generally contraindicated in patients with completed strokes.[6,61]

REHABILITATIVE MANAGEMENT

Rehabilitation begun early in the acute stage optimizes the patient's potential for functional recovery. Early mobilization prevents or minimizes the harmful effects of deconditioning and the potential for developing contractures. Functional reorganization is promoted through use of the affected side. Maladaptive patterns of movement and poor habits can be prevented. Mental deterioration can be reduced through the development of a positive outlook and an early, organized plan of care that stresses resumption of normal, everyday activities. In the acute care setting, patients may be referred for rehabilitation services or may be admitted to a specific stroke rehabilitation unit. Both groups have consistently demonstrated significantly improved functional outcomes when compared with patients not receiving those services.[63-65]

Patients with mild residual deficits may be discharged with a home program or referred for outpatient rehabilitation services. Patients with moderate or severe residual deficits may be referred to a regional rehabilitation facility for comprehensive services, usually within 3 to 6 weeks after the stroke. Optimal timing of rehabilitation based upon individual patient readiness is an important consideration. A number of factors appear to be related to rehabilitation readiness, including the side of lesion. There is some evidence to suggest that patients with right hemiplegia may respond more favorably to earlier comprehensive rehabilitation efforts. Patients with left hemiplegia who suffer more cognitive-perceptual deficits and generally have longer rehabilitation stays may benefit from the additional preadmission time to allow for cognitive and perceptual-motor reorganization. Equally important factors that might influence the timing of rehabilitation efforts include medical stability, motivation, patient endurance, stage of recovery, and ability to learn. In an era of time-limited payment for comprehensive rehabilitation services, selecting the optimal time for rehabilitation training may prevent unnecessary patient failures and may improve long-term functional outcomes.[66,67]

Comprehensive services for the patient with stroke can best be provided by a team of rehabilitation specialists including the physician, nurse, physical therapist, occupational therapist, speech therapist, and medical social worker. Additional disciplines may include a neuropsychologist, audiologist, dietician, or ophthalmologist. Coordinated interaction among all professionals is necessary to formulate and to implement an integrated plan of care designed to meet the patient's individual needs.[68]

Assessment

The physical therapy assessment of a patient who has had a stroke will be determined by each patient's unique needs and problems. A comprehensive battery for assessing neurologically impaired patients (presented in Table 17–5) presents an appropriate database for the selection of appropriate procedures.

MENTAL STATUS

One of the first procedures performed should be an assessment of mental function. This will include tests for memory, orientation, ability to follow instructions, **perseveration,** and attention span. Memory impairments typically involve short-term recall while long-term memory is usually preserved. Questions might be posed to the patient regarding what he or she had for breakfast as opposed to questions regarding the date and location of birth. Orientation can be assessed by eliciting responses to questions about the day of the week, month, location of the hospital, and identification of self, staff, and/or

Table 17–5 ASSESSMENT BATTERY FOR NEUROLOGICALLY IMPAIRED PATIENTS

Demographic information
Medical history
Psychosocial history
Patient's chief complaint
Impact of disability on lifestyle
Mental status
Communication ability
Mobility
  Range of motion (ROM)
  Joint play
  Soft tissue
    Skin condition
    Compliance of muscle and connective tissue
    Edema
Motor control
  Muscle tone
  Strength
  Abnormal reflexes
  Voluntary movement patterns
  Motor planning ability
  Coordination
  Balance—static/dynamic
  Developmental sequence
  Automatic postural and equilibrium reactions
Vital functions
Autonomic nervous system
Sensation
Perception
Pain
Posture
Gait
Functional abilities
Equipment
Endurance/cardiorespiratory status

From Wolf, S: *Clinical Decision Making in Physical Therapy.* FA Davis, 1985, p 193, with permission.

family members. Ability to follow instructions (retention span) should be tested by directing the patient to perform activities at increasing levels of difficulty. For example, a one-level command would instruct the patient to "pick up the glass"; a two-level command would instruct the patient to "pick up the glass and place it on the table." Patients with short retention spans will respond only to short, simple commands during therapy. **Perseveration** is the meaningless repetition of a word or movement after the stimulus for a response has been removed. Thus the patient will repeat a response to a question or a movement response several times and require instruction or physical assistance to stop. Attention span should be assessed in terms of the specific time the patient is able to concentrate on a task. Generalization deficits also may limit performance. A patient with this problem will be unable to transfer learning from one setting to another: The patient can transfer safely in the physical therapy department but becomes totally unsafe when attempting the same transfer in the hospital room. **Emotional lability** (excessive crying or laughing) should be assessed by observing the behaviors in the context in which they occur. Labile behaviors are often not related directly to the situation and can be diverted by directing the patient's attention to something else.[32]

COMMUNICATION ABILITY

Close collaboration with the speech therapist will be important in determining an accurate analysis of the patient's communication deficits. One of the critical aspects of this and other exchanges with team members will be the development of collaborative goals and treatments that are mutually reinforced in all therapies. Impairments in receptive language (reading comprehension, word recognition, auditory comprehension) and/or expressive language function (word finding, fluency, writing, spelling) should be noted. Orofacial sensorimotor dysfunction should be carefully assessed as well. Communication deficits may severely limit the validity of other assessments, and patient comprehension should be fully ascertained before proceeding. It is not uncommon for staff to overestimate the patient's abilities to understand speech. A quick assessment to check an individual's level of understanding can be performed by saying one thing to the patient and gesturing another (e.g., "It's hot in here" and putting on a sweater). Alternate forms of communication (gestures, movements, pantomime) should be well established before additional testing begins.[32]

SENSORY AND PERCEPTUAL ABILITIES

Significant information on sensory and perceptual deficits will be provided by close communication with the occupational therapist. Many assessments and formalized test batteries have been developed to test such areas as hemianopsia, limits of peripheral vision, left-sided neglect, depth perception, figure-ground disturbance, topographic orientation, perception of body image, and spatial relations. These are discussed fully in chapter 7. During testing, the uninvolved limbs may be used as guides to normal function, although dysfunction in the so-called normal extremities is possible.[30] Because the patient with left hemiplegia may behave in ways that tend to minimize disabilities, it is easy for staff to overestimate the patient's spatial-perceptual abilities. The use of gestures or visual cues may decrease this patient's ability to perform, whereas verbal cues (either your own or the patients) may permit success. Carefully structuring the environment (minimizing clutter and activity, using clear reference points, a well-lit room) will improve patient performance.[29,32]

JOINT MOBILITY

An assessment of joint mobility should include an assessment of range of motion (ROM), joint play, and soft tissue compliance. Problems with spasticity may result in inconsistent passive ROM findings as alterations in tone are common from one testing session to the next. Thus tonal abnormalities should be noted at the time of examination. Active ROM tests may be invalid, because synergy dominance may influence performance and may not correspond with standard testing. Only those patients who demonstrate selective motor control associated with advanced recovery may be appropriately tested using active ROM techniques.

MOTOR CONTROL

The neurologically impaired patient may exhibit a number of deficits in motor control, including tonal abnormalities, alterations in strength, and dominance of primitive and tonic reflexes with decreased function of higher-level postural reactions (righting, equilibrium, protective extension). Voluntary movement patterns may be stereotyped (in synergy) with a corresponding loss of selective movement control. Movements demonstrating selective control may be uncoordinated and affected by timing deficits. Thus the muscles are slow to develop tension and are also slow in decreasing tension. These items are fully discussed in chapter 9, Motor Control Assessment. The traditional motor function test (manual muscle test) which assesses strength in isolated joint movements is an *invalid measure* to use with a neurologic patient who presents with problems of sensory or perceptual loss, spasticity, reflex dominance, positional alterations in tone, and stereotyped movement patterns.[69,70]

The assessment tools of Brunnstrom and Bobath have been widely used or adapted for assessment and management of adult hemiplegia. The Brunnstrom assessment[19] is based upon sequential recovery stages and carefully plots the emergence, dominance, and variation of the motion synergies. Both synergy and isolated movements are assessed in terms of the active ROM completed. Gross sensory changes and tone alterations (flaccidity or spasticity) by stage of recovery are also determined. Late-stage control is assessed by timed tasks in which the patient is asked to complete test items as quickly as possible. This test also presents a complete analysis of hand function and lower extremity control in sitting, standing, and walking activities.

The Bobath assessment[21] is based upon a qualitative assessment of postural and movement patterns. Tonal abnormalities (flaccidity or spasticity) are assessed during both passive and active movements. The therapist may place the limbs in various positions and observe the patient's responses during attempts to hold the position (placing and holding). Tests for active movements are divided into two groups: advanced movement combinations (out of synergy movements) progressing from easiest to most difficult and tests for balance and other automatic protective responses. All the assessment items can be used as a basis for treatment using this approach, inasmuch as they represent an advanced recovery progression. Bobath emphasizes the need for *daily* assessments because the state and general function of many patients may vary considerably from one treatment session to the next.

GAIT

The normal gait pattern is usually altered following a stroke, owing to a number of factors, including impairments in sensation, perception, mobility, and motor control. Some of the more common problems in hemiplegic gait and their possible causes are summarized in Table 17–6. Assessment of gait may be done using a subjective rating system and/or objective measures (see chapter 11). Individual rating systems may bias the examiner to iden-

Table 17–6 GAIT PROBLEMS COMMONLY SEEN FOLLOWING STROKE

Stance Phase

Trunk/pelvis
  Unawareness of affected side: poor proprioception
  Forward trunk:
    Weak hip extension
    Flexion contracture
Hip
  Poor hip position (typically adduction or flexion): poor proprioception
  Trendelenburg limp: weak abductors
  Scissoring: spastic adductors
Knee
  Flexion during forward progression
    Flexion contracture combined with weak knee extensors and/or poor proprioception
    Ankle dorsiflexion range past neutral, combined with weak hip and knee extension or poor proprioception at knee and ankle
    Weakness in extension pattern or in selective motion of hip and knee extensors and plantarflexors
    Slow contraction of knee extensors/knee remains flexed 20 to 30 degrees during forward progression
  Hyperextension during forward progression
    Plantarflexion contracture past 90 degrees
    Impaired proprioception: knee wobbles or snaps back into recurvatum
    Severe spasticity in quadriceps
    Weak knee extensors: compensatory locking of knee in hyperextension
Ankle/foot
  Equinus gait (heel does not touch the ground); spasticity or contractures of gastroc-soleus
  Varus foot (patient bears weight on the lateral surface of the foot): hyperactive or spastic anterior tibialis, post tibialis, toe flexors, and soleus
  Unequal step lengths: hammer toes caused by spastic toe flexors prevent the patient from stepping forward onto the opposite foot because of pain/weight bearing on flexed toes
  Lack of dorsiflexion range on the affected side (approximately 10 degrees is needed)

Swing Phase

Trunk/pelvis
  Insufficient forward pelvic rotation (pelvic retraction): weak abdominal muscles
  Inclination to sound side for foot clearance: weakness of flexor muscles
Hip
  Inadequate flexion
  Weak hip flexors, poor proprioception, spastic quadriceps, abdominal weakness (hip hikers), hip abductor weakness of opposite side
  Abnormal substitutions include circumduction, external rotation/adduction, backward leaning of trunk/dragging toes; momentum/uncontrolled swing
  Exaggerated hip flexion: strong flexor synergy
Knee
  Inadequate knee flexion
  Inadequate hip flexion and poor foot clearance; spastic quadriceps
  Exaggerated but delayed knee flexion: strong flexor synergy
  Inadequate knee extension at weight acceptance: spastic hamstrings or sustained total flexor pattern
  Weak knee extensors or poor proprioception
Ankle/foot
  Persistent equinus and/or equinovarus: plantarflexor contracture or spasticity; weak dorsiflexors, delayed contraction of dorsiflexors/toes drag during midswing
  Varus: spastic anterior tibialis, weak peroneals, and toe extensors
  Equinovarus: spasticity of post tibialis and/or gastroc-soleus
  Exaggerated dorsiflexion: strong flexor synergy pattern

From educational materials used at Rancho Los Amigos Medical Center, Downey, CA, and Spaulding Rehabilitation Hospital, Boston, MA.

tify problems in specific areas. For example, the Brunnstrom form assesses independence from synergies based on a normal recovery sequence. The Bobath assessment stresses qualitative control and balance reactions, and the Barthel index stresses functional independence and endurance.[71] The accuracy of rating scales for observational gait analysis is highly dependent upon the skill of the examiner and the consistency and endurance of the patient, which may be limited following a stroke.[73] Subjective systems can be improved by the addition of videotaping, which allows the permanent recording of gait patterns. The therapist can then replay the tape and reexamine gait deficits without tiring the patient. Depending upon the complexity of the equipment, the speeds can be adjusted and the action stopped at a point at which further investigation is warranted.[71,73] Objective systems (walkways, foot switches, grid systems) have been used to assess temporal gait factors accurately in neurologic patients.[74] Data obtained from both types of assessments can provide meaningful insight into the type and degree of gait deviations seen with hemiplegia as well as the specific cause of the problem.

FUNCTIONAL ACTIVITY LEVEL

At varying stages of recovery, bed mobility, transfers, self-care (feeding, hygiene, dressing), communication, and locomotion (wheelchair mobility, ambulation) should be assessed carefully (see chapter 12, Functional Assessment). Functional testing frequently serves as a measure of outcome of stroke rehabilitation and thus becomes the primary instrument in studies assessing treatment effectiveness. The Barthel Activities of Daily Living Scale appears as one of the more commonly used ADL scales in stroke studies.[57,75–78] Outcome studies using other functional scales also have been reported.[70–81]

Rehabilitation During Early Recovery (Stages 1 and 2)

Rehabilitation during the acute stage can begin as soon as the patient is medically stabilized, typically within 24 to 36 hours. General goals during the early recovery stages include those listed below.
1. Minimize the effects of tonal abnormalities.
2. Maintain normal ROM and prevent deformity.
3. Improve respiratory and oromotor function.
4. Mobilize the patient in early functional activities involving bed mobility, sitting, standing, and transfers.
5. Prevent deconditioning.
6. Promote awareness, active movement, and use of the hemiplegic side.
7. Improve trunk control and sitting balance.
8. Initiate self-care activities.

POSITIONING

Positioning of the patient can be instituted early even before full consciousness is regained. An effective positioning program seeks to prevent the development of postures that can lead to increased spasticity, contractures, or decubitus ulcers. Because most patients with

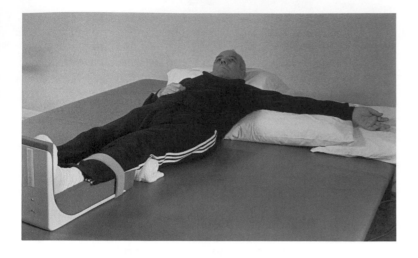

Figure 17–5. Positioning for the acute stroke patient: lying supine.

stroke develop spasticity, the program is aimed at positioning out of tone- and reflex-dependent postures.[21,82,83] The following postures are commonly assumed and should be *avoided:*

1. Lateral flexion of the head and trunk toward the affected side, with head rotation toward the unaffected side

2. Depression and retraction of the scapula, internal rotation and adduction of the arm, elbow flexion and forearm pronation, wrist and finger flexion

3. Retraction and elevation of the hip, with hip and knee extension and hip adduction; or hip and knee flexion with hip abduction. Ankle plantarflexion is common to both.

Prolonged positioning in the supine position may facilitate extensor tone through the action of the **symmetric tonic labyrinthine reflex (STLR),** whereas prolonged positioning of the head out of its normal midline position may facilitate tonal responses associated with the **asymmetric** and **symmetric tonic neck reflexes (ATNR, STNR).** Abnormal extensor responses of the foot and leg may be stimulated through the use of a footboard, which provides a contact stimulus to the ball of the foot and can activate a positive supporting response.

A positioning program should encourage maximum awareness of the hemiplegic side. This can be accomplished by positioning the patient's bed so that the main part of the room, door, and other objects of interest are on the patient's affected side. However, this may be contraindicated in cases of severe neglect or anosognosia, inasmuch as the arrangement may contribute to sensory deprivation and withdrawal. Attention should be directed to the hemiplegic shoulder, which may be flaccid at this stage of recovery. Correct positioning protects the shoulder from downward displacement by controlling scapula and arm position and providing approximation forces through the shoulder joint whenever possible. The patient should be placed on a turning schedule and rotated through a series of postures at least every 2 hours. Common positions that should be *promoted* include those described below.

Lying in Supine Position.   The supine position facilitates extensor tone and should be used with great care. The head and trunk should be flexed slightly toward the sound side to elongate muscles on the hemiplegic side. The arm rests on a supporting pillow with the scapula upwardly rotated and protracted. The elbow is extended with forearm supinated. The pelvis is protracted (on a small pillow or towel roll) with the leg in a neutral position relative to rotation. The affected knee is slightly flexed (Fig. 17–5).

Lying on the Sound Side.   When the patient is lying on the unaffected side, the trunk should be straight or slightly elongated. A small pillow under the rib cage can

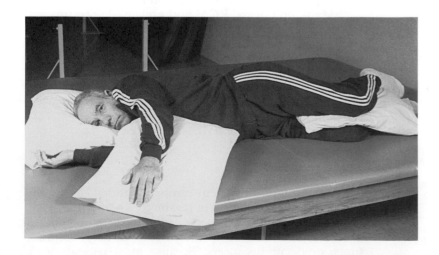

Figure 17–6. Positioning for the acute stroke patient: on the unaffected side.

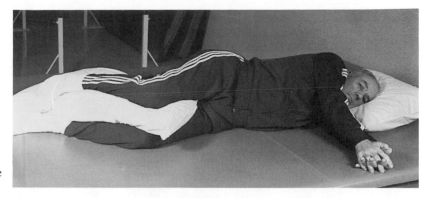

Figure 17–7. Positioning for the acute stroke patient: on the affected side.

be used to elongate the hemiplegic side. The affected shoulder is protracted and the arm is well forward on a supporting pillow with elbow extended and forearm in neutral or supinated position. The pelvis is protracted, and the affected leg is flexed slightly. The hip is maintained in neutral rotation supported by a pillow (Fig. 17–6).

Lying on the Affected Side. When the patient is lying on the affected side, the trunk should be straight. The affected shoulder is positioned well forward with the elbow extended and forearm supinated. The affected leg is positioned in hip extension and slight knee flexion. An alternate position is slight hip and knee flexion with pelvic protraction. The unaffected leg is positioned in flexion on a supporting pillow (Fig. 17–7).

Sitting (in Bed or in a Wheelchair). The patient should be upright with trunk and head in midline alignment. Symmetrical weight bearing on both buttocks should be encouraged. The legs should be in neutral with respect to rotation. When sitting in a chair, the hips and knees should be positioned in 90 degrees of flexion, each with a moderate amount of weight bearing on the posterior thighs. The hemiplegic arm should be supported on a pillow (bed) or wheelchair device (arm board or lap board) with the scapula in slight upward rotation and protraction, elbow slightly flexed and wrist and fingers in a functional open position. Weight bearing and compression through the shoulder joint can be achieved optimally through the use of a lap board. A small pillow behind the affected shoulder/scapula and/or pelvis can be used to help keep them protracted and to assist in maintaining trunk alignment.

RANGE OF MOTION

Range of motion (ROM) exercises during early recovery serve to maintain normal range in flaccid, nonfunctional limbs and mobility of the joint capsule. In the upper extremity, correct ROM techniques should include careful attention to scapular mobilization and upward rotation during shoulder elevation activities (Fig. 17–8). If normal scapulohumeral rhythm is not simulated, the patient is likely to experience shoulder pain or rotator cuff injury. Poor ROM technique also can lead to the development of shoulder-hand syndrome.[84] The use of overhead pulleys for self ROM is generally contraindicated for the above reasons. Tightness and swelling of the wrist and finger flexors is a common finding. Daily

ROM, elevation, massage, ice dipping, or compression wrapping may improve the status of the hand. Splinting in a functional position can be considered. Either dorsal or volar resting pan splints are commonly used, incorporating the forearm, wrist, and hand.[22,30,44]

During position changes, care must be taken not to pull on the arm or to let it hang unsupported, increasing the risk of a traction injury. Although slings may assist in supporting the flaccid shoulder mechanically during these activities, prolonged use may encourage the development of adhesive capsulitis and static posturing of the upper extremity. Contractures are likely to develop in shoulder adductors, internal rotators, and pronators when the arm is held close to the body. Slings also impair trunk mobility and balance reactions and body image. An alternate approach to the traditional sling is proposed by Bobath, who suggests a soft roll in the axilla or a humeral cuff maintained by a figure-eight harness. This device supports the upper arm and shoulder and allows free elbow extension (Fig. 17–9). Careful monitoring of circulation, lateral humeral displacement, and nerve compression is necessary when using this type of sling.[21,50,85]

As spasticity emerges, the use of a sling is generally contraindicated. Care must be taken to mobilize the arm

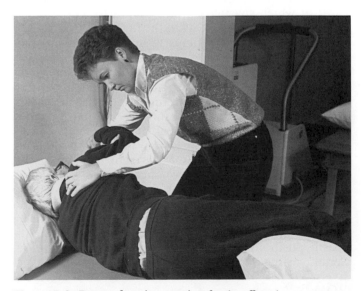

Figure 17–8. Range of motion exercises for the affected upper extremity. The therapist carefully mobilizes the scapula during arm elevation.

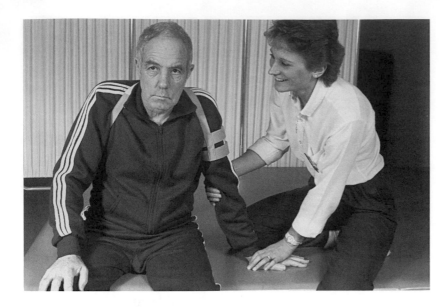

Figure 17–9. Sitting, with extended arm support. The patient is wearing a Bobath arm sling with humeral cuff to prevent subluxation of the shoulder. The therapist assists in stabilizing the elbow and fingers in extension.

and to prevent prolonged posturing, especially in internal rotation and adduction with pronation and wrist and finger flexion. Full ROM in shoulder elevation activities (stressing elongation of the pectoralis major and latissimus dorsi with scapular rotation) should be maintained. Exercise procedures should concentrate on the action of the serratus anterior, emphasizing scapula upward rotation. This can be accomplished in a number of postures (supine, sidelying, or sitting) using the techniques of placing and holding or modified hold-relax-active movement (HRAM) with the arm externally rotated and extended with an open hand. Alternately holding in a more flexed and abducted (in synergy) position may help initiate contraction of the serratus anterior. Weight bearing on the affected arm with joint approximation also will improve the stabilizing responses of the shoulder muscles and decrease spasticity. This can be accomplished by using an on-elbow posture (prone on elbows, sidelying, or sitting using a padded stool) or extended arm. Finger abduction splints or finger spreaders may be used in cases in which spasticity predominates to reduce flexor tone and to maintain ROM in the fingers.[19,21,85]

Inasmuch as most patients regain some use of their lower extremities early in recovery, ROM techniques should focus on specific areas of deficit. For many patients the foot and ankle remain nonfunctional and tone quickly progresses from initial flaccidity to spasticity, typically in the plantarflexors. Techniques designed to activate or to strengthen weak dorsiflexors may prove more successful in both lessening tone and promoting movement than passive ROM. Weight bearing (i.e., in modified plantigrade) or prolonged static positioning using adaptive equipment (i.e., tilt table or splints) also can inhibit hypertonus, gain motion, and facilitate activity in the foot evertors. Johnstone[82] suggests using orally inflated pressure splints to maintain limbs in antispasm positions and to promote sensory reeducation. Serial casting techniques also have been used effectively in cases of persistent spasticity and decreased ROM.[87–89]

MOTOR CONTROL TRAINING

Motor Relearning

Recovery from stroke is based upon the brain's capacity for reorganization and adaptation. An effective rehabilitation plan capitalizes on this potential and encourages movement patterns closely linked to normal performance. Function should be stressed at all times, and the function should be meaningful and important to the patient. Optimal motor learning can be ensured through attention to a number of factors. Demonstrate the desired task and the ideal performance speed. Manually guide the patient through the desired movement to assist in the understanding of the task and its components. Encourage early active participation of the affected side. Practicing the movements on the unaffected side first can yield important transfer effects to the affected side. Simultaneous practice of similar movements on both sides (bilateral activities) can improve learning while promoting integration of both sides of the body.

Visualization of the movement components (mental practice) can help some patients in initially organizing the movement. During early learning, visual guidance is extremely important. This can be facilitated by having the patient watch the movement. If the patient needs glasses, make sure they are worn during therapy. If field defects are present, the patient will need to compensate by turning the head fully to follow the movement. Use of a mirror can be an effective technique for many patients to improve visual feedback, especially during postural activities.

During later learning, proprioception becomes important for movement refinement. This can be encouraged by early and carefully reinforced weight bearing (approximation) on the affected side in upright activities. Additional proprioceptive inputs (manual contacts, tapping, stretch, tracking resistance, antigravity postures, or vibration) can be used to improve movement feedback and to stimulate the necessary movement components. The patient should be encouraged to "feel the movement" and to learn to recognize correct movement responses from incorrect ones. Assist the patient in learning to eliminate the unnecessary movement components. Extereoceptive inputs (light rubbing, brushing, ice application) may provide additional sources of information, particularly where distortions of proprioception exist. However, great care must be taken to avoid sensory bombardment or feedback dependence. This requires careful assessment during each treatment session. Pain and fatigue (either mental or physical) should be avoided, because each will be associated with a decrease in motor performance.

Careful attention to the learning environment also will yield important therapeutic gains. Reduce distractions and provide a consistent and comfortable place in which the patient can exercise. Provide clear, simple verbal instructions; don't overload the patient with excessive or wordy commands. Monitor performance carefully and give accurate feedback. Reinforce correct performance and intervene when movement errors become consistent. Organize the patient's schedule so that practice sessions are relatively short and frequent. Coordinate staff efforts to ensure that the patient is being asked to perform the task consistently with the same performance expectations. Progress and challenge the patient with a new task as soon as the previous one has been mastered. Encourage the patient to be self-sufficient and to develop goals and problem-solving abilities. Begin and end treatment sessions on a positive note, ensuring the patient success in treatment and continuing motivation. Finally, communicate, support, and encourage the patient; recovery from stroke is an extremely stressful experience and will challenge the abilities of both patient and therapist.[19,21,41,90-92]

Treatment Techniques

In the early stages of recovery the patient with hemiplegia will generally demonstrate impaired mobility in most activities and poor stability in upright postures. Thus early treatment should focus on improving function in the beginning stages of motor control. The loss of sensory and motor function on one side will present tremendous problems for the patient struggling to adjust, to relearn movement on the affected side, and to integrate movements using both sides of the body. Initial treatment strategies to improve mobility should include the use of passive or guided movement, quickly progressing to active assisted movement (AAM). The patient should be given only as much assistance as needed and should be encouraged to participate actively in movement. The technique of rhythmic initiation (RI) can be helpful when persistent motor learning problems exist or when spasticity emerges as an obstacle to mobility function.[85]

If the patient is hypotonic or unable to initiate movement, effective strategies may include direct facilitation of movement using a variety of different stimuli. Extereoceptive, proprioceptive, and reflex stimulation techniques have been used.[19,71,85,93-95] Some disagreement exists, however, over the type of movements that ought to be stimulated. Brunnstrom advocates the use of reflexes and synergies as a bridge to functional recovery

for those patients locked in an early recovery stage. Reflex reinforcement and practice of synergistic patterns may be helpful in a small group of select patients when used in moderation to regain early control of movement and to bridge the gap between flaccidity and early movement. These patterns are then quickly replaced by practice of isolated movement patterns out of synergy. Because reflexes are viewed as the basic language of the CNS and its motor programs,[96] and as intermediate steps in recovery from hemiplegia,[97-102] there is some theoretic base for this type of training. Its appropriateness, however, depends upon the individual characteristics of the patient. Patients who already demonstrate voluntary control of movement and spasticity (stage 2 recovery or beyond) would be inappropriate candidates for these techniques.

For the recovering patient, emphasis on synergistic movements can lead to an increase in spasticity, poor control of selective movement patterns, and widespread abnormal reactions (e.g., associated reactions, tonic reflexes). Tone reduction and the promotion of "normal" movement responses (out of synergy) are, therefore, important to emphasize in treatment through the use of appropriate handling techniques.[21] The approach to the patient in the middle and late stages of recovery is clear. Isolated movements out of synergy, using techniques that stress reciprocal action and reversals of movement (e.g., slow reversals, placing and holding, agonistic reversals) are emphasized.[19,21,85]

Very few attempts have been made to validate these approaches through controlled research trials.[78] Because patients have variable symptoms, rigid application of any one technique generally will yield unsatisfactory results. The therapist must consider the needs of each individual patient, select those procedures which have the greatest chance of success, and monitor patient responses carefully. It is clear that the patient with hypotonia may respond effectively to a broader range of techniques, whereas far greater care must be taken with the patient with hypotonia by selecting techniques that do not produce increased tone. See chapter 14 for a more complete discussion of strategies for improving motor control.

Techniques designed to improve stability (tonic holding, alternating isometrics, rhythmic stabilization, weight bearing, and approximation) can be used to develop early control in antigravity postures. Sitting with a stable, symmetrical posture is an important early treatment activity. Stability of the shoulder and arm can be encouraged by early weight bearing either with an extended arm (see Figure 17-9) or with the arm flexed and weight bearing in sidelying or on a stool. Resistance during stability work should be minimal and graded carefully, especially when spasticity is present.

Early Activities

Early bed activities should focus on rolling, sitting up, bridging, sitting balance, and transfers. Rolling and sitting up should be encouraged in both directions: onto the sound side to promote early independence and onto the affected side to encourage functional reintegration of

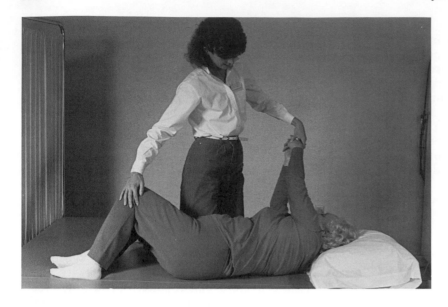

Figure 17-10. Early mobility activities: rolling onto the unaffected side. The patient pushes off with her affected left extremity and brings her hip forward. The therapist assists the movement and the inhibitory pattern (prayer position) of the upper extremities.

the hemiplegic side. Extremity movement patterns can facilitate improved rolling through momentum and the fostering of segmental trunk patterns. With both hands clasped together in a prayer position, the patient can be actively assisted by flexing and rotating the upper trunk into a sidelying on-elbow posture. In addition to promoting early weight bearing on the hemiplegic shoulder and hip, this posture also elongates the lateral trunk flexors, which may be spastic. The patient can then be assisted in moving the legs over the edge of the bed and pushing up to a full sitting position using both arms. The lower extremity (LE) can assist in rolling by pushing off from a flexed and adducted, hooklying, position (Fig. 17-10). This encourages an important advanced limb pattern needed for gait, hip extension with knee flexion, and also facilitates early weight bearing in the supine position.[21] An alternate method involves using a proprioceptive neuromuscular facilitation (PNF) chopping pattern that also encourages upper trunk rotation and flexion with upper extremity (UE) diagonal movement. The

patient can be taught to use the leg to assist by pulling the hip and knee up and across the body in an LE D_1 flexion pattern (flexion, adduction, external rotation).[85,103]

Bridging activities develop control in important functional tasks, including the use of a bedpan and initial bed mobility in scooting. They also develop pelvic control, advanced limb control (hip extension with knee flexion and foot eversion) and early LE weight bearing (Fig. 17-11). Bridging activities should include assisted and independent assumption of the posture, holding in the posture, and moving in the posture (side to side). If the affected lower extremity is unable to hold in a hooklying position, the therapist will need to assist by stabilizing the foot during the bridge activity.

Early upright activities should include sitting and sit-to-stand activities and transfers to a chair or wheelchair. Postural responses can be developed through a progression of techniques that promote first trunk stability, controlled mobility (rocking or weight shifts), and finally balance reactions. The unstable patient can be assisted in

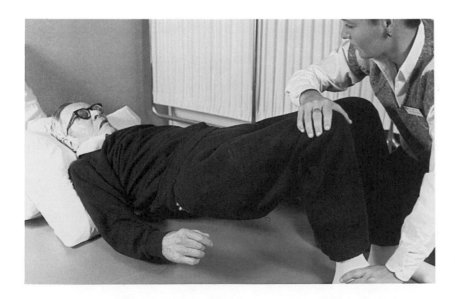

Figure 17-11. Early mobility activities: bridging. The patient combines hip extension with knee flexion. The therapist assists in stabilizing the affected leg in flexion.

maintaining the sitting posture by using the arm for support. If only one arm is needed, then the affected arm should be used. Rocking movements should incorporate leaning forward, backward, side-to-side weight shifts, trunk rotation, and diagonal movement and may be combined with UE shoulder ROM using an arms-cradled position. Once this control is achieved, the patient is ready to practice sitting balance reactions in response to alterations in position. The therapist removes support and gently displaces the patient. Normal adjustments include responses in the trunk (rotation and/or lateral flexion) and counterbalancing movements of the extremities. Patients with stroke typically exhibit delayed, incomplete, or absent postural responses in response to such stimuli. The therapist will need to proceed slowly, to give the patient enough time to respond, to provide support when needed, and gradually to increase both the range and the speed of the stimulation to tolerance. Having the patient's feet in contact with the floor will assist balance, overall sense of security, and provide lower extremity weight bearing in the sitting position.

During early transfers, staff often emphasize the sound side by placing the chair to that side and having the patient stand and pivot a quarter turn on the unaffected leg before sitting down. Although this promotes early and safe independence in transfers, this compensatory technique neglects the affected side and makes subsequent training more difficult. Having the patient transfer to the hemiplegic side encourages active use of that side and promotes postural reintegration (Fig. 17–12). When

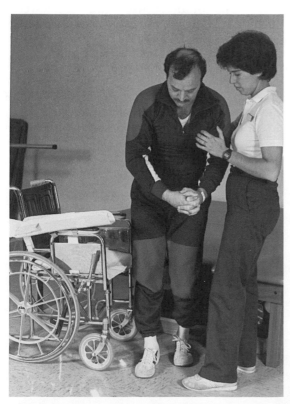

Figure 17–12. Transferring to the affected side. The patient learns to control standing up and pivoting with the affected leg leading. The therapist assists in balance.

transferring to the affected side, the patient's affected arm can be stabilized in extension and external rotation against the therapist's body. Alternately, the patient's arm (hands in prayer position) can be placed on the therapist's shoulders. The therapist can then assist in the forward weight shift by using manual contacts either at the upper trunk or pelvis. The affected leg may be stabilized by exerting a counterforce on the patient's knee with the therapist's knee, if needed.[21]

Oromotor Activities

The goals of early oromotor training include normalizing respiratory, facial, swallowing, and chewing functions. Patients on prolonged bedrest with marked deconditioning or with marked paralysis affecting the trunk musculature may experience impaired or shallow breathing patterns. Improved chest expansion can be achieved by effective use of manual contacts, resistance, and stretch to various chest wall segments. Several postures can be used, including supine, sidelying, sidelying on elbow, and sitting. Diaphragmatic, basal, and lateral costal expansion should be stressed. A prespeech activity consists of having the patient maintain a vocal expression (e.g., "ah") during the entire expiratory phase, inasmuch as poor breath control often contributes to soft or vacillating production of sounds.[41] Respiratory activities should be combined with other movement patterns whenever possible (e.g., inspiration with reverse chopping and expiration with chopping). During any sustained activity (isometric holding), breath control should be emphasized and the Valsalva maneuver always avoided. This is especially important in patients with documented concomitant cardiovascular problems.

Facial movements should be encouraged and facilitated whenever necessary. This may include the use of stretch, resistance, or quick ice to stimulate the desired function. Emphasis should be placed on the affected muscles in order to regain a balance of function. The use of a mirror may be helpful in treatment, provided the patient does not have visuospatial dysfunction.

Problems in chewing (mastication) and swallowing (deglutition) should receive early attention in therapy. An upright sitting posture with the head stabilized and slightly flexed is mandatory to begin oromotor training. This position reduces the changes of aspiration and promotes normal swallowing through appropriate alignment of the necessary structures. Additional components necessary for successful function include jaw opening and closure, lip closure, and tongue control. Normal sensation, reflex activity (gag, sucking, and swallowing), and control of breathing are also essential to normal oromotor function. The goals of oromotor retraining are to (1) improve strength, coordination, and range of oral musculature; (2) promote normal feeding through graduated resumption of activities; and (3) promote volitional control through effective verbal coaching. Facilitation techniques (quick ice, quick stretch, resistance) can be used to stimulate the muscles responsible for jaw opening and closing. Jaw movements can be stimulated by vibrating or pressing above the upper lip for closure and under the lower lip for opening. Jaw closure can be assisted when necessary during feeding by holding the jaw firmly closed using a jaw control technique (e.g., thumb on jaw line, index finger between lower lip and chin and middle finger under chin applying firm pressure). Tongue movements (forward, lateral, or diagonal) can be resisted manually (using a sterile gauze or glove to cover finger) or with a moist tongue depressor. Firm pressure on the front of the tongue can be used to stimulate the posterior elevation of the tongue necessary for swallowing. Sucking control and saliva production can be stimulated using small amounts of ice water or an ice cube. The therapist also can apply deep pressure on the neck above the thyroid notch to stimulate sucking. Resisted sucking can be promoted using a straw and very thick liquids (slushes, shakes) or by holding the open end of the straw against your finger. As sucking control proceeds, thinner liquids can be substituted. Patients with a hypoactive gag reflex may be stimulated briefly with a cotton swab to develop this response. At first food should be semimoist (e.g., pureed food, pasta, boiled chicken), progressing to foods rich in taste, smell, and texture, which assist in facilitating the swallowing reflex. Additional considerations for successful feeding include providing an environment free from distraction. The patient's full attention and cortical control should be directed to the task at hand, using appropriate verbal cues.[103–105]

Rehabilitation During Middle Recovery (Stages 3 and 4)

Many treatment activities begun during early recovery are continued throughout the course of the patient's rehabilitation. Some are modified appropriately to challenge and to progress the patient to optimal recovery. During the middle stages, the patient is out of bed and involved in a variety of activities and therapies. It is important to monitor cardiorespiratory endurance carefully and to avoid overtiring the patient. Because synergies and spasticity reach a peak during this period, isolated (out-of-synergy) movement patterns and tone

reduction techniques become an important part of a treatment program. General goals include those listed below.

1. Minimize the effects of spasticity and promote a balance of antagonists.
2. Maintain normal ROM and prevent deformity.
3. Promote functional use and reintegration of the hemiplegic side and selective movement control out of synergy.
4. Improve postural control and independent balance.
5. Improve cardiorespiratory endurance.
6. Develop independence in bed mobility and transfers.
7. Develop wheelchair independence and/or ambulation with assistive devices as necessary.
8. Develop independence in self-care and ADL with assistive devices as necessary.

TONE REDUCTION

Patients who demonstrate strong spasticity typically seen during this phase of recovery may benefit from a number of techniques designed to modify or to reduce tone. These include positioning out of reflex-dependent postures, reflex-inhibiting movement patterns which encourage movement of the weak and hypotonic antagonists, and avoiding excess effort and heavy resistance.[21,106] Rhythmic rotation of the limbs with slow steady passive movement out of the spastic pattern may also serve to decrease tone while providing ROM exercises to the spastic limb. A reduction in truncal tone can be promoted through techniques of rhythmic initiation or slow reversals combined with upper and lower trunk rotation (Fig. 17–13). Postures of sidelying, sitting, or hooklying are frequently used. Proprioceptive neuromuscular facilitation extremity or trunk patterns (chopping or lifting), which emphasize diagonal and rotational movements, combined with techniques designed to reduce tone (e.g., rhythmic initiation) may be helpful.[85] Local facilitation techniques (muscle tapping, vibration) may prove successful in stimulating weak antagonists

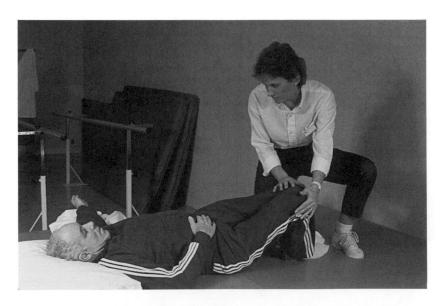

Figure 17–13. Inhibition of truncal tone through lower trunk rotation. The therapist uses the technique of rhythmic initiation to increase mobility.

and reducing spasticity in some patients. However, as Bobath points out, reciprocal relationships are not always normal, particularly in the presence of strong spasticity. Therefore, these techniques may be ineffective, serving to increase rather than to decrease tone in the spastic muscles.[21] Exercise procedures that take advantage of prolonged pressure on long tendons and the resultant inhibition are also effective in reducing tone. A common exercise for patients involves weight bearing on an extended, abducted, and externally rotated arm with the wrist and fingers extended (see Figure 17–9). Slow rocking movements add to the inhibitory effect on the spastic wrist and finger flexors. Spasticity in the quadriceps can be similarly inhibited through weight bearing in a kneeling or quadruped position. Orally inflated pressure splints also have been used effectively to position limbs and to provide prolonged stretch and inhibition to spastic muscles.[107]

Techniques that produce a generalized reduction in tone by decreasing CNS arousal mechanisms include slow stroking down the posterior primary rami and soothing verbal commands.[108,109] Gentle rocking (sidelying, rolling, rocking chair) works through the vestibular system to produce a generalized reduction in tone.[110]

Prolonged icing using ice wraps, ice packs, or ice massage may decrease spasticity by slowing conduction in nerves and muscles and decreasing muscle spindle activity. Once tone is reduced, the therapist should emphasize active movement out of the positions of spasticity. This can enhance the inhibitory effects and produce a longer lasting result.[111–113]

MOTOR CONTROL TRAINING

General Considerations

Training should focus on improving motor control by stressing selective (out-of-synergy) movement patterns. Movement combinations that allow the completion of feeding, dressing, gait, or other functional tasks should be emphasized. Synergy movements are inappropriate to practice during this stage of recovery and should not be permitted. Patients frequently respond to movement commands with gross or mass patterns of movement. The initiation of the proper components and the refinement of isolated control require a great deal of mental concentration and volitional control. Inhibition of unwanted activity is crucial to the patient's success.[114] Movements that are performed too quickly or too strongly will be ineffective in producing the control needed. Initially the therapist should select postures that assist the motion and/or reduce tone and reflex interference. Reflex-inhibiting-patterns are specifically designed with this focus in mind.[21] As control develops, postures can be progressed to more difficult ones that challenge developing control. Resistance to movement should be minimal.[115] Often the resistance of gravity or slight manual resistance is enough to initiate or to facilitate the correct muscular responses. Strengthening is *not* an appropriate goal during this stage of training owing to the presence of spasticity. Normal function implies a tremendous variability in movement performance. Muscles

need to be activated in a variety of patterns and using different types of contraction patterns. Eccentric contractions are generally easier to perform than concentric (more tension can be generated with decreased metabolic cost).[116] Isometric contractions (holding in mid or shortened ranges) are also important because increased recruitment of static gamma motoneurons occurs, providing additional facilitation for weak or hypotonic muscles. Thus the clinician should stress holding or letting-go movements before shortening ones. Weak muscles (antagonistic to strong spastic ones) should be activated first in unidirectional patterns followed by activities that stress reciprocal movements. This emphasis on balanced interaction of both agonists and antagonists is crucial for normal coordination and effective function.[19,21,41,103]

Trunk/Postural Control

Activities begun during early training that emphasize weight bearing and trunk control during movement transitions and upright postures should be continued and progressed. Sitting trunk control can be challenged by the addition of static-dynamic activities (e.g., PNF chopping or lifting patterns). Sit-to-stand transitions should be practiced, emphasizing symmetrical weight bearing and controlled responses of the hemiplegic side. Trunk rotation can be increased by having the patient stand up and shift the pelvis to one side or the other before sitting down. By using a platform mat for this activity, the patient can move all the way around the mat first in one direction, then in the other. Arms should be clasped and held straight ahead in order to prevent a stiff, total trunk response during this activity[21] (Fig. 17–14). Modified plantigrade is also an ideal posture to practice lower trunk control first in symmetrical standing, then in stride position. Techniques of rhythmic initiation or slow reversals are ideal to assist the patient.[85,103,117]

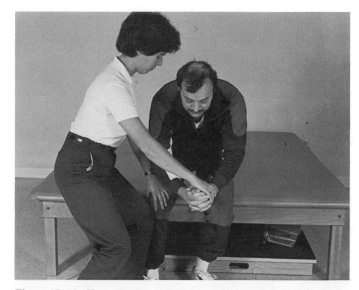

Figure 17–14. Sit-to-stand movement transitions. The therapist assists the patient in straightening his knee while he brings his center of gravity forward.

Upper Extremity Control

Initial mobility of the upper extremity can be achieved by focusing first on scapular motions. Inasmuch as the typical spastic pattern is one of retraction and fixation, protraction should be emphasized. This is typically performed in a sidelying or supine position with the patient's arm supported in flexion, adduction, external rotation with elbow extension. The arm is mobilized forward and the patient is asked to hold this position. If holding is successful, then eccentric movements and slow reversals are attempted (using techniques of hold-after positioning, push-pull, modified hold-relax-active movement, or slow reversals). Once initial control is achieved, the posture can be altered to a more challenging one (e.g., sitting) and more active control of shoulder and elbow components added through increasing range (e.g., PNF D_1 thrust pattern; arm raising to forward or side horizontal, arm overhead).

Movements that should be stressed include hand to mouth and hand to opposite shoulder, inasmuch as they have important functional implications in feeding and dressing. Elbow extension movements combined with shoulder abduction or flexion also should be stressed to counteract the effects of the dominant flexion synergy. This can be achieved through extension (weight-bearing) activities performed in sitting, modified plantigrade (Fig. 17–15), or standing. The quadruped posture provides the greatest challenge for upper extremity weight bearing but may be too difficult for many patients. Control should be progressed from initial stability or holding in the posture to controlled mobility using rocking movements.

Training of hand function should emphasize forearm, wrist, and finger movements independent of shoulder and elbow motions. Excessive shoulder adduction, elbow flexion, pronation, and finger flexion are the typical spastic patterns which must be counteracted. Voluntary release is generally much more difficult to achieve than voluntary grasp, and inhibitory techniques may be necessary before extension movements are successful. Prehension patterns should be practiced and manipulation of common objects (pencil, fork, toothbrush) attempted. The therapist needs to observe these movements carefully and to assist the patient in eliminating those aspects of performance which interfere with effective control.

Lower Extremity Control

Training of the lower extremity during this phase of recovery essentially prepares the patient for ambulation. Pregait mat activities should concentrate on working muscles in the appropriate combinations needed for gait. For example, hip and knee extensors need to be activated with abductors and dorsiflexors for early stance. Strong synergy combinations also need to be broken up (e.g., hip and knee extension). A variety of activities can be used, including bridging, supine-knee flexion/hip extension over the side of the mat, or standing/modified prone, knee flexion. Hip adduction should be stressed during flexion movements of the hip and knee, and abduction should be stressed during extension movements (e.g., supine, PNF D_1 lower extremity diagonal; sitting—crossing and uncrossing the hemiplegic leg). Pelvic control is important and can be promoted through lower trunk rotation activities that emphasize forward pelvic rotation (protraction) in a number of postures; for example, sidelying, modified hooklying with the hemiplegic leg pushing off (see Fig. 17–10), kneeling, or standing.

An effective progression increases the challenge to the patient gradually by modifying postures until synergy influence is completely lacking; for example, hip abduction can be first performed in hooklying, supine, sidelying, modified plantigrade, then standing. Contraction patterns should also be varied. Thus, dorsiflexors can be activated first in a sitting posture using a holding contraction, followed by an eccentric letting go, and finally a shortening response. This simulates the functional expectations of the normal gait cycle as the foot goes from swing phase through stance.

Voluntary control of eversion is often difficult to achieve because these muscles do not function in either synergy. The application of stretch and resistance to these muscles during a pattern that activates dorsiflexors may be effective in initiating a response.[19] Postural responses (e.g., hooklying, lower trunk rotation, standing-balance responses) also may elicit these muscles automatically, even though voluntary control (upon command) is lacking. Control of knee function is also problematic. Reciprocal action (smooth reversals of flexion and extension movements) should be stressed early, beginning first in sitting, hooklying, prone, modified plantigrade, or supported standing (Fig. 17–16) and progressing to standing and walking. Dissociation of arm movements during lower extremity training is also an important consideration and may be achieved through the use of prepositioning and voluntary control (e.g., having the patient hold clasped hands together overhead in a "prayer position" during a lower extremity activity).[21]

Figure 17–15. Early weight bearing in modified plantigrade with extended arms. The therapist assists elbow and finger extension.

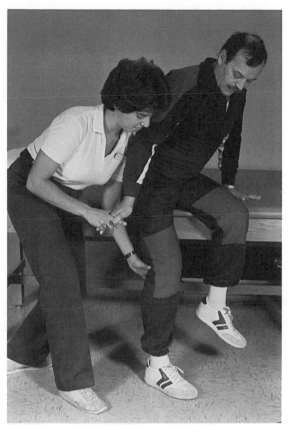

Figure 17-16. Early weight bearing on the affected leg. The therapist assists controlled, small-range flexion and extension movements of the knee. The affected arm is maintained in an inhibitory pattern.

Balance-Ambulation Training

Control of balance can be developed by progressing the patient through a series of upright postures, including sitting, quadruped, kneeling (Fig. 17-17), modified kneeling (hemiplegic knee flexed and placed on platform mat), or standing (symmetrical and in stride positions). Displacement of the patient's center of gravity outside of the

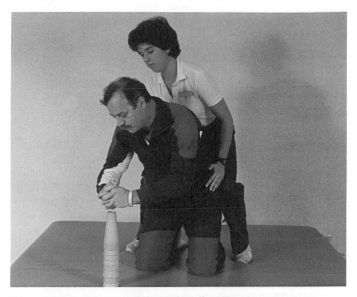

Figure 17-17. Balance training in kneeling. The therapist uses protective guarding at the hips while the patient reaches over and touches the stacked cones.

base of support should be controlled and gradual with emphasis on normal responses of trunk (rotation and lateral flexion). Supported standing can be achieved in the parallel bars, in modified plantigrade, or over a large gymnastic ball (Fig. 17-18). Weight shifting and bearing full weight on the hemiplegic side should precede unweighting and stepping movements of the sound side. Crossed standing and walking (e.g., braiding) also can be used to stimulate balance responses.

Walking should emphasize controlled movements performed at average speeds. Pelvic-shoulder rhythm (trunk counterrotation) can be assisted by effective use of the therapist's manual contacts on the patient's pelvis. Persistent posturing of the upper extremity in flexion and adduction during gait can be controlled through inhibitory techniques aimed at positioning the hemiplegic arm in extension and abduction with the hand open (Fig. 17-

Figure 17-18. Balance training in supported standing using a large gymnastic ball. One therapist stimulates mediolateral balance reactions while the other therapist supports and assists the patient.

Figure 17–19. Assisted ambulation. The therapist provides support on the patient's affected side. The arm is maintained in elevation, extension and abduction to inhibit the typical flexed and adducted arm posture.

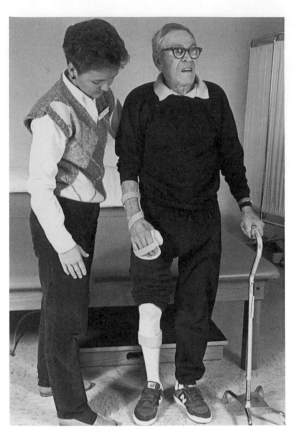

Figure 17–20. Assisted ambulation using a plastic ankle-foot orthosis and quad cane.

19). Movement deficiencies should be identified, and the patient should be instructed to correct faulty responses. Initially this may require exaggerating the deficiencies (e.g., trunk rotation or knee flexion) and practicing them first in standing or stepping and then during gait until they become a consistent part of the patient's gait pattern. Early walking before balance and normal control is obtained may restore motivation but increases the risk of developing persistent and faulty habits. Although ambulation aids such as quad canes allow for early mobilization, they may distort balance, promote an excessive weight shift onto the unaffected side, and create poor habits. The therapist must balance the advantages and disadvantages of each before deciding on an effective course of action. Often the patient who is recovering more quickly and has a better prognosis for normal function may benefit from delayed ambulation and use of assistive devices.

Orthoses are required when persistent problems prevent safe ambulation. Prescription will depend upon the unique problems each patient presents. The pattern of weakness and mediolateral instability at the ankle, and the extent and severity of spasticity and sensory deficits of the limb, are the major factors considered when prescribing an orthosis. However, other factors such as hemispheric laterality (persistent cognitive and perceptual disturbances) or incoordination may influence the type of device prescribed. Temporary devices (e.g., dor-

siflexion assists) may be used during the early stages while recovery is proceeding to allow the patient to practice standing, weight shifting, and early walking in the parallel bars. Permanent devices are prescribed once the patient's status is relatively stable (generally between 8 and 12 weeks). Extensive bracing using a knee-ankle-foot orthosis (KAFO) is rarely indicated or successful. Ankle-foot orthoses (AFO) such as a conventional double-bar AFO with stops or plastic devices (polypropylene AFO; plastic spiral AFO; solid ankle AFO) are commonly prescribed to control deficient knee and ankle/foot function (Fig. 17–20). See chapter 27 for a more complete description of these and other devices. Therapists must frequently reassess the patient's motor function and the need for the orthosis, inasmuch as additional recovery may not warrant continued use of the device.[118]

Rehabilitation During Late Recovery (Stages 5 and 6)

During the advanced recovery stages, the patient has regained many or most of the movements initially lost. Tone is approaching normal. Timing and coordination are the essential deficits noted during this time. Training should focus on refinement of control of many of the activities begun during the course of rehabilitation. Because patients can plateau at any stage of recovery, many will not reach this level of recovery. General goals are outlined below.

1. Promote skill levels of motor control
   a. Normal timing and coordination of movement patterns
   b. Normal gait, including elevation and community activities
   c. Normal manipulation and dexterity, including independence in self-care and ADL
2. Promote normal cardiorespiratory endurance

MOTOR CONTROL TRAINING

Coordinated movement can be promoted using advanced movement patterns. For example, PNF patterns might be selected on the basis of individual patient deficiencies (e.g., if incomplete knee flexion with hip extension was present, the therapist might select D_1 extension—extension, abduction, internal rotation—with the knee flexing). Eventually all movement combinations or variations should be practiced. Appropriate techniques might include timing for emphasis or repeated contractions if components are deficient, or slow reversals/slow reversal-hold with an emphasis on normal timing to promote balanced control. Mat activities should focus on controlled mobility or skill level activities. For example, agonistic reversals are important in developing the eccentric control necessary for normal function. These are typically practiced in bridging, stand-to-sit or in kneeling-to-heel-sitting transitions. Rocking or weight shifting can be practiced in advanced or more difficult postures such as half kneeling. Trunk counterrotation is an extremely difficult skill level activity and can be promoted first in sidelying then standing, using techniques of rhythmic initiation or slow reversals.[85,103]

BALANCE-AMBULATION TRAINING

Balance training is important during late recovery. The patient continually should be challenged with weight-bearing and balance reactions that emphasize normal movements and reintegration of the hemiplegic side. Stepping activities with the sound foot, crossed standing, and protective extension reactions of both upper and lower extremities should be facilitated by challenging balance. Both the range and the speed of these reactions should be tested and increased. Engaging the patient in an activity like ball throwing also challenges balance and stimulates the patient to respond automatically. Ball gymnastics (e.g., patient sitting on a gymnastic ball and displacing the patient's center of gravity in all directions) may prove helpful. Advanced gait training should continue to emphasize selective movement control of the trunk and extremities and should promote normal timing. Gait can be practiced forward, backward, sideward, and in a crossed pattern (braiding). Elevation activities (stair climbing—step over step; over and around obstacles) and community activities (on different terrains) should be practiced. Rhythm can be improved through the use of a resisted progression technique, stimulating music, or a treadmill. At this point in recovery the patient should be able to monitor his or her own performance and to recognize and to initiate corrective actions. The patient should be able to vary the speed of walking and to maintain performance while cognitively engaged in other activities such as carrying on a conversation. The patient should also feel confident walking in all types of situations likely to be encountered in daily life.

BIOFEEDBACK

Electromyographic (EMG) feedback may be used to improve motor function in patients with hemiplegia during the middle or late recovery stages. This technique allows patients to alter motor unit activity based upon audio and visual feedback information. Thus firing frequency can be decreased in spastic muscles or increased along with recruitment of additional motor units in weak, hypoactive muscles (see chapter 29 for a more complete description of this topic). Patients in the chronic stage (typically defined as 1 year post stroke) or patients in late recovery for whom spontaneous recovery is more or less complete (4 to 6 months post stroke) have demonstrated favorable results that may be attributed to biofeedback. Benefits have been demonstrated in terms of ROM, motor control, function, and relaxation. Most studies indicate that its greatest effectiveness is achieved when used as an adjunctive treatment in a combined therapeutic approach.[119,120] Successful biofeedback applications to the trunk and lower extremity have focused on improving posture and balanced control of ankle and knee muscles.[121,122] Program considerations include beginning training in the more dependent postures such as supine or sitting and gradually progressing to more upright postures. Dynamic control using feedback during gait also should be emphasized. Electromyographic or electrogoniometric information can improve control of the limb and eliminate problematic gait deviations such as genu recurvatum or limited dorsiflexion in swing.[123] Limb load devices that provide feedback about the amount of loading or weight bearing on the hemiplegic limb also have been effective in improving the timing of the gait cycle. Patients receiving this training demonstrate more normal weight-bearing and stance times on their affected limb and increased swing times on their unaffected limb.[124] Monitoring devices that assess loading on assistive devices (e.g., a straight aluminum cane fitted with a strain gauge) also have been described.[125]

Upper extremity applications have focused on relaxation of spastic muscles such as pectoralis major, biceps, or wrist and finger flexors. Significant improvements in tone and other neuromuscular measures have been noted. The greatest functional gains were achieved in patients with superior initial abilities. Initial voluntary finger extension and minimal hyperactivity in muscles typically spastic were associated with the largest gains following upper extremity biofeedback training.[126-128]

ISOKINETICS

Isokinetic devices such as the Kinetron may be used to improve the timing of rapid alternating movements of the lower extremities required for gait. Both lower

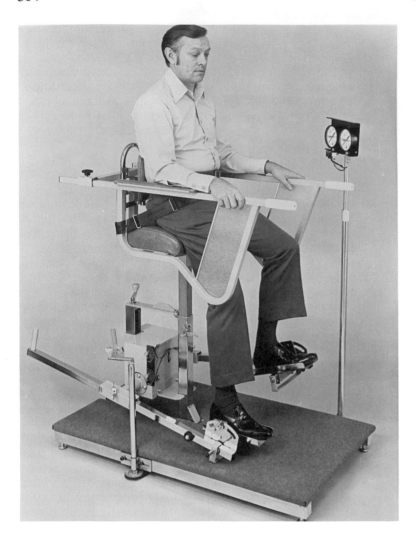

Figure 17–21. Isokinetic training. (From Rosenthal, M, et al: *Rehabilitation of the Head-Injured Adult.* FA Davis, 1983, p 323 with permission.)

extremities pedal at predetermined speeds. The therapist initially should use slow speeds and progress to more rapid speeds as control improves. If consistency in maintaining a steady rhythm is problematic, a metronome can be used to pace the activity. Gradually the patient's position should be modified to approach a more upright standing position (Fig. 17–21). Pelvic rotation can then be practiced in this position in combination with the reciprocal movements of the legs to stimulate normal walking. A rate of movement approaching 1 cycle per second which is within normal parameters for heel-strike to heel-strike should be the desired end point of treatment.[129]

CARDIORESPIRATORY ACTIVITIES

Patients who have had a stroke demonstrate decreased levels of physical conditioning following periods of prolonged immobility and reduced activity. The energy costs to complete many of the functional tasks in their daily lives may be higher because of the abnormal ways in which they perform these activities.[130,131] Many patients also demonstrate concomitant cardiovascular disease and may be recovering from acute cardiac events at the same time.[3] All these patients can benefit from an organized approach to improving cardiovascular fitness as part of their rehabilitation program.[132] Considerations

for prescription should be based upon the individual abilities and interests of the patient. Cycle ergometry or a walking program (treadmill, gym, home) can be expected to produce measureable results when based upon appropriate prescriptive elements. These include (1) a frequency of three to five days a week; (2) an intensity of 60 to 70 percent of maximum HR (HRmax), or 40 to 60 percent of VO$_2$max; and (3) a duration of 15 to 60 minutes, depending upon the intensity of the activity.[133] Conditioning programs for patients with hemiplegia can yield significant improvements in physical fitness, functional status, and self-concept.[134]

Patient and Family Education

Stroke represents a major health crisis for many patients and their families. Ignorance about the cause of illness or the recovery process and misconceptions concerning the rehabilitation program and potential outcome can negatively influence coping responses. Frequently the problems seem unmanageable and overwhelming for the family, especially when faced with alterations in the patient's behavior, cognition, and emotion. Patients may feel depressed, isolated, irritable, or demanding. Families often demonstrate reactions including initial relief and hope for full recovery, followed by feelings of entrapment, depression, anger, or guilt when complete recovery does not occur. These changes and feelings can strain even the best of relationships.[36] Psychologic, sexual, leisure, and vocational counseling can assist in improving the overall quality of life and should be implemented as needed. Therapists can often have a dramatic influence on this situation because of the high frequency of contact and often close relationships which develop with patients and their families. Important guidelines to follow when planning interactions and educational sessions with patients and their families are provided below.

1. Give accurate, factual information; counsel family members about the patient's capabilities and limitations; *avoid* predictions that categorically define expected function or future recovery.

2. Structure interventions carefully, giving only as much information as the patient or family needs or can assimilate; be consistent and repeat information.

3. Provide a forum for open discussion and communication.

4. Be supportive and sensitive and maintain a hopeful manner.

5. Assist patients and families in confronting alternatives and developing problem-solving abilities.

6. Motivate and provide positive reinforcement in therapy; enhance patient satisfaction and self-esteem.

7. Refer to support and self-help groups such as the American Heart Association Stroke Clubs.[36,135]

Discharge Planning

Family members should regularly participate in therapy sessions to learn proper techniques and exercises designed to support the patient's independence. Home visits should be made prior to discharge to assess physical structure and accessibility. Potential problems can be identified and corrective measures initiated. Home adaptions, assistive devices, and supportive services should be in place before the patient is discharged home. Several trial stays may be helpful in smoothing the transition from rehabilitation center to home. Patients with residual stroke deficits who will be receiving outpatient or home therapy should be given all the necessary information concerning these services. Long-term follow-up at regularly scheduled intervals should be initiated in order to maintain a patient at the highest possible level.

Rehabilitation Outcome

Rehabilitation programs for patients who have had strokes have been shown to improve functional outcome and to allow a significant percentage of patients to return home. In one study of 248 patients, 80 percent of patients with severe stroke deficits were able to return home after a rehabilitation stay averaging 43 days. Most of these patients were ambulatory (85 percent) and able to perform their own self-care without assistance (56 percent).[136] Health care costs are also minimized when compared with long-term placement in hospitals or nursing homes.[136–138]

Stroke outcome studies have not always yielded consistent results, however. Some studies have found a positive relationship between rehabilitation and functional gains,[139–141] whereas others found no treatment effects, with gains primarily attributed to spontaneous recovery.[84,142,143] Moreover, studies attempting to delineate differences between facilitation and traditional exercise approaches have failed to yield any significant differences.[78,144] Major difficulties in these and other studies appear to be related to subject selection and confounding maturation (recovery)/treatment effects.[145]

Most patients are able to maintain their independent living status following discharge. Severity of physical disability, age, and persistent emotional problems (anxiety and depression) are the primary factors related to quality of life and continued success in independent living. Other key factors identified include marital status (a helpful spouse), home barriers, and transportation problems.[58,59]

Effective rehabilitation should take advantage of spontaneous recovery. Rehabilitation also seeks to prevent or to lessen complications and to provide an effective environment for learning. The major emphasis should be on improving function and behavior.[146] From a practical standpoint, patients with strokes present a tremendous challenge for clinicians because of their diffuse problems affecting widespread areas of function.

SUMMARY

Stroke can result from a number of different vascular events which interrupt cerebral circulation and impair brain function. These include cerebral thrombosis, emboli, or hemorrhage. The location and size of the ischemic process, the nature and functions of the structures involved, and the availability of collateral blood flow all influence the symptomatology that evolves. For many patients, stroke represents a major cause of disability with diffuse problems affecting widespread areas of function. From a practical standpoint, patients with strokes present a tremendous challenge for clinicians. Effective rehabilitation should take advantage of spontaneous recovery. Rehabilitation also seeks to prevent or to lessen complications and to provide an effective environment for learning. The major emphasis should be on improving function and behavior.

QUESTIONS FOR REVIEW

1. Differentiate between occlusive lesions in each of the major cerebral arteries in terms of the symptoms produced. What are the hemispheric differences?

2. What are the major causes of stroke? Define and explain each.

3. What diagnostic measures are used to confirm stroke?

4. Describe the normal recovery process in stroke. What are the typical stages? Prognosis?

5. What are the major sensory, motor, language, perceptual, and mental deficits produced with stroke?

6. Describe the dynamics and causative factors of shoulder dysfunction in hemiplegia. How should this knowledge influence your assessment and treatment?

7. Outline the medical management of the patient with stroke.

8. A mental status examination should include what essential components?

9. Assessment of communication ability poses what problems for the therapist? How should they be assessed? How should they be managed during treatment?

10. Differentiate between common hemiplegic assessments, including those of Brunnstrom and Bobath.

11. What are the key strategies in positioning the patient with stroke during the acute stage?

12. Identify and describe common orthotic devices used in stroke rehabilitation. What are the major indications and contraindications for each?

13. Identify critical motor learning strategies for treating the patient with stroke.

14. List four activities that could be used in the early phases of rehabilitation to mobilize the patient.

15. Oromotor training should focus upon key functions. What are they?

16. Describe three strategies to reduce muscle tone.

17. What is the principal focus of motor control training during the middle stages of recovery? During the late stages?

18. How can timing deficits in ambulation be overcome? Identify two strategies.

19. What factors should be considered when teaching the patient and the family about stroke and stroke rehabilitation?

20. What are the major factors affecting stroke outcome?

REFERENCES

1. American Heart Association: Heart Facts 1981. American Heart Association, Dallas, 1981.
2. Kurtzke, J: Epidemiology of Cerebrovascular Disease. In Office of Scientific Health Reports, NINCDS, NIH: The National Survey of Stroke. Stroke 12, Suppl 1 Mar/Apr 1981.
3. Kannel, W and Wolf, P: Epidemiology of cerebrovascular disease. In Russel, R (ed): Vascular Diseases of the Central Nervous System, ed 2. Churchill Livingstone, Edinburgh, 1983.
4. Gilroy, J and Holliday, P: Basic Neurology. Macmillan, New York, 1982.
5. Toole, J: Diagnosis and Management of Stroke. American Heart Association, Dallas, 1979.
6. Russell, R: Vascular Disease of the Central Nervous System, ed 2. Churchill Livingstone, Edinburgh, 1983.
7. Sacco, R, et al: Survival and recurrence following stroke—the Framingham study. Stroke 13:290, 1982.
8. Schoenberger, J: Stroke Risk Handbook. American Heart Association, Dallas, 1974.
9. Cohen, M: Cerebrovascular disease. In Weiner, W and Goetz, C (eds): Neurology for the Non-Neurologist. Harper & Row, Philadelphia, 1981.
10. Hachinski, V and Norris, J: The Acute Stroke. FA Davis, Philadelphia, 1985.
11. Fieschi, C and Lenzi, G: Cerebral blood flow and metabolism in stroke patients. In Russell, R (ed): Vascular Diseases of the Central Nervous System, ed 2. Churchill Livingstone, Edinburgh, 1983.
12. Haerer, A: Clinical manifestations of occlusive cerebrovascular disease. In Smith, R (ed): Stroke and the Extracranial Vessels. Raven Press, New York, 1984.
13. Meadows, J: Clinical features of focal cerebral hemisphere infarction. In Russell, R (ed): Vascular Diseases of the Central Nervous System, ed 2. Churchill Livingstone, Edinburgh, 1983.
14. Toole, J: Cerebrovascular Disorders, ed 3. Raven Press, New York, 1984.
15. Leo, K and Soderberg, G: Relationship between perception of joint position sense and limb synergies in patients with hemiplegia. Phys Ther 61:1433, 1981.
16. Marshall, J: Types of hemiplegia, Physiotherapy 60:334, 1974.
17. Twitchell, T: The restoration of motor function following hemiplegia in man. Brain 47:443, 1951.
18. Brunnstrom, S: Motor testing procedures in hemiplegia based on recovery stages. J Am Phys Ther Assoc 46:357, 1966.
19. Brunnstrom, S: Movement Therapy in Hemiplegia. Harper & Row, New York, 1970.
20. Fugl-Meyer, A, et al: The post stroke hemiplegic patient. I. A method for evaluation of physical performance. Scand J Rehabil Med 7:13, 1976.
21. Bobath, B: Adult Hemiplegia: Evaluation and Treatment, ed 2. William Heinemann Medical Books, London, 1978.
22. Michels, E: Synergies in hemiplegia. Clinical Management 1:9, 1981.
23. Bobath, B: Abnormal Postural Reflex Activity Caused by Brain Lesions, ed 3. William Heinemann Medical Books, London, 1985.
24. Mulley, G: Associated reactions in the hemiplegic arm. Scand J Rehab Med 14:17, 1982.
25. Mills, V and DiGenio, M: Functional differences in patients with left or right cerebrovascular accidents. Phys Ther 63:481, 1983.
26. Boller, F: Strokes and behavior: Disorders of higher cortical functions following cerebral disease. Disorders of language and related functions. Stroke 12:532, 1981.
27. Butler, R and Benson, F: Aphasia: A clinical-anatomical correlation. Br J Hosp Med (August) 211, 1974.
28. Benson, D and Geschwind, N: The aphasias and related disturbances. In Baker, A and Baker, L (eds): Clinical Neurology, Vol 1. Harper & Row, New York, 1971.
29. Siev, E, Freishtat, B, and Zoltan, B: Perceptual and Cognitive Dysfunction in the Adult Stroke Patient. Slack, Inc., Thorofare, NJ, 1986.
30. Trombly, C: Stroke. In Trombly, C (ed): Occupational Therapy for Physical Dysfunction, ed 2. Williams & Wilkins, Baltimore, 1983.
31. Diller, L: Perceptual and intellectual problems in hemiplegia: Implications for rehabilitation, Med Clin North Am 53:575, 1969.
32. Fowler, R and Fordyce, W: Stroke: Why Do They Behave That Way? American Heart Association, Dallas, 1974.
33. Pearce, J: Dementia in cerebral arterial disease. In Russell, R: Vascular Disease of the Central Nervous System, ed 2. Churchill Livingstone, Edinburgh, 1983.
34. Cocito, L, Fafale, E, and Reni, L: Epileptic seizures in cerebral arterial occlusive disease. Stroke 13:189, 1982.
35. Zane, M: Psychiatric rehabilitation of stroke. Sandoz Panorama (August) 18, 1970.
36. Binder, L: Emotional problems after stroke. Stroke 15:174, 1984.
37. Robinson, R and Szetela, B: Mood change following left hemispheric brain injury. Ann Neurol 9:447, 1981.
38. Robinson, R and Price, T: Post-stroke depressive disorders: A follow-up study of 103 patients. Stroke 13:635, 1982.
39. Fell, G and Strandness, D: Management of vascular disease. In Kottke, F, Stillwell, G, and Lehmann, J (eds): Krusen's Handbook of Physical Medicine and Rehabilitation, ed 3. WB Saunders, Philadelphia, 1982.

40. Veis, S and Logemann, J: Swallowing disorders in persons with cerebrovascular accident. Arch Phys Med Rehabil 66:372, 1985.
41. Carr, J and Shephard, R: A Motor Relearning Programme for Stroke. Aspen, Rockville, MD, 1983.
42. Bruton, J: Shoulder pain in stroke—patients with hemiplegia or hemiparesis following cerebrovascular accident. Physiotherapy 71:2, 1985.
43. Griffin, J and Reddin, G: Shoulder pain in hemiplegia. Phys Ther 61:1041, 1981.
44. Calliet, R: The Shoulder in Hemiplegia. FA Davis, Philadelphia, 1980.
45. Tepperman, P, et al: Reflex sympathetic dystrophy in hemiplegia. Arch Phys Med Rehabil 65:442, 1984.
46. Solzi, J, et al: Hemiplegics after a first stroke: Late survival and risk factors. Stroke 14:703, 1983.
47. Bishop, B: Neural plasticity. Part 4. Lesion-induced reorganization of the CNS. Recovery phenomena. Phys Ther 62:1442, 1982.
48. Craik, R: Clinical correlates of neural plasticity. Phys Ther 62:1452, 1982.
49. Finger, S and Stein, D: Brain Damage and Recovery. Academic Press, New York, 1982.
50. Delisa, J, et al: Stroke rehabilitation: Part II. Recovery and complications. Am Fam Physician 26:143, 1982.
51. Dove, H, Schneider, K, and Wallace, J: Evaluating and predicting outcome of acute cerebral vascular accident. Stroke 15:858, 1984.
52. Freed, M and Wainapel, S: Predictors of stroke outcome. Am Fam Physician 28:119, 1983.
53. Kusoffsky, A, Wadell, I, and Nilsson, B: The relationship between sensory impairment and motor recovery in patients with hemiplegia. Scand J Rehabil Med 14:27, 1982.
54. Lundgren, J, et al: Site of brain lesion and functional capacity in rehabilitated hemiplegics. Scand J Rehabil Med 1982.
55. Botvin, J, Keith, R, and Johnston, M: Relationship between primitive reflexes in stroke patients and rehabilitation outcome. Stroke 9:256, 1978.
56. Prescott, R, Garraway, W, and Akhtar, A: Predicting functional outcome following acute stroke using a standard clinical examination. Stroke 13:641, 1982.
57. Wade, D, Hewer, R, and Wood, V: Stroke: Influence of patient's sex and side of weakness on outcome. Arch Phys Med Rehabil 65:513, 1984.
58. DeJong, G and Branch, L: Predicting the stroke patient's ability to live independently. Stroke 13:648, 1982.
59. Ahlsio, B, et al: Disablement and quality of life after stroke. Stroke 15:886, 1984.
60. Barnett, H and the EC/IC Bypass Study Group: Failure of extracranial-intracranial arterial bypass to reduce the risk of ischemic stroke. N Engl J Med 313:1191, 1985.
61. Smith, R (ed): Stroke and the Extracranial Vessels. Raven Press, New York, 1984.
62. Strand, T, et al: A non-intensive stroke unit reduces functional disability and the need for long-term hospitalization. Stroke 16:29, 1985.
63. McCann, B and Culbertson, R: Comparisons of 2 systems for stroke rehabilitation in a general hospital. J Am Geriatr Soc 24:211, 1976.
64. Hamrin, E: Early activation in stroke: Does it make a difference? Scand J Rehabil Med 14:101, 1982.
65. Garraway, M: Stroke rehabilitation units: Concepts, evaluation, and unresolved issues. Stroke 16:178, 1985.
66. Johnston, M and Keister, M: Early rehabilitation for stroke patients: A new look. Arch Phys Med Rehabil 65:437, 1984.
67. Novack, T, Satterfield, W, and Connor, M: Stroke onset and rehabilitation: Time lag as a factor in treatment outcome. Arch Phys Med Rehabil 65:316, 1984.
68. Feigenson, J and McCarthy, M: Guidelines for establishing a stroke rehabilitation unit. NY State J Med 34:1430, 1977.
69. Evans, C: The practical evaluation of handicap after severe stroke. Physiotherapy 67:199, 1981.
70. Ashburn, A: A physical assessment for stroke patients. Physiotherapy 68:109, 1982.
71. Turnbull, G and Wall, J: The development of a system for the clinical assessment of gait following a stroke. Physiotherapy 71:294, 1985.
72. Professional Staff Association: Normal and Pathological Gait Guide. Rancho Los Amigos Hospital, 1978.
73. Pink, M: High speed video application in physical therapy. Clinical Management 5:14, 1985.
74. Holden, M, et al: Clinical gait assessment in the neurologically impaired: Reliability and meaningfulness. Phys Ther 64:35, 1984.
75. Mahoney, F and Barthel, D: Functional evaluation: Barthel Index. Md State Med J 14:61, 1965.
76. Delong, G and Branch, L: Predicting the stroke patient's ability to live independently. Stroke 13:648, 1982.
77. Wade, D, Silbeck, C, and Hewer, R: Predicting Barthel ADL score at 6 months after an acute stroke. Arch Phys Med Rehabil 64:24, 1983.
78. Logigian, M, Samuels, M, and Falconer, J: Clinical exercise trial for stroke patients. Arch Phys Med Rehabil 64:364, 1983.
79. Spence, J: Toward a uniform assessment of outcome. Stroke 6:873, 1982.
80. Spence, J and Donner, P: Problems in design of stroke treatment trials. Stroke 13:94, 1982.
81. Feigenson, J, et al: Burke Stroke Time-Oriented Profile (BUS-TOP): An overview of patient function. Arch Phys Med Rehabil 60:508, 1979.
82. Johnstone, M: The Stroke Patient: Principles of Rehabilitation. Churchill Livingstone, Edinburgh, 1976.
83. Todd, J: Physiotherapy in the early stages of hemiplegia. Physiotherapy Nov 1974.
84. Brocklchurst, J, et al: How much physical therapy for patients with stroke? Br Med J 1:1307, 1978.
85. Voss, D, Ionta, M, and Myers, B: Proprioceptive Neuromuscular Facilitation, ed 3. Harper & Row, Philadelphia, 1985.
86. Smith, R and Okamoto, G: Checklist for the prescription of slings for the hemiplegic patient. Am J Occup Ther 35:91, 1981.
87. Cherry, D and Weigand, G: Plaster drop-out casts as a dynamic means to reduce muscle contracture. Phys Ther 61:1601, 1981.
88. Zachazewski, J, Eberle, E, and Jefferies, M: Effect of tone-inhibiting casts and orthoses on gait. Phys Ther 62:453, 1982.
89. Booth, D, Doyle, M, and Montgomery, J: Serial casting for the management of spasticity in the head-injured adult. Phys Ther 63:1960, 1983.
90. Sage, G: Introduction to Motor Behavior—A Neuropsychological Approach, ed 2. Addison-Wesley, Reading, MA, 1977.
91. Schmidt, R: Motor Control and Learning. Human Kinetics, Champaign, IL, 1982.
92. Marteniuk, R: Motor skill performance and learning: Considerations for rehabilitation. Physiotherapy (Can) 31:187, 1979.
93. DeSouza, L: The effects of sensation and motivation on regaining movement control following stroke. Physiotherapy 69:238, 1983.
94. Rood, M: The use of sensory receptors to activate, facilitate, and inhibit motor response, autonomic and somatic in developmental sequence. In Sattely, C (ed): Approaches to Treatment of Patients with Neuromuscular Dysfunction. Wm Brown, Dubuque, IA, 1962.
95. Knott, M and Voss, D: Proprioceptive Neuromuscular Facilitation: Patterns and Techniques, ed 2. Harper & Row, New York, 1968.
96. Easton, T: On the normal use of reflexes. Am Sci 60:591, 1972.
97. Hellebrandt, F, et al: Physiological effects of simultaneous static and dynamic exercise. Am J Phys Med 35:106, 1956.
98. Magnus, R: The regulation of movements by the central nervous system. Pfluger Arch Physio 130:219, 1909.
99. Magnus, R and De Kleijn, A: The influence of the position of the head on tone of the muscles of the extremities. Pfluger Arch Physiol 145:455, 1912.
100. Marie, P and Foix, C: Synkinesis in hemiplegia. Rev Neurol 29:3, 1916.
101. Sherrington, C: Flexion reflex of the limb, crossed extension reflex and reflex stepping in standing. J Physiol 40:28, 1910.
102. Tokizane, T, et al: Electromyographic studies of tonic neck, lumbar, and labrynthine reflexes in normal persons. Jpn J Physiol 2:130, 1951.
103. Sullivan, P, Markos, P, and Minor, M: An Integrated Approach to Therapeutic Exercise. Reston, Reston, VA, 1982.
104. Zimmerman, J and Oder, L: Swallowing dysfunction in the acutely ill patient. Phys Ther 61:1755, 1981.
105. Larsen, G: Rehabilitation for dysphagia paralytica. J Speech Hear Disord 37:187, 1972.
106. Bobath, B: Treatment of adult hemiplegia. Phsyiotherapy 63:310, 1977.

107. Johnstone, M: Control of muscle tone in the stroke patient. Physiotherapy 67:198, 1981.
108. Heiniger, M and Randolph, S: Neurophysiological Concepts in Human Behavior. CV Mosby, St Louis, 1981.
109. Stockmeyer, S: An interpretation of the approach of Rood to the treatment of neuromuscular dysfunction. Am J Phys Med 46:900, 1967.
110. Pederson, D: The soothing effect of rocking as determined by the direction and frequency of movement. Can J Behav Sci 7:237, 1975.
111. Eldred, E, Lindsley, D, and Buchwald, J: The effect of cooling on mammalian muscle spindles. Exp Neurol 2:144, 1960.
112. Michalski, W and Seguin, J: The effect of muscle cooling and stretch on muscle spindle secondary endings in the cat. J Physiol 253:341, 1975.
113. Knutsson, E: Topical cryotherapy in spasticity. Scand J Rehabil Med 2:159, 1970.
114. Kottke, F, et al: The training of co-ordination. Arch Phys Med Rehabil 59:567, 1978.
115. Norton, B and Sahrmann, S: Reflex and voluntary electromyographic activity in patients with hemiparesis. Phys Ther 58:951, 1978.
116. Rothstein, J: Muscle biology clinical considerations. Phys Ther 62:1823, 1982.
117. Lane, R: Facilitation of weight transference in the stroke patient. Physiotherapy 64:260, 1978.
118. Post-Graduate Medical School, Prosthetics and Orthotics: Lower-Limb Orthotics. New York University, New York, 1986.
119. Brundy, J, et al: EMG feedback therapy: Review of treatment of 114 patients. Arch Phys Med Rehabil 57:55, 1976.
120. Wolf, S: Electromyographic biofeedback applications to stroke patients—a critical review. Phys Ther 63:1448, 1983.
121. Earnshaw, J, Lubbock, G, and Ellis, R: Clinical application of the exeter posture monitor. Physiotherapy 67:326, 1981.
122. Wolf, S and Binder-Macleod, S: Electromyographic biofeedback applications to the hemiplegic patient—changes in lower extremity neuromuscular and functional status. Phys Ther 63:1404, 1983.
123. Hogue, R and McCandless, S: Genu recurvatum: Auditory biofeedback treatment for adult patients with stroke or head injuries. Arch Phys Med Rehabil 64:368, 1983.
124. Binder, S, Moll, C, and Wolf, S: Evaluation of electromyographic biofeedback as an adjunct to therapeutic exercise in treating the lower extremities of hemiplegic patients. Phys Ther 61:886, 1981.
125. Baker, M, Hudson, J, and Wolf, S: A "feedback" cane to improve the hemiplegic patient's gait. Phys Ther 59:170, 1979.
126. Prevo, A, Visser, S, and Vogelaar, T: Effect of EMG feedback on paretic muscles and abnormal co-contraction in the hemiplegic arm, compared with conventional physical therapy. Scand J Rehab Med 14:121, 1982.
127. Basmajian, J, Gowland, C, and Brandstater, M: EMG feedback treatment of upper limb in hemiplegic stroke patients: A pilot study. Arch Phys Rehabil 63:613, 1982.
128. Wolf, S and Binder-Macleod, S: Electromyographic biofeedback applications to the hemiplegic patient—changes in upper extremity neuromuscular and functional status. Phys Ther 63:1393, 1983.
129. Nelson, A: Strategies for improving motor control. In Rosenthal, M, et al: Rehabilitation of the Head-Injured Adult. FA Davis, Philadelphia, 1983.
130. Corcoran, P, et al: Effects of plastic and metal braces on speed and energy cost of hemiparetic ambulation. Arch Phys Med Rehabil 51:69, 1970.
131. Hirschberg, G and Ralston, H: Energy cost of stair climbing in normal and hemiplegic subjects. Am J Phys Med 44:165, 1965.
132. Atwood, J and Nielsen, D: Scope of cardiac rehabilitation. Phys Ther 65:1812, 1985.
133. American College of Sports Medicine: Position statement on the recommended quantity and quality of exercise for developing and maintaining fitness in healthy adults. Med Sci Sports Exerc 10:vii, 1978.
134. Brinkmann, J and Hoskins, T: Physical conditioning and altered self-concept in rehabilitated hemiplegic patients. Phys Ther 59:859, 1979.
135. Mulhall, D: Stroke: A problem for patient and family. Physiotherapy 67:195, 1981.
136. Feigenson, J: Stroke rehabilitation: Outcome studies and guidelines for alternative levels of care. Stroke 12:372, 1981.
137. Feigenson, J: Stroke rehabilitation: Effectiveness, benefits, and costs. Some practical considerations. Stroke 10:1, 1979.
138. Johnston, M and Keith, R: Cost-benefits of medical rehabilitation: Review and critique. Arch Phys Med Rehabil 64:147, 1983.
139. Bourestom, N: Predictors of long term recovery in cerebrovascular disease. Arch Phys Med 52:415, 1971.
140. Katz, S, et al: Prognosis after stroke, Part II: Long term course of 159 patients. Medicine 45:236, 1966.
141. Lehmann, J, et al: Stroke: Does rehabilitation affect outcome? Arch Phys Med 56:375, 1975.
142. Waylonis, G, Keith, M, and Aseff, J: Stroke rehabilitation in a midwestern county. Arch Phys Med 54:151, 1973.
143. Feldman, D, et al: A comparison of functionally oriented medical and formal rehabilitation in management of patients with hemiplegia due to cardiovascular disease. J Chron Dis 15:297, 1962.
144. Stern, P, et al: Factors influencing stroke rehabilitation. Stroke 2:213, 1971.
145. Lind, K: A synthesis of studies on stroke rehabilitation. Chronic Dis 35:133, 1982.

SUPPLEMENTAL READINGS

Anderson, R and Kottke, F: Stroke rehabilitation: A reconsideration of some common attitudes. Arch Phys Med 59:175, 1978.
Bach-y-Rita, P: Recovery of Function: Theoretical Considerations for Brain Injury Rehabilitation. University Park Press, Baltimore, 1980.
Carr, J and Shephard, R: Early care of the stroke patient—a positive approach. Wm Heinemann Medical, London, 1980.
Carr, J, et al: Investigation of a new motor assessment scale for stroke patients. Phys Ther 65:175, 1985.
Delisa, J, et al: Stroke rehabilitation: Part I. Cognitive deficits and prediction of outcome. Am Fam Physician 26:207, 1982.
Gordon, W, et al: Perceptual remediation in patients with right brain damage: A comprehensive program. Arch Phys Med Rehabil 66:353, 1985.
Isaacs, B: Stroke research and the physiotherapist. Physiotherapy 63:366, 1977.
Office of Scientific Health Reports, NINCDS, NIH: The National Survey of Stroke, Stroke 12(2), Suppl 1 Mar/Apr 1981.
Ruskin, A: Understanding stroke and its rehabilitation. Stroke 14:438, 1983.
Sarno, M and Levita, E: Recovery in treated aphasia in the first year post-stroke. Stroke 10:663, 1979.
Sahs, A, Hartman, E, and Aronson, S: Stroke Cause, Prevention, Treatment and Rehabilitation. Castle House, London, 1979.
Weinberg, J, et al: Training sensory awareness and spatial organization in people with right brain damage. Arch Phys Med Rehabil 60:491, 1979.

GLOSSARY

Agnosia: The inability to recognize familiar objects with one sensory modality, while retaining the ability to recognize the same object with other sensory modalities.

Agraphia: Loss of the ability to write.

Alexia: Loss of the ability to read; word blindness.

Anomia: Inability to remember and to express names (nouns) of persons and objects.

Apraxia: A disorder of voluntary learned movement characterized by an inability to perform purposeful movements, which can not be accounted for by inadequate strength, loss of coordination, impaired sensation, attentional deficits, or lack of comprehension.

Associated reactions: Automatic responses of the limbs resulting from action occurring in some other part of the body, either by voluntary or reflex stimulation. In hemiplegia, these reactions are stereotyped and abnormal.

Asymmetric tonic neck reflex (STNR): Head rotation to the left causes extension of the left arm and leg (skull limbs) with flexion of the right arm and leg (jaw limbs); head rotation to the right causes the reverse pattern.

Arteriovenous malformation (AVM): An abnormality in embryonal development leading to a skein of tangled arteries and veins, usually without an intervening capillary bed. Commonly occurs along the distribution of the middle cerebral artery. Rupture produces cerebral hemorrhage.

Atherosclerosis: A form of arteriosclerosis characterized by a variable combination of changes of the intima of arteries.

Berry aneurysm: Small saccular congenital aneurysm of a cerebral vessel; communicates with the vessel by a small opening.

Body image: A visual and mental image of one's body that includes feelings about one's body, especially in relation to health and disease.

Body scheme: A postural model of one's body, including the relationship of one's body parts to each other and the relationship of the body to the environment.

Broca's aphasia (nonfluent, expressive, or motor aphasia): Decreased ability to communicate owing to deficits of the motor speech areas of the brain.

Cerebral embolus (CE): A blood clot that forms in the blood vessels in one part of the body and travels to cerebral vessels.

Cerebral thrombosis: Formation of a blood clot in a blood vessel leading to the brain.

Cerebral hemorrhage: Escape of blood into tissues of the brain.

Circle of Willis: Union of the anterior and posterior cerebral arteries (branches of the carotid artery) forming an anastomosis at the base of the brain.

Computerized axial tomography (CAT, CT scanning): Computerized radiographic examination by transmission of x-ray photons and computer analysis.

Dementia: Irrecoverable deteriorative mental state with absence or reduction of intellectual faculties; associated with organic brain disease.

Dysphagia: Inability to swallow or difficulty in swallowing.

Emotional lability: Unstable or changeable emotional state.

Endartectomy: Surgical removal of the intima, subintimal atheroma, and part of the media layer of a diseased vessel.

Forced gaze deviation: Deviation of the eyes secondary to unopposed action of eye muscles.

Global aphasia: Severe expressive and receptive language dysfunction.

Hemianopsia: Inability to see half the field of vision in both eyes.

Hemiplegia: Paralysis of one half of the body.

Hemiparesis: Partial or incomplete paralysis affecting only one half of the body.

Hemispheric disconnection: Lack of coordinated function of the two cerebral hemispheres owing to impairment of the corpus callosum.

Intracerebral hemorrhage (IH): Rupture of one of the cerebral vessels with subsequent bleeding into the brain.

Neologisms: Made-up words that are meaningless, typically seen in the patient with **Wernicke's aphasia.**

Perseveration: Continued repetition of a meaningless word or movement.

Reflex sympathetic dystrophy (RSD, shoulder-hand syndrome): Sympathetic vasomotor symptoms secondary to prolonged immobility of the shoulder or hand.

Spatial relations sydrome: A constellation of deficits that have a common difficulty in perceiving the relationship between objects in space, or the relationship between self and two or more objects.

Stroke: An impeded blood supply to some part of the brain caused by hemorrhage, embolus, or thrombus (SYN: Apoplexy, cerebrovascular accident [CVA]).

Subarachnoid hemorrhage, (SH): Rupture of one of the cerebral vessels with subsequent bleeding into the subarachnoid space.

Subclavian steal syndrome: Shunting of blood, which was destined for the brain, away from the cerebral circulation. This occurs when the subclavian artery is occluded. Blood then flows from the opposite vertebral artery across to and down the vertebral artery on the side of the occlusion.

Symmetric tonic labyrinthine reflex (STLR): Positioning in the supine position produces an increase in extensor tone, whereas the prone position increases flexor tone.

Symmetric tonic neck reflex (STNR): Flexion of the neck results in flexion of the arms and extension of the legs; extension of the neck produces the opposite responses.

Thalamic pain: Continuous, unpleasant sensation on the hemiplegic side.

Transient ischemic attack (TIA): Temporary interference with blood supply to the brain. Symptoms of neurologic deficit may last for only a few minutes or several hours. After the attack no evidence of residual brain damage or neurologic damage remains.

Verbal apraxia: Difficulty in forming and organizing intelligible words, although the musculature responsible for speech remains intact.

Verbal paraphasias: Inappropriate substitution of one word for another; commonly seen in the patient with **Wernicke's aphasia.**

Wernicke's aphasia (receptive or **sensory):** Normal or greater than normal amount of communication output with marked impairment of comprehension.

Chapter 18

PERIPHERAL VASCULAR DISEASE

JOSEPH McCULLOCH

OBJECTIVES

1. Define terms pertinent to the study of peripheral vascular disease.

2. Describe the epidemiologic factors that contribute to peripheral vascular disease.

3. Describe the pathophysiologic factors that cause and complicate peripheral vascular disease.

4. Identify the component parts of the examination of a patient with peripheral vascular disease.

5. Identify the role of the physical therapist in the rehabilitative management of patients with peripheral vascular disease.

INTRODUCTION

When one thinks about peripheral vascular disease (PVD), the clinical picture of a patient with arterial insufficiency, cramping, and gangrene frequently comes to mind. Involvement of the arterial system certainly is a major component in peripheral vascular disease. One must also give serious consideration to the clinical presentation and treatment resulting from the involvement of the venous and lymphatic systems. In a general sense, peripheral vascular disease can be considered as any of a number of conditions that may affect the circulatory system, external to the heart. Peripheral vascular disease is most commonly thought of, however, as affecting the extremities. Because PVD encompasses such a diverse group of diseases, it is difficult, if not impossible, to discuss their etiologic bases in a global sense. It is much more appropriate to discuss etiologic factors as they relate to each specific subsystem, as will be done in this chapter. Many patients referred for rehabilitation present with peripheral vascular disease as a secondary or complicating diagnosis. These can include patients with

stroke, amputation, or spinal cord injury. Patients who have been on prolonged bedrest and inactivity are also likely to experience vascular complications of the peripheral system. The reader should be aware that environment and lifestyle are major factors in the development of many of the diseases to be discussed. Nicotine and high-cholesterol diets are probably the most frequently reported causative or contributory factors.

ANATOMIC CONSIDERATIONS

Considering the cardinal principle of the circulatory system put forth by John Hunter over a century ago, it is quite understandable that the circulatory system is laid out in the manner in which it is. Hunter stated that "to maintain a circulation sufficient for the part and no more" is the primary function of the circulatory system.[1] When examined in a simplistic manner, it is apparent that pathologic processes arising in the circulatory system basically result from problems with supplying nutrients and removing waste products.

371

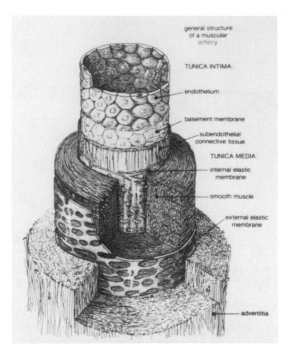

Figure 18–1. Structure of the arterial walls.

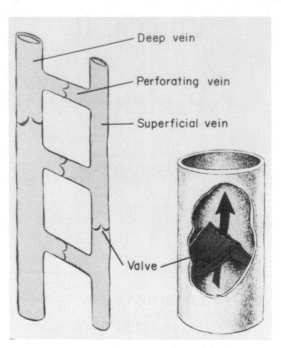

Figure 18–2. The venous valves of the legs.

Arterial System

Blood enters the peripheral arterial system from the left ventricle after having been oxygenated in the pulmonary system. Structurally, arteries are divided into three layers, or tunics; the tunica intima, tunica media, and tunica adventitia, which course from within the artery to the outside (Fig. 18–1). These layers are composed of varying amounts of smooth muscle cells, connective tissue, and other differentiated and undifferentiated cells, depending on the specific location and function of the artery. The more elastic arteries are found closer to the heart, and the more muscular ones reside more peripherally.[2] The arterial system appears to function without the assistance of valves, with the exception of the heart valves. The geometric layout of the system greatly influences blood flow and, as shall be discussed later, plays a major role in pathology. As the larger arteries course through the body, they continually **bifurcate,** or branch, resulting in successively smaller arterial subunits until reaching the **capillary** beds, where gaseous exchange occurs.

Venous System

Although the walls of veins, like those of arteries, can be divided into three layers, these layers tend to be less distinct. The venous walls are thinner than their arterial counterparts and therefore more transparent.[2] The innermost layer, or tunic, forms periodic folds along its course. These folds make up the venous valves, which provide the functional foundation of the system[8] (Fig. 18–2). Although delicate in appearance and structure, the valves, or cusps, can withstand rather strong forces without failure.

Poorly oxygenated blood leaving the capillary bed enters the venous system through the **venules.** The venules in turn empty into the collecting veins and finally into the superior and inferior vena cavae. Veins course in company with arteries and have a similar branching pattern. At several places in the body, including below the elbows and knees, paired veins are found. These veins are located one on each side of the artery and are joined by short **anastomotic** bridges along their course.[3]

Inasmuch as most venous problems seen by physical therapists occur in the lower extremities, a few moments will be spent discussing the functional layout of the leg veins. Each leg has three basic sets of veins, termed *subcutaneous or superficial, deep or intramuscular,* and *perforating or communicating.* The superficial veins have rather thick and muscular walls and occur in pairs of two in each extremity. The perforating veins serve the function of connecting the superficial and deep systems. Both the perforating and deep veins have thin walls. The deep veins course along with their corresponding arteries, as mentioned previously. Each lower extremity is served by two major venous systems, the great and small saphenous veins.[4]

Lymphatic System

The lymphatic system is comprised of three major components: the *capillaries and peripheral plexuses,* the *collecting vessels,* and the *lymph nodes.* The *lymphatic capillaries* are the most peripheral structures in the system and anastomose to form what are termed peripheral plexuses. These plexuses, consisting solely of a layer of endothelial cells, lie in direct contact with the adjacent tissues and give rise to short channels that lead to the collecting ducts.

Three types of *collecting ducts* exist. The main differences in the ducts are the number of muscular layers each possesses. They range in complexity from those with a single muscular layer to two and finally three layers of muscle. The second type, with two muscular layers, is most common.[5] The walls of these vessels are only 0.5 to 1 millimeter in diameter, and although they are more plentiful than veins, they tend to accompany the veins as they course through the body.[3,4] Their thin walls make them more delicate than arteries and veins and therefore more susceptible to trauma. Any injury significant enough to affect venous return most likely inflicts damage to the lymphatic vessels. The ramifications for edema become apparent.

Lymph nodes range in size from several millimeters to greater than one centimeter and consist of small accumulations of lymphocytes housed in an encapsulated network of connective tissue.[3,5] The nodes serve two basic purposes. The first is that of a filtering and phagocytosis system whereby the nodes work to rid the body of unwanted substances that have been deposited into their dense network. The second function of the node is that of lymphocyte production. After being cleansed of unwanted particulate matter by the lymph nodes, almost all lymph, with its newly acquired lymphocytes, proceeds through the thoracic duct into the systemic circulation.

The lymphatic and venous systems work in harmony to absorb the arterial capillary filtrate. It is estimated that approximately 10 percent of this filtrate and almost all protein molecules are handled via the lymphatic system.[4] The roles of the venous and lymphatic systems in edema production and control will be discussed later.

PATHOPHYSIOLOGICAL CONSIDERATIONS

Most forms of peripheral vascular disease encountered in physical therapy practice occur in the lower extremities. Because older individuals are more commonly

Table 18–1 COMMON PERIPHERAL VASCULAR DISEASES

ARTERIAL DISEASE
Chronic
    Arteriosclerosis obliterans
    Thromboangitis obliterans
Acute
    Arterial thrombosis
    Embolic occlusion
    Vasospastic disease
VENOUS DISEASE
Chronic
    Varicose veins with or without venous stasis
    Chronic venous insufficiency
Acute
    Venous thrombosis
LYMPHATIC DISEASE
    Primary (congenital) lymphedema
    Secondary (acquired) lymphedema

affected by these disorders, other complicating conditions may be encountered such as diabetes, stroke, and heart failure. Table 18–1 provides a brief classification of the more common conditions. Each will be discussed briefly.

Arterial Dysfunction

ARTERIOSCLEROSIS OBLITERANS

By far, the most common form of chronic occlusive vascular disease affecting the lower extremities is *arteriosclerosis obliterans*. Arteriosclerosis obliterans is known by various names such as chronic occlusive arterial disease, obliterative arteriosclerosis, and atherosclerotic occlusive disease. It is a peripheral manifestation of the generalized disease atherosclerosis.[6] Approximately 95 percent of all cases of chronic occlusive arterial disease are of this type.[7] Being a slowly developing degenerative process, its manifestations occur insidiously. Pathologically, the disease develops by the formation of an atheromatous plaque in the intima of the artery. As the plaque increases in size, the result is a narrowed lumen and impaired linear flow of blood.

One of the earliest presenting symptoms in this disease is **intermittent claudication.** This is characterized by severe pain in the lower extremity that occurs with activity but subsides with rest. It is frequently associated with walking and is the result of inadequate arterial blood supply to the exercising muscles. As the disease progresses, arterial flow may become impaired to the point of pain being present even at rest. The clinical assessment of a patient with this pathology reveals diminished or absent pedal pulses and positive signs of **rubor** of dependency, which will be discussed later. As the disease becomes more pronounced, **trophic changes** begin to occur as a result of impaired growth and nourishment of tissues. Skin color and pigmentation changes occur. The foot becomes cold to the touch. In late stages of the disease, tissue necrosis and ulceration may develop as a result of prolonged ischemia. This occurs even more frequently in persons whose disease is complicated by diabetes.[6]

THROMBOANGIITIS OBLITERANS

Thromboangiitis obliterans (Buerger's disease) is the second most common form of chronic occlusive arterial disease.[6] The disease process is similar to that of arteriosclerosis obliterans but is unique in that it tends to occur predominantly in young male smokers. The disease is first manifested in the distal aspects of the extremities and progresses proximally. It has been demonstrated that cessation of smoking arrests the disease.[8] The pathology responsible for the clinical symptoms of decreased tissue temperature (cold distal extremities) and eventual tissue necrosis is an inflammatory process in the veins and arteries that appears to be directly related to tobacco use. Nicotine is also a very potent vasoconstrictor and is therefore responsible for the decrease in skin temperature seen in smokers.

ACUTE ARTERIAL DISEASE

Physical therapists are less likely to be involved in the treatment of individuals with acute arterial disease. Nevertheless, it is important that these diseases and their signs and symptoms be recognized should they occur during therapy for some other problem. The sudden loss of blood flow to an extremity, regardless of cause, is an emergency that requires immediate attention. The most common forms of acute arterial occlusion are arterial embolism, thrombosis, and vasospastic disease. Any of these conditions can result in the classic signs and symptoms of pain, **pallor,** loss of pulses, paresthesia, and paralysis.[9]

Arterial Embolism

Arterial embolism is probably the most frequently encountered form of acute arterial disease. Emboli can arise from any of numerous sites and can be composed of various substances. Probably one of the most frequently occurring types results from the dislodging of a preexisting thrombus in the heart, which migrates to an arterial **bifurcation.**

Arterial Thrombi

Arterial thrombi occur less frequently than emboli and usually occur in the area of a previously existing atherosclerotic lesion. In the normal individual, blood flows through the arteries in a laminar, or straight, manner. When the arterial lumen narrows in the presence of an atherosclerotic lesion, the blood flow becomes turbulent. This swirling motion of the blood slows its passage through the area and permits platelets to collect. This platelet aggregation, together with significant amounts of fibrin, leads to the development of the thrombus. The severity of the problems that ensue are related to the location of the thrombus. Severe ischemia is usually the result of thrombi development at the aortic bifurcation, whereas thrombi in other areas, well served by collateral flow, may manifest only minor problems.

Vasospastic Disease

Vasospastic disease in the extremities, although including such processes as **livedo reticularis** and **acrocyanosis,** is most frequently referred to as **Raynaud's phenomenon.** Vasospastic disorders are characterized by changes in skin color and temperature. This is in contrast to the findings of **intermittent claudication** and tissue necrosis seen in other arterial disorders. The arterial spasm that occurs appears localized to the small arteries and **arterioles.**[10]

Raynaud's phenomenon can be precipitated by exposure to cold or by emotional stress. The phenomenon is manifested by changes in skin color of the digits. The color changes range from **pallor** to **cyanosis** and **rubor.** Pain and numbness tend to occur with the pallor and cyanosis. The condition can occur secondarily with such conditions as **scleroderma, thoracic outlet syndrome,** and occlusive arterial disease.

Venous Dysfunction

CHRONIC VENOUS INSUFFICIENCY

Chronic venous insufficiency is probably one of the most frequently seen vascular problems in the physical therapy clinic. This is due both to its high incidence—12 percent of the adult population—and the success of therapy.[11] Chronic venous insufficiency results from dysfunction in venous outflow resulting from defective venous valves. The valvular defect, combined with obesity and inactivity, results in a significant pooling of blood in the lower extremities. The signs and symptoms are varied and range from tiredness in the legs to aching, dependent edema, brownish discoloration in the skin, and ultimately ulceration.

VARICOSE VEINS

Many patients may manifest varicose veins with or without the presence of stasis. The varicosities may be hereditary or acquired in nature. Acquired or secondary varicosities result from proximal obstruction to venous return, as seen with pregnancy or a pelvic mass. The increased pressure placed on the venous system leads to valve failure and the tortuous appearance noted in the more superficial veins.

ACUTE VENOUS DISEASE

Like arterial thrombosis, acute venous thrombosis is the formation of a clot within the vessel wall and is not a condition treated by the physical therapist. An understanding of the clinical features of this process are of importance to the therapist, should they appear during treatment. Acute venous thrombosis results in a bursting type of pain from obstruction to venous outflow.[12] Several types of patients predisposed to development of acute venous thrombosis are dehydrated elderly individuals on bedrest, individuals who apply elastic wraps inappropriately after a musculoskeletal injury, and patients on estrogen therapy.

PHLEBITIS: THROMBOPHLEBITIS

Phlebitis is inflammation of the veins characterized by pain and tenderness along the course of the vein. It can result in inflammatory swelling and acute edema below the level of obstruction. Patients may also experience a rapid pulse, mild elevation in temperature, and pain in the joints. When the inflammation of a vein occurs in conjunction with the formation of a thrombus, it is termed **thrombophlebitis.**

THROMBOEMBOLISM

A venous thrombosis that becomes dislodged forms an embolism, which can travel to the right side of the heart and reach the lung (pulmonary embolism). Clinical signs during the acute stage include pain, shortness of breath, and tachycardia. Death may occur if the pulmonary emboli are large or if they occur in patients with preexisting cardiopulmonary disease. Predisposing factors that contribute to the development of thromboembolic complications include immobilization (venous stasis), local vessel trauma, and hypercoagulability.

Lymphatic Dysfunction

LYMPHEDEMA

Lymphedema is manifested by an excessive accumulation of edema in the tissues brought about by disruption of the lymph channels. Lymphedema can be classified as primary (congenital) or secondary (aquired), depending on whether it is congenital or acquired. Persons with congenital lymphedema have a faulty lymphatic system resulting from a complete failure of lymph vessels to develop **(agenesis)** or poorly developed vessels **(aplasia).**[13] Secondary lymphedema results from the same situations that lead to secondary varicosities (i.e., pelvic masses or other space occupying lesions). If the lymphatic drainage system is blocked, fluid accumulates.

Gangrene

Gangrene is necrosis or death of tissue, usually resulting from deficient or absent blood supply. Tissues deprived of adequate blood supply suffer anoxia (loss of oxygen) to the part, become diseased, and finally die. Gangrene can develop as a result of severe vascular pathology, including inflammatory processes, injury, or degenerative changes. It is common in diseases such as diabetes mellitus and Raynaud's disease.

THE SUBJECTIVE EXAMINATION

The examination should be initiated by taking a complete history. In addition to ascertaining the patient's reasons for seeking medical attention, other baseline information should be obtained. This should include the patient's age, sex, race, height, weight, and occupation.

The patient should be asked to describe in detail the problems that led to or coincided with the current problem. It is important to ascertain how the body responds to such factors as cold, heat, dependent positions, and minor or severe trauma. Any past history of varicosities, pulmonary emboli, or other systemic conditions affecting limb circulation (diabetes, hypertension, atrial fibrillation, congestive heart failure, or myocardial infarction) should be noted.

Other questions should focus on social habits, especially tobacco use. The type, frequency, and duration of smoking should be noted. Detailed information should be obtained on any previous surgical procedures that may have involved the vascular system (e.g., **sympathectomy, vascular prosthesis, endarterectomy,** amputation).

The patient should next describe the current problems being experienced. Careful documentation should be made of episodes of intermittent claudication, rest pain, swelling, and numbness and tingling. A sample of a gen-

eral vascular examination worksheet is presented in Appendix A.

OBJECTIVE EXAMINATION

Trophic Changes and Pigmentation

The patient's skin should be examined, and any evidence of abnormal pigmentation, **stasis dermatitis,** ulceration, and effects of position on skin color should be noted. Skin color is produced primarily by blood in the superficial venules. The skin will take on a chalky white appearance if the arterial flow is absent or decreased. When partial but inadequate arterial flow is present, the skin may be either red or cyanotic, depending on temperature and oxygenation.

Loss of hair over the digits, combined with dry skin and thickened nails, indicates poor vascular nutrition. This situation is one quite likely to lead to tissue breakdown.

Discoloration of the tissues, if present, will frequently be brownish in nature. The discoloration is caused by **hemosiderin,** a pigment released from lysed red cells. The pigment stains the tissues permanently and thus serves as an indicator of previous stasis problems. If varicosities are present, an attempt should be made to determine whether they are primary or secondary in nature.

Temperature

Gross variation in skin temperature can be noted by palpation. If a discrepancy does appear to exist, objective clinical measurements should be made with a **thermistor** or a **radiometer. Thermistors** (Fig. 18–3) are essentially electronic thermometers that measure temperature via a probe placed directly on the skin. **Radiometers** (Fig. 18–4), on the other hand, measure the infrared radiations emitted by the body. Although radiometers provide a quick means of scanning the area to assess temperature changes, their higher costs often make them less practical.

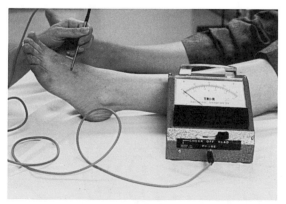

Figure 18–3. Temperature measurement using a thermistor.

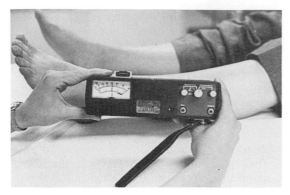

Figure 18–4. Temperature measurement using a radiometer.

Pulses

The quality and presence of pulses should be determined for every patient with vascular problems. Although the radial and carotid pulses are most frequently monitored, the therapist must be able to locate and to assess all palpable pulses including the temporal, external carotid, brachial, radial, ulnar, abdominal, common iliac, femoral, popliteal, dorsalis pedis, and posterior tibial pulses. Pulses can be graded as $2+$ = normal, $1+$ = diminished, and 0 = absent. Variations in patient size can frequently make palpation of pulses difficult. In these instances, the use of sophisticated equipment, such as the doppler ultrasound, may be necessary. The doppler unit will be discussed later in this chapter.

Auscultation

Blood flow is usually laminar in nature. If you were to listen over an artery by use of a stethoscope while blood is flowing in this direct fashion, you would not be able to detect any signs of blood flow. When the motion becomes turbulent, as when the arterial lumen is narrowed, a swishing sound will be detected. This sound is known as a **bruit** and is very similar to the sound heard through a stethoscope when taking a blood pressure measurement. All large arteries in the neck, abdomen, and limbs should be examined for bruits. If one is noted that

has not been brought to the attention of a physician, the physician should be notified. It is also advisable to listen over large scars for possible **arteriovenous fistulas,** which result when blood is improperly shunted between the arterial and venous systems.

Blood Pressure

Routine blood pressure measurements should be taken prior to the initiation of therapy. The patient should be placed in the sitting position and the pressure determined in both upper extremities. A properly fitting cuff should be placed around the upper arm, with the lower edge of the cuff approximately one inch above the elbow. The suggested method for recording blood pressure measurements for vascular patients is to use three recording intervals.[14] This helps avoid confusion, inasmuch as there often is a discrepancy in what individuals record as the diastolic reading. Many examiners record the muffling of the sound, but others record the disappearance. Using all three recording points listed below will help avoid this confusion.
1. First audible sound (systolic pressure)
2. Muffling of sound (first diastolic pressure)
3. Disappearance of sound (second diastolic pressure)

Edema

There are four main causes of edema:
1. Increased capillary permeability
2. Decreased osmotic pressure of plasma proteins
3. Increased pressure in venules and capillaries
4. Obstruction to lymphatic flow
Edema, if not corrected, can lead to tissue necrosis. It is therefore extremely important that objective measurements be made to judge whether extremities are increasing or decreasing in size. Several methods exist for monitoring girth and volume. *Girth measurements* are usually made with the patient supine. Using a skin pencil, the therapist locates a bony landmark and then makes measurement marks every two inches above and below this point. The circumference is measured at each marking (Fig. 18–5).

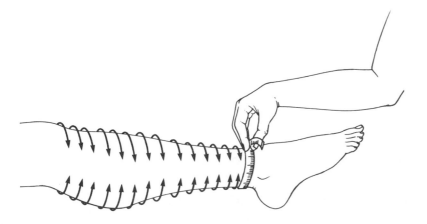

Figure 18–5. Circumferential measurement of girth.

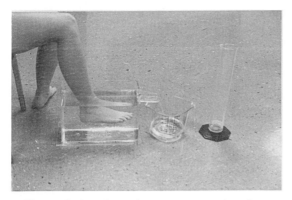

Figure 18–6. Volumetric measurement of the foot.

Volumetric measurement is a more accurate, yet more time-consuming, means of assessing limb size. It is particularly valuable when measuring irregular surfaces such as the feet, where use of a tape measure is unreliable. To perform a volumetric measurement, one needs a volumeter. The volumeter (Fig. 18–6) is a specially designed tank with an overflow spout. A graduated cylinder is also required. The patient is positioned so that the extremity to be assessed can be submerged into the volumeter. The volumeter previously should have been filled to overflowing and allowed to sit until all dripping from the spout has ceased. As the extremity is placed into the container, all displaced water is collected and measured. The amount of water (in milliliters) is recorded. Because the volume that water occupies is different at different temperatures, it is suggested that careful attention be paid to assuring that the same temperature water is used with each subsequent measurement.

Tests of Peripheral Arterial Circulation

RUBOR OF DEPENDENCY

This test is used to assess the adequacy of arterial circulation by determining the skin color changes that occur with elevation and dependency of the extremity. The test is performed by placing the patient supine and noting the color of the soles of the feet. In normal individuals, they will be pinkish in appearance. The legs are then elevated to about 45 degrees. This may result in a slight blanching of the extremities. If a quick loss of color occurs, resulting in a dead grayish white appearance, arterial involvement may be suspected. After returning the legs to a dependent position, normal individuals will display a quick pink flush in the feet. If the arterial circulation is impaired, the color change may take longer than 30 seconds to occur and will be a very bright red. This is due to the fact that arterial flow is insufficient and can not overcome gravity when the legs are elevated. Inasmuch as venous blood leaves the leg, the next blood into the leg after it is returned to the examining table is pure arterial blood.

VENOUS FILLING TIME

This test measures the time necessary for the superficial veins to refill after emptying. The test is only of use in persons with a normal venous system, because any valvular problems could permit retrograde venous flow and not give a good picture of filling via the normal arterial pathway. The patient is also placed supine for this test, and the legs are elevated and milked of venous blood. After this has been accomplished, the patient hangs the legs over the edge of the table, and the time necessary for the veins to refill is noted. A time greater than 10 to 15 seconds indicates arterial insufficiency.

CLAUDICATION TIME

Intermittent claudication is a fairly subjective yet valuable source of information when assessing a patient's response to therapy. One means of objectifying this information is to have the patient walk at 1 mile per hour on a level (0°) treadmill. The amount of time walked before claudication prevents further activity is recorded. Because the environment is controlled, the same test can be repeated at future times to assess functional improvement.

Tests of Peripheral Venous Circulation

PERCUSSION TEST

This test is designed to assess the competence of the greater saphenous vein. The test is performed by having the patient stand so that any varicosities present will fill with blood. A segment of the vein below the knee is palpated while the vein above the knee is percussed simultaneously. Detecting a fluid wave under the palpating finger indicates that the valves are incompetent and that an essentially continuous column of blood is present. If the valves were competent, the fluid wave would have been dampened.

TEST FOR DEEP VEIN THROMBOPHLEBITIS

To check for deep vein **thrombophlebitis,** the therapist should squeeze the gastrocnemius while forcefully dorsiflexing the patient's ankle. In acute thrombophlebitis, this manuever causes a great deal of pain. This is reported as a positive *Homan's sign.* Another test for this problem is to apply a blood pressure cuff around the calf and to record how high the cuff can be inflated. Patients in acute distress can not tolerate pressures greater than 40 mmHg (Fig. 18–7).

Other Special Tests

DOPPLER ULTRASOUND

Doppler ultrasound provides a noninvasive means for the therapist to assess arterial flow (Fig. 18–8). The Dop-

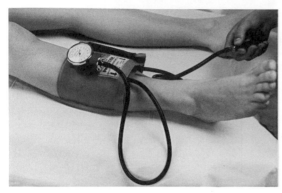

Figure 18–7. Cuff test for assessing acute thrombophlebitis.

pler unit is a transcutaneous detector of blood flow in a vessel. As the name implies, the unit uses the Doppler principle to determine flow. Working in a manner similar to a clinical ultrasound unit, the Doppler transmits a 5 to 10 MHz signal into a blood vessel. If blood cells are moving through the vessel, the sound waves are reflected back to the Doppler unit at a different frequency. This frequency shift is presented to the examiner via an audible signal. Though this test can not be fully explained in this short space, the following serves as a brief explanation of the process. Those wishing a more extensive explanation of the procedure are referred to an article by MacKinnon.[15]

To perform the test, a blood pressure cuff is placed around the lower extremity at varying sites along the calf or thigh and inflated until blood flow ceases. As the cuff is released, the examiner listens over a distal artery such as the dorsalis pedis. When a signal is detected, the reading in millimeters of mercury is noted. The process is repeated at several points along the leg, specifically a high thigh, low thigh, high calf and low calf measurement, and the results are compared with readings from the brachial artery.

Being very sensitive, the Doppler unit can measure a systolic pressure sooner than it can be detected audibly with a stethoscope. The measurements obtained with a Doppler examination are recorded as an index comparing upper and lower extremity measurements. This means, therefore, that if the systolic pressure obtained in the lower extremity is divided by that obtained in the

upper extremity, a value greater than or equal to 0.9 should be noted. This value is termed the *Doppler index.* Persons with indices less than 0.5 are likely to have severe arterial disease.

ADJUNCTIVE TESTING

Numerous other diagnostic studies performed by physicians can provide information valuable to the therapist in establishing a treatment program. The therapist should become familiar with the results of some of these tests, such as venography, arteriography, and lymphangiography. All of these tests involve the injection of a contrast medium into the respective system. This is then followed by a roentgenographic examination to detect occlusions or other pathologic processes within the vessel.

TREATMENT

Acute Arterial Disease

The treatment of acute arterial disease requires medical and/or surgical intervention. The patient is typically started on heparin to prevent further thrombus formation. Once a patient is stabilized medically, the usual treatment of choice is a thromboembolectomy.[16]

Postoperative care by the physical therapist centers on preventing pressure on the surgical area, monitoring pulse and temperature, and enhancing venous return. The patient should be checked to make sure that there is no binding clothing impeding blood flow. Although the patient is in bed, a turning schedule should be instituted, making sure that the surgical site is always visible. The patient should never be positioned such that pressure is applied to the surgical area.

Patients run the risk of recurrence of emboli during recovery. Because of this, pulses and skin temperature should be monitored and recorded. A Doppler unit is useful in detecting poorly palpable pulses, but a blood pressure cuff is not used unless the surgeon specifically wishes to obtain a systolic pressure reading. Any significant changes in pulse character or skin temperature should be reported immediately.

Venous stasis in the calf can pose problems postoperatively. The physical therapist should use conservative measures such as gentle massage and passive dorsiflexion of the ankles to assist venous return and to prevent stasis. The lower extremities should not be elevated.

Chronic Arterial Disease

The primary goals of treatment for patients with chronic arterial disease are to improve circulation and to instruct the patient in management at home. Although the exact mechanism is not clearly understood, there is general agreement in the literature that exercise leads to reduction of claudication.[17–20] The reported studies involved exercise programs ranging from 8 weeks to 6 months in duration and included both walking and bicy-

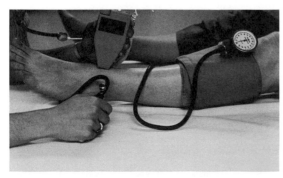

Figure 18–8. Doppler examination of the lower extremity.

cling activities. In 1924, Buerger[21] developed an exercise program aimed at enhancing the formation of collateral circulation. His exercise program and modifications of it (Buerger-Allen exercises) consisted of a systematic series of exercises in which the legs were alternately raised and then placed in a dependent position for varying periods of time. These exercises were performed several times per session and then several times throughout the day. These exercises have been advocated for years in the treatment of chronic arterial insufficiency, in spite of the fact that they were proven ineffective as far back as 1953.[22]

Home programs for patients can include walking and/ or bicycling protocols, in addition to a generalized aerobic workout. Such programs can—and should—be very simple in design. The primary purpose of the programs is to increase walking or cycling times and, in so doing, to "stress" the circulatory system gradually. The purpose of the exercises is to make progressive demands on the circulatory system in the hope that collateral sprouting will be encouraged. Patients should be requested to keep a log of their exercise times and distances and to try to improve on each every day. Patients with complicating neurologic involvement, resulting in insensitivity in the feet, should be instructed in techniques of inspection and proper foot care. A set of general instructions for footcare instructions for patients with peripheral vascular disease is found in Table 18–2.

Acute Venous Disease

Physical therapists are not frequently involved in the treatment of acute venous disease. However, they are frequently the first to note its presence and therefore should be able to recognize the early symptoms and to initiate an immediate medical referral. Because thrombophlebitis is a potentially fatal disease, patients are usually placed on bedrest and anticoagulant therapy. Occasionally the physical therapist will be requested to provide moist heat to the extremities. As the patient's condition

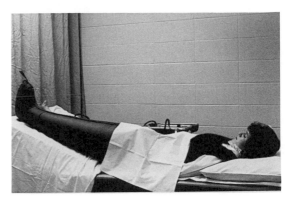

Figure 18–9. Patient receiving treatment with Jobst intermittent compression pump.

improves, the therapist may play a role in reinstituting exercise and ambulation.

Chronic Venous Disease

The goals of treatment for patients with chronic venous disease are to decrease edema, to prevent and/or to heal ulcerations, and to provide patient education. Physical therapy has a great deal to offer the patient with chronic venous insufficiency. Proper intervention can delay, and often can prevent, the need for surgery.

Secondary to venous stasis, edema can be effectively treated by use of an intermittent compression pump and custom-fitted stockings (Figs. 18–9 and 18–10). The compression pump and stockings serve the purpose of providing an external force to assist in the removal of edema from tissues. Pumping should always precede fitting of the patient for custom-fabricated stockings. These stockings are of value only once the edema has been removed. Patients who are fitted prematurely tend to continue to remain edematous and eventually develop stasis ulcerations. During the stages at which the patient is still receiving treatment on the intermittent compression pump and stockings have not been fitted, the girth reductions gained by therapy can be maintained by use of tubular elastic gauze, such as Tubigrip.* Tubular gauze

---

*Seton, Tubiton House, Oldham OL13HS, England.

Table 18–2 GENERAL INSTRUCTIONS FOR PATIENTS WITH PERIPHERAL VASCULAR DISEASE AND PRINCIPLES OF FOOT CARE

1. Feet should be washed each night with a mild soap and warm water.
2. While the feet are still wet, apply a liberal amount of petroleum jelly and then pat off remaining water.
3. Wear clean socks daily. White socks are preferable because the dyes used in colored socks may be irritating.
4. Shoes should be loose fitting and preferably custom fitted.
5. Cut toenails straight across or have your podiatrist cut them for you.
6. Do not cut corns or calluses—see your podiatrist.
7. Be careful not to impede blood flow in the extremities. Do not wear tight or constricting clothing.
8. Do not put medications or ointments on your feet unless they have been medically prescribed.
9. Do not use tobacco in any form.

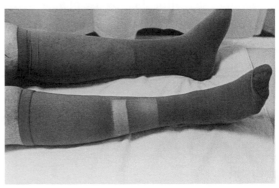

Figure 18–10. Patient wearing custom-fitted support stocking.

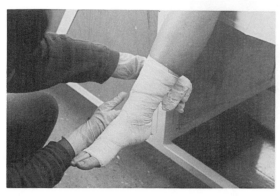

Figure 18–11. Unna's boot being applied to the lower extremity.

ile saline solution. Placing the extremity into a warm whirlpool for 20 minutes in a dependent position certainly only invites more swelling. Intermittent compression therapy has a role in ulcer treatment because it is only after edema is removed that healing will occur. The ulcer should be dressed with gauze to prevent the compression sleeve from becoming soiled.[23] The Unna's boot* (Fig. 18–11) is an excellent dressing to apply between treatment sessions. The Unna's boot consists of a wide mesh cotton gauze that has been impregnated with zinc oxide, calamine, and gelatin. The "boot" is applied in a manner similar to an elastic bandage. Once the bandage sets, it forms a semirigid dressing, and because it does not give like an elastic bandage, it does not permit swelling to recur. The zinc oxide and calamine have also been advocated for the treatment of venous stasis ulcerations. At one time it was believed that topically applied zinc would facilitate wound healing. This is not the case, unless the person is zinc deficient. In such cases, orally administered zinc would be most desirable. The calamine functions as a drying agent.

comes in graded pressures and is far superior to any temporary prefabricated support garment. Once girth measurements stabilize, the patient can be fitted with a custom-made elastic garment such as the Jobst† stocking. Care should be taken to reorder stockings well in advance of needing replacement, to avoid a relapse of edema.

In any situation in which one is considering the use of compression therapy, care should be taken to make sure that the patient does not have acute thrombophlebitis or arterial insufficiency. In thrombophlebitis there is the risk of causing an embolism, whereas in arterial insufficiency the concern is further impeding arterial flow in an already compromised area.

Exercise programs are of great benefit to patients with chronic venous disease. However, the patient should be carefully instructed to elevate the extremities after exercise until the heart rate returns to normal. The increased blood flow caused by exercise could otherwise lead to stasis if the extremities are allowed to remain in a dependent position.

The more information the patient has about the disease process, its implications and precautions, the more likely the patient is to follow a treatment protocol. Proper patient education should also include information about foot care, as mentioned previously.

Venous stasis ulcerations unfortunately are inevitable in many patients. Should these develop, local wound care and pressure dressings are indicated. Care should be taken to avoid the overzealous use of whirlpool. Venous stasis wounds are usually soupy in nature, so further hydration is seldom necessary. Instead, cleansing is indicated. This can be accomplished by use of a basin of ster-

Lymphatic Disease

Because the lymphatic system works in synergy with the venous system, the techniques mentioned previously are appropriate in treating edema secondary to lymphatic dysfunction. The goals of therapy are the same: to decrease swelling and to provide patient education. The therapist should be aware, however, that lymphedema often is due to carcinoma or other serious pathology. Any treatment technique used should be selected with consideration to possible adverse secondary effects.

SUMMARY

This chapter has provided an overview of the more commonly encountered peripheral vascular diseases. The means by which they are assessed and suggested mechanisms of management also have been discussed. An emphasis has been placed on the importance of examining the peripheral vascular system of any patient whose symptoms indicate vascular involvement, regardless of the current diagnosis. Many of the vascular problems encountered in practice can be improved by treatment, and more serious problems avoided, if treatment is initiated early.

†Jobst Incorporated, Toledo, Ohio.

*Miles Pharmaceuticals, 1127 Myrtle Street, Elkhart, IN.

QUESTIONS FOR REVIEW

1. Compare and contrast the presenting clinical symptoms of patients with the three major types of peripheral vascular disease.

2. When assessing a patient with arterial insufficiency, which tests would be unreliable if a concurrent venous insufficiency is present?

3. Discuss the signs and symptoms that should indicate to a physical therapist the need to refer a patient for further medical assessment.

4. Having assessed a patient who presents with a classical picture of venous insufficiency, discuss short- and long-term goals and available therapeutic intervention.

5. Explain how persistent edema prevents the resolution of a venous stasis ulcer.

REFERENCES

1. Palmer, JF: The Works of John Hunter, F.R.S., Vol 3. Longman Group, London, 1835.
2. Stehbens, WE: Hemodynamics and the Blood Vessel Wall. Charles C Thomas, Springfield, IL, 1979.
3. Basmajian, JV: Grant's Method of Anatomy, ed 10. Williams & Wilkins, Baltimore, 1980.
4. Sabiston, DC (ed): David-Christopher Textbook of Surgery, ed 11. WB Saunders, Philadelphia, 1977.
5. Battezzati, M and Donini, I: The Lymphatic System. John Wiley & Sons, New York, 1972.
6. deWolfe, VG: Chronic Occlusive Arterial Disease of the Lower Extremities. In Spittell, JA (ed): Clinical Vascular Disease. FA Davis, Philadelphia, 1983.
7. Juergens, JL, Spittell, JA, and Fairbairn, JF: Peripheral Vascular Disease, ed 5. WB Saunders, Philadelphia, 1980.
8. Correlli, F: Buerger's disease: Cigarette smoker disease may always be cured by medical therapy. J Cardiovasc Surg 14:28, 1973.
9. Hollier, LH: Acute Arterial Occlusion. In Spittell, JA (ed): Clinical Vascular Disease. FA Davis, Philadelphia, 1983.
10. Spittell, JA: Clinical Vascular Disease. FA Davis, Philadelphia, 1983.
11. Coon, WW, Willis, PW, and Keller, JB: Venous thromboembolism and other venous disease in the Tecumseh community health study. Circulation 48:839, 1973.
12. Hume, M: Acute Venous Thrombosis. In Spittell, JA (ed): Clinical Vascular Disease. FA Davis, Philadelphia, 1983.
13. Kinmouth, JB, Taylor, GW, and Tracy, GD: Primary lympho-edema: Clinical and lymphangiographic studies of a series of 107 patients in which lower limbs were affected. Br J Surg 45:1, 1957.
14. DeGowin, EL and DeGowin, RL: Bedside Diagnostic Examination, ed 3. Macmillan, New York, 1976.
15. MacKinnon, JL: Study of doppler ultrasonic peripheral vascular assessment by physical therapists. Phys Ther 63:30–34, 1983.
16. Fairbairn, JF, Joyce, JW, and Pairolero, PC: Acute Arterial Occlusion of the Extremities. In Juergen, JL, Spittell, JA, and Fairbairn, JF (eds): Peripheral Vascular Diseases. WB Saunders, Philadelphia, 1980.
17. Ruell, PA, et al: Intermittent claudication: the effect of physical training on walking tolerance and venous lactate concentration. Eur J Appl Physiol 52:420, 1984.
18. Jonason, T, et al: Effect of physical training on different categories of patients with intermittent claudication. Acta Med Scand 206:253, 1979.
19. Sorlie, D and Myhre, K: Effects of physical training in intermittent claudication. Scand J Clin Lab Invest 38:217, 1978.
20. Ekroth, R, et al: Physical training of patients with intermittent claudication: Indications, methods and results. Surgery 84:640, 1978.
21. Buerger, L: The Circulatory Disturbances of the Extremities. Philadelphia, 1924.
22. Wisham, LH, Abramson, AS, and Ebel, A: Value of exercise in peripheral arterial disease. JAMA 153:10, 1953.
23. McCulloch, JM: Intermittent compression for treatment of a chronic stasis ulceration. Phys Ther 61:1452, 1981.

SUPPLEMENTAL READINGS

1. Ellis, H: Varicose Veins: How They Are Treated and What You Can Do to Help. Arco, New York, 1982.
2. Barker, WF: Peripheral Arterial Disease, ed 2. WB Saunders, Philadelphia, 1975.
3. Holling, HE: Peripheral Vascular Diseases: Diagnosis and Management. JB Lippincott, Philadelphia, 1972.
4. Kappert, A and Winsor, T: Diagnosis of Peripheral Vascular Disease. FA Davis, Philadelphia, 1972.

GLOSSARY

Acrocyanosis: Cyanosis of the extremities owing to a vasomotor disturbance; seen in catatonia and hysteria.

Agenesis: Congenital absence of an organ or part of an organ.

Anastamotic: Pertaining to the natural communication between two vessels.

Aplasia: Failure of an organ or tissue to develop normally.

Arteriole: Smallest arterial branch of the vascular system.

Arteriovenous fistula: An abnormal connection between the arterial and venous systems.

Bifurcation: A point of branching or forking of a vessel.

Bruit: An adventitious sound, heard in a blood vessel during auscultation, which is caused by the turbulent flow of blood.

Capillary: A small blood vessel that connects arterioles to venules.

Cyanosis: A slightly bluish-gray or purple discoloration of the skin caused by a decreased hemoglobin content in the blood.

Endarterectomy: An excision or removal of the thickened, atheromatous intimal layer of an artery.

Fistula: An abnormal connection between two areas.

Gangrene: Tissue death or necrosis which is usually due to impaired or absent blood supply.

Hemosiderin: A pigment released from hemoglobin owing to red cell lysis.

Intermittent claudication: A severe pain in the lower extremity that occurs with activity but subsides with rest; the result of inadequate arterial blood supply to the exercising muscles.

Livedo reticularis: A semipermanent bluish discoloration of the skin which is aggravated by exposure to cold.

Pallor: Paleness or absence of coloration in the skin.

Radiometer: A temperature-measuring device designed to measure infrared radiation.

Raynaud's phenomenon: A vasospastic disorder; attacks are initiated by exposure to cold or emotional disturbance; results in intermittent episodes of pallor followed by cyanosis then redness of the digits before returning to normal. Etiology is unknown.

Rubor: Redness of the skin; a primary sign of inflammation.

Scleroderma: A chronic disease of unknown etiology resulting in a sclerosis, or hardening, of the skin and other internal organs.

Stasis dermatitis: An inflammatory condition of the skin; associated with pooling of venous blood.

Sympathectomy: An excision of a portion of the sympathetic nervous system.

Thermistor: A temperature-measuring device designed to measure contact temperature of the skin.

Thoracic outlet syndrome: A condition caused by compression of the brachial plexus nerve trunks; clinical features may include vascular compromise, pain, weakness, and paresthesias of distal segments of the upper extremity.

Thrombophlebitis: Inflammation of a vein in conjunction with the formation of a thrombus; usually occurs in an extremity, most frequently in a leg. Clinical features include swelling, erythema, and heat (SYN: phlebitis).

Trophic changes: Tissue changes that result from impaired growth and nourishment; may include abnormal pigmentation, changes in skin color, loss of hair, dry skin, thickened nails, **stasis dermatitis,** or ulceration.

Vascular prosthesis: Any artificial component placed into the vascular system to perform a function previously carried out by a unit of the system (e.g., an artificial heart valve).

Venule: Smallest venous branch of the vascular system.

APPENDIX A VASCULAR EXAMINATION WORKSHEET

Patient's Name _____ Age _____
Occupation _____ Sex _____
PROBLEM
History and Subjective Examination
When did problem begin? _____
How did it begin (onset)? _____
  Was it sudden/gradual? _____
  Was there an associated injury (mechanism)? _____
  Was it spontaneous (nontraumatic)? _____
  What was first noticed? _____
  Were there predisposing factors? _____
How has the problem progressed since onset? _____
  Is it better or worse? _____
What relevant family history exists? _____
What relevant personal history exists? _____
Has the patient been treated for this problem previously?
_____
  If yes, what has the treatment been?
  What was the response to treatment? _____
What are the present symptoms? (area, depth, intensity,
  type) _____
  Are they constant? _____
  Do they vary in intensity? _____
  When are they present? _____
  What brings them on? _____
  What makes them increase? _____
  What relieves them? _____
  How long do they last? _____
  Are there associated paresthesias/anesthesias? _____
What is the patient's state of health? _____
Have any diagnostic studies been performed? _____
  If yes, what were the results? _____
Has the patient noticed any color changes in the extrem-
  ities? _____
How is the condition affected by rest/activity? _____
What medications is the patient currently taking? ____
_____

Objective Examination
Observations
  Gait _____
  How does the person move? _____
  Overall appearance? _____
  Weight? _____
Range of motion of affected areas: _____
Palpation
  Skin temperature? _____
  Pulses? _____
  Sensory examination? _____
Clinical Measurements
  Temperature (oral)? _____
  Blood pressure (supine/sitting)? _____
  Deep tendon reflexes? _____
  Auscultation for bruits? _____
  Test for rubor of dependency? _____
  Venous filling time? _____
  Percussion test? _____
  Cuff test for deep vein thrombophlebitis? _____
  Claudication time? _____
  Doppler measurements? _____
  Other tests? _____
_____

Assessment
Do the objective findings correlate with the subjective
  complaints?
Is the nature of this problem such that the physical ther-
  apist should not be treating this patient?
Are findings consistent with diagnosis for which the
  patient was referred?
Plan
What are your short- and long-term goals for this
  patient?
What treatment measures do you wish to use to achieve
  these goals?
What will be the frequency, duration, and intensity of
  treatment?
What home program might you recommend for this
  patient?

Chapter 19

PREPROSTHETIC MANAGEMENT FOR LOWER EXTREMITY AMPUTATION

BELLA J. MAY

OBJECTIVES

1. Identify the major etiologic factors involved in lower extremity amputation.

2. Describe the major concepts involved in amputation surgery.

3. Describe the major methods of postoperative amputation management.

4. Develop an assessment plan for a patient with a lower extremity amputation.

5. Develop a postoperative positioning program for a patient with a lower extremity amputation.

6. Identify the major concepts of proper residual limb bandaging.

7. Develop an exercise program for a patient with a lower extremity amputation.

8. Recognize the psychologic impact of lower extremity amputation.

INTRODUCTION

Lower extremity amputations secondary to some form of peripheral vascular disease are a leading cause of disability among the elderly population today. In 1964, Glattly studied 12,000 individuals with recent amputations and reported that the major cause of amputation was peripheral vascular disease (58 percent), the majority were in the 61-to-70 age group, and 77 percent were male. Ten years later, Kay and Newman replicated the Glattly study for the Committee on Prosthetic Research and Development and the Committee on Prosthetic-Orthotic Education with over 5000 cases and found that 70 percent of the amputations had been done for peripheral vascular disease, the majority were still in the 61-to-70 age group, and 72 percent were male (Table 19–1).[1,2] As individuals continue to live well into their eighth and ninth decades, the incidence of lower extremity amputations among the elderly is expected to rise. The elderly person with a lower extremity amputation is not content to sit in a wheelchair for the rest of life but seeks effective rehabilitation services and a meaningful lifestyle. Physical therapists have a major role in the rehabilitation of these individuals, and early onset of appropriate treatment influences the eventual outcome of rehabilitation.

Some of the content of this chapter appeared in Sanders, GT: *Lower Limb Amputations: A Guide to Rehabilitation*. FA Davis, Philadelphia, 1986. Used here with permission of the publisher.

Table 19–1 PERCENTAGE OF AMPUTATIONS OWING TO TUMOR, TRAUMA, AND DISEASE, BY AGE

Age Group	Tumor		Trauma		Disease	
	Glattly Study (1961–1963)	CPRD-CPOE Study (1973–1974)	Glattly Study (1961–1963)	CPRD-CPOE Study (1973–1974)	Glattly Study (1961–1963)	CPRD-CPOE Study (1973–1974)
0–10	4.9	2.7	3.6	4.2	1.1	0.1
11–20	28.3	33.5	11.0	19.7	1.3	0.9
21–30	12.1	13.8	17.4	25.7	1.3	0.8
31–40	14.0	10.0	18.8	16.9	3.7	2.1
41–50	13.4	11.5	20.7	14.2	10.0	7.7
51–60	13.6	12.7	15.7	10.4	22.6	21.7
61–70	9.1	10.0	9.2	6.8	35.9	36.8
71–80	3.8	5.4	3.0	1.8	20.3	23.9
81–90	0.8	0.4	0.6	0.3	3.7	5.7
91+	0	0	0	0	0.1	0.3

The boxed numerals indicate the age group of highest incidence from each study.

LEVELS OF AMPUTATION

Traditionally, levels of amputation have been identified by anatomic considerations such as above-knee and below-knee. In 1974, the Task Force on Standardization of Prosthetic-Orthotic Terminology developed an international classification system to define amputation levels. Table 19–2 defines the major terms commonly in use today.

Amputations may be performed at any level. The surgeon tries to maintain the greatest bone length and save all possible joints. Amputations for vascular diseases are generally performed at partial-foot, below-knee, or above-knee levels. Until recently, amputations for vascular disease routinely were performed at above-knee levels as surgeons were guided by the presence or absence of popliteal pulses. In 1967, Warren and Record[3] advocated performing below-knee amputations on patients

Table 19–2 LEVELS OF AMPUTATION

Partial toe	Excision of any part of one or more toes
Toe disarticulation	Disarticulation at the metatarsal phalangeal joint
Partial foot/ray resection	Resection of the 3rd, 4th, 5th metatarsals and digits
Transmetatarsal	Amputation through the mid section of all metatarsals
Symes	Ankle disarticulation with attachment of heel pad to distal end of tibia. May include removal of malleoli and distal tibial/fibular flares.
Long below-knee	More than 50% tibial length
Short below-knee	Less than 20% tibial length
Below-knee	Between 20 and 50% of tibial length
Knee disarticulation	Amputation through the knee joint; femur intact.
Long above-knee	More than 60% femoral length
Above-knee	Between 35 and 60% femoral length
Short above-knee	Less than 35% femoral length
Hip disarticulation	Amputation through hip joint; pelvis intact.
Hemipelvectomy	Resection of lower half of the pelvis
Hemicorporectomy	Amputation of both lower limbs and pelvis below L4/5 level

with ischemic feet regardless of popliteal pulses. They stated that bleeding at the amputation site was a better indicator of the potential for healing. In 1967, Sarmiento[4] documented that viability of the skin flaps at the level of amputation was a better indicator of vascular supply than popliteal pulses. Sarmiento advocated performing below-knee amputations for the majority of patients with vascular diseases, emphasizing that elderly individuals with below-knee amputations have a much higher incidence of successful rehabilitation than those with amputations above the knee. In recent years it has become generally accepted that those with unilateral below-knee amputation regardless of age, are more likely to become functional prosthetic users than those with above-knee amputations. Many patients with bilateral below-knee amputations can be successfully rehabilitated, whereas most with bilateral above-knee amputations do not become functional prosthetic users.[5–9] Generally, hip disarticulation, **hemipelvectomy,** and **hemicorporectomy** are performed for tumors and represent a small percentage of the amputee population. Modern surgical and prosthetic techniques have led to greater flexibility in amputation surgery and a higher level of rehabilitation among all patients, regardless of the cause of amputation.

SURGICAL MANAGEMENT

The specific type of amputation surgery used is at the discretion of the surgeon and is often determined by the status of the extremity at the time of amputation. In general, the surgeon must remove part of the limb, allow for primary or secondary wound healing, and construct a residual limb for optimum prosthetic fitting and function. Numerous factors affect the decision on the level of amputation. Conservation of residual limb length is important, as is uncomplicated wound healing. Surgical techniques vary with the level and cause of amputation, and a description of each type of surgical procedure is beyond the scope of this book. However, the physical therapist needs to understand the general principles of amputation surgery.

Skin flaps are as broad as possible, and the scar should

be pliable, painless, and nonadherent. For most above-knee and below-knee amputations, equal length anterior and posterior flaps are used, placing the scar at the distal end of the bone. More recently, long posterior flaps have been used with the **dysvascular** below-knee amputee patients because the posterior tissues have a better blood supply than anterior skin tissues. This places the scar anteriorly over the distal end of the tibia. Care must be taken to ensure that the scar does not become adherent to the bone (Fig. 19–1). Stabilization of major muscles allows for maximum retention of function. Muscle stabilization may be achieved by **myofascial closure, myoplasty, myodesis,** or **tenodesis.** In most below-knee and above-knee amputations, a combination of *myoplasty* (muscle-to-muscle closure) and *myofascial closure* (muscle-to-fascia closure) is used to ensure that the muscles are properly stabilized and do not slide over the end of the bone. In some centers, *myodesis* (muscle attached to periosteum or bone) is employed, particularly in the below-knee amputation. Whatever the technique, muscle stabilization under some tension is desirable.

Severed peripheral nerves may form **neuromas** in the residual limb. It is important for the neuroma to be well surrounded by soft tissue so as not to cause pain and to interfere with prosthetic wear. Surgeons identify the major nerves, pull them down under some tension, then cut them cleanly and sharply and allow them to retract into the soft tissue of the residual limb. Neuromas that form close to scar tissue or bone generally cause pain and may require later resection or revision.

Hemostasis is achieved by ligating major veins and arteries; **cauterization** is used only for small bleeders. Care is taken not to compromise circulation to distal tissues, particularly the skin flaps which are important to uncomplicated wound healing.

Bones are sectioned at a length to allow wound closure without excessive redundant tissue at the end of the residual limb and without placing the incision under great tension. Sharp bone ends are smoothed and rounded; in the below-knee amputation, the anterior portion of the distal tibia is **beveled** to reduce the pressure

between the end of the bone and the prosthetic socket. Care is taken to ensure that the bone is physiologically prepared for the pressures of prosthetic wear.

The closure follows the principles of good surgical management in that tissue layers are approximated under normal physiologic tension. Drainage tubes may be inserted as necessary.

In a traumatic amputation, the surgeon attempts to save as much bone length and viable skin as possible. Proximal joints are preserved while providing for appropriate healing of tissues without secondary complications such as infection. Usually the incision will be left open with the proximal joint immobilized in a functional position for 5 to 9 days to prevent invasive infection. Secondary closure also allows the surgeon to shape the residual limb appropriately for prosthetic rehabilitation.

Amputation for vascular disease is generally considered an elective procedure; the surgeon determines the level of amputation by assessing tissue viability through a variety of measures. Segmental limb blood pressures can be determined by Doppler ultrasound or plethysmography. Determination of tissue oxygen supply by transcutaneous oxygen measurement and determination of skin blood flow by radioisotope have been advocated as more accurate methods of selecting the level of amputation.[10]

REHABILITATION GOALS

The earlier the onset of rehabilitation, the greater the potential for success. The longer the delay, the more likely the development of secondary complications such as joint contractures, general debilitation, and a depressed psychologic state. The postoperative program can be arbitrarily divided into two phases: the *preprosthetic phase,* which is the time between surgery and fitting with a definitive prosthesis or until a decision is made not to fit the patient; and the *prosthetic phase,* which starts with delivery of a permanent replacement limb. The major goal of the preprosthetic period is to prepare the individual physically and psychologically for prosthetic rehabilitation.

The long-term goals of the total rehabilitation program focus on regaining the presurgical level of function. For some, it will mean return to gainful employment with an active recreational life. For others, it will mean independence in the home and community. For still others, it may mean living in the sheltered environment of a retirement center or nursing home. If the amputation resulted from long-standing chronic disease, the goal may be to help the person function at a higher level than immediately before surgery.

Long-term goals include those listed below.

1. Independent in all ambulation and self-care activities.

2. Competent in caring for residual limb and other lower extremity.

3. Determine the individual's physical and emotional suitability for prosthetic use.

4. Help the individual adjust physically and mentally to the loss of a limb.

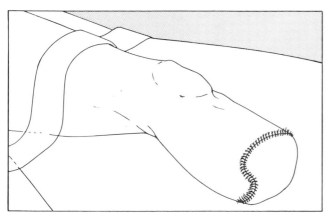

Figure 19–1. Amputation site postsurgery with anterior placement of scar.

5. Maintain the viability of the uninvolved lower extremity.

Goals with bilateral amputations or individuals with other disabilities will vary accordingly.

Specific short-term goals will depend on the results of the assessment and the status of each patient. Generally, it is desirable to achieve the following goals within the first 2 or 3 weeks after surgery, in addition to reducing any specific problem that may exist.

1. Promote healing of the incision and reduction of postoperative edema if a rigid dressing has not been applied.

2. Achieve independence in bed mobility, self-care and transfer activities.

3. Maintain or regain strength in the affected lower extremity.

4. Maintain or increase strength in the remaining extremities.

5. Prevent the development of joint contractures in the residual limb or any extremity; reduce any existing contractures.

6. Initiate instruction in care of the residual limb, including residual limb bandaging if indicated.

7. Assist with adjustment to loss of a body part.

8. Gain initial skill in ambulation with crutches if possible, or a walker.

9. With **peripheral vascular dysfunction,** instruct in care of the remaining lower extremity and provide information to facilitate patient understanding of the disease process.

The success of the rehabilitation program is determined to some extent by the individual's psychophysiologic status and the physical characteristics of the residual limb. The longer the residual limb, the better potential for successful prosthetic ambulation regardless of level of amputation. A well-healed, cylindrical limb with a nonadherent scar is easier to fit than one that is conical or has redundant tisssue distally or laterally. The vascular status of the remaining extremity will affect the rehabilitation program, as will the age of the individual. The presence of conditions such as diabetes, cardiovascular disease, visual impairment, limitation of joint motion, and muscular weakness may affect the eventual level of function.

THE CLINIC TEAM

The majority of amputations today are performed by orthopedic surgeons who may or may not be knowledgeable about prosthetic rehabilitation. Referral to an amputee clinic or to physical therapy may be delayed for many weeks as the surgeon waits until the residual limb heals completely and the postoperative edema has been absorbed. Such delays are undesirable and may limit the eventual outcome of rehabilitation. Ideally, the clinic team should become involved before surgery, or at least immediately after. Unfortunately, many amputations are performed in hospitals without the services of an amputee clinic or a well-trained team which can develop and supervise the program. The physical therapist may be the only person with competence in prosthetic rehabilita-

tion. Close contact with the surgeons in one's facility may serve to increase the likelihood of early referrals.

Members

The amputee clinic team plans and implements comprehensive rehabilitation programs designed to meet the physical, psychologic, and economic needs of the patient. Most amputee clinic teams are located in rehabilitation facilities or university health centers. The team generally includes a physician, physical therapist, occupational therapist, prosthetist, social worker, and vocational counselor. Other health professionals who often contribute to the team are the nurse, dietitian, psychologist, and, possibly, administrative coordinator. Table 19–3 outlines the major functions of team members. Clinic frequency is dictated by the caseload; patients are seen regularly and decisions are made using input from all team members. A screening clinic held by the physical and occupational therapists prior to the actual amputee clinic allows for the careful assessment of each person to be seen and improves the effectiveness of the clinic function.[11]

Residual Limb Care

Surgeons today have several options regarding the postoperative dressing, including (1) immediate postoperative fitting or rigid dressing, (2) semirigid dressing, (3)

Table 19–3 AMPUTEE CLINIC TEAM FUNCTIONS

Physician	Clinic chief; coordinates team decision making; supervises patient's general medical condition; orders appliances.
Physical therapist	Assesses and treats patients through preprosthetic and prosthetic phases; makes recommendations for prosthetic components and whether or not to fit the patient. May be clinic coordinator.
Prosthetist	Fabricates and modifies prosthesis; recommends prosthetic components; shares data on new prosthetic developments.
Occupational therapist	Assesses and treats patients through preprosthetic and prosthetic phases; special emphasis on functional training and management of upper extremity amputations. May be clinic coordinator.
Social worker	Financial counselor and coordinator; liaison with third-party payers and community agencies; helps patient and family cope with social and financial problems.
Dietitian	Consultant for patients with diabetes or those needing diet guidance.
Vocational counselor	Assesses client's employment potential; helps with education, training, and placement.

controlled environment, or (4) soft dressing. Regardless of the type of dressing used, the limb must not be allowed to remain uncovered for any length of time between dressing changes because edema will result. Excessive edema in the residual limb can compromise healing and cause pain.

RIGID DRESSING

In the early 1960s, orthopedic surgeons in the United States started experimenting with a technique developed in Europe that consisted of fitting the patient with a socket made of plaster of Paris in the configuration of the definitive prosthesis. In some instances, a foot and pylon were attached and the patient was allowed to walk with limited weight bearing within 48 hours of surgery. Application techniques varied to some extent. In some centers the dressing was brought above the knee to prevent possible movement between the residual limb and the socket, and in another center the dressing was wrapped below the knee with the knee joint temporarily immobilized by a soft dressing.[12,13] Regardless of the method of suspension, the **immediate postoperative prosthesis** applied in the operating room provides several advantages over the more traditional soft dressing:

1. It greatly limits the development of postoperative edema in the residual limb, thereby reducing postoperative pain and enhancing wound healing.
2. It allows for earlier ambulation with the attachment of a pylon and foot.
3. It allows for earlier fitting of the definitive prosthesis by reducing the length of time needed for shrinking the residual limb.
4. It is configured to each individual residual limb.
The major disadvantages are:
1. It requires careful application by individuals knowledgeable about prosthetic principles.
2. It requires close supervision during the healing stage.
3. It does not allow for daily wound inspection and dressing changes.

After several years, research indicated that early ambulation did not influence wound healing positively and, in fact, might interfere with healing if the patient could not control the amount of weight borne on the amputated extremity.[4,11] Since then, the immediate postoperative prosthesis (intended to allow early ambulation) generally has been replaced by the molded rigid dressing. This rigid dressing also is applied in the operating room but is not intended for early weight-bearing activities. In addition to the surgeon, the prosthetist, physical therapist, nurse, or cast technician can, after training, apply the rigid dressing, which consists of a total contact plaster of Paris socket padded over bony prominances and suspended so as to prevent any motion between the skin and the cast. Individuals interested in learning casting techniques should attend a course given for that purpose.

Like the postoperative prosthesis, the rigid dressing limits the development of postoperative edema, thereby decreasing pain and improving potential for healing. Studies indicate that healing takes place, even in limbs wihout circulation through the major vessels, if there is good bleeding through the skin flaps at the time of surgery.[4,13] The absence of edema allows for good skin circulation in the surgical site, thereby allowing surgeons to perform more amputations at below-knee levels. The rigid dressing is considered the most effective postoperative treatment available today.

SEMIRIGID DRESSINGS

Semirigid dressings include the **Unna paste,** the air splint, and the controlled environment treatment (CET). The **Unna paste dressing,** a compound of zinc oxide, gelatin, glycerin, and calamine, is applied in the operating room. Once dry, it is light, semirigid, and controls postoperative edema. Depending on the length of the residual limb, the dressing may be applied to midthigh or to just below the knee for a below-knee amputation. The above-knee dressing may include a hip spica, if necessary, for suspension. The major advantages of the Unna paste dressing are

1. Good control of postoperative edema.
2. Self-suspension without additional straps.
3. Can be changed easily if there is much wound exudate.
4. Allows freedom of motion in the proximal joint of long residual limbs.
5. Conforms to the shape of the residual limb.
The major disadvantages are
1. It may loosen before being fully dry and allow some edema to develop.
2. It is less rigid than the plaster of Paris dressing and therefore does not protect the residual limb as well.
3. It needs more frequent changing than the plaster of Paris dressing.
The Unna paste dressing has occasionally been used with a temporary prosthesis as a covering for the residual limb.

Little first reported the use of an air splint to control postoperative edema as well as to aid in early ambulation[14,15] (Fig. 19–2). The air splint is a plastic double wall bag that is pumped to the desired level of rigidity. It has a zipper and encases the entire extremity, which is covered with an appropriate postsurgical dressing. The advantages of the air splint are

1. Better edema control than the soft dressing, but not as effective as the rigid dressing.
2. The incision is available for inspection.
3. Bipedal support for the patient in the upright position.
4. Relatively inexpensive, inasmuch as it can be reused.
5. It can be applied by most health care personnel, with minimal training.
The disadvantages are
1. Once applied, the pressure is constant and does not intimately conform to the shape of the residual limb.
2. The environment of the plastic is hot and humid, requiring frequent cleaning.
3. Thickness of the inflated walls encourages hip abduction.
Pressure is measured in millimeters of mercury and can be varied. The system appears to be more effective for

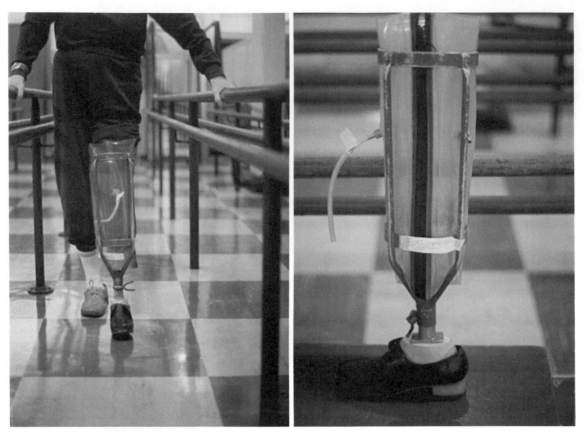

Figure 19–2. Air splint. (From Sanders, GT: *Lower Limb Amputations: A Guide to Rehabilitation.* FA Davis, Philadelphia, 1986, p 363, with permission.)

patients with below-knee than above-knee amputations because of the difficulty in suspending the appliance with the shorter residual limb.

The controlled environment treatment (CET) was developed at the National Biomechanical Research and Development Unit of Reohampton, England, and has been used in some centers in the United States.[16,17] The CET is composed of a console and a polyvinyl bag. The console controls pressure, temperature, and humidity, and sterilizes the air in the unit. The polyvinyl transparent bag encases the residual limb. Bags are available in a variety of sizes and can be used with long above-knee limbs as well as below-knee and Symes amputations. In a preliminary report of 20 patients, Kegel indicated that the CET decreased postsurgical edema and pain and appeared to improve circulation to the wound as a result of the cyclical pressure changes.[10] The bag's flexibility allowed active exercises of the involved extremity as well as standing at bedside. The hose connecting the bag to the console made ambulation somewhat difficult. Kegel indicated that, in addition to the advantages of the rigid dressing for control of edema and pain, the CET allowed some 60 degrees of active knee motion and gave the therapist and nursing staff an excellent opportunity to observe the condition of the wound. On the negative side, the size of the equipment keeps the patient in the hospital room, and the bag interferes with lying prone so that a definitive program of hip extension must be undertaken. In addition, the nursing staff must pay particular

attention to skin care because these patients spend more time in bed than those with other types of postsurgical dressing.

SOFT DRESSINGS

The soft dressing is the oldest method of postsurgical management of the residual limb. The major advantages are

1. It is relatively inexpensive.
2. It is lightweight and readily available.
3. It can be laundered.

The major disadvantages are

1. Relatively poor control of edema.
2. Requires skill in proper application.
3. Needs frequent reapplication.
4. Can slip and form a tourniquet.

A dressing is applied to the incision, followed by some form of gauze pad, then the compression wrap. The soft dressing is indicated in cases of local infection but is not the treatment of choice for most individuals. The patient should learn to apply the wrap as soon as possible after wound care is no longer necessary. Many elderly persons, especially those with above-knee amputations, do not have the necessary balance and coordination to wrap the residual limb effectively.

Some surgeons prefer delaying elastic wrap until the incision has healed and the sutures have been removed. Leaving the residual limb without any pressure wrap allows for full development of postoperative edema. The limb may be quite uncomfortable, and edema may interfere with circulation in the many small vessels in the skin and soft tissue, thereby potentially compromising healing. The therapist can discuss the benefits of early wrapping if no other form of rigid dressing is used.

One of the major drawbacks of the elastic wrap is that it needs frequent rewrapping. Movement of the residual limb against the bedclothes, bending and extending the proximal joints, and general body movements will cause slippage and changes in pressure. Covering the finished wrap with a stockinet helps reduce some of the wrinkling. However, careful and frequent rewrapping is the only effective way to prevent complications. Nursing staff, family members, and the patient, as well as the physical therapist, need to assume responsibility for frequent inspection and rewrapping of the residual limb. Residual limb wrapping is described in detail later in this chapter.

ASSESSMENT

Careful assessment of each individual is an integral part of preprosthetic management. Assessment data are obtained continuously throughout this period as the incision heals and the person's tolerance improves. Data regarding the condition of the residual limb, strength of the affected extremity, joint range of motion, condition of the other extremity, and the patient's feeling about the amputation are used in establishing treatment activities and in setting priorities and terminal expectations. The availability of some of this data will depend in part on the treatment of the residual limb by the surgeon.

Range of Motion

Gross range of motion estimations are adequate for assessment of the uninvolved extremity, but specific goniometric measurements are necessary for the amputated side. Hip flexion and extension, abduction and adduction measurements are taken early in the postoperative phase following below-knee amputation. Measurement of knee flexion and extension are taken, if the dressing allows, after some incisional healing has occurred. Hip flexion and extension and abduction and adduction range of motion measurements are taken several days after surgery, when the dressing allows, with an above-knee amputation. Measurement of internal and external hip rotation is difficult to obtain and unnecessary if no gross abnormality or pathology is evident. Joint range of motion is monitored throughout the preprosthetic period.

Muscle Strength

Gross manual muscle testing of the upper extremities and uninvolved lower extremity is performed early in the postoperative period. Manual muscle testing of the involved lower extremity must usually wait until most healing has occurred. With a below-knee amputation

good strength is needed in the knee extensors and flexors as well as in the hip extensors and abductors for satisfactory prosthetic ambulation. The patient with an above-knee amputation uses the hip extensors and abductors to a great extent during ambulation and requires at least good strength in these muscles. The strength of these muscles should be monitored throughout the preprosthetic program.

Residual Limb

Circumferential measurements of the residual limb are taken as soon as the dressing will allow, then regularly throughout the preprosthetic period. Measurements are made at regular intervals over the length of the residual limb. Circumferential measurements of the below-knee or Syme residual limb are started at the medial tibial plateau and taken every 2.5 to 3.2 inches (5 to 8 cm), depending on the length of the limb. Length is measured from the medial tibial plateau to the end of the bone.

Circumferential measurements of the above-knee or through knee residual limb are started at the ischial tuberosity or the greater trochanter, whichever is most palpable, and taken every 3.2 to 4 inches (8 to 10 cm). Length is measured from the ischial tuberosity or the greater trochanter to the end of the bone. If there is considerable excess tissue distal to the end of the bone, then length measurements are taken to both the end of the bone and the incision line. For accuracy of repeat measurements, exact landmarks are carefully noted. If the ischial tuberosity is used in above-knee measurements, hip joint position is noted as well. Other information gathered about the residual limb includes its shape (conical, bulbous, redundant tissue), skin condition, joint proprioception, and tactile sensation.

The Phantom Limb

The majority of amputee patients over the age of six years will experience a **phantom limb** sensation, the sensation of the limb which is no longer there. The phantom, which usually occurs initially immediately after surgery, is often described as a tingling, pressure sensation, sometimes a numbness. The distal part of the extremity is the most frequently felt, although occasionally the person will feel the whole extremity. The sensation is responsive to external stimuli such as bandaging or rigid dressing. It may dissipate over time, or the person may have the sensation throughout life. Phantom sensation is painless and usually does not interfere with prosthetic rehabilitation. It is important that the patient be aware of the possibility of phantom limb sensation.

Phantom pain occurs less frequently and is usually characterized as either a cramping or squeezing sensation, a shooting pain, or a burning pain. Some patients report all three. The pain may be localized or diffuse; it may be continuous or intermittent and triggered by some external stimuli. It may diminish over time or may become a permanent and often disabling condition.

There is little agreement as to the cause of either phantom sensation or pain. Although phantom sensation rarely interferes with prosthetic rehabilitation, phantom pain frequently does.

The residual limb should be carefully examined to differentiate phantom pain from any other condition such as a neuroma. Sometimes, wearing a prosthesis will ease the phantom pain. Noninvasive treatments such as ultrasound, icing, TENS, massage, or exercise have been used with varying success. Mild nonnarcotic analgesics have been of limited value with some individuals, and no particular narcotic analgesic has proven effective. Occasionally, in the presence of trigger points, injection with steroids or a local anesthetic has reduced the pain temporarily. A variety of surgical procedures such as **chordotomies, rhizotomies,** and peripheral **neurectomies** have been tried with limited success. The treatment of phantom pain can be very frustrating for the clinic team and the patient. Treatment is individualized and can include psychotherapy on an ongoing basis.

Other Data

The vascular status of the uninvolved lower extremity should be determined. The condition of the skin, presence of pulses, sensation, temperature, edema, pain on exercise or at rest, presence of wounds, ulceration, or other abnormalities should be assessed.

Activities of daily living, including transfer and ambulatory status, are assessed and documented. Information on the patient's home situation, including any constraints or special needs, is valuable in establishing an individually relevant treatment program. Data regarding

Table 19–4 PREPROSTHETIC ASSESSMENT GUIDE

Medical status	1. Cause of amputation (disease, tumor, trauma, congenital) 2. Associated diseases/symptoms (neuropathy, visual disturbances, cardiopulmonary disease, renal disease, congenital anomalies) 3. Medications
Skin	1. Scar (location; healed, unhealed; adherent, mobile; invaginated, flat, thickened, keloid; from other surgery or a burn) 2. Open lesions (size, shape, exudate) 3. Moisture (moist, dry, crusting) 4. Sensation (absent, diminished, hypersensitive to touch or pressure) 5. Grafts (location, type, degree of healing) 6. Dermatologic lesions (psoriasis, eczema, acne vulgaris, dermatitis, boils, epidermoid cysts)
Length	1. Bone length 2. Soft tissue, redundant tissue length 3. The length of the below-knee limb is usually measured from the medial tibial plateau, and the above-knee limb from the ischial tuberosity or the greater trochanter
Shape	1. Cylindrical, conical, hourglass, "dog-ears," bulbous 2. Above-knee adductor roll
Vascularity (Both limbs if cause of amputation is vascular disease)	1. Pulses (femoral, popliteal, dorsalis pedis, posterior tibial) 2. Color (cyanotic, redness) 3. Temperature (cool, warm) 4. Edema (circumference measurements, water displacement measurement, diameter measurement using calipers) 5. Pain (in dependent position, throbbing, claudication) 6. Tropic changes (shininess, dryness, loss of hair)
Range of motion (ROM)	1. Hips (flexion, abduction, or external rotation contracture) 2. Knee (flexion, extension contracture) 3. Ankle (plantarflexion contracture)
Strength	1. Major muscle groups 2. Adaptation must be made for shortened lever arm
Neurologic	1. Neuroma (location, tenderness) 2. Phantom (sensation; pain; description: throbbing, burning, electrical; duration) 3. Diabetic neuropathy (touch, joint proprioception, nerve conduction velocity, electromyogram) 4. Mental status (alert, senile; intelligent, limited ability to understand)
Activities of daily living	1. Transfers (bed to wheelchair, to toilet, to tub, to automobile; independent, dependent) 2. Ambulatory status (with crutches, walker; type of gait; independent, dependent) 3. Home (architectural barriers, safety rails; stairs; other hazards, such as small rugs, unsturdy rails) 4. Self-care (independent, dependent; includes residual limb care)
Psychologic	1. Emotional status (depression, denial, cooperativeness, enthusiasm, motivation) 2. Family situation (interest, support, level of understanding, ability to help) 3. Work situation (job opportunity) 4. Prosthetic goals (desire for a prosthesis, anticipated activity level and lifestyle)
Prior prosthesis	1. Type, components 2. Problems, gait deviations

presurgical activity level and the person's own long-range goals are obtained through interview.

The person's apparent emotional status and degree of adjustment are noted. Exploration of the patient's suitability and desire for a prosthesis is begun and continues throughout the preprosthetic period. Any other problems that may affect the rehabilitation program and goals are assessed and documented. Table 19–4 illustrates an assessment guide.

EMOTIONAL ADJUSTMENT

Initial reaction to the loss of a limb is usually grief and depression. If the amputation is traumatic, the immediate reaction may include disbelief. The person may experience insomnia, restlessness, and have difficulty concentrating. Some individuals may actually mourn the possible loss of a job or the ability to participate in a favorite sport or other activities rather than the lost limb per se. In the early stages, the sense of grief may alternate with feelings of hopelessness, despondency, bitterness, and anger. Socially patients may feel lonely, isolated, and the object of pity or horror. Concerns about the future, about body image and function, about the responses of family and friends, and about employment all affect the individual's reactions.

Long-term adjustment depends to a great extent on the individual's basic personality structure, sense of accomplishment, and place in the family, community, and world. In general, many individuals make a satisfactory adjustment to the loss of a limb and are reintegrated into a full and active life. In achieving final acceptance, the individual may go through a number of stages, including denial, anger, euphoria, and social withdrawal.

Some individuals may try to avoid distressing thoughts of the lost limb through conscious self-control or by avoiding situations or people that remind them of the lost limb. Others may display temper tantrums or irrational resentment. A few may revert to childlike states of helplessness and dependence.

Many individuals are not fully aware of the consequences of amputation and may fear other physical limitations as a result of the surgery. Fear of impotence or sterility may lead some men to make grandiose statements or display reckless behavior to mask the fear. Thorough explanations of the amputation process and implications by the surgeon, physical therapist, or other health worker may alleviate many of these fears.

Generally, following amputation, individuals dream of themselves as not being amputated. This image may be so vivid that persons who have lost a leg fall as they get up at night and attempt to walk to the bathroom without a prosthesis or crutches. Individuals who have lost a limb through injury may dream about the accident in which they were injured. Such reenactments may lead to insomnia, trembling fits, speech impediments, and difficulty with concentration. In general, individuals with congenital amputations or who acquire amputations before the age of 5 do not have some of the problems mentioned above because their amputation is part of their developed self-image.

Psychologic Support

The patient with an amputation needs to receive reassurance and understanding from the entire rehabilitation team. The staff should create an open and receptive environment and be willing to listen. The patient should know what to expect during the entire process. The steps of rehabilitation and the goals should be carefully explained by the surgeon and therapists. Audiovisual media such as films or slides may be helpful in patient orientation and education.

Others with amputations who have made satisfactory adjustments in their lives and successfully completed rehabilitation may provide support and encouragement to the new patient in private or group sessions. Professionals skilled in group dynamics should be present, especially for medical or technical advice regarding such issues as diabetes, medications, or peripheral vascular disease. Family and friends should be invited to attend. The atmosphere should be nonthreatening so that patients can express their feelings and frustrations.

Patients have various attitudes toward the prosthesis. Many are particularly concerned about its appearance, hoping that it will conceal their disability and give the illusion of an intact body. Others claim to be concerned primarily with the restoration of function. When the artificial limb is fitted, the person must face the fact that the natural limb has been lost irrevocably. If the patient is told that the prosthesis will "replace" the amputated limb, then there may be unrealistic expectations that appearance and function will be as good as in the nonamputated leg. Realistic adjustment will be necessary as the individual learns to use the artificial substitute. Good predictors for adjustment to the prosthesis are motivation to master the prosthesis and return to an active lifestyle.

The Elderly

The elderly individual's immediate reaction to amputation is no different than that of any other individual, except that the amputation will usually not come as a surprise. The reaction may depend in part on the severity of preoperative pain and the extent of attempts to save the diseased limb. Individuals who have suffered considerable pain may be grateful that the pain has ended. Patients who underwent extensive medical and surgical procedures to save the limb may have a sense of failure that the efforts were not successful. Some may feel a sense of hopelessness and despair and have a preoccupation with impending death. Others may suffer insomnia, loss of appetite, and be withdrawn. Some elderly individuals may experience a loss of self-esteem and be afraid of becoming dependent. In some instances, they may express that they have nothing to live for and desire death. Occasionally suicide may be attempted. Elderly persons seldom use denial, and are more likely to dream that the amputation has taken place than are younger individuals. The elderly person may view the amputation as impending death because the rest of the body is vulnerable.

If preoperative attitudes are unrealistically hopeful, then postoperative disturbances may be more severe. The elderly person should not be misled to expect a total cure. Learning to use an artificial limb may be a slow and discouraging ordeal, and the patient may not express distress or depression in front of the optimism of others. Sharing and support from other elderly persons with amputations can be quite helpful, as can a realistic attitude by rehabilitation team members.

Complete rehabilitation includes not only preparation of the individual physically and psychologically for the community but also preparation of the community for the individual. Public education media can be used to inform the community of the potentials of persons with amputations in society and employment. As with any other physically challenged individual, those with amputations need to be accepted and integrated into the community because of their abilities and not their disabilities.

RESIDUAL LIMB CARE

Individuals not fitted with a rigid dressing or a temporary prosthesis use elastic wrap or **shrinkers** to reduce the size of the residual limb. The patient or a member of the family applies the bandage which is worn 24 hours a day, except when bathing.

Removable rigid dressings for use with below-knee amputations are also available. This type of dressing may be an important alternative to the elastic wrap for some patients. Regretfully, there are fewer alternatives for the above-knee amputation; rigid dressings and inexpensive temporary prostheses are more difficult to fabricate, and elastic wraps or shrinkers are only minimally effective. It may be advisable to fit the amputated limb with a definitive prosthesis early and then to adjust for shrinkage by using additional socks or a liner.

There may be difficulty controlling edema in the residual limb owing to complications of diabetes, cardiovascular disease, or hypertension. Therapeutically, an intermittent compression unit can be used to reduce edema on a temporary basis. Above- and below-knee sleeves are commercially available.

Proper hygiene and skin care are important. Once the incision is healed and the sutures removed, the person can bathe normally. The residual limb is treated as any other part of the body; it is kept clean and dry. Individuals with dry skin may use a good skin lotion. Care must be taken to avoid abrasions, cuts, and other skin problems. Friction massage, in which layers of skin, subcutaneous tissue, and muscle are moved over the respective underlying tissue, can be used to prevent or to mobilize adherent scar tissue. The massage is done gently, after the wound is healed and no infection is present. Patients can learn to perform a gentle friction massage to help decrease hypersensitivity of the residual limb to touch and pressure. Vibration is also an effective measure for decreasing hypersensitivity. Early handling of the residual limb by the patient is an aid to acceptance and is encouraged, particularly for individuals who may be repulsed by the limb.

The patient is taught to inspect the residual limb with a mirror each night to make sure there are no sores or impending problems, especially in areas not readily visible. If the person has diminished sensation, careful inspection is particularly important. Because the residual limb tends to become a bit edematous after bathing as a reaction to the warm water, nightly bathing is recommended, particularly once a prosthesis has been fitted. The elastic bandage, shrinker, or removable rigid dressing is reapplied after bathing. If the person has been fitted with a temporary prosthesis, the residual limb is wrapped at night and any time the prosthesis is not worn. Sometimes, individuals fitted in surgery with a rigid dressing then transferred immediately into a temporary prosthesis do not know how to bandage and encounter difficulties with edema after they remove the prosthesis at night. Learning proper bandaging is part of the rehabilitation program for all patients, because most people need to wrap the limb at one time or another.

Patients have been known to apply a variety of "home and folk remedies" to the residual limb. Historically it was believed that the skin had to be toughened for prosthetic wear by beating it with a towel-wrapped bottle. Various ointments and lotions have been applied; residual limbs also have been immersed in substances such as vinegar, salt water, and gasoline to harden the skin. Although the skin does need to adjust to the pressures of wearing an artificial limb, there is no evidence to indicate that "toughening" techniques are beneficial. Such methods may actually be deleterious, inasmuch as research indicates that soft pliable skin is better able to cope with stress than tough dry skin. Patient education on proper skin care can reduce the use of home remedies.

The skin of the residual limb may be affected by a variety of dermatologic problems such as eczema, psoriasis, or radiation burns. A few of these conditions may mitigate against fitting or wrapping. Treatment may include ultraviolet irradiation, whirlpool, reflex heating, hyperbaric oxygen, or medication. Care must be taken in using ultraviolet or heat in the presence of vascular dysfunction. The whirlpool may not be the treatment of choice because it increases circulation and edema in the treated limb. The advantages of the whirlpool as a cleansing agent for skin problems, infected wounds, or incidences of delayed healing must be balanced against its disadvantages before effectiveness can be determined for any individual person.

Residual Limb Wrapping

There are many methods of wrapping the residual limb, and most therapists will adapt a method to their own needs. Without proper instruction and supervision, patients tend to wrap the residual limb in a circular manner, often creating a tourniquet which may compromise healing and foster the development of a bulbous end. Although the below-knee residual limb can be wrapped effectively in a sitting position, it is difficult to wrap and anchor the above-knee limb properly while sitting. Elderly patients often cannot balance themselves in the standing position while wrapping. An effective bandage will be smooth and wrinkle free, will emphasize angular turns, will provide pressure distally, and will encourage proximal joint extension. The ends of bandages should be fastened with tape, safety pins, or velcro rather than clips, which can cut the skin and do not anchor well. A system of wrapping that uses mostly angular or figure-eight turns was developed specifically to meet the needs of the elderly and has been in use for the past 20 years.[18] Figures 19–3 and 19–4 illustrate the techniques.

THE BELOW-KNEE BANDAGE

Two 4-inch elastic bandages will usually be enough to wrap most below-knee residual limbs. Very large residual limbs may require three bandages. The below-knee bandages should not be sewn together, so that the weave of each bandage can be brought in contraposition to each other to provide more support. Although an elastic wrap does not provide as much pressure as a rigid dressing, it should be used as effectively as possible to help deter the development of postsurgical edema as much as possible; therefore, a firm even pressure against all soft tissues is desirable. If the incision is placed anteriorly, then an attempt should be made to bring the bandages from posterior to anterior over the distal end.

The first bandage is started at either the medial or lateral tibial condyle and brought diagonally over the anterior surface of the limb to the distal end. One edge of the bandage should just cover the midline of the incision in an anterior-posterior plane. The bandage is continued diagonally over the posterior surface then back over the beginning turn as an anchor. At this point, there is a choice: The bandage may be brought directly over the beginning point as indicated in Figure 19–3, or it may be brought across the front of the residual limb in an *X* design. The latter is particularly useful with long residual limbs and aids in bandage suspension. An anchoring turn over the distal thigh is made, making sure that the wrap is clear of the patella and is not tight around the distal thigh.

After a single anchoring turn above the knee, the bandage is brought back around the opposite tibial condyle and down to the distal end of the limb. One edge of the bandage should overlap the midline of the incision and the other wrap by at least ½ inch to ensure adequate distal end support. The figure-eight pattern is continued as depicted in Figure 19–3 until the bandage is used up. Care should be taken to cover the residual limb completely with a firm and even pressure. Semicircular turns are made posteriorly to bring the bandage in line to cross

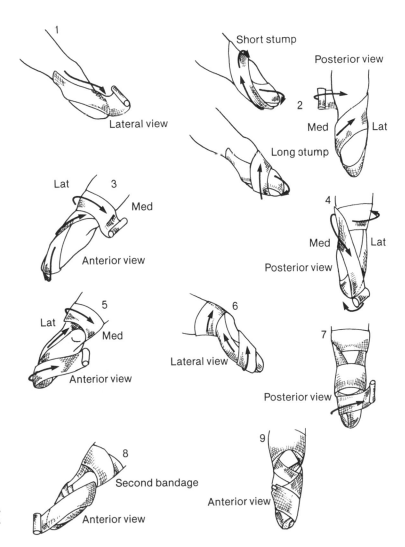

Figure 19–3. Below-knee residual limb wrapping. (From Sanders, GT: *Lower Limb Amputations: A Guide to Rehabilitation.* FA Davis, Philadelphia, 1986, p 365, with permission.)

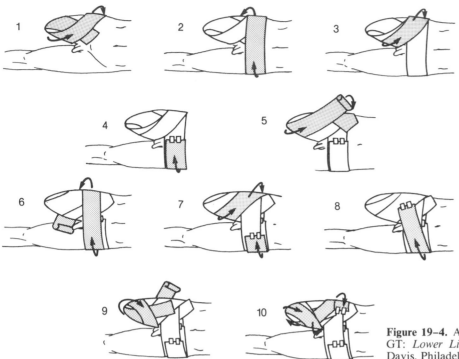

Figure 19–4. Above-knee residual limb wrapping. (From Sanders, GT: *Lower Limb Amputations: A Guide to Rehabilitation.* FA Davis, Philadelphia, 1986, p 366, with permission.)

the anterior surface in an angular line. This maneuver provides greater pressure on the posterior soft tissue while distributing pressure anteriorly where the bone is close to the skin. Each turn should partially overlap other turns so that the whole residual limb is well covered. The pattern is usually from proximal to distal and back to proximal, starting at the tibial condyles and covering both condyles as well as the patellar tendon. Usually the patella is left free to aid in knee motion, although with extremely short residual limbs it may be necessary to cover it for better suspension.

The second bandage is wrapped like the first, except that it is started at the opposite tibial condyle from the first bandage. Bringing the weave of each bandage in contraposition exerts a more even pressure. With both bandages, an effort is made to bring the angular turns across each other rather than in the same direction.

THE ABOVE-KNEE BANDAGE

For most residual limbs, two 6-inch and one 4-inch bandages will adequately cover the limb. The patient is depicted in a sidelying position in Figure 19–4, which allows a family member or therapist easy access to the residual limb. The patient with good balance on the remaining limb can self-bandage in the standing position, but it is difficult for the patient to self-bandage correctly in the sitting position.

The 6-inch bandages are used first. The first bandage is started in the groin and brought diagonally over the anterior surface to the distal lateral corner, around the end of the residual limb, and diagonally up the posterior side to the iliac crest and around the hips in a spica. The bandage is started medially so that the hip wrap will encourage extension. After the turn around the hips, the bandage is wrapped around the proximal portion of the residual limb high in the groin, then back around the hips. Although this is a proximal circular turn, it does not create a tourniquet as long as it is continued around the hips. Going around the medial portion of the residual limb high in the groin ensures coverage of the soft tissue in the adductor area and reduces the possibility of an adductor roll, a complication that can seriously interfere with comfortable prosthetic wear. In most instances, the first bandage ends in the second spica and is anchored with tape or a pin.

The second 6-inch bandage is wrapped like the first but is started a bit more laterally. Any areas not covered with the first bandage must be covered at this time. The second bandage is also anchored in a hip spica after the first figure-eight turn and after the second turn high in the groin. As more of the first two bandages are used to cover the proximal residual limb, care must be taken that no tourniquet is created. Bringing the bandage directly from the proximal medial area into a hip spica helps keep the adductor tissue covered and prevents rolling of the bandage to some degree.

The 4-inch bandage is used to exert the greatest amount of pressure over mid and distal areas of the residual limb. It is usually not necessary to anchor this bandage around the hips because friction with the already applied bandages and good figure-eight turns provide adequate suspension. The 4-inch bandage is generally started laterally to bring the weave across the weave of previous bandages. Regular figure-eight turns in varied patterns to cover all the residual limb are the most effective.

Bandages are applied with firm pressure from the onset. Elastic bandages can be wrapped directly over a soft postsurgical dressing so that bandaging can begin immediately after surgery. The elastic wrap controls edema more effectively if minimal gauze coverage is used over the residual limb. Several gauze pads placed just over the incision usually provide adequate protection without compromising the effect of the wrap. Care must be taken to avoid any wrinkles or folds, which can cause excessive skin pressure, particularly over a soft dressing.

SHRINKERS

Shrinkers are socklike garments knitted of heavy rubber-reinforced cotton; they are conical in shape and come in a variety of sizes (Fig. 19–5). Shrinkers are an alternative to the elastic wrap and can be used to control edema of the residual limb. The below-knee shrinker is rolled over the residual limb and is designed to be self-suspending. Individuals with heavy thighs may need additional suspension with garters or a waist belt. Currently available above-knee shrinkers incorporate a hip spica, which provides good suspension except with obese individuals. Care must be taken that the patient understands the importance of proper suspension because any rolling of the edges or slipping of the shrinker can create a tourniquet around the proximal part of the residual limb. Although easier to apply than the elastic wrap, there is some controversy regarding the effectiveness of shrinkers. A recent study reported shrinkers to be more effective than an elastic wrap in decreasing limb volume in below-knee residual limbs; however, others have not shared this experience.[19] Shrinkers are more expensive to use than elastic wrap; the initial cost is greater, and then

new shrinkers of smaller sizes must be purchased as the limb volume decreases. However, shrinkers are a viable option for individuals who are not able to wrap the residual limb properly.

Positioning

One of the major goals of the early postoperative program is to prevent secondary complications such as contractures of adjacent joints. Contractures can develop as a result of muscle imbalance or fascial tightness, from a protective withdrawal reflex into hip and knee flexion, from loss of plantar stimulation in extension, or as a result of faulty positioning such as prolonged sitting. The patient should understand the importance of proper positioning and regular exercises in preparing for eventual prosthetic fit and ambulation (Fig. 19–6).

With the below-knee amputation, full range of motion in the hips and knee, particularly in extension, is needed. While sitting, the patient can keep the knee extended by using a posterior splint or a board attached to the wheelchair. With an above-knee amputation, full range of motion in the hip, particularly in extension and adduction, is needed. Prolonged sitting is to be avoided, especially for individuals who have difficulty walking on crutches. Some time each day should be spent in the prone position. Though beneficial for edema control, elevation of the residual limb on a pillow can lead to the development of hip flexion contractures and so should be avoided. The early postoperative period is critical in establishing positive patterns of activity which will aid the patient throughout the rehabilitative period. Taking the time to teach the patient to assume responsibility for self-care can reap later benefits.

Exercises

The exercise program is designed individually and includes strengthening and coordination activities. The postsurgical dressing, degree of postoperative pain, and healing of the incision will determine when resistive exercises for the involved extremity can be started. There are a great variety of exercises that can be used to achieve the desired goals. The hip extensors and abductors and knee extensors and flexors are particularly important for prosthetic ambulation. A general strengthening program that includes the trunk and all extremities is indicated, particularly for the elderly person who may have been quite sedentary prior to surgery.

Immediately after surgery and until incisional healing has occurred, only mild active range of motion exercises are indicated for the joint immediately proximal to the incision. No pulling or stretching of the incisional area is allowed. If the immediate postoperative dressing limits joint motion, isometric contractions can be initiated. Isometric quadricep and gluteal exercises can be taught prior to surgery and started early after amputation.

Active and resistive exercises for the uninvolved lower extremity, trunk, and upper extremities are initiated immediately after surgery. There are a variety of

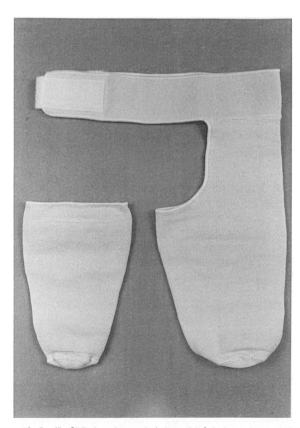

Figure 19–5. *(Left)* Below-knee shrinker, *(right)* above-knee shrinker.

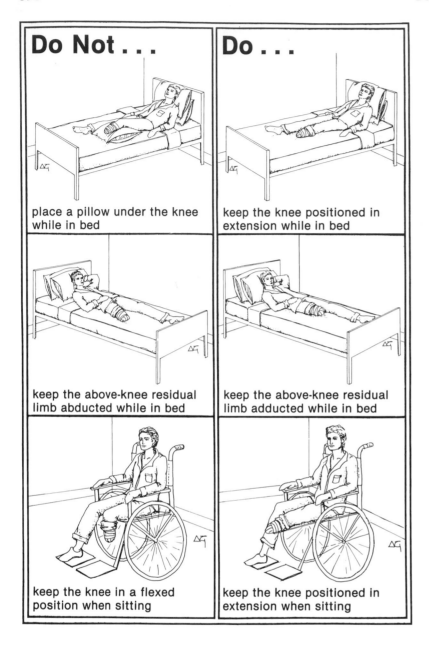

Do Not . . .

place a pillow under the knee while in bed

keep the above-knee residual limb abducted while in bed

keep the knee in a flexed position when sitting

Do . . .

keep the knee positioned in extension while in bed

keep the above-knee residual limb adducted while in bed

keep the knee positioned in extension when sitting

Figure 19–6. Correct and incorrect positioning for below- and above-knee amputations. (From Sanders, GT: *Lower Limb Amputations: A Guide to Rehabilitation.* FA Davis, Philadelphia, 1986, p 370, with permission.)

approaches that can be used to help the patient regain strength and coordination. Proprioceptive neuromuscular facilitation techniques are particularly valuable because they use combination movements and total body involvement in appropriate patterns. Such exercises can be started to the patient's tolerance early in the program as long as care is taken to prevent stress or trauma to the involved limb.

An exercise program that emphasizes coordinated activities between parts of the body and muscle groups is more effective than one that works only individual muscles. Eisert and Tester[20] published a program of dynamic exercises which emphasized coordination action between the residual limb and the rest of the body. The exercises help the individual adjust to the changed body alignment and balance. Figures 19–7 to 19–10 depict some sample exercises that can be done with above-knee amputations. Many can be adapted for the below-knee amputation as

well. Supine residual limb extension over a pillow as well as hip abduction and adduction on a pillow can be incorporated in the home program inasmuch as most patients can perform these alone with minimal practice. Exercises for range of motion and strength of hip musculature must not be forgotten when treating patients with amputations below the knee.

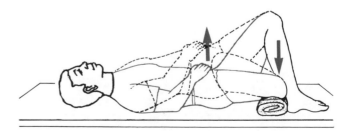

Figure 19–7. Residual limb extension in supine position.

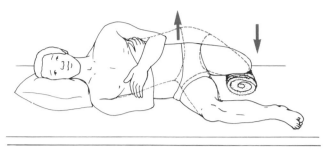

Figure 19–8. Residual limb adduction in sidelying position with involved extremity uppermost.

The younger, more active, patient with a traumatic amputation does not usually lose a great deal of muscle strength. Many elderly individuals, however, are relatively sedentary after surgery and need encouragement to develop good strength, coordination, and cardiopulmonary endurance for later ambulation.

Ideally, the exercise program should be sequenced for progressive motor control, increasing coordination and function. The patient should be progressed gradually through a program of bed then mat exercises that emphasizes both specific muscle strengthening as well as coordinated functional movements. Each program must be individualized. The patient's status and rehabilitation needs will be determined to a great extent by the preoperative status, the length of time of disability, other medical problems, and the effects of the surgery itself. A postoperative and long-term rehabilitation program that allows concentrated therapy and appropriate sequencing is desirable. Unfortunately, the majority of patients are not referred to rehabilitation centers from the acute care hospitals and current reimbursement patterns may lead to an early discharge, often within a week of amputation. Home health services, if available, are also restricted in time and scope. Therefore it is important to emphasize functional activities and to teach the patient or family a home program early after amputation.

Early mobility is important to total physiologic recovery. The patient needs to become independent in bed mobility and to resume the upright position as soon as feasible. This is particularly important for the elderly individual who may have more difficulty adapting to a changed body alignment. Movement transitions (supine-to-sit and sit-to-stand) and wheelchair transfers are preliminary to later gait-training activities. Bed mobility can

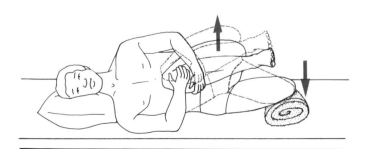

Figure 19–9. Residual limb abduction in sidelying position with uninvolved extremity uppermost.

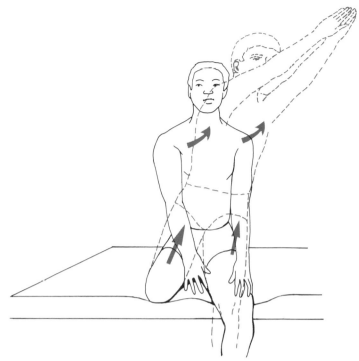

Figure 19–10. Residual limb extension, rising to a semistanding position.

be started early after surgery, but care must be taken to protect the residual limb from any trauma. The patient must be advised not to push on the residual limb when turning from side to side or coming to sitting. The patient must be cautioned against spending too much time in any one position to prevent the development of joint contractures or skin breakdowns.

Most patients with unilateral amputations have little difficulty adjusting to the change in balance point. Stability and rocking should precede sitting balance activities. Upper extremity strengthening exercises using weights, elastic bands, or resisted exercises (i.e., PNF patterns) are important. Shoulder depression and elbow extension are particularly necessary to provide the patient with a means of lifting the body from place to place. Those with bilateral below-knee amputations who have one healed residual limb often use that limb as a prop for bed activities and transfers. If the individual has a prosthesis for one of the residual limbs, it may be used to aid in transfers. Often an elderly person with bilateral amputations who is unable to lift the body for bed to wheelchair transfers will become independent when allowed to use the old prosthesis to push on.

Use of the tilt table and standing in the parallel bars may be indicated in some instances to help the person regain standing balance. Walking is an excellent exercise and necessary for independence in daily life. Gait training can start early in the postoperative phase, and the individual with a unilateral lower extremity amputation can become quite independent using a swing-through gait on crutches. Many elderly individuals have difficulty learning to walk on crutches. Many are afraid, others lack the necessary balance and coordination, and still others lack endurance. Studies have indicated that walking with crutches without a prosthesis requires a greater expenditure of energy than walking with a prosthesis.[8,21]

Contractures

Some individuals will present with hip or knee flexion contractures. Mild contractures may respond to manual mobilization and active exercises, but it is almost impossible to reduce moderate to severe contractures by manual stretching, especially hip flexion contractures. Although it is desirable for the patient to spend some time every day in the prone position, reality makes this impractical, and many elderly individuals can not assume the prone position at all. Prevention is the most effective method of coping with a hip flexion contracture, inasmuch as there is little that can be done to reduce a true contracture of the hip flexors. Prolonged, low-load static stretching may also be successful in improving range of motion. Active stretching techniques are more effective than passive stretching; these include hold-relax or contract-relax followed by active movement into the new range. A small hip flexion contracture can be accommodated in the above-knee socket, but a major contracture may mitigate against prosthetic fitting.

Knee flexion contractures are a bit easier to reduce, and one of the more effective ways is to fit the patient with a patellar tendon-bearing (PTB) prosthesis aligned in a manner that places the hamstrings on stretch with each step. Such prosthetic alignment provides an active stretch that is quite effective. A slight hip or knee flexion contracture is not usually a problem. Prevention, however, continues to be the best treatment for contractures.

Ambulation

Independent crutch walking is a goal worthy of considerable therapy time. The individual who can ambulate with crutches will develop a greater degree of general fitness than that of the person who spends most of the time in a wheelchair. Crutch walking is good preparation for prosthetic ambulation, and the person who can learn to use crutches will have less difficulty learning to use a prosthesis. However, the individual who can not learn to walk with crutches independently but is able to stand and to balance on one extremity, to transfer, and to ambulate with a walker will usually become a functional walker, particularly with a below-knee amputation.

There are advantages and disadvantages to using a walker for support during the preprosthetic period. Certainly walking with a walker is physiologically and psychologically more beneficial than sitting in a wheelchair, but the walker should be used only if the person can not learn to walk with crutches. A walker is sturdier than crutches but can not be used on stairs and curbs. It is sometimes difficult for the person who has used a walker during the preprosthetic period to switch to one crutch or cane when fitted with a prosthesis, and the gait pattern used with a walker is not appropriate with a prosthesis. Early hospital discharge often dictates that walker ambulation be taught rather than crutch walking.

All individuals with lower extremity amputations need to learn some form of mobility without a prosthesis for use at night or when the prosthesis is not worn for some reason. Some patients try to get up in the middle of the night, forgetting they do not have a leg; they fall and may injure themselves. The patient should be taught some method of moving about without a prosthesis, or the use of a bedside commode at night may be recommended.

TEMPORARY PROSTHESES

Many patients are not fitted with a definitive prosthesis until the residual limb is free from edema and much of the soft tissue has shrunk, a process that can take many months of conscientious limb wrapping and exercises. Early fitting with a temporary prosthesis can greatly enhance this postsurgical rehabilitation period. Ambulation with crutches or a walker can be initiated and wheelchair mobility encouraged. Most individuals must delay a return to work and a few activities of daily living may be limited while waiting for the residual limb to mature. Once fitted with a definitive prosthesis, the residual limb continues to change in size, and a second prosthesis is often required within the first year. Early fitting with a temporary prosthesis can greatly enhance the postsurgical rehabilitation program.

A temporary prosthesis includes a socket designed and constructed according to regular prosthetic principles and attached to some form of pylon, a foot, and some type of suspension strap. A temporary prosthesis can be fitted as soon as the wound has healed.

There are many advantages to using a temporary prosthesis:

1. It shrinks the residual limb more effectively than the elastic wrap.

2. It allows early bipedal ambulation.

3. Many elderly people who otherwise would not be ambulatory can walk safely with a temporary prosthesis and crutches during the preprosthetic period.

4. Certain individuals can return to work.

5. It provides a means of assessing the rehabilitation potential of individuals with a questionable prognosis.

6. It is a positively motivating factor by providing a replacement for the missing part of the body.

7. It reduces the need for a complex exercise program, because many people can return to full active daily life.

8. It can be used by individuals who may have difficulty obtaining payment for a definitive prosthesis.

The below-knee temporary socket may be simply constructed of plaster of Paris, or it may be prosthetically fabricated from plastic materials. In all instances the socket design should follow regular prosthetic principles and should incorporate the use of a regular prosthetic foot attached to the socket with an aluminum pipe for proper gait pattern and weight distribution. A crutch tip, frequently used in earlier days, does not adequately distribute the forces transmitted from the floor to the end of the residual limb and is now contraindicated, particularly for the dysvascular person. Many temporary sockets today are made of lightweight thermoplastic materials which can be formed over a positive cast of the residual limb; some are constructed of a fiberglass material which can be formed directly over the residual limb. The prosthesis is usually suspended by a supracondylar cuff to which a waist belt can be added if necessary. The prosthesis is worn with a wool sock of appropriate thickness. When the residual limb has shrunk so that three heavy wool socks are needed to maintain socket fit, a new socket needs to be constructed. The socket is commonly fabricated by a prosthetist but can involve contributions by the therapist, physician, or any individual who understands the application of prosthetic principles of socket design. Prosthetic components such as feet of various sizes, suspension straps, knee joints, and pylons are now generally available.

It is easier to fabricate a below-knee socket than an above-knee one, but the use of a temporary prosthesis is very important in the rehabilitation of the person with an above-knee amputation. There is a commercially available training leg which has an adjustable canvas socket with a pipe and crutch tip for support. Although it allows bipedal activities, this pylon does not fit well enough to aid in shrinking the residual limb. It also does not allow for good distribution of weight-bearing forces, and it encourages the development of an awkward, energy-consuming stiff-legged gait. The temporary prosthesis for an above-knee amputation should incorporate the regular quadrilateral socket, articulated knee joint, foot, and pylon. Suspension may be with Silesian bandage or pelvic band.

PATIENT EDUCATION

Patient education is an integral and ongoing part of the rehabilitation program. Information on the care of the residual limb, proper care of the uninvolved extremity, positioning, exercises, and diet, if the patient is a diabetic, is necessary for the patient to be a full participant in the rehabilitation program.

Many individuals with vascular disease who lose one leg will be concerned about the other leg and receptive to learning proper care. An understanding of the physiologic and functional implications of **peripheral vascular disease (PVD)** helps the individual assume responsibility for the care of the unamputated extremity (see chapter 18). A patient education program must be individually designed to be relevant and may include the following:

1. A discussion of the disease process and the physiologic effects of the symptoms experienced.
2. Information on the benefits of exercises, lower extremity cleanliness, proper foot care, and proper shoe fitting.
3. Methods of edema control.
4. The use of exercise to improve circulatory status.

Edema, pain, changes in skin color or temperature may indicate impending problems. If the person is ambulatory on the remaining extremity, these symptoms may indicate too much stress; if the person spends considerable time sitting with the leg in a dependent position, it may be necessary to elevate the extremity. Cramping (intermittent claudication) during activity is an indication of a need to rest. The endurance of the remaining extremity is developed slowly through a progressive program of exercises and ambulation. It is important to remember that too much activity may be as harmful as too little.

The educational program is individually developed to meet specific needs. Care must be taken not to overwhelm the patient with too much information at one time, inasmuch as information overload results in noncompliance. It is more effective to prioritize the information and ask the person to remember one new thing each session rather than to try to develop a complex program at one time. The same approach can be used for the home exercise program. Once the patient is discharged, weekly visits throughout the preprosthetic phase provide a check on home activities, on the condition of the residual limb, and is supportive to the patient and family.

BILATERAL AMPUTATION

The preprosthetic program for the individual with bilateral lower extremity amputations is similar to the program developed for unilateral amputation except, possibly, ambulation. If the individual was previously fitted and ambulated with a unilateral amputation, the prosthesis is useful for transfer activities and limited ambulation in the parallel bars. Occasionally, the individual may be able to use the prosthesis with external support to get around the house more easily, particularly for bathroom activities. Fitting with a temporary prosthesis, as previously mentioned, is advisable, particularly if the amputations are at below-knee levels. The higher the initial level of amputation, the more difficult ambulation becomes.

All individuals with bilateral amputations require the use of a wheelchair on a permanent basis. The chair should be as narrow as possible with removable desk arms and removable leg rests. Amputee wheelchairs with offset rear wheels and no leg rests are recommended only when the therapist is sure that the person will never be fitted with prostheses, even cosmetically. It is easier to add antitipping devices to the rear of the wheelchair or to attach small weights to the front uprights for use when the foot rests are removed.

The preprosthetic program includes mat activities designed to help the person regain a sense of body position and balance, upper extremity and residual limb strengthening exercises, wheelchair transfers, and regular range of motion exercises. With bilateral amputations, individuals spend considerable time sitting and are therefore more prone to develop flexion contractures, particularly around the hip joints. The patient should be encouraged to sleep prone if possible, or at least to spend some time in the prone position each day. The therapy program also emphasizes range of motion of the residual limbs. Some people move about their homes on their knees, the ends of the residual limbs, or the buttocks. Knee pads made of heavy rubber used by field workers are effective protectors for the residual limbs. Protectors also can be fabricated from foam or felt.

Temporary prostheses are of great value in rehabilitation with bilateral below-knee amputations. Temporary prostheses are used to assess ambulation potential and as an aid to balance and transfer activities. If the individual was initially fitted with a unilateral prosthesis, the temporary prosthesis will allow some resumption of ambulation. The ambulatory potential with bilateral above-knee amputations is uncertain, particularly among the elderly.

The bilateral above-knee amputated limbs can be fitted with shortened prostheses called **stubbies** (Fig. 19–11). Stubby prostheses have quadrilateral sockets, no articulated knee joints or shank, and modified rocker bottoms turned backward to prevent posterior falls. Inasmuch as the patient's center of gravity is much lower to the ground and the prostheses are nonarticulated, they are relatively easy to use. **Stubbies** allow the person to acquire erect balance and to participate in ambulatory activities quickly and with only moderate expenditures of energy. Their acceptance by patients, however, is quite variable; some like to use them for activities of daily living in the home but rely on a wheelchair outside the home. Although prescribed rather rarely, they are most effective for individuals with short residual limbs or who will not be able to ambulate with regular prostheses. Temporary prostheses of different heights can be used to determine ambulatory potential, but care must be taken to ensure that the temporary limbs are constructed well enough to tolerate the stresses generated in walking.

NONPROSTHETIC MANAGEMENT

The preprosthetic period is designed to determine the individual's suitability for prosthetic replacement. Not all those with amputations are candidates for a prosthesis, regardless of personal desire. The cost of the prosthesis and the energy requirements of prosthetic training

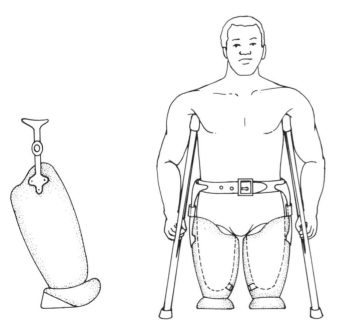

Figure 19–11. Stubbies.

require that the clinic team use some judgment in selecting individuals for fitting.

There is no general rule that can safely be applied to all patients in making the decision to fit or not to fit. The patient is part of the decision-making process, but the fact that the individual wants a prosthesis is not enough. Many people are not aware of the physiologic demands of prosthetic ambulation, particularly at above-knee levels. The development of lightweight prostheses, safety knees, and hydraulic mechanisms have made it possible to fit successfully many more individuals than in the past. However, some consideration for nonfitting is necessary.

Below-Knee Levels

Most individuals amputated at any below-knee level can be fitted with a prosthesis successfully. Flexion contractures, scars, poorly shaped residual limbs, and adherent skin are not necessarily contraindications for fitting, even though such problems will create difficulty with socket fit. Circulatory problems in the nonamputated extremity, unless so severe as to preclude any ambulation, are indications for fitting at the earliest possible time because bipedal ambulation reduces stress on the remaining extremity. Additionally, the individual who has learned to ambulate with a unilateral amputation is more likely to be able to ambulate with bilateral amputations. There are few contraindications to fitting a prosthesis to a below-knee amputation other than contraindications to ambulation itself. Individuals who were not ambulatory prior to amputation for reasons other than the problems leading to the amputation will probably not be ambulatory with an amputation. However, individuals who were nonambulatory and debilitated because of infection, uncontrolled diabetes, and ulcers will probably regain the necessary strength and coordination for ambulation after the diseased limb has been removed. Generally, individuals requiring nursing or custodial care will not be able to use a prosthesis; often equipment sent to a nursing home becomes lost, and fitting such individuals may be a poor use of limited resources.

Above-Knee Levels

The vast majority of individuals with unilateral above-knee amputations can become relatively functional prosthetic users with or without external support. The physiologic demands of walking with an above-knee prosthesis are considerably higher than walking with a below-knee prosthesis, and not all individuals have the necessary balance, strength, and energy reserves.[8] Severe hip flexion contractures, weakness, or paralysis of hip musculature, poor balance and coordination may mitigate against successful ambulation. The person's level of activity and participation in the preprosthetic program help in determining potential for prosthetic ambulation. A temporary prosthesis is a good assessment tool.

Most individuals amputated at hip levels are younger

and learn to use a prosthesis relatively easily. Although early fitting is physically and psychologically beneficial, active involvement in chemotherapy or radiation therapy will delay fitting. Radiation therapy often burns the skin, making fitting impossible until the skin has healed. Patients undergoing chemotherapy are often ill, lose weight, and usually do not have the energy to participate in a prosthetic training program. The preprosthetic program is individually adjusted and supportive until the chemotherapy is complete. If the person has lost considerable weight, fitting may have to be delayed inasmuch as it is difficult to adjust a prosthesis for increases in weight.

Bilateral Amputations

Fitting or not fitting the individual with bilateral amputations is a difficult decision. Young, agile individuals are generally good candidates for prosthetic fitting. Most patients with bilateral below-knee amputations can become quite functional with prostheses. With bilateral above-knee amputations, patients have considerable difficulty learning to use two prostheses. Patients with one above-knee amputation and one below-knee amputation generally can learn to use two prostheses if the first amputation was at the above-knee level, and if the person successfully used an above-knee prosthesis before losing the other leg.

Bilateral amputations require that the person have more strength, better coordination, better balance, and greater cardiorespiratory reserves than unilateral amputations. The decision to fit or not to fit is made after careful individual assessment of the person's total potential and needs.

Physical Therapy Intervention

Individuals who are not fitted with a prosthesis need to become as independent as possible in a wheelchair. The physical therapy program includes strengthening, training in all transfers and activities of daily living, and education in the proper care of the residual limb. Wrapping the residual limb is no longer necessary unless the person is more comfortable with the limb covered. The program emphasizes sitting balance, moving safely in and out of the wheelchair, and other activities to support as independent a lifestyle as the person's physical and psychologic condition allows.

SUMMARY

Most individuals with lower extremity amputations can be helped to return to a full and useful life following the loss of a limb. A program of postoperative care that includes consideration of physical and emotional needs will enable most patients to become functional prosthetic users. Many prosthetic problems can be avoided by properly preparing the individual for prosthetic wear. In this chapter, concepts related to the postoperative management of the individual with a lower extremity amputation have been presented. The role of the physical therapist during this phase of care has been emphasized. Through a process of careful assessment and open communication among the patient, family, and rehabilitation team members, a comprehensive program designed to meet the needs of an individual patient can be achieved. This approach will facilitate maximum functional prosthetic use and successful reintegration into the community.

QUESTIONS FOR REVIEW

1. Discuss the advantages and disadvantages of the following methods of postsurgical residual limb management:
   a. Rigid dressing
   b. CET
   c. Air splint
   d. Soft dressing
2. Discuss the proper methods of wrapping the below-knee and the above-knee residual limbs.
3. A 72-year-old man with a history of diabetes, cardiovascular disease, and peripheral vascular disease has been referred for physical therapy 24 hours after right below-knee amputation for gangrene. What assessment data are needed to plan an appropriate treatment program? Which are the most critical to obtain on the first visit?
4. Design an exercise program for an 82-year-old patient with a left above-knee amputation who is referred 2 weeks postamputation.
5. Which preprosthetic activities are more important with bilateral amputations than with unilateral amputation? How might you teach these activities?

REFERENCES

1. Glattly, HW: A statistical study of 12,000 new amputees. South Med J 57:1373, 1964.
2. Kay, HW and Newman, JD: Relative incidences of new amputations: Statistical comparisons of 6,000 new amputees. Orth Pros 29:3, 1975.
3. Warren, R and Record, EE: Lower Extremity Amputations for Arterial Insufficiency. Little, Brown & Co, Boston, 1967.
4. Sarmiento, A, Urricchio, JV, and May, BJ: Experiences with patellar tendon bearing prostheses in geriatric amputees. Clin Orthop 50:181, 1967.

5. Kerstein, MD, et al: Amputations of the lower extremity: A study of 194 cases. Arch Phys Med Rehabil 55:454, 1974.

6. Kegel, B, Carpenter, ML, and Burgess, EM: Functional capabilities of lower extremity amputees. Arch Phys Med Rehabil 59:109, 1978.

7. Kerstein, MD, et al: What influence does age have on rehabilitation of amputees? Geriatrics 30(12):67, 1975.

8. Waters, RL, et al: Energy cost of walking of amputees: The influence of level of amputation. J Bone Joint Surg 58-A:42, 1976.

9. Steinberg, FU, Sunsoo, I, and Roettger, RF: Prosthetic rehabilitation of geriatric amputee patients: A follow-up study. Arch Phys Med Rehabil 66:742, 1985.

10. Spence, VA, et al: Assessment of tissue viability in relation to the selection of amputation level. Prosth Orth Int 8:67, 1984.

11. May, BJ: A statewide amputee rehabilitation programme. Pros Orth Int 2(1):24, 1978.

12. Burgess, EM: Amputations of the lower extremities. In Nickel, VM (ed): Orthopedic Rehabilitation. Churchill Livingstone, New York, 1982, p 377.

13. Sarmiento, A, et al: Lower-extremity amputation: The impact of immediate postsurgical prosthetic fitting. Clin Orth 68:22, 1970.

14. Little, JM: A pneumatic weight-bearing temporary prosthesis for below-knee amputees. Lancet 1(7693):271, 1971.

15. Little, JM: The use of air splints as immediate prostheses after below-knee amputation for vascular insufficiency. Med J Aust 2(19):870, 1970.

16. Burgess, EM: Wound healing after amputation: Effect of controlled environment treatment, a preliminary study. J Bone Joint Surg 60-A:245, 1978.

17. Kegel, B: Controlled environment treatment (CET) for patients with below-knee amputations. Phys Ther 56:1366, 1976.

18. May, BJ: Stump bandaging of the lower extremity amputee. Phys Ther 44:808, 1964.

19. Mueller, MJ: Comparison of removable rigid dressing and elastic bandages in preprosthetic management of patients with below-knee amputations. Phys Ther 62:1438, 1982.

20. Eisert, O and Tester, OW: Dynamic exercises for the lower extremity amputee. Arch Phys Med Rehabil 35:695, 1954.

21. Pagliarulo, MA, Waters, R, and Hislop, HJ: Energy cost of walking of below-knee amputees having no vascular disease. Phys Ther 59:538, 1979.

SUPPLEMENTAL READINGS

Banerjee, SN (ed): Rehabilitation management of amputees. Williams & Wilkins, Baltimore, 1982.

Beekman, C and Hunt, A: Change in function and equipment use in lower extremity amputees discharged to nursing homes. Phys Ther 59:1374, 1979.

Friedmann, LW: The Psychological Rehabilitation of the Amputee. Charles C Thomas, Springfield, IL, 1978.

Karacoloff, LA: Lower Extremity Amputation: A Guide to Functional Outcomes in Physical Therapy Management. Aspen, Rockville, MD, 1985.

Kostuik, JP (ed): Amputation Surgery and Rehabilitation: The Toronto Experience. Churchill Livingstone, New York, 1981.

Levy, SW: Skin Problems of the Amputee. WH Green, St Louis, 1983.

Little, JM: Major Amputations for Vascular Disease, Churchill Livingstone, New York, 1975.

Manella, KJ: Comparing the effectiveness of elastic bandages and shrinker socks for lower extremity amputees. Phys Ther 61:334, 1981.

Melzack, R and Wall, PD: The Challenge of Pain. Basic Books, New York, 1983.

Nowroozi, F, Salvanelli, ML, and Gerber, LH: Energy expenditure in hip disarticulation and hemipelvectomy amputees. Arch Phys Med Rehabil 64:300, 1983.

Siegfried, J and Zimmerman, M (eds): Phantom and Stump Pain. Springer-Verlag, New York, 1981.

Troup, IM: Controlled environment treatment (CET). Prosth Orth Int 4:15, 1980.

Volpicelli, LJ, Chambers, RB, and Wagner, FW: Ambulation levels of bilateral lower-extremity amputees. J Bone Joint Surg 65-A:599, 1983.

Wu, Y, et al: An innovative removable rigid dressing technique for below-the-knee amputation. J Bone Joint Surg 61-A:724, 1979.

GLOSSARY

Beveling (of bone): The process of smoothing the cut ends of bone to prevent rough edges and spurring that would interfere with prosthetic management.

Cauterization: Destruction of tissue by use of a caustic agent such as heat, cold, electricity, or corrosive chemicals.

Chordotomy (or cordotomy): Division of the anterolateral tracts of the spinal cord; used to relieve pain.

Dysvascular: Having abnormality of the peripheral vascular system, commonly arteriosclerosis.

Hemicorporectomy: Translumbar amputation; surgical removal of the lower half of the body.

Hemipelvectomy: Amputation of one half of the pelvis and entire lower extremity.

Hemostasis: Arrest of bleeding.

Immediate postoperative prosthesis: Application of a temporary prosthesis immediately following amputation; consists of a plaster of Paris socket, pylon, and foot.

Myodesis: Method of muscle stabilization following amputation in which the cut muscle is sutured to periosteum or bone.

Myofascial closure: Method of muscle stabilization following amputation in which muscle is sutured to fascia; often used in combination with myoplasty.

Myoplasty: Method of muscle stabilization following amputation in which muscle is sutured to muscle; the cut flexor and extensor muscles are surgically attached; often used in combination with myofascial closure.

Neurectomy: Partial or total excision or resection of a nerve.

Neuroma (amputation): Collection of nerve cells which develop following transection of a nerve.

Peripheral vascular disease (PVD): A general term used to describe any disorder that interferes with arterial or venous blood flow of the extremities.

Phantom limb: The sensation, following amputation, that the limb is still present.

Phantom pain: The sensation of pain originating from a removed (amputated) limb.

Rhizotomy: Division or severance of a nerve root.

Shrinker: Commercially made socklike garment of heavy rubber-reinforced cotton; used to control edema of the residual limb following amputation.

Stubbies: Short prostheses used with bilateral above-knee amputation; consist of quadrilateral sockets, no articulated knee joints or shank, and modified rocker bottoms turned backward.

Tenodesis: Surgical attachment of a tendon to a bone.

Unna's paste dressing: A semirigid dressing consisting of zinc oxide, gelatin, glycerin, calamine, and figure-eight spiral bandages; used in management of stasis ulcers and control of postoperative edema following amputation.

Chapter 20

PROSTHETIC ASSESSMENT AND MANAGEMENT

JOAN E. EDELSTEIN

OBJECTIVES

1. Relate various levels of amputation to prosthetic restoration.

2. Describe the major components of below-knee and above-knee prostheses, including advantages and disadvantages of alternative components and materials.

3. Describe the distinctive features of knee and hip disarticulation prostheses.

4. Outline the maintenance program for each prosthetic element.

5. Identify the principal features of below-knee and above-knee prostheses assessed during the checkout procedure.

6. Recognize the therapist's role in management of individuals with lower-limb amputation.

INTRODUCTION

A *prosthesis* is a replacement of a body part. A *prosthetist* is the health care professional who designs, fabricates, and fits prostheses. In the broadest sense, prostheses include dentures, wigs, and plastic heart valves. The physical therapist, however, is concerned primarily with limb prostheses (i.e., artificial legs and arms) and the management of individuals with lower- and upper-limb amputation.

Lower-limb amputation is much more prevalent than loss of the upper limb. The major causes of amputation are peripheral vascular disease, trauma, malignancy, and congenital deficiency. Vascular disease accounts for most leg amputations in individuals older than 50. Trauma is responsible for the majority of amputations in younger adults and adolescents and affects both upper and lower limbs. Trauma and vascular disease are more common among men than among women. Bone and soft tissue tumors are sometimes treated by removal of the limb;

adolescence is the peak period of incidence. *Congenital deficiency* refers to absence or abnormality of a limb evident at birth. Tumors and congenital deficiencies affect the upper and lower limbs in approximately equal numbers.[1,2]

This chapter focuses on lower-limb prosthetics because more patients have lost a portion of the leg, as compared with the arm, and because the physical therapist is expected to assume a greater role in management of the lower-limb, rather than the upper-limb, amputation patient. Prostheses will be described, together with a program for training patients in their use.

LOWER EXTREMITY PROSTHETIC DEVICES

The concept of replacing a missing limb is very old. Prostheses, such as the forked stick to support a below-knee amputated limb, were known in antiquity. The

407

Roman historian Herodotus reported in 484 BC of a Persian who escaped from leg irons by cutting off his foot and replacing it with a wooden one. The oldest prosthesis to survive to modern times was a copper and wood leg dating from the third century BC.[3] The Talmud, antedating the sixth century, contains references to a padded peg leg.[4]

The principal lower-limb prostheses are partial foot, below-knee, and above-knee, as well as knee and hip disarticulation. The physical therapist should be familiar with their characteristics, as well as with their maintenance.

Partial Foot Prostheses

The purpose of partial foot prostheses are (a) to restore, as much as possible, foot function, particularly in walking, and (b) to simulate the shape of the missing foot segment. The patient who has lost one or more toes may simply pad the toe section of the shoe to improve appearance of the upper portion of the shoe. Standing will not be affected, assuming the metatarsal heads remain. Push-off will be less forceful, particularly if the phalanges of the great toe are absent.

Transmetatarsal amputation disturbs foot appearance more noticeably. A prosthesis prevents the shoe from developing an unnatural crease in the forefoot area. The patient bears most weight on the heel and reduces the amount of time spent on the affected foot during walking. A particularly useful prosthesis consists of a plastic socket for the remainder of the foot affixed to a rigid plate which extends the full length of the inner sole of the shoe, completed with a cosmetic toe filler. The socket protects the amputated ends of the metatarsals, while the rigid plate restores full foot length so that the person can spend more time during stance phase of gait on the affected side than would otherwise be the case. To aid push-off, the bottom of the prosthesis or the sole of the shoe may have a slight rocker bar.

Amputation or disarticulation through the tarsals poses the additional problem of retaining the small foot segment in the shoe. Foot length is apt to be diminished further by an equinus deformity of the amputation limb, resulting from unbalanced contraction of the triceps surae. Consequently, the prosthesis as described for the transmetatarsal amputation may be augmented with a plastic calf shell which is strapped around the leg.

Below-Knee Prostheses

The below-knee level refers to an amputation in which the tibia and fibula are transected. The patient retains the anatomic knee and its motor and sensory functions. This is the prevalent site of amputation, particularly for individuals with vascular disease. From a functional and prosthetic viewpoint, the **Syme's amputation** is similar; amputation is through the malleoli, with all foot bones removed and the calcaneal fat pad retained. The amputation limb is longer than the below-knee, improving prosthetic control; in addition, the individual with a Syme's amputation may be able to tolerate significant weight bearing through the end of the limb. Prostheses for these levels consist of four elements: (a) foot-ankle assembly, (b) shank, (c) socket, and (d) suspension.

FOOT-ANKLE ASSEMBLIES

The prosthetic foot (Fig. 20–1) serves to restore the general contour of the patient's foot, absorbs shock at heel strike, plantar flexes in early stance, and simulates metatarsophalangeal hyperextension (toe-break action) in the latter part of the stance phase. Some feet also provide slight mediolateral and transverse motion.

Nonarticulated Feet

Most feet prescribed in the United States present a one-piece external appearance, without a cleft between the foot and the lower portion of the shank. As compared with articulated feet, they are lighter in weight, more dur-

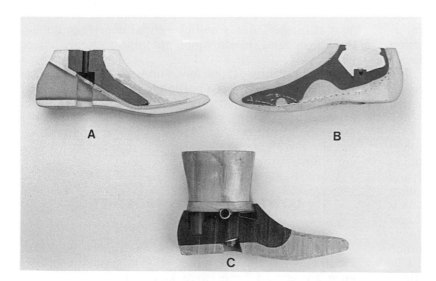

Figure 20–1. Cross-section of foot-ankle assemblies: (*A*) SACH, (*B*) SAFE, (*C*) single-axis.

able, and more attractive; some versions are made to suit low- and high-heeled shoes. These feet, however, are not readily adjustable to accommodate for changes in gait pattern.

SACH Foot. The **SACH (solid ankle cushion heel)** assembly predominates in current practice (see Figure 20–1A). It consists of a wood or aluminum **keel,** which terminates at a point corresponding to the metatarsophalangeal joint. The rigid section is covered by rubber; the posterior portion is resilient to absorb shock and to permit plantarflexion in early stance. Anteriorly, the junction of the keel and rubber allows toe breaking at push-off. The SACH foot is manufactured in a large range of sizes to accommodate children and adults, and with heel cushions of varying degrees of compressibility for individuals who strike the floor with different amounts of force, as well as in several plantarflexion angles to fit diverse shoe heel heights. The heel cushion allows a very small amount of mediolateral motion.

Other Nonarticulated Feet. A new version of the SACH foot is the **stationary attachment flexible endoskeleton (SAFE)** foot[5] (see Figure 20–1B). It has a rigid ankle block joined to the posterior portion of the keel at an angle comparable to the anatomic subtalar joint. The junction permits the SAFE foot wearer to maintain contact with uneven terrain, because of the greater range of mediolateral motion permitted at the heel. The SAFE foot, however, is somewhat heavier, more expensive, and less durable than the SACH foot. The Seattle foot incorporates a slightly flexible plastic keel which bends somewhat at heel strike, storing energy. At push-off, the keel recoils as the foot is unloaded, releasing energy for a forceful termination to stance. The Seattle foot is particularly effective in assisting the individual to run.[6] Other energy storage/release designs involve the same principle.

Articulated Feet

These assemblies are manufactured with separate foot and lower shank sections, joined by a metal bolt or cable. The ease of foot motion is controlled by bumpers. In the rear is a resilient rubber bumper to absorb shock and to control plantarflexion excursion. Anterior to the ankle bolt is a relatively firm dorsiflexion stop. The bumpers are easily changed to regulate the amount of foot motion. At early stance, the slightest loading of the heel causes the foot to plantarflex, to ensure that the wearer achieves the stable foot-flat position.[7] Articulated feet are subject to eventual loosening, which may sometimes be signalled by a squeaking noise.

Single-Axis Feet. The most common example of an articulated foot is the **single-axis foot** (see Figure 20–1C). It permits plantarflexion and dorsiflexion, as well as toe-break action. Some versions can be adjusted to accommodate shoes of various heel heights. Single-axis feet do not provide mediolateral or transverse motion.[8]

Multiple-Axis Feet. Multiple-axis feet are sometimes called functional feet. They permit a slight amount of motion in all planes to aid the wearer in maintaining maximum contact with the walking surface, even if the surface slopes or presents slight irregularities. Multiple-axis feet are heavier and less durable than single-axis feet.

Rotators. A rotator is a prosthetic component placed over the prosthetic foot to absorb shock in the transverse plane. This action protects from chafing which would otherwise occur if the socket were permitted to rotate against the skin. Rotators are most commonly used with single-axis feet, and by very active individuals with above-knee amputations.[9]

SHANKS

Adjacent to the foot-ankle assembly, or the rotator, is the shank. It restores leg length and transmits load from the socket to the foot. Two types of shanks are used: **exoskeletal** and **endoskeletal.** The Syme's prosthesis does not have a shank because the socket encasing the amputated limb extends to the foot-ankle assembly.

Exoskeletal Shank

The most common type of **exoskeletal shank** presents a rigid exterior, shaped to simulate the contour of the leg, and finished with **polyester laminate** tinted to match the wearer's skin color (Fig. 20–2). The exoskeletal shank, sometimes called **crustacean,** is very durable and, with the laminate finish, impervious to liquids and most abrasives.

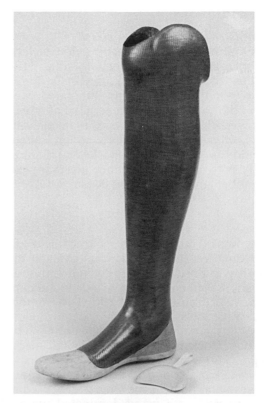

Figure 20–2. Below-knee prosthesis with SACH foot, exoskeletal shank, patellar-tendon-bearing socket, and supracondylar wedge suspension.

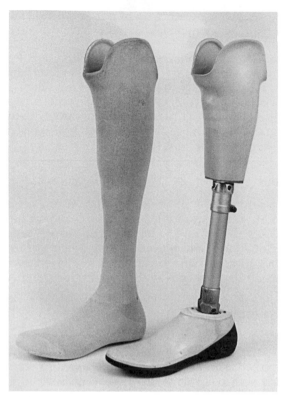

Figure 20-3. Below-knee prosthesis with SACH foot, endoskeletal shank, patellar-tendon-bearing socket, and supracondylar suspension with and without foam rubber covering.

Endoskeletal Shank

In contrast, the **endoskeletal shank** may consist of a central aluminum or rigid plastic pylon covered with foam rubber and a sturdy stocking (Fig. 20-3). The endoskeletal, or **modular,** shank presents a more lifelike appearance than does the shiny laminated exoskeletal shank. In addition, the pylon generally has some means for making slight adjustment of the angulation of the prosthesis, which may contribute to improvement in comfort and ease of walking. Endoskeletal shanks are less commonly prescribed because they are more expensive and the rubber covering is less durable.

SOCKET

The amputated limb fits into a receptacle called the *socket.* Ordinarily the socket is total contact; that is, it contacts all portions of the limb for maximum distribution of load, as well as to assist venous blood circulation and to provide sensory feedback. The contours and materials of the socket are the major determinants of the comfort of the prosthesis. Several materials have been used to make sockets. Wood, the original medium for this design, is rarely used currently because it is virtually impossible to carve wood to achieve total contact distally. Polyester laminate is the most widely used material today. Compared with wood, laminated materials are less bulky and can be molded to contact all portions of the amputated limb. The rigid laminate socket is now being superseded by a combination of flexible socket

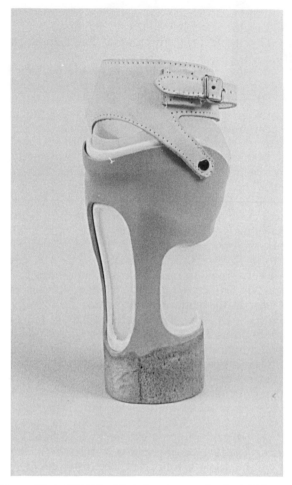

Figure 20-4. ISNY flexible below-knee socket in rigid frame.

encased in a rigid frame, such as the ISNY (Icelandic-Swedish-New York University) design (Fig. 20-4). The socket portion is made of very thin **polyethylene,** a thermoplastic that can be spot-heated to facilitate alteration of socket fit. The thin plastic adheres to the skin better and thereby improves suspension, dissipates body heat more effectively, and affords the wearer sensory input from external objects, such as chairs. The flexible socket nests in a carbon-fiber-reinforced laminated frame which transmits load to the distal portion of the prosthesis.

Patellar-Tendon-Bearing Socket

The standard socket for the below-knee prostheses is the patellar-tendon-bearing (PTB) socket (Fig. 20-5).[10] It includes a convexity (build-up) at the patellar tendon to increase loading on the pressure-tolerant structure, as well as build-ups on the posterior aspect and medial tibial flare, corresponding to the pes anserinus. The PTB socket has concavities (reliefs) over the fibular head, tibial crest, and other sensitive tissues. The posterior brim includes reliefs for the medial and lateral hamstring tendons, which are especially important when the patient sits.

When viewed from above, the PTB socket resembles a triangle, the apex of which is formed by the relief for the

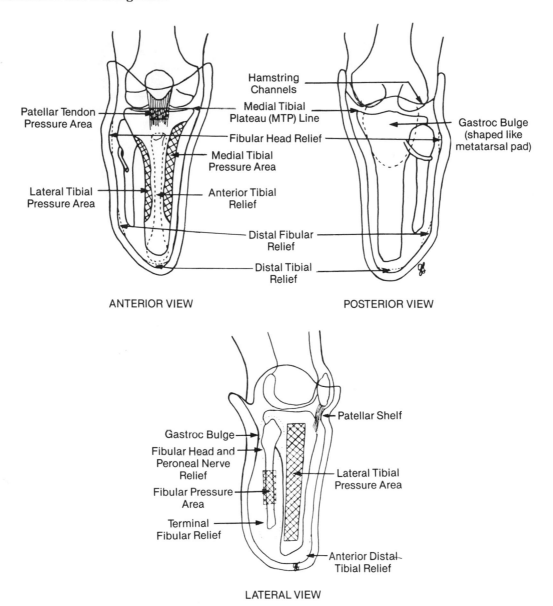

Figure 20–5. Patellar-tendon-bearing socket. (From Sanders, GT: *Lower Limb Amputations: A Guide to Rehabilitation.* FA Davis, Philadelphia, 1986, p 176, with permission.)

tibial tubercle and crest, and the base angles being the hamstring reliefs. The anterior wall terminates at the patella, or above. The medial and lateral walls extend to the femoral epicondyles, or above, for mediolateral stabilization. The posterior wall lies at the popliteal fossa, at a level slightly above the patellar tendon build-up.

The PTB socket is aligned on the shank in slight flexion to enhance loading on the patellar tendon, as well as to prevent genu recurvatum, to resist the tendency of the amputated limb to slide down the socket, and to facilitate contraction of the quadriceps muscle. The socket is also aligned with slight lateral tilt to reduce loading on the fibular head.

Soft Socket. The PTB socket generally includes a resilient liner, usually of polyethylene foam. In addition to cushioning the amputation limb, the liner facilitates alteration of socket size; the prosthetist can add material to the outside of the liner, reducing the volume of the socket while preserving smooth interior contours. The liner, however, adds to the bulk of the prosthesis and acts as a heat insulator, which the wearer may find uncomfortable in the summer. The Syme's prosthesis has a liner that assists entry of the bulbous distal end of the amputation limb, enabling the wearer to don the prosthesis easily.

Unlined Socket. Although the unlined socket is sometimes referred to as a hard socket, that term is a misnomer, for the wearer derives cushioning from socks worn with the unlined socket. Occasionally a resilient pad is placed in the bottom of the unlined socket to protect the distal end of the amputated limb. The unlined socket is more satisfactory for the individual whose limb has stabilized in volume, because the socket shape is more difficult to alter than the lined, soft socket.

Syme's Socket

Because the individual with a Syme's amputation usually can bear significant weight through the distal end of the amputation limb, the Syme's socket need not rely on a patellar tendon build-up for loading. The socket trimlines are slightly lower, and the frontal and sagittal plane alignment less tilted (Fig. 20–6). Relief for the tibial crest remains an important feature of the socket. If the distal end of the Syme's limb is markedly bulbous, the lower part of the medial wall may be made removable; the patient dons the socket, then fastens the wall section in place.

SUSPENSIONS

The prosthesis is retained on the limb by means of a cuff, or various designs of the prosthetic brim, or with a thigh corset.[11]

Cuff

The PTB socket originated with a supracondylar cuff, still a widely used mode of suspension. The cuff, a leather strap encircling the thigh immediately above the femoral condyles, permits the wearer to adjust the snugness of suspension easily (Fig. 20–7). Some individuals, however, object to the profile of the distal thigh created by use of the cuff.

Brim Designs

In place of the cuff, the PTB socket may be suspended by its socket walls extended proximally. Neither the cuff

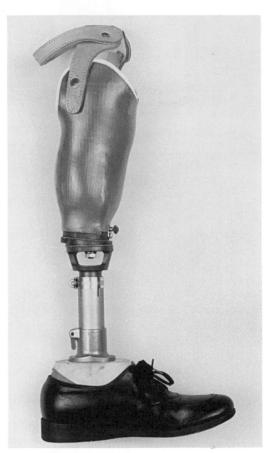

Figure 20–7. Below-knee temporary prosthesis with cuff suspension. Socket is mounted on an adjustable pylon shank with SACH foot.

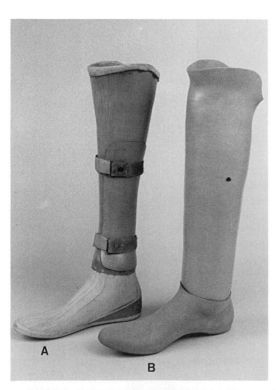

Figure 20–6. Syme's prostheses. (*A*) Socket with medial opening, (*B*) socket with continuous walls and flexible liner.

nor brim suspension interferes with knee motion during walking and sitting.

Supracondylar Suspension. With supracondylar (SC) suspension, the medial and lateral walls extend above the femoral epicondyles (see Figure 20–2). The medial wall is fitted with a wedge, which is removed to don the socket. Then the wedge is placed between the socket and the medial side of the amputated limb to retain the prosthesis on the limb. Alternatively, the wedge can be incorporated in a liner; for donning, the wearer applies the liner, then inserts the amputated limb with liner into the socket. Supracondylar suspension increases mediolateral stability of the prosthesis, presents a pleasing contour at the knee, and eliminates the need to engage a buckle or cuff loop. Its disadvantages are that it is more difficult to fabricate, hence more expensive, and not readily adjustable.

Supracondylar/Suprapatellar Suspension. Presenting a similar contour of medial and lateral walls, the **supracondylar/suprapatellar (SC/SP)** suspension also features an anterior wall which terminates immediately above the patella (Fig. 20–8). The short amputated limb is accommodated by SC/SP suspension. The high anterior wall may interfere with kneeling and presents a conspicuous appearance when the wearer sits.

Syme's Suspension. The Syme's prosthesis is generally suspended by the contour of its brims. Because the amputated limb is relatively long, the Syme's prosthesis

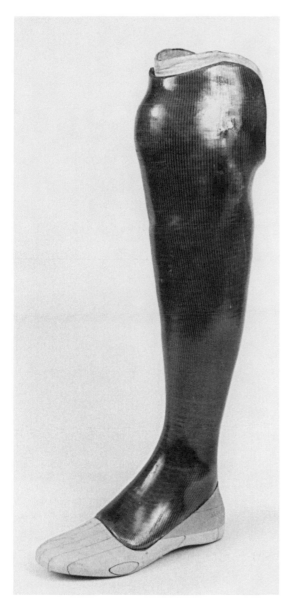

Figure 20–8. Below-knee prosthesis with supracondylar/suprapatellar suspension.

usually dispenses with the cuff and supracondylar projections.

Thigh Corset

Some individuals with very sensitive skin on the amputation limb may benefit from thigh corset suspension (Fig. 20–9). Metal hinges are attached distally to the medial and lateral aspects of the PTB socket and proximally to a leather corset. The corset may be low, terminating at the distal third of the thigh, or it may be high, sometimes reaching the ischial tuberosity for maximum weight relief on the amputated limb. The hinges increase frontal plane stability, and the corset leather increases area for load distribution. The resulting prosthesis is heavier and apt to foster **piston action** because the hinges have a single pivot joint which does not articulate colinearly with the anatomic knee. Prolonged use of a thigh corset causes atrophy of the thigh. Corset suspen-

sion is more difficult to don because the wearer must fasten laces or a series of Velcro loops.

Above-Knee Prostheses

Individuals with amputation between the femoral epicondyles and the greater trochanter are fitted with above-knee prostheses. Those whose limbs include the distal part of the femur can wear a knee disarticulation prosthesis that differs primarily in the type of knee unit. If the amputation is proximal to the trochanter, the patient cannot retain or control an above-knee prosthesis and is therefore a candidate for a hip disarticulation limb. The above-knee prosthesis consists of (a) a foot-ankle assembly, (b) a shank, (c) a knee unit, (d) a socket, and (e) a method of suspension.

The SACH and single-axis feet are most commonly used for above-knee prostheses. Because the single-axis foot reaches the foot-flat position with minimal application of load, it is somewhat more frequently prescribed for above-knee amputations than for below-knee prostheses. Nevertheless, the SACH unit is the prodominant foot for above-knee limbs.

The exoskeletal shank is typical, for it is sturdy and economical. The endoskeletal shank, however, is another option, not only because of its more attractive appearance but also because the above-knee endoskeletal prosthesis is somewhat lighter than one with a crustacean

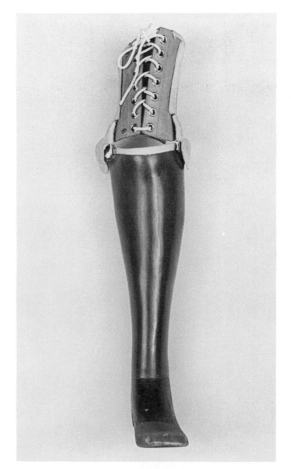

Figure 20–9. Below-knee prosthesis with thigh corset suspension.

shank. Problems of durability remain, particularly at the knee, where the constant bending of the joint tends to deteriorate the rubber cover.

KNEE UNITS

The prosthetic knee enables the user to bend the knee when sitting or kneeling and, in most instances, also permits knee flexion during the latter portion of stance phase and throughout swing phase. Commercial knee units may be described according to four attributes: (a) **axis,** (b) **friction mechanism,** (c) **extension aid,** and (d) **mechanical stabilizer.** Many combinations of features are found, and not every knee unit has all these attributes.[12]

Axis Systems

The thigh piece can be connected to the shank either by a single-axis hinge (Fig. 20–10), the usual arrange-

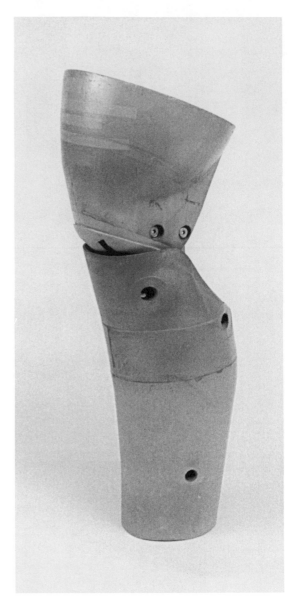

Figure 20–11. Polycentric knee unit.

ment, or by **polycentric linkage** (Fig. 20–11). The single-axis design is simpler and, in most cases, satisfactory. Polycentric systems provide greater stability to the knee, inasmuch as the momentary center of knee rotation is posterior to the wearer's weight line during most of stance phase; this style is less common because of its greater complexity and because other means are available to stabilize the knee.

Friction Mechanisms

In the simplest sense, the above-knee prosthesis is a pendulum swinging about the knee. For the elderly individual who walks slowly, for short distances a basic pendulum is adequate. For more energetic walkers, however, adjustable **friction mechanisms** that modify the pendular action of the knee are desirable. If the knee does not have sufficient friction to retard its natural pendular action, the individual who walks rapidly experiences high heel rise at the beginning of swing phase and **terminal swing**

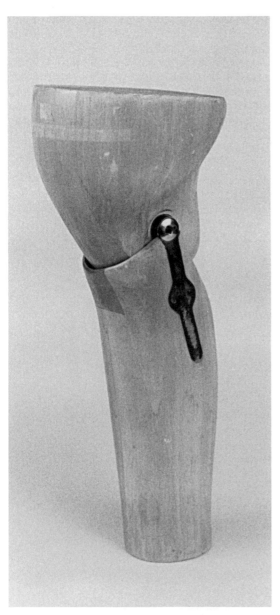

Figure 20–10. Single-axis knee unit.

impact of the knee (sudden, forceful stopping of the shank) at the end of the swing phase.

Friction mechanisms change the knee swing by modifying the speed of knee motion during various times in swing phase and by affecting knee swing according to the walking speed.

Time. The most popular knee unit has **constant friction,** generally consisting of a clamp that grasps the knee bolt. Throughout a given swing phase, the amount of friction is unvarying. It is easy to loosen or to tighten the clamp to change the ease of knee motion.

A more sophisticated device applies **variable friction,** in which the amount of friction changes during a given swing phase. At early swing, high friction is applied to retard heel rise; during mid swing, friction diminishes to permit the knee to swing easily; at late swing, friction increases to dampen impact.

Media. The medium through which friction is applied influences performance. The usual medium is **sliding friction,** such as when a clamp slides about a bolt. This method is simple, but it does not accommodate automatically as the walking speed changes. A more complex approach uses fluid, either oil **(hydraulic friction)** or air **(pneumatic friction).**[13] Unlike sliding friction, fluid friction varies directly with velocity. Thus, with a hydraulic or pneumatic unit, if the wearer suddenly walks faster, the knee increases friction instantly, to prevent high heel rise and terminal impact. Consequently, the movements of the prosthetic and sound limbs are more symmetrical than would be the case with sliding friction.[14] Oil or air is contained in a cylinder in the knee unit. A piston descends in the cylinder during early swing, causing the knee to flex. The speed of piston descent depends on the type of fluid and the walking speed. Later, the piston ascends, extending the knee.

Hydraulic units provide more friction than do pneumatic devices. Both types are more expensive than the simpler sliding friction designs.

Various combinations of friction designs are manufactured, such as constant sliding friction, variable sliding friction, and variable fluid friction.

Extension Aids

Many knee units have a mechanism to assist knee extension during the latter part of swing phase. The simpler type is an external aid, consisting of elastic webbing located in front of the knee axis. The elastic is stretched when the knee flexes in early swing and recoils to extend the knee in late swing. The webbing is easily adjusted but tends to pull the knee into extension when the wearer sits. The internal extension aid is an elastic band or spring within the knee unit. It functions identically to the external aid during walking, but, unlike the external aid, the internal type keeps the knee flexed when the individual sits. Acute knee flexion causes the band or spring to pass posterior to the knee axis, maintaining the flexed attitude.

Stabilizers

Most knee units do not have a special device to increase stability. The patient controls knee action by hip motion, aided by the alignment of the knee in relation to the other components of the prosthesis. Specifically, the prosthetic knee joint is aligned posterior to the trochanter-knee-ankle (TKA) line. Elderly or debilitated patients, however, may benefit from additional mechanical security.

Manual Lock. The simplest stabilizer is a manual lock, in which a pin lodges in a receptacle and is released only when the wearer manipulates an unlocking lever. When engaged, the manual lock prevents knee flexion. The user is secure during early stance but is hampered through the rest of the gait cycle when knee flexion is desirable. To compensate for the difficulty in advancing the locked prosthesis, the shank should be shortened approximately ½ inch (1 cm). Another problem inherent with the manual lock is the need to disengage it when the wearer sits.

Friction Brake. The **friction brake,** a more elaborate stabilizing system, provides very high friction during early stance, resisting any tendency the knee may have to flex. One design, incorporated in a sliding friction unit, involves the mating of a wedge and groove upon loading, assuming the knee is flexed less than 25 degrees. Another version of friction brake is found in a hydraulic unit; during early stance additional fluid resistance markedly retards piston descent.

From midstance through heel strike, friction brakes do not interfere with knee motion. In addition, they do not impede the patient during seated transfers. Such devices add to the cost of the prosthesis and, if improperly designed, may not protect the patient from falling.

SOCKETS

Although several socket designs are in current use for above-knee prostheses, the standard remains the quadrilateral total contact socket (Fig. 20–12). When viewed from above, the socket resembles a rectangle. Custom molded of plastic, the socket features a horizontal posterior shelf for the ischial tuberosity and gluteal musculature, a medial brim at the same level as the posterior shelf, an anterior wall 2½ to 3 in (6 to 8 cm) higher to apply a posteriorly directed force to the thigh to retain the tuberosity on its shelf, and a lateral wall the same height as the anterior wall to aid in mediolateral stabilization. Concave reliefs are: (a) anteromedial for the pressure-sensitive adductor longus tendon, (b) posteromedial for the sensitive hamstring tendons, (c) posterolateral to permit the gluteus maximus to contract and to bulge without being crowded, and (d) anterolateral to allow extra room for the rectus femoris. The anterior wall has a convexity, Scarpa's bulge, to maximize pressure distribution in the vicinity of the femoral triangle. The lateral wall may have reliefs for the greater trochanter and the distal end of the femur. The quadrilateral socket is designed to fit snugly.[15]

The total contact above-knee socket brings the wearer the comparable advantages as described for the total contact below-knee socket; namely, maximum area for load distribution, counterpressure to assist venous return and to prevent distal edema, and enhancement of sensory feedback to foster better control of the prosthesis.

Slight socket flexion on the distal thigh section of the

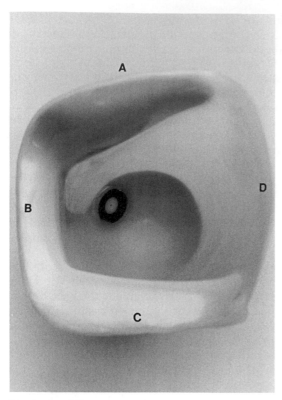

Figure 20–12. Quadrilateral ISNY flexible socket viewed from above. (*A*) Anterior wall, (*B*) medial wall, (*C*) posterior wall, (*D*) lateral wall.

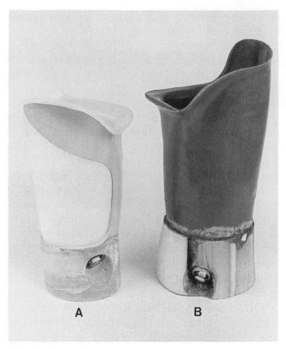

Figure 20–13. Quadrilateral total suction sockets. (*A*) ISNY flexible socket in rigid frame, (*B*) rigid polyester laminate socket.

prosthesis is desirable for several reasons: (a) to increase loading on the posterior shelf, (b) to facilitate contraction of the hip extensors, (c) to reduce lumbar lordosis, and (d) to provide a zone through which the thigh may be extended in order to permit the wearer to take steps of approximately equal length.

Three means are used to suspend the above-knee prosthesis: (a) total suction, (b) partial suction, and (c) no suction.

Suction Suspension

Suction refers to the pressure difference inside and outside the socket. With suction suspension, internal socket pressure is less than external pressure; consequently, atmospheric pressure causes the socket to remain on the thigh (Fig. 20–13). The socket brim must fit snugly, and a one-way air release valve must be located at the bottom of the socket. With total suction, the wearer uses a pulling sock to don the prosthesis. After the sock-encased amputated limb is inserted into the socket, the sock is pulled out through the valve hole, and the wearer installs the valve. Total suction, which affords maximum control of the prosthesis without any encumbering auxiliary suspension, can be achieved only if the socket fits snugly; if the patient experiences changes in amputated limb volume, suction will be lost. Some individuals have difficulty pulling the donning sock off the amputation limb. Before abandoning attempts to use suction suspension, the wearer should try donning by substituting elastic bandage for the cotton stockinet pulling sock. The bandage

is wound around the thigh and the distal tail of bandage pulled through the valve hole, generally an easier maneuver than using the stockinet.

Partial Suction. A socket that is slightly looser may enable partial suction suspension (Fig. 20–14). The wearer dons a sock, pulls it slightly through the valve opening to smooth superficial thigh tissues into the socket. The wearer then replaces the valve and the sock remains inside the prosthesis. Because socket fit is looser,

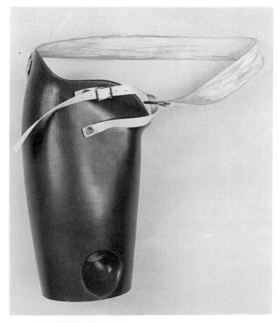

Figure 20–14. Quadrilateral partial suction socket with Silesian bandage.

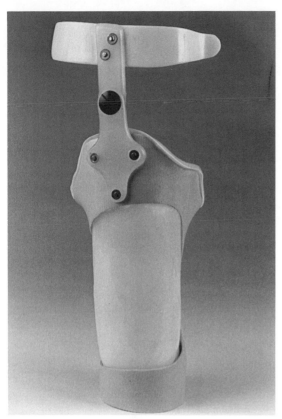

Figure 20-15. Quadrilateral partial suction socket with rigid plastic pelvic band attachment.

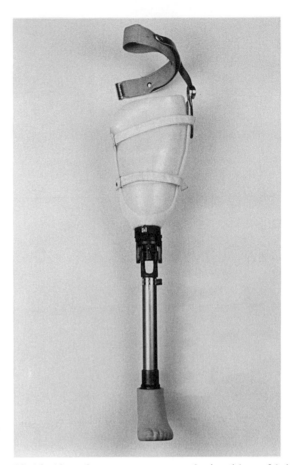

Figure 20-16. Above-knee temporary prosthesis with prefabricated adjustable polypropylene socket, pelvic band, and adjustable pylon shank with SACH foot.

auxiliary suspension aids are needed—either a fabric Silesian bandage or a rigid plastic or metal hip joint and pelvic band (Fig. 20-15). These aids encircle the pelvis.

No Suction. Suspension without any pressure differential requires a socket that is looser than suitable for partial suction suspension. The patient wears one or more socks and does not use a suction valve (Fig. 20-16). Auxiliary suspension, usually a pelvic band, is essential. The relatively loose socket makes donning easy but hinders control of the prosthesis. Some individuals dislike the pressure of the pelvic band against the back during sitting. It should also be noted that donning ease will be affected by socket size and type of closure.

Disarticulation Prostheses

Individuals with knee or hip disarticulation wear prostheses that include the same distal components as for prostheses for lower levels; that is, identical foot selection pertains to knee disarticulations and below-knee amputations, and foot and knee units are common for both hip disarticulations and above-knee amputations. The major distinction, therefore, is in the proximal portion of the prostheses.

KNEE DISARTICULATION PROSTHESES

When amputation is at or distal to the femoral epicondyles, the patient should have excellent prosthetic con-

trol because (a) thigh leverage is maximum, (b) most of body weight can be borne through the distal end of the femur, and (c) the broad epicondyles provide rotational stability. The problem presented by knee disarticulation is primarily cosmetic; when the individual sits, the thigh on the amputated side may protrude slightly, particularly if a bulky knee unit is worn. Consequently, the knee disarticulation prosthesis has a streamlined knee with a specially designed socket (Fig. 20-17).

Sockets

Two types of socket are in current use. Both are usually made of plastic and terminate below the ischial tuberosity. No additional suspension aids are needed. One version features an anterior opening to accommodate a bulbous amputation limb. After the limb is inserted, the wearer closes the socket with lacing or Velcro straps. The other design has no anterior opening and is suitable for limbs that are not bulbous.

Knee Units

Several units are specifically manufactured for knee disarticulation. All have a thin proximal attachment plate to minimize added thigh length. One may choose among hydraulic, pneumatic, and sliding friction units,

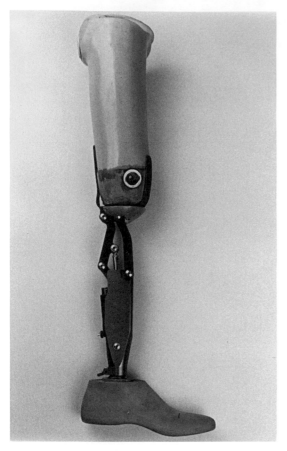

Figure 20–17. Knee disarticulation prosthesis.

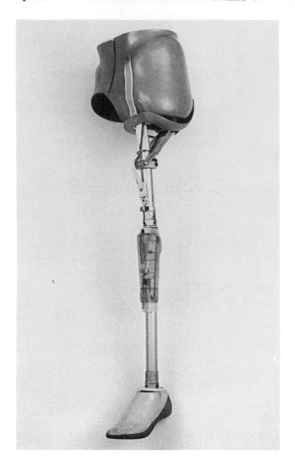

Figure 20–18. Hip disarticulation prosthesis.

with or without polycentric linkage. Even with a special knee unit, however, the thigh may project farther forward on the amputated side. Consequently, the shank is shortened equivalently, so that when the person stands, the pelvis is level. When the individual sits, slight thigh protrusion on the prosthetic side may be evident.

HIP DISARTICULATION PROSTHESES

A hip disarticulation prosthesis (Fig. 20–18) is fitted to one with amputation above the greater trochanter (very short above-knee), removal of the femoral head from the acetabulum (hip disarticulation), or removal of the femur and some portion of the pelvis (hemipelvectomy). Prostheses for proximal levels share common hip, knee, and foot assemblies but differ with regard to socket design. The endoskeletal thigh and shank predominate, because they afford appreciable weight saving in these massive prostheses.

Sockets

The basic socket is the plastic Canadian hip disarticulation socket. For very short above-knee amputation and hip disarticulation, the socket provides weight bearing on the ipsilateral ischial tuberosity and both iliac crests. The

person with a hemipelvectomy who does not retain the ipsilateral tuberosity or crest has a socket with a higher proximal trimline, sometimes encompassing the lower thorax. This person supports weight on the remainder of the pelvis, on the abdomen, and perhaps on the lower ribs.

Hip Unit

Various joints are available to simulate hip flexion. They have an extension aid to bias the prosthesis toward the stable neutral position. Positioning the mechanical hip anterior to a point corresponding to the anatomic hip also contributes to hip stability. The joint is located inferior to the normal hip, so that with sitting, the prosthetic thigh will not protrude unattractively.

Stability

Several attributes combine to make the Canadian hip disarticulation prosthesis very stable, namely, the hip extension aid, anterior placement of the hip joint, and posterior placement of the knee unit, which usually has an extension aid. The unit may be shortened slightly, primarily to aid clearance during swing phase but also to encourage the wearer to apply maximum weight to the prosthesis.

Socks

All individuals with lower-limb amputations, except those wearing above-knee prostheses suspended by suction, require a supply of clean socks of appropriate fabric, size, and shape. It is expeditious to include an order of at least a dozen socks at the time the prosthesis is ordered, so that third-party payment may cover this relatively inexpensive but important accessory.

Socks are knitted of unbleached mercerized cotton, wool, orlon/lycra, or nylon. Cotton absorbs perspiration better than the other materials, is rarely allergenic, and is often worn next to the skin. Cotton may shrink if washed in very hot water or dried in high heat. Cotton is knitted in two-, three-, and five-ply, the last being the thickest; ply refers to the number of threads knitted together.

Wool is the most resilient material, routinely woven in three-, five-, and six-ply. It requires the most care when laundering to avoid shrinkage. Wool socks are the most expensive.

Orlon/lycra socks are somewhat elastic. They are manufactured in two- and three-plies. This synthetic fabric combination affords considerable resilience but does not absorb much perspiration. They can be washed easily without shrinking.

Nylon is an alternative for wear against the skin. The fabric's exceptional smoothness minimizes shear at the socket-skin interface, thus reducing the risk of skin abrasion, especially in hot weather and among those with much scarring. Some below-knee prosthesis wearers are able to use a woman's knee-high nylon stocking if the amputation limb is rather slender. Nylon sheaths are woven specifically for use with a prosthesis. Because nylon does not absorb perspiration, liquid passes through the weave to be absorbed by an outer sock of wool, cotton, or orlon/lycra.

Regardless of material, the shape of the sock is important for comfort. A sock of proper size fits smoothly without wrinkling or undue stretching. The sock should be long enough to terminate above the most proximal part of the socket or thigh corset.

It is common practice to add more socks as the amputated limb shrinks. Nevertheless, more than 15 ply of socks will convert the triangular below-knee socket or the quadrilateral above-knee socket into a round, plug fit, losing the effect of strategically placed socket build-ups and reliefs. When the limb reduces this much, the socket needs alteration or replacement.

Prosthetic Maintenance

Optimal function depends on proper care of the socks, prosthesis, amputated limb, and intact limb. Guidelines for personal hygiene are presented in the preceding chapter. In addition to ensuring cleanliness, the individual should wear a well-fitting sock and shoe on the sound foot, the mate to the shoe on the prosthesis. Both shoes should have heels and soles in excellent condition.

Like any mechanical device, the prosthesis benefits from simple regular maintenance, which generally avoids costly, time-consuming repairs. Printed instructions pertaining to prosthesis and sock care for patient education are helpful.

SOCKET AND SUSPENSION

Plastic sockets should be washed with a cloth dampened in warm water that has a very small amount of mild soap dissolved in it. The socket is then wiped with a damp, soap-free cloth and dried with a fresh towel. In warm climates, the socket should be washed every evening so that it will be completely dry when the patient dresses the following morning.

The above-knee suction valve should be brushed daily to remove talcum and lint which would clog the tiny aperture. The valve should be inserted and removed only with one's finger, for tools are apt to damage the internal mechanism or outer threads.

Leather corsets should be kept dry. Use of saddle soap will keep leather clean. If incontinence is present, the individual with a below-knee amputation who requires a thigh corset should have one made of flexible polyester laminate, which is impervious to urine.

Socket liners made of polyethylene foam can be washed by hand in tepid water with mild soap and air dried overnight.

KNEE UNITS

Sliding friction mechanisms tend to loosen with walking and thus require periodic tightening to retain the original adjustment. The frequency of tightening depends on how much the wearer walks. Most units have a pair of screws in front or in the rear of the knee unit which can be turned clockwise with an Allen wrench or common screwdriver. After turning each screw a quarter turn, the person should walk for at least 5 minutes to ascertain the effectiveness of the adjustment. Squeaking at the knee or articulated ankle indicates the need for oil.

The rubber or felt extension bumper in the knee unit will erode after prolonged vigorous use, and the wearer will then notice that the knee begins to hyperextend. The bumper, visible when the knee is flexed, must be replaced by the prosthetist.

The external kick strap extension aid may lose its elasticity after several years. The wearer will then experience high heel rise and slow knee extension at the end of swing phase. The simplest approach is to tighten the strap through its buckle. Eventually, the prosthetist will need to replace the elastic. Internal elastic extension aids are not subject to rubbing from the trouser leg or skirt and thus do not lose elasticity as readily. Steel spring internal aids retain their effectiveness for the life of the prosthesis.

Pneumatic and hydraulic units must be protected against tears of the rubber shield protecting the piston. It is most important that the piston not be scratched and thereby allow air and debris to enter the cylinder. Air bubbles in the unit will cause a spongy feeling and possibly noise with walking. The prosthesis should be stored upright with the knee extended to exclude air from the cylinder.

FEET

Usual precautions should be taken to avoid getting the prosthetic foot wet, especially if the foot is a wood articulated model. If this happens, the shoe and sock should be removed to allow the foot to dry completely, away from direct heat. The wearer should also avoid stepping into sand and similar materials which might enter the cleft between the foot and shank section and restrict the excursion of the foot. The prosthetist would have to disassemble the foot to clean it.

The individual should inspect the foot periodically to spot cracking at the toe-break or at the tip of the keel, which will curl the toes and prevent smooth transition during push-off. A deteriorated heel cushion or plantar bumper will cause the wearer to appear to be walking in a hole.

Socks wear much more quickly on the prosthetic side, because the hard foot assembly and shank rub against the fabric. Stair risers also scuff the sock. Some find that wearing two socks helps cushion the outer one against premature formation of holes.

The individual must be instructed regarding wearing shoes of the same heel height as was the case when the prosthesis was aligned. Too low a heel interrupts push-off; an unduly high heel makes the knee less stable. If the wearer wishes to wear flat-heeled sneakers, a ½ inch (1 cm) shim should be placed inside the sneaker at the heel. High-heeled shoes require that the foot be changed either by unbolting it and replacing it with a foot with an appropriate plantarflexion angle or by adjusting the heel-height screw found in certain single-axis models. Boots and other footwear with stiff upper sections restrict the action of any foot assembly which is designed to provide substantial dorsiflexion and plantarflexion.

Removing the shoe is easier if the prosthesis is not worn. With the shoe unlaced completely, the counter is grasped, and the heel of the shoe pushed off the back of the foot. The shoe is then pulled upward and off the forefoot. The shoe should be donned with the aid of a shoehorn.

EXTERIOR FINISHES

The usual finish of polyester laminate is impervious to most liquids. It needs only to be wiped periodically with a cloth dampened with dilute detergent to remove surface soil. Marks can be scoured with kitchen cleanser, but excessive abrasion will dull the finish.

The soft foam cover of the endoskeletal prosthesis requires reasonable caution against exposure to direct heat, penetrating objects, and solvents. The outer covering will need replacement whenever it becomes unacceptably soiled or torn. The above-knee version tends to deteriorate at the knee, especially if the wearer kneels a great deal.

PHYSICAL THERAPY MANAGEMENT

Physical therapists participate in amputation management at several key stages: (a) preoperative, (b) postop-erative-preprosthetic, (c) prosthetic prescription, (d) prosthetic assessment, and (e) prosthetic training.

The first two stages are described in the preceding chapter. Our discussion emphasizes the responsibilities of the physical therapist with regard to the patient and prosthesis. Ideally, the therapist works as a member of a **clinic team,** together with the physician and prosthetist. Others, such as a vocational counselor, a psychologist, and a social worker, may participate in the team on a regular basis or as needed. The clinic team provides the best environment for exchange of information and viewpoints regarding the patient, fostering a coordinated pattern of treatment. The team meets to formulate the prosthetic prescription, to assess the newly delivered prosthesis, and to reassess the patient and prosthesis upon completion of prosthetic training. The therapist, therefore, has an integral part to play in these critical points in rehabilitation, as well as conducting prosthetic training. If a formal clinic team is not established in the therapist's work setting, then the therapist must seek to coordinate the recommendations of the physician and prosthetist.

With either administrative situation, the physical therapist

1. Performs preprescription assessment
2. Contributes to prosthetic prescription
3. Assesses the prescribed prosthesis
4. Facilitates prosthetic acceptance
5. Trains the patient to don, to use, and to maintain the prosthesis

Preprescription Assessment

Successful prosthetic rehabilitation depends on matching the individual's physical and psychologic characteristics to a prosthesis composed of carefully selected components.

PHYSICAL EXAMINATION

The physical therapist should measure and record the patient's physical attributes such as active and passive range of motion of all lower extremity joints on both limbs. Knee and hip flexion contractures compromise prosthetic alignment and appearance. A knee lock may be needed with an above-knee amputation and an alternate socket design for a below-knee amputation. Severe contractures preclude fitting with conventional components, or may contraindicate provision of *any* prosthesis. The deleterious effects of contractures are especially serious with bilateral amputations.

Amputated limb length must be measured. The individual with a short below-knee amputation may require SC/SP suspension. Every attempt should be made to fit the patient with a short above-knee amputation with suction or partial suction suspension to retain the prosthesis on the limb.

Muscle strength should be assessed. Frequently, the geriatric patient with vascular disease experiences reduced physical activity levels as leg pains and foot ulceration develop. Such an individual may present marked debility, which would interfere with prosthetic use or necessitate use of a locking knee unit.

Proprioception is another factor requiring assessment. For example, an individual with impaired joint position sense at the knee will need extra prosthetic stability in the form of higher medial and lateral walls or side joints attached to a thigh corset on the below-knee prosthesis. Other sensory changes influence prescription. Blindness does not preclude fitting but poses problems with regard to selecting components easy to don, as well as altering the training program.

Other neurologic changes, such as cerebrovascular accident, complicate fitting and training. Ipsilateral hemiplegia is not as detrimental to prosthetic rehabilitation as contralateral paralysis.[18] In both instances, the prosthesis should be designed for maximum stability.

Circulatory status of the amputated and sound limbs requires scrutiny. Prosthetic fitting may benefit the dysvascular contralateral limb by transferring some stress from it. In addition, should the person come to bilateral amputation, previous experience with donning and controlling a unilateral prosthesis is invaluable in adjusting to a pair of prostheses.

Prosthetic prescription also hinges on the patient's cardiopulmonary condition. The clinic team must formulate a realistic goal based on the individual's physical capacity, particularly as related to exercise tolerance and endurance. The individual who is not expected to walk rapidly is an unlikely candidate for an energy-storing foot or a fluid-controlled knee unit.

Obesity is another factor to be considered in the preprescription assessment. Socket design for the flabby thigh differs from that for a firmer above-knee amputation limb. In addition, the obese individual is more apt to fluctuate in body weight, necessitating provision of socket liners and several socks to compensate for changing limb circumference. Similarly, those who have renal disease, especially if managed with kidney dialysis, experience volume changes which need prosthetic accommodation.

Arthritic changes affect prescription. Diminished lower-limb mobility or deformity compromises prosthetic alignment. Hand and wrist stiffness and malalignment affect the mode of donning; a laced corset should be avoided. Canes and crutches may require special modification.

PSYCHOSOCIAL ASSESSMENT

The physical therapist ordinarily treats the patient more frequently than other members of the clinic team and so is more likely to be attuned to the individual's attitudes. The patient and family who are excessively fearful will be best served by prosthetic rehabilitation beginning with a **temporary prosthesis.** Motivation is a cardinal determinant of prosthetic outcome. Again, strong motivation demonstrated through use of a temporary prosthesis and compliance with other elements of the rehabilitation program are generally good predictors of prosthetic success. One should guard against the family or patient who portrays unrealistic expectations. Involving them in group situations with other persons with amputation, in the physical therapy department and in social environments, will help foster appropriate attitudes.

The therapist should also weigh the likelihood that the patient will be able to care for complex mechanisms and have the means to obtain prosthetic servicing, especially on components, such as the rubber covering of the endoskeletal shank, that are less durable.

Prosthetic Prescription

Because no prosthetic component, or combination of components, is ideal for all patients, it is necessary to select components that are most apt to meet the individual's needs. Alternatives for every element of the prosthesis have advantages and disadvantages. The task of the physical therapist, in conjunction with other team members, is to judge the relative merits of the various feet, shanks, and other components in light of objective and subjective information pertaining to the prosthetic candidate.

Some individuals can be expected to function best with a sophisticated prosthesis that enhances the ability to engage in vigorous walking and athletics. Others are best served by a simple, inexpensive device. The most accurate predictor of future function is the patient's performance with a previous prosthesis. For the wearer who seeks a replacement prosthesis, the clinic team should consider the extent of use of the previous limb, together with any changes in the patient's physique and lifestyle. For example, if the person fitted with one prosthesis now returns with bilateral amputation, never having used the original prosthesis, that person is a very poor candidate for bilateral prosthetic fitting. In contrast, another patient who had been fitted with a simple above-knee prosthesis expresses the wish to engage in sports. By demonstrating good use of the original prosthesis, that individual is likely to derive considerable benefit from a new prosthesis with an energy-storing foot.

The task of prescription for the new patient is more difficult. Depending on the interval between amputation surgery and prescription, the amputated limb may not have stabilized in volume, nor the patient achieved the maximum benefit of the preprosthetic program. The best criterion for prosthetic prescription in such an instance is performance with a temporary prosthesis. This appliance includes a well-fitting socket; suitable suspension, pylon, and foot; and, with the above-knee amputation, a knee unit. The temporary prosthesis also serves for preliminary gait and activities training. The major difference between the temporary and definitive prosthesis is appearance. The temporary socket is designed for easy alteration to accommodate reduction in amputated limb volume. Little attention ordinarily is paid to the color and shape of the temporary prosthesis.

BELOW-KNEE TEMPORARY PROSTHESES

Most below-knee temporary prostheses have a plaster of Paris socket molded to the amputated limb. Plaster is inexpensive, readily available, and easy to use. The resulting socket, however, is likely to be heavy and bulky. Alternatively, sockets can be made of thermoplastic material, such as Orthoplast and Aquaplast, which become malleable at temperatures low enough to permit forming directly on the patient.[19] Suspension is usually by a cuff or thigh corset. The pylon can be an aluminum component manufactured for this purpose; such a pylon has a proximal fixture permitting small changes in prosthetic alignment. A simpler pylon can be made with polyvinylchloride piping, such as that used by plumbers. The pipe is lightweight and can be spot heated to enable slight alteration in alignment. A SACH foot is customary on temporary prostheses.

ABOVE-KNEE TEMPORARY PROSTHESES

The easiest approach is to use a prefabricated polypropylene socket, which is manufactured in several sizes and which has a series of Velcro straps for adjustment of circumferential fit (see Figure 20–16). The socket can be suspended by a Silesian bandage or pelvic band, and is mounted on a knee unit which may include a manual lock. Alternatively, a custom-fabricated socket of plaster or low-temperature thermoplastic can be used. Some individuals with bilateral above-knee amputations use a different system, namely, a pair of stubbies (see chapter 19). These are nonarticulated prostheses; the sockets are mounted on short platforms, drastically reducing the wearer's height in order to increase hip stability. The platforms have rearward projections to protect the wearer from a backward fall.

Prosthetic Assessment

Checkout is one of the most important functions of the clinic team. The prosthesis should be assessed before the patient engages in prosthetic training and should be reassessed at the conclusion of training. The checkout procedure is intended to determine the adequacy of prosthetic fit and function, as well as the wearer's opinion of appearance.

In many institutions, the physical therapist assesses the prosthesis and presents a summary of findings to the clinic team. The team makes the final determination regarding the acceptability of the prosthesis. At initial checkout, the team has three options: (a) pass, (b) provisional pass, and (c) fail. Pass indicates that no changes are needed in the prosthesis and the patient can proceed to training. Provisional pass signals one or more minor problems requiring correction, none of which will interfere with basic training. Failure is the clinic team's judgment that the prosthesis has a major fault which should be corrected to the team's satisfaction prior to commencement of prosthetic training. For example, poor finishing of the prosthetic foot merits a provisional pass, whereas a socket that abrades the amputated limb should be graded as fail.

If the therapist intends to train a patient who is not managed by a formal clinic team, it is especially critical that the therapist assess the prosthesis prior to initiating training to discover any problems that would negate the future program.

At final checkout, two ratings are available; pass indicates that no problems exist and the patient uses the prosthesis in a manner commensurate with the individual's physical capacity. Fail means that major or minor problems remain which require correction.

No special materials are needed for checkout, except for a form and a straight chair. Appendices A and B contain checkout forms referred to in the following sections.

BELOW-KNEE CHECKOUT

Most items on the checkout form (Appendix A) are self-explanatory. Each contributes to forming an accurate judgment of the adequacy of the prosthesis.

Static Assessment

The prosthesis is assessed as the wearer stands and sits. In addition, the amputated limb and details of the prosthesis will be examined. The prosthesis should be compared with the prescription. Departures from the original specifications must be approved by the individual(s) who developed the prescription.

The new wearer should stand in the parallel bars or other secure environment and should attempt to bear equal weight on both feet. The therapist should solicit subjective comments about comfort. Estimates of anteroposterior and mediolateral alignment are aided by slipping a sheet of paper under various parts of the shoe. Ideally, the patient should stand with the heel and sole flat on the floor. Malalignment, indicated by excessive bearing on a portion of the shoe, may be confirmed by subsequent analysis of gait.

Most prostheses are constructed so that when the individual stands, the pelvis is level. If the pelvis tilts, the therapist should place thin lifts under the foot on the shorter side to restore a level attitude. If the lifts measure ½ inch (1 cm) or less, no attention is needed. For greater discrepancy, the therapist should seek causative factors. An amputated limb that sinks too far into the socket will make the prosthetic side appear short, and the wearer will probably complain of distal discomfort.

Piston action (or pistoning) refers to vertical motion of the socket when the patient elevates the pelvis. It is evident during gait as an up-and-down movement of the socket on the limb. This socket slippage is caused by looseness and/or inadequate suspension.

Socket walls should be of proper height for the individual and should fit snugly, as should the thigh corset if it is part of the prosthesis.

Comfortable sitting is a primary need, especially for older individuals. The posterior brim should not impinge into the popliteal fossa, and hamstring reliefs should be adequate, especially on the medial side. Placement of the tabs of the cuff or the joints of the corset also influence sitting comfort.

Dynamic Assessment

Checkout includes appraisal of the gait pattern and performance of other activities. The new wearer will have had brief experience walking in the prosthesis during the course of fabrication. Nevertheless, gross departure from the usual gait exhibited with below-knee amputations[20] should be noted and causes pursued. Table 20–1 summarizes the prosthetic and anatomic causes of gait deviations. In particular, below-knee analysis focuses on action of the knee during stance phase. As with a nonamputated limb, the knee should flex in a controlled manner during early and late stance phase. Excessive flexion indicates that the socket is aligned too far anterior in relation to the foot or is aligned in excessive flexion; this deviation may cause the patient to fall. If the knee flexes excessively only during early stance, the cause may be a heel cushion that is too firm for the individual. Conversely, insufficient flexion results from posterior displacement of the socket or inadequate socket tilting. When viewed in the frontal plane, the socket brim should maintain reasonable contact with the leg; excessive lateral thrust of the prosthetic brim suggests that the prosthetic foot has been positioned too far medially.

At initial checkout, performance on stairs and inclines may be omitted because the patient has not had training in these activities.

Assessment with the Prosthesis off the Patient

After conducting the dynamic assessment, the therapist should examine the amputated limb for signs of proper loading. The posterior wall should be at the same level as the build-up for the patella tendon when the patient stands. Because one can not ascertain this relationship when the prosthesis is being worn, a substitute check is performed. Stand the prosthesis on a table; place the end of a long pencil or ruler on the patellar bulge and rest the stick on the posterior brim. In a well-constructed prosthesis, the stick will slant upward toward the rear, indicating that when the individual stands in the prosthesis and compresses the heel cushion, the wall will be at the proper height.

Check and fork straps are rarely used with PTB sockets. If present, they should provide reasonable adjustability. General workmanship is a guide to future durability, as well as contributing to acceptable appearance of the prosthesis.

ABOVE-KNEE CHECKOUT

The same format is used to assess the above-knee prosthesis (Appendix B). It is most important to recognize that seldom is one item on the form of major significance. The therapist and the entire team should look for patterns that herald future difficulty. For example, malalignment detected in static analysis should be confirmed during dynamic gait analysis.

Static Assessment

The checkout form is designed to assess the fit of the quadrilateral socket, whether of rigid polyester laminate

Table 20–1 BELOW-KNEE PROSTHETIC GAIT ANALYSIS

Deviation	Prosthetic Causes	Anatomic Causes
Excessive knee flexion in early stance	Insufficient plantarflexion Stiff heel cushion or plantar bumper Excessive socket flexion Socket malaligned too far anteriorly Excessive posterior placement of cuff tabs	Knee flexion contracture Weak quadriceps
Insufficient knee flexion in early stance	Excessive plantarflexion Soft heel cushion or plantar bumper Insufficient socket flexion Socket malaligned too far posteriorly	Pain at anterodistal aspect of amputation limb Weak quadriceps Extensor spasticity Knee arthritis
Excessive lateral thrust	Excessive inset of foot Excessive socket adduction	
Medial thrust	Outset of foot Insufficient socket adduction	
Early knee flexion in late stance "drop off"	Insufficient plantarflexion Distal end of keel or toe break misplaced posteriorly Soft dorsiflexion stop Excessive socket flexion Socket malaligned too far anteriorly Excessive posterior placement of cuff tabs	Knee flexion contracture
Delayed knee flexion in late stance "walking uphill"	Excessive plantarflexion Distal end of keel or toe break misplaced anteriorly Stiff dorsiflexion stop Insufficient socket flexion Socket malaligned too far posteriorly	Extensor spasticity Knee arthritis

or flexible polyethylene. Proper location of the adductor longus tendon and ischial tuberosity ensures that the patient has donned the socket correctly. The prosthetic knee should be stable enough to withstand a blow delivered by the therapist to the posterior aspect of the unit. Stability is influenced by the alignment of the knee in relation to the hip and prosthetic ankle. The farther posterior the knee bolt, the more stable the knee. Polycentric linkage and mechanical stabilizers also contribute to stability. A horizontal posterior brim allows weight to be borne on the gluteal musculature as well as the ischial tuberosity. Perineal pressure results from sharpness of the medial brim or insufficiency of the adductor longus relief. If the socket is opaque, the only way to judge its snugness is by palpating tissue protruding through the valve hole when the valve is removed.

The Silesian bandage is a fabric webbing generally used to augment partial suction suspension. The lateral attachment is superior and posterior to the greater trochanter for best control of prosthetic rotation. Anteriorly, the attachment should be at the level of the ischial seat, or slightly below to aid in adducting the prosthesis.

The pelvic joint and band should fit the torso snugly for best control of the prosthesis and least bulkiness.

The patient should be able to sit comfortably with the prosthesis. Posterior discomfort may indicate inadequate hamstring relief or a sharp posterior brim.

Dynamic Assessment

Gait analysis enables the clinic team members to assess the adequacy of socket fit and prosthesis alignment and adjustment. The patient also influences the walking pattern by the timing and force of muscular contraction and the presence or absence of contractures.[21] See Table 20–2 for a summary of above-knee prosthetic gait deviations.

Deviations Best Viewed from Behind. Many patients with above-knee amputations abduct the prosthesis, indicating poor frontal plane balance. Hip abduction contracture predisposes to this deviation seen in stance phase. Inadequate socket adduction, socket looseness, or medial discomfort compel the fault. Lateral trunk bending toward the prosthetic side during stance phase gen-

Table 20–2 ABOVE-KNEE PROSTHETIC GAIT ANALYSIS

Deviation	Prosthetic Causes	Anatomic Causes
Lateral trunk bending	Short prosthesis Inadequate lateral wall adduction Sharp or excessively high medial wall Malalignment in abduction	Weak abductors Abduction contracture Hip pain Very short amputation limb Instability
Wide walking base (abducted gait)	Long prosthesis Excessive abduction of hip joint Inadequate lateral wall adduction Sharp or excessively high medial wall Malalignment in abduction	Abduction contracture Adductor tissue roll Instability
Circumduction	Long prosthesis Excessive stiffness of knee unit Inadequate suspension Small socket Excessive plantarflexion	Abduction contracture Poor knee control
Medial (lateral) whip	Faulty socket contour Malrotation of knee unit	
Rotation of foot on heel strike	Stiff heel cushion or plantar bumper Malrotation of foot	
Uneven heel rise	Inadequate knee friction Lax or taut extension aid	
Terminal swing impact	Insufficient knee friction Taut extension aid	Excessively forceful hip flexion
Foot slap	Soft heel cushion or plantar bumper	
Uneven step length	Faulty socket contour Inadequate knee friction Lax or taut extension aid	Weak hip musculature Hip flexion contracture Instability
Lordosis	Inadequate support from posterior brim Inadequate socket flexion	Hip flexion contracture Weak hip extensors
Vaulting	Long prosthesis Inadequate suspension Inadequate knee friction Excessive plantarflexion Small socket	Walking speed exceeding that for which friction in a sliding friction knee unit was adjusted

erally accompanies abducted gait. If the prosthesis is too long, the patient is apt to abduct; if it is too short, one will see lateral bending without abduction. Alternatively, the patient may circumduct the prosthesis during swing phase, especially if the prosthesis is too long or if the patient is reluctant to allow the knee to bend; socket looseness also may result in circumduction.

Whips refer to rotation of the heel at the time of heel off. If the socket does not fit well, contraction and bulging of hip musculature will cause the prosthesis to rotate abruptly as it is being unloaded at the end of stance phase. Less likely, malrotation of the knee unit may contribute to whipping. Rotation of the foot on heel strike is a much more serious flaw. It indicates inadequate compression of the heel cushion or plantar bumper and can result in a fall.

Deviations Best Viewed from the Side. Improper adjustment of the knee unit gives rise to uneven heel rise and terminal swing impact. If both deviations are present, the probable cause is insufficient friction. If the knee exhibits impact without undue heel rise, more likely the extension aid is too tight. Foot slap indicates that the heel cushion or plantar bumper is too resilient for the amount of force applied by the walker. With a hip flexion contracture or inadequate balance, the patient is apt to take a longer step with the prosthesis than with the sound limb. The longer prosthetic step gives the individual more time on the sound limb. A flexion contracture prevents the sound limb from passing the prosthetic side during swing phase on the sound side. Lumbar lordosis results from inadequate socket flexion, aggravated by a hip flexion contracture. Vaulting is excessive plantar flexion of the sound foot to afford extra room to clear the prosthesis during prosthetic swing phase.

Assessment with the Prosthesis off the Patient

Following the static assessment the therapist should examine the prosthesis and limb as indicated on the checkout form. A resilient back pad is unnecessary with the flexible socket, which enables the patient to sit quietly without undue trouser or skirt abrasion.

Facilitating Prosthetic Acceptance

Amputation is generally viewed as a grievous occurrence, with its visibility a constant reminder of the individual's abnormality. The physical therapist can assist the patient and family to accept the reality of amputation and the prosthesis by verbal and nonverbal communication. The therapist's calm respect for the patient as a worthy human being, regardless of limb condition, should set a model for the attitudes of others. Clinic team management accords not only the benefits of better prosthetic provision but also brings the individual in contact with clinicians who convey experience and confidence in dealing with problems that the individual may consider unique.[22]

As soon as possible, the hospitalized patient should be treated in the physical therapy department, rather than on the ward. The bustle of the department should help dispel despondency. Although postoperative mourning is to be expected, prolonged depression is not constructive. Peer support groups are often effective in aiding acceptance of the prosthesis and in learning special procedures for accomplishing activities. Observation and eventual participation in sports programs for the physically challenged is another way patients learn to cope and gain the most from prosthetic rehabilitation.

The physical therapist, by virtue of close daily contact with the patient, is also in a position to recommend to the clinic those who might profit from psychologic counseling and psychiatric services.

Prosthetic Training

Learning to use a prosthesis effectively involves being able to don it correctly, to develop good balance and coordination, to walk in a reasonably symmetrical manner, and to perform other ambulatory and self-care activities safely. Treatment goals depend on the individual's physical status, preprosthetic experience, and quality of prosthesis. Using the prosthesis only to assist in transferring from the wheelchair to the toilet may be an appropriate goal for the elderly, multidisabled individual, whereas the program for the young person with a traumatic amputation might extend to involving the individual in a full range of sports.

DONNING

Correct application of the prosthesis and frequent inspection of the amputated limb are very important, especially for the beginner and those with poor circulation. Those with partial foot, Syme's, and below-knee amputations can don the prosthesis while seated, after having applied the correct number and sequence of socks. In most instances, the individual simply inserts the amputated limb into the socket. Those with SC/SP suspension should apply the liner to the amputated limb, then insert limb and liner into the socket. The initial entry into the socket with corset suspension may be made while sitting; however, final tightening of laces or straps should be done in the standing position to ensure that the amputated limb is well lodged in the socket.

Individuals with above-knee amputations also can begin the donning process while seated. Those who use partial suction or no suction apply the sock, making certain the proximal margin of the sock extends to the inguinal ligament. The patient then introduces the amputated limb into the socket, taking care that the adductor longus tendon resides in its anteromedial relief. The partial suction user pulls the distal end of the sock down through the valve hole enough to ensure that skin is smooth, then inserts the valve. Finally, the pelvic band or Silesian bandage is secured.

Total suction wearers begin by applying a pulling sock, approximately 30 inches (76 cm) long, or a roll of elastic bandage or a nylon stocking. Whatever the donning aid, it should be placed high in the inguinal region (to pull in proximal tissues) and be drawn through the valve hole. A light dusting of talcum powder reduces friction to ease donning. Although it is possible to complete the donning process while seated, most wearers are accustomed to standing while pulling the sock or other aid out through the valve hole. By leaning forward, the body's weight line will prevent the prosthetic knee from flexing. Finally, the patient inserts the valve.

BALANCE AND COORDINATION

Exercises are similar for all patients with lower-limb amputations, although the individual with an above-knee amputation may be expected to encounter more difficulty controlling the mechanical knee as compared with those who need only to deal with the anatomic knee. All must become accustomed to bearing weight on the amputated side. A graduated program for increasing prosthetic tolerance minimizes the danger of skin abrasion, particularly if the amputated limb presents skin grafts, poor circulation, or diminished sensation. Exercise and rest should be alternated, with cardiopulmonary monitoring a routine part of the program, especially for high-risk individuals.[23]

Some clinicians eschew parallel bars because the fearful patient pulls on them, which will be fruitless when progressing to canes. When bars are used, the therapist should encourage use of an open-handed grip for support, rather than viselike gripping. A sturdy plinth offers the triple advantages of providing good support on only one side, ordinarily the contralateral side, and unidirectional control, because the patient can only push, never pull, for balance.

Static balance, simply standing erect, reintroduces the novice to bipedal posture. The patient should strive for level pelvis and shoulders, vertical trunk without excessive lordosis, and equal weight bearing. The therapist should guard and assist the patient; standing near the prosthesis encourages the patient to shift onto it. To suggest symmetrical performance, refer to the limbs as "right" and "left" or "sound" and "prosthetic," rather than discouraging the patient with "good" and "bad." The patient must learn to exploit proximal sensory receptors to maintain balance and to perceive the position of the prosthesis without looking at the floor. Some patients respond well to use of a mirror for visual feedback.

Dynamic exercises improve mediolateral, sagittal, and rotary control. The patient learns that hip flexion causes the knee to bend, and hip extension stabilizes the knee. Placing the sound foot ahead of the prosthesis makes the prosthetic knee more stable. Patients should be instructed in weight shifting in both symmetrical and stride positions and in stepping movements. Symmetrical performance is fostered by having all exercises performed rhythmically with both the right and left lower extremities.

GAIT TRAINING

Walking is a natural progression from dynamic balance exercises, as the patient takes successive steps. Heel-toe progression can be assisted by a biofeedback limb-load monitor which has a heel switch which buzzes upon heel contact and a toe switch which signals toe-off.[24] Some patients respond well to viewing themselves on videotape; the cassettes also form a valuable record of patient performance and progress.[25,26] Rhythmic counting and walking in time with music in 4/4 time are other ways of improving gait symmetry and speed.

A cane or forearm crutches are appropriate aids for the individual who is unable to achieve a safe gait without undue fatigue. Sometimes the cane is used only outdoors to aid in negotiating curbs and other ground irregularity and to signal oncoming traffic. Ordinarily the cane is used on the contralateral side to enhance frontal plane balance. If bilateral assistance is required, a pair of forearm crutches is preferable to two canes. The crutches remain clasped around the forearms when the user opens a door. Axillary crutches tempt the patient with leaning on the axillary bars, impinging on the radial nerve, and are inconvenient when climbing stairs.

FUNCTIONAL ACTIVITIES

The prosthetic wearer who is learning to walk also should gain experience in performing other skills involving the prosthesis. Activities, such as transferring to various chairs, vary the program and, for some individuals, may be more important than long-distance ambulation. The training program for vigorous individuals includes stair climbing, negotiating ramps, retrieving objects from the floor, kneeling, sitting on the floor, running, driving a car, and engaging in sports. The fundamental difference between these functional activities and walking is the way each leg is used. Walking stresses symmetrical usage, but the other activities are done asymmetrically, with greater reliance on the strength, agility, and sensory control of the sound limb.

Generally the patient should have the opportunity to analyze a new situation, rather than depending on directions from the therapist. Most tasks can be accomplished safely in several ways. The learner may profit from observing other prosthesis wearers as well as from professional instruction.

Transfers

Rising from different chairs, the toilet, and car are primary skills even for patients who are elderly or generally debilitated. Most patients enter the physical therapy department in a wheelchair. Initially, the patient can park the chair at the parallel bars or at a sturdy plinth. After raising the foot rests, the patient can sit forward and transfer weight to the intact leg, then push down on chair armrests. Later, the individual will realize that placing the sound foot close to the chair will enable rising by extending the knee and hip on the sound side.

Sitting is accomplished by placing the sound foot close to the chair and lowering oneself by controlled hip and knee flexion on the sound side.

For both rising and sitting, the beginner should have the advantage of a chair with armrests which enable use of the hands to control and to assist trunk movement. Later the person should attempt sitting in deep upholstered sofas and low chairs, as well as benches, the toilet, and other seats that do not have armrests. Transfer into an automobile should be an integral part of the training regimen; otherwise, the person faces a gloomy future, confined to home or dependent on special transportation systems. To enter the right, passenger, side, the prosthetic wearer faces toward the front of the car. The person with a right amputation puts the right hand on the door post and the left hand on the back of the seat, then swings the prosthesis so that its foot is on the car floor. The patient slides onto the car seat, finally placing the intact foot into the car. The person with a left amputation must swing the prosthesis to position it on the car floor, then slide sideward until seated, and finally put the intact right foot inside the car.

Climbing

Patients with Syme's and below-knee amputations generally ascend and descend stairs and inclines with steps of equal length in step-over-step progression. All those with unilateral above-knee amputation, in contrast, ascend by leading with the sound side and learn to descend by first placing the prosthesis on the lower step. A few with above-knee amputations subsequently learn to control prosthetic knee flexion in order to descend step-over-step.

Curbs present a different problem, for there is no hand rail. The techniques are basically the same, however. If the stairs, ramp, or curb are too steep, the individual may climb diagonally, or side step with the prosthesis kept on the downhill side.

FINAL CHECKOUT AND FOLLOW-UP CARE

Economic strictures may compel the therapist to conclude the training program after the patient is able to walk and to negotiate basic transfers and climbing activities. Prior to discharge, the patient and the prosthesis should be reassessed to make certain that socket fit, prosthetic appearance, and function are acceptable.

The new prosthetic wearer should return to the training site at regular intervals so that the clinic team may check for socket fit. Most will require major socket revision or replacement during the first year to accommodate shrinkage. Follow-up visits are good opportunities to augment training and to encourage the individual to engage in the widest range of activities.

Functional Capacities

Functional capacities refer to the individual's ability to walk, to transfer from chairs, to climb stairs, and to perform other ambulatory activities, including recreational endeavors. A primary responsibility of the clinic team is to predict the probable function of the person with a new amputation, in order to determine whether the individual would benefit from a prosthesis and what degree of activity is likely. Because the majority of those with lower-limb amputations are elderly with several medical problems, the need for accurate forecasting and ongoing monitoring is especially critical.

Walking with a prosthesis increases energy costs. Compared with those with two sound limbs, the individual with a unilateral below-knee amputation requires slightly more oxygen when walking at a comfortable speed, but nearly 50 percent more oxygen than normal is consumed by the person with an above-knee amputation. The prosthesis wearer should choose a comfortable pace, because at a speed that is natural for the individual the energy cost per minute is similar to that of a person without a prosthesis, although the speed is at least one third slower.[28] The lower the amputation level, the less the metabolic disadvantage. Among persons with below-knee amputations older than 40, those with long amputated limbs average a minimal increase in energy, but persons with shorter limbs work much harder. Those with bilateral below-knee amputations expend less energy than those with unilateral above-knee amputations.[29] Those whose amputation was traumatic perform better than those whose amputation was dysvascular in origin, at every amputation level. They walk faster and use less oxygen than their dysvascular counterparts.[30]

The metabolic toll results in part from the socket which surrounds semifluid tissue, giving imperfect anchorage. The foot-ankle assembly transmits no plantar tactile or proprioceptive sensation, does not move through as large an excursion as the normal foot, and does not initiate the dynamic push-off characteristic of normal gait. The above-knee prosthesis also incorporates a knee unit which provides no proprioception to the wearer. The problem is aggravated by the fact that a prosthesis is operated by remotely located muscles which contract longer and more forcefully than would occur without amputation. With above-knee amputation, for example, the prosthetic foot is placed by hip motion. The resulting alteration of motion is reflected in asymmetry of timing, further disturbing gait smoothness. Individuals with prostheses walk with greater vertical movement, inasmuch as the knee, whether prosthetic for the above-knee or anatomic in the below-knee wearer, does not flex as much as the contralateral knee during stance phase.[20]

For many of those with amputations, function is not limited to walking. They participate in a wide array of sports, most of which require little or no prosthetic modification, such as bowling, tennis, golf, and baseball. Sometimes minor adaptions are helpful; for example, bicycle toe clips purchased at a sporting goods store enable the individual to lift the pedal as well as to push it. Other activities, such as swimming, are generally performed without a prosthesis. Ski programs are conducted at many resorts; most with unilateral amputations ski "three track"; that is, without a prosthesis but with small rudders on the ski poles. Acquainting the individual with recreational clubs and with simple techniques for engaging in sports is a superb way of enhancing that person's functional capacity.

SUMMARY

This chapter has focused on lower-limb prosthetics. Characteristics and function of the principal lower-limb prostheses and prosthetic components have been discussed. In addition, the responsibilities of the physical therapist in prosthetic management have been emphasized.

Successful prosthetic rehabilitation depends on close collaboration among the patient, physician, physical therapist, prosthetist, and other team members involved in care of the individual patient. This will provide an environment for information exchange and will foster a coordinated pattern of treatment. The result will be an optimum match between the patient's physical and psychologic characteristics and a prosthesis capable of fulfilling its intended purpose.

QUESTIONS FOR REVIEW

1. What are the principal causes of amputation in the elderly? In the young?

2. Describe appropriate prostheses for individuals with various partial foot amputations.

3. Distinguish between the Syme's and the below-knee amputated limbs and prostheses.

4. What prosthetic feet are especially suitable for geriatric amputees? Why?

5. Name the reliefs and build-ups in the PTB and quadrilateral sockets.

6. Contrast the modes of suspension for the below-knee prosthesis. Which suspension is indicated for an individual with a short amputated limb? For one with fragile skin?

7. Classify knee units according to friction mechanisms.

8. Describe the modes of suspension of the quadrilateral socket. In which type(s) does the amputee wear a sock?

9. How is the wearer of a hip disarticulation prosthesis prevented from inadvertently flexing the hip and knee?

10. Compare various materials used for prosthetic socks.

11. Outline a maintenance program for an above-knee prosthesis with hydraulic knee unit and endoskeletal shank.

12. What factors should be assessed prior to formulating a prosthetic prescription?

13. How can the physical therapist assess and improve the patient's psychologic status?

14. What features of the below-knee prosthesis are considered in static assessment?

15. Delineate the training program for a patient with a new above-knee amputation.

REFERENCES

1. Goldberg, RT: New trends in the rehabilitation of lower extremity amputees. Rehabil Lit 45:2, 1984.
2. Friedmann, LW: The Surgical Rehabilitation of the Amputee. Charles C Thomas, Springfield, IL, 1978.
3. Friedmann, LW: Amputations and prostheses in primitive cultures. Bull Prosthet Res 10–17:131–132, 1972.
4. American Academy of Orthopaedic Surgeons: Orthopaedic Appliances Atlas, vol 2. JW Edwards, Ann Arbor, 1960.
5. Campbell, JW and Childs, CW: The SAFE foot. Orthot Prosthet 34:3–16, 1980.
6. Burgess, E, et al: The Seattle prosthetic foot: A design for active sports. Orthot Prosthet 37:25–31, 1983.
7. Doane, NE and Holt, LE: A comparison of the SACH and single axis foot in the gait of unilateral below-knee amputees. Prosthet Orthot Int 7:33, 1983.
8. Goh, JCH, et al: Biomechanical evaluation of SACH and uniaxial feet. Prosthet Orthot Int 8:147–154, 1984.
9. Racette, W and Breakey, JW: Clinical experience and functional considerations of axial rotators for the amputee. Orthot Prosthet 31:29–33, 1977.
10. Radcliffe, C: The biomechanics of below-knee prostheses in normal, level bipedal walking. Artif Limbs 6:16–24, 1962.
11. Veterans Administration: Variants of the PTB (patellar-tendon-bearing) below-knee prosthesis. Bull Prosthet Res 10–13:120–134, 1970.
12. Veterans Administration: Selection and application of knee mechanisms. Bull Prosthet Res 10–18:90–158, 1972.
13. Erback, JR: Hydraulic prostheses for above-knee amputees. J Am Phys Ther Assoc 43:105–110, 1963.
14. Murray, MP, et al: Gait patterns in above-knee amputee patients: Hydraulic swing control vs constant friction knee components. Arch Phys Med Rehabil 64:339–345, 1983.
15. Anderson, MH, Bray, JJ, and Hennessy, C: Prosthetic Principles: Above Knee Amputations. Charles C Thomas, Springfield, IL, 1959.
16. Kristinsson, O: Flexible above-knee socket made from low density polyethylene suspended by a weight transmitting frame. Orthot Prosthet 37:25–27, 1983.
17. Staff, Prosthetics and Orthotics: Fabrication Procedures for the ISNY Above-Knee Flexible Socket. New York University, Post-Graduate Medical School, 317 E 34th Street, New York, NY, 10016, 1984.
18. Varghese, G: Rehabilitation outcome of patients with dual disability of hemiplegia and amputation. Arch Phys Med Rehabil 59:121–123, 1978.
19. Vagias, G and Hurwitz, R: Method of making a patellar tendon bearing pylon. J Am Phys Ther Assoc 42:253–255, 1962.
20. Breakey, J: Gait of unilateral below-knee amputees. Orthot Prosthet 30:17–24, 1976.
21. Zuniga, EN, et al: Gait patterns in above-knee amputees. Arch Phys Med Rehabil 53:373–382, 1972.
22. Foort, J: Amputee management procedures. Orthot Prosthet 28:3–11, 1974.
23. Clarke, C: Radioelectrocardiogram monitoring during ambulation training of patients with amputations. Phys Ther 51:906–913, 1971.
24. Gapsis, J: Limb load monitor: Evaluation of a sensory feedback device for controlled weight bearing. Arch Phys Med Rehabil 63:38–41, 1982.
25. Alexander, J and Goodrich, R: Videotape immediate playback. Arch Phys Med Rehabil 59:141–144, 1978.
26. Netz, P, Wersen, K, and Wetterberg, M: Videotape recording: A complementary aid for the walking training of lower limb amputees. Prosthet Orthot Intl 5:147–150, 1981.
27. Huang, C, et al: Amputation: Energy cost of ambulation. Arch Phys Med Rehabil 60:18–24, 1979.

28. Ralston, HJ: Dynamics of the Human Body during Locomotion. University of California, San Francisco, 1971.
29. Gonzales, EG, Corcoran, PJ, and Reyes, RL: Energy expenditure in below-knee amputees: Correlation with stump length. Arch Phys Med Rehabil 55:111–119, 1974.
30. Waters, RL, et al: Energy cost of walking of amputees: Influence of level of amputation. J Bone Joint Surg 58-A:42–46, 1976.

SUPPLEMENTAL READINGS

American Academy of Orthopaedic Surgeons: Atlas of Limb Prosthetics, CV Mosby, St Louis, 1981.

Banerjee, SN (ed): Rehabilitation Management of Amputees. Williams & Wilkins, Baltimore, 1982.

Batzdorff, J and Frankel, B: Initial gait training of the patient with an above-knee amputation. Phys Ther 58:575, 1978.

Convery, P, et al: A clinical evaluation of an ultralightweight polypropylene below-knee prosthesis, Orthot Prosthet 40:30, 1986.

Culham, EG, Peat, M, and Newell, E: Below-knee amputation: A comparison of the effect of the SACH foot and single axis foot on electromyographic patterns during locomotion. Prosthet Orthot Int 10:15, 1986.

Friberg, O: Biomechanical significance of the correct length of lower limb prostheses: A clinical and radiological study. Prosthet Orthot Int 8:124, 1984.

Hanak, R and Hoffman, ES: Specifications and fabrication details for the ISNY above-knee socket system. Orthot Prosthet 40:38, 1986.

Karacoloff, LA: Lower Extremity Amputation: A Guide to Functional Outcomes in Physical Therapy Management. Aspen, Rockville, MD, 1985.

Kawamura, I and Kawamura, J: Some biomechanical evaluations of the ISNY flexible above-knee system with quadrilateral socket. Orthot Prosthet 40:17, 1986.

Kegel, B: Physical fitness: Sports and recreation for those with lower limb amputation or impairment. Journal of Rehabilitation Research and Development Clinical Supplement No 1, 1985.

Kostuik, JP: Amputation Surgery and Rehabilitation. Churchill Livingstone, New York, 1981.

Narang, IC, et al: Functional capabilities of lower limb amputees. Prosthet Orthot Int 8:43, 1984.

Rubin, G, Fischer, E, and Dixon, M: Prescription of above-knee and below-knee prostheses. Prosthet Orthot Int 10:117, 1986.

Sanders, GT: Lower Limb Amputations: A Guide to Rehabilitation. FA Davis, Philadelphia, 1986.

Staff, Prosthetics and Orthotics: Lower-Limb Prosthetics, rev ed. New York University, New York, 1981.

Van Griethuysen, C: Gait training for the below-knee amputee. Prosthet Orthot Int 3:163, 1979.

Vittas, D, Larsen, TK, and Jensen, EC: Body sway in below-knee amputees. Prosthet Orthot Int 10:139, 1986.

GLOSSARY

Axis (prosthetic): Component of the prosthetic knee joint; creates the connection between the thigh piece (socket) and shank; may be either a single-axis hinge or polycentric linkage.

Check strap: A posterior strap extending from the thigh corset or socket to shank; functions to control forward motion of shank and to prevent terminal impact.

Clinic team: A group of health care professionals that conducts prosthetic (and/or orthotic) rehabilitation. The basic team consists of a physician who serves as chief, physical (and/or occupational) therapist, and prosthetist (and/or orthotist).

Endoskeletal (modular, pylon): A prosthetic shank in which the support consists of a rigid pipe usually covered with resilient material to simulate the shank of the intact leg. **Modular** refers to the ease of interchanging foot and knee units. **Pylon** is the pipe itself, although pylon is also used to signify a temporary prosthesis.

Exoskeletal (crustacean): A prosthetic shank in which the support consists of rigid material at the periphery, usually covered with a thin layer of polyester laminate. **Crustacean** refers to the placement of the supporting structure externally, as is the case with animals such as the lobster.

Extension aid: Mechanism designed to assist prosthetic knee extension during the latter part of swing phase; may consist of elastic webbing placed externally or an elastic band or spring within the knee unit.

Fork strap: Prosthetic suspension and knee extension aid; consists of a fork-shaped strap attached to the prosthetic shank which is attached to the waist belt via an elastic strap.

Friction brake: A device in a prosthetic knee unit that resists knee flexion during early stance phase, commonly a spring-loaded wedge which is forced into a groove upon transfer of body weight to the prosthesis.

Friction mechanism: A device that permits adjusting the resistance to swing of the prosthetic knee unit.

    Constant friction: A mechanism that applies uniform resistance throughout swing phase; may be incorporated in sliding or hydraulic friction mechanisms.

    Hydraulic friction: A mechanism consisting of an oil-filled cylinder in which a piston connected to the knee hinge moves up and down; the oil resists piston motion, and hence knee swing.

    Variable friction: A mechanism that applies greater friction at early and late swing than at mid swing; may be incorporated in **sliding, hydraulic,** or **pneumatic** friction mechanisms.

    Sliding friction: A mechanism consisting of solid structures that resist motion, commonly a clamp which rubs against the knee bolt.

    Pneumatic friction: A mechanism consisting of an air-filled cylinder in which a piston connected to the knee hinge moves up and down.

Keel: The rigid longitudinal portion of a prosthetic foot, terminating distally at a point corresponding to the metatarsophalangeal joints.

Mechanical stabilizer: Devices or methods used to increase stability of the prosthetic knee joint; may be accomplished by the alignment of the prosthetic knee joint posterior to the trochanter-knee-ankle (TKA) line, by use of manual locks or a friction brake.

Multiple axis: Describing a mechanism in a prosthetic foot that permits sagittal, frontal, and transverse plane motion.

Piston action (pistoning): Vertical motion of the prosthetic socket on the residual limb; evident during gait as an up-and-down movement of the prosthesis; caused by looseness of the socket (poor fit) and/or inadequate suspension.

Polycentric linkage: Describing linkage in a knee unit that permits the momentary axis of knee flexion to change through the arc of motion.

Polyester laminate: A thermosetting plastic used for rigid prosthetic sockets and for finishing the exterior of exoskeletal shanks. Polyester resin saturates layers of fabric, producing a hard, durable material.

Polyethylene: A thermoplastic material used for flexible prosthetic sockets; the plastic becomes malleable when heated, permitting its contour to be changed.

Single-axis foot: A prosthetic joint articulation that permits motion in one plane at a fixed point. The single-axis foot permits plantarflexion and dorsiflexion at a point corresponding to the anatomic ankle. The single-axis knee permits flexion and extension at a point corresponding to the suprapatellar level.

Solid ankle cushion heel (SACH): A prosthetic foot in which the posterosuperior portion of the keel is attached to the shank without a definite ankle joint, and a posteroinferior compressible wedge permits plantarflexion during early stance. The distal end of the keel permits hyperextension of the foot during late stance.

Stationary attachment flexible endoskeleton (SAFE): A prosthetic foot that has a rigid ankle block attached to the shank without a definite ankle joint: the anterior portion of the block terminates at a 45 degree angle, abutting a somewhat more flexible keel, to simulate subtalar motion. The distal end of the keel permits hyperextension of the foot during late stance. The posteroinferior surface has compressible material to permit plantarflexion during early stance.

Suction: A mode of prosthetic suspension in which an airtight socket is held on the amputation limb by atmospheric pressure greater on the outside than on the inside of the socket. Commonly, suction suspension is used on above-knee prostheses, in which the snug socket has an air-release valve.

Supracondylar cuff: A mode of prosthetic suspension by which a below-knee socket is held on the amputation limb by snug contact immediately above the femoral epicondyles. Commonly, supracondylar suspension employs a plastic wedge inserted between the medial epicondyle and the proximomedial socket wall.

Supracondylar/suprapatellar suspension: A mode of prosthetic suspension by which a below-knee socket is held on the amputation limb by supracondylar suspension augmented by the anterior margin of the socket which terminates immediately above the patella.

Syme's amputation: An amputation procedure involving removal of the foot at the supramalleolar level; the calcaneal fat pad is attached to the anterior skin flap to cushion the distal end of the limb.

Temporary prosthesis: A device consisting of a socket designed to accept full weight bearing, attached to a pylon and foot. Unlike a definitive prosthesis, the temporary one may not be cosmetically finished. For the above-knee amputee, the pylon usually is surmounted by a knee unit.

Terminal swing impact: Sudden, abrupt, forceful stopping of the prosthetic shank (above-knee prosthesis) at the end of swing phase of gait; often accompanied by an auditory impact; caused by insufficient knee friction or a knee extension aid that is too strong.

APPENDIX A PROSTHETIC CHECKOUT: BELOW-KNEE*

Date _____

Patient _____
Amputation type: _____
_____

_____
Initial checkout ( )   Final checkout ( )
Pass ( )   Provisional pass ( )   Fail ( )
  If the patient needs further attention, please indicate the type of treatment required:
Medical-surgical _____( )   Training _____( )
Prosthetic _____( )   Other _____( )
                    (Vocational, psychologic, etc.)

Recommendations and comments: _____
_____
_____
_____
_____
_____

_____
Clinic chief

_____ 1. Is the prosthesis as prescribed? If a recheck, have previous recommendations been accomplished?
_____ 2. Can the patient don the prosthesis easily?

Check with the Patient Standing

_____ 3. Is the patient comfortable while standing with the midlines of the heels not more than 6 inches apart?
_____ 4. Is the anteroposterior alignment of the prosthesis satisfactory? (The patient should not feel that the knee is unstable nor that the knee is being forced backward.)
_____ 5. Is the mediolateral alignment satisfactory? (The shoe should be flat on the floor and there should be no uncomfortable pressure at the lateral or medial brim of the socket.)
_____ 6. Is the prosthesis the correct length?
_____ 7. Is piston action minimal when the patient raises the prosthesis?
_____ 8. Are the anterior, medial, and lateral walls of adequate height?
_____ 9. Do the medial and lateral walls contact the epicondyles, and with the patellar-tendon-bearing variants, the areas immediately above?

_____
*From Staff, Prosthetic and Orthotics: *Lower-Limb Prosthetics,* rev ed. New York University, New York, 1981, with permission.

Thigh Corset
_____10. Do the uprights conform to the flares above the epicondyles?
_____11. Are knee joints close to the epicondyles (about ⅛ to ¼ inch)?
_____12. Does the thigh corset fit properly, with adequate provision for adjusting corset tension?
_____13. Do the length and construction of the thigh corset appear to be appropriate for its intended function of weight bearing or stabilization?

Check with the Patient Sitting

_____14. Can the patient sit comfortably with minimal bunching of soft tissues in the popliteal region, when the knees are flexed to 90 degrees?

Check with the Patient Walking

_____15. Is the patient's performance in level walking satisfactory? Indicate below the gait deviations that require attention.

_____16. Is piston action between the stump and socket minimal?
_____17. Does the patient go up and down inclines and stairs satisfactorily?
_____18. Are the socket and suspension system comfortable?
_____19. Does the knee cuff maintain its position?
_____20. Is the patient able to kneel satisfactorily?
_____21. Does the prosthesis function quietly?
_____22. Are size, contours, and color of the prosthesis approximately the same as those of the sound limb?
_____23. Does the patient consider the prosthesis satisfactory?

Check with Prosthesis off the Patient

_____24. Is the patient's stump free from abrasion, discolorations, and excessive perspiration immediately after the prosthesis is removed?
_____25. Does weight bearing appear to be distributed over the proper areas of the stump?
_____26. Is the posterior wall of the socket of adequate height?
_____27. Do the check strap and fork strap have adequate provision for adjustment?
_____28. Is the general workmanship satisfactory?

APPENDIX B PROSTHETIC CHECKOUT: ABOVE-KNEE*

Date _____

Name of Patient _____
Amputation Type _____
_____
_____

Initial Checkout ( )   Final Checkout ( )
Pass ( )   Provisional Pass ( )   Fail ( )
If the patient needs further attention, please indicate the type of treatment required:
Medical-surgical _____( )   Training _____( )
Prosthetic _____( )   Other _____( )
                          (Vocational, psychologic, etc.)
Recommendations and comments: _____
_____
_____
_____
_____
_____

_____
                    Clinic Chief

_____ 1. Is the prosthesis as prescribed?
           If a recheck, have previous recommendations been accomplished?

Check with the Patient Standing

Fit and Alignment
_____ 2. Is the patient comfortable while standing with the midlines of the heels not more than 6 inches apart?
_____ 3. Is the adductor longus tendon properly located in its channel, and is the patient free from excessive pressure in the anteromedial aspect of the socket?
_____ 4. Does the ischial tuberosity rest properly on the ischial seat?
_____ 5. Is the prosthesis the correct length?
_____ 6. Is the knee stable on weight bearing (without the patient using excessive effort in pressing backward with the stump)?
_____ 7. Is the brim of the posterior wall approximately parallel to the ground?
_____ 8. Is the patient free from vertical pressure in the area of the perineum?
_____ 9. When the valve of a total-contact socket is removed, does stump tissue protrude slightly into the valve hole and have satisfactory consistency (approximately that of the thenar eminence)?
Suspension
_____ 10. Are the lateral and anterior attachments of the Silesian bandage correctly located?

_____
*From Staff, Prosthetic and Orthotics: *Lower-Limb Prosthetics,* rev ed. New York University, New York, 1981, with permission.

_____ 11. Does the pelvic band accurately fit the contours of the body?
_____ 12. Is the center of the pelvic joint set slightly above and ahead of the promontory of the greater trochanter?
_____ 13. Is the valve located to facilitate pulling out the pull sock and the manual release of pressure?

Check with the Patient Sitting

_____ 14. Does the socket remain securely on the stump?
_____ 15. Does the shank remain in good alignment?
_____ 16. Is the center of the knee bolt ½ to ¾ inch above the level of the medial tibial plateau?
_____ 17. Can the patient remain seated without a burning sensation in the hamstring area?
_____ 18. Can the patient rise to a standing position without objectionable air noise from the socket?

Check with the Patient Walking

Performance
_____ 19. Is the patient's performance in level walking satisfactory? Indicate below the gait deviations that require attention.
           a. Abducted gait   ( )
           b. Lateral bending of trunk   ( )
           c. Circumduction   ( )
           d. Medial whip   ( )
           e. Lateral whip   ( )
           f. Rotation of foot on heel strike ( )
           g. Uneven heel rise   ( )
           h. Terminal swing impact   ( )
           i. Foot slap   ( )
           j. Uneven length of steps   ( )
           k. Lumbar lordosis   ( )
           l. Vaulting   ( )
           m. Other   ( )
Comments and recommendations: _____
_____
_____ 20. Is suction maintained during walking?
_____ 21. With a total-contact socket, does the patient have the sensation of continued contact between the stump and socket in both swing and stance phases?
_____ 22. Does the patient go up and down inclines satisfactorily?
_____ 23. Does the patient go up and down stairs satisfactorily?
Socket
(Check these items *after* the performance evaluation has been done.)
_____ 24. Does the ischial tuberosity maintain its position on the ischial seat?
_____ 25. Is any flesh roll above the socket minimal?
_____ 26. Does the lateral wall of the socket maintain firm and even contact with the lateral aspect of the stump?

Miscellaneous

_____27. Does the prosthesis operate quietly?

_____28. Are the size, contours, and color of the prosthesis approximately the same as those of the sound limb?

_____29. Does the patient consider the prosthesis satisfactory as to comfort, function, and appearance?

Check with the Prosthesis off the Patient

Examination of the Stump

_____30. Is the patient's stump free from abrasions, discoloration, and excessive perspiration immediately after the prosthesis is removed?

Examination of the Prosthesis

_____31. Are the anterior and lateral walls at least 2 inches higher than the posterior wall?

_____32. Does the inside of the socket have a smooth finish?

_____33. Is there satisfactory clearance at knee and ankle articulations?

_____34. Are the posterior surfaces of the thigh and shank shaped so that there is minimal concentration of pressure when the knee is flexed fully?

_____35. With the prosthesis in the kneeling position, can the thigh piece be brought to at least the vertical position?

_____36. In the total-contact socket, is the bottom of the valve hole at the level of the bottom of the socket? (It may be lower, particularly with a soft insert.)

_____37. Is a back pad attached to the posterior wall of the socket?

_____38. Is the general workmanship satisfactory?

_____39. Do the components function properly?

Chapter 21

RHEUMATOID ARTHRITIS

ANDREW A. GUCCIONE

OBJECTIVES

1. Describe the epidemiology, pathology, pathogenesis, disease course, and common clinical manifestations of rheumatoid arthritis.

2. Identify the medical diagnostic procedures commonly used in the assessment of rheumatoid arthritis, including laboratory tests and radiography.

3. Describe the medical management of the individual with rheumatoid arthritis.

4. Explain the procedures commonly used in assessing the individual with rheumatoid arthritis.

5. Discuss the rehabilitation management of the individual with rheumatoid arthiritis.

6. Describe psychosocial factors associated with rheumatoid arthritis that affect achievement of rehabilitation goals.

7. Explain the importance of a team approach with the individual with rheumatoid arthritis.

INTRODUCTION

The terms *arthritis* and **rheumatism** are generic references to an array of over 100 diseases, which are divided into 10 classification categories. **Rheumatoid arthritis** (RA) is a major subclassification within the category of diffuse connective tissue diseases that also includes juvenile arthritis, **systemic lupus erythematosus,** progressive systemic sclerosis or scleroderma, polymyositis, and dermatomyositis. The first clinical description of the disease is attributed to AJ Landre'-Beauvais in 1800, although analysis of pictorial art of the late Renaissance has provided some evidence for the existence of RA in earlier times. Early descriptive comparisons of patient symptomatology were complicated by the lack of uniform agreement about the distinguishing characteristics of the disease, a difficulty that persists even today, given the wide spectrum of clinical presentations associated with

the disease. Although the term *rheumatoid arthritis* was first used by Garrod in 1858, it was not accepted by the American Rheumatism Association (ARA) as the official terminology until 1941.[1] The ARA has revised the diagnostic terminology and criteria for rheumatoid arthritis several times in the last 30 years and continues to monitor them for accuracy and validity.[1]

CLASSIFICATION CRITERIA

Clinically, the differential diagnosis of RA is predicated upon the patient's signs and symptoms and careful exclusion of other disorders. When conducting epidemiologic and other kinds of research studies, it is often necessary to identify homogeneous groups of individuals with relatively similar signs and symptoms of RA. Although other criteria sets exist for this purpose, the

ARA classification criteria are most often used to identify the criteria with which an individual's clinical presentation has been counted as a case of RA. There are four classifications of RA: classical, definite, probable, and possible (Table 21–1). The criteria for each classification include a combination of signs, symptoms, and laboratory findings that have persisted for a specified period of time. Classification is difficult in the early course of the disease when articular symptoms are accompanied only by constitutional symptoms such as fatigue and loss of appetite, which are common to a number of chronic diseases. A full array of clinical signs and symptoms may not manifest itself for one to two years.[1] A diagnosis of *classical* RA is established upon the presentation of 7 of the 11 listed criteria with a duration of joint signs and symptoms for at least 6 weeks. A diagnosis of *definite* RA is made upon observation of five of these criteria with a similar duration of joint complaints. *Probable* RA is defined as the presentation of any three

criteria with continuing joint signs and symptoms over a 6-week period. A diagnosis of *possible* RA is made in the instance in which an individual presents with two of the following criteria lasting three weeks: morning stiffness, a history of pain or joint swelling, subcutaneous nodules, an elevated sedimentation rate, or C-reactive protein.[1,2]

EPIDEMIOLOGY

Prevalence rates can be confounded by the "type" of RA a person had at the time the epidemiologic survey was conducted as well as the criteria used. When the prevalence of RA in Sudbury, Massachusetts, was studied using both the ARA criteria and the more stringent New York criteria,[3] remarkable differences in the rates of definite and probable RA at follow-up were reported, emphasizing the difficulty with prevalence studies that have used less stringent inclusion criteria such as those

Table 21–1 AMERICAN RHEUMATISM ASSOCIATION CRITERIA FOR THE CLASSIFICATION OF RA

Eleven criteria available. For three different degrees of certainty of diagnosis, different numbers of criteria must be met. Unlike the Jones criteria for rheumatic fever, there are no major and minor criteria.
   Classic RA—7 criteria needed
   Definite RA—5 criteria needed
   Probable RA—3 criteria needed
To meet criteria 1 to 5, symptoms or signs must be present for at least 6 weeks.

Criteria	Comments
1. Morning stiffness	This symptom is very useful as an indicator of inflammation; the absence of morning stiffness in a chronically painful joint is good evidence that synovial inflammation is minimal or absent.
2. Pain on motion or tenderness in at least one joint	Criteria 2 to 6 must be observed by a physician.
3. Swelling of one joint, representing soft tissue or fluid	Bony overgrowth is usually representative of a degenerative process, not synovial inflammation.
4. Swelling of at least one other joint (soft tissue or fluid) with an interval free of symptoms no longer than 3 months	
5. Symmetrical joint swelling (simultaneous involvement of the same joint, right and left)	Terminal interphalangeal joints are rarely involved in RA and therefore are not acceptable for this or other criteria.
6. Subcutaneous nodules over bony prominences, extensor surfaces or near joints	See exclusions in second footnote below.
7. Typical roentgenographic changes which must include dimineralization in periarticular bone as an index of inflammation; degenerative changes do not exclude diagnosis of RA	Demineralization may result from disease of muscles around inflamed joints as well as from release of prostaglandins by inflamed synovial tissue
8. Positive test for rheumatoid factor in serum	Laboratory quality control is essential here; in general, positive tests should be in a titer of 1:64 or greater
9. Synovial fluid; a poor mucin clot formation on adding synovial fluid to dilute acetic acid	This is strictly a qualitative test and can be used only as a crude estimate of sustained joint inflammation.

10. Synovial histopathology consistent with RA
  a. Marked villous hypertrophy
  b. Proliferation of synovial cells
  c. Lymphocyte/plasma cell infiltration in subsynovium
  d. Fibrin deposition within or upon microvilli
Characteristic histopathology of rheumatoid nodules biopsied from any site
	These are nonspecific; granuloma annulare is indistinguishable on routine histological preparations from the rheumatoid nodule.

A diagnosis of *possible* RA requires that morning stiffness, history of pain or swelling of joints, subcutaneous nodules, an elevated ESR, or C-reactive protein—any two of these criteria—be present for a least 3 weeks.
Exclusions are based principally on presence of evidence for other diseases that have criteria for their own diagnosis (e.g., systemic lupus erythematosus, scleroderma) or more specific diagnostic techniques (e.g., the crystal deposition diseases). Some may be inappropriate. For instance, it is known that gout and RA can be present in the same patient.
From Harris, ED, Jr: Rheumatoid arthritis: The clinical spectrum. In Kelley, WN, et al: *Textbook of Rheumatology*, ed 2. WB Saunders, Philadelphia, 1985.

for probable and possible RA.[4] Using ARA criteria for definite or classical RA, it has been estimated that in 1984 there were 4 to 6 million cases of RA with an incidence of 100,000 to 200,000 new cases of definite or classic RA that year.[2] Rheumatoid arthritis affects women three times more often than men in the typical years of onset between the ages of 20 and 60. Men and women over the age of 65 appear to be affected at the same rate.[5] There is a general increase in prevalence for both sexes as age increases. Age- and sex-specific prevalence rates are nearly equal in black and white populations. There is also some indication that prevalence rates are higher in lower social classes. Despite common folklore to the contrary, climate and geography do not appear to affect the prevalence rate, thus giving RA global distribution. Population-based studies have demonstrated relatively similar prevalence rates worldwide despite some minor variations that appear to be more a function of differences in study criteria than an indication of actual population differences.[1,5]

ETIOLOGY

Like that of many other chronic diseases, the etiology of RA is unknown. Current research into the causes of RA is based on a complex, but as yet incomplete, appreciation of the functions of the immune system which is beyond the scope of this chapter. Briefly, an **antigen** is a substance, usually foreign to the host, that provokes the immune system into action. The immune system may respond to the antigen directly (cellular immunity) or by the production of **antibodies** that circulate in the serum (humoral immunity). These responses involve two general kinds of lymphocytes: T cells, which are responsible for cellular immunity; and B cells, which produce circulating antibodies specific to the antigen. Antibodies are a type of serum protein that are referred to as immunoglobulins. Based upon the current understanding of humoral and cellular immunity, two hypotheses concerning the pathogenesis of RA have been developed. One proposal is that an antigen-antibody reaction initiates the inflammatory process in RA as a humoral-type immune response. The alternative proposal suggests that a cell-mediated immune response can occur as a result of contact between sensitized T lymphocytes and an antigen, thus activating the complement system, which is one of the enzymatic protein systems that mediate the process of inflammation. This activation of complement triggers the inflammatory process through an alternative pathway, which does not require the production of antibodies.[1,6]

Based on the fact that individuals with RA produce antibodies to their own immunoglobulins, there is some reason to believe that RA is an *autoimmune* disorder. It is not clear, however, whether this antibody production is a primary event or results as a response to a specific antigen from an external stimulus. A specific etiologic agent for RA has not been identified even though investigators have been able to identify that specific external etiologic agents may produce an inflammatory arthritis in instances such as **Lyme arthritis.** The disease that is

finally manifested may be more dependent on the host's manner of response than on the agent or the mechanism involved.[7]

Current evidence suggests that a variety of agents may initiate an arthritis through a number of different mechanisms. A number of bacterial organisms have been suggested, including streptococcus, clostridia, diptheroids, and mycoplasmas, but no connections have been definitely proven. There also has been discussion of a viral etiology, particularly surrounding the evidence that the serum of patients with RA reacts with cells infected by the Epstein-Barr virus (EBV). The EBV can initiate lymphoid proliferation, which suggests that it has the ability to alter the regulation of the immune system. As with other investigations that seek to identify a viral etiology for RA, research in this area still remains speculative.[7,8]

Rheumatoid factors (RF) have received considerable attention in the search for a causative agent in RA because they are found in the sera of approximately 70 percent of all patients with RA.[1] Rheumatoid factors are antibodies specific to IgG, one of the five classes of immunoglobulins. Current theory suggests that RF arise as antibodies to "altered" autologous (the patient's own) IgG. Some modification of IgG changes its configuration and renders it an autoimmunogen, stimulating the production of RF. Another type of immunoglobulin, IgM, is the first class of immunoglobulins formed after contact with an antigen, and most RF are of this class, although RF may be of any immunoglobulin class.[1,6] Although RF may be important in the pathogenesis of RA, their exact biologic role is unknown. Rheumatoid arthritis occurs in the absence of RF in a substantial number of individuals. Individuals with RA, however, who do have RF, or seropositive disease, have increased frequency of subcutaneous nodules, vasculitis, and polyarticular involvement.[1,9]

Recent studies have sought to establish a genetic predisposition to the development of RA. Human leukocyte antigens (HLA) are found on the cell surface of most human cells and are capable of generating an **immune response** when genetically incompatible tissues are grafted to each other (e.g., during organ transplants). Genes controlling these HLA are found on the sixth chromosome. Four loci have been described: HLA-A, HLA-B, HLA-C, and HLA-D. Rheumatoid arthritis has been associated wtih increased HLA-D and HLA-DR (D-related) antigens, suggesting that certain genes determine whether a host is prone to an immunologic response that leads to RA.[5,9,10]

PATHOLOGY

Long-standing RA is characterized by the grossly edematous appearance of the **synovium** with slender villous or hairlike projections into the joint cavity. There are distinctive vascular changes including venous distention, capillary obstruction, neutrophilic infiltration of the arterial walls, and areas of thrombosis and hemorrhage. Synovial proliferation of vascular granulation tissue, known as **pannus,** dissolves collagen as it extends over the joint cartilage. Eventually, if RA continues, the granulation tissue will result in adhesions and fibrous or bony **ankylosis** of the joint. Chronic inflammation also can weaken the joint capsule and its supporting ligamentous structures, altering joint structure and function. Tendon rupture and fraying tendon sheaths may produce imbalanced muscle pull on these pathologically altered joints, resulting in the characteristic musculoskeletal deformities seen in advanced RA.[1]

Pathogenesis

The key features that differentiate synovial joints from other kinds of joints are exactly those features that make them susceptible to persistent inflammation. Rapid changes in the cellular content and volume of the synovial fluid may occur following alterations in blood flow. This infiltration occurs as a result of low pressure in the joint space and the lack of a limiting membrane between the joint space and the synovial blood vessels. High molecular weight substances such as macroglobulins and fibrinogens can pass through the synovial capillaries during periods of inflammation and are not easily cleared.[9] Because the cartilage is avascular, antigen-antibody complexes may be sequestered within the joint cavity and may facilitate the process of phagocytosis and further development of pannus. Although it is accepted that sustained **synovitis** requires the proliferation of new blood vessels, the exact mechanism of capillary growth is not currently understood. One attractive hypothesis is that activated macrophages, responding to antigen-antibody complexes, may stimulate this development.

In established synovitis, polymorphonuclear (PMN) leukocytes are chemotactically drawn into the joint cavity and contribute to the inflammatory destruction of the synovium, although the exact mechanism of this destruction is unknown.[9] It is known that the lysosomal enzymes which are released from these leukocytes can directly injure synovial tissues. IgM RF, produced earlier during this process, also may play a substantial role in further activating the complement system. Complement can then combine with PMN leukocytes, enhancing the inflammatory process.[1,9]

CLINICAL DIAGNOSTIC CRITERIA

The clinical diagnosis of RA is based upon careful consideration of three factors: the clinical presentation of the patient, which is elucidated through history taking and physical examination; the corroborating evidence gathered through laboratory tests and radiography; and the exclusion of other possible diagnoses.[1,2]

Signs and Symptoms

SYSTEMIC MANIFESTATIONS

Morning stiffness lasting more than 30 minutes is a hallmark symptom of RA. Difficulty in moving upon awakening and generalized stiffness despite morning activity help differentiate this sign from the stiffness seen in **degenerative joint disease** (DJD) following inactivity.[14] Morning stiffness can be qualified in terms of its severity and duration, both of which are directly related to the degree of disease activity. As with other systemic diseases, anorexia, weight loss, and fatigue also may be present.[1,2,11]

JOINT INVOLVEMENT

Rheumatoid arthritis is most often marked by a bilateral and symmetrical pattern of joint involvement. Clinically the patient presents with immobility and the cardinal signs of inflammation: pain, redness, swelling, and heat.[1] The joint examination also may reveal **crepitus**, which is audible or palpable grating or crunching as the joint is moved through its range of motion (ROM). Crepitus is the result of uneven degeneration of the joint surface.

CERVICAL SPINE

The cervical spine is often involved in RA. The atlantoaxial joint and the mid-cervical region are the most common sites of inflammation, which leads to decreased ROM, particularly in rotation, 50 percent of which takes place at the C1-C2 level. Involvement of these two vertebrae may produce life-threatening situations if the transverse ligament of the atlas should rupture or if the odontoid process should fracture or herniate through the foramen magnum. Cervical involvement also may produce radiating pain and nerve and cord compression, which is most likely to be seen in the lower cervical spine where the cervical lordosis is greatest.[1]

TEMPOROMANDIBULAR JOINT

Involvement of this synovial joint results in an inability to open the mouth fully (approximately 2 inches) with normal side-to-side gliding and protrusion. In resting position, the normal approximation of the upper and lower teeth may be reduced following persistent inflammation.[1]

SHOULDERS

Shoulder involvement may be seen in the glenohumeral, sternoclavicular, or acromioclavicular joints. These joints may demonstrate degeneration, pain, and loss of ROM. The scapulothoracic articulation may secondarily exhibit a loss of ROM as well. Chronic inflammation of the shoulders causes the capsule and the ligaments to become distended and thinned. Joint surfaces may be eroded until the shoulder eventually becomes unstable. Additionally, rotator cuff damage, **tendinitis**, and **bursitis** may complicate management.[1,11,12]

ELBOWS

Inflammation, capsular and ligamentous distension, and joint surface erosion may lead to elbow instability and irregular or catching movements. Flexion contractures frequently develop as the outcome of persistent spasm secondary to pain.[1,11]

WRISTS

Early synovitis between the eight carpal bones or at the distal ulna leads to a fairly rapid development of a flexion contracture, which ultimately diminishes the individual's ability to execute power grasp. Chronic inflammation of the proximal row of carpals can lead to a volar **subluxation** of the wrist and hand on the radius, accentuating the normal 10 to 15 degrees of volar inclination of the carpus on the distal radius (Fig. 21-1). Chronic inflammation leads to the loss of radial ligamentous support and destruction of the extensor carpi ulnaris and the fibrocartilage on the distal side of the ulna. The attentuation of these restraining structures allows the proximal carpals to slide down the distal radius toward the ulna, creating a radial deviation of the distal row of carpals in the wrist relative to the two bones of the forearm, where normally there are 5 to 10 degrees of ulnar deviation (Fig. 21-2).[11]

HAND JOINTS

Metacarpophalangeal (MCP)

Soft tissue swelling around the metacarpophalangeal (MCP) joints is very common. The volar subluxation and ulnar drift of the MCPs frequently seen in RA are thought to result from accentuation of the normal structural shapes of these joints, which tilt the proximal phalanges in an ulnar direction. The anatomic placement and length of the collateral ligaments, which are most stretched during MCP flexion, and the insertions of the intrinsics, which also pull from an ulnar direction, contribute to ulnar drift at the MCPs during hand motion. Weakened ligaments can not resist a pull toward volar subluxation during power pinch or grasp when flexor tendons "bowstring" across MCPs through frayed tendon sheaths damaged by long-term synovitis.[11] The bowstring effect results from moving the fulcrum of the flexor tendons distally, which places an ulnar and volar pull on the proximal phalanges (Fig. 21-3). Radial deviation of the

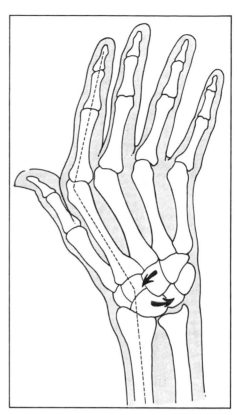

Figure 21-2. Relationship between wrist and metacarpophalangeal joint deformity. (From Melvin, J,[11] p 214, with permission.)

carpals will further enhance MCP ulnar drift as the phalanges try to compensate for the loss of normal ulnar deviation at the wrist. Known as the **zig-zag effect,** forces in the hand try to move the index finger back into its normal functional position in line with the radius (see Figure 21-2).[11,13-17]

Proximal Interphalangeal (PIP)

Swelling of these joints produces a fusiform or sausagelike appearance in the fingers. There are two characteristic deformities seen at the proximal interphalangeal (PIP) joint in individuals with RA. The first of these is known as **swan-neck deformity** and consists of PIP hyperextension and distal interphalangeal (DIP) flexion. Swan-neck deformities arise in three distinct ways, depending on the site of initial involvement.[11,17] Most commonly, swan-neck deformity follows from initial synovitis of the MCP, where the pain of chronic synovitis leads to reflex muscle spasm of the intrinsics (Fig. 21-4). The biomechanical force of the intrinsics then combines with the hypermobility found in the chronically inflamed and structurally changed PIP, resulting in volar subluxation and PIP hyperextension. Swan-neck deformity also may result when the volar capsule of the PIP is stretched. In this situation the lateral bands move dorsally, and tension is placed on the flexor digitorum profundis with the combined flexion of the PIP and the DIP (Fig. 21-5). In these instances, a rupture of the flexor digitorum sublimus further predisposes an individual to

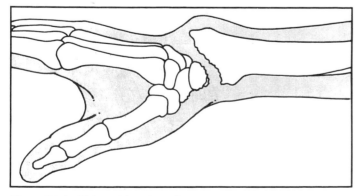

Figure 21-1. Volar subluxation of the carpus on the radius as a result of erosive synovitis of the radiocarpal joint. (From Melvin, J,[11] p 213, with permission.)

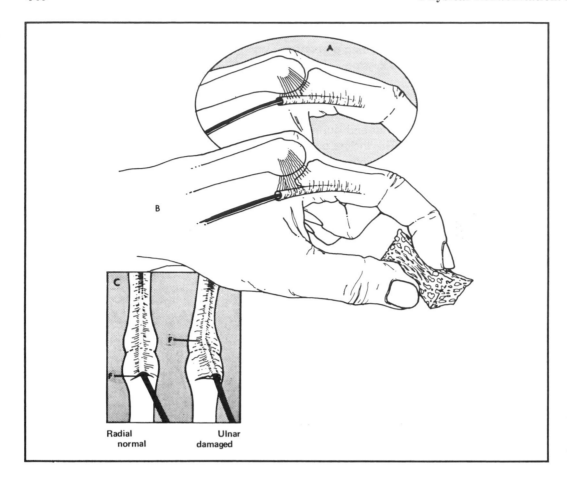

Radial   Ulnar
normal   damaged

Figure 21–3. Influence of the long flexors in metacarpophalangeal drift deformity. (From Melvin, J,[11] p 216, with permission.)

swan-neck deformity. A third mechanism for developing swan-neck deformity involves a rupture of the extensor digitorum communis at its insertion on the DIP resulting in DIP flexion and PIP hyperextension due to unrestrained pull by the flexor digitorum profundis (Fig. 21–6).[11]

The other characteristic deformity of the PIP is known as a **boutonniere deformity** and consists of DIP extension with PIP flexion (Fig. 21–7). As a result of chronic synovitis, the insertion of the extensor digitorum com-

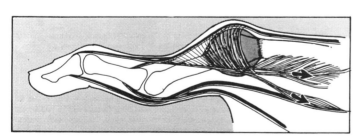

Figure 21–4. Swan-neck deformity with initial synovitis at the metacarpophalangeal joint. (From Melvin, J,[11] p 219, with permission.)

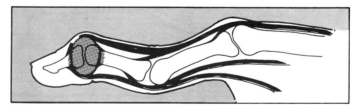

Figure 21–6. Swan-neck deformity with initial synovitis at the distal interphalangeal joint. (From Melvin, J,[11] p 220, with permission.)

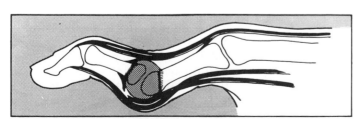

Figure 21–5. Swan-neck deformity with initial synovitis at the proximal interphalangeal joint. (From Melvin, J,[11] p 219, with permission.)

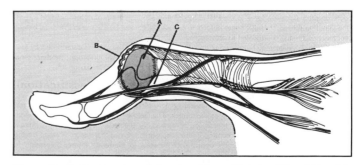

Figure 21–7. Boutonniere deformity. (From Melvin, J,[11] p 221, with permission.)

munis into the middle phalanx known as the central slip lengthens and the lateral bands slide volarly to force the PIP into flexion. Bony formation or outgrowths around the end of a joint are termed **osteophytes.** Those found at the PIP are known as **Bouchard's nodes** and may be seen in DJD, which is also known as **osteoarthritis.** They are unrelated to RA, although an individual may have both kinds of arthritis at the same time.[11]

Distal Interphalangeal (DIP)

The distal interphalangeal (DIP) joint is often uninvolved in RA. Osteophytes are, however, common in DJD and are called **Heberden's nodes.** Occasionally the tendon of the extensor digitorum communis will rupture, and the unopposed pull of the flexor digitorum profundis will pull the DIP into flexion. This condition is known as **mallet finger** deformity.[11]

Thumb

As in the other digital joints, the primary cause of deformity in the thumb is synovial swelling. The fibers of the dorsal hood mechanism over the MCP, the joint capsule and the collateral ligaments, and the tendons of the extensor policis brevis and extensor pollicis longus are particularly affected. The exact mechanism of thumb deformities depends on the particular combination of affected structures and may be classified according to the criteria elaborated by Nalebuff.[18] Similar to other hand deformities, the actual presentation depends on the site of initial synovitis, the direction of imbalanced muscle forces, and the integrity of the surrounding joint structures. A type I deformity, consisting of MCP flexion with interphalangeal (IP) hyperextension without involvement of the carpometacarpal (CMC) joint, is most commonly seen. Type II classifications are assigned when the CMC is subluxed and the IP is held in hyperextension. Carpometacarpal subluxation with MCP hyperextension is classified as a Type III deformity and is more commonly found in RA than a type II deformity.[11,18]

Mutilans Deformity (Opera-glass Hand)

Grossly unstable thumbs and severely deformed phalanges are indicative of **mutilans type deformity.** Also known as opera-glass hand, the transverse folds of the skin of the thumb and fingers resemble a folded telescope. Radiographic study of the bones of the hand reveals severe bone resorption, erosion, and shortening of the MCP, PIP, radiocarpal, and radioulnar joints especially. The negative impact of this deformity on hand function and activities of daily living is significant.[2,11]

HIP

Although patients may have early complaints of pain in the groin, often related to trochanteric bursitis, the hip is less commonly involved in RA than in other kinds of arthritis. Radiographic hip disease is seen in about half of all patients with RA. Severe inflammatory destruction of the femoral head and the acetabulum may push the acetabulum into the pelvic cavity, a condition known as **protrusio acetabuli.**[1,2,11]

KNEES

Because of the relatively large amount of synovium in the knee, it is one of the most frequently affected joints in RA. Chronic synovitis results in distension of the joint capsule, attentuation of the collateral and cruciate ligaments, and destruction of the joint surfaces. Painful knees may be rested in flexed positions, ultimately resulting in flexion contractures.[1,2,10]

ANKLES AND FEET

Chronic synovitis accentuates the natural tendency of the talus to glide medially and in a plantar direction, resulting in pressure on the calcaneus and leading to hindfoot pronation. The spring ligament is also stretched by these occurrences, flattening the medial longitudinal arch (Fig. 21-8). The calcaneus may erode or develop bony **exostoses,** known as spurs. As synovitis weakens the transverse arch, the metatarsals spread and a splayed forefoot **(splayfoot)** may develop (Fig. 21-9). Synovitis of the metatarsophalangeal (MTP) joints is extremely common. A **hallux valgus** may also be present. When volar subluxation of the MTP combines with flexion of the proximal interphalangeal and hyperextension of the distal interphalangeal joints, this condition is commonly referred to as **hammer toes** (Fig. 21-10). The MTPs also may exhibit volar subluxation of the metatarsal head with flexion of the proximal and distal interphalangeal

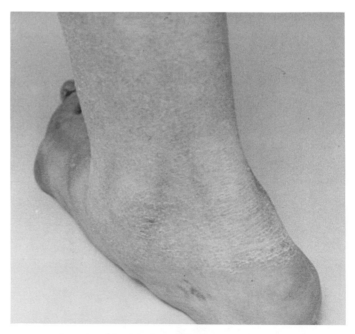

Figure 21-8. Posteromedial view of the foot and ankle showing calcanelavalgus, pes planus (flatfoot) and hallux valgus. (From the Arthritis Teaching Slide Collection copyright 1980. Used by permission of the Arthritis Foundation.)

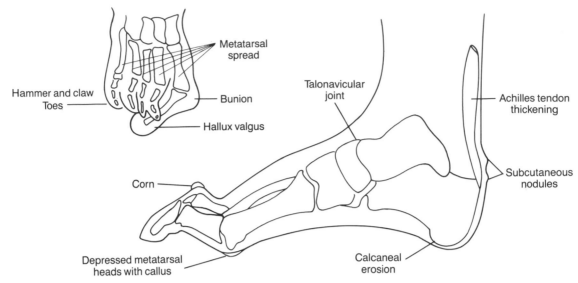

Figure 21–9. Major foot and ankle deformities seen in rheumatoid arthritis. (From Dimonte, P and Light, H.[75] Used by permission of the American Physical Therapy Association.)

joints, known as **cock-up** or **claw toes** (Fig. 21–11). As the capsule and intertarsal ligaments are weakened and stretched, the proximal phalanges move dorsally on the metatarsal heads (Fig. 21–12). Similar to conditions observed in the hand, the long toe extensors bowstring over the proximal interphalangeal joints while the flexors are displaced into the intertarsal spaces.[1,2,11,19,20]

MUSCLE INVOLVEMENT

Muscle atrophy around affected joints may be present early. It is not definitively known, however, if this atrophy is the result simply of disuse or selective attrition of

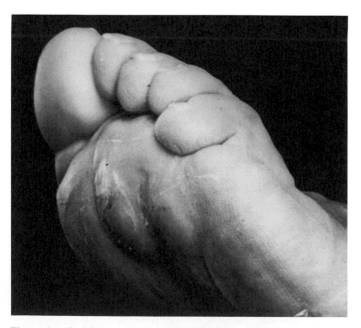

Figure 21–10. Metatarsophalangeal subluxation. (Reprinted from the Revised Clinical Slide Collection on the Rheumatic Diseases, copyright 1981. Used by permission of the American Rheumatism Association.)

muscles owing to some unknown mechanism specifically related to the disease itself. Atrophy in the intrinsic muscles of the hand and in the quadriceps is particularly evident in long-standing disease, although the mechanisms for these changes may not be the same. It appears that individuals with RA experience selective attrition of type II (phasic) muscle fibers through some unknown mechanism.[21,22] There is also some evidence that type I (tonic) muscle fibers of the quadriceps will selectively undergo atrophy following anterior cruciate damage.[23] Loss of muscle bulk may be the result of a peripheral neuropathy, myositis, or steroid-induced myopathy. Muscle weakness may be due to either reflex inhibition secondary to pain, or atrophy.[21–23]

TENDONS

Inflammation of the synovial lining of the tendon sheaths results in a tenosynovitis that interferes with the smooth gliding of the tendon through the sheath and may directly damage the tendon itself. Eventually the tendon may rupture. A patient with tendon damage or muscle weakness may exhibit a lag phenomenon, which refers to a substantial difference in passive versus active ROM. This is a nonspecific finding which therapists need to assess carefully in order to determine the cause and appropriate treatment.[2,11]

Laboratory Tests

Two concepts are essential to a full understanding of the use of laboratory tests in the detection of RA. The first is the concept of the *sensitivity* of a test, which indicates the proportion of truly diseased individuals who have a positive test. The clinical value of sensitive tests is particularly evident in those instances in which a negative diagnosis would be deleterious to the health of the patient who actually had the disease. In research terms,

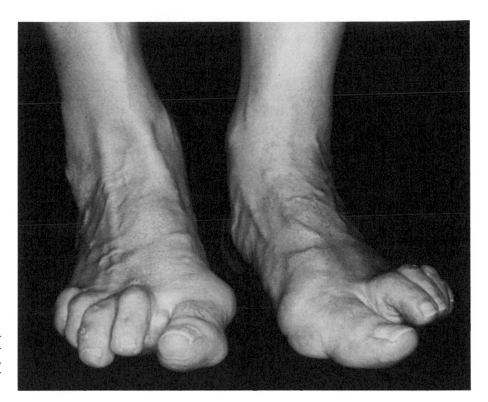

Figure 21–11. Common deformities in the rheumatoid foot. (Reprinted from the Revised Clinical Slide Collection on the Rheumatic Diseases, copyright 1981. Used by permission of the American Rheumatism Association.)

this is equivalent to the laboratory test's ability to avoid a false-negative result. The concept of *specificity,* on the other hand, refers to the proportion of truly nondiseased individuals who have a negative test. In other words, the specificity of a laboratory test is a measure of its ability to avoid false-positives. The clinical diagnostician will usually choose a mix of both sensitive and specific tests to confirm clinical impressions during the diagnostic process.

The erythrocyte sedimentation rate (ESR) is highly nonspecific but exceptionally sensitive to inflammatory processes. Therefore, it is a good test to choose when the clinician wishes to confirm the presence or absence of any inflammation irrespective of the underlying pathology or disease. A normal ESR makes it unlikely that an inflammatory process underlies a patient's complaints. The ESR in individuals with RA is typically elevated and is a reasonable marker of overall disease activity. A return toward normal usually signals the success of medical management and can be used by physical therapists as an indicator to commence more aggressive treatment.

There are two different tests to determine the presence of RF. The sheep cell agglutination test (SCAT) and the latex fixation test identify the proportion of RF in the sera following repetitive dilutions. The greatest dilution that produces a positive test is known as a *titer.* High titers after repeated dilutions indicate greater proportions of RF. In general, the SCAT is regarded as the more

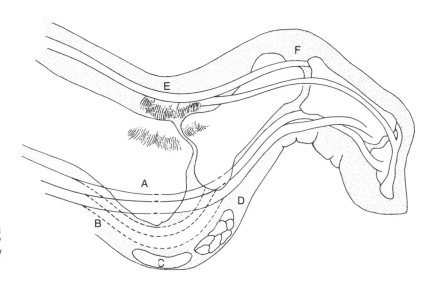

Figure 21–12. Relationship of structures to the metatarsal heads in metatarsalgia. (From Moncur, C and Shields, M.[19] Used by permission of *Clinical Management in Physical Therapy.*)

specific test, yielding fewer false-positive results, and the latex fixation is thought to be more sensitive, yielding fewer false-negatives. The SCAT is usually used as an initial screening test.

A complete blood count is also routinely ordered. Red blood cell counts are usually decreased. Anemia is found in approximately 20 percent of individuals with RA. The white blood cell count, by comparison, is usually normal. An increase in platelets, called thrombocytosis, is not unusual in active RA.

A synovial fluid analysis can greatly enhance the process of differential diagnosis. Normal synovial fluid is transparent, yellowish, viscous, and without clots. Synovial fluid from inflamed joints is cloudy, less viscous owing to a change in hyaluronate proteins, and will clot. Significant inflammation will also increase the number of proteins in the fluid. A culture can be done to identify potential bacterial agents as the cause of the joint inflammation. If the joint is inflamed, there will be an elevation of white blood cells in the fluid, 90 percent of which may be PMN leukocytes. Normal fluid has a low cell count with only 25 percent PMN representation. The presence of crystals may confirm the diagnosis of gout (urate crystals) or pseudogout (calcium pyrophosphate crystals). A mucin clot is formed in synovial fluid by mixing it with acetic acid. If the synovial fluid is normal, a ropelike mass will form in a clear solution after mixing. Shredding indicates fair mucin clotting, whereas the formation of small masses with shreds is indicative of a poor mucin clot. Poor clotting accompanies acute infectious arthritis. Inflammatory arthritis produces fair to poor mucin clotting. Good mucin clotting of the synovial fluid is found in a joint that presents with a noninflammatory arthritis.[1,2]

Radiography

Radiographic assessment is an essential component of the diagnostic work-up for RA. Physical therapists working in rheumatology should be avid consumers of the radiographic information available in a patient's record. They also should develop a basic proficiency in identifying abnormalities in joint structure and the surrounding soft tissues that influence the course and outcome of rehabilitation. The ability to identify abnormalities assumes that the therapist has a firm notion of how a normal joint appears on x-ray film. Therapists can orient themselves to an x-ray examination by considering the following parameters: alignment, bone density and surface, and cartilagenous spacing (Figs. 21–13 and 21–14). In assessing the alignment, the therapist should note whether the long axes of the proximal and distal bones of the joint are in their normal spatial relationships and whether the convex surface of one fits well with the concavity of the other. Bone density, in the absence of **osteoporosis,** should be somewhat opaque and milky and appear evenly distributed throughout. The cortices of each bone should be distinct, appropriately thick, and well defined. The soft tissues surrounding the joints should conform to known anatomic shape. The therapist should note any soft tissue swelling evident on the x-ray

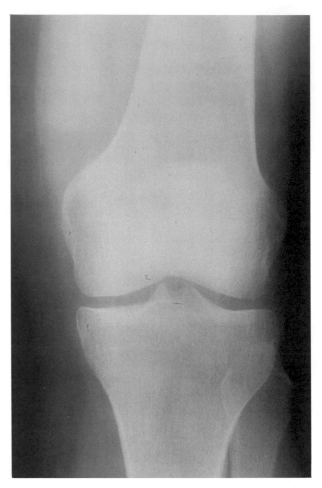

Figure 21–13. Frontal view of the normal knee. (Reprinted from the Revised Clinical Slide Collection on the Rheumatic Diseases, copyright 1981. Used by permission of the American Rheumatism Association.)

Table 21–2 CLASSIFICATION OF PROGRESSION OF RHEUMATOID ARTHRITIS

Stage 1, Early
*1. No destructive changes on roentgenographic examination
2. Roentgenologic evidence of osteoporosis may be present.

Stage II, Moderate
*1. Roentgenologic evidence of osteoporosis, with or without slight subchondral bone destruction; slight cartilage destruction may be present.
*2. No joint deformities, although limitation of joint mobility may be present.
3. Adjacent muscle atrophy
4. Extraarticular soft tissue lesions, such as nodules and tenosynovitis may be present.

Stage III, Severe
*1. Roentgenologic evidence of cartilage and bone destruction, in addition to osteoporosis
*2. Joint deformity, such as subluxation, ulnar deviation, or hyperextension, without fibrous or bony ankylosis.
3. Extensive muscle atrophy
4. Extraarticular soft tissue lesions, such as nodules and tenosynovitis may be present.

Stage IV, Terminal
*1. Fibrous or bony ankylosis
2. Criteria of stage III

*The criteria prefaced by an asterisk are those that must be present to permit classification of a patient in any particular stage or grade.

From *Primer on the Rheumatic Diseases,* ed 8. Arthritis Foundation, 1983. Used by permission of the Arthritis Foundation, Atlanta.

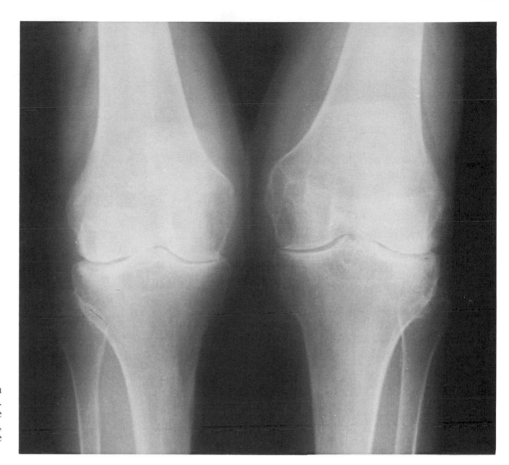

Figure 21–14. Frontal view of the knee with characteristics of rheumatoid arthritis. (Reprinted from the Revised Clinical Slide Collection on the Rheumatic Diseases, copyright 1981. Used by permission of the American Rheumatism Association.)

film that might limit function. Finally, the therapist should note whether there is even spacing between the joint surfaces. Uneven, reduced, or absent spacing suggests loss of cartilage or erosion of the joint surfaces. Overall the joint surface should be smooth and conform to known anatomic shape without osteophytes. The progression of the disease can be characterized along four stages following periodic radiographic assessment (Table 21–2). The radiographic changes seen early in the disease are nonspecific and usually limited to swelling in the surrounding soft tissues, joint effusions, and periarticular demineralization. Diagnostic confirmation is available only later in the disease process when the typical joint space narrowing and erosions in the hands and feet are seen in the characteristic bilateral distribution.[24]

SECONDARY PROBLEMS AND COMPLICATIONS

Rheumatoid Nodules

Rheumatoid nodules are the most common extra-articular manifestations of RA and occur in approximately 25 percent of patients. They are most commonly found in the subcutaneous or deeper connective tissues in areas subjected to repeated mechanical pressure such as the olecranon bursae, the extensor surfaces of the forearms, and the Achilles tendons. Nodules are usually asymptomatic, although they can be tender and may cause skin breakdown or become infected.[1]

Vascular Complications

Most forms of vascular lesions associated with RA are silent, although the fulminant form of rheumatoid arthritis can be life-threatening and accompanied by malnutrition, infection, congestive heart failure, and gastrointestinal bleeding. Foot or wrist drop may occur as a result of vasculitis of the vasa arteriosum to the nerve supply of the radial or superficial peroneal nerves.[1,2]

Neurologic Manifestations

Mild peripheral neuropathies are often seen in RA, particularly in elderly patients, and are unrelated to vasculitis. Most neuropathies result from nerve compression or entrapment such as tarsal tunnel and **carpal tunnel** syndromes.[1,2]

Cardiopulmonary Complications

Pericarditis has been demonstrated during autopsy in about 40 percent of patients, but clinically detectable heart disease from RA is rare. Similarly, pleuropulmonary manifestations are most commonly asymptomatic, although pleuritis is commonly found on autopsy.[1,2]

Ocular Manifestations

Ocular lesions are most usually associated with the dry eyes of **Sjogren's syndrome,** which is an inflammatory disorder of the lacrimal and salivary glands. Scleritis and the relatively more benign episcleritis also can be present and require careful medical treatment.[1,25]

CLINICAL MANIFESTATIONS OF RHEUMATOID ARTHRITIS

Disease Onset and Course

Disease onset in RA is most usually insidious with complaints of generalized joint pain and stiffness. Men who develop RA past the age of 60 typically present without stiffness and swelling in the upper extremities.[2] The question of whether elderly onset RA represents a distinct disease remains controversial. Comparisons of elderly onset RA with early onset RA have revealed that abrupt onset and large joint involvement, particularly of the shoulder girdle, were more common in the older group. The elderly onset group also more commonly had features of **polymyalgia rheumatica,** a distinct disease affecting the shoulder and pelvic girdles, with which elderly onset RA can be confused.[26] Older adolescent women may present with a chronic erosive arthritis of the knees without other joint involvement or systemic manifestations. It is not known whether this presentation is a variation of juvenile arthritis, adult-onset RA, or a distinct form of arthritis involving only a few joints.[2]

Acute onset is seen in 8 to 15 percent of patients. Onset is intermediate in approximately 15 to 20 percent of patients. Disease progression is highly variable. High titers of RF can indicate a more severe disease course. Spontaneous remissions can occur, usually within the first two years, most typically in those patients who met only the criteria for possible or probable RA. Twenty to 30 percent of patients experience an intermittent course characterized by partial to complete remissions longer than the periods of exacerbations. A third group of patients experiences the full destructive process of progressive RA. Of these, less than 3 percent do not respond to any aggressive therapy.[1,2]

PROGNOSIS

Although systemic vasculitis and atlantoaxial subluxation can be fatal, RA itself is not usually a cause of death. Long-term inflammation ultimately results in joint destruction and significant functional loss. Almost 50 percent of individuals with RA will eventually have marked restrictions in activities of daily living (ADL) or will be incapacitated.[1] Individuals with elderly onset RA appear to have a better functional outcome than those with early onset RA, but it is unclear whether this is the result of having the disease for a shorter period of time

or of having a different form of the disease itself.[26] A broad classification of functional disability has been developed by the ARA to characterize the progressive impacts of the disease (Table 21–3). The most severe social loss, income, is directly attributable to work disability secondary to loss of physical function.[27,28]

MEDICAL MANAGEMENT

Drug Therapy

The overall goal of medical management in RA is to control inflammation and to retard the long-term progression of the disease. Although a curative drug for RA does not exist, many of the available medications do reduce inflammation, and some are believed to prevent the erosive effects of the disease. Drugs are usually prescribed sequentially, beginning with aspirin, which has both an **analgesic** and an antiinflammatory effect. It is prescribed in a large dose, often 12 or more 325 mg tablets per day, which results in a serum salicylate level in the range of 20 to 25 mg/dl. **Tinnitus** is the major symptom of aspirin toxicity, which may be reported by a patient to the physical therapist. If aspirin therapy fails to produce the desired therapeutic effects, or if the side effects of aspirin, such as gastrointestinal bleeding, become unmanageable, the patient will be placed on one of the currently approved nonsteroidal anti-inflammatory drugs (NSAIDs), which are differentiated according to their chemical derivation (Table 21–4). Although NSAIDs are more costly than aspirin, they require less frequent administrations each day and may have fewer side effects. There is no evidence, however, that they are more effective than aspirin in controlling inflammation.

If the patient fails to respond to either aspirin or NSAIDs, a physician will consider using antimalarials, gold salts, or penicillamine. Positive effects from their administration may not be noticed for 10 to 12 weeks. Antimalarials carry the remote risk of severe side effects to the retina and require that the patient receive periodic eye examinations. Gold may be administered either orally or intramuscularly and is thought to prevent ero-

Table 21–3 CLASSIFICATION OF FUNCTIONAL CAPACITY IN RHEUMATOID ARTHRITIS

Class I:	Complete functional capacity with ability to carry on all usual duties without handicaps
Class II:	Functional capacity adequate to conduct normal activities despite handicap of discomfort or limited mobility of 1 or more joints
Class III:	Functional capacity adequate to perform only few or none of the duties of usual occupation or of self care
Class IV:	Large or wholly incapacitated with patient bedridden or confined to wheelchair, permitting little or no self care

From Steinbrocker O, Traeger CH, Batterman RC: Therapeutic criteria in rheumatoid arthritis. JAMA 140:659–662, 1949. Reprinted from the *Primer on the Rheumatic Diseases,* ed 8. Arthritis Foundation, 1983. Used by permission of the Arthritis Foundation, Atlanta.

Table 21–4 COMMON NONSTEROIDAL ANTI-INFLAMMATORY DRUGS

Class and Drug	Usual Supply	Usual Daily Dose
Salicylates and related drugs		
Aspirin or buffered aspirin*	250–325-mg tabs	3–6 g
Ascriptin	325 mg aspirin and 150 mg Maalox	3–6 g
Choline magnesium trisalicylate (Trilisate*)	500-mg tabs	2–6 g
Enteric-coated aspirin (Ecotrin*)	325-mg tabs	2–6 g
Diflunisal (Dolobid*)	250, 500-mg tabs	500–1000 mg
Choline salicylate (Arthropan*)	Liquid	1–1½ tsp q.i.d.
Salicylsalicylic Acid (Disalcid*)	500, 750 mg	3000 mg
Indoles (and related drugs)		
Indomethacin (Indocin*)	25, 50, 75-mg (timed-release) capsules	75–200 mg
Sulindac (Clinoril*)	150, 200-mg tabs	300–400 mg
Tolmetin (Tolectin*)	200-mg tabs	600–2000 mg
Propionic acids		
Ibuprofen (Motrin*)	200, 300, 400, 600, 800-mg tabs	1.4–3.2 g
Fenoprofen (Nalfon*)	300, 600-mg capsules	1–3 g
Naproxen (Naprosyn) (Anaprox)	250, 375, 500-mg tabs	0.75–1 g
Oxicams		
Piroxicam (Feldene*)	10, 20-mg capsules	20 mg
Anthranilic acids		
Meclofenamate (Meclomen*)	50, 100-mg capsules	1.5–2 g
Pyrazoles		
Phenylbutazone (Butazolidine*)	50, 100 mg	300–400 mg
Oxyphenbutazone (Tandearil*)	50, 100 mg	300–400 mg

Modified from Simon, Mills LS, Mills JA: Drug therapy: Nonsteroidal anti-inflammatory drugs (two parts). N Engl J Med 302:1179, 1237, 1980.

*Trade name.

From Goldenberg, DL and Cohen, AS: *Drugs in the Rheumatic Diseases.* Grune & Stratton, Orlando, FL, 1986.

sions. Side effects are not rare, the most common of which is skin rash. Penicillamine, which is a chelating agent that binds with metal ions, appears to have immunomodulating effects. Its major side effect is bone marrow depression. Other multiple side effects have led to its decreased usage.

If a patient has failed to respond to all other drugs, the final step in the sequence will place the patient on cytotoxic or immunosuppressive drugs, most commonly methotrexate, azathioprine, or cyclophosphamide. Methotrexate has the least serious side effects. Cyclophosphamide has potentially the most serious side effects, including a predisposition to malignancy and leukopenia and may additionally cause alopecia. Six

months or more may be required in order to determine the effectiveness of one of these drugs.[1,29–32]

Surgical Management

Surgery represents one of the greatest advances in the management of RA in the last 25 years. Surgery is not appropriate, however, for every individual with RA, and the careful selection of the patient and the timing of the procedure are critical. The primary indications for surgery are pain, loss of function, and progression of deformity, although the last two are not always correlated. Surgical outcomes are greatly affected by the personal characteristics of the individual patient, such as motivation and the quality of postoperative rehabilitation. The postoperative rehabilitation goals are to restore mobility to the affected joint, to promote stability within the joint, and to regain active control of joint motion.

In general there are three surgical procedures that may be performed on soft tissues: synovectomy, soft tissue release, and tendon transfers. Similarly, there are three general bone and joint procedures: **osteotomy,** prosthetic **arthroplasty,** and **arthrodesis.** The choice of specific postoperative physical therapy procedures will depend upon the particular surgical intervention, the extent of joint involvement prior to surgery, and individual characteristics of the patient.[33]

REHABILITATIVE MANAGEMENT

Because RA is a chronic, progressive disease, rehabilitation team members must always concern themselves with the long-range trajectory of the illness beyond the particular point in time that the care is provided. Rheumatoid arthritis is a systemic disease with multiple impacts on all facets of the individual's life. Although each professional regards the individual as a whole person, the expertise of each professional addresses only certain aspects of the complex and interconnected problems faced by that person. Without a broad range of expertise, none of these problems can be adequately solved. Therefore, the rehabilitation of the individual with RA requires the intense and coordinated efforts of a variety of health professionals, including physical therapists. Although a therapist may provide services to assist a person in adjusting to the effects of systemic illness, it is the individual with RA who must live within the constraints imposed by the illness each day and who is the ultimate authority on the goals of therapy in whatever setting services are provided.

The overall rehabilitation goals are specific to the three stages of inflammation: acute, subacute, and chronic. During the acute stage, the primary goal is to reduce pain and inflammation by resting affected joints and applying pain-relief modalities. Other goals are to maintain ROM, strength, and endurance, and to promote independence in ADL. As the inflammation subsides and the individual enters the subacute stage, efforts should be directed toward increasing ROM, strength, and endurance and regaining independence in a broader range of ADL.

Affected joints should continue to be protected through proper positioning and reduced biomechanical stress. Once the inflammatory process has been controlled, the goals of rehabilitative management will change. Expanded goals will include the independent resumption of previous levels of ADL, including work. The rehabilitation program also will seek to maintain optimal levels of physical, psychologic, and social functioning with particular emphasis on patient education that enables the individual to reestablish a sense of control over his or her life despite chronic illness.[11,34]

Physical Therapy Assessment

The primary functional limitations of the individual with RA result from impairment to the musculoskeletal system. Therefore, an extensive and careful assessment of the musculoskeletal system as it contributes to the overall functional disability of the patient is imperative. Because quality care of the individual with RA involves an entire team of professionals, the physical therapist must carefully review the chart and consult with all other caregivers to ascertain their proposed plans and goals of treatment. The physical therapist should begin the assessment by taking a patient history. This will orient the therapist to the nature and extent of the current problem and relate that problem to the patient's past medical history. During the interview the therapist should elicit from the patient that individual's understanding of the disease and what is personally seen as the major problem at hand. In the acute and subacute stages, the patient is most often concerned with pain, which should be assessed in terms of its location, duration, and intensity along with the other signs of inflammation: heat, **erythema**, and swelling. In the chronic stages, individuals are usually more concerned with loss of function, deformity, and the prevention of further deterioration. Specific information on joint symptoms, morning stiffness, previous level of activity, pattern and degree of fatigue, and current medication regimen also should be gathered. Although the majority of test procedures to be used in assessing the individual with RA are generic to the practice of physical therapy, many of these procedures require particular adaptations, owing to the nature of joint involvement.

RANGE OF MOTION

Goniometric measurement of passive ROM is indicated at all affected joints following a gross ROM assessment. Common wisdom suggests that a complete goniometric baseline is useful for documenting the progression of a chronic disease. Unless the method of measurement for each joint has been standardized in the clinical setting and used in every assessment, the potential variations in intrarater and interrater reliability of goniometry call this practice into question, particularly given the considerable time that gathering such a database requires.[35-37] Although such a database may be useful in terms of a particular course of physical therapy treatment, it is of questionable value when compared

with data collected by another therapist using a different instrument and method of measurement. If joint pain or poor activity tolerance prohibit measurement of passive ROM, the therapist may consider substituting a functional ROM test by asking the patient to touch various body parts (e.g., the top of head and small of the back) in order to determine the ROM available for performing self-care activities. During the ROM assessment, the therapist should note any tenderness, crepitus, or pain on movement.

STRENGTH

Application of standard manual muscle tests to assess strength in RA may be inappropriate because of pain at various points in the range. A patient may be strong in the pain-free portion of the range but weak secondary to reflex inhibition in the very portion of the range that is essential to a functional activity. Individuals with severe deformity and deranged joints are inappropriate candidates for traditional tests of strength. A functional test of strength, therefore, is more indicative of rehabilitation needs and will identify the required functional outcomes of strengthening programs prior to initiating treatment. An additional complicating factor in the application of conventional muscle tests is the frequent display of the **lag phenomenon**. Because the patient is able to move only partway through the available range, traditional grading systems are not sensitive to recording changes as the gap between active and passive ROM closes as a result of treatment. A therapist may want to comment specifically on the degrees of active motion and the grade of strength exhibited in that arc of motion. If a traditional muscle-testing method is used, therapists should also document the particular approach to testing used (e.g., break testing, isometric holding at the end of range, and/or resistance throughout the ROM), which will clarify the meaning of the grade assigned. Break testing generally yields higher grades than would be received if full range testing were done. It is also important to record whether the patient was receiving any medications that might alter performance or exercise tolerance. The therapist also may wish to document the time of day to account for the effects of morning stiffness.

JOINT STABILITY

The ligamentous laxity of any affected joint should be fully investigated. Ligamentous instability of upper and lower extremity joints may be a significant deterrent to ADL and ambulation. Improper loading of an unstable joint may further contribute to its deformation.

ENDURANCE

Fatigue is one of the systemic manifestations of RA and should be carefully assessed both during the course of a single day and over several days in order to obtain a full understanding of its pattern. The decreased cardiovascular fitness of individuals with RA demands specific attention.[38] Heart rate, respiratory rate, and blood pressure should be measured during a functional activity that is reasonably stressful for the patient's current level of fitness. Excessive increases in any of these parameters may indicate the need for more extensive and sophisticated testing. Because the costosternal and costovertebral articulations are synovial joints, chest expansion, breathing, and coughing may be compromised and should be assessed.

FUNCTIONAL ASSESSMENT

As with any long-term disease process, a number of different functional tests may be indicated. Functional assessments may include ADL, work, and leisure activities (see chapter 12). The choice of a functional assessment instrument is influenced by several factors, including the characteristics and needs of the individual patient, the level and depth of information required, and its predictive value in gauging the efficacy of treament.[39] As with goniometric measurement, the reliability and validity of the instrument should be known if the data are to be used for comparative purposes. The Functional Status Index, which was designed expressly to be used in outpatient rheumatologic settings, is an instrument that is known to be reliable and valid as well as to provide sufficient baseline data to be an effective screen of patient performance (see Appendix A).[40,41] This instrument is used to investigate a statistically derived representative sample of typical ADL along the parameters of the pain, difficulty, and dependence experienced by the individual in performing these activities. Another arthritis-specific instrument, the Arthritis Impact Measurement Scales, expands the concept of function to include performance in psychologic and social domains as well as in the physical areas.[42]

FUNCTIONAL MOBILITY AND GAIT

A complete assessment of bed mobility and transfers is essential, particularly in the initial acute stage or later recurrence of multiple joint inflammation. A complete and detailed gait analysis is one of the most important contributions of the physical therapist to the rehabilitation team's understanding of the individual's functional abilities and serves to identify additional areas for assessment and treatment (Table 21–5).

SENSORY ASSESSMENT

Any indication of peripheral neuropathy or nerve involvement should be investigated using standard assessment procedures (see chapter 6). Sensory changes that are concomitant with other conditions such as diabetes or normal aging should be considered when appropriate.

PSYCHOLOGIC STATUS

Despite folklore to the contrary, there is no personality type specific to individuals with RA that has been demonstrated in any scientifically acceptable way.[43–48] Reports of pain are, however, significantly correlated with self-reports of depression but not correlated with functional level.[49] The overall psychologic status of the individual with RA is generally similar to those individuals with other chronic diseases that threaten a severe change in body image and disruption of social integration. Individuals respond to these threats with various coping strategies to maintain psychologic equilibrium. No single strategy is better than another, although some strategies ultimately facilitate the achievement of positive outcomes and others will hinder an individual's progress toward self-professed goals. Assessment of the patient's attitude toward rehabilitation as well as that of family members can assist the therapist in achieving the goals of treatment as well as instill a realistic, yet positive, orientation to future functional ability. The individual with RA is requested to implement a series of changes in daily life with respect to medications, exercise, and self-care. Failure to comply with professional recommendations is often interpreted as a rejection of the care provider's assistance or psychologically maladaptive behavior. The physical therapist must avoid using one's professional authority as a reason to exert control over another person. Allowing the individual to set the direction of treatment and to use the expertise of the care provider to attain these self-chosen goals offers the greatest opportunity for responsible and humane care.

ARCHITECTURAL BARRIERS

The therapist should be aware of physical barriers in the home and work environments that might require specific assessment and recommendations for change (see chapter 13). A discussion about the home and work environments may reveal conditions that impede regaining complete independence and make the individual aware of the possibilities for altering these environments. The costs of such changes may be a limiting factor in implementing these recommendations.

TREATMENT

The general goals of physical therapy treatment for the individual with RA include the following:
1. Decrease pain
2. Increase or maintain the ROM of all joints sufficient for all functional activities
3. Increase or maintain muscle strength sufficient for the patient's level of function
4. Increase joint stability and decrease biomechanical stress on all affected joints
5. Increase endurance for all functional activities
6. Promote independence in all ADL, including bed mobility and transfers
7. Improve efficiency and safety of gait pattern
8. Educate the patient, family, and other personnel to promote the individual's capacity for self-management
The particular goals identified for each patient will depend on individual circumstances. Although programs for individuals with chronic diseases usually stress self-reliance, therapists must be accountable for their own professional actions. This includes determining the plan of care, implementing that plan safely and effectively,

Table 21–5 ANALYSIS OF GAIT DEVIATIONS, PHYSICAL EXAMINATION FINDINGS, AND TREATMENT GOALS

	Gait Deviations	Physical Examination Findings	Treatment Goals
Pronated foot	Shuffled progression Decreased step length Initial contact with medial border of foot Decreased single-limb balance Prolonged double-support phase Late heel rise Plantarflexion of ipsilateral ankle in swing Genu valgus with weight bearing	Tenderness over subtalar midtarsal area Limited inversion range Weak and painful posterior tibialis muscle Pronated weight-bearing posture of foot Lax medial collateral ligament of knee	Relieve subtalar and midtarsal joint stresses Increase ankle inversion Strengthen posterior tibialis muscle Stabilize hypermobile joints with rigid orthosis Maintain neutral alignment in stance by foot positioning
Hallux valgus	Lateral and posterior weight shift Late heel rise Decreased single-limb balance	Lateral deviation of great toe Swelling of first MTP joint Shortening of flexor hallucis brevis muscle Tenderness of great toe Weakness of great toe abduction	Accommodate foot with wide toe box shoe Increase extension of great toe Relieve weight-bearing stresses
Metatarsophalangeal joint subluxation	Diminished roll off Decreased single-limb stance Apropulsive progression Decreased single-limb balance	Painful MTP heads with weight bearing Callus formation over MTP heads Ulcerations over MTP heads Limited MTP flexion Prominent MTP heads	Redistribute pressure with metatarsal bar Relieve pressure with soft cutout shoe insert Increase flexion mobility of MTP joints Accommodate foot with extra-depth shoe
Hammer or claw toes	Diminished roll off Decreased single-limb stance Apropulsive progression Decreased single-limb balance	Posture of MTP joint hyperextension with proximal and distal interphalangeal joint flexion Posture of MTP and distal interphalangeal joint hyperextension with proximal interphalangeal flexion Callus formation at plantar tips and dorsum of proximal interphalangeal joint Limited MTP flexion	Improve toe alignment with metatarsal bar Accommodate foot with extra-depth shoe Diminish pressure with soft insert Increase toe mobility
Painful heel	Toe-heel pattern No heel contact in stance Decreased stride length Decreased velocity Plantar flexion of ankle in swing Increased hip flexion in swing Decreased step length of contralateral limb	Painful active plantar flexion Painful passive and active dorsiflexion Swelling and pain at Achilles insertion Tenderness over spur Decreased ankle dorsiflexion range	Decrease inflammation with steroid injection or modalities Relieve weight-bearing stress Decrease pressure over spur with soft shoe insert Maintain ankle mobility

From Dimonte, P and Light, H: Pathomechanics, gait deviations and treatment of the rheumatoid foot. Phys Ther 62:1148, 1982, with permission of the American Physical Therapy Association.

and delegating responsibility appropriately. One component of professional accountability is documentation of treatment goals that allows an outside party to determine the purposes of treatment and the degree to which the therapist realized these objectives. The therapist should also be able to ensure that these objectives are attained in the most expedient manner. Treatment goals should be specifically tailored to meet the needs of the patient and should be stated clearly in terms of measurable outcomes and the time period proposed for achievement; for example, increase ROM of the left shoulder in three weeks, and independent ambulation with platform crutches for at least 500 yards without fatigue within one month. Stating time frames for achievement of goals serves as a check for the therapist. Failure to achieve a certain outcome in a proposed period of time suggests that the therapist needs to reassess the nature of the prob-

lem or to reformulate the treatment program along different lines to produce the desired effect. Goals should be revised to reflect changes in anticipated outcomes owing to other factors that may affect progress or alter the proposed time frames.

Treatment Procedures

MODALITIES FOR PAIN RELIEF

Therapists may choose from a variety of physical agents that provide superficial and deep heat as well as superficial cold to affected joints. The primary purpose of using any of these modalities is to suppress and to control the symptoms of inflammation. Superficial heat is used to produce localized analgesia and to increase local circulation in the area to which it is applied. It penetrates only a few millimeters, however, and does not enter the depth of the synovial cavity. Superficial heat can be delivered through a number of means: moist hot pack, dry heating pads and lamps, paraffin, and hydrotherapy. There is no conclusive evidence that any one method of application achieves a significantly better therapeutic effect, but patients often report a greater tolerance for and comfort derived from moist heat. Paraffin is particularly useful in delivering superficial heat to irregularly shaped joints or to individuals who can not tolerate the weight of a moist hot pack. Although paraffin mixtures can be concocted at home by the patient, instructions for its use should be provided cautiously because of the high flammability of the wax. Although hydrotherapy is one of the most expensive and time-consuming methods for delivering superficial heat, it does have the added advantage that the therapist can combine heat with exercise. It may also orient the patient to the value of a therapeutic swimming program that can be undertaken in conjunction with or following treatment.[50] Deep-heating modalities may affect the viscoelastic properties of collagen and increase the plastic stretch of ligaments. Their use in treating individuals with RA during the acute stage of inflammation is contraindicated in that they may stimulate collagenase activity within the joint, furthering its destruction.[51–54]

Local applications of cold also will produce local analgesia and increase superficial circulation at the site of application following an initial period of vasoconstriction. It is particularly useful around joints that are swollen, a condition that usually worsens with the application of superficial heat modalities. Therapists may use either wet or dry application techniques. Superficial cold is contradicted in patients with Raynaud's phenomenon or cryoglobulinemia, an abnormal protein in the blood that forms gels at low temperatures. Both may be associated with RA.[53,54]

Therapists also may wish to consider using other modalities for pain relief in treating the individual with RA, including relaxation training and transcutaneous electrical nerve stimulation (TENS), although the value of the latter as reported in the literature is controversial.[55,56] Splints may be used to immobilize specific joints and to help reduce pain and swelling by providing local rest. They may have a negative impact on function during the times they are worn and should be used judiciously.[11] Complete bedrest may similarly be beneficial but should be weighed against the deleterious systemic effects on the musculoskeletal and cardiopulmonary systems its overuse can produce.[53,54,57–59]

JOINT MOBILITY

A major factor affecting joint mobility in individuals with RA is the position in which they are kept when not in motion. Patients should be taught proper positioning when resting and should be encouraged to self-perform ROM to the extent possible, especially when any joint has been immobilized. In the acute state, joint motion should be kept to a minimum inasmuch as repetitive motion aggravates inflammation and delays recovery.[60] Although it may take two to five movements through the available range to reach the end point, only one complete motion to the end of range is necessary to maintain that range. In the less acute stages an additional three to five repetitions may be necessary to increase ROM.[54] Static stretch of sufficient intensity and duration, such as standing on a tilt table with appropriate positioning, may be used to increase range in the lower extremities.[61] Therapists may apply neurophysiologic principles of therapeutic exercise to lengthen shortened muscles.[62] Patients should be given the opportunity to rest frequently when performing these exercises. Pain should be respected at all times and should be minimal after exercise. Exercise-induced pain should subside within 1 hour. If the patient reports discomfort in excess of 1 hour, it is a good indicator that either the intensity or the duration of the exercise was too great and should be reduced at the next treatment session. Patients should be encouraged to exercise on their own during those times of the day when they feel best. Therapists should coordinate their treatment sessions with a patient's medication schedule so that treatment will be administered during a period of maximum analgesia. Local pain-relief modalities prior to or following treatment are important considerations and should be used as indicated. Splints and casts may be used to maintain newly gained ROM following treatment.[53,54]

STRENGTHENING

The role of isometric exercise in the treatment of individuals with RA during the acute stage is well accepted because of the low increase in intra-articular pressure and minimal joint movement involved.[54,63,64] It appears that as few as six maximal isometric contractions held for 6 seconds each will effectively increase strength.[54,65] Isometrics should be done throughout the range in order to ensure the ability of the muscle to hold throughout the range during functional activities.[66] There is little evidence, however, that isometric strengthening will carry over to isotonic function, which also requires endurance.[67] The literature has not expressly addressed the disease-specific problems of isotonic strengthening in RA. Can muscle really be strengthened in light of the known selective fiber atrophy that occurs with this disease and that is unrelated to disuse? If a muscle must be fatigued in order to be strengthened, can the individual with systemic fatigue work at the appropriate intensity and duration? Muscle function is specific to its training and use. The most important consideration for the therapist, then, is the kinds of contraction required by the patient's functional activity. Most functional activities require combinations of isotonic as well as isometric contractions. Isotonic and isokinetic exercise should be instituted as soon as the symptoms of inflammation subside.

JOINT STABILITY

Splints may be used to relieve pain, to reduce inflammation, to protect weak joints, to preserve anatomic alignments, and to enhance function. There is no conclusive evidence, however, that they prevent deformities beyond the degree they help to relieve inflammation during acute periods.[11] Therapists should target functional activities that require specific techniques of joint protection.[68] Patients should be encouraged to incorporate joint care into all ADL in order to minimize pain and to conserve energy (see Appendix B).

Splinting of the lower extremity joints may provide relief during periods of acute inflammation and pain.[69] When the patient is ready to resume functional activities and ambulation, foot orthoses may similarly be thought of as having the dual purpose of relieving biomechanical stresses and enhancing function.[19] Finding the proper shoe can be a vexing problem for the individual with RA, particularly as cosmesis evaporates with each additional recommendation for a shoe modification. The cost of special shoes may be formidable for some individuals and may not be reimburseable under many insurance programs. A good shoe will provide support and eliminate unnecessary joint motion in the talocalcaneal joint with a firm and wide heel counter. It should also help to maintain normal bony alignment and accommodate all existing foot deformities within a toe box of adequate dimensions. Pressure should be evenly distributed along the plantar surface of the foot during weight bearing. The latter goal may require the fabrication of orthoses.

ENDURANCE TRAINING

The cardiovascular fitness of individuals with RA may be compromised. Several studies have attested to the ability to improve this impairment through regular cardiovascular conditioning without aggravating joints. Programs similar to those designed for patients with cardiac conditions can be instituted for individuals with RA by adapting the method of conditioning to a non-weight-bearing apparatus such as a bicycle ergometer. Furthermore, patients who have engaged in such a program often report an increase in self-esteem and psychologic outlook.[70-74]

FUNCTIONAL TRAINING

Functional training for the individual with RA proceeds in the same fashion as it would be accomplished for other individuals with similar deficits. Therapists may choose to reduce the functional demands of an activity either temporarily, such as under conditions of acute inflammation, or permanently by incorporating a variety of aids into ADL that substitute for lost ROM and strength. These modifications can include long-handled appliances and devices with built-up handles for easier grasp. There are aids for dressing and grooming as well as personal hygiene.

Upper extremity involvement, particularly of the wrist and hands, may complicate the choice of an ambulation aid by barring any weight bearing on these affected joints. In these instances, platform attachments can be used to transform the forearm into a weight-bearing surface. Rearranging the home or work environment also can improve a person's functional abilities. Raising beds or chairs can reduce the effort needed to stand up. Railings placed around the bed, bath, and along stairways also can help increase an individual's independence.

GAIT TRAINING

Specific gait deviations will be evident throughout the gait cycle. These will include decreased velocity, cadence, and stride length, prolonged period of double support, inadequate heel strike and toe off, and diminished joint excursion through both swing and stance. Gait deviations owing to progressive foot deformities also will be evident (Table 21–5).[75] Therapists should address the underlying joint and muscle impairments that contribute to these deviations prior to initiating gait training.

The degree to which the gait of an individual with RA should, or can, approximate normal gait is one of the most difficult questions in designing a therapeutic program. Some "abnormalities" such as antalgic limping may in fact reduce joint loading. Joint destruction may necessitate the introduction of ambulation aids as cumbersome as platform crutches or rolling walkers with platform attachments. The gait of the individual with RA should be safe, functional, and cosmetically acceptable to the patient rather than an unattainable idealized version of the norm.

EDUCATION

The goals for teaching will be as varied as the individuals who seek treatment. The Arthritis Foundation can supply the clinician or the individual with a variety of educational materials, pamphlets, and self-help courses that will increase cognitive understanding of the disease process and self-management skills. Many local chapters of the foundation hold individual and family support groups to increase psychosocial adaptation as well. The Arthritis Health Professions Association, the professional section of the Arthritis Foundation, can provide the therapist with scientific and clinical enrichment for enhanced practice as well as provide access to a network of professional colleagues who work in rheumatology.

SUMMARY

Rheumatoid arthritis is a chronic, progressive disease that affects women more commonly than men in the typical years of onset between the ages of 20 and 60. Its etiology is currently unknown. The key disease process in RA is inflammation. Rheumatoid arthritis is marked by a bilateral and symmetrical pattern of joint involvement which eventually exhibits characteristic deformities. Long-standing inflammation can weaken the joint capsule and supporting ligamentous structures as well as erode the joint itself. Loss of joint mobility and muscle atrophy and weakness may be present early in the disease. The overall goals of medical management are to control inflammation and to slow the disease's progression. The primary functional limitations of the individual with RA result from musculoskeletal impairments. The physical therapist is well suited to assess and to treat these impairments and to remediate the disability they cause.

QUESTIONS FOR REVIEW

1. What epidemiologic factors are related to RA?
2. What are the major pathologic changes seen in RA?
3. State two hypotheses concerning the pathogenesis of RA.
4. Name at least two laboratory tests used in the diagnosis of RA and state their purposes.
5. Explain three parameters for orienting oneself to radiographs.
6. Describe the changes seen in each joint in the individual with RA.
7. Define ulnar drift, swan neck, boutonniere, hammer toes, cock-up tocs, and hallux valgus.
8. Describe the overall goals of medical management in RA.
9. What are the primary indications for surgery in RA?
10. Describe the key points to be covered in taking a history on the individual with RA.

11. What sort of adaptations of standard test procedures should be made in assessing the individual with RA?
12. What are the general goals of physical therapy in treating individuals with RA?
13. Explain the progression of a strengthening program and the purpose of each kind of exercise.
14. Discuss treatment alternatives for increasing ROM.
15. State at least four principles of joint protection and give a practical application of each.
16. What criteria guide the selection of shoes for the individual with RA?
17. What are the purposes of splints?
18. Describe gait deviations commonly associated with RA.
19. Describe what kinds of assistive devices and ambulation aids are most suited to the individual with RA.

REFERENCES

1. Rodnan, GP and Schumacher, HR (eds): Primer on the Rheumatic Diseases, ed 8. Arthritis Foundation, Atlanta, 1983.
2. Harris, ED, Jr: Rheumatoid arthritis: The clinical spectrum. In Kelley, WN, et al (eds): Textbook of Rheumatology, ed 2. WB Saunders, Philadelphia, 1985.
3. Bennett, PH and Burch, TA: New York symposium on population studies in the rheumatic diseases: New diagnostic criteria. Bull Rheum Dis 17:453, 1967.
4. O'Sullivan, JB and Cathcart, ES: The prevalence of rheumatoid arthritis. Follow-up evaluation of the effect of criteria on rates in Sudbury, Massachusetts. Ann Intern Med 76:573, 1972.
5. Kelsey, JL: Epidemiology of Musculoskeletal Disorders. Oxford University Press, New York, 1982.
6. Fan, PT: Inflammatory mechanisms in rheumatic disease. In Bluestone, R (ed): Rheumatology. Houghton Mifflin, Boston, 1980.
7. Bennett, JC: The etiology of rheumatoid arthritis. In Kelley, WN, et al (eds): Textbook of Rheumatology, ed 2. WB Saunders, Philadelphia, 1985.
8. Fox, RI, et al: Epstein Barr virus in rheumatoid arthritis. Clin Rheum Dis 11:665, 1985.
9. Harris, ED, Jr: Pathogenesis of rheumatoid arthritis. In Kelley, WN, et al (eds): Textbook of Rheumatology, ed 2. WB Saunders, Philadelphia, 1985.
10. Miller, ML and Glass, DN: The major histocompatibility complex antigens in rheumatoid arthritis and juvenile arthritis. Bull Rheum Dis 31:21, 1981.
11. Melvin, JL: Rheumatic Disease: Occupational Therapy and Rehabilitation, ed 2. FA Davis, Philadelphia, 1983.
12. Gibson KR: Rheumatoid arthritis of the shoulder. Phys Ther 66:1920, 1986.
13. Hakstian, RW and Tubiana, R: Ulnar deviation of the fingers. J Bone Joint Surg 49(A):299, 1967.
14. Pahle, JA and Raunio P: The influence of wrist position on finger deviation in the rheumatoid hand. J Bone Joint Surg 51(B):664, 1969.
15. Swezey, RL and Fiegenberg, DS: Inappropriate intrinsic muscle action in the rheumatoid hand. Ann Rheum Dis 30:619, 1971.
16. Smith, EM, et al: Role of the finger flexors in rheumatoid deformities of the metacarpophalangeal joints. Arthritis Rheum 7:467, 1964.
17. English, CB and Nalebuff, EA: Understanding the arthritic hand. Am J Occup Ther 7:352, 1971.
18. Nalebuff, EA: Diagnosis, classification and management of rheumatoid thumb deformities. Bull Hosp Joint Dis 24:119, 1968.
19. Moncur, C and Shields, M: Clinical management of metatarsalgia

in the patient with arthritis. Clin Management Phys Ther 3(4):7, 1983.
20. Kirkup, JR, Vidigal, E, and Jacoby, RK: The hallux and rheumatoid arthritis. Acta Orthop Scand 48:527, 1977.
21. Edstrom, L and Nordemar, R: Differential changes in Type I and Type II muscle fibers in rheumatoid arthritis. Scand J Rheum 3:155, 1974.
22. Nordemar, R, et al: Changes in muscle fiber size and physical performance in patients with rheumatoid arthritis after 7 months' physical training. Scand J Rheum 5:233, 1976.
23. Edstrom, L: Selective atrophy of red muscle fibers in the quadriceps in long-standing knee-joint dysfunction. J Neurol Sci 11:551, 1970.
24. Forrester, DM and Brown, JC: The radiographic assessment of arthritis: The plain film. Clin Rheum Dis 9:291, 1983.
25. Tessler, HH: The eye in rheumatic disease. Bull Rheum Dis 35(5):1, 1985.
26. Deal, CL, et al: The clinical features of elderly-onset rheumatoid arthritis. Arthritis Rheum 28:987, 1985.
27. Meenan, RF, et al: The impact of chronic disease. A sociomedical profile of rheumatoid arthritis. Arthritis Rheum 24:544, 1981.
28. Yellin, E, et al: Work disability in rheumatoid arthritis: Effects of disease, social and work factors. Ann Intern Med 93:551, 1980.
29. Roth, SR: Drug therapy and the rehabilitation process: A necessary interaction. In Ehrlich, GE (ed): Rehabilitation Management of Rheumatic Conditions. Williams & Wilkins, Baltimore, 1986.
30. Hunder, GG and Bunch, TW: Treatment of rheumatoid arthritis. Bull Rheum Dis 32:1, 1982.
31. Klinefelter, HF: Drug treatment of rheumatoid arthritis. Clin Rheum Pract 3:100, 1985.
32. Goldenberg, DL and Cohen, AS: Drugs in the Rheumatic Diseases. Grune & Stratton, Orlando, FL, 1986.
33. Bayley, I and Parry, CBW: Rehabilitation following sugery in arthritis. Clin Rheum Dis 7:497–533, 1981.
34. Swezey, RL: Rehabilitation in arthritis and allied conditions. In Kottke, FJ, Stillwell, GK, and Lehmann, JF (eds): Krusen's Handbook of Physical Medicine and Rehabilitation, ed 3. WB Saunders, Philadelphia, 1982.
35. Miller, PJ: Assessment of joint motion. In Rothstein, JM (ed): Measurement in Physical Therapy. Churchill Livingstone, New York, 1985.
36. Gogia, PP, et al: Reliability and validity of goniometric measurements at the knee. Phys Ther 67:192, 1987.
37. Riddle, DL, Rothstein, JM, and Lamb, RL: Goniometric reliability in a clinical setting: Shoulder measurements. Phys Ther 67:668, 1987.

38. Ekblom, B, et al: Physical performance in patients with rheumatoid arthritis. Scand J Rheum 3:121, 1974.
39. Liang, MH, et al: Comparative measurement efficiency and sensitivity of five health status instruments for arthritis research. Arthritis Rheum 28:542, 1985.
40. Jette, AM: Functional capacity evaluation: An empirical approach. Arch Phys Med Rehabil 61:85, 1980.
41. Jette, AM: Functional Status Index: Reliability of a chronic disease evaluation instrument. Arch Phys Med Rehabil 61:395, 1980.
42. Meenan, RF, Gertman, PM, and Mason, JH: Measuring health status in arthritis: The Arthritis Impact Measurement Scales. Arthritis Rheum 23:146, 1980.
43. King, SH: Psychosocial factors associated with rheumatoid arthritis. J Chron Dis 3:287, 1955.
44. Scotch, NA and Geiger, HJ: The epidemiology of rheumatoid arthritis. J Chron Dis 15:1037, 1962.
45. Moos, RH: Personality factors associated with rheumatoid arthritis: A review. J Chron Dis 17:41, 1964.
46. Meyerowitz, S: The continuing investigation of psychosocial variables in rheumatoid arthritis. In Hill, AGS (ed): Modern Trends in Rheumatology. Appleton-Century-Crofts, New York, 1971.
47. Wolff, BB: Current psychosocial concepts in rheumatoid arthritis. Bull Rheum Dis 22:656, 1972.
48. Hoffman, AL: Psychological factors associated with rheumatoid arthritis. Nurs Res 23:218, 1974.
49. Bradley, LA: Psychological aspects of arthritis. Bull Rheum Dis 35(4):1, 1985.
50. Haralson, K: Therapeutic pool programs. Clin Management Phys Ther 2(5):10, 1985.
51. Feibel, A and Fast, A: Deep heating of joints: A reconsideration. Arch Phys Med Rehabil 57:513, 1976.
52. Harris, ED, Jr and McCroskery, PA: The influence of temperature and fibril stability on degradation of cartilage collagen by rheumatoid synovial collagenase. New Engl J Med 290:1, 1974.
53. Gerber, LH: Rehabilitation of patients with rheumatic diseases. In Kelley, WN, et al (eds): Textbook of Rheumatology, ed 2. WB Saunders, Philadelphia, 1985.
54. Swezey, RL: Arthritis: Rational therapy and rehabilitation. WB Saunders, Philadelphia, 1978.
55. Griffin, JW and McClure, M: Adverse responses to transcutaneous electrical nerve stimulation in a patient with rheumatoid arthritis. Phys Ther 61:354, 1981.
56. Mannheimer, C and Carlsson, C: The analgesic effect of transcutaneous electrical nerve stimulation (TNS) in patients with rheumatoid arthritis. A comparative study of different pulse patterns. Pain 6:329, 1979.
57. Partridge, REH and Duthie, JJR: Controlled trial of the effects of complete immobilization of the joints in rheumatoid arthritis. Ann Rheum Dis 22:91, 1963.
58. Gault, SJ and Spyker, JM: Beneficial effects of immobilization of joints in rheumatoid arthritis and related arthritides. Arthritis Rheum 12:34, 1969.
59. Mills, JA, et al: The value of bedrest in patients with rheumatoid arthritis. New Engl J Med 284:453, 1971.
60. Michelsson, JE and Riska, EB: The effect of temporary exercising of a joint during an immobilization period: An experimental study on rabbits. Clin Orthop Rel Res 144:321, 1979.
61. Guccione, AA and Peteet, JO: Standing wedge for increasing ankle dorsiflexion. Phys Ther 59:766, 1979.
62. Cherry, DB: Review of physical therapy alternatives for reducing muscle contracture. Phys Ther 60:877, 1980.
63. Deusinger, RH: Biomechanics in clinical practice. Phys Ther 64:1860, 1984.
64. Jayson, MI and Dixon, AS: Intra-articular pressure in rheumatoid arthritis of the knee. Pressure changes during joint use. Ann Rheum Dis 29:401, 1970.
65. Muller, EA: Influence of training and of inactivity on muscle strength. Arch Phys Med Rehabil 51:449, 1970.
66. Lindh, M: Increase of muscle strength from isometric exercises at different knee angles. Scand J Rehab Med 11:33, 1979.
67. Grimby, G, et al: Muscle strength and endurance after training with repeated maximal isometric contractions. Scand J Rehabil Med 5:118, 1973.
68. Cordery, JC: Joint protection, a responsibility of the occupational therapist. Am J Occup Ther 19:285, 1965.
69. Nicholas, JJ and Ziegler, G: Cylinder splints: Their use in arthritis of the knee. Arch Phys Med Rehab 58:264, 1977.
70. Harkcom, TM, et al: Therapeutic value of graded aerobic exercise training in rheumatoid arthritis. Arthritis Rheum 28:32, 1985.
71. Ekblom, B, et al: Effect of short-term physical training on patients with rheumatoid arthritis I. Scand J Rheum 4:80, 1975.
72. Ekblom, B, Lovgren, O, Alderin, M, Fridstrom, M, and Satterstrom, G: Effect of short-term physical training on patients with rheumatoid arthritis II. Scand J Rheum 4:87, 1975.
73. Nordemar, R, Ekblom, B, Zachrisson L, and Lundqvist, K: Physical training in rheumatoid arthritis: A controlled long-term study. I. Scand J Rheum 10:17, 1981.
74. Nordemar, R: Physical training in rheumatoid arthritis: A controlled long-term study. II. Functional capacity and general attitudes. Scand J Rheum 10:25, 1981.
75. Dimonte, P, and Light, H: Pathomechanics, gait deviations, and treatment of the rheumatoid foot. Phys Ther 62:1148, 1982.

SUPPLEMENTAL READINGS

Barnard, RJ, et al: Effects of exercise on skeletal muscle. I. Biochemical and histochemical properties. J Appl Physiol 28:762, 1970.
Barnard, RJ, et al: Effect of exercise on skeletal muscle. II. Contractile properties. J Appl Physiol 28:767, 1970.
Gollnick, PD, et al: Enzyme activity and fiber composition in skeletal muscle of untrained and trained men. J Appl Physiol 33:312, 1972.
Jarvinen, M: Immobilization effect on the tensile properties of striated muscle: An experimental study in the rat. Arch Phys Med Rehabil 58:123, 1977.

Lehman, JF, et al: Effect of therapeutic temperatures on tendon extensibility. Arch Phys Med Rehabil 51:481, 1970.
Lehman, JF (ed): Therapeutic Heat and Cold. Williams & Wilkins, Baltimore, 1982.
Salter, RB, et al: The biological effect of continuous passive motion on the healing of full-thickness defects in articular cartilage. JBJS 62A:1232, 1980.
Woo, SL, et al: Connective tissue response to immobility. Arthritis Rheum 18:257, 1975.

GLOSSARY

Analgesic: Medication or modality used to relieve pain.

Ankylosing spondylitis: Chronic bone and joint disease in which the inflammatory process primarily affects the sacroiliac, spinal facet, and costovertebral joints.

Ankylosis: Immobility or fixation of a joint.

Antibody: A protein developed in response to an antigen, belonging to one of the immunoglobulin classes.

Antigen: Any substance that induces the formation of antibodies that will react specifically to that antigen.

Arthralgia: Pain in a joint.

Arthrodesis: Surgical procedure designed to accomplish fusion of a joint.

Arthroplasty: Any surgical reconstruction of a joint; may or may not involve prosthetic replacement.

Avascular necrosis: Necrosis of part of a bone secondary to ischemia; most commonly seen in the femoral or humeral head.

Baker's cyst: Cystic swelling behind the knee in the popliteal fossa.

Bouchard's nodes: Osteophyte formation around the proximal interphalangeal joints typical of degenerative joint disease; similar to Heberden's nodes.

Boutonniere deformity: Finger deformity with flexion of the proximal interphalangeal joint and hyperextension of the distal interphalangeal joint.

Bunion: Hallux valgus with a painful bursitis over the medial aspect of the first metatarsophalangeal joint.

Bursitis: Inflammation of a bursa which can be due to frictional forces, trauma, or rheumatoid diseases.

Calcific tendonitis: Inflammatory involvement of a tendon associated with calcium deposits; commonly affects the supraspinatus and biceps tendons in the shoulder.

Carpal tunnel syndrome: Compression of the median nerve in the carpal flexor space; commonly seen in patients with flexor tenosynovitis.

Cock-up toe (claw toe): Deformity with hyperextension of the metatarsophalangeal joint and flexion of the proximal and distal interphalangeal joints.

Crepitus: A grating, crunching, or popping sensation (or sound) that occurs during joint or tendon motion.

Degenerative joint disease: Noninflammatory slowly progressive disorder of joints caused by deterioration of articular cartilage with secondary bone formation.

deQuervain's disease: Stenosing tenosynovitis of the first dorsal compartment of the wrist, involving the abductor pollicis longus and the extensor pollicis brevis.

Edema: Perceptible accumulation of excess fluid in the tissues.

Effusion: Excess fluid in the joint indicating irritation or inflammation of the synovium; escape of fluid into a body cavity.

Erythema: Redness of the skin.

Exostoses: Ossification of muscular or ligamentous attachments.

Fibrosis: Abnormal formation of fibrous tissue.

Gout: Disease characterized by acute episodes of arthritis with the presence of sodium urate crystals in the synovial fluid and deposits of urate crystals in or about the joints and other tissues.

Hammer toe: Deformity with hyperextension of the metatarsophalangeal joint, flexion of the proximal interphalangeal, and hyperextension of the distal interphalangeal joints.

Hallux valgus: Valgus deformity at the first metatarsophalangeal joint.

Heberden's nodes: Bony enlargement of the distal interphalangeal joint; characteristic of primary degenerative joint disease.

Immune response: The reaction of the body to substances that are foreign or interpreted as foreign. A cell-mediated immune response involves the production of lymphocytes by the thymus (T cells) in response to an antigen. A humoral immune response involves the production of plasma lymphocytes (B cells) in response to an antigen and results in the formation of antibodies.

Lag phenomenon: Difference between active and passive range of motion.

Lyme arthritis: An epidemic, systemic inflammatory disorder characterized by recurrent episodes of polyarthritis, skin lesions, and involvement of the cardiac and nervous systems following a tick bite. Named after the Connecticut town where it was first discovered in 1975.

Mallet finger deformity: Deformity involving only flexion of the distal interphalangeal joint; secondary to disruption of the insertion of the extensor tendon into the base of the distal phalanx.

Metatarsal bar: Ridge on the sole of the shoe to relieve metatarsal pressure and pain.

Metatarsal pad: Pad placed inside the shoe proximal to the metatarsal heads to relieve metatarsal pressure and pain.

Metatarsalgia: Pain over the metatarsal heads on the plantar aspect of the foot.

Morning stiffness: This term describes the prolonged generalized stiffness that is associated with inflammatory arthritis upon awakening. The stiffness is indicative of systemic involvement. The duration of the stiffness correlates with the intensity of the disease. This generalized stiffness is in contrast to the localized stiffness seen in degenerative joint disease, which results from inactivity.

Morton's neuroma: A neuroma of the plantar digital nerve caused by trauma to the nerve as it passes between the metatarsal heads.

Mutilans deformity: Severe bony destruction and resorption in a synovial joint. In the fingers it results in a telescopic shortening (opera-glass hand).

Myalgia: Muscle pain.

Myositis: Inflammatory disease of striated muscle.

Osteoarthritis: The most common term used for degenerative joint disease.

Osteophyte: Bone growth at joint margins.

Osteoporosis: Condition characterized by a loss of bone cells. It can be a primary condition or associated with other diseases, drug therapies (steroids), or disuse; can be improved or minimized with exercise.

Osteotomy: Surgical cutting of a bone.

Pannus: Excessive proliferation of synovial granulation tissue that invades the joint surfaces.

Polymyalgia rheumatica: Relatively common condition most typically found in women over the age of 50. Characterized by marked pain of the shoulder and pelvic girdle muscles, elevated sedimentation rate, and absence of muscle disease.

Protrusio acetabulae: Condition in which the head of the femur pushes the acetabulum into the pelvic cavity.

Pseudogout: Similar to gout clinically but a condition in which the synovitis is due to deposits of pyrophosphate crystals.

Rheumatism: General term for acute and chronic conditions characterized by inflammation, muscle stiffness and soreness, and joint pain.

Rheumatoid arthritis: A systemic disease characterized by a bilateral, symmetrical pattern of joint involvement and chronic inflammation of the synovium.

Rheumatoid factor: An immunoglobulin found in the blood of a high percentage of adults with rheumatoid arthritis; may be described as sero-negative or sero-positive. A latex fixation or sheep cell agglutination test is used to determine if the factor is present.

Rocker sole: Shoe sole curved at the toe to facilitate push off for limited ankle motion.

Sjogren's syndrome: Disease of the lacrimal and parotid glands, resulting in dry eyes and mouth; frequently occurs with rheumatoid arthritis, systemic lupus erythematosus, and systemic sclerosis.

Splayfoot: Transverse spreading of the forefoot.

Subluxation: Incomplete or partial dislocation.

Swan-neck deformity: Finger deformity involving hyperextension of the proximal interphalangeal joint and flexion of the distal interphalangeal joint.

Synovectomy: Surgical procedure to remove the synovial lining of joints or tendon sheaths.

Synovium: Tissue lining synovial joints, tendon sheaths, and bursa. In the joint it produces fluid for lubrication and is the part of the joint that becomes inflamed in inflammatory joint disease.

Synovitis: Inflammation of the synovium.

Systemic: A condition that affects the body as a whole.

Systemic lupus erythematosus: Systemic inflammatory disease characterized by small vessel vasculitis and a diverse clinical picture.

Tinnitus: Subjective ringing or buzzing sensations in the ear; used as an indicator of aspirin toxicity.

Tophi: Deposits of sodium biurate crystals near joints, in the ear, or in bone.

Zig-zag effect: Ulnar drift at the metacarpophalangeal joints associated with radial deviation of the wrist.

APPENDIX A FUNCTIONAL STATUS INDEX

KEY: ASSISTANCE: 1 = independent; 2 = uses devices; 3 = uses human assistance; 4 = uses devices and human assistance; 5 = unable or unsafe to do the activity

PAIN: 1 = no pain; 2 = mild pain; 3 = moderate pain; 4 = severe pain

DIFFICULTY: 1 = no difficulty; 2 = mild difficulty; 3 = moderate difficulty; 4 = severe difficulty

Time frame: On the average during the past 7 days

ACTIVITY	ASSISTANCE (1-5)	PAIN (1-4)	DIFFICULTY (1-4)	COMMENTS
Mobility				
Walking inside	_____	_____	_____	
Climbing up stairs	_____	_____	_____	
Rising from a chair	_____	_____	_____	
Personal care				
Putting on pants	_____	_____	_____	
Buttoning a shirt/blouse	_____	_____	_____	
Washing all parts of the body	_____	_____	_____	
Putting on a shirt/blouse	_____	_____	_____	
Home chores				
Vacuuming a rug	_____	_____	_____	
Reaching into low cupboards	_____	_____	_____	
Doing laundry	_____	_____	_____	
Doing yardwork	_____	_____	_____	
Hand activities				
Writing	_____	_____	_____	
Opening container	_____	_____	_____	
Dialing a phone	_____	_____	_____	
Social activities				
Performing your job	_____	_____	_____	
Driving a car	_____	_____	_____	
Attending meetings/ appointments	_____	_____	_____	
Visiting with friends and relatives	_____	_____	_____	

Used by permission of the author, Alan M. Jette.

APPENDIX B JOINT PROTECTION, REST, AND ENERGY CONSERVATION

JOINT PROTECTION

Why Is Joint Protection Important?

Overuse and abuse of arthritic joints may lead to progressive deterioration of the joint and its surrounding tissues. Positive action is necessary to protect joints, to conserve energy, and to preserve function.

During activity, a normal joint is protected by the muscles around it that absorb the forces on the joint, preventing undue strain on the tendons, ligaments, and cartilage. A diseased joint is mechanically weak and poorly stabilized, which can contribute to the overstretching of the tendons and ligaments and damage to the cartilage. This increased stress can increase the destruction of the joint and cause increased pain.

How Can Joints Be Protected?

The main idea in joint protection is to minimize the strain on joints in daily activities. Joint protection techniques try to reduce the force on the joint, to slow down the joint damage. Good posture and positioning, changing the method of an activity, and pacing all help to protect the joint.

Which Joints Need Protection?

People with a local type of arthritis, like osteoarthritis, need to pay close attention to the joints that are involved with the arthritis. People with a systemic or whole body type of arthritis, like rheumatoid arthritis, need to reduce the stress on all their joints. In addition to the joint protection principles and examples listed below, people with rheumatoid arthritis should look at the section entitled Care of Rheumatoid Arthritis in the Hands.

In planning your joint protection, start by concentrating on the joints that are currently giving you the most trouble. Check off the principles that apply most strongly to you, and list several examples of how you can apply that principle to your problem joints.

JOINT PROTECTION PRINCIPLES

Your Examples

☐ 1. *Respect Pain*
   a. It is important to distinguish between discomfort and pain.   _____
   b. Pain that lasts for more than 1 to 2 hours after an activity indicates that the activity is
      too stressful and needs to be modified.   _____
   c. If there is a sharp increase in pain during activity, stop and rest, then modify the activity.   _____
   d. If there is unusual pain or stiffness the next day, look back at the previous day's activities
      to see if they were too strenuous.   _____

☐ 2. *Avoid Positions of Deformity*
   The foremost position of deformity for most joints is flexion, bending of the joint. Maintaining a bent position increases the possibility of deformity.
   a. Stand erect, with weight evenly divided on both feet.   _____
   b. Lay as flat as possible in bed, do not curl up or prop yourself up on several pillows.   _____
   c. Work with your hands flat.   _____
   d. Avoid tight grip or squeezing.   _____

☐ 3. *Avoid Awkward Positions*
   Use each joint in its most stable and functional position: Extra strain is placed on a joint
   when it is twisted or rotated.   _____
   a. Rise straight up from sitting, rather than leaning to one side for support.   _____
   b. Reposition feet rather than twisting trunk or knees.   _____
   c. Stand on stool to reach overhead.   _____
   d. Reposition yourself closer to object rather than stretch your reach.   _____
   e. Sit to clean or garden, rather than squatting or kneeling down.   _____
   f. Use good posture when you stand, sit, and lie down.   _____

☐ 4. *Use Strongest Joints or Distribute the Force over Several Joints*
   The stress on each individual joint is less if it is divided over several joints. The larger joints
   have greater muscles surrounding them to absorb the stress.   _____
   a. Use two hands whenever possible.   _____
   b. Carry packages in both arms rather than in one.   _____
   c. Carry shoulder purse, or purse handle over forearm rather than in fingers.   _____
   d. Use knapsack to carry packages on back.   _____
   e. Lift objects from underneath, using wrist and elbow, rather than pinch gripping the sides.   _____
   f. Lift objects with your knees bent, your back straight.   _____
   g. Move large objects with body weight behind it, the push coming from the legs.   _____
   h. Push with open palm or forearm rather than fingers.   _____

☐ 5. *Use Adapted Equipment*
   Find equipment that will reduce the stress on the joint or make the job easier.
   The Self-Help Manual for People with Arthritis
   A catalog of adapted equipment is available from the local Arthritis Foundation.   _____
   a. Equipment can be modified by
      1. Building up the handle so it is easier to grasp.   _____
      2. Extending the handle so it is easier to reach.

    b. Equipment available:
       Walking aids
       Self-care aids
       Bathroom safety
       Homemaking equipment
       Job modification equipment

Joints that need protection: _____
_____
_____
Activities to be modified: _____
_____
_____
_____
_____
_____
_____

ADDITIONAL REMINDERS FOR THE PROTECTION OF THE RHEUMATOID HAND

1. Through exercise, maintain wrist extension (ability to pick hand up off table) to ensure power grip.
2. Through exercise, maintain supination (ability to turn palm up) to ensure ability to hold and to carry objects.
3. Avoid positions of deformity
    a. Finger flexion
      1. Avoid making fist or tight grip—use built-up handles.
      2. Work with hand flat—use dust mitts, sponges.
      3. Avoid prolonged holding of objects: pen, book, pan, needle.
      4. Avoid putting any pressure on bent knuckles.
    b. Ulnar deviation (tendency of fingers to slide to little finger side)
      1. Avoid pressure toward little finger side of hand.
      2. Any twisting of hand, open door knobs, jars, etc., should be turned toward thumb.
      3. Grip objects parallel across palm, not diagonal; for example, hold utensil like dagger to cut food, stir with wooden spoon.
4. Avoid stress on small joints of hand.
    a. Use two hands whenever possible.
    b. Substitute larger stronger joints: for example, lift or carry with palms or forearm, not small finger joints; carry bag over elbow or shoulder, not in fingertips.
    c. Avoid activities involving pinching motions.
    d. Avoid twisting and squeezing motions with hands.

GETTING ADDITIONAL REST

Rest is important because it reduces the pain and fatigue that accompany arthritis. In addition, it aids the body's healing process and helps control the inflammation. Rest also may reduce the stress on joints and protect them from further damage. All of these benefits are important in managing arthritis.

Each day you need to make sure you get enough whole body rest, local joint rest, and emotional rest. There are many options: Mark off the options that may be possible for you.

☐ 1. *Plenty of Nightly Rest*
    Get the usual 8 to 10 hours of nightly rest. It is not as important that you sleep for that length of time, but make sure you stretch out with your joints supported, so that your body can rest.

_____

☐ 2. *Daily Rest Periods*
    Ideally, several times a day you can stretch out for 15 to 60 minutes with your joints supported. Again, it is the body rest, not sleep, that is most important.
☐ 3. *Five-Minute "Breathers"*
    Partway through a task, sit back and take it easy for a few minutes. This will allow you to finish the task almost as quickly but more comfortably and with less fatigue.
☐ 4. *Local Joint Rest*
    When a joint hurts, stop and rest it. If your hip or knee hurts while walking, sit down for a few minutes with your legs supported; if your hand hurts while writing, stop and lay it flat for a few minutes. Splints can be used to rest painful wrists or fingers. If your neck hurts, lay down with just a small pillow supporting the curve of your neck. Any painful joint can be given extra rest.
☐ 5. *Take Time for Relaxing Activities*
    Listening to music, reading, playing cards, or other light leisure activities all can be a pleasant change of pace and can be restful and refreshing for you.

There are unlimited options for getting additional rest. It takes creativity to find ways to fit extra rest into your schedule; then it takes self-discipline to make sure you follow through, incorporating the additional rest in your activities. Making the effort to get more rest can pay off in a reduction of pain and fatigue.

Ways to get more rest:
Systemic, whole body rest _____
Local joint rest _____
Emotional rest _____

ENERGY CONSERVATION TO REDUCE FATIGUE

Why Is Energy Conservation Important?

One of the major symptoms of arthritis may be fatigue—getting tired very easily. In the inflammatory types of arthritis, fatigue may be part of the disease process. In all types of arthritis, pain and difficult movement may use up energy, so you tire more easily.

It is important to avoid getting overtired. Fatigue may increase the possibility of a flare-up in inflammatory types of arthritis like rheumatoid arthritis. In all types of arthritis, fatigue may make the pain and stiffness seem worse, and it will make activities more difficult. We hope to reduce this fatigue by conserving energy and using it carefully.

How Can You Reduce Fatigue?

Some people try to conserve energy and reduce fatigue by staying in bed all day. Others stop doing anything that is not absolutely necessary each day. Unfortunately, the activities that are usually cut out are the leisure activities—the enjoyable things people do for themselves or for fun. These are not good ideas.

You can conserve energy and reduce fatigue by modifying and simplifying your activities, pacing yourself, getting additional rest, and using adapted equipment.

Energy Conservation

By conserving your energy, you may be able to do as much or more activity with less pain and fatigue. We are trying to avoid both overactivity and underactivity. Conserving your energy and simplifying your work is *not* being lazy. It is not sensible to overtire yourself. Overwork will not keep your joints mobile, but it may damage your joints further.

It is not so much *what* you do, but *how* you do it that can help control your fatigue. An attempt should be made to modify any activities that leave you overly tired or cause pain that continues for more than 1 to 2 hours.

You will need to identify ways that your own daily activities can be simplified. As you read through the energy conservation strategies, check off strategies that may work for you, and list several of your own examples.

☐ 1. *Plan the Task*   Your Examples
    a. Think the task through.   ————————
    b. Decide when and where the job is best done.   ————————
    c. Plan out the simplest approach to the job.   ————————
    d. Gather all supplies before you begin.   ————————
    e. Arrange step sequence so that it moves in one direction (usually left to right). ————————
    f. Use fewer, more efficient movements to complete task.   ————————

☐ 2. *Eliminate Extra Trips*
    a. Organize your shopping list according to how the store is laid out.   ————————
    b. Stay in the laundry room until your laundry is finished.   ————————
    c. Clean one area at a time.   ————————

☐ 3. *Use Good Posture and Body Mechanics*
    a. Sit to work; you will be more stable and use your strength more efficiently.   ————————
    b. Use large strong muscle groups, rather than straining individual muscles and joints. ————————
    c. Lift with your knees bent, your back straight.   ————————
    d. Carry objects close to your body.   ————————
    e. Push objects, with body weight behind it, rather than pulling or carrying.   ————————
    f. Avoid awkward bending, reaching, and twisting.   ————————

☐ 4. *Don't Fight Gravity*
    a. Slide, rather than lift objects.   ————————
    b. Use wheeled cart.   ————————
    c. Use lightweight equipment.   ————————
    d. Stabilize pitcher on surface and tilt to pour, rather than picking it up.   ————————

☐ 5. *Pace Yourself*
    a. Get plenty of nightly rest.   ————————
    b. Plan several rest periods during the day.   ————————
    c. Rest before you get tired.   ————————
    d. Avoid a rush.   ————————
    e. Work at a steady rate with rest periods.   ————————
    f. Develop a rhythm to your movements.   ————————

☐ 6. *Use Energy-Saving Devices*
    a. Convenience foods.   ————————
    b. Adapted equipment.   ————————

Strategies to be tried: ————————————————
————————————————————————————
————————————————————————————
————————————————————————————
————————————————————————————

Activities to be modified: ————————————————
————————————————————————————
————————————————————————————
————————————————————————————
————————————————————————————

————————

Excerpted from Brady, TJ: *Home Management of Arthritis: Developing Your Own Plan.* Arthritis Foundation, Minnesota Chapter, Minneapolis, 1983. Used by permission of the author.

Chapter 22

MULTIPLE SCLEROSIS

SUSAN B. O'SULLIVAN

OBJECTIVES

1. Define the pathology, epidemiology, etiology, course, and clinical symptoms of multiple sclerosis.

2. Describe the diagnostic and assessment procedures commonly used for patients of multiple sclerosis.

3. Describe the medical management of the patient with multiple sclerosis.

4. Describe the rehabilitative management of the patient with multiple sclerosis.

5. Value the role and contribution of the physical therapist in the long-term management of patients with multiple sclerosis.

INTRODUCTION

Multiple sclerosis (MS) is a demyelinating disease of the central nervous system affecting mostly young adults and often referred to as the "great crippler of young adults." It was described as early as 1822 in the diaries of an English nobleman and further depicted in an anatomy book in 1858 by a British medical illustrator. Dr. Jean Cruveibier, a French physician, first used the term *islands of sclerosis* to describe areas of hardened tissue discovered upon autopsy. However, it was Dr. Jean Charcot in 1868 who defined the disease by its characteristic clinical and pathologic findings. His findings included paralysis and the cardinal symptoms of intention tremor, scanning speech, and nystagmus, later termed **Charcot's triad.** Using autopsy studies he identified areas of hardened plaques and termed the disease "sclerosis in plaques."[1] Since this time, it has been the subject of intense study and investigation.

The onset of symptoms typically occurs between the ages of 10 and 40 years. The disease is rare in children, as is the onset of symptoms in adults over the age of 50 years. The sexes are affected about equally. Clinically MS is characterized by multiple signs and symptoms and by fluctuating periods of **remissions** and **exacerbations.** The symptoms are highly variable, and the course of the disease is unpredictable. In the early stages a relatively complete remission of initial symptoms may occur; however, as the disease progresses the remissions become less complete and neurologic dysfunction increases. Among the most common clinical features of MS are spasticity, decreased motor function, ataxia, intention tremor, impaired sensation, visual defects, speech problems, and bowel and bladder dysfunctions.[2-4]

PATHOLOGY

The disease is characterized by demyelinating lesions known as plaques that are scattered throughout the central nervous system (CNS) white matter. Though widely disseminated, there are certain areas of predilection, such as the periventricular areas of the cerebrum, cerebellar peduncles, brainstem, and dorsal spinal cord. Lesions tend to be symmetrical and have a perivenous distribution, containing lymphocytes, macrophages, and plasma cells. In the initial stages inflammation is accompanied by a reduction in oligodendroglia (the myelin-producing cells). The myelin membrane breaks down with relative sparing of the axons themselves. Myelin serves as an insulator, speeding up the conduction along nerve fibers from one node of Ranvier to another (termed *saltatory conduction*). It also conserves energy for the axon, inasmuch as depolarization occurs only at the nodes.[5] **Demyelinization** impairs neural transmission and causes nerves to fatigue rapidly. Marked infiltration of mononuclear cells consisting largely of T cells and macrophages has been found in the plaques, suggesting an immunologically mediated pathogenesis.[6,7] Infiltrates surround the acute lesion and further interfere with the conductivity of the nerve fiber. Conceivably, this infiltration (which gradually subsides) may, in part, account for the multiple remissions and exacerbations characteristic of this disease. The myelin sheath is ultimately replaced by fibrous scarring produced by glial cells (**gliosis**). Inasmuch as the sclerotic plaques may occur anywhere in the brain or spinal cord, symptoms will vary considerably among individual patients.

EPIDEMIOLOGY

Epidemiologic studies have revealed a worldwide distribution of MS with areas of high, medium, and low frequency. High-frequency areas include northern United States, northern Europe, southern Canada, New Zealand, and southern Australia, with the incidence reported at rates of 30 to 80 (or more) per 100,000 population. Areas of medium frequency (southern United States and Europe, and the rest of Australia) have a reported incidence of 10 to 15 per 100,000. Low-frequency areas (Asia and Africa) have reported rates of under 5 per 100,000. Multiple sclerosis affects predominately white populations; blacks demonstrate approximately half the risk of acquiring the disease. Migration studies indicate that the geographic risk of an individual's birthplace is retained if migration occurs after the age of 15. Individuals migrating before this age assume the risk of their new location. Two epidemics of MS have been reported in the literature; one in the Faroe Islands off the coast of Norway and one in Iceland following occupation by soldiers during World War II. These epidemiologic studies have lent support to the theory that MS is an acquired and transmittable disease.[8,9]

ETIOLOGY

The cause of MS is unknown. Major causative theories currently focus on an infectious origin, on an immune-mediated pathogenesis, or a combination of the two. Numerous epidemiologic studies provide the most convincing evidence of MS as an acquired and transmittable disease. Geographic distributions, migrant data, and epidemic studies all suggest an infectious origin. Pathologic studies of inflammatory reactions in the CNS and serologic studies of antiviral antibodies in MS serum also lend support to this theory. The identification of increased immunoglobulin (IgG) and oligoclonal bands in the cerebrospinal fluid (CSF) of 65 to 95 percent of MS patients also provides convincing evidence of a persistent viral infection or a CNS autoantigen. The causative agent most frequently suggested is a slow virus, though no specific agent has been identified. Numerous viruses have been linked to MS (canine distemper, rabies, measles, herpes-simplex). It has been proposed that the virus may exist in a genomic or proviral form not currently recognizable by standard laboratory techniques. The virus may be acquired during childhood, lie dormant, and become activated many years later. It is also possible that multiple agents may initiate the disease. Genetic predisposition and familial tendency also have been identified. Susceptibility to MS appears dependent upon the genetically linked HLS antigen system.[7,10,11]

Immunopathogenesis of MS also has been a long-proposed theory. Evidence of active immune responses in immunoglobulin production in the CNS serum and in the CSF (IgG and oligoclonal bands) is abundant. Activated T cells have been found in the blood and CSF of MS patients in both clinically active and inactive stages of the disease. The exact role of these immune-control mechanisms, however, remains unclear. They have been suggested as the direct cause of the demyelination or as the result of the disease process itself. Thus the viral infection may be the initial causative factor in producing demyelination. Inflammatory reactions and the production of antibodies then occur as the body's reaction to the primary infection. Alternately, the infection may institute an autoimmune reaction against the CNS itself, thereby initiating the demyelination process.[6,7,10,11]

DIAGNOSTIC CRITERIA

The diagnosis of MS is based upon clinical findings, historical evidence, and supportive laboratory tests. Clinical criteria include multiple signs of neurologic dysfunction occurring on more than one occasion and at more than one site that can not be attributed to other causes.[10] Thus the patient may present with blurred vision and tingling in the arms occurring sporadically over several months. A detailed neurologic exam is performed to confirm the symptoms and to rule out other causes. A reliable patient history helps pinpoint the episodic bouts. To confirm a definite diagnosis of MS, attacks must involve different areas of the CNS, last longer than 24 hours, and be separated by a period of at least 1 month.[13] Laboratory studies are commonly used to assist in the diagnosis.[7,10,13–15] These include those described below.

Lumbar Puncture and Cerebrospinal Fluid Analysis

Typical changes seen in MS patients include a mild increase in protein and/or lymphocytes, an elevation in the level of IgG above normal values of 11 in CSF (seen in 70 percent of patients), and oligoclonal banding (seen in 90 percent of patients). These immunoglobin abnormalities are not unique to MS, however, and can be seen in other viral and occasionally bacterial disorders. Elevated levels of myelin basic protein or myelin proteolytic fragments indicate active demyelination and are useful diagnostic indicators during acute episodes.

Computerized Axial Tomography (CAT Scan)

Computerized axial tomography is helpful in detecting multiple lesions and during acute exacerbations. Contrast enhancement techniques are necessary to enhance detection of lesions. Nuclear-magnetic-resonance imaging (NMR) also has been used in diagnosing MS lesions and appears more sensitive than CAT scans in detecting small plaques.

Electrophysiologic Testing

The presence of lesions also can be confirmed by visual-, auditory-, and somatosensory-evoked potentials. The rate of nerve impulse transmission is measured and compared with normal rates. Slowed conduction time is evidence of demyelination (see chapter 10).

Blood

Changes in blood lymphocytes in the distribution of T and B cells have been described in MS patients, particularly during acute exacerbations. Reports of increased activated T cells in peripheral blood delineate abnormal immune activation occurring outside the CNS.[6] Changes in lymphocyte subpopulations have also been noted.[10,13-15]

CLINICAL MANIFESTATIONS OF MULTIPLE SCLEROSIS

Course

Multiple sclerosis is an unpredictable disease with sporadic occurrence of symptoms over a period of many years. At one end of the continuum the course can be benign with mild symptoms and very little if any disability, whereas at the other end of the continuum it can be rapidly progressing, leading to severe disability or death within a few years. Four main types of clinical courses have been recognized.[14,16] These are briefly described below.

1. Benign. The benign course affects approximately 20 percent of patients and is characterized by one or two initial attacks with complete or nearly complete remission. These individuals usually experience little or no functional disability and may remain relatively symptom free.

2. Exacerbating-remitting. Approximately 20 to 30 percent of patients experience this type of course, which is characterized by a sudden onset of symptoms with par-

tial or complete remissions. Patients remain relatively stable for long periods.

3. Remitting-progressive. Affecting 40 percent of patients, this course is similar to the exacerbating/remitting course, but symptoms do not remit as completely, and lasting physical disability develops.

4. Progressive. The progressive course, which affects 10 to 20 percent of patients, progresses without remitting and leads to severe disability. The rate can be very rapid (acute, fulminating), resulting in early death, or slow (gradual, insidious) resulting in progressive loss of function over a number of years.

Because patients may alter their clinical presentation (e.g., moving from one clinical course to another), clinicians must be alert to changes in symptoms, the rate of progression, and the frequency of relapses. This will allow the clinician to assess the effects of treatment better inasmuch as it becomes extremely difficult to differentiate them from spontaneous neurologic recovery.[4,10,14,16]

Clinical Signs and Symptoms

Symptoms vary considerably in character, intensity, and duration. The onset of symptoms can develop rapidly over a course of minutes or hours; less frequently the onset may be insidious, occurring over a period of weeks or months. Symptoms will depend on the location of lesions, and early symptoms often demonstrate involvement of the sensory, pyramidal, cerebellar, and visual pathways or disruption of cranial nerves and their linkage to the brainstem.

SENSORY DISTURBANCES

Sensory symptoms are common and often unpredictable in MS patients. Tingling paresthesias or numbness may be present in any area of the body. **Lhermitte's sign** (an electric shocklike sensation running down the spinal cord and lower extremities produced by flexing the neck) is frequently present and is indicative of posterior column damage in the spinal cord. Disturbances in position sense are also frequent, as are lower extremity impairments of vibratory sense. Complete loss of any single sensation is rare.

Approximately 10 to 20 percent of these patients experience pain. The causes are variable. Burning pain along the distribution of a nerve (pseudoradicular pain) may result from MS lesions in spinothalmic tracts or in sensory roots. Trigeminal **neuralgia** is characterized by short attacks of severe pain and results from demyelination of the sensory tracts of the trigeminal nerve. Pain also may result from painful reflex spasms, spasticity, or abnormal positioning of limbs. Increased frequency of headaches also has been reported in some MS patients.[14,17,18]

WEAKNESS

Signs of muscle weakness secondary to damage of the motor cortex or its pyramidal tracts may vary from mild paresis to total paralysis of the involved extremities.

Involvement usually occurs first or is most pronounced in the lower extremities, though the upper extremities may be involved. Weakness secondary to disuse atrophy and prolonged inactivity also may occur.[2,14]

SPASTICITY

Spasticity occurs from demyelinating lesions in the pyramidal tracts, resulting in hyperactivity of spinal gamma motoneurons. It is characterized by increased muscle tone and hyperactive stretch reflexes and is extremely common in MS patients, occurring in 90 percent of all cases. Spasticity may range from mild to severe in intensity, depending upon the progression of the disease. Typical signs include ankle clonus, exaggerated stretch reflexes, spontaneous spasms, reflex irradiation, and a positive Babinski sign. Because the stretch reflexes are velocity dependent, muscle tone is greatly increased with rapid movements. Primitive reflex mechanisms also predominate with the loss of cortical control. Thus static postural reflexes such as the asymmetrical and symmetrical tonic neck reflexes (ATNR, STNR) or the tonic labyrinthine reflex (TLR) may be present and also interfere with voluntary movement.[5,18–20]

FATIGUE

Fatigue patterns in the patient with MS are among the most common complaints and one of the few predictable clinical symptoms. The patient usually wakes relatively refreshed but by early afternoon gradually experiences increasing fatigue and exhaustion. An increase in neurologic symptoms and physical dysfunction is usually noted at this time. Some recovery of energy may occur by early evening. Fatigue may be brought on more frequently and more rapidly by excessive physical activity, muscle weakness and strain, underlying depression, or elevated body temperature.[3,4,14]

CEREBELLAR DISTURBANCES

Demyelinating lesions in the cerebellum and cerebellar tracts are common in MS. Intention tremors or action tremors occur when voluntary movement is attempted and result from the inability of the cerebellum to dampen motor movements. Intention tremors vary in severity from slight quivering to massive involuntary oscillatory movements during purposeful activity. Severe tremors will impose significant limitations in performance of functional activities, particularly in such areas as personal hygiene, eating, and dressing activities.

Dysmetria, dysdiadochokinesia, and ataxia are also classic findings of cerebellar disease. Dysmetria is an inability to fix the range of movement. Rapid movements are typically made with more force than necessary. Dysdiadochokinesia is the inability to perform rapidly alternating movements. Ataxia refers to incoordinated movement. Progressive ataxia of the trunk and lower limbs is often apparent. During gait activities ataxia is demonstrated by a staggering, wide-based pattern with poor foot placement and slow, uncoordinated progression of reciprocal lower extremity movement. Ataxia

during speech production results in dysarthria or slurred speech.[5,14]

Vertigo can occur in varying degrees of intensity. Patients may experience nausea, vomiting, and general feelings of unsteadiness.[21]

VISUAL DISTURBANCES

Visual symptoms are common with MS, affecting approximately 80 percent of the patients. Involvement of the optic and occulomotor nerves can produce loss of vision (scotoma and/or blindness), field defects, **diplopia,** or blurred vision. Optic neuritis can produce pain upon movement of the eyes. Nystagmus is tremor of the eyeballs. The rapid, involuntary oscillations are usually bilateral and frequently more apparent when the eyes attempt to focus in a lateral or vertical direction. Visual disturbances frequently remit and are seldom the primary cause of disability, although reading and visual tracking activities are difficult for many patients.[5,18,21]

COMMUNICATION DISTURBANCES

Speech and swallowing defects secondary to demyelinating lesions of the cranial nerves are also common in MS. Dysarthria is characterized by slurring and incoordination during phonation with scanning of syllables and low speech volume. Dysphagia is characterized by swallowing difficulties and may result in impaired feeding, choking, or aspiration. Poor coordination of breath control; poor posture; and spasticity, weakness, ataxia, or fatigue of oral muscles can all contribute to these difficulties.[22]

BLADDER AND BOWEL DISTURBANCES

Urinary bladder disturbances are a frequent complaint in MS, affecting 54 to 78 percent of patients. Common symptoms include urinary frequency, urgency, incontinence, retention, or hesitancy and may result from suprasacral neurologic lesions or from mechanical outlet obstruction. Neurogenic disorders also may impair bowel function, resulting in incontinence or constipation, and sexual function, producing impotence or retrograde ejaculation. These disturbances have tremendous functional and social implications for the patient and rehabilitation specialist.[18,23–27]

COGNITIVE AND BEHAVIORAL DISTURBANCES

Significant mental deterioration is associated with extensive cerebral lesions in acute fulminating cases or in the later stages of progressive disease and is relatively rare. In these patients, memory, conceptual thinking, and abstract reasoning may be adversely affected. Emotional or psychotic derangements also may occur.[18]

Behavioral alterations such as depression are common. Anxiety, denial, anger, aggression, or dependency can occur in response to the stress of a chronic and unpredictable disease.

Patients with MS face issues related to the ambiguity

of their health status, the presence of borderline or non-visible symptoms, the uncertainty of future status, and the loss of effective functioning during young adulthood.[28] Moreover, many of the symptoms of MS (tremor, scanning speech, incontinence) are humiliating and embarrassing.[29]

Emotional instability or lability is also common. This involuntary response is most often characterized by **euphoria** (an exaggerated feeling of well-being). Excessive laughing or crying also can occur. This instability results from bilateral demyelinating lesions in the supranuclear pathways to the brainstem.[14,18]

Secondary Problems and Complications

Numerous secondary problems and complications can result from prolonged inactivity, bedrest, or static positioning in a wheelchair. These are summarized in Figure 22–1. Although the effects are not directly attributable to the disease itself, they may become primary limiting factors in the rehabilitation of these patients.[18,30–32]

PSYCHOSOCIAL

Prolonged inactivity typically intensifies feelings of anxiety or depression and can lead to despondency or detachment. These feelings can then further compound the problems of inactivity by decreasing the patient's desire to move or to interact with the environment. Withdrawn and detached individuals also may demonstrate deficits in intellectual functioning.

NEUROMUSCULAR

A decrease in the overall level of sensory input is concomitant with prolonged inactivity. Decreased motor activity results in *neuromuscular disassociation,* which is characterized by impaired processes of motor control and movement coordination. The autonomic nervous system also may demonstrate instability, rendering the individual unable to maintain a stable level of performance (homeostasis). Autonomic processes (sympathetic and parasympathetic functions) and somatic control (via interaction with the reticular activating system) may be hypoactive or hyperactive.

MUSCULOSKELETAL

Significant functional limitations develop as MS symptomatology increases. The majority of patients experience a restriction in their mobility. Inactivity, poor positioning, and neglected spasticity will contribute to progressive deformity. Typically, hip and knee flexion contractures and foot deformities develop if the patient

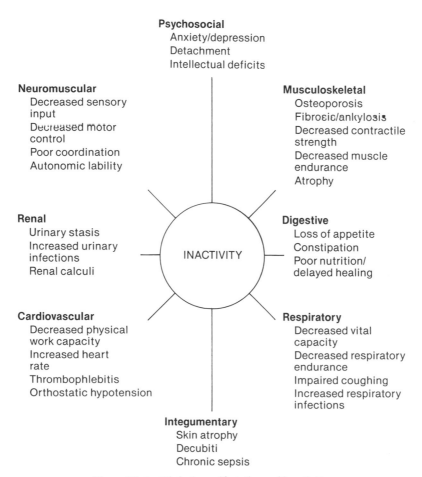

Figure 22–1. Clinical manifestations of inactivity.

is confined to bed or wheelchair and the limbs not regularly moved through their normal ranges. Progressive calcium loss in bones (osteoporosis) can lead to spontaneous fractures, hypercalciuria, and deposition of calcium in soft tissues (heterotopic ossification). Joints may become fibrotic or ankylosed. The loss of contractile strength and endurance of muscles is often dramatic within a very short period, and muscle atrophy becomes visually apparent.

RENAL

Loss of calcium from bones can lead to the formation of renal calculi (kidney stones). Urinary stasis, urinary infection, and urinary obstruction are serious problems for the inactive patient.

DIGESTIVE

Loss of appetite accompanied by a general decrease in gastrointestinal activity can lead to poor nutritional intake, delayed healing, and persistent problems with constipation.

CARDIOVASCULAR

Cardiovascular deconditioning results in a decrease in the overall physical work capacity, increased heart rate response to effort, orthostatic hypotension, decreased circulating blood volume, and increased likelihood of thrombophlebitis.

RESPIRATORY

Respiratory changes include a decrease in lung volume and vital capacity, a decrease in respiratory endurance, decreased efficiency of the coughing mechanism, and increased likelihood of respiratory infections. These changes may be life-threatening for the bedridden patient.

INTEGUMENTARY

With decreasing activity, skin atrophy and decubitus ulcers become a major concern. Changes in skin turgor, static posturing, and prolonged pressure over bony prominences increase the likelihood of skin breakdown. Complicating these problems are sensory impairments, which decrease the patient's awareness of limb position and pressure sensation, contractures, spasticity, and/or involuntary movements which may cause friction effects between the patient's skin and supporting surfaces.

Exacerbating Factors

Several factors have been identified with the exacerbation of symptoms in MS. The avoidance of these aggravating factors is important in ensuring the patient's optimal function.[4,14,23]

HEAT

Individuals with MS typically demonstrate an adverse reaction to heat. External heat, either in the form of climatic conditions (summer heat) or therapeutic modalities (hot baths, hot packs), may cause an exacerbation of clinical symptoms and rapidly induce fatigue. Internal heat (fever, increased body temperature following prolonged exercise) may produce similar effects.

STRESS

Emotional stress has frequently been implicated by patients in the worsening of their symptoms, though controlled studies are lacking. Stress events (competition, job-related anxiety, divorce, death) are similar to those implicated in the pathogenesis of other chronic illnesses such as cardiovascular disease or ulcers.

TRAUMA

Patients often identify trauma with the onset of MS or an exacerbation of symptoms. Unrelated physical injury or related diagnostic procedures (lumbar puncture) frequently have been reported as precipitating factors. The first few months following pregnancy and birth also have been found to increase the risk of exacerbation, though the long-term outcome is generally considered nondeleterious. The related psychologic stresses associated with these events are an important consideration.

Prognostic Indicators

The mean survival rate is 22 to 25 years, with the cause of death typically resulting from either respiratory or urinary infection.[33] Several prognostic indicators have been identified in predicting the later course of the disease and are listed below. These remain general guidelines and do not necessarily fit the outcome of individual patients.

1. Onset with only one symptom. This is one of the strongest indicators of a favorable prognosis.
2. An acute onset rather than a slow, insidious onset. A progressive course is generally considered ominous, whereas benign and exacerbating–remitting courses are more favorable.
3. Onset before the age of 35. Onset after 35 is more frequently associated with a rapid progressive course and increased incidence of death.
4. Neurologic status at 5 years. Significant pyramidal and cerebellar signs and multiple system involvement at 5 years is associated with a poorer prognosis and more severe impairment.[16,30]

MEDICAL MANAGEMENT

Medical management of the patient with MS is directed at the overall disease process itself and at the specific symptoms that emerge. There is currently no treatment that can prevent or cure MS. Acute attacks can be partially influenced by pharmacologic treatments aimed at suppressing immunologic reactions. Adreno-corticotrophin hormone or steroids (prednisone) can shorten the duration of exacerbations, though numerous side effects limit their use to short-term or intermittent regimens. Other **immunosuppressive agents** (axathio-prine, cylophosphamide, lomustine) and interferon are currently being used in experimental situations. Plas-mapheresis and hyperbaric oxygen treatment are also under investigation.[7,10,14,34]

Symptomatic treatment includes careful monitoring of function, and prompt treatment of infections and other problems with pharmacologic and/or surgical manage-ment. Medications commonly used in the symptomatic management of MS are presented in Table 22–1. A vari-ety of drugs have been used to treat a number of symp-toms, including incoordination, pain, sensory distur-bances, and mood disturbances, sometimes with limited success. The clinician should have a thorough under-standing of the effects, side effects, and interactions of each of the drugs a patient is taking.

Urinary problems require a complete urodynamic assessment to identify the specific cause of the problem and to arrive at the appropriate course for treatment. Treatment for a spastic (uninhibited neurogenic bladder) typically involves pharmacologic management with anti-cholinergic drugs (oxybutynin, propantheline, or atro-pine), voiding maneuvers (Crede voiding or Valsalva), and may include intermittent catheterization. Perma-nent catheterization (Foley) or surgical urinary diversion (suprapubic catheter) may be necessary with elevated residual urines or persistent infections. The flaccid neu-rogenic bladder is usually managed with intermittent self-catheterization. If this is not possible, permanent catheterization is instituted.[25–27] A bowel program typi-cally consists of a high-fiber diet, increased water intake, manipulation of the patient's environment, and sup-positories, while avoiding long-term use of laxatives and enemas.[35]

Medical management of spasticity includes pharma-cologic, surgical, and selective regional management. Commonly used drugs are baclofen (Lioresal), dantro-lene sodium (Dantrium), clonazepam (Clonopin), and diazepam (Valium). Numerous side effects, including drowsiness, fatigue, weakness, and dizziness, accompany the use of these drugs and usually preclude long-term use. Functional implications also must be considered in the prescription of these drugs. Many patients are able to use their spasticity to achieve stability and functional control (e.g., standing) or as an assist to lower extremity circu-lation. Without this hypertonus, muscle weakness may predominate, rendering function impossible. Thus lack of specificity is the greatest problem in the pharmaco-logic approach. **Nerve blocks** injected either epidurally or at motor end points have been used successfully to block spasticity. Chemical or surgical **rhizotomy** also can alle-viate spasticity or spontaneous spasms in chronic, non-ambulatory patients. Using neurophysiologic principles, motor function can be modified using functional electri-cal stimulation and is commonly used in ambulatory patients to block ankle clonus via stimulation of the per-oneal nerve. An accurate assessment of an intact func-tional reflex arc is crucial to the success of this technique. Spinal cord stimulation (dorsal column stimulator) has been used to successfully modify bladder function and spasticity in selected patients.[36] Surgical procedures (ten-otomies, nerve sectioning) may be indicated in cases of severe spasticity and contracture.[37]

Table 22–1 MEDICATIONS USED IN SYMPTOMATIC THERAPY OF MULTIPLE SCLEROSIS

Symptom	Drug	Usual Dosage Range	Expected Benefit	Potential Adverse Effects
Spasticity	Baclofen	10 mg–20 mg tid or qid	Decreased hypertonus; improved movement	Weakness; liver dysfunction; sedation
	Clonopin	0.5 mg tid		
	Valium	5 mg–10 mg tid or qid		
	Dantrium	25 mg–50 mg tid or qid		
Cerebellar incoordination	INH	300 mg/day	Decreased tremor; improved truncal stability	Liver dysfunction (INH); cardiac effects (Inderal)
	Inderal	10 mg–20 mg tid or qid		
	Clonopin	0.5 mg–1 mg tid		
Urinary urgency	Ditropan	5 mg bid or tid	Improved bladder control; decreased urgency	Increased hesitancy of bladder; constipation
	Pro-Banthine	15 mg bid or tid		
Painful sensory disturbance	Tegretol	200 mg bid or tid	Decreased painful dysesthesia	Bone marrow suppression
Depression	Tricyclic antidepressants (Aventyl, Elavil)	25 mg bid or tid	Decreased insomnia; improved mood	Dry mouth; constipation; urinary hesitancy; weight gain

From Maloney, F, Burks, J, and Ringel, S: Interdisciplinary Rehabilitation of Multiple Sclerosis and Neuromuscular Disorders. JB Lippincott, Philadelphia, 1985, with permission.

PHYSICAL THERAPY MANAGEMENT

Long-range planning is critical in the effective management of MS. A coordinated interdisciplinary team approach is needed to address the many diverse problems and unpredictable course of this chronic neurologic disability. Professionals need to maintain a positive, caring attitude and to use a problem-solving approach for the management of complex and often multifaceted problems. Effective management also requires an organized continuum of care from hospital to home and community settings.[38,39]

The long-term goals of a physical therapy program may include the following.

1. Improve the status of presenting neurologic symptoms of MS.

2. Improve or maintain optimal level of physical and psychologic function.

3. Prevent or retard the development of secondary complications.

Assessment

Because many areas of the CNS may be affected, it is imperative that a careful assessment be performed to determine the extent of neurologic and functional involvement. Subsequent reassessment at specified intervals should attempt to distinguish a change in status as well as the effects of treatment. It may not always be possible to differentiate the treatment results from a remission of symptoms. Considering the variability of symptoms of any individual patient, it is often beneficial to perform assessment procedures over a period of several days in order to obtain a representative sample of baseline functioning. Fatigue patterns and exacerbating factors should be taken into account when planning testing sessions.

Historical data can be gained from a review of the patient's chart and from a discussion with the patient and the family. There are a number of assessment procedures that are appropriate to a physical examination:

1. Range of motion, assessment of joint limitation and postural deformity.

2. Sensation, including pain.

3. Muscle tone, including factors that influence tonal quality such as positioning, stress, and so forth.

4. Muscle strength and motor control: If spasticity is severe, traditional manual muscle testing procedures will be inappropriate, and strength should be assessed in terms of functional movement patterns and availability of selective movements.

5. Coordination and balance.

6. Gait.

7. Fatigue patterns.

8. Skin integrity and condition.

9. Respiratory patterns.

10. Cognitive abilities.

11. Visual defects.

12. Functional status.

In 1955, Kurtzke developed a scale for assessing disability in MS (the **Disability Status Scale** or **DSS**) which was modified in 1965 and again in 1982, resulting in an expanded version (EDSS). This scale has been widely used to measure maximum function as limited by neurologic deficits. Patients are first graded on the basis of presenting symptoms in eight different functional systems (FS). They are then classified into one of 20 steps in the EDSS based upon the grades obtained in the FS assessment. For example, patients classified in EDSS step 2.5 (minimal disability) may have grade 2 involvement in two FS categories (Table 22–2).[40,41] Other currently popular scales to measure severity of disability include the Pulses Profile and the Barthel Index.[42] The use of standardized tests allows for comparison between similar groups of patients and within a group, monitoring the progression of the disease and the effects of treatment over time. Inasmuch as these measures were developed as quantitative and not qualitative measures, their use must be augmented by other more qualitative assessments of function.

A sample physical therapy assessment form is provided in Appendix A.

Treatment

Although the individual needs of patients will vary considerably, the following generic short-term goals are often appropriate for physical therapy management of multiple sclerosis patients:

1. Increase or maintain range of motion in all joints.

2. Improve sensory feedback.

3. Educate on skin care for the patient with sensory loss.

4. Diminish abnormal spastic patterns and tonal influences on movement.

5. Improve muscle strength.

6. Improve motor control.

7. Improve coordination.

8. Improve gait pattern.

9. Improve function in activities of daily living.

    a. Teach problem-solving skills.

    b. Teach compensatory training.

    c. Teach energy conservation.

    d. Provide appropriate mobility aids and adaptive equipment.

10. Assist with psychologic adjustment of patient and family.

    a. Promote understanding of disease, its symptoms and management.

    b. Emphasize realistic expectations while maintaining hope.

    c. Focus on remaining abilities.

    d. Inform patient about support groups and the MS society.

Each of these goals will not be appropriate for every patient or at every phase of the disease process. Goal setting and treatment selection should be carefully planned around the patient's individual abilities and needs. Full involvement of the patient in all stages of planning will

TABLE 22–2 AN EXPANDED DISABILITY STATUS SCALE (EDSS) FOR EVALUATING PATIENTS WITH MULTIPLE SCLEROSIS

FUNCTIONAL SYSTEMS

Pyramidal Functions
0. Normal
1. Abnormal signs without disability
2. Minimal disability
3. Mild or moderate paraparesis or hemiparesis; severe monoparesis
4. Marked paraparesis or hemiparesis; moderate quadriparesis; or monoplegia
5. Paraplegia, hemiplegia, or marked quadriparesis
6. Quadriplegia
V. Unknown

Cerebellar Functions
0. Normal
1. Abnormal signs without disability
2. Mild ataxia
3. Moderate truncal or limb ataxia
4. Severe ataxia, all limbs
5. Unable to perform coordinated movements due to ataxia
V. Unknown
X. Is used throughout after each number when weakness (grade 3 or more on pyramidal) interferes with testing

Brain Stem Functions
0. Normal
1. Signs only
2. Moderate nystagmus or other mild disability
3. Severe nystagmus, marked extraocular weakness, or moderate disability of other cranial nerves
4. Marked dysarthria or other marked disability
5. Inability to swallow or speak
V. Unknown

Sensory Functions (revised 1982)
0. Normal
1. Vibration or figure-writing decrease only, in one or two limbs
2. Mild decrease in touch or pain or position sense, and/or moderate decrease in vibration in one or two limbs; or vibratory (c/s figure writing) decrease alone in three or four limbs
3. Moderate decrease in touch or pain or position sense, and/or essentially lost vibration in one or two limbs; or mild decrease in touch or pain and/or moderate decrease in all proprioceptive tests in three or four limbs
4. Marked decrease in touch or pain or loss of proprioception, alone or combined, in one or two limbs; or moderate decrease in touch or pain and/or severe proprioceptive decrease in more than two limbs
5. Loss (essentially) of sensation in one or two limbs; or moderate decrease in touch or pain and/or loss of proprioception for most of the body below the head
6. Sensation essentially lost below the head
V. Unknown

Bowel and Bladder Functions (revised 1982)
0. Normal
1. Mild urinary hesitancy, urgency, or retention
2. Moderate hesitancy, urgency, retention of bowel or bladder, or rare urinary incontinence
3. Frequent urinary incontinence
4. In need of almost constant catheterization
5. Loss of bladder function
6. Loss of bowel and bladder function
V. Unknown

Visual (or Optic) Functions
0. Normal
1. Scotoma with visual acuity (corrected) better than 20/30
2. Worse eye with scotoma with maximal visual acuity (corrected) of 20/30 to 20/59
3. Worse eye with large scotoma, or moderate decrease in fields, but with maximal visual acuity (corrected) of 20/60 to 20/99
4. Worse eye with marked decrease of fields and maximal visual acuity (corrected) of 20/100 to 20/200; grade 3 plus maximal acuity of better eye of 20/60 or less
5. Worse eye with maximal visual acuity (corrected) less than 20/200; grade 4 plus maximal acuity of better eye of 20/60 or less
6. Grade 5 plus maximal visual acuity of better eye of 20/60 or less

V. Unknown
X. Is added to grades 0 to 6 for presence of temporal pallor

Cerebral (or Mental) Functions
0. Normal
1. Mood alteration only (does not affect DSS score)
2. Mild decrease in mentation
3. Moderate decrease in mentation
4. Marked decrease in mentation (chronic brain syndrome—moderate)
5. Dementia or chronic brain syndrome—severe or incompetent
V. Unknown

Other Functions
0. None
1. Any other neurologic findings attributed to MS (specify)
V. Unknown

EXPANDED DISABILITY STATUS SCALE (EDSS)

0 = Normal neurologic exam (all grade 0 in Functional Systems [FS]; Cerebral grade 1 acceptable)

1.0 = No disability, minimal signs in one FS (i.e., grade 1 excluding Cerebral grade 1)

1.5 = No disability minimal signs in more than one FS (more than one grade 1 excluding Cerebral grade 1)

2.0 = Minimal disability in one FS (one FS grade 2, others 0 or 1)

2.5 = Minimal disability in two FS (two FS grade 2, others 0 or 1)

3.0 = Moderate disability in one FS (one FS grade 3, others 0 or 1), or mild disability in three or four FS (three/four FS grade 2, others 0 or 1) though fully ambulatory

3.5 = Fully ambulatory but with moderate disability in one FS (one grade 3) and one or two FS grade 2; or two FS grade 3; or five FS grade 2 (others 0 or 1)

4.0 = Fully ambulatory without aid, self-sufficient, up and about some 12 hours a day despite relatively severe disability consisting of one FS grade 4 (others 0 or 1), or combinations of lesser grades exceeding limits of previous steps. Able to walk without aid or rest some 500 meters.

4.5 = Fully ambulatory without aid, up and about much of the day, able to work a full day, may otherwise have some limitation of full activity or require minimal assistance; characterized by relatively severe disability, usually consisting of one FS grade 4 (others 0 or 1) or combinations of lesser grades exceeding limits of previous steps. Able to walk without aid or rest for some 300 meters.

5.0 = Ambulatory without aid or rest for about 200 meters; disability severe enough to impair full daily activities (eg, to work full day without special provisions). (Usual FS equivalents are one grade 5 alone, others 0 or 1; or combinations of lesser grades usually exceeding specifications for step 4.0.)

5.5 = Ambulatory without aid or rest for about 100 meters; disability severe enough to preclude full daily activities. (Usual FS equivalents are one grade 5 alone, others 0 or 1; or combinations of lesser grades usually exceeding those for step 4.0.)

6.0 = Intermittent or unilateral constant assistance (cane, crutch, or brace) required to walk about 100 meters with or without resting. (Usual FS equivalents are combinations with more than two FS grade 3+.)

Constant bilateral assistance (canes, crutches, or braces) required to walk about 20 meters without resting. (Usual FS equivalents are combinations with more than two FS grade +.)

Unable to walk beyond about 5 meters even with aid, essentially restricted to wheelchair; wheels self in standard wheelchair and transfers alone; up and about in w/c some 12 hours a day. (Usual FS equivalents are combinations with more than one FS grade 4+; very rarely, pyramidal grade 5 alone.)

Unable to take more than a few steps; restricted to wheelchair; may need aid in transfer; wheels self but cannot carry on in standard wheelchair a full day; may require motorized wheelchair. (Usual FS equivalents are combinations with more than one FS grade 4+.)

Essentially restricted to bed or chair or perambulated in

Table 12–2 *Continued*

wheelchair, but may be out of bed itself much of the day; retains many self-care functions; generally has effective use of arms. (Usual FS equivalents are combinations, generally grade 4+ in several systems.)	Helpless bed patient; can communicate and eat. (Usual FS equivalents are combinations, mostly grade 4+.)
Essentially restricted to bed much of the day; has some effective use of arm(s); retains some self-care functions. (Usual FS equivalents are combinations, generally 4+ in several systems.)	Totally helpless bed patient; unable to communicate effectively or eat/swallow. (Usual FS equivalents are combinations, almost all grade 4+.)
	Death due to MS.

From Kurtzke, J,[41] with permission of the publisher.

help ensure the patient's cooperation, motivation, and self-reliance. At all times, specific attention should be given to fatigue patterns and exacerbating factors. Optimizing function is a goal of treatment, but overexertion must be carefully avoided.[18]

RANGE OF MOTION

Passive range of motion exercises for immobilized parts should be performed several times each day. This usually requires the involvement of nursing staff and family members in order to provide an effective prevention program. The patient should be instructed in self-range of motion exercises and active limb movements, if possible, to help maintain joint mobility. Exercise programs should stress strengthening of weak agonist muscles and moving out of positions of deformity or reflex dependency. Splinting may be a necessary adjunct to treatment in order to maintain optimal position. If specific muscle tightness has developed, the proprioceptive neuromuscular facilitation (PNF) techniques of hold-relax and contract-relax may be useful in gaining increased joint range through use of neurophysiologic inhibitory mechanisms. Capsular tightness should be addressed using manual techniques of joint mobilization. If spasticity is an apparent cause of joint tightness or limitation in range, inhibitory techniques should be employed prior to exercise (see treatment suggestions for spasticity). Fixed contractures usually require more aggressive management, including manual passive stretching or prolonged static stretching using weights or positioning. In one study of chronic immobilized patients, low-load prolonged stretch using modified Buck's skin traction and weights proved more effective in reducing contracture than a brief, manually applied high-load stretch.[43] Surgical releases may become necessary in situations unresponsive to more conservative treatment approaches.[44–47]

SENSORY DISTURBANCES

Sensory feedback training should be instituted to improve and/or to compensate for sensory impairments. Patients with diminished sensation may respond favorably to sensory stimulation techniques (repeated or vigorous rubbing or brushing) with a temporary increase in sensory awareness of their limbs. Patients with proprioceptive losses will demonstrate impaired motor learning and motor control. Effective strategies to compensate for this deficit include the use of verbal cues to reinforce correct movements or increased visual guidance of movement through appropriate positioning or mirrors. Biofeedback also provides an augmented source of either visual or auditory feedback and may be effective for selected patients. Eye patching is frequently used to reduce double vision, although some depth perception will be sacrificed. This requires a necessary adjustment in the performance of motor activities.[48]

SKIN CARE

Awareness of sensory deficits and compensatory activities to protect desensitized parts should be taught early in the rehabilitation process and be consistently reinforced by all personnel. The patient should be educated in the cardinal rules of skin care:

1. Keep the skin clean and dry.
2. Follow a good diet and drink plenty of fluids.
3. Inspect skin regularly (at least twice a day).
4. Provide regular pressure relief.

Decubitus ulcers are one of the primary complications of inactivity and prolonged positioning in a bed or wheelchair. Patients should change their position or be changed frequently, typically every 2 hours in bed and every 15 minutes when sitting in a wheelchair. Water, gel, or air mattresses, and wheelchair cushions, are helpful in distributing the body weight. Protective aides (sheepskins, air or foam cushions) may be necessary to protect areas prone to breakdown (shoulder blades, elbows, ischial tuberosities, sacrum, trochanters, knees, malleoli, or heels). Clothing should be comfortable, not too loose (wrinkled) or too tight. Seams, buttons, and pockets should not press on the skin, particularly in weight-bearing areas. Clothing should be "breathable" and smooth or soft. The patient must be cautioned against activities or stimuli that might traumatize the skin. Thermal injury may result from cigarette ashes, hot water, or hot objects. Dragging, bumping, or scraping body parts during a transfer also may traumatize the skin.

If skin redness develops (lasting longer than 30 minutes), patients should be instructed to stay off the area until the redness disappears. Blisters, blue areas, or open sores indicate more serious injury. Ulceration should be exposed to the air to maximize healing and may be treated with medications, ultraviolet light, or surgical debridement.[18,23,49]

SPASTICITY

Muscle tone and abnormal movement patterns may be decreased using a variety of physical therapy treatment approaches. These include the use of modalities, therapeutic exercise, positioning, or any combination thereof.

Local application of cold (ice packs, cold wraps, ice massage) or immersion in cold water reduces spasticity by directly lowering the firing of the muscle spindle[50,51] and by delaying or blocking conduction of impulses in nerves and muscles.[52] The effects of cryotherapy can last a relatively long time, and patients will experience an enhanced ability to move once freed from the static limitations of spastic muscles.[53,54]

Functional electrical stimulation has been used to reduce spasticity and clonus by utilizing mechanisms of reciprocal inhibition. Because ankle clonus is a common problem for ambulatory patients, peroneal stimulation can be an effective measure to improve function. An intact reflex arc and intersegmental reciprocal relationships are prerequisites for using this type of therapy.[37]

Therapeutic exercises begun early in the course of the disease and continued through regularly scheduled sessions can help the patient maintain mobility and controlled mobility function effectively. Developmental activities aimed at reducing tone should concentrate on trunk and proximal movements inasmuch as many patterns of hypertonus seem to arise from these key areas.[55,56] Trunk activities should include both log and segmental rolling performed in sidelying and hooklying postures. Upper and lower trunk rotation can then be performed in more difficult postures such as sitting, quadruped, modified plantigrade, and standing. A further progression might include rotation in combination with extremity patterns or in a reciprocal trunk pattern (counterrotation in sidelying). Extensor tone seems to predominate, so activities that stress flexion with trunk rotation are generally most effective. For example, chopping and reverse chopping combined with rolling is often effective in initiating or maintaining independent rolling. Movement transitions and spiral or diagonal extremity patterns which incorporate rotation should be stressed. Specific techniques that are effective include active assisted movement, using neurodevelopmental treatment (NDT) techniques of handling,[55,56] or PNF techniques of rhythmic initiation or slow reversals.[46,57] Finally, patterns of motion that encourage or use spasticity should be discouraged. This generally includes any of the primitive reflex patterns such as the asymmetric tonic neck reflex (ATNR) or the tonic labyrinthine reflex (TLR).

Positioning out of reflex-dependent postures is an important adjunct to exercise. Sidelying is preferable as oppposed to the prone and supine positions which can activate the TLR reflex. Head position (full flexion or extension or side head turning) can activate the STNR or ATNR reflexes and produce an increase in hypertonus. Pressure on the ball of the foot (sitting or standing) can increase extensor responses through the action of the positive supporting response. In general, prolonged or static positioning in any fixed posture can be deleterious to the patient with spasticity and should be avoided.

Local facilitation techniques such as muscle tapping, vibration, or light touch may prove useful in facilitating the antagonist of a spastic muscle, thereby reducing tone in the spastic muscle. However, it should be noted that in the presence of spasticity, reciprocal relationships may not be normal.[56] Resistance to facilitate contraction in a weakened antagonist must be used cautiously, because overflow or irradiation may result in an increase in tone in the spastic agonist muscle. Prolonged stretch or pressure on long tendons of spastic muscles also decreases tone owing to action of peripheral receptors (Golgi tendon organ, muscle spindle secondary endings, joint receptors). Therapeutically this can be achieved through inhibitory techniques such as manual contacts, splinting, or inhibitory casting techniques. A more generalized decrease in tone can be achieved through techniques aimed at decreasing CNS arousal mechanisms (slow stroking down the posterior primary rami, inverted or tonic labyrinthine position, or soothing verbal commands).[58-60] Slow vestibular stimulation achieved through rolling or slow rocking movements also has been effective in reducing muscle tone.[61] These techniques are reviewed more thoroughly in chapter 14.

MUSCLE WEAKNESS AND FATIGUE

Muscle weakness will vary considerably from patient to patient. Exercise techniques will therefore vary depending upon the patient's symptoms. In cases of mild weakness, a resistive training sequence (PRE, isokinetics) may be appropriate. When spasticity is a major presenting symptom, strengthening can best be achieved using an exercise program designed to promote tone reduction while increasing mobility. Proprioceptive neuromuscular facilitation patterns are ideal because of their emphasis on diagonal movement (helpful in reducing tone) and on combining the action of major muscle groups (helpful when the patient fatigues easily). Because the patient typically has a limited amount of energy to expend, exercises must be chosen judiciously, accomplishing the greatest number of goals with the fewest exercises. Functional activities should always be stressed. Scheduling the exercise session in the morning before fatigue sets in and balancing exercise with frequent rest periods should be major considerations.[18,48]

ATAXIA

Improvement of ataxia may be achieved by emphasizing postural stability (tonic holding and cocontraction) of proximal musculature. This can be accomplished by using antigravity postures in the developmental sequence (prone on elbows, sitting, quadruped, kneeling, modified plantigrade, and standing) and techniques designed to stimulate tonic holding (shortened held resisted contraction) and cocontraction of proximal muscles (joint approximation, alternating isometrics, rhythmic stabilization). Patients with significant ataxia may benefit from the application of the technique of slow reversals progressing through decrements of range. As improvement occurs, postural reactions (righting, equilibrium, protective extension) can be challenged by using controlled mobility activities (gentle rocking, moving out of positions of stability). The last step in a progression should be the addition of distal extremity movements superimposed on proximal stability. Ataxic limb movements have sometimes been helped by the application of Velcro weight cuffs (wrist or ankle). Weighted cuffs increase proprioceptive feedback during activity and may serve to decrease extraneous movement.[46,55–57,62]

Frenkel's exercises were originally developed in 1889 to treat patients with problems of incoordination and cerebellar ataxia owing to a loss of proprioception from tabes dorsalis. They have been widely applied in the treatment of MS to remediate similar problems. These exercises are designed to substitute the use of vision and hearing for the loss of sensation and require a high degree of mental concentration, visual control of movements, and repetition. They are, therefore, not appropriate for all patients with MS. For those patients with the prerequisite abilities, they can be effective in reducing ataxia and regaining some control of functional movement. Patients with partial sensation may progress to practicing these exercises with eyes closed. Frenkel's exercises are presented in Appendix B.[63,64]

A successful exercise program is dependent upon a number of factors essential for motor learning, including practice, adequate feedback, and knowledge of results. The patient with MS is often restricted in practice by neuromuscular fatigue and by neurologic deficits which impair sensory feedback, attention, memory, and motivation. The successful therapist will need to identify the patient's resources and abilities carefully and to capitalize on them to maximize the patient's chances for functional improvement. Concomitant with this is the ability to recognize treatment goals that are not realistic considering the patient's remaining abilities.[65–67]

Symptomatic treatment may require the application of conflicting techniques, such as techniques to decrease tone and to increase strength. Careful monitoring of treatment results is essential in looking at the overall therapeutic outcome. Intensive physical therapy that exhausts the patient and raises internal temperatures may actually produce a transient worsening of symptoms. This may have adverse effects on motivation and stress-related relapses. An alternate approach discussed by DeSouza is the use of group classes and self-paced, voluntary exercises.[68] The therapist's primary role in this approach is one of educator. Successful management of group classes requires careful, individualized assessment of group members with specific predetermined goals. The therapist concentrates on effective use of verbal instructions instead of manual skills. Significant improvement in function, balance, and daily living skills in a group of 40 patients not in active exacerbation was obtained using this approach.

GAIT

Early gait problems often include poor balance and heaviness of one or more limbs. Later problems center around clonus, spasticity, increasing weakness, sensory loss, and/or ataxia. A well-designed mat program of tone reduction and postural and preambulatory activities is an essential prerequisite for gait training (see chapter 15). Standing and walking activities generally should stress adequate weight transfer, trunk rotation, an appropriate base of support, and a controlled progression.

Ambulatory aids and orthoses may become necessary to maintain function and are prescribed in the early stages of the disease. In one study of 1145 patients with MS, 4 percent were using crutches, 6 percent leg braces, and 12 percent were using walkers or canes. Long-term function was more often maintained through the use of wheelchairs, seen in more than 40 percent of the patients.[69] Ankle-foot stability can be achieved by the addition of an ankle foot orthoses (AFO). The presence or absence of spasticity will determine the type of device selected. **Rocker shoes** (modified Danish clogs) have been successful in selected patients in compensating for lost ankle mobility. Gait patterns with these shoes appeared more normal with a significant savings in energy cost (150 percent over ambulation without rocker shoes).[70] The addition of weights to a cane or a walker may help stabilize the device and diminish the excursion of ataxia.[23]

FUNCTIONAL CONSIDERATIONS

Functional training should focus on the development of problem-solving skills, appropriate compensatory techniques, and energy conservation. Full participation of the patient in all phases of rehabilitation and problem solving will increase personal involvement and self-worth while decreasing dependency and passivity.[29,39]

Because many patients will depend upon the wheelchair as their primary means of mobility, appropriate prescription of the chair and its components is extremely important (see chapter 28). The stage and progression of the disease and presenting symptoms should be taken into consideration when deciding upon a wheelchair. For example, if the disease is rapidly progressing, a reclining back and elevating legrests may be appropriate. A power-drive wheelchair or other motorized devices such as the Amigo may be indicated if fatigue problems are severe. Patients should be instructed carefully in the use of all parts of the chair and in its maintenance. Attention to good posture and pressure relief are important considerations. Patients should be encouraged to balance time in the wheelchair with other activities such as walking or exercise and should be extra diligent in stretching muscles that tend to contract from prolonged sitting.[71]

The majority of patients with MS use multiple devices.[69] This requires careful attention to prescription of appropriate devices and to environmental modification. Adaptive equipment should assist the patient in conserving energy and maintaining function. Mobility aids may include the use of bed or toilet grab bars, an overhead trapeze, raised seats, sliding boards, or lifts. Adapted or weighted eating utensils or ball-bearing feeders can assist the patient while eating. Long-handled shoe horns, reachers, button hooks, sock aids, or other devices can assist in dressing. Effective communication may require built-up writing utensils, typewriter, or an electronic communication system. The clinician needs to recognize when a device is indicated and to assist the patient in learning how to use it before significant deterioration of function occurs. Assisting the patient in acceptance of the device also requires skill and understanding.[18,72]

A significant number of patients (one out of every two patients) also require the assistance of another person.[69] This places an extra burden on family members and/or on the financial resources of the patient if outside attendants must be used. The clinician will need to devote considerable time to an educational program aimed at instructing these individuals and coordinating home management. Organized team involvement in teaching with full active participation of the patient is usually the best approach to achieving this goal. A positive attitude and an honest, open presentation are important. Instruction should be kept appropriately brief, proceeding from simple to more complex procedures. The patient's abilities should be emphasized, stressing the need for optimal function while providing a realistic appraisal of the problems.[73,74]

RESPIRATORY/EATING AND SWALLOWING PROBLEMS

Breathing exercises are an important consideration in treatment during all stages of the disease. Shallow respiratory patterns may contribute to speech difficulties and recurrent respiratory infections. Specific involvement of respiratory muscles should be ascertained. These muscles may be weak, ataxic, or spastic. Diaphragmatic breathing, resistive breathing, effective coughing, and postural drainage are all vital components of treatment. Segmental expansion should be facilitated through proper placement of manual contacts and resistance. When speech or eating difficulties are apparent, these efforts should be coordinated with a speech therapist.

Eating and swallowing difficulties may be alleviated by improved sitting posture, head control, balance, eye-hand coordination, and voluntary control of the muscles of mastication. Adaptive equipment may be necessary. An upright posture and a slightly flexed head position is essential for good swallowing. Stretch and resistance can be used to facilitate and to strengthen muscle action (jaw opening or closing, lip closure, tongue mobility). Sucking reflexes and saliva production can be stimulated by using an ice cube or a water popsicle. Resistive sucking through a straw can also be helpful. Brief icing of the tongue and laryngeal area of the neck may stimulate swallowing reflexes. Thicker liquids which provide some resistance and therefore some facilitation of muscle action are generally easier to swallow than thin liquids. Soft foods are easier to swallow than firm ones. Fatigue patterns also affect eating, and patients may benefit from having their main meal in the morning or from eating multiple small meals. Feeding tubes may be necessary in the more chronic stages of the disease.[22]

PSYCHOLOGIC FACTORS

Patients with MS may show a variety of behavioral adaptations associated with the stress of a chronic disease. The primary role of clinicians is to assist the individual and family in their understanding of the disease and in their psychosocial adjustment. The unique feature of a disease with an exacerbating-remitting course is that it requires continual readjustment every time a new set of symptoms appears. Patients who appear well adjusted at one stage may regress as the disease worsens. In addition, the unknown and unpredictable future creates a tremendous amount of stress for these individuals. Matson and Brooks[75] point out that living with MS requires not only initial acceptance but also a tremendous flexibility to deal with this lack of closure.

In the initial stages of the disease, denial is common and can sometimes be helpful. However, the patient should not be allowed to continue with this coping mechanism for extended periods of time.[29] Major depressions or anxiety are often handled medically with the use of tranquilizers (Valium). A positive, affirmative attitude can have a direct impact on the patient's attitude. Clinicians should relay to their patients a strong belief that treatment can be beneficial. This maintenance of therapeutic hope is extremely important. Treatment should focus on remaining abilities and should carefully build in successful experiences. As in any long-term care situation, a relationship of trust and caring is crucial in ensuring treatment success.[74]

A mutual support group also can provide a necessary psychologic base for patients and their families. Within this environment individuals can gain accurate and useful information about the disease, can discuss common problems and methods of coping, and can share anxieties. Thus it provides the necessary forum to assist in the continual adjustment process. Successful group counseling programs have been reported in the literature.[28,76] The National Multiple Sclerosis Society also provides a valuable resource for patients and their families.

SUMMARY

Multiple sclerosis is a chronic demyelinating disease of the central nervous system characterized by widespread lesions and multiple symptoms. Although the cause is unknown, major theories focus on an infectious viral origin, an immune-mediated pathogenesis, or a combination of the two.

The diagnosis is usually based upon clinical findings, including multiple signs of neurologic dysfunction occurring over time. Additional laboratory tests supportive of the diagnosis include lumbar puncture, computerized tomography, electrophysiologic testing, and blood changes.

Multiple sclerosis is an unpredictable disease, typically presenting with an exacerbating-remitting course, although other clinical courses have been recognized. Common clinical findings include disturbances in sensation, muscle strength, tone, fatigue, coordination, vision, communication, bladder and bowel function, and cognitive and behavioral function. Numerous secondary problems can arise from prolonged inactivity. Exacerbating factors in MS include heat, stress, or trauma. The prognosis is variable, although most patients live an average of 25 years with the disability.

Medical management is directed at the disease process itself or at its symptoms. There is no specific preventive or curative treatment. Interventions typically include pharmacologic and surgical measures.

Rehabilitation of the patient with MS is centered around decreasing symptoms, improving function, preventing secondary complications, and promoting successful psychosocial adjustment. It requires the comprehensive efforts of a health care team to provide coordinated and continuing care.

QUESTIONS FOR REVIEW

1. What is the principal structure in the central nervous system impaired in MS? How is the function altered?

2. What are the most common signs and symptoms?

3. What are the two major causative theories? How might these two theories interact to explain the pathogenesis of MS?

4. What are the diagnostic measures used to confirm MS? What are the immunologic factors present in this disease?

5. Differentiate between the four main types of clinical course.

6. What are the clinical effects of inactivity for the chronic, immobilized patient?

7. What are the major exacerbating factors in MS? What is the impact of these factors on the patient with MS?

8. What is the typical prognosis for the patient with MS? Name three factors that indicate a poor prognosis.

9. Why is adrenocorticotrophin hormone or prednisone used in the treatment of MS?

10. Describe the major drugs used in the treatment of spasticity. What other medical procedures are used?

11. What are the major components of a physical therapy assessment? How might some of the standard assessments have to be modified?

12. How do stretching techniques vary in the presence of spasticity? Name four tone-reducing techniques.

13. What developmental activities should receive primary emphasis in the treatment of the patient with MS? Why?

14. Describe Frenkel's exercises. What motor learning principles do they incorporate?

15. What are the major functional devices likely to be used by the patient with MS? In ordering this equipment, what should be kept in mind?

16. What physical therapy procedures can be helpful in treating the patient with eating difficulties?

17. What are the major considerations in facilitating psychosocial adjustment to MS?

REFERENCES

1. Dean, G: The multiple sclerosis problem. Scientific American 223:40, 1970.
2. Field, E (ed): Multiple Sclerosis. University Park Press, Baltimore, 1977.
3. Field, E, Bell, T, and Carnegie, P: Multiple Sclerosis. North Holland Publishing, Amsterdam, 1972.
4. McAlpine, D, Lumsden, C, and Acheson, E: Multiple Sclerosis—A Reappraisal, ed 2. Longman Group, Edinburgh, 1973.
5. Guyton, A: Basic Neuroscience. WB Saunders, Philadelphia, 1987.
6. Hafler, D, et al: In vivo activated T lymphocytes in the peripheral blood and cerebrospinal fluid of patients with multiple sclerosis. N Engl J Med 312:1405, 1985.
7. Ellison, GW (moderator): Multiple sclerosis. Ann Intern Med 101:514, 1984.
8. Kurtzke, J: Epidemiological contributions to multiple sclerosis: An overview. Neurology 30:61, 1980.
9. Scheinberg, L: Demyelinating diseases. In Beeson, P and McDermott, W (eds): Textbook of Medicine, ed 14. WB Saunders, 1975.
10. McFarlin, D and McFarland, H: Multiple sclerosis. N Engl J Med 307:1183, 1982.
11. Cook, S and Dowling, P: Multiple sclerosis and viruses: An overview. Neurology 30:80, 1980.
12. Lisak, R: Multiple sclerosis: Evidence for immunopathogenesis. Neurology 30:99, 1980.
13. Poser, C, et al: New diagnostic criteria for multiple sclerosis: Guidelines for research protocols. Ann Neurol 13:227, 1983.
14. Franklin, G and Burks, J: Diagnosis and medical management of multiple sclerosis. In Maloney, FP, Burks, J, and Ringel, S (eds): Interdisciplinary Rehabilitation of Multiple Sclerosis and Neuromuscular Disorders. JB Lippincott, Philadelphia, 1985.

15. Johnson, K: Cerebrospinal fluid and blood assays of diagnostic usefulness in multiple sclerosis. Neurology 30:106, 1980.
16. Kraft, G, et al: Multiple sclerosis: Early prognostic guidelines. Arch Phys Med Rehabil 62:54, 1981.
17. Dolan, B: Multiple sclerosis. J Neurosurg Nurs 11:83, 1979.
18. Bauer, H: A Manual on Multiple Sclerosis. International Federation of Multiple Sclerosis Societies. Vienna, 1977.
19. Burke, D: Stretch reflex activity in the spastic patient. Kyoto Symposia (EEG Suppl) 36:172, 1982.
20. Bishop, B: Spasticity: Its physiology and management. Phys Ther 57:371, 1977.
21. Weiner, W and Goetz, C (eds): Neurology for the Non-neurologist. Harper & Row, Philadelphia, 1981.
22. Ruttenberg, N: Assessment and treatment of speech and swallowing problems in patients with multiple sclerosis. In Maloney, F, Burks, J, and Ringel, S (eds): Interdisciplinary Rehabilitation of Multiple Sclerosis and Neuromuscular Disorders. JB Lippincott, Philadelphia, 1985.
23. Schneitzer, L: Rehabilitation of patients with multiple sclerosis. Arch Phys Med Rehabil 59:430, 1978.
24. Kelly-Hayes, M: Guidelines for rehabilitation of multiple sclerosis patients. Nurs Clin N Am 15:245, 1980.
25. Blaivas, J: Management of bladder dysfunction in multiple sclerosis. Neurology 30:12, 1980.
26. Felder, L: Neurogenic bladder dysfunction. J Neurosurg Nurs 111:94, 1979.
27. Augspurger, R: Bladder dysfunction in multiple sclerosis. In Maloney, F, Burks, J, and Ringel, S: Interdisciplinary Rehabilitation of Multiple Sclerosis and Neuromuscular Disorders. JB Lippincott, Philadelphia, 1985.
28. Hartings, M, Pavlou, M, and Davis, F: Group counseling of MS

patients in a program of comprehensive care. J Chron Dis 29:65, 1976.

29. Weinstein, E: Behavioral aspects of multiple sclerosis. Mod Treat 7:961, 1970.
30. Kurtzke, J, et al: Studies on the natural history of multiple sclerosis. J Chron Dis 30:819, 1977.
31. Vallbona, C: Bodily responses to immobilization. In Kottke, F, Stillwell, G, and Lehmann, J (eds): Krusen's Handbook of Physical Medicine and Rehabilitation, ed 3. WB Saunders, Philadelphia, 1982.
32. Salten, B, et al: Response to submaximal and maximal exercise after bedrest and training. Circulation 38:7, 1968.
33. Gilroy, J and Holliday, P: Basic Neurology. Macmillan, New York, 1982.
34. Ellison, G and Myers, L: Immunosuppressive drugs in multiple sclerosis: pro and con. Neurology 30:28, 1980.
35. Catanzaro, M: MS—Nursing care of the person with MS. Am J Nurs 80:286, 1980.
36. Berg, V, et al: The value of dorsal column stimulation in multiple sclerosis. Scand J Rehabil Med 14:183, 1982.
37. Dimitrijevic, M and Sherwood, A: Spasticity: Medical and surgical treatment. Neurology 30:19, 1980.
38. Slater, R: A model of care: Matching human services to patients' needs. Neurology 30:39, 1980.
39. Kottke, F: Philosophic consideration of quality of life for the disabled. Arch Phys Med Rehabil 63:60, 1982.
40. Kurtzke, J: On the evaluation of disability in multiple sclerosis. Neurology 11:686, 1961.
41. Kurtzke, J: Rating neurological impairment in multiple sclerosis: An expanded disability status scale (EDSS). Neurology 33:1444, 1983.
42. Granger, C, Albrecht, G, and Hamilton, B: Outcome of comprehensive medical rehabilitation: Measurement by Pulses Profile and the Barthel Index. Arch Phys Med Rehabil 60:145, 1979.
43. Light, K, et al: Low-load prolonged stretch vs high-load brief stretch in treating knee contractures. Phys Ther 64:330, 1984.
44. Cherry, D: Review of physical therapy alternatives for reducing muscle contracture. Phys Ther 60:877, 1980.
45. Sady, S, Wortman, M, and Blanke, D: Flexibility training: Ballistic, static or proprioceptive neuromuscular facilitation? Arch Phys Med Rehabil 63:261, 1982.
46. Voss, D, Ionta, M, and Myers, B: Proprioceptive Neuromuscular Facilitation, ed 3. Harper & Row, Philadelphia, 1985.
47. Kaltenborn, F: Mobilization of the Extremity Joints: Examination and Basic Treatment Techniques. Olaf Norlis Bokhandel, Oslo, Norway, 1980.
48. Pal Brar, S and Wangaard, C: Physical therapy for patients with multiple sclerosis. In Maloney, F, Burks, J, and Ringel, S: Interdisciplinary Rehabilitation of Multiple Sclerosis and Neuromuscular Disorders. JB Lippincott, Philadelphia, 1985.
49. Cardi, M: Skin Care for the Patient with Sensory Loss. Helen Hayes Hospital, West Haverstraw, NY, 1982.
50. Eldred, E, Lindsley, D, and Buchwald, J: The effect of cooling on mammalian muscle spindles. Exp Neurol 2: 144, 1960.
51. Michalski, W and Seguin, J: The effect of muscle cooling and stretch on muscle spindle secondary endings in the cat. J Physiol 253:341, 1975.
52. Miglietta, O: Action of cold on spasticity. Am J Phys Med 52:198, 1973.
53. Knutsson, E: Topical cryotherapy in spasticity. Scand J Rehabil Med 2:159, 1970.
54. Watson, C: Effects of lowering body temperature on the symptoms and signs of multiple sclerosis. N Eng J Med 261:1253, 1959.
55. Bobath, K and Bobath, B: The facilitation of normal postural reactions and movements in the treatment of cerebral palsy. Physiotherapy 50:246, 1964.
56. Bobath, B: The treatment of neuromuscular disorders by improving patterns of co-ordination. Physiotherapy 55:18, 1969.
57. Sullivan, P, Markos, P, and Minor, M: An Integrated Approach to Therapeutic Exercise. Reston Publishing, Reston, VA, 1982.
58. Rood, M: The use of sensory receptors to activate, facilitate, and inhibit motor response, autonomic and somatic, in developmental sequence. In Sattely, C (ed): Approaches to the Treatment of Patients with Neuromuscular Dysfunction. WC Brown, DuBuque, IA, 1962.
59. Heiniger, M and Randolph, S: Neurophysiological Concepts in Human Behavior. CV Mosby, St Louis, 1981.
60. Stockmeyer, SA: An interpretation of the approach of Rood to the treatment of neuromuscular dysfunction. NUSTEP Proceedings. Am J Phys Med 46(1):900, 1967.
61. Pederson, D: The soothing effect of rocking as determined by the direction and frequency of movement. Can J Behav Sci 7:237, 1975.
62. Block, J and Kester, N: Role of rehabilitation in the management of multiple sclerosis. Mod Treat 7:930, 1970.
63. Hollis, M: Practical Exercise Therapy, ed 2. Blackwell Scientific Publications, Oxford, 1981.
64. Kottke, F: Therapeutic exercise to develop neuromuscular coordination. In Kottke, F, Stillwell, G, and Lehmann, J: Krusen's Handbook of Physical Medicine and Rehabilitation. WB Saunders, Philadelphia, 1982.
65. Kottke, F, et al: The training of coordination. Arch Phys Med Rehabil 59:567, 1978.
66. Schmidt, R: Motor Control and Learning. Human Kinetics, Champaign, IL, 1982.
67. Sage, G: Introduction to Motor Behavior—A Neuropsychological Approach, ed 2. Addison-Wesley, Reading, MA, 1977.
68. DeSouza, L: A different approach to physiotherapy for multiple sclerosis patients. Physiotherapy 70:428, 1984.
69. Baum, H and Rothschild, B: Multiple sclerosis and mobility restriction. Arch Phys Med Rehabil 64:591, 1983.
70. Perry, J, Gronley, J and Lunsford, T: Rocker shoe as walking aid in multiple sclerosis. Arch Phys Med Rehabil 62:59, 1981.
71. Todd, J: Multiple sclerosis—physiotherapy. In Downie, P (ed): Cash's Textbook of Neurology for Physiotherapists, ed 3. Faber & Faber, London, 1982.
72. Wolf, B: Occupational therapy for patients with multiple sclerosis. In Maloney, F, Burks, J, and Ringel, S (eds): Interdisciplinary Rehabilitation of Multiple Sclerosis and Neuromuscular Disorders. JB Lippincott, Philadelphia, 1985.
73. Price, G: The challenge to the family. Am J Nurs 80:283, 1980.
74. Slater, R and Yearwood, A: MS—facts, faith, and hope. Am J Nurs 80:276, 1980.
75. Matson, R and Brooks, N: Adjusting to multiple sclerosis: An exploratory study. Soc Sci Med 11:245, 1977.
76. Scheinberg, L, et al: Comprehensive long-term care of patients with multiple sclerosis. Neurology 31:1121, 1981.

GLOSSARY

Charcot's triad: Cardinal symptoms of multiple sclerosis: intention tremor, scanning speech, and nystagmus.

Demyelinization: Destruction or removal of the myelin sheath of nerve tissue.

Diplopia: Double vision.

Disability Status Scale: A commonly used scale devised by Kurtzke and used to measure the severity of functional impairment in multiple sclerosis.

Euphoria: An exaggerated feeling of well-being.

Exacerbation: An aggravation of symptoms or increase in the severity of a disease.

Fatigue pattern: Characteristic pattern of afternoon exhaustion which occurs in multiple sclerosis.

Frenkel's exercises: Exercises designed to improve incoordination and cerebellar ataxia resulting from a loss of proprioception.

Gliosis: Proliferation of neuroglial tissue in the central nervous system.

Immunosuppressive agent: A substance that suppresses or interferes with the normal immune response, used in the control of autoimmune diseases.

Lhermitte's sign: An electric shocklike sensation running down the spinal cord and legs produced by flexing the neck.

Nerve block: The induction of regional anesthesia to prevent sensory nerve impulses from reaching centers of consciousness.

Neuralgia: Severe sharp pain along the course of a nerve.

Remission: A lessening of symptoms or decrease in the severity of a disease.

Rhizotomy: Surgical cutting of a nerve root.

Vertigo: Sensation of movement of one's body or of objects moving about the body.

APPENDIX A   RMMSC PHYSICAL THERAPY EVALUATION FORM (AND EXPLANATIONS)*

Hospital-number_____-__   Date: Year 19 ___ Mo ___ Day ___
Name_____   Sex: __ (M = Male, F = Female)
     (Last, First)
Date of birth   Year 19 ___ Mo ___ Day ___   Hand dominance __ (R = Right, L = Left)
Age at first symptom ___   Year of diagnosis 19 ___
Physical status __ (R = remission, E = exacerbation, P = progression, S = stable, U = other)
  (Definitions below.)
Most involved extremity . . . UE ___ . . . LE __ (R = Right, L = Left, E = Equal)
Have you ever received physical therapy before? __ (Y = Yes, N = No)
Current sensory symptoms (check all that apply):
Paresthesia/numbness   Right UE __   Left UE __   Right LE __   Left LE __   Trunk __
Dysesthesia/pain   Right UE __   Left UE __   Right LE __   Left LE __   Trunk __
Definitions of Items Regarding Physical Status
Remission: Patient has recovered from an exacerbation and has resumed normal function.
Exacerbation: Patient is in an acute attack.
Progression: Patient is experiencing slowly or rapidly progressing MS.
Stable: Patient is in a stable condition with some residual symptoms of MS remaining.

Functional Movement Evaluation
(Use standard scale of 0 to 5. For + or −, use second box.) (If strength in an extremity is normal, record only for extremity as a whole. If not normal, record individual muscle groups.)

Right UE __-__   Left UE __-__   Right LE __-__   Left LE __-__

Right	Muscle Groups	Left	Right	Muscle Groups	Left
__-__	Shoulder flexors	__-__	__-__	Hip flexors	__-__
__-__	Shoulder extensors	__-__	__-__	Hip abductors	__-__
__-__	Shoulder abductors	__-__	__-__	Hip extensors	__-__
__-__	Elbow flexors	__-__	__-__	Knee extensors	__-__
__-__	Elbow extensors	__-__	__-__	Knee flexors	__-__
__-__	Wrist flexors	__-__	__-__	Ankle dorsiflexors	__-__
__-__	Wrist extensors	__-__	__-__	Ankle plantarflexors	__-__
__-__	Back extensors	__-__	__-__	Abdominals	__-__

Range of Motion
(Check functional range in each extremity below. 0 = Absent, 5 = Normal. If ROM is abnormal, check the appropriate range for the categories given.)
Right UE __   Left UE __   Right LE __   Left LE __
Shoulder abduction   Right UE __   Left UE __
  (A = 0–90, B = 90–180)
Ankle dorsiflexion/plantarflexion   Right LE __   Left LE __
  (A = 10–15 of dorsiflexion, B = neutral to +5 or −5, C = 10–20 plantarflexion, D = 25–35 plantarflexion)
List specific contractures (e.g., 20-degree hip flexion in contracture): _____
_____

Sensation
Proprioceptive loss (1 = none, 2 = mild, 3 = severe. Explanation below.)
Right UE __   Left UE __   Right LE __   Left LE __
Definitions of Sensation Classifications
None: No loss of proprioception
Mild: Any loss at PIP joints in upper extremities and MP joint in toes.
Severe: Any loss at ankles or wrists

---

*From Maloney, F, Burks, J, and Ringel, S: *Interdisciplinary Rehabilitation of Multiple Sclerosis and Neuromuscular Disorders.* JB Lippincott, Philadelphia, 1985, with permission.

Muscle Tone

<table>
<tr>
<td align="center">Tone Grade
(1 = normal, 2 = hypotonic, 3 = spastic)</td>
<td align="center">Spasticity Grade
(1 = mild, 2 = moderate, 3 = severe)</td>
</tr>
</table>

Right UE . . . . __	Left UE . . . . __	Right UE . . . . __	Left UE . . . . __
Right LE . . . . __	Left LE . . . . __	Right LE . . . . __	Left LE . . . . __

(If spasticity exists, check appropriate categories to indicate amount of spasticity.)

Gait

Does vision affect your gait? __ (Y = Yes, N = No)
    If Yes, check all that apply: Blurred vision __ Double vision __ Loss of vision __
Patient ambulatory? __ (Y = Yes, N = No)
Appliances used for ambulation (Check all that apply.)
    Shoes/braces __   Crutches __   Walker __   Cane __

(Check all listed items that definitely are present.)

	With Appliances and Shoes		Without Appliances or Shoes	
	Right	Left	Right	Left
Independent reciprocal gait	—	—	—	—
Recurvatum at mid stance	—	—	—	—
Toes in/out at mid stance	—	—	—	—
Circumduction on swing	—	—	—	—
Lack of reciprocal arm swing	—	—	—	—
Footdrop	—	—	—	—
Wide base	—	—	—	—
Ataxic	—	—	—	—

Additional comments: _____

Explanation of Gait Evaluation

Most items of gait are evaluated by checking whether a type of gait, gait component, or structural change is present or absent. Gait is observed front, back, and side for all determinants. Patients are assessed with and without shoes, with and without aids, wearing clothing that permits easy view of the trunk, hips, and legs. Rather than setting up a several-point scale, the items that are used are assessed as definitely present, which means that mild tendencies on items that may cause disagreement among evaluators as to their presence would usually be termed absent. Also, for the item to be listed as present, it must be observed for at least 5 to 10 consecutive complete strides (heel strikes of the same foot).

Specifics of gait are as follows: Write "Y" if patient is ambulatory and "N" if nonambulatory. If nonambulatory, go on to "Balance." Check the appropriate numbers for appliances used. Please evaluate gait with shoes and appliances and without either.

1. Independent reciprocal gait is defined as the absence of all the factors evaluated.
2. Recurvatum is present when the knee is obviously thrown back on weight bearing or is curved more than 180 degrees visually at mid to late stance.
3. Toes in and out are judged from the front by watching the plane of the foot during stance as the foot strikes a line on the floor. A neutral or greater adduction posi-

tion is considered toe in, and an angle greater than 15 degrees of toe out is marked as toe out.
4. Circumduction is determined by obvious pattern of swing phase. Very mild and equivocal circumduction is termed as absent.
5. Person walks without reciprocal swing.
6. Foot drag assessment is either absent or present.
7. Wide base is present if the patient walks with greater than 9 inches between feet. The 9″ is measured using the standard 9″ floor tile width. This may be due to mild limb ataxia or proprioceptive loss.
8. Ataxic—present if for any reason other than weakness the person cannot keep balance during gait especially during sharp turns, or base is wide because of balance impairments; equivocal assessments are listed as absent. This would indicate a more severe form of incoordination.

Balance

Sitting balance __ (G = good, F = fair, P = poor, N = none)
Standing balance __ (G = good, F = fair, P = poor, N = none)
    Standing on right foot __ (A = 1 min, B = 10 sec, C = 1–9 sec, D = N/A or 0 sec)
    Standing on left foot __ (A = 1 min, B = 10 sec, C = 1–9 sec, D = N/A or 0 sec)

Romberg Test (see definition below): Positive _____
  Negative _____

Balance
  Independent sitting and standing balance are evaluated:
Good—maintains balance in all directions even with moderate pushing from evaluator
Fair—cannot maintain balance with moderate push in any direction
Poor—cannot maintain balance with mild push in any direction
None—no balance

For evaluating one-leg standing balance choose one of the listed categories.

Romberg Test: Patient stands with comfortable stance with eyes open.
  Positive Romberg is moderate to marked worsening of standing balance with eyes closed.
  Negative Romberg is no change in patient's standing balance. The Romberg tests proprioceptive loss rather than cerebellar ataxia.

ADL Status
ADL status determined by __ (D = demonstration, H = history) (use ADL scale below)

Roll side to side   __ 5 = independent and in optimal manner
Sit up in bed   __ 4 = independent, but less than optimal manner
Transfers
  Bed–W/C   __ 3 = independent, but impractical

W/C–Toilet   __ 2 = with standby attendant only
W/C–Car   __ 1 = with human assistance
Operate W/C   __ 0 = unable to perform

Functional mobility grade __ (range 0–12, use scale below)

Functional Mobility Grade:

(Choose one or more items to signify present functional level. Use "Comments" space for further explanation of functional mobility level.)

1. No restrictions; minimal status
2. Definite impairment, but fully ambulatory without aids
3. Limited ability (distance) without aids; able to climb stairs
4. Needs cane and/or brace; stair-climbing equivocal
5. Requires crutches or walker
6. Uses wheelchair, but may use crutches or walker in the home
7. Wheelchair independent
8. Wheelchair independent, but cannot transfer
9. Requires motorized wheelchair (or could manage motorized chair)
10. Wheelchair dependent (specialized chairs)—cannot manage motorized
11. Bed-ridden, but still has arm and hand functions
12. Bed-ridden, helpless
Comments on functional mobility grade: _____
_____

Additional comments: _____
_____

Recommendations: _____
_____
_____

APPENDIX B FRENKEL's EXERCISES

General instructions: Exercises can be performed with the part supported or unsupported, unilaterally or bilaterally. They should be practiced as smooth, timed movements, performed to a slow even tempo by counting out loud. Consistency of performance is stressed, and a specified target can be used to determine range. Four basic positions are used: lying, sitting, standing, and walking. The exercises progress from postures of greatest stability (lying, sitting) to postures of greatest challenge (standing, walking). As voluntary control improves, progress to stopping and starting on command, increasing the range, and performing the same exercises with eyes closed. Concentration and repetition are the keys to success.
Examples of exercises include the following:

1. Half lying:* hip and knee flexion and extension of each limb, foot flat on plinth
2. Half lying: hip abduction and adduction of each limb with the foot flat, knee flexed; then extended
3. Half lying: hip and knee flexion and extension of each limb, heel lifted off plinth

_____
*Half lying refers to the supine position with the head and upper trunk elevated to allow visual feedback for movement.

4. Half lying: heel of one limb to opposite leg (toes, ankle, shin, patella)
5. Half lying: heel of one limb to opposite knee, sliding down crest of tibia to ankle
6. Half lying: Hip and knee flexion and extension of both limbs, legs together
7. Half lying: Reciprocal movements of both limbs: flexion of one leg during extension of the other
8. Sitting: Knee extension and flexion of each limb; progress to marking time
9. Sitting: hip abduction and adduction
10. Sitting: alternate foot placing to a specified target (using floor markings or a grid)
11. Standing up and sitting down: to a specified count
12. Standing: foot placing to a specified target (floor markings or grid)
13. Standing: weight shifting
14. Walking: sideward or forward to a specified count (a Frenkel mat, parallel lines, or floor markings may be used as targets to control foot placement, stride length, and step width)
15. Walking: turning around to a specified count (floor markings can be helpful in maintaining a stable base of support)

A similar progression of exercise can be developed for the upper extremities.

Chapter 23

PARKINSON'S DISEASE

SUSAN B. O'SULLIVAN

OBJECTIVES

1. Define terms associated with the pathology and management of Parkinson's disease.

2. Describe the etiology, pathophysiology, symptomatology, and sequela of Parkinson's disease.

3. Describe the procedures commonly used in the assessment of Parkinson's disease.

4. Describe the rehabilitative management of the patient with Parkinson's disease.

5. Value the role and contribution of the physical therapist in the management of patients with Parkinson's disease.

INTRODUCTION

Parkinson's disease is a chronic, progressive disease of the nervous system involving the **basal ganglia** and resulting in disturbances of tone, abnormal postures, and involuntary movements. Clinically, the patient usually exhibits some combination of three classic signs: **rigidity, bradykinesia,** and **tremor.** The appearance of these signs is believed to be neurochemical in origin and caused by a deficiency of the neurotransmitter **dopamine** within the corpus striatum. This deficiency is secondary to a degeneration of the substantia nigra neurons that send their axons to the caudate nucleus and putamen. Significant changes in striatal dopamine receptors may occur, resulting in decreased binding of dopamine in the basal ganglia. Failure of dopaminergic synapses results in an imbalance in the basal ganglia's mutually antagonistic systems. The cholinergic system, acting through its neurotransmitter acetylcholine, is theorized to permit activity of the short-axon striatal interneurons, and the dopaminergic system is believed to provide tonic inhibition of these cholinergic interneurons. When dopamine is lacking, excessive excitatory output results in a generalized activation of skeletomotor and fusimotor systems

by corticospinal, reticulospinal, and rubrospinal pathways.[1,2] The dopamine deficiency may underlie the appearance of rigidity and bradykinesia. The production of tremor also may be related to the reduced levels of serotonin found in the basal ganglia. This explains why **levodopa** or, more commonly, **sinemet,** medications used to maintain striatal levels of dopamine in patients with parkinsonism are more effective in large doses for alleviating rigidity and bradykinesia than for tremor (Fig. 23–1).[3–8]

Parkinson's disease occurs in about 1 percent of the population over 50 years of age and becomes increasingly more common with advancing age, reaching proportions of 2.6 percent of the population by age 85. The mean age of onset is between 58 and 60 years, though a small percentage may develop the disease as early as the 30s and 40s. Men have a greater incidence of the disease than women by a ratio of 3:2.[9] The etiology is unknown, although several different causes of parkinsonism are suspected:

1. Idiopathic parkinsonism. This term implies that the etiology is unknown. This group includes the true Parkinson's disease or paralysis agitans first described by James Parkinson in 1817 and is the most common form

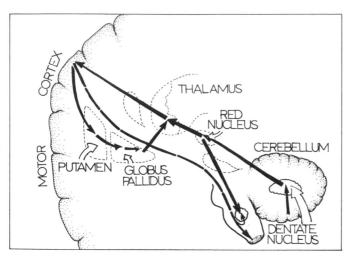

Figure 23–1. The basal ganglia in relation to other central nervous system structures.

excess activation of alpha motoneurons in both agonist and antagonist muscle groups. Rigidity occurs throughout the range of motion. This is in contrast to the clasped-knife phenomenon seen in spasticity, in which resistance increases to a point and then suddenly releases. Rigidity may be unequal in distribution and frequently begins in one limb or side, eventually spreading to involve the whole body. Loss of reciprocal arm swing during gait may be due to truncal rigidity. Active movement, mental concentration, or emotional tension may increase the amount of rigidity present. Two variations are possible, either **cogwheel** or **leadpipe. Cogwheel rigidity** is a jerky, rachetlike response to passive movement as muscles alternately contract and relax. This is theorized to be the result of autogenic reflex inhibition from the Golgi tendon organs, or it may result from the superimposition of tremor on rigidity. **Leadpipe rigidity** is a smooth uniform resistance with no fluctuations to passive movement.[3–6,9,15]

occurring in middle-aged or elderly persons. Current theories of etiology include premature or accelerated aging, or metabolic defect.[10–13]

2. Postinfectious parkinsonism. This type of parkinsonism is theorized to be casued by a viral encephalitis. The influenza epidemics of encephalitis lethargica that occurred from 1917 to 1926 produced the greatest number of these patients. The onset of symptoms of parkinsonism typically occurs after many years, giving rise to a theory of slow virus infection of the brain. There has been no recent reoccurrence of this influenza and the incidence of this type of parkinsonism is now greatly diminished.[10–13]

3. Toxic parkinsonism. Parkinsonian symptoms occur in individuals exposed to certain industrial poisons and chemicals (manganese, carbon disulfide, carbon monoxide). Reports have also described severe and lasting Parkinson symptoms in individuals who ingested a synthetic heroin containing the chemical MPTP.[14] Certain drugs such as powerful tranquilizers like chlorpromazine (largactil) can also cause Parkinson symptoms, though these effects are not necessarily permanent and may be reversed once medications are withdrawn.[11]

4. Arteriosclerotic parkinsonism. Arteriosclerotic involvement and infarction of the brainstem involving the substantia nigra, the nigrostriatal pathways, or the basal ganglia also may produce parkinsonian symptoms. Typically other symptoms of stroke also appear, such as weakness on one side of the body or lability. The separate classification of this type of parkinsonism has been abandoned by some authorities.[4,10–13]

CLINICAL SIGNS

Rigidity

One of the first major clinical signs of parkinsonism is **rigidity.** Rigidity may be defined as an increased resistance to passive motion which affects all striated muscle. It represents an increase in static stretch reflexes and

Bradykinesia

Bradykinesia refers to the difficulty in initiating movement and the slowness and paucity of movement that these patients exhibit. Voluntary and automatic movements are reduced in speed, range, and amplitude **(hypokinesia).** The rotary component to movement is reduced, resulting in movement typically in one plane of motion. Often considerable time elapses between the patient's desire to move and the actual movement response (reaction time). Similarly, the time it takes to complete an activity is also increased (movement time). Overall coordination is impaired, particularly in fine motor tasks such as writing or handling small objects. Movements must now be cortically controlled, requiring intense mental effort and additional expenditure of energy. Bradykinesia is theorized to result from a lack of integration of sensory information by the **basal ganglia** with a resultant alteration in motor planning and the facilitation of movement.[16,17] The basal ganglia are responsible for the automatic execution of selected motor plans, allowing the execution of slow movement patterns. Thus the patient with Parkinson's disease moves slowly and constantly checks progress along the way. Fast ballistic movements may be difficult owing to the patient's inability to initiate sufficient force of contraction.[18,19] Electromyography studies reveal that motor unit recruitment is delayed and once initiated is characterized by pauses and an inability to increase firing rate as contraction continues.[20] Bradykinesia may or may not be associated with rigidity and often is among the most disabling symptoms. When bradykinesia is severe, it is termed **akinesia,** which implies a complete inability to initiate or to execute movement. The term **freezing** also has been used to describe this lack of movement.[8]

Tremor

Tremor is defined as involuntary, rhythmic, alternating bursts of movement of antagonistic muscle groups occurring at a rate of about 4 to 7 oscillations per second. The parkinsonian tremor is described as a resting, static, or nonintention tremor, inasmuch as it is usually present at rest and disappears with voluntary movement. This is not always the case, however, for as the disease progresses, tremor can occur with movement. It is theorized that tremor results from enhanced activity in the basal ganglia-thalamic-cortical circuit, with resultant rhythmic discharge of the alpha motoneurons by the ventrolateral nucleus of the thalamus.[4,6] Tremor tends to be less severe when the patient is relaxed and unoccupied, it is diminished by voluntary effort, and it can disappear completely during sleep. It is aggravated by emotional tension, excitement, or fatigue. Tremors affect about two thirds of the patients with parkinsonism and may precede rigidity in onset. In the early stages of the disease tremor may occur for only short periods, whereas in later stages tremor fluctuates more in terms of frequency and intensity. The most frequent type of tremor seen is the pill-rolling movement of the hand, which is characterized by alternate flexion and extension movements of the fingers and thumb. Tremors most commonly develop in the limbs but may be seen in the jaw and tongue.[8-10]

CLINICAL MANIFESTATIONS

Postural changes include the development of abnormal postural fixation, typically in a flexed or stooped posture (Fig. 23–2). Flexor and adductor muscles become selectively more contracted in both upper and lower extremities. In addition, pronators, plantar flexors, neck and thoracic flexors are involved. Postural reflexes (righting, equilibrium, and protective extension reactions) are all diminished. When balance is lost, the immediate compensatory adjustments needed to regain equilibrium are reduced. If the patient does fall, protective responses may be lacking, resulting in frequent injury. Automatic postural responses are particularly impaired if rigidity of the trunk is severe.[3,18] Patients with parkinsonism may be

Figure 23–2. Patients with Parkinson's disease develop a flexed or stooped posture which contributes to the problems of a festinating gait.

unable to perceive the upright or vertical position with their eyes closed.[21] This may indicate an abnormality in processing vestibular and proprioceptive information contributing to balance.[22] Rotatory movements around the longitudinal axis are also impaired. Thus the patient finds turning and rolling movements difficult, if not impossible. Deficits in axial rotation are particularly disabling, impairing many simple functional activities such as rolling over and getting out of bed.[23]

Automatic or unconscious movements are impaired or lost. An example of this is the loss of reciprocal arm swing during gait. The patient is required to think about each movement in order to execute it successfully. Constantly combating the effects of bradykinesia and rigidity can lead to mental fatigue and loss of motivation.

In patients with fully developed parkinsonism, fatigue is one of the most common symptoms reported. The patient has difficulty in sustaining activity and experiences increasing weakness and lethargy as the day progresses. Repetitive motor acts may start out strong but decrease in strength as the activity progresses. Thus the first few words spoken may be loud and strong but audibility of succeeding words diminishes rapidly as speech continues. Performance decreases dramatically after great physical effort or mental stress. Rest or sleep may restore mobility. When levodopa therapy is initiated, the patient may notice a dramatic improvement by feeling significantly less fatigued, whereas in long-standing drug therapy fatigue may reappear.[24]

The gait pattern of the patient with parkinsonism is highly stereotyped and characterized by an impoverishment of movement. Lower limb, hip, knee, and ankle motions are decreased with a generalized lack of extension at all three joints. Trunk and pelvic motions also are diminished, resulting in a decrease in step length and reciprocal arm swing. Patients characteristically walk with a slow and shuffling gait. Persistent posturing of a forward head and trunk typically displaces the patient's center of gravity forward and may result in a **festinant gait pattern.** The patient takes multiple short steps in order to avoid falling forward and may eventually break into a run or trot. **Propulsive gait pattern** has a forward accelerating quality, and a **retropulsive gait** has a backward accelerating one. Many patients are able to stop only when they come in contact with an object or a wall. Patients who are toe walkers owing to plantarflexion contractures exhibit an additional postural instability because of a narrowing of their base of support. Movements that involve turning or changing direction are particularly difficult to accomplish.[25]

Facial expression is described as **masklike** with infrequent blinking and lack of expression. Smiling may be possible only on command or with volitional effort. Drooling, **sialorrhea,** may be present along with impaired swallowing (dysphagia). Speech also may be disturbed. The predominant finding is usually hypophonia or decreased volume of speech secondary to rigidity and bradykinesia of the speech musculature and decreased excursion of the chest. In some advanced cases, the patient speaks in whispers, if at all, and the speech is slurred and monotonous.[26]

Autonomic nervous sytem dysfunction also may occur

with symptoms of postural dizziness, excessive perspiration, greasy skin, or uncomfortable sensations of heat. Problems with constipation, or urinary frequency or retention, may be present.[9]

Mental changes occur in about 25 percent of the patients and may result from severe parkinsonism, drug toxicity, or from concurrent multiple cerebrovascular accidents. Consistent deficits have been reported in short-term memory and in problem solving, which tends to be slow and confused (termed bradycognition).[8] Many patients also demonstrate apathy, passivity, loss of ambition or enthusiasm, and dependency. In severe cases, behavioral changes also may result from the sensory deprivation caused by the marked paucity of movement.[9] Delusions and visual hallucinations are common complications of drug toxicity. Similarities of the population with Parkinson's disease to the aging population in general and more specifically to those with Alzheimer's disease have been studied. Serious losses in neurotransmitter synthesis may account for the difficulties in movement many older individuals experience. Parkinsonlike problems such as a shuffling gait are common in the elderly. Some features of parkinsonism may appear with Alzheimer's disease.[10,21,23,27]

Although patients with Parkinson's disease do not suffer from primary sensory deficits, many experience discomfort or pain that is cramplike and poorly localized. These sensations may result from lack of movement, sustained muscle spasms, faulty posture, or ligamentous strain. Many patients experience paresthesias in the limbs. Perceptual motor deficits also may be present in this disease. Patients demonstrate significantly more errors on visual perceptual tasks involving spatial organization. The basal ganglia appear to play an important role in the integration of sensory information used in the feedback system. Deficits in tasks involving gestural movements, delayed response, simultaneous double tasks, tracking, construction, and body scheme have been reported.[9,17,18,21,28]

SECONDARY PROBLEMS AND COMPLICATIONS

Most patients with parkinsonism are elderly and show the effects of generalized musculoskeletal deconditioning. The more severe the symptoms, the greater the inactivity and resultant deconditioning. Widespread rigidity also produces additional gastrointestinal and circulatory problems. Secondary problems and complications include those described below.

1. Muscle atrophy and weakness secondary to disuse.
2. Respiratory changes. Vital capacity is usually markedly reduced owing to decreased thoracic expansion, resulting from rigidity of the intercostals and the upper trunk and upper extremity positions of flexion and flexion-adduction. Energy consumption is increased, and hyperpnea often results secondary to the increased muscular effort required for normal breathing. These patients are in constant danger of respiratory complications such as pneumonia, which is one of the leading causes of death in patients with this disease.

3. Nutritional changes. Patients with Parkinson's disease notoriously have an excellent appetite and yet tend to lose weight. Late in the disease, many of these patients become malnourished because of problems in eating, chewing, and swallowing. This contributes to the fatigue and exhaustion they often experience from ordinary activities of daily living. Constipation is also a problem, and most patients need to be on a regular bowel program.

4. Osteoporosis. This is often a serious problem with parkinsonism because of prolonged inactivity and typical age. Poor diet also may contribute to the development of osteoporosis. Loss of automatic movement, poor balance reactions, and osteoporosis result in frequent falls and fractures. Fracture healing may be delayed or disordered.

5. Circulatory changes. The lower extremities exhibit circulatory changes secondary to the venous pooling that results from decreased mobility. These patients can present with edema of the feet and ankles during the day, which disappears when in bed.

6. Contracture and deformity. Lack of movement in any body segment leads to shortening of muscles and soft tissue deformity. Typical contractures occur in hip and knee flexors; hip adductors; plantarflexors and toe flexors; upper chest, dorsal spine and neck flexors; shoulder adductors and internal rotators; forearm pronators; and wrist and finger flexors. Kyphosis is the most common postural deformity, although some patients tend to lean to one side when walking or sitting, possibly owing to unequal distribution of rigidity in the trunk.

7. Decubitus ulcers. In advanced cases, prolonged inactivity and bedrest may lead to the development of decubitus ulcers. This is a serious complication, because healing is often delayed. If a prolonged infection occurs, it may become life-threatening.

TREATMENT

The treatment of patients with parkinsonism involves both medical and rehabilitative management. The diagnosis is usually made on the basis of history and clinical examination. Blood tests, electroencephalography, and computerized axial tomography (CAT scan) may aid in the differential diagnosis by excluding other causes. An estimate of the stage and severity of the disease can be made using existing scales (Table 23–1). These provide a useful measure of the progression of the disease and the long-term response to treatment.[8] A carefully planned program of drug therapy and nutritional intervention is a typical component of both early and long-term care. Intensive exercise and activity programs are designed to keep the patient mobile and functionally independent. Finally, counseling by all members of the multidisciplinary team assists the patient and family in the difficult adjustment to chronic disability. They should be helped to maintain realistic expectations about what therapy can and can not achieve. In cases of marked depression and poor motivation, a psychiatric consultation may be indicated. Intervention is symptomatic. A cure for Parkinson's disease is currently not available, and the disease is progressive in nature. With early and vigorous treatment, the effects of the disease can be minimized and the

Table 23–1 PROGNOSTIC CLASSIFICATION OF PARKINSON DISEASE

Schwab Classification of Progression*			Hoehn and Yahr Classification of Disability†	
Grade	Chronology of Disease Manifestations	Comments	Stage	Character of Disability
1	Symptoms generally remain stable for at least 5 years after diagnosis.	Diagnosis may be uncertain. Minimal therapy is required. Ability to live independently is usually not threatened.	I	Minimal or absent; unilateral if present.
2	Some evidence of progression may be observed after 5 years. Disease may remain unilateral.	With appropriate pharmacotherapy, most patients can remain independent.	II	Minimal bilateral or midline involvement. Balance not impaired.
3	Marked progression is observed after 3 to 5 years. Disease may remain unilateral.	Partial incapacitation is likely, but most patients are still able to live independently 10 years after diagnosis.	III	Impaired righting reflexes. Unsteadiness when turning or rising from chair. Some activities are restricted, but patient can live independently and continue some forms of employment.
4	Disease progresses to severe tremor and rigidity after 3 to 5 years. Manifestations are usually bilateral after 8 to 10 years.	Patient may remain ambulatory, but serious disability may supervene.	IV	All symptoms present and severe. Requires help with some activities of daily living.
5	Onset of disease is abrupt. Severe bilateral tremor, rigidity, and akinesia are present within a few months. Marked incapacity and motor deficiency are present within 1 year.	Outlook is for severe or total disability.	V	Confined to bed or wheelchair unless aided.

*Adapted from Schwab, RS: *Progression and prognosis in Parkinson's disease.* J Nerv Ment Dis 130:556, 1960.
†Adapted from Hoehn, MM, and Yahr, MD: *Parkinsonism: Onset, progression, and mortality.* Neurology 17:433, 1967.
From Feldman, R,[8] with permission.

secondary complications prevented or minimized. Treatment is very often least effective in older patients with more advanced disease. In late or severe cases, the patient may be wheelchair dependent or bedridden.

Medical Management

Drugs are prescribed to control rigidity, bradykinesia, tremor, and depression. These drugs are summarized in Table 23–2. None is completely successful in alleviating all the symptoms, for these patients seem to develop a tolerance for drugs, necessitating a change in prescription from time to time. Often it is the therapist who first notices a change in the patient's status as the patient's system adapts to either the amount or the type of drug prescribed. Accurate observation and reporting of these changes will greatly assist the physician in modifying a drug prescription.

Levodopa, or **L-dopa,** was first introduced in 1961 as an experimental drug and was used widely in clinical practice by 1967.[29] It is currently the standard treatment for Parkinson's disease. Levodopa is a metabolic precursor of dopamine that is able to cross the blood-brain barrier. It raises the level of striatal dopamine in the basal ganglia, thus attempting to correct the neurochemical imbalance. L-dopa is most commonly administered in combination with decarboxylase inhibitor that doesn't enter the brain (e.g., **Sinemet** or Madopar). Its primary effect is in alleviating bradykinesia and rigidity with less effect on tremor. Often the initial functional improvement is dramatic. It is less effective in treating patients with long-standing disease, because there is a progressive loss of dopamine receptors in the striatal neurons as the disease progresses. There are numerous side effects to levodopa therapy, which usually do not present serious problems and which can be controlled by adjusting the dosage or administering it in combination with other drugs. Among them are (1) gastrointestinal disturbances (nausea and vomiting); (2) dyskinesias (facial grimacing with twitching of the lips, face, and tongue protrusion; choreoathetoid movements of the arms and legs); (3) mental disturbances (restlessness, general overactivity, anxiety or depression, disorientation, hallucinations, or memory disturbance); (4) orthostatic hypotension (dizziness and fainting); (5) painful spasms or cramps; and (6) rarely, cardiac arrythmias. L-dopa is usually contraindicated in patients with acute myocardial infarction and must be monitored closely in patients with generalized cardiovascular insufficiency. Patients may feel so much better while taking L-dopa that they may engage in sudden heavy physical activity, seriously overtaxing their cardiovascular system. The therapist needs to watch for this and to pace the patient accordingly.[10]

End-of-dose deterioration (as effects of individual dose wears off) occurs owing to the brain's loss of storage

Table 23–2 ANTIPARKINSONISM DRUGS

Drug	Dosage	Precautions and Remarks
Anticholinergic drugs Trihexyphenidyl (Artane)	1–5 mg 3 times daily, starting at low dosage and slowly increasing. For oculogyric crisis use 10 mg 3 times daily.	May precipitate acute glaucoma in elderly persons and are contraindicated in patients with glaucoma. Blurred vision, dryness of mouth, vertigo, and tachycardia are early toxic symptoms; late symptoms are vomiting, dizziness, mental confusion, and hallucinations. The synthetic drugs are apt to cause more dizziness than the natural alkaloids and are somewhat less potent parasympatholytics.
Biperiden (Akineton)	2 mg 3–4 times daily.	
Procyclidine (Kemadrin)	2.5–5 mg 3 times daily after meals.	
Benztropine mesylate (Cogentin)	0.5 mg 1–2 times daily, increasing by 0.5 mg at intervals of several days to 5 mg daily or toxicity. Often most effective as single dose at bedtime.	Side effects similar to those of trihexyphenidyl.
Dopaminergic drugs Levodopa (Dopar, Larodopa, etc)	250 mg 3 times daily. Increase to tolerance (4–8 g daily).	Nausea, vomiting, postural hypotension, choreiform movements.
Levodopa and carbidopa (Sinemet)	3–6 tablets daily of Sinemet 25/250.	Nausea, vomiting, postural hypotension, dyskinesias.
Armantadine (Symmetrel)	100 mg twice daily.	Jitteriness, insomnia, depression, confusion, hallucinations, livedo reticularis.
Bromocriptine mesylate (Parlodel)	1.25 mg twice daily with food. Increase slowly as necessary by adding 2.5 mg daily at 2- to 4-week intervals.	Nausea, abnormal involuntary movement, hallucinations, confusion, drowsiness.

From Chusid, JG: *Correlative Neuroanatomy and Functional Neurology,* ed 19. Lange Medical Publications, Los Altos, CA, 1985, with permission.

capacity. Off episodes (a sudden episode of immobility) may appear usually at the end of dose. Long-term use of levodopa therapy may result in a deterioration of the overall therapeutic effect. This may be due to a progressive unresponsiveness of the dopamine receptors or progressive loss of dopamine neurons. Fluctuations in performance and drug response ("on-off" phenomenon) occurs in about 50 percent of the patients treated for more than 2 years. After 3 to 5 years, most patients gradually worsen. Dyskinesias, or off episodes, become more common and end-of-dose deterioration may occur earlier. An increase in parkinsonian fatigue or loss of sleep benefit also may be noted.[24,30–32] Patients with decreased responsiveness to levodopa therapy may be given a period of transient levodopa withdrawal. This drug holiday averages 7 to 10 days and may enhance motor responsiveness to the drug and decrease levodopa-induced side effects. The beneficial effects of a drug holiday may last as long as 6 months to a year. Approximately 20 to 30 percent of patients do not benefit from a drug holiday.[33,34] Hospitalization is common to monitor the effects of the drug holiday and to facilitate reinstitution of drug therapy. During this time patients may have a dramatic worsening of symptoms, and the secondary effects of immobility must be carefully monitored.

Patients with advanced Parkinson's disease may benefit from administration of striatal dopaminergic agonist drugs such as bromocriptine. These drugs are thought to improve function of dopamine receptors and are generally used in combination with levodopa/carbidopa to prolong the effectiveness of levodopa therapy.[8,35] Additional new drugs designed to maintain drug effectiveness are also undergoing clinical trials.[36,37] The therapist needs

to be fully aware of each medication the patient is on and of its potential side effects. Therapists also may be involved in the monitoring of patient performance during clinical drug trials.

Another major group of drugs used, often in conjunction with L-dopa, are the **anticholinergic agents**. These drugs block the excessive cholinergic activity in the basal ganglia and are most effective in controlling tremor.[8] Trihexyphenidyl hydrochloride (Artane), benztropine (Cogentin), and biperiden (Akineton) are commonly prescribed drugs in this group. Side effects include dry mouth, constipation, urinary retention, and impairment of memory or judgment. Additional drugs to control tremor, depression, edema, and other secondary problems may also be prescribed.[4,9]

Nutritional management consists of a high-caloric, low-protein diet. Research suggests that a high-protein diet can block the effectiveness of levodopa and therefore may be contraindicated in some patients.[38] In addition, the patient may be given a vitamin supplement (without B_6) and placed on a bowel program. A vigorous training program in activities of daily living to improve eating and swallowing skills is also of considerable importance in helping maintain the nutrition and general health of these patients.

Surgical Management

For years, **stereotaxic surgery** to alleviate the symptoms of parkinsonism was a major form of therapy for these patients. It involves producing destructive lesions in the basal ganglia or thalamus by cryosurgery or chemosurgery. Recent advances in microelectrode techniques allow for precise subcortical localization of the lesions. The principal effects are to decrease or to abolish tremor and to reduce rigidity, and it is effective in approximately 90 percent of the cases. The effects of bradykinesia are not improved by stereotaxic surgery. The combined effects of surgery and levodopa therapy may be beneficial for a few patients.[39,40]

Rehabilitative Management

The long-term goals of a physical therapy program include the following:

1. Delay or minimize the progression and effects of the disease symptoms.

2. Prevent the development of secondary complications and deformity.

3. Maintain the functional abilities of the patient to the fullest extent.

The attainment of these goals is dependent upon a thorough and accurate plan that maximizes movement and engages the patient's full cooperation. It also requires a comprehensive team approach involving the coordinated effort of all members of the rehabilitation team, including the family.

ASSESSMENT

The examination begins with a thorough assessment of the tone problems the patient exhibits and their impact on movement. The therapist needs to determine the degree of rigidity in response to passive movement as well as the limitations imposed upon active and automatic movements. Movement transitions (e.g., rising from a chair or rolling in bed) should be stressed. Inasmuch as the distribution of tone is very often unequal, it is important to determine which body segments are most affected. Close attention must be paid to the tone changes in the trunk, because rigidity here can often be the most disabling in terms of loss of function. Postural reactions will be diminished or absent. A thorough assessment of righting, equilibrium, and protective reactions is indicated. Unequal distribution of tone also leads to contracture and deformity. Objective measurement of both active and passive range of motion using goniometry is helpful in quantifying these deficits. Postural and gait assessments are also routinely performed.

An assessment of the patient's functional abilities can be determined using a disability scale. The influence of rigidity, bradykinesia, and tremor on functional performance should be noted for each skill tested. Problems will often be noted in those activities having a rotational component, such as rolling or turning. Fine motor skills, such as feeding or dressing, will also be more difficult. The time it takes to initiate and to complete an activity should be recorded. Scored performance on disability scales are frequently used to monitor the patient's responses to drug and rehabilitation therapy. Because these patients experience increased fatigue with resultant fluctuations in performance, examinations should be kept brief (i.e., 10 to 15 minutes) and repeated at different times during the day. A videotape of functional movement patterns can provide an objective record of dysfunction. Table 23–3 presents a sample assessment form. Functional assessment in the home environment is also indicated.

More complicated and objective methods of studying movement also have been used to study patients with Parkinson's syndrome. Torque output (isokinetic testing) and electromyography (EMG) have been used to quantify the effects of rigidity and bradykinesia on motor performance. Long latency responses (50 to 120 msec) have been observed in the EMG responses to muscles subjected to sudden stretch. Abnormal patterns of motor unit recruitment are also present.[20] Tests for **reaction time** (**RT,** the interval between the presentation of a stimulus and the start of movement) and **movement time** (**MT,** the interval between the beginning and end of movement) have been used to study motoric slowing. Instruments that measure RT and MT usually employ a response key and chronoscopes (which record time in hundreths of seconds) activated by a stimulus (typically a buzzer or light).[41] Patients with parkinsonism have significant increases in MT, whereas RT is essentially normal. These results suggest hypokinesia may represent a deficit of autoevoked arousal mechanisms (individual will) rather than exoevoked mechanisms (response to external stimuli).[42,43] Timed tests for rapidly alternating movements (alternate pronation-supination) and complex tasks (tapping tests, pegboards, and other coordination tests) also have been used.[44]

The therapist should focus particular attention on assessing the patient's cardiorespiratory status. Cardiovascular endurance is usually decreased from long-standing inactivity and poor respiratory function. Excessive fatigue, shortness of breath, and high heart rate response to exercise are all indices of marked deconditioning and exercise intolerance. Diaphragmatic movements and thoracic expansion and mobility also should be assessed. Respiratory function tests (vital capacity and forced expiratory volume) and screening for dysphagia should be routinely considered. Finally, it is important to assess the patient's premorbid interests, abilities, and daily activities in order to translate them into a treatment program that will engage the patient's full cooperation.

FORMULATING A TREATMENT PLAN

The following short-term goals are relevant to the treatment of the patient with parkinsonism.

1. Maintain or increase range of motion in all joints.

2. Prevent contractures and correct faulty posture.

3. Prevent disuse atrophy and muscle weakness.

4. Promote and improve motor function and mobility.

5. Improve gait pattern.

6. Improve speech, breathing patterns, chest expansion and mobility.

7. Maintain or increase functional independence in activities of daily living.

8. Assist in psychologic adjustment to chronic disability and lifestyle modification.

Inasmuch as each patient is unique and presents a different set of problems, these goals will vary accordingly.

Table 23-3 PHYSICAL THERAPY FLOW SHEET: PARKINSON PROGRAM

Date Time										
Last Med. Time										
Video tape										
Bradykinesia										
TREMOR — Type										
TREMOR — Severity										
RIGIDITY — Type										
RIGIDITY — Severity										
Vital Capacity										
SPECIFY IN TIME — Supine to sitting										
SPECIFY IN TIME — Sitting to standing										
SPECIFY IN TIME — Ambulation 50 feet										
SPECIFY IN TIME — Side step 10 times										
SPECIFY IN TIME — Backwalking 10 steps										
Assistive Device										

Key (Refer to Full Evaluation for Additional Information)

BRADYKINESIA
0 = None
1 = Minimal slowness
2 = Moderate slowness; poverty of movement
3 = Marked slowness; poverty of movement, hesitation on initiation of movement, arrests of ongoing movement
4 = Severe slowness and poverty; inability to perform four-limb simultaneous movement

1 = Supervision
2 = Contact guarding
3 = Minimal assistance
4 = Moderate assistance
5 = Maximal assistance

TREMOR
0 = Absent
1 = Minimal amplitude
2 = Moderate amplitude
3 = Marked amplitude but only intermittently present
4 = Severe; marked amplitude constantly present

I = Intention
R = Resting

RIGIDITY
0 = Absent
1 = Minimal
2 = Moderate
3 = Marked, but full range of motion easily achieved
4 = Severe; full ROM with difficulty

C = Cogwheel
L = Leadpipe

From University Hospital, Department of Rehabilitation Medicine, Boston, with permission.

Early intervention with patients with mild disease is critical in the prevention of the devastating musculoskeletal deformities that these patients are so prone to develop. In general, each treatment session should encourage as much activity and movement as possible. However, movement must be carefully balanced with adequate rest periods to ensure that the patient does not reach the point of fatigue and exhaustion. Thus, frequent, short periods of physical activity are preferable.

RELAXATION EXERCISES

Gentle rocking and rhythmic techniques that emphasize slow vestibular stimulation can be used to produce generalized relaxation of the total body musculature. This effect was described almost 100 years ago by Professor Charcot in Paris, who noted dramatic improvement in patients with parkinsonism after rides in bumpy, horsedrawn carriages. Following this observation, he constructed a vibrating chair to use with his patients.[10] More recent work has substantiated the beneficial effects of repetitive vestibular stimulation on hypertonicity.[45,46] Clinically, a rocking chair or rotating chair may provide an effective aid in reducing tone and improving mobility.[47] Slow rhythmic rolling also can be accomplished on a mat. The inverted head position (positioning with head down, e.g., prone over a stool or large ball) can produce a generalized relaxation through activation of the carotid sinus reflex and depression of the medullary centers. This technique must be used for only a short duration, however, for prolonged head-down positioning could result in a drop in blood pressure and an increase in intracranial pressure.[48,49] Finally, yoga is an effective relaxation technique for many patients and may be particularly effective for these patients because of its emphasis on combining relaxation with deep breathing and slow, steady stretching.[50]

RANGE OF MOTION EXERCISES

Both active and passive range of motion exercises ideally should be completed several times a day. Active exercises should focus on strengthening the patient's weak, elongated extensor muscles while stretching the shortened, tight flexor muscles. Because the patient will be limited in the amount of active movement possible, it is usually necessary to use active assistive and passive movement as well. Specific muscle contractures may respond to autogenic inhibition techniques, such as the proprioceptive neuromuscular facilitation (PNF) contract-relax technique, which combines inhibition from active movement with rotation of the limb.[51,52] Prolonged, passive stretching at the maximum tolerated length of muscle also increases range through autogenic inhibition and may be accomplished through manual or mechanical stretching (inhibitory casting, splints, traction, tilt table).[53] The resistance to stretch in patients with parkinsonism is constant and present at all speeds of stretch, unlike spasticity, in which resistance is velocity dependent. The therapist should avoid excessive stretching and pain, which can stimulate pain receptors and cause a rebound muscle contraction. Excessive stretching also can cause tearing of the tissue, scar formation, and more shortening. These patients must be considered suspect of osteoporosis and therefore must be exercised accordingly. Ideally, range of motion exercises should be combined with other exercises using functional patterns that stress total reciprocal movements, including trunk, scapula, and pelvic components. Joint mobilization techniques are helpful in patients with tightness of the joint capsule or ligaments around a joint. By using selected grades of accessory movement, both range and pain can be improved.[54] Home range of motion exercise often can be accomplished by adaptive equipment such as wall pulleys if the bradykinesia is not severe. Hanging from an overhead bar also may be used to provide a maintained stretch on the upper trunk and extremity flexors.[55] Thus an effective range of motion program utilizes a variety of treatment techniques and is based on careful assessment to identify the underlying causes of restricted movement.

MOBILITY EXERCISES

An exercise program for the patient with parkinsonism should be based upon functional movement patterns that engage several body segments at once. Extensor, abductor, and rotary movements should be stressed. Movements should be rhythmic and reciprocal and should progress toward full range of motion. Exercises that are related to functional skills, such as self-care, and premor-bid skills will help increase motivation and reduce the apathy and depression that is commonly seen in these patients. The use of verbal, auditory, and tactile stimulation provides sensory reinforcement and helps increase patient awareness of movement. Verbal commands, music, clapping, marching, metronomes, mirrors, and floor markings are all examples of effective aids in promoting successful performance of an activity. These techniques are consistent with research findings describing an increased dependence on external stimuli for movement control.[42,56,57]

Several specific exercise techniques and approaches have been found particularly effective in the treatment of the patient with parkinsonism. These include PNF,[51,58] Bobath's neurodevelopmental treatment (NDT),[59-60] and rhythmic activities.[61-64] The use of diagonal limb and trunk PNF patterns accomplishes several exercise goals at once. Because these patients have a minimum of energy to expend and multiple clinical problems, they benefit from exercising in total-body, physiologic patterns that combine several motions at once. Proprioceptive neuromuscular facilitation patterns also emphasize rotation, a movement component that is typically lost early in Parkinson's disease. Extremity patterns should emphasize smooth movement, using slow reversals through increments of range. Particular emphasis should be placed on activating extensor muscles to counteract the tendency for a flexed, stooped posture. In the upper extremities, bilateral symmetrical D_2 flexion patterns (shoulder flexion, abduction, external rotation) are useful in promoting upper trunk extension and in counteracting kyphosis. During this exercise, coordination with respiratory movements emphasizing increased chest expansion should be encouraged. In the lower extremities, hip and knee extension should be emphasized, ideally in a D_1 extension pattern (hip extension, abduction, internal rotation) to counteract the typical flexed, adducted posture. The PNF technique of choice is rhythmic initiation, which is aimed specifically at overcoming the debilitating effects of bradykinesia. The therapist begins by moving the limb through the pattern passively, gradually increasing the range and setting up a rhythm to the movement. As relaxation occurs and the movements are more easily accomplished, the patient is asked to participate in the movement, first with assistance and then gradually against slight resistance. After several repetitions, the patient then moves actively through the pattern. This "pumping up" sequence can be used as an effective start to many activities. For example, in activities of daily living such as standing up, the patient can begin by swaying back and forth until a rhythm is set up and tone reduced. The active movement of standing up can then be superimposed upon the more relaxed body state. Thus the patient progresses from passive reversals to active assistive to resistive and finally to active movement.

Developmental mat activities that emphasize the mobility stage of motor control, rotational movements, and extensor antigravity muscles are also helpful. Upper trunk extension with rotation (lifting) is an example. This activity may become a useful component in teaching rolling or upright sitting. Rolling is a problematic activity which should receive early and intensive emphasis in treatment. Active rolling can be facilitated using rhythmic initiation and segmental (either upper or lower trunk) rotation in the sidelying posture. Once control is achieved in sidelying, rolling from full prone to the supine position and reverse can be practiced. Head and neck patterns, particularly extension with rotation, also may be helpful. Standing balance may be improved with the use of rhythmic stabilization, a technique designed to improve imbalances in postural muscles through isometric reversals of antagonists and cocontraction. The grading of resistance is extremely important, for high levels of resistance are not appropriate for patients with hypertonia. Resistive techniques should be discontinued if they lead to an increase in rigidity.

Facilitating movement of facial, hyoid, and tongue muscles is another important goal, inasmuch as the patient may have limited social interaction and poor eating skills in the presence of marked rigidity and bradykinesia. These factors can greatly influence the patient's overall psychologic state and motivation. Use of stretch, manual contacts, resistance, and verbal commands may enhance facial movement greatly. Movement reversals and repeated contractions should be stressed. In cases in which eating is impaired by immobility, the movements of opening and closing the mouth and chewing combined with neck control (stabilization in a neutral position) should be stressed. Icing to tongue, facial and hyoid muscles may facilitate more normal function. Eating should be done in a sitting position, and the therapist should ensure that the head and neck are in good position. The patient also can be instructed to practice deliberate articulations and facial movements such as smiling, frowning, and so forth, using a mirror for visual feedback.

In NDT, righting, equilibrium, and protective extensor reactions through the use of automatic patterns of movement are emphasized. Movement transitions that use rotational patterns help break up the total flexor patterns commonly seen in these patients. Effective handling by the therapist promotes active and automatic postural adjustment. Helpful activities include active trunk rotation in both sitting and standing. Transitions from sidesitting to all fours and back to sidesitting are helpful in developing lower trunk mobility. Manual contacts should be on the hips as a key point of control. Rolling, sit to stand, and standing balance activities also should be addressed.

RESPIRATORY EXERCISES

The patient is taught breathing exercises to increase the mobility of the chest wall and to improve lung ventilation. Diaphragmatic breathing and basal chest expansion should be emphasized. Chest wall mobility can be increased by using stretch and resistance to the intercostals and by combining arm and upper trunk patterns with breathing exercises. Pressure and manual contacts can be used to emphasize areas of poor chest expansion. Improving postural alignment in kyphotic patients is also important. Control of breathing can be facilitated greatly by using verbal and tactile stimuli. Inasmuch as control is very often achieved only with conscious effort, carry-over into daily activities can be limited. In order to prevent further respiratory complications from develop-

ing, these exercises should receive major emphasis in treatment.[65]

GAIT TRAINING

Gait training attempts to overcome the following primary deficits: a festinant and shuffling gait, poor postural alignment, and defective postural reflexes. Specific goals are to lengthen the stride, to broaden the base of support, to increase contralateral trunk movement and arm swing, to encourage a heel-toe gait pattern, to increase postural reactions, and to provide a program of regular walking. Stride and width may be controlled through the use of floor markings; for example, walking lanes, transverse lines, or footprints. Small blocks of about 2 inches (5 cm) to 3 inches (7.5 cm) may be used to encourage picking up the feet and avoiding a shuffling gait. Two poles or sticks (held by the patient and therapist, one in each hand) may facilitate reciprocal arm swing during gait. The therapist uses his or her arm swing to assist the patient's. Stopping, starting, changing direction and type of movement pattern should be emphasized. Balance reactions in standing and walking should be practiced daily. Turning movements emphasizing small steps and a wide base also should be stressed. Because these patients may fall frequently, treatment should include instruction and practice in getting up from the floor. The overall rhythm of the gait pattern can be improved greatly by using voice commands (counting), music (Sousa's marches) or a metronome. A festinant gait sometimes may be partially alleviated by the addition of shoe wedges. A toe wedge may slow down a propulsive gait, and a heel wedge may diminish a retropulsive gait pattern.

For those postural defects that do not respond to exercise, other measures may have to be employed. A neck collar may help control the forward head position but will inhibit active head movement. Carrying a bag in one arm may help control listing of the trunk to the opposite side. These should be considered last-step measures to be employed when active or automatic postural control is impossible.

GROUP EXERCISES

Group exercise classes are often organized for patients with Parkinson's disease. Patients benefit from the positive support, camaraderie, and communication the group situation offers. Careful assessment of each patient prior to admission into a group is essential. Patients should be able to perform the therapeutic core of the class. Selecting patients with similar levels of disability is often advisable, because the sense of competition frequently can be a key factor in motivating groups. The ratio of staff to patients should be kept small (ideally 1:8 or 1:10), and extra staff should be added if patients are unable to work on their own. A variety of activities can be used to stimulate and to motivate patients. Warm-up activities or calisthenics involving large joints should be used to help patients limber up and get going. Exercise stations (e.g., stationary bicycle, mats, pulleys) are often devised. Exercises done by the whole group together should focus on important exercise goals (e.g., improve ROM, mobility). Games or activities can follow the exercise portion using such activities as dancing, singing, or marching to recorded music, ball playing, bean-bag toss, and so forth. The activities selected should be interesting and varied. The class should then end on a quiet note with a discussion of home recommendations and everyday problems. The therapist's approach needs to be enthusiastic and supportive. Teaching style should incorporate a stimulating voice, careful observation, and gentle corrections.[66,67]

PATIENT AND FAMILY EDUCATION

The key element in patient and family education is ensuring they understand that prolonged periods of inactivity should be avoided. Movement and ways to stimulate movement are the primary focus. Family members can be taught rhythmic rotation and pumping-up procedures. Early morning warm-up exercises are helpful in reducing the increased stiffness patients may experience upon rising. Environmental aids or adaptions should be used as needed to help patients overcome specific problems. Clothing adaptions or adapted eating utensils may improve function. From bed, the patient can be helped to assume a sitting position by elevating the head of the bed with blocks of approximately 4 inches (10 cm) or by attaching a knotted rope to the end of the bed to pull on. The bed should be firm. Rocking movements also help initiate movement. In sitting, the patient can rock or be rocked forward and backward, combining these movements with arm swing to bring the weight forward over the feet. A favorite, firm chair also can be raised about 4 inches (10 cm) with blocks, or a rocking chair can be helpful. The patient should never be dragged from a chair by the arms but, rather, should be assisted to standing by a slight push on the back. Once in the standing position, forward progression can sometimes be initiated by having the patient dorsiflex the toes, shifting the weight either forward or to the side or by marking time in place. Arm movements (e.g., shifting a hankerchief from one hand to the other) may be helpful in initiating movement, or, sometimes, dropping in front of the patient a small object that has to be stepped over has been found to work. The patient can learn to use these triggering techniques to initiate movement. Other times a family member must be instructed in the proper way to best assist the patient.[68]

LONG-TERM CARE

Patients with parkinsonism typically are seen on an outpatient basis and are given home programs to attain or to maintain the therapeutic goals of treatment. These should include exercises that the patient can master either alone or with the aid of a family member. They should be realistic and of moderate duration and inten-

sity. The patient should be cautioned against overdoing activity, resulting in excessive fatigue. Exercises should be done daily and often. Patients successfully treated with levodopa will exhibit a dramatic decrease in rigidity and bradykinesia. The alleviation of these symptoms does not always produce a similar amount of improvement in their function, however, for poor habits and faulty posture may persist. These patients usually will respond quite well to a treatment program designed to facilitate more normal movement patterns and posture. The excellent results achieved with L-dopa and rehabilitation are quite gratifying for both patient and therapist.

Patients with advanced disease or who do not respond well to medical or rehabilitation management will require continual supervision in activities of daily living and mobility. These patients should be encouraged to move as much as possible and not to let everything be done for them. Often, environmental adaptations may mean the difference between total dependence and partial independence. The entire rehabilitation team should be supportive of the patient's efforts, no matter how small they may be. This group of patients is one of the more debilitated populations seen in rehabilitation. One of the most frustrating aspects of working with them is that there seems to be very little carry-over outside the clinic. Movement achieved with a great deal of conscious control and stimulation in treatment soon disintegrates or disappears when those influences are removed. Home programs are effective only if the family becomes actively involved. In order to provide continued support and effective management, therapists and families need to maintain a realistic but positive outlook.

SUMMARY

Parkinson's disease is a chronic, progressive disorder of the basal ganglia characterized by a classic triad of symptoms: rigidity, bradykinesia, and tremor. Clinical manifestations include the development of abnormal fixed postures, diminished automatic postural reactions, festinating gait pattern, fatigue, masklike facial expression, and autonomic nervous system dysfunction. These patients are prone to develop any one of a number of secondary problems and complications owing to their progressive inactivity. Pharmacologic management of the disease focuses on control of specific symptoms. Levodopa or its derivative remains the mainstay of drug therapy. Effective rehabilitation programs focus on the maintenance of the functional abilities of the patient within the limitations imposed by the disease. Programs also seek to delay or to minimize disease progression while preventing the development of secondary complications and deformity. A comprehensive team approach including active involvement of family members can provide optimal benefits.

QUESTIONS FOR REVIEW

1. What are the major central nervous system structures involved in Parkinson's disease? How is the function of these structures altered? What is the primary effect on the motor system?

2. Name the three main clinical signs of parkinsonism. What are the major clinical manifestations?

3. How is Parkinson's syndrome diagnosed? What are the key elements of an assessment? What objective assessments are available?

4. Describe the drug therapy used in Parkinson's disease. How might a physical therapy program be influenced by drug management?

5. What are the major components of an exercise program? Name three techniques to increase range of motion. Name three techniques to increase mobility.

6. What types of activities should a gait training program stress? A home program?

7. What type of therapeutic program would you structure for the patient with advanced disease who is relatively unresponsive to drugs?

8. What are the major considerations in patient and family education?

REFERENCES

1. Burke, D, Hagbarth, K, and Wallin, G: Reflex mechanisms in Parkinsonian rigidity. Scand J Rehab Med 9:15, 1977.
2. Somjen, G: Neurophysiology: The Essentials. Williams & Wilkins, Baltimore, 1983.
3. Eyzaguirre, C and Fidone, S: Physiology of the Nervous System 2. Year Book Medical Publishers, Chicago, 1975.
4. Gilroy, J and Holliday, P: Basic Neurology. Macmillan Publishing, New York, 1982.
5. Brooks, VB: Roles of cerebellum and basal ganglia in initiation and control of movements. Can J Neurol Sci 2:265, 1975.
6. Guyton, A: Basic Neuroscience. WB Saunders, Philadelphia, 1987.
7. Lindsley, D and Holms, J: Basic Human Neurophysiology. Elsevier, New York, 1984.
8. Feldman, R: Parkinson disease: Individualizing therapy. Hosp Prac 20:80A, 1985.
9. Ilson, J, Bressman, S, and Fahn, S: Current concepts in Parkinson's disease. Hosp Med 19:33, 1983.
10. Stern, G: Parkinson's Disease. Oxford University Press, Oxford, 1982.
11. Weiner, W and Goetz, C: Neurology for the Non-neurologist. Harper & Row, Philadelphia, 1981.
12. Marttila, R: Etiology of parkinson's disease. In Rinne, UK, Klinger, M, and Stamm, G (eds): Parkinson's Disease: Current Progress, Problems and Management. Elsevier/North-Holland Biomedical Press, New York, 1980.
13. Duvoisin, R: Problems in the treatment of parkinsonism. In Messiha, F and Kenny, A (eds): Parkinson's Disease Neurophysiological, Clinical and Related Aspects. Plenum Press, New York, 1977.
14. Langston, JW and Ballard, P: Chronic Parkinsonism in humans due to a product of meperidine-analog synthesis. Science 219:976, 1983.
15. Torre, JC: Neurophysiology of movement disorders. In Messiha, F and Kenny, A (eds): Parkinson's Disease Neurophysiological, Clinical and Related Aspects. Plenum Press, New York, 1977.
16. Denny-Brown, D and Yanagisawa, N: The role of the basal ganglia in the initiation of movement. In Yahr, MD (ed): The Basal Ganglia. Raven Press, New York, 1976.
17. Sharpe, M, Cermak, S, and Sax, D: Motor planning in parkinson patients. Neuropsychologia 21:455, 1983.
18. Marsden, CD: The mysterious motor function of the basal ganglia: The Robert Wartenberg lecture. Neurology (NY) 32:514, 1982.
19. Evarts, EV: Brain mechanisms in movement. Scientific American 229:96, 1973.
20. Milner-Brown, H, et al: Electrical properties of motor units in Parkinsonism and a possible relationship with bradykinesia. J Neurol Neurosurg Psychiatry 42:35, 1979.
21. Bowen, FP: Behavioral alterations in patients with basal ganglia lesions. In Yahr, MD (ed): The Basal Ganglia. Raven Press, New York, 1976.
22. Melnick, M: Basal ganglia disorders: Metabolic, hereditary, and genetic disorders in adults. In Umphred, D: Neurological Rehabilitation. CV Mosby, St Louis, 1985.
23. Lakke, JP, deJong, R, et al: Observations on postural behavior: Axial rotation in recumbent position in parkinson patients after L-Dopa treatment. In Rinne, UK, Klinger, M, and Stamm, G: Parkinson's Disease: Current Progress, Problems, and Management. Elsevier/North-Holland Biomedical Press, New York, 1980.
24. Marsden, CD: On-off phenomena in Parkinson's disease. In Rinne, UK, Klinger, M, and Stamm, G: Parkinson's Disease: Current Prog-

ress, Problems and Management. Elsevier/North-Holland Biomedical Press, New York, 1980.
25. Murray, P, et al: Walking patterns of men with Parkinsonism. Am J Phys Med 57:278, 1978.
26. Berger, J: Impaired swallowing and excessive drooling in Parkinson's disease. Parkinson Report III (IV):1, 1985.
27. McGeer, P, McGeer, E, and Suzuki, J: Aging and extrapyramidal function. J Arch Neurol 34:33, 1977.
28. Stern, Y: Behavior and the Basal Ganglia. Adv Neurology (The Dementias) 38:195, 1983.
29. Stern, PH, et al: Levodopa and physical therapy in the treatment of patients with Parkinson's disease. Arch Phys Med 51:273, 1970.
30. Markhan, D and Diamond, S: Evidence to support early levodopa therapy in Parkinson disease. Neurology 31:125, 1981.
31. Klawans, H, et al: Recent advances in the biochemical pharmacology of extrapyramidal movement disorders. In Messiha, F and Kenny, A (eds): Parkinson's Disease: Neurophysiological, Clinical and Related Aspects. Plenum Press, New York, 1977.
32. Lang, A: Motor fluctuations in Parkinson's disease. Parkinson Report, II (IV):1, 1985.
33. Koller, W, et al: Complications of chronic levodopa therapy: Long-term efficacy of drug holiday, Neurology (NY) 31:373, 1981.
34. Direnfeld, L, et al: The L-dopa on-off effect in Parkinson disease: Treatment by transient drug withdrawal and dopamine receptor resensitization. Ann Neurol 4:573, 1978.
35. Lieberman, A, et al: Bromocriptine in Parkinson disease: Further studies. Neurology 29, 363, 1979.
36. White, J: Drug abuse yields important clues to Parkinson's disease. Drug Topics (Sept):32, 1985.
37. Weiner, W: Sinemet and Parlodel in the treatment of Parkinson's disease. Parkinson Report III (IV):3, 1985.
39 Mena, I and Cotzias, G: Protein intake and treatment of Parkinson's disease with levodopa. N Engl J Med 292:181, 1975.
39. Cooper, I, et al: Bilateral parkinsonism: Neurosurgical rehabilitation. J Am Geriatr Soc XVI:11, 1968.
40. Kelly, P and Gillingham, F: The long-term results of stereotaxic surgery and L-dopa therapy in patients with Parkinson's disease. J Neurosurg 53:332, 1980.
41. Sage, G: Introduction to Motor Behavior—A Neuropsychological Approach, ed 2. Addison-Wesley, Reading, MA, 1977.
42. Heilman, M, et al: Reaction times in Parkinson disease. Arch Neurol 33:139, 1976.
43. Terabavainen, H and Calne, DB: Assessment of hypokinesia in Parkinsonism. J Neural Tranm 51:149, 1981.
44. Terabavainen, H and Calne, D: Quantitative assessment of Parkinsonian deficits. In Rinne, UK, Klinger, M, and Stamm, G: Parkinson's Disease: Current Progress, Problems and Management. Elsevier/North-Holland Biomedical Press, New York, 1980.
45. Pederson, D: The soothing effects of rocking as determined by the direction and frequency of movement. Can J Behav Sci 7:237, 1975.
46. Peterson, B, et al: Changes in response of medial pontomedullary reticular neurons during repetitive cutaneous, vestibular, cortical and rectal stimulation. J Neurophysiol 39:564, 1976.
47. Stockmeyer, S: An interpretation of the approach of Rood to the treatment of neuromuscular dysfunction. Am J Phys Med 46:900, 1967.
48. Heineger, M and Randolph, S: Neurophysiological Concepts in Human Behavior. CV Mosby, St Louis, 1981.

49. Rood, M: The use of sensory receptors to activate, facilitate, and inhibit motor response, automatic and somatic, in developmental sequence. In Satterly, C (ed): Approaches to The Treatment of Patients with Neuromuscular Dysfunction. Wm C Brown, DuBuque, IA, 1962.

50. Vishnudenananda, S: The Complete Illustrated Book of Yoga. Pocket Books, New York, 1972.

51. Voss, D, Ionta, M, and Myers, B: Proprioceptive Neuomuscular Facilitation, ed 3. Harper & Row, New York, 1985.

52. Markos, P: Ipsilateral and contralateral effects of proprioceptive neuromuscular techniques on hip motion and electromyographic activity. Phys Ther 59, 1366, 1979.

53. Cherry, D: Review of physical therapy alternatives for reducing muscle contracture. Phys Ther 60:877, 1980.

54. Kaltenborn, F: Mobilization of the Extremity Joints: Examination and Basic Treatment Techniques. Olaf Norlis Bokhandel, Oslo,1980.

55. Scott, A: Degenerative diseases. In Trombly, C: Occupational Therapy for Physical Dysfunction, ed 2. Williams & Wilkins, Baltimore, 1983.

56. Cooke, J, Brown, J, and Brooks, V: Increased dependence on visual information for movement control in patients with Parkinson's disease. Can J Neurol Sci 5:413, 1978.

57. Stefaniwsky, L and Bilowit, D: Parkinsonism: Facilitation of motion by sensory stimulation. Arch Phys Med Rehabil 54:75, 1973.

58. Sullivan, P, Markos, P, and Minor, M: An Integrated Approach to Therapeutic Exercise. Reston Publishing, Reston, VA, 1982.

59. Bobath, B: Abnormal Postural Reflex Activity Caused by Brain Lesions. William Heinemann Medical Books, London, 1965.

60. Bobath, B: The treatment of neuromuscular disorders by improving patterns of coordination. Physiotherapy 55:18, 1969.

61. Ball, J: Demonstration of the traditional approach in the treatment of a patient with parkinsonism. Am J Phys Med 46:1034, 1967.

62. Doshay, L and Feitelberg, S: Exercises for the Parkinson Patient. United Parkinson Foundation, Chicago (undated).

63. Wroe, M, and Greer, M: Parkinson's disease and physical therapy management. Phys Ther 53:631, 1973.

64. Harrison, H: Parkinsonism—physiotherapy. In Downie, P (ed): Cash's Textbook of Neurology for Physiotherapy, ed 3. Faber & Faber, London, 1982.

65. Humbersone, N: Respiratory treatment. In Cardiopulmonary Physical Therapy. CV Mosby, St Louis, 1985.

66. Davis, J: Team management of Parkinson's disease. Am J Occup Ther 31:300, 1977.

67. Hollis, M: Practical Exercise Therapy, ed 2: Blackwell Scientific, Oxford, 1981.

68. National Parkinson Foundation: The Parkinson Handbook: A Guide for Parkinson Patients and Their Families. The National Parkinson Foundation, Miami, 1985.

GLOSSARY

Akinesia: Inability to initiate or to execute movement.

Anticholinergic agents: Drugs used to block excessive cholinergic activity in patients with Parkinson's disease. Commonly used drugs include artane, cogentin, or akineton.

Basal ganglia: Masses of gray matter located beneath the cerebral cortex and just lateral to the dorsal thalmus; includes the caudate nucleus and putamen (corpus striatum), globus pallidus, substantia nigra, and subthalmus.

Bradykinesia: Extreme slowness of movement.

Dopamine: An inhibitory neurotransmitter secreted by neurons that are located in the substantia nigra and terminate in the striate region of the basal ganglia.

Festinant gait pattern (festination): Abnormal and involuntary increase in speed of walking in an attempt to catch up with a displaced center of gravity.

Freezing: A sudden episode of immobility.

Hypokinesia: Movements that are reduced in speed, amplitude, and range.

Levodopa (L-dopa): A drug used in the treatment of Parkinson's disease used to raise the level of striatal dopamine in the basal ganglia.

Masklike face: A lack of facial expression and blinking.

Movement time (MT): The interval between initiation and completion of movement.

Propulsive gait: A gait pattern with a forward accelerating quality.

Reaction time (RT): The interval between the presentation of a stimulus and the start of movement.

Retropulsive gait: A gait pattern with a backward accelerating quality.

Rigidity: Muscle stiffness or hypertonia; sustained contraction of muscle resulting in an inability to bend or to be bent.

  Cogwheel rigidity: A jerky, rachetlike resistance to passive movement.

  Leadpipe rigidity: A smooth, uniform resistance to passive movement.

Sialorrhea: Increased drooling.

Sinemet: A drug used in the treatment of Parkinson's disease to raise the level of striatal dopamine in the basal ganglia; a combination of levodopa with carbidopa.

Stereotaxic surgery: The precise location and destruction of localized areas in the brain.

Tremor: An involuntary movement of a part or parts of the body resulting from alternate contractions of opposing muscles.

Chapter 24

TRAUMATIC HEAD INJURY

VIRGINIA M. MILLS

OBJECTIVES

1. Describe the epidemiology and pathophysiology of traumatic head injury.

2. Define the difference between local and diffuse injuries to the brain.

3. Describe acute complications associated with head injury.

4. Name and describe three different clinical rating scales used to define recovery from traumatic head injury.

5. Describe the different functional outcomes of a severe head injury.

6. Describe the significant factors that should be considered when assessing and treating individuals with head injury.

7. Explain how cognitive deficits can have impact on the physical therapist's interactions with an individual recovering from head injury.

8. Value the role of the physical therapist in head-injury rehabilitation.

INTRODUCTION

A **traumatic head injury** can have a devastating impact on the lives of the injured person and the family. The human brain guides all thoughts, behaviors, motivations, personal traits, talents, movement abilities, cognitive abilities, and social skills. Severe head injury can cause deficits in all of these areas. Rarely is the individual with head injury the only person affected by the problems resulting from the head injury. Often the family also suffers losses and carries the burden of permanently changed life goals and expectations for their family member. Physical therapists are closely involved with head-injury rehabilitation. Management of this population draws heavily on general physical therapy neurologic strategies and interventions. Considerations unique to

this diagnostic group will be discussed in this chapter, including (1) diffuse and focal brain injuries caused by trauma, (2) the anticipated clinical course of recovery, and (3) the implications of these factors to physical therapy assessment and treatment.

EPIDEMIOLOGY

Trauma is the leading cause of death in the United States for persons under 34 years. Each year there are 22 to 25 fatal head injuries per 100,000 persons, and over 500,000 injuries are significant enough to require hospitalization.[1] Of those who survive the traumatic event, many sustain serious head injury and are left with physical, cognitive, and behavioral deficits that significantly alter premorbid lifestyle. The majority of these people are under the age of 30, with a normal life expectancy.[1]

The Vital Statistics of the United States indicate that accidents are the fourth most common cause of death for all ages.[2,3] Fifty percent of all accidental deaths result from motor vehicle accidents. In 62 percent of the motor vehicle accidents, head injury was the cause of death.[3,4] Head injury occurs more frequently in men than in women. Patients sustaining head injury often have been using alcohol at the time of the accident.[3,4] Advances in medicine over the last few decades have made it more probable that persons with severe head injuries will survive. Rehabilitation professionals require specialized training to develop the programs and treatment needed to meet the diverse and challenging long-term problems of this population.

PATHOPHYSIOLOGY

Mechanisms of Injury

LOCAL (FOCAL) BRAIN DAMAGE

It is important to understand the mechanisms of head injury inasmuch as the sensorimotor, cognitive, behavioral, and social consequences follow directly from the injury. Any movement of the head that is suddenly halted or a direct blow to the skull produces displacement and distortion of brain tissues. The nature and direction of the forces—that is, acceleration, deceleration, or rotation—and the magnitude of the forces determine the degree of primary or impact (secondary) damage to the brain. Because the brain is not rigid but, rather, gelatinous, momentum causes it to shift until it is resisted by the dural septa or the skull. Focal injuries refer to damage under the point of impact and are characterized by **cerebral contusions** of the gray matter, with resulting parenchymal and surface hemorrhage. Contusions may be mild or severe. In the case of a severe blow to the head, damage to the brain can occur at two sites: (1) at the point of impact, and (2) at a point opposite the impact where the tissue makes contact with the skull, termed **contrecoup injury.**[5-7]

Lacerations are also a major form of local brain damage. The skull is made of rigid and dense bone, with irregular contours on its interior surface concentrated largely in the frontal and temporal areas. When the interior bony irregularities of the skull abrade the surface of the brain, surface lacerations result. Depressed skull fractures are another major cause of local contusions and lacerations and are associated with a high incidence of fatality.[5]

The tearing of vascular structures can result in epidural, subdural, or intracerebral **hematomas.** A **hematoma** is a swelling or mass of blood caused by the break in a blood vessel. In an **epidural hematoma,** the blood accumulates on top of the dura mater, whereas in a **subdural hematoma** the blood accumulates beneath the dura. **Intracerebral hematomas** are characterized by the formation of a blood mass within the brain tissue at the site of contusion. Hematomas occupy space and compress brain tissue. If severe enough, they can result in additional brain damage, brain shift, or **herniation** of brain tissue. **Herniation** of the uncus and hippocampal gyrus through the tentorial notch is termed **uncal herniation** and is characterized by decreasing levels of consciousness with progressive motor dysfunction. Initially hemiparesis develops, followed by tonic posturing, either decorticate or decerebrate rigidity, and ipsilateral third nerve palsy. The latter results in dilation of the ipsilateral pupil. **Herniation of the brainstem** through the foramen magnum results in vegetative disturbances, with decreased respiration leading to apnea, slowed heart rate, and increased blood pressure. These are potentially fatal complications.[6,8,9] Computerized axial tomography (CAT) scans will show a shift of normal anatomic structures in the brain away from the pressure of the hematoma.[10]

The neurologic signs that result from local brain damage are directly related to the extent and location of the injury. For example, damage to the primary motor area may produce a contralateral loss of motor function. When swelling occurs, the patient may demonstrate a deterioration in the level of consciousness or prolongation of **coma.** Herniation is associated with the development of a new set of neurologic signs, termed **false-localizing signs.** These are the result of compression of the brainstem and selected cranial nerve nuclei.[8]

DIFFUSE BRAIN DAMAGE

In addition to the local damage, rotational and shaking forces on the brain can result in **diffuse lesions,** characterized by widely scattered shearing of axons within their myelin sheaths. The result is severe, widespread degeneration of white matter. Structural disruption of the brain is usually not macroscopically visible but occurs microscopically. When damage is extensive, brainstem injury occurs. Lesions of the corpus callosum and superior cerebellar peduncle are common.[9] Diffuse injury is evident on a CAT scan by the presence of **punctate hemorrhages,** or tiny spots or points of hemorrhage.[11]

The neurologic picture of the patient with diffuse white matter shearing injury is fairly typical. The patient is deeply comatose with abnormal extensor posturing of the limbs and usually some autonomic dysfunction.[5] The patient may persist in a **vegetative state** for many weeks or months. If recovery progresses to the point at which the patient regains consciousness, there is widespread disruption of function. A few clinical features that characterize patients recovering from diffuse head injury include deficits in attention, endurance, coordination, speed, judgment, and insight.[11,12]

SECONDARY BRAIN DAMAGE

Secondary insults to the injured brain evolve over time and are the direct result of events set in motion by the initial injury (Fig. 24–1). They pose an additional threat to the brain and can impair function, cause additional neuronal loss, and may prove fatal. Secondary insults include (1) raised **intracranial pressure,** (2) arterial **hypoxia** and brain ischemia, (3) **cerebral edema,** (4) arterial hypotension, (5) impaired salt and water balance

DYNAMIC PATHOLOGY

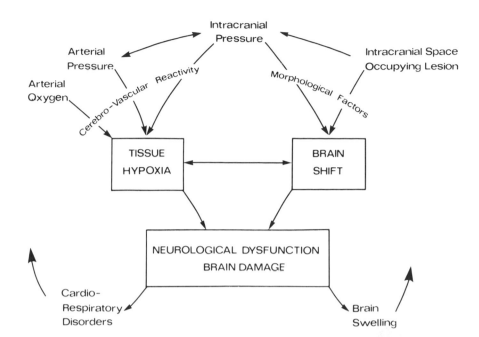

Figure 24–1. Dynamic interactions after head injury. Several pathologic processes can interact and lead to brain damage. (From Jennett, B and Teasdale, G: *Management of Head Injuries.* FA Davis, Philadelphia, 1981, p 71, with permission.)

(hyponatremia), (6) intracranial infection, or (7) hydrocephalus.[8,13–15]

COMPLICATIONS

The most frequent delayed complication from head injury is posttraumatic **epilepsy. Epilepsy** can begin months or years after the initial injury. Once a patient has a seizure, there is a high probability that the seizures will continue.[5] Numerous other complications are likely to develop. Concomitant injuries resulting from multiple trauma are a frequent occurrence in head injury. Lifesaving medical procedures such as tracheostomies, catheters, and drugs may lead to additional complications. Finally, prolonged bedrest and inactivity can lead to a large group of complications, including respiratory problems, muscle atrophy, contractures, osteoporosis, heterotopic ossification, decubitus ulcers, edema, infections, thrombophlebitis, and urinary tract disorders.

Concussion

Cerebral **concussion** is the loss of consciousness, either temporary or permanent, resulting from an injury or blow to the head. It implies impaired function of the reticular activating system in the brainstem. Additional signs of brainstem dysfunction may be present, including changes in pulse rate, blood pressure, and respiration. Concussion may range from mild to severe, depending upon the injury.

Mild concussion syndrome represents the least severe type of injury, with only momentary loss of **consciousness** or confusion after the injury.[9] **Retrograde amnesia,** a loss of memory that goes back in time before the injury occurred, may occur with mild concussion. For example,

a person would not remember what was happening during the 5 to 10 minutes before the injury. Although most patients fully recover in a very brief time, about one third suffer posttraumatic symptoms that may last weeks or months. These can include persistent headaches, dizziness, and incoordination.[8] Many mild concussion injuries are not brought to medical attention. Examples include those experienced during the course of normal sports activities of boxers or football players.[9]

Classical cerebral concussion is moderate in severity, and causes a loss of consciousness that is transient and mostly reversible within 24 hours. Retrograde and **posttraumatic amnesia** are present. **Posttraumatic amnesia (PTA)** is **anterograde amnesia,** or the loss of memory for events after the traumatic event. It is the interval of time from the injury until continuous memory returns. Mild and classical cerebral concussions are thought to be caused by physiologic dysfunction of the brain rather than any observable pathologic or structural damage.[8,9]

Loss of consciousness for longer than 24 hours is **severe concussion** and is associated with diffuse brain injury. Many patients will be unconscious for days or weeks. Purposeful movements are present only in response to painful stimuli, and patients may appear restless. The injury represents a combination of both physiologic and anatomic dysfunction. Permanent deficits in cognitive, behavioral, and motor abilities are to be anticipated and may range from mild to severe.[8,9]

RECOVERY STAGES FROM HEAD INJURY

The recovery from head injury often appears variable and complex. In an effort to systematize the clinical description of the recovery process and to facilitate communication among different specialties, various recovery scales have been developed. The different rating scales primarily describe the stages of recovery seen immediately following trauma and during the acute phase of recovery. There are no well-accepted scales for subacute rehabilitation programs at this time. Rating scales that describe the cognitive recovery of patients from head injury are useful because they allow for staff with different backgrounds to communicate in a similar language about patient behavior and progress. They are also useful teaching tools for individuals learning head-injury rehabilitation.

The Glasgow Coma Scale

The most widely used clinical rating scale during the acute stage of recovery is the **Glasgow Coma Scale,** developed by Jennett and Teasdale.[5] The **Glasgow Coma Scale** assesses the patient's level of consciousness. This scale allows clinicians to rate the severity of the injury and to monitor the patient's recovery from the unconscious state to the conscious state. Change in the degree of impairment of consciousness is a good indicator of improved brain function. The degree and duration of coma are reflections of the severity of the diffuse brain injury. The length of coma and posttraumatic amnesia are important factors in predicting the overall outcome. **Focal lesions** do not usually cause any impairment of consciousness.

The Glasgow Coma Scale rates three types of responses: eye opening, best motor responses, and verbal response (Table 24–1). Eye opening is observed and rated as occurring spontaneously, in response to speech, to pain, or not at all.[16]

Within the motor category, the patient's best motor response is used for the rating scale rather than a median score or the poorest motor response. The following is a description of how patients with progressively greater motor involvement would be scored using a scale of 0 to

Table 24–1 GLASGOW COMA SCALE

	Score
EYE OPENING	
spontaneous	4
to speech	3
to pain	2
no response	1
BEST MOTOR RESPONSE	
follows motor commands	6
localizes	5
withdraws	4
abnormal flexion	3
extensor response	2
no response	1
VERBAL RESPONSE	
oriented	5
confused conversation	4
inappropriate words	3
incomprehensible sounds	2
no response	1

From Jennett and Teasdale,[5] p 78, with permission.

6. A patient who can *obey* motor commands is given the highest score (a score of 6). For those patients who can not respond to instructions, a painful stimulus is given to the nailbeds or supraorbital region. If the hand moves toward the painful stimulus, the response is rated as *localizing* (a score of 5). A patient who demonstrates a *withdrawal* response from a stimulus is scored a 4. Responses in any of these top three categories are indicative of intact descending pathways. *Abnormal flexor posturing* is a decortication response characterized by flexion of the arms and extension of the legs. It is scored a 2 and indicates a functional level of injury between the cortex and red nucleus. *Abnormal extensor posturing* of all four limbs represents decerebration and is scored a 1. The functional level of injury is between the red nucleus and the vestibular nucleus. *No motor response* (scored 0) reflects a functional level of injury below the vestibular nucleus.[16]

The patient's speech is classified as the following: normal with *oriented conversation, confused, inappropriate words, sounds* (such as grunts and groans), or *no vocalization* at all. Sometimes a verbal response is not possible owing to endotracheal tubes. The capacity of the patient to speak a few words indicates a higher level of brain functioning.[16]

The *procedure* for using the Glasgow Coma Scale is relatively simple and can be administered several times a day to the patient in the intensive care unit. It is reliable, and with training, members of the team can administer the scale with consistent results. The *coma score* is a summary of the ratings achieved on each of the three parts of the scale (eye opening, motor, verbal). Within the range of coma scores between 3 and 15 there is no clear point at which it can be said the patient is no longer in coma. The authors of the scale reported that 90 percent of all patients with a score of 8 or less are in coma (unable to open the eyes, to make any recognizable sound, or to follow any commands), whereas all patients with a score of 9 or more are out of coma.[5]

The Glasgow scale demonstrates that patients with traumatic head injury do not just "wake up" from a coma. Some clinicians may dispute whether a patient is actually comatose, semicomatose, or stuperous. None of these terms may clearly describe the patient's neurologic state. The Glasgow scale uses a more objective approach to the description of the transition of the patient from coma to consciousness.

The Rancho Los Amigos Cognitive Scale

Clinicians involved in acute care have developed rating scales to describe patients' behaviors as they continue their recovery from head injury. The most widely known of these scales is the **Rancho Los Amigos Cognitive Scale.**[17] The Rancho Scale has eight levels (Table 24–2). The levels are 1, no response; 2, generalized response; 3, localized response; 4, confused–agitated; 5, confused–inappropriate; 6, confused–appropriate; 7, automatic–appropriate; and 8, purposeful and appropriate.

In a general way the levels describe a patient's behavior as the patient emerges from coma and progresses

Table 24–2 RANCHO LOS AMIGOS LEVELS OF COGNITIVE FUNCTIONING

I NO RESPONSE Patient appears to be in a deep sleep and is completely unresponsive to any stimuli.

II GENERALIZED RESPONSE Patient reacts inconsistently and nonpurposefully to stimuli in a nonspecific manner. Responses are limited and often the same regardless of stimulus presented. Responses may be physiologic changes, gross body movements, and/or vocalization.

III LOCALIZED RESPONSES Patient reacts specifically but inconsistently to stimuli. Responses are directly related to the type of stimulus presented. May follow simple commands in an inconsistent, delayed manner, such as closing eyes or squeezing hand.

IV CONFUSED-AGITATED Patient is in heightened state of activity. Behavior is bizarre and nonpurposeful relative to immediate environment. Does not discriminate among persons or objects; is unable to cooperate directly with treatment efforts. Verbalizations frequently are incoherent and/or inappropriate to the environment; confabulation may be present. Gross attention to environment is very brief; selective attention is often nonexistent. Patient lacks short-term and long-term recall.

V CONFUSED-INAPPROPRIATE Patient is able to respond to simple commands fairly consistently. However, with increased complexity of commands or lack of any external structure, responses are nonpurposeful, random, or fragmented. Demonstrates gross attention to the environment but is highly distractible and lacks ability to focus attention on a specific task. With structure, may be able to converse on a social automatic level for short periods of time. Verbalization is often inappropriate and confabulatory. Memory is severely impaired; often shows inappropriate use of objects; may perform previously learned tasks with structure but is unable to learn new information.

VI CONFUSED-APPROPRIATE Patient shows goal-directed behavior but is dependent on external input or direction. Follows simple directions consistently and shows carry-over for relearned problems but appropriate to the situation; past memories show more depth and detail than recent memory.

VII AUTOMATIC-APPROPRIATE Patient appears appropriate and oriented within hospital and home settings; goes through daily routine automatically, but frequently robot-like with minimal to absent confusion and has shallow recall of activities. Shows carry-over for new learning but at a decreased rate. With structure is able to initiate social or recreational activities; judgment remains impaired.

VIII PURPOSEFUL AND APPROPRIATE Patient is able to recall and to integrate past and recent events and is aware of and responsive to environment. Shows carry-over for new learning and needs no supervision once activities are learned. May continue to show a decreased ability relative to premorbid abilities, abstract reasoning, tolerance for stress, and judgment in emergencies or unusual circumstances.

From Professional Staff Association, Rancho Los Amigos Hospital,[17] pp 87–88, with permission.

through and beyond a **confusional state.** A patient with impaired cognition typically demonstrates an inability to pay attention, to process environmental stimuli adequately, to respond appropriately, or to remember events. Memories from one moment to the next are not formed, and, therefore, there is no continuity of thought. During early recovery agitation is a common response to cognitive disorganization.

Clinicians can gain some understanding of cognitive processing deficits if they can imagine what it would be like to try to talk to someone on the telephone, to answer someone nearby asking a question, to write a letter, and to listen to the radio all at the same time. To complete any of these tasks successfully, the individual must be able to pay attention to only the relevant stimuli while screening out irrelevant stimuli and to organize a sequence of behaviors necessary to complete the task. The individual with a head injury is unable to screen out irrelevant from relevant stimuli or to organize the sequence of steps necessary to complete a task, even for simple, everyday tasks (e.g., washing, eating, dressing). Instead, all stimuli are weighed equally and are equally distracting.

One of the major objectives of assessment using the Rancho scale is the observation and categorization of behavior in both structured and unstructured environments. Stimuli are carefully manipulated. For example, the patient may be placed in a structured environment that minimizes irrelevant stimuli, creating an advantageous situation for the patient to process relevant cognitive and motor requests. The amount of assistance in organizing and sequencing the steps to an activity also may vary. As the patient improves, the amount of assistance decreases.

The Cognitive Continuum

Another example of a rating scale is the Cognitive Continuum developed at Braintree Hospital.[18] This scale has five stages (Table 24–3): 1, arousal; 2, attention; 3,

Table 24–3 BRAINTREE HOSPITAL COGNITIVE CONTINUUM

1 AROUSAL The patient has difficulty initiating attention to purposeful tasks. The patient's behavior is purposeless, reflexive, inconsistent, and dependent in all functional areas. They may show some visual tracking and are usually not vocal.

2 ATTENTION
Low Level The patient initiates attention but has difficulty sustaining attention. Patient is able to follow one-step commands, but inconsistently. The patient may function automatically in overlearned behaviors. Patient does not initiate activities and may wander if left unsupervised.
High Level The patient's main deficit area is in sustaining and switching attention. The patient is distractible and perseverative. He or she may recall pieces of information but is unable to integrate information.

3 DISCRIMINATION Patient is able to sustain and to switch attention sufficiently to integrate small amounts of information. Patient initiates activities but may still show some perseveration and impulsivity. Behavior can be partly modified by feedback. Recall over time is improved.

4 ORGANIZATION
Low Level Patient can integrate multiple pieces of information for a task but tends to be concrete and have difficulty sequencing the task. Patient can begin simple problem solving.
High Level Patient can use selective attention to perceive stimuli or task elements accurately, select a strategy, and reach a solution. Patient continues to be concrete, has trouble generalizing and carrying over learning from one setting to another. In stressful situations, shows breakdown in cognitive function.

5 HIGHER LEVEL COGNITIVE FUNCTION The patient is able to do complex problem solving but is limited owing to limited flexibility, insight, social behavior, and endurance. The patient is susceptible to breakdown of behavior outside of a structured setting (e.g., school or work). In stressful situations, shows preserved cognitive functions. Cognitive processing is slow.

From Professional Staff, Braintree Hospital,[18] with permission.

discrimination; 4, organization; 5, higher-level cognitive functions. It also reflects neurologic recovery from diffuse head injury and is one alternative to the Rancho Los Amigos Scale. All disciplines can use this scale to describe behaviors that are exhibited during their interactions with the patient. Patients may be rated at different levels on the continuum, depending on the environment in which they are placed. The patient may behave very well with the speech pathologist in a closed environment, such as an office, but be much more difficult to manage with the physical therapist in a noisy, open treatment area. Understanding how the patient performs and behaves in different environments is useful for maximizing treatment efforts and influencing the patient's behavior.

MEDICAL MANAGEMENT

Diagnosis

The diagnosis of traumatic head injury is usually made when the patient is first seen in the emergency room. Pertinent history is taken. In lethargic or comatose patients, reliable witnesses can be questioned. In the absence of a conscious patient or reliable witness, head injury is assumed. A neurologic examination is given with emphasis on state of consciousness, pupillary reaction, eye movements, occular reflexes, motor responses, and breathing patterns. Additional diagnostic procedures can include computerized axial tomography (CAT), radioisotope imaging, x-ray examination, cerebral angiography, ultrasound encephalography, electroencephalography (EEG), evoked cerebral potentials, and cerebrospinal fluid (CSF) analysis. Continuous monitoring of physiologic functions is initiated, including intracranial pressure (ICP), ventilatory and pulse rates, arterial blood gases, serum electrolyte concentrations and osmolality, and cerebral blood flow.[5]

Mild head injury may be overlooked in many cases in which the individual either does not lose consciousness or only loses consciousness for a brief period of time. These patients may be released from the hospital without any medical treatment or may never seek medical attention.[19] If the minor head injury is significant, the person may experience problems with concentration and memory, therefore, school or job performance may suffer. The individual's difficulties may never be recognized as related to the initial head injury.[19]

Treatment

Medical management following a traumatic head injury is directed toward immediate lifesaving measures and close observation for secondary complications that could threaten life. One of the first measures taken in the emergency room is to ensure an adequate airway. Nasotracheal or endotracheal intubation may be initiated. Oxygen is administered because hypoxia can cause additional brain damage and neurologic deficits. Ventilation is controlled to maintain Pa_{CO_2} between 25 and 30 mmHg. This helps lower intracranial pressure by inducing a state of relative hypocarbia. A central venous catheter may be placed to help monitor hypovolemic shock and to determine hematocrit and central venous pressure.[7] Treatment is initiated to prevent or to reduce complications such as hypotension, respiratory insufficiency, hypovolemia, seizures, hematomas, intracranial pressure, intracranial mass lesions, brain swelling, fractures, and lacerations.[20] Steroids or osmotic diuretics may be used to help reduce cerebral edema and intracranial pressure. Barbiturate coma may be induced to reduce intractable intracranial hypertension. Table 24–4 presents some of the more common pharmacologic agents and their effects used in the treatment of patients with head injury. Many times surgical or orthopedic procedures are delayed until a determination is made that the patient will survive and becomes medically stable.[5,7]

Once the patient becomes stable, medical management focuses on continued neurologic assessment, prognosis, orthopedic procedures, and secondary complications such as infections and seizures. Physical therapy and occupational therapy intervention may be requested to prevent deterioration. If the patient remains in a persistent vegetative state, chronic coma management and nursing care will be required. Coma stimulation has never been proven to affect outcome. However, during the first year after trauma this approach is a useful way of systemically assessing a patient's wakefulness and responses.

If alert and able to participate in therapy, the patient is usually referred for rehabilitation. Many patients recover and are discharged to their homes, where they may be followed and/or receive treatment on an outpatient basis. The team members working with the patient usually recommend what continued care the patient should receive. The patient's insurance coverage can significantly affect the range of available medical and rehabilitation services in both the acute and subacute recovery stages.

Prognosis/Outcome

As with other central nervous system lesions, recovery from traumatic head injury is dependent on a number of factors. These include age, size of the lesion or lesions, extent of diffuse injury, premorbid skills, intelligence and behaviors, genetic inheritance, neural plasticity, nutritional history, and environment.[9,21] Outcome from traumatic head injury is not easily predicted. With head injury, individual outcome is related not only to the severity of the initial injury but also to early medical management, rehabilitation, family involvement, and the availability of support services.

Scales that attempt to define and to describe outcome following head injury are also available. One such scale is the **Glasgow Outcome Scale**, which describes five different categories of outcome following head injury and is based on overall social, physical, and cognitive sequelae.[22,23] These categories are *death, persistent vegetative state, severe disability, moderate disability,* and *good recovery.* The ratings from the Glasgow Coma Scale

Table 24–4 COMMON PHARMACOLOGIC AGENTS AND INTERACTIONS PERTINENT TO PATIENTS WITH HEAD INJURY

Name	Purpose	Contraindications	Side Effects	Comments
Elavil	Antidepressant Level II/III to heighten arousal; with higher levels to decrease agitation	Arrhythmias Urinary retention	Change in BP, change in blood sugar, sweating, dry mouth, weakness, fatigue, tingling, tremors, ataxia, arrhythmias, initial sedation, breast enlargement or testicular swelling	Is a central nervous system depressant that acts to decrease psychologic depression
Tofranil	Antidepressant	Myocardial infarction	Change in blood pressure, confusional states, numbness, tingling, ataxia, tremors, dry mouth, blurred vision, change in blood sugar	Stimulation of central nervous system
Ritalin	Stimulation to heighten alertness	Hypertension, history of drug dependency	Ataxia, insomnia, cardiac arrhythmia, nausea, anorexia, blurred vision, skin rash	Monitor blood pressure "tolerance" to drug effect
Phenobarbital	Anticonvulsant (seizure prevention)	Severe trauma, severe hypotension, uncontrolled diabetes, drug dependence	Lethargy/sedation, skin rash, ataxia, nystagmus, osteomalacia, habit-forming	Drug discontinuance should be done gradually
Thorazine	Tranquilization Management of psychotic disorders	Comatose states Presence of large amounts of CNS depressants	Drowsiness, jaundice, hypotension (usually transient), neuromuscular extrapyramidal reactions, dystonias, pseudo-parkinsonism, potential for hepatotoxicity	Precise mechanisms unknown
Haldol	Tranquilization Management of psychotic disorders	Severe toxic CNS depression or comatose states Parkinson's disease	Neuromuscular extrapyramidal reactions, Parkinsonlike symptoms, restlessness, dystonia, akathisia, drowsiness	Dopamine blocker
Mellaril	Tranquilization Management of manifestations of psychotic disorders	Severe CNS depression or comatose strokes	Drowsiness (infrequently) Extrapyramidal symptoms	
Navane	Tranquilization Management of manifestations of psychotic disorders	Patients with circulatory collapse, comatose states, CNS depression, blood dyscrasias	Drowsiness, restlessness, agitation	May precipitate convulsions
Artane	Adjunct in treatment of all forms of parkinsonism Control of extrapyramidal disorders caused by CNS drugs	Cautious use for patients with cardiac, liver, or kidney disorders or with hypertension	Dryness of mouth, blurring of vision, dizziness, mild nausea, or nervousness	Size and frequency of dosage to control extrapyramidal reactions to tranquilizers must be determined empirically
Dilantin	Anticonvulsant	Previous hypersensitivity	Skin rash, hyperglycemia, osteomalacia, nystagmus, ataxia, gum hyperplasia	Drug discontinuance should be done gradually
Tegretol	Anticonvulsant temporal lobe	Liver abnormality	CBC abnormalities, rash, cardiac effects, (arrhythmia, edema, CHF) sedation	Long-term therapy is associated with hepatic complications
Dantrium	To control spasticity	Liver abnormalities	Drowsiness, dizziness, weakness, fatigue, diarrhea Potential for hepatotoxicity (with greater than 800 mg daily)	Discontinue if no change in 45 days Directly interferes with the contractile mechanism of the muscle
Lioresal (Baclofen)	To control spasticity General CNS depressant	Diabetes, epilepsy (should be monitored)	Transient drowsiness, dizziness, fatigue, frequent urge to urinate, constipation, nausea, impaired renal function	Should not exceed 80 mg/d Abrupt withdrawal can lead to hallucinations (interferes with the release of excitatory transmitters)

Table 24–4 *Continued*

Name	Purpose	Contraindications	Side Effects	Comments
Valium	To control spasticity Skeletal muscle relaxant	Children under 6 months of age	Drowsiness, fatigue, ataxia, headaches, confusion, depression, blurred vision or double vision, skin rashes, urinary incontinence, constipation	May enhance effectiveness of Dilantin Physical/psychologic dependence Lowers blood pressure

Developed by Marion Miller, RPT, for New England Rehabilitation Hospital Brain Injury Unit Orientation Packet for Staff Physical Therapists. Orientation packet compiled by Marion Miller, RPT, and Mary Evens, RPT.
From Slater, B,[47] pp 161–163, with permission.

along with other information were correlated with the outcome scale for 1000 patients 6 months after injury.[24,25] The data showed that 48 percent of the patients died. The other categories presented the following results: vegetative, 2 percent; severe disability, 10 percent; moderate disability, 17 percent; and good recovery, 23 percent. This study showed that 29 percent of the patients survived with less than a good recovery. The good recovery category includes those who have neurologic and psychologic deficits but could return to leisure interests, or some type of work. The Glasgow Outcome Scale is a gross measure of overall outcome. Each patient can be measured only by the degree of return to their premorbid status in social, cognitive, behavioral, physical, and vocational abilities. What may be considered a satisfactory outcome to clinicians may be totally unacceptable to the patient and the family.

Many authors have assessed sensorimotor outcome and resulting physical disability from traumatic head injury. Two studies found that the ability to ambulate after a head injury was most often regained within 6 months after the injury.[26,27] Another study showed that 90 percent of the patients studied were ambulatory after 1 year.[28] Many authors have documented cerebellar imbalance and incoordination as major sequelae of head injury.[29-32] Other studies suggest that a significant amount of sensorimotor recovery occurs during the time the patient is in a rehabilitation service.[23,33] Long-term follow-up of patients with penetrating head injuries shows that those individuals who had selective movement impairments were largely functionally independent.[34] Overall, the literature suggests that patients experience a significant amount of sensorimotor recovery following head injury and that most patients regain functional independence in the area of mobility. This does not imply that patients have normal sensorimotor function but, rather, that they may be able to compensate for residual sensorimotor impairment in basic mobility skills.

REHABILITATION MANAGEMENT

The treatment for a significant traumatic head injury requires a comprehensive rehabilitation team approach. Patients with head injury have a very complicated mixture of needs. Almost all require the expertise of the entire rehabilitation team inasmuch as their limiting deficits can be physical, cognitive, perceptual, communica-

tion, behavioral, and social. The majority of head-injury programs tend to be acute and outpatient rehabilitation programs. Subacute programs that involve day treatment, transitional living, group homes, and long-term supported living have been developed and are growing in numbers, but they are few, and funding for these programs is limited. Rehabilitation professionals in acute care and acute rehabilitation settings provide the majority of the treatment. Therefore, the patients' and their families' understanding of the long-term consequences of head injury is largely dependent on these professionals.[35]

Rehabilitation During the Acute Stages

During very early recovery from head injury, the patient is in the intensive care unit where emphasis is placed on managing primary injuries and reducing secondary complications. Positioning, skin care, range of motion exercises, and pulmonary hygiene are important components of early care. After becoming conscious, medically stable, and able to follow some commands, the patient should be referred to a rehabilitation program specializing in traumatic head injury. The primary goal of acute head-injury rehabilitation should be the provision of an environment and daily structure in which the patient is best able to process stimuli cognitively. It is the rehabilitation team's responsibility to create an environment in which the patient is not agitated or distracted and thus able to pay attention. In this way, the patient's behaviors are shaped and influenced positively without inadvertent reinforcement of disruptive behaviors. In those instances in which the brain injury causes severely agitated or abnormal behaviors, this type of team approach allows for behavior programs to be easily integrated into all of the patient's therapy sessions and daily routine.

A major consequence of traumatic head injury after the individual regains consciousness is loss of memory. The individual not only is unable to remember events prior to the injury but also is unable to form new memories of moment to moment or of day-to-day events after the injury. As mentioned earlier, this latter type of memory deficit is called posttraumatic amnesia.[36,37] Posttraumatic amnesia often has been used to predict outcome[38] and is associated with a disabling outcome.[39] Acute rehabilitation programs must focus on management while the patient is still experiencing posttraumatic amnesia inasmuch as most patients are not discharged from inpatient rehabilitation programs until posttraumatic amnesia clears.

The severity and individual aspects of the pathology of the patient's head injury will have impact on the extent of attentional, behavioral, and cognitive deficits. Ultimately, it is these deficits which will limit the physical therapist's goals for the patient.

Patients with mixed motor and cognitive deficits require therapy that focuses on compensation, functional, and community activities. Patients with focal injury to the frontal lobes demonstrate predominently behavioral problems and limited motor deficits. They require behavioral intervention to gain a good recovery because they have severely impaired motivation, judgment, and insight. Other focal injuries should be rehabilitated on the basis of the specific neurologic deficits presented (see Table 24–5).

ASSESSMENT

The physical therapy assessment of the patient with traumatic head injury is basically the same as for other neurologic patients. Emphasis must be placed on the importance of cognitive and behavioral deficits as they relate to sensorimotor function. Assessment approaches must be selected that are appropriate to the patient's cognitive and behavioral statuses. An analogy to this concept is that therapists do not ask patients with aphasia for extensive verbal information during their assessment but, rather, concentrate on the patient's ability to understand what performance is required for the assessment process. Similarly, the therapist can not expect the patient with head injury to remember, to follow complicated instructions, to transfer learned skills, to act socially appropriate, or to pay attention if these behaviors are beyond the patient's abilities. In addition, the patient's behavioral abilities change during recovery, and therefore the therapist's assessment approach must also change on a regular basis.

Table 24–5 TYPES OF HEAD INJURY AND RELATED TREATMENT CONSIDERATIONS

Injury	Clinical Consequences	Treatment Consideration
Diffuse	Coma, persistive vegetative state	Treatment and activity should be related to cognitive status
	Confusion, cognitive stages (e.g., Rancho levels)	
	Mixed sensory and motor deficits	Emphasize movement, functional activities; deemphasize component deficits
Local	Frontal lobe: confusion; impaired insight, judgment; safety, behavioral problems	Behavioral focus, safety training
	Other areas of the brain: mixed sensory, motor, and language deficits	Sensory integration, compensation, function

The therapist should also consider the environment in which the patient is being assessed. The patient may perform very differently in a noisy, distracting setting than in a quiet one. The patient also may perform very differently in the clinic as compared with a real-life situation. The more automatic or overlearned a skill becomes, the more likely the individual will have improved performance for that particular activity. As the complexity of the environment increases, the difficulty of the task increases for the patient. An understanding of premorbid skills will guide the clinician's understanding of the patient's performance during both assessment and treatment.

The physical therapy assessment will also depend on the status of the patient, the time available, the type of health care facility, and the availability of other professionals. The purpose of the assessment is (1) to determine the initial and ongoing recovery status of the patient, (2) to aid in determining prognostic considerations, and (3) to develop treatment goals and plans. The overall written report should be geared to all the users of the information. Table 24–6 provides an outline of the components of the physical therapy assessment.[40]

The patient with a head injury presents a challenge to the therapist's skills. The patient can have involvement of different sensorimotor systems, and each patient can look very different from every other with head injury. The patient may have hemiparsis on one side of the body and incoordination on the other side. The patient may have spasticity and hypotonicity mixed in unusual patterns. The synergies characteristically seen during recovery from a stroke may not develop or may be hybrid patterns. For example, the patient may have a completely paralyzed shoulder with a functional hand.

Traditional models of motor control are based on the reflex model and the hierarchical model. The *reflex model* implies that motor control is based on stimulus-response reflexes and that movement is the sum of individual reflex circuits working together.[41–42] The *hierarchical model* of motor control is based on higher cortical centers overseeing and inhibiting lower level reflexes to allow movement.[43] There is increasing evidence that these models may not describe sensorimotor control and organization adequately. Another model, called the *systems model* of motor control, attempts to account for both the complexity and the simplicity of movement.[44] This model defines the central nervous system as a circular network of subsystems which act together but shift in dominance, depending on the movement requirements. In the systems model, sensory information is used in different ways and has different roles in terms of influencing motor control and depends, in part, on environmental conditions. For example, vestibular, visual, and proprioceptive information can all be used as sensory signals assisting balance function. Each may dominate motor responses, depending upon the environmental condition and the required balance function.

The systems model of motor control can provide the clinician with insight into patient assessment findings. Patients may have motor control deficits secondary to impaired central nervous system integration of sensory information. Each sensory system may function nor-

**Table 24–6 COMPONENTS OF
THE PHYSICAL THERAPY
ASSESSMENT**

MEDICAL INFORMATION
History, onset, and etiology
Results of diagnostic tests (e.g., CAT scan, X-rays)
Precautions
Respiratory status
Dysphagia status
Bowel and bladder
Skin integrity
Medications
PSYCHOLOGIC INFORMATION
Previous function
Neuropsychologic or psychologic assessments
Educational and vocational status
SOCIAL INFORMATION
Family and supportive others
Economic and insurance information
Home or discharge environment
COGNITIVE/COMMUNICATIVE/BEHAVIORAL STATUS
Level of alertness
Attention
Orientation
Memory function
Communicative ability
Behavior status
Higher level cognitive abilities
SENSORIMOTOR FUNCTIONS
Visual and auditory ability
Visual—spatial ability
Sensation—kinesthesia, proprioception, light touch, pressure, pain
Muscle tone
Abnormal movement patterns
Abnormal reflexes
Equilibrium responses
Strength
Coordination
Praxis
Posture
Speed of movement
Quality of movement
Strategies of movement to maintain posture and balance
Functional movement (movement may be abnormal but compensate
for deficit)
Endurance
FUNCTIONAL STATUS
Bed mobility
Transfers
Sitting and standing ability
Balance
Ambulation
Gait
Stairs
Outside terrain
Higher-level physical activities (may include sports)
Functional abilities in differing environments
Endurance
Work or school capacity

Adapted from Mills and Wusteney.[40]

mally when tested individually. Yet when the nervous
system attempts to consolidate the various sensory
inputs to accomplish postural control and balance, it is
deficient. Thus the individual may have good strength,
proprioception, kinesthesia, and coordination but still
have difficulty with balance and ambulation. This type
of patient profile is consistent with a motor control defi-

cit related to inadequate integration of sensory and
motor systems. The therapist must carefully observe and
objectively measure integrated function when analyzing
deficits in postural control. Several examples of assessments that focus on integrated function follow. Figure
24–2 shows a patient performing head and eye movements while performing high-level balance activities.
This activity requires integration of eye, head, and neck
movements and static balance. Figure 24–3 shows the
same patient performing high-level balance and coordination activities on a gymnastic ball. This activity
requires coordinated limb movements with dynamic balance. In Figure 24–4 a therapist is testing a patient on an

Figure 24–2. Static-dynamic activity: balancing on one hand and one
knee while holding the opposite limbs in a non-weight-bearing position.

Figure 24–3. Dynamic balancing on a gymnastic ball.

Figure 24–4. Balance testing using an Equitest machine.

Equitest machine (Equitest Neurocom International, Clarkamos, OR). This instrument assesses the patient's ability to use sensory information during systematized balance testing. The information gained with these tests can contribute to a more complete understanding of the patient's deficits and the formulation of an appropriate treatment program.

During assessment, the therapist must also consider whether the abnormal movements or postural control strategies are functional. If so, they may not require remediation, and, if they are eliminated, the patient may lose function.[45] For example, the patient may use excessive ataxic arm movements in order to maintain balance. Attempts to diminish these ataxic movements may result in decreased function. In such a case, the movements may be a compensatory strategy and should not be eliminated. Abnormal movements and synergies may reflect the only strategies available to obtain function.

GOAL SETTING

Dramatic changes may occur from the initial assessment over the course of recovery. It follows that treatment goals should be reformulated frequently during recovery, especially during the early stages. Improvement will depend largely on the patient's stage of recovery. Most recovery occurs within the first 6 months after head injury.[5] Thus, following a serious head injury changes in status can be rapid and take place over days and weeks. Later, changes in status or function may be progressively slow and may require longer periods of time. For example, a patient 2 years postinjury may benefit from physical therapy for improving posture, coordination, or balance, but the changes will be far less dramatic than would be anticipated early after the injury.

Long-term goals should always be related to functional outcomes, whereas short-term goals are geared to specific areas of abilities such as strength, coordination, range of motion, balance, and posture. In the early stages of recovery, short-term goals should address areas such as bed mobility and transfers. Later, the therapist's goals should concern mobility and safety in the home and community. The goals of management should be interdisciplinary. For example, all members of the team should concentrate their efforts on similar areas; for example, cognitive and behavioral deficits.

Setting accurate predictive goals for the patient with a head injury is very difficult. Experienced clinicians who have had the opportunity to follow patients for years over the full course of recovery are a good resource to the new clinician in head-injury rehabilitation. A clinician who stays in the field will have the opportunity to keep in touch with some patients for years. Following individual patients over time helps give the therapist a perspective as to the importance of any particular intervention in relation to eventual outcome. Therapists must achieve a balanced approach that does not exaggerate or underestimate the importance of any particular treatment intervention. For example, if the patient has significant spasticity in the upper extremity but the main barrier to being able to function in home and community settings is behavioral deficits, the therapist can concentrate efforts on behavioral control while trying to decrease spasticity. If the patient improves in behavior but not in tone, the intervention was still successful.

TREATMENT

Treatment of patients with head injury is focused on the functional deficits that result from impairment of one or more body systems. Therapists can use any number of intervention strategies designed to improve cardiopulmonary, integumentary, musculoskeletal, or neurologic function. Each patient is unique and presents a highly individualized set of functional deficits. All treatment is influenced by the patient's cognitive and behavioral status during recovery. For example, in the acute stages of recovery, a patient who is confused and agitated will be unable to cooperate in an intensive program. A clinical report of 24 patients with head injury treated by physical therapists in a rehabilitation setting revealed that patients rated at levels 3 and 4 on the Rancho Los Amigos Cognitive Scale tolerated many fewer types of treatments in physical therapy as compared with patients at levels 5, 6, 7, and 8. Patients at level 3 and 4 were unable to attend and to follow commands and were often restless. The types of treatments that were tolerated were range of motion, tilt table activities, and assisted ambulation activities. Patients at level 5 were able to participate in a much wider range of therapeutic activities. This was probably the result of their ability to pay adequate attention in a structured and controlled environment. Patients at levels 6, 7, and 8 tolerated the same number of different therapy activities, but those at levels 7 and 8 were also able to participate in advanced motor activities.[46] This clinical report emphasizes that therapists should consider cognitive and behavioral status when selecting treatment techniques. Many patients with cognitive impairments can benefit from physical therapy when the activity is simple, relatively few demands are made, and the patient is allowed to function within his or her own cognitive limits.

Strategies for Behavioral Management

All disciplines should incorporate behavioral management strategies into their interactions with the patient. Clinicians are constantly attempting to modify or to influence motor, perceptual, cognitive, or social behaviors. If the patient has a behavioral problem such as inappropriate interactions with people, then it is imperative that all team members approach these abnormal behaviors in a consistent manner. For example, a patient becomes overstimulated in physical therapy and strikes out at the therapist. In response to this behavior the therapist gives the patient "time out" in a quiet area of the room. Later, the same patient strikes out at the nurse and speech pathologist and they use two different behavioral interventions in response to the patient's aggressive behavior. This type of inconsistent behavioral management is a common problem in rehabilitation settings and can be destructive. Without a coordinated behavioral program to influence the patient positively, the patient may become more confused and will not easily learn how to control behavioral outbursts when overstimulated. Lack of a consistent approach also enables the patient to manipulate therapists. The patient learns to comply to therapeutic demands in some situations and not in others.

General management strategies also should include treating the patient as an adult and not as a child. Therapists should not talk down to an individual with head injury but, rather, allow the patient as much dignity, responsibility, and control as possible. Behavioral interventions should be initiated early in order to prevent the development of persistent undesirable behavioral patterns. Not all behavioral problems can be changed. Those that can generally require a long, slow time frame in order to ensure a permanent change. Therapists need to demonstrate patience when working with these individuals and to serve as role models for patient behavior. A therapist who is calm and controlled is far more effective than one who becomes upset when a patient becomes agitated or combative. When disruptive behaviors occur, the therapist should reduce sources of stimulation and/or stress and redirect the patient's attention to another topic, stimulus, or person.[17,47,48] Appendix A to this chapter presents some sample behavioral problems and intervention strategies.

Strategies for Motor Learning

Successful rehabilitation involves the learning or relearning of motor skills. Effective motor learning strategies should be employed to assist the patient in the learning process (see also chapter 14). During early learning, the patient must develop an understanding of the task. Therapists should demonstrate the task at ideal performance speeds. The practice environment should be carefully structured to promote a closed environment, free of distractors and irrelevant stimuli. Early practice attempts should be performed with the patient looking at the movement, because vision is the main error-correcting mechanism during this stage. Manual guidance techniques can be used to help the patient "preview the movement" and succeed in initial attempts. Fatigue should be avoided inasmuch as it may influence the quality of movements produced. For this reason many patients with head injury require multiple short treatment sessions rather than extended therapy sessions. Reinforcements and praise should be given for correct performance, but errors, which are largely inconsistent at this stage, should not be emphasized. During the intermediate stages of learning as motor skills become organized, the therapist should continue to structure the practice sessions, providing feedback as errors become consistent. Both knowledge of results and knowledge of performance are important factors in promoting motor learning. Emphasis should be on the "feel of the movement" based on proprioceptive feedback. The environment can be gradually modified as learning progresses to include more distractors. Thus the progression from a closed environment to a more open environment becomes a goal of treatment. Some patients with head injury never reach this stage of learning and continue to require a closed environment in order to perform motor skills successfully. Finally, motor skill acquisition is dependent upon continued practice and reinforcement of behaviors.[49,50]

Strategies to Improve Motivation

Motivation is a key element during treatment. The patient must not only understand the purpose of the activity attempted but also must feel that the task is important, desirable, and realistic to learn. Because goals initiate behaviors, it is important to involve the patient in goal setting. Communication, support, and encouragement can go a long way in reducing the fear and apprehension patients may feel when beginning a new series of tasks. Motivational strategies such as setting time limits or counting to the completion of an activity should be applied consistently. For example, if a therapist determines that an activity will be completed at the count of 10, then the activity should be stopped when the count is reached. Asking for one more attempt may prove counterproductive during follow-up practice sessions because the patient has learned not to rely on the therapist's word. The development of trust between patient and therapist is crucial to continuing motivation and sustaining the therapeutic relationship. Arousal or ready state influences both motivation and performance and requires careful monitoring and modification of central nervous system function. Calming stimuli such as gentle rocking or slow stroking can be used to reduce excessive sympathetic responses and to promote homeostatic balance. Finally, support groups for individuals recovering from head injury and their families may provide an additional source of inspiration, comfort, and motivation.

Strategies to Improve Attention

Attention deficits are difficult to deal with during therapy. In order to ensure that the important parts of the skill are attended to, the therapist needs to help the patient identify and focus on key task elements. Information presented to the patient should be limited. Many patients can respond to only one or two level commands. Absolute consistency in the treatment setting, including the time, daily routine, and approach, can help keep the patient focused and productive. Sudden or unexpected changes such as a change of room or therapist can be disruptive and can result in marked deteriorations in behavior. Pain and discomfort interfere with attention mechanisms and should be kept to a minimum whenever possible. Sometimes small adjustments in things that annoy patients such as tubes or restraints can yield significant improvements in attention during therapy.[17,48]

Strategies to Improve Memory

Memory deficits also pose complex problems during therapy. Patients perform better when instructions and verbal descriptions are kept to a minimum. The rate of instruction should be controlled and the responses to commands carefully monitored. Keep unrelated activities to a minimum, thereby reducing interference when-

ever possible. The speed, length, and complexity of the movement task can all interfere with memory. Thus, the slower the movement, the shorter the task, or the simpler the skill, the easier it will be for the patient to remember. Practice should always follow soon after demonstration and instruction. Any delay between the initial explanation and the practice attempt can result in decreased performance. Common strategies to enhance memory include verbal cuing, rehearsal, repetition, counting, and coding. Memory boards or logs are used in some facilities to help the patient maintain a schedule or remember sequences. Spacing therapeutic sessions will help keep mental or physical fatigue to a minimum. As memory improves, aids should be gradually withdrawn.[17,48]

Strategies to Improve Motor Control

Treatment should always be directed toward improving function as a priority over diminishing abnormal signs or symptoms. For example, hypertonicity may be a persistent problem. The therapist might direct efforts to decreasing this abnormal tone and find that the patient is less able to function; for example, to stabilize in a particular position. If the hypertonicity does not interfere with function or with joint biomechanics, treatment should not be geared to inhibit it. Some abnormal motor responses may prove functional and should be allowed.

Patients should be encouraged to perform functional movements similar to the way they were performed before the injury. For example, a therapist may teach the patient to sit up from bed by rolling onto one side and then pushing up with one arm. Compensatory functional patterns that deviate from the normal pattern should not be emphasized unless absolutely necessary. If it becomes apparent that the patient cannot master the normal movement strategy for whatever reason, then substitute strategies can be initiated. Function thus becomes the primary goal of treatment.

In general, early after an injury patients tend to respond best to activities that are well learned and automatic in nature, such as ambulation, cycling a stationary bike, stair climbing, and throwing or kicking a ball. Complex verbal instruction is not required, and many can be accomplished with only minimal physical assistance. For example, a patient usually will try to catch a thrown ball but may be unable to reach the arm out when verbally instructed to do so. Often, confused patients can tolerate passive treatment such as joint mobilization, tilt table, and stretching but can not participate actively in exercise. Later, when the patient is able to follow a series of verbal commands, more complex activities, such as developmental mat exercises, can be initiated. These higher-level activities require the patient to cooperate actively and to pay attention to the treatment intervention for some period of time.

A developmental approach to sequencing activities based on a progression of normal motor skill development is an important therapeutic strategy (see chapter 14).[51] For example, mobility and stability activities are attempted before controlled mobility and skilled activities. When sequences are not followed, activities may prove too difficult and patients may be unsuccessful. For example, stability in sitting is essential before learning to lean forward, stand up, and transfer to a wheelchair (controlled mobility activities). Skilled hand activities such as eating or dressing are dependent upon proximal stabilization of the shoulder and trunk. Appropriate sequencing of activities can not be overemphasized. Incorrect sequencing will lead to continued failures in therapy, which will interfere with both learning and motivation. Activities should be chosen carefully, providing the right amount of challenge while ensuring successes in treatment. Treatment sessions should end on a positive note, whenever possible, in order to ensure continuing motivation of the patient. Games and recreational activities are important considerations in developing a well-rounded therapeutic program.

Other Rehabilitative Procedures

Serial Casting. **Serial casting** is repeated cast fabrication for the purposes of (1) ensuring a statically aligned joint position, (2) stretching out contractures, and (3) preventing tightness and contractures. In the early recovery stages when abnormal posturing and tone are exhibited, serial casts can be used to prevent contractures. Later, casting can be used to correct deformities and to maximize normal anatomic alignment to regain normal joint function. Serial casting also may contribute to decreasing muscle tone.[52] Other evidence suggests that this allows the limb to be held in a more extended, anatomically aligned position without altering muscle activity and tone.[53]

Figure 24–5 shows a patient's foot in an inverted and plantarflexed posture. At one time during recovery, the patient's foot was fixed in this position as a result of soft tissue and joint tightness. Bivalued serial casts were used to stretch out the abnormal foot posture. Figure 24–6

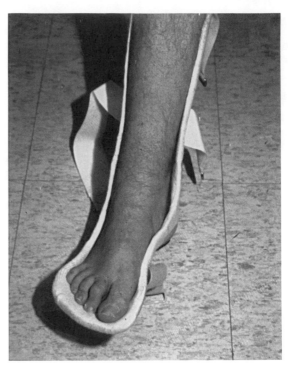

Figure 24–6. Improved foot alignment in a bivalved cast.

shows the improvement in the patient's foot alignment in the cast.

Phenol Blocks. A **phenol block** is a procedure in which an injection of phenol is given at motor points of mixed nerves, causing demyelination of axons (mostly sensory) and resulting in decreased spasticity. The use of phenol blocks to eliminate hypertonicity that interferes with function is very useful during all stages of recovery. For example, the patient may have increased tone in the plantarflexors of the ankle, even though full active movement in the dorsiflexors is present. During walking, the abnormal plantarflexor tone results in weight bearing on the ball of the foot throughout stance and consequently a functionally longer limb during walking. An abnormal gait pattern develops. A phenol block to the gastrocsoleus muscle group can often ameliorate the abnormal foot posture during gait and allow improved function.

Tilt Table. The tilt table may be part of a primary maintenance program for low level patients. Very confused patients can be positioned to achieve stretching and lower extremity weight bearing in standing. Stimulation of joint receptors can decrease pain in the lower extremities, and resumption of an upright posture can prevent the development of orthostatic hypotension.

Wheelchair Positioning Devices. Positioning in correct postural alignment with normal weight bearing through the body surfaces helps inhibit abnormal tone and movements. It also helps preserve joint alignment and range of motion. For example, a normal individual placed in a wheelchair without sufficient lumbar support and laterally displaced to one side without upper quarter support would become very uncomfortable within a very short period of time. Poorly positioned patients are sim-

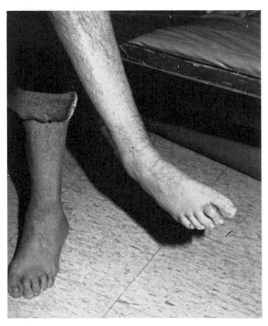

Figure 24–5. A fixed inverted and plantarflexed foot posture.

ilarly uncomfortable and develop tightness, commonly in the lower back and neck. Positioning devices should strive to place patients in as near normal alignment as possible within realistic limits. Figure 24–7 shows a patient sitting in a wheelchair with an exaggerated forward head posture. Figure 24–8 shows the improved pos-

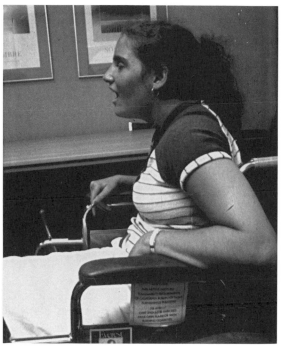

Figure 24–7. Abnormal forward head posture while sitting in a wheelchair.

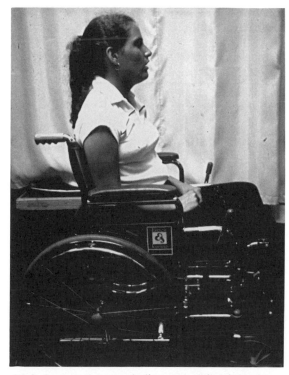

Figure 24–8. Improved postural alignment while sitting in a wheelchair. Head and trunk are upright instead of forward.

tural alignment achieved with positioning devices. The improved posture allowed this young woman additional function.

Equipment, Assistive Devices, and Orthoses. Prescription of equipment is usually necessary early after the injury. The use of equipment, assistive devices, and orthoses should be reassessed routinely because these patients show recovery over a long period of time. For example, the need for an orthosis may decrease over time and may eventually be discontinued as the patient becomes more independent in function.

FAMILY EDUCATION

Family involvement in the patient's rehabilitation is extremely important. Family members need a clear understanding of the patient's capabilities, overall prognosis, and stages of recovery. Behavioral intervention and other management strategies also should be taught. At discharge, it is very often family members who carry out the patient's ongoing care and provide therapy. Their close interaction with the patient and staff throughout the entire rehabilitation process is vital.

Long-Term Planning

After discharge from the acute rehabilitation setting, the individual with a head injury may still show recovery over the next few years.[54] Initially the patient should continue rehabilitation in a structured outpatient or day treatment program. Outpatient care may last several months or years, depending on the severity of the head injury. Patients with severe and moderate disabilities will require periodic reassessment, revision of home program, and limited treatment for the remainder of life. Patients with few residual deficits will not require therapy for more than a limited time span. For many patients in later stages, cognitive and behavioral deficits far outweigh physical disabilities. Low endurance levels are also a fairly common problem with this patient group. Cardiovascular endurance should be carefully assessed. A prescribed fitness program with periodic monitoring can be very beneficial to these patients.

Long-term and residential transitional programs usually have physical therapy involvement. The role of the therapist is to consider the patient's overall level of function and fitness and to foster the patient's mobility in the community. Many patients will never become competitive in the job market. It is important that the patient find some daily routine to enjoy.

Individuals with head injury are different from the mentally ill or retarded and should not share sheltered workshops and placements with these groups.[55] Unless these individuals can derive some satisfaction from their daily routine, the lack of recreational, vocational, and social opportunities will have a psychologically destructive effect on the individual and the family. The best rehabilitation program can be undermined if it does not incorporate constructive daily routine activities.

There are insufficient community-based programs for the head injured. Adequate day care, sheltered workshops, supported work programs, and social groups need to be developed to ensure successful rehabilitation and community reintegration.[55]

Additional Factors Affecting Treatment Outcomes

An important factor affecting treatment outcome is patient resources. The patient needs appropriate medical insurance coverage or other financial resources to obtain the services necessary to achieve and to maintain an optimal functional level. Institutionalization may be the only option remaining when all other resources have been exhausted.

As mentioned earlier, family support and involvement also influence outcome. A dedicated and involved family that follows through with recommendations and treatment interventions can have positive impact on the patient's outcome. The patient's premorbid personality characteristics influence performance in rehabilitation. If

the patient was a wild, uncontrolled teenager prior to the accident, it usually will be harder to gain cooperation during the rehabilitation process. The individual who had good work habits and social skills prior to injury will be able to build on these strengths during rehabilitation.[56]

SUMMARY

Head injury is the leading cause of death for persons under the age of 34 in the United States and can cause devastating deficits in an individual's sensorimotor, cognitive, perceptual, communication, and behavioral abilities. Physical therapists are integrally involved in the rehabilitation of these individuals. It is therefore important that therapists gain a clear understanding of the pathophysiology, medical intervention, rehabilitation process, and outcome from head injury. Because head injury rehabilitation is a relatively new and developing field, physical therapists also have a vital role in helping shape its further development.

QUESTIONS FOR REVIEW

1. What kind of cerebral lesions can be caused by tramatic head injury?

2. What is a diffuse injury? A local injury?

3. Name and describe three types of secondary complications from traumatic head injury.

4. Describe a scale that is used in the intensive care unit to describe the patient waking up from coma. Why are recovery scales useful?

5. What is a concussion? Describe three types of postconcussion syndromes.

6. For how long do patients recover from head injury?

7. What significant factors should a therapist take into consideration when assessing and treating a patient with head injury?

8. What types of physical therapy treatments are routinely used during the early stages of recovery from head injury?

9. How does the patient's cognitive status affect the physical therapist's treatment choice? What kind of treatments can be used with low-level cognitive performance? High-level cognitive performance?

10. How is the physical therapist involved in behavior modification of the patient with head injury?

11. What factors affect the patient's outcome from a severe head injury?

12. How do the pathology, clinical consequences, and implications for physical therapy treatment relate to one another?

REFERENCES

1. Jennett, B and MacMillan, R: Epidemiology of head injury. Br Med J 282:101, 1981.
2. US Department of Health, Education, Welfare: National Center for Health Statistics. Vital Statistics of the United States—1975. Hyattsville, MD, 1979.
3. Cooper, P: Epidemiology of head injury. In Cooper, P (ed): Head Injury. Williams & Wilkins, Baltimore, 1982.
4. National Safety Council: Accident Facts. National Safety Council, Chicago, 1978.
5. Jennett, B and Teasdale, G: Management of Head Injuries. FA Davis, Philadelphia, 1981.
6. Friedman, W: Head Injuries. Ciba Clinical Symposia 35(4):1, 1983.
7. Gilroy, J and Holliday, P: Basic Neurology. Macmillan, New York, 1982.
8. Miller, J: Early evaluation and management. In Rosenthal, M, et al (eds): Rehabilitation of the Head-Injured Adult. FA Davis, Philadelphia, 1983.

9. Gennarelli, T: Cerebral concussion and diffuse brain injuries. In Cooper, P (ed): Head Injury. Williams & Wilkins, Baltimore, 1982.
10. Cooper, P: Post-traumatic intracranial mass lesions. In Cooper, P (ed): Head Injury. Williams & Wilkins, Baltimore, 1982.
11. Ommaya, A and Gennarelli, T: Cerebral concussion and traumatic unconsciousness: Correlations of experimental and clinical observations on blunt head injuries. Brain 97:633, 1974.
12. Mitchell, D and Adams, J: Primary focal impact damage to the brainstem in blunt head injuries: Does it exist? Lancet 2:215, 1973.
13. Marshall, L and Bowers, S: Medical management of intracranial pressure. In Cooper, P (ed): Head Injury. Williams & Wilkins, Baltimore, 1982.
14. Katzman, R, et al: Brain edema in stroke. Stroke 8:510, 1977.
15. Langfitt, T and Kassell, N: Acute brain swelling in neurosurgical patients. J Neurosurg 24:975, 1966.
16. Jennett, B and Teasdale, G: Aspects of coma after severe head injury. Lancet 1:878, 1978.

17. Professional Staff Association of Rancho Los Amigos Hospital. Rehabilitation of the Head Injured Adult: Comprehensive Physical Management. Rancho Los Amigos Hospital, Downey, CA, 1979.
18. Professional Staff: Cognitive Continuum. Braintree Hospital, Braintree, MA.
19. Ruff, R: Neuropsychological outcome of mild head injury. Presented at the Braintree Hospital, Sixth Annual Traumatic Head Conference, Braintree, MA, 1986.
20. Tabaddor, K: Emergency care; initial evaluation. In Cooper, P (ed): Head Injury. Williams & Wilkins, Baltimore, 1982.
21. Finger, S and Stein, D: Brain Damage and Recovery: Research and Clinical Perspectives. Academic Press, New York, 1982.
22. Jennett, B: Prognosis after severe head injury. Clin Neurosurg 19:200, 1971.
23. Teasdale, G, et al: On comparing series of head injured patients. Acta Neurochir Suppl 28:205, 1979.
24. Jennett, B, et al: Prognosis in series of patients with severe head injury. Neurosurg 4:283, 1979.
25. Jennett, B, et al: Severe head injuries in three countries. J Neurol Neurosurg Psychiatry 40:291, 1977.
26. Bond, MR and Brooks, NJ: Understanding the process of recovery as a basis for the investigation of rehabilitation for the brain damaged. Scand J Rehab Med 8:127, 1976.
27. Najenson, TH, et al: Prognostic factors in rehabilitation after severe head injury. Scand J Rehab Med 7:101, 1975.
28. McKinlay, WW, et al: The short term outcome of severe blunt head injury as reported by relatives of the injured persons. J Neurol Neurosurg Psychiatry 44:527, 1981.
29. Panting, A and Merry, PH: The long term rehabilitation of severe head injuries with particular reference to the need for social and medical support for the patient's family. Rehabilitation 82:33, 1972.
30. Fahy, TJ, Irving MH, and Millac, P: Severe head injuries. A six year follow-up. Lancet 2:475, 1967.
31. Roberts, AH: Patterns of residual central neural lesions and associated disabilities. In Severe Accidental Head Injury, Macmillan, London, 1979.
32. Mills, VM: Sensorimotor deficits in the traumatically head injured patient. Neurology Report 9:11, 1985.
33. Talmage, EW, and Collins, GA: Physical abilities after severe head injury: A retrospective study. Phys Ther 63:2010, 1983.
34. Sweeney, J and Smutok, MA: Vietnam head injury study: Preliminary analysis of the functional and anatomical sequelae of penetrating head trauma. Phys Ther 63:2018, 1983.
35. Howard, M: Santa Clara Valley Medical Center Eighth Annual Conference, Coma to Community, April, 1986.
36. Russell, W: The Traumatic Amnesias. Oxford Press, London, 1971.
37. Brooks, N: Closed Head Injury. Oxford Medical Publications, Oxford, 1984.
38. Russell, W and Smith, A: Post traumatic amnesia in closed head injury. Arch Neurol 5:16, 1961.
39. Brooks, N: Wechsler memory scale performance and its relationship to brain damage after severe closed head injury. J Neurol Neurosurg Psychiatry, 39:593, 1976.
40. Mills, V and Wusteney, E: Physical therapy and the rehabilitation of patients with cerebrovascular accidents. In Kaplan, P and Cerullo, L (eds): Stroke Rehabilitation. Butterworths, Stoneham, MA, 1986.
41. Magnus, R: Some results of studies in the physiology of posture. Lancet 2:531, 1926.
42. Sherrington, C: The Integrative Action of the Central Nervous System. Yale University Press, New Haven, 1906.
43. Jackson, J: Selected Writings of John Hughlings Jackson. Vol I, II, Edited by J Taylor. Hodder & Stoughter, London, 1932.
44. Bernstein, N: The Coordination and Regulation of Movement. Pergammon, London, 1967 (Russian edition, 1947).
45. Nasher, L, Woollacott, M, and Tuma, G: Organization of rapid responses to postural and locomotor-like perturbations of standing man. Exp Brain Res 36:463, 1979.
46. Mills, V: Physical therapy and cognitive impairments in traumatically head injured patients: A clinical report. Neurology Report 9:51, 1985.
47. Slater, B: A Positive Approach to Head Injury. George B Slack, Thorofare, NJ, 1987.
48. Howard, M and Bleiberg, J: A Manual of Behavior Management Strategies for Traumatically Brain-Injured Adults. Education and Training Center, Rehabilitation Institute of Chicago, Chicago, 1983.
49. Schmidt, R: Motor Control and Learning. Human Kinetics, Champaign, IL, 1982.
50. Kelso, J and Clark, J: The Development of Movement Control and Coordination. John Wiley & Sons, New York, 1982.
51. Sullivan, P, Markos, P, and Minor, M: An Integrated Approach to Therapeutic Exercise. Reston, Reston, VA, 1982.
52. Booth, B, Doyle, M, and Montgomery, J: Serial casting for the management of spasticity in the head-injured adult. Phys Ther 63:1960, 1983.
53. Mills, V: Electromyographic results of inhibitory splinting. Phys Ther 64:190, 1984.
54. Thompsen, I: A long-term psychosocial follow-up of severe head injury. Presented at the Braintree Hospital Fifth Annual Traumatic Head Injury Conference, Braintree, MA, 1984.
55. Hackler, E and Tobis, J: Reintegration into the community. In Rosenthal, et al (eds): Rehabilitation of the Head-Injured Adult. FA Davis, Philadelphia, 1982.
56. Gilchrist, E and Wilkinson, M: Some factors determining prognosis in young people with severe head injuries. Arch Neurol 36:355, 1979.

GLOSSARY

Amnesia: Loss of memory.

Anterograde amnesia: Loss of memory for events occurring after the precipitating trauma.

Posttraumatic amnesia (PTA): Amnesia resulting from sudden physical injury. New memories are not formed (anterograde amnesia); exists until the patient can remember waking up and forming new memories of daily events.

Retrograde amnesia: Loss of memory for events occurring before the precipitating trauma.

Cerebral contusion: A bruise to cerebral tissue.

Cerebral edema: Brain substance that is expanded because of an increase in tissue fluid.

Coma: A state of unconsciousness in which the patient cannot be aroused by external stimuli.

Concussion: Loss of consciousness either temporary or permanent resulting from an injury or blow to the head.

Mild concussion syndrome: Momentary loss of consciousness or confusion following a head injury.

Classical cerebral concussion: Loss of consciousness that is transient and mostly reversible within 24 hours.

Severe concussion: Loss of consciousness for longer than 24 hours.

Confusional state: A mental state in which the patient is unable to attend to the environment from one moment to the next and is therefore unable to form new memories.

Consciousness: A state of awareness.

Contrecoup injury: Damage to the brain at a point opposite to the initial impact.

Decerebrate rigidity (decerebrate posturing): Sustained contraction of the extensor muscles of the extremities.

Decorticate rigidity (decorticate posturing): Sustained contraction of the extensor muscles of the lower extremities and the flexor muscles of the upper extremities.

Diffuse lesion (diffuse white matter shearing lesion): Scattered lesions occurring throughout the brain, resulting in severe, widespread degeneration of white matter.

Epilepsy: Recurrent transient nervous system dysfunction resulting from disturbed electrical function of the brain.

False-localizing signs: A set of neurologic signs associated with brain swelling and herniation.

Glascow coma scale: A clinical rating scale used to assess level of consciousness during coma.

Glascow outcome scale: A clinical rating scale used to assess outcome following head injury.

Hematoma: An extravascular blood mass or abnormal swelling caused by a break in a blood vessel.

Epidural hematoma: Extravascular blood mass located between the dura and the skull.

Subdural hematoma: Extravascular blood mass located beneath the dura.

Intracerebral hematoma: Extravascular blood mass located within the brain tissue at the site of injury.

Herniation: Protrusion of an organ or part of an organ through a surrounding wall or cavity.

Brainstem herniation: Protrusion of the brainstem through the foramen magnum.

Uncal herniation: Protrusion of the uncus and hippocampal gyrus of the brain through the tentorial notch.

Hypoxia: Decreased oxygen.

Intracranial pressure: Measure of pressure inside the cranium.

Laceration: A wound or irregular tear of tissue.

Local lesion (focal lesion): A limited, localized lesion to brain tissue.

Phenol block: Injection of phenol at motor points to mixed nerves to block transmission; used to decrease spasticity.

Punctate hemorrhage: Tiny spots or points of hemorrhages.

Rancho Los Amigos Cognitive Scale: A clinical rating scale used to assess patient behaviors during recovery from head injury.

Serial casting: The repeated fabrication of casts for the purposes of improving joint alignment, preventing or stretching contractures, correcting deformity or reducing spasticity.

Traumatic head injury: An injury or blow to the head caused by an external force.

Vegetative state (persistent vegetative state): An unconscious state in which the patient shows no meaningful response and demonstrates characteristic sleep/wake rhythms with periods of eye opening and abnormal motor responses.

APPENDIX A BEHAVIORAL MANAGEMENT STRATEGIES*

Problems in the area of behavior are often present in patients who have sustained an injury to the brain. Behavior problems may be a direct result of the injury, occur as a secondary effect, or as an exaggeration of pre-morbid personality traits. Behavior problems tend to interfere with all aspects of therapy and tend to endure over time.

Behavior Problems

AGGRESSION

a. Verbal: shouting obscenities and insults.
b. Physical: striking out at a person or at the environment.

SEXUAL PROVOCATION

a. Verbal: harassment and/or inappropriate seductive comments or jokes.
b. Physical: exposing genitals or masturbation. Inappropriate touching of others.

SOCIAL DISINHIBITION

Poor control of impulses in social situations. Lack of social judgment in conversation, e.g., rude or insulting comments or gestures. Overfamiliarity (verbal or physical). General lack of awareness of how behavior affects others.

DENIAL

Blaming others for deficits or lack of progress. Also, aggressive behaviors or refusal to participate in treatment.

DEPRESSION

Despondency, apathy, passive/aggressive behaviors, neglecting one's self-care (eating, hygiene), tearful.

AGITATION/IRRITABILITY

Impatience, restlessness, low frustration tolerance, disagreeable, combative with little provocation.

Developed by Charlene Arthur Greirard, OTR-L and Jane Kenig, OTR-L for New England Rehabilitation Hospital Brain Injury Unit Orientation Packet for Staff Physical Therapists. Compiled by Marion Miller, RTP, and Mary Evens, RPT.
*From Slater, B,[47] with permission.

PASSIVITY/DEPENDENCY

Low self-esteem, following therapist around, requires excessive positive reinforcement, childlike dependency; asks for permission to do things. May show "poor me" attitude.

Treatment Strategies

1. Consistency is the key in reducing disruptive behavior. It establishes predictability for the patient. For example, treat in the same environment. Give consistent responses to behavior. Have a consistent primary and covering therapist. Use a consistent schedule, explaining what is going to happen and why if appropriate.

2. Gear treatment towards positive experiences. At times it may be necessary to begin and end sessions which provide less challenge to the patient. This would allow for a successful experience especially important for patients who show depression, low frustration tolerance, or passivity.

3. Set firm limits and give patient clear feedback about the effect of his or her behavior on others. Allow for role playing or repeating the situation, so that patients may receive a positive response from their environment.

4. Attempt to give the patient some control over treatment planning by offering choices of therapeutic activities and by allowing for breaks or time out as needed. Build responsibility into the treatment program to increase investment and self-esteem. Avoid power struggles.

5. Whenever possible incorporate patient's interests in an attempt to promote self-motivation and investment in treatment.

6. Do not force the patient to remain in an uncomfortable environment. Switching treatment environments may be appropriate.

7. Avoid surprises, quick movements, unanticipated or uncomfortable touching. Warn the patient when a treatment modality may be painful or noxious.

8. A familiar contact may be helpful in extreme phases of agitation or irritability, or simply to increase patient cooperation in treatment.

9. Attempt to reduce stimulation for the patient by responding in a calm voice, which should be consistent with body language.

10. Redirect patient's attention away from source or cause of frustration.

11. Be careful of your body language. Be aware of patient's ego boundaries or concept of personal body space.

12. Either write or verbally contract with patient prior to treatment which behaviors are permissible and which are not. Include length of time specific behaviors will be required.

Chapter 25

BURNS

JEFFREY E. FALKEL

OBJECTIVES

1. Define the terms associated with the pathology and management of burn injuries.

2. Describe the etiology, pathophysiology, symptomatology, and sequelae of burn injuries.

3. Describe the anatomy and physiology of the skin as an organ both in health and following a burn injury.

4. Describe the management of the patient with various degrees of burn in relation to resuscitation, surgery, medical management, and rehabilitation.

5. Describe the nature of contractures following burn injury and the treatment and rehabilitation of these conditions.

6. Value the physical therapist's role in the team management of the patient with burn injuries.

INTRODUCTION

One of the major health concerns in the world today is the injury that occurs as a direct result of burn or thermal damage of the skin. Burn injuries are one of the major health problems of the industrial world, and the United States annually records the highest incidence of burn injury in the world.[1] Survey data from 1982 indicated that more than 2 million persons required medical attention and that 10,000 deaths related to burn injury occurred.[2,3] In addition, it has been estimated that there is a 1 in 70 chance of an American being burned in his or her lifetime of a serious enough nature as to require hospitalization.[1]

Although these data dramatically illustrate the degree of the health care problem caused by burn injury, recent medical advances have significantly reduced the number of deaths from burn injuries and have improved the prognosis and functional abilities of the patients who are surviving burn injuries. The survival rate improves annually owing to improved resuscitation techniques, the acute medical and surgical care that are now available, and continued research into the management and care of the patient with burn injury.

This chapter introduces the problems that occur with the different degrees of burn injuries and the complications that result from thermal destruction of the skin. Current techniques used in the medical, surgical, and rehabilitative management of the patient who has been burned are described. For more in-depth and detailed information on assessment and treatment of the patient with burn injuries, the reader is referred to several excellent reviews and texts[1,4–6] cited throughout and listed at the conclusion of this chapter.

EPIDEMIOLOGY OF BURN INJURIES

Although the prognosis and life expectancy of individuals with burn injuries have dramatically increased in

515

recent years, the epidemiology of burns remains basically the same. There is a peak incidence in children 1 to 5 years of age owing primarily to burns from hot liquids. The primary cause of burn injuries in adolescents and adults is due to accidents with flammable liquids, and men between the ages of 17 and 30 have the highest incidence of injury.[1,7] Fires that occur in homes and other structural dwellings are responsible for less than 5 percent of the hospital admissions for burn injuries but account for nearly 45 percent of the burn-related deaths in this country. Most of these deaths are due to smoke and other inhalation injuries.

The number of burn-related accidents has been decreased somewhat by better preventative measures such as smoke detectors, education, and more stringent fire codes. One of the major reasons for the improved prognosis and survival of severe thermal injury and burns is the increased number of specialized burn center facilities. There are over 150 specialized centers for burn care consisting of 1700 burn-care beds in the United States today, compared with only 12 specialized burn centers 20 years ago.[1] DeGregorio[8] describes the classification established by the American Burn Association for those burns that are routinely treated in burn centers:

1. Second degree burns of 25 percent or more of total body surface area in adults, or 20 percent in children
2. Third-degree burns of 10 percent or more of the total body surface area
3. Burns involving specialized areas: hands, feet, face, eyes, or perineum
4. Burns complicated by inhalation injuries
5. Burns complicated by fractures or other trauma
6. High-voltage electrical burns
7. Burns in poor-risk groups of patients that have additional significant medical problems

As of 1980, the average length of stay in the specialized burn center was 22.4 days, with an average hospitalization of 55.2 days for patients older than 30 years of age.[9] This number of days of hospitalization is significantly greater than for most other conditions. However, the advent of the burn center and the concentrated care and research that have been generated by these centers has drastically reduced the average hospital stay in most cases, as well as improved the prognosis and survival of patients with severe burns. The burn center team is made up of physicians, nurses, physical therapists, occupational therapists, nutritionists, psychologists, social workers, vocational rehabilitation specialists, and other support personnel that direct all their energies to the care, treatment, and rehabilitation of the burn patient.

PATHOPHYSIOLOGY OF BURNS

Before the discussion of the pathophysiologic consequences of burn injuries can begin, an understanding of the physiology of the skin as an organ needs to be established. The skin consists of two layers of distinctive tissue: the **epidermis,** which is the outermost layer, exposed to the environment, and the **dermis,** which contains the growth and vital functions of the skin. A third layer involved in the anatomic consideration of the skin is the subcutaneous fat cell layer directly under the dermis and above the muscle fascial layers.

These three layers can be seen in Figure 25–1. The **epidermis** performs several vital functions. There are two primary layers of the epidermis which are critical to an understanding of the burn wound. The stratum corneum gives the skin its waterproof function and serves in the role of protection from infection. The stratum granulosum is the layer responsible for water retention and heat regulation. This layer also contains keratin cells and melanocytes, which determine the coloration of the epidermis. The under surface of the epidermis which con-

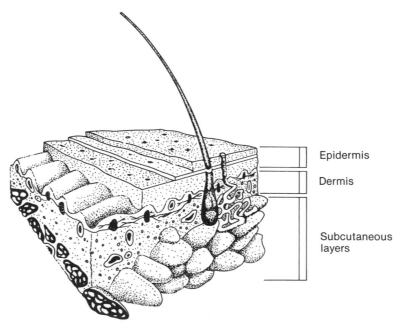

Epidermis

Dermis

Subcutaneous layers

Figure 25–1. Cross-section of skin.

tacts the dermis consists of an extensive series of inter-papillary ridges which serve to increase the surface area between the epidermis and the dermis. These ridges are needed to overcome the frictional forces that the skin is exposed to in daily activity. Lack of these ridges in the burn wound will result in the abrasion and poor adherence of the new epidermis tissue when it comes in contact with clothing or other surfaces and thus is critical in the healing and recovery phases.

The **dermis** is the component of the skin tissue that contains a tremendous network of vascular beds, blood vessels, lymphatic structures, sweat glands, hair follicles, nerve endings, and the cells from which epidermal elements regenerate. The dermis is twenty to thirty times thicker than the epidermis. The dermis is primarily collagen in structure, and these collagenous fibers are woven and interwoven in a parallel plane for the most part. The orientation of normal collagen in the dermis is different from that seen in the fibrous scar tissue that results from burn injury. The dermis is connected to the subcutaneous tissue with an irregular interlacing network of fibrous connective tissue into the facial aponeurosis of the muscle.

In addition to the functions outlined above, the skin also serves as the largest organ of the body, comprising 15 percent of the body weight. It serves in the regulation and conservation of body fluids, regulation of temperature, excretion of sweat and electrolytes, secretion of oils that lubricate the skin, synthesis of vitamin D, sensation, and cosmetic appearance and individualization. As a result of a burn injury, some or all of these functions will be impaired and/or lost and the patient's defense mechanisms will be compromised. As this chapter progresses, the consequences of the destruction of epidermal and dermal tissue will be elaborated upon.

The basic pathophysiologic consideration in the burn injury is the destruction of the capillary and vascular integrity, which results in the formation of edema with the concomitant loss of protein-rich intravascular fluid into the intercellular spaces.[5] The destruction of the vascular integrity and the edema formation occur in the area of the burn as well as in adjacent tissues. One of the major concerns of the physical therapist on the burn team is the patient's splinting of the injured part to prevent movement, owing to pain. This results in an even greater accumulation of edema in the area as well as stiffness of the joints and immobility of tendons and muscle within the burned area. From the protein-rich exudate, collagen fibers will attempt to form and to organize into adhesions that will further limit the range of motion and movement of the involved tissues if active physical therapy intervention is not implemented.[5]

The Burn Wound

The amount of tissue destruction is based on the temperature and the time of exposure of the skin to that temperature. The type of insult (i.e., flame, liquid, chemical, or electrical) will also have impact on the amount of tissue destruction. A tremendous amount of heat is not required to cause damage and injury. At temperatures

below 111°F (44°C), local tissue damage will not occur unless the exposure is for prolonged periods of time. In the temperature range between 111°F and 124°F (44°C and 51°C), the rate of cellular death doubles with each degree rise in temperature, and short exposures will lead to cell destruction.[10] At temperatures in excess of 124°F (51°C), exposure time needed to damage tissue is extremely brief. The burn wound consists of three zones, illustrated in Figure 25–2.[11] In the zone of coagulation, cells are irreversibly damaged and skin death occurs. The zone of stasis contains injured cells that will die within 24 to 48 hours without specialized treatment. It is in this zone of stasis that infections and/or drying of the wound will result in conversion of potentially salvageable tissue to completely necrotic tissue if treatment is not provided. Finally, the zone of hyperemia is the site of minimal cell damage which should recover within seven days with no lasting effects.[10,11]

Definition and Classifications of Burn Injuries

Until recent years and the advances in burn research, burn injuries were classified as **first degree,** which was a superficial sunburn type of injury to the outer epidermis only; **second degree,** which resulted in blister formation and damage to the epidermis and part of the dermis; and **third degree,** in which damage occurred completely through the dermal layers. Although these classifications are still used, most of the literature now classifies and defines burn injuries by both depth and degree of thickness of the tissue destroyed.

SUPERFICIAL BURN (FIRST DEGREE)

In this burn, cell trauma and injury occurs only to the outer epidermis. Because of the avascular nature of the outer epidermis, no bleeding will result. There will be an erythemic reaction owing to the irritation of the underlying dermis, but there is no injury to the dermal tissue.

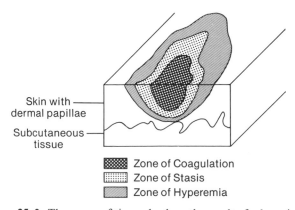

Skin with dermal papillae

Subcutaneous tissue

▓ Zone of Coagulation
▒ Zone of Stasis
▨ Zone of Hyperemia

Figure 25–2. The zones of tissue death as the result of a burn injury. The zone of coagulation is the site of irreversible skin death. The zone of hyperemia is the site of minimal cell involvement and early spontaneous recovery. The zone of stasis involves conversion of the wound from viable tissue to necrotic tissue due to infection. (From Artz, CP, et al,[4] p 25, with permission of the publisher.)

Normally, a mild inflammatory reaction occurs and the skin will be painful to the touch, but there will be no blisters formed and healing will normally occur within 2 to 5 days. There will also be some peeling, or **desquamation,** of the outer epidermis.

SUPERFICIAL PARTIAL THICKNESS BURNS (SECOND DEGREE)

With a superficial partial thickness burn, as illustrated in Figure 25–3, the damage occurs through the epidermis and into the upper layers of the dermis. The epidermal layer is destroyed completely, but the dermal layer sustains only mild to moderate damage. Owing to the vascular dilatation to help dissipate the heat from the thermal exposure, blisters will form, and edema will occur in the localized area of the burn. This type of burn is extremely painful because of the irritation of the nerve endings and pain sensors that survive the thermal insult. The wound and injured tissue are protected by a cellular barrier, the blister, which is sterile and will resist infection. As the wound heals and the blister ruptures, the dermal layers will have healed sufficiently to retain the infection barrier function of the skin, and complete healing should occur in 5 to 21 days. There may be some residual skin coloration changes owing to destruction of some melanocytes, but under normal circumstances no grafting or other therapeutic intervention is needed.

DEEP PARTIAL THICKNESS BURN (DEEP SECOND DEGREE)

This burn injury, illustrated in Figure 25–4, involves destruction of the epidermis and severe damage of the dermal layer as well. Most of the nerve endings, hair follicles, and sweat glands will be injured as most of the der-

mis is destroyed. The burn appears red, tan, or white and dull looking, depending on the depth of injury. The deeper the injury, the more white and dull it will appear. The vascular network and capillary bed will be damaged, and thus bleeding will occur with more widespread edema at the dermal-epidermal junctions. This is still a painful injury because not all the nerve endings have been destroyed; however, the tissue may be anesthetic immediately post burn trauma. **Eschar,** or the dead tissue that results from the injury and destruction of tissue, develops as a result of plasma and necrotic cells. There will be a tremendous amount of evaporation, 15 to 20 times normal through the area, owing to tissue and vascular destruction. Regeneration of normal tissue is possible depending on the extent of injury. By definition, the dermis is only partially destroyed, therefore there should remain some epithelial islands which will serve as the sources for new skin growth. The new skin will be thin and normally will lack the usual sebaceous secretions to keep the skin moist. Thus the new tissues will be dry, itchy, and scaling. It is easily abraded, and the surface is typically protected by creams to lubricate the new surface artificially. Sensation usually will be diminished, and the number of active sweat glands will be decreased initially and may remain reduced, depending on the extent of injury. The tissue will generally heal in 3 to 5 weeks if it does not get infected. Infection in a deep partial thickness burn can cause it to convert to a full thickness burn.

FULL THICKNESS BURN (THIRD DEGREE)

In the full thickness burn, as illustrated in Figure 25–5, all of the epidermal and dermal layers are destroyed completely. In addition, the subcutaneous fat layer will be damaged to some extent. All of the covering epithe-

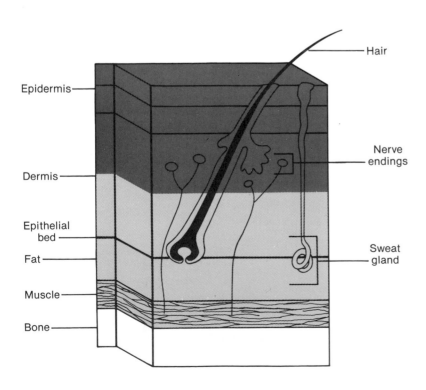

Figure 25–3. Superficial partial thickness burn. (From Malick, MH and Carr, JA,[69] p 3, with permission of the publisher.)

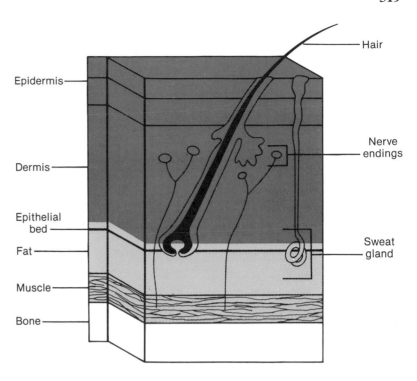

Figure 25–4. Deep partial thickness burn. (From Malick, MH and Carr, JA,[69] p 4, with permission of the publisher.)

lium at the site of the burn will be destroyed and discarded. Because of the depth of the burn, there will be no viable area for regeneration of dermal and epidermal tissue in the area of full thickness burn. The extent of the injury leads to coagulation necrosis of cells, destruction of blood vessels, massive edema, and cellular infiltration into the wound. The eschar will appear dry and leathery to the touch. The wound will be rigid and nonpliable. Because of the complete destruction of the nerve endings in the area, the wound will be relatively pain free. The wound will not **blanch.** Blanching refers to the tissue color response to pressure. If pressure is exerted against the eschar with a finger, the white spot present due to dissipation of blood in the capillaries under pressure will return to a pink or reddish tint. However, this does not occur with a full thickness burn. This is a useful diagnostic test to determine if a burn is a partial or full thickness burn. Because of the extent of tissue destruction with a full thickness burn, it will not blanch, whereas a partial thickness burn will blanch under pressure. Due to the

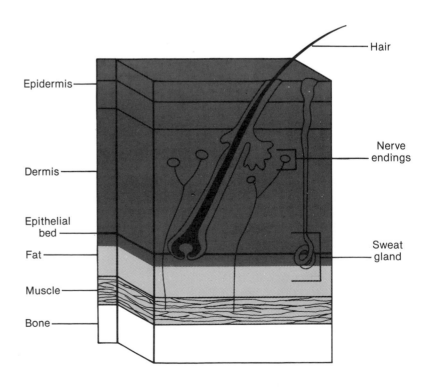

Figure 25–5. Full thickness burn. (From Malick, MH and Carr, JA,[69] p 5, with permission of the publisher.)

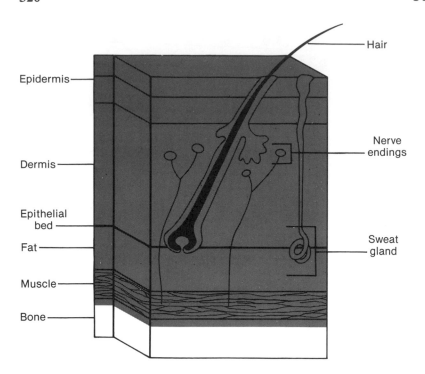

Epidermis

Dermis

Epithelial bed

Fat

Muscle

Bone

Hair

Nerve endings

Sweat gland

Figure 25–6. Classic electric burn. (From Malick, MH and Carr, JA,[69] p 6, with permission of the publisher.)

destruction of the epithelial bed, tissue regeneration will occur only from the margins or borders of the damaged tissue. Therefore grafting of tissue over this full thickness area will be necessary. Infection is highly probable, and every effort must be made to keep infection at a minimum. If not, the full thickness burn can convert to include destruction of the underlying fascia, muscle, and/or bone.

ELECTRICAL BURN (FOURTH DEGREE)

A fourth-degree burn, illustrated in Figure 25–6, involves complete destruction of all tissue from the epidermis down to and including the underlying bone tissue. This type of burn normally occurs as a result of contact with electricity. Classically there will be an entrance wound which will be charred and depressed. Where the electricity left the body there will also be an exit wound, which normally exhibits explosive wound edges. If the current is strong enough, fractures of the underlying bone also may occur. Skin along the course of the burn will not blanch. Extensive surgical excision and possible amputation will be needed to return the patient to some degree of functional ability. In addition to the local tissue damage, there may be extensive internal damage, or there may be no internal complications. Electrical burns are extremely unpredictable and make treatment and prognosis very difficult.

DIAGNOSIS AND DETERMINATION OF BURNED AREA

There are two major concerns in the determination of the seriousness and amount of burned area. The first is the percent of the total body surface area that has been burned. In addition, the depth of the burned areas needs to be assessed. Lund and Browder[12] modified the percentages of the body surface area that Berkow first described in 1924 to allow for the accurate means of determining the extent of burn injury. Figures 25–7 and 25–8 show the relative percentages of burned area for infants and adults according to the Lund-Browder charts. Although these charts provide an accurate assessment, they are not practical in triage of the burn patient in an emergency situation. In an attempt to allow a more rapid estimate of the percent of total body surface area burned and the depth and degree of burned area, Polaski and Tennison[13] developed the **rule of nines.** The rule of nines divides the body surface area into segments that are approximately 9 percent of the total. Figure 25–9 shows the percentages using the rule of nines for adults and children.

The **burn index** was developed to further assist in the initial assessment of the amount and degree of burn and also has been used to assess the mortality of patients. The burn index assigns one point for full thickness burns and one half point for partial thickness burns. These points are then multiplied by the percent of each area burned, and the burn index is established. This index is only that—an index—for it fails to take into account any preexisting medical condition or health problem that the patient might have. For example, an elderly patient with concomitant cardiovascular disease and a burn index of 20 is probably at much greater risk than an adolescent with a burn index of 40.

CLINICAL SIGNS AND SYMPTOMS

Each of the different classifications of burns will present with a different clinical picture, and each will change dramatically during the course of the treatment. In addi-

BURN SHEET

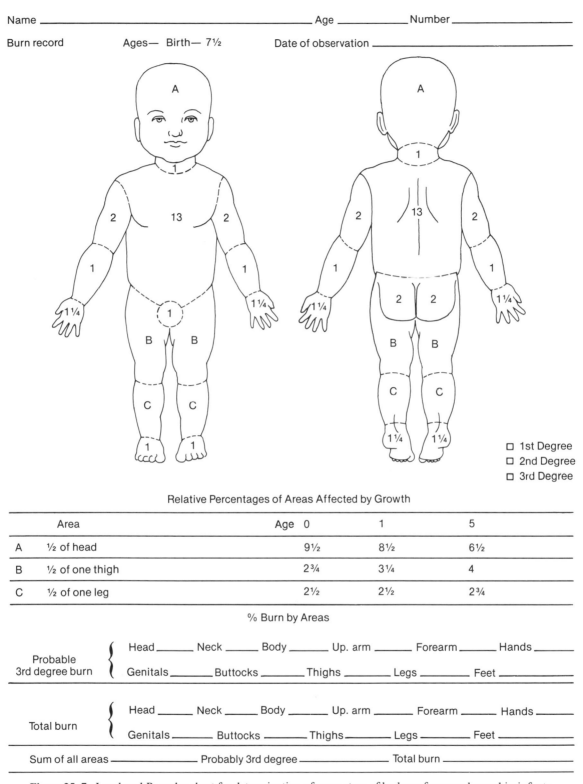

Name _____ Age _____ Number _____

Burn record   Ages— Birth— 7½   Date of observation _____

☐ 1st Degree
☐ 2nd Degree
☐ 3rd Degree

Relative Percentages of Areas Affected by Growth

	Area	Age 0	1	5
A	½ of head	9½	8½	6½
B	½ of one thigh	2¾	3¼	4
C	½ of one leg	2½	2½	2¾

% Burn by Areas

Probable 3rd degree burn {
Head _____ Neck _____ Body _____ Up. arm _____ Forearm _____ Hands _____
Genitals _____ Buttocks _____ Thighs _____ Legs _____ Feet _____

Total burn {
Head _____ Neck _____ Body _____ Up. arm _____ Forearm _____ Hands _____
Genitals _____ Buttocks _____ Thighs _____ Legs _____ Feet _____

Sum of all areas _____ Probably 3rd degree _____ Total burn _____

Figure 25–7. Lund and Browder chart for determination of percentage of body surface area burned in infants.

tion to the amount of tissue damage from the burn directly, the patient's metabolic status, physiologic conditions, degree of infection, and psychologic outlook all interact and have impact on the patient's clinical status.

This section presents general clinical signs and symptomatology seen in each of the various classifications and describes the various signs with the underlying pathophysiologic process that accompanies them.

BURN SHEET

Name_____ Age_____ Number_____

Burn record   Ages 7 to adult   Date of observation_____

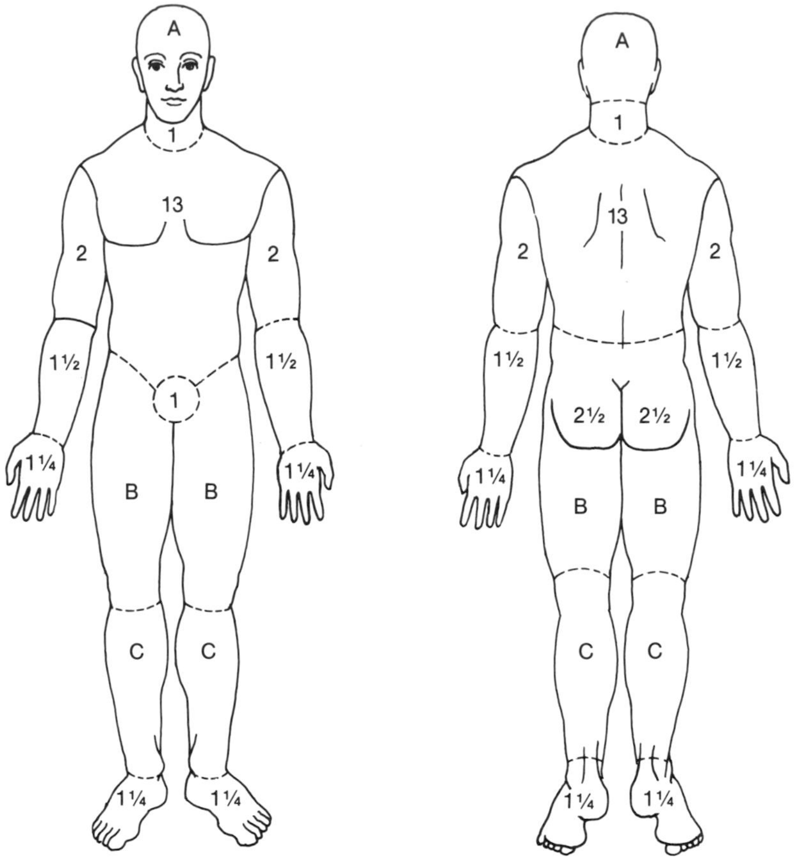

☐ 1st degree
☐ 2nd degree
☐ 3rd degree

Relative Percentages of Areas Affected by Growth

	Area	Age	10	15	Adult
A	½ of head		5½	4½	3½
B	½ of one thigh		4¼	4½	4¾
C	½ of one leg		3	3¼	3½

% of Burn by Areas

Probable 3rd degree burn	{	Head _____ Neck _____ Body _____ Up. arm _____ Forearm _____ Hands _____
		Genitals _____ Buttocks _____ Thighs _____ Legs _____ Feet _____

Total burn	{	Head _____ Neck _____ Body _____ Up. arm _____ Forearm _____ Hands _____
		Genitals _____ Buttocks _____ Thighs _____ Legs _____ Feet _____

Figure 25–8. Lund and Browder chart for determination of percentage of body surface area burned in adults.

Superficial Burns

The classic sunburn is the best example of a superficial burn. Sunburn is a reaction that follows exposure to ultraviolet light of wavelengths of 2900 to 3200 Å.[14] The degree of burning depends on many factors, including the duration and intensity, the area exposed, and the individual's pigmentation and genetic makeup. Clinically, mild reactions begin to occur 6 to 12 hours after exposure and will reach peak intensity within 24 hours.[15] The first signs are erythema of the exposed tissue, which may be associated with itching and a burning sensation. The ery-

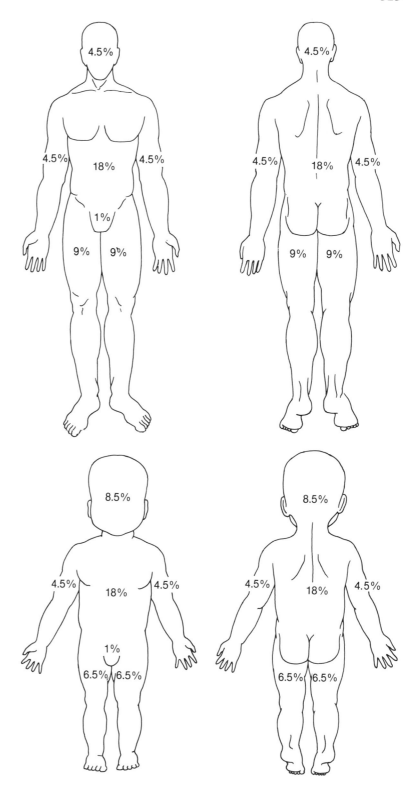

Figure 25–9. Rule of nines for determining percentage of body surface area burned in children and adults.

thema is a direct result of the epidermal damage to the vascular endothelium with the diffusion of inflammatory mediators from the sites of epidermal damage and release of vasoactive substances from mast cells.[16–19] The most severe cases develop acute erythema with some edema in the skin. In the absence of infection and areas of superficial partial thickness burns, the inflammatory reaction will cease, the injured skin will desquamate, and

the injured epidermis will peel off in a matter of 48 to 64 hours in most cases.[15]

In addition to these signs and symptoms, the patient also may suffer some nausea, headache, and general malaise if the exposure has been prolonged and the area of burn extensive. Only in severe cases will fever become manifested, and if this occurs, prompt medical attention is needed for further assessment and treatment.

Superficial Partial Thickness Burns

The most common sign and symptom of the superficial partial thickness, or second-degree, burn is the formation of blister over the area that has been injured. Blisters also may be present in the deep partial thickness burns. The blister signals the presence of edema at the dermal-epidermal junction. The underlying tissue will present a reddened erythema indicative of the inflammatory process that is the result of the thermal insult. As the burned tissue begins to heal, the area will develop a gelatinlike eschar, which will eventually peel off, similar to the desquamation of the first-degree sunburn. This eschar is the product of the topical antibiotic used to prevent infection and the coagulum that seeps from the wound as a function of the insult to the capillary integrity.

The fluid loss from a partial thickness burn is much more evident than that seen in a full thickness burn. Blisters that are debrided will contain fluid, and the blister should be left alone for as long as possible. The internal environment is sterile, and the outer covering of injured epidermis forms an ideal biologic covering over a burn wound. Healing will occur more rapidly than if the skin is removed and antibiotic agents are applied. However, if the blister becomes contaminated, it more than likely will delay healing, and if additional blisters develop in the area after 48 hours postburn, the probability of infection from staphylococcal bacteria is significantly increased. In this case, the blister is removed. In patients with significant areas of partial thickness burns that require daily hydrotherapy, the blister will also be removed. Although the initial fluid loss from the opening of the blister will be great, the majority of fluid loss does not come from the superficial blister but, rather, from beneath the coagulum of the deeper areas of the burn. Eschar that has a leathery appearance and feel to it usually has 20 times more fluid loss than normal skin.[20] The composition of the fluid loss is critical to the healing process and to measures taken to prevent excessive electrolyte losses. The importance of electrolyte and nutritional monitoring will be discussed in the section on medical management of burns.

In most cases, these burns may be more painful than any of the other classifications of burns in the initial period postburn. If there are infected areas, the patient will probably have fever and other subjective symptoms that accompany infection.

Deep Partial Thickness Burns

It may be difficult to differentiate between deep and superficial partial thickness burns from a clinical standpoint. Vascular morphologic changes of deep partial thickness burns are characterized by arterial occlusion with evidence of arterial patency only to the deeper structures of muscle and bone. Focal cellular deprivation and growth of granulation tissue has the possibility of primary healing if infection can be controlled. The function of the topical medication that is applied to the deep partial thickness burn is to provide a relatively infection-free environment that will allow for epithelial regeneration of skin from the remaining, surviving epithelial islands. Although the vascular integrity to most of the dermis has been destroyed, the amount of edema and fluid loss must be controlled. In addition, it is critical to keep the wound free of infection if at all possible, for until all the eschar is removed, infection will destroy the remaining epithelial islands and convert the deep partial thickness burn into a full thickness burn.[2,21,22]

The eschar will be relatively anesthetic in the initial stages, despite the fact that this type of burn has good potential for regeneration. Because the depth of the injury is difficult to determine, demarcation of the wound during the first few days is difficult. Many burns that might be expected to be full thickness and require grafting are capable of potential regenerative activity. Demarcation becomes evident after several days as the eschar begins to loosen. Hair follicles that penetrate into the deeper dermal regions should still be viable. They are of clinical importance in that the wound is typically shaven upon admission. Preservation of the hair follicle and the new growth of the hair will indicate a deep partial rather than a full thickness burn and greater potential for spontaneous healing. The differentiation line between the epidermal structures that survive and those that die may be based on the thickness of the skin in the particular location and/or the distance from the source of the heat.[23]

The local cutaneous defense mechanisms against infection by various bacteria are a normal function of the skin. In the patient who has been burned, this normal function may be altered and/or destroyed. In addition, there will be systemic responses to the trauma of the burn. Organ system failure in conjunction with infection constitute the leading cause of mortality from burns.[24] Bacteria in the hair follicles and glands that survive the heat and trauma of the burn will be in large quantities (normally in the range of 10^3 per gram of tissue). The rich vascularity of the inflammatory phase of the early burn with the vast amount of edema formed and the destruction of the bacteria defensive mechanisms make the wound very susceptible to streptococcal infections. The use of penicillin in the early stages of the burn treatment has decreased the infection from this source. However, as one bacteria is destroyed, another organism becomes resistant to topical medication used and infects the wound area. Virulent strains of Pseudomonas aeruginosa and staphylococcus aureus which are antibiotic-resistant strains have been responsible for epidemic infections in burn centers.[1] Systemic antibiotics are now used to treat both burn and general system infections once they have been documented by analyses of the burn biopsy.[24] A bacterial count in excess of 10^5 per gram of tissue constitutes "burn wound sepsis" and levels of 10^7 to 10^9 are usually associated with lethal burns. In the patient treated with systemic antibiotics, the plasma levels of the medication need to be assessed frequently owing to the fluid losses from the burn and the increased metabolic rate of the burned patient.[25] Most wounds are still treated with topical antibiotics, and these will be discussed in the section on medical care of burns.

The other major problems from deep burns are the risks imposed from the destruction of the vascular integrity and the damage to the peripheral vascular system. Owing to the destruction of the dermal and epidermal tissues and the increased amount of fluid loss and edema, the extravascular spaces become filled with fluid which will restrict and even constrict the deep vascular branches to the point of occlusion of blood flow. In an attempt to maintain the vascular flow so critical to the healing process of the burn as well as the viable tissues downstream from the burn, many times it is necessary to perform an **escharotomy.** An **escharotomy** is a midlateral incision of the burned eschar.[26] Figure 25–10 shows an escharotomy and the amount of edema that forces the incision line open even farther. Because the eschar does not have the normal elastic qualities of normal skin, edema that forms in the area as a result of the direct vascular and lymphatic injury will cause compression of the remaining vascular bed. If this compression is not relieved by escharotomy, it will lead to further edema and eventual occlusion, with possible necrosis to the tissue.[26] Following the escharotomy, pulses are monitored frequently. If the escharotomy is successful, there will be a marked improvement in the peripheral blood flow, as documented by normal pulses distal to the wound, with normal temperature, sensation, and movement of the distal extremity.

Full Thickness Burns

Although it may be difficult to differentiate the deep partial burn from the full thickness burn in the early postburn period, after several days, as the eschar begins to loosen, the differences will become evident. With the full thickness burn, there are no sites available for the reepithelialization of the wound and eventual closure with new regenerated tissue. All epithelial islands have been destroyed, and the only therapy to gain closure will be the grafting of tissue over the wound. (Grafting will be discussed in detail in the section on surgical intervention in the treatment of burns.)

The signs and symptoms of the full thickness burn are very similar to the deep partial thickness burn, with the complications discussed above being even more of a risk to the patient. Full thickness injury is characterized by a translucent, parchment-like dry, hard anesthetic burn which includes thrombosis of the subcapillary beds. This signifies a more severe pathologic consequence owing to the diffuse arterial involvement, the lack of epithelial regeneration, and the prolonged and deeper eschar. The full thickness burn is characterized within 24 hours with having complete vascular occlusion, lack of subcutaneous cellular infiltration, and significantly marked edema. Because of the lack of viable epithelial beds and the depth of the eschar, the risk of infection is increased tremendously. In many circumstances, if the infection is not controlled, the full thickness burn can be converted to resemble a classic electrical burn with cell death and necrosis of the underlying fascia, muscle, and bone in the area. The conversion of one classification of burn to the next most severe owing to infection can occur with any type of burn. Thus careful monitoring of infection, the use of antibiotics, and the constant treatment and care of the patient in specialized burn centers are paramount.

The relative anesthesia in full thickness burns is due to the destruction of the nerve endings in the dermal tissue. If the burn is severe enough to be lethal, there will be a period of hours in which the patient will feel essentially no pain and yet will die soon owing to the severity of the burn injury. This is a very difficult situation for both the patient and the family to comprehend. It is important that the nature of the injury and the prognosis for the patient be discussed. However, with recent advances in

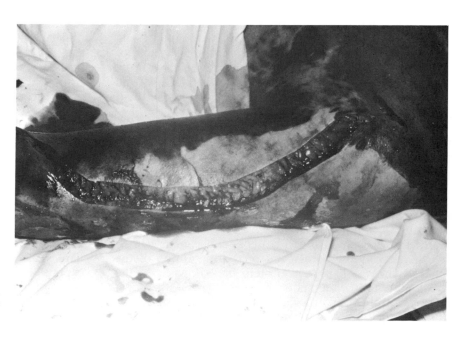

Figure 25–10. Escharotomy of the upper extremity. (From DiGregorio, VR,[5] p 19, with permission of the publisher.)

the surgical removal of eschar and new grafting techniques, there will be many more survivors of burns that were once lethal.

Electrical Burns

The electrical burn will be extremely variable in its signs and symptoms. This is due to the variability of the injury, type of current, intensity of the current, and the area the electrical current passes through. There are three types of electrical burns: the true electrical burn, in which the current passes through the body; the second type, which is produced by an arc current burn; and the third, which is due to flame burn from electrical sparks.[27]

TRUE ELECTRICAL BURN

This type of burn is due to an electric current passing through the skin and tissue after the skin has made contact with an electrical conductor. The burn will have an entrance and an exit wound. The entrance wound is located where the conductor came in contact with the body. The entrance wound will be charred and depressed and many times will be smaller than the exit wound. There will be edema formation immediately proximal to the entrance wound. The skin will appear yellow, and it will be ischemic. The exit wound will appear as if there has been an explosion out of the tissue at the site. It will be depressed but dry.[27] The underlying tissues will be damaged by the current and the heat that it developed. An extremity or area that appears viable after the injury may become necrotic and gangrenous in a few days. The electric current follows the course of the blood vessels, and as a result it is possible to have thrombosis formation at a distance from the wounds. The arteries will undergo spasm, and there will be necrosis of the vascular wall which will probably extend well beyond the area of injury. The internal configuration of the blood vessels will be altered and/or destroyed, and severe hemorrhage most likely will follow. As the blood supply to the surrounding tissues is altered, so, too, will be the underlying muscle tissue. Damaged muscle will feel soft. Because of the unpredictable course of the tissue destruction, there will be unequal and uneven muscle damage.[27] Only time will tell which tissues will remain viable and which will not.

There are other consequences of the electricity passing through the body. The cardiac effects will include electrocardiographic arrhythmias; in fact, the major cause of death from electrical burns is ventricular fibrillation and anoxia. Several excellent sources are available that describe the electrocardiographic changes.[28-30] Briefly, these are due to intraventricular conduction defects resulting in bundle branch blocks, ectopic activity, and tachycardia. There also will be renal consequences leading to renal failure as a result of the disruption of the renal artery, the excessive protein breakdown, and the shock that follows a major trauma. One of the most severe complications of electrical current injury to the kidney is acute tubular damage and eventual necrosis. Breakdown and catabolic activity of muscle myoglobin

from the injured muscle tissue most likely causes the tubular failure.[27] Spinal cord damage is frequently seen. It is usually incomplete and is not necessarily associated with the path of the current or any particular vertebral fracture. Clinically, these patients will have spastic paresis but may or may not have sensory pathway changes over concomitant areas of spasticity.[27] Many times the spinal cord and nervous changes will not manifest themselves immediately and may take months or years to become symptomatic. Finally, abdominal complications may occur as a result of the vascular destruction and hemorrhage into and from the area.

THE ARC ELECTRICAL BURN

This burn occurs as electrical current passes external to the body from the point of contact to a ground. The burns that result from an electrical arc are mostly caused by high-tension electrical current, which has a temperature of about 4532°F (2500°C).[27] The depth of burn is contingent upon how close the skin was to the arc. Generally these burns are very deep and have all the symptomatology of the true electrical burn.

THE FLAME BURN ASSOCIATED WITH ELECTRICAL ACTIVITY

Burns of this type are due to ignition of clothing from sparks or arcing. The area and extent of the burn may be extensive and usually is very severe. Typically, the prolonged exposure to the flame secondary to the patient's becoming dazed or unconscious from the electrical phenomena is responsible for the severity of the burn.[27]

SECONDARY PROBLEMS AND COMPLICATIONS OF BURN INJURIES

Depending on the extent of burn injury, the depth of the burn, and the type of burn, there usually will be secondary systemic complications. In addition, the health, age, and psychologic status of the patient who becomes burned will have impact on secondary problems and complications as the result of burn trauma. This section will concentrate on the major complications and problems to the various other body systems and organs that follow a significant burn injury.

Pulmonary Complications After Burn Injury

The probability of some form of pulmonary complication after a significant burn injury is extremely high. In addition to having been exposed to the heat of the flames, the patient who has been burned in a fire has been exposed to the smoke, which contains carbon monoxide, sulfur dioxide, hydrocarbons, and other possible harmful gases.[31] As the burn patient begins to form edema, the extra vascular fluid causes a contraction of the vascular space which results in a fall in cardiac output and concomitant ventilation-perfusion imbalances. Then, when the patient is resuscitated with large volumes of fluid, the vascular permeability is increased and additional fluid may fill the lung fields.[31] Therefore pulmonary complications are numerous and may have an important impact on the success or failure of a rehabilitation program. Several studies have indicated that the incidence of pulmonary complications following severe burns ranges from 24 to over 84 percent of all burn accidents and that death owing to pneumonia alone may account for over one third of the deaths of burn victims.[31-33]

There are three primary complications of pulmonary origin: restrictive disease, inhalation injury, and later complications. Most patients who have burns over 40 percent of the body surface area will have some degree of restrictive lung disease as a result of the burn. If these patients already have some form of restrictive lung disease from other causes, their condition will be more complicated.[31] Table 25-1 shows some of the restrictive changes that occur in pulmonary function measurements after burns.[31] Vital capacity is significantly lower, but pulmonary resistance is higher. Patients with burns of the chest wall will have decreased chest movement with respiration, which lowers vital capacity and other pulmonary function parameters. The varying degrees of restrictive disease will lead to pulmonary complications such as pneumonia, atalectasis, and pulmonary edema. Active chest physical therapy procedures will be necessary to reduce these problems throughout the course of the patient's hospitalization.

Inhalation injury from noxious gases and smoke may be the single most lethal aspect of the burn injury.[31] Among individuals who sustained burns, the incidence of smoke inhalation may be in excess of 33 percent, and that figure does not include patients who died at the site of the fire or on the way to the burn center or hospital.[34] Any patient who has been burned in a closed space should be suspected of having an inhalation injury.[35] Patients who present with facial burns, singed nasal hairs, harsh cough, hoarseness, abnormal breath sounds, respiratory distress, and/or hypoxemia are likely to have inhalation injury.[36] The incidence of inhalation injury in patients with facial burns has been reported to be as high as 66 percent.[37] In order to determine the extent of the inhalation injury, several diagnostic procedures are attempted. The most reliable is bronchoscopy.[38] Xenon lung scanning and serial pulmonary function testing also are done to first determine the extent of the lung damage and the status of pulmonary function, and then to monitor how successful interventions are in improving lung and pulmonary function.[39-41] The primary complications associated with inhalation injury are carbon monoxide poisoning, tracheal damage, upper airway obstructions, pulmonary edema, and pneumonia.[31]

The other problems associated with pulmonary diseases resulting from burns are those that take place later in the recovery phases. The patient may have either restrictive disease and/or inhalation problems, and the relatively low level of activity may further complicate these conditions by the formation of pulmonary edema, pulmonary emboli, and pneumonia. Sulfamylon, a topical agent used in the infection control treatment of burns, may act to inhibit carbonic anhydrase activity, which will cause an increased ventilatory demand from a patient who already has a low pulmonary reserve.[31] To conclude, pulmonary complications can be life-threatening for the burn patient during the initial insult or at any time during the convalescence and recovery process. A significant part of the treatment plan will include pulmonary parameters, of which active and aggressive chest physical therapy will be one of the most important components.

Metabolic Complications of Burns

Thermal injuries cause a significant metabolic and catabolic challenge to the body. Most of the advances in burn resuscitation and rehabilitation have come directly from the increased understanding of the metabolic demands of a burn injury and the ability to improve the patient's nutritional status to meet these demands. The consequences of the increased metabolic and catabolic activity following a burn are a rapid decrease in body weight, negative nitrogen balance, losses of intracellular components, and a decrease in energy stores which are so vital to the healing process.[42] Figure 25-11 graphically shows the changes that occur in various metabolic events following a thermal injury. It should be noted that these

Table 25-1 PULMONARY FUNCTION TEST CHANGES AS THE RESULT OF INHALATION INJURY SECONDARY TO TRUNK BURNS

	Inhalation Injury (Positive ^{133}Xenon Scan)	Controls	p
VC (% predicted)	80.8 (15.6)	85.3 (19.4)	NS
FRC (% predicted)	96.0 (18.3)	89.6 (22.1)	NS
TLC (% predicted)	76.0 (13.3)	80.5 (13.5)	NS
Peak flow (% predicted)	61.9 (17.0)	99.1 (15.1)	<0.01
Flow at 50% VC (% predicted)	41.6 (14.3)	98.7 (25.7)	<0.01
C_{STAT} (L/cm H_2O)	0.281 (.113)	0.324 (.159)	NS
C_{DYN} (L/cm H_2O)	0.290 (.160)	0.224 (.188)	NS
R_{PULM} (cm H_2O/liter/second)	4.85 (.31)	3.08 (1.01)	<0.01

From Artz, CP, et al: *Burns: A Team Approach.* WB Saunders, Philadelphia, 1979, p 100, with permission.

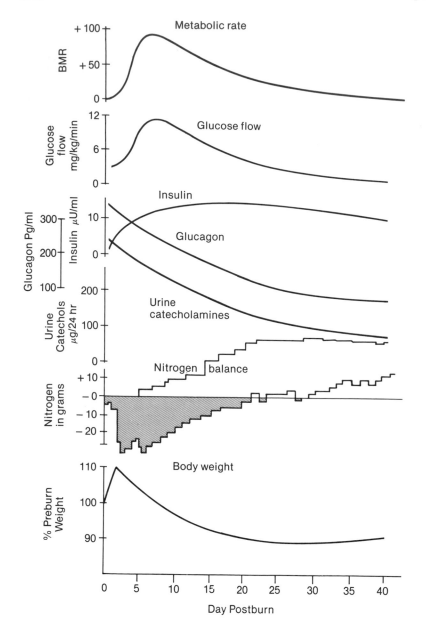

Figure 25–11. Metabolic changes that occur as a result of burn injuries. (From Artz, CP, et al,[4] p 121, with permission of the publisher.)

metabolic changes occur for a prolonged period post-burn. One of the many ramifications of the altered metabolic state is changes in glucose kinetics, resulting in hyperglycemia and the complications that it manifests.[42] In particular, an individual with diabetes who has been burned will be in a critical metabolic condition owing to the altered metabolism of insulin and glucogen and hyperglycemia. Other hormonal imbalances in the catecholamines and regulatory hormones account for much of the altered metabolic state seen in the burn victim.[44,45]

As a result of the increased metabolic activity, there will be a 1° to 2°C increase in core temperature that seems to be due to a resetting of the hypothalamic temperature centers in the brain.[1] Wilmore and associates[46] have hypothesized that there is a significant relationship between the increased evaporative heat loss from the impaired skin barrier over the burn and the hypermetabolic state. In any event, if the patient with a burn is placed in a room with normal ambient temperature, excessive heat loss will be exhibited, which will further

exaggerate the stress response seen in these patients.[1,46] Therefore it has been recommended, and is now practiced extensively in burn centers, that the room temperature for the burn victim be kept at 86°F (30°C), which will significantly lower the metabolic rate.

Much of the improved management of burns has been attributed to the greater focus of research on the nutritional needs of the patient. Because it is beyond the scope of this chapter to detail nutritional supplementation, the interested reader is referred to several excellent reviews of burn nutrition.[47–50]

Cardiac Function and Circulatory Complications

As has been evident from earlier sections of this chapter, there will be significant reductions in the plasma and extracellular fluid volume after a burn. Following these changes there will be a tremendous decrease in cardiac output in the initial stages of the burn, which may reach a 30 percent decrease in cardiac output within 30 minutes of injury.[10] Cardiac output will then slowly return to normal levels within 36 hours and may indeed rise to above normal levels and be maintained there for prolonged periods of time in many patients.[51] One of the suspected causes of the depressed and altered cardiac function has been labeled "myocardial depressant factor."[52] The exact mechanism of this factor is not fully known yet, but it appears to be present in patients who have 40 to 60 percent body surface area burns, and it may be the primary reason for resuscitative failures in burns that are in excess of 60 percent of total body surface area.[52]

Hemotologic and circulatory changes also occur following a severe burn injury. These changes include alterations in platelet concentration and function, clotting factors, white blood cell components, and red blood cell dysfunction.[53] These, coupled with the cardiac changes and injured vascular beds, will have significant impact on initial resuscitation efforts and, if the patient survives, on how rapidly he or she will recover.

Table 25–2 presents a brief overview of some of the

Table 25–2 PHYSIOLOGIC AND BIOCHEMICAL CHANGES FOLLOWING BURN INJURY

Free fatty acids	Elevated proportional to burn size for short time.
Triglycerides	Elevated proportional to burn size for short time.
Cholesterol	Depressed proportional to burn size.
Phospholipids	Depressed proportional to burn size.
Fibrinogen	Initial fall with prolonged rise following. Consumption great but production greater.
Renin	Increase proportional to burn size, especially in children.
Angiotensin	Increase proportional to burn size, especially in children.
ACTH	Increase proportional to burn size, especially in children.
Protein	Rapid and persistent drop.
Albumin	Prompt and persistent drop persisting until wound closed. Production depressed and catabolism 2 to 3 times normal.
Globulin	Initial drop with rise to supranormal levels by 5 to 7 days. Catabolism 2 to 3 times normal, but production vastly increased.
IgG	Immediate depression followed by slow rise.
IgM	Altered little by burn in adults but in children follows pattern of IgG.
IgA	Altered little by burn in adults but in children follows pattern of IgG.
Red blood cells	Immediate loss proportional to burn size and depth. Life span 30% of normal due to plasma factor.
White blood cells	Initial and prolonged rise. May drop with sepsis.
Cardiac output	Precipitous drop to 20 to 40% of normal with slow spontaneous recovery in 24 to 36 hours. Myocardial depressant factor demonstrated.
Blood viscosity	Sharp rise proportional to hematocrit.
Carboxyhemoglobin	Not significant after 72 hours (<2%). Most prominent with inhalation injury (80%). Exists with or without surface burns.
BSP	Retention proportional to burn size with rapid rise and persistence for several weeks.
Cortisol	Prompt rise to 2 to 4 times normal.
Aldosterone	Usually returns to normal by end of first week but may remain elevated for long periods. Varied response to ACTH often nil in early period.
Peripheral resistance	Rises sharply—slow fall.
Pulmonary vascular resistance	Rises sharply—slow fall.
Pulmonary artery pressure	Prompt rise and slow return.
Left aterial pressure	Normal or low. High with failure.
PO$_2$	Low with delay or inadequate therapy.
PH	Prompt response to therapy.
Pco$_2$	Initial alkalosis or hyperventilation promptly resolves.
Blood lactate	May rise to high levels with hyperventilation or poor perfusion.
Excess lactate	Mild elevations characteristic but may rise to high levels with inadequate or delayed resuscitation.
SGOT	Prompt rise with peak at 2 to 3 days and persistence for several weeks owing to liver damage, not release of
SGPT	skin enzymes.
A–P	
Renal function	Renal plasma flow depressed more than glomerular filtration rates. Free water clearances down. All values promptly return to normal with adequate resuscitation.
Evaporative water loss	Donor sites and partial thickness burns have intermediate loss rates. Full thickness burns lose at same rate as open pan of water. Estimate (25 + % burn) × M^2 body surface. Fifteen to 20 times normal skin rates.
Pulmonary function (in absence of pneumonia)	Proportional to magnitude of burn. Independent of inhalation injury. Minute ventilation (V$_e$) increased up to 500%. Peak at 5 days. Static compliance (C$_{stat}$) usually normal but may change with onset pneumonia. Lung clearance index (LCI) normal until terminal. Oxygen consumption greatly increased. Forced vital capacity (FVC) normal even with V$_e$ increase. May drop with pneumonia.

physiologic and biochemical complications that lead to the secondary problems of burn injury. It is these concomitant problems combined with the degree and extent of burn that make treatment such a complicated and comprehensive task requiring the skills of an entire team of health care professionals.

PHYSIOLOGY OF BURN WOUND HEALING

The burn wound has been identified, and the causes and complications of burn injury have been reviewed. The remaining sections of this chapter concentrate on the various types of therapeutic intervention and rehabilitation of the burn patient. However, before discussing the medical, surgical, and physical therapy aspects of burn treatment, a knowledge of the physiology of the healing process of the burn wound is needed.

The two layers of the skin, the epidermis and the dermis, will heal by separate mechanisms. The physiology of each component will be described with the clinical implications demonstrated.

Healing of the Dermis

The basic reaction at the surface of the functioning viable tissue surrounding the wound is inflammation, which results in exudation and cellular infiltration. Coagulation of the exudate results in the formation of fibrin fibers. Fibrin serves a threefold function: It partially retains body fluids, it provides a firm coagulum substance from which cells coming up from lower areas can infiltrate, and it protects the underlying cells from dessication. Therefore, fibrin can be thought of as forming a "ladder" from which cells can climb and work themselves into the healing structure.

One of the first tissue components that must heal before any other is the vasculature. The vasculature is restored by the deposition of granulation tissue which serves as a vehicle to transport collagen-forming cells and their constituents into the space. Intimal cells of capillaries immediately adjacent to the wound invade the exudate fibrin lining the wound. They form new and larger capillaries, creating a rich blood supply within the area. As free blood flow is established and there is more organization of fibrin deposited into the capillaries, these new structures become a source from which new capillaries grow and extend. Capillary advancement continues into the surface fiber coagulum in a continual manner, which provides the granular bed from which wound healing can proceed. The expanding vascular bed is evident by the increased bleeding in areas where eschar has been removed.

Deposition of granulation tissue is vast and a necessary precursor to epithelial coverage. Granular tissue deposition is also the precursor to collagen deposition, which will provide strength and the ability of the new tissue to withstand the stresses of daily living. Clinically, the survival and protection of the epithelium is critical. The patient sees that the wound is closed and may assume that with the wound being healed, additional pre-

cautions are unnecessary. However, the application of medication, the donning of clothes, or any irritation of the area may quickly lead to blister formation and eventual tearing away of the newly healed epithelium. This is due to the loss of the interpapillary ridges that normally provide protection against shear forces applied to the skin. Deposition of granulation tissue continues even with the lack of epithelial covering. If epithelialization is delayed, granulation tissue will continue to be laid down, producing a more difficult surface for future epithelial covering as well as decreasing the vascular supply needed for the formation of epithelium. When epithelialization finally occurs, granulation tissue formation will cease. The deposition of the granular substance is seen clinically by a change in the appearance of the wound from gray or yellow to bright red and a granular appearance. Excessive granulation is clinically evident by granulation tissue that becomes pale pink and over which epithelialization is difficult. It is paradoxic that what is so vital to wound healing in the proper quantities is so detrimental when it is formed in excess. Granulation tissue is effective as a barrier for infection and the beginning of the reformation of the defense mechanisms, but it is not an effective method of permanent wound coverage.

Epithelial Healing

The stimulus to epithelial growth is the presence of an open wound, exposing subepithelial tissue of the body to the environment. The intact epithelium attempts to cover the exposed wound. Covering with epithelium takes place through the ameboid movement into the wound of cells from all layers of the surrounding epithelium. The process is completed by the union of membranes from opposite sides of the wound, which is followed by rearrangement and multiplication of the cells. Although epithelial cells move about the wound site, they maintain a connection with the normal epithelium at the wound margin. A suitable base for the epithelial healing tissue to continue must be provided by adequate nutrition and blood supply or the new cells will die. The outermost cells will quickly cornify, and in doing so they provide a fairly stable "roof" from which cells on the underside can adhere and along which they can move out into the wound. The formation of a basal cell layer under an extension membrane of epithelial cells is dependent upon the presence of an adequate fibrous tissue formation under the extension membrane.

Protection of the epithelial extensions is critical. If there are multiple occurrences of epithelial cell loss by any means over a long period of time, the available cells at the margin of the wound will become reduced in number so that continued outgrowth of the extending epithelium will be either delayed or stopped all together.

The process of epithelialization is most evident clinically in the partial thickness wound that has intact hair follicles and glands. Although the eschar will adhere to the hair follicles and make **debridement** more difficult, epithelial tissue can be seen and will flourish. The epithelial cells provide islands from which the wound may close from within the margins and the healing will spread peripherally from these islands in the wound. This is an exciting phenomenon to watch for all members of the burn team, the patient, and the family, because skin growth and coverage can actually be seen over time from these epithelial islands.

The reversion of these epidermal appendages are responsible for the dryness and itching of the healing wound. The itching begins as soon as the sebaceous glands stop producing oil secretions in order to provide epidermal cells for healing. Lubrication can be a problem, and the skin is characteristically dry, and it may crack. This dryness may continue for a long time, because many of the sebaceous glands do not return to their normal function after the wound is epithelialized. The dryness problem is further compounded by the poor absorption qualities of many topical substances. Patients need to be educated about the type, frequency, and techniques of applications of external creams to lubricate the new tissue.

Collagenous Healing

The deposition of granulation tissue provides the method by which the collagen-producing cells and their substances are deposited in the wound. At the time the epithelium succeeds in covering the wound, the deposition of granulation tissue and its precollagen tissue constituents ceases. If granulation tissue is allowed to accumulate over time, collagen will be deposited the entire time. Precollagen fibrils and then collagen fibers are rapidly formed and regrouped. The collagen will form with no alignment similar to that seen in the wound healed by granulation tissue. The collagen tissue has no true architectural arrangement of fibers. Stresses coming through the area are propagated variously along the surfaces, and the fibers are formed in various patterns along these variable stresses. Although the wound is considered healed from the time the epithelium covers the wound, reorganization of both its collagenous fibers and its epithelial components will continue for up to 2 years postburn. This is due, for the most part, to the continuing contraction of the underlying new collagen scar. It is for this reason that active exercise and splinting must be continued for some time even after the patient leaves the hospital. Range of motion can be lost very quickly owing to the tendency of the collagen to contract and to retain its shortest possible length. Consequently, contractures are easily developed and may result in not only limitations in the range of motion available but, more importantly, the degeneration of this layer of tissue and the disruption of the healing process.

Maturation of the Burn Wound

Over a period of many months, the inflammatory response and hypervascularity characteristics of a deep burn will begin to recede, and the skin will become more pliable. There also may be a color change as the vascular component of the granulation tissue recedes and the epithelial covering increases in depth, which will present as a paler wound. However, the color depends on many other factors, such as the number of melanocytes. The final component of the wound healing is the potential for hypertrophic collagen scarring as time progresses. These scars result in the raised discolored tissue classically seen after a burn injury. The treatment of these hypertrophic regions will be discussed in depth later in the chapter under physical therapy management.

MEDICAL MANAGEMENT

Advances in the medical management of burns have enabled the survival of thousands of patients in recent years who 10 or 15 years ago would not have survived. The research base and techniques available today have enabled patients to receive better care and more sophisticated techniques for treatment of major burns. This section of the chapter will discuss the emergency and initial treatment of patients with burns, the medical management of burns, and the surgical procedures associated with the debridement and grafting of new skin onto the burn wound.

Emergency Management and Resuscitation

This phase of care can be defined as the first 6 to 12 hours postburn. The goals of this phase address the major life-threatening problems and stabilize the patient through procedures designed to accomplish the following:

1. Establish and maintain an airway.
2. Prevent cyanosis, shock, and hemorrhage.
3. Establish baseline data on the patient and the amount of burned surface area.
4. Prevent or reduce fluid losses.
5. Clean the patient and wounds.
6. Assess injuries.
7. Prevent pulmonary and cardiac complications.
8. Prevent deformities.

The triage through these procedures applies only to major burn trauma.

Initially, the patient must be transported from the site of the injury to a treatment facility. If possible, transportation will be directly to the burn center rather than to a hospital emergency room. The goal of the treatment in transit is to stabilize the patient and to maintain an airway. Most burns are relatively stable immediately after injury, and only in circumstances in which burns have occurred to the face or chest will an emergency procedure be necessary to establish an artificial airway. Also during the initial transportation phase, patient history and personal data are gathered if possible. The type of agent causing the burn is noted, and initial assessment of the burn injury takes place. The emergency medical personnel will use the rule of nines (see Figure 25–9) to chart the areas and types of burns.

One of the major advances in burn resuscitation has been in the area of volume replacement initially and throughout the patient's treatment. Information about the physiologic changes responsible for the shifts in body fluids and protein changes have led to new solutions to improve the survival and welfare of the patient with a burn injury.[1,54-57] This research has led to a new understanding of the physiologic changes that occur following a burn and the volume replacement therapy necessary to improve the chances for survival.

After the patient arrives at the burn center and the team has assessed the type and degree of injury, the first procedure after starting an intravenous line (IV) to begin fluid replacement will be the initial cleaning and removal of the eschar. This is usually done in a large tank or whirlpool where the patient can be totally immersed. The water temperature should be between 98.6°F and 104°F (37°C and 40°C). The initial tanking allows the team to examine the patient fully, to remove hair, to establish body weight, to remove any loose skin, and to start the **debridement** process. **Debridement** is the removal of the eschar, or necrotic tissue, from the patient. There are several methods for debridement: (1) occlusive dressings with topical solutions or creams, (2) exposure with topical creams, and (3) primary excision.[58]

Occlusive dressings serve three purposes: (1) they hold medications on the skin, (2) they mechanically debride the wound when they are removed, and (3) they protect the burn wound and reduce the fluid loss from the wound. Dressings are often changed once or twice a day, depending on the size and type of wound and also depending on the type of medication used. Table 25-3 presents the most common topical medications used in the treatment of burns. The dressings consist of several layers. The first layer is fine gauze, followed by cotton padding such as Kerlix or Kling. The final layer consists of positioning splints wrapped on with more bandaging. Dressings may be soaked and removed in the tubbing procedure described below, or they may be removed dry. Dry mechanical debridement is extremely painful and should be avoided if possible.

The technique of applying topical ointment without dressings allows for some ongoing inspection of the wound and an assessment of the healing progress. The ointment must be removed every day, normally in a daily immersion of the patient in a large whole-body whirlpool. The ointment must be constantly reapplied throughout the day. The patient is placed in warm— 98.6°F to 104°F (37°C to 40°C)—water to cover the entire burn. If the face is involved, a swimming snorkel may be used to allow breathing while the face is submerged. The whirlpool tub will have some form of disinfectant in the water to assist in infection control, as well as some salt solution to prevent the osmotic losses of fluid to the water from the patient. While the patient is in the water, the dressings are removed. Care must be taken in the removal of the dressings to ensure the removal of loose eschar with minimal if any bleeding. The removal of the dressings in the water is less painful than the dry removal, but it is still extremely painful, and most patients require pain medications prior to the procedure. All wound care is carried out using a sterile technique. If **sharp debridement,** or the use of surgical scissors and forceps to remove the eschar, is to be done, the loose epidermis and eschar are removed and pockets of pus are exposed, but bleeding should be kept at a minimum. The goal of immersion and debridement is to remove any eschar or nonhealing epithelium that will come off, to promote healing and to allow for the revascularization of the area for reepithelialization to begin. NOTE: The removal of dressings and the sharp debridement are very painful and frightening experiences for the patient. Even the most stoic and medicated patient normally will cry out in pain during the procedure. It can not be emphasized enough that skilled care and compassion play a critical role in the physical and mental healing process of the patient. The physical therapist is normally involved in hydrotherapy and debridement. The therapist should strive to take extreme care in the debridement and provide as much support for the patient as possible. After debridement, the wound is carefully inspected. The appearance, depth, size, granulation tissue, exudate, and odor are noted. Infection is heralded by such signs as a thick purulent drainage, odor, fever, a brownish-black discoloration, rapid separation of eschar, boils in the adjacent tissue, and the conversion of a deep partial

Table 25-3 COMMON TOPICAL MEDICATIONS USED IN TREATMENT OF BURNS

Medication	Description	Method of Application
Furacin (nitrofurazone)	Antibacterial cream used in less severe burns; indicated to decrease bacteria growth; may be used to prepare wound for graft and/or used prophylactically	Applied directly; may be in rolled form or applied as gauze pad
Garamycin (gentamicin)	Antibiotic used against gram-negative organism and staphyloccal and streptococcal bacteria	Cream or ointment applied with sterile glove and covered with gauze
Silver sulfadiazine	Topical antibacterial agent effective against Pseudomonas infections; it may also cause the adherence of eschar, thus delaying separation	Cream applied with sterile glove in a film 2–4 mm thick; may be left uncovered
Sulfamylon (mafenide acetate)	Topical antibacterial agent effective against gram-negative and gram-positive organisms; diffuses easily through eschar; may prevent conversion of burns	Cream applied directly to wound in thin $\frac{1}{16}$ inch layer BID; may be left undressed or used with thin layer of gauze; must be completely removed before reapplied or may cause bacterial growth in old sulfamylon
Silver nitrate	Caustic antiseptic germicide and astringent; will penetrate only 1–2 mm of eschar; used only for surface bacteria	Small sticks used to cauterize small areas; dressings or soaks also used every 2 hours; not used with full thickness burns
Travase	Enzyme debrider has no bacterial control action; used with silver sulfadiazine	Applied to eschar with moist occlusive dressing

thickness burn to a full thickness burn. Wounds are then cleaned, and once the patient is removed from the tub, medications and/or dressings are reapplied as the patient is being warmed. One additional therapeutic procedure, active or passive range of motion, may be carried out by the physical therapist while the patient is still in the water. It is critical to maintain as much range of motion as possible during the healing of the tissue around the joints, because the more range that can be maintained throughout the initial phases of the recovery, the less difficult it will be to fully rehabilitate the patient once all wounds are healed and closed.

The third type of debridement is the primary excision of the eschar surgically. Much of the increased survival rate of patients with extensive burns—greater than 65 percent body surface area—has been due to the early primary excision of the burn wound in surgery. Normally the patient will be taken to surgery within 24 hours of the burn, the surgeons waiting only long enough to allow the patient to be stabilized, if possible. The patient is then anesthetized and all of the eschar is removed at one time. Proponents of primary early excision feel that the approach is easier on the patient than repeated debridement and that it promotes more rapid healing, reduces infection and scarring, and is more economic in terms of staff and hospital time.[59]

Surgical Grafting of the Burn Wound

In many burn centers, the wound is closed with a graft at the time of the primary excision. There are many types of grafts that can be used to close the wound. An **autograft** is the patient's own skin, taken from an unburned area and transplanted to cover the burned area. The site from which the skin graft is taken is called the **donor site.** Common donor sites include the thighs, buttocks, and trunk. Autografts are desirable because they tend to be rejected less often and provide permanent coverage and thus healing of the wound. An **allograft,** or **homograft,** is the skin taken from an individual of the same species, usually cadaver skin. The skin can be kept in skin banks for prolonged periods. **Allografts** are temporary grafts used to cover large burns when there is insufficient autograft available. **Xenograft** (also called a **heterograft**) is the donation of skin for coverage of the burned wound from another species, usually pigskin or **porcine.** Artificial skin is a temporary graft used when large areas of burn exist and coverage is done for survival. Allografts or xenografts are used until there is sufficient normal skin available for an autograft. Several reports have shown great success with allografts when primary excision and grafting were done within the first days postburn[60] and when the patient received the antirejection drug **cyclosporin.**[61] These advances add hope for the survival of extensively burned patients today, whereas survival was not even considered feasible 10 years ago.

Perhaps the most exciting advance in the care of the burn patient comes in the use of artificial skin for the coverage of the excised wound. The use of artificial skin was initiated by Dr. John Burke and Dr. Ioannis Yannas at Massachusetts General Hospital in Boston, Massachusetts.[62,63] The artificial skin consists of a bilayer membrane of distinct epidermal and dermal portions, with each portion physiologically resembling its counterpart in normal skin. The epidermal portion is a homogenous layer of **Silastic,** a Dow–Corning material, which is approximately $\frac{1}{10}$ mm thick. It controls water flux approximately equal to normal skin, provides a bacteria-free layer, and makes a firm bond with the artificial dermal layer. The dermal portion consists of bovine hide and chondroitin-6-sulfate from shark cartilage. The artificial skin is grafted onto the patient, normally within 24 hours postburn after the primary surgical excision of the eschar. The Silastic epidermis is a temporary measure being replaced by autoepidermis at a time of clinical convenience. The Silastic is easily peeled from the artificial dermis, leaving a partly vascularized "neodermis" with a granular surface for the adherence of the new graft. The artificial dermis remains on the patient, thus it saves additional surgical grafting and allows for quicker healing and discharge from the hospital. In one study, 10 patients with third-degree burns over 50 to 90 percent of their body surface areas were treated with the artificial skin.[64] These patients had up to 64 percent of the burned areas covered with the artificial skin. All 10 patients survived and recovered normally following the use of artificial skin as graft material to cover extensive burns. The authors cite several advantages to the use of artificial skin. It significantly reduced the average hospital stay. The patients needed significantly fewer pain medications, and the need for medications was lower. The healing was primary, as opposed to secondary healing with scar tissue, which resulted in less hypertrophic scarring. There was little or no infection owing to the early removal of all sources of bacteria and dead tissue. The neodermis provided the physical and cosmetic properties of normal dermis and led to improved functional and cosmetic results. Finally, the patients were able to return to exercise and functional activities much more rapidly.[64]

SKIN GRAFTING PROCEDURES

The removal of skin for use in grafting is done in surgery under anesthesia. The skin used for the graft is usually removed with a dermatome, which is an instrument for cutting thin layers of donor skin. This allows the surgeon to obtain a larger sheet of graft, and a more consistent depth of graft. The dermatome removes a predetermined depth of skin, either a **split thickness skin graft (STSG)** or a **full thickness skin graft (FTSG).** The split thickness skin graft contains only the superficial layers of the dermis from the donor site, as opposed to the full thickness graft, which consists of the full dermal thickness. The split thickness graft will adhere to the graft site but may contract more than the full thickness graft. The full thickness graft has the disadvantage of leaving a full thickness lesion in the donor site, which will essentially behave as an additional burned area until it, too, reepithelializes.

Most commonly, and most advantageous from cosmetic and functional viewpoints, the skin graft is applied as it is removed from the dermatome. The face, neck, and flexor surfaces are normally covered with a solid sheet graft, and most other areas are covered with a **mesh graft.** The meshing of a graft consists of running the sheet graft through a machine that makes tiny parallel incisions in a linear arrangement. This allows the graft to be stretched to three times its size before it is applied to the wound bed. It covers a larger area, and once it "takes," the interstices close in from the multiple meshes. Figure 25–12 shows the transfer of the meshed graft to the burn wound.

The thickness of the graft varies from 0.0008 to 0.012 inches; this is sufficient to obtain a graft containing the epidermis and some percentage of the dermis. Generally, the thinner the graft, the better the take; the thicker the graft, the better the cosmetic result. Selection of depth depends on many factors, including whether or not the donor site needs to be used again for another crop of skin as soon as possible. Taking a thicker sheet graft adversely affects the possibility of taking another graft from the same site for a prolonged period of time. Crops from STSG sites may be repeated in 10 to 14 days, depending on the healing rate of the donor site.

The graft is sutured to the margins of the burn wound. Once the graft is fixed in position, any blood or serum that might have become located between the graft and the capillary bed should be removed. Application of a pressure dressing facilitates total continuity of the graft to the bed but does not necessarily hasten fibrin fixation of the graft. Fixation of the graft to the host bed by fibrin occurs spontaneously.

One of the basic criteria for successful "take" of a graft is sufficient vascularity within the wound bed. The intent is, therefore, to apply the graft while the granulation tissue is young and is most vascular. Delay means more collagen deposition and more heaped-up granulation tissue, which lacks the necessary vascularity upon which the success of the graft depends. Once the graft has been applied, separation of the graft bed owing to excessive motion, mechanical trauma, or exudate formation must be prevented. Initially the area is immobilized, and the dressing applied needs to provide firm, even compression around the wound.

Survival of the skin graft depends on several nutritive factors: (1) plasmatic circulation, which provides a promotive nutritive supply to the graft via absorption of exudate from the host vascular bed; (2) inosculations or the process by which a direct connection is established between the graft and the host vessels; and (3) penetration of the host vessels into the graft site. Grafts that are commonly white and blanched at the time of transplantation begin to show pinkish coloration within a matter of hours following their placement on an adequate vascular bed.

The reestablishment of circulation in the graft site will take place through the formation of direct anastomosis between respective vessels, invasion from the host bed forming new channels, or by a combination of both. At approximately 6 hours postgraft, there is activity of the host endothelium. Twenty-four hours postgraft, numerous host vessels are seen to penetrate the graft. The invasion of new capillaries seems to be the most important consideration in vascularization, inasmuch as the pattern of ingrowing vessels generally differs radically from the original vascular pattern present in the graft. However, capillary transfer across the host graft separation will not be sufficient to keep the graft unless fibrin con-

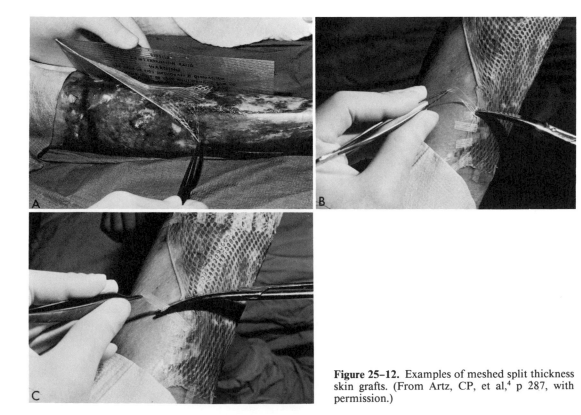

Figure 25–12. Examples of meshed split thickness skin grafts. (From Artz, CP, et al,[4] p 287, with permission.)

nections are made. Initially, structural connections are fibrous. Precollagen material will next be delivered via ingrowing capillaries. The collagen is then laid down to secure the attachment of the graft. Normally, within 48 hours there is organization of the fibrous reticulum, and by 72 hours granulation has proceeded so far that it is impossible to distinguish the graft from the host.

PHYSICAL THERAPY MANAGEMENT

The rehabilitation of the burn patient begins the moment the patient arrives at the hospital, and it is an everchanging process that is modified on a daily basis. The preceding sections of this chapter have discussed the pathophysiologic changes and alterations of the skin that occur in the burn wound and the closure of that wound with various types of graft materials. While the skin is healing, it is imperative that the patient's rehabilitation occur concurrently. With hard work and dedication to the rehabilitation program, the burned patient can indeed return to a normal productive life. For most patients, the most difficult phase of rehabilitation occurs after the wounds have healed. If the physical therapist is actively involved in early care and can establish a program of movement in conjunction with the wound healing process, the posthealing rehabilitation can be much less traumatic and more successful. The remainder of this chapter is dedicated to the physical therapist's role in the patient's active rehabilitation and return to functional activity.

Assessment

After reviewing the initial assessment of the depth of the burns and the total amount of body surface area involved, the physical therapist will begin to assess the patient's ability to move and will measure the patient's available range of motion. The range may be limited owing to swelling and edema, but an initial baseline measure can be obtained. In addition, the physical therapist needs to get an accurate history from the patient and family as to any predisposing limitations or old injuries that may confound the rehabilitation potential.

During each of the hydrotherapy sessions, it is appropriate and necessary to use the buoyancy of the water to help maintain the range of motion in each limb and joint. The water acts as a buoyant medium to reduce the weight of the limb, and it also serves to keep the healing skin wet, which will facilitate movement. While the patient is in the tub, active and passive range of motion must be monitored and carefully documented to ensure that the patient is not losing range of motion.

The other musculoskeletal examination techniques discussed in chapter 5 should also be included in the initial assessment and ongoing reassessments of the patient. Because the healing of the burn wound is a daily, dynamic process, and because changes occur so frequently, the physical therapist needs to assess and to monitor the changes and to perform various assessment procedures almost daily. This will keep the other members of the burn care team abreast of potential problems so that intervention can begin before the potential problem becomes a real one.

While working with the patient the physical therapist needs to monitor the patient's vital signs (chapter 4) continually in order to assess the cardiovascular and respiratory response to the treatment. As previously mentioned, insults to the cardiovascular and respiratory systems are common. In addition, the cardiovascular strain associated with the healing process is significant. When exercise is performed on top of this increased cardiovascular effort, it may cause the patient to become overexerted. Monitoring of pulse, blood pressure, and respiratory rate before, during, and after exercise, during the recovery period, will yield valuable information as to the recovery and healing of the cardiorespiratory system.

The assessment of cardiovascular or aerobic endurance will normally not take place until most of the burn wounds are completely healed. Once they are healed and the patient is able to ambulate and/or to ride a cycle ergometer, a modified exercise assessment can be performed in a supervised, monitored exercise test. Workloads should be increased by no more than one MET increments, and the work period per workload should be either 1 or 2 minutes in duration. It may be difficult to obtain a 12-lead exercise electrocardiogram from the patient, particularly if there are extensive burns of the chest, but the patient should have as many monitored leads as feasible to obtain the most complete picture of the cardiac response to the exercise.

One of the major complications of extensive burns is the destruction of the sweating mechanisms. Thus the burned patient may be at a distinct disadvantage in thermoregulation during exercise, particularly exercise in the heat. Previous research has shown that although the areas of deep full thickness burns do not sweat at all, the nonburned areas will sweat excessively and inefficiently.[65] As of this writing, a series of investigations are in progress that will examine the thermoregulation problems associated with sunburn[66] and the concerns associated with patients who have extensive areas of artificial skin grafts.

The changes in body composition also need to be assessed by the physical therapist. Owing to the increased metabolic demand of burn wound healing, patients will lose a great deal of body weight. The patient will lose not only fat weight but also lean body mass. The physical therapist can assess changes in body composition either by underwater weighing[67] or more easily by skinfold anthropometry.[68] It should be noted that skinfold estimation of body composition is most accurate when done on a population similar to that from which the regression equations were generated. An area of needed research is the establishment of skinfold estimation of body composition changes in patients with burns correlated with underwater weighing.

Another area that warrants extensive assessment is hand function in patients who have sustained burns of the hands. Depending on members of the burn care team, either a physical or occupational therapist will have responsibility for the assessment of hand function, and all members will assist in the hand rehabilitation. Hands and fingers will lose motion and function very quickly and need to be assessed daily to prevent further losses of movement.

Other areas such as psychologic, mental, emotional, and vocational assessments will be performed by professionals in those areas. The physical therapist will have to be cognizant of these other assessments because they will have significant impact on the patient's progress and outlook toward the future and rehabilitation.

Goal Setting

Based on the assessment, the amount and degree of the burn, the patient's current health status, age, and physical and mental condition, the prognosis for the patient will be determined by the burn care team. The goals for rehabilitation and physical therapy management are contingent on the patient's prognosis and potential. It is difficult to give specific goals because of the varied nature of each burn injury, but typical goals include the following:

1. Attain clean burn wound for healing and grafting.
2. Maintain range of motion.
3. Prevent or reduce scar contractures.
4. Prevent pulmonary complications.
5. Promote independence in ambulation.
6. Promote independence in activities of daily living.
7. Improve cardiovascular endurance and strength.

The ultimate goal of rehabilitation is return of the patient to normal function and to life as it was before the burn injury.

Treatment

Physical therapy treatment will begin on the day of admission. The initial assessment of the patient will determine which areas need to be addressed first. The physical therapy concerns in wound cleaning and hydrotherapy have been addressed earlier. The attainment of the other physical therapy goals outlined above are covered here.

ACTIVE AND PASSIVE EXERCISE

Active exercise is encouraged in all burned areas. Active exercise begins on the first day. Other forms of exercise should be used only if confusion, pain, or other complications prevent active exercise. All joints, even those in unburned areas, should go through active, full range exercise. In most cases, active range of motion should be done at least three times a day. Resistive devices such as free weights, pull cord, pulleys, and so forth can be used to prevent loss of strength in the areas not burned. During tubbing is the best time for the most aggressive active exercise session because the dressings will be removed and the skin will be moist. If the patient has just received a skin graft, active and passive exercise of the area is discontinued for 7 to 10 days to allow the graft site to take. After the surgeon determines it is safe to begin exercise again, gentle range of motion, first active, and then passive if needed, will be reinstituted.

Active assistive and passive exercises will have to be initiated if the patient can not achieve full range of motion with active exercise. Exercise over healing burned areas will be extremely painful, and most patients will indicate they would rather lose their motion than be subjected to the additional pain that occurs with movement. It can be, and usually is, extremely hard and mentally draining on the physical therapist, who must push patients to exercise in and through pain, but it is critical for the therapist to be persistent. Timing exercise sessions with pain medication effects will lessen the problems, and there will be times when the therapist needs to "give in" to the needs of the patient. However, the patient and family need to be educated as to the complications of NOT EXERCISING, and the therapist should elicit the assistance of the family in keeping the patient moving as much as possible. The burn patient will require a lifetime of exercise to prevent contractures and losses of movement. The patient must be encouraged and educated to accept this and actively to begin aggressive rehabilitation.

As the patient continues with physical therapy, resistive and strengthening exercises are incorporated into the treatment plan. Burn patients lose a tremendous amount of body weight, and lean muscle mass decreases rapidly. Exercise can consist of isokinetic, isotonic, or other resistive training devices. General principles of exercise training and strength improvement should be followed but may need to be modified based on the patient's condition and stage of wound healing.

Patients should be encouraged to begin active exercise that will stress the cardiovascular system such as walking from the burn unit to the physical therapy department to exercise. Cycle ergometry, rowing ergometry, or other forms of stationary exercise should be encouraged. These exercises will not only work to increase cardiovascular endurance, but also can have the benefit of improving range of motion of the extremities. In addition, it introduces some variety into the rehabilitation program. The physical therapist working with burn patients needs to be creative and innovative to keep patients motivated and striving to increase their exercise capacity.

Ambulation should always be initiated at the earliest appropriate time, and stationary exercise may serve to prepare the patient for ambulation. If the legs are grafted, ambulation should be discontinued for approximately 10 days until the physicians feel that it is safe to continue. When early ambulation is initiated, the legs should be wrapped in Kerlix and in elastic supports to support the new grafts and to promote venous return. If the patient can not tolerate the upright position owing to orthostatic hypotension, gradual increases in tilt table treatment time will assist in preparing the patient for ambulation. Initially, the patient may require assistive devices to ambulate. However, independent ambulation without devices should be achieved as soon as possible.

The physical therapist will spend a great deal of time with each patient in exercise sessions. The time is necessary, and the rewards are tremendous when a patient who had life-threatening burns is able to walk out of the hospital and to return to productive community involvement.

POSITIONING AND SPLINTING OF BURN WOUNDS

Positioning and splinting begin on the day of admission and require constant care and attention to prevent contractures. The patient is prone to the development of contractures owing to the hypertrophic scarring and formation of collagen across the joints. In addition, because of such great pain, if left alone, the patient will not move the burned area, which further results in contracture development. There are several excellent sources available on the proper positioning and designing of splints to prevent burn contractures[69,70] and the reader is referred to these resources for more detailed positioning and splinting information which is beyond the scope of this chapter. However, general principles are discussed and some examples provided in the appendix.

Burn surfaces should be positioned in a stretched or neutral position of function. Burns over the flexor surface will tend to be held flexed and thus must be splinted in an extended position. Splints should not be left on continuously except after grafting. They are appropriate to be worn continuously only at night. Splints should conform to the body parts, and care must be taken to ensure that there are no pressure points that may cause a breakdown in the healing or in normal skin. Active motion is important, and splints and positioning are intended to serve only as adjuncts until full active motion can be achieved.

Most splinting has been of the static nature. Dynamic splints have also been used in the care of burn patients.[71] This offers great potential for the earlier return of active function in those areas of extensive burn and grafting. Although no research has been found that utilized the continuous passive motion devices, it would seem that these may be appropriate for certain burn patients.

In patients who have to be splinted, the physical therapist will need to institute some form of stretching to maintain the range of motion. Passive stretching can cause reflex muscle spasm and additional pain, so, if possible, active forms of stretching techniques should be utilized. Proprioceptive neuromuscular facilitation (PNF) techniques of contract-relax and hold-relax can be used very effectively. Care should be taken around areas of grafts, and the stretch should be gentle, prolonged, and gradual. The burned area should be lubricated prior to exercise, if appropriate, to keep the skin moist, similar to exercise in the water. If the burns are well healed, heating modalities may be used to increase further the elastic components of collagen prior to stretching.

PREVENTION AND TREATMENT OF SCAR CONTRACTURE

Although measures to prevent a contracture can be undertaken with the best intention, there will be patients who develop a scar contracture for one reason or another. There are several nonsurgical and surgical methods available to aid in the prevention and/or treatment of scar contracture.

Nonsurgical Scar Contracture Treatments

The hypertrophic scar that forms across the burn wound is made up of immature collagen formation, as was discussed earlier. These areas will continue to form and the scar contracture will continue to grow unless action is taken against this growth. There are three relatively simple procedures that have proven very effective in halting the growth of hypertrophic scars: splinting, constant pressure, and exercise. Splinting and exercise have already been addressed; therefore, this section focuses on the concepts of constant pressure.

Constant pressure dressing or garments exerting pressure exceeding 25 mmHg will decrease the vascularity, depress the tissue partial pressure of oxygen, decrease the amount of mucopolysaccharides (especially chondroitin sulfate A), decrease the cellular response as well as the collagen deposition, and significantly lessen localized lymphedema.[72] The early hypertrophic scar is readily influenced by mechanical forces and thus will respond to pressure garments. The earlier the scar formation is exposed to the pressure, the better the result. Usually, if the scar is less than 6 months old, it will respond to the pressure garments. The scar conforms to the pressure and will lie flat on the surface, not developing into a contracture. However, even if the scar is still active, or shows evidence of high vascularity (red color) for up to a year, pressure garments have proven successful.

The most common pressure garment used in the treatment of scar contracture formation is the Jobst Pressure Garment, available from the Jobst Company in Toledo, Ohio.[73] The Jobst garments are specifically fitted for the individual patient and made usually within 24 to 48 hours after receipt of the measurements at the factory. The physical therapist uses specially designed circumferential tape measures to assess the circumference of each limb every inch and a half in order to fit the garment exactly to the limb with the proper pressure. The garments are very tight and difficult to get on, but the pressure is needed in order to prevent the scar formation. Garments can be ordered for any or all body parts, and the garments are usually worn 23 hours a day for up to 12 to 18 months, if necessary, to prevent the scar formation.

Two other nonsurgical interventions can reduce scar formation. Deep friction massage may loosen scar tissue by mobilizing cutaneous tissue from underlying tissue and breaking up adhesions. When massage of this type is used in conjunction with stretching and exercise, the mature scar tissue may be stretched and contracture corrected. Secondly, the use of ultrasound on the scar has shown promising results. Ultrasound is well documented in its ability to increase circulation and to separate collagen fibers which form in the scar. If ultrasound is used in dosages of 1 to 2 w/cm^2 continuously and directly over the scar for 6 to 8 minutes, it can facilitate increases in range of motion and can decrease the pain associated with the scar. Ultrasound works most effectively if it is used while the scar is less than 1 year old.

Surgical Correction of Scar Formation

Surgery is usually not indicated in the active, immature phase of the scar formation, when it is most vascu-

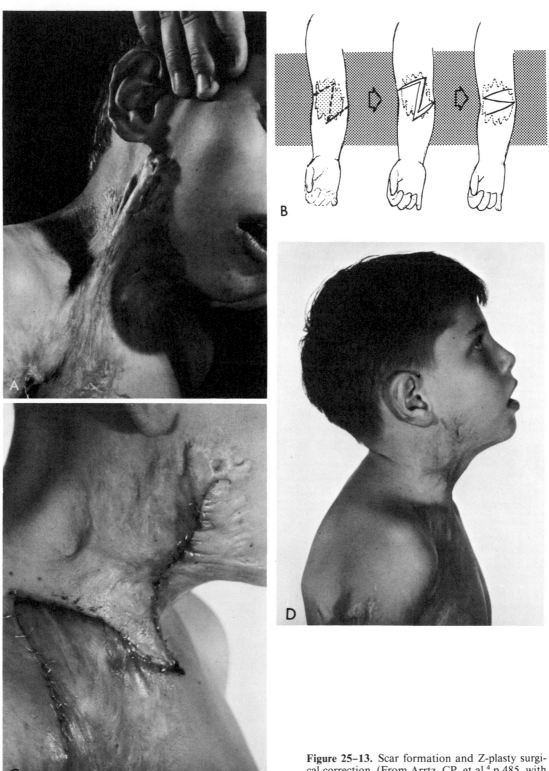

Figure 25–13. Scar formation and Z-plasty surgical correction. (From Arrtz, CP, et al,[4] p 485, with permission.)

lar, because the final results will be less than optimal owing to the local response to the surgical trauma.[72] Each patient's scar will require individualized treatment. One common component of many surgical revisions is release of tension created by scar tissue. Figure 25–13 shows the technique and result of **Z-plasty surgery** used for the release of scar formation of the neck and elbow. The **Z-plasty** serves to lengthen the scar. Following surgery, the patient is treated with skin grafting if needed, as well as pressure garments to prevent additional hypertrophic scarring. This procedure is very effective and may be the only alternative available to treat the disfiguring limitations of scar formation.

Factors Affecting Treatment Outcomes

The rehabilitation of the burn patient has made tremendous strides in recent years secondary to many advances in our understanding of the care and resuscitation of the burn wound through all stages of recovery. The increased number of specialized burn units in hospitals all over the country has resulted in the survival of patients with extensive burns. The advances in emergency treatment and fluid resuscitation during transit have decreased mortality significantly. In addition, skin-grafting techniques and the introduction of artificial skin have had great impact on the success of treatment of burn wounds. There are numerous support groups, such as the Shriners' Institutes, that care for burned children, not only in the acute phase but into the rehabilitation and recovery phases as well. Burn patients and their families may need psychosocial counseling and help in adjustment to overcome the cosmetic disfigurement. Burn care teams typically include psychologists who have aided patients to return successfully to society as functioning members.

SUMMARY

Burn injuries represent a major health problem in terms of management and care of surviving patients. Specific problems and complications vary according to the degree of thermal destruction of the skin. The classification of burn injuries is based on both the depth and the degree of thickness of the tissue destroyed and includes superficial burn (first degree), superficial partial thickness burn (second degree), deep partial thickness burn (deep second degree), full thickness burn (third degree), and electrical burn (fourth degree). The rule of nines and the burn index were developed to assist in the initial assessment of the amount and degree of burn injury. The specific clinical signs and symptoms that result from a burn injury vary according to the different classifications. Secondary problems can include pulmonary, metabolic, and cardiac/circulatory complications. Epithelial healing is dependent upon the deposition of granulation tissue and subsequent collagen production. Continued maturation of the burn wound results in a reduction of the hypervascularity characteristics with the potential for hypertrophic collagen scarring. Medical management addresses life-threatening problems and stabilization of the patient. Debridement, or removal of the eschar, occlusive dressings with topical drugs, and surgical excision and grafting are primary treatment measures. Physical therapy management focuses on the prevention of scar contracture, the maintenance of normal range of motion, the development of muscular strength, the improvement of cardiovascular endurance, and the return to function and activities of daily living. Although burn trauma and subsequent recovery can be one of the most devastating life occurrences, a comprehensive medical team can assist individuals with burn injury and their families to return to as normal a lifestyle as possible.

QUESTIONS FOR REVIEW

1. Describe the differences between first-, second- (superficial and deep partial thickness), third-, and fourth-degree burns.

2. Explain how a second-degree burn can convert to a third-degree burn.

3. Outline the pathophysiologic changes that occur with deep, partial thickness burns.

4. Compare the difference in pathophysiology and treatment between deep partial thickness burns and full thickness burns.

5. What additional complications can result from an electrical burn?

6. Describe the three primary complications of the pulmonary system caused by extensive burns.

7. What are the major metabolic problems associated with burns and their treatment?

8. List the events that occur in the healing of the burn wound.

9. What are the goals of the emergency management and resuscitation of the acute burn patient?

10. Compare the methods of debridement.

11. Define the various types of skin grafts.

12. What is the function of mesh grafts and when are they used as opposed to full thickness skin grafts?

13. What are some of the primary considerations necessary for a successful "take" of the skin graft?

14. Discuss the need for active exercise in the rehabilitation of burn patients.

15. What steps can be undertaken to maintain ROM and to prevent burn wound scar contracture formation?

REFERENCES

1. Demling, RH: Medical progress: Burns. N Engl J Med 313:1389, 1986.
2. Accident Facts. National Safety Council, Chicago, 1983.
3. Fick, G and Baptiste, M: The epidemiology of burn injury. Public Health Rep 94:312, 1979.
4. Artz, CP, Moncrief, JA, and Pruitt, BA: Burns: A Team Approach. WB Saunders, Philadelphia, 1979.
5. DiGregorio, VR (ed): Clinics in Physical Therapy Series, vol 5. Rehabilitation of the Burn Patient. Churchill Livingstone, New York, 1984.
6. Fisher, SV and Helm, PA: Comprehensive Rehabilitation of Burns. Williams & Wilkins, Baltimore, 1984.
7. MacKay, A, et al: A comparison of age-specific burn injury rate in five Massachusetts communities. Am J Publ Health 69:1146, 1979.
8. DeGregoro, VR: The burn problem, the burn team and the physical therapist. In DiGregoro, VR (ed): Clinics in Physical Therapy: Rehabilitation of the Burn Patient. Churchill Livingstone, New York, 1984.
9. Feller, I, Tholen, D, and Cromwell, RD: Improvements in burn care: 1965–1979. JAMA 244:2074, 1980.
10. Moncrief, JA: The body's response to heat. In Artz, CP, Moncrief, JA, and Pruitt, BA: Burns: A Team Approach. WB Saunders, Philadelphia, 1979.
11. Zawacki, BE: Reversal of capillary stasis and prevention of necrosis in burns. Ann Surg 180:98, 1974.
12. Lund, CC and Browder, NC: Estimation of area of burns. Surg Gynecol Obstet 79:352, 1955.
13. Polaski, GR and Tennison, AC: Estimation of the amount of burned surface area. JAMA 103:34, 1948.
14. Maegarith, BG: Clinical effect of exposure to heat and sunlight. Br Med J 98:1402, 1952.
15. Mochelle, AB, Pillsbury, RE, and Hurley, HH (ed): Dermatology. WB Saunders, Philadelphia, 1975.
16. Gilchrest, BA, et al: The human sunburn reaction: Histologic and biochemical studies. J Ann Acad Dermatol 5:411, 1981.
17. Johnson, BE and Daniels, F: Lysosome and the reaction of skin to ultraviolet radiation. J Invest Dermatol 53:85, 1969.
18. Sams, WM and Wendelman, RK: The effect of ultraviolet light on isolated cutaneous blood vessels. J Invest Dermatol 53:79, 1969.
19. Voltonene, EJ: The effect of erythemal reaction caused by ultraviolet irradiation on mast cell degradation in the skin. Acta Dermatol Veneral 44:269, 1964.
20. Baxter, CR: Fluid volume and electrolyte changes in the early post burn period. Clin Plast Surg 1:693, 1974.
21. Teplitz, C: The pathology of burns and the fundamentals of burn wound sepsis. In Artz, C, et al: Burns: A Team Approach. WB Saunders, Philadelphia, 1979.
22. Salisbury, RE, et al: Postburn edaema of the upper extremity: Evaluation of present treatment. J Trauma 13:857, 1973.
23. Teplitz, C: The pathology of burns and the fundamentals of burn wound sepsis. In Artz, C, et al: Burns: A Team Approach. WB Saunders, Philadelphia, 1979.
24. Marvin, JA, et al: Usefulness of blood cultures in confirming septic complications in burn patients: Evaluation of a new culture method. J Trauma 15:657, 1975.
25. Zaski, DE, et al: Increased dosage requirements of gentamycin in burn patients. J Trauma 16:824, 1976.
26. Zane, LJ: Evaluation of the acutely ill burn patient. In DiGregoro, VR (ed): Clinics in Physical Therapy: Rehabilitation of the Burn Patient. Churchill Livingstone, New York, 1984.
27. Artz, CP: Electrical injury. In Artz, CP, et al: Burns: A Team Approach, WB Saunders, Philadelphia, 1979.
28. Taylor, PH, Pugsley, LQ, and Vogel, EH: The intriguing electrical burn. J Trauma 2:309, 1962.
29. Proceedings of the International Symposium on Electrical Accidents. International Occupational Safety and Health Information Center, International Labour Office, Geneva, Switzerland, 1964.
30. Baxter, CR: Present concepts in the management of major electrical injuries. Surg Clin N Am 50:1401, 1970.
31. Petroff, PA and Pruitt, BA: Pulmonary disease in the burn patient. In Artz, CP, et al: Burns: A Team Approach. WB Saunders, Philadelphia, 1979.
32. Cahalane, M and Demling, RH: Early respiratory abnormalities from smoke inhalation. JAMA 251:771, 1984.
33. Davies, LK, Poulton, TJ, and Modell, JH: Continuous positive airway pressure is beneficial in treatment of smoke inhalation. Crit Care Med 11:726, 1983.
34. Greenberg, MI and Walter, J: Axioms on smoke inhalation. Hosp Med 19:13, 1983.
35. Moylan, JA: Smoke inhalation and burn injury. Surg Clin N Am 60:1530, 1980.
36. Scheulen, JJ and Munster, AM: The Parkland formula in patients with burns and inhalation injury. J Trauma 22:869, 1982.
37. Chu, CS: New concepts of pulmonary burn injury. J Trauma 21:958, 1981.
38. Stephensen, BA: Smoke inhalation: The invisible injury. RN 47:36, 1984.
39. Moylan, JA: Smoke inhalation: Diagnostic techniques and steroids. J Trauma 19:971, 1979.
40. Trunkey, DD: Inhalation injury. Surg Clin N Am 58:1133, 1978.
41. Venus, B, et al: Prophylactic intubation and continuous positive airway pressure in the management of the inhalation injury in burn victims. Crit Care Med 9:519, 1981.
42. Wilmore, DW: Metabolic changes in burns. In Artz, CP, et al: Burns: A Team Approach. WB Saunders, Philadelphia, 1979.
43. Wilmore, DW, Aulick, LH, and Becker, RA: Hormones and the control of metabolism. In Fischer, JE (ed): Surgical Nutrition. Little, Brown & Co, Boston, 1983.
44. Wilmore, DW and Aulick, LH: Metabolic changes in burned patients. Surg Clin N Amer 58:1173, 1978.
45. Shamoon, H, Hendler, R, and Sherwin, RS: Synergistic interactions among anti-insulin hormones in the pathogenesis of stress hyperglycemia in humans. J Clin Endocrinol Metab 52:1235, 1981.
46. Wilmore, DW, et al: Effect of ambient temperature on heat production and heat loss in burn patients. J Appl Physiol 38:593, 1975.
47. Pelham, LD: Rational use of intervenous fat emulsions. Am J Hosp Pharm 38:198, 1981.
48. Alexander, JW, et al: Beneficial effects of aggressive protein feeding in severely burned children. Ann Surg 192:505, 1980.
49. Dominioni, L, et al: Prevention of severe postburn hypermetabolism and catabolism by immediate intragastric feeding. J Burn Care Rehab 5:106, 1984.
50. Matsuda, T, et al: The importance of burn wound size in determining the optimal calorie:nitrogen ratio. Surgery 94:562, 1983.
51. Moncrief, JA: Effect of various fluid regimens and pharmacologic agents on the circulating hemodynamics of immediate postburn period. Ann Surg 164:723, 1966.
52. Brand, ED, Cowgill, R, and Lefer, AM: Further characterization of a myocardial depression factor present in hemorrhagic shock. J. Trauma 9:216, 1969.
53. Eurenius, K: Hematologic changes in burns. In Artz, CP, et al: Burns: A Team Approach. WB Saunders, Philadelphia, 1979.
54. Baxter, CR: Fluid volume and electrolyte changes in early postburn period. Clin Plast Surg 1:693, 1974.
55. Arturson, G: Microvascular permeability to macromolecules in thermal injury. Acta Physiol Scand (Suppl) 463:111, 1979.
56. Kramer, GC, et al: Mechanisms for reduction of plasma protein following acute protein depletion. Am J Physiol 243:803, 1982.
57. Leape, LL: Initial changes in burns: Tissue changes in burned and unburned skin of rhesus monkeys. J Trauma 10:488, 1970.
58. VonPrince, K and Yeakel, MH: The Splinting of Burns. Charles C Thomas, Springfield, MA, 1974.
59. Burke, JF: Primary excision and prompt grafting as routine therapy for the treatment of thermal burns in children. Surg Clin N Am 56:477, 1976.
60. Cuono, C, Langdon, R, and McGuire, J: Use of cultured epidermal autografts and dermal allografts as skin replacement after burn injury. Lancet 8490:1123, 1986.
61. Achauer, BA, et al: Long-term skin allograft survival after short-term cyclosporin treatment in a patient with massive burns. Lancet 8471:14, 1986.
62. Yannus, IV and Burke, JF: Design of an artificial skin. I. Basic design principles. J Biomed Mater Res 14:65, 1980.
63. Yannus, IV, et al: Design of an artificial skin. II. Control of chemical composition. J Biomed Mater Res 14:107, 1980.
64. Burke, JF, et al: Successful use of a physiologically acceptable artificial skin in the treatment of extensive burn injury. Ann Surg 193:413, 1981.

65. Shapiro, Y, et al: Thermoregulatory responses of patients with extensive healed burns. J Appl Physiol 53:1019, 1982.
66. Falkel, JE, et al: Effect of sunburn on thermoregulation during exercise in the heat and cold. Protocol submitted to US Army Research Institute of Environmental Medicine, 1986.
67. Durnin, JV and Wormersley, J: Body fat assessed from total density and its estimate from skinfold thickness on 481 men and women aged 16 to 72 years. Br J Nutr 32:77, 1974.
68. Jackson, AE and Pollack, MK: Estimation of body composition, percent fat and lean body weight from skinfold measurements. Med Sci Sport 10:23, 1979.
69. Malick, MH and Carr, JA: Manual on Management of the Burn Patient. Harmarville Rehabilitation Center, Pittsburgh, 1982.
70. American Physical Therapy Association: Burn Care: Educational Resource Guide. APTA, Alexandria, VA, 1984.
71. Richard, RL: Use of Dynasplint to correct elbow flexion burn contracture: A case report. J Burn Care 7:151, 1986.
72. Larson, D, et al: Prevention and treatment of burn scar contracture. In Artz, CP, et al: Burns: A Team Approach. WB Saunders, Philadelphia, 1979.
73. Jobst Institute: Burn Scar Management. Jobst Institute, Toledo, OH, 1981.

GLOSSARY

Allograft (or homograft): Skin used to cover a burn wound that is taken from the same species—usually from cadaver skin.

Autograft: Skin taken from an unburned area of the patient and transplanted to cover the wound.

Blanch: Presence of a white spot seen on the skin when pressure is applied against the eschar. This is an indication of the presence of viable capillary beds; the blanched area will become pink if the capillary bed is perfused.

Burn index: An assessment tool used to estimate the extent of the body surface area burned, as well as the depth of the burn. One point is given for full thickness burns, and one half point given for partial thickness burns.

Cyclosporin: Antirejection drug used to reduce the risk of rejection of transplanted organs (i.e., heart, kidney, liver, and now used with skin organ transplantation).

Debridement: The removal of eschar and/or any loose tissue from the burn wound.

Dermis: Growth and vital functions layer of the skin; contains the vascular bed, blood vessels, lymphatics, sweat glands, hair follicles, nerve endings, and epidermal cells.

Desquamation: The peeling off of the outer layers of the epidermis.

Donor site: Site from which a skin graft is taken.

Epidermis: Outermost layer of the skin.

Epithelial islands: Areas in the burn wound that are viable, surviving tissue from which the new cell growth will originate.

Eschar: The dead, necrotic tissue from the burn wound.

Escharotomy: Midlateral incision of the burned eschar used to relieve pressure in the extremity.

First-degree burn: Superficial or sunburn type of thermal injury involving only the epidermal layer.

Full thickness skin graft: Graft containing full dermal thickness from the donor site.

Mesh graft: Process whereby the skin taken from the donor site is passed through a device creating holes in the skin; this allows stretching of the graft, increasing the surface area of the graft threefold.

Rule of nines: A method of estimating the amount of total body surface area that has been burned. It divides the body into segments that are approximately 9 percent of the total.

Second-degree burn: Blister-forming thermal injury with damage to epidermis and part of the dermal layer. Also called superficial partial thickness burn or deep partial thickness burn, depending on the amount of dermal damage.

Sharp debridement: Use of sterile scissors and forceps to remove the eschar.

Silastic: Epidermal component of artificial skin that is eventually removed once the dermal layer of the artificial skin "takes."

Split thickness skin graft (STSG): Graft containing only superficial layers of the dermis from the donor site.

Third-degree burn: A thermal injury with damage occurring completely through the dermal layer. Also called full thickness burn.

Xenograft (or heterograft): Skin donation to cover the burn wound from another species of animal, usually pigskin or porcine.

Z-plasty surgery: Procedure used to lengthen a burn scar contracture surgically to allow for greater range of motion.

APPENDIX A POSITIONING STRATEGIES FOR COMMON DEFORMITIES

Joint	Common Deformity	Motions to Be Stressed	Suggested Approaches
Anterior neck	Flexion	Hyperextension	Use double mattress—position neck in extension (Fig. 25–14); with healing—rigid cervical orthosis
Shoulder-axilla	Adduction and internal rotation	Abduction, flexion and external rotation	Position with shoulder flexed and abducted (Fig. 25–15) Airplane splint (Fig. 25–16)
Elbow	Flexion and pronation	Extension and supination	Splint in extension
Hand	Claw hand (also called burn claw hand or intrinsic minus hand)	Wrist extension: metacarpophalangeal flexion, proximal interphalangeal and distal interphalangeal extension, Thumb opposition	Wrap fingers separately (Fig. 25–17) Elevate to decrease edema. Position in *intrinsic plus* position, wrist in extension, metacarpophalangeal in flexion, proximal interphalangeal and distal interphalangeal in extension, thumb in opposition with large web space (Fig. 25–18)
Hip and groin	Flexion and adduction	All motions, especially hip extension and abduction	Hip neutral (0°), extension with slight abduction
Knee	Flexion	Extension	Posterior knee splint
Ankle	Foot drop (equinovarus)	All motions—especially dorsiflexion	Plastic ankle-foot orthosis with cutout at Achilles tendon and ankle positioning in 0° dorsiflexion (Fig. 25–19)

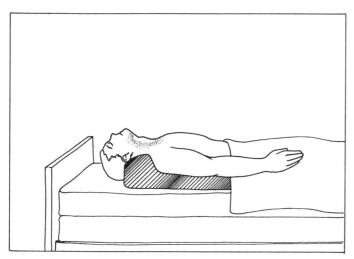

Figure 25–14. Positioning in bed of patient with burns of the anterior neck.

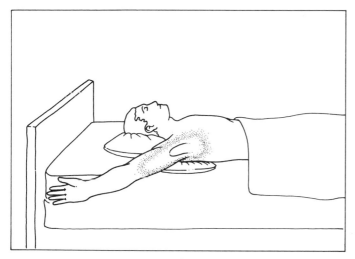

Figure 25–15. Positioning in bed of patient with burns of the axilla or shoulder.

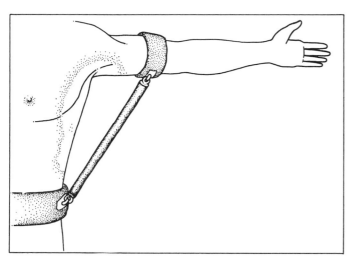

Figure 25–16. Airplane splint.

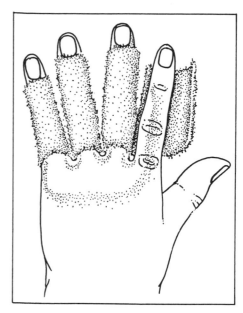

Figure 25–17. Wrapping the fingers separately prior to dressing the hand.

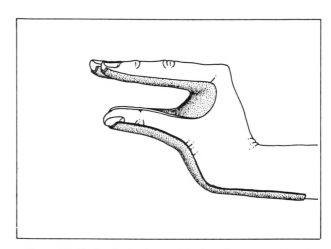

Figure 25–18. Intrinsic plus positioning of the burned hand.

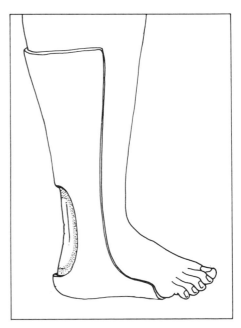

Figure 25–19. Adapted ankle-foot orthosis for burns of the ankle.

Chapter 26

TRAUMATIC SPINAL CORD INJURY

THOMAS J. SCHMITZ

OBJECTIVES

1. Identify the major etiologic factors involved in traumatic spinal cord injury.

2. Describe the clinical features following damage to the spinal cord.

3. Describe the potential secondary complications associated with spinal cord injury.

4. Identify the anticipated functional expectations for spinal cord patients at various lesion levels.

5. Identify and describe appropriate assessment and treatment procedures for both the acute and chronic phases of management.

INTRODUCTION

Spinal cord injury (SCI) has been identified as a low-incidence, high-cost disability requiring tremendous changes in a patient's lifestyle.[1] It is estimated that approximately 11,000 new cases of spinal cord impairment occur in the United States annually. A gross estimate indicates that there are about 200,000 individuals with spinal cord dysfunction currently living in the United States.[2]

DEMOGRAPHICS

Statistics from the National Spinal Cord Injury Data Research Center (NSCIDRC) provide important demographic information related to traumatic spinal cord injury.[3] The NSCIDRC project was organized to determine the true incidence of traumatic SCI in the United States. The results of this project represent information obtained on over 6000 patients collected between 1973 and 1981 from 17 regional SCI care systems located throughout the country. The sample is representative of approximately 10 percent of the annual incidence of SCI

in the United States for the years during which data were collected. All information obtained related to traumatic injuries.[4] Data from this program are a frequently cited source of demographic information on SCI and will provide the statistical references reported in the following sections.

Etiology

Spinal cord injuries can be grossly divided into two broad etiologic categories: traumatic injuries and non-traumatic injuries. *Traumatic* influences are by far the most frequent cause of injury in adult rehabilitation populations. They result from damage caused by a traumatic event such as a motor vehicle accident, fall, or gunshot wound. Considering their higher incidence, management of traumatic injuries will be described in this chapter. However, the treatment principles discussed will have direct application to nontraumatic lesions as well.

Statistics from the NSCIDRC indicate motor-vehicle-related accidents to be the most frequent cause of traumatic SCI: automobile, 38 percent; motorcycle, 7 percent; and other vehicles, 1 percent. Jumps and falls

Table 26–1 FREQUENCY DISTRIBUTION BY ETIOLOGY

Etiology	Cases	
	N	*%*
Auto Accident	2264	38
Motorcycle Accident	397	7
Other Vehicular Accident	36	1
Boat Accident	7	<1
Fixed Wing Aircraft	37	1
Helicopter	13	<1
Snowmobile	6	<1
Bicycle	43	1
Gunshot	782	13
Other Penetrating	41	1
Person-to-Person	32	1
Explosion	3	<1
Diving	564	9
Football	63	1
Trampoline	32	1
Snow Skiing	26	<1
Water Skiing	11	<1
Other Sports	16	<1
Wrestling	23	<1
Baseball	5	<1
Basketball	6	<1
Surfing	23	<1
Fall or Jump	952	16
Falling/Flying Object	298	5
Pedestrian	100	2
Med/Surg. Complication	76	1
Other	51	1
Horseback	16	<1
Gymnastics	18	<1
Rodeo	9	<1
Track/Field	2	<1
Field Sports	10	<1
Hang Gliding	17	<1
Air Sports	5	<1
Winter Sports	19	<1
Skateboard	1	<1
Unknown	10	<1
TOTAL	6014	100

From Young, JS, et al,[3] p 26, with permission.

ranked second (16 percent), followed by gunshot wounds (13 percent), diving accidents (9 percent), and injuries sustained from falling or flying objects (5 percent). The remaining injuries were largely related to other forms of sport activities and penetrating wounds (other than gunshot). Table 26–1 presents the type and incidence of all accidents reported to the NSCIDRC during the years of the data collection.

Nontraumatic injuries in adult populations generally result from a disease or pathologic influence. Several examples of nontraumatic conditions that may damage the spinal cord are vascular malfunctions (arterial venous malformation [AVM], thrombosis, embolus, or hemorrhage), vertebral subluxations secondary to rheumatoid arthritis or degenerative joint disease, infections such as syphilis or tranverse myelitis, spinal neoplasms, syringomyelia, abcesses of the spinal cord, hysterical paralysis, and neurologic diseases such as multiple sclerosis and amyotrophic lateral sclerosis. Statistics are not currently available that detail the incidence of nontraumatic cord damage. However, it is estimated that nontraumatic etiologies account for 30 percent of all spinal cord injuries.[2]

DISTRIBUTION BY NSCIDRC VARIABLES

The NSCIDRC project collected data on multiple preinjury and postinjury patient variables. The most salient statistics are presented here. Of the 6014 patients from which data were collected, 82 percent were male and 18 percent female. Almost one half of the population were in the 15-to-24-year-old age group, with 80 percent of all injuries occurring under the age of 40 (Fig. 26–1). Seventy-eight percent had only a high school education or less, and 54 percent were single at the time of injury. The data also indicated that a proportionately higher incidence of injuries (31.6 percent) occurred during the three summer months (June, 9.7 percent; July, 11.7 percent; and August, 10.2 percent) and that 38.6 percent of the injuries occurred on weekends (Saturday, 19.8 percent; and Sunday, 18.8 percent).

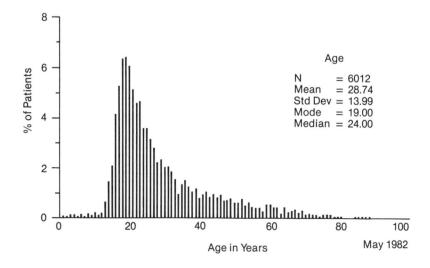

Age
N = 6012
Mean = 28.74
Std Dev = 13.99
Mode = 19.00
Median = 24.00

May 1982

Figure 26–1. Frequency distribution at age of spinal cord injury demonstrating high concentrations in young adults. (From Young, JS,[3] p 17, with permission.)

**Table 26–2 NUMBER OF DAYS HOSPITALIZED AND
HOSPITAL CHARGES DURING INITIAL MEDICAL/
REHABILITATION PERIOD**

Neurologic Category	Days Hospitalized			Hospital Charges, 1981 Dollars		
	Mean	*Std. Dev.*	*Median*	*Mean*	*Std. Dev.*	*Median*
Paraplegic						
Incomplete	110	54	101	$38,700	$21,818	$34,355
Complete	123	55	113	45,400	24,699	39,710
Quadriplegic						
Incomplete	149	78	139	$55,200	$33,161	$49,608
Complete	184	100	166	75,300	51,626	65,145

From Young, JS, et al,[3] p 123, with permission.

Cost

The financial impact of SCI is extremely high. The disability is characterized by extended periods of initial hospitalization, medical complications, extensive follow-up care, and recurrent hospitalizations. Medical cost analysis data were available on 6111 patients during the 1973–1981 period of the NSCIDRC project. It should be noted that this information is presented in 1981 dollars. Adjusting these data for inflation will provide estimates of charges for other calendar years. The mean hospital charges for the initial medical/rehabilitation period (defined as the period from initial onset of SCI until discharge to a living situation) were $75,300 for complete quadriplegia and $45,400 for complete paraplegia. Twenty percent of those with complete quadriplegia in this study had initial costs of over $100,000. Table 26–2 presents mean hospital charges and mean and median number of days for the initial/rehabilitation period for patients with quadriplegia and those with paraplegia.

Follow-up hospitalization charges are also available from this study. During follow-up years, individuals with complete quadriplegia spent between $9,100 and $14,000 annually on hospital care. Those with complete paraplegia spent between $8,500 and $11,800. These figures are not comprehensive estimates of follow-up costs, inasmuch as they include only hospital charges without consideration to outpatient or in-home care, medications, supplies, equipment purchased after discharge, environmental modifications, and so forth.

This brief presentation of demographic information provides some important general perspectives on characteristics of SCI patients. It is a relatively low-incidence disability affecting a predominately young population and is associated with lengthy and costly care. Spinal cord injury costs in the United States are now estimated at three billion dollars annually.[3]

CLASSIFICATION OF CORD INJURIES

Functional Classification

Spinal cord injuries typically are divided into two broad functional categories: quadriplegia and paraplegia. **Quadriplegia** refers to partial or complete paralysis of all four extremities and trunk, including the respiratory muscles, and results from lesions of the cervical cord. **Paraplegia** refers to partial or complete paralysis of all or part of the trunk and both lower extremities, resulting from lesions of the thoracic or lumbar spinal cord or sacral roots.[5]

DESIGNATION OF LESION LEVEL

Several methods of identifying the specific level of lesion are used throughout the world.[6] The most commonly used method is to indicate the most distal uninvolved nerve root segment with normal function together with the skeletal level. The term *normal function* has a precise meaning used in this context.[7] The muscles innervated by the most distal nerve root segment must have at least a fair+ or 3+ grade on manual muscle testing. This grade generally indicates sufficient strength for functional use. For example, if the patient has an intact C-7 nerve root segment (with no sensory or motor function below C-7), the condition would be classified as a *C-7 complete quadriplegia*. However, if spotty sensation and some muscle function (with less than a fair+ muscle grade) were evident below the C-7 nerve root segment, the lesion would be classified as a *C-7 incomplete quadriplegia*.

Oblique injuries to the cord present asymmetric sensory and/or motor function. These lesions are classified in the same manner. However, they require designating the most distal nerve root segment with normal function *on each side* of the patient's body. For example, the designation for an oblique lesion would be recorded as C-6 complete on the right and C-7 complete on the left. This designation may be abbreviated to read *C-6(R) complete* and *C-7(L) complete*.

In considering designation of spinal cord lesions it is useful to review briefly the anatomic relationship of the spinal cord and nerve roots to the vertebral bodies (Fig. 26–2). There are 31 pairs of spinal nerves: 8 cervical, 12 thoracic, 5 lumbar, 5 sacral, and 1 coccygeal. The upper cervical nerves are relatively horizontal as they exit the intervertebral foramina. However, the remaining nerves exit in a downward direction and do not emerge at the corresponding vertebral level. During fetal development the cord fills the entire length of the vertebral canal, and the spinal nerves run in a horizontal direction. As the

FUNCTIONAL LEVEL   MUSCLES PRESENT

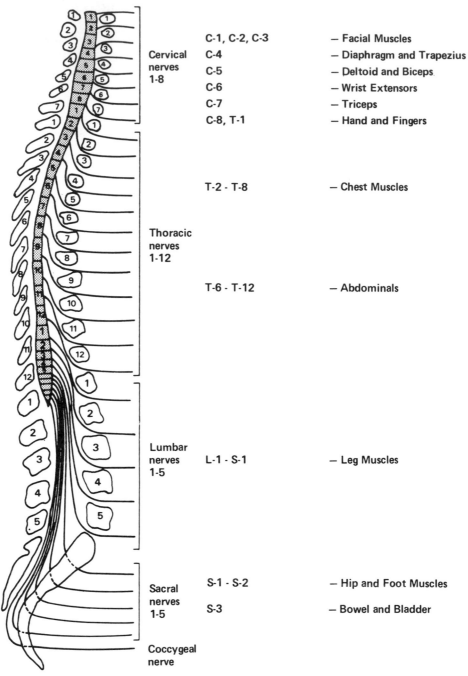

Functional Level	Muscles Present
C-1, C-2, C-3	— Facial Muscles
C-4	— Diaphragm and Trapezius
C-5	— Deltoid and Biceps
C-6	— Wrist Extensors
C-7	— Triceps
C-8, T-1	— Hand and Fingers
T-2 - T-8	— Chest Muscles
T-6 - T-12	— Abdominals
L-1 - S-1	— Leg Muscles
S-1 - S-2	— Hip and Foot Muscles
S-3	— Bowel and Bladder

Cervical nerves 1-8
Thoracic nerves 1-12
Lumbar nerves 1-5
Sacral nerves 1-5
Coccygeal nerve

Figure 26–2. Relationship between the spinal cord and nerve roots to vertebral bodies and innervation of major muscle groups. (From Coogler, CE,[7] p 150, with permission.)

vertebral column elongates with growth, the spinal cord, which does not elongate, is drawn upward. The roots assume an increasingly oblique and downward direction, running in an almost vertical direction in the lumbar area, giving the appearance of a "horse's tail" (cauda equina).

COMPLETE LESIONS

In a *complete lesion* there is no sensory or motor function below the level of the lesion. It is caused by a com-

plete transection (severing), severe compression, or extensive vascular impairment to the cord.

INCOMPLETE LESIONS

Incomplete lesions are characterized by preservation of some sensory or motor function below the level of injury. This preservation of function indicates that some viable neural tissue is crossing the area of injury to more distal segments.[8] Incomplete lesions often result from **contusions** produced by pressure on the cord from displaced bone and/or soft tissues[9] or from swelling within the spinal canal. Some or even complete recovery from contusion is possible when the source of pressure is relieved. Incomplete lesions also may result from partial transection of the cord.

The clinical picture presented by incomplete lesions is unpredictable. There is a mixture of sensory and motor function below the level of lesion, with variable patterns of recovery. Early return of function is generally considered a good prognostic sign.

Despite the uncertainty associated with recovery of incomplete lesions, several syndromes have emerged with consistent clinical features. Information related to the anticipated sensory and motor functions of these syndromes is useful in establishing long-term goals and treatment planning. The area of cord damage of each syndrome is presented in Figure 26–3.

Brown-Sequard Syndrome

The **Brown-Sequard syndrome** occurs from hemisection of the spinal cord (damage to one side) and is typically caused by stab wounds.[8] Partial lesions occur more frequently; true hemisections are rare.[10] The clinical features of this syndrome are asymmetrical.[11,12] On the *ipsilateral (same)* side as the lesion, there is loss of sensation in the dermatome segment corresponding to the level of the lesion. Owing to lateral column damage, there are decreased reflexes, lack of superficial reflexes, clonus, and a positive Babinski's sign. As a result of dorsal column damage, there is loss of proprioception, kinesthesia, and vibratory sense. On the side *contralateral (opposite)* to the lesion, damage to the spinothalamic tracts results in loss of sense of pain and temperature. This loss begins several dermatome segments below the level of injury. This discrepancy in levels occurs because the lateral spinothalamic tracts ascend two to four segments on the same side before crossing.[13]

Anterior Cord Syndrome

The **anterior cord syndrome** is frequently related to flexion injuries of the cervical region with resultant damage to the anterior portion of the cord and/or its vascular supply from the anterior spinal artery. There is typically compression of the anterior cord from fracture dislocation or cervical disk protrusion.[13] This syndrome is characterized by loss of motor function (corticospinal tract damage) and loss of sense of pain and temperature (spinothalamic tract damage) below the level of the lesion.[12] Proprioception, kinesthesia, and vibratory sense are generally preserved, because they are mediated by the posterior columns with a separate vascular supply from the posterior spinal arteries.

Central Cord Syndrome

The **central cord syndrome** most commonly occurs from hyperextension injuries to the cervical region. It also has been associated with congenital or degenerative narrowing of the spinal canal.[8] The resultant compressive forces give rise to hemorrhage and edema, producing damage to the most central aspects of the cord.[14] There is characteristically more severe neurologic involvement of the upper extremities (cervical tracts are more centrally located) than of the lower extremities (lumbar and sacral tracts are located more peripherally).

Varying degrees of sensory impairment occur[15] but tend to be less severe than motor deficits.[16] With complete preservation of sacral tracts, normal sexual, bowel, and bladder function will be retained.[17]

Patients with central cord syndrome typically recover the ability to ambulate with some remaining distal arm weakness. Surgical intervention to relieve the source of compression has produced significant improvement in some patients.[15]

Posterior Cord Syndrome

The **posterior cord syndrome** is an extremely rare syndrome resulting in deficits of function served by the posterior columns.[9] The clinical picture includes preservation of motor function, sense of pain, and light touch.[8] There is loss of proprioception and epicritic sensations (e.g., two-point discrimination, graphesthesia, stereognosis) below the level of lesion. A wide-based steppage gait pattern is typical. In the past, this syndrome was seen with tabes dorsalis, a condition found with late-stage syphilis.

Sacral Sparing

Sacral sparing refers to an incomplete lesion in which the most centrally located sacral tracts are spared. Varying levels of innervation from sacral segments remain intact. Clinical signs include perianal sensation, rectal sphincter contraction, cutaneous sensation in the "saddle area," and active contraction of the sacrally innervated toe flexors. These are important neurologic findings and often the first signs of an incomplete cervical lesion.[8,13]

Cauda Equina Injuries

The spinal cord tapers distally to form the conus medullaris at the lower border of the first lumbar vertebra. Although some anatomic variations exist, this is the typ-

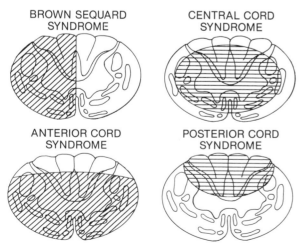

Figure 26–3. Areas of spinal cord damage in incomplete cord syndromes. (From Rieser, TV,[8] p 14, with permission.)

ical termination point of the spinal cord.[18] Below this level is the collection of long nerve roots known as the *cauda equina.* Complete transections in this area may occur. However, **cauda equina lesions** are frequently incomplete owing to the great number of nerve roots involved and the comparatively large surface area they encompass (i.e., it would be unlikely that an injury to this region would involve the entire surface area and all the nerve roots).

Cauda equina lesions are peripheral nerve injuries. As such, they have the same potential to regenerate as peripheral nerves elsewhere in the body.[19] However, full return of innervation is not common since (1) there is a large distance between the lesion and the point of innervation, (2) axonal regeneration may not occur along the original distribution of the nerve, (3) axonal regeneration may be blocked by glial-collagen scarring, (4) the end organ may no longer be functioning once reinnervation occurs, and (5) the rate of regeneration slows and finally stops after about one year.

Root Escape

Peripheral nerve roots at or above the lesion site may also be damaged following SCI. As with other peripheral nerve injuries, the potential for regeneration of nerve roots exists, and some improved function may be evident. The term **root escape** refers to the preservation or return of function of nerve roots at or near the level of the lesion. Although frequently associated with incomplete cauda equina injuries, root escape may occur at any lesion level.

MECHANISMS OF INJURY

Various mechanisms, often in combination, produce injuries to the spinal cord. Spinal cord injury most frequently occurs from indirect forces produced by movement of the head and trunk and less often from direct injury to a vertebra.[20] Common mechanisms operating in SCI include flexion, compression, hyperextension, and flexion-rotation. These forces result in either a fracture and/or dislocation. The intensity and combination of forces imposed have direct influence on the type and location of fracture(s), the amount of dislocation, and the extent of soft tissue damage.

The spine demonstrates various degrees of susceptibility to injury. Some areas are inherently more vulnerable owing to their high mobility and relative lack of stability as compared with other segments of the spine (e.g., the rigid thoracic region). The areas of the spine that demonstrate the highest frequency of injury are between C-5 and C-7 in the cervical region and between T-12 and L-2 in the thoracolumbar region.[21]

Table 26–3 presents a summary of the major mechanisms of injury involved in SCI. Although these forces typically occur *in combination,* they are presented individually inasmuch as each has characteristic patterns of primary and associated injuries.

Two additional contributing mechanisms involved in SCI are **shearing** and **distraction. Shearing** occurs when a horizontal force is applied to the spine relative to the adjacent segment.[13] Shearing frequently disrupts ligaments and is associated with fracture dislocations of the thoracolumbar region.[20] **Distraction** involves a traction

Table 26–3 MECHANISMS OF INJURY[20,22–24]

Force	Etiology	Associated Fractures	Potential Associated Injuries
Flexion	1. Head-on collision in which head strikes steering wheel or windshield. 2. Blow to back of head or trunk. 3. Most common mechanism of SCI.	1. Wedge fracture of anterior vertebral body (vertebral body compressed). 2. High percentage of injuries occur from C-4 to C-7 and from T-12 to L-2.	1. Tearing of posterior ligaments. 2. Fractures of posterior elements: spinous processes, laminae, or pedicles. 3. Disruption of disk. 4. Anterior **dislocation** of vertebral body.
Compression	1. Vertical or axial blow to head (diving, surfing, or falling objects). 2. Closely associated with flexion injuries.	1. Concave fracture of endplate. 2. Explosion or **burst fracture** (comminuted). 3. **Teardrop fracture.**	1. Bone fragments may lodge in cord. 2. Rupture of disk.
Hyperextension	1. Strong posterior force such as a rear-end collision. 2. Falls with chin hitting a stationary object (more commonly seen in elderly populations).	1. Fractures of posterior elements: spinous processes, laminae, and facets. 2. **Avulsion** fracture of anterior aspect of vertebrae.	1. Rupture of anterior longitudinal ligament. 2. Rupture of disk. 3. Associated with cervical lesions; only of minor influence in thoracolumbar injuries.
Flexion-rotation	Posterior to anterior force directed at rotated vertebral column (e.g., rear-end collision with passenger rotated toward driver).	Fracture of posterior pedicles, articular facets, and laminae (fracture is very unstable if posterior ligaments rupture).	1. Rupture of posterior and interspinous ligaments. 2. **Subluxation** or dislocation of facet joints. 3. In thoracic and lumbar regions, facets may "lock."

force and is the least common mechanism. It occurs when significant momentum of the head is created, as in whiplash injuries. This momentum creates a tensile force in the cervical spine as the head is pulled away from the body.[13,20]

CLINICAL PICTURE

Spinal Shock

Immediately following SCI there is a period of areflexia called **spinal shock.** This period of transient reflex depression is not clearly understood. It is believed to result from the very abrupt withdrawal of connections between higher centers and the spinal cord.[25] It is characterized by absence of all reflex activity, flaccidity, and loss of sensation below the level of the lesion. It may last for several hours to several weeks but typically subsides within 24 hours.[26] Early resolution of spinal shock is an important prognostic sign. One of the first indicators that spinal shock is resolving is the presence of a positive **bulbocavernosus reflex.** This test is part of the neurologist's examination. During a digital rectal examination, this reflex is elicited by pressure applied to the glans penis or glans clitoris or by intermittently "tugging" on an indwelling catheter. If positive, a reflex contraction of the anal sphincter around the examining digit will be evident.[27] A positive bulbocavernosus reflex indicates that spinal shock has terminated. This reflex may be present several weeks before deep tendon reflexes are apparent in the lower extremities.[26] However, if this reflex is positive without some evidence of accompanying sensory or motor return (particularly in the perianal region), spinal shock has subsided, and it usually indicates the presence of a complete lesion.[26]

Motor Deficits and Sensory Loss

Following spinal cord injury there will be either complete or partial loss of muscle function below the level of the lesion. Disruption of the ascending sensory fibers following SCI results in impaired or absent sensation below the lesion level.

The clinical presentation of motor and sensory deficits is dependent on the specific features of the lesion. These include the neurologic level, the completeness of the lesion, the symmetry of the lesion (transverse or oblique), and the presence or absence of sacral sparing or root escape.

Impaired Temperature Control

After damage to the spinal cord the hypothalamus can no longer control cutaneous blood flow or level of sweating. This autonomic (sympathetic) dysfunction results in loss of internal thermoregulatory responses. The ability to shiver is lost, vasodilation does not occur in response to heat nor vasoconstriction in response to cold. There is absence of thermoregulatory sweating, which eliminates

the normal evaporative cooling effects of perspiration in warm environments. This lack of sweating is often associated with excessive compensatory **diaphoresis** above the level of lesion. Patients with incomplete lesions may also demonstrate "spotty" areas of localized sweating below the lesion level.[28,29]

Changes in thermal regulation result in body temperature being significantly influenced by the external environment. This is a more frequent problem with cervical lesions than with thoracic or lumbar involvement. Patients must rely heavily on sensory input from the head and neck regions to assist in determining appropriate environmental temperatures. Although some improvement in thermoregulatory responses occur over time, patients with quadriplegia typically experience long-term impairment of body temperature regulation, especially in response to extreme environmental changes.[13]

Respiratory Impairment

Respiratory function varies considerably, depending on the level of lesion. With high spinal cord lesions between C-1 and C-3, phrenic nerve innervation and spontaneous respiration are significantly impaired or lost. An artificial ventilator or phrenic nerve stimulator is required to sustain life. In contrast, lumbar lesions present with full innervation of both primary (diaphragm) and secondary (neck, intercostal, and abdominal) respiratory muscles.

All patients with quadriplegia and those with high-level paraplegia demonstrate some compromise in respiratory function. The level of respiratory impairment is directly related to the lesion level and residual respiratory muscle function, additional trauma sustained at time of injury, as well as premorbid respiratory status. Respiratory involvement represents a particularly serious and life-threatening feature of SCI. Pulmonary complications (especially bronchopneumonia and pulmonary embolism) are responsible for a high incidence of mortality during the early stages of quadriplegia.[13]

There is a progressively greater loss of respiratory function with increasingly higher lesion levels. Multiple respiratory changes occur related to both the inspiratory and expiratory phases of ventilation. The primary muscles of *inspiration* are the diaphragm and external intercostals. As the diaphragm contracts and descends, the intercostals normally elevate the ribs and increase the lateral anteroposterior diameter of the thorax.[30] Paralysis of the intercostals results in decreased chest expansion and a lowered inspiratory volume. With progressively higher level lesions, increased involvement of the accessory muscles of respiration will be noted. These muscles assist with elevation of the ribs and include the sternocleidomastoid, trapezii, scaleni, pectoralis minor, and serratus anterior.

The primary muscles of *expiration* are the abdominals and internal intercostals. Normally, relaxed expiration is essentially a passive process which occurs through elastic recoil of the lungs and thorax. However, the abdominals and internal intercostals contribute several important functions related to movement of air out of the lungs. Loss of these muscles significantly decreases expiratory efficiency. When fully innervated, the abdominal muscles play an important role in maintaining intrathoracic pressure for effective respiration. They support the abdominal viscera[31,32] and assist in maintaining the position of the diaphragm. They also function to push the diaphragm upward during forced expiration.[13] With paralysis of the abdominals this support is lost, causing the diaphragm to assume an unusually low position in the chest.[33] This lowered position and lack of abdominal pressure to move the diaphragm upward during forced expiration results in a decreased expiratory reserve volume.[13] This subsequently decreases cough effectiveness and the ability to expel secretions.

Paralysis of the external obliques also influences expiration. Their normal function is to depress the ribs and to compress the chest wall to assist with forceful expulsion of air.[31,34] With higher-level lesions this function becomes less efficient, with further reduction in the patient's ability to cough and to expel secretions. These factors combine to make the SCI patient particularly susceptible to retention of secretions, atelectasis, and pulmonary infections.[13]

Paralysis also results in the development of an altered breathing pattern.[30,35] This pattern (Fig. 26–4) is characterized by some flattening of the upper chest wall, decreased chest wall expansion, and a dominant epigastric rise during inspiration. With relaxation of the diaphragm a negative intrathoracic pressure gradient moves air into the lungs.[30,35] Over time, this breathing pattern will lead to permanent postural changes.

Two additional factors may further impair the respiratory status of the patient: *additional trauma* sustained at the time of injury, and *premorbid respiratory problems*. Fractures (e.g., ribs, sternum, or extremities), lung contusions, or soft tissue damage will also compound respiratory problems. These secondary injuries are particularly problematic if long periods of immobility are required for healing or if pain inhibits full lung expansion. Premorbid respiratory problems such as existing pulmonary disease, allergies, asthma, or a history of smoking will further compromise respiratory function.[13]

Spasticity

Spasticity results from release of intact reflex arcs from central nervous system control and is characterized by hypertonicity, hyperactive stretch reflexes, and clonus. It typically occurs below the level of lesion after spinal shock subsides. There is a gradual increase in spasticity during the first six months and usually reaches a plateau one year after injury.[26] Spasticity is increased by multiple internal and external stimuli, including positional changes, cutaneous stimuli, environmental temperatures, tight clothing, bladder or kidney stones, fecal impactions, catheter blockage, urinary tract infections, decubitus ulcers, and emotional stress.[13,36]

Spasticity varies in degree of severity. Patients with minimal to moderate involvement may learn to trigger the spasticity at appropriate times to assist in functional activities. However, strong spasticity interferes with many aspects of rehabilitation and can be a deterrent to independent function. In these situations spasticity is often managed first through drug therapy. Drugs typically used include muscle relaxants and spasmolytic agents such as diazepam (Valium), baclofen (Lioresal),

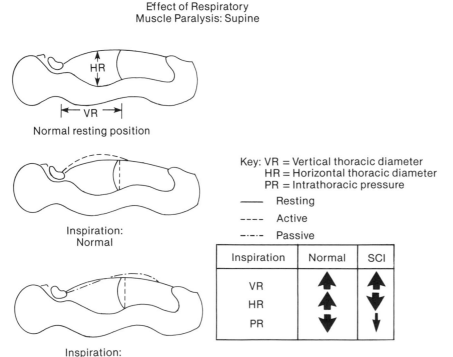

Effect of Respiratory
Muscle Paralysis: Supine

Normal resting position

Inspiration:
Normal

Inspiration:
Spinal cord injury

Key: VR = Vertical thoracic diameter
HR = Horizontal thoracic diameter
PR = Intrathoracic pressure

——— Resting
- - - - Active
—··— Passive

Inspiration	Normal	SCI
VR	↑	↑
HR	↑	↓
PR	↓	↓

Figure 26–4. Effect of paralysis on thoracic volume and breathing pattern. (From Alvarez, SE, et al,[30] p 1738, with permission.)

and dantrolene sodium (Dantrium).[37] Drug management is usually not completely successful in alleviating spasticity, and its benefits must be weighed against potentially harmful side effects. Additionally, patients often develop a tolerance to prolonged use of individual drugs.

Injected chemical agents also have been used to decrease spasticity. Generally, these are considered only if results obtained from drug management are deemed inadequate. The two approaches used are **peripheral nerve blocks** and **intrathecal injections.**

In nerve blocks, the chemical injection is used peripherally to block selectively transmission of the motor nerve to a spastic muscle and therefore to interrupt the intact reflex arc peripherally. This procedure provides a temporary reduction in spasticity. These procedures include (1) phenol peripheral nerve blocks, and (2) phenol motor point blocks.[26,37]

Intrathecal (within the spinal canal) **injections** are used to interrupt the reflex arc mechanism and subsequently to reduce spasticity. Intrathecal approaches provide a more permanent abatement of spasticity. These procedures include intrathecal phenol or alcohol injections.[26,37] Intrathecal injections are used only rarely because they interfere with bladder and sexual function.[5,37]

Surgical approaches also have been used to combat spasticity in more severe cases. They range from relatively simple orthopedic procedures to complex neurosurgery. Orthopedic surgical procedures used include **myotomy,** which is a sectioning or release of a muscle; **neurectomy,** a partial or complete severance of a nerve; or **tenotomy,** a sectioning of a tendon which allows subsequent lengthening (e.g., heel cords). Each of these procedures decreases spasticity by altering the contraction potential of the muscle.[5,26]

A number of more radical neurosurgical interventions are used to eliminate extremely severe spasticity. These destructive approaches (neural tissue is damaged) result in permanent and profound alterations in spasticity. These procedures are useful when spasticity is at an intolerable level and prohibits or significantly limits functional activities. Examples of these interventions include severance of nerve roots (**rhizotomy**) or of spinal cord nerve fibers (**myelotomy**).

ALTERATIONS IN BLADDER AND BOWEL FUNCTION

BLADDER DYSFUNCTION

The effects of bladder dysfunction following SCI pose a serious medical complication requiring consistent and long-term management. Data from the NSCIDRC project indicated urinary tract infections (UTI) to be the most frequent medical complication during the initial medical/rehabilitation period. The incidence of UTI was 66 percent with paraplegia and 70 percent with quadriplegia.[3]

During the stage of spinal shock, the urinary bladder is flaccid. All muscle tone and bladder reflexes are absent. Medical considerations during this period are focused on establishing an effective system of drainage and prevention of urinary retention and infection.[5]

The spinal integration center for **micturition** is the conus medullaris. Primary reflex control originates from the sacral segments of S-2, S-3, S-4. Following spinal shock, one of two types of bladder conditions will develop, depending on location of the lesion. Patients with lesions that occur within the spinal cord above the conus medullaris typically develop a *reflex* neurogenic bladder. Following a lesion of the conus medullaris or cauda equina, an *autonomous,* or *nonreflex,* neurogenic bladder develops.

Reflex (upper motor neuron) bladders contract and reflexly empty in response to a certain level of filling pressure. The reflex arc is intact. This reflex emptying may be triggered by manual stimulation techniques such as stroking, kneading, or tapping the suprapubic region[5] or thigh, and lower abdominal stroking, pinching, or hair pulling.[38]

Autonomous or nonreflex (lower motor neuron) bladders are essentially flaccid because there is no reflex action of the detrusor muscle. This type of bladder can be emptied by increasing intra-abdominal pressure using a *Valsalva maneuver* or by manually compressing the lower abdomen using the **Crede maneuver.**[39]

Bladder Training Programs

The primary goal of bladder training programs is to allow the patient to be free of a catheter and to control bladder function.[40] Because urinary incontinence has very strong psychosocial implications for the patient, a coordinated approach to this problem is particularly important. Knowledge of and participation in the bladder training program is an important consideration for the physical therapist.

The bladder training program most frequently used with reflex bladders is *intermittent catheterization.* The purpose of this program is to establish reflex bladder emptying at regular and predictable intervals in response to a certain level of filling. Briefly, the program involves establishing a fluid intake pattern restricted to approximately 2000 ml per day. Fluid intake is monitored at 150 to 180 ml per hour from morning until early evening. Intake is stopped late in the day to reduce the need for catheterization during the night. Initially, the patient is catheterized every 4 hours. Prior to catheterization, the patient attempts to void in combination with one or more of the manual stimulation techniques. The catheter is then inserted and residual volume drained. A record is maintained of voided and residual urine. As bladder emptying becomes more effective, residual volumes will decrease and time intervals between catheterizations can be expanded.[40,41]

A *timed voiding program* is another method of bladder training and is indicated for autonomous or nonreflex bladders. This program involves first establishing the patient's pattern of incontinence. The residual urine volume is then checked to ensure that it is within safe limits. Once the occurrence of incontinence has been established, it is compared with the patterns of intake. This information provides the basis for establishing a new intake and voiding schedule. The bladder gradually becomes accustomed or "trained" to empty at regular, predictable intervals. As incontinence decreases, the schedule is readjusted to expand the intervals between voiding. Fluid intake is avoided late in the day to decrease the risk of **nocturia**. Stimulation techniques are also incorporated into this type of training program.[40]

It should be noted that not all bladder training programs are successful. Some patients will require long-term use of either an external (condom) or indwelling catheter. For male patients, the condom catheter is preferred because it provides decreased risk of infection. For female patients, an indwelling catheter is currently the only option.

BOWEL DYSFUNCTION

Similar to the bladder, two types of neurogenic bowel conditions develop after spinal shock subsides. In cord lesions above the conus medullaris there is a *reflex* bowel, and in conus medullaris or cauda equina lesions an *autonomous,* or *nonreflex,* bowel develops.[40]

Bowel Programs

Typically, reflex bowel management requires use of suppositories and digital stimulation techniques to initiate defecation.[42] Digital stimulation involves manual stretch of the anal sphincter either with a gloved finger or an orthotic digital stimulator. This stretch stimulates peristalsis of the colon and evacuation of the rectum (mediated by S-2, S-3, S-4).[37] Nonreflex bowel management relies heavily on straining with available musculature and manual evacuation techniques.

The major goal of a bowel program for the patient with a SCI is establishment of a regular pattern of evacuation. This is achieved through multiple interventions, including diet, fluid intake, stool softeners, suppositories, digital stimulation, and manual evacuation.

As with bladder programs, bowel management is an emotionally laden issue and an extremely high priority for most patients. Lack of bowel control may negate other rehabilitation efforts because it will seriously limit the patient's involvement.[40]

Sexual Dysfunction

"Sexual information is as vital and as 'normal' a part of the rehabilitation process as is providing other information to enable the patient to better understand and adapt to his medical condition."[43] For many years physical disability was assumed to depress or to eliminate sex drives. This erroneous attitude fostered considerable neglect of sexual function as a component of the rehabilitation process.[1] Today, sexual disturbances are recognized as a complex rehabilitation issue characterized by physiologic dysfunction, sensory and motor impairment, often accompanied by social and psychologic distress.[44] Greater numbers of SCI care centers now include a sexual counselor as a component team member. This individual may be a physician or a psychologist with a specialty in this area or a nonphysician specialist trained in sexual dysfunction.[44] Many rehabilitation centers also offer structured programs to assist patients with sexual adjustment.[43,45,46] Although the format of these programs varies, common shared goals include (1) direct patient care including assessment, prognosis, treatment, and counseling; (2) education of the patient and his or her partner; and (3) preparation of staff members to deal with sexual concerns.

THE MALE RESPONSE

Sexual response is directly related to level and completeness of injury. As with bowel and bladder function, sexual capabilities are broadly divided between upper motor neuron (UMN) lesions (damage to the cord above the conus medullaris) and lower motor neuron (LMN) lesions (damage to the conus medullaris or cauda equina).

A slowly expanding body of research is available on the male sexual response following SCI. Statistics related to sexual capacity provide important general information regarding anticipated function following a given type of injury. However, these statistics must be considered cautiously. Owing to the inherent methodologic difficulties in collecting these types of data and the close relationship between sexual activity and self-image, some discrepency may exist between reported and actual sexual function.[1,47]

Erectile Capacity

In a review of the literature on sexual response after SCI, Higgins[47] presented two consistent findings: (1) erectile capacity is greater in UMN lesions than in LMN lesions and (2) greater in incomplete lesions than in complete lesions.

There are two types of erections: *reflexogenic* and *psychogenic.* Reflexogenic erections occur in response to external physical stimulation of the genitals or perineum. An intact reflex arc is required (mediated through S-2, S-3, S-4). Psychogenic erections occur through cognitive activity such as erotic fantasy. They are mediated from the cerebral cortex either through the thoracolumbar or sacral cord centers.[48]

Comarr[17] reported on erectile capability in 525 patients with UMN lesions. His findings indicated that 93 percent of the patients with complete lesions and 98 percent of those with incomplete lesions had reflexogenic erections. Data were also collected on 154 patients with LMN lesions. In the group with complete LMN lesions, 74 percent had no erections and 26 percent had erections only by psychogenic stimuli. With incomplete LMN lesions, 83 percent had erections, but all by psychogenic means.

Ejaculation

Available data indicate that there is a higher incidence of ejaculation with (1) LMN lesions than with UMN lesions, (2) lower-level versus higher-level cord lesions, and (3) in incomplete as compared with complete lesions.[17,47] Comarr[17] also presented data on ejaculation capability from the same total of 679 patients (525 UMN lesions and 154 LMN lesions). In the UMN group, 3 percent with complete and 28.5 percent with incomplete lesions were able to ejaculate. In the LMN group, 16.5 percent with complete and 60 percent with incomplete lesions achieved ejaculation.

Orgasm

Orgasm and ejaculation are two separate events. Orgasm is a cognitive, psychogenic event, whereas ejaculation is a physical occurrence. Relatively little information is available related to the effects of SCI on orgasm. This again relates to inherent difficulties in collecting such data. Higgins[47] also suggests that the few studies that have been done have demonstrated serious methodologic flaws. He identifies the major problems in these studies as a lack of criteria for defining orgasm, considering ejaculation and orgasm as identical events, and a lack of reported data on how subjects achieved orgasm. Currently, accurate data on the effects of SCI on male orgasm are not available.

Fertility

Relatively few SCI patients are able to sire children. In a group of 529 patients followed to determine progeny, only 3 percent sired children, with patients in the LMN incomplete lesion group being most successful.[17] This low level of fertility results primarily from impaired spermatogenesis and secondarily from an inability to ejaculate.[48]

THE FEMALE RESPONSE

There is a scarcity of literature and systematic reports of data collection related to sexual dysfunction in women with SCI. This may be a function of women's remaining capable of sexual intercourse following SCI. It also may be related to the fact that fertility is unaffected, or, perhaps, because of the proportionately lower number of female patients.[49] Trieschmann[1] also believes that this relates to the traditionally passive sexual roles ascribed to women. Consequently, sexual functions of women following SCI have been considered relatively unimpaired and given comparatively little attention. Studies that have been completed have been criticized as lacking in desired degree of sophistication.[47] The current available information does not clearly delineate the effects of SCI on female orgasm.

Female sexual responses also follow a pattern related to location of lesion. In patients with UMN lesions the reflex arc will remain intact. Therefore, components of sexual arousal (vaginal lubrication, engorgement of the labia, and clitoral erection) will occur through reflexogenic stimulation, but psychogenic response will be lost. Conversely, with LMN lesions, psychogenic responses will be preserved and reflex responses lost.[49,50]

Menstruation

The menstrual cycle typically is interrupted for a period of one to three months following injury. After this time normal menses return.

Fertility and Pregnancy

The potential for conception remains unimpaired. Pregnancy is possible under close medical supervision inasmuch as the patient is placed at high risk for impaired respiratory function. In addition, owing to impaired sensation the initiation of labor may not be perceived. Labor also may precipitate the onset of autonomic dysreflexia (see the following section on potential secondary complications). Consequently, patients are frequently hospitalized for a period of time prior to the expected delivery date to monitor cervical dilation.[49] Although uterine contractions are hormonally controlled and not affected by paralysis, patients with an inability to bear down during the final stages of delivery[49] or who experience prolonged or difficult labor may be candidates for cesarean section.[27]

A major consideration for the physical therapist regarding sexual dysfunction is that a patient will often direct questions to the individuals with whom he or she feels most comfortable. It is not uncommon for such a discussion to arise during a physical therapy session. These questions or issues should be addressed openly and honestly. However, the therapist must anticipate and be prepared for these situations by (1) obtaining accurate information about the patient's physiologic state and anticipated sexual function and (2) by having knowledge of referral options and support services available to the patient for appropriate assessment and counseling.[13]

POTENTIAL SECONDARY COMPLICATIONS

Pressure Sores

Pressure sores are ulcerations of soft tissue (skin or subcutaneous tissue) caused by unrelieved pressure and shearing forces. They are subject to infection, which can migrate to bone. Pressure sores are a serious medical complication, a major cause of delayed rehabilitation, and they may even lead to death.[51] Among the most frequent medical complications following SCI,[52,53] pressure sores were found in one study to be the single most important factor in increasing duration and subsequently cost of hospital stay.[3]

Impaired sensory function and the inability to make appropriate positional changes are the two most influential factors in the development of pressure sores. Other important factors are (1) loss of vasomotor control, which results in a lowering of tissue resistance to pressure; (2) spasticity, with resultant shearing forces between bony surfaces; (3) skin maceration from exposure to moisture (e.g., urine);[54] (4) trauma, such as adhesive tape or sheet burns; (5) nutritional deficiencies (low serum protein and anemia will reduce tissue resistance to pressure); (6) poor general skin condition; and (7) secondary infections.[55] Another primary factor in the development of pressure sores is the intensity and duration of the pressure. The higher the intensity of pressure, the shorter the time required for anoxia of the skin and soft tissues to occur.[54,56]

Pressure sores will develop over any bony prominence subjected to excessive pressure. Among the more common sites of involvement are the sacrum, heels, trochanters, and ischium. Other areas susceptible to skin breakdown are the scapula, elbows, anterior iliac spines, knees, and malleoli.

By far the most important intervention for eliminating the potential development of pressure sores is *prevention*. This will involve a coordinated approach, and it is a shared responsibility among the rehabilitation team. Initially, the patient will be turned every 2 hours by the nursing staff on a 24-hour schedule. Skin condition should be monitored on a continual basis. If a reddened area occurs, the patient's position must be altered immediately to alleviate the pressure. As the rehabilitation program progresses, the patient gradually assumes responsibility for skin care. Preparation for assumption of this responsibility will include patient education as to the potential risks of pressure sores and instruction in skin inspection techniques and in the use of pressure relief equipment and procedures.

Autonomic Dysreflexia

Autonomic dysreflexia (or **hyperreflexia**) is a pathologic autonomic reflex that occurs in lesions above T-6 (above sympathetic splanchnic outflow). Reported incidence of this problem varies. One study[57] found a 48 percent occurrence in a group of 213 patients. Rosen[58] estimates that as many as 85 percent of those with quadriplegia and high-level paraplegia experience this problem during the course of rehabilitation. Episodes of autonomic dysreflexia gradually subside over time and are relatively uncommon, but not rare, three years following injury.[58]

This clinical syndrome produces an acute onset of autonomic activity from noxious stimuli below the level of the lesion. Afferent input from these stimuli reach the lower spinal cord (lower thoracic and sacral areas) and initiate a mass reflex response resulting in elevation of blood pressure. Normally, the impulses stimulate the receptors in the carotid sinus and aorta, which signal the vasomotor center to readjust peripheral resistance. Following SCI, however, impulses from the vasomotor center can not pass the site of the lesion to counteract the hypertension by vasodilation.[58–60] This is a critical, emergency situation. Owing to lack of inhibition from higher centers, hypertension will persist if not treated promptly. Death may result.

INITIATING STIMULI

The most common cause of this pathologic reflex is bladder distention. Other precipitating stimuli include rectal distention, pressure sores, urinary stones, bladder infections, noxious cutaneous stimuli, kidney malfunction, urethral or bladder irritation, and environmental temperature changes.[13,57] Episodes of autonomic dysreflexia also have been reported following passive stretching at the hip.[61]

SYMPTOMS

The symptoms of autonomic dysreflexia include hypertension, bradycardia, headache (often severe and pounding), profuse sweating, increased spasticity, restlessness, vasoconstriction below the level of lesion, vasodilation (flushing) above the level of the lesion, constricted pupils, nasal congestion, piloerection (goose bumps), and blurred vision.[13,57,62]

TREATMENT

The onset of symptoms should be treated as a *medical emergency*. Because bladder distention is a primary cause of autonomic dysreflexia, the drainage system should be assessed immediately. If the patient is wearing a clamped catheter, it should be released. The drainage tubes also should be checked for internal or external blockage or twisting. If lying flat, the patient should be brought to a sitting position, inasmuch as blood pressure will be lowered in this position. The patient's body should be checked for irritating stimuli such as tight clothing, restricting catheter straps, or abdominal binders.

If symptoms do not subside, or if the source of irritation can not be located, medical/nursing assistance should be sought for possible bladder irrigation (a higher-level block may exist) and assessment for bowel impaction. Drug therapy (antihypertensives) may be indicated to control these episodes if more conservative approaches are unsuccessful.

The attending physician, nursing staff, and other team members should always be notified of occurrences of autonomic dysreflexia. This will allow careful monitoring of the patient for several days following the episode and will alert others to the risk of future occurrences. The individual patient's symptoms, precipitating stimuli, and methods of relief should be documented.

Postural Hypotension

Postural hypotension is a decrease in blood pressure which occurs when a patient is moved from a horizontal position to a vertical position. It is caused by a loss of sympathetic vasoconstriction control. The problem is enhanced by lack of muscle tone, causing peripheral venous and splanchnic bed pooling. Reduced cerebral flow and decreased venous return to the heart also may occur.[37]

Inasmuch as many patients are immobilized for up to 6 to 8 weeks, episodes of postural hypotension are a fairly common occurrence during early progression to a vertical position. They tend to occur more frequently with lesions of the cervical and upper thoracic regions. Patients will often describe the onset as feelings of "dizziness," "faintness," or impending "black out." Although the exact mechanism is not clearly understood, the cardiovascular system, over time, gradually reestablishes sufficient vasomotor tone to allow assumption of the vertical position.[63]

A related problem is edema of the legs, ankles, and

feet, which is usually symmetric and pitting in nature. It occurs secondary to the above problems and is complicated by decreased lymphatic return.[37]

To minimize these effects the cardiovascular system should be allowed to adapt gradually by a slow progression to the vertical position. This frequently begins with elevation of the head of the bed and progresses to a reclining wheelchair with elevating leg rests and use of a tilt table. Vital signs should be monitored carefully, and the patient should always be moved very slowly. Use of compressive stockings and an abdominal binder will further minimize these effects. Drug therapy such as ephedrine[37,59] may be indicated to increase blood pressure or low-dose diuretics[37] to relieve persistent edema of legs, ankles, or feet. As vasomotor stability returns, tolerance to the vertical position will gradually improve.

Heterotopic (Ectopic) Bone Formation

Heterotopic bone formation is osteogenesis in soft tissues below the level of the lesion.[56,64] The etiology of this abnormal bone growth is unknown. However, multiple theories have been proposed, including tissue hypoxia secondary to circulatory stasis,[65] abnormal calcium metabolism, local pressure,[66] and microtrauma related to too aggressive range of motion exercises.[67,68]

Heterotopic bone formation is always extra-articular and extracapsular.[69] It may develop in tendons, in connective tissue between muscle, in aponeurotic tissue, or in the peripheral aspects of muscle.[56,67,69] It must be differentiated from *myositis ossificans,* which results from injury to a muscle and is characterized by bony deposits *within* muscle tissue. No relationships have been found between the development of heterotopic bone formation and level of injury, amount of exercise, or degree of spasticity or flaccidity.[65,70,71]

Heterotopic bone formation typically occurs adjacent to large joints, with the hips and knees most commonly involved.[64] Other joints that have demonstrated involvement include the elbows,[56] shoulders, and spine.[64] Early symptoms of heterotopic ossification resemble those of thrombophlebitis, including swelling, decreased range of motion, erythema, and local warmth near a joint. Early onset is also characterized by elevated serum alkaline phosphatase levels and negative radiographic findings.[72] During later clinical stages, soft tissue swelling subsides and radiographic findings are positive.[72]

For many patients the development of heterotopic ossification will pose no significant functional limitations.[13] However, a serious complication affecting 20 percent of patients is joint ankylosis, with which the hip is most commonly affected.[56]

Management of ectopic bone formation utilizes several approaches, including drug therapy, physical therapy, and, with severe functional limitations, surgery.[13] Drug therapy (diphosphates) has been used to inhibit the formation of calcium phosphate and to prevent ectopic bone formation.[56] These drugs, however, have no effect on mature ectopic bone.[13] Physical therapy is important in maintaining range of motion and preventing deformity. Early research[68,69] discouraged the use of range of motion, indicating that the exercise increased ectopic bone formation. However, later studies[64,65,71] have shown no increase in the formation of bone deposition with range of motion exercises. A logical approach to maintaining functional range of motion appears to be a combination of drug therapy with regular exercises during the early formation stages of ectopic development.[13] Finally, surgery is used when extreme limitations in function impede rehabilitation. This generally involves resection of the ectopic bone.[56]

Contractures

Contractures develop with prolonged shortening of structures across and around a joint, resulting in limitation in motion. Contractures initially produce alterations in muscle tissue but rapidly progress to involve capsular and pericapsular changes.[13] Once the tissue changes have occurred, the process is irreversible. A combination of factors places the patient with SCI at particularly high risk for developing joint contractures. Lack of *active muscle function* eliminates the normal reciprocal stretching of a muscle group and surrounding structures as the opposing muscle contracts.[56] *Spasticity* often results in prolonged unopposed muscle shortening in a static position. *Flaccidity* may result in gravitational forces maintaining a relatively consistent joint position. In addition, faulty positioning, ectopic bone formation, edema, and imbalances in muscle pull (either active or spastic) will contribute to the specific direction and location of contracture development.

Contractures are strongly influenced by the existing pattern of spasticity and the positioning methods used. The hip joint is particularly prone to flexion deformities and typically includes components of internal rotation and adduction. The shoulder may develop tightness in flexion or extension (depending on early positioning). Both patterns at the shoulder are associated with internal rotation and adduction. All joints of the body are at risk for contractures, including the elbows, wrist and fingers, knees, ankles, and toes.

The most important management consideration related to the potential development of contractures is *prevention.* Maintenance of joint motion is effectively achieved by a consistent and concurrent program of range of motion exercises, positioning, and, if appropriate, splinting.

Deep Venous Thrombosis (Thrombophlebitis)

Deep venous thrombosis (DVT) results from development of a *thrombus* (abnormal blood clot) within a vessel. The occurrence of such a clot is a dangerous medical complication. It has the potential to break free of its attachment and to float freely within the venous blood stream. Such mobile clots are known as *emboli.* They are particularly likely to block pulmonary vessels[28] (pulmonary emboli), which can result in death.

The most important factor contributing to the development of DVT following SCI is loss of the normal "pumping" mechanism provided by active contraction of lower extremity musculature. This slows the flow of blood, allowing higher concentrations of procoagulants (e.g., thrombin) to develop in localized areas. This in turn results in a predisposition to thrombus formation. Normally, these procoagulants are rapidly mixed with large quantities of blood and removed in the liver.[28] The risks of DVT are heightened with age and from prolonged pressure (e.g., extended contact against the bed or supporting surface).[54] Prolonged pressure can damage the vessel wall and precipitate initiation of the clotting process. In addition, loss of vasomotor tone and immobility further enhance the potential development of DVT.

The most frequent occurrence of DVT is within the first two months following injury.[54] The clinical features include local *swelling, erythema,* and *heat.* These signs are similar to those of early ectopic bone formation and long bone fractures.[56] Differential diagnosis is made on the basis of venous flow studies and venography.[56,73]

The clinical manifestations of DVT have been estimated to occur in approximately 15 percent of SCI patients.[73] However, one study reported an incidence as high as 40 percent.[74] Studies using iodine 125 fibrinogen scanning have yielded a much higher incidence. Fibrinogen scanning is sensitive to fibrin deposits and can detect the presence of an active thrombotic process[75] in the absence of clinical manifestations. Using this technique, incidence in patients with acute SCI has been reported at 90 percent in one group of 10 patients[76] and 100 percent in a group of 14 patients.[75]

Management of this secondary complication focuses on prevention. Prophylactic anticoagulant drug therapy is typically initiated following the acute onset of injury and routinely continued for 2 to 3 months[74] or up to 6 months for patients at high risk.[77] Other preventative measures include (1) a turning program designed to avoid pressure over large vessels, (2) passive range of motion exercises, (3) elastic support stockings, and (4) positioning of the lower extremities to facilitate venous return.

Pain

Pain is a common occurrence following SCI.[78] Several classification systems have been developed to describe this pain.[13,79-81] These classifications are related to the source and type of pain as well as to the length of time since onset (acute versus chronic pain).

TRAUMATIC PAIN

Initially, pain experienced following acute traumatic injury is related to the extent and type of trauma sustained as well as to the structures involved. Pain may arise from fractures, ligamentous or soft tissue damage, muscle spasm, or from early surgical interventions. This acute pain generally subsides with healing in 1 to 3 months.[13] Typical management includes immobilization and use of analgesics.[37] Transcutaneous electrical nerve stimulation (TENS) also has been found effective in reducing this type of acute, postinjury pain.[82]

NERVE ROOT PAIN

Pain or irritation may arise from damage to nerve roots at or near the site of cord damage. Pain can be caused by acute compression or tearing of the nerve roots,[83] or it may arise secondary to spinal instability, periradicular scar tissue and adhesion formation, or improper reduction.[37,54] Nerve root pain is often described as sharp, stabbing, burning, or shooting and typically follows a dermatomal pattern.[13] It is most common in cauda equina injuries, in which a high distribution of nerve roots is present.[78]

Management of nerve root pain is a challenging clinical problem. Multiple approaches have been suggested, with varying degrees of success. Conservative management involves drug therapy[83] and transcutaneous electrical nerve stimulation.[81] Surgical interventions for more severe, debilitating pain include nerve root sections (neurectomy) and posterior rhizotomies.[37]

SPINAL CORD DYSESTHESIAS

It is not uncommon for patients to experience many peculiar, often painful sensations **(dysesthesias)** below the level of the lesion. The sensations tend to be diffuse and usually do not follow a dermatome distribution.[37] They occur in body parts that otherwise lack sensation and are often described by the patient as burning, numbness, pins and needles, or tingling feelings. Occasionally they involve abnormal proprioceptive sensations, causing the individual to perceive a limb in other than its actual position.[13,54] Dysesthesias have been described as "phantom" pains or sensations similar to those experienced following amputation.[84] The exact etiology of this pain is not well understood. However, it is theorized to be related to scarring at the distal end of the severed spinal cord.[29,37] These sensations are present following the acute onset of injury and typically subside over time. However, they tend to be more persistent and long-standing in cauda equina lesions.[54]

Dysesthesia pain is particularly resistant to treatment. It is important that the complaints be acknowledged as real and that the patient be educated as to the legitimacy of the pain. Gentle handling of the patient's limbs and careful positioning frequently make the pain more tolerable.[29] Drug management using carbamazepine (Tegretol) and phenytoin (Dilantin) has been found effective in reducing dysesthesia pain.[83] Narcotic analgesics are usually discouraged because of the danger of addiction.[29,79,83] Other forms of treatment have not been found effective in managing this type of pain.[83]

MUSCULOSKELETAL PAIN

Pain also may occur above the level of lesion and frequently involves the shoulder joint.[85,86] Pathologic changes at the shoulder often are related to faulty positioning and/or inadequate range of motion exercises, resulting in tightening of the joint capsule and surrounding soft tissue structures. In addition, the shoulder muscles are excessively challenged in their role as tonic stabilizers to substitute for lack of trunk innervation. This situation may be complicated by muscle imbalances around the joint, inflammation, or upper extremity fractures sustained at the time of injury.

Prevention of secondary shoulder involvement is critical, considering the importance of this joint in self-care and functional activities. Shoulder pain and limitation of range of motion will significantly delay the rehabilitation process. The most important preventative measures include a regular program of range of motion exercise and a positioning program designed to facilitate full motion at the shoulder. To achieve this latter goal, several useful additions to traditional positioning programs have been suggested for the acute patient.[85] The first involves use of arm boards, which can be attached to a turning frame or can be slid under a mattress with pillows used to alter the height of the supporting surface. With the patient in a supine position, the side boards will allow positioning of the shoulders in 90 degrees of abduction with the elbows extended. A second suggestion, also with the patient in a supine position, is to place the arm above the patient's head for a short period of time. This will encourage external rotation and abduction beyond 90 degrees. The elbows should be in approximately 80 degrees of flexion. Finally, in sidelying, with the lower arm in 90 degrees of shoulder flexion, it is suggested that an axillary pillow be placed under the chest to help relieve pressure on the acromion process and head of the humerus. When the patient is positioned in sidelying, the uppermost arm can be extended and abducted and supported on a pillow.

Osteoporosis and Renal Calculi

Changes in calcium metabolism following SCI lead to **osteoporosis** below the level of the lesion and development of renal calculi. Normally, there is a dynamic balance between the bone resorption activity of osteoclasts and the role of osteoblasts in laying down new bone. Following SCI there is a net loss of bone mass as greater resorption occurs relative to the rate of new bone formation.[56] Consequently, there is a greater susceptibility to fracture. As a result of this resorption there are large concentrations of calcium present in the urinary system (hypercalciuria), creating a predisposition to stone formation.

The highest incidence of bone mass changes and hypercalciuria occurs during the first 6 months following SCI.[87,88] After this period, changes gradually diminish and assume a constant low normal level after approximately 1 year.[87,89]

The exact mechanism causing bone mass changes following paralysis is not clearly understood. However, immobility and lack of stress placed on the skeletal system through dynamic weight-bearing activities are well accepted as major contributing factors.

Treatment consists primarily of dietary management and early mobility activities. Dietary considerations include calcium-restricted foods and vigorous hydration (especially increased amounts of water). Excessive intake of foods such as milk, ice cream, and other dairy products high in calcium are generally discouraged.[90,91] High-protein foods such as meats, whole-grain products, eggs, and cranberries or dried fruit (e.g., prunes or plums) are encouraged.[41] In addition, the risk of calculi formation will be reduced by prevention of urinary tract infections and careful maintenance of bladder drainage to prevent urinary stasis.[41]

PROGNOSIS

The potential for recovery from SCI is directly related to the extent of damage to the spinal cord and/or nerve roots. Donovan and Bedbrook[22] have identified three primary influences on potential for recovery: (1) the degree of pathologic changes imposed by the trauma, (2) the precautions taken to prevent further damage during rescue, and (3) prevention of additional compromise of neural tissue from hypoxia and hypotension during acute management.

Formulation of a prognosis is initiated only after spinal shock has subsided and is guided by whether or not the lesion is complete. Following spinal shock, a lesion is generally considered *complete* in the absence of any sensory or motor function below the level of cord damage. Early appearance of reflex activity in these instances is considered a poor prognostic indicator.[24] In complete lesions, no motor improvement is expected other than that which may occur from nerve root return.

With *incomplete* lesions some evidence of sensory and/or motor function is noted below the level of the cord lesion after spinal shock subsides. Early signs of an incomplete lesion may be indicated by sacral sparing (perianal sensation, rectal sphincter tone, or active toe flexion). Incomplete lesions also may present with areas of spotty or scattered sensory and motor function throughout.

It is important to note that with most incomplete lesions improvement begins almost immediately following cessation of spinal shock. Many patients will have some progressive improvement of muscle return. It may be minimal or, less frequently, dramatic and usually becomes apparent during the first several months following injury. With a consistent progression of returning function (daily, weekly, or even monthly) further recovery can be expected along the same rate or slightly slower. Meticulous and frequent assessment of sensory and motor functions during this period will provide important information about the progression of recovery.

In time, the rate of recovery will decrease, and a plateau will be reached. When the plateau is reached and no new muscle activity is observed for several weeks or months, no additional recovery can be expected in the future.

MANAGEMENT

The remainder of this chapter is divided into the acute and subacute phases of rehabilitation. The section on acute management addresses treatment interventions from the onset of injury until the fracture site is stable and upright activities can be initiated. The rehabilitation phase includes suggested treatment activities following initial orientation to the vertical position through preparation for discharge from the rehabilitation facility.

Acute Phase

EMERGENCY CARE

Ideally, management of SCI begins at the location of the accident. Techniques used in moving and managing the patient immediately following the trauma can influence prognosis significantly. Rescue personnel must be adept at questioning and assessing for signs of spinal injury before moving the individual.[13] When a spinal injury is suspected, efforts should be made to avoid both active and passive movements of the spine.[22] Movement of the spine can be averted by strapping the patient to a spinal back board, use of a supporting cervical collar, and assistance from multiple personnel in moving the patient to safety. These measures will assist in maintaining the spine in a neutral, anatomic position and will prevent further neurologic damage.[22]

On arrival at the emergency room initial attention is focused on stabilizing the patient medically. A complete neurologic examination is performed. Radiographic studies, tomograms, and myelography assist in determining the extent of damage and plans for management.[22] Attention is directed toward preventing progression of neurologic impairment by restoration of vertebral alignment and early immobilization of the fracture site. A catheter typically is inserted, and secondary injuries are addressed.

Unstable spinal fractures require early reduction and fixation. Symptoms of instability may include pain and tenderness at the fracture site, radiating pain, increasing neurologic signs, and decreasing motor function.

FRACTURE STABILIZATION

Cervical Injuries

Immobilization of unstable cervical fractures is achieved via skeletal traction. Traction can be applied by use of tongs attached to the outer skull (Fig. 26–5) or by a halo device (Fig. 26–6).

Tongs. Several types of tongs are available (e.g., Crutchfield, Barton, Vinke, Gardner-Wells), each with a slightly different design. The tongs or calipers are inserted laterally on the outer table of the skull. Traction is accomplished by attachment of a traction rope to the skull fixation. With the patient in a supine position, this rope is threaded through a pulley or traction collar with weights attached distally. The weights hang freely without touching the floor. With the selection of tongs as the method of skeletal traction the patient is generally immobilized for about 12 weeks until healing occurs.

Turning Frames and Beds. Several types of frames and beds are used during this period of immobilization. Each has different design characteristics and functions. Among the most commonly used turning frame is the Stryker frame. It consists of an anterior and posterior

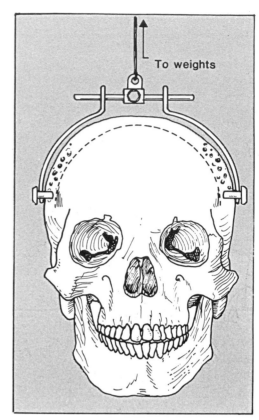

Figure 26–5. Cervical tongs. (From Judd, E (ed): *Nursing Care of the Adult.* FA Davis, Philadelphia, 1983, p 482, with permission.)

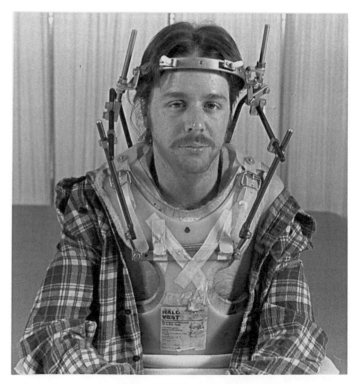

Figure 26–6. Halo device.

frame attached to a turning base (Fig. 26–7). In turning from a supine position, the anterior frame is placed on top of the patient. A circular ring clamps in place to secure the two frames during turning. Additional security is provided by safety straps. Rotation to the prone position is accomplished by manually turning the two frames as a unit. The uppermost frame is then removed. Return to the supine position is accomplished in the same manner. The primary benefit of these devices is that they allow positional changes while maintaining anatomic alignment of the spine. Turning can be accomplished without interruption of the cervical traction. A disadvantage of turning frames is that positioning is limited to prone and supine. This is particularly problematic for patients with a low tolerance for the prone position (e.g., cardiac or respiratory involvement). In addition, these frames can not accommodate obese patients.

The Roto Rest Kinetic Treatment Table (Roto Rest Bed) is an electronically operated unit that provides continuous side-to-side rotation along its longitudinal axis (Fig. 26–8). Its basic components include an oscillating base frame and a series of bolsters, pads, and supports for patient positioning. The primary advantage of this system for patients with SCI is the ability to maintain cervical traction with reduction of the secondary complica-tions of bedrest. The continuous oscillation provides the important advantages of improved pulmonary and kidney drainage as well as assisting with prevention of pressure sores via continual redistribution of tissue pressure.

It should be noted that some patients can not tolerate the continuous oscillation provided by this unit and develop motion sickness. These symptoms may be successfully treated by drug intervention (e.g., Dramamine). If symptoms persist, it may be necessary to discontinue use of the bed. In addition, severe claustrophobia is generally considered a contraindication for use of this bed.

Circular frame beds (Fig. 26–9) are also electronically powered. They provide positional changes from supine to prone and reverse by a vertical (upright) turn. An anterior frame is placed on the patient before turning. This type of bed is no longer used for patients with acute SCI, because of the excessive loading of the spine in a vertical position.[92]

Finally, in some facilities standard hospital beds are used. Any of a variety of special mattresses (gel, sand, water, air, or foam) are used for pressure relief. Positional changes are accomplished by log rolling.

Halo Devices. Currently, halo devices are being used with much greater frequency to immobilize cervical fractures. These traction devices (see Figure 26–6) consist of

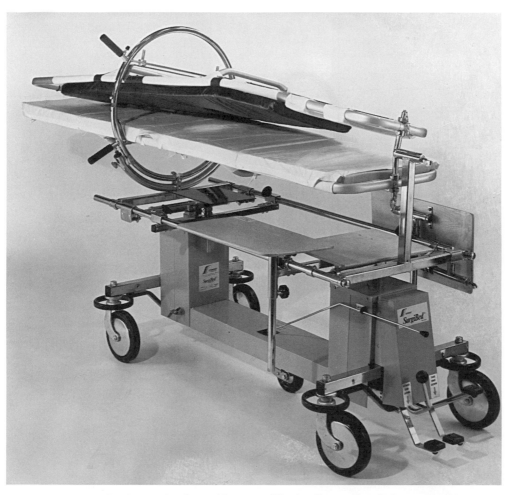

Figure 26–7. Stryker turning frame. (Courtesy of Stryker Corporation, Kalamazoo, MI.)

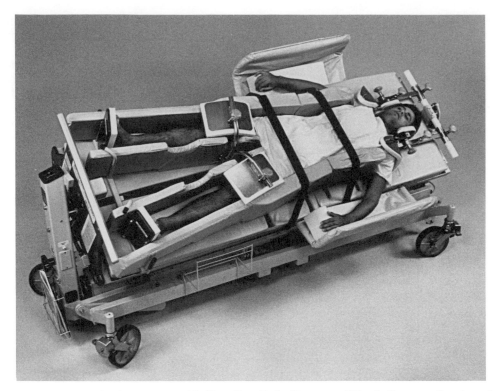

Figure 26–8. Roto Rest kinetic treatment table (Roto Rest Bed). (Courtesy of Kinetic Concepts, San Antonio, TX.)

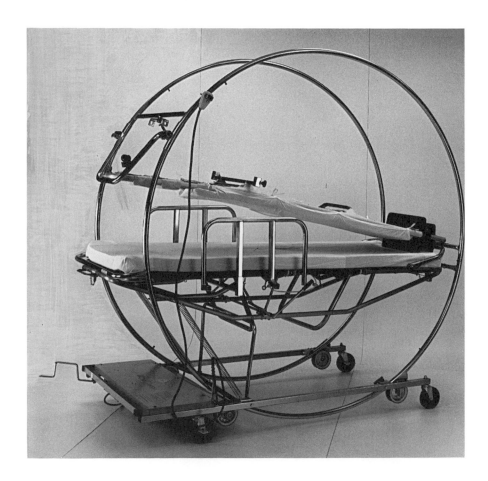

Figure 26–9. Circle electric bed. (Courtesy of Stryker Corporation, Kalamazoo, MI.)

a halo ring with four steel screws that attach directly to the outer skull. The halo is attached to a body jacket or vest by four vertical steel posts. The introduction of halo devices has generally been considered a major advance in managing cervical fractures. They provide several important advantages over use of tongs and prolonged confinement to a bed or turning frame. These devices reduce the secondary complications of prolonged bedrest, permit earlier progression to upright activities, allow earlier involvement in a rehabilitation program, and reduce the length and cost of hospital stay.[93] In addition, for patients without neurologic involvement, discharge from the hospital may occur several days after application of the halo device. These patients are then followed closely on an outpatient basis.[94]

Skeletal traction devices are left in place until radiographic findings indicate stability has been achieved (approximately 12 weeks). Following removal, a cervical orthosis is applied during a transitional period (approximately 4 to 6 weeks) until unrestricted movement is allowed. The SOMI (sterno-occipital-mandibular-immobilizer) cervical orthosis, Philadelphia collar, or custommade plastic collars are frequently used during this period with progression to a soft foam collar prior to resuming unsupported movement.

Thoracic and Lumbar Injuries

Fractures of the thoracic and lumbar area are typically managed by immobilization through bedrest or by application of a body cast or jacket. Bedrest is achieved by use of a turning frame or a standard bed, maintaining a log-roll technique for positional changes.

The expanded use of spinal orthotics also has allowed for earlier mobility activities following thoracic and lumbar injuries. Plaster or plastic body jackets (Fig. 26–10) function to immobilize the spine while allowing earlier involvement in a rehabilitation program. Body jackets are typically bivalved to allow for removal during bathing and skin inspection.

SURGICAL INTERVENTION

Surgery may be indicated to restore bony anatomic alignment, to prevent further damage to the cord, and to stabilize the fracture site.[22] Compared with spontaneous healing times, surgical stabilization allows earlier initiation of rehabilitation activities.[22]

Surgical interventions for cervical fractures may include decompression (anterior or posterior) and fusion. Fusion is achieved by bone grafting and may be combined with posterior wiring of the spinous processes.[95]

Frequently, surgery for thoracic and lumbar fractures requires use of an internal fixation device, which may be used in combination with bone grafts. The three most common devices used for achieving spinal realignment, stability, and internal fixation are Harrington distraction rods, Harrington compression rods, and Weiss compression springs.[96] Following thoracic or lumbar surgery, the

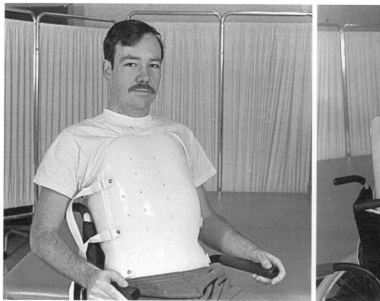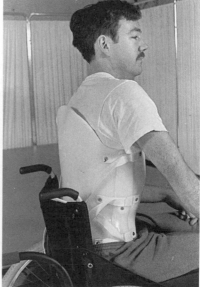

Figure 26–10. Anterior and lateral view of bivalved, plastic body jacket.

patient is placed in a spinal orthosis (e.g., Knight-Taylor orthosis, Jewett hyperextension orthosis; or a custom-made, plastic, bivalved body jacket) for a minimum of 3 months.[96]

PHYSICAL THERAPY ASSESSMENT DURING THE ACUTE PHASE

A general assessment of the patient is indicated, including respiratory function, muscle strength and tone, and skin condition. Results will assist the therapist in determining the lesion level, identifying general functional expectations, and formulating appropriate treatment goals. As noted earlier, the lesion level is considered to be the lowest segmental level in which muscle strength is present at a fair+ grade. During the acute stage, spinal instability often precludes a complete and thorough physical therapy assessment. However, gross screening will provide important initial data until the patient is cleared for further activity.

1. Respiratory assessment. Details of respiratory status and function are essential. The areas listed below should be assessed:

a. Function of respiratory muscles. Muscle strength and tone, and atrophy of the diaphragm, abdominals, and intercostals should be assessed; respiratory rate should be noted.

b. Chest expansion. Circumferential measurements should be taken at the level of the axilla and xiphoid process using a cloth tape measure. Chest expansion is recorded as the difference in measurement between maximum exhalation and maximum inhalation. Normally, chest expansion is approximately 2.5 to 3 inches at the xiphoid process.[33]

c. Breathing pattern. A determination should be made of muscles that are functioning and their contributions to respiration. This may be accomplished by manual palpation over the chest and abdominal region or by observation. Particular attention should be directed toward use of accessory neck muscles and alteration in breathing pattern when the patient is talking or moving.[30]

d. Cough. Coughing allows the patient to remove secretions. Ineffective cough function will necessitate suctioning to avoid pulmonary complications. Alvarez and coworkers[30] have defined three cough classifications: (1) *functional*: strong enough to clear secretions; (2) *weak functional*: adequate force to clear upper-tract secretions in small quantities; assistance is required to clear mucus secondary to infection; and (3) *nonfunctional*: unable to produce any cough force.

e. Vital capacity. Initial measures may be taken with a handheld spirometer.[30] Vital capacity measures also can be used as a baseline for defining respiratory muscle weakness.[33]

2. Skin assessment. During the acute phase, meticulous and regular skin inspection is a shared responsibility of the patient and the entire subacute team. As management progresses into the rehabilitation phase, the patient will gradually assume greater responsibility for this activity. Patient education related to skin care is crucial and should be initiated early. Frequent position changes and

skin inspection may be viewed by the patient as bothersome or distracting to sleep without adequate knowledge of the importance and purpose of these activities.

Skin inspection combines both visual *observation* and *palpation*.[97] The patient's entire body should be observed regularly with particular attention to areas most susceptible to pressure (Table 26-4). Palpation is useful for identifying skin temperature changes which may be indicative of a hyperemic reaction. This is particularly important in assessing dark-skinned individuals, inasmuch as early skin responses to pressure may not be readily apparent. Skin reactions to excess pressure include redness, local warmth, local edema, and small open or cracked skin areas. Careful attention should be directed toward accidental skin abrasions or bruises which increase the potential for skin breakdown.[97] If the patient is wearing a halo, vest, or other orthotic device, contact points between the body and the appliance must also be inspected.

3. Sensory assessment. A *detailed* assessment of superficial, deep, and combined sensations should be completed (see chapter 6). It should be noted that the sensory level of injury may not correspond to the motor level of injury (i.e., incomplete lesions).

4. Tone and deep tendon reflexes. Muscle tone should be assessed (see chapter 9) with reference to quality, muscle groups involved, and factors that appear to increase or to decrease tone. An assessment of deep tendon reflexes is indicated. The specific tendons selected for testing will be influenced by the lesion level. The deep tendon reflexes most commonly assessed and their levels of innervation are the biceps (C-6), triceps (C-7), quadriceps (L-3-4), and gastrocnemius (S-1).[49]

5. Manual muscle test (MMT) and range of motion (ROM) assessment. Standard techniques should be used for MMT[98] and ROM.[99] Inasmuch as mobility will be limited during the acute phase, deviations from standard positioning will be necessary and should be carefully documented. In cases of spinal instability, *extreme* caution should be used when performing gross muscle and ROM tests, because movements of this sort may place undue stress on the fracture site. Discretion should be used in applying resistance around the shoulders in quadriplegia and around the lower trunk and hips in paraplegia.

Table 26-4 AREAS MOST SUSCEPTIBLE TO PRESSURE IN RECUMBENT POSITIONS

Supine	Prone	Sidelying
Occiput	Ears (head rotated)	Ears
Scapulae		Shoulders (lateral aspect)
Vertebrae		Greater trochanter
Elbows	Shoulders (anterior aspect)	Head of fibula
Sacrum	Iliac crest	Knees (medial aspect
Coccyx	Male genital region	from contact between
Heels	Patella	knees)
	Dorsum of feet	Lateral malleolus
		Medial malleolus
		(contact between
		malleoli)

6. Functional assessment. Accurate and specific determination of functional skills usually must be delayed until the patient is cleared for activity. Once activity is allowed, a more detailed assessment of function can be made (see chapter 12).

7. Sacral sparing. Periodic checks should be made for the presence of sacral sparing, which may not have been evident on admission (e.g., perianal sensation, rectal sphincter tone, or active toe flexion).

PHYSICAL THERAPY TREATMENT DURING THE ACUTE PHASE

During the acute phase of rehabilitation, emphasis is placed on respiratory management, prevention of secondary complications, maintaining range of motion, and facilitating active movement in available musculature. Pending orthopedic clearance, limited strengthening activities also may be initiated during this early phase.

1. Respiratory management. Respiratory care will vary according to the level of injury and individual respiratory status. Primary goals of management include improved ventilation, increased effectiveness of cough, prevention of chest tightness and of ineffective substitute breathing patterns.[30] Depending on the individual patient, the following treatment activities may be appropriate:

a. Deep breathing exercises. Diaphragmatic breathing should be encouraged. To facilitate diaphragmatic movement and to increase vital capacity, the therapist can apply light pressure during both inspiration and expiration. Manual contacts can be made just below the sternum. This will assist the patient to concentrate on deep breathing patterns even in the absence of thoracic and abdominal sensation. To facilitate expiration, manual contacts are made over the thorax with the hands spread wide. This creates a compressive force on the thorax, resulting in a more forceful expiration followed by a more efficient inspiration.[5] Patients immobilized in traction devices or limited to recumbent positions may benefit from use of a mirror to provide visual feedback during these activities. Inflation hold and incentive spirometry are also useful adjuncts to deep breathing exercises.[100]

b. Glossopharyngeal breathing. This activity is often appropriate for patients with high-level cervical lesions. The technique utilizes accessory muscles of respiration to improve vital capacity. The patient is instructed to inspire small amounts of air repeatedly, using a "sipping" or "gulping" pattern, thus utilizing available facial and neck muscles. By using this technique, enough air is gradually inspired to improve chest expansion despite paralysis of the primary muscles of respiration.

c. Airshift maneuver. This technique provides the patient with an independent method of chest expansion. This maneuver is accomplished by closing the glottis after a maximum inhalation, relaxing the diaphragm and allowing air to shift from the lower to upper thorax. Airshifts can increase chest expansion by 0.5 to 2 inches (1.3 to 5.1 cm).

d. Strengthening exercises. Progressive resistive exercises can be used to strengthen the diaphragm. This can be accomplished by manual contacts over the epigastric area below the xiphoid or by use of weights. Strengthening exercises for innervated abdominal and accessory musculature are also indicated.

e. Assisted coughing. To assist with coughing and movement of secretions, manual contacts are placed over the epigastric area. The therapist pushes quickly in an inward and upward direction as the patient attempts to cough.[5]

f. Abdominal support. An abdominal corset or binder is indicated for patients whose abdomens protrude, allowing the diaphragm to "sag" into a poor position for function. The corset will support the abdominal contents and improve the resting position of the diaphragm. In addition, abdominal supports provide the secondary benefits of maintaining intrathoracic pressure and decreasing postural hypotension.

g. Stretching. Mobility and compliance of the thoracic wall can be facilitated by manual stretching of pectoral and other chest wall muscles.

In addition to these respiratory approaches, intermittent positive pressure breathing may be utilized to assist in maintenance of lung compliance. Modified postural drainage and percussion techniques also may be indicated to assist with mobilizing and eliminating secretions.

2. Range of motion and positioning. While the patient is immobilized in bed or on a turning frame, full ROM exercises should be completed daily except for those areas which are contraindicated or require selective stretching. With paraplegia, motion of the trunk and some motions of the hip are contraindicated. Generally, straight-leg raising greater than 60 degrees and hip flexion beyond 90 degrees (during combined hip and knee flexion) should be avoided. This will avert strain on the lower thoracic and lumbar spine. If possible, ROM exercises should be completed in both the prone and supine positions (prone positioning may be contraindicated for some patients secondary to fracture and/or respiratory compromise in this position). In the prone position, attention should be directed toward shoulder and hip extension and knee flexion. With quadriplegia, motion of the head and neck is contraindicated pending orthopedic clearance. Stretching of the shoulders should be avoided during the acute period; however, the patient should be positioned out of the usual position of comfort, which is internal rotation, adduction and extension of the shoulders, elbow flexion, forearm pronation, and wrist flexion. Full ROM exercises are generally included for both lower extremities.

Patients with spinal cord injuries do not require full ROM in all joints. In some instances, allowing tightness to develop in certain muscles will enhance function. For example, with quadriplegia, tightness of the lower trunk musculature will improve sitting posture by increasing trunk stability; tightness in the long finger flexors will provide an improved tenodesis grasp. Conversely, some muscles require a fully lengthened range. After the acute phase, the hamstrings will require stretching to achieve a straight leg raise of approximately 120 degrees. This ROM is required for many functional activities such as sitting, transfers, lower extremity dressing, and self-

ROM exercises. This process of understretching some muscles and full stretching of others is referred to as *selective stretching*.

Positioning splints for the wrist, hands, and fingers are an important early consideration. Alignment of the fingers, thumb, and wrist must be maintained for functional activities or future dynamic splinting.[101] For high-level lesions the wrist is positioned in neutral, the web space is maintained, and the fingers are flexed.[101] If the wrist extensors are functional (fair muscle grade), a C-bar or short-opponens splint is usually sufficient.

Ankle boots or splints are indicated to maintain alignment and to prevent heel cord tightness and pressure sores. Sandbags or towel rolls also may be required to maintain a position of neutral hip rotation.

Following orthopedic clearance, the patient typically is placed on a schedule to increase tolerance to the prone position. For patients wearing a halo device, one or two pillows under the chest will allow assumption of the prone position. The ankles should be positioned at a 90 degree angle. Tolerance to the prone position should be increased gradually until the patient is able to sleep all, or at least part, of the night in this position. This routine will assist with prevention of pressure sores on posterior aspects of the body and development of flexor tightness at the hips and knees. Proning schedules also are considered to promote improved bladder drainage.

3. Selective strengthening. During the course of rehabilitation, all remaining musculature will be strengthened maximally. However, during the acute phase, certain muscles must be strengthened very cautiously to avoid stress at the fracture site. During the first few weeks following injury, application of resistance may be contraindicated to (1) musculature of the scapula and shoulders in quadriplegia and (2) musculature of the hips and trunk in paraplegia.

An important consideration in planning exercise programs during the acute phase is to emphasize bilateral upper extremity activities because these will avoid asymmetric, rotational stresses on the spine. Several forms of strengthening exercises are appropriate during this early phase: bilateral manually resisted motions in straight planes; bilateral upper extremity proprioceptive neuromuscular facilitation (PNF) patterns; and progressive resistive exercises using cuff weights or dumbbells. Biofeedback training also may be a useful adjunct during early exercise programs. With quadriplegia, emphasis should be placed on strengthening the anterior deltoid, shoulder extensors, biceps, and lower trapezius. If present, the radial wrist extensors, triceps, and pectorals should also be emphasized because they will be of key importance in improving functional capacity. With paraplegia, all upper extremity musculature should be strengthened, with emphasis on shoulder depressors, triceps, and latissimus dorsi, which are required for transfers and ambulation.

Early involvement in functional activities should be stressed. In addition to their intrinsic value, many activities afford the important benefit of progressive strengthening. For example, self-feeding and involvement in limited personal care activities will assist with strengthening the shoulder and elbow flexors. Another example of a functional activity (although not appropriate during the acute phase) with important strengthening benefits is wheelchair propulsion (deltoids, biceps, and shoulder rotators).

4. Orientation to the vertical position. Once radiographic findings have established stability of the fracture site, or early fracture stabilization methods are complete, the patient is cleared for upright activities. As discussed earlier, the patient typically will experience symptoms of postural hypotension if approach to management has required prolonged immobility. A *very gradual* acclimation to upright postures is most effective. The use of an abdominal binder and elastic stockings will retard venous pooling. During early upright positioning, elastic wraps are often used in combination with (placed over) the elastic stockings.

Initially, upright activities can be initiated by elevating the head of the bed and progressing to a reclining wheelchair with elevating leg rests. Use of the tilt table provides another option for orienting the patient to a vertical position. Vital signs should be monitored carefully and documented during this acclimation period.

Patients who have been immobilized in halo devices or undergone surgical spine stabilization will not be confined to recumbent positions for prolonged periods. For these patients, the same progression is used, although a more rapid advance to the vertical position can be anticipated.

Subacute Phase

FUNCTIONAL EXPECTATIONS

A spinal cord injury will require that specific long-term functional goals be established as part of overall rehabilitation planning. Table 26–5 presents reasonable functional expectations, at various lesions levels, for a young, healthy patient unimpaired by secondary complications. This information may be a useful guide in establishing realistic goals. However, it is important not to adhere too closely to established "norms" and, hence, to limit the patient by your own expectations. Goals should be established individually for each patient on the basis of assessment findings in accordance with the level and extent of injury.

The term *key muscles* is a common expression in the management of these patients and is used in Table 26–5. Key muscles are the muscles that add significantly to a patient's functional capability at each successive level of lesion. It is also important to note that the neurologic level of innervation may vary slightly from source to source.

PHYSICAL THERAPY ASSESSMENT DURING THE SUBACUTE PHASE

All the assessment procedures completed during the acute phase will be continued at regular intervals during the subacute phase of rehabilitation. Inasmuch as greater patient mobility is now allowed, more specific testing of muscle strength, ROM, and functional skills can be com-

Table 26–5 FUNCTIONAL EXPECTATIONS FOR SPINAL CORD INJURED PATIENTS*

Most Distal Nerve Root Segments Innervated and Key Muscles	Available Movements	Functional Capabilities	Equipment and Assistance Required
C-1,C-2,C-3 Face and neck muscles (cranial innervation)	Talking Mastication Sipping Blowing	1. Total dependence in ADL	Respirator dependent; may use phrenic nerve stimulator during the day[102] Full-time attendant required
		Activation of light switches, page turners, call buttons, electrical appliances, and speaker phones	Environmental control units
		2. Locomotion	Electric wheelchair (typical components include a high, electrically controlled reclining back, a seatbelt and trunk support); a portable respirator may be attached; microswitch or sip-and-puff controls may be used[100]
C-4 Diaphragm Trapezius	Respiration Scapular elevation	1. ADL a. Limited self-feeding	Mobile arm supports (possibly with powered elbow orthosis), powered flexor hinge hand splint Adapted eating equipment (long straws, built-up handles on utensils, plate guards, and so forth) Plexiglass lapboard[101]
		b. Typing	Electric typewriter using head or mouth stick or sip-and-puff controls; another option is a rubber-tipped stick held in hand by a splint (in combination with mobile arm supports and powered splints)
		c. Page turning	Head or mouth stick Environmental control unit for powered page turner
		d. Activation of light switches, call buttons, electrical appliances, and speaker phone	Environmental control units
		2. Locomotion	Electric wheelchair with mouth, chin, breath, or sip-and-puff controls
		3. Pressure relief	Electric reclining back on wheelchair
		4. Transfers and bed mobility	Dependent
		5. Skin inspection	Dependent
		6. Cough with glossopharangeal breathing	Dependent
		7. Recreation a. Table games such as cards or checkers	Head or mouth stick Built-up playing pieces
		b. Painting and drawing	Full-time attendant required
C-5 Biceps Brachialis Brachioradialis Deltoid Infraspinatus Rhomboid (major and minor) Supinator	Elbow flexion and supination Shoulder external rotation Shoulder abduction to 90 degrees Limited shoulder flexion	1. ADL: able to accomplish all activities of a C-4 quadriplegic with less adaptive equipment and more skill a. Self-feeding	Assistance is required in setting up patient with necessary equipment; patient can then accomplish activity independently Mobile arm supports Adapted utensils
		b. Typing	Electric typewriter Hand splints Adapted typing sticks Some patients may require mobile arm supports or slings
		c. Page turning	Same as above
		d. Limited upper extremity dressing	Assistance required
		e. Limited self-care (i.e., washing, brushing teeth, and grooming)	Hand splints Adapted equipment (wash mitt, adapted toothbrush, and so forth)

Table 26–5 *continued.*

Most Distal Nerve Root Segments Innervated and Key Muscles	Available Movements	Functional Capabilities	Equipment and Assistance Required
		2. Locomotion	Manual wheelchair with handrim projections
			Electric wheelchair with joystick or adapted upper extremity controls
		3. Transfer activities	Overhead swivel bar
			Sliding board
			Dependent
		4. Skin inspection and pressure relief	Dependent
		5. Cough with manual pressure to diaphragm	Assistance required
		6. Driving	Van with hand controls
			Part-time attendant required
C-6	Shoulder flexion, extension, internal rotation, and adduction	1. ADL	
Extensor carpi radialis		a. Self-feeding	Universal cuff
Infraspinatus			Intertwine utensils in fingers
Latissimus dorsi			Adapted utensils
Pectoralis major (clavicular portion)	Scapular abduction and upward rotation	b. Dressing	Utilizes momentum, button hooks, zipper pulls,[101] or other clothing adaptations; dependent on momentum to extend limbs
Pronator teres	Forearm pronation		
Serratus anterior	Wrist extension (tenodesis grasp)		Can not tie shoes
Teres minor			
		c. Self-care	Flexor hinge splint
			Universal cuff
			Adaptive equipment
		d. Bed mobility	Independent
		2. Locomotion	Manual wheelchair with projection or friction surface handrims
		3. Transfer activities	Independent with sliding board
		4. Skin inspection and pressure relief	Independent
		5. Bowel and bladder care	Can be independent, depending on bowel and bladder routine
		6. Cough with application of pressure to abdomen	Independent
		7. Driving	Automobile with hand controls and U-shaped cuff attached to steering wheel
			Usually requires assistance in getting wheelchair into car
		8. Wheelchair sports	Limited participation
C-7	Elbow extension	1. ADL	
Extensor pollicus longus and brevis	Wrist flexion	a. Self-feeding	Independent
	Finger extension	b. Dressing	Independent
Extrinsic finger extensors			Button hook may be required
		c. Self-care	Shower chair
Flexor carpi radialis			Adapted hand shower nozzle
Triceps			Adapted handles on bathroom items may be required
		2. Locomotion	Manual wheelchair with friction surface handrims
		3. Transfers	Independent (usually without sliding board)
		4. Bowel and bladder care	Independent with appropriate equipment (digital stimulator, suppositories, raised toilet seat, urinary drainage device, and so forth)
		5. Manual cough	Independent
		6. Housekeeping	Light kitchen activities
			Requires wheelchair-accessible kitchen and living environment
			Adapted kitchen tools
		7. Driving	Automobile with hand controls
			Able to get wheelchair in and out of car

Table 26–5 *continued.*

Most Distal Nerve Root Segments Innervated and Key Muscles	Available Movements	Functional Capabilities	Equipment and Assistance Required
C-8 to T-1 Extrinsic finger flexors Flexor carpi ulnaris Flexor pollicis longus and brevis Intrinsic finger flexors	Full innervation of upper extremity muscles	1. ADL 2. Locomotion 3. Housekeeping 4. Driving 5. Employment	Independent in all self-care and personal hygiene Some adaptive equipment may be required (e.g., tub seat, grab bars, and so forth) Manual wheelchair with standard handrims Independent in light housekeeping and meal preparation Some adaptive equipment may be required (e.g., reachers) Requires a wheelchair-accessible living environment Automobile with hand controls Able to work in a building free of architectural barriers
T-4 to T-6 Top half of intercostals Long muscles of back (sacrospinalis and semispinalis)	Improved trunk control Increased respiratory reserve	1. ADL 2. Physiologic standing (not practical for functional ambulation) 3. Housekeeping 4. Curb climbing in wheelchair 5. Wheelchair sports	Independent in all areas Standing table Bilateral knee-ankle orthoses with spinal attachment Some patients may be able to ambulate for short distances with assistance Independent with routine activities Requires a wheelchair-accessible living environment Able to negotiate curbs using a "wheelie" technique Full participation
T-9 to T-12 Lower abdominals All intercostals	Improved trunk control Increased endurance	1. Household ambulation 2. Locomotion	Bilateral knee-ankle orthoses and crutches or walker (high energy consumption for ambulation) Wheelchair used for energy conservation
L-2,L-3,L-4 Gracilis Iliopsoas Quadratus lumborum Rectus femoris Sartorius	Hip flexion Hip adduction Knee extension	1. Functional ambulation 2. Locomotion	Bilateral knee-ankle orthoses and crutches Wheelchair used for convenience and energy conservation
L-4,L-5 Extensor digitorum Low back muscles Medial hamstrings (weak) Posterior tibialis Quadriceps Tibialis anterior Posterior tibialis Quadriceps Tibialis anterior	Strong hip flexion Strong knee extension Weak knee flexion Improved trunk control	1. Functional ambulation 2. Locomotion	Bilateral ankle-foot orthoses and crutches or canes Wheelchair used for convenience and energy conservation

*This table presents general functional expectations at various lesion levels. Each progressively lower segment includes the muscles from the previous levels. Although the key muscles listed frequently receive innervation from several nerve root segments, they are listed here at the neurologic levels where they add to functional outcomes.

pleted. A high level of skill in MMT is needed for the therapist to distinguish accurately between true voluntary contraction and movement associated with spasticity or substitution.

During this phase of management, the patient will be instructed gradually to assume responsibility for skin inspection. This will involve practice in use of long-handled (Fig. 26–11) or adapted mirrors to allow inspection of areas not easily visible. Wall mirrors adjacent to the bed may assist in achieving independence with this activity. Patients with high-level lesions may be incapable of skin inspection. It is important that these patients be instructed in how to direct others to complete this assessment. Continued emphasis by the therapist should be

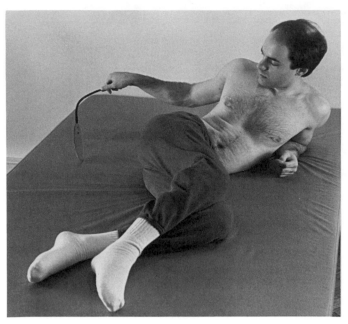

Figure 26–11. Skin inspection with use of long-handled mirror.

placed on the importance of skin inspection and the rationale for pressure relief. Skin inspection must become a regular and lifelong component of the patient's daily routine.

Once some wheelchair mobility has been achieved, assessment of cardiovascular endurance is indicated (see chapter 16). The patient's age, sex, and cardiac history should be taken into account. Upper extremity stress testing or telemetry monitoring during wheelchair propulsion may be indicated for patients who are suspected of having impaired cardiovascular adaption to exercise.

PHYSICAL THERAPY TREATMENT DURING THE SUBACUTE PHASE

Continuing Activities

During this phase of management many of the treatment activities initiated during the acute period will be continued. Emphasis will remain on respiratory management, ROM, and positioning. The patient also will be involved in a continuing and expanded program of resistive exercises for all muscles that remain innervated (e.g., PNF, PRE using manual resistance, weights, wall pulleys, sling suspension, group exercise classes). Development of motor control and muscle reeducation techniques directed at appropriate muscles (depending on lesion level) are indicated. This phase of treatment will also emphasize regaining postural control and balance by substituting upper body control and vision (for lost proprioception).

Mat Programs. Mat activities constitute a major component of treatment during the rehabilitation phase. The sequence of activities typically progresses from achievement of stability within a posture and advance through controlled mobility to skill in functional use. Early activities are bilateral and symmetrical. A progression is then made to weight shifting and movement

within the posture. A gradual emphasis is placed on improved timing and speed.

Mat activities are often individual components of more complex functional skills. They should be sequenced from easiest to most difficult so that the patient is performing activities within, or almost within, the sphere of mastery. As mastery of the various components of more complex and difficult activities is achieved, the patient should be asked to perform these tasks in the current living environment (i.e., hospital room, or, eventually, home on weekends).

The therapist must determine the appropriate mat activities for each patient based on level of injury and medical status. It is important to note that complete mastery of an activity is not always necessary before moving on to the next. At some points in treatment, several components of the mat progression will be worked on concurrently.

Mat activities should be initiated as soon as the patient is cleared for activity. Progression through the sequence of mat activities develops improved strength and functional ROM, improves awareness of the new center of gravity, promotes postural stability, facilitates dynamic balance, and assists with determining the most efficient and functional methods for accomplishing specific tasks. It also provides the opportunity to develop functional patterns of movement (e.g., use of innervated musculature or momentum to move body parts that lack active movement).

The following section represents a sample progression of selected mat activities. The degree to which they can be performed independently and the time needed to learn them vary considerably with the level of lesion. Each component of the mat progression is presented with its functional implications and several suggested treatment activities to facilitate accomplishment of the activity. Chapter 14 should also be consulted for additional treatment suggestions.

1. Rolling. The functional significance of rolling is related to improved bed mobility, preparation for independent positional changes in bed (for pressure relief), and for lower extremity dressing.

Rolling is a frequent starting point of mat programs for these patients and provides an early lesson in developing functional patterns of movement. It requires the patient to learn to use the head, neck, and upper extremities as well as momentum to move the trunk and/or lower extremities. It is usually easiest to begin rolling activities from the supine position, working toward the prone position. If asymmetric involvement exists, rolling should be initiated with movement *toward* the weaker side.

The activity is initially taught on a mat. However, rolling must be mastered also on the surface of a bed, similar to the one that the patient will use at home. To develop maximum independence, bed rails, ropes, or overhead devices should be avoided, if possible. In addition, the patient should achieve independent rolling when covered by sheets and blankets.

Mat activities. To begin training and to facilitate rolling, several approaches can be used.

a. Flexion of the head and neck with rotation may be used to assist movement from supine to prone positions.

b. Extension of the head and neck with rotation may be used to assist movement from prone to supine positions.

c. Bilateral, symmetrical upper extremity rocking with outstretched arms produces a pendular motion when moving from supine to prone positions. The patient rhythmically rocks the outstretched arms and head from side to side and then forcefully "tosses" them to the side to which the patient is rolling. The trunk and hips will follow (Fig. 26–12). Use of wrist cuff weights (2 to 3 lbs) may be used initially to increase kinesthetic awareness and momentum.

d. Crossing the ankles will also facilitate rolling (see Figure 26–12). The therapist crosses the patient's ankles such that the upper limb is toward the direction of the roll (e.g., the right ankle would be crossed over the left when rolling toward the left). Rolling can be promoted further by flexing the hip and knee of the top lower extremity and placing it over the opposite limb (e.g., the hip and knee of the right lower extremity would be flexed and placed over the left when rolling toward the left).

e. In moving from the supine position to the prone position, pillows may be placed under one side of the pelvis (or scapula, if needed) to create initial rotation in the direction of the roll. The activity can be started with two pillows, progress to one, and then to rolling without the use of pillows. If difficulty is encountered in initiating the roll, the activity can be started from sidelying. To facilitate movement from prone to supine positions, pillows may be placed under one side of the chest and/or pelvis. Again, the number and height of pillows should be reduced gradually and eventually eliminated.

f. Several proprioceptive neuromuscular facilitation (PNF) patterns are useful during early rolling activities. The upper extremity patterns of D_1 flexion, D_2 extension, and reverse chop will facilitate *rolling toward the prone position*. The upper extremity lifting pattern will facilitate *rolling toward the supine position* from sidelying.[103–105]

2. Prone-on-elbows position. The functional implications of this activity are improved bed mobility and preparation for assuming the quadruped and sitting positions.

This component of the mat progression facilitates head and neck control as well as proximal stability of the glenohumeral and scapular musculature via cocontraction. Scapular strengthening exercises also can be accomplished in this position. At first, the patient may require the therapist's assistance in assuming the prone-on-elbows position. To assume this position independently (from prone), the patient places the elbows close to the trunk and the hands near the shoulders and pushes the elbows down into the mat while lifting the head and upper trunk. From this position, one of two maneuvers can be used: (a) weight shifting from elbow to elbow will allow progressive movement of the elbows forward until they are under the shoulders; (b) or body weight can be shifted posteriorly until the elbows are under the shoulders.[33]

Mat Activities. The prone-on-elbows position must be used with caution, particularly following thoracic and lumbar injuries. Some patients may find it difficult to tolerate the increased lordotic curve imposed by this position.

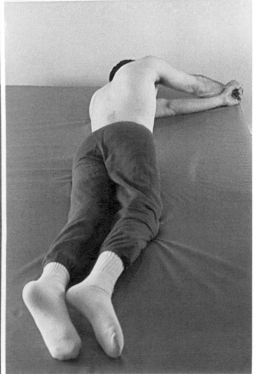

Figure 26–12. Rolling from supine position to prone position facilitated by upper extremity momentum and crossing of the ankles.

a. Weight bearing in the prone-on-elbows position will improve stability through increased joint approximation. Weight shifting assists with the development of controlled mobility and is usually easiest in a lateral direction with a progression to anterior or posterior movements.

b. Rhythmic stabilization may be used to increase stability of the head, neck, and scapula.[103]

c. Manually applied approximation can be used to facilitate tonic holding of proximal musculature.

d. Unilateral weight bearing onto one elbow (static-dynamic activity) can be achieved in the prone-on-elbows position by having the patient lift one arm. This further facilitates cocontraction in the weight-bearing limb.

e. Movement within this posture can be achieved by an on-elbows forward, backward, and side-to-side progression.

f. Strengthening of the serratus anterior and other scapular muscles can be completed in the prone-on-elbows position. This is accomplished by having the patient push the elbows down into the mat and tuck the chin while lifting and rounding out the shoulders and upper thorax (Fig. 26–13). This is similar to the "cat/camel" maneuver used in the quadruped position. The patient lowers the chin and upper chest to the mat again by allowing the scapula to adduct.

3. Prone-on-hands (with paraplegia). The functional carry-over of this position (Fig. 26–14) includes development of the initial hyperextension of the hips and low back for patients who will require this postural alignment during ambulation, and standing from a wheelchair or rising from the floor with crutches and bilateral knee-ankle-foot orthoses (KAFOs).

Some patients may have difficulty assuming this posi-

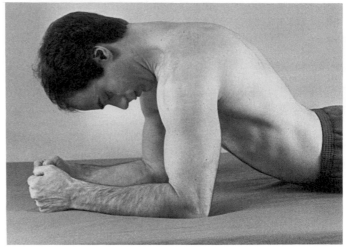

Figure 26–13. Prone-on-elbows position can be used for strengthening the serratus anterior and other scapular muscles.

tion initially, and a gradual acclimation may be indicated (strong pectoralis major and deltoid muscles are required to accomplish this activity). A gradual progression can be made by supporting the patient's upper trunk with a wide, firm bolster or a sling suspension system. As the patient gradually becomes accustomed to the new position, the height of the support can be increased and eventually removed.

Hand placement for the prone-on-hands position is similar to a standard push-up position except that the hands are slightly more lateral and the arms are externally rotated.

Figure 26–14. Prone-on-hands position.

Mat activities. It should be noted that this position will not be appropriate for every patient with paraplegia owing to the excessive lordosis required to assume and to maintain the position.

    a. Lateral weight shifting with weight transfer between hands will increase joint approximation.

    b. Additional approximation force can be applied through manual contacts to facilitate tonic holding of proximal musculature further.

    c. Scapular depression and prone push-ups may be utilized as strengthening exercises.

4. Supine-on-elbows position. The purpose of this activity is to assist with bed mobility and to prepare the patient to assume a long sitting position (Fig. 26–15). There are several approaches to assuming the supine-on-elbows position.[33] If abdominal muscles are present, the patient may have sufficient strength to achieve the position by pushing the elbows into the mat and lifting into the position.

A more common technique is for the patient to "wedge" the hands under the hips or to hook the thumbs into pants pockets or belt loops. By contracting the biceps and/or wrist extensors, the patient can pull up partially into the posture. By shifting weight from side to side, the elbows can then be positioned under the shoulders.

Finally, some patients may find it easiest to assume this position from sidelying. The lower elbow is first positioned and pushed into the mat. The patient then rolls toward the supine position and quickly extends the upper arm, landing on the elbow as close to the shoulder as possible. By weight shifting, placement of the elbows can then be adjusted.

Mat activities. Much of the inherent benefit of this activity is achieved in learning to assume the posture. In addition to its direct functional significance, this activity is also an important strengthening exercise for shoulder extensors and scapular adductors.

    a. Lateral weight shifting can be practiced in this position.

    b. Side-to-side movement in this posture will enhance the patient's ability to align the trunk over the lower extremities when in bed or in preparation for positional changes.

5. Pull-ups (with quadriplegia). The purpose of this activity is to strengthen the biceps and shoulder flexors in preparation for wheelchair propulsion.

Mat activity. The patient is positioned in the supine position. The therapist assumes the high-kneeling position with one lower extremity on each side of the patient's hips. The therapist grasps the patient's supinated forearms just above the wrists. The patient pulls to sitting and then lowers back to the mat.

6. Sitting. Both long (Fig. 26–16) and short (Fig. 26–17) sitting positions are essential for many activities of daily living, such as dressing, self-ROM, transfers, and wheelchair mobility. Good sitting balance and the ability to move within this posture are also critical prerequisite skills to standing.

Patients with quadriplegia require at least 100 degrees of straight-leg ROM to assume a long sitting position. Without this available motion, hamstring tension will cause a posterior tilting of the pelvis. This will result in the patient's sitting on the sacrum with resultant stretching of the lower-back musculature.

It is important to note that sitting posture will vary considerably with lesion level. Patients with low thoracic lesions can be expected to sit with a relatively erect trunk. Individuals with low cervical and high thoracic lesions will maintain sitting balance by forward head displacement and trunk flexion. Patients with high cervical lesions will demonstrate poor sitting posture.

For patients with triceps and abdominal musculature (paraplegia), the sitting position can generally be assumed without difficulty. Patients with quadriplegia initially are taught to assume a stable sitting position by placing the shoulders in hyperextension and external rotation, the elbows and wrists in extension with the fingers flexed (flexion of the fingers is particularly important to avoid overstretching, which will interfere with a func-

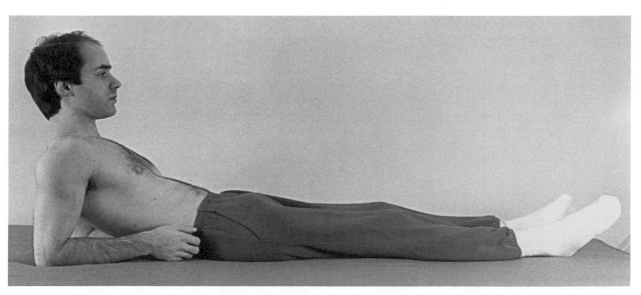

Figure 26–15. Supine-on-elbows position.

Figure 26–16. Individual with a T-4 complete paraplegia in long sitting position without upper extremity support.

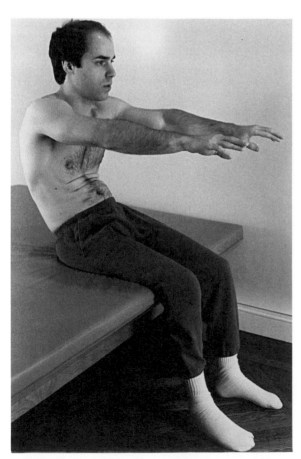

Figure 26–17. Sitting without upper extremity support.

tional tenodesis grasp). Weight is then borne on the base of the hand. Patients without triceps function can be taught to lock the elbows mechanically, using shoulder girdle musculature. The patient first tosses the shoulder into hyperextension with the forearm supinated. Once the base of the hand makes contact with the mat, the shoulder is quickly elevated to extend the elbow followed by rapid shoulder depression to maintain elbow extension. This technique will stabilize the arm in hyperextension and external rotation.

There are two basic approaches to instructing the patient to assume the sitting position.[33] Starting in the supine-on-elbows position, the patient is instructed to shift weight from side to side. Once sufficient momentum is achieved, the patient tosses one arm behind and shifts the weight onto that extended arm. The opposite arm is then tossed behind into an extended position. From this point, the patient "walks" the arms forward until a stable sitting position is achieved.

From a prone-on-elbows position the patient creeps sideward, using the elbows and forearms. This will position the trunk in flexion and allow the patient to reach the lower extremities. The patient then hooks the uppermost forearm under the knee and pulls forward with this arm, using the biceps, and then quickly tosses the opposite extremity behind. The upper extremity originally placed under the knee is then also thrown into an extended position. The patient then "walks" forward until a stable sitting position is achieved.

Numerous patients have developed their own variations on these basic techniques. Often patient-devised approaches may be the most appropriate for the individual and should be assessed in terms of safety, function, and energy expenditure. In addition, during the early stages of rehabilitation, adaptive equipment such as an overhead trapeze, rope ladders, or graduated loops hanging from over-bed frames may be used to facilitate movement into sitting.

Mat activities. Several suggestions follow which can be utilized in a sitting position.

a. Initial activities will focus on practice in maintaining the position. During early sitting, a mirror may provide important visual feedback.

b. Manual approximation force may be used at the shoulders to promote cocontraction.

c. A variety of PNF techniques may be used. Specifically, alternating isometrics and rhythmic stabilization are important in promoting early stability in this posture.[104]

d. Balancing activities may be practiced in sitting. The base of support provided by the upper extremities can be gradually decreased, progressed to single limb support, or, with some patients, eliminated (see Figures 26–16 and 26–17). The patient's balance can be challenged progressively in each position. Activities such as ball throwing or tapping a balloon between the patient and therapist (with or without cuff weights) also may be incorporated into a progression of sitting activities.

e. Sitting push-ups are an important preliminary activity for transfers and ambulation. For quadriplegia, the patient is positioned with the shoulders in extension, the elbows locked, and the hands posterior to the hips. The patient leans forward and depresses the shoulders to clear the buttocks. Initially this activity may be facilitated by manual assistance from the therapist and/or by use of sandbags or small, hard bolsters to provide a firmer weight-bearing surface for the upper extremities (Fig. 26–18). For paraplegia, a progression can be achieved by initiating the activity with weight bearing on the base of the hands placed directly on the mat and then using push-up blocks with graded increments in height.

f. Movement within this posture can be accomplished by using a sitting push-up in combination with momentum created by movement of the head and upper body. This momentum is created by throwing the head and shoulders forcefully in the direction opposite to the desired direction of motion. For example, while performing a sitting push-up on the mat, simultaneous rapid and forceful extension of the head and shoulders will move the lower extremities forward; movement in a posterior direction can be achieved by use of a sitting push-up with simultaneous rapid and forceful flexion of the head and trunk. This same progression of movement is used with the swing-to and swing-through gait patterns. Early mobility activities in sitting should emphasize adequate clearance of the buttock for skin protection.

7. Quadruped position (in paraplegia). The functional implication of this all-fours position is its importance as a lead-up activity to ambulation. It is the first position in the mat sequence that allows weight bearing through the hips and is useful for facilitating initial control of the available musculature of the lower trunk and hips.

Generally the patient is instructed to assume a quadruped position from the prone-on-elbows position. From this position the patient can "walk" backward on elbows, progressing to weight bearing on hands, one at a time. Forceful flexion of the head, neck, and upper trunk while pushing into the mat with the elbows or hands will assist with elevating the pelvis. The patient continues to "walk" backward until the hips are positioned over the knees.

A second technique is to assume the quadruped posture from long sitting. In this approach the patient rotates the trunk to allow weight bearing on the hands

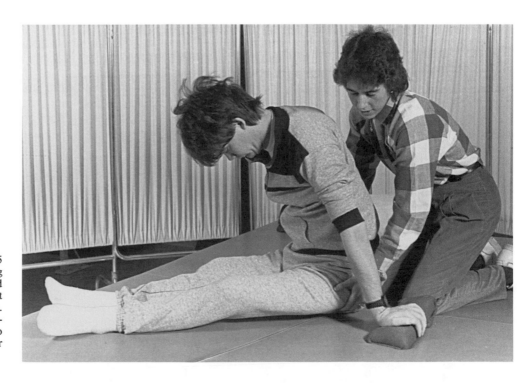

Figure 26–18. Individual with a C-5 incomplete quadriplegia in long sitting position. Pushups are initially facilitated by manual assistance from the therapist with use of sandbags for weight bearing. Note that hand placement maintains finger flexion during wrist extension to avoid stretching of the long finger flexors.

with the elbows extended. From this sidesitting position the patient then moves into the quadruped position by a combination of upper extremity and available trunk strength and momentum from the head and shoulders (moving opposite the direction of the hips).

Mat activities. Several suggested activities follow which can be utilized in the quadruped position.

    a. Initial activities will involve practice in maintaining the position; rhythmic stabilization can be used to facilitate cocontraction.

    b. Manual application of approximation force also can be used to facilitate cocontraction.

    c. Weight shifting can be practiced in a forward, backward, and side-to-side direction.

    d. Rocking through increments of range (forward, backward, side to side, and diagonally) will promote development of equilibrium responses.[103,104]

    e. Alternately freeing one upper extremity from a weight-bearing position may be used in the quadruped position. This will provide greater joint approximation forces on the supporting extremity and increase tonic holding of the available postural muscles (e.g., moving the dynamic limb in a diagonal pattern).

    f. Movement within the quadruped position (creeping) has important implications for ambulation. Creeping can be used to improve strength (resisted forward progression), to facilitate dynamic balance reactions, and to improve coordination and timing.

8. Kneeling (in paraplegia). This position is particularly important for establishing functional patterns of trunk and pelvic control and for further promoting upright balance control. It is an important lead-up activity to ambulation using crutches and bilateral knee-ankle orthosis.

It is usually easiest to assist the patient into the kneeling position from the quadruped position. From the quadruped position, the patient moves or "walks" the hands backward until the knees further flex and the pelvis drops toward the heels. The patient will be "sitting" on the heels. From this position the patient may be assisted to kneeling by using the upper extremities to climb stall bars while the therapist guides the pelvis. Another method is for the therapist to assume a heel-sitting position directly in front of the patient. The patient's upper extremities are supported on the therapist's shoulders while the therapist manually guides the pelvis. In time, the patient will be taught to assume a kneeling position using mat crutches (Figure 26–19).

Mat activities. Several suggested activities follow which can be utilized during kneeling.

    a. Initial activities will concentrate on maintaining the position using available musculature and postural alignment (hips fully extended with the pelvis slightly anterior to the knees).

    b. The patient's balance may be challenged in this position. Balancing activities may be progressed from support with both upper extremities to support from only one.

    c. A variety of mat crutch activities can be used in the kneeling position; examples include weight shifting anteriorly, posteriorly, and laterally, with emphasis on lower trunk and pelvic control; placing the crutches for-

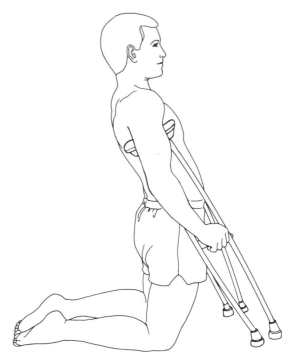

Figure 26–19. Kneeling position with use of mat crutches.

ward, backward, and to the side with weight shifts in each direction; alternately raising one crutch at a time and returning it to the mat; hip hiking; instruction in gait pattern and forward progression using crutches.

Transfers

Transfer training is generally initiated once the patient has achieved adequate sitting balance. It is a necessary prerequisite skill to many other functional activities, such as tub transfers, ambulation, and driving.

Training is usually initiated on a firm mat surface and progresses to alternate surfaces such as a bed, toilet, bathtub, car, chair to floor (and reverse), and so forth. The technique most frequently used by patients with spinal cord injury is some variation of a sliding transfer (with or without the use of a sliding board) (Fig. 26–20). Some experimentation and problem solving between the patient and therapist is generally required to determine the most efficient and safest method for an individual patient.

As with all functional skills, the patient is instructed in the component parts of the activity (e.g., locking the brakes, removing the armrests, placing the sliding board) before the entire sequence is attempted.

Wheelchair Prescription and Management

Most patients with spinal cord injuries will use a wheelchair as the primary means of mobility. Even the patient with paraplegia who has mastered ambulation with crutches and orthoses will choose to use a wheelchair on many occasions inasmuch as it provides a lower energy expenditure and greater speed and safety.

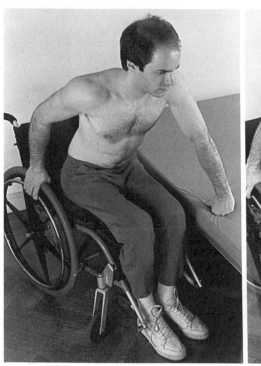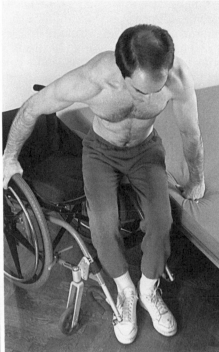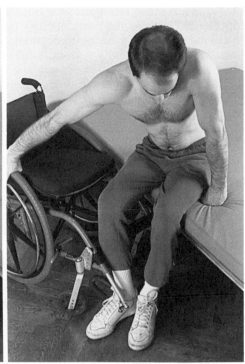

Figure 26–20. Individual with a T-4 complete paraplegia transferring from wheelchair to mat without use of a sliding board.

Prescription. Because most patients will be using a wheelchair extensively, it should be custom ordered for each individual. A wheelchair prescription will vary according to the level and extent of injury. More specific information is presented in chapter 28; however, some general considerations follow:

1. Seat depth should be as close as possible to 1 inch (2.5 cm) back from the popliteal space to allow an even weight distribution on the thighs and to prevent excessive pressure on the ischial tuberosities.

2. Floor-to-seat height is important. A seat cushion will be required. The type and dimensions of the cushion must be known so that seat height can be measured accurately, allowing adequate (2 inches [5.1cm]) clearance from the floor to the foot pedals and provide 90 degree angles at the knees.

3. Back height is also a consideration. If the patient will not be pushing the wheelchair, a high back may be desired for added comfort and stability. A patient with quadriplegia who will be pushing the wheelchair requires a back height that is below the inferior angle of the scapula, so that the axilla is free of the handles during functional activities. Most patients with paraplegia prefer a lower back height, especially if they have intact abdominal muscles.

4. Seat width is variable. Wheelchairs come in narrow (16 inch [40.6 cm]) or adult (18 inch [46 cm]) sizes. The patient should be fitted in the narrowest chair possible as long as there is at least a hand's width between the hips and the sides of the chair. The patient's previous weight should be considered, especially if there has been a significant loss since the initial injury and potential exists to regain the weight. If orthoses are worn, they must also be included in the consideration of width.

5. Patients with lower extremity spasticity may require heel loops and/or toe loops on the footrests to keep the feet in place. Elevating footrests may be necessary if circulatory problems are present.

6. Removable armrests and detachable swing-away legrests should be considered standard components on most wheelchairs used by patients with SCI. On some chairs (especially the newer models with tubular designs), the legrests do not detach. The suitability of these legrests must be considered with respect to the transfer capabilities and techniques used by the individual patient.

7. Additional wheelchair accessories may be required to meet specific patient needs. Several features that warrant consideration include enlarged release mechanisms on the legrests, a friction surface on the handrims (rubber tubing wrapped around the handrim is often effective), brake extensions, antitipping devices, and grade-aids (which decrease backward movement of the chair while ascending inclined surfaces).

8. Electric wheelchairs are indicated for all patients with C-4 lesions and above. Many patients with C-5 level lesions also elect to use electric wheelchairs, particularly for long-distance travel. Controls are usually either joystick or puff-and-sip types. Hydraulic reclining units are available to allow patients with quadriplegia or high thoracic lesions to manage independent reclining and pressure relief.

9. Some patients may require more than one wheelchair. Many standard lightweight chairs currently available are suitable for sport and recreational activities. However, depending on the interests of the patient, a second chair specifically designed for a particular sport may be required (e.g., racing chairs).

Management. The patient should be taught how to operate all the specific parts of the wheelchair. Management of the brakes, arms, and pedals is crucial for all transfer activities. Many patients with limited hand function are able to propel the wheelchair by using the base of the hand against the handrim. Some patients require assistive devices to aid in propulsion. Vertical or horizontal handrim projections (Fig. 26–21) are useful for patients with poor hand function. The use of leather hand cuffs (or cycling gloves) will protect the skin and also will improve the patient's grip on the handrims.

Wheelchair mobility activities should begin on level surfaces (including doorways and elevators) and progress to outdoor, uneven surfaces. Patients with sufficient upper extremity strength and upper trunk control also should be instructed in "wheelies," which involve balancing on the back wheels of the chair with the casters off the floor. Wheelies are required for independent curb climbing. Many facilities utilize canvas straps secured to the ceiling to assist with teaching this technique. The distal end of each strap has a C-clamp, which attaches to the push handle of the wheelchair. This allows safe practice by eliminating the danger of a posterior fall.

The patient should be instructed in pressure relief techniques from a sitting position. Ten to 15 seconds of pressure relief (or tissue redistribution) for every 5 to 10 minutes of sitting should become part of the patient's daily routine. Although many patients will develop their own techniques, several common approaches to these activities include (1) wheelchair push-ups; (2) hooking an elbow or wrist around the push handle and leaning toward the opposite wheel (Fig. 26–22); and (3) hooking one elbow or wrist around the push handle and leaning forward (if triceps are available, hooking the elbow or wrist will be unnecessary).

Those patients who will be driving a car must learn how to fold the wheelchair and slide it in and out of the car as well as learn to drive with hand controls. Transfer techniques should be considered with respect to the type of car the patient will drive. Vans with self-contained lifting platforms are a great asset for patients with quadriplegia and can increase their functional independence significantly.

Ambulation for Patients with Paraplegia

After the patient has mastered bed, mat, and wheelchair activities, ambulation can be initiated. The goals of such training include (1) teaching functional ambulation, or (2) increasing physiologic standing tolerance. Most patients expect that they will become functional ambulators.

A number of factors will influence the success or failure in attaining this goal. Patients must possess adequate muscle strength, postural alignment, range of motion, and sufficient cardiovascular endurance to be considered a candidate for ambulation. Patients who become functional ambulators are those whose trunk muscles (abdominals and erector spinae) grade fair or better. This usually excludes patients with high thoracic lesions (T-2 to T-8) who lack the ability to stabilize the trunk and pelvis and, in addition, who demonstrate poor respiratory reserve. Patients with incomplete lesions who demonstrate some residual strength in one or both hip flexors and/or quadriceps are more likely to achieve success in ambulating functionally.[106]

Inasmuch as spinal bracing is too restrictive, heavy, and impractical for functional ambulation, adequate range of motion and postural alignment are crucial in achieving stability of the trunk. Full range of motion in hip extension is essential in attaining balance in the upright position. The patient learns to lean into the anterior ligaments of the hip in order to stabilize the trunk or

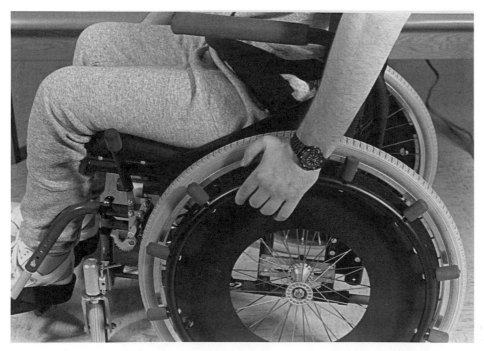

Figure 26–21. Handrim projections assist with forward propulsion of wheelchair for patients with limited grip.

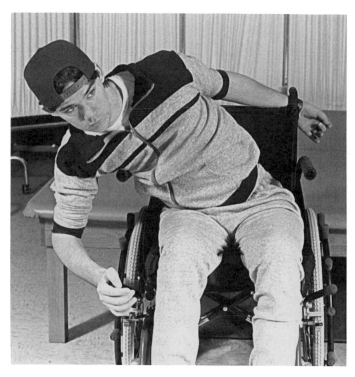

Figure 26–22. Lateral weight shift for pressure relief.

pelvis. The absence of knee flexion and plantarflexion contractures is also important in attaining upright standing balance.

Adequate cardiovascular endurance also is a criterion for functional ambulation. Because the energy cost of paraplegic ambulation is two to four times greater than normal walking, endurance becomes an important factor in determining success or failure as a functional ambulator.[107] Although some training effects can be attained with a program of endurance training for the upper extremities, the patient's age, body weight, history of cardiovascular disease or respiratory problems can restrict the amount of training that can be achieved. Other factors that may restrict ambulation include severe spasticity, loss of proprioception (particularly at the hips and knees), pain, and the presence of secondary complications such as decubitus ulcers, heterotopic bone formation at the hips, or deformity. In addition, the patient's motivation plays a key role in determining success or failure in ambulation. A highly motivated patient can learn to ambulate with limited residual function. However, these patients may eventually find that the energy cost of ambulation is too great.

Follow-up studies of long-term continuation of ambulation have not been extensive. Mikelberg and Reid[108] surveyed 60 individuals with SCI for whom orthoses had been prescribed between 1973 and 1977. They received a total of 35 replies. From this group, 60 percent used their wheelchairs as the primary means of mobility. Thirty-one percent completely discarded their orthoses. Those that did use their orthoses reserved them primarily for standing and exercise activities. Considering the high cost of orthoses and ambulatory training, the authors

suggest careful individual consideration of each patient before orthoses are prescribed. They also suggest delaying decisions about ambulation; training might reasonably occur during a later, follow-up readmission.

Orthotic Prescription and Ambulation Potential. The orthotic prescription varies according to the lesion level. Usually only ankle and/or knee control bracing is necessary. Patients with low thoracic lesions, T-9 to T-12, will require knee-ankle-foot-orthoses (KAFOs). Conventional KAFOs include bilateral metal uprights, posterior thigh and calf bands, an anterior knee flexion pad, drop-ring or bail locks, adjustable locked ankle joints, a heavy-duty stirrup, and a cushion heel. The ankle joints are usually locked in 5 to 10 degrees of dorsiflexion to assist hip extension at heel strike. Orthotic hip control is not necessary, because the braces allow the patient to balance weight over the feet with the hips hyperextended (Fig.26–23). The center of gravity is kept posterior to the hip joints but anterior to the ankles.

The Scott-Craig orthosis[109] is another type of KAFO that is frequently prescribed for patients with paraplegia (see chapter 27). These orthoses consist of standard double uprights, an offset knee joint providing improved biomechanical alignment, bail locks, a posterior thigh band, an anterior tibial band, adjustable ankle joint, and a sole plate which extends beyond the metatarsal heads.[110] A modification of this orthosis (Fig. 26–24) includes a plastic solid ankle section in place of the metal ankle joint and sole plate.[111] This change decreases overall weight of the orthosis, improves cosmesis, and eliminates the need for custom-made shoes.[111]

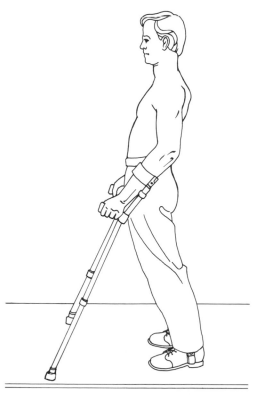

Figure 26–23. Standing alignment using bilateral knee-ankle-foot orthoses. Note that the upright position is maintained by "leaning" into the anterior Y ligaments, creating hyperextension at the hips.

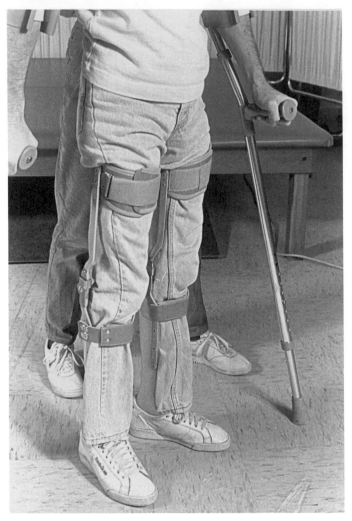

Figure 26-24. New England Regional Spinal Cord Injury Center (NERSCIC) orthosis (modification of the Craig-Scott orthosis). Note: Patient is wearing orthoses over clothing for purposes of demonstration.

An addition to the types of orthotic devices available to SCI patients are the reciprocating gait orthoses (see chapter 27). These orthoses have cable attachments which transmit forces from one lower extremity to the other. The dual cable system allows control of both flexion and extension. This cable functions to "coordinate" action between the two extremities during ambulation. As the advancing leg is unloaded, it is assisted into flexion while the stance leg is simultaneously pushed into extension. Thus, the orthosis allows for unilateral leg advancement and a reciprocating gait pattern.[112]

Pelvic bands and spinal attachments are rarely prescribed. These attachments severely restrict dressing activities, movement from sitting to standing, and ambulation by reducing trunk and pelvis flexibility and by adding extra weight (often as much as 4 lb). Furthermore, the use of these components makes gait slow, laborious, and usually nonfunctional. Patients who would require these attachments (T-2 to T-8 lesions) are usually not candidates for orthotic prescription. Instead, these

patients can achieve physiologic standing with the use of posterior splints or a tilt table.

Ankle-foot-orthoses (AFOs) are often appropriate for lower level lesions (e.g., L-3 and below). Either a conventional metal-upright or plastic AFO may be indicated.

Patients with lesions of L-3 and below often demonstrate a maximus-medius gait pattern. The absence of gluteal muscles and hamstrings result in a sharp posterior movement of the trunk at heel strike. Lateral trunk flexion also will be noted at midstance. Crutches or canes are typically prescribed to improve the patient's gait pattern.

Functional Electrical Stimulation (FES). Electrical stimulation has been used with some frequency to enhance both standing and ambulatory activities with SCI patients.[113-115] It has also been used with cycle ergometry to improve endurance. The gait patterns achieved have been unrefined and allow for only short-distance ambulation. Both surface and implanted electrodes have been used. A major disadvantage of this technique is the muscle fatigue that develops secondary to continuous stimulation.

Currently this work is largely confined to clinical research settings. However, electrical stimulation may hold future potential for functional, cost-effective ambulation for some SCI patients.

Preparation for Ambulation. A swing-through type of gait pattern (Fig. 26-25) should be the ultimate goal for functional ambulators with KAFOs. In teaching this pattern, it is important to stress a smooth, even cadence. Crutches should be placed equidistant from both toes at toe-off and the heels at heel strike. It is important to establish an overall rhythm, inasmuch as improved timing will result in improved energy efficiency and cosmesis. Relevant training activities include those described below.

1. Putting on and removing orthoses. The patient is first taught the correct way to apply the orthoses. The entire procedure is usually done in the supine or sitting position. The patient must be cautioned to check constantly for pressure areas, particularly after brace removal.

2. Sit-to-stand activities. These activities should be practiced in the parallel bars using a wheelchair. The patient must learn to slide to the edge of the chair and to lock and to unlock the orthoses. Initially, the patient is taught to pull to standing using the parallel bars (a progression is made to using the wheelchair armrests to push to standing). Once in an upright position, the patient pushes down on the hands and tilts the pelvis forward in front of the shoulders. Return to sitting is a reversal of this procedure.

3. Trunk balancing. The patient learns to balance the trunk in the hips-extended position, keeping the weight balanced over the feet, learning to remove first one hand then both from the support. Placing hands forward and backward behind the hips while maintaining a stable position should also be practiced. Chapter 15 should be consulted for a more detailed description of suggestions for early parallel bar activities.

4. Push-ups. This includes lifting the body off the floor using shoulder depression, ducking the head to gain added height, and controlled lowering of the body.

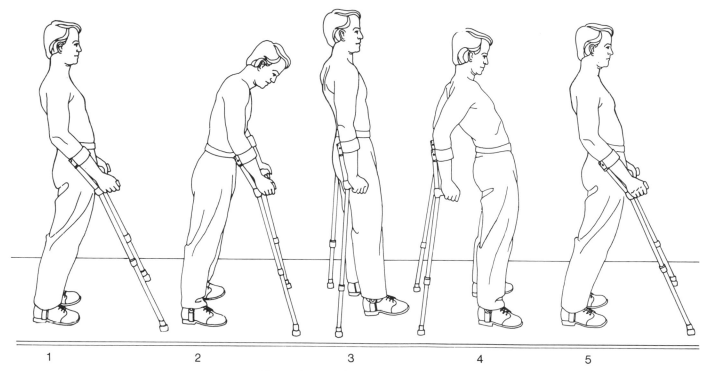

Figure 26–25. Swing-through gait pattern.

5. Turning around. This involves lifting and lowering the body in 90-degree turns and changing hands from one bar to another.

6. Jackknifing. This entails controlling the pelvic position using upper extremity support and positioning the head and shoulders forward ahead of the pelvis. This is an unstable position, and the patient must be taught recovery in order to overcome and/or to prevent this from happening during ambulation.

7. Ambulation activities in the parallel bars. Four-point and two-point gaits require hip flexion or hip hiking. Patients with high lesions may learn this movement using the secondary hip hikers (internal and external obliques and latissimus dorsi). Those with low lesions will have the quadratus lumborum intact. Trunk rotation on the swing side or lateral flexion toward the stance side will facilitate forward progression.

Swing-to and swing-through gaits require varying degrees of body elevation and push-off. These gait patterns involve some jackknifing and recovery. At push-off, the head ducks to gain increased height, and at foot contact the head and back arch to help regain stability.

Crutch Training. Forearm crutches are most often selected for patients with paraplegia. These crutches provide several advantages. They are lightweight; they allow use of the hand without the crutch becoming disengaged; they fit more easily into an automobile; and, most important, they improve function in ambulation and stair climbing by allowing unrestricted movement at the shoulders.

1. Standing from the wheelchair with crutches. To begin this activity the patient first places the crutches behind the chair, leaning against the push handle(s). To assume a standing position with crutches, the patient moves forward in the chair, locks both knee joints, crosses one leg over the other (Fig. 26–26), and then rotates the trunk and pelvis. Hand placements on the armrest are reversed and the patient pushes to standing by pivoting around to face the chair. The reverse of this technique is used to return to the chair.

2. Crutch balancing. Initially, the patient must learn to become secure in the tripod stance. This is best achieved by first balancing in the parallel bars or against a wall. Weight shifting, alternating lifting one crutch off the floor and jackknifing should be practiced.

3. Ambulation activities. Four-point, two-point, swing-to, and swing-through gaits should be practiced. They demonstrate a progression from a slow, steady gait pattern to a faster, more unstable one. A gradual emphasis should be placed on improved timing and speed.

4. Travel activities. The patient should become proficient in walking sideward and backward, in turning, and in walking through doorways. Changes in floor surface (e.g., carpeting, tile) and terrain (sidewalks and grass) may present problems for the patient if they are not introduced during training. All patients will require proficiency in ambulation on level surfaces in order to master these more difficult activities successfully.

5. Elevation activities. The easiest pattern of ascent or descent of stairs is usually upstairs backward (Fig. 26–27) and downstairs forward (Fig. 26–28). Most patients will use a handrail, for it is only the very exceptional patient who can manage stairs without one. Once some degree of proficiency is attained, going upstairs forward and downstairs backward can be practiced as well. The use of graduated steps will help make the initial task of learning eas-

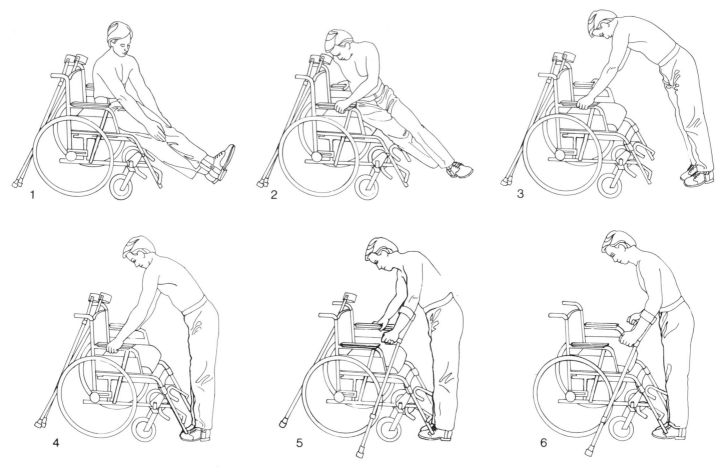

Figure 26–26. Standing from wheelchair using crutches and bilateral knee-ankle-foot orthoses. The reverse sequence is used to return to the chair.

ier. The therapist needs to guard and to support the patient adequately. The use of a properly fitting guarding belt is essential. Curbs should be attempted last, because this is usually the most difficult elevation activity. Using graduated platforms or curbs will assist the patient in mastery of this task. A four-point gait pattern, going up backward and down forward is the slower, more stable method. Swinging both legs up together takes considerable balance and is for the more advanced ambulator.

6. Falling. Controlled falling and getting up from the floor are important considerations for patients expected to become functional ambulators.

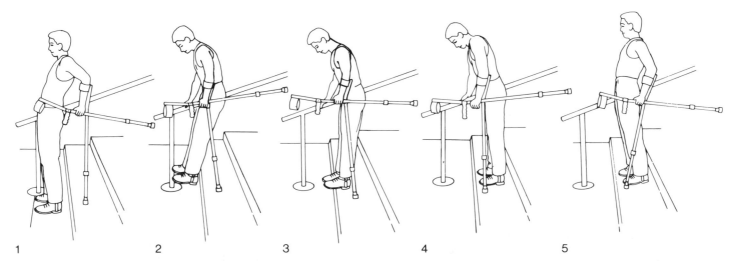

Figure 26–27. Ascending stairs backward. The crutch is placed on the step to which the patient is ascending. The head and trunk are forcefully flexed while depressing the shoulders and extending the elbows. This maneuver unweights the lower extremities and creates momentum for movement to the next higher step. Postural alignment is then regained.

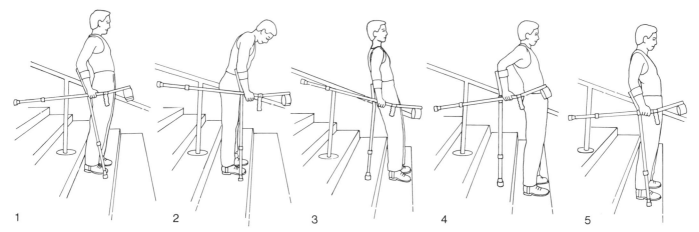

1   2   3   4   5

Figure 26–28. Descending stairs forward. To begin, the crutch remains on the step that the patient is leaving. Initial flexion of the head and trunk is immediately followed by forceful extension while depressing the shoulders and extending the elbows. This procedure unweights the lower extremities and creates momentum for movement to the next lower step. The crutch is then lowered and postural alignment regained.

LONG-RANGE PLANNING

An important aspect of long-range rehabilitation planning involves educating the patient in life-long management of the disability. This will focus on community reintegration and methods of maintaining the optimal state of health and function achieved during rehabilitation. Consideration must be given to multiple issues, including housing, nutrition, transportation, finances, maintaining functional skills and level of physical fitness, employment or further education, and methods for involvement in desired social or recreational activities. Each of these issues must be addressed early in the course of rehabilitation in consultation with the patient, the family, and appropriate team members. The patient also should be encouraged to contact and to explore the resources available through the local chapter of the National Spinal Cord Injury Association. Publications such as *Accent on Living, Paraplegia News, Sports'n Spokes,* and the National Spinal Cord Injury Association's *National Resource Directory* will provide the patient with current information on a variety of topics such as research related to SCI, legislative activities, conferences, housing, transportation, new adaptive equipment, and sporting and recreational activities. Resource addresses for these publications are included in the appendix to this chapter. Finally, a coordinated plan must be developed for long-term periodic rehabilitation follow-up visits.

SUMMARY

This chapter has presented the principal clinical features and secondary complications of traumatic SCI. Emphasis has been placed on physical therapy intervention during both the acute and subacute phases of rehabilitation. Anticipated goals and treatment considerations have been addressed. These general goals and treatment suggestions must be tailored to meet the needs of an individual patient. This will be achieved through a process of careful assessment with specific attention to length of time since onset, lesion level, method(s) of fracture stabilization, premorbid interests, psychosocial factors, and presence of secondary complications.

Management of the patient with SCI is a complex and challenging task in which continuity of care is critical to achieving the overall goals of rehabilitation. Frequent and open communication among team members, patient, and family is vital to maintaining an organized and highly individualized approach to both rehabilitation and reintegration of the patient into the community.

QUESTIONS FOR REVIEW

1. Identify the clinical features of Brown-Sequard, anterior, central, and posterior cord syndromes.
2. Define spinal shock.
3. Describe the clinical picture associated with spinal cord injury. Your description should address alterations that occur in each of the following areas:
   a. Motor function
   b. Sensory function
   c. Temperature control
   d. Respiratory function
   e. Muscle tone
   f. Bladder and bowel function
   g. Sexual function
4. What is autonomic dysreflexia? Describe the initiating stimuli and symptoms of this syndrome. What action would you take if a patient experienced an onset of symptoms during a physical therapy treatment?
5. What is heterotopic bone formation? Describe the early symptoms. Where does it most commonly develop following SCI?

6. Describe the clinical features of deep venous thrombosis. Why are patients with SCI at risk for development of this secondary complication?

7. Suggest a positioning program to prevent limitations in ROM at the shoulders for a patient with quadriplegia during the acute phase of management.

8. Identify three primary influences affecting prognosis following spinal cord injury.

9. Describe the major advantages of halo devices as compared with tongs for immobilizing cervical fractures.

10. What is included in a physical therapy assessment during the acute phase of management? How might some of the standard assessment techniques have to be modified?

11. What is meant by the term *selective stretching?*

12. Identify the primary goals of respiratory care during the acute phase of management. Suggest potential treatment activities to meet these goals.

13. What forms of strengthening exercises are appropriate during the acute phase? Why are bilateral upper extremity activities emphasized?

14. Outline sample mat progressions for two patients, one with a C-6 quadriplegia and one with a T-12 paraplegia. Assume that both patients have complete lesions. Describe the specific mat sequence and activities you would include. Identify the functional significance of each. What type of progressive strengthening activities would you suggest for each patient as an adjunct to the mat progression?

REFERENCES

1. Trieschmann, RB: Spinal Injuries: Psychological, Social and Vocational Adjustment. Pergamon Press, Elmsford, NY, 1980.
2. Young, JS and Northrup, NE: Statistical information pertaining to some of the most commonly asked questions about SCI (monograph). National Spinal Cord Injury Data Research Center, Phoenix, 1979.
3. Young, JS, et al: Spinal Cord Injury Statistics: Experience of the Regional Spinal Cord Injury Systems. Good Samaritan Medical Center, Phoenix, 1982.
4. Young, JS: Personal communication, June 30, 1986.
5. Bromley, I: Tetraplegia and Paraplegia: A Guide for Physiotherapists, ed 3. Churchill Livingstone, New York, 1985.
6. Michaelis, LS: International inquiry on neurological terminology and prognosis in paraplegia and tetraplegia. Paraplegia 7:1, 1969.
7. Coogler, CE: Clinical decision making among neurologic patients: Spinal cord injury. In Wolf, SL (ed): Clinical Decision Making in Physical Therapy. FA Davis, Philadelphia, 1985.
8. Rieser, TV, Mudiyam, R, and Waters, RL: Orthopedic evaluation of spinal cord injury and management of vertebral fractures. In Adkins, HV (ed): Spinal Cord Injury. Churchill Livingstone, New York, 1985.
9. Hardy, AG and Rossier, AB: Spinal Cord Injuries: Orthopedic and Neurologic Aspects. Publishing Science Group, Acton, MA, 1975.
10. Ruge, D: Neurologic evaluation. In Ruge, D (ed): Spinal Cord Injuries, Charles C Thomas, Springfield, IL, 1969, p 51.
11. Chusid, JG: Correlative Neuroanatomy and Functional Neurology, ed 19. Lange Medical Publications, Los Altos, CA, 1985.
12. Gilman, S and Winans, SS: Manter and Gatz's Essentials of Clinical Neuroanatomy and Neurophysiology, ed 6. FA Davis, Philadelphia, 1982.
13. Schneider, FJ: Traumatic spinal cord injury. In Umphred, DA (ed): Neurological Rehabilitation. CV Mosby, St. Louis, 1985, p. 314.
14. Bose, B, et al: Reanalysis of central cervical cord injury management, Neurosurgery 15:367, 1984.
15. Brodkey, JS, Miller, CF, and Harmody, RM: The syndrome of acute central cervical spinal cord injury revisited. Surg Neurol 14:251, 1980.
16. Raynor, RB and Koplik, B: Cervical cord trauma: The relationship between clinical syndromes and force of injury. Spine 10:193, 1985.
17. Comarr, AE: Sexual function in patients with spinal cord injury. In Pierce, DS and Nickel, VH (eds): The Total Care of Spinal Cord Injuries. Little, Brown & Co, Boston, 1977, p 171.
18. Bedbrook, GM: Examination. In Bedbrook, G (ed): The Care and Management of Spinal Cord Injuries. Springer-Verlag, New York, 1981, p 8.
19. Pierce, DS: Acute treatment of spinal cord injuries. In Pierce, DS and Nickel, VH (eds): The Total Care of Spinal Cord Injuries. Little, Brown & Co, Boston, 1977, p 1.

20. Rogers, LF: Fractures and dislocations of the spine. In Calenoff, L (ed): Radiology of Spinal Cord Injury. CV Mosby, St Louis, 1981, p 85.
21. Calenoff, L, et al: Multiple level spinal injuries: Importance of early recognition. Am J Roentgenol 130:665, 1978.
22. Donovan, WH and Bedbrook, G: Comprehensive management of spinal cord injury. Ciba Clin Symp 34(2), Ciba Pharmaceutical, 1982.
23. English, E: Mechanisms of cervical spine injuries. In Tator, CH (ed): Early Management of Acute Spinal Cord Injury. Raven Press, New York, p 25.
24. Holdsworth, F: Fractures, dislocations, and fracture-dislocations of the spine. J Bone Joint Surg 52-A:1534, 1970.
25. Guttman, L: Spinal shock and reflex behaviour in man. Paraplegia 8:100, 1970.
26. Stauffer, ES: Long-term management of traumatic quadriplegia. In Pierce, DS and Nickel, VH (eds): The Total Care of Spinal Cord Injuries. Little, Brown & Co, Boston, 1977, p 81.
27. Edibam, RC: Medical management. In Bedbrook, G (ed): The Care and Management of Spinal Cord Injuries. Springer-Verlag, New York, 1981, p 109.
28. Guyton, AC: Human Physiology and Mechanisms of Disease, ed 4. WB Saunders, Philadelphia, 1987.
29. Thomas, EL: Nursing care of the patient with spinal cord injury. In Pierce, DS and Nickel, VH (eds): The Total Care of Spinal Cord Injuries. Little, Brown & Co, Boston, 1977, p 249.
30. Alvarez, SE, Peterson, M, and Lunsford, BR: Respiratory treatment of the adult patient with spinal cord injury. Phys Ther 61:1737, 1981.
31. Romanes, GJ (ed): Cunningham's Textbook of Anatomy, ed 11. Oxford University Press, New York, 1972.
32. Moore, KL: Clinically Oriented Anatomy. Williams & Wilkins, Baltimore, 1980.
33. Nixon, V: Spinal Cord Injury: A Guide to Functional Outcomes in Physical Therapy Management. Aspen Systems Corporation, Rockville, MD, 1985.
34. Goss, CM: Gray's Anatomy of the Human Body. Lea & Febiger, Philadelphia, 1973.
35. Wetzel, J: Respiratory Evaluation and Treatment. In Adkins, HV: Spinal Cord Injury. Churchill Livingstone, New York, 1985, p 75.
36. Seidel, AC: Spinal cord injury. In Logigian, MK (ed): Adult Rehabilitation: A Team Approach for Therapists. Little, Brown & Co, Boston, 1982, p 325.
37. Rosen, JS: Rehabilitation process. In Calenoff, L (ed): Radiology of Spinal Cord Injury. CV Mosby, St Louis, 1981, p 309.
38. Cardenas, DD, Kelly, E, and Mayo, ME: Manual stimulation of reflex voiding after spinal cord injury. Arch Phys Med Rehabil 66:459, 1985.
39. Finkbeiner, AE, Bissada, NK, and Redman, JF: Urologic care of the patient with a spinal cord injury. J Arkansas Med Soc 74:30, 1978.

40. Pires, M and Kelly-Hayes, M: Collaborative nursing therapies for clients with neurological dysfunction. In Umphred, DA (ed): Neurological Rehabilitation. CV Mosby, St Louis, 1985, p 632.

41. Zejdlik, CM: Maintaining urinary function. In Zejdlik, CM (ed): Management of Spinal Cord Injury. Wadsworth Health Sciences Division, Monterey, CA, 1983, p 269.

42. Kiser, C and Herman, C: Nursing considerations: Skin care, bowel and bladder training, autonomic dysreflexia. In Adkins, HV (ed): Spinal Cord Injury. Churchill Livingstone, New York, 1985, p 155.

43. Comarr, AE and Vigue, M: Sexual counseling among male and female patients with spinal cord and/or cauda equina injury (part I). Am J Phys Med 57:107, 1978.

44. Miller, S, Szasz, G, and Anderson, L: Sexual health care clinician in an acute spinal cord injury unit. Arch Phys Med Rehabil 62:315, 1981.

45. Romano, MD and Lassiter, RE: Sexual counseling with the spinal-cord injured. Arch Phys Med Rehabil 53:568, 1972.

46. Eisenberg, MG and Rustad, LC: Sex education and counseling program on a spinal cord injury service. Arch Phys Med Rehabil 57:135, 1976.

47. Higgins, GE: Sexual response in spinal cord injured adults: A review of the literature. Arch Sex Behav 8:173, 1979.

48. Gott, LJ: Anatomy and physiology of male sexual response and fertility as related to spinal cord injury. In Sha'ked, A (ed): Human Sexuality and Rehabilitation Medicine: Sexual Functioning Following Spinal Cord Injury. Williams & Wilkins, Baltimore, 1981, p 67.

49. Hanak, M and Scott, A: Spinal Cord Injury: An Illustrated Guide for Health Care Professionals, Springer–Verlag, New York, 1983.

50. Geiger, RC: Neurophysiology of female sexual response in spinal cord injury. In Sha'ked, A (ed): Human Sexuality and Rehabilitation Medicine: Sexual Functioning Following Spinal Cord Injury. Williams & Wilkins, Baltimore, 1981, p 74.

51. Thiyagarajan, C and Silver, JR: Aetiology of pressure sores in patients with spinal cord injury. Br Med J 289:1487, 1984.

52. Richardson, RR and Meyer, PR: Prevalence and incidence of pressure sores in acute spinal cord injuries. Paraplegia 19:235, 1981.

53. Seymour, RJ and Lacefield, WE: Wheelchair cushion effect on pressure and skin temperature. Arch Phys Med Rehabil 66:103, 1985.

54. Guttman, L: Spinal Cord Injuries: Comprehensive Management and Research. Blackwell Scientific, London, 1973.

55. Constable, JD and Pierce, DS: Pressure sores. In Pierce, DS and Nickel, VH (eds): The Total Care of Spinal Cord Injuries. Little, Brown & Co, Boston, 1977, p 187.

56. Hendrix, RW: Soft tissue changes after spinal cord injury. In Calenoff, L (ed): Radiology of Spinal Cord Injury. CV Mosby, St Louis, 1981, p 438.

57. Lindan, R, et al: Incidence and clinical features of autonomic dysreflexia in patients with spinal cord injury. Paraplegia 18:285, 1980.

58. Rosen, JS: Autonomic dysreflexia. In Calenoff, L (ed): Radiology of Spinal Cord Injury, CV Mosby, St Louis, 1981, p 554.

59. Comarr, AE: Autonomic dysreflexia. In Pierce, DS and Nickel, VH (eds): The Total Care of Spinal Cord Injuries. Little, Brown & Co, Boston, 1977, p 181.

60. Yeo, JD: Recent research in spinal cord injuries. In Bedbrook, G (ed): The Care and Management of Spinal Cord Injuries. Springer-Verlag, New York, 1981, p 285.

61. McGarry, J, Woolsey, RM, and Thompson, CW: Autonomic hyperreflexia following passive stretching to the hip joint. Phys Ther 62:30, 1982.

62. Erickson, RP: Autonomic hyperreflexia: Pathophysiology and medical management. Arch Phys Med Rehabil 61:431, 1980.

63. Belson, P: Autonomic nervous system dysfunction in recent spinal cord injured patients: A physical therapist's perspective. In Eisenberg, MG and Falconer, JA (eds): Treatment of the Spinal Cord Injured: An Interdisciplinary Perspective. Charles C Thomas, Springfield, MA, 1978, p 34.

64. Wharton, GW: Heterotopic ossification. Clin Orthop 112:142, 1975.

65. Stover, SL, Hataway, CJ, and Zeiger, HE: Heterotopic ossification in spinal cord-injured patients. Arch Phys Med Rehabil 56:199, 1975.

66. Abramson, AS: Bone disturbances in injuries to the spinal cord and cauda equina (paraplegia): Their prevention by ambulation. J Bone Joint Surg 30-A:982, 1948.

67. Rossier, AB, et al: Current facts on para-osteo-arthropathy (POA). Paraplegia 11:36, 1973.

68. Silver, JR: Heterotopic ossification: A clinical study of its possible relationship to trauma. Paraplegia 7:220, 1969.

69. Damanski, M: Hetertopic ossification in paraplegia: A clinical study. J Bone Joint Surg 43-B:286, 1961.

70. Hardy, AG and Dickson, JW: Pathological ossification in traumatic paraplegia. J Bone Joint Surg 45-B:76, 1963.

71. Wharton, GW and Morgan, TH: Ankylosis in the paralyzed patient. J Bone Joint Surg 52-A:105, 1970.

72. Nicholas, JJ: Ectopic bone formation in patients with spinal cord injury. Arch Phys Med Rehabil 54:354, 1973.

73. Neiman, HL: Venography in acute spinal cord injury. In Calenoff, L (ed): Radiology of Spinal Cord Injury. CV Mosby, St Louis, 1981, p 298.

74. van Hove, E: Prevention of thrombophlebitis in spinal injury patients. Paraplegia 16:332, 1978.

75. Todd, JW: Deep venous thrombosis in acute spinal cord injury: A comparison of ^{125}I fibrinogen leg scanning, impedance plethysmography and venography. Paraplegia 14:50, 1976.

76. Brach, BB, et al: Venous thrombosis in acute spinal cord paralysis. J Trauma 17:289, 1977.

77. El Masri, WS and Silver, JR: Prophylactic anticoagulant therapy in patients with spinal cord injury. Paraplegia 19:334, 1981.

78. Nepomuceno, C, et al: Pain in patients with spinal cord injury. Arch Phys Med Rehabil 60:605, 1979.

79. Burke, DC: Pain in paraplegia. Paraplegia 10:297, 1973.

80. Waisbrod, H, Hansen, D, and Gerbershagen, HG: Chronic pain in paraplegics. Neurosurgery 15:933, 1984.

81. Davis, R and Lentini, R: Transcutaneous nerve stimulation for treatment of pain in patients with spinal cord injury. Surg Neurol 4:100, 1975.

82. Richardson, RR, Meyer, PR, and Cerullo, LJ: Transcutaneous electrical neurostimulation in musculoskeletal pain of acute spinal cord injuries. Spine 5:42, 1980.

83. Davis, R: Pain and suffering following spinal cord injury. Clin Orthop 112:76, 1975.

84. Bors, E: Phantom limbs of patients with spinal cord injury. Arch Neurol Psychiatry 66:610, 1951.

85. Scott, JA and Donovan, WH: The prevention of shoulder pain and contracture in the acute tetraplegic patient. Paraplegia 19:313, 1981.

86. Ohry, A, et al: Shoulder complications as a cause of delay in rehabilitation of spinal cord injured patients: Case reports and review of the literature. Paraplegia 16:310, 1978.

87. Claus-Walker, J, et al: Calcium excretion in quadriplegia. Arch Phys Med Rehabil 53:14, 1972.

88. Burr, RG: Urinary calculi composition in patients with spinal cord lesions. Arch Phys Med Rehabil 59:84, 1978.

89. Hancock, DA, Reed, GW, and Atkinson, PJ: Bone and soft tissue changes in paraplegic patients. Paraplegia 17:267, 1979.

90. Maynard, FM and Imai, K: Immobilization hypercalcemia in spinal cord injury. Arch Phys Med Rehabil 58:16, 1977.

91. Wilson, DR: Renal calculi: Diagnosis and medical management. Primary Care 5:41, 1978.

92. Bohlman, HH: Complications and pitfalls in the treatment of acute cervical spinal cord injuries. In Tator, CH (ed): Early Management of Acute Spinal Cord Injury. Raven Press, New York, 1982, p 373.

93. Tator, CH, et al: Halo devices for the treatment of acute cervical spinal cord injury. In Tator, CH (ed): Early Management of Acute Spinal Cord Injury. Raven Press, New York, 1982, p 231.

94. Edmonds, VE and Tator, CH: Coordination of a halo program for an acute spinal cord injury unit. In Tator, CH (ed): Early Management of Acute Spinal Cord Injury. Raven Press, New York, 1982, p 263.

95. Cerullo, LJ: Surgical stabilization of spinal cord injury: Section A: Cervical spine. In Callenoff, L (ed): Radiology of Spinal Cord Injury. CV Mosby, St Louis, 1982, p 202.

96. Meyer, PR: Surgical stabilization of spinal cord injury: Section B: Thoracic and lumbar spine. In Calenoff, L (ed): Radiology of Spinal Cord Injury. CV Mosby, St Louis, 1981, p 202.

97. Zejdlik, CM: Maintaining protective functions of the skin. In Zej-

dlik, CM (ed): Management of Spinal Cord Injury. Wadsworth Health Sciences Division, Monterey, CA, 1983, p 399.

98. Daniels, L and Worthingham, C: Muscle Testing: Techniques of Manual Examination, ed 5. WB Saunders, Philadelphia, 1986.

99. Norkin, CC and White, DJ: Measurement of Joint Motion: A Guide to Goniometry. FA Davis, Philadelphia, 1985.

100. Clough, P, et al: Guidelines for routine respiratory care of patients with spinal cord injury: A clinical report. Phys Ther 66:1395, 1986.

101. Trombly, CA: Spinal cord injury. In Trombly, CA (ed): Occupational Therapy for Physical Dysfunction, ed 2. Williams & Wilkins, Baltimore, 1983, p 385.

102. Van Steen, H: Treatment of a patient with a complete C1 quadriplegia. Phys Ther 55:35, 1975.

103. Sullivan, PE, Markos, PD, and Minor, MAD: An Integrated Approach to Therapeutic Exercise: Theory and Clinical Application. Reston Publishing, Reston, VA, 1982.

104. Voss, DE, Ionta, MK, and Myers, BJ: Proprioceptive Neuromuscular Facilitation: Patterns and Techniques, ed 3. Harper & Row, Philadelphia, 1985.

105. Voss, DE: Proprioceptive neuromuscular facilitation (NUSTEP Proceedings). Am J Phys Med 46:838, 1967.

106. Hussey, RW and Stauffer, ES: Spinal cord injury: Requirements for ambulation. Arch Phys Med Rehabil 54:544, 1973.

107. Corcoran, PJ: Energy expenditure during ambulation. In Downey, J and Darling, R (eds): Physiological Basis of Rehabilitation Medicine. WB Saunders, Philadelphia, 1971, p 185.

108. Mikelberg, R and Reid, S: Spinal cord lesions and lower extremity bracing: An overview and follow-up study. Paraplegia 19:379, 1981.

109. Scott, BA: Engineering principles and fabrication techniques for the Scott-Craig long leg brace for paraplegics. Orth Pros 25:14, 1971.

110. Huang, CT: Energy cost of ambulation in paraplegic patients using Craig-Scott braces. Arch Phys Med Rehabil 60:595, 1979.

111. Lobley, S, et al: Orthotic design from the New England Regional Spinal Cord Injury Center: Suggestion from the field. Phys Ther 65:492, 1985.

112. Durr-Fillauer Medical, Inc: LSU Reciprocating Gait Orthosis: A Pictoral Description and Application Manual. Durr-Fillauer Medical, Chattanooga, 1983.

113. Bajd, T, et al: Use of a two-channel functional electrical stimulator to stand paraplegic patients. Phys Ther 61:526, 1981.

114. Vodovnik, L, et al: Functional electrical stimulation for control of locomotor systems. CRC Crit Rev Bioeng 6:63, 1981.

115. Brindley, GS, Polkey, CE, and Rushton, DN: Electrical splinting of the knee in paraplegia. Paraplegia 16:428, 1978.

SUPPLEMENTAL READINGS

Bajd, T, et al: Electrical stimulation in treating spasticity resulting from spinal cord injury. Arch Phys Med Rehabil 66:515, 1985.

Bartlow, S: Driver's ed: A program for the patient with spinal cord injury. Clinical Management in Physical Therapy 3 (2):6, 1983.

Bedbrook, GM (ed): Lifetime Care of the Paraplegic Patient. Churchill Livingstone, New York, 1985.

Berczeller, PH and Bezkor, MF (eds): Medical Complications of Quadriplegia. Year Book Medical Publishers, Chicago, 1986.

Buchanan, LE and Nawoczenski, DA (eds): Spinal Cord Injury: Concepts and Management Approaches. Williams & Wilkins, Baltimore, 1987.

Collins, WF: A review of spinal cord injury. Br J Surg 71:974, 1984.

Corbet, B (ed): National Resource Directory: An Information Guide for Persons with Spinal Cord Injury and Other Physical Disabilities. National Spinal Cord Injury Association, 149 California Street, Newton, MA, 02158, 1985.

Crotti, FM, et al: Surgical indications and results in spinal injuries. J. Neurosurg Sci 28:185, 1984.

Curtis, KA: Physical therapist role satisfaction in the treatment of the spinal cord-injured person. Phys Ther 5:197, 1985.

Curtis, KA and Hall, KM: Spinal cord injury community follow-up: Role of the physical therapist. Phys Ther 66:1370, 1986.

DeVivo, MJ and Fine, PR: Spinal cord injury: Its short-term impact on marital status. Arch Phys Med Rehabil 66:501, 1985.

Donovan, WH and Dwyer, AP: An update on the early management of traumatic paraplegia (nonoperative and operative management). Clin Orthop 189:12, 1984.

Ford, JR and Duckworth, B: Physical Management for the Quadriplegic Patient, ed 2. FA Davis, Philadelphia, 1987.

Gerhart, KA: Increasing sensory and motor stimulation for the patient with quadriplegia. Phys Ther 59:1518, 1979.

Green, BC, Pratt, CC, and Grigsby, TE: Self-concept among persons with long-term spinal cord injury. Arch Phys Med Rehabil 65:751, 1984.

Hansebout, RR, Tanner, JA, and Romero-Sierra, C: Current status of spinal cord cooling in the treatment of acute spinal cord injury. Spine 9:508, 1984.

Jacobs, RR and Casey, MP: Surgical management of thoracolumbar spinal injuries. Clin Orthop 189:22, 1984.

McAdam, R and Natvig, H: Stair climbing and ability to work for paraplegics with complete lesions: A sixteen-year follow-up. Paraplegia 18:197, 1980.

Mollinger, LA, et al: Daily energy expenditure and basal metabolic rates of patients with spinal cord injury. Arch Phys Med Rehabil 66:420, 1985.

Millington, PJ, et al: Thermoplastic minerva body jacket—A practical alternative to current methods of cervical spine stabilization: A clinical report. Phys Ther 67:223, 1987.

Nacht, MB, Wolf, SL, and Coogler, CE: Use of electromyographic biofeedback during the acute phase of spinal cord injury. Phys Ther 62:290, 1982.

Nutt, RL: Halo traction and the halo vest for cervical fracture patients without neurological deficit. Clinical Management 4(6):6, 1984.

O'Daniel, WE and Hahn, HR: Follow-up usage of the Scott-Craig orthosis in paraplegia. Paraplegia 19:373, 1981.

Professional Staff Association: Interdisciplinary Model for Management of a Person with a Spinal Injury. Ranch Los Amigos Hospital, Downey, CA, 1981.

Rabin, BJ: The Sensuous Wheeler: Sexual Adjustment for the Spinal Cord Injured. Barry J Rabin, 2844 E. 3rd St, Suite 106, Long Beach, CA 90814, 1980.

Stanton, GM: A needs assessment of significant others following the patient's spinal cord injury. J Neurosurg Nurs 16:253, 1984.

Sugarman, B: Medical complications of spinal cord injury. Q J Med 54:3, 1985.

Sullivan, PE and Markos, PD: Clinical Procedures in Therapeutic Exercise. Appleton & Lange, Norwalk, CT, 1987.

Tator, CH: Relationships between spinal cord lesions and vertebral lesions. J Neurosurg Sci 28:157, 1984.

Wager, FC and Cheharzi, B: Neurological evaluation of cervical cord injuries. Spine 9:507, 1984.

Webb, DR, Fitzpatrick, JM, and O'Flynn, JD: A 15-year follow-up of 406 consecutive spinal cord injuries. Br J Urol 56:614, 1984.

White, AA and Panjabi, MM: The role of stabilization in the treatment of cervical spine injuries. Spine 9:512, 1984.

Woolsey, RM: Rehabilitation outcome following spinal cord injury. Arch Neurol 42:116, 1985.

Yeo, JD: First-aid management of spinal-cord injuries. Med J Aust 2:531, 1979.

GLOSSARY

Anterior cord syndrome: Incomplete spinal cord lesion with primary damage in anterior cord; loss of motor function, sense of pain and temperature; perseveration of proprioception, kinesthesia, and vibration below level of lesion.

Autonomic dysreflexia (or hyperreflexia): A pathologic autonomic reflex seen in patients with high-level spinal cord injuries. It is precipitated by a noxious stimulus below the level of the lesion and produces an acute onset of autonomic activity. It is considered an emergency situation; symptoms include hypertension, bradycardia, headache, and sweating.

Avulsion: Pulling or tearing of a piece of bone away from the main bone.

Brown-Sequard syndrome: Incomplete spinal cord lesion caused by hemisection of the cord; loss of motor function, proprioception, and kinesthesia on side of lesion; loss of sense of pain and temperature on opposite side.

Bulbocavernous reflex (positive): Pressure on the glans penis or glans clitoris elicits a contraction of the external anal sphincter.

Burst (explosion) fracture: A comminuted vertebral fracture associated with pressure along the long axis of the vertebral column; also associated with flexion injuries; bone fragments are displaced centripetally.

Cauda equina lesion: Damage to peripheral nerve roots below the first lumbar vertebra; some regeneration is possible.

Central cord syndrome: Incomplete spinal cord lesion producing greater neurologic involvement in upper extremities (cervical tracts more centrally located) than in the lower extremities (lumbar and sacral tracts more peripheral).

Complete lesion (SCI): No sensory or motor function below the level of lesion.

Compression fracture: A vertebral fracture resulting from pressure along the long axis of the vertebral column; closely associated with flexion injuries.

Contusion (SCI): Damage to the spinal cord produced by pressure from displaced bone and/or soft tissues or swelling within the spinal canal.

Crede maneuver: Technique for emptying urine from a flaccid bladder; pressure is placed between the umbilicus and symphysis pubis in an upward and downward direction.

Diaphoresis: Profuse sweating.

Dislocation: Displacement of a bone or vertebral body from its normal position.

Distraction: Traction force; separation of joint surfaces.

Dysesthesias (SCI): Bizarre, painful sensations experienced below the level of lesion following spinal cord injury; often described as burning, numbness, pins and needles, or tingling sensations.

Heterotopic bone formation: Abnormal bone growth in soft tissues; a potential secondary complication following spinal cord injury; occurs below the level of the lesion. SYN: ectopic bone.

Incomplete lesion (SCI): Some preservation of sensory or motor function below the level of lesion.

Intrathecal injection: Central (within the spinal canal) chemical injection that interrupts the reflex arc; used to decrease severe spasticity.

Maceration: Softening of a solid by exposure to water or other fluid; usually pertains to the skin.

Micturation: Voiding of urine. SYN: urination.

Myelotomy: Severance of nerve fibers of the spinal cord; used to reduce severe spasticity.

Myotomy: Surgical sectioning or release of a muscle; used to reduce spasticity.

Neurectomy: Partial or total excision or resection of a nerve; used to reduce severe spasticity.

Nocturia: Excessive urination during the night.

Osteoporosis: Decreased density or softening of bone.

Paraplegia: Refers to partial or complete paralysis of all or part of the trunk and both lower extremities from lesions of the thoracic or lumbar spinal cord or sacral roots.

Peripheral nerve block: Local chemical injection (e.g., phenol) used to block transmission of a motor nerve selectively; used to decrease spasticity.

Posterior cord syndrome: A rare incomplete lesion with primary damage to the posterior cord; preservation of motor function, sense of pain and light touch with loss of proprioception and epicritic sensations below the level of lesion.

Postural hypotension: A decrease in blood pressure that occurs when moving toward an upright posture. This occurs normally but may be severe following prolonged bedrest.

Pressure sore: Ulceration of soft tissue caused by unrelieved pressure and shearing forces. SYN: decubitus ulcer, bed sore.

Quadriplegia: Partial or complete paralysis of all four extremities and trunk, including the respiratory muscles from lesions of the cervical cord.

Rhizotomy: Division or severance of a nerve root; used to reduce severe spasticity.

Root escape: Preservation of peripheral nerve roots at the level of a spinal cord injury.

Sacral sparing: Incomplete lesion in which some sacral innervation remains intact; complete loss of motor function and sensation in other areas below the level of lesion.

Shearing: Application of a horizontal or parallel force relative to adjacent structures; opposite to force which is normally present; associated with fracture dislocations of the thoracolumbar region.

Spinal shock: Period immediately following injury to the spinal cord; characterized by absence of all reflex activity, flaccidity, and loss of sensation below the level of the lesion; generally subsides within 24 hours.

Subluxation: Incomplete or partial dislocation.

Teardrop fracture: Bursting type of fracture of cervical region; produces a characteristic anterior-inferior bone chip; fragment resembles a "teardrop" on x-ray film; associated with flexion and compression forces.

Tenotomy: Surgical section of a nerve; used to reduce spasticity.

APPENDIX A

Accent on Living (periodical)
PO Box 700
Bloomington, Illinois 61701

Paraplegia News and *Sports'n Spokes* (periodicals)
Paralyzed Veterans of America
5201 N 19th Ave, Suite 111
Phoenix, Arizona 85015

*National Resource Directory: An Information Guide for
Persons with Spinal Cord Injury and Other Physical
Disabilities*
National Spinal Cord Injury Association
149 California Street
Newton, Massachusetts 02158

Chapter 27

ORTHOTIC ASSESSMENT AND MANAGEMENT

JOAN E. EDELSTEIN

OBJECTIVES

1. Relate the major parts of the shoe to the requirements of individuals fitted with lower-limb orthoses.

2. Describe the main components of foot, ankle-foot, knee-ankle-foot, hip-knee-ankle-foot, and spinal orthoses.

3. Identify the principle features of ankle-foot and knee-ankle-foot orthoses assessed during the check-out procedure.

4. Recognize the therapist's role in management of individuals fitted with lower-limb and spinal orthoses.

INTRODUCTION

An *orthosis* is an external appliance worn to restrict or to enhance motion, or to reduce load on a body segment. The older term, brace, can be used synonymously. A *splint* connotes an orthosis intended for temporary use. The alternative terms, *walking irons* and **calipers,** give insight into orthotic materials and designs. An *orthotist* is the health care professional who designs, fabricates, and fits orthoses.

This chapter focuses on lower-limb orthotics and includes descriptions of the most frequently prescribed orthoses, together with programs for training patients in their use. Because individuals with spinal cord injury often require orthoses, the principal appliances for the trunk also will be included.

HISTORICAL PERSPECTIVE

Archeologic evidence indicates that orthoses have been used for fracture management at least since the fifth

Egyptian dynasty, 2750–2625 BC. Claudius Galen, a Greek physician residing in Rome in the second century, developed orthoses for scoliosis. The French barber-surgeon Ambroise Pare (1510–1590) published an orthotics text in 1575 which included fracture braces, weight-relieving orthoses, and shoe modifications. Fabricius Hildanus (1560–1624) invented a traction splint in Germany to correct contractures resulting from burns, a knee contracture appliance, and a clubfoot brace. Nicholas Andry declared in his *Orthopaedia,* which appeared in 1740, that orthoses were useful for preventing deformities.

The term *orthosis* appears to have been coined soon after World War II. The professional organization of prosthetists and orthotists became the American Orthotics and Prosthetics Association in 1960.

TERMINOLOGY

Current practice reflects the trend toward generic terminology, rather than the identification of orthoses by the names of their inventors or publicizers. Functional terms aid communication among those not familiar with local usage. Orthoses are named by the joints they encompass. Thus, foot orthoses (FO) are appliances applied to the foot and placed inside or outside the shoe, such as metatarsal pads, arch supports, and heel lifts. Ankle-foot orthoses (AFO) encompass the shoe and terminate at some point below the knee. The term replaces the older nomenclature, *short leg brace* and *below-knee orthosis*. The knee-ankle-foot orthosis (KAFO) extends from the shoe to the thigh; the term is preferable to *long leg brace* or *above-knee orthosis*. A hip-knee-ankle-foot orthosis (HKAFO) is a KAFO with an extension, such as a pelvic band, surrounding the pelvis. A trunk-hip-knee-ankle-foot orthosis (THKAFO) controls the thorax as well as the lower limb. A knee orthosis (KO) and a hip orthosis (HO) are other applications of the same terminology system.

TYPES OF ORTHOSES

Characteristics and functions of the principal FOs, AFOs, KAFOs, HKAFOs, and spinal orthoses, together with the important attributes of shoes, will be described. Although physical therapists also encounter KOs, HOs, and orthoses for special purposes, such as management of Legg Calve Perthes' disease, these braces are not included because they are used less often than the appliances that appear in this chapter.

Shoes

The shoe is the foundation for most lower-limb orthoses. Each part of the shoe contributes to the efficacy of orthotic management and offers many options for selection. Shoes transfer body weight to the ground and protect the wearer from the bearing surface and the weather. The ideal shoe should distribute bearing forces so as to preserve best function and appearance of the foot. For the individual with an orthopedic disorder, footwear serves two additional purposes: (1) reducing pressure on sensitive deformed structures by redistributing weight toward pain-free areas, and (2) serving as the foundation of the lower-limb orthosis. Unless the shoe is correctly fitted and appropriately modified, the alignment of the orthosis will not provide the desired pattern of weight bearing. The major parts of a shoe are the upper, sole, heel, and linings and reinforcements.

UPPER

The portion of the shoe over the dorsum of the foot is the *upper*. It consists of an anterior component called the *vamp* and a posterior section called the *quarters*. The vamp contains the lace stays which have the eyelets for shoe laces. For most orthotic purposes, a lace stay in the Blucher pattern is preferable; it is distinguished by the separation between the anterior margin of the lace stay and the vamp (Fig. 27–1). This style provides a wide inlet, making the shoe easy to don and easy to adjust. The alternative is the Bal, or Balmoral, lace stay, in

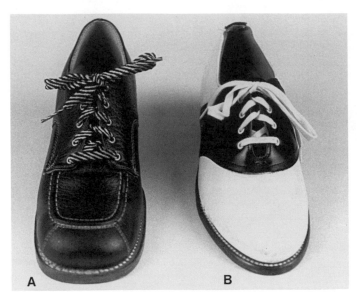

Figure 27–1. Low quarter shoes: (*A*) Blucher, (*B*) Bal (Balmoral).

which the lace stay is continuous with the vamp. This type of shoe cannot be opened as widely as the Blucher, and vamp stitching restricts the amount of tightening or loosening of the upper.

Quarter height is another consideration in shoe prescription. Low quarters are those which do not cover the malleoli. This type is generally considered more attractive and does not restrict ankle or intertarsal motion. If the patient will be wearing a plastic orthosis molded about the ankle, it should not be necessary to go to the additional expense of providing a high-quarter shoe for ankle support. A high-quarter shoe may be required to contain the foot fixed in equinus deformity or for mild ankle instability.

SOLE

The sole is the bottom portion of the shoe. For use with an orthosis with a riveted metal attachment to the shoe, the sole should consist of two parts—the outer and the inner sole, both made of leather. Between the two lies a metal reinforcement which receives the rivets. The outer sole should not contact the floor at the distal end; the slight rise of the sole is known as *toe spring*, which allows a rocker effect for push-off (Fig. 27–2). If a lift is added to the sole to compensate for leg length discrepancy, the lift should be beveled to achieve toe spring. A leather outer sole is necessary if external modifications are to be applied to the shoe, such as a **metatarsal bar** (Fig. 27–3).

If the shoe is to be worn with an orthosis that includes a foot plate, then a leather outer sole is not essential. A resilient rubber sole is effective with an insert orthosis; the sole absorbs shock and improves traction.

HEEL

The heel is the portion of the shoe adjacent to the outer sole, under the anatomic heel. It is generally composed of a rigid base and a rubber plantar surface. For most

Figure 27–2. Toe spring of anterior portion of sole.

orthotic purposes, a broad, low heel is suitable. For an adult, a heel 1 inch or lower tilts the center of gravity slightly forward to aid transition through stance phase but does not disturb knee and hip alignment significantly. A higher heel causes the ankle to exceed its normal plantarflexion range and forces the tibia forward. The wearer compensates either by retaining slight knee and hip flexion or by extending the knee and exaggerating lumbar lordosis. High heels transmit more stress to the metatarsals. A heel lift is indicated for patients with fixed pes equinus, leg shortening, or calcaneal pain.

LININGS AND REINFORCEMENT

For orthotic purposes, one should select a shoe that is lined to shield the foot from abrasion and reactions to the dyes and other substances used in the fabrication of the rest of the shoe. A cotton lining is hypoallergenic and takes moisture from the foot and permits it to evaporate. A leather lining eventually dries and cracks from accumulated perspiration. All linings should be perfectly smooth.

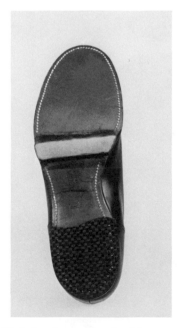

Figure 27–3. Leather outer sole with metatarsal bar.

Reinforcements located at strategic points preserve the shape of the shoe. *Toe boxing* strengthens the anterior vamp, serving to protect the toes against trauma. The shoe should have toe boxing high enough to clear all the toes; if the patient has hammer toes or other deformities, a pair of shoes with high toe boxing must be ordered. The **counter** reinforces the quarters in the region of the anatomic heel. The counter is made of stiff leather or other firm material and is placed between the lining and the outside of the shoe. It functions to increase stability and to maintain the shape of the posterior aspect of the shoe. The individual with pes planovalgus should have a shoe with a long medial counter which will resist the tendency of the foot to collapse medially. The *shank* is a rigid plate that reinforces the space between the anterior border of the heel and the widest part of the sole, called the *ball*. If an orthosis is to be riveted to the shoe, a corrugated steel shank is optimal. Because the reinforcements are not visible in the finished shoe, it is important that the physical therapist become familiar with details of construction of the shoes that are being considered for orthotic wearers.

Foot Orthoses

Foot orthoses may be affixed to the interior or exterior of the shoe or may consist of a separate **insert** worn inside the shoe. All these appliances improve function by relieving pain and improving foot balance. Pain may be lessened by transferring weight-bearing stresses to pressure-tolerant sites, and by protecting painful areas from contact with the shoe and with adjacent portions of the foot. Shoes also may be modified to equalize foot and leg lengths on both limbs. Comfort and mobility can be improved by correcting alignment of a flexible segment, or by accommodating fixed deformity by altering the contour of the shoe.

In many instances, a particular therapeutic aim can be achieved by various devices. Generally the closer the modification is to the foot, the more effective. An **insert** is placed over the surface of the inner sole inside the shoe and may be removable or stationary. Internal corrections reduce shoe volume, so proper shoe fit must be judged with these components in place. If the patient's ordinary shoes will be too tight, extradepth shoes are needed; these are shoes manufactured with a larger upper and two inner soles. One inner sole is discarded if a custom insert is to be used. Occasionally, modifications are sandwiched between the inner and outer soles; for example, the patient with marked arthritic changes in the forefoot will probably be more comfortable if the shoe has a long steel spring sandwiched between the soles to eliminate motion at the painful joints. An *overlay* is a modification cemented or nailed to the bottom of the outer sole. It will not reduce shoe volume, but it will erode as the patient walks and is somewhat more conspicuous.

If a basic or extradepth shoe cannot accommodate the deformed foot and the intended shoe modifications, then a pair of specially constructed shoes have to be obtained. The individual with fixed severe pes valgus may require a shoe manufactured on an outflare last. The **last,** the form over which the shoe is made, determines the shape and volume of the shoe. Consequently, an outflare last provides extra room in the lateral portion of the shoe. An inflare last presents the opposite shape. Custom-molded shoes are another option for the markedly deformed foot.

EXTERNAL MODIFICATIONS

Among the most frequently prescribed external shoe modifications is the heel wedge. It alters alignment of the calcaneus. A medial wedge is incorporated in the **Thomas heel,** intended for flexible pes valgus. The anterior border of the Thomas heel extends forward on the medial side to augment the effect of the medial wedge to support the longitudinal arch.

A *cushion heel* is made of resilient material to absorb shock at heel strike. Because it provides slight plantarflexion, the cushion heel is indicated when the patient wears an orthosis with a rigid ankle.[1]

Sole wedges alter mediolateral metatarsal alignment. A lateral wedge shifts weight bearing to the medial side of the forefoot. It compensates for fixed forefoot valgus, allowing the entire forefoot to contact the floor.

A **metatarsal bar** is a flat piece of leather placed across the sole immediately posterior to the ball of the sole (see Figure 27-3). The ball is the widest part of the sole, lying below the metatarsophalangeal joints. At push-off, the metatarsal bar transfers stress from the joints to the metatarsal shafts. A rocker bar is also located posterior to the ball of the sole. The *rocker bar* has a convexity on its plantar surface to reduce the distance through which the foot must travel during stance phase, improving push-off as well as shifting load from the metatarsophalangeal joints to the metatarsal shafts.

The patient with a leg length discrepancy of more than ½ inch (1 cm) will probably walk better with a shoe lift. Approximately ⅜ inch (0.8 cm) of the elevation can be accommodated inside the shoe at the heel.

INTERNAL MODIFICATIONS

Longitudinal arch supports are intended to prevent depression of the subtalar joint. The minimum support is a rubber **scaphoid pad** positioned at the medial border of the insole with the apex between the sustantaculum tali and the navicular tuberosity. For more realignment of the flexible flat foot, the **University of California Biomechanics Laboratory (UCBL) insert** is effective. Custom-made on a plaster model of the foot taken with the foot in maximum correction, the plastic insert applies medialward force on the calcaneus and lateral and upward force to the medial portion of the midfoot.[2] As with all inserts, the UCBL insert must fit both the patient's foot and the interior of the shoe to prevent rocking inside the shoe.

The **metatarsal pad** may be incorporated in an insert or may be a separate rubber convex piece glued to the insole. The apex is slightly posterior to the painful metatarsophalangeal joints.

Ankle-Foot Orthoses

The ankle-foot orthosis (AFO) is composed of a shoe or foot attachment, ankle control, one or two uprights, and a proximal leg band.

SHOE ATTACHMENTS

The traditional foundation for the AFO is a steel fixture in the form of a **stirrup** or **caliper** joined to the shoe. These attachments still provide advantages for selected patients.

Stirrups

Of the metal attachments, the **stirrup** is most common. It is a U-shaped piece of steel. The base is riveted to the sole of the shoe through the shank. The arms of the stirrup join the brace uprights at the level of the anatomic ankle, providing congruency between orthotic and anatomic joints. The solid stirrup is a one-piece attachment that provides maximum stability of the orthosis on the shoe (Fig. 27-4). The **split stirrup** consists of a box caliper, a rectangular receptacle riveted to the shank, and separate medial and lateral arms which fit into the box caliper (Fig. 27-5). The split stirrup simplifies donning the orthosis and enables the wearer to interchange shoes, assuming that the other shoes also have a box caliper. In addition to being slightly less stable than the solid stirrup, the split stirrup is also bulkier and heavier.

Calipers

A **caliper** is a tonglike attachment (Fig. 27-6). The arms of the brace upright fit into a tube in the shoe heel. Brace donning and shoe interchange are very easy with the caliper. The major objection is the marked incongruity between the orthotic and anatomic ankle joints. If the AFO permits dorsiflexion, the calf band will press the calf whenever the wearer dorsiflexes while walking.

Figure 27-4. Solid stirrup.

Figure 27–5. Split stirrup.

FOOT ATTACHMENTS

A plastic shoe insert (Fig. 27–7) or a plastic (Fig. 27–8) or metal foot plate can also serve as the foundation for the AFO.[3] Both offer the advantages of incorporating a metatarsal pad, and in the case of the shoe insert, medial longitudinal arch support, without need to modify the shoe. The patient has a much wider choice of shoes that may be worn with the AFO, assuming that all shoes selected have been made on the same last, so that the orthosis exerts the intended effect on the leg. Less expensive shoes, such as sneakers, can be worn, because the foot attachment does not depend on being fixed to a shank located between inner and outer soles. Foot attachments are inappropriate if the patient cannot be relied upon to wear the orthosis with a shoe of proper heel height. They also reduce interior shoe volume; consequently, shoes with adequate adjustment are necessary. These custom-molded attachments are more expensive than shoe attachments.

ANKLE CONTROLS

Most AFOs are prescribed to control ankle motion by limiting plantarflexion or dorsiflexion or motion in both directions, or by assisting motion. The most common control is a posterior stop that limits plantarflexion; for example, so the patient with drop foot will not catch the toe and stumble during swing phase. A metal posterior stop can be incorporated in joints used with the shoe or foot attachments. An anterior stop limits dorsiflexion, aiding the individual with paralysis of the triceps surae to achieve push-off.[4] A limited motion stop is a metal

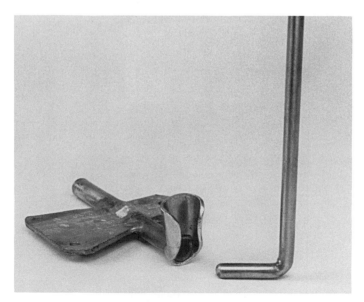

Figure 27–6. Caliper.

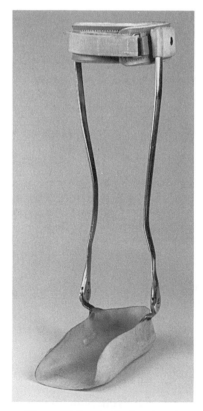

Figure 27–7. Plastic shoe insert.

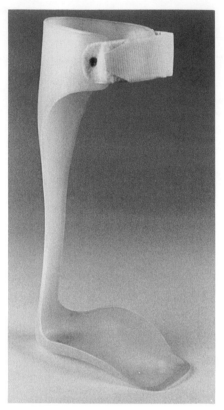

Figure 27–8. Plastic foot plate on posterior leaf spring ankle-foot orthosis.

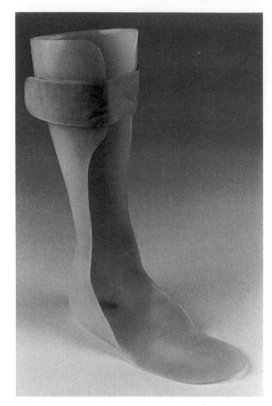

Figure 27–9. Plastic solid ankle ankle-foot orthosis.

joint that restricts both plantarflexion and dorsiflexion.

The plantarflexion and dorsiflexion stops are connected to medial and lateral metal uprights which also tend to limit foot inversion and eversion.

Varus or valgus at the ankle can be controlled by a leather correction strap. This accessory is sewn to either the lateral or the medial side of the shoe. A varus correction strap is sewn to the lateral side of the shoe and is buckled around the medial upright. The valgus strap is applied in reverse.

The plastic solid ankle AFO (Fig. 27–9) limits all motion of the ankle and posterior foot. The orthosis with its foot attachment fits into the shoe.[5,6]

Ankle controls that assist motion may be selected. The dorsiflexion spring assist is a metal component that has a spring that is stretched at heel strike and recoils at push-off to dorsiflex the foot, maintaining dorsiflexion throughout swing phase. Unlike the posterior stop, the dorsiflexion spring assist permits slight plantarflexion at heel strike to absorb shock. Bichannel adjustable ankle locks **(BiCAAL)** consist of a pair of joints, each of which has an anterior and a posterior spring (Fig. 27–10). Ordinarily the springs are replaced by metal pins, the length of which determines the amount of motion and thus the attitude of the AFO or other orthosis.

The flexibility of plastic may be used to assist dorsiflexion, as is the case with the plastic posterior leaf spring AFO (see Figure 27–8). The foot plate and calf shell are a continuous piece of polyethylene or **polypropylene.** At

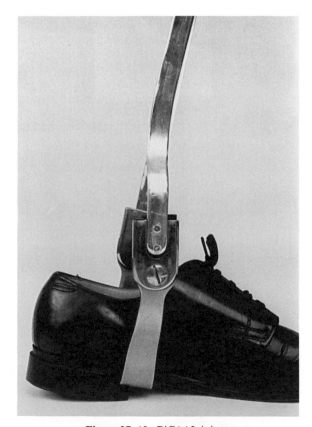

Figure 27–10. BiCAAL joints.

heel strike the wearer bends the plastic slightly backward. The plastic returns to its neutral position at push-off. The amount of dorsiflexion assistance and plantarflexion resistance depends on the width and thickness of the plastic at the back of the ankle. Wider, thicker material limits motion more.[7,8]

UPRIGHTS

Metal AFOs ordinarily have a pair of aluminum or steel uprights that extend from the ankle control along the midline of the medial and lateral aspects of the leg to terminate at the leg band. Aluminum uprights can be made to equal the strength of steel at half the weight, if the upright is of thicker metal. Although bilateral uprights are more conspicuous, they make a sturdier brace than do unilateral uprights.

Plastic AFOs may have a single upright. The solid ankle AFO has a sheet of plastic extending from the medial to the lateral midline of the leg, thus providing excellent mediolateral control. The posterior leaf spring AFO has a single posterior upright and thus does not contribute to frontal or transverse plane control.[9] The spiral AFO is a design now made in **nylon acrylic** or polypropylene in which the single upright spirals from the foot plate around the leg, terminating in a proximal band[10] (Fig. 27–11). This orthosis is designed to provide modest assistance to plantarflexion and dorsiflexion, as well as to control foot inversion. Orthoses with plastic uprights are molded over a cast of the patient's leg and are designed to fit snugly for maximum control and least conspicuousness. Such AFOs are contraindicated for the individual whose ankle and leg volume fluctuate markedly, inasmuch as they cannot be adjusted readily.

PROXIMAL LEG BANDS

The AFO terminates in a *leg band*. The usual band for the AFO with metal uprights is an upholstered metal calf band (Fig. 27–12). The farther the band is from the ankle joint, the more effective the leverage of the orthosis; however, the band must not extend so far proximally as to impinge on the peroneal nerve. An anterior calf band used in association with a solid ankle AFO is very effective in applying a posteriorly directed force which enables the AFO to resist knee flexion. If the AFO is intended to reduce weight transmitted through the foot, the band may be **patellar tendon bearing,** resembling a below-knee prosthetic socket.[11–13] Unlike the prosthesis, the patellar-tendon-bearing band or brim has a less prominent build-up at the patellar tendon and does not support all weight proximally.

Knee·Ankle·Foot Orthoses

Individuals with more extensive paralysis or limb deformity may benefit from KAFOs, which consist of a shoe or foot attachment, ankle control, uprights, knee joint, and leg and thigh bands. The shoe and distal com-

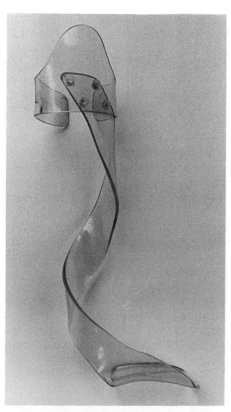

Figure 27–11. Spiral ankle-foot orthosis.

Figure 27–12. Ankle-foot orthosis with stirrup attachment, limited motion ankle joints, bilateral uprights, and upholstered metal calf band.

ponents of the KAFO may be selected from the components already described.

KNEE JOINTS

The simplest knee joint is a *hinge* (Fig. 27–13). Inasmuch as most KAFOs include a pair of uprights, the orthosis also would have a pair of knee hinges that provide mediolateral and hyperextension restriction. The pathway of rotation of the anatomic knee is more complex than that of the hinge; consequently, if the KAFO is used without any knee lock, the brace may slide on the leg. The alternate orthotic knee joint is a **polycentric unit;** it rotates in a J-shaped pathway, more nearly tracking with the anatomic knee in the sagittal plane. No orthotic joint, hinge or polycentric, follows the transverse plane rotation of the anatomic knee.

The **offset joint** (see Figure 27–13) is a hinge placed posterior to the midline of the leg. The patient's weight line falls anterior to the joint, stabilizing the knee during the early stance phase of gait. Because the offset joint usually does not have a mechanical lock, the knee is free to bend during swing phase and when the patient sits. The joint is contraindicated in the presence of knee flexion contracture.

For total protection against flexion, a knee lock is required. The most common type is the *drop ring lock* (Fig. 27–14). This simple device slips into position when the brace upright is straight. Both medial and lateral joints should be locked for maximum stability. A pair of drop ring locks is thus inconvenient, unless each upright

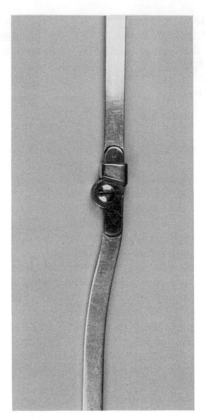

Figure 27–14. Hinge with drop ring lock.

is equipped with a spring-loaded retention button. They permit the wearer to unlock one upright, then attend to the other one without having the first lock drop again. The buttons also enable the physical therapist to give the patient a trial period of walking with the knee joints unlocked.

The **pawl lock** provides simultaneous locking of both uprights (Fig. 27–15). The mechanism has a spring-loaded bar that fits into a notched disk. The user unlocks the brace by pulling upward on a **bail** projecting posteriorly from the medial and lateral locks; a few are agile enough to be able to nudge the bail by pressing it against a chair. The bail segment is somewhat conspicuous and may be jostled to the unlocked position inadvertently. Both the drop ring and the pawl lock require the patient to extend the knee completely for both locking and unlocking.

The individual with a knee flexion contracture must use a knee joint designed to accommodate the contracture. Such joints have a drop ring lock for stability in the partially flexed attitude.

Sagittal stability is augmented by a knee cap (Fig. 27–16) or an anterior band (Fig. 27–17). The leather knee cap is the traditional component. It has four straps buckled to both uprights above and below the orthotic knee joint and applies a posteriorly directed force to oppose any tendency of the knee to flex. The disadvantages of the knee cap are that it increases the time the patient needs to don the KAFO, and when tight enough for knee stability during standing and walking, the cap restricts the knee when the user sits. Alternatives are prepatellar

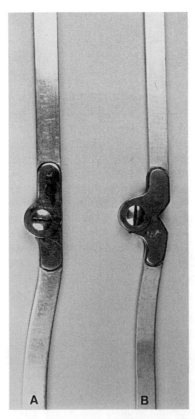

Figure 27–13. Knee joints: (*A*) hinge, (*B*) offset hinge.

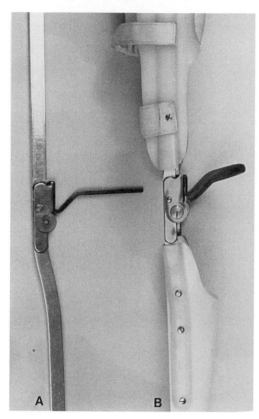

Figure 27–15. Pawl lock: (*A*) basic component, (*B*) pawl lock installed in knee-ankle-foot orthosis with bail shaped to curve posteriorly.

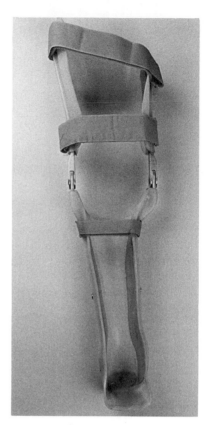

Figure 27–17. Knee-ankle-foot orthosis with Velcro anterior prepatellar and supracondylar bands.

and supracondylar bands, both of which also apply posteriorly directed force but do not interfere with sitting and are easier to don. The bands are generally molded of plastic and are not readily adjustable. The prepatellar band rests over the bony proximal portion of the leg and requires careful contouring to be comfortable. The supracondylar band fits over the fleshy anterodistal thigh.

LEG AND THIGH BANDS OR SHELLS

The KAFO includes a series of posterior bands or shells. Upholstered metal calf and distal thigh bands contribute to stability of the orthosis, and the proximal thigh band, located at the upper edge of the uprights, determines the leverage that the KAFO exerts (see Figure 27–16). Polypropylene calf and thigh shells serve the same purpose (see Figure 27–17). They are impervious to urine and abrasion and apply pressure over a much larger area than do the metal bands. Plastic shells can be shaped to apply corrected force for genu valgus or varum. A few patients find that the shells retain too much body heat, especially in the summer.

CRAIG-SCOTT KAFOS

A pair of **Craig-Scott KAFOs** (Fig. 27–18) are commonly prescribed for adults with paraplegia. The original design included shoes reinforced with long steel springs sandwiched between the inner and outer soles and transverse metal plates, BiCAAL ankle joints locked in slight

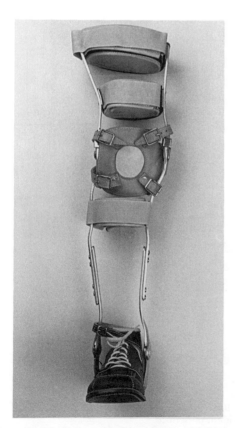

Figure 27–16. Knee-ankle-foot orthosis with knee cap.

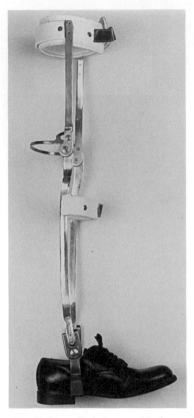

Figure 27–18. Scott-Craig knee-ankle-foot orthosis.

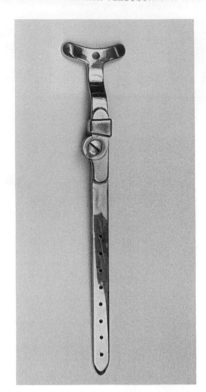

Figure 27–19. Hip joint with drop ring lock.

dorsiflexion, pretibial band, pawl locks with bail release, and a single thigh band.[14] A more recent version substitutes a plastic solid ankle section for the reinforced shoe and metal ankle joint.[15] The orthosis enables the patient to stand with posterior lean of the trunk, with the iliofemoral ligaments resisting a backward fall.

Hip·Knee·Ankle·Foot Orthoses

For hip control, in addition to ankle and knee control, a hip-knee-ankle-foot orthosis (HKAFO) is indicated. The orthosis consists of a pair of KAFOs with hip joints and a pelvic band.

HIP JOINTS

The usual hip joint is a metal hinge (Fig. 27–19) that connects the lateral upright of the KAFO to a pelvic band. The arrangement controls hip rotation as well as abduction and adduction. If flexion control is also required, a drop ring lock is added to the hip joint. A two-position lock stabilizes the patient in hip extension for standing and walking and at 90 degrees for sitting.

PELVIC BAND

An upholstered metal band may be fabricated to anchor the HKAFO to the pelvis (Fig. 27–20). The band is designed to lodge between the greater trochanter and

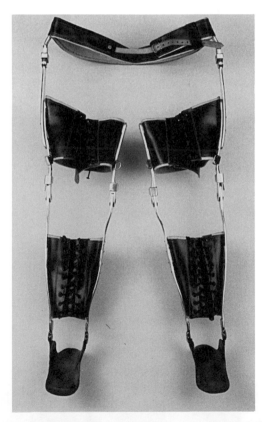

Figure 27–20. Hip-knee-ankle-foot orthoses. Laced thigh cuffs and leg cuffs are seldom prescribed.

iliac crest on each side. Hip-knee-ankle-foot orthoses are not used very often because they are much more difficult to don than KAFOs, and they restrict gait to a swing-to or swing-through pattern.

Trunk·Hip·Knee·Ankle·Foot Orthoses

Patients who need more stability than that provided by Craig-Scott KAFOs or HKAFOs may be fitted with trunk-hip-knee-ankle-foot orthoses (THKAFOs) (Fig. 27–21) which incorporate a lumbosacral orthosis attached to KAFOs. The pelvic band of the trunk brace takes the place of the pelvic band used on HKAFOs. Because the THKAFO is very difficult to don and is heavy and cumbersome, it is seldom worn after the patient is discharged from the rehabilitation program. Alternative orthoses that provide standing stability, with or without provision for walking, include the **reciprocating gait orthosis,** the standing frame, and the **parapodium.**

RECIPROCATING GAIT ORTHOSIS

Another orthotic option for paraplegia is the **reciprocating gait orthosis,** a version of THKAFO in which the hips are joined by two metal cables[16] (Fig. 27–22). When the wearer shifts weight onto the right leg, the cables advance the left leg. When the patient shifts weight onto

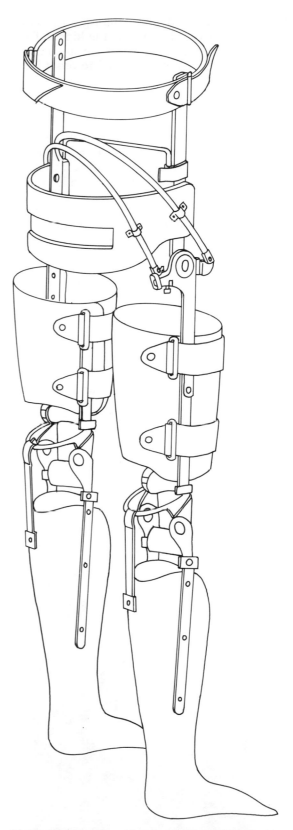

Figure 27–22. Reciprocating gait orthosis. (From *LSU Reciprocating Gait Orthosis: A Pictorial Description and Application Manual.* Durr-Fillauer Medical, Chattanooga, TN, 1983, p 14, with permission.)

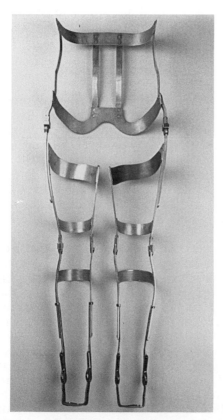

Figure 27–21. Trunk-hip-knee-ankle-foot orthoses.

the left leg, the cable advances the right leg. For sitting, both cables are released to enable the hips to flex. In the reciprocating gait orthosis, the feet are stabilized in solid ankle orthoses which are connected to offset knee joints for knee security.

STANDING FRAME

Designed for children, particularly those with spina bifida, the standing frame consists of a broad base, posterior nonarticulated uprights extending from the base to the midtorso, anterior leg and chest bands, and a posterior thoracolumbar band (Fig. 27–23). The child wears ordinary shoes without any special attachments. The shoes are strapped to the base of the frame. The prefabricated frame is less expensive than custom-made orthoses and accommodates easily to the child's growth. It permits the child to stand without crutch support, freeing the hands for play activities.

PARAPODIUM

The **parapodium** (Fig. 27–24) differs from the standing frame by virtue of articulations that permit the wearer to sit.[17] The stabilizing points on the two orthoses are the same. The newest version of the parapodium also has provision for keeping the knees stable while the child unlocks the hips for leaning forward to pick up objects from the floor.[18] Crutchless ambulation in the parapodium is achieved by rotating the trunk to rock the base along the floor. For walking longer distances, the para-

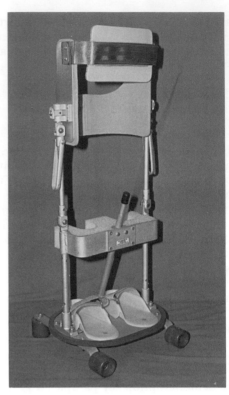

Figure 27–24. Parapodium. (Courtesy of Variety Village, Electro Limb Production Centre, Scarborough [Toronto], Ontario, Canada.)

podium wearer uses crutches or a walker in the swing-to or swing-through pattern. The parapodium is worn on the outside of the clothing, which most children older than 6 years find too conspicuous.

Spinal Orthoses

Although THKAFOs are infrequently prescribed for paraplegia, alternate means are needed to support the paralyzed trunk. Patients with spinal cord injury benefit from spinal orthoses in two ways: (1) the orthoses impart control of motion of the lumbar region, with or without thoracic control, and (2) they provide compression of the abdomen to improve respiration. Those with cervical lesions may need to wear an orthosis that restrains neck motion until stability is achieved by surgery or other means.

If abdominal compression is the sole goal, a corset may suffice. It is a fabric orthosis that has no horizontal rigid structures, although frequently it has vertical rigid reinforcements. The corset may cover only the lumbar region, or it may extend superiorly as a thoracolumbosacral corset. The primary effect of a corset is to increase intra-abdominal pressure.

A few individuals with low-back disorders find that corsets relieve pain. The increase in anterior, intra-abdominal pressure reduces stress on posterior spinal musculature, thus diminishing the load on the lumbar intervertebral disks. Although temporary reduction of abdominal and erector spinae muscular activity is therapeutic, long-term reliance on a corset can promote mus-

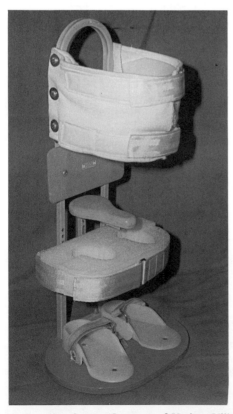

Figure 27–23. Standing frame. (Courtesy of Variety Village, Electro Limb Production Centre, Scarborough [Toronto], Ontario, Canada.)

cular atrophy and contracture, as well as psychologic dependence on the appliance.

Most lumbosacral and thoracolumbosacral orthoses include a corset or a fabric abdominal front to compress the abdomen. Rigid orthoses are distinguished by the presence of horizontal, as well as vertical, metal or rigid plastic components. A typical example is the lumbosacral flexion, extension, lateral control orthosis (LSFELO) (Fig. 27–25) also known by its older name, Knight spinal orthosis. This appliance includes a pelvic band, which should provide firm anchorage over the midsection of the buttocks, and a thoracic band, which is intended to lie horizontally over the lower thorax without impinging on the scapulae. The bands are joined by a pair of posterior uprights, which lie on either side of the vertebral spines, and a pair of lateral uprights placed at the lateral midline of the torso. A corset or abdominal front completes the LSFELO. The orthosis restrains flexion by a three-point system consisting of posteriorly directed force from the top and bottom of the abdominal front or corset and an anteriorly directed force from the midportion of the posterior uprights. Extension is controlled by posteriorly directed force from the midsection of the abdominal front or corset and anteriorly directed force from the thoracic and pelvic bands. The lateral uprights resist lateral flexion.

The thoracolumbosacral flexion-extension control orthosis, TLSFEO, also designated as a Taylor brace, consists of a pelvic band, posterior uprights terminating at midscapular level, an abdominal front or corset, and axillary straps attached to an interscapular band (Fig. 27–26). This orthosis reduces flexion by a three-point system consisting of posteriorly directed force from the axillary straps and the bottom of the abdominal front or corset and anteriorly directed force from the midportion of the posterior uprights. Extension resistance is provided by posteriorly directed force from the midsection of the abdominal front or corset and anteriorly directed force from the pelvic and interscapular bands.

Cervical orthoses are classified according to design characteristics. Minimal motion control is provided by collars, which encircle the neck with fabric or resilient

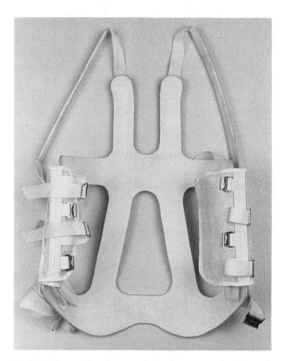

Figure 27–26. Thoracolumbosacral flexion-extension-lateral control orthosis.

material or with rigid plastic. A few collars encompass the chin and posterior head for slightly greater restraint. For moderate control, a four-poster appliance is used (Fig. 27–27). Usually it has two anterior adjustable posts joining a sternal plate to a mandibular plate and two pos-

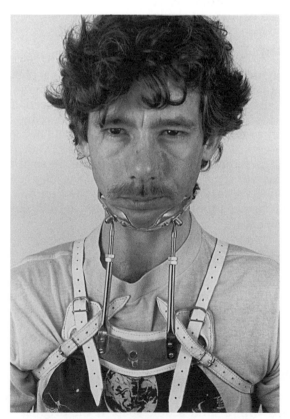

Figure 27–27. Four-poster cervical orthosis.

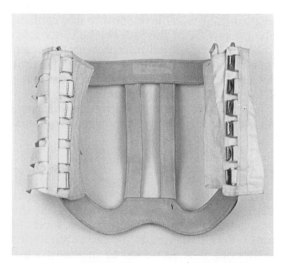

Figure 27–25. Lumbosacral flexion-extension-lateral control orthosis.

terior uprights connecting a thoracic plate to an occipital plate. The sternal plate is strapped to the thoracic plate, and the occipital plate is strapped to the mandibular plate. Maximum orthotic control of the neck requires a *halo*. The halo is a circular band of metal that is fixed to the skull by four tiny screws. Uprights connect the halo to a thoracic orthosis.

Orthotic Maintenance

For best service from orthoses, the patient should learn basic routine inspection and care procedures. Written instructions help reinforce the orthotist's and therapist's recommendations.

SHOES

Whether or not the shoe is attached directly to the orthosis, it is important that footwear be kept in good condition, with replacement of the sole and heel as soon as moderate wear is evident. The replacements should include whatever wedges, bars, or elevations were originally prescribed. The patient who tends to strike on the toe may need metal toe plates to preserve the sole. Shoes that are outgrown or distorted will not afford the wearer best function from the orthosis. If a stirrup is attached to the shoe, the patient should inspect the rivets to make certain that none have separated; if so, the shoe should be returned to the orthotist for repair.

Clean hose without holes or repairs should be worn. In addition, long hosiery or cotton stockinette leggings shield the leg from pressure at the edges of the brace uprights, bands, and shells.

UPRIGHTS

In a metal/leather AFO or KAFO for a child, the uprights are overlapped so that as the child grows, the brace may be lengthened. Overlapping sections are secured with screws which may work loose, reducing the stability of the orthosis. This problem should be reported to the orthotist. In a plastic/metal KAFO, the metal upright is screwed or riveted to the plastic shell and is less likely to separate. A child's KAFO is lengthened by removing the fasteners and inserting them in new holes drilled farther up on the calf shell and farther down on the thigh shell.

JOINTS AND LOCKS

Metal components should be kept away from sand, liquids, and other foreign substances. If the joints do not articulate smoothly or if the locks do not engage properly, then cleaning and lubrication may remedy the problem. Otherwise professional attention is required.

BANDS AND STRAPS

Leather bands require periodic cleaning and can be washed with a mild saddle soap. If the original leather deteriorates such that portions of the underlying metal are exposed, new leatherwork may be required. Leather straps eventually become brittle and may break. One should watch for loss of flexibility and replace the straps before they break.

PHYSICAL THERAPY MANAGEMENT

Physical therapists participate in management of the wearer of an orthosis (a) prior to orthotic prescription, (b) at orthotic prescription, (c) upon delivery of the orthosis, and (d) during training to facilitate proper use and care of the orthosis.

In an optimal situation the therapist is a member of an orthotic clinic team, working directly with the physician and orthotist to develop the orthotic prescription and to assess the patient and orthosis before and after training. The physical therapist is also responsible for training the patient.

Whether or not the hospital or rehabilitation center has a clinic team, the physical therapist will be expected to accomplish the following.

1. Perform preorthotic assessment.
2. Contribute to orthotic prescription.
3. Assess the prescribed orthosis.
4. Facilitate orthotic acceptance.
5. Train the patient to don, to use, and to maintain the orthosis.

Preprescription Assessment

Matching the patient's biomechanical requirements to the appropriate orthosis requires careful physical assessment.

JOINT MOBILITY

A thorough goniometric examination, including both active and passive range of motion, is a prerequisite to orthotic prescription. If the patient presents with a fixed foot deformity, the shoe will have to be modified to accommodate the foot, or an insert fabricated. In either instance, the goal is to achieve comfortable contact of the entire plantar surface of the foot on the inner sole of the shoe. Knee flexion contracture necessitates prescription of accommodative joints, because the usual drop ring and pawl locks can be used only with a knee that can be brought to the fully extended position. Hip flexion contracture negates prescription of orthoses that depend on alignment for stability, such as the offset knee joint or the Craig-Scott KAFOs.

LIMB LENGTH

The therapist should ascertain whether there is a leg length discrepancy. If the patient can stand, the therapist can check the pelvis to ascertain if it is level. For the recumbent individual, one can measure each leg from the anterior superior iliac spine to the medial malleolus. A difference of more than ½ inch (1 cm) should be compensated for by a shoe elevation. For the patient with weakness in one limb, a ½-inch (1-cm) lift on the contralateral shoe will aid clearance of the paralyzed leg during swing phase.

MOTOR FUNCTION

The manual muscle test should be augmented by a functional activities assessment to determine what substitutions the patient is able to make to accomplish standing and walking. Even though the muscle test may reveal marked weakness, if the patient can manage without an orthosis, it is unlikely that one will be accepted. For example, the individual with dorsiflexor paralysis who is able to walk by exaggerating hip flexion during swing phase may not agree to an AFO with a posterior stop. An important consideration in assessment of motor function is that traditional manual muscle tests are inappropriate in the presence of spasticity. In these instances, functional tests of motor performance are indicated.

SENSATION

The therapist should record the extent of any sensory loss, for this information will guide later assessment of the fit of the orthosis. Intimately fitted plastic orthoses are satisfactory for individuals with sensory loss if the edges of the orthosis are properly smooth and the orthosis does not pinch the patient's flesh. Proprioceptive loss may indicate the need for orthotic stabilization, such as a solid ankle AFO to control a Charcot neuropathic ankle.

UPPER LIMBS

Although the patient is being considered as a candidate for lower-limb orthoses, the therapist must determine the mobility and motor power of the upper limbs. Significant weakness, stiffness, or deformity will interfere with donning the orthosis. Substitution of Velcro straps for leather buckles may be sufficient. If the individual can not ambulate without canes or crutches, the therapist should determine whether standard aids will be satisfactory or whether modification of the handpiece is required. If the upper limbs are very weak, the patient will not be able to use the lower-limb orthoses for walking. Alternate standing arrangements may be preferable, such as the use of a standing frame or standing table to provide weight-bearing stress.

PSYCHOLOGIC STATUS

Realistic orthotic prescription assumes that the patient is willing to wear the orthotic device. The patient with a recent spinal cord injury may still deny the permanence of paralysis and thus be adverse to wearing orthoses, which are visible reminders of disability. The adolescent with spina bifida may prefer to sit unbraced in a wheelchair rather than to struggle with donning orthoses and walking slowly, in a manner very different from the individual's peers. The individual who has suffered a cerebrovascular accident resulting in severe perceptual deficiency may not be able to ambulate, even with orthotic assistance. An orthosis for prevention of deformity may be prescribed, rather than one that is designed to aid walking. The therapist should judge the extent to which the patient will comply with instructions pertaining to orthotic use. For example, if the individual is unlikely to wear appropriate shoes with an insert orthosis, then the prescription should specify stirrup attachment to suitable shoes.

Orthotic Prescription

Lower-limb orthoses benefit individuals with a wide variety of musculoskeletal disorders. The particular diagnosis is less important in formulating the prescription, as compared with consideration of the patient's disability. Prognosis does influence prescription. The patient who is likely to recover partial or full function should have an orthosis that can be adjusted to accommodate the changing status. A patient with new hemiplegia, for example, may exhibit marked spasticity, indicating need for limited motion at the ankle. As the patient regains voluntary control, the ankle can be adjusted to permit more movement.

The individual's lifestyle has a bearing on orthotic selection. One who is very active requires an orthosis made of exceptionally sturdy materials. Split stirrups, for example, may not be indicated because they can spring loose from the box caliper if excessive mediolateral stress is applied. The patient's concern with appearance is another practical factor that may dictate use of a shoe insert so that reasonably fashionable shoes may be worn. Similarly, plastic shells are less bulky than metal uprights and calf bands, and they do not present a shiny metal appearance.

ANKLE-FOOT ORTHOSES

The primary candidates for AFOs are those with peripheral neuropathy—especially peroneal lesions—and hemiplegia. Those with foot drag can be fitted with an AFO with a posterior stop; this design, however, tends to cause the knee to flex excessively in early stance when controlled plantarflexion is normally achieved. In the absence of plantarflexion, the patient may flex the knee to effect foot flat. The alternative is an AFO with a dorsiflexion spring assist in the form of a metal joint or a plastic leaf spring, both of which permit controlled plantarflexion early in stance to prevent knee stress.[19]

Orthotic management of hemiplegia depends on the extent of spasticity and paralysis.[20] If the motor loss is confined to poor dorsiflexion, the simple posterior leaf spring orthosis suffices. Those with mediolateral and sagittal plane disability require an AFO with limited motion ankle joints, or a plastic spiral AFO. With pain or severe instability, a solid ankle AFO is required. In the presence of moderate or severe spasticity, a spring assist for joint motion is contraindicated because it may serve to increase spasticity. This is a common problem in patients with spasticity of the plantarflexor muscles.

KNEE-ANKLE-FOOT AND OTHER ORTHOSES

Paralysis of the entire leg may be compensated by a KAFO. The physical therapist should assess the patient with a temporary orthosis in order to proceed more confidently with prescription of an expensive, custom-made orthosis. Several versions of temporary KAFOs are manufactured and prove exceedingly useful in demonstrating whether the patient is likely to benefit from knee control.

Craig-Scott KAFOs, KAFOs with unrestrained dorsiflexion, HKAFOs, and the reciprocating gait orthosis are options for paraplegia. For the juvenile individual, the orthotic program should start with a simple standing frame and progress to the parapodium before involving the child in the greater expense of form-fitting KAFOs or more extensive bracing.

Orthotic Assessment

Check-out is an essential element of orthotic management. The physical therapist should be certain that the orthosis fits and functions properly before attempting to train the patient to use it. Check-out may be conducted under the aegis of a formal orthotic clinic team. If so, at initial check-out, conducted when the orthosis is delivered, the team will assess the suitability of the orthosis as *pass, provisional pass,* or *failure. Pass* indicates that the orthosis is altogether satisfactory and the patient is ready for training. *Provisional pass* means that minor faults exist, generally having to do with the cosmetic finishing of the orthosis; the patient can wear the orthosis in the training program without harmful effect. *Failure* signifies that the orthosis has a major defect that would interfere with training; for example, shoes that are too tight for the patient. The problem must be resolved before training can begin. If the orthosis is not prescribed by a clinic team, then the therapist should use the check-out procedure to assure that the orthosis meets the patient's needs. Final check-out is performed at the conclusion of training to reassess the fit and function of the orthosis and the patient's skill in using it.

ANKLE-FOOT ORTHOTIC CHECK-OUT

The therapist should respond to every question on the checkout form (Appendix A), although a few items will be marked not applicable for particular individuals. The static check-out is useful for assessing both metal/leather and plastic AFOs.

Static Assessment

The orthosis is assessed as the wearer stands and sits. The patient's skin and the workmanship of the orthosis are checked with the orthosis off the patient. The orthosis should be compared with the prescription. Departures from the original specifications must be approved by the individual(s) who developed the prescription.

The patient should stand in parallel bars, or other secure environment, and should attempt to bear equal weight on both feet. The shoe should fit satisfactorily, particularly in length, width, and snugness of the counters. Whether or not wedges or lifts have been added to the shoe, the sole and heel should rest flat on the floor. The ankle joint should be at the distal tip of the medial malleolus, in order to be congruent with the anatomic ankle and to avoid vertical motion of the orthosis on the leg.

The calf band should terminate below the fibular head to avoid impingement on the peroneal nerve. If a patellar-tendon-bearing brim is used, it should have a concave relief for the fibular prominence. This component does not eliminate distal weight bearing; therefore, one should judge whether the shoe heel is somewhat unloaded. This can be estimated by placing a ribbon in the shoe before the patient stands. One end of the ribbon hangs out the back of the shoe. When the patient stands with the shoe and orthosis on, the therapist should be able to pull the ribbon out of the shoe. The calf band or patellar-tendon-bearing brim should not intrude on the popliteal fossa so that the patient has difficulty flexing the knee when sitting. It should also be noted that donning ease will be affected by the type of closure of both the shoe and bands.

When the brace is off the patient, the therapist should move the ankle joints slowly to check the range of motion. Binding refers to tilting of the distal portion of the ankle joint in relation to the proximal member which interferes with movement. If the medial and lateral stops do not contact their respective stops at the same time, the stop that contacts first will erode rapidly and may contribute to twisting of the orthosis.

Dynamic Assessment

Check-out includes analysis of the patient's gait and performance of other ambulatory activities (see also chapter 11). The check-out form includes a list of 16 common deviations that may be observed as the patient walks. It should be noted, however, that observational gait analysis is a moderately reliable assessment; sagittal plane deviations are easier to judge than are those which occur in the frontal or transverse plane.[21]

Most of the deviations have both anatomic and orthotic causes (Table 27–1). Lateral trunk bending in early stance phase may be the result of hip abductor weakness or hip instability; however, uncompensated shortness of the limb will also give rise to this problem. Hip hiking occurs when the hip flexors are weak, as well as when the extremity is functionally longer than the contralateral limb. Increased leg length may be produced by a faulty posterior stop that no longer limits plantarflexion. Internal or external hip rotation may be caused by motor imbalance between medial and lateral musculature; the orthotic causes relate to malalignment of the brace. Similarly, excessive medial or lateral foot contact may indicate that the orthosis does not track the way the patient's limb does. A walking base that is abnormally wide can be caused by a limb that is longer than that on the opposite side. Anterior and posterior trunk bending

Table 27–1 ORTHOTIC GAIT ANALYSIS

Deviation	Orthotic Causes	Anatomic Causes
Lateral trunk bending	Excessive height of medial upright of KAFO Excessive abduction of hip joint Insufficient shoe lift to compensate for leg shortening	Weak abductors Abduction contracture Dislocated hip Hip pain Instability
Hip hiking	Hip or knee lock uncompensated by contralateral shoe lift Pes equinus uncompensated by contralateral shoe lift Inadequate plantarflexion stop or dorsiflexion spring	Weak hip flexors Hip extensor spasticity
Internal (external) hip rotation	Transverse plane malalignment	Weak lateral (medial) hip musculature
Circumduction	Hip or knee lock uncompensated by contralateral shoe lift Pes equinus uncompensated by contralateral shoe lift Inadequate plantarflexion stop or dorsiflexion spring	Weak hip flexors Abduction contracture
Wide walking base	Excessive height of medial upright of KAFO Excessive abduction of hip joint Knee lock uncompensated by contralateral shoe lift	Weak abductors Abduction contracture Instability Genu valgum
Excessive medial (lateral) foot contact	Transverse plane malalignment	Weak invertors (evertors) Pes valgus (varus) Genu valgum (varum)
Anterior trunk bending	Inadequate knee lock	Weak quadriceps
Posterior trunk bending		Weak hip extensors
Lordosis	Inadequate support from the brim of a weight-relieving KAFO	Hip flexion contracture Weak hip extensors
Hyperextended knee	Genu recurvatum inadequately controlled by plantar stop and excessively concave calf band Pes equinus uncompensated by contralateral shoe lift	Weak quadriceps Lax knee ligaments Extensor spasticity
Knee instability	Inadequate knee lock Inadequate dorsiflexion stop	Knee flexion contracture Weak quadriceps
Inadequate dorsiflexion control	Inadequate plantarflexion stop or dorsiflexion spring	Weak dorsiflexors Extensor spasticity
Vaulting	Hip or knee lock uncompensated by contralateral shoe lift Pes equinus uncompensated by contralateral shoe lift Inadequate plantarflexion stop or dorsiflexion spring	Weak hip flexors Abduction contracture

are seen at early stance when the patient attempts to control a weak knee or hip. The patient who fears that the knee may collapse may benefit from an AFO with a solid ankle and an anterior leg band. Lordosis indicates hip flexion contracture or a KAFO that does not fit properly.

Knee hyperextension or excessive flexion indicates that the orthosis is not applying adequate control. A posterior stop on the AFO should prevent the lax knee from hyperextending. Excessive genu valgum or varum suggests the need for a KAFO that provides mediolateral control. Inadequate dorsiflexion control results from dorsiflexor weakness and is particularly troublesome in swing phase when the dragging toe may cause the patient to stumble. The posterior ankle stop or dorsiflexion spring assist should be adjusted to prevent this problem. Insufficient push-off, originating with plantarflexor paralysis, can be mitigated with an anterior stop and a rocker bar. Vaulting refers to exaggerated plantarflexion on the contralateral limb during swing phase of the affected side.

Vaulting occurs because the braced leg is functionally too long, possibly because the posterior stop has eroded.

KNEE-ANKLE-FOOT CHECK-OUT

The same format is used to assess the KAFO (Appendix B).

Static Assessment

In addition to the checkpoints applicable to the AFO, the therapist should examine the proximal portions of the KAFO. The mechanical knee joints should be congruent with the anatomic knee; for the adult, the usual placement is approximately ¾ inch (2 cm) above the medial tibial plateau. The knee lock check is a critical element in the assessment process, because the major reason for wearing a KAFO is to stabilize the knee. The medial upright should terminate approximately 1½ inches (5 cm) below the perineum. The calf and distal thigh bands should be equidistant so that when the orthosis is flexed, as in sitting, the bands will contact one another, rather than pinch the back of the wearer's leg.

If the KAFO has a quadrilateral brim to reduce weight bearing through the skeleton, the brim should have adequate provision for the sensitive adductor longus tendon and should provide a sufficient seat for the ischial tuberosity.

The pelvic joint is set above the greater trochanter to compensate for the usual angulation of the femoral neck; setting the joint anterior to the trochanter takes into account the medial rotation of the femur.

Dynamic Assessment

In addition to the causative factors noted for deviations that might be exhibited by wearers of AFOs, the physical therapist should pay particular attention to several problems more apt to occur with the KAFO. Lateral trunk bending can result if the medial upright is too high, or if the HKAFO user has a pelvic band and joint that are excessively abducted. The presence of a knee lock effectively lengthens the limb and may cause the patient to bend laterally, to hike the hip, to circumduct, to walk with a wide base, or to vault. These problems should be anticipated, and, for the unilateral KAFO wearer, can be prevented by adding a ½-inch (1-cm) lift to the contralateral shoe. Anterior trunk bending may indicate the need for a knee lock to provide needed stability. Lordosis may result if the individual has a weight-bearing KAFO with an ischial ring, a narrow strip of upholstered metal that offers very little support. The KAFO should control genu recurvatum; if the wearer exhibits this problem while walking, the stops at the knee joint are set improperly or have eroded; the calf and distal thigh bands, or corresponding plastic shells should be made shallow to apply an anteriorly directed force to counteract the problem. Knee instability suggests that a knee lock is required.

Facilitating Orthotic Acceptance

The care with which the therapist conducts check-out is an important element in impressing the patient with the good function to be derived from the orthosis, assuming that no major problems have emerged. Clinic team management also is valuable for allying several clinicians who join efforts to help the patient realize the maximum benefit from orthotic rehabilitation. Bringing the new wearer of an orthosis in contact with other users by scheduling the beginner for treatment in the physical therapy department when other brace wearers will be present can help the new patient recognize that orthotic use is not a strange occurrence. Peer support groups for patients and their families are valuable in facilitating sharing concerns and anxieties and reaching workable solutions to common problems. The physical therapist can serve constructively to guide some meetings of the group. The physical therapist works most closely with the patient, usually on a daily basis, and thus is able to identify those individuals whose response to disability is sufficiently aberrant as to require psychologic attention.

Orthotic Training

Orthoses are designed to provide the patient with a maximum of function with a minimum of discomfort and effort. No single training program suits every orthosis wearer because of the wide range of disorders for which orthotic management may be indicated. To the extent possible, however, the physical therapist should instruct the patient in the correct manner of donning the orthosis, developing standing balance, walking safely, and performing other ambulatory activities.

Optimal performance depends on the favorable interaction of many factors. Foremost is the extent of skeletal and neuromuscular involvement. The mobility, strength, and coordination of all joints, especially in the lower extremities and trunk, are important, as is the individual's muscle tone, cardiovascular and pulmonary health, psychologic status, and chronologic age. The quality of the orthosis also influences the patient's achievements.

Most orthosis wearers have chronic conditions, such as rheumatoid arthritis, or permanent sequelae from trauma, such as paraplegia following spinal cord injury. Orthotic management enhances function without necessarily influencing the underlying pathology. Training prepares the patient for lifelong activity with a brace. Persons with reversible disorders, such as fracture, often benefit from temporary use of an orthosis. Such individuals should learn proper use of the orthosis to prevent secondary disorders and should receive reassessment so that the orthosis may be altered as the condition changes. Progressive disorders, such as muscular dystrophy, require vigilant reassessment so that the extent of physical deterioration may be reflected in orthotic changes, as well as continual training to cope with altered functional abilities. For all situations, a carefully devised exercise and activity program should enable the patient to manage efficiently for maximum independence.

DONNING ORTHOSES

Regardless of type of orthosis, the patient should wear clean, properly fitting hose. The AFO with shoe insert is most easily donned by applying the orthosis to the foot and leg, prior to placing the braced limb in the shoe. If the AFO has a split stirrup, the shoe should be donned first, then the orthosis fitted into the box caliper on the shoe. Similarly, an AFO with a caliper is donned by first applying the shoe, then inserting the caliper into the heel.

The same procedures are useful with KAFOs. The patient may find donning simpler if the brace is applied while the individual lies in bed or on a mat table. If the KAFO is donned while the patient sits, the therapist should check the tightness of the knee cap, if this component is part of the orthosis. A knee cap that is comfortable for sitting will probably be too loose for effective knee control when the wearer stands. Donning HKAFOs is much more arduous. The beginner should lie on a mat table alongside the orthoses. By rolling to one side, the patient should be able to pull the brace under the legs to permit lying in them. Then the patient dons the shoes and fastens the various straps on the HKAFO.

STANDING BALANCE

The problem of standing safely is most difficult for the individual who wears a pair of KAFOs or more extensive bracing. In ordinary standing, all weight passes through the feet, whereas when standing and walking with orthoses and crutches, the patient must learn to distribute weight partly on the hands and partly on the feet. The center of gravity falls within a triangle bounded by the hands and feet. The tripod is a compromise between leaning too far forward on the hands (initially placed on parallel bars, to increase stability at the price of fatiguing the arms) and leaning too far backward, which reduces arm strain but makes balance precarious. As balance improves, the patient uses the hands only for balance, rather than for substantial weight bearing.

The bilateral KAFO wearer will need crutches or other aids for independent gait. A prerequisite for crutch ambulation is the ability to shift weight in the sagittal plane. Shifting weight to the heels takes pressure off the hands so they can be moved. The beginner shifts all weight to the feet and raises and lowers one hand, then the other hand. The goal is to be able to lift both hands simultaneously, as will be done with crutches. Once able to shift weight from the feet to the hands and back to the feet confidently, the same exercise should be done with crutches. Advanced skills such as moving the hands, and eventually the crutches, behind the body, should be practiced.

GAIT TRAINING

The various standard crutch gaits differ in the sequence of crutch and foot steps. Patterns differ in speed, safety, and amount of energy required. The patient should learn as many gaits as possible, enabling one to modify walking in crowds, long distances, and in situations in which speed is desired. In addition to walking forward, the patient needs to be able to walk sideward, to turn corners, and to maneuver on different surfaces, such as rugs, gravel, grass, and through doors. A repertoire of gaits permits the patient to adjust to environmental requirements.

Criteria for gait selection depend on the individual's disability:

1. Step ability. Can the patient take steps with either or both lower extremities?

2. Weight-bearing and balance ability. Can the patient bear weight and remain balanced on one or both lower extremities?

3. Upper-limb power. Can the patient push the body off the floor by pressing down on the hands?

Reciprocal Gaits

The four-point and two-point gaits require that one move the lower extremities alternately by hip flexion or pelvic elevation. The patient shifts weight as each limb is moved. The four-point sequence is (a) right hand, (b) left foot, (c) left hand, and (d) right foot. The two-point sequence requires greater balance and coordination but is a faster mode of walking; (a) right hand and left leg; (b) left hand and right leg.

These gaits are suited to persons with lack of coordination, poor balance, or fear of falling. The patterns are also useful when one is confronted with crowds or slippery surfaces.

Simultaneous Gaits

If both lower limbs are moved simultaneously, the patient places considerable stress on the upper limbs. The series includes the drag-to, swing-to, and swing-through patterns. They enable the individual with paraplegia to get to places inaccessible in a wheelchair, such as traversing a narrow doorway. They are very fatiguing, for the upper limbs are poorly adapted for ambulatory function; a sizable amount of nonfunctioning bodily structure must be controlled by a smaller muscular apparatus. The weight of the orthoses, and in the case of spinal cord lesion, absence of peripheral sensation, aggravates the problem of simultaneous ambulation.

The drag-to gait is the most elementary of the group, but it is very slow. The sequence is (a) advance both hands, then (b) push on the crutches enough to drag the feet forward. The feet, however, do not pass ahead of the hands. The swing-to pattern is more rapid, for the patient swings rather than drags the lower limbs. Swinging is accomplished by extending the elbows and depressing the shoulder girdle to elevate the trunk and lower limbs. The swing-through gait is the most advanced pattern, requiring much balance, strength, and coordination of the upper limbs, because the patient swings the legs beyond the hands, or crutch tips. The sequence is (a) advance both hands, (b) swing both legs to a point in front of the hands to reverse the basic tripod position, and (c) advance both hands to the starting position. The swing-through gait requires extensive preliminary training, including push-ups to strengthen the arms. The gait is rapid but requires more floor space than the other patterns, to permit alternate swinging of legs and crutches. Detailed instructions in gait training are provided in chapters 15 and 26.

The ultimate test of walking proficiency is the ability to conduct a conversation while ambulating, indicating some degree of automatic functioning. Practice in the clinical setting should be extended to walking on various terrain, indoors and outdoors, if walking is to be a useful skill.

ACTIVITIES

The patient should learn as many activities of daily living as the physical condition permits. Daily life usually involves the need to negotiate stairs, curbs, and ramps, as well as transferring from the chair to the upright position, and into an automobile. Instruction in driving a suitably equipped car is an important part of the rehabilitation process. Not all individuals who wear orthoses achieve the full range of ambulatory activities, yet they benefit from partial independence in accomplishing tasks, at least from the psychologic and physiologic values attendant to ambulatory activity.

FINAL CHECK-OUT AND FOLLOW-UP CARE

Prior to discharge, the orthosis wearer and the brace should be reassessed to make certain that fit, function, appearance, and patient use are acceptable.

The patient should return to the hospital or rehabilitation center at regular intervals so that the clinic team can check for continued good function of the orthosis and can monitor for incipient abrasions or other signs of misfit. The follow-up visit also enables the physical therapist to reinforce skills taught in the intensive program and to address any new problems the patient may present.

Functional Capacities

The patient's ambulatory ability and capacity for other physical activities reflect both orthotic and anatomic factors. Energy measurement is a valuable guide to functional capacity. Energy cost is calculated from the amount of oxygen consumed as the subject ambulates. Consumption may be determined either per distance traversed or per unit time. One tends to select a walking speed that requires the least energy per distance. If energy cost is too high, the patient will realize that ambulation is not a practical mode of locomotion. Sometimes, high energy cost is tolerable for short distances, as in household ambulation. Community ambulation, however, demands sustained effort for longer distances, plus the ability to maneuver over curbs and other irregularities in the walking surface. Many energy studies have been conducted with the two largest groups of patients who wear orthoses, namely those with paraplegia and those with hemiplegia.

PARAPLEGIA

The level of spinal cord damage is a critical determinant of functional capacity. Investigators generally conclude that functional ambulation is not feasible for those with lesions above the 11th thoracic segment of the spinal cord.[22-25] Patients with thoracic injuries consume nine times the energy per meter expended by normal individuals, while those with lumbar lesions require triple the normal amount of oxygen, when walking at self-selected speeds.[22] Those with high-level paraplegia use three times their own basal oxygen rate ambulating with Craig-Scott KAFOs; they choose a very slow walking pace.[26] Subjects with lesions between T-11 and L-2 wearing bilateral KAFOs select walking speeds less than half that of nondisabled persons, with oxygen uptake six times normal. Wheelchair propulsion by the same group increases oxygen uptake less than 10 percent more than normal, with considerably faster speed.[27] The very high energy cost may be accounted for by the fact that the lower-limb paralysis requires that the individual must move by upper limb and thoracic action, usually in a swing-to or swing-through gait. This pattern is extremely strenuous, taxing normal adults at least 75 percent more energy than normal walking.[28-29]

Of far less significance in determining functional capacity is the type of orthosis. Restraining both plantarflexion and dorsiflexion, as provided by Craig-Scott KAFOs, reduces energy demand very slightly.[30-31] Ankle restraint, however, makes no appreciable difference in energy required to negotiate stairs and ramps.[32] Performance is somewhat more efficient with molded plastic KAFOs, which weigh somewhat less than the traditional metal/leather version.[31]

One must not lose sight of the principal purpose of ambulation; namely, to get from one place to another, rather than to execute an exhausting physical stunt. The near universal abandonment of braces by spinal cord injured individuals upon discharge from the rehabilitation center attests to the fact that most decide that accomplishing vocational and recreational tasks is more important than struggling with brace donning and awkward ambulation.

HEMIPLEGIA

Although the increased energy demand occasioned by hemiplegic ambulation is not nearly as dramatic as that for paraplegic gait, the cost should be considered in planning reasonable goals. Energy cost rises in proportion to the amount of spasticity.[33] The increase ranges from no appreciable difference for persons without hemiplegia[34] to a 100 percent increase for relatively inexperienced hemiplegic walkers.[35] On average, comfortable gait is approximately half the speed of that for normal individuals.

The type of orthosis does not appear to make much difference in functional capacity, although patients with hemiplegia perform more efficiently with some design of AFO than without any bracing.[36] Investigation of the factors that influence energy expenditure, especially physical status, help the clinician plan the most appropriate rehabilitation program and to forecast long-term performance.

SUMMARY

This chapter has focused on lower-limb orthotics. The more frequently prescribed orthoses and orthotic components have been presented. In addition, the responsibilities of the physical therapist in orthotic management have been emphasized.

Ideally, an orthosis is prescribed by an orthotic clinic team composed of a physician, a physical therapist, and an orthotist. The prescription should be based on a thorough assessment, with particular attention to the specific factors discussed in this chapter. Input from the patient and all team members during the decision-making process is critical. This approach will ensure an optimum match between the patient's biomechanical requirements and an appropriate orthosis capable of providing its intended function.

QUESTIONS FOR REVIEW

1. What is meant by the terms *ankle-foot orthosis* and *knee-ankle-foot orthosis?*

2. Describe the major parts of the shoe. What is the advantage of the Blucher opening? A low quarter?

3. Describe appropriate shoes for an individual with severe pes valgus.

4. Specify the purpose and placement of a metatarsal bar.

5. What are the advantages and disadvantages of the solid stirrup as compared with the shoe insert?

6. Indicate the clinical usages of a posterior leg band, an anterior leg band, and a patellar-tendon-bearing brim.

7. What orthotic knee joint is indicated for the individual with knee flexion contracture?

8. How do Craig-Scott KAFOs support an individual with paraplegia?

9. What orthoses permit the person with paraplegia to stand without the aid of crutches?

10. Outline a maintenance program for a metal/leather KAFO with split stirrups and pawl lock.

11. What factors should be assessed prior to formulating an orthotic prescription?

12. What features of the ankle-foot orthosis are considered in static assessment?

13. Delineate the training program for a person with paraplegia fitted with bilateral KAFOs.

REFERENCES

1. McIlmurray, W and Greenbaum, W: The application of SACH foot principles to orthotics. Orthot Prosthet Appl J 13:37–40, 1959.
2. Doxey, GL: Clinical use and evaluation of molded thermoplastic foot orthotic devices. Phys Ther 65:1679–1682, 1985.
3. Dolan, CE, Mereday, C, and Hartmann, G: Evaluation of the NYU Insert Brace. Post-Graduate Medical School, New York, 1969.
4. Lehmann, J, et al: Ankle-foot orthoses: Effect on gait abnormalities in tibial nerve paralysis. Arch Phys Med Rehabil 66:212–218, 1985.
5. Glancy, J and Lindseth, R: The polypropylene solid ankle orthosis. Orthot Prosthet 26:14–26, 1972.
6. Showers, DC and Strunck, ML: Sheet plastics and their applications in orthotics and prosthetics. Orthot Prosthet 38:41–48, 1984.
7. Engen, T: The TIRR polypropylene orthosis. Orthot Prosthet 26:1, 1972.
8. Lehmann, J, et al: Plastic ankle-foot orthoses: Evaluation of function. Arch Phys Med Rehabil 64:402–407, 1983.
9. Stills, M: Thermoformed ankle-foot orthoses. Orthot Prosthet 29:41, 1975.
10. Lehneis, HR: Plastic spiral ankle-foot orthoses. Orthot Prosthet 28:3, 1974.
11. Bowers, JA and Klassen, EG: Use of short leg braces with patellar tendon bearing cuffs. Arch Phys Med Rehabil 46:436–437, 1965.
12. Lehmann, JF and Warren, CG: Ischial and patellar tendon weight bearing braces: Function, design, adjustment and training. Bull Prosthet Res 10:6, 1973.
13. Rubin, G: The patellar tendon bearing orthosis. Bull Hosp Joint Dis 33:155, 1972.
14. Scott, BA: Engineering principles and fabrication techniques for the Scott-Craig long leg brace for paraplegics. Orthot Prosthet 25:14–19, 1971.
15. Lobley, S, et al: Orthotic design from the New England Regional Spinal Cord Injury Center. Phys Ther 65:492–493, 1985.
16. Motloch, W: The parapodium: An orthotic device for neuromuscular disorders. Artif Limbs 15:36, 1971.
17. Gram, M, Kinnen, E, and Brown, J: Parapodium redesigned for sitting. Phys Ther 61:657–660, 1981.
18. Durr-Fillauer Medical, Inc: LSU Reciprocating Gait Orthosis: A Pictoral Description and Application Manual. Durr-Fillauer Medical, Inc, Chattanooga, 1983.
19. Lehmann, J: Biomechanics of ankle-foot orthoses: Prescription and design. Arch Phys Med Rehabil 60:200–207, 1979.
20. Sarno, JE: Below-knee orthosis: A system for prescription. Arch Phys Med Rehabil 54:548–552, 1973.
21. Krebs, DE, Edelstein, JE, and Fishman, S: Reliability of observational kinematic gait analysis. Phys Ther 65:1027–1033, 1985.
22. Clinkingbeard, JR, Gersten, JW, and Hoehn, D: Energy cost of ambulation in traumatic paraplegia. Am J Phys Med 43:157–165, 1964.
23. Gordon, EE and Vanderwalde, H: Energy requirements in paraplegic ambulation. Arch Phys Med Rehabil 37:276–285, 1956.
24. Long, C and Lawton, EB: Functional significance of spinal cord lesion level. Arch Phys Med Rehabil 36:249–255, 1955.
25. Rosman, N and Spira, E: Paraplegic use of walking braces: Survey. Arch Phys Med Rehabil 55:311–314, 1974.
26. Huang, CT, et al: Energy cost of ambulation in paraplegic patients using Craig-Scott braces. Arch Phys Med Rehabil 60:595–600, 1979.
27. Cerny, K, et al: Walking and wheelchair energetics in persons with paraplegia. Phys Ther 60:1133–1139, 1980.
28. McBeath, AA, Bahrke, M, and Balke, B: Efficiency of assisted ambulation determined by oxygen consumption measurement. J Bone Joint Surg 56-A: 994–1000, 1974.
29. Fisher, SV and Patterson, RP: Energy cost of ambulation with crutches. Arch Phys Med Rehabil 62:250–256, 1981.
30. Lehmann, JF, et al: Biomechanical evaluation of braces for paraplegics. Arch Phys Med Rehabil 50:179–188, 1969.
31. Lehneis, HR, Bergofsky, E, and Frisinia, W: Energy expenditure with advanced lower limb orthoses and with conventional braces. Arch Phys Med Rehabil 57: 20–24, 1976.
32. Miller, NE, et al: Paraplegic energy expenditure during negotiation of architectural barriers. Arch Phys Med Rehabil 65:778–779, 1984.
33. Bard, G: Energy expenditure of hemiplegic subjects during walking. Arch Phys Med Rehabil 44:368–370, 1963.
34. Bard, G and Ralston, HJ: Measurement of energy expenditure during ambulation, with special reference to evaluation of assistive devices. Arch Phys Med Rehabil 40:415–420, 1959.
35. Gersten, JW and Orr, W: External work of walking in hemiparetic patients. Scand J Rehabil Med 3:85–88, 1971.
36. Corcoran, PJ, et al: Effects of plastic and metal leg braces on speed and energy cost of hemiparetic ambulation. Arch Phys Med Rehabil 51:69–77, 1970.

SUPPLEMENTAL READINGS

American Academy of Orthopaedic Surgeons: Atlas of Orthotics, ed 2. CV Mosby, St Louis, 1985.

Bunch, WH and Keagy, RD: Principles of Orthotic Treatment. CV Mosby, St Louis, 1976.

Kennedy, JM: Orthopaedic Splints and Appliances. Williams & Wilkins, Baltimore, 1974.

Nixon, V: Spinal Cord Injury: A Guide to Functional Outcomes in Physical Therapy Management. Aspen, Rockville, MD, 1985.

Redford, JB (ed): Orthotics Etcetera, ed 3. Williams & Wilkins, Baltimore, 1986.

Staff, Prosthetics and Orthotics: Lower-Limb Orthotics. New York University Post-Graduate Medical School, New York, 1986.

GLOSSARY

Bail: The posteriorly protruding semicircular handle of a pair of knee locks, usually pawl locks. Moving the bail upward releases the locks.

Bichannel adjustable ankle lock (BiCAAL): An ankle joint having posterior and anterior receptacles with springs which can be compressed to assist motion or can be replaced by pins to alter the attitude of the joint and thus the uprights attached to the joint.

Caliper: A shoe attachment consisting of a steel tube placed transversely in the shoe heel, into which can be inserted a rod projecting perpendicularly from the orthotic upright, so that the patient can remove the orthosis from the shoe.

Counter: A shoe component consisting of stiff leather or other firm material placed between the lining and the outside of the posterior aspect of the shoe; reinforces the quarter and increases stability of the back of the shoe.

Craig-Scott knee-ankle-foot orthosis: A knee-ankle-foot orthotic design intended for persons with paraplegia, invented by Bruce Scott, an orthotist at the Craig Rehabilitation Center, Denver, Colorado. Each of the pair of orthoses consists of bilateral uprights attached to a shoe by a stirrup, BiCAAL ankle joints, pretibial band, pawl locks with bail release, and a single thigh band.

Insert: Material, usually removable, placed in the shoe, extending from the posterior margin of the sole to an area immediately posterior to the point corresponding to the metatarsophalangeal joints, or farther anterior.

University of California Biomechanics Laboratory (UCBL) insert: A plastic insert that includes a wall covering the medial, posterior, and lateral margins of the foot. The insert is fabricated over a cast of the foot in a maximally corrected position.

Last: The wood or plastic foot-shaped form over which a shoe is made.

Metatarsal bar: A strip of leather attached transversely to the outer sole of a shoe immediately posterior to a point corresponding to the metatarsophalangeal joints, intended to relieve weight bearing at those joints.

Metatarsal pad: Resilient dome-shaped material placed on the inner sole of a shoe, with the apex immediately posterior to one or more painful metatarsophalangeal joints. A resilient or rigid metatarsal pad may be incorporated in a shoe insert.

Nylon acrylic: Transparent thermoplastic material that is molded at 140° C (284° F), and that is very rigid with high-impact and high-flexural strength.

Offset joint: A knee joint in which the axis is located posterior to the midline of the leg. The offset joint provides greater knee stability during early stance as compared with a nonoffset joint.

Parapodium: A prefabricated orthotic frame intended for standing and sitting. It consists of a base connected to a thoracolumbar band by lateral uprights that are hinged and locked at the knees and at the trunk. Chest and anterior leg bands stabilize the device on the patient, who can lock and unlock the knees and hips.

Patellar tendon bearing: Describing the proximal termination of an ankle-foot orthosis that is molded of plastic to resemble the proximal margin of a below-knee prosthesis. The patellar-tendon-bearing brim of an orthosis is intended to support part of the patient's weight proximally, especially on the patellar tendon.

Pawl lock: The locking portion of a knee joint, consisting of a proximal segment having a pivoted bar that lodges in a notch in the distal segment.

Polycentric unit: A knee joint that permits the axis of knee flexion to change through the arc of motion, intended to simulate anatomic knee motion in the sagittal plane.

Polypropylene: Translucent thermoplastic material that is molded at 200° C (392° F), and that is somewhat rigid with high-impact and high-fatigue strength.

Reciprocating gait orthosis: A trunk-hip-knee-ankle-foot orthosis consisting of a pair of knee-ankle-foot orthoses to which is attached a mechanism having two steel cables passing from the right to the left hip joint. When the patient rotates the trunk toward the left, the left lower limb advances while the right limb is held stable by the cable system. Upon transfer of weight to the left limb, the patient then rotates the trunk toward the right to advance the right limb.

Scaphoid pad: Resilient dome-shaped material placed at the junction of the inner sole and medial quarter of the shoe, with the apex located between the navicular tuberosity and the sustentaculum tali of the calcaneus.

Stirrup: A shoe attachment used to connect the orthotic uprights to the shoe.

Solid stirrup: A shoe attachment consisting of a steel plate riveted to the sole at the anterior margin of the heel; the medial and lateral portions of the plate are bent perpendicular to the midsection and are connected to the orthotic uprights at a point corresponding to the anatomic ankle joint. The solid stirrup does not permit the patient to remove the orthosis from the shoe.

Split stirrup: A three-piece stirrup, the central section having a rectangular transverse channel into which the medial and lateral sections can be inserted to permit the patient to remove the orthosis from the shoe.

Thomas heel: A shoe heel designed by Hugh Owen Thomas in which the anterior margin is curved, such that its medial border curves anteriorly, usually with a slight medial wedge. The heel is intended to support flexible pes valgus.

APPENDIX A   ORTHOTIC CHECK-OUT: BELOW-KNEE (AFO)*

Date _____

Patient _____
Diagnosis _____
Disability/deformity _____

Initial check-out ( )   Final check-out ( )
Pass ( )   Provisional Pass ( )   Fail ( )
If the patient needs further attention, please indicate the type of treatment required:
Medical-surgical _____ ( ) Training_____ ( )
Orthotic _____ ( ) Other _____ ( )
                                          (Vocational, psychologic, etc.)
Recommendations and comments: _____
_____
_____

_____
                                          Clinic Chief

_____ 1. Are the orthosis and shoe as prescribed? If a recheck, have previous recommendations been accomplished?
_____ 2. Can the patient don the orthosis without difficulty?

CHECK WITH PATIENT STANDING

Shoe

_____ 3. Is the shoe satisfactory and does it fit properly?
_____ 4. Are the sole and heel of the shoe flat on the floor?

Ankle

_____ 5. Are the mechanical ankle joints aligned so that they coincide approximately with the anatomic ankle and is there adequate clearance?
_____ 6. Is sufficient force exerted by the varus or valgus correction strap or shoe insert to produce the desired support without causing significant discomfort?
_____ 7. Is there minimal rocking between the shoe insert and shoe?

Uprights

_____ 8. Do the uprights (or plastic shell) conform to the contour of the leg?
_____ 9. Do the uprights provide adequate clearance and are they at the midlines of the leg?
_____ 10. In a child's orthosis, is there adequate provision for lengthening uprights?

Bands and Brims

_____ 11. Is the band or shell comfortable, of proper width, and does it conform to the contours of the leg?
_____ 12. Is there sufficient clearance or relief for the head of the fibula?

_____ 13. If a patellar-tendon-bearing brim is used, is there adequate reduction in weight bearing at the heel?

Stability

_____ 14. Is the patient stable?

CHECK WITH PATIENT WALKING

_____ 15. Is there adequate clearance between the malleoli and the mechanical ankle joints?
_____ 16. Does the varus or valgus correction strap or shoe insert provide the desired support?
_____ 17. Is the patient's performance in level walking satisfactory? Indicate any gait deviations that require attention.
_____ a. Lateral trunk bending
_____ b. Hip hiking
_____ c. Internal (external) limb rotation
_____ d. Circumduction
_____ e. Abnormal walking base
_____ f. Excessive medial (lateral) foot contact
_____ g. Anterior trunk bending
_____ h. Posterior trunk bending
_____ i. Lordosis
_____ j. Hyperextended knee
_____ k. Excessive knee flexion
_____ l. Excessive genu valgum or varum
_____ m. Inadequate dorsiflexion control
_____ n. Insufficient push-off
_____ o. Vaulting
_____ p. Rhythmic disturbances
_____ q. Other, including arm motion, noises, etc. (describe) _____
_____
_____

CHECK WITH PATIENT SITTING

_____ 18. Can the patient sit comfortably with the knees flexed approximately 105 degrees?

CHECK WITH ORTHOSIS OFF THE PATIENT

_____ 19. Are the foot and leg free from signs of irritation immediately after the orthosis is removed?
_____ 20. Do the ankle joints move without binding and provide the prescribed range of motion?
_____ 21. Do medial and lateral stops of the ankle joint make simultaneous contact when the joint is fully flexed and extended?
_____ 22. Is the general workmanship of the orthosis satisfactory?
_____ 23. Is the general appearance of the orthosis satisfactory?
_____ 24. Does the patient consider the orthosis satisfactory as to weight, comfort, function, and appearance?

_____
*From Staff, Prosthetics and Orthotics: Lower-Limb Orthotics. New York University Postgraduate Medical School, 1986, p 252, with permission.

APPENDIX B ORTHOTIC CHECK–OUT: ABOVE–KNEE (KAFO)*

Date _____

Patient _____

Diagnosis _____

Disability/deformity _____

Initial check-out ( )   Final check-out ( )

Pass ( )   Provisional Pass ( )   Fail ( )

If the patient needs further attention, please indicate the type of treatment required:

Medical-surgical _____ ( ) Training _____ ( )

Orthotic _____ ( ) Other _____ ( )

(Vocational, psychologic, etc.)

Recommendations and comments: _____

_____

_____

_____

_____

_____

_____ Clinic Chief

_____ 1. Is the orthosis as prescribed? If a recheck, have previous recommendations been accomplished?

_____ 2. Can the patient don the orthosis without difficulty?

CHECK WITH PATIENT STANDING

Shoe

_____ 3. Is the shoe satisfactory and does it fit properly?

_____ 4. Are the sole and heel of the shoe flat on the floor?

Ankle

_____ 5. Are the mechanical ankle joints aligned so they coincide approximately with the anatomic ankle?

_____ 6. Is there satisfactory clearance between the anatomic ankle and the medial and lateral mechanical ankle joints?

_____ 7. If a varus or valgus strap or shoe insert is used, is sufficient force exerted to produce the desired support without causing significant discomfort?

_____ 8. If a shoe insert is used, is there minimal rocking between insert and shoe?

Knee

_____ 9. Are the mechanical knee joints aligned so they coincide approximately with the anatomic knee?

_____ 10. When the patient stands with most of the weight on the braced leg, is there satisfactory clearance between the mechanical knee joint and the patient's knee on both the medial and lateral sides?

_____ 11. Is the knee lock secure and easy to operate?

Uprights

_____ 12. Do the uprights conform to the contours of the leg and thigh?

_____ 13. Is there satisfactory clearance between the medial upright and the perineum?

_____ 14. Is the lateral upright below the head of the trochanter but at least 1 inch higher than the medial upright?

_____ 15. Are the uprights at the midline of the leg and thigh?

_____ 16. In a child's orthosis, is there adequate provision for lengthening all uprights?

Bands and Cuffs

_____ 17. Are the bands and cuffs of proper width, and do they conform to the contours of the leg and thigh?

_____ 18. Are the bands and cuffs comfortable?

_____ 19. Is there sufficient clearance between the top of the calf band and the head of the fibula?

_____ 20. Are the distal thigh band and the calf band equidistant from the knee?

Quadrilateral Brim (when prescribed)

_____ 21. Is the adductor longus properly located in its channel and is the patient free from excessive pressure in the anteromedial aspect of the brim?

_____ 22. Does the ischial tuberosity rest properly on the ischial seat?

_____ 23. Is any flesh roll above the brim minimal?

_____ 24. Is the brim of the posterior wall approximately parallel to the ground?

_____ 25. Is the patient free from vertical pressure in the area of the perineum?

Hip

_____ 26. Is the center of the pelvic joint slightly above and ahead of the greater trochanter?

_____ 27. Is the hip lock secure and easy to operate?

_____ 28. Does the pelvic band fit the contours of the body accurately?

Special Attachments

_____ 29. If a special attachment, such as a torsion shaft, is used, are the intended forces exerted without subjecting the limb to undesirable force?

Stability

_____ 30. Is the patient stable?

CHECK WITH PATIENT WALKING

_____ 31. Is the shoe flat on the floor during the midstance phase of walking?

_____ 32. Is there adequate clearance between the patient's ankle and knee and the corresponding mechanical joints?

_____ 33. Does the varus or valgus strap or shoe insert provide the desired support?

_____ 34. Is the patient's performance in level walking

*From Staff, Prosthetics and Orthotics: *Lower Limb Orthotics*. New York University Postgraduate Medical School, New York, 1986, p 264, with permission.

satisfactory? Indicate below the gait deviations that require attention.

_____ a. Lateral trunk bending
_____ b. Hip hiking
_____ c. Internal (external) hip rotation
_____ d. Circumduction
_____ e. Wide walking base
_____ f. Excessive medial (lateral) foot contact
_____ g. Anterior trunk bending
_____ h. Posterior trunk bending
_____ i. Lordosis
_____ j. Hyperextended knee
_____ k. Knee instability
_____ l. Inadequate dorsiflexion control
_____ m. Insufficient push-off
_____ n. Vaulting
_____ o. Rhythmic abnormalities
_____ p. Other, including arm motion, noises, etc. (Describe)_____
_____
_____
_____

_____ 35. Is the orthosis sufficiently strong and rigid?
_____ 36. Does the orthosis operate quietly?

CHECK WITH PATIENT SITTING

_____ 37. Can the patient sit comfortably with the knees flexed 90 degrees, and can the patient flex the knee an additional 15 degrees without undue pressure?
_____ 38. Do the mechanical ankle joints provide the prescribed range of motion?

_____ 39. Are the mechanical knee joint adjustments adequate?
_____ 40. Are the sole and heel of the shoe flat on the floor?

CHECK WITH ORTHOSIS OFF THE PATIENT

_____ 41. Is the limb free from signs of irritation immediately after the orthosis is removed?

Orthosis

_____ 42. Is the shoe firmly attached to the orthosis, and is the shoe shank strong enough for its anticipated use?
_____ 43. Is the heel flat and firmly nailed to the shoe, and are wedges and lifts as neat and inconspicuous as possible?
_____ 44. Do the ankle and knee joints move without binding?
_____ 45. Do both medial and lateral stops of the ankle and knee joints make simultaneous contact when the joints are fully flexed and extended?
_____ 46. Is the calf band adequately and smoothly lined and padded?
_____ 47. Is there adequate provision for adjustment of the straps and cuffs?
_____ 48. Are the metal parts of the orthosis smooth and free from sharp edges and sharp bends?
_____ 49. Is the leatherwork neat?
_____ 50. Is the general appearance of the orthosis satisfactory?
_____ 51. Does the patient consider the brace satisfactory as to comfort, function, and appearance?

Chapter 28

THE PRESCRIPTIVE WHEELCHAIR: AN ORTHOTIC DEVICE

ADRIENNE FALK BERGEN

OBJECTIVES

1. Identify the postural support components of a wheelchair system.

2. Identify the components that make up a wheeled mobility base.

3. Describe the function of an orthotic wheelchair in the rehabilitation process.

4. Identify the team members who contribute to problem solving during a wheelchair assessment and prescription.

5. Identify the measurements that are needed for correct wheelchair fitting.

INTRODUCTION

Physical therapists are often called upon to prescribe wheelchairs. A properly prescribed wheelchair can be a useful device in reintegrating a differently abled individual into the mainstream, whereas a poorly prescribed one can actually exacerbate the problems associated with a disability. This chapter presents a systematic approach to providing a prescriptive wheelchair. First, attention will be directed toward the seating system required to provide the proper support for the individual patient. Second, the features available to create a proper mobility base for the seating system will be described. The seating system and mobility base combine to create a prescriptive wheelchair.

A wheelchair is truly a mobility orthosis. An *orthosis* is a device used to provide support or to straighten or to correct a deformity. It is typically some type of brace made of metal or plastic that increases or maintains a patient's level of function. If properly prescribed, a wheelchair will provide sufficient support to help deter the effect of deforming forces or weakened structures on function of the system. In simpler terms, it should sup-

port the patient as needed to allow maximum functional potential. Inasmuch as it is on wheels, the system can be called a mobility orthosis, providing appropriate support to allow maximum mobility.

Like a well-made orthosis, the wheelchair should fit correctly. It should be reasonably cosmetic to the user. It should also be as lightweight and yet as strong as possible. It can be obtained from a stock supply when that type of device works, but most often individual modifications for the patient's special needs are required.

Like a well-made orthosis, a well-fitted wheelchair should be prescribed by a qualified professional(s). The decision making around a prescriptive wheelchair should be done by the entire team. It is important that all those concerned with the patient's present and future function be a part of this team. This includes the patient, therapists, family members, nurses, physicians, and vocational counselors. The team must have a clear idea of where this chair will be used and who will be using it to ensure that the most suitable device is obtained.

A prescriptive wheelchair is a combination of a *postural support system* and a *mobility base*. The support system is made up of the seat and any additional components such as torso supports, adductors, abductors, and lap belt needed to maintain postural alignment. The mobility base consists of the tubular frame, legrests and armrests, foot supports and wheels. Once the decisions are made about the type of support system needed, the team must then decide what type of mobility base best suits the user's functional level and environmental and caretaking needs. Clear information will be needed to ensure that the postural support system and the mobility base interface properly. The most cost-effective approach is to have one support system interface with all the mobility bases. Sometimes it is best to have the individual use the support system in the chair used most frequently, and then to forego optimum postural support in the backup system in order to facilitate transport for short trips.

THE POSTURAL SUPPORT SYSTEM

A thorough assessment of the patient's posture, cardiopulmonary function, range of motion, skin condition and tone must be completed prior to decision making regarding the postural support system. This information will assist in determining whether the patient is functioning at the highest potential or whether additional support would be helpful in freeing distal body parts to improve function. It will also assist in assessing the consequences of poor posture on skin condition, respiratory function, speech, and general functioning.

During this assessment the patient should be positioned in various sample wheelchairs. The patient's mode of propulsion, method of transfer, and interaction with the environment should be observed. Performance in each of these areas will be influenced by the individual's strength, posture, and tone and can be modified by support system intervention. Proper intervention may

enhance function (e.g., respiratory or motor), whereas improper intervention (e.g., poorly placed wheels or excessive chair width) may interfere with function.[1-5]

In choosing chair properties, careful attention must be given to possible secondary problems that may be created. For example, if the intervention includes a high seat cushion for pressure relief, will the user be able to get under tables and desks, transfer, or reach the wheels for self-propulsion? If the prescription includes a custom support system, will the weight preclude easy self-propulsion? Will the bulk make automobile transport difficult or impossible?

The components of the system that will directly effect comfort and maintenance of posture are the seat surface, seat back, lap belt, armrests and foot supports. These areas should be addressed together. The team must also address interfacing these components with the rest of the wheeled mobility system.

Seat Surface

Most wheelchairs come with a sling seat. This type of surface reinforces a poor pelvic position with the hips tending to slide forward, creating a posterior pelvic tilt. The thighs typically move toward adduction and internal rotation (Fig. 28–1A). Most patients can benefit from a firm sitting surface (Fig. 28–1B).[6] Total contact between the under surface of the thigh and the seating surface will enhance sitting ability by providing a stable base of support on which to mount upper body function. The front of the seat can actually extend into the popliteal fossa, provided that the front edge is well padded and contoured to provide relief for hamstring tendons and/or calf bulk. This surface may require specialized foam in one or varying densities, or a specific contour. The patient also may require a special cushion for comfort,

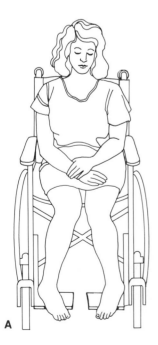
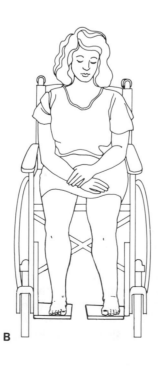

A   **B**

Figure 28–1. (*A*) A sling seat often results in poor pelvic positioning, with the thighs moving toward adduction and internal rotation. (*B*) A firm seating surface provides stable pelvic positioning and will improve upper body function. (Adapted from Bergen, AF and Colangelo, C,[6] p 7, with permission.)

control, and/or pressure relief. Cushions are generally made of foam, gel, liquid, pockets of air, or a combination of these elements.

The depth of the seat should be measured carefully, because an overly deep seat will encourage a posterior pelvic tilt and a resultant tendency toward **kyphotic posturing.** A seat that is too shallow will not provide enough support, making maintenance of lower extremity alignment more difficult.

For patients with neuromuscular problems (e.g., multiple sclerosis, muscular dystrophy, cerebral palsy), the seat may require an **abductor pommel, adductor cushions,** or groin strap to maintain alignment of the lower extremities. The chair must be prepared for these additions before being upholstered. The seat also may require angling to modify tone at the hips. This can be done with varying foam densities, **contouring, control blocking,** or with specialized hardware.

Back Surface

Patients who have fair to good trunk control usually require only a midscapula back height. Many prefer it lower; however, evidence exists that although some lower back supports work well in the short run, they may cause problems over longer periods of use.[7] For patients who have poor trunk control and those who tend to push into extension, the back height should be to the shoulders (approximately to the level of the acromion process). This is especially critical if any type of shoulder support is to be used. This higher back may make it more difficult for caretakers to adjust the patient's posture, but the added control offered will make frequent postural adjustments unnecessary.

Many individuals will not be provided adequate support from the standard fabric seat back that comes with a wheelchair. In these situations a back insert is indicated. The insert is fabricated from a firm base such as wood, plastic, or triwall cardboard and padded foam. The foam can vary in thickness and density. The team must assess the patient's response to a back insert and vary the foam according to postural needs and comfort level. A very firm foam may work well for individuals with low central tone by encouraging more extension, but those with prominent bony protuberances may not tolerate this type of surface.

For patients with extensor tone it will be critical that the insert maintains a 90 degree angle to the sitting surface. The interface between the seat back insert and the wheelchair back tubes must be assessed. Modifications to either the back uprights or the back of the insert may be needed to keep the insert braced at this 90 degree angle.

Lap Belt

A lap belt may be needed for safety or for assistance with postural control. Attention must be given to style, size, direction of pull, and placement to achieve maximum effectiveness. Generally, the lap belt should form a 45 degree angle with the sitting surface (Fig. 28–2). If excessive extensor tone is present (e.g., cerebral palsy, multiple sclerosis), a 90 degree angle of pull may be more effective in providing postural control and alignment.

Arm Supports

ARMRESTS

Wheelchair armrests have many important functions. They provide assistance for pushing up to standing, a support surface for arms and lap boards, a mechanism

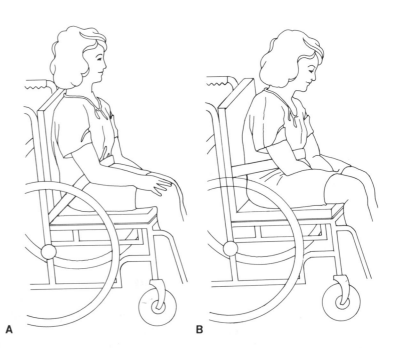

Figure 28–2. (*A*) The lap belt should ideally form a 45-degree angle with the seating surface. (*B*) A lap belt that crosses the pelvis at the level of the ASIS will encourage a posterior pelvic tilt. (From Bergen, AF and Colangelo, C,[6] p 11, with permission.)   **A**   **B**

for relief of ischial pressure (sitting pushup), and some small amount of lateral stability. Attention should be directed to the height of the armrests and the length and size of the support surface. It may be necessary for the patient to use the armrests to support the upper extremities and thus to decrease pull on the shoulders and trunk. This approach is often used with very weak individuals such as those with high spinal cord injuries or muscular dystrophy. For many patients the armrests will be used to mount a lap board (tray).

LAP BOARDS

Lap boards provide several important functions. They can be used to achieve symmetrical positioning of the upper extremities, to maintain corrected alignment of the glenohumeral joint and scapula, and to serve as a work or communication surface. They also can act as an adjunct to the postural control system by supporting the weight of the arms and decreasing their pull on the shoulders and trunk. In addition, high (elevated) lap boards can be used to inhibit tone around the shoulders and neck. In extreme cases, the arms of individuals with athetosis may be trapped purposely beneath the lap board to decrease interference of involuntary movement when using a head pointer or during feeding activities.[8]

Foot Supports

Style and position are important considerations when selecting wheelchair foot support systems. Placement of the foot support system will directly effect the position of the entire lower body, affecting tone and posture in the trunk, head, and arms. Ninety degrees of hip flexion will help keep the pelvis well positioned on the sitting surface. A proper support height and style is required for maintenance of this position. Foot supports that are too low will result in lower knees, placing the hips in less than 90 degrees of flexion. Elevating foot support systems may place excessive stretch on tight hamstrings, pulling the pelvis into a posterior tilt, also placing the hips in less than 90 degrees of flexion. Decisions on straps and foot positioners also must be made early, in order to ensure placement on the final unit.

Several special wheelchair systems are available with component parts that provide specific levels of support. Examples include the Mulholland and Orthokinetics chairs. For patients who do not fit well into a specialized seating system, the dealer may have to work with several manufacturers to create a customized seating unit (Fig. 28–3). The use of multiple manufacturers to create a single seating and mobility system increases the level of difficulty for the team and requires ever-increasing amounts of planning and research to ensure that the end result will be satisfactory.

MEASURING THE PATIENT

It is important to take complete measurements when preparing to order a wheelchair. This may be time-consuming. However, it is well worth the investment

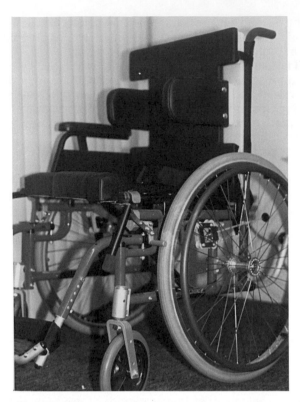

Figure 28–3. Component seating systems can be mounted on standard wheelchairs to create a custom seating unit. (Courtesy of Medco Adaptive Equipment, Merrick, NY.)

because it provides a permanent record of why certain decisions were made. During the ordering or manufacturing process, additional decisions on modifications may be needed. If accurate measurements are on file, decisions can often be made without recalling the patient to the clinic.

To create a properly fitted system, accurate measurements will be needed of thigh/hip length, leg length, distance from seat to the midback, midscapula, and shoulder, distance from hanging elbow to seat surface, and the width across the hips (Fig. 28–4).

Thigh/Hip Length

Measurement of the thigh/hip length is required to determine seat depth (see Figure 28–4A). It is usually taken in the sitting position. For patients with tone problems (e.g., cerebral palsy, hemiplegia, multiple sclerosis), this may be inaccurate because of the posterior tilt of the pelvis during uncorrected sitting. In addition, sitting may create subtle or obvious asymmetries in pelvic position which are difficult to assess in this position.

To ensure an accurate measurement of seat depth, it is helpful to take this measurement in two positions. The first is the traditional upright seated position with as much correction as possible. This may require an additional person to assist with controlling the pelvis while the measurement is taken. The second measurement should be taken with the patient supine on a firm surface (a mat or carpeted floor works well; a bed is not firm enough). Both hips and knees should be flexed to 90

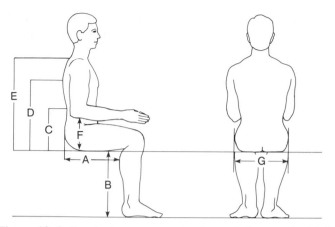

Figure 28–4. Required measurements for ordering a wheelchair include (*A*) thigh/hip length, (*B*) leg length, (*C*) distance from the seating surface to the midback, (*D*) midscapula, (*E*) to the top of the shoulder, (*F*) hanging elbow, and (*G*) across the hips.

degrees. Care should be taken to neutralize the pelvic tilt if at all possible. This can be accomplished by using tone reduction techniques while keeping the fingers on the anterior superior crests of the pelvis. If the pelvis is asymmetrical with the knees pointed upright, this may indicate limited range of hip abduction or adduction. In some cases it will be necessary to allow the legs to rotate off to the side (**windblown position**) to achieve good pelvic alignment. If this occurs during measurement, consideration must be given to how the windblown position will be accommodated in the final wheelchair (e.g., wider wheelchair, offset armrests).

The actual measurement is taken by holding the lower extremities in the optimal position in both sitting and supine positions (hips and knees flexed to 90 degrees if possible). A second person measures the undersurface of the thigh from the popliteal fossa to the back of the buttocks (this is considered to be the supporting surface in the supine position; and to the edge of the skin surface in sitting). This should be done for each leg individually, obtaining a left and right measurement. If discrepancies in the measurement are obtained between the supine and sitting positions, a halving of the difference will usually provide a correct measurement for seat depth.

Leg Length

This measurement (see Figure 28–4B) is needed to determine the correct height for the foot plate. Most wheelchairs have a standard range of adjustment which relates to the overall size of the chair. Many patients will fall outside of this range, necessitating a custom modification. This measurement is obtained with the patient either seated or in the supine position. It is taken from the popliteal fossa to the bottom of the heel with the patient wearing customary footwear.

Seat Back Height

During a complete assessment, measurement of seat back height should be taken in a corrected sitting posi-

tion. This measurement is taken from the seating surface to the midback (see Figure 28–4C), midscapula (see Figure 28–4D), and to the top of the shoulder (see Figure 28–4E). These measurements will provide a detailed record should decisions regarding back height be needed after the assessment is completed.

Hanging Elbow

This measurement (see Figure 28–4F) will be needed to determine proper armrest height. With the patient in a corrected sitting position, the upper extremity is positioned at the side of the body with 90 degrees of elbow flexion, and the shoulder in a neutral position. A measurement is taken from the bottom of the elbow to the seating surface.

Across the Hips

With the patient in a corrected sitting position, a measurement (see Figure 28–4G) is taken across the hips at the widest point (from the most lateral aspect of skin surface on each side). The usual recommendation in determining seat width is to add 1 to 2 inches to this measurement. Attention should be directed to the orthoses, which may be worn when seated, and to any user preferences (which do not detract from function) as to the fit of the chair.

THE WHEELED MOBILITY BASE: WHEELCHAIR FEATURES AND ACCESSORIES

The wheeled base forms the mobility structure for the seating system. Mobility bases include dependent systems, independent systems activated manually, and independent systems activated under battery power.

Dependent systems include strollers, push chairs, and many of the elaborate postural systems used with individuals who are severely physically and mentally impaired. These systems have small wheels not intended for self-propulsion. When considering a dependent mobility system it is important to determine the function of the unit. Is this a primary mobility system or a backup for the patient who has powered mobility? If the ability to use any independent movement exists, the patient should be assessed for either a manual or powered wheelchair as the primary mobility system. Sophisticated technology now allows even the most severely physically impaired individual to achieve independent mobility. This should be encouraged and assisted by the proper wheeled mobility base. If at all possible, even very young children (12 months and older) and the elderly should be provided with a means of independent mobility that allows them to extend beyond the boundary of the physical impairment. Research supports the beneficial impact of independent functioning on all aspects of cognitive and psychosocial well-being.[9]

When preparing the specifications for a wheeled mobility base, many features have to be carefully studied

(Fig. 28–5). There are dozens of bases available. Each have subtly different features. The team will be challenged in their effort to make the correct patient–product match.

Seat

SEAT DEPTH

Correct seat depth is particularly important to achieving maximum postural support and tone control. Wheelchairs are readily available from manufacturers in various seat depths. The depth measurements given in the catalog usually correspond to the depth of the upholstery itself from the back to the front edge. Depending on the manufacturer, the upholstery depth may be equal to, less than, or greater than the metal seat rail. The team must be aware of different manufacturers' features. If the patient does not fit a listed size, modifications can be made incorporating one or more of the following methods: a back insert, frame construction, or upholstery modifications.

Back Insert

To decrease the overall depth of the sitting surface, a *back insert* can be used to bring the user forward in the seat. This back insert, or cushion, can be ordered with any specified overall thickness and usually consists of a piece of wood or plastic, and foam.

When ordering standard back inserts it is imperative that one know the manufacturer's standard thickness and density of foam. With most styles of wheelchairs one can specify whether the insert is to be positioned between the back tubes or in front of them. This choice will effect the impact of the back insert on overall available sitting surface. It is important to note whether the upholstery is mounted in front of the back tubes, between the back tubes, or half and half, inasmuch as this will directly affect the placement of the back insert. It is also critical to note whether the back tube has a bend, which will affect the vertical orientation of the back insert. If the insert must be vertical (perpendicular to the seat surface) for postural control, either a straight back tube will be required or the insert will require adaption to brace it in position.

Frame Construction

Seat depth also can be modified (increased or decreased) by frame construction. Modifications *by construction* should be considered with short wide or very tall patients or long-legged individuals who have slowed or completed their growth cycle. An important factor to

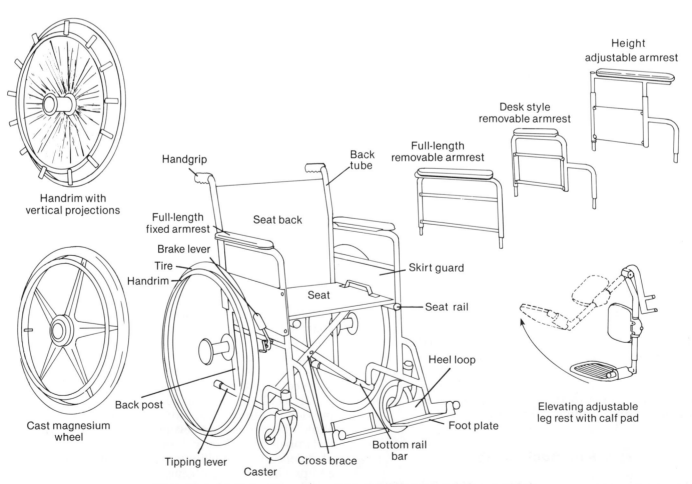

Figure 28–5. Multiple options are available in creating a prescriptive wheelchair.

consider is that lengthening the chair frame will increase the turning radius and may prevent the user from maneuvering the chair in small spaces. A few manufacturers supply seat extension kits which extend the seat rail a few inches without changing the overall length of the frame.

Upholstery Modifications

Wheelchair seat depth may also be altered by *upholstery changes*. This can be achieved symmetrically if leg length is equal, or asymmetrically if leg length is unequal. Seat depth can be increased or decreased within specific dimensions set by the manufacturer. Generally, a seat insert can be extended at least 1 inch beyond the front end of the seat rail without creating an unstable sitting surface. The seat upholstery or inserts also can be cut back several inches. The effects on foot placement of any of these modifications must be assessed. Subsequent footplate adjustments may be required.

Working on the upholstery of the chair requires detailed knowledge of what each manufacturer considers standard. For instance, is upholstery depth as listed in the catalog the same as seat rail length, 1 inch shorter or 1 inch longer? Are standard footplates a large or small size, and how close are they to the front end of the frame? Careful assessment of various wheelchairs will reveal wide discrepancies in available parts and interfaces, depending on wheelchair style and manufacturer.

SEAT WIDTH

The width of the sitting surface, as well as the overall width of the wheelchair, is important to functional use. For individuals who wear orthoses, require control blocks at the hip, wear bulky clothing, or experience weight fluctuations, special considerations will be needed. The natural tendency is to increase the width of the seat. Such a solution must be approached cautiously, however, inasmuch as this will also increase the overall width of the chair, creating difficulty for those needing to reach the wheels for self-propulsion, or for those who must maneuver in tight places.

The goal is to create a chair that fits as closely to the user's body as reasonable. This will make the chair easy to wheel and easier to maneuver. It also will make the chair seem, visually, more congruent with the user's body lines.

Seat width can be changed in several ways. *Widening* can be accomplished by use of fixed offset or removable arms; by construction on a new chair; or by changing the cross braces on an existing chair. Seat *narrowing* can be achieved by upholstery or by construction. Narrowing a chair by upholstery essentially creates a "growing" chair out of any size chair. The chair is simply folded a bit, and narrower upholstery is mounted, preventing full width opening. It must be recognized, however, that narrowing a chair by upholstery will raise the seat height.

The overall outside width of the chair should be as narrow as possible for maximum function. Excessive width makes the chair difficult to maneuver through doorways and in small areas. It is also more difficult to propel the chair if the arms must be widely abducted to reach the wheels. This wide abduction requires the patient to use available muscular strength around the shoulder girdle for stability and posture, leaving less to use for functional push. The width can be modified by several means. The modifications include various hand rim and armrest options; use of internal mounting of the wheel axle plate on some ultralight wheelchairs; and wheelchair narrowing devices. The narrowing devices are useful only for individuals who have sufficient coordination to rock the chair forward and back while turning the crank handle of the device. The device will not work with solid seat inserts, or with reclining wheelchairs that have spreader bars to reinforce the back. If there is enough room to use the wheelchair narrowing device comfortably, perhaps the wheelchair should have been narrower in the first place.

SEAT HEIGHT

The height of the wheelchair sitting surface is important for maximum independent functioning in foot-assisted self-propulsion, transfers, approaching working surfaces, relating with peers, and transfer into a van via lift or ramp. Seat height must be assessed with respect to the entire chair, inasmuch as it may alter the patient's position relative to the armrests, back height, wheel locks, wheels, and footrests.

Seat height can be altered by one or more methods, including altering the frame construction on ordering the chair, altering the thickness of the seat inserts or cushions, removing the seat upholstery and using solid hook-out seat boards with varying depth hardware.

SEAT SURFACE

A firm sitting surface will provide a more symmetrical sitting base. This firm surface will provide the patient with a more stable base of support for the upper body, usually resulting in improved function. A firm sitting surface can be achieved in a variety of ways, with or without specialized cushions.

Prior to deciding on an intervention that is other than standard, the team should inspect what the manufacturer considers a standard seat. Some manufacturers use extremely taut fabric for their seat slings (notably some of the ultralight wheelchairs). In combination with a firm foam cushion, no other support is needed. Others use a fabric design that allows the sling component to be adjusted. This works adequately for some patients, allowing them to adjust the tension as the sling becomes slack with extended use.

If a firm seat board is needed, there are several ways this can be achieved. The simplest is to incorporate a clinic or vendor-made board into the foam cushion that comes with the chair; or into a foam cushion that comes with a removable cover (Fig. 28–6A). It is possible that this lightweight unit may slide about in the chair, producing an asymmetrical sitting surface. A few cushions do have special fabric or velcro strips on the underside, which discourages slipping.

A second option for a firm seat is to order the wheelchair with a standard hammock seat with a solid seat insert on top. This type of insert adds little to no weight to the wheelchair system. It is usually made of foam and wood and is covered with vinyl to match the chair. The standard thickness and density of the foam varies with each manufacturer. The individual supplier of durable medical equipment will provide information on standard foam characteristics so that alterations can be made as needed. Custom thickness and density are available if requested, either directly from the primary manufacturer or from a manufacturer of wheelchair component parts.

This solution has several drawbacks. The insert may slip about in the seat, especially when the armrests are spaced away from the seat, creating an asymmetrical sitting surface. The insert must be removed to fold the chair, which may result in its elimination or loss after several foldings.

Another option for firm seating is a solid folding seat (see Figure 28–6B). This type of seat is an integral part of the frame. It is permanently hinged to one seat rail, folding up when the chair is folded and dropping down into place as it is opened. When the chair is folded, this style of seat alters the shape of the chair. It is important to determine whether this shape will fit into the family car. When this folding seat is in the opened position, it rests between the seat rails, leaving the rails exposed. If it is 1 inch thick overall, its top surface will be level with the seat rails. If fabricated with thicker foam, the solid folding seat surface will be above the seat rails. In a 16-inch-wide wheelchair, for instance, there will be 14 inches of upholstered and padded seating surface and 1 inch of rail exposed on each side. Some patients find this uncomfortable if they are using the full seat width as a sitting surface.

The advantage of a solid folding seat is that it cannot get lost or eliminated from the seating system for convenience. The Everest and Jennings (E&J) hardware for solid folding seats actually adds some strength to the frame but, will also add 7 to 10 pounds to the weight of the chair. This style of seat on other manufacturer's wheelchairs has a simpler mechanism, which adds neither weight nor additional strength to the frame of the chair.

A fourth option for providing a solid seating surface is the solid hook-on seat (see Figure 28–6C). This is a separate seat board which has hook-type hardware along both sides. These hooks clip onto the seat rail, securing the seat in the chair. The seat can hook on level with the seat rails or above them. With this variability and the different thicknesses of foam available for the insert and/or separate seat cushions, it is possible to change the height of the sitting surface without altering the frame. When the seat is removed to fold the chair, there is no sitting surface on the chair frame and there is no extra hardware. The hook-on seat does not add weight to the frame, except a small amount for the hardware. Care should be taken in providing this alternative to patients who drive and use the seat upholstery as a handle for pulling the chair into the car.

In addition to the standard bent hooks, the solid hook-on seat can be equipped with specialized hardware that allows the seat surface to be angled. Many styles of hardware are available from different manufacturers. Several wheelchair manufacturers (e.g., Poirier, E&J, Meyra) include angle-adjustable seats in their catalogs.

THE SEAT BACK

To determine height of the seat back, the degree of back support needed to achieve maximum function must be ascertained. The wheelchair back can be ordered to specification. Until patient status is stable, consideration should be given to ordering add-on or removable parts such as (1) a seat back with an extension piece; (2) a sectional height seat back that can be removed and replaced later (tubes and upholstery); or (3) an adjustable height seat back.

The effect of the additional back height on the overall dimensions of the chair may make the chair too large to fit into a car or may not allow adequate clearance for entering a van. In such cases, or in cases in which a custom chair is not possible or an existing chair is in good condition, a high back insert may suffice.

When increasing or decreasing the back height, attention should be directed to the level of the push handles. On many chairs these can be mounted at a height most useful for the caretakers. An extra reinforcement cap of upholstery may provide additional strength to the upper edge of the upholstery. A few wheelchairs are upholstered with the top edge of the back upholstery wrapped around the front of the back tubes; on other chairs the upholstery forms a sleeve around the back tubes.

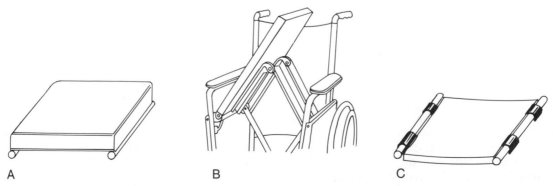

Figure 28–6. A firm seating surface can be provided by (*A*) a cushion with a solid internal board, (*B*) a solid folding seat, or (*C*) a solid hook-on seat.

On standard wheelchairs the back tubes rise straight to midback level and then angle backward. When a patient leans on these for support, they tend to facilitate shoulder retraction and back extension. Patients often need this leeway to feel comfortable. If a solid back insert is used, the user may push on the top edge until it rests on the tubes, forcing the bottom edge to push the pelvis forward on the wheelchair seat (Fig. 28–7A). If this problem is anticipated, it is possible to order the chair with straight tubes instead of the standard angled ones. It is also possible to add a wedge to the back of the solid insert to maintain a vertical position (see Figure 28–7B).

THE LAP BELT

The lap belt is one of the simplest features on a prescription wheelchair. Most clinicians know that a lap belt should cross the pelvis at a 45 degree angle, and many understand that the closure style is often critical. There is more than this involved, however, in deciding on a proper lap belt.

The style of closure is important in facilitating independent use. Many patients can only manage Velcro, but others can manage only buckles. If the patient is not able to use the belt independently, and/or if significant postural control is required, the style of belt is limited. Some Velcro lap belts are not strong enough for use by patients with severe extensor tone. For these, and for others who require a great deal of control, a Velcro and D-ring style belt, or a belt with a cinching-style buckle arrangement, is the most suitable. Cinching-style buckles similar to those on automobile seat belts are available in push-button and flipper styles. The critical feature on all styles is that once the initial contact is made with the fastener, the belt can be adjusted further to increase tightness.

The direction of pull of the belt is important if patterns of spasticity tend to be asymmetrical. For example, if one hip tends to pull forward consistently, it may be useful to have the belt tighten by pulling it down toward that hip. The angle of pull to the seating surface should form a 45-degree angle (a slightly larger angle may be beneficial for some patients). Mounting the belt to the seat rail about 4 inches forward of the seat–back junction will create a downward pull across the upper thighs or just at the thigh–abdomen interface. Caution should be used with patients who push into excessive extension. This type of belt placement may cause the wheelchair to fold as the patient pushes upward on the belt. In such situations, a custom-made piece of hardware may be needed to allow mounting the belt at a specific point on the lower wheelchair rail.

The width of the belt and size of the buckle will effect the level of control offered. The belt and buckle must be proportioned to the user's body correctly. Small children should have 1-inch-wide belts, larger children 1.5-inch-wide belts, and adults 2-inch-wide belts. The buckles should be compatible. Plastic buckles may be more comfortable for some users.

The Legrest and Foot Support

Legrest size is determined by measuring the leg length from the popliteal fossa to the heel and subtracting 1 inch. The corresponding measure on the wheelchair is called the *minimum footboard extension (MinFBX)*. This measure is the distance from the seat rail to the footplate. If separate cushions or an insert with or without special foam thickness has been added, or if the seat itself must be angled, the MinFBX measurement must be modified accordingly when the chair is ordered from the manufacturer. For example, if the distance from the popliteal fossa to the heel measures 16 inches and the patient is to sit on a 2-inch-thick cushion, a MinFBX of approximately 14 inches will be needed if the seat is firm, or 15 inches if the seat is soft foam.

Optimum foot placement may be difficult to achieve in the presence of postural control problems or abnormal tone. Proper sitting posture for maximum control calls for 90 degrees of flexion at the hips and knees and a neutral ankle position. Many times this knee-foot alignment is imperative in maintaining total body alignment. For small individuals this is rather simple. When dealing with larger patients it may be necessary to raise them on cushions, to order special smaller casters, or to use a special extended wheelchair frame to allow the knees to be flexed to 90 degrees without the feet interfering with caster movement.

There are several styles of foot support: a one-piece footboard, tubular foot supports, or two individual foot plates. These supports can be mounted directly to the frame, on clip-off hangers, on swing-away hangers, or on elevating hangers. The style of hardware the particular manufacturer uses will change the orientation of the foot support to the frame of the chair and to the patient's body. Swing-away hangers, for example, may place the foot plate parallel to the floor, or at an angle, and may locate them close to the chair frame or as much as 3 to 4 inches anterior to the front upright. Many manufacturers

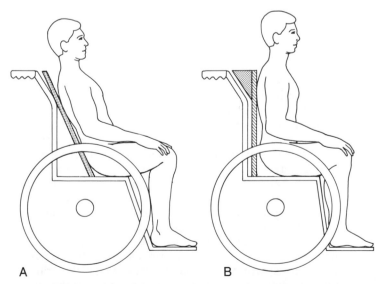

Figure 28–7. (*A*) When the patient leans back on a solid insert, it may push the pelvis forward. (*B*) A wedge can be added to the back of the insert to maintain a vertical position.

will alter this as a custom modification, but specific information must be supplied on the original order.

The mounting hardware should be chosen for function as well as posture. For individuals with edema, detachable elevating legrests may be required (see Figure 28–5). For patients with increased hamstring tone or tightness (e.g., cerebral palsy, multiple sclerosis, muscular dystrophy), elevating legrests are usually not recommended because opening the knee angle will stretch the hamstrings and may pull the pelvis out of alignment. Detachable swing-away footrests do not elevate but do swing away to assist in transfers and better approach to the front of the wheelchair. When ordering front-rigging styles, consideration must be given to both present and future function so that the patient will be able to progress within the chair and not have a chair that actually exacerbates problems of management.

The size of the foot plate surface can vary. A few manufacturers offer three different sizes, others offer only one or two. The ultralight wheelchairs are often available with open or filled-in foot plates. The foot plate should accommodate the length of the foot as well as the width of orthoses, splints, or oversized shoes. Narrowing a chair for a better fit around the hips and better hand placement on the rims also will decrease the available space between the front tubes for the foot plates. Some of the flip-up style foot plates have additional hardware, which further limits the available space in this area.

A calf strap or pad can be used to help keep the feet on the foot plates. Heel loops and/or ankle straps may be needed to control the feet on the foot plate. Heel loops are available in webbing, single width; vinyl, single or double width; and plastic, single or double width. Although plastic and double-width style heel loops offer more control, they can prevent the foot plates from being flipped up, interfering with some transfer styles.

Ankle straps control the heel position on the foot plate. The straps should make a 45 degree angle with the foot plate surface, causing weight to be placed into the heel. These straps can be simple Velcro, Velcro with D-rings, or straps with buckles. Crossed ankle straps or figure-eight strapping also can be effective.

A few patients also may benefit from toe loops (or straps). Toe loops are generally fabricated from canvas webbing and attach in a half-circle pattern to the anterior portion of the foot plate. Many toe loops are solid; others have Velcro or buckle openings. Toe loops are used to assist control of severe involuntary movements or spasticity (especially extensor spasms).

Armrests

Fixed armrests offer no specific benefits for a wheelchair user unless it is likely that removable armrests will be lost. They are often ordered in an attempt to reduce the overall width of the chair. This can be achieved with wrap-around armrests (Fig. 28–8), which are removable and allow for transfers, sitting without armrests, use of special adapted inserts, changing from fixed height to adjustable height armrests, and so forth. Although adjustable and wrap-around armrest styles may be more

Figure 28–8. Wrap-around armrests. The posterior upright of the armrest inserts behind the seat back tube, decreasing overall width of the chair. (Courtesy of Invacare Corporation, Elyria, OH.)

costly on the initial frame, they provide for a more flexible system that can be altered as the patient's functional needs change.

Wrap-around armrests reduce the overall outside width of the chair 1.5 inches by bringing the wheels in closer. This is accomplished by structural placement of the posterior upright of the armrest *behind* ("wrapped around") the seat back tube. This narrows the chair for easier maneuverability and places the wheels closer for better hand access. Removal and repositioning of this style armrest may be difficult for some individuals, and a careful assessment is needed.

Height-adjustable armrests (see Figure 28–5) are important for children, especially those whose chair frames have been ordered with built-in growth allowance. This type of adjustability also is useful for patients who need more or less support depending on the time of day or activity. They permit placement of a lap board without extensive custom modifications.

Full-length arm pads give more room for a lap board to be secured. They also afford the user a larger surface to grasp for push-ups and transfers. Standard full-length armrests, however, may prevent the user from getting close to tables or work surfaces. Shorter-length desk arms can be ordered to allow for this function. Alternatively, full-length height-adjustable armrests allow the user to remove the armrest top or to raise it above the table surface, allowing the front jog feature to be used in a manner similar to a desk arm (Fig. 28–9).

Many of the wheelchairs in use today have nontraditional armrest styles. Some armrests are tubular, with rounded tops rather than flat armrest pads. Several of these styles have only one point of mounting on the chair and may not be stable enough for weight bearing (e.g., for pressure relief or depression transfers). Others mount in

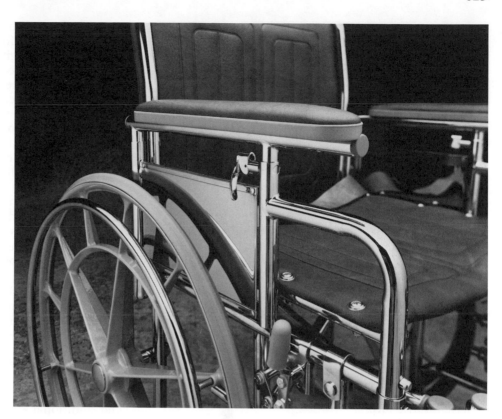

Figure 28–9. Full-length height-adjustable armrests provide the benefit of full-length arm support while the desk notch allows easy access to tables. (Courtesy of Invacare Corporation, Elyria, OH.)

two places, a few on the outside of the chair frame and others into housings, which provide more stability. A few of the newer styles flip up but do not remove, and others swing out to the side. Some have skirt guards, and others do not. It is important to examine all available options with function in mind to be certain which product will best suit the consumer's need.

When ordering a specific armrest style, the height of the armrest from the seat rail should be checked. After comparing this to the measurement obtained for the hanging elbow, a custom-ordered armrest height may be required. Wheelchair armrest height is determined by adding 1 inch to the hanging elbow measure. Armrests that are too high will cause shoulder elevation, and those that are too short may encourage leaning. Those spaced too far apart may interfere with the person's ability to wheel the chair.

Wheels, Handrims, and Tires

Wheels are available in 20-, 22-, 24-, and 26-inch diameters and are available through wheelchair manufacturers as well as through specialty companies. They are available with standard or heavy-duty spokes and in a spokeless style. The spokeless styles are growing in popularity because they are easier to maintain and do not add more than a pound or so to the overall weight of the chair. When quick-release wheels are available as an option, they may be desirable because their removal reduces the weight of the chair by 8 pounds, making it more readily lifted or stored.

Wheel size and location may be critical to the patient's

ability to self-propel. Generally, the 24-inch wheel is adequate. This size may need to be specially ordered on small chairs. Although these large wheels often look strange on small chairs, they can add significantly to function because of their proximity to the user's hands. Patients who are weak or poorly coordinated may be able to self-propel if a choice of axle positions allows for a personalized wheel placement. This often is justification to order an ultralight wheelchair with a multiposition axle plate.

For patients who are unable to manage dual wheel propulsion, one-arm drive systems are available. These units use a double handrim on one wheel to drive both wheels (Fig. 28–10). Operation can be confusing and difficult to coordinate for those with limited cognitive or perceptual ability. Patients with increased tone may demonstrate spastic overflow and asymmetry when using one hand to propel the chair. When supplying this type of chair, attempts should be made to use one of the units with a very lightweight frame and precision wheel bearings which decrease rolling resistance.

Separate chrome handrims are standard on most wheels. They can be spaced further from the wheel if requested, but this will add width to the chair. Some patients have difficulty propelling the wheelchair because of poor hand control or a weak grip. A leather glove or coated handrim will add friction between the hand and rim, making wheeling easier. Special hand rims can be ordered in increased diameter, sponge coatings, and with knobs or projections (see Figure 28–5).

Standard hard rubber tires are useful for most individuals. They are durable and cared for easily. Pneumatic (air filled) tires are standard on some models and are

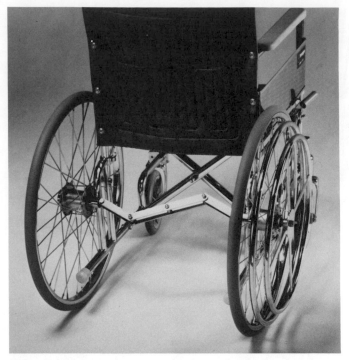

Figure 25–10. A one-arm drive wheelchair has a double handrim on one side, allowing one-hand propulsion. (Courtesy of Theradyne Corporation, Lakeville, MN.)

available as a special order on others. These require more maintenance but provide a smoother ride and improved traction in some instances. Zero pressure tubes, or flat proof liners can be substituted for the tube to create a flat proof tire with the appearance of a pneumatic. The ride with these liners is not as smooth, and in some cases the life of the tire may be shortened.

The Frame

Most people with wheelchairs use *outdoor frames*. This means that the large wheels are in the back and the casters are in the front. Chairs with large wheels in the front are called *indoor chairs*. They are sometimes ordered for individuals with severe knee flexion contractures, and for those whose upper extremity range of motion is limited. Although access to the wheels may be easier with the indoor model, overall maneuverability may be more difficult, and transfers may present a problem.

Chair frames are available in heavy-duty, standard, lightweight, active-duty lightweight, and ultra-lightweight construction. Patients who are functioning in the community should be offered the lightest, strongest possible frame whenever feasible. The lighter frames are easier for the user to propel and easier for caretakers to manage. For individuals in institutions, or when caretakers do not have to lift and to carry the unit, the issue of weight may be secondary to the issue of price. To justify the added expense of an active-duty lightweight or ultra-lightweight chair, explanation for its necessity must usually be provided to the third-party payer.

For patients who are not capable of using one or both upper extremities for functional self-propulsion, consideration should be given to some form of powered mobility. Motorized wheelchairs are available in many styles with varying degrees of portability, power, and levels of electronic sophistication (Figs. 28–11 and 28–12). In all cases it would be ideal if a proportional drive system could be used. **Proportional drives** respond to pressure similar to an automobile accelerator; the more pressure, the more speed. Because the speed and degree of acceleration are controlled by the patient's hand movement, this type of system affords the user the greatest degree of control. If fine hand function is not available, the team may want to consider using head or foot operation before selecting a **microswitching system**.

A **microswitching system** is an all-or-none drive system. The speed is preset. The operator applies any degree of pressure, and as soon as the switch is activated the system runs at top speed. Individual switches are provided for the four directions (forward, reverse, right, left), and a series of individual movements are required to maneuver in tight places. Individual microswitches can be arranged around a joystick in a control box, or they can be placed anywhere around the body in order to allow the patient to drive the chair. For example, there might be two switches on a tray for gross pressing with the hand and additional switches at the head, knees, or feet to allow mobility in all four directions. Control of acceleration must be achieved through some type of acceleration modifier either built into the chair or as an add-on accessory.

Many accessories are available to personalize the chair

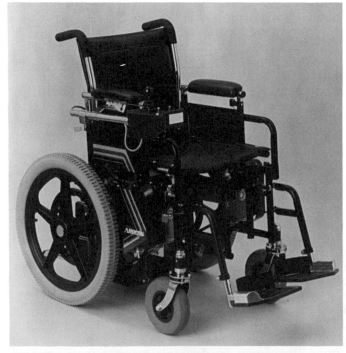

Figure 28–11. Standard configuration motorized wheelchairs are operated through a joystick. (Courtesy of Invacare Corporation, Elyria, OH.)

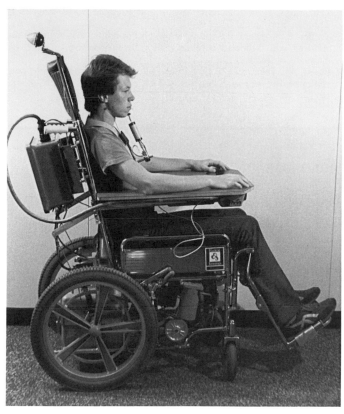

Figure 28–12. Motorized wheelchairs can be outfitted with special controls and even on-board computers for severely disabled patients. (Courtesy of DU-IT Control Systems Group, Shreve, OH.)

for functional and aesthetic reasons. Crutch holders, antitippers, utility bags and trays all may serve a functional purpose. Frame and upholstery color, usually at no extra cost, will help personalize the chair.

Making the perfect match between consumer and product will require a careful determination of the patient's needs and then matching these to the product features. Something as simple as the style of arm lock or the type of push handle may have important long-term functional or caretaking implications.

SUMMARY

A systematic approach to providing a prescriptive wheelchair has been presented. The individual components of both the postural support and the wheeled mobility base have been described. The primary goal in developing any prescriptive wheelchair is maximum patient function and independence. It must be the result of a thorough assessment using a problem-solving approach, with attention to the specific factors discussed in this chapter. Input from the user and all team members during the decision-making phase is critical. This process will result in an optimally designed chair capable of achieving its intended purpose. This problem-solving approach, with open communication among team members, patient, family, and manufacturer will ensure that each prescriptive wheelchair is designed to meet the needs of the individual patient.

QUESTIONS FOR REVIEW

1. Describe the following seating components and give two reasons why each is needed.
   A. Firm seat
   B. Firm back
   C. Lap board
   D. Lap belt
2. Describe the following wheelchair components; compare and contrast their functional benefits:
   A. Detachable swing-away footrests/elevating legrests.
   B. Fixed-height armrests/adjustable-height armrests.
   C. Single-axle placement/multiple-axle placement.
   D. Proportional drive/microswitching system.

3. When measuring seat depth, what two positions would you place the patient in and why?
4. Identify landmarks and measurements needed to help determine the size of the following parts of a wheeled mobility system:
   A. Seat width.
   B. Seat depth.
   C. Seat back height.
   D. Armrest height.
   E. Minimum footrest extension (MinFBX).

REFERENCES

1. Smith, PD, et al: Effect of adaptive seating on speech intelligibility in children who have cerebral palsy. Presentation at 1985 Annual Meeting of the American Academy of Cerebral Palsy and Developmental Medicine.
2. Nwaobi, OM, Hobson, D, and Trefler, E: Hip angle and upper extremity movement time in children with cerebral palsy. In Proceedings of RESNA Annual Conference, 1985.
3. Nwaobi, OM and Smith, PD: Effect of adaptive seating on pulmonary function of children with cerebral palsy. Dev Med Child Neurol 28:351, 1986.

4. Perkash, I, et al: Seating systems for body support and prevention of tissue trauma. Research in Progress, VA Medical Center, Palo Alto, CA, 94304.
5. Hartigan, JD: The dangerous wheelchair. J Am Geriatr Soc 30:572, 1982.
6. Bergen, AF and Colangelo, C: Positioning the Client with Central Nervous System Deficits: The Wheelchair and Other Adapted Equipment, ed 2. Valhalla Rehabilitation Publications, Valhalla, NY, 1985.
7. Zackarkow, D: Wheelchair Posture and Pressure Sores. Charles C Thomas, Springfield, IL, 1984.
8. Trefler, E, Monahan, L, and Nwaobi, O: Functional arm restraint for children with athetoid cerebral palsy. In Proceedings of RESNA Annual Conference, 1985.
9. Breed, AL, Ibler, I: The motorized wheelchair: New freedom, new responsibility and new problems. Dev Med Child Neurol 24:366, 1982.

SUPPLEMENTAL READINGS

Brammell, CA and Maloney, FP: Wheelchair prescriptions. In Maloney, FP, Burks, JS, and Ringel, SP (eds): Interdisciplinary Rehabilitation of Multiple Sclerosis and Neuromuscular Disorders. JB Lippincott, Philadelphia, 1985, p 364.
Cochran, GVB and Palmieri, V: Development of test methods for evaluation of wheelchair cushions. Bulletin of Prosthetics Research 17(1):9, 1980.
Downey, J and Low, N (eds): The Child with a Disabling Illness: Principles of Rehabilitation. WB Saunders, Philadelphia, 1973.
Enders, A: Technology for Independent Living Sourcebook. Rehabilitation Engineering Society of North America, Washington, DC, 1984.
Hulme, JB, et al: Perceived behavioral changes observed with adaptive seating devices and training programs for multihandicapped, developmentally disabled individuals. Phys Ther 63:204, 1983.
Kamenentz, HL: The Wheelchair Book. Charles C Thomas, Springfield, IL, 1969.
McClay, I: Electric wheelchair propulsion using a hand control in C4 quadriplegia: A case report. Phys Ther 63:221, 1983.
Palmieri, VR, Haelen, GT, and Cochran, GVB: A comparison of sitting pressures on wheelchair cushions as measured by air cell transducers and miniature electronic transducers. Bulletin of Prosthetics Research 17(1):5, 1980.
Pritham, CH and Leiper, CI: A method for custom seating of the severely disabled. Orthotics and Prosthetics 35(4), 1981.
Scott, AD: Wheelchair measurement and prescription. In Trombly, CA (ed): Occupational Therapy for Physical Dysfunction, ed 2. Williams & Wilkins, Baltimore, 1983, p 300.
Trefler, E: Seating for Children with Cerebral Palsy: A Resource Manual. The University of Tennessee Center for Health Sciences, Rehabilitation Engineering Program, Memphis, 1984.
Wilson, AB: Wheelchairs: A Prescription Guide. Rehabilitation Press, Charlottesville, VA, 1986.

GLOSSARY

Abductor pommel (abductor): An upholstered block or wedge placed on the front of the wheelchair seating surface; used to maintain abduction of the lower extremities.

Adductor cushion: An upholstered block or pad placed on the lateral aspect of the wheelchair seating surface; used to control excessive adduction of the lower extremities.

Contouring (of seat): Method of creating a custom molded seating surface; a mold is taken directly from the patient, hardened and appropriately upholstered or padded.

Control blocks (blocking): Use of upholstered supports or pads attached to the seating system to enhance postural alignment.

Kyphotic posturing (kyphosis): Excessive convex curvature of the thoracic spine as viewed laterally.

Microswitching system: Type of power switch mechanism on a motorized wheelchair that produces an all-or-none response; any degree of pressure will activate the system to a preset speed.

Mobility base: A wheelchair support and movement system; consists of the tubular frame, the legrests and armrests, foot supports, and wheels.

Postural support system: A wheelchair seating, support, and postural alignment system; consists of the seat surface, seat back, and any additional components such as a torso support, adductor cushion, abductor pommel or lap belt needed to maintain alignment.

Proportional drive: Type of power switch mechanism on a motorized wheelchair that responds to level of pressure; the greater the pressure, the more speed.

Windblown position: Movement of the knees away from midline during corrected pelvic alignment.

Chapter 29

BIOFEEDBACK

DAVID E. KREBS

OBJECTIVES

1. Describe the purposes of biofeedback techniques.

2. Describe the motor learning principles underlying biofeedback techniques.

3. Describe technical requirements and limitations of biofeedback equipment.

4. Identify differences in electromyographic biofeedback techniques used for spastic versus paretic muscle groups.

5. Describe the application of kinematic and kinetic biofeedback techniques to gait training.

INTRODUCTION

Biofeedback has matured from its early cult-cure-all days to its current status as a legitimate adjunctive technique for specific neuromuscular and behavioral disorders. Biofeedback can be used to inform the patient about movement, muscle activity, force, joint displacement, skin temperature, heart rate, blood pressure, or other physiologic information by amplifying and displaying this information so that the patient can learn to control these signals. To quote John Basmajian,[1] biofeedback is a "technique to reveal to human beings some of their internal physiological events, normal and abnormal, in the form of visual and auditory signals in order to teach them to manipulate these otherwise involuntary or unfelt events by manipulating the displayed signals." Most often, biofeedback techniques are used for the patient who has difficulty accessing the information through normal physiologic mechanisms such as proprioception or visual cues (Fig. 29–1).

Muscle activity or electromyographic (EMG) biofeedback is most frequently employed in clinical physical therapy settings, so this chapter will focus primarily on EMG feedback. Joint position and force feedback will be considered less comprehensively.

GENERAL PRINCIPLES

The goal of biofeedback in physical therapy is to improve motor performance by facilitating motor learning. To use biofeedback correctly and effectively, therapists must understand the principles of motor learning and the technical limitations of biofeedback machines.

Motor Learning

Excellent reviews of normal motor control are available to the student and clinician, many of them substantial and comprehensive (e.g., Herman, et al,[2] and Brooks[3]), so concepts will be considered here only briefly. The motor control literature, however, has few unifying theories, and the limited work that has been done on abnormal populations tends to contradict the remaining areas of agreement. Thus, although it is accepted that motor control requires information from the external world as well as proprioception, how that information is processed is presently unknown. Attempts to view biofeedback dogmatically as a substitute for proprioceptive pathways are therefore at best a naive misunderstanding

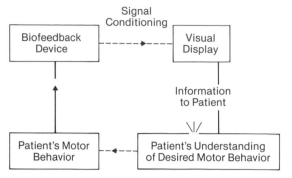

Figure 29–1. Schematic relationship of biofeedback device to patient.

of the extremely sophisticated human control systems that have evolved.

A behavioral positive reinforcement or "reward" model is usually employed with biofeedback techniques. Simply stated, when patients generate appropriate motor behaviors, they are positively reinforced. The audio and visual feedback stimuli and other nonverbal information are usually much faster and more accurate than the therapist's comments. Unlike other forms of treatment, the benefits of accomplishing small changes in motor behavior in the desired direction can be reinforced, which should speed the rehabilitation process. In behavioral learning terminology, the therapist uses the biofeedback signal to shape the motor behavior by reinforcing the patient's successive approximations to the goal behavior or functional outcome (see Mulder and Hulstyn[4]).

When the patient succeeds in controlling the signal, the therapist must relate it to the underlying motor behavior and then reset the goals. Reinforcing already learned behaviors is, of course, futile, so the machine's threshold should be monitored frequently, increasing the task's difficulty as motor skills progress.

PHYSIOLOGIC FEEDBACK

The fastest cortical feedback circuits (i.e., those which can take into account changes in environmental conditions) have at least 100 to 200 msec latencies. For example, a fast pianist performing a "run" cannot possibly rely on visual or auditory feedback during the "run." The performance is therefore "open loop": if a mistake is made, several notes will be played before the performer is even aware that the mistake has occurred and several more notes will be played (i.e., about two-tenths of a second of music) before any adjustments to the motor plan can be made.

Ambulation also requires a series of preplanned motor events. If a disruption occurs, feedback of the "mistake" can be acted upon and built into the plan only for *ensuing* steps. Normal walking speed is about 1 cycle per second. Ankle dorsiflexors, for example, must resist foot-slap from heel strike to foot-flat for about 60 msec. Therapists attempting to encourage normal gait in patients with hemiplegia by using feedback from dorsiflexor EMG should not, therefore, request the patient to correct inadequate dorsiflexor motor unit activity *within* each gait cycle. At best, patients will use that information

during the next gait cycle, but the information is merely that EMG activity was inadequate during the past gait cycle. The therapist and patient must determine the correct neurophysiologic strategy to increase dorsiflexor motor unit activity in anticipation of ensuing heel strikes.

BIOFEEDBACK IN REHABILITATION

When using biofeedback, the patient must (1) understand the relationship of the electronic signal to the desired functional task, (2) practice controlling the biofeedback signal, and (3) perform the functional task until it is mastered and the patient no longer needs the biofeedback. Biofeedback techniques thus require that patients engage in "closed-loop" learning, using ongoing feedback (Fig. 29–2), until motor skills develop sufficiently so that "open-loop" movements (where no feedback is required) can be accomplished.*

Conventional neuromuscular reeducation is based heavily upon providing patients with helpful comments (feedback) to assist their recovery of previously acquired skills. The therapist's job is to focus the patient's attention on the underlying motor programs and biomechan-

---

*The reader should be aware that this oversimplified dichotomy of open- and closed-loop movements is included here for its heuristic value, not because it is a physiologically validated motor control paradigm.

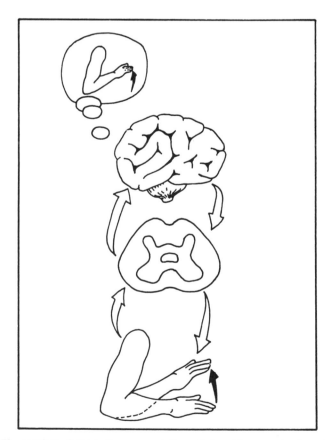

Figure 29–2. Schematic representation of closed-loop motor learning theory.

ical schema required to recoup those skills. If a postmeniscectomy patient cannot straight-leg-raise, for example, then gait training will be impeded, and the therapist usually prescribes quadriceps-setting exercise. Biofeedback-assisted quad-setting, however, might improve the patient's information processing and result in more rapid progress by augmenting knee joint or quadriceps proprioception with electronic feedback, supplying "knowledge of results" that were inhibited by the meniscectomy.[5,6] As shown schematically in Figure 29–3, if the patient's normal proprioception and other physiologic mechanisms are disrupted, normal movement control and relearning of motor skills are restricted.

Biofeedback is simply one technique that therapists may employ to help convey their message about motor programs and biomechanical schema to the patient. Biofeedback can assist the rehabilitation process by the following:

1. Providing a clear goal (motor behavior or outcome) that the patient should accomplish.

2. Permitting the therapist and patient to experiment with various strategies (processes) that generate motor patterns to achieve the goal.

3. Reinforcing appropriate motor behavior.

4. Providing a process-oriented, timely, and accurate knowledge of results of the patient's efforts.

By attending to the biofeedback signal, the patient can "close the loop," as shown in Figure 29–4. Many patients become more motivated when biofeedback is employed

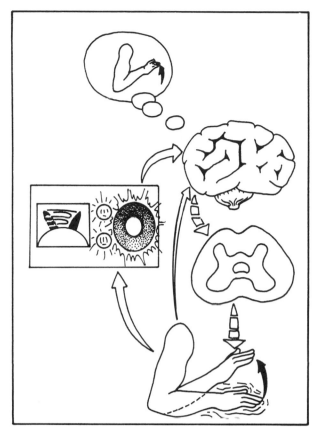

Figure 29–4. Abnormal feedback loop augmented by biofeedback signal.

because they know the machine won't be falsely encouraging. Therefore, both the therapist and the patient must understand the meaning of the biofeedback signal, and appropriate goals must be set.

The therapist must explain what the machine's signals mean to the patient and what constitutes "success." The machine should be set to give auditory or visual feedback that corresponds to the motor behavior desired. For example, if spastic antagonist muscles are monitored, the patient should be instructed to decrease the EMG activity; the biofeedback device is set to flash a light to signal accomplishment of this goal. Alternatively, an **electrogoniometer** might be employed that changes the pitch of a buzzer as the joint is moved in the proper direction.

MOTOR LEARNING SUMMARY

Biofeedback techniques are used to augment the patient's sensory feedback mechanisms through precise information about body processes that might otherwise be inaccessible. Positive reinforcement is the operative learning model.

Technical Limitations

Feedback must be relevant, accurate, and rapid in order to enhance motor learning. If any of these three ele-

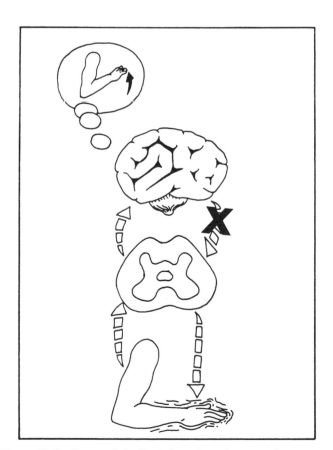

Figure 29–3. Abnormal feedback loop impedes normal movement control.

ments is missing, traditional verbal feedback is probably just as useful and is certainly more convenient.

RELEVANCY

Useful information is pertinent to the desired motor outcome: Neither too much nor too little information is given, and the information is immediately applicable to the behavior. Although therapists may describe the location of agonist and antagonist muscles verbally, and even make attempts to describe the "feelings" patients should experience if the muscles are used appropriately, there is no way to communicate which motor units to activate. Electromyographic biofeedback can provide relevant information regarding motor unit activity which patients do not otherwise have available.

ACCURACY

It should come as no surprise that disagreement exists regarding the utility of biofeedback, because today's technology is quite crude and most forms of feedback (especially EMG feedback) merely communicate "more" or "less" activity. The information provided to patients via current technology is decidedly unsophisticated and incomplete compared with that which intact nervous systems can provide during normal movement. Many therapists prefer to work with devices that measure force or joint range of motion (ROM) directly. These therapists feel that EMG signals are not sufficiently informative or sophisticated to be true "process" feedback and that EMG does not adequately reflect actual outcome (e.g., limb displacement or torque) to provide accurate knowledge of results. In order to maximize the use of biofeedback, the therapist must be certain the type of device and the way in which it is attached provide accurate information.

SPEED OF INFORMATION

Feedback must be timely to be useful. While feedback is employed, the movements necessarily are closed loop, as described above.

In addition to **endogenous,** physiologic latencies, most EMG biofeedback instruments have built-in integrators or averagers, which further slow the signal output. In addition, all EMG processors delay electrical events during signal amplification and conversion to the audio speaker and visual meter, owing to inherent delays from the electrical circuits. Most commercial EMG feedback instruments introduce 50 to 100 msec delays before the signal can even reach the ears and eyes of patients, and further delays ensue within the patients' neural "circuits."

TECHNICAL SUMMARY

Information to be fed back to patients must be accurate, relevant, and timely in order to be of any therapeutic use. Therapists must choose the instrument or device that provides the most meaningful information to patients. Commercially available EMG instruments, for example, can provide timely feedback if the motor

behavior being monitored is at least ½ second in duration. Thus, for feedback during a 5-second isometric contraction, adequate time may be available for patients to adjust the motor program and to change the motor strategy being employed. During most functional activities, therefore, the "feedback" acts as an error signal to provide knowledge of results, which is used in planning future movements.

USING EMG FEEDBACK FOR NEUROMUSCULAR REEDUCATION

General Introduction

The basic EMG biofeedback device includes one ground and two active surface electrodes, an amplifier, an audio speaker, and a video display. The EMG signal (which is on the order of millionths of a volt, or microvolts) is transmitted from the muscle through the skin, through the electrode paste, through the electrodes and wires, and thence to the amplifier.

Surface electrodes are metal disks that should be ½ inch or less in diameter (Fig. 29–5). Electrode paste is a gel that reduces the resistance between the electrodes and the skin. Some modern biofeedback units do not require the use of electrode paste or gel because they have very high input impedance (more on impedance later in this section). Those that do, however, require the user to apply the paste carefully so that it "just covers" the electrode. Excess paste is not only sloppy, it will affect the apparent amplitude of the EMG signal, perhaps even short-circuiting the two active electrodes. Therapists generally should place one electrode on the motor point, where most of the endplates are located, and the other distal to it and parallel to the direction of the fibers.

The rest of the equipment is somewhat more complex and requires a fairly thorough understanding of the EMG signal's characteristics.

In this section, the origins of the EMG signal will be reviewed briefly and its progress followed from the

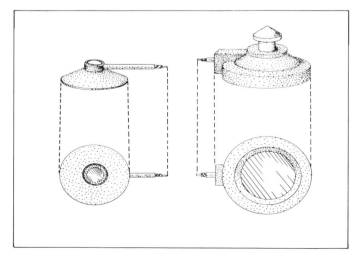

Figure 29–5. EMG surface electrodes. Center area is concave and should be filled flush to its surface with electrode paste.

patient (starting with the intention to move) through the monitoring instrumentation, and back to the patient for error correction.

Muscle Physiology: Where Does the EMG Signal Come From?

After the central nervous system (CNS) signals its intention to move, and the signal travels down the spinal cord, the anterior horn cell discharges. The motor nerve then depolarizes, conducting its electrical current toward the muscle at 40 to 60 m/sec. Because a motor unit is, by definition, the anterior horn cell, its nerve, and all the muscle fibers it innervates, the amount of muscle that is activated depends upon the size of the motor unit field (i.e., the number of muscle fibers innervated by each anterior horn cell and its axon).

After all motor nerve terminal branches have discharged, the action potential hits the neuromuscular junction. The distal-most end of the nerve contains acetylcholine, which diffuses across the synaptic cleft. The acetylcholine receptors cause a second action potential to occur, this time in the sarcolemma, or jacket, surrounding the muscle (from the Greek, sarcos = flesh; lemma = sheath). The sarcolemnal depolarization, or action potential, conducts more slowly than the nerve action potential propagation. The EMG device registers this sarcolemnal depolarization; it does not register muscle tension. After the electrical excitation travels through the muscle, the action potential reaches a storage area for calcium ions. Only after the electrical depolarization reaches this storage area and causes calcium to be released does the mechanical event, muscle contraction, occur. The muscle's electrical action potential normally, although not always, results in tension (force) production by the muscle.[7,8]

In EMG feedback, surface electrodes are most often used. Surface electrodes summate all potentials beneath their surfaces. Therefore, an increase in observed EMG activity may result from more muscle cells discharging, or from changes in electrode placement. The surface electrodes' summation masks the precise source of the signal. Electromyographic activity may be from a muscle immediately below the electrodes or from a distant source. Furthermore, the EMG signal will increase whether patients are developing increased activation of small motor units more rapidly and synchronously or if a greater number of units are being recruited.

It should be understood from the preceding paragraphs that measuring electrical activity of a muscle, as is done with EMG, is not the same as measuring muscle tension. The important point for understanding biofeedback is that the EMG signal arises prior to, and occasionally independent of, muscle mechanical activity, so blind reliance on EMG output can be deceiving.

EMG Biofeedback Equipment and Technical Specifications

The EMG biofeedback device is at heart a very sensitive **voltmeter** with a speaker and meter attached. Like any "differential" voltmeter, EMG instruments can sense electrical signals only if one pole experiences a voltage different from the other; one pole of the instrument must be negative with respect to the other pole to register any activity. After the electrical signal is detected, most biofeedback instruments condition the signals so that positive and negative impulses are "rectified" (the machine finds the signal's absolute amplitude); then the device "smooths" (filters) the signal prior to display to decrease the normal fluctuations present in the muscle's electrical output. (See chapter 10 for further details on signal conditioning.) Thus, although the muscle's electrical event occurs prior to its mechanical contraction, by the time the EMG machine produces the feedback signal, the mechanical event is over. The quality of the machine and, therefore, its output are chiefly indicated by its input **impedance, common mode rejection ratio,** frequency response, **noise** level, and ability to cope with non-EMG **artifacts**.

INPUT IMPEDANCE

Ohm's law indicates that resistance **(impedance)** is inversely related to voltage. At the muscle fiber level, muscle action potentials are several thousandths of a volt. The summated current passes through the resistive subcutaneous tissues and skin, reducing the voltage, sometimes by 100-fold. Therefore, EMG signals from obese patients or limb sites with above-average amounts of adipose tissue will appear less than normal, even if the signals at the muscle fiber level are equivalent to that from other muscles with less intervening tissue. In fact, all intervening tissues, including bone and atrophic, necrotic, or especially oily skin, resist the muscles' electrical signals. Because skin resistance varies but internal resistance from fat and other tissues probably remains constant, only skin resistance is typically a concern.

If the EMG machine's impedance is much greater than skin impedance, skin resistance becomes trivial in comparison, and the biofeedback signal reflects more valid muscle EMG activity. As a rule of thumb, EMG instruments should have at least 1000 times as much input impedance as that measured between the two active electrodes. The therapist can easily measure skin electrode impedance by attaching an **ohm meter** to the surface electrode after it is attached to the skin. Generally, a standard, careful skin preparation to remove dead surface skin and excess oil will decrease resistance to 1000 ohms or less, as much as is necessary with contemporary instruments with high (at least 100 meg-ohm) input impedance.

Electrode size also alters the effective resistance seen by the amplifier. Larger electrodes have lower resistances. Greatest resistance is measured in the use of needle electrodes, because their surface area is so small. Therefore, changing electrodes may cause an ostensible change in the EMG signal—but the therapist must realize that this is an artifact.

COMMON MODE REJECTION RATIO

Contemporary EMG instruments almost always use a differential amplifier, comparing the voltage at one active electrode with that of the other active electrode. The ground electrode in a good EMG machine may be placed almost anywhere on the patient. If the voltage travels down the muscle and arrives at both electrodes simultaneously, no difference between the electrodes is registered and the instrument would reflect no change of activity. Therefore, therapists must choose electrode placements that maximize the likelihood that EMG signals will first reach one active electrode and later reach the other active electrode.

The advantage of the differential recording system is its "rejection" of extraneous voltages. Although we may not be aware of it, patients' skin receives a great many voltages, such as from lights, motors, and other hospital appliances which produce currents that travel through the air and can affect the recordings on the skin. Other muscles (e.g., the heart) also produce voltages. If the electricity from these other sources reaches the two active electrodes simultaneously, a differential amplifier with a high **common mode rejection ratio** (CMMR) will "reject" those artifactual signals.

The voltage from lights and other exogenous generators nearly always reaches the two skin electrodes simultaneously, so room current (60 Hz) interference is often minimal. Myocardial activity, however, is frequently a problem when electrodes are on the chest or upper back, near the heart. The presence of a regularly alternating signal in the "feedback" signal, unrelated to the muscle(s) being monitored, indicates that the electrodes should be re-placed perpendicular to the progression of the electrocardiographic (ECG) wave, so that the ECG signal arrives at both electrodes concurrently.

Electronic common mode rejection is not perfect. If a signal of 60 Hz interferes with a treatment session, turn off the room lights or look for a nearby whirlpool or diathermy machine as the culprit. An ungrounded appliance operating from the same electrical circuit as the EMG feedback instrument occasionally will interfere with EMG recordings. If the EMG instrument cannot operate by batteries, then disconnect the ungrounded appliance or install an outlet for the EMG that is isolated from other appliances.

As with input impedance, higher is better. Common mode rejection ratios should be at least 200,000:1. If the muscles being monitored are especially paretic and generate only a few microvolts, then larger amplifier gains are required; large gains, unfortunately, also amplify the artifacts. Therefore, high CMRR is especially desirable when using biofeedback for the low myoelectric signals common in neuromuscular reeducation.

FREQUENCY RESPONSE (BANDWIDTH)

Bandwidth is the difference between the lowest and highest **frequency responses** of an EMG instrument. Most of the power at surface kinesiologic EMG recordings is between 20 and 200 Hz, so manufacturers often dictate that their EMG instruments need no more than 200 Hz as its highest cutoff frequency. However, instrument responsiveness relates not only to the frequency of the monitored signal but also to how quickly the signal changes. Optimally, the high end of the machine's band-

width should exceed 1000 Hz to enable the machine to respond to all components of the signal. In general, a frequency response of 32 to 1000 Hz is adequate for surface kinesiologic EMG feedback.

NOISE LEVEL

In general, the lower the noise, the better. If, for example, the noise level of the device is 5 microvolts, a muscle contraction of 4 microvolts would be lost within the machine. Modern devices using high-quality electronic components typically have acceptable noise levels of 2 microvolts or less.

OTHER ARTIFACTS

False readings can be traced to many sources, but the most common **artifacts** in EMG biofeedback are volume-conduction and movement.

A volume-conducted artifact results when signals from nearby muscles are inadvertently sampled by the surface electrodes. The easiest solution is to bring the active electrodes closer to one another. The therapist also might palpate the suspected muscle during the movement, keeping in mind that tendons and muscle bellies become palpably tense simply from being passively stretched. A better solution is to use a second set of electrodes to monitor the offending muscle's activity on another channel.[9]

For example, when treating a patient with hemiplegia, a reasonable plan might be to increase elbow extension by increasing triceps EMG amplitude. The therapist should realize that spastic elbow flexors may be contracting. Although the EMG signal may appear to increase, the elbow still does not extend. The increase in EMG registered by the biofeedback device in this case might result from spastic biceps muscle activity, which in turn explains why the elbow does not extend. The solution, therefore, would be to attempt first to relax the biceps brachii, then to facilitate triceps motor activity using the EMG biofeedback.

Patients with paretic muscles from lower motor neuron disorders sometimes use similarly incorrect strategies. Because paretic muscles, for example, those resulting from peroneal palsy, have too few activated motor units, the low EMG signals must be amplified greatly, perhaps by using an EMG scale of 0 to 10 microvolts. By using the biofeedback machine at such high gains, therapists can discern practically any amount of motor unit activity. Unfortunately, patients often try to please their therapists and to show themselves that "there is life in my muscle," so they clench their teeth and cocontract throughout the limb. In so doing, they are successful in increasing the response of the biofeedback instrument, but in this case, biofeedback reinforces functionally inappropriate motor behavior. Therefore, it is the therapist's responsibility to ensure that the feedback is valid.

Many patients are referred for biofeedback because, according to the referring clinician, "The patient can increase the muscle's EMG but can't achieve any functional gains." The problem is virtually always volume-conduction EMG artifact. As indicated above, multichannel biofeedback is employed to monitor all the muscles in the limb, to allow understanding of the strategy the patient is employing to increase the EMG signal. The goal of therapy becomes inhibition of the antagonists and facilitation of the agonists. Many patients require as many as three or more sessions to reverse the effects of previous "biofeedback" (which was in fact artifact feedback!).

Movement artifacts are one of the most vexing problems in EMG biofeedback. Particularly when muscles are weak and amplification perforce is high, movement artifacts, whose greatest power is below 20 Hz, can be easily mistaken for EMG signals. Whenever movement occurs, the cables move and "signals" are fed back, even if the muscles are not generating electrical activity. Of course, a high CMRR can decrease this problem, but the best solution is to eliminate the cables altogether by putting the preamplifier at the electrode site. A few commercially available biofeedback instruments provide this electrode/preamplifier combination for application at the skin site (Fig. 29–6).

Clinical Application

In the most general terms, EMG feedback can be used only to help the patient increase or decrease muscle activity.[10,11] Thus, for paretic muscles the goal is usually to increase the EMG signal, and for spastic muscles the goal is to decrease the EMG signal. Note that the etiology of paresis or spasticity is not mentioned: Biofeedback techniques to date make no distinction among the various diagnostic categories. Biofeedback applications distinguish only between paresis and spasticity; that is, *functional* classifications. As a result, typical physical therapy intervention includes:

1. Patient assessment.
2. Problem identification and treatment goal setting.
3. Therapeutic application of biofeedback.

Patient assessment is performed in the usual way: Tests and measurements are conducted to determine the status of motor performance. Attention is directed toward assessment of sensation, motor control, functional capabilities, cognition, perception, and other relevant functions. The therapist should be especially observant of cooperation and attention because they are critical to successful implementation of biofeedback techniques.

Problem identification flows from assessment, and goal setting follows from the problem list thus generated. After determining the functional deficit, the therapist performs a kinesiologic assessment to identify the muscle(s) that require(s) intervention. The EMG device can be connected to enhance further the information gathered at this time, which can be particularly helpful in identifying goals of initial treatment sessions. If the therapist's kinesiologic assessment is correct, then therapeutic interventions to augment control of the muscle group(s) should lead directly to enhanced function.

Therapeutic interventions in EMG feedback typically require the therapist to accomplish the following:

1. Select the muscle(s) to be monitored.
2. Prepare the skin at the surface electrode site.
3. Prepare the electrodes and apply them to the skin.
4. Determine the maximum and minimum EMG readings *without* patient feedback, to determine baseline readings. At this time, be sure that the signal reaching the patient is artifact free and valid.
5. Set the goals for the session and be sure the patient understands them. Typically, goal setting at each session requires the audio and visual thresholds to be set.
6. Teach the patient to manipulate the controls of the machinery, to involve patient participation in the intervention maximally. The more responsibility the patient assumes for the treatment, the greater the chances of success.
7. Use facilitation or other neuromuscular reeducation techniques. In so doing, both the therapist and the patient react to the EMG feedback to monitor their success.

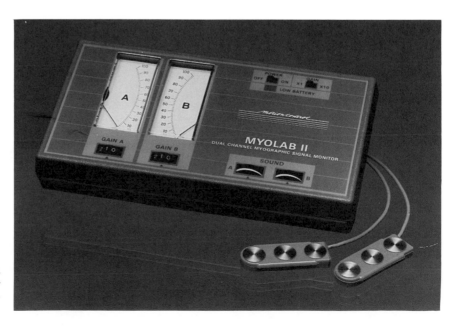

Figure 29–6. Electrode/preamplifier combination in a commercially available biofeedback instrument for neuromuscular re-education. (Courtesy of Motion Control, Salt Lake City, UT.)

8. Remove and clean the device and the patient's skin after the session's end.

The initial session is structured to permit *the therapist* to understand the motor dysfunction and to permit the patient to understand the equipment. Therefore, simple tasks are given to the patient, and following mastery, more difficult tasks are given. After explaining to the patient the purpose of biofeedback techniques and after choosing the appropriate muscle, the therapist will demonstrate what the patient should make the biofeedback device do by placing the electrodes on the patient's sound, contralateral limb. If both limbs are affected, the therapist will use his or her own limb for the demonstration.

Prepare the skin according to the recommendations indicated above; use alcohol or other skin abrasives if the device's input impedance is not optimal.

Choice of electrode size is essentially a decision based upon the quality of the equipment to be used. In general, smaller electrodes are better: They are less likely to transmit volume-conducted artifact and permit wider choice in electrode site selection, because few sites are too small to seat them well. Be aware, however, that impedance varies inversely with electrode size, so unless the amplifier has high input impedance, small electrodes may induce signal artifacts. The preferred electrode size is about 10 mm in diameter, as shown at left in Figure 29–5.

Prepare the electrodes as shown in Figure 29–7. The adhesive collars shown are only one way of attaching the electrodes to the skin; one also may use adhesive tape, rubber or elastic bands, nonelastic velcro-fastening bands, spring-loaded clips, or adhesive electrode paste*—in any combination—as long as the electrodes remain securely attached to the skin. When applying the electrode paste, it is most important to fill the concave "well" only to the point that the gel is level with its surface. Too little gel leaves gaps between the electrode and the skin, decreasing the effective electrode size; too much gel oozes out onto the surrounding skin, increasing the effective electrode size and possibly even creating a short circuit if the gels from both electrodes touch.

The closer the electrodes are to one another, the more confidence the therapist has that the signal is coming from the target muscle. Wider electrode spacing yields greater signal amplitude (more apparent voltage), but today's electronic amplifiers do not need assistance from widely spaced electrodes. For the same reason, if the signal amplitude recordings are made to help chronicle the patient's progress, the therapist should also register the electrode locations and separation distance.

When treating in-patients, the therapist can mark the patient's skin, tracing the electrode locations for replication on ensuing days. Otherwise, specify the electrode locations in the treatment record according to anatomic markers on that patient: A mole, blemish, or any other permanent skin marker is optimal. The closer the reference point to the electrode site, the easier the replication will be at the next visit.

PATIENT CONSIDERATIONS

After the equipment is in place and the therapist is satisfied that the feedback signal is accurate, the patient should be taught to master the movement. Generally, the therapist should begin by requesting a simple isometric contraction, setting the amplification gains so the patient achieves the criterion for feedback (the audio or video threshold) on about two of three contractions. Thus, the gains are set quite high for paretic muscles and low for spastic muscles.

Use of imagery, proprioceptive neuromuscular facilitation (PNF), ice, vibration—indeed, even electrical stimulation—in conjunction with biofeedback can enhance the patient's motor performace—as long as the adjunctive treatment (e.g., melting ice) does not induce artifactual "feedback." Probably the most useful technique is to have the patient imagine the motor activity and—while the electrodes monitor the muscle and the therapist gives verbal reinforcement and manual assistance such as tapping, tendon pressure, or putting the muscle on stretch—then attempt to perform that activity.[12]

EXAMPLE

Consider the patient with hemiplegia who has a classic foot-drop gait. Initial sessions should concentrate on

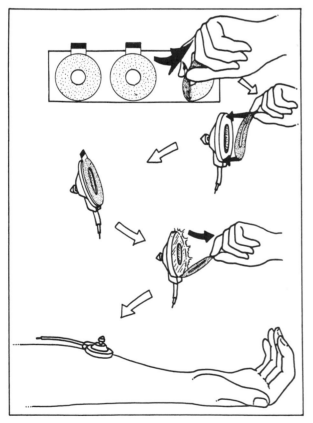

Figure 29–7. Preparation and placement of EMG biofeedback electrodes.

---

*Tac-Gel adhesive electrode paste. Pharmaceutical Innovations, 897 Frulinghuysen Avenue, Newark, NJ, 07114.

recruiting more dorsiflexor activity (and/or less plantar-flexor spasticity, if present) until the patient can isolate dorsiflexion reliably. Positional differences are important: most patients will be able to dorsiflex most easily in sitting, with the knee at about 70 to 80 degrees flexion and the foot flat on the floor. The task should be incremented to require the patient to dorsiflex with the knee flexed to 90 degrees and then with the knee in progressively less flexion until dorsiflexion is possible in sitting with the knee at full extension. The patient should now be able to dorsiflex while standing, so the next task is to introduce this skill during walking. As indicated previously, dorsiflexion must be rapid to be helpful in clearing the foot, so the patient should be trained from the outset to contract the dorsiflexors explosively while keeping the plantarflexors relatively quiet.

To help relax spastic muscles, use the EMG device to monitor muscle activity during slow passive stretch, then increase the challenge by more rapid stretch. Finally, progress to active-assisted movement and then to independent movement. The patient must keep the EMG levels below a certain threshold—for example, 20 microvolts—at first. As the patient improves the ability to control spastic muscle activity during passive or active stretch, increment the task difficulty by lowering the detection threshold to perhaps 17 or 15 microvolts.

During gait training, the patient should walk with the dorsiflexor EMG feedback acting as an error signal, telling the patient which strategies have been successful in eliciting the appropriate motor activity. The therapist should, of course, continue to treat the entire patient, including the "nonaffected limb," whether or not these muscles participate directly in the feedback session.

Note that little clinical research has been done to delineate the usefulness of providing EMG feedback for spasticity, so the above example should be considered only as a guide.[1,13,14] Furthermore, there is no agreement among gait analysis experts on what constitutes normal EMG activity for a given muscle group[15,16] nor even on the best way to analyze and to present the EMG signal.[17] Therefore, use and interpretation of EMG biofeedback signals for gait training in general should be undertaken with circumspection, but particularly for patients with spastic muscles, the therapist should not rely upon the EMG signal alone for signs of functional progress.

Patients with paretic muscles present a different challenge. Rather than strategies to control the muscle or its antagonist, the challenge is to recruit more motor units or to use the motor units more effectively. Patients with weak muscles whose manual muscle test (MMT) values are fair+ or less are good candidates for EMG feedback. If some resistance can be accommodated (i.e., good− or greater MMT value), then resistive exercises should be given: Biofeedback can enhance muscle control, but no research to date has shown that EMG feedback plus resistive exercises is better than the latter alone. Experimental research has, however, shown that EMG feedback plus isometric quad-setting is substantially more effective than the quad-setting exercises alone in increasing muscle power following knee arthrotomy.[5]

GENERAL RELAXATION

Relaxation therapy techniques sometimes combine EMG feedback with Jacobson's progressive relaxation,[18] Schultz's autogenic imagery,[19] and other psychologic techniques.[20] In these sessions, the EMG is typically monitored from frontalis or forearm muscle sites. The patient sits quietly while passively attempting to decrease the EMG signal, attending to the psychologic and behavioral correlates of relaxation.[21] Very deep relaxation can be induced, so nonpsychologists must be wary of their comments and actions around patients whose defenses are so relaxed.

Relaxation sessions also may include finger temperature, skin impedance, blood pressure, or heart rate feedback. Particularly with respect to skin temperature feedback, the therapist's knowledge of physiology is an important determinant of whether or not the patient's experience can be successful. Most important, however, is the therapist's approach: Support of the patient's goals, warmth, compassion, and belief in the techniques have been demonstrated to be as important as technical capabilities in relaxation therapies.

Patients who find it difficult to relax, or those with stress-related disorders, may benefit from relaxation biofeedback techniques. Temperature feedback for Raynaud's disease may be a treatment of choice.[22] Occasionally, patients with spasticity recalcitrant to the interventions described above will benefit from a session or two of general relaxation. It is frequently amazing to realize the general population's ignorance of tension-related stigmata. Many patients literally don't realize that when they clench their fists, grind their teeth, or otherwise tense their muscles they are increasing their muscle tension. These patients find it quite difficult to relax their spastic muscles because they don't know how to relax their normal muscles.

CLINICAL APPLICATION SUMMARY

No matter what the diagnosis, the biofeedback technique treatment approach is similar:
1. Select a muscle the EMG signal of which is relevant to the functional activity.
2. Have the patient practice controlling the signal.
3. Withdraw the feedback as function is gained.

EMG Biofeedback Summary

Electromyographic biofeedback has probably been employed since the first diagnostic EMG examination was performed, asking the patient to watch the oscilloscope and to listen to the speaker to relax or to increase muscle activity. EMG biofeedback has been found to be of benefit in treating patients with dystonic or idiopathic torticollis[23] and patients with neurogenic or orthopedic muscle paresis.[10] Patients with hemiplegia, spinal cord injuries, ataxia, and other movement disorders are more difficult to help with EMG biofeedback, but at minimum the addition of EMG information provides the clinician greater insight.[24] Table 29–1 presents a list of neuromus-

38638

2Physical Rehabilitation: Assessment and Treatment

**TABLE 29–1 LIST OF
NEUROMUSCULAR DISORDERS
CONSIDERED AMENABLE TO
BIOFEEDBACK APPLICATION**

Foot drop owing to stroke
Muscle tendon transfer
Hemiplegia/hemiparesis
Pain, chronic (owing to muscle spasm)
Peripheral nerve injury
Bell's palsy
Lower-motor neuron lesions
Paretic muscles
Spastic muscles
  Torticollis
  Immobilization (following orthopedic trauma)
  Low-back pain (owing to muscle spasm)
  Spinal cord lesion, incomplete
  Joint repair
  Paralysis, residual (owing to polio)
  Blepharospasm
  Cerebral palsy
  Parkinson's disease
  Writer's cramp

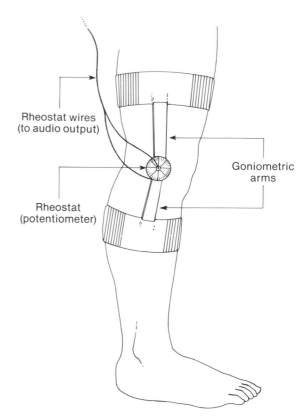

Figure 29–8. Electrogoniometer. Note that its arms attach to patient's limb segments.

cular disorders "for which there exists sufficient evidence to justify the use of biofeedback."[25] This list is not intended to be exhaustive but is provided merely to give the reader an idea of the breadth of diagnoses and disabilities currently considered amenable to biofeedback interventions.

KINEMATIC (JOINT MOTION) FEEDBACK

Joint motions are commonly measured by using a goniometer. An **electrogoniometer,** or el-gon (Fig. 29–8) is an electronic version of the manual goniometer that employs a **potentiometer** (i.e., a variable resistor, or **rheostat**) attached to the proximal and distal arms. The arms move just as they do in a conventional goniometer; they correspond to the position of the limb segments.[26]

How Electrogoniometers Work

Rheostats are commonly used as the volume control knob on stereos or as room light dimmers. Rotating the rheostat changes its resistance, which in turn increases or decreases the current from the signal of the feedback device. If a volume control knob or room light dimmer were connected to an el-gon on a knee, for example, each step would cause the audio signal or lights to fluctuate.

It is important to be sure that the feedback is indeed linearly related to joint motion. For the same reason that a 20-degree turn of a volume control knob on a stereo should always result in the same audio volume change, so should a 20-degree knee flexion always result in the same electrogoniometer feedback change. The voltage through the electrogoniometer is provided by a battery; joint movement causes the rheostat's pitch or volume to change proportionately.[27,28]

Clinical Application

As in all biofeedback techniques, the therapist should first demonstrate the desired behavior by attaching the electrogoniometer to the patient's uninvolved limb or to one's own corresponding limb segments.[29] The other principles of biofeedback techniques also apply to **kinematic** feedback, such as positive reinforcement and establishing a criterion for success described above. The therapist should begin by setting the error signal range to be quite forgiving during early stages of training and then increment the difficulty of the task as mastery is achieved. The baseline position on the el-gon is generally set for silence (no feedback), but movement in the desired direction is reinforced with sound.

Children with orthopedic disorders can be especially easy to treat, by making the volume of the TV or radio contingent upon movement in the proper direction. For example, louder volume could be used to indicate increased knee flexion, and the child's postsurgical recovery can be hastened by allowing cartoons to be watched and heard as long as knee flexion is above a criterion level.

Patients with above-knee amputations need to learn to keep their prosthetic knee extended during stance. Fernie and colleagues[30] and Wooldridge and associates[31] described the use of an el-gon to facilitate this learning by providing audio feedback that indicated when the knee was safe for weight bearing.

The therapist must, however, have a good working

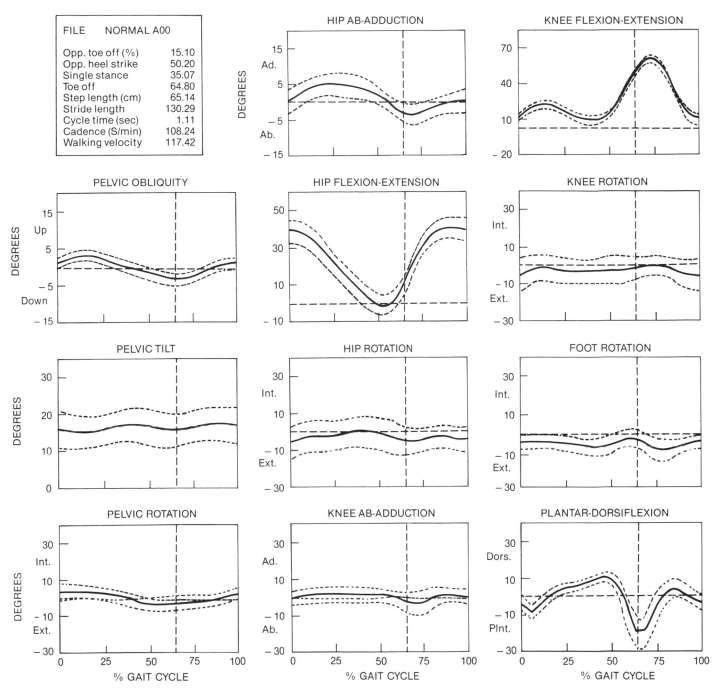

FILE	NORMAL A00
Opp. toe off (%)	15.10
Opp. heel strike	50.20
Single stance	35.07
Toe off	64.80
Step length (cm)	65.14
Stride length	130.29
Cycle time (sec)	1.11
Cadence (S/min)	108.24
Walking velocity	117.42

Figure 29–9. Normal adult kinematics. Solid line is average joint angle; dashed line represents $+/-1$ standard deviation. Note particularly the dorsiflexion angle. (Data collected at Newington Children's Hospital Gait Analysis Laboratory, Newington, CT.)

knowledge of normal kinematics (Fig. 29–9) and of the kinematics expected of patients with a particular diagnosis. It is, for example, inappropriate to ask a patient with hemiplegia to dorsiflex beyond neutral during the swing phase, or to ask the individual with an above-knee amputation to employ normal knee kinematics during prosthetic stance phase (Fig. 29–10).[32]

The same logic applies to orthotic rehabilitation. Orthoses are frequently prescribed to support or to restrict joint motions quite distant from the device itself. For example, setting the orthotic ankle joint in slight plantarflexion encourages knee extension during stance.

Patients using such devices should not be expected to attain normal knee motions, and kinematic biofeedback should not be used to encourage flexion when such ground reaction orthoses are being employed.

Construction

DeBacher[28] provides detailed instructions on the use and construction of electrogoniometers.[28] Therapists can easily and inexpensively fabricate a simple el-gon: The electrical parts are available from the local electronics

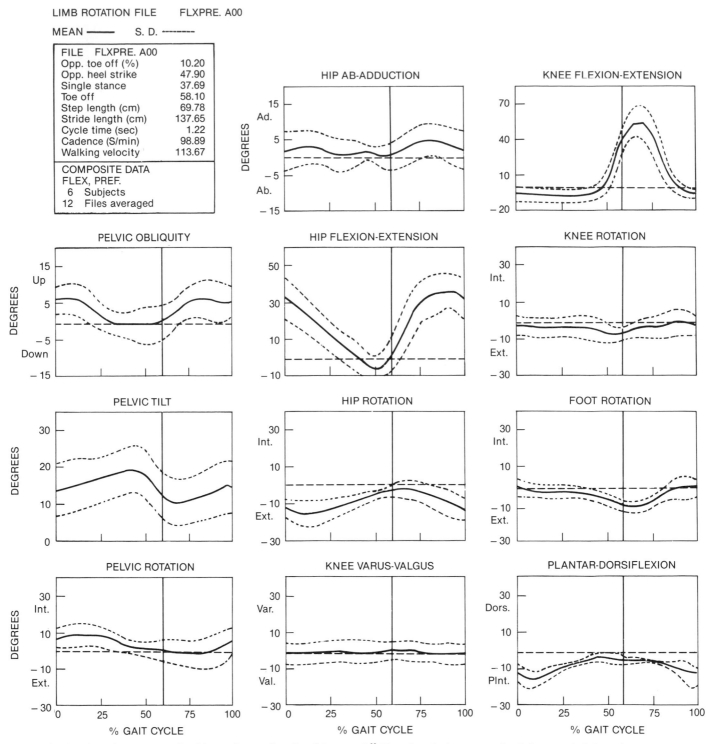

Figure 29–10. Above-knee amputation kinematics, preferred walking speed.[32] Note that the knww remains fully extended throughout stance. (Data collected at Newington Children's Hospital Gait Analysis Laboratory, Newington, CT.)

store, and the remainder consists essentially of a manual goniometer.[27] The potentiometer should have at least 90 percent linearity, but almost all commercially available rheostats today satisfy that requirement. Also, it should be noted that most isokinetic devices have a built-in electrogoniometer: Asking the patient to monitor the printed goniometric channel is often a good method of encouraging joint mobility through kinematic biofeedback techniques. Finally, as with all electrical/electronic devices,

electrogoniometers should be assessed for compliance with both federal and local safety standards.

KINETIC (DYNAMIC FORCE) FEEDBACK

Kinetic, or dynamic force, feedback renders information regarding the amount or rate of loading through the limbs. As in other types of biofeedback, an audio or visual feedback signal is used. In kinetic feedback, the goal is usually one of informing the patient that weight bearing is correct, excessive, or insufficient (limb load feedback). Limb load feedback requires the therapist to be familiar with the same general motor learning strategies (the time sequence, positive reinforcement, and establishing a success ratio) as discussed previously under EMG and kinematic biofeedback. Understanding the goals of kinetic feedback is also required.

Types of Kinetic Feedback Devices

The most familiar type of kinetic feedback is a bathroom scale, which can be used to habituate patients to the weight-bearing requirements of their fracture, prosthesis, or orthosis during static standing. The bathroom scale, however, is not useful for dynamic force feedback in part because it will register artifactually high forces during the loading phase as in the stance phase of gait. Another familiar, but little-appreciated, kinetic feedback device is the force reading from isokinetic devices like the Cybex machine.

FOOTSWITCH

A simple footswitch can be used for kinetic feedback. It is easily fabricated in the physical therapy clinic. A buzzer and a battery connected to a footswitch can warn the patient not to bear weight on a fractured limb, or it may help encourage heel-strike from a patient with hemiplegia or cerebral palsy. When the metal parts of the footswitch contact during the stance phase, the buzzer sounds, giving audible biofeedback. Two footswitches could be used bilaterally to provide stance time symmetry biofeedback. Of course, the weight-bearing force is unknowable using this simple system, but footswitches have the benefit of convenience.

One advantage of footswitches is that they can be used to record the patient's progress in achieving heel contact by attaching them to a strip chart recorder. This technique was previously used in gait laboratories before more sophisticated methods were devised.

LIMB LOAD MONITOR

A **limb load monitor** (LLM) is most frequently used to provide kinetic feedback in the clinic because it gives feedback concerning the *amount* of weight born on a limb.[33] Limb load monitors generally have a strain gauge built into an insole or the sole of a sandal. The strain gauge works by decreasing its electrical resistance as the force on the foot increases.[34] Less resistance, in turn, permits more electricity to reach the audio speaker, which beeps faster or at a higher pitch as greater loads are applied.

The feedback threshold is set according to the amount of weight required to be applied on the limb. For example, if no weight bearing is required, the therapist might set the audio signal to respond as soon as 2 lb or more is sensed by the LLM. When weight bearing exceeds the threshold, an audible tone warns the patient and informs the therapist or orthopedist that the protocol is being violated.[35,36]

In other applications, the therapist may want to encourage weight bearing. For patients being encouraged to bear weight, the LLM can be used to inform them when they have achieved the criterion weight bearing set by the therapist.[37] Again, modest goals are set initially, and then increments are added as success is achieved consistently. When the patient achieves full weight bearing on the limb, feedback is withdrawn and the patient attempts to maintain the treatment effect without supervision. The LLM then can be used to monitor the patient's success surreptitiously.

Technical Limitations

Only the vertical ground reaction component is registered by LLMs: fore-aft, torsional, and horizontal sheer forces are not monitored separately in present devices. Therefore, limb load monitors may feed back invalid signals, especially if the patient uses a pathologic gait pattern, as is typically true with lower-limb disability. The greatest danger of artifact occurs during heel strike, particularly during fast walking.

Until technology improves, the prudent therapist employs limb-load feedback only as an indication of gross errors in timing and weight bearing.

Clinical Application

Gait training is tiring. Gait training with kinetic feedback is probably more tiring, owing to the additional cognitive demands. The patient not only must exercise but also must concentrate on the feedback signal. Therefore the therapist must provide frequent rest periods and occasionally reassess the patient's progress to ensure that treatment goals are accomplished. Fatigue interferes with learning no less in biofeedback than in other neuromuscular reeducation.

The therapist will start a treatment session usually by reviewing the goals for that day with the patient. If it is the patient's first exposure to the LLM, the therapist demonstrates the task on himself or herself and then on the patient's "uninvolved" limb.

The first session usually consists of static weight shifting. Next, the patient practices walking in place, usually in the parallel bars. If the patient cannot understand the LLM feedback, the therapist can use bathroom scales combined with the LLM to show the relationship of the LLM feedback to a familiar load monitor.[38]

After consistently successful static performance, the patient should be asked to walk in place while generating the appropriate biofeedback signal. Weight shifting and balance should be encouraged by stance- and swing-phase biofeedback. After roughly two thirds or more of the trials are successful, introduce short-distance ambulation with biofeedback.

After approximately five sessions, reassess the patient's progress. Are the therapy goals appropriate? Is biofeedback enhancing or interfering with progress in other areas of therapy? Review sessions occasionally should be provided, including static weight shifting and dynamic gait activities, to ensure that the basic skills are not forgotten.

Most importantly, assess the patient's performance without biofeedback. Normal gait is a smooth, automatic, and subconsciously controlled activity; that goal should retain priority above all else. In contrast, biofeedback compels voluntary attention to the tasks to be practiced. Hesitation or slow gait may indicate excessive reliance on the biofeedback, which in fact detracts from normal gait.

To develop normal locomotor skills, the therapist must encourage normal walking speed. Many patients with hemiplegia, for example, can look fairly normal while using biofeedback, but when asked to walk at a normal pace, about one cycle per second, their control is rendered asunder. Biofeedback is only a tool: The therapist retains responsibility for the correct timing and speed of movement training.

Effective kinematic and kinetic biofeedback depends upon appropriate goal setting. The person with hemiplegia generally should be encouraged to flex the affected knee during stance, but an individual with an above-knee amputation should not. The patient's diagnosis and prosthetic/orthotic appliances will manifest differences in gait requirements, which modify treatment goals and functional expectations. Any therapeutic technique, including biofeedback, should achieve the most efficient gait possible, consistent with safety and stability.

NEW CONCEPTS AND AREAS FOR FURTHER RESEARCH

The necessity for further research in biofeedback cannot be overemphasized. The great potential of biofeedback techniques is that they put the responsibility for healthy behavior squarely upon the patient. The paradigm of therapist or doctor as healer becomes a paternal relic if the patient takes the role of healer. To realize this potential, however, self-regulation techniques such as biofeedback need to be subjected to the scrutiny of critical thinkers and tested empirically through clinical research.

Perhaps the chief impediment to giving patients more direct control of their rehabilitation is our current inability to understand deeply the rules and mechanisms governing human orthopedic and neurologic recovery. We can hardly translate to layman's terms that which scientists do not understand. The challenge to the therapist, then, is to understand the rules of human behavior better. Biofeedback techniques can be used to monitor physiologic results and to help patients gain access to these otherwise unfelt concomitants of recovery. But unless professionals first understand the underlying physiology, technical applications are hopelessly futile.

One area of interest is adaptation of computers to rehabilitation. The addition of microcomputers to biofeedback-assisted therapy may improve information processing (Fig. 29–11). With the enormous memories of computers, storing normal movement templates in the microcomputer and subsequently requesting patients to approximate those movement patterns has been widely advertised to be effective in teaching neuromuscular skills. Absolutely no research, however, can be presented now to substantiate those claims. Indeed, excess information can overwhelm patients and therapists with its sheer volume.

Perhaps the most pressing deficiency in the rehabilitation biofeedback literature is the lack of controlled studies involving patients. Most of the evidence that supports the use of biofeedback techniques is based on normal subjects.

Figure 29–11. Example of computer-assisted biofeedback device. Note that cartidges in foreground supply movement "games" to facilitate patient participation in therapy. (Courtesy of Self-Regulation Systems, Redmond, WA.)

It is abundantly clear that electronic advances should be utilized clinically to the advantage of our patients. The therapist must assume the responsibility for exploring their potential and validating biofeedback techniques through clinical research, particularly on patient populations.

SUMMARY

The primary use of biofeedback in physical therapy is to improve motor performance by facilitating motor learning. It can be used to inform the patient about movement, muscle activity, force, joint displacement, blood pressure, heart rate, and other physiologic information. Effective use of biofeedback is contingent upon an understanding of the principles of motor learning and the technical capabilities of the biofeedback equipment. It is clearly evident that biofeedback holds important potential as an adjunctive treatment for specific neuromuscular and behavioral disorders. Its capabilities should be used clinically to the advantage of our patients. The need for additional evidence to support its clinical use is also clear. Physical therapists must assume responsibility for exploring further applications of biofeedback and validating its use through clinical research, particularly on patient populations.

QUESTIONS FOR REVIEW

1. Provide examples of physiologic events and components of human movement that potentially can be influenced by biofeedback.

2. What is the primary psychologic/motor learning model employed in biofeedback?

3. What benefits does biofeedback provide to assist the rehabilitation process of neuromuscular disorders?

4. Differentiate between volume conduction and movement artifacts.

5. Describe the general procedure for therapeutic application of biofeedback.

6. What is the most likely source of an artifactual, rhythmically repeating EMG interference when the electrodes are on the patient's back?

7. Why is input impedance important to therapists using EMG feedback?

8. What type of biofeedback, kinetic or kinematic, is represented by a limb load monitor?

REFERENCES

1. Basmajian, JV: Introduction: Principles and background. In Basmajian, JV (ed): Biofeedback: Principles and Practice for Clinicians. Williams & Wilkins, Baltimore, MD, 1983.
2. Herman, RM, et al (eds): Neural Control of Locomotion. Plenum, New York, 1976.
3. Brooks, VB (ed): Handbook of Physiology: Sec.1: The Nervous System, Vol.2: Motor Control (Part 1). American Physiological Society, Bethesda, MD, 1981.
4. Mulder, T and Hulstyn, W: Sensory feedback therapy and theoretical knowledge of motor control and learning. Am J Phys Med 63:226–244, 1984.
5. Krebs, DE: Clinical electromyographic feedback following meniscectomy: A multiple regression experimental analysis. Phys Ther 61:1017–21, 1981.
6. Krebs, DE, et al: Knee joint angle: Its relationship to quadriceps femoris activity in normal and postarthrotomy limbs. Arch Phys Med Rehabil 64:441–447, 1983.
7. Lenman, JAE: Quantitative electromyographic changes associated with muscular weakness. J Neurol Neurosurg Psychiatry 22:306–310, 1959.
8. Lippold, OCJ: Relation between integrated action potentials in human muscle and its isometric tension. J Physiol 117:492–499, 1952.
9. Wolf, SL: Essential considerations in the use of EMG biofeedback. Phys Ther 58:25–31, 1978.
10. Inglis, J, Campbell, D, and Donald, MW: Electromyographic biofeedback and neuromuscular rehabilitation. Can J Behav Sci 8:299–323, 1976.
11. Keefe, FJ and Surwit, RS: Electromyographic feedback: Behavioral treatment of neuromuscular disorders. J Behav Med 1:13–25, 1978.
12. Cataldo, ME, Bird, BL, and Cunningham, CE: Experimental analysis of EMG feedback in treating cerebral palsy. J Behav Med 1:311–322, 1978.
13. Wolf, SL: Electromyographic feedback for spinal cord injured patients: A realistic perspective. In Basmajian, JV (ed): Biofeedback: Principles and Practice for Clinicians. Williams & Wilkins, Baltimore, MD, 1983.
14. Balliet, R, Levy, B, and Blood, KMT: Upper extremity sensory feedback therapy in chronic cerebrovascular accident patients with impaired expressive aphasia and auditory comprehension. Arch Phys Med Rehabil 67:304–310, 1986.
15. Shiavi, R, et al: Variability of electromyographic patterns for level-surface walking through a range of self-selected speeds. Bull Prosthet Res 10(35):5–14, 1981.
16. Winter, DA: Pathologic gait diagnosis with computer-averaged electromyographic profiles. Arch Phys Med Rehabil 65:393–398, 1984.
17. Yang, JF and Winter DA: Electromyographic amplitude normalization methods: Improving their sensitivity as diagnostic tools in gait analysis. Arch Phys Med Rehabil 65:517–521, 1984.
18. Jacobson, E: Progressive Relaxation, ed 2. University of Chicago Press, Chicago, 1938.
19. Schultz, JH: Das Autogene Training: Konzentrative Selbstent-spannung. Georg Thieme Verlag, Stuttgart, Germany, 1932.
20. Stoyva, JM: Guidelines in cultivating general relaxation: Biofeedback autogenic training combined. In Basmajian, JV (ed): Biofeedback: Principles and Practice for Clinicians. Williams & Wilkins, Baltimore, MD, 1983.
21. Collins, GA, et al: Comparative analysis of paraspinal and frontalis EMG, heart rate and skin conductance in chronic low back pain patients and normals to various postures and stress. Scand J Rehab Med 14:39–46, 1982.
22. Sedlacek, K: Biofeedback for Raynaud's Disease. Psychosomatics 20:537–541, 1979.
23. Korein, J and Brudny, J: Integrated EMG feedback in the management of spasmodic torticollis and focal dystonia: A prospective study of 80 patients. In Yahr, MD (ed): The Basal Ganglia. Raven Press, New York, 1976.
24. Health and Public Policy Committee, American College of Physicians: Biofeedback for neuromuscular disorders. Ann Intern Med 102:854–858, 1985.

25. Biofeedback Society of America, Committee on Legislation and Public Policy: The Efficacy of Biofeedback in the Treatment of Specified Medical Disorders. Biofeedback Society of America, Wheat Ridge, CO, 1982.
26. Binder, SA: Assessing the effectiveness of positional feedback to treat an ataxic patient: Application of a single-subject design. Phys Ther 61:735–736, 1981.
27. Gilbert, JA, et al: Technical note: Auditory feedback of knee angle for amputees. Prosthet Orthot Internat 6:103–104, 1982.
28. DeBacher, G: Feedback goniometers for rehabilitation. In Basmajian, JV (ed): Biofeedback: Principles and Practice for Clinicians. Williams & Wilkins, Baltimore, MD, 1983.
29. Koheil, R and Mandel, AR: Joint position biofeedback facilitation of physical therapy in gait training. Am J Phys Med 59:288–297, 1980.
30. Fernie, G, Holden, J, and Soto, M: Biofeedback training of knee control in the above-knee amputee. Am J Phys Med 57:161–166, 1978.
31. Wooldridge, CP, Leiper, C, and Ogston, DG: Biofeedback training of knee joint position of the cerebral palsied child. Physiotherapy (Canada) 28:138–143, 1976.

32. Krebs, DE: Effect of Variations in Residuum Environment and Walking Rate on Residual Limb Muscle Activity of Selected Above-Knee Amputees. Doctoral Dissertation; University Microfilms International, Ann Arbor, MI, 1986.
33. Gapsis, JJ, et al: Limb load monitor: Evaluation of a sensory feedback device for controlled weight bearing. Arch Phys Med Rehabil 63:38–41, 1982.
34. Wolf, SL and Binder-Macleod, SA: Use of the Krusen limb load monitor to quantify temporal and loading measurements of gait. Phys Ther 62:976–982, 1982.
35. Craik, RL and Wannstedt, GT: The limb load monitor: An augmented sensory feedback device. In Proceedings of a Conference on Devices and Systems for the Disabled. Krusen Research Center, Philadelphia, PA, 1975, pp 19–24.
36. Wannstedt, GT and Herman, RM: Use of augmented sensory feedback to achieve symmetrical standing. Phys Ther 58:553–559, 1978.
37. Kegel, B and Moore, AJ: Load cell: A device to monitor weight bearing for lower extremity amputees. Phys Ther 57:652–654, 1977.
38. Peper, E and Robertson J: Biofeedback use of common objects: The bathroom scale in physical therapy. Biofeedback Self Regul 1:237–240, 1976.

SUPPLEMENTAL READINGS

Azrin, N, et al: Behavioral engineering: Postural control by a portable apparatus. J Appl Behav Anal 1:99, 1968.
Ball, T, McCrady, R, and Hart, A: Automated reinforcement of head posture in two cerebral palsied, retarded children. Percept Mot Skills 40:619, 1975.
Basmajian, JV, et al: Biofeedback treatment of foot-drop after stroke compared with standard rehabilitation technique: Effects on voluntary control and strength. Arch Phys Med Rehabil 56:231, 1975.
Bjork, L and Wetzel, A: A positional biofeedback device for sitting balance. Phys Ther 63:1460, 1983.
Block, JD, et al: Hemiplegic hand spasticity: Amelioration by assisted extension practice with augmented feedback. Arch Phys Med Rehabil 52:573, 1971.
Bohannon, RW and Short, D: Compact device for positional biofeedback. Phys Ther 64:1235, 1984.
Bowman, BR, Baker, LL, and Waters, RL: Positional feedback and electrical stimulation: An automated treatment for the hemiplegic wrist. Arch Phys Med Rehabil 60:497, 1979.
Brown, DM, DeBacher, GA, and Basmajian, JV: Feedback goniometers for hand rehabilitation. Am J Occup Ther 33(7):458, 1979.
Catanese, AA and Sandford DA: Head-position training through biofeedback: Prosthetic or cure? Dev Med Child Neurol 26:369, 1984.
Driscoll, B: Creative technological aids for the learning-disabled child. Am J Occup Ther 29:102, 1975.
Dworkin, B: Instrumental learning for the treatment of disease. Health Psychol 1:45, 1982.
Greenberg, S and Fowler, RS: Kinesthetic biofeedback: A treatment modality for elbow range of motion in hemiplegia. Am J Occup Ther 34:738, 1980.
Hallum, A: Subject-induced reinforcement of head lifting in the prone position. Phys Ther 64:1390, 1984.
Hallum, A: How to build simple, inexpensive biofeedback systems. Phys Ther 64:1235, 1984.
Harris F, Spelman, F, and Hymer, J: Electronic sensory aids as treatment for cerebral palsied children. Phys Ther 54:354, 1974.
Harris, FA: Treatment with a position feedback-controlled head stabilizer. Am J Phys Med 58:169, 1979.
Huggins, M and Gallen, D: A training program for operation of a head-controlled electric wheelchair. Physiotherapy (Canada) 36:204, 1984.
Hurd, WW, Pegram, V, and Nepomuceno, C: Comparison of actual and simulated EMG biofeedback in the treatment of hemiplegic patients. Am J Phys Med 59:73, 1980.
Ince, LP, Leon, MS and Christidis, D: Experimental foundations of EMG biofeedback with the upper extremity: A review of the literature. Biofeedback Self Regul 9:371, 1984.
Ince, LP, Leon, MS, and Christidis, D: EMG biofeedback for improve-

ment of upper extremity function: A critical review of the literature. Physiotherapy (Canada) 37:12, 1985.
Inglis, J, et al: Electromyographic biofeedback and physical therapy of the hemiplegic upper limb. Arch Phys Med Rehabil 65:755, 1984.
Lee, K-H, et al: Myofeedback for muscle retraining in hemiplegic patients. Arch Phys Med Rehabil 57:588, 1976.
Leiper, CI, et al: Sensory feedback for head control in cerebral palsy. Phys Ther 61:512, 1981.
Maloney, FP: A simplified mercury switch head-control biofeedback device. Biofeedback Self Regul 5:257, 1980.
Middaugh, SJ: EMG feedback as a muscle re-education technique: A controlled study. Phys Ther 58:11, 1978.
Middaugh, SJ and Miller, MC: Electromyographic feedback: Effects on voluntary muscle contractions in paretic subjects. Arch Phys Med Rehabil 61:24, 1980.
Morris, A and Brown, M: Electronic training devices for hand rehabilitation. Am J Occup Ther 30:376, 1976.
Mroczek, N, Halpern, D, and McHugh, R: Electromyographic feedback and physical therapy for neuromuscular retraining in hemiplegia. Arch Phys Med Rehabil 59:258, 1978.
O'Brien, F and Azrin, N: Control of posture by informational feedback. J Appl Behav Anal 3:235, 1970.
Prevo, AJH, Visser, SL, and Vogelaar, TW: Effect of EMG feedback on paretic muscles and abnormal co-contraction in the hemiplegic arm, compared with conventional physical therapy. Scand J Rehabil 14:121, 1982.
Tiller, J, et al: Treatment of functional chronic stooped posture using a training device and behavior therapy. Phys Ther 62:1597, 1982.
Turczynski, B, Hartje, W, and Sturm, W: Electromyographic feedback treatment of chronic hemiparesis: An attempt to quantify treatment effects. Arch Phys Med Rehabil 65:526, 1984.
Walmsley, RP, Crichton, L, and Droog, D: Music as a feedback mechanism for teaching head control to severely handicapped children: A pilot study. Develop Med Child Neurol 23:739, 1981.
Wolf, SL: Electromyographic biofeedback applications to stroke patients: A critical review. Phys Ther 63:1448, 1983.
Wolf, SL and Binder-MacLeod, SA: Electromyographic biofeedback applications to the hemiplegic patient: Changes in lower extremity neuromuscular and functional status. Phys Ther 63:1404, 1983.
Wolf, SL and Binder-MacLeod, SA: Electromyographic biofeedback applications to the hemiplegic patient: Changes in upper extremity neuromuscular and functional status. Phys Ther 63:1393, 1983.
Wooldridge, CP and Russel, G: Head position training with the cerebral palsied child: An application of biofeedback techniques. Arch Phys Med Rehabil 57:407, 1976.
Zimnicki, BZ and Fernie, GR: Biofeedback and the lower extremity amputee: A new training aid. Physiotherapy (Canada) 28:79, 1976.

GLOSSARY

Artifact: A voltage signal generated by a source other than the one of interest.

Biofeedback: Method of augmenting awareness of movement or physiologic events by amplifying and displaying this information so that the patient can learn to control these functions.

Common mode rejection ratio (CMRR): A proportion expressing an amplifier's ability to reject unwanted noise while amplifying the wanted signal.

Electrogoniometer: Rheostat, or variable resistor, with extended attachments for limb segments. Joint rotation changes the resistance of the device to a current passing to a recorder or speaker for kinesiologic recording or biofeedback, respectively.

Endogenous: Produced or caused by factors within a cell or organism.

Impedance: The property of a substance that offers resistance to current flow in an alternating current.

Kinematic: Description of the movement and displacement of objects (usually limb segments) in motion without reference to the forces that cause the motion.

Kinetics: Description of the movement, displacement, and forces involved with objects (usually limb segments) in motion.

Limb load monitor: Device to measure and report the forces experienced by the lower limbs during walking or other weight-bearing activities.

Noise: An unwanted electrical signal that is detected along with the desired signal.

Ohmmeter: A device that measures electrical resistance; measured in ohms.

Ohm's law: The strength of an electrical current is equal to the voltage divided by the resistance; expressed in ohms.

Potentiometer: An instrument used to measure voltage.

Rheostat: A mechanism for regulating the resistance in an electrical circuit; controls the amount of electrical current entering a circuit; variable resistor.

Voltmeter: An instrument for measuring electromotive force; measured in volts.

Chapter 30

TRANSCUTANEOUS ELECTRICAL NERVE STIMULATION

GERALD LAMPE

OBJECTIVES

1. Define transcutaneous electrical nerve stimulation (TENS).

2. State the purposes of TENS.

3. Explain patient selection criteria.

4. Describe patient education components.

5. Explain TENS system "application" techniques.

6. Describe related neurophysiology and electrophysiology.

INTRODUCTION

Transcutaneous electrical nerve stimulation (TENS) is a valuable clinical procedure for the symptomatic relief of **pain** (Fig. 30–1). Combine a little box (generator), a few wires (lead wires/cables), and patches (electrodes), add a battery and some control buttons, knobs, or switches, and one sees the external, superficial components of a sophisticated and carefully modulated electrotherapy called TENS. Within the unit are miniaturized electronics, circuit boards, and computer chips that represent a linking of modern engineering with our current medical understanding of pain. For perhaps 150,000 to 200,000 people a year, TENS provides relief of pain. Sometimes TENS is used adjunctively to medication, psychologic interventions, nursing care, and/or physical therapy procedures. Other times TENS is used alone to control pain, frequently after multiple other attempts have failed.

The indications for use of TENS can be categorized into two major areas: (1) relief of acute pain, and (2) treatment of chronic pain. For controlling acute pain, TENS frequently augments concurrent therapy administered to correct the cause of the pain (Fig. 30–2). For chronic benign pain sufferers, the safe, noninvasive, nonaddictive TENS therapy may "turn down" or "turn off" the painful signals and allow the individual to carry out normal personal and occupational activities comfortably. Similarly, such interventions as rest, ice, compression, elevation, or medications do not treat the cause of pain directly. However, they do allow the resolution of pain and provide comfort during healing.

Transcutaneous electrical nerve stimulation systems reflect both scientific and technologic discovery relative to **sensory pacing** for the relief of pain with electrical stimulation. The knowledge and skill of the health care professional who prescribes the therapy and/or applies it is critical to the effectiveness of TENS.

Figure 30–1. Primary typical acute/chronic pain cycle.

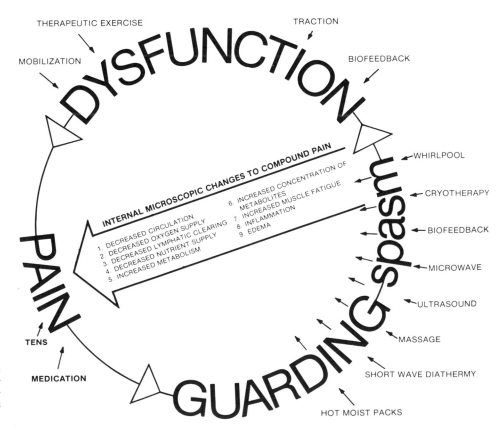

Figure 30–2. Pain cycle and interventions. (From Mannheimer, J and Lampe, G: *Clinical Transcutaneous Electrical Nerve Stimulation.* FA Davis, Philadelphia, 1984, p 21, with permission.)

Although there may be several reasons patients do not obtain adequate pain relief with TENS, not all of which are yet fully understood, the two primary causes of failure appear to be (1) failure to assess the patient properly, and (2) failure to instruct the patient properly. Proper assessment is an inarguable tenet of good clinical practice. Equally, the need for good patient instruction is as essential. High technology, as reflected by many TENS systems, must be complemented by "high touch" human element factors as well.

Although the Egyptians may have used a crude form of electrical stimulation for medical treatment as early as AD 46,[1] the publication of the gate control theory of pain by Melzack and Wall[2] in 1965 has done more than any other single event in history to advance the use of electricity in conventional medical circles for controlling acute and chronic pain. Their thinking revealed the possibility that special stimulation could be put into the nervous system to block pain.

Transcutaneous electrical nerve stimulation of the peripheral nervous system has become the one available treatment that can be used safely and inexpensively over a long period of time for the patient with pain of benign origin. It has been found to provide relief for patients with pain following surgical procedures and for those suffering pain associated with acute trauma, with success rates ranging from 70 to 90 percent.[3-5]

Optimal benefit is becoming more possible and more likely now that we can integrate our knowledge and experience regarding the nature of pain, with the electrotherapeutic management of its symptoms. We now know from our understanding of electrophysiology and pain that TENS electrodes do not need to be placed randomly or blindly; and that impulse amplitude, rate, and width can be selected with sound rationale. There also exists a logical approach in selecting the mode of stimulation so that **conventional,** high-rate, low-rate, **burst, brief intense, modulation, strength-duration,** or combined modes can be used with reasonable order and purpose.

DESCRIPTION OF TERMS

The term **transcutaneous** describes how the therapy is applied. An interfacing conduction medium is applied to electrodes, if they aren't pregelled, to transmit electrical impulses to the skin. The electrodes then are applied to the skin. The impulses are transmitted across the skin without disruption of the skin barrier. Once impulses reach the nerve, sensory pacing is achieved for pain control.

Electrical refers to the procedure of passing controlled, low-voltage electrical impulses through the skin to the underlying tissue to act as a stimulus.

Nerve receives and transmits signals. *Pain* is a sensation initiated at the receptors of the nervous system and is transmitted by peripheral nerves. Painful stimuli enter the central nervous system via the dorsal horn of the spinal cord, are received by the thalamus, and finally are projected to the cerebral cortex (Figure 30–3). There they are integrated, interpreted, and a response is formu-

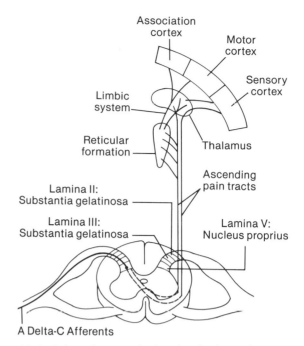

Figure 30–3. Pain pathways: spinal cord and mixed spinal nerve with contralateral afferent projection of pain impulses. (From Lampe, G: *TENS Technology and Physiology.* Codman & Shurtleff, Randolph, MA, 1984, p 6, with permission.)

lated—it hurts! Pain is a perception mediated by the nervous system through a series of electrochemical events. Therefore, to affect pain we must effectively modulate activity in the nervous system to reduce or to abate the transmission of pain. Thus the term **neuromodulation** is used with TENS.

The message unit of the nervous system is the evoked potential—a tiny electrical impulse. Therefore it is logical that if TENS (an electric generator and delivery system) is properly positioned to effectively recruit the appropriate peripheral nerve(s), and if the impulse characteristics are properly set to recruit appropriate fiber types within the peripheral nervous system (PNS), then TENS will produce effective electrochemical neuromodulation for the person experiencing pain. As a result, the patient will suffer less and probably receive optimal benefit. Transcutaneous electrical nerve stimulation achieves optimal effect when the electrodes are placed over the PNS. Neuromodulation also influences both the ascending and descending central nervous system (CNS) pathways related to the transmission and perception of pain.

GENERAL PRINCIPLES

The primary goal of TENS is to relieve pain. Although other recommendations, claims, and applications have been related to TENS, approval by the Food and Drug Administration remains specific and limited. Thus the use of TENS is limited to pain relief as a class II medical service.[6] Therefore, applications of TENS outside of this purpose should be avoided until specific formal approval has been granted for such exceptional use, or exceptional use should be limited to approved investigational protocols.

Equipment

TENS equipment consists of a pulse generator voltage source, electrodes, and interconnecting **lead wires** (Fig. 30–4).

ENERGY SOURCE

Transcutaneous electrical nerve stimulation **generators** may receive their primary energy source from a conventional electrical wall outlet. This 60-cycle alternating current (AC) source is then "modified" by the TENS generator to produce one of the typical TENS waveforms. More often, however, TENS generators receive their primary energy from disposable or rechargeable batteries. The most common battery source used through the 1970s was a set of AA batteries. Very frequently, TENS systems were provided with nickel cadmium (NICAD) rechargeable AA batteries and a recharging unit. As the circuitry of the TENS unit continued to improve through the 1980s, it became possible to utilize a 9-volt battery source, rechargeable or disposable. The utilization of either AA or 9-volt energy sources is not a reflection of the level of sophistication of the TENS circuitry but of the availability of progressively smaller units. The integration of the two battery types has allowed increased flexibility in the design of the TENS generator hardware.

The use of disposable batteries is rather straightforward. Put new ones in, use them until they run down, and then throw them away. The use of the rechargeable systems can be somewhat less handy than the throwaway method, but they offer the potential to save considerable money on the long term. Opinions differ regarding the proper charging and discharging method for rechargeable (NICAD) batteries. The best advice is the manufacturer's instructions related to the proper use and storage of the NICAD batteries. This information should be read carefully by both clinician and patient and then discussed to ensure proper understanding.

LEAD WIRES

The stimulating impulse created by the TENS generator must be transmitted to electrodes and then to the skin before the impulse can affect the human nervous system. **Lead wires,** sometimes called cables, are required between the generator and the electrodes. There are many different lead wire systems which vary in length, thickness, tensile strengths, and degree of flexibility. Generally, the quality of the lead wire systems has advanced so that they rarely break. Therefore, considerations in selection are based on cosmetic and functional factors.

ELECTRODES

The skin is the largest organ of the body and provides the very essential function of providing a barrier to protect the inside of our bodies from its outside environment. The skin does not generally function well when something is firmly attached for long periods of time, even a Band-Aid. Therefore, when electrodes for TENS systems are attached to skin, there is an inherent problem.

However, TENS systems require that electrodes be

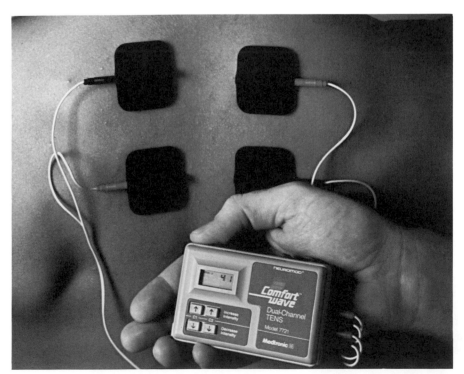

Figure 30–4. TENS equipment system consists of a pulse generator voltage source, electrodes, and interconnecting lead wires.

attached to the skin. They further require that an electrode system must include a coupling medium for the transmission of the generated impulse. When a gel medium is used, it provides a slippery and unstable electrode–skin connection. Hence the electrodes must be fastened to prevent slipping. Usually they are secured with adhesive tape. Because of the mechanical stresses the adhesive tape can cause to the superficial skin layers, selection of the proper tape is an important consideration for long-term repeated application of TENS for pain management. Inasmuch as skin irritation can become a problem associated with repeated adhesive tape applications, all TENS users should be well aware of the options that exist. More and more electrode systems are available that are self-conducting, self-adhesive, and extremely flexible.

Allergies to electrodes and conducting media have been abated with few exceptions. However, occluding the skin with gels, electrodes, and tapes has resulted in skin rash problems. The skin problems that have been encountered were sometimes unavoidable, but perhaps many of them could have been prevented. A few of the ways that thermal and/or mechanical stresses have caused the skin rashes include poor or improper patient instruction, careless spreading of the gels, improper contact of the electrode with the skin, selecting a tape that is too irritating, taping with disregard for body segment motion, improper tape application techniques, improper skin hygiene, or improper tape removal techniques. A **tension loop procedure** can be used to reduce shearing stresses at the electrode sites. This consists of coiling a small loop of lead wire about 6 to 10 inches from the electrodes and taping this loop to the skin.

There are many electrode types available to match a patient's combined need of simplicity, safety, cost, and convenience. If appropriate attention is given to electrode selection, placement, and care, relatively few patients will experience skin problems related to TENS.

It has been common for new TENS hardware (generators) to appear at every American Physical Therapy Association national convention. The rate of change in the accessory (electrode) industry occurs even more rapidly. Inasmuch as electrodes are extremely important, and because they remain the weakest part of TENS systems, change is good. Touring the exhibit areas in conjunction with professional meetings is a good place to learn of advances in electrode design and function. Medical equipment suppliers and manufacturer representatives can be valuable resources for monitoring change as well. Skin and electrode care inservice programs should be a periodic component of continuing education for therapists using TENS systems. In addition, patients should be educated carefully regarding proper use of electrodes and tape and how to protect skin from avoidable stress.

Electrode Placement

Electrode placement is one of the most critical factors that can influence the success rate and benefit from TENS. Because our concern is limited to noninvasive (surface) stimulation, our choice of effective stimulation sites is immediately narrowed. In order for an area of the body to be labeled as an optimal stimulation site, the following criteria must be met:

1. The site selected should allow stimulation to be easily directed into the peripheral nervous system (PNS) and central nervous system (CNS).

2. The region must be conducive to TENS electrode placement. This eliminates most bony prominences and areas primarily covered with hair that may be accessible only to a needle or a probe.

3. The area selected should be anatomically or physiologically related to the source of pain.

4. The site should have anatomic markers that can be repeatedly and distinctly located.

Optimal stimulation sites at motor points and/or a superficial aspect of a major peripheral nerve may prove to be the best areas at which to stimulate when performing acupuncturelike, pulse-train, or **brief intense** TENS.[9–12] These three methods of TENS require strong, visible muscle contractions in segmentally related myotomes and may prove beneficial in more severe pain syndromes or when conventional TENS is not effective.

Conventional TENS (without muscle contraction) may be applied best at optimal stimulation sites where motor points are not found. However, all three methods of TENS can be performed successfully at all optimal stimulation sites that are segmentally related to the source of pain.[13]

Optimal stimulation sites that also possess motor points will probably provide for stronger stimulation because the stimulus will be conducted through a greater number of nerve fibers entering the spinal cord at several segments (sensory plus motor innervation). It is thus possible that the stronger and more widespread stimulation obtained with acupuncturelike, pulse-train, or brief intense TENS may in part help explain the liberation of endogenous opiates that has been shown to occur with these methods.[14–16]

The intermediate tissues between the electrode and the underlying nerve(s) are also important to consider when attempting to examine the effects of electrotherapy. All the tissues, including skin, adipose tissue, muscle, nerve, blood vessels, and bone, can be represented in terms of electrical circuits composed of resistors and capacitors. The resistance to the flow of the applied TENS current by the combined tissues is known as *impedance*. The higher the moisture content of a tissue, the lower the impedance of that tissue.

Electrodes for TENS are applied to the skin near or above the peripheral nerve and its branches. It is somewhat ironic that the electrodes must be placed on the skin. The outermost layer of the skin, the epidermis or stratum cornium, has a very low fluid content, so it offers more resistance to the passage of stimulating current than any of the other tissues involved. This suggests that if electrical stimulation is to be applied serially, special precautions should be taken to protect the integrity of the skin. In order to optimize the effects of the stimulating current, a few simple procedures should be employed to prepare the skin to receive the electrodes and the stimulating current so that impedance is reduced. These include gentle cleaning with clear fluids and moistening.

NEUROPHYSIOLOGIC MECHANISMS IN PAIN MODULATION

Electrical Nerve Stimulation

The modulation of normal nervous system function (neuromodulation) by externally applied electrical energy has been a prominent area of scientific interest and application since Galvani first demonstrated the phenomenon in the 1770s. During the following 200 years, electricity never achieved the clinical therapeutic benefits expected by its proponents. This resulted from a lack of understanding of the interaction of electrical stimulation with human tissue. With advances in technology and the advent of modern pain theories, greater understanding and applications have been developed.

What happens between the presentation of a stimulus and the signaling of this stimulus to the CNS (Fig. 30–5)? At rest, an uninjured nerve fiber has a resting potential which indicates a voltage gradient of 70 to 90 mv inside (negative) versus outside (positive) (Fig. 30–6A). The sodium-potassium pump maintains this resting potential (Fig. 30–6B). However, if a threshold stimulus is applied to the fiber, the capacity of the sodium-potassium pump will be exceeded and an explosive influx of sodium will occur at the point of stimulation. A disturbance of potential known as a nerve impulse, or evoked potential, will occur (Fig. 30–7). The impulse will then be propagated along the afferent or efferent fiber in both directions away from the stimulus. It is sustained without decrement by the metabolic inertia of the nerve. The

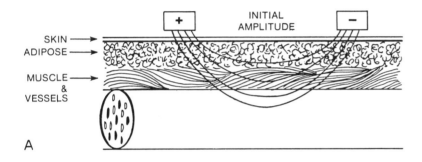

A

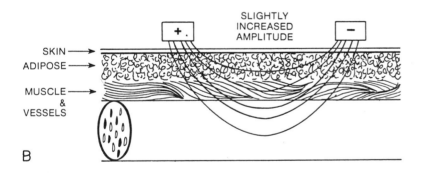

B

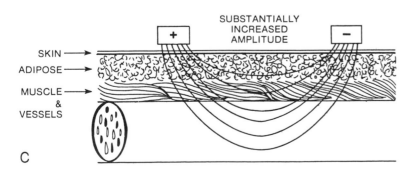

C

Figure 30–5. Stimulus strength and progressive nerve fiber recruitment. (From Mannheimer, J and Lampe, G: *Clinical Transcutaneous Electrical Nerve Stimulation.* FA Davis, Philadelphia, 1984, p 208, with permission.)

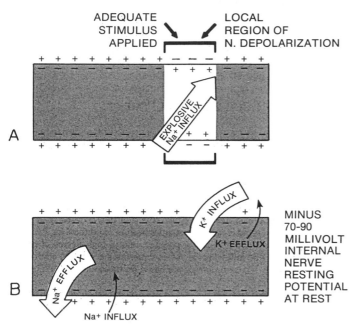

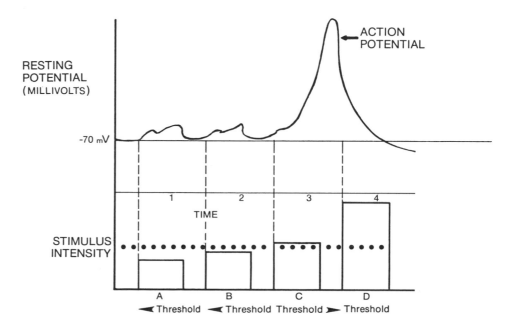

Figure 30-6. (*A*) Nerve resting potential and dynamic sodium-potassium pump. (*B*) Adequate stimulus causes capacity of sodium-potassium pump to be exceeded, and a reversal of potential occurs (positive inside and negative outside). An action potential is evoked. (From Mannheimer, J and Lampe, G: *Clinical Transcutaneous Electrical Nerve Stimulation.* FA Davis, Philadelphia, 1984, p 206, with permission.)

electrical potential is an all-or-none phenomenon and passes to the CNS.

The stimulation of nerve fibers should not be viewed as impulses moving through a wire. The bioelectric nature of the events in nerves is much different:

1. The nerve is an active conductor. Its sodium–potassium pump maintains a measurable resting potential. A wire is a passive conductor.

2. Propagation of a potential along a nerve occurs without decrement, and the evoked potential amplitude is maintained at a constant level. Much differently, as a charge moves along a wire, the resistance causes its potential to decline gradually.

3. When a nerve is warm, it is both a conductor and a propagator of nerve impulses. However, if a nerve is cooled sufficiently, it is incapable of propagating nerve impulses even though it remains a conductor. There is not a similar property known to metals.

4. The energy of a propagated nerve impulse is derived from the nerve's own metabolic potential (and metabolic inertia). The energy from the battery or other electric energy source serves only to depolarize a narrow segment of the nerve initially. In contrast, a potential passing in a wire must continuously be created and driven by the energy of the battery or electrical source.

5. The impulses within a nerve may travel at speeds up to 100 meters per second; the impulses in a wire may travel three million times as fast.

6. Nerves demonstrate refractory periods after depolarization. During this time they may be absolutely or relatively incapable of responding to a subsequent stimulus, no matter how strong the stimulus.

Central Nervous System Transmission of Pain Signals

Sensory information generated by high-intensity stimuli are mediated in the PNS by small A-delta and C-afferent fibers and terminate in the dorsal gray matter of the spinal cord (A-delta to lamina I and lamina V and C fibers to lamina II to lamina III of the substantia gelatinosa) (Fig. 30–8). Synaptic transmission of impulses from these small primary afferents depends on chemical transmitters. Substance P has been identified as one essential synaptic neurotransmitter associated with small fiber afferents and the transmission of "pain." Once the sensory impulses enter the CNS, they project to the

Figure 30-7. Stimulus intensity needed to evoke an action potential. (From Mannheimer, J and Lampe, G: *Clinical Transcutaneous Electrical Nerve Stimulation.* FA Davis, Philadelphia, 1984, p 207, with permission.)

A

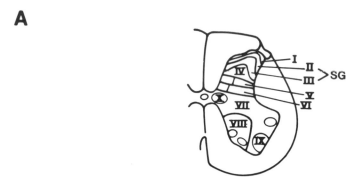

B

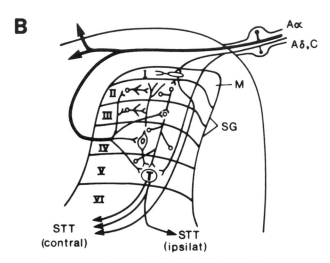

Figure 30–8. (*A*) Typical organization of laminae within gray matter of the spinal cord. (*B*) A schematic representation of primary afferent fiber projections into the dorsal horn. SG = substantia gelatinosa, M = marginal zone (lamina I), T = location of transmission cells (lamina V), STT = spinothalamic tract. (From Mannheimer, J and Lampe, G: *Clinical Transcutaneous Electrical Nerve Stimulation.* FA Davis, Philadelphia, 1984, p 45, with permission.)

higher centers by a number of second-order pathways. There are at least two components of the long ascending tracts to the brainstem: (1) spinothalamic and (2) spinoreticular.

The pain messages are transmitted by ascending afferent neurons in the lateral division of the anterolateral sensory system and remain differentiated and processed according to the specific characteristics of the stimulus. Acute **fast pain** will cross to the opposite side and ascend in the lateral, or neospinothalamic, tract. The information is transmitted to the thalamus and somatosensory cortex without significant synaptic projections to the reticular formation or limbic system and subserves the sensory-discriminative aspect of pain.. Chronic **slow pain** projects contralaterally and ipsilaterally in the paleospinothalamic tract and projects to widespread brainstem and cortical areas, including the reticular formation, limbic system, and frontal lobes. This explains the more diffuse nature of chronic pain and its greater affective-motivational aspects.

Sensory information generated by low-intensity stimuli is mediated by the large afferent A fibers (primarily A-beta) and terminates in the dorsal gray matter of the spinal cord in the lamina II-lamina III substantia gelatinosa. Unlike the A-delta, C-fiber afferents, the large A-fiber afferents ascend in the second-order neurons of the dorsal column on the ipsilateral side. In the spinal-cephalic course of impulses of this afferent information, fibers cross to the contralateral side in the brainstem, probably at the level of the medulla, and project with all other sensory input in the medial lemniscus to the thalamus and sensory cortex on that side.

Afferent Modulation

Information that travels to the brain is dependent not only on the afferent drive-stimulus, but also on the modulatory influences that act on the system. If transmission of nociceptive input can be modulated at the spinal cord level, the rostral transmission of pain can be blocked (e.g., intrathecal administration of local anesthetic may be given to block all sensory input). Transcutaneous electrical nerve stimulation may be administered to block pain, leaving all other sensation intact.

Spinal modulation appears to be under the influence of two different systems: (1) a supraspinally organized system originating in the brain and descending to the spinal cord; and (2) a segmental, spinal cord organized system.

All of the subregions of the nervous system involved in processing somatosensory information are subject to the influences from the reticular formation (descending control). Depending on circumstances, the effects may be presynaptic or postsynaptic, facilitatory or inhibitory. Although the neurotransmitter(s) that are preferential to the spinal cord are not well known, it is well known that the supraspinal system relies on serotoninergic and noradrenergic neurotransmitters. It is also well known that exogenous opiates like morphine act preferentially on the small A-delta/C fibers at opiate receptors and act to block the discharge of A-delta/C-fiber pain impulses (Fig. 30–9).

More recently, researchers[17–19] have discovered that the body has its own endogenous substances named **endorphins.** These substances have the same action as exogenous opiate alkyloids to block A-delta/C-fiber evoked activity. Successful activation of afferent input into the spinal cord could generate activity in certain intrinsic systems such as the endogenous enkephalin-endorphin systems which are found in segmental neurons of the spinal cord and in descending pathways that release seratonin and noradrenalin. This would result in the endorphin-enkephalin inhibition of A-delta/C-fiber-evoked activity and selective inhibition of pain. This effect has been demonstrated with certain deep brain stimulation trials, and the pain relief obtained has been reversible by the administration of the known opiate antagonist, naloxone. An endorphin-mediated inhibition of pain has been reported by a few investigators[11,16] using **low-frequency, acupuncturelike TENS.** This author has

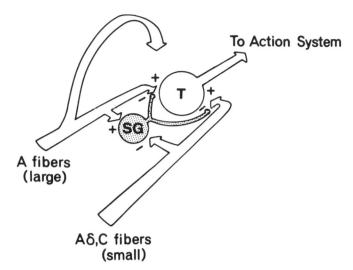

Figure 30–9. Schematic representation of primary afferent and interneuronal interactions implicated in gate control theory. SG = substantia gelatinosa, T = transmission cells, − = inhibitory synapse; + = facilitatory synapse. (From Mannheimer, J and Lampe, G: *Clinical Transcutaneous Electrical Nerve Stimulation.* FA Davis, Philadelphia, 1984, p 49, with permission.)

not been able to duplicate the claims or effects without stimulating through acupuncture needles and knows of no one else who has duplicated them clinically. Therefore, it is suggested that the scientific method be applied to further assess the possible endorphin-mediated changes associated with TENS therapy. While assessing this possible endorphin effect, it would serve the clinician well to assess claims by providers of TENS systems critically. Just as there *is* some doubt surrounding the TENS-endorphin causal relationship, there is *no* doubt that low-rate TENS does provide significant clinical benefit for a small but significant number of patients. The mechanism of action is poorly understood and, perhaps, erroneously assigned at this time, given that an opiate-mediated pain relief response has not been reproducible with surface electrodes and low-rate TENS as generally accepted. Figure 30–10 presents a summary of the factors involved in the transmission, modulation, and perception of pain.

TENS: CURRENT CHARACTERISTICS

In order to stimulate irritable tissue with a single pulse of current, three criteria must be fulfilled: (1) the stimulus must have an adequately abrupt onset (pulse rise time); (2) the impulse must have an adequate duration (pulse width); (3) the impulse intensity must be equal to or above threshold (amplitude).

For a given current waveform threshold, there is a specific relationship between the intensity and the duration. A graphic plotting of points showing this relationship is called the **strength-duration curve.** The relationship between intensity and duration is known as the law of excitability. All excitable tissue will respond to stimuli throughout a range of variables of intensity and duration

of the stimulating pulse. Each type of irritable tissue will respond most optimally to a relatively specific pulse shape with its own discrete intensity and duration. Thus, we commonly refer to the chronaxie and rheobase for each class or group of excitable tissue. In nerve tissue, it is known that the larger the fiber diameter, the lower its threshold of response and the shorter its chronaxie. The larger fibers have a briefer latent period and shorter refractory period. The differences in the stimulus-response characteristics between the larger fiber populations and small fibers make it possible to generate impulses of certain shapes. These impulses can preferentially stimulate the large A-fiber afferents which will act to block the discharge of A-delta/C-fiber "pain" impulses.

PAIN

NOT A PRIMARY SENSATION FROM SPECIFIC NERVE ENDINGS OR RECEPTORS

RESULT OF WHOLE INPUT PATTERN (PERIPHERAL AND CENTRAL)

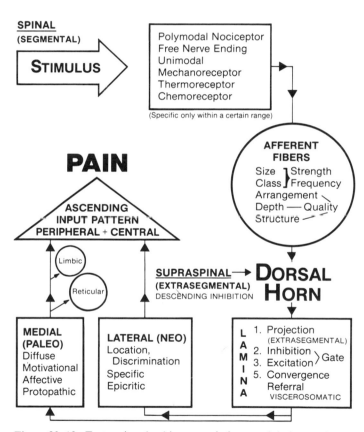

Figure 30–10. Factors involved in transmission, modulation, and perception of pain. The ultimate quality and location of pain depend on the nature of the stimulus, size of the excited afferent fibers, depth and arrangement of the involved structure, dorsal horn interactions, and ascending pathways. Receptors are specific only within a certain range. A thermoreceptor provides information on temperature change. However, if heat greater than 45°C or cold lower than 10°C comes in contact with the skin, the thermoreceptor becomes a nociceptor. Strong mechanical pressure or deformation also can be perceived as pain. (From Mannheimer, J and Lampe, G: *Clinical Transcutaneous Electrical Nerve Stimulation.* FA Davis, Philadelphia, 1984, p 65, with permission.)

Difficulty exists in integrating the use of TENS generators such that stimulus parameters can be easily and effectively set to take advantage of the different stimulus-response characteristics of various nerve fiber classes. Some TENS systems, for example, have not indicated the relationship between the numbers on the external dial or knob and the internal range available for each parameter. Other TENS systems have made erroneous claims for the meanings of their dial settings. Others have provided the clinician with one or more direct and obvious means to know the output characteristics of each generated impulse. Still, the majority of the TENS systems have not met this clinical need satisfactorily. Consequently, the "How to Adjust the Output Parameters" instructions are as variable and inconsistent as the systems' colors and shapes, and even as variable, perhaps, as the quality of TENS hardware from the numerous manufacturers.

As a result of these inconsistencies, only a small population of clinicians may use TENS to produce pain control; there are probably more clinicians who utilize TENS to provide control of pain with random and episodic success; and there are other clinicians who have used TENS to provide pain control on only rare occasions. Standardized procedures are mandatory if the health care team is to provide the greatest possible benefit to a maximum number of patients who suffer from pain. The standardization of procedures will require, however, that objective methods be provided with which each TENS treatment can be administered accurately. This will require full disclosure of the amplitude of the generated impulse, its pulse width, and rate of output. As with all therapeutic interventions, a reasonable approach and knowledge must guide the dose-frequency-duration relationships characteristic of effective electroanalgesia with TENS.

Waveforms

Electric current is the flow of a small electrical charge in a conductor. Small negatively charged electrons flow between the cathode $(-)$ or anode $(+)$ of a battery. The number of electrons that flow past a given point in a conductor in one second is called *amperage* (amps). The force that "pushes" electrons to flow is called *voltage* or electromagnetic force (EMF). One volt is the electromagnetic force that, when applied to a conductor with a resistance of one ohm, produces a one ampere current. The electric potential (voltage) moves a single electron. That electron will flow with gradually diminishing energy until it comes into contact with one or more "resting electrons" which will in turn be set into motion by contact with the first electron. The "obstacles to movement" of an electron in a conductor is called electrical resistance. **Ohm's law** describes the relationship between voltage, amperage current, and resistance with the formula

$$E = IR$$

where E is electromotive force *or* voltage, I is amperage, and R is resistance. Electrical currents can be either **monophasic** (unidirectional) or **biphasic** (alternating) (Fig. 30–11). Transcutaneous electrical nerve stimulation generators almost universally produce biphasic pulses. Monophasic pulses will be reviewed briefly in order to compare and contrast their characteristics and effects with those of biphasic TENS pulses.

MONOPHASIC, UNIDIRECTIONAL PULSES

A **monophasic, unidirectional, direct current** is the flow of current in one direction from the isoelectric point or

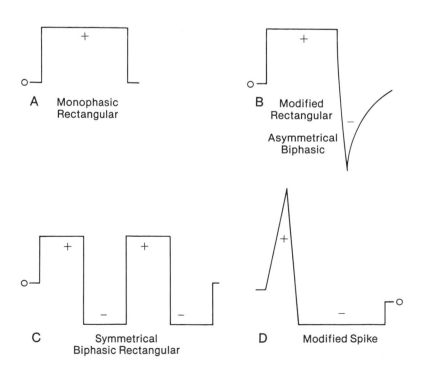

A Monophasic Rectangular

B Modified Rectangular

Asymmetrical Biphasic

C Symmetrical Biphasic Rectangular

D Modified Spike

Figure 30–11. TENS waveforms. *A* is monophasic. *B, C, D* are biphasic.

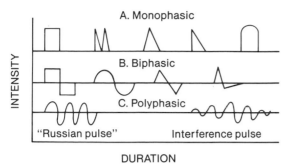

Figure 30–12. Basic TENS waveforms.

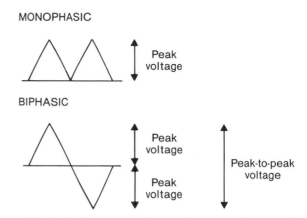

Figure 30–13. Peak current/voltage of monophasic and biphasic waveforms.

line (Fig. 30–12). Originally the term *current flow* was used to describe current flow from a positive pole to the negative pole. This is opposite the more contemporary view. This historical perspective reflected the belief that current resulted from the movement of positive charges. However, in defining current flow to be the flow of electrons in a conductor, the present-day view is that electrical current is produced when negative electrons flow from a negative (cathode) terminal to a positive (anode) terminal. Monophasic pulses move in one direction from the zero charge or isoelectric line. A monophasic pulse remains entirely above the baseline (conventionally described as a positive pulse) or below it (a negative pulse). Many different waveforms can be monophasic. Sawtooth, rectangle, and spike waveforms are only three examples, but they are representative of the different shapes that may remain unidirectional or monophasic as they are repeated in series. The maximum amplitude or

peak current occurs at the point of a pulse's maximum deviation above or below its isoelectric line (Fig. 30–13).

Pulsed Direct Current

Direct current is also referred to as galvanic current. Strong polar (positive and/or negative) effects are *not* produced by pulsed DC currents unless the pulse durations are 300 miliseconds or longer. In physical therapy, what has been called *high voltage galvanic stimulation* (HVGS) has twin peaked spike pulses with pulse durations measured in microseconds (Fig. 30–14). Therefore, HVGS is a monophasic pulse source without substantial

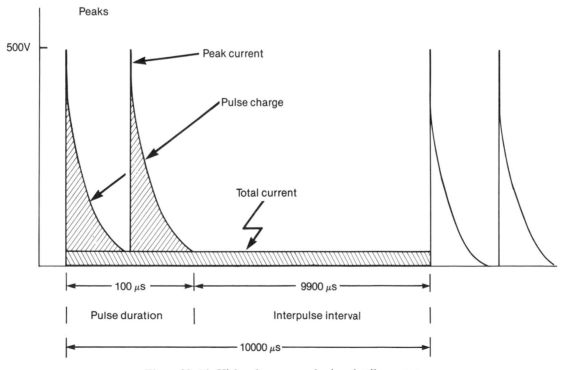

Figure 30–14. High-voltage monophasic pulsatile current.

polar effects. Although HVGS is acclaimed for its ability to reduce edema, this benefit probably is not secondary to alleged polar effects beneath the electrodes. A special note is included here for two reasons: First, to negate confusion regarding claims of strong polar effects with HVGS; second, to clarify that the brief duration of the twin peaked monophasic spike pulses of HVGS make it possible to use that modality for many minutes without producing chemical burns on the skin. Therefore, HVGS is used as a TENS system to reduce pain.

Chemical effects from polarization are largely absent with TENS. However, TENS effectively stimulates nerve tissue. To stimulate nerve tissue, an effective stimulus must have (1) an adequate amplitude that is sustained for a minimum period of time (strength-duration), and (2) the final intensity must be achieved in a minimum amount of time. Thus, an extremely short rise time is appropriate for TENS.

In a monophasic pulse the width or duration is easy to measure. The period is easily measured as well. It is a combination of the pulse width and the interval from the beginning of one pulse to the beginning of the next (Fig. 30–15). The interpulse interval is the time between pulses. Restated, then, the period is the interpulse interval plus the pulse width.

BIPHASIC PULSES

Most transcutaneous electrical nerve stimulation pulses are biphasic. These waveforms may be symmetrical or asymmetrical. When considering biphasic pulses, pulse width is less simple than with monophasic waveforms. Symmetrical biphasic rectangular waveforms have two component pulse widths; one phase above and one phase below the isoelectric line which combine as the total pulse width. Although technically the pulse width is equal to the sum of both pulse phases, a few writers of TENS literature loosely refer to the term *pulse width* to describe either the pulse phase duration above the isoelectric line or that below it (Fig. 30–16). Biphasic waveforms may be generated with or without an intrapulse interval. When there is an intrapulse interval, the tendency to describe the pulse width separately as either the positive ($+$) or the negative ($-$) increases. In this example, the pulse width is the *sum* of the widths of the positive pulse phase, the intrapulse interval, and the negative pulse phase (Fig. 30–17).

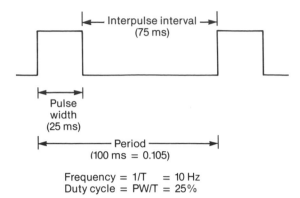

Frequency = 1/T   = 10 Hz
Duty cycle = PW/T = 25%

Figure 30–15. 10 Hz square wave.

PULSE WIDTH

The pulse width of the electrical wave is one of the most important factors involved in coupling to the A-beta fiber. Clinical studies and field testing have shown that narrow pulse width waveforms in the region of 125 microseconds have provided maximum coupling to the A-beta fiber and a minimum coupling to C and motor fibers. In addition to proper pulse width, the waveform of the stimulator also should have a negative component to prevent ionization of the skin, which is often responsible for reddening of the skin under the pads.

PULSE RATE

The pulse rate is generally adjusted for maximum patient comfort. The rate control can increase or decrease the number of pulses that the patient receives every second. Sometimes on longer applications the pulses are turned on and off as groups. This is referred to as **modulation** or as a surge-type current. **Modulation** reduces muscle tetanus and nerve fatigue during long stimulation sessions.

OUTPUT

The output of the device should produce a constant current into a typical skin-electrode load. This is important because the electrode contact and the skin resistance of the patient change over time. Generally these increase owing to loss of moisture and desensitization by the elec-

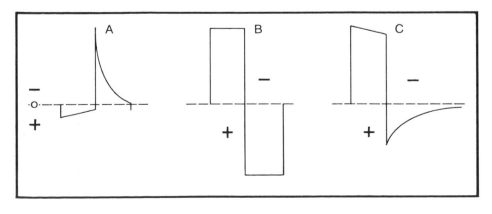

Figure 30–16. TENS waveforms: Each is balanced-biphasic with zero net DC component. (*A*) Spike, (*B*) asymmetric rectangular/square, (*C*) symmetric biphasic rectangular. (From Mannheimer, J and Lampe, G: *Clinical Transcutaneous Electrical Nerve Stimulation.* FA Davis, Philadelphia, 1984, p 214, with permission.)

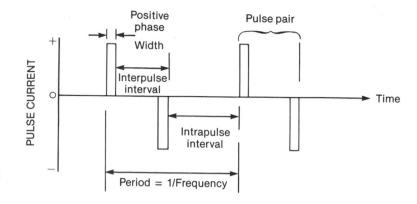

Figure 30–17. Biphasic waveform with intrapulse pulse and interpulse intervals.

trical current. Constant current devices will automatically increase or decrease the voltage to ensure an even current flow, thus maintaining good stimulation. A few devices produce a constant voltage stimulus, and as skin impedance on electrode contact changes, the voltage is held constant and the amperage automatically varies—a less desirable clinical feature.

Electroanalgesia with TENS

Electrical stimulation for the control of pain usually occurs via a nonopioid mechanism and is not naloxone-reversible. Transcutaneous electrical nerve stimulation shows no cross-tolerance with opiates. Therefore, it can suppress pain in patients under exogenous opiate medication therapy and there is no evidence of development of tolerance to peripheral TENS. For at least a few patients, TENS can produce permanent pain relief, perhaps suggesting that a memorylike mechanism mediates analgesia. This central control may play an important part in the long-term duration of pain relief following TENS therapy.

Stimulation Modes

There have developed no less than six modes of stimulation that may be selected and administered with today's TENS systems:
1. Conventional (high-rate-continuous)
2. Low-rate (acupuncturelike)
3. Burst
4. Brief intense
5. Modulated
6. Strength-duration

PROTOCOLS FOR DIFFERENTIATING STIMULATION MODES

Conventional

Conventional, high-rate stimulation may be defined as a continuous, uninterrupted chain of generated high-rate impulses of short duration and low amplitude (Fig. 30–18). More specifically, this stimulation is provided at impulse rates of 75 to 150 Hz and at pulse widths that

are specifically less than 200 microseconds (μsec) and that may be as brief as 40 to 60 microseconds (μsec) in their initial preset form. Amplitude is a more subjective parameter and should be provided to ensure that stimulation remains within the sensory stimulation ranges only, with a strong but very comfortable sensation resulting.

The majority of patients who have received adequate pain control from TENS have received this benefit from conventional high-rate stimulation. In the high-rate conventional and brief intense modes of stimulation, TENS preferentially recruits large afferent-A fibers. Preferential large-fiber recruitment establishes a control system over small-fiber pain. Through the interneuron in the dorsal horn at the substantia gelatinosa "gate," this mode of stimulation produces modulating effects on pain behavior, and the effect is enhanced by inhibitory cross-over between the lateral and medial thalamus in the brain. Although mechanism of action of this mode is not fully understood, there is an overwhelming suggestion that nonendorphinergic pathways produce the powerful analgesia. This mode of stimulation can be provided continuously for 24 hours without adverse side effects. However, constant stimulation is rarely appropriate or necessary. Instead, a program that integrates brief applications of TENS therapy into the activities of daily living when necessary has been most useful in providing the

CONVENTIONAL STIMULATION

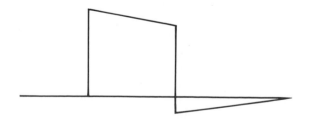

Amplitude: Strong comfortable stimulus
Pulse width: 50 μsec (microseconds)
Pulse frequency: 75 to 150 Hz (pulses per second)

Figure 30–18. Conventional stimulation. (From Lampe, G: *TENS Technology and Physiology.* Codman & Shurtleff, Randolph, MA, 1984, p 10, with permission.)

necessary pain relief and in preventing unwanted dependency. (This does not imply chemical dependency.)

Electrodes must be placed accurately so that the stimulating current from the TENS generator recruits peripheral nerve fibers which influence the segmentally related spinal cord systems implicated in the pain problem. Patient assessment will establish the somatovisceral components (structures) of the pain pattern, and, thereafter, it is a straightforward process to identify the spinal cord segment/peripheral nerve innervation of the involved structures. By integrating the trigger points located relative to the pain pattern, and points along the peripheral nerve which can be stimulated transcutaneously, the selections for electrode sites can be effectively established.

The generated impulse rate should be preset at about 85 pps so that each fiber recruited will be paced appropriately. The pulse width should be preset at 40 to 60 microseconds. The patient should make all subsequent adjustments to the TENS generator to reduce anxiety.

Upon the clinician's direction, the patient should slowly advance the amplitude/intensity setting until perception of the stimulus is noted in the area of the electrodes. Then the amplitude/intensity should be adjusted to provide a strong, comfortable stimulus sensation. If there is no burning sensation between electrode-skin interfaces, the process may continue. If the patient describes a tingle, buzz, or vibration within the body tissues at or near the area of pain, this suggests that the electrodes have been properly placed and that the amplitude/intensity setting is essentially correct.

Attention should shift to the pulse width setting. Careful, slow advancement should produce the perception that the sense of stimulation is stronger, even though the amplitude/intensity control was not changed. That is normal. The width advancement will also, however, produce another distinct and helpful perception for most patients—it will cause the tingle to spread deeper into the area of pain or to spread wider to better "fill" the area of pain. This manual scan of the underlying nerve will optimize the analgesic benefits of TENS. If good pain relief is produced but some discomfort remains, advancing the pulse rate may accelerate the pacing of the peripheral nerve fibers and thereby increase the afferent projections to the CNS.

Low-Frequency (Low-Rate) TENS

Low-frequency, acupuncturelike stimulation occurs at rates of less than 10 Hz and optimally between 1 and 4 Hz (Fig. 30–19). The amplitude/intensity is greater than that of the high-rate mode and is somewhat more objective. In this mode of stimulation it is mandatory that visible low-rate muscle contractions (twitch) be produced. Inasmuch as sensory and motor stimulation are both required in this mode, the stimulus-response characteristics of the involved nerve tissue are different from that of the conventional mode. A pulse width of 200 microseconds or greater is effective for recruiting both sensory and motor nerve fibers. Therefore it can be observed that when differentiating conventional and low-frequency modes, all parameters—the rate, the width, and the

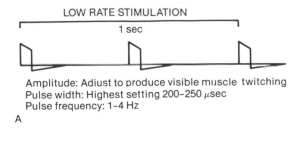

LOW RATE STIMULATION

Amplitude: Adjust to produce visible muscle twitching
Pulse width: Highest setting 200–250 μsec
Pulse frequency: 1–4 Hz

A

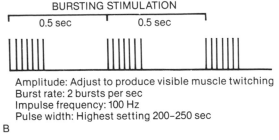

BURSTING STIMULATION

Amplitude: Adjust to produce visible muscle twitching
Burst rate: 2 bursts per sec
Impulse frequency: 100 Hz
Pulse width: Highest setting 200–250 sec

B

Figure 30–19. (*A*) Low rate stimulation. (*B*) Bursting stimulation. (From Lampe, G: *TENS Technology and Physiology.* Codman & Shurtleff, Randolph, MA, 1984, p 10, with permission.)

amplitude/intensity—are inversely proportional. Low-frequency stimulation may be provided by individual impulses generated at specified low rates or by interrupted "trains" or "bursts" of generated impulses. In the latter instance, it has been observed conventionally that cycles of two bursts per second have been provided. With each burst-train there are seven impulses. Each burst-train is followed by an off period, and then another burst of seven impulses. Less conventionally, several TENS systems have allowed the number of impulses per burst to be varied by the practitioner so that the internal frequency of each burst might be more or fewer than seven. The rationale for the less conventional configuration is poorly understood, sparsely documented and research has not indicated improved clinical response for controlling pain.

Low-rate acupuncturelike stimulation has provided pain relief to a certain portion of the patient population, but that proportion is significantly less than that associated with pain relief by the conventional mode. It must be emphasized that the pain relief that has been obtained with low-rate stimulation is no less important or gratifying than pain relief with the conventional mode. It simply does not occur in as great a population. The mechanism of action that produces analgesia with low-rate stimulation has been described as being opiate mediated. Liberation of the opioid peptides that might result in analgesia should be either partly or completely reversed by the administration of naloxone because, in this instance, it would be hypothesized that opiate receptors mediated the analgesia. This author has not noted the reversal of pain relief by naloxone associated with low-rate TENS stimulation. Therefore, we should remain at least open to the possibility that pain relief with low-rate TENS is mediated by an as yet undefined nonopioid mechanism.

Bursting TENS

Bursting stimulation, as previously described, is very similar to the low-rate stimulation (see Fig. 30–19). The rates, two bursts per second, have clinical effects similar to those of two impulses per second. The net pulse width of each burst is wider than the pulse width of an individual impulse, and therefore the impulse intensity required to produce visible motor twitching tends to be less with the burst mode than with the low-rate mode. For many patients, this has resulted in subjectively more acceptable and tolerable motor stimulation when utilizing burst stimulation. Both the bursting mode stimulation and the low-rate mode stimulation have the clinical limitation that each can be administered for no longer than 30 to 45 minutes per session without inducing some slight discomfort from muscle fatigue associated with prolonged twitching. Electroanalgesia provided by either of these modes is sometimes observed to have longer duration after stimulation is terminated than does conventional mode stimulation.

The pulse width is usually preset to the highest setting since the chronaxie for motor efferent fibers is approximately 200+ microseconds. Muscle fiber recruitment must occur to produce low-rate muscle twitches. With a wider pulse width, the law of excitability in strength-duration proportions allows us to presuppose that motor fiber recruitment will occur at lower amplitude/intensity settings than with a narrow pulse.

Many TENS devices have a discrete control that automatically delivers bursts at a rate of two per second. The amplitude/intensity should be increased to produce visible muscle twitches. Motor points would have been selected as sites for electrode placement, and neuromuscular pacing in this mode may proceed for 30 to 45 minutes comfortably. The burst mode at 1 to 4 Hz is essentially the same except that many TENS generators have a discrete switch-dial setting which activates this feature. Pain relief with this mode tends to occur with significant latency, but after it does occur, it tends to persist for substantial periods.

Brief Intense TENS

The **brief intense mode of stimulation** is very similar to the conventional mode in that the stimulus is provided by an uninterrupted chain of impulses at very high rates, moderate widths, and moderate intensity (Fig. 30–20). It is recommended that the pulse rate be set at the highest rate available from a given TENS generator, that the pulse width be at or near 200 microseconds, and that the amplitude/intensity be adjusted to provide a very strong but tolerable stimulation in the area of application. Electrodes are placed as in the conventional mode. A brief intense stimulation for 15 minutes should be used to reduce pain. After 15 minutes, it should be discontinued for 2 to 3 minutes and repeated as necessary.

Modulation TENS

The **modulation mode of TENS stimulation** may indicate a single parameter modulation: the rate alone, pulse

BRIEF INTENSE STIMULATION

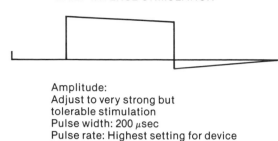

Amplitude:
Adjust to very strong but
tolerable stimulation
Pulse width: 200 μsec
Pulse rate: Highest setting for device

Figure 30–20. Brief intense stimulation. (From Lampe, G: *TENS Technology and Physiology.* Codman & Shurtleff, Randolph, MA, 1984, p 11, with permission.)

width alone, or pulse intensity alone (Fig. 30–21). Modulation is defined by some unit manufacturers as multi-modulation in which two of the parameters are cyclically modulated simultaneously.

An effective stimulus needs a certain intensity (threshold stimulus intensity) and a certain duration (pulse width). The energy per pulse is determined by the interrelationship between the stimulus intensity and duration. The recent integration of microprocessors into some TENS systems has made it possible for programmed modulation of amplitude/intensity and width simultaneously while maintaining a more constant energy per pulse throughout the modulation range. Calculations and recalculations by a microprocessor will occur automatically with any change to either amplitude/intensity or pulse width.

Within the limited assessments of the modulation mode it has been noted that some patients have expressed a subjective preference for modulation for several reasons. First, the modulation mode produces a massagelike sensation. For most, the variable modulation provided *some* distractions which would make it difficult to use this mode at all stimulation times. Most patients indicated that occasionally the massagelike sensation was highly preferred (e.g., at the end of the day the massagelike stimulation seemed to help them relax). In addition, a very small number of patients have indicated that the modulation mode significantly enhanced pain relief.

Its relatively new appearance logically indicates why the potential value of this modulation mode has not been

MODULATED STIMULATION

Simultaneous modulation of
amplitude and pulse width

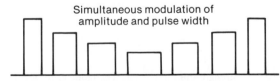

Figure 30–21. Modulated stimulation. As amplitude is decreased, pulse width is automatically increased to deliver more consistent energy per pulse. While the above cycle is being repeated, the rate can also be modulated. (From Lampe, G: *TENS Technology and Physiology.* Codman & Schurtleff, Randolph, MA, 1984, p 11, with permission.)

fully or adequately assessed. Although early indications certainly suggest that modulation is not a panacea, the same assessments have indicated a periodic subjective preference for this mode by a significant number of patients. Features and benefits claims associated with modulation, whether explicit or implied, may or may not be borne out with more extensive, scientific, clinical investigation. Claims of a causal relationship between modulation and accommodation are probably nonsense, as are claims of deeper penetration. Early enthusiasm may have caused unsubstantiated claims to slip forth. Perhaps the greatest hazard of overstatement is that when early trials fail to substantiate the claims, any or all modes of TENS therapy may be improperly condemned. Cautious optimism would be appropriate in assessing the value of each new mode of stimulation.

The subjective preference by many patients for the massaging sensations may be an appropriate guide to establishing the settings of modulation generators. Patient compliance may be enhanced by adjusting the generator to produce the most comfortable massage as subjectively defined by each patient. Use may be indicated as desired or as needed for 15 to 60 minutes for each application. Electrode placement is guided in the same manner as for the conventional mode.

Strength-Duration TENS

The **strength-duration (S-D) mode of stimulation** is another development in TENS therapy (Fig. 30–22). As the name implies, this mode of stimulation has a direct relationship with the **strength-duration curve** which is the basis for the law of excitability. The recent integration of microprocessors enables some TENS systems to regulate generator output and to match technology with neurophysiology. The law of excitability, which is graphically described by the strength-duration curve, can be plotted by application of the following equation:[18]

$$AMP = \frac{Irh}{1 - e - (PW/K)}$$

Legend: Irh: rheobase
　　　　AMP: amplitude
　　　　e: mathematical constant
　　　　PW: duration/pulse width
　　　　K: constant as a function of chronaxie

The microprocessor responds to certain information from the clinician's determination and input. The human element sets inside limits for pulse width and intensity. The microprocessor calculates the plotted curve along which the generated impulses fall during stimulation, following the strength-duration guidelines of excitability with constant current, constant energy per pulse rectangular impulses. Early clinical assessment of S-D stimulation curves has indicated that the use of this TENS mode allows a more systematic investigation of optimal parameters by its protocol of implementation. It also enables an accurate identification of the discrete pulse width and pulse amplitude combinations which provide optimal stimulation for each patient and each separate area of application. The pulse rate should be selected using the same criteria as for conventional mode. The frequency and duration of treatment should be similarly selected. Complete accuracy (± 2 percent), the programmed S-D plotting, and the objectivity of measurement and recording are representative of the highest technology applied to TENS generators. Perhaps the greatest value of the S-D mode of modulation is that it marks a new trend in efforts to establish measureable, reproducible, and recordable data specifically related to transcutaneous stimulation of the PNS for pain control. If the technology provided by the S-D mode of stimulation is accompanied by a commitment from the clinical community to integrate the recording and reporting of information provided by the technology, the relative value of each and every mode of TENS stimulation will be greatly enhanced.

CLINICAL APPLICATION

Phases of Delivery

There should be three phases to the delivery system of TENS to its patient users:

1. A prescription that includes specifications for
   a. the TENS system (hardware and software)
   b. adequate instruction and supervision by the physical therapist
2. The patient-user should be assessed and appropriately instructed regarding the safe, effective use of

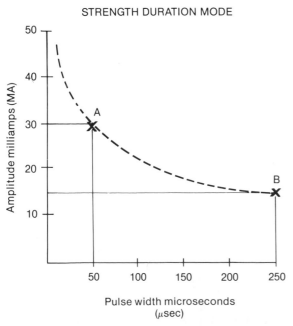

STRENGTH DURATION MODE

Figure 30–22. Strength-duration mode. The clinician inputs points A and B. The microprocessor calculates the curve using the reference equation. The clinician can automatically "scan" impulse probabilities on that curve and determine the patient's settings for amplitude and pulse width. (From Lampe, G: *TENS Technology and Physiology.* Codman & Shurtleff, Randolph, MA, 1984, p 12, with permission.)

TENS—including, but not limited to, instructions regarding the safe and proper use and care of the generator, its battery, the lead wires, the optional choice of electrodes, and of appropriate skin care. For the initial trial period, the patient should be allowed to borrow or to rent a TENS system to determine both the short-term and probable long-term effects of TENS intervention. When used for acute pain sufferers, the painful condition will usually be self-limiting. Thus, the use of TENS will be limited to a few days or weeks. The purchase of a TENS device would, in most instances, be inappropriate in this application. Instead, a short-term rental agreement with the supplier should be effected.

3. When it becomes obvious that the painful condition is chronic and unretractable, and that TENS has been found to provide substantial benefit, then a TENS system may be prescribed appropriately for purchase. Such prescription should include the TENS unit and accessories. It must also provide for ongoing supplies such as electrodes, tapes, and gels.

Indications

Because the TENS systems are safe, practical, and non-addictive, TENS therapy has grown in popularity. It is widely used to control a wide spectrum of aches and pains from simple sprains and strains to more difficult chronic pain, even to that associated with terminal cancer. Although less widespread, the use of TENS is expanded to include control of some of the discomfort associated with childbirth labor and delivery. Except when specific contraindications preclude such trials or uses, TENS may be used to treat clinical pain at the therapist's discretion.

Contraindications and Precautions

There are circumstances that prohibit or limit the applications of TENS for certain individuals.

PACEMAKER PATIENTS

Many patients with cardiac pacemakers may also require pain therapy through the application of TENS. Few problems have been reported. This does not mean there is an absence of effects of TENS interference on pacemakers, because many patients can tolerate these influences without noticeable effects.

In the worst conceivable case, total inhibition of the pacemaker may occur with fatality. Additional, theoretical calculations imply that if very high TENS currents were applied directly over a unipolar pulse generator, the generator and lead may transfer sufficient TENS current to the heart to induce ventricular arrhythmias. *As a result, TENS may be contraindicated for pacemaker patients.*

A moderate view contends that the risk may be reduced to an acceptable level by observing proper techniques. The issuance of these techniques does not imply endorsement. Rather, it recognizes that careful use of TENS can reduce the likelihood of a problem. TENS interference will not cause any damage to the pacemaker and will end when the TENS unit is turned off or disconnected. Bipolar pacemakers are much less affected by interference than are unipolar pacemakers. Bipolar pacemakers should be considered for patients known in advance to use TENS.

Clinicians who apply TENS or who have a patient desiring to use TENS should consider the potential effects of inhibition and/or reversion on the patient. The following recommendations should be considered.

1. The two electrodes of each pair of TENS electrodes should be positioned as close together as possible. This will reduce spreading of the TENS current.

2. The TENS electrodes should be placed on the body as far from the heart area and pacemaker as possible. Stimulation via an electrode pair on an extremity is unlikely to affect pacing. Stimulation on the torso, however, and especially on the thorax, is likely to affect pacing.

3. The orientation of the TENS electrode pair relative to the pacemaker electrode pair affects how much TENS interference will be picked up by the pacemaker electrodes. In general, the least interference transfer will occur when the TENS pair is oriented perpendicular to the pacemaker pair.

4. The lowest TENS power or current setting that is clinically effective should be used.

5. A TENS frequency should be selected with regard to inhibition or reversion. In general, frequencies above 30 per second may cause reversion; frequencies below 10 per second may cause inhibition.

6. Monitoring heart rate is desirable during TENS use.

7. If the patient reports lightheadedness or dizziness, the TENS should be turned off until the situation is assessed.

8. The TENS electrodes should not be handled while the TENS unit is on.[19]

Because stimulation over the carotid sinuses may elicit a vagovagal reflex and hypotensive responses, the use of TENS therapy over the carotid sinuses in any individual is contraindicated.

There are several situations, described below, that dictate that TENS should be used advisedly and with caution:

PREGNANCY

Except in the case of attempts to control discomfort related to childbirth labor and delivery, TENS should be used over the pregnant uterus with special caution. The safety of using TENS during pregnancy has not been established and therefore should be used with caution during all other stages of pregnancy. Close medical supervision by the obstetrician-gynecologist, nurse, and the physical therapist are the important ingredients to make the use of TENS safe for pregnant women who suffer from low-back pain or sacrococcygeal pain. The locally confined effects of pain control with TENS may be highly preferable to the systemic effects of pain medication for both the childbearer and the fetus.

SELECTED LOCATIONS

Transcutaneous electrical nerve stimulation should not be used directly over the eyes and should not be applied internally. One exception to the latter might be the application of pulsed high-voltage stimulation with microamperage output. Although technically the high-voltage stimulation units are TENS systems, they are sometimes recommended for intraoral, vaginal, and/or rectal stimulation.

CARDIAC PROBLEMS

There are no known complications recorded to limit the use of TENS on the thorax of patients with cardiac disease. However, in the presence of a history of cardiac problems TENS should be applied directly to the thorax with caution.

STROKE

The effects of transcranial stimulation are not yet well understood. Therefore, TENS should not be used on the head or face if a history of recent cerebral vascular accident (CVA), transient ischemic attack (TIA), epilepsy, or other seizure disorder is present.

COGNITIVE IMPAIRMENTS

For the patient who may not be able to understand the safe, correct use of TENS, and for the person who can not safely and correctly apply TENS because of physical limitations, the prescription and application of this treatment requires special consideration. If support person-nel, or a significant other, is available to administer and to monitor its use, then TENS trials and/or ongoing TENS therapy may be appropriate. Otherwise, it would be professionally and fiscally irresponsible to attempt TENS therapy.

SUMMARY

Transcutaneous electrical nerve stimulation has experienced a typical profile for a new, developing clinical treatment form. What is it? How does it work? How is it used properly? Which patients are appropriate candidates for TENS therapy? Research, experience, and education have answered each of these questions adequately, and TENS has become a safe, simple, and effective adjunctive therapy for managing postoperative, acute, and chronic pain symptoms. Electrode placement selection is determined directly so that TENS elicits modulated activity in the excitable nerve tissues related to the source and/or radiated pain. Four or five modes of stimulation provide alternate protocols for treating multiple clinical syndromes with TENS. Use with certain cardiac pacemakers is the only clear contraindication for TENS therapy. Use for patients who are pregnant should be limited to precautionary status, and, as such, can be very helpful for safe pain management. Minor skin irritations may occur associated with electrodes being fastened to the skin. However, skin irritations can usually be prevented or minimized with good hygiene and adaptive procedures. Transcutaneous electrical nerve stimulation symptomatically relieves pain and may be used as an adjunct to other pain management procedures or as an alternative. Its noninvasive, nonaddictive characteristics are valuable, especially for use by patients suffering from chronic pain.

QUESTIONS FOR REVIEW

1. There are many different types of pain associated with clinical diagnoses. What are the different modes of TENS? How may they be integrated to reduce or to abate pain symptoms successfully for individual needs?

2. Briefly describe why TENS relies on the excitability of the nervous system to moderate painful symptoms.

3. Describe the indications and contraindications for TENS therapy.

4. What are the principles of electrode placement?

How are they applicable to most conditions in which TENS is an appropriate clinical procedure?

5. There are several electrical waveforms that can be selected for TENS. However, the characteristics of an effective stimulus are the same for each. List the common waveforms used in TENS, and describe the components of an effective stimulus as they exist with each waveform.

6. Differentiate pulse period from pulse width, and an intrapulse interval from an interpulse interval.

REFERENCES

1. Stillings, D: A short history of electrotherapy in England to about 1880. Museum of Electricity in Life at Medtronic, Minneapolis, MN, 1974.
2. Melzack, R and Wall, P: Pain mechanisms: A new theory. Science 150:971, 1965.
3. Loeser, J, Black, R, and Christman, A: Relief of pain by transcutaneous stimulation. J Neurosurg 22:308, 1975.
4. Chapman, C, Wilson, M, and Gehring, J: Comparative effects of acupuncture and transcutaneous stimulation on the perception of painful dental stimuli. Pain 2:265, 1976.

5. Daugherty, R: TENS: An alternative to drugs in the treatment of chronic pain. Presented at 30th Annual Scientific Assembly American Academy of Family Physicians. San Francisco, Sept. 25-28, 1978.
6. FDA Drug Bulletin, July–August, 1975.
7. Cheng, R and Pomeranz, B: Electroanalgesia could be mediated by at least two pain relieving mechanisms: Endorphins and non-endorphin systems. Life Sci 26:631, 1980.
8. Sjolund, B, Terenius, L, and Eriksson, M: Increased cerebrospinal fluid levels of endorphin after electro-acupuncture. Aeta Physical Scand 100:382, 1977.
9. Eriksson, M and Sjolund, B: Pain relief from conventional versus acupuncturelike–TNS in patients with chronic facial pain. Pain Abstracts. Second World Congress on Pain IASP, Montreal, 1978, p 128.
10. Melzack, R: Prolonged relief of pain by brief, intense transcutaneous somatic stimulation. Pain 1:357, 1975.
11. Mannheimer, J: Electrode placement for transcutaneous electrical nerve stimulation. Phys Ther 58:1455, 1978.
12. Sojolund, B and Eriksson, M: Electro-acupuncture and endogenous morphines. Lancet 2:1085, 1976.
13. Anderson, S and Holmgren, E: An acupuncture analgesia and the mechanisms of pain. Am J Clin Med 3:311, 1975.
14. Sjolund, B and Eriksson, M: Endorphins and analgesia produced by peripheral conditioning stimulation. Pain Abstracts, Second World Congress on Pain. IASP, Montreal, 1978, p 15.
15. Hughes, J and Kosterlitz, H: Opioid peptides. Br Med Bull 33:157, 1977.
16. Snyder, S: Opiate receptors and internal opiates. Sci Am 236:44, March, 1977.
17. Goldstein, A: Opioid peptides (endorphins) in pituitary and brain. Science 193:1081, 1976.
18. Aidley, D. The Physiology of Excitable Cells. Cambridge University Press, New York, 1971.
19. Tech Note. Medtronic, April 1982.

SUPPLEMENTAL READINGS

Basbaum, A and Fields, H: Endogenous pain control mechanisms: Review and hypothesis. Ann Neurol 4:451, 1978.

Berlant, S: Method of determining optimal stimulation sites for transcutaneous electrical nerve stimulation. Phys Ther 64:924, 1984.

Bishop, B: Pain: Its physiology and rationale for management. Part I. Neuroanatomical substrate of pain. Phys Ther 60:13, 1980.

Bishop, B: Pain: Its physiology and rationale for management. Part II. Analgesic systems of the CNS. Phys Ther 60:21, 1980.

Boivie, J and Meyerson, B: A correlative anatomical and clinical study of pain suppression by deep brain stimulation. Pain 13:113, 1982.

Bonica, J, et al (eds): Advances in Pain Research and Therapy, Raven, New York, 1979.

Campbell, J: Examination of possible mechanisms by which stimulation of the spinal cord in man relieves pain. Appl Neurophysiol 44:181, 1981.

Fields, H: Pain. McGraw-Hill, New York, 1987.

Fields, H and Basbaum, JA: Brainstem control of spinal pain-transmission neurons. Ann Rev Physiol 40:217, 1978.

Gersh, M and Wolf, S: Applications of transcutaneous electrical nerve stimulation in the management of patients with pain: State-of-the-art update. Phys Ther 65:314, 1985.

Goldner, J, Nashold, B, and Hendrix, P: Peripheral nerve electrical stimulation. Clin Orthop 163:33, 1982.

Lampe, G: TENS Technology and Physiology. Codman Shurtleff, Randolph, MA, 1984.

Mannheimer, J and Lampe, G: Clinical Transcutaneous Electrical Nerve Stimulation. FA Davis, Philadelphia, 1984.

Melzack, R and Wall, P: Pain mechanisms: A new theory. Science 150:971, 1965.

Melzack, R: Recent concepts of pain. J Med 13:147, 1982.

Melzack, R, Vetere, P, and Finch, L: Transcutaneous electrical nerve stimulation for low back pain: A comparison of TENS and massage for pain and range of motion. Phys Ther 63:489, 1983.

Meyerson, B: Electrostimulation procedures, effects, presumed rationale and possible mechanisms. Advances in Pain Research and Therapy 5:495, 1983.

Nelson, R and Currier, D: Clinical Electrotherapy. Appleton & Lange, Norwalk, CT, 1987.

Ng, LKY and Bonica, JJ (eds): Pain Discomfort and Humanitarian Care. Elsevier, New York, 1980.

O'Brien, W, et al: Effect of transcutaneous electrical nerve stimulation on human blood beta-endorphin levels. Phys Ther 64:1367, 1984.

Pert, A: Mechanisms of opiate analgesia and the role of endorphins in pain suppression. Adv Neurol 33:107, 1982.

Richardson, D and Akil, H: Pain reduction by electrical brain stimulation in man. Part 1 and 2. J Neurosurg 47:178, 1977.

Richardson, R, et al: Transcutaneous electrical neurostimulation in functional pain. Spine 6:185, 1981.

Santiestehan, A and Sanders, B: Establishing a postsurgical TENS program. Phys Ther 60:789, 1980.

Soper, W, and Melzack, R: Stimulation-produced analgesia: Evidence for somatotopic organization in the midbrain. Brain Res 251:301, 1982.

Terenius, L: Endogenous peptides and analgesia. Annu Rev Pharmacol Toxicol 18:189, 1978.

Wall, D: The gate control theory of pain mechanisms: A re-examination and re-statement. Brain 101:2, 1978.

Wolf, S: Perspectives on central nervous system responsiveness to transcutaneous electrical nerve stimulation. Phys Ther 58:1443, 1978.

Wolf, S, Gersh, M, and Rao, V: Examination of electrode placements and stimulating parameters in treating chronic pain with conventional transcutaneous electrical nerve stimulation. Pain 11:157, 1981.

Wong, R and Jette, D: Changes in sympathetic tone associated with different forms of transcutaneous electrical stimulation in healthy subjects. Phys Ther 64:478, 1984.

GLOSSARY

Biphasic current (alternating current, AC): An electrical current of short duration with two component phases contained in a single pulse.

Brief intense TENS: A form of TENS stimulation that uses high-frequency (greater than 100 Hz) impulses with moderate pulse widths and moderate intensities.

Bursting TENS: A form of TENS stimulation that uses a combination of high- and low-frequency TENS with rates of 2 bursts per second.

Conventional TENS: A form of TENS stimulation that uses high-frequency (50 to 100 Hz) impulses of short pulse widths (20 to 60 ms) and low amplitudes.

Endorphins: Endogenous substances secreted by the central nervous system that block A-delta- and C-fiber-evoked activity.

Fast pain (acute): Pain that is transmitted by myelinated A-delta fibers and centrally via the anterolateral system (neospinothalamic tract).

Generator: A unit that produces a stimulating electrical impulse from a primary energy source (AC current or battery).

Lead wires: Insulated conducting cables that transmit a generated electrical impulse to electrodes for TENS.

Low-frequency TENS (low-rate, acupuncturelike): A form of TENS stimulation that uses low-frequency (1 to 4 Hz) impulses of wide pulse widths (150 to 250 ms).

Modulation TENS: A form of TENS stimulation with a built-in automatic increase or decrease of phase parameters: pulse rate, pulse width or intensity.

Monophasic current (pulsating DC current): An electrical current of short duration with only one phase to each pulse.

Neuromodulation: The modulation of nervous system activity to reduce or to abate the transmission of pain.

Ohm's law: A description of the relationship between voltage, amperage (current), and resistance.

Pain: A sensation in which a person experiences discomfort, distress, or suffering owing to provocation of sensory nerves.

Sensory pacing: The control of afferent, ascending nerve signals by externally applied electrical stimulation which induces altered nervous system activity.

Slow pain (chronic, burning, aching pain): Pain signals that are transmitted by nonmyelinated, slow-conducting C fibers and centrally via the anterolateral system (paleospinothalamic tract).

Strength-duration curve: The graphic plotting of the relationship between stimulus intensity and duration.

Strength-duration TENS: A form of TENS stimulation that uses a microprocessor to program the variables of stimulus strength and duration.

Tension loop procedure: A coil or small loop of lead wire placed 6 to 10 inches from electrodes and taped to the skin.

Transcutaneous: Transmitted across the skin without disruption of the skin barrier.

INDEX